W9-DEU-563

THE K&W GUIDE TO
COLLEGES

FOR STUDENTS WITH LEARNING DISABILITIES OR ATTENTION DEFICIT DISORDER

8TH EDITION

One of the wonderful things about this *K&W Guide* is that it helps students and their parents plan the best ways to find and use help. With this guide you can map out new, essential connections: with colleges and universities who understand your needs; with appropriate support services on campus; with departments and faculty members who will understand, challenge and respect you.

Edward M. Hallowell, MD and David Keevil, PsyD

The Hallowell Center

My first exposure to *The K&W Guide to Colleges for Students with Learning Disabilities or Attention Deficit Disorder*, was on a booklist in a college admissions and career planning class…When I first sat down in the quiet evening hours at home, when everyone else was asleep and I do my best thinking, I had the heart thumping and mesmerizing experience one gets when you read something that you feel was written just for you by someone who really understands. The 47 page introduction before the college profiles fits the books dedication: "This book is a labor of love written to help individuals throughout the world who have been identified as having learning disabilities or attention deficit disorder. Just as important, it is for those students who have never been officially identified as learning disabled. And of course, it is an educational tool for all the families, professionals, and friends who know someone who has a learning disability."

Parent of children with learning disabilities and attention deficit disorder

San Francisco, California

You have an excellent resource right at your fingertips! *The K&W Guide to Colleges for Students with Learning Disabilities or Attention Deficit Disorder* is an excellent starting point for exploring the wide spectrum of assistance provided by DSS offices in every state. Keep in mind that the goal of college is not just getting in, but getting out successfully. Finding an appropriate DSS office to student match can be the key to that success. *The K&W Guide to Colleges for Students with Learning Disabilities or Attention Deficit Disorder* can help direct you in that roadmap to success.

Dr. Kendra Johnson, Director of the Office for Accessibility at the University of Toledo and president of Transition Game Educational Consultants, Toledo, Ohio

"Many colleges have programs and services for students with learning disabilities. A very informative guidebook you might want to consult is the *The K&W Guide to Colleges for Students with Learning Disabilities or Attention Deficit Disorder*.

Jeffrey Zaslow

Reporter

K&W is a "godsend"

Dodge Johnson

College Planning

Malvern, PA

If you are a student using *The K&W Guide* as part of your college search, you are taking an important step towards a successful transition to college.

Kathleen Lynch, Dean of Admission, Dean College

The Princeton Review

THE K&W GUIDE TO
COLLEGES

FOR STUDENTS WITH LEARNING DISABILITIES OR ATTENTION DEFICIT DISORDER

8TH EDITION

MARYBETH KRAVETS, MA

AND IMY F. WAX, MS

RANDOM HOUSE, INC.

NEW YORK

www.PrincetonReview.com

The Princeton Review, Inc.
2315 Broadway
New York, NY 10024
E-mail: bookeditor@review.com

ISBN: 0-375-76495-X

Manufactured in the United States of America on partially recycled paper.

9 8 7 6 5 4 3 2

8th Edition

DEDICATION

This book is a labor of love written to help individuals throughout the world who have been identified as having learning disabilities or attention deficit disorder. Just as important, it is for those students who have never been officially identified as learning disabled. And of course, it is an educational tool for all of the families, professionals, and friends who know someone who has a learning disability.

ACKNOWLEDGMENTS

To the families of Marybeth Kravets and Imy F. Wax for their patience and support in this endeavor: Alan, Wendy, Steve, Allison, Connor, Isabel, Mark, Sara, David, Robert, Bennett, Cathy, Cliff, Christina, Amanda, Dan, Andrea, Howard, Lisa, Bill, Niaya, Ellis, Gary, Debrah, and Greg.

To Deerfield High School and High School District 113 for their ongoing support of learning disability programs and services and their belief in promoting the development of independence of all students and guiding them toward making good decisions about life after high school.

To all of the colleges who provide services and programs to promote the educational endeavors and dreams of students with learning disabilities or Attention Deficit Disorder.

To all of the contributors in the "Thoughts From..." section of the K&W Guide for sharing their thoughts and experiences with learning disabilities and Attention deficit/hyperactivity disorder.

To Stephanie Gordon, learning disability specialist, Deerfield High School, Deerfield, Illinois, for her professional assistance.

To Karen Rodgers Photography for the authors' pictures.

CONTENTS

FOREWORD

Going to college is a rite of passage. The time for college finally arrives, and with considerable fanfare our children go; they go away from home, friends, and family and go toward a "grown up" life of freedom and independence.

As this time arrives, parents and children often have powerful and competing urges on both sides: to hold on tight and never let go, or to sever all connections and begin anew. Of course many parents tend toward the former urge, while their adolescents yearn for the latter.

When you're a parent, so many instincts protest against letting go. The world is often a cruel and dangerous place, and you are all too aware of your children's newness—their youth and fragility. When you're young, it's blissful to dream of a new life that is entirely yours. And so much in our world supports that dream—songs, sitcoms, the exalted fables of popular culture.

If your child has ADD or LD, you may feel even more acutely the urge to hold tight. Your child may be impulsive; he or she may seem emotionally unprepared for the challenges ahead and may have only a vague understanding of the sometimes tedious and always disciplined work required at college. You may be particularly aware of all the effort "behind the scenes" that went into getting your child even this far—the homework assistance, the teachers' meetings, the evaluations and treatments—the countless hours of "extra help" along the way.

Your child with ADD or LD may yearn particularly for the independence of college life. He or she may be awfully tired of feeling dependent on all the help you and others have offered. College may feel like a chance to "throw off the yoke" and finally succeed on one's own, free of dependence.

This tension—between the urge to hold on and the urge to let go—is very real for all of us who are parents, and it is very real for our children. I suppose the good and bad news is that this tension is life-long; we never really outgrow these competing urges. They just take on different shapes and sizes as we all continue to grow and mature.

What I want to tell you here—something I'm sure you already understand—is that the way to resolve this conflict is not to choose one side or the other, not to hold on even tighter, or pull away so hard that you are impossibly out of reach, but to mix them together, to balance them. In order to do this, you need to stay connected.

What do I mean by "stay connected"? I mean three things. First, hold on to what you have. Second, stay flexible. And third, grow new connections. Let me tell you a little more about each of these ideas.

HOLD ON TO WHAT YOU HAVE

Maybe it looks as if I'm saying that you shouldn't let go. Actually, some letting go will be essential, for both parent and child. Parents will probably unpack the car, move things into their child's room, get a last hug, and drive away. Students will spend their first night in a college dorm, go to their first campus party, register for classes, and set their own study schedule. But in the midst of all this necessary letting go, remember to hold on to what's important from the past as well.

What is important from the past? Every new college student will have his or her own list, but I hope most lists will include these themes:

- Your parents love you, and will continue to love you no matter what
- You have a home to return to where you are welcome
- You have friends who care about you
- You have specific strengths and abilities you carry with you
- You have learned many essential skills for coping with your ADD or LD, and college is a tremendous opportunity to learn and use many more

Here's an idea for parents: As your child with ADD or LD prepares for college, devote some time to making a detailed, truthful, loving, and relentlessly supportive list of what your child will "carry" to college, and offer it to your child as a gift. And here's an idea for new college students with ADD or LD: Make your own list of what you will carry with you—make this list as a personal, intimate reminder of what is strong and sustaining in your life.

Each list is a testament to the connections that will endure and sustain.

STAY FLEXIBLE

In nature, the best connections—the strongest and most sustaining—are flexible. Think of how a tree sways in the wind, allowing it to stay connected both to the ground and to the air, through its branches and leaves. Connections that are rigid tend to snap and crack apart under strain. Flexibility allows us to grow and flourish.

What does this mean for parents, and for their child with ADD or LD? It means not to attach too rigidly to any one thing—to any one expectation, to any one vision of the future, to any one marker of "success." Think "trial and error"; think "a different drummer"; think "two steps forward, one-and-a-half steps back."

One of the exciting and dismaying things about people with ADD is that we do not always follow the pack. We may act impulsively, or "forget" to act at all. We may make associative connections between seven different ideas, but drop the one that's on next Monday's test. These and many other behaviors can lead to difficulty and risk. And they can lead to creativity and discovery.

Parents: If your child goes off to college and marches through in four years with a high grade point average, then good for your child! But this may well not happen. And if you tie your happiness to such expectations—if your expectations are too rigid—then you may well be disappointed, or unhappy, or angry, or dismissive. As a result, the connection between you and your child, and between your child and his or her positive self-understanding, may snap and crack apart. And that's not a good thing for anyone. Keep the connections flexible, pliant, and resilient. Cut each other slack, practice forgiveness, and keep your sense of humor.

And expect surprises. Life is always a dress rehearsal, and people flub their lines and miss their cues all the time. People with ADD or LD may play a love scene when we expected tragedy, or start tap dancing during the soliloquy. There's nothing to be gained by throwing them off the stage. Rather, find out how your script might be rewritten, and how they can accustom themselves to the action around them. Stay flexible!

GROW NEW CONNECTIONS

Many adolescents with ADD or LD who head off to college have already received a great deal of help over the years. They may be sick of help! But if they avoid help at college they will be missing one of the most important lessons college has to teach: how to find and use help. Think of preparing for college as preparing to find and use help—from teachers, from tutors, from other students, from administrators, from friends and family.

Finding and using help is not the same thing as offering excuses, or getting others to do your work. It is the same thing as growing new connections. College is a community of learners. The vast majority of human beings learn best in community—we learn from others and with others. A student who has something to prove by "going it alone" is mistaking a lack of connections for maturity.

One of the wonderful things about *The K&W Guide* is that it helps students and their parents plan the best ways to find and use help. With this guide, you can map out new, essential connections with colleges and universities who understand your needs; with appropriate support services on campus; with departments and faculty members who will understand, challenge, and respect you. Use this guide to start planning now, and to further develop your ability to find and use help. Ask yourself, What kind of help might I need? How will I recognize when I need it? How will I go about finding it? How will I ask, and whom will I ask? The answers you discover will change and grow as you change and grow. Remember, stay connected and stay flexible!

IN CLOSING

Bon voyage! You have an exciting trip ahead of you, climbing to the top of your own mountain. If you have ADD or LD, the path may be particularly challenging, and the air may be particularly thin at times. But you will get there. The people who love and respect you will not stand on the summit with you—that is yours alone. But I hope and trust they will help you along the paths you choose (and the paths that choose you), by remaining connected with you, assisting you in ways you find helpful, and sharing with you the wonder and excitement of your discoveries.

Edward M. Hallowell, MD, and David Keevil, PsyD, of The Hallowell Center

The Hallowell Center in Sudbury, Massachusetts, is dedicated to promoting cognitive and emotional well-being in children and adults. For more information, visit www.DrHallowell.com.

INTRODUCTION

The K&W Guide was conceived independently by the authors more than 20 years ago, but it took until 1987 for the paths of the authors to cross.

Imy Wax is a licensed psychotherapist and educational consultant. She is also the mother of four children—two with learning disabilities and one who also has attention deficit/hyperactivity disorder (ADD). The truth is that this book is really a dedication to Imy's daughter, who at the age of two was identified as having multiple learning disabilities, a large delay in her language skills, and a dismal prognosis for her future. Several professionals indicated that a traditional public elementary and high school experience would not be possible, and college was never even mentioned.

Imy was always optimistic, however, and she absolutely refused to accept such a diagnosis. She set goals, became a visionary, and exerted significant influence to allow her daughter to compensate for her limitations. She became an advocate for her daughter. She researched, read every book and every article she could find, and gave herself hope to believe in her child and in herself. Imy made it her goal to understand the learning disability and the strategies that would best contribute to her daughter's well-being.

Imy's daughter ultimately attended both public school and a special private school for students with learning disabilities (LD). When her daughter was in the eighth grade in a private school, Imy volunteered in the College Resource Center at Deerfield High School so that she could get a better grasp on what might be in store for her daughter if she were to enroll in the local public high school. This was in 1987, and the paths of the two authors crossed for the first time.

Marybeth Kravets is the college consultant at Deerfield High School, where Imy volunteered. Deerfield High School is a public high school that has comprehensive programs and services for students with learning disabilities and attention deficit/hyperactivity disorder. Deerfield High School is also a school from which 98 percent of students matriculate to college, including those students identified as having LD or ADD. Imy discovered that her daughter could be accommodated in the high school, and that the professionals there had hopes of mainstreaming her into regular college preparatory courses with appropriate accommodations and modifications.

Hidden under Imy's "coat of hope," however, lived the growing anxiety that she experienced every time she listened to a college representative visiting with students at the high school. It seemed to her that all colleges were after the same student—one with at least a 3.0 GPA, an ACT score of 24 or an SAT score of 1100, a ranking in the top 50 percent of the class, and a four-year curriculum consisting of every subject at Deerfield High School. Imy's daughter had begun the ninth grade with only special education courses, which were individualized to meet her special needs. By junior year, she had mainstreamed into college preparatory courses in English, science, fine arts, and social studies, but was still enrolled in special education classes in math. She was not even close to learning about algebra (the typical freshman curriculum), and she had never taken a foreign language.

One day, Imy asked to meet with Marybeth to talk about her concern that there was not enough information about colleges that were prepared to accommodate students with learning disabilities. As the two began to explore the available resources for information, they realized most guidebooks only offered computer-generated information that said almost the same thing about every college regarding special services and special admissions. Thus began their search for more pertinent information to help Imy in her quest for a possible match for her daughter, and to help Marybeth provide better college counseling for the students at her high school.

The first edition of this book included extensive information about 150 colleges. The next seven editions grew. The eighth edition of *The K&W Guide* has expanded to include more college profiles with detailed information about what these schools do and do not provide. It also gives specific information about documentation guidelines for students with LD or ADD and important information highlighting how, at the college level, services and accommodations are individually tailored for each student.

Through the information in this book, students can determine if the services or programs offered at a particular school match their individual needs. In this edition, you'll find:

- Facts about special programs and services for students with multiple learning disabilities and/or ADD, or for those needing limited accommodations

- Information that professionals need to know in order to help advise and counsel students and parents in their college search process

- Data on general and special admission procedures, the application process, services, programs, accommodations, remedial or developmental courses, and opportunities for basic skills classes

- Policies and procedures regarding course waivers or substitutions

- General profiles of colleges and universities

- A listing of student rights and responsibilities from the U.S. Department of Education

- Information about independent living options for nontraditional learners

The main focus of *The K&W Guide* is to provide comprehensive information about the services or programs available at colleges and universities for students with learning disabilities or attention deficit/hyperactivity disorder. Many colleges and universities will include students with LD or ADD in their structured programs or special services. In most high schools, students identified as having only ADD are categorized under "other health-related disabilities" and protected by Section 504 of the Rehabilitation Act of 1973. These students can request and receive accommodations in high school and college, as long as they present current and appropriate documentation from a certified professional.

It is extremely important that readers understand that the availability of a service or accommodation does not necessarily mean that every student with LD/ADD can access it. After a student self-discloses, requests accommodations, and then submits current and appropriate documentation, the disability support personnel at the college will determine what accommodations are "reasonable." Too often, students assume that because they received specific services or accommodations in high school, they will receive the same level of services in college. This is not the case for all students. Colleges have the right to independently examine the documentation and identify the services they feel are reasonable and appropriate.

Fortunately, most colleges are happy to provide descriptions of the level of support and accommodations available on their campuses, whether they are basic services complying with the mandates of Section 504 or enhanced services that go beyond the mandates. As long as students have access to complete and accurate information from the colleges, students will have the opportunity to choose colleges where the services match their needs.

In addition to reviewing the college profiles in this book, students and their parents are encouraged to read the college catalogs, talk to the admissions staff and the directors of the special support services, and visit the campuses. Campus visits are an ideal time for the student to provide documentation and to ask about the services and/or accommodations that are offered by the college. Before planning a trip, however, students should begin with a thorough reading of this guide. If students take the time to think about what they want and need from a college, they will be in a good position to ask thoughtful questions when they visit college campuses.

Students with unique learning needs should search for colleges that meet all of their individual needs—educational, cultural, and social. There is more than one "right" college for any student, learning disabled or not. No single source can provide all of the information needed to help students make educated decisions about appropriate college choices, but this book is a great place to start. The ultimate goal of *The K&W Guide* is to give equal access to descriptive and honest information. This guide is the first place to look for colleges providing:

- **Structured Programs:** Colleges with structured programs offer specific programs for students with LD/ADD that go well beyond mandated services. These services might include special admissions procedures, specialized and trained professionals, compensatory strategies, one-on-one tutoring, additional fees, compulsory participation, and monitoring.

- **Coordinated Services:** Colleges with coordinated services offer programs for students with LD/ADD that might be somewhat involved with the admissions decisions and might include voluntary participation, services beyond those that are mandated, low or no fees, and less structure.

- **Services:** Colleges with basic services comply with Section 504 mandates but rarely have specialized LD staff, do not have monitoring, and are totally dependent on student advocacy.

The authors gratefully acknowledge the time and effort of all the service providers at the colleges and universities who responded to our request for current information about their services and programs. The staffs at these colleges, and others like them, work closely with learning disabled students, believe in empowering students to articulate their own needs, and help students to become independent and successful learners.

It is essential that college services and accommodations for individuals with learning disabilities and ADD be visible, honored, funded, maintained, and expanded to meet the needs of identified students. When this happens, learning disabilities are identified earlier, which gives diagnosed students the opportunity to be provided with individualized educational plans to meet their needs. Diagnosed students can then become self-advocates, learn compensatory skills, and make the transition in greater numbers from high school to college.

This must be a joint effort. The colleges and universities need to support the efforts and the ongoing learning process of these individuals. Those who believe in the merit of helping these individuals should reach out to those who do not understand. Those who do not understand should open their minds to the fact that learning disabilities are neurological and are life-long; they do not go away.

The authors of this guide applaud these students. No children choose to be born with learning disabilities or ADD. However, if they hold fast to their dreams and aspirations and look beyond the imperfections and hidden handicaps, they can make things happen for themselves.

Marybeth Kravets and Imy Wax

THOUGHTS FROM . . .

A Parent: A paradigm shift occurred when I read the chapter heading in the book, Colleges That Change Lives by Loren Pope, which was titled "The Learning Disabled of Today Will Be the Gifted of Tomorrow." I am the parent of several children, each with different learning disabilities, or, as I now prefer to say, "learning differences." One child has Asperger Syndrome. Although she has exceptionally high intelligence, she has great difficulty dealing with everyday social situations (i.e. school!), has intense interests which border on obsessive/compulsive, has trouble processing and expressing emotions appropriately, finds direct eye contact painful, and has a unique learning style. This all can lead to isolation, inappropriate educational placement, misdiagnosis, and high risk for anxiety, depression, and even suicide (*The Oasis Guide to Asperger Syndrome*; Patricia R. Bashe and Barbara L. Kirby). With her sheer determination and her parent's support, however, she recently graduated from a highly selective college and is working in marketing—with plans to attend business school.

Another child has ADD and severe dyslexia. This child spent two years with a vision therapist working on three-dimensional vision so the written word would sit flat on a page instead of popping up. This child is highly visual, spatial, artistic, and has bounding, often out of control, energy levels. As a teenager, this child was fortunate to attend a small private high school that supported him educationally, but because of a very low reading and comprehension level, college was not attempted.

Another child currently in college has ADD with inattention and mild dyslexia and is an advocate for educational rights. With all the difficult family issues we had to deal with, this child was often overlooked in high school. Sadly enough, although I have diagnoses for my children now, I was always a step behind in finding appropriate and adequate information, access to support professionals, and correct and thorough diagnoses. Recently, I have delved deeply into all of these issues and am finally accessing wonderful and extremely helpful information. I know that it is never too late to help my own children and our family, and I want to help other families so they can avoid the pitfalls and challenges that were a daily part of the fabric of our lives.

This is my history. Amazingly enough, for I am compulsive information and book gatherer, my first exposure to *The K&W Guide to Colleges for Students with Learning Disabilities* was on a booklist in a College Admissions and Career Planning class.

Why had I not noticed it in the bookstore or on the pages of Amazon.com after years of collecting this type of book? When I first sat down in the quiet evening hours at home— when everyone else was asleep and I do my best thinking—I had the heart thumping and mesmerizing experience one gets when you read something that you feel was written just for you by someone who really understands. The 50-page introduction before the college profiles fits the books dedication: "This book is a labor of love written to help individuals throughout the world who have been identified as having learning disabilities or Attention deficit disorder. Just as important, it is for those students who have never been officially identified as learning disabled. And of course, it is an educational tool for all the families, professionals, and friends who know someone who has a learning disability."

Before I continue on, let me just say that my one criticism with the book was the title, but that occurred before my paradigm shift. In fairness to students, family, and teachers and in light of the revelation that is to come, I would greatly prefer if the title said "learning differences" and not "learning disabilities." However, I have researched this topic more thoroughly now, and the term "learning disabilities" needs to be used in professional settings to take advantage of the federal mandate under the Americans with Disabilities Act to provide equal rights and services to all citizens with a documented disability.

One of the most important things to realize when you are looking into colleges is that the services that were provided to children in the K–12 public educational system under Individuals with Disabilities Education Act (IDEA)—which places direct responsibility on the schools to identify students with disabilities and provide them services—changes dramatically under Section 504 of the Rehabilitation Act of 1073 and the American with Disabilities Act (ADA), which governs post-secondary school education and places the burden on students to self-identify and request reasonable accommodations. Almost all colleges require recent documentation from trained and certified professionals. Now, more than every before, the student must become his/her own advocate (with parental support if available) and politely demand the services that are their right and will make the difference in a successful college experience.

Before my children entered college I had little familiarity with the wide range of programs that were available to students with documented LDs. (I have since learned that they could have qualified for SAT/ACT accommodations, such as extended testing time.) I was unclear if there should be any mention of special needs on admissions documents (we thought that it might negatively affect the chance of admissions) and did not talk with LD staff at any of the colleges. We believed that with enough hard work our children could make it through their freshman year without any additional support.

We soon discovered that to survive without additional support would result in unnecessary stress and lower grades. That's when we discovered the disabilities resource center that provided extended time on tests in a quiet room, use of a spellchecker, private communication with professors regarding the learning differences and needs, and a variety of other services, many of which were not taken advantage of as yet. Although we didn't know it at the time of my child's acceptance to college and decision to attend college, one of the colleges my child selected had one of the finest structured programs for students with learning differences in the United States. As of 2004, only three other state universities offered similar programs. At this school, students must submit a general application to the university admission office and another application to the program. This particular child, who never before wanted to discuss or reveal the learning differences, is now applying to the program to get help with the educational goal of graduating and perhaps continuing on for a medical degree.

When I "consumed" the information in the *K&W Guide*, I was specifically interested in colleges and universities that offered a "structured programs" because my daughter had higher educational needs, and if my son with ADD and severe dyslexia ever wanted to attend college, he would need to be at a school with a very highly structured program. Just a few days ago, I thought a college education was out of the questions for students like him, but slowly the paradigm shift was occurring and I began to think it was possible. I decided to look at programs that were offered at small colleges that I had never heard of before. For example, in the K&W Guide I read about tiny University of the Ozarks, a school with an undergraduate enrollment of 703 students in Clarksville, Arkansas, in the Arkansas River Valley. Students who are admitted to the Jones Learning Center are automatically admitted to the university and NO ACT or SAT scores are required. The school believes that all students are entitled to an education that allows them to compete with other students, and the Jones Center provides a total learning environment with individualized personalized instruction with a 4:1 student/staff ratio. The goal is to allow each student to realize his or her true academic potential, find a personal learning style by utilizing strengths and circumventing deficits, and become an independent learner and self-advocate.

The thrill at discovering colleges such as University of the Ozarks and exploring their websites was palpable. That night I sat down once again to read, but this time it was Loren Pope's exceptional book, *Colleges that Change Lives*. He is the epitome of a novel and forward thinker, and his views on the college experience in modern day America are more than revealing about our culture and how it reflects our angst and anxiety. When I came to the chapter entitled, "The Learning Disabled of Today Will Be the Gifted of Tomorrow," my heart did stop. I had just been reading about the myriad of colleges and universities who recognized the gifts and the talents of the LDs and Asperger's of the world and I thought they are the new breeding ground of talent and creativity in our country. Aside from the fact that history has proven that some of our greatest minds (Leonardo da Vinci, Albert Einstein) had great trouble with words but were visual, conceptual, and spatial thinkers, as Pope contends, these are the same gifts that our modern world needs to foster now. We are entering a new era which has been called the "post-literate" era and the adage "a picture is worth a thousand words" will take on new meaning (Pope, 2000). As the computer's artificial intelligence multiplies and takes on all forms of computations and routine knowledge, the human gift will be the ability to bring imagination, creativity, intuition, serendipity and connectivity to the task at hand. This is where dyslexics are outstanding (Pope, 2000).

Rather than hide an LD on the application process, the student should be honest and remember that many of these colleges want to help you. Remember, many of the world's geniuses come from this group, which includes Lewis Carroll, Winston Churchill, William Butler Yeats, and Thomas Edison. My paradigm shift was complete when I realized that day Adelphi University in Garden City, NY, tiny Mitchell College in New London, CT, Westminster College in Fulton, MO, and Finlandia University in the rugged Upper Peninsula of Michigan could be the breeding ground for some of our most creative and talented students.

When the revelation hit me, I shared my enthusiasm with my out-of-the-box, brilliant child with Asperger's, who responded, "If this disorder is so wonderful, why don't they call it 'spatial ability' rather than 'dyslexia'?" and I wondered why myself. Just as the new political correctness prefers "learning different" to "learning disabled," why call these original and creative thinkers, "dys" (abnormal) and "lexia" (lexicon or vocabulary)? Why not rename them "pro-spatial" and see what changes occur in their self-confidence and how society now values their unique and sought after gifts? I will now embark on a "pro-spatial" campaign and see where my efforts lead me. This is my unexpected and wonderful discovery.

◆　◆　◆

Michael Barron, Director of Admissions, University of Iowa: More than 37 years ago, when I first became an admission officer at a medium-size public university in Texas, my mentors and colleagues suggested that I would encounter applicants who had not performed very well in high school. I was told to expect that some of those students would "claim" to have a reading problem and others would actually use the term dyslexia. It seems that many of my admission colleagues were somewhat dubious about the true extent of such a disability (although the term dyslexia was not in widespread use at the time). It is with horror that I look back on those times when many of us simply discounted such students as just being lazy, dumb, or under-prepared.

We are blessed today with greater knowledge about learning disabilities, and more important, with compassionate understanding of those individuals who cope with one or more of the growing list of what we now call learning disabilities. Often these students exhibit superior intellectual capacity, but lack the ability to mark the appropriate bubble or write an answer on paper in the prescribed time period. They are a resource that cannot be overlooked or swept aside by our application of some of the more odious and inappropriate labels used in the past.

We must take risks along with these students in order to help them develop their potential. We have learned that there are many disorders that impact an individual's ability to learn, but do not impair their intellectual capacity. I am pleased to say that now there are many more of my colleagues who understand these needs and, working carefully with disabilities specialists and faculty, are developing ways to provide these students with the opportunity for higher education.

At Iowa, the Office of Admissions has a special relationship with the Office of Services for Disabled Students, and has operated a very successful program of alternative admission consideration for such students. We seek students with learning disabilities who have used the resources available to them to their fullest potential.

A diverse student body with a variety of talents, interests, and backgrounds is necessary in a university. Iowa welcomes applications from students with documented learning disabilities and/or attention deficit disorder. The staff in the Office of Services for Disabled Students, as well as that in the Office of Admissions, carefully evaluates the overall academic performance of these students for evidence that they will be able to successfully pursue a demanding and rigorous collegiate program. We keep in mind that we are looking for students with the ability to do college work that is reflected in the strength of the courses they have taken, as well as the compensatory strategies that they have employed during their high school years.

Some students fulfill all of our regular admission requirements despite documented learning disabilities. This does not mean that they no longer need compensatory strategies or a special office to assist them in advising faculty of their special needs. They do. We have also had excellent success at Iowa with our special admission process for students with learning disabilities who do not meet our regular admission requirements, and recent data suggest that with proper attention, as many as eight out of ten such students succeed at the university. Faculty members are recruited to be partners in this process.

We recognize that the decision for students to self-identify themselves as learning disabled is a personal choice. A student's decision not to self-identify is respected. However, it has been our experience that students with learning disabilities who acknowledge the existence of a disability and seek assistance early are more likely to achieve academic success than those who wait for problems to develop. It was not too long ago that such students probably would never graduate from high school. Even if they did, they could not look forward to a future with very many options for employment.

Thankfully, we are making breakthroughs for many of these students and are now providing them with access to and opportunities for higher education. While there are programs like Iowa's that are beginning to achieve success, we have by no means provided a paradigm that is consistently accepted and used throughout the country. That will only come through public discussion of the successes and failures of those of us who have met the challenge and taken the risk. This book, *The K&W Guide to Colleges for Students with Learning Disabilities or Attention Deficit Disorder*, is certainly one of the resources I hope will be widely used in that effort.

While we are working to educate our colleagues, to modify our systems to accommodate these students, and to provide them with the opportunity to obtain the education that they desire, we also must begin to work as partners with industry. It will not be enough to provide an environment where an individual can complete a university degree and yet fail miserably in the world of work because of its lack of understanding and inappropriate job placement procedures. Our experience at Iowa is that these students desperately want to succeed, and they want to stand on the merits of their own achievements. To deny them the opportunity to be an asset at the highest level of their ability is to squander a valuable human resource, creating an unnecessary and unwanted liability for society. I urge students with learning disabilities and their families to demand the services they need and to be patient with those of us in the education establishment, as we seek to understand. I also encourage educators at all levels to be sensitive to and aware of these individuals as a resource not to be wasted, and to work diligently to provide educational opportunity to all.

◆　◆　◆

Jane Benson, Director of Learning Disabilities Services, University of North Carolina at Chapel Hill

Learning Through Lived Experience

When I went off to college, I remember how I wanted more than anything to leave behind all the academic difficulties that went along with my learning disability. Somehow I had hoped that college would afford the opportunity for a fresh start, where if I just didn't tell anyone about my LD, then maybe, just maybe, the academic difficulties that so often plagued my school work would just magically disappear!

Twenty-five years ago when I went to college, it was still fairly new territory for kids with learning disabilities to be entering post-secondary schools. At the time, the unspoken assumption was that anyone with a disability, particularly a hidden disability, wouldn't be able to make it in college.

Although this was never directly talked about, believe me, I somehow had become privy to this unspoken rule. And of course knowing this only contributed to my desire to keep my LD to myself! What was also true around the time I went to college was that the number of schools that had any type of services in place for students with LD/ADD was few at best.

Being a fairly resourceful person, I had learned long ago that one way to get help in areas that I struggled with was to quickly assess the other kids in my classes, and identify who I thought the "smart" kids were and who seemed nice enough to give me some help. Once I had that figured out, I would make an effort to start a friendship with them.

Starting friendships with this unspoken motive had some pretty big personal costs associated with it. I often felt as if I was giving up a piece of myself by initiating friendships for this reason. Each time I did, I felt dishonest since I wasn't divulging what was really going on for me, thereby only magnifying the shame I felt in having a learning disability and in feeling the need to keep it a secret. I also felt an obligation to keep these sorts of friendships alive, since I felt that the only way I could "do" college was by having their help.

Another cost associated with this approach to relationships centered on the specific ways in which I allowed friends to help me. For example, when I would struggle for hours on a paper and finally call a "friend" for help, what seemed easiest for them was to just take my paper and "edit" it for me. Editing in this case often meant reworking my paper to the point that my voice was no longer present. I hated this, but I also felt that I didn't have the ability to write, and that the only option was to keep depending on "friends" for help, which in turn seemed to perpetuate my assumption that LD kids really can't make it in college.

It wasn't until my junior year that I began to see that no matter how much help I got from my peers, or how many hours I would put into doing homework or studying for tests, it never was enough—at least as reflected by my grades. Clearly I needed to find another way to approach college, or I wouldn't be there much longer. If there was one thing I knew for sure it was that I wanted to be a special education teacher and someday be able to make a difference for kids with LD who wanted to go to college. I knew I had to have a college degree in order to do this, so leaving just wasn't an option to me. As scared as I was to look at other ways of getting through college, I was willing to try and do it.

Perhaps it was fitting, or certainly gratifying, that a professor ended up being the one who was instrumental in helping me see that it was really okay to seek help. What drew the attention of this professor was the significant difference she saw between my participation in class and my writing ability. I was asking good questions and making strong contributions to discussions, but my test performance and my writing didn't reflect the level of understanding that my class participation did.

My professor seemed to think that she was dealing with two completely different students: the one in the room and the one on the pages of the tests. It was through her willingness to be a curious learner, and to see me as smart and capable of doing the work, not to mention her love of teaching, that enabled her to meet with me for hours on end. We focused on how I could approach writing and studying for tests in a way that built upon what I did well. It amazed me how she could zero in on a strength of mine for which I had little appreciation. She then asked me a lot of questions about my writing process, and through this active and interpersonal process we designed strategies that capitalized on my strengths.

It was amazing how freed up I became once I was able to talk out my ideas and not get bogged down with trying to hold them long enough in my head to get them down on paper. (I was in college well before computers came along!) Talking out loud became the way I studied for tests too, again playing on a strength. I'd find an empty classroom and would stand in front of the class and pretend I was giving a lecture on whatever I was studying. I'd use the board to draw diagrams or to write out the important points I was making.

The incredible gift this professor gave me was to see that I had strengths that I could use, and to see that I could use these to find my own way of approaching my school work. The biggest impact this experience had on me was discovering that I didn't need to depend on others to complete school work successfully. By using the strengths, I came to experience learning as (sometimes) fun, as I tried to figure out new ways of capitalizing on them. It was also through this experience that I gained the confidence to seek accommodations and other forms of help—since I now had discovered that I actually had much to offer as a student and could see that it was in fact possible for me to succeed.

Certainly my experience of having no preparation for the transition to college has fueled my commitment to, and strong belief in, the need for students to develop a working understanding of their disability and other life skills necessary for college adjustment. This development, which needs to start prior to college, obviously needs to continue at the college level and beyond. Thus, I strongly believe that high schools and college programs that work with students who have learning disabilities and/or attention deficit disorders need to include this focus on self learning and the skills that ensue from this psychological growth.

The Transition Process and Potential Pitfalls

Over the years, I've seen many students enter college with varying levels of readiness in terms of their preparation for the transition from high school. There are some noteworthy attributes that I've observed as either roadblocks to a positive transition, or alternatively, that provide for a smoother transition into the vastly different college environment.

Some of my insights regarding transition issues come from meetings I've had with families, as well as from my own work with students. Some examples of roadblocks that I've seen are when parents, with the best of intentions, struggle to let go of the majority of responsibilities associated with areas that are directly impacted by the student's disability. One way I've seen this impact a student in the long run is when parents take on the main responsibility of establishing a relationship with the college office that provides services for students with LD/ADD. Parents will submit documentation on the student's behalf, as well as collect information on how their kids can access services, all without any involvement from the student. Although at the time this may appear to be the most efficient way of taking care of these matters, I believe this mode of entry is sometimes associated with an ongoing limited amount of involvement on the student's part; that is, it may set a tone that makes it harder for a student to independently seek services later on.

Often for many of these same students, their secondary education has not provided them ample opportunities to develop life skills/behaviors such as understanding themselves as a learner; appreciating the impact of their disability across both academic and non-academic settings; exploring what accommodations may assist them in demonstrating their knowledge; and learning self-advocacy skills.

When coming from the high school setting, it often appears that priority has been placed solely on the student's current academic performance. Although the goal for doing well academically is usually so the student has good college options, by not focusing on the life skills associated with a more positive transition, we are selling students short by holding them to what, in retrospect, appear to be short-sighted goals. Instead, a longer, developmental view should be taken that encompasses the level of self-knowledge the student will need to independently negotiate a new learning and social environment.

I've seen how detrimental it can be for students who lack broader life skills and who respond by hiding the difficulties they're having, or by taking a "wait and see" approach, just as I did in college. This often places students even deeper into academic jeopardy. I've also encountered students who have not had opportunities to develop these skills but at the same time have needed little academic support in high school. It is not surprising that these students assume that they won't need accommodations/services in college but often end up needing them as urgently as the student who struggled in high school.

Often high school students seem unfamiliar with the significant differences between high school and college. These differences are likely to impact the student in ways not experienced in high school. Therefore, it is likely that accommodations that have not been used previously may now be called for given the increased academic demands, differences in the structure of classes, and the relative lack of external structures often found in college.

Even though services and accommodations have been in place for some time now at the post-secondary level for students with LD/ADD, the perception of some teachers and students still exists that utilizing accommodations is a "crutch" or an "unfair advantage," when in truth, if one were to consider the specific nature and impact of LD/ADD that a student experiences, together with the increased academic demands and loss in structure, it stands to reason that the impact of a learning disability or attention deficit would likely increase. Preparing students for these changes would perhaps make accessing such services and accommodations easier once in college.

Since I always like to go directly to the source, I've collected quotes from students who attend UNC and who have learning disabilities and/or attention deficit disorders. I asked students to complete a brief survey about their transition to college and what they would have liked to have experienced differently. Here's what some of these students shared:

"I wish my high school teachers had read over my report with me, so I really understood what my disability was."

John, UNC sophomore

"Parents need to stop being the experts about their kids' disability, and instead help them learn about him or herself."

Mary, UNC senior

"Before going to college, students need to know who they are and what they'll need to succeed."

Jaci, UNC freshman

"Let kids practice being independent and making their own decisions so they can learn from their mistakes in high school."

Louisa, UNC senior

"Teachers need to make sure that the accommodations they give in high school will be available in college. I was shocked that my professors wouldn't give me extensions on papers and that my spelling errors could be counted off my grade, also that I couldn't have my tests untimed."

Kevin, UNC freshman

"I wish my Mom would have stopped helping me and reminding me so much. I didn't know how to function when she wasn't there my freshman year."

Katelyn, UNC junior

Facilitating Successful Transitions

I'd like to share with you some factors that I believe contribute to a smooth transition from high school to college for students with LD/ADD. What I will share comes from several different places: the experts—students in college who have LD/ADD, my personal experiences, and my professional background over the past 20 years or so.

Self-awareness and the development of advocacy skills have long been reported as critically important life skills for students with LD/ADD to develop before heading off to college. Certainly I agree with these findings, but I believe the development of these skills cannot be accomplished in a vacuum and often need to involve the efforts of many members within a student's community. Typically this may include a student's parents, teachers, coaches, and perhaps an employer.

The development of these life skills is achieved neither automatically nor by a "cookbook" approach. Instead, these skills must be developed gradually and as a process that occurs over the student's high school (if not earlier) education. This skill development needs to be tailored to the student's specific strengths and weaknesses, all while keeping in mind where the student is with respect to self-awareness and acceptance of his or her disability.

Further, what's paramount to the success of developing these life skills is the commitment from the student's community to maintain a broader view of the student's life. This entails looking beyond high school and coming to see what skills will play an increasingly critical role in the student's ability to navigate through the world once out of high school. Therefore, the goal of this process should be building toward an increasing independence and the creation of opportunities to practice these skills within the student's current community. In working toward a successful transition, it is only when these skills are fully incorporated into the student's sense of self that they can serve as a foundation when academic or other types of demands increase. The student will then have the internal resources needed to meet these demands.

The following are general areas for consideration when focusing on the development of these life skills:

- Developmental issues can surface in adolescence—be ready to recognize these changes.
- If needed, obtain a current evaluation by a psychologist who has done evaluations for students who are transitioning to college.
- Often, teachers and parents seem to have a general understanding about disabilities, but they may struggle to understand how best to integrate all of the issues with which a student is dealing. In these cases, there is a need to identify professionals within the community who can provide information about how best to help the student develop the skills needed for a positive transition.
- Explore with students their views about their disabilities, within the context of themselves—socially, emotionally and academically.
- Explore with students their strengths, both academic and non-academic.
- Develop an understanding of how students feel about medication to ensure their continued compliance once leaving home.
- Collect data about the impact of medicine from others who have regular contact with the student, possibly at various times and settings within the day. This may provide useful information to students as it may allow them to fully see the impact of medicine in their lives.
- Keep the student centrally involved in decisions about their educational plan and current accommodations as well as their future plans for life after high school.

It Takes a Community

Including people who are part of a student's community, both in and out of school, can provide powerful "lab" opportunities, in which students can try out new behaviors/skills. Ideally, students can begin to explicitly examine life skills in their home communities where they already feel safe and have established and trusted relationships. This creates a perfect "playing field" for students to try new behaviors and skills, knowing that even if they don't work as planned, the impact is likely to be less detrimental than if they were in a brand new setting with less established supports.

Here are some suggestions for how the community could best be utilized to foster these skills, keeping in mind that this is a process that must occur over time. It is not suggested that any of this can happen quickly, and it's important to recognize that this will change as the student gets older and is faced with different challenges.

How Teachers Can Take the Longer View:
- Individualize decisions about accommodations.
- Link decisions to the student's area(s) impacted by disability.
- Incorporate gradually accommodations that reflect what students will encounter at the post-secondary level. In so doing, reconsider accommodations such as: unlimited extended test time, spelling not taken into account as part of grade, and/or extensions on written assignments because of disability.
- Involve students in the process of determining and negotiating accommodations.
- Explore technology to find ways to accommodate the disability that can transition with a student to college.
- Facilitate the student's development of external structures so as to increase independence and accountability. This may include designing ways to keep deadlines, remember things that need to come to and from school, initiating meetings with teachers, and be punctual for appointments

Parents' Roles in the Development of Teenager's Life Skills for Transition:
- Anticipate times of confusion, concern, and frustration.
- Identify resources to assist you with the acceptance of your teen's disability.
- Develop an understanding of the specific nature of your teen's disability.
- Look at a teenager's whole life and possible areas of disability impact outside of academics
- Get curious with your teenager—they are experts on themselves.
- Recognize strengths and encourage further expansion of areas enjoyed.
- Consider how you feel about the use of medicine.
- Utilize resources to learn more about the potential role of medicine.
- Notice where and when you're "managing" your teenager's life and consider: Are you waking her up in the morning, scheduling appointments and making sure she gets to them, keeping track of assignments due, and providing reminders for long term projects?
- What are the ways you can begin to relinquish your management of the foregoing tasks?
- Look to collaborate with the school to carry over structures into your home.
- Work together with your teenager to expand the areas of responsibility, including increased responsibilities at home.

Utilizing the Community

Keeping a broader developmental view can play out within the student's community beyond home and school and serve as terrific "learning labs" in which new life skills can be developed and practiced.

One example of such a lab may be with a coach if the student plays a sport. Let's assume that a student has difficulty getting to practice on time. Instead of having the coach come up with how the student is going to get there on time, the student and perhaps a teacher might meet with the coach to discuss a student-developed reminder system and then work with the coach to design a plan around accountability for the student's use of their reminder system and what will take place if either it isn't used or if it isn't working sufficiently. The goal here is to have the student in the driver's seat for determining what system is most likely to work in this situation. Since he or she has created it, often the student becomes more invested in its success.

Self-awareness and acceptance play a pivotal role here, since part of a student's awareness may likely be in recognizing that the "doing" or "using" of a system can be the very place that is most problematic for them. Once becoming more accountable, the student is inclined to view the created structures, not as punishment, but as helpful aids to their continued success.

Another way to utilize the community and to facilitate a high school student's understanding about the differences between high school and a post-secondary setting is to contact a nearby college that has a program for students with LD/ADD. Invite a panel of students from the college program to come and speak with high school kids who have LD/ADD. On our campus, when students have gone into area high schools to put on such programs, we have been amazed by how transforming the experience has been for both the college and the high school participants. The impact on high school kids, when they can hear directly from college students who are closer to their age, is that they are much more willing to ask questions and seem more open to having follow-up conversations with teachers after this type of experience.

For college students, this experience is equally powerful, in that it affirms all that students have learned about their own self-acceptance and provides terrific opportunities for college students to share the ways they have developed to compensate for areas of difficulty, and to discuss the types of accommodations that are making a significant difference for them.

Facilitating such a panel is truly a win-win situation for all involved. The experience makes a profound and lasting impact all of the students involved and arranging such a panel is fairly easy to do.

Admissions: To Disclose or Not to Disclose

Over the years as Director of LD Services, I've met with many families who continue to report that they're being cautioned not to disclose a student's disability when applying for admission to a competitive university. That's extremely unfortunate to hear and continues to perpetuate the perception that it's best to keep hidden disabilities hidden. In my experience of reviewing applications for admission, I find that without information about a student's disability and the accommodations he has received, it's often quite difficult to determine if in fact the student's grades are representative of his true potential. Keeping in mind that the intent of accommodations is to minimize the impact of a student's disability and therefore provide a more accurate reflection of his ability, it is easy to see what an important role such information can have on a student's application.

In light of this, consider letting go of the misconception that "it looks better" to colleges if you don't use accommodation. Instead, consider this: If an accommodation allows a student to demonstrate what they know, and therefore minimizes the impact of his disability, then wouldn't it make sense for a college to have this information in order to make a more informed decision?

As you begin applying to colleges, it's likely that you'll come to find that there's no standard procedure that all colleges follow when a student discloses a disability. That's why contacting each college a student is considering applying to is a necessary step to take before making any decision regarding disclosure.

Some Questions to Ask When Contacting a College:

- What is the area of expertise of the person(s) who review information submitted about a student's disability?
- How is this information integrated to derive a complete understanding of the student?
- If accepted, is the student then eligible for services, or is eligibility for services a separate process?
- If a student chose not to disclose, and then was not accepted to the college, is there an appeals process such that the student can then submit documentation for review?
- Once information pertaining to disability has been provided, does it become part of the student's academic record?

When visiting a college campus, arrange to meet with a staff member in the office that works directly with students with LD/ADD. Although at our university there's no requirement for such a meeting, I recommend it because I believe families, as consumers, can get the best sense of how an office feels by going and seeing the physical space as well as meeting with a staff member.

On a personal note, I love it when I get a call from a high school student who wants to meet with me and asks if they can meet with a student who uses our services! Think of all the great information a student can gather when given the opportunity to hear it directly from the source! See if you can put something like that together for visits that you make, and you will likely gain a wealth of information.

In closing, the good news is that the number of students succeeding in college who have learning disabilities and/or attention deficit disorders are equally good as the number students without learning disabilities and/or attention deficit disorders!

Keep the following in mind: If you're a student and reading this book, you're already on the path to a successful transition to college—good for you! Keep asking for help when you need it, and remember that you've worked hard to get into college, and you've earn your place there! Now it's about bringing all that you've come to understand about yourself to the next level. In college, keep learning about yourself and exploring accommodations/services as your needs change.

I wish all of you good luck as you move forward in realizing your dreams! Remember that I'm a resource for you, and if you'd like to contact me, feel free to do so at jsbenson@email.unc.edu.

◆ ◆ ◆

Lydia S. Block, PhD, Educational Consultant, Block Educational Consulting: For many students the idea of attending a large university is very intriguing. These schools offer large sports programs, many majors, different types of living situations, and a multitude of cultural and social activities. Successfully negotiating the large university setting also requires a considerable amount of initiative on the student's part. How do students and their parents know when a large school is a good match? How does a student know that he or she will be able to get what is necessary in terms of academic support and accommodations from a large university? These are important things to find out before applying. *The K&W Guide* is the best resource available to provide families with information gleaned first-hand both from school visitations and directly from the schools' Disability Service Providers.

With few exceptions, most large universities have disability service programs to serve students with all disabilities. Some campuses have limited staff to work with students, and students will find that it is up to them to seek the help that they need. By the nature of their size, there is far less personal attention at a large university then at a small school and students must learn to advocate for themselves. Students at large schools must be very independent. The classes are generally large the first year or two, some are taught by graduate students, and it is less likely that a faculty member will be able to get to know a student well. Students must know what they need in terms of academic support and accommodations and be prepared to ask for it. Generally, students are responsible for filing paperwork with the appropriate office to receive accommodation, and for meeting with faculty members to explain their disability.

In addition to knowing what they need in terms of accommodations, students at large universities must also be able to identify when they do not understand material or an assignment. This is true at any school, but a large university offers fewer opportunities for class discussion and often less access to faculty members than a small school. So it is up to the students to seek help when they need it.

Students with attention deficit/hyperactivity disorder sometimes find it difficult to structure their academic and social lives at a large university. Students must rely on motivation and their ability to independently make decisions and follow them through. This is a challenge for all college freshmen, but it is particularly difficult for some students with LD and ADD.

For students who have been successfully involved in activities in high school, and shown the ability to structure their lives and advocate for themselves, a large institution can be full of wonderful opportunities. For certain majors, large schools offer the best programs, noted faculty, and research and internship opportunities. It is important for students to consider what being a student at a large campus environment will be like. When the student visits a large university, it is essential that she sit in on large lecture classes and meet with the disability service provider. These are important steps in realistically evaluating what life would be like in a setting where everything will not always be clearly defined.

◆ ◆ ◆

Kathleen Lynch, Dean of Admission, Dean College: Congratulations! If you are a student using *The K&W Guide* as part of your college search, you are taking an important step toward a successful transition to college. You already know that there are many wonderful colleges and universities to choose from, and you want to be prepared to find a good match for your individual needs. Here are some points you may want to consider as you go through the college selection and application process.

If you are still selecting courses for high school, work with your counselor to build a schedule that is as challenging as possible without being overwhelming. Check on the admission requirements for the schools on your dream list. Is there a foreign language requirement? Does the college expect to see three or four years of math? What are the average SAT and/or SAT Subject Test scores? How do your scores measure up? Can you and/or should you take the ACT instead? Are there any provisions for alternative assessments such as submission of an academic portfolio? If an interview is either required or recommended, would that be a plus or minus for you?

As you begin the college search process, it is critical that you understand as much as possible about yourself and the nature of your learning difference. What does your individualized educational plan actually say about you? Are you familiar with the diagnostic testing in your file? (Most colleges will want testing that has been done within the three years before you enroll.) Can you explain clearly to someone what accommodations or modifications you need and how you can best accomplish your academic goals? Do you know your learning style? As you look at colleges and universities, how important will it be for you to know whether most first-year classes are in a lecture hall or in a small-class setting?

If you are taking any medication, do you understand why you take it, and what an overdose or forgetting to take it will mean? Will the social adjustment of sharing a room with someone present any special challenges for you? Ask about the counseling services and health services on campus.

During the application process, let the college know that you have learning differences. Often a personal statement or an interview is a good way to disclose this information. Remember that this is not an excuse for poor performance, but an honest assessment of what challenges you face and what compensatory skills you have developed or are working to develop. Colleges have a wide range of help available, from extended time on tests to highly structured programs. Unless you are willing and able to discuss your needs and their services during the college search, you risk missing a chance for the best match. Getting admitted is only the first step. Research has shown that the most critical period for college success is the first semester. The admission staff can put you in touch with learning services on campus before the academic year begins, and you can start the critical first semester with services in place and a good understanding of how to access all the help available. Even if you have gradually become less dependent on services in high school, the first year of college is not the best time to try to go it alone. Real independence lies in learning to be your own advocate.

Discuss with your parents and counselor the differences between the special education services required by law at the high school level and the limits of what must be provided in a college setting. Know your rights and also your responsibilities.

Large or small, urban or rural, colleges and universities want you to succeed and are ready to work with you. Improving your skills as a self-advocate will prepare you to work with them.

◆ ◆ ◆

Julie T. Steck, PhD, HSPP; and Dennis Ray Kinder, PhD, HSPP; Children's Resource Group:

Dear Parents:

As soon as our adolescents enter high school, most of us begin to worry about what they will do after high school. Increasingly, a parent's dream for their child includes a college education. As parents strive to assist their adolescent in traversing the rocky path through high school, college begins to seem more like a nightmare than a dream. It somehow seems like an insurmountable task. How can a student who loses homework in their backpack be expected to organize, complete, and turn in a term paper? How can a student who misses the bus on a regular basis ever make it to an 8 A.M. class without a parent to awaken him? How can a student who forgets the combination to her locker keep track of a dorm key?

These are the scenarios that haunt families of students with attention deficit/hyperactivity disorder (ADD). So, is a college education a realistic expectation? Yes, but it takes a great deal of planning, thought, commitment, and (most importantly) patience. All too often the goal of families with students with ADD is to get the student into college. But if a college education is the goal, the goal must also include staying on path to complete a college education, finding some enjoyment in the process, and becoming a successful adult. Leaving home and going to college does not mean that the characteristics of ADD are left behind. It only means that the parents no longer see evidence of the disability on a daily basis. The young adult must still deal with the disorder, and he or she will be doing it in an environment with much less internal structure and with many more distractions.

What can parents do to prepare their student to be successful in college? The first step toward achieving the dream is to confront the problem. If you suspect that your student has ADD or if he or she has been diagnosed but not adequately addressed, you and your child need to recognize the disorder and develop an appreciation for how it impacts his or her progress. The impact of ADD is far-reaching and often has social, educational, emotional, and organizational implications. Just as with any other medical disorder, a young adult must become increasingly responsible for managing his or her own care. For example, students with asthma must know how much they should exercise, what type of weather and climate is best for them, and when and how much medication to take. Similarly, students with ADD need to know how to structure their day, what type of classes and social situations are best for them, and how to appropriately use their medications. All too often, parents have willingly provided these supports for their student with ADD without the student realizing why they needed to be done. As students approach young adulthood, parents need to assist in educating their student about ADD and the potential impact of the disorder on the young person's life.

The second step toward the dream of college is to ensure that the disorder is appropriately diagnosed. The evaluation should be conducted by a qualified medical provider or psychologist who has been trained in ADD. In order to meet the criteria required by most colleges and universities for special programs, accommodations, or adaptations, the evaluation must include the use of standardized measures which document the disability and its impact on educational performance. In addition, the report should contain specific recommendations for accommodations and programming. This evaluation should not be considered just another hurdle to cross, but should be viewed by the parent and student as an opportunity to obtain information regarding the student's performance and levels of functioning. The evaluation should also serve as a forum to gain insight into the student's strengths and needs, providing helpful information for both the parent and the student.

The third step toward the dream is to review the student's elementary, junior high, and high school career objectively. How has the student performed overall? In what types of classes did the student do well? What types of classes were difficult for the student? If medication has been used, how did it impact grades and performance? What types of learning environments did the student prefer? Did he or she do well in the environments they preferred? It is likely that these factors will impact college performance just as they have previously. The best predictor of the future is often a realistic assessment of the past.

The fourth step in achieving the dream of college is to choose a college or university in which the student can be successful. Most students with ADD have experienced a great deal of frustration in high school largely because there were so few choices available to them regarding their school environment. Selecting an appropriate college provides an opportunity to choose an environment more tailored to the student's needs. In general, students with ADD do best when they chose colleges with the following:

- Smaller classroom environments
- Opportunities to interact directly with instructors and professors
- Structured support services for students with disabilities
- Academic expectations that will not be a "reach" for the student
- An adult mentor within the university or living nearby
- On-campus living environments
- Tutoring services in areas of weakness
- Academic counselors knowledgeable about ADD

The most important step in achieving the dream of a college education is for parents to work jointly with their young adult to build a plan for success. Most students with ADD do not complete a four-year college program in four years. Generally, this is due to the student dropping out of college (or being asked to leave) due to frustration or failure. It is far better to anticipate college taking longer and build in a five-year (or longer) plan. Many students benefit from taking a class in the summer at a local college prior to starting their freshman year. This provides an opportunity for the student to experience a college-level class before leaving home. Most students will do better with a slightly lighter class load than normal. Instead of starting with five classes and dropping one, start with four classes that will require a realistic amount of time and study. If the student will be working to support themselves, the course load may need to be even lighter.

In working with high school and college students with ADD, we have typically observed that these students seldom consistently achieve grades at a level at which they, or others, expect they are capable. Thus, it's usually preferable to set goals that are attainable and to focus on completion. If completion of a degree is viewed as success, students with ADD and their families can achieve success. If success is viewed as a consistent level of high performance there is a likelihood of failure that may result in a decision to abort the dream. In our experience, it is far better to set realistic expectations and succeed than it is to reach for the stars and fail.

◆ ◆ ◆

Dr. Kendra Johnson, Director of the Office for Accessibility at the University of Toledo; president of Transition Game Educational Consultants, an educational consulting firm specializing in assisting students with disabilities with the transition to college; and co-author of the book, *100 Things Every College Student With a Disability Ought to Know*.

The Ten Most Commonly Asked Questions by Parents of College-Bound Students with Disabilities © Copyrighted. Reprinted with permission from Dr. Kendra Johnson.

1. **Will the disability support services (DSS) provided in college be the same as those provided in high school?**

    It is important to know that colleges and universities provide accommodations under the requirements of the Americans with Disabilities Act and Section 504 of the 1973 Rehabilitation Act. Neither act requires post-secondary institutions to provide accommodations that fundamentally alter the essential requirements of a course, alter the core curriculum of an academic program, or provide assistance that is considered to be "personal" in nature. Therefore, it is feasible that some accommodations provided in high school may not be provided in post-secondary education. For a detailed explanation of the ADA and Section 504 as it pertains to college and university requirements, visit http://postitt.org//frame/legal/compare.htm.

2. **When should we make contact with the disability support (DSS) office?**

    Because the services provided by a DSS office can vary from minimal to extensive, it is important to determine whether the DSS office can meet individual student need before the student enrolls in the institution. Students and parents are strongly encouraged to visit the DSS office as early as their junior year in high school. Each college visit should include a scheduled meeting with the campus DSS office for a detailed investigation of its service offerings.

3. **Is my child's written Individualized Education Program (IEP) sufficient to establish college eligibility for disability support services?**

    An Individualized Education Program (IEP) is a function of the Individuals with Disabilities Education Act (IDEA), a K–12 special education statute. The IDEA does not apply to post-secondary institutions. Thus the IEP, while helpful in establishing a history of using accommodations, does not apply in the post-secondary setting. Colleges will typically require more detailed information of the disability to determine eligibility–information that usually far exceeds what exists within the IEP. A recent psychosocial assessment by a licensed professional will likely be required to establish eligibility for college disability support services. For an example of the most common documentation requirements for students with learning disabilities and Attention deficit disorder seeking college accommodations, visit www.ets.org/.

4. **Should my son or daughter disclose his or her disability on the admission application?**

    College admissions applications are generally prohibited from asking students if they have a disability however, whether to disclose the existence of a disability is a personal decision that should be considered carefully. For example, if a student has overcome significant odds and achieved academically, disclosing the disability in a personal statement highlights their record of accomplishment and could be a benefit. If electing to disclose, the goal is to highlight your academic strengths, not your weaknesses. Whether you choose to disclose or not, post-secondary institutions are not required to waive or lower its admission criteria because a student has a disability.

5. **Are there existing scholarships specifically for students with disabilities?**

Colleges and universities typically offer scholarships for students meeting a wide variety of criteria and characteristics, including disability status. Check with both the college's office of financial aid and scholarship, as well as the DSS office to inquire what is available. Many national organizations serving individuals with disabilities offer scholarships and thus, parents and students should also inquire directly with these organizations. For a comprehensive listing of organizations, review the free listing of Web Resources for Assisting College Students with Disabilities at http://das.kucrl.org/iam/resources.html

6. **Will my son or daughter's disability qualify him or her for a single residence hall room?**

As with all accommodation requests at the post-secondary level, qualification for a single residence hall room will be evaluated on an individualized basis. Students should make their request known to the DSS office before they enroll. The exact nature of the student's disability and the resulting impact on both the student and the potential roommate(s) will be one of the determining factors.

7. **Will the DSS staff have expertise in my child's disability?**

The professional training and background of the DSS office professional staff can vary immensely from campus to campus. Some may have specific certification in learning disabilities and cognitive disorders, while others may have a generalist background in such fields as counseling, education, or social work, to name a few. When investigating the service offered by the DSS office, do not hesitate to inquire about the expertise, training, and credentials of the professional staff.

8. **Are private tutors available?**

The U.S. Department of Education Office of Civil Rights has been consistent in its findings that tutoring is a "personal service" and, therefore, post-secondary institutions are under no obligation to provide it. On most college campuses however, some form of tutoring will be available. Students with disabilities will have access to existing tutoring services on the same basis as other students. Some campuses with comprehensive DSS services may indeed provide specialized, private professional tutoring for students with disabilities, although there may be a fee associated with this specialized service.

9. **Will the college keep me informed of my child's academic progress?**

Colleges and University view enrolled students as adults and will generally place limits on divulging personal information of its students. Further, the Family Educational Rights and Privacy Act (FERPA) limits some of the information the college and DSS office can share with parents without written permission from the student. Therefore, parents should assume that neither the DSS office nor the college will release information relating to a student's academic progress. For a detailed explanation of FERPA, visit www.ed.gov/offices/OM/fpco/ferpa.

10. **Is there a centralized resource that can provide me with detailed information on the DSS offices throughout the country as we begin the college selection process?**

Yes! You have an excellent resource right at your fingertips! *The K & W Guide to Colleges for Students with Learning Disabilities or Attention Deficit Disorder* is an excellent starting point for exploring the wide spectrum of assistance provided by DSS offices in every state. Keep in mind that the goal of college is not just getting in, but getting out successfully. Finding an appropriate DSS office to student match can be the key to that success. *The K & W Guide to Colleges for Students with Learning Disabilities or Attention Deficit Disorder* can help direct you in that roadmap to success.

◆ ◆ ◆

Jeanne M. Kincaid, Esq. Due Process Special Education Hearing Officer, New Hampshire; Adjunct Faculty Member of the University of New Hampshire's Graduate School of Education and the Franklin Pierce Law Center; co-author of Section 504, the ADA and the Schools; contributing author to the publication Disability Compliance for Higher Education; and **Brooke R. Whitted—, Esq.**, Adjunct Faculty, University of Illinois at Chicago (Medical School), practicing special education attorney.

The K&W Guide offers potential students and their families the opportunity to make an educated decision when selecting the proper college or university to meet the student's needs, in light of his or her learning disability. Although nearly every college in the country is subject to Section 504 of the Rehabilitation Act and many also fall within the coverage of the Americans with Disabilities Act (ADA) (both of which prohibit discrimination on the basis of disability), the range of accommodations and services offered by each institution varies considerably.

The following information is designed to assist the student and family in helping to understand what the law minimally requires, determining if the student requires more, and learning what other services might be available. The requirements at the post-secondary level are not the same as those imposed on elementary and high school districts by the Individuals with Disabilities Education Act.

Admissions

Generally, institutions of higher education may not inquire about one's disability prior to acceptance, unless the inquiry is made for affirmative action purposes. However, students and families should consider contacting the college's Section 504/ADA Coordinator, or the Disabled Student Services (DSS) Office, to determine what services the student is likely to receive if accepted by the college. The DSS office may also be helpful in advising the student whether to disclose the presence of a disability in the application. Additionally, should the student choose to enroll at the college, the DSS office can advise the student as to what documentation he may need, in order to ensure that he or she receives timely and effective services are obtained.

Documentation

Documentation serves two important purposes: 1) It establishes that the student has a disability as defined by Section 504 and the ADA; and 2) It guides the college in providing appropriate accommodations for the adult learner. Many colleges require that documentation be no more than three years old. Moreover, as federal law does not obligate a college to conduct assessments, a student should consider requesting that the high school update the assessment, consistent with any requirements of the college in which the student seeks enrollment. For example, some colleges have established guidelines for the type of documentation they require. Checking with the DSS office in advance, however, may yield information about what assessments the college may provide the student free of charge.

Accommodations

At a minimum, a student with a learning disability should be able to expect the following accommodations if the nature of the disability requires such adjustments and is supported by the documentation: a reduced course load, extended time to complete tests and assignments, extended time to complete degree requirements, a note-taker, course substitution of nonessential courses, a quiet testing room, books on tape, the right to tape-record classes, and in some cases, an alternate format for taking tests.

The law does not obligate an institution of higher education to provide all recommended accommodations, but rather effective accommodations. A student should therefore not presume that what he or she received in high school will necessarily be honored at the post-secondary level. However, documentation reflective of a long-standing disability (i.e. since at least sixth or seventh grade) is more effective and speaks louder than a document trail that is relatively recent.

With respect to course load, often students with disabilities benefit greatly from taking less than the average number of courses, particularly during the first year, as the student makes the transition to the rigors of higher education. Nonetheless, as many students with learning disabilities may take five or more years to complete an undergraduate degree, it is important to consider the impact a reduced courseload may have upon financial aid. Although most loans and scholarships should be prorated, rather than lost entirely, colleges handle this issue in a variety of ways. Again, the DSS office should be able to apprise the student of the college's policy.

A critical consideration for college selection is determining the college's general education requirement imposed on all students in order to obtain a degree as well as requirements for graduating with a particular major. Many colleges and universities require one or more courses in foreign language and mathematics. For some students with learning disabilities, no amount of accommodation will result in their successful completion of such requirements. It cannot be emphasized enough how vital it is to review such requirements before selecting your college, as such requirements typically need not be waived based upon disability.

Services

Beyond the accommodations mentioned above, colleges often provide a vast array of additional services. Although a college may not charge for legally mandated accommodations, it may impose a fee for services that go beyond the minimal legal requirements. For example, as discussed throughout this guide, some colleges provide tutoring by personnel specifically trained in working with students with learning disabilities. As tutoring is considered a personal service and not an accommodation, a college may generally charge for such services, to the extent they go beyond the minimum legal standard. Other such services may include assessments, study-skills training, priority registration, counseling, and case management services.

Securing Accommodations

Each campus has its own unique system for providing students with disability-related accommodations. Many give the student a letter detailing recommended accommodations, with instructions to the student to approach the professors in each course so that classroom accommodations are provided in a timely fashion. Some DSS offices send the letter directly to the student's professors. However, the former approach is the trend, as it promotes self-advocacy, a necessary skill for the student's long-term success, both as a student and, in the future, as an employee. Although many professors have received training on the ADA and Section 504, many have not. Therefore, should a professor fail to agree to the recommendations or neglect to carry them out, it is imperative that the student promptly notifies the DSS office, which should intervene accordingly. Unlike public high school, civil rights laws in institutions of higher education do not require that the institution monitor the student's progress to ensure that the accommodations are provided and effective. *It is up to the student to take affirmative steps when problems arise.* Remember, no one is likely to ever know if a note-taker fails to consistently show for a class unless the student notifies the DSS office.

A Final Cautionary Note

Students with hidden disabilities, such as learning disabilities, often wish to attempt college without accommodation. Many students have been "labeled" their entire educational lives and are committed to attempting college on their own terms, without special assistance. Although some succeed without accommodation, court and agency rulings have consistently held that a student who fails to take advantage of available disability-related accommodations does so at his or her peril. Although the ADA is based on promoting success, it also gives individuals with disabilities the right to fail. Before making a decision to forego accommodations, prospective students to consult with the applicable office handling disability issues.

GUIDELINES FOR DOCUMENTATION

Students with disabilities may arrive as freshmen knowing what strategies have worked best for them in a previous learning environment, or they may become injured or diagnosed after they arrive at college and face some unanticipated adjustments to learning and living in a dormitory. In either case, they are asked by institutions of higher learning to provide clinical documentation to assist the school in determining what, if any, accommodations are appropriate now: The mere history of services at an earlier age and in a previous setting may not reflect the intellectual functioning, demands and routines of the new environment.

Rather than expect clinicians to guess how little or how much information is needed, documentation guidelines have been developed over time which are designed to capture the current functional strengths and limitations of each student seeking accommodations. It gives the disability service provider the opportunity to start a conversation with students based on solid information, and promotes communication with professionals to clarify the information, leading to the best opportunity to serve students well.

Our documentation guidelines are designed to parallel those of testing agencies and professional licensure examinations to minimize the need for frequent, expensive retesting. Whatever postsecondary setting the student may enter, this information can lead to excellent self-advocacy skills designed to work with schools and employers to provide the most productive environment possible.

Louise H. Russell, Director
Student Disability Resources, Harvard University

One of the more confusing things about applying to college as a student with a learning disability is answering the questions "What documentation should I send?" and "How will the college use that documentation?" It is important to keep in mind that documentation of your disability cannot be considered during the admission process unless you are requesting special consideration of your application. In cases of special consideration, your disability documentation may help the review committee understand the nature of your learning disability and how it impacted your high school studies. It may also help to explain why you did not complete some high school classes commonly required for admission to your favorite college or university.

Though documentation may be important during the admission process, for most students current, comprehensive documentation becomes critical for receiving appropriate accommodations guaranteed under either the ADA or Section 504.

The Individuals with Disabilities Education Act (IDEA) no longer requires that a disability be reevaluated every three years. It is true that learning disabilities do not go away with age, but the nature of the disability may change and functional limitations may result in difficulties not experienced until college. For this reason, many colleges and universities are requiring that documentation of disability be "current," in many cases within the last three years.

Comprehensive documentation, including measures of aptitude, achievement, and information processing are essential for any college or university to implement the best possible academic accommodation plan. Accommodations are to be provided based on the individual student's functional limitations and each evaluation should point to a link between the test scores and the recommendations the evaluator is making regarding the student's needs. Students sometimes believe that because an evaluator made recommendations in his or her documentation report that those recommendations will be followed. This may not be true. The post-secondary service provider must be able to identify how the functional limitations of the disability necessitate a particular accommodation.

Documentation of learning disabilities should include results of a clinical interview with a medical, family, school, and psychosocial history. This information not only helps to add to the credibility of a diagnosis of learning disability, it frequently helps the service provider to understand the full scope of a student's needs.

Providing comprehensive, current documentation of your learning disability in the form of a report compiled by a well-trained professional will help to assure you the most appropriate support services in college. Make sure you do everything you can to set the stage for your success!

Diane C. Quinn, Ed. Director,
The SALT Center, The University of Arizona

GUIDELINES FOR DOCUMENTATION OF LEARNING DISABILITIES

INTRODUCTION

This section describes standard criteria for documenting learning disabilities (LD) that can be used to determine appropriate accommodations for individuals with learning disabilities in postsecondary settings. The two official nomenclatures designed to outline the criteria used in making these diagnoses are the *Diagnostic and Statistical Manual of Mental Disorders*, Fourth Edition, Text Revision, published by the American Psychiatric Association (DSM-IV-TR) and *The International Statistical Classification of Diseases and Related Health Problems*, Tenth Revision, published by the World Health Organization (ICD-10). In instances where there may be multiple diagnoses including AD(H)D disabilities and psychiatric disabilities, evaluators should consult the appropriate companion guidelines that can be found at the Continuing Education website, www.dce.harvard.edu. The guidelines provide students, professional diagnosticians, and service providers with a common understand-ing and knowledge base of those components of documentation which are necessary to validate a learning disability and the need for accommodation in this postsecondary setting. The information and documentation to be submitted should be comprehensive in order to avoid or reduce time delays in decision-making related to the provision of services.

This section presents guidelines in four important areas:
1. Qualifications of the evaluator
2. Recentness of documentation
3. Appropriate clinical documentation to substantiate the learning disability
4. Evidence to establish a rationale supporting the need for accommodation(s)

Under the Americans with Disabilities Act (ADA) and Section 504 of the Rehabilitation Act of 1973, individuals with disabilities are guaranteed certain protections and rights to equal access to programs and services. In order to establish that an individual is covered under the ADA, the documentation must indicate that the disability substantially limits one or more major life activity, and supports the request for accommodations, academic adjustments, and/or auxiliary aids. A diagnosis of a disorder/condition alone does not automatically qualify an individual for accommodations under the ADA. The following documentation guidelines are provided in the interest of assuring that a clinically documented learning disability appropriately verifies eligibility and may support some or all requests for accommodations, academic adjustments, and/or auxiliary aids.

Clinical documentation of a learning disability which is submitted to the Division of Continuing Education for the purpose of seeking accommodations is expected to meet the standards set forth in these guidelines. All clinical documentation is reviewed by the Division of Continuing Education and its consultants, as required, to determine what, if any, accommodations are appropriate to the settings for which they are intended. Although a previous history of accommodation may provide valuable insight into the student's ability to integrate into a previous setting, the Division of Continuing Education makes an independent judgment about Harvard settings and the appropriateness, if any, of accommodation requests.

Appendix A provides consumers with recommendations for finding and working with a qualified professional. A suggested listing of standardized tests for assessing adolescents and adults with suspected learning disabilities is included in Appendix B.

Documentation Guidelines

I. A Qualified Professional Must Conduct the Evaluation
   Professionals conducting assessments and rendering diagnoses of specific learning disabilities and making recommendations for appropriate accommodations must be qualified to do so. Comprehensive training and relevant experience with an adolescent and adult LD population are essential. Competence in working with culturally and linguistically diverse populations is also essential.

The name, title, and professional credentials of the evaluator, including information about license or certification (e.g., licensed psychologist) as well as the area of specialization, employment, and state in which the individual practices, must be clearly stated in the documentation. For example, the following professionals would generally be considered qualified to evaluate specific learning disabilities provided that they have additional training and experience in evaluating adolescent/adult learning disabilities: clinical or educational psychologists; school psychologists; neurophysiologists; learning disabilities specialists; and medical doctors with training and experience in the assessment of learning problems in adolescents and adults.

Use of diagnostic terminology indicating a specific learning disability by someone whose training and experience are not in these fields is not acceptable. It is not appropriate for professionals to evaluate members of their own families. All reports should be on letterhead, they should be typed, dated, signed, and otherwise legible.

II. Testing Must Be Current

Because the provision of all reasonable accommodations and services is based upon assessment of the current impact of the student's disabilities on his or her academic performance, it is in a student's best interest to provide recent and appropriate documentation. In most cases, it is recommended that testing have been conducted within the past three years.

III. Documentation Necessary to Substantiate the Learning Disability Must Be Comprehensive

Prior documentation may have been useful in determining appropriate services in the past. However, documentation must validate the need for services based on the individual's current level of functioning in the educational setting. A school plan such as an individualized educational plan (IEP) or a 504 plan is insufficient documentation in and of itself, but can be included as part of a more comprehensive assessment battery. A comprehensive assessment battery and the resulting diagnostic report should include a diagnostic interview, assessment of aptitude, academic achievement, and information processing.

A. Diagnostic Interview

Because learning disabilities are commonly manifested during childhood, though not always formally diagnosed, relevant historical information regarding the student's academic history and learning processes in elementary, secondary, and postsecondary education must be investigated and documented. An evaluation report should include the summary of a comprehensive diagnostic interview by a qualified evaluator.

By using a combination of student self-report, interviews with others, and historical documentation such as transcripts and standardized test scores, the diagnostician should provide a summary of the following:

1. A description of the presenting problem(s)
2. Developmental history
3. Relevant medical history including the absence of a medical basis for the present symptoms
4. Academic history including results of prior standardized testing; reports of classroom performance
5. Relevant family history, including primary language of the home, and the student's current level of fluency of English
6. Psychosocial history
7. Relevant employment history
8. A discussion of dual diagnosis, alternative or coexisting mood, behavioral, neurological, and/or personality disorders along with any history of relevant medication and current use which may impact the individual's learning; and exploration of possible alternatives which may mimic a learning disability when, in fact, one is not present.

B. Assessment

The neuropsychological or psychoeducational evaluation for the diagnosis of a specific learning disability must provide clear and specific evidence that a learning disability does or does not exist. Assessment, and any resulting diagnosis, must consist of and be based upon a comprehensive assessment battery that does not rely on any one test or subtest.

Objective evidence of a substantial limitation to learning must be provided. A list of acceptable tests is included in Appendix A. Minimally, the domains to be addressed must include the following:

1. Aptitude/Cognitive Ability—A complete intellectual assessment with all subtests and standard scores reported is essential.

2. Academic Achievement—A comprehensive academic achievement battery is essential with all subtests and standard scores reported for those subtests administered. The battery must include current levels of academic functioning in relevant areas such as reading (decoding and comprehension), mathematics, and oral and written language.

3. Information Processing—Specific areas of information processing (e.g., short- and long-term memory; sequential memory; auditory and visual perception/processing; processing speed; executive functioning; motor ability) should be assessed.

4. Other Assessment Measures—Non-standard measures and informal assessment procedures or observations may be helpful in determining performance across a variety of domains. Other formal assessment measures may be integrated with the above instruments to help rule in or rule out the learning disability to differentiate it from coexisting neurological and/or psychiatric disorders, i.e., to establish a differential diagnosis. The evaluator should address why these assessments were included in addition to the standard measures. In addition to standardized tests, it is also very useful to include informal observations of the student during the test administration.

C. The Documentation Must Include a Specific Diagnosis

Nonspecific diagnoses, such as individual "learning styles," "learning differences," "academic problems," "computer phobias," "slow reader," and "test difficulty or anxiety," in and of themselves do not constitute a learning disability. It is important to rule out alternative explanations for problems in learning, such as emotional, attentional, or motivational problems that may be interfering with learning but do not constitute a learning disability. The diagnostician is encouraged to use direct language in the diagnosis and documentation of a learning disability, avoiding the use of such terms as "suggests" or "is indicative of."

If the data indicates that a learning disability is not present, the evaluator must state that conclusion in the report.

D. Actual Test Scores From Standardized Instruments Must Be Provided

Standard scores and/or percentiles must be provided for all normed measures. Reports of grade equivalents must be accompanied by standard scores and/or percentiles. The data must logically reflect a substantial limitation to learning for which the student is requesting the accommodation. The particular profile of the student's strengths and weaknesses must be shown to relate to functional limitations that may necessitate accommodations.

The tests used should be reliable, valid, and standardized for use with an adolescent/adult population. The test findings must document both the nature and severity of the learning disability. Informal inventories, surveys, and direct observation by a qualified professional may be used in tandem with formal tests in order to further develop a clinical hypothesis.

E. Each Accommodation Recommended by the Evaluator Must Include a Rationale

It is important to recognize that accommodation needs can change over time and are not always identified through the initial diagnostic process. Conversely, a prior history of accommodation, without demonstration of a current need, does not in and of itself warrant the provision of a like accommodation.

The diagnostic report must include specific recommendations for accommodation(s), as well as a detailed explanation of why each accommodation is recommended. The evaluator(s) must describe the impact the diagnosed learning disability has on a specific major life activity, as well as the degree of significance of this impact on the individual. The evaluator(s) should support recommendations with specific test results or clinical observations. If no prior accommodation(s) has been provided, the qualified professional and/or the student should include a detailed explanation of why no accommodation(s) was used in the past and why an accommodation(s) is needed at this time.

If an accommodation(s) is not clearly identified in the diagnostic report, the Division of Continuing Education will seek clarification, and if necessary, more information. The division will make the determination as to whether appropriate and reasonable accommodations are warranted and can be provided to the individual.

IV. A Clinically Interpretive Summary Must be Provided

A well-written diagnostic summary based on a comprehensive evaluative process is a necessary component of the report. Assessment instruments and the data they provide do not diagnose; rather, they provide important elements that must be integrated with background information, observations of the client during the testing situation, and the current context. It is essential, therefore, that professional judgment be used in the development of a clinical summary.

A. The clinical summary must include:

1. Indication that the evaluator ruled out alternative explanations for academic problems such as poor education, poor motivation and/or study skills, emotional problems, attentional problems, and cultural/language differences

2. Indication of how patterns in cognitive ability, achievement, and information processing are used to determine the presence of a learning disability

3. Indication of the substantial limitation to learning presented by the learning disability and the degree to which it affects the individual in the learning context for which accommodations are being requested

4. Indication of why specific accommodations are needed and how the effects of the specific disability are mediated by the accommodation.

V. Accountability and Confidentiality

Reasonable accommodation(s) may help to ameliorate the disability and to minimize its impact on the student's clinically documented difficulties in this particular setting.

The determination of reasonable accommodation(s) rests with the Division of Continuing Education in collaboration with the individual with the disability and, when appropriate, faculty, all of whom have a responsibility to maintain confidentiality of any information. The student is responsible for obtaining and providing the division with all relevant materials in a timely manner. Continuing Education may not release any part of the documentation without the individual's informed consent. If the requested accommodations are not clearly identified in the diagnostic report, the Division of Continuing Education reserves the right to seek additional clinical information pertaining to determination of eligibility for requested accommodations.

Appendix A—Recommendations for Consumers

1. For assistance in finding a qualified professional:

   a) Contact the disability services coordinator at the institution you attend or plan to attend to discuss documentation needs.

   b) Discuss your future plans with the disability services coordinator. If additional documentation is required, seek assistance in identifying a qualified professional.

2. In selecting a qualified professional:

   a) Ask what his or her credentials are.

   b) Ask what experience he or she has had working with adults with learning disabilities.

   c) Ask if he or she has ever worked with the service provider at your institution or with the agency to which you are sending material.

3. In working with the professional:

   a) Take a copy of these guidelines to the professional.

   b) Encourage him or her to clarify questions with the person who provided you with these guidelines.

c) Be prepared to be forthcoming, thorough, and honest with requested information.

d) Know that professionals must maintain confidentiality with respect to your records and testing information.

4. As follow-up to the assessment by the professional:

a) Request a written copy of the assessment report.

b) Request the opportunity to discuss the results and recommendations.

b) Request additional resources if you need them.

c) Maintain a personal file of your records and reports.

Appendix B—Tests for Assessing Adolescents and Adults

When selecting a battery of tests, it is critical to consider the technical adequacy of instruments including their reli-ability, validity and standardization on an appropriate norm group. The professional judgment of an evaluator in choosing tests is important.

The following list is provided as a helpful resource, but it is not intended to be definitive or exhaustive.

Aptitude

- Wechsler Adult Intelligence Scale–Revised (WAIS–R)
- Woodcock-Johnson Psychoeducational Battery–Revised: Tests of Cognitive Ability
- Kaufman Adolescent and Adult Intelligence Test
- Stanford-Binet Intelligence Scale (4th Ed.)
- The Slosson Intelligence Test–Revised and the Kaufman Brief Intelligence Test are primarily screening devices that are not comprehensive enough to provide the kinds of information necessary to make accommodation decisions.

Academic Achievement

- Scholastic Abilities Test for Adults (SATA)
- Stanford Test of Academic Skills
- Woodcock-Johnson Psychoeducational Battery–Revised: Tests of Achievement
- Wechsler Individual Achievement Test (WIAT)

Or Specific Achievement Tests Such As:

- Nelson-Denny Reading Skills Test
- Stanford Diagnostic Mathematics Test
- Test of Written Language–3 (TOWL–3)
- Woodcock Reading Mastery Tests–Revised

Specific achievement tests are useful instruments when administered under standardized conditions and interpreted within the context of other diagnostic information. The Wide Range Achievement Test–3 (WRAT–3) is not a comprehensive measure of achievement and therefore is not useful if used as the sole measure of achievement.

Information Processing

Acceptable instruments include the Detroit Tests of Learning Aptitude–3 (DTLA–3), the Detroit Tests of Learning Aptitude–Adult (DTLA–A), information from subtests on WAIS–R, Woodcock-Johnson Psychoeducational Battery–Revised: Tests of Cognitive Ability, as well as other relevant instruments.

Adapted from Ad Hoc Committee on Learning Disabilities, Revised July 2001, ©Educational Testing Service 1999; Loring Brinckerhoff, Ad Hoc Committee Chairperson, ©Educational Testing Service; Joan McGuire, Ad Hoc Committee Liaison to the Board, University of Connecticut–Storrs; Kim Dempsey, Law School Admission Council; Cyndi Jordan, University of Tennessee–Memphis; Shelby Keiser, National Board of Medical Examiners; Catherine Nelson, ©Educational Testing Service; Nancy Pompian, Dartmouth College; Louise H. Russell, Harvard University. AHEAD—Guidelines for Documenting LD—July 1997.

GUIDELINES FOR DOCUMENTATION OF ATTENTION DEFICIT (HYPERACTIVITY) DISORDER (ADD)

INTRODUCTION

Under the Americans with Disabilities Act (ADA) and Section 504 of the Rehabilitation Act of 1973, individuals with disabilities are protected from discrimination and may be entitled to reasonable accommodations and rights to equal access to programs and services. To establish that an individual is covered under the ADA, the documentation must indicate that the disability substantially limits one or more major life activity, and supports the request for accommodations, academic adjustments, and/or auxiliary aids. A diagnosis of a disorder/condition alone does not automatically qualify an individual for accommodations under the ADA.

These guidelines are based on the AHEAD (Association on Higher Education and Disability) guidelines as recommended by the Consortium on AD(H)D Documentation © 1998. The mission of the Consortium was to develop standard criteria for documenting attention deficit disorders, with or without hyperactivity (AD(H)D). Modified versions of these guidelines can be used by postsecondary personnel, examining, certifying, and licensing agencies, and consumers who require documentation to determine reasonable and appropriate accommodation(s) for individuals with AD(H)D. Although the more generic term, attention deficit disorder (ADD), is frequently used, the official nomenclature in the *Diagnostic and Statistical Manual of Mental Disorders*, Fourth Edition (DSM-IV-TR) (American Psychiatric Association, © 2000) is attention deficit/hyperactivity disorder (AD(H)D), which is used in these guidelines. The guidelines provide consumers, professional diagnosti-cians, and service providers with an understanding and knowledge base of the components of documentation that are necessary to validate the existence of AD(H)D, its impact on the individual's educational performance, and the need for accommodation(s). The information and documentation to be submitted should be comprehensive in order to avoid or reduce unnecessary time delays in decision-making related to the provision of services.

Clinical documentation of AD(H)D that is submitted to the Division of Continuing Education for the purpose of seeking accommodations is expected to meet the standards set forth in these guidelines. All clinical documentation is reviewed by the Division and its consultants, as required, to determine what, if any, accommodations are appropriate to the settings for which they are intended. Although a previous history of accommodation may provide valuable insight into the student's ability to integrate into a previous setting, the Division of Continuing Education makes independent judgment about Harvard settings and the appropriateness, if any, of accommodation requests.

In the main section of the document, the Consortium presents guidelines in four important areas:

1) Qualifications of the evaluator
2) Recentness of documentation
3) Comprehensiveness of the documentation to substantiate the AD(H)D
4) Evidence to establish a rationale to support the need for accommodation(s)

Appendix A provides diagnostic criteria for AD(H)D reprinted with permission from the *Diagnostic and Statistical Manual of Mental Disorders*, Fourth Edition, Text Revision (DSM-IV-TR), Copyright 2000 American Psychiatric Association. Appendices B, C, and D provide recommendations for consumers, suggestions for assessment, and a listing of resources and organizations, respectively.

This document provides guidelines necessary to establish the impact of AD(H)D disabilities on the individual's educational performance and participation in other university programs and activities, and to validate the need for accommodations. The two official nomenclatures designed to outline the criteria used in making these diagnoses are the *Diagnostic and Statistical Manual* (DSM-IV-TR) and the ICD-10 (*The International Statistical Classification of Diseases and Related Health Problems*, Tenth Revision, published by the World Health Organization). In instances where there may be multiple diagnoses including learning disabilities and psychiatric disabilities, evaluators should consult the appropriate companion guidelines available from the Division of Continuing Education. Information and documentation submitted by students to verify accommodation eligibility must be comprehensive in order to avoid unnecessary delays in decision making related to the provision of requested accommodations.

Documentation Guidelines

I. A Qualified Professional Must Conduct the Evaluation

    Professionals conducting assessments and rendering diagnoses of AD(H)D must have training in differential diagnosis and the full range of psychiatric disorders. The name, title, and professional credentials of the evaluator, including information about license or certification as well as the area of specialization, employment, and state or province in which the individual practices, should be clearly stated in the documentation. The following professionals would generally be considered qualified to evaluate and diagnose AD(H)D provided they have comprehensive training in the differential diagnosis of AD(H)D and direct experience with an adolescent or adult AD(H)D population: clinical psychologists, neurophysiologists, psychiatrists, and other relevantly trained medical doctors. It may be appropriate to use a clinical team approach consisting of a variety of educational, medical, and counseling professionals with training in the evaluation of AD(H)D in adolescents and adults.

    Use of diagnostic terminology indicating an AD(H)D by someone whose training and experience are not in these fields is not acceptable. It is also not appropriate for professionals to evaluate members of their own families. All reports should be on letterhead, typed, dated, signed, and otherwise legible. The receiving institution or agency has the responsibility to maintain the confidentiality of the individual's records.

II. Documentation Must be Current

    Because the provision of all reasonable accommodations and services is based upon assessment of the current impact of the disability on academic performance, it is in an individual's best interest to provide recent and appropriate documentation. In most cases, this means that a diagnostic evaluation has been completed within the past three years. Flexibility in accepting documentation that exceeds a three-year period may be important under certain conditions if the previous assessment is applicable to the current or anticipated setting. If documentation is inadequate in scope or content, or does not address the individual's current level of functioning and need for accommodation(s), reevaluation may be warranted. Furthermore, observed changes may have occurred in the individual's performance since previous assessment, or new medication(s) may have been prescribed or discontinued since the previous assessment was conducted. In such cases, it may be necessary to update the evaluation report. The update should include a detailed assessment of the current impact of the AD(H)D and interpretive summary of relevant information and the previous diagnostic report.

III. Documentation Should be Comprehensive

    A. Evidence of Early Impairment

        Because AD(H)D is, by definition, first exhibited in childhood (although it may not have been formally diagnosed) and manifests itself in more than one setting, relevant historical information is essential. The following should be included in a comprehensive assessment: clinical summary of objective, historical information establishing symptomology indicative of AD(H)D throughout childhood, adolescence, and adulthood as garnered from transcripts, report cards, teacher comments, tutoring evaluations, past Psychoeducational testing, and third party interviews when available.

    B. Evidence of Current Impairment

        In addition to providing evidence of a childhood history of impairment, the following areas must be investigated:

        1. Statement of Presenting Problem—A history of the individual's presenting attentional symptoms should be provided, including evidence of ongoing impulsive/hyperactive or inattentive behaviors that significantly impair functioning in two or more settings.

2. Diagnostic Interview—The information collected for the summary of the diagnostic interview should consist of more than self-report, as information from third party sources is critical in the diagnosis of AD(H)D. The diagnostic interview with information from a variety of sources should include, but not necessarily be limited to, the following:

- History of presenting attentional symptoms, including evidence of ongoing impulsive/ hyperactive or inattentive behavior that has significantly impaired functioning over time
- Developmental history
- Family history for presence of AD(H)D and other educational, learning, physical, or psychological difficulties deemed relevant by the examiner
- Relevant medical and medication history, including the absence of a medical basis for the symptoms being evaluated
- Relevant psychosocial history and any relevant interventions
- A thorough academic history of elementary, secondary, and postsecondary education
- Review of prior psychoeducational test reports to determine whether a pattern of strengths or weaknesses is supportive of attention or learning problems
- Relevant employment history
- Description of current functional limitations pertaining to an educational setting that are presumably a direct result of problems with attention
- Relevant history of prior therapy

C. Rule Out Alternative Diagnoses or Explanations

The evaluator must investigate and discuss the possibility of dual diagnoses, and alternative or coexisting mood, behavioral, neurological, and/or personality disorders that may confound the diagnosis of AD(H)D. This process should include exploration of possible, alternative diagnoses, and medical and psychiatric disorders, as well as educational and cultural factors impacting the individual that may result in behaviors mimicking an attention deficit/hyperactivity disorder.

D. Relevant Testing Information Must Be Provided

The assessment of the individual must not only establish a diagnosis of AD(H)D, but must also demonstrate the current impact of the AD(H)D on an individual's ability to take standardized tests. In addition, neuropsychological or psychoeducational assessment is important in determining the current impact of the disorder on an individual's ability to function in academically related settings. The evaluator must objectively review and include with the evaluation report relevant background information to support the diagnosis and its impact within the current educational environment. If grade equivalents are reported, they must be accompanied by standard scores and/or percentiles.

Test scores or subtest scores alone should not be used as a sole measure for the diagnostic decision regarding AD(H)D. Selected subtest scores from measures of intellectual ability, memory functions tests, attention or tracking tests, or continuous performance tests do not in and of themselves establish the pres-ence or absence of AD(H)D. Checklists and/or surveys can serve to supplement the diagnostic profile but in and of themselves are not adequate for the diagnosis of AD(H)D and do not substitute for clinical observations and sound diagnostic judgment. All data must logically reflect a substantial limitation to learning for which the individual is requesting accommodation.

E. Identification of DSM–IV–TR Criteria

According to the DSM–IV–TR, "the essential feature of AD(H)D is a persistent pattern of inattention and/or hyperactivity-impulsivity that is more frequent and severe than is typically observed in individuals at a comparable level of development" (page 85). A diagnostic report should include a review and discussion of the DSM–IV–TR criteria for AD(H)D both currently and retrospectively and specify which symptoms are present (see Appendix A for DSM–IV–TR criteria). In diagnosing AD(H)D, it is particularly important to address the following criteria: symptoms of hyperactivity/impulsivity or inattention that cause impairment which must have been present in childhood; current symptoms that have been present for at least the past six months; impairment from the symptoms present in two or more settings (for example, school, work, and home); clear evidence of significant impairment in social, academic, or occupational functioning; and symptoms that do not occur exclusively during the course of a pervasive developmental disorder, schizophrenia, or other psychotic disorder and are not better accounted for by another mental disorder (e.g., mood disorder, anxiety disorder, dissociative disorder, or a personality disorder).

F. Documentation Must Include a Specific Diagnosis

The report must include a specific diagnosis of AD(H)D based on the DSM–IV diagnostic criteria. The diagnostician should use direct language in the diagnosis of AD(H)D, avoiding the use of terms such as "suggests," "is indicative of," or "attention problems." Individuals who report only problems with organization, test anxiety, memory, and concentration in selective situations do not fit the proscribed diagnostic criteria for AD(H)D. Given that many individuals benefit from prescribed medications and therapies, a positive response to medication by itself does not confirm a diagnosis, nor does the use of medication in and of itself either support or negate the need for accommodation(s).

G. An Interpretative Summary Should Be Provided

A well-written interpretative summary based on a comprehensive evaluative process is a necessary component of the documentation. Because AD(H)D is in many ways a diagnosis that is based upon the interpretation of historical data and observation, as well as other diagnostic information, it is essential that professional judg-ment be utilized in the development of a summary, which should include:

- Demonstration of the evaluator having ruled out alternative explanations for inattentiveness, impulsivity, and/or hyperactivity as a result of psychological or medical disorders or non-cognitive factors
- Indication of how patterns of inattentiveness, impulsivity, and/or hyperactivity across the life span and across settings are used to determine the presence of AD(H)D
- Indication of whether or not the student was evaluated while on medication, and whether or not there is a positive response to the prescribed treatment
- Indication and discussion of the substantial limitation to learning presented by the AD(H)D and the degree to which it impacts the individual in the learning context for which accommodations are being requested. Indication as to why specific accommodations are needed and how the effects of AD(H)D symptoms, as designated by the DSM–IV–TR, are mediated by the accommodation(s).

IV. Each Accommodation Recommendation by the Evaluator Should Include a Rationale

The evaluator(s) should describe the impact, if any, of the diagnosed AD(H)D on a specific major life activity as well as the degree of impact on the individual. The diagnostic report should include specific recommendations for accommodations that are realistic and that postsecondary institutions examining, certifying, and licensing agencies can reasonably provide. A detailed explanation should be provided as to why each accommodation is recommended and should be correlated with specific functional limitations determined through interview, observation, and/or testing. Although prior documentation may have been useful in determining appropriate services in the past, current documentation should validate the need for services based on the individual's present level of functioning in the educational setting. A school plan such as an individualized education program (IEP) or a 504 plan is insufficient documentation in and of itself but can be included as part of a more comprehensive evaluative report. The documentation should include any record of prior accommodations or auxiliary aids, including information about specific conditions under which the accommodations were used (e.g., standardized testing, final exams, licensing or certification examinations) and whether or not they benefitted the individual. However, a prior history of accommodations, without demonstration of a current need, does not in itself warrant the provision of a like accommodation. If no prior accommodations were provided, the qualified professional and/or the individual should include a detailed explanation as to why no accommodations were used in the past and why accommoda-tions are needed at this time.

Because of the challenge of distinguishing normal behaviors and developmental patterns of adolescents and adults (e.g., procrastination, disorganization, distractibility, restlessness, boredom, academic underachieve-ment or failure, low self-esteem, and chronic tardiness or inattendance) from clinically significant impairment, a multifaceted evaluation should address the intensity and frequency of the symptoms and whether these behaviors constitute an impairment in a major life activity.

If an accommodation(s) is not clearly identified in the diagnostic report, the Division of Continuing Education will seek clarification, and, if necessary, more information. The Division of Continuing Education will make the determination as to whether appropriate and reasonable accommodations are warranted and can be provided to the individual.

V. Accountability and Confidentiality

Reasonable accommodation(s) may help to ameliorate the disability and to minimize its impact on the student's clinically documented difficulties in this particular setting. The determination for reasonable accommodation(s) rests with the Division of Continuing Education in collaboration with the individual with the disability and, when appropriate, faculty, all of whom have a responsibility to maintain confidentiality of any information. The student is responsible for obtaining and providing the Division of Continuing Education with all relevant materials in a timely manner. The Division of Continuing Education may not release any part of the documentation without the individual's informed consent, except in the case of a court ordered subpoena. If the requested accommodations are not clearly identified in the diagnostic report, the Division of Continuing Education reserves the right to seek additional clinical information pertaining to determination of eligibility for requested accommodations.

Appendix A—DSM–IV–TR Diagnostic Criteria for AD(H)D

Permission is required to reproduce the DSM–IV–TR. The following excerpt, that comprises appendix A, is reprinted with permission from the *Diagnostic and Statistical Manual of Mental Disorders*, Fourth Edition, Text Revision, Washington, DC, American Psychiatric Association, 2000, pp. 92–93.

Diagnostic criteria for Attention-Deficit/Hyperactivity Disorder

A. Either (1) or (2):

    (1) Six (or more) of the following symptoms of inattention have persisted for at least 6 months to a degree that is maladaptive and inconsistent with developmental level:

Inattention

    a) Often fails to give close attention to details or makes careless mistakes in schoolwork, work, or other activities

    b) Often has difficulty sustaining attention in tasks or play activities

    c) Often does not seem to listen when spoken to directly

    d) Often does not follow through on instructions and fails to finish schoolwork, chores, or duties in the workplace (not due to oppositional behavior or failure to understand instructions)

    e) Often has difficulty organizing tasks and activities

    f) Often avoids, dislikes, or is reluctant to engage in tasks that require sustained mental effort (such as schoolwork or homework)

    g) Often loses things necessary for tasks or activities (e.g., toys, school assignments, pencils, books, or tools)

    h) Is often easily distracted by extraneous stimuli

    i) Is often forgetful in daily activities

    (2) Six (or more) of the following symptoms of hyperactivity-impulsivity have persisted for at least 6 months to a degree that is maladaptive and inconsistent with developmental level:

Hyperactivity

    a) Often fidgets with hands or feet or squirms in seat

    b) Often leaves seat in classroom or in other situations in which remaining seated is expected

    c) Often runs about or climbs excessively in situations in which it is inappropriate (in adolescents or adults, may be limited to subjective feelings of restlessness)

    d) Often has difficulty playing or engaging in leisure activities quietly

    e) Is often "on the go" or often acts as if "driven by a motor"

    f) Often talks excessively

Impulsivity

    g) Often blurts out answers before questions have been completed

    h) Often has difficulty awaiting turn

    i) Often interrupts or intrudes on others (e.g., butts into conversations or games)

B. Some hyperactive-impulsive or inattentive symptoms that caused impairment were present before age 7 years.

C. Some impairment from the symptoms is present in two or more settings (e.g., at school [or work] and at home).

D. There must be clear evidence of clinically significant impairment in social, academic, or occupational functioning.

E. The symptoms do not occur exclusively during the course of a pervasive developmental disorder, schizophrenia, or other psychotic disorder and are not better accounted for by another mental disorder (e.g., mood disorder, anxiety disorder, dissociative disorder, or a personality disorder).

The DSM–IV–TR specifies a code designation based on type:

314.01 Attention Deficit/Hyperactivity Disorder, Combined Type:

If both Criteria A1 and A2 are met for the past 6 months.

314.00 Attention Deficit/Hyperactivity Disorder, Predominantly Inattentive Type:

If Criterion A1 is met but Criterion A2 is not met for the past 6 months.

314.01 Attention Deficit/Hyperactivity Disorder, Predominantly Hyperactive-Impulsive Type:

If Criterion A2 is met but Criterion A1 is not met for the past 6 months.

Coding note: For individuals (especially adolescents and adults) who currently have symptoms that no longer meet full criteria, "In Partial Remission" should be specified.

314.9 Attention Deficit/Hyperactivity Disorder Not Otherwise Specified

This category is for disorders with prominent symptoms of inattention or hyperactivity-impulsivity that do not meet criteria for Attention-Deficit/Hyperactivity Disorder.

Examples include

1. Individuals whose symptoms and impairment meet the criteria for attention deficit/hyperactivity disorder, predominately inattentive type but whose age at onset is 7 years or after

2. Individuals with clinically significant impairment who present with inattention and whose symptom pattern does not meet the full criteria for the disorder but have a behavioral pattern marked by sluggishness, daydreaming, and hypoactivity

Appendix B—Recommendations for Consumers

For assistance in finding a qualified professional:

Contact the disability services coordinator at a college or university for possible referral sources; and/or contact a physician who may be able to refer you to a qualified professional with demonstrated expertise in AD(H)D.

In selecting a qualified professional:

- Ask what experience and training he or she has had diagnosing adolescents and adults;
- Ask whether he or she has training in differential diagnosis and the full range of psychiatric disorders. Clinicians typically qualified to diagnose AD(H)D may include clinical psychologists, physicians, including psychiatrists, and neuropsychologists;
- Ask whether he or she has ever worked with a postsecondary disability service provider or with the agency to whom you are providing documentation;
- Ask whether you will receive a comprehensive written report.

In working with the professional:

- Take a copy of these guidelines to the professional;
- Be prepared to be forthcoming, thorough, and honest with requested information.

As follow-up to the assessment by the professional:

- Schedule a meeting to discuss the results, recommendations, and possible treatment;
- Request additional resources, support group information, and publications if you need them;
- Maintain a personal file of your records and reports;
- Be aware that any receiving institution or agency has a responsibility to maintain confidentiality.

Appendix C—Suggestions for Assessment

The diagnosis of AD(H)D is strongly dependent on a clinical interview in conjunction with a variety of formal and informal measures. Since there is no one test, or specified combination of tests, for determining AD(H)D, the diagnosis of an attention deficit/hyperactivity disorder (AD(H)D) requires a multifaceted approach. Any tests that are selected by the evaluator should be technically accurate, reliable, valid, and standardized on the appropriate norm group. The following list includes five broad domains that are frequently explored when arriving at an AD(H)D diagnosis. This listing is provided as a helpful resource but is not intended to be definitive or exhaustive.

1. Clinical interview

   The evaluator should:

   a) Provide retrospective confirmation of AD(H)D;

   b) Establish relevant developmental and academic markers;

   c) Determine any other coexisting disorders; and

   d) Rule out other problems that may mimic AD(H)D.

   Specific areas to be addressed include:

   - Family history
   - Results of a neuromedical history
   - Presence of AD(H)D symptoms since childhood
   - Presence of AD(H)D symptoms in last six months
   - Evidence that symptoms cause a "significant impairment" over time
   - Results of clinical observation for hyperactive behavior, impulsive speech, distractibility
   - Extent of functional impairment across settings (e.g., academic, occupational, social)
   - An accounting for periods in which student was symptom-free
   - Presence of other psychiatric conditions (mood or anxiety disorders, substance abuse, etc.)
   - Indication that symptoms are not due to other conditions (e.g., depression, drug use, neuromedical problems)
   - Relevant medication history
   - Determination of which remediation approaches and/or compensating strategies are and are not currently effective
   - Determination of what accommodations, if any, have alleviated symptoms in the past or in the present setting

2. Rating scales

   Self-rater or interviewer-rated scales for categorizing and quantifying the nature of the impairment may be useful in conjunction with other data. Selected examples include:

   - Wender Utah Rating Scale
   - Brown Attention-Activation Disorder Scale
   - Beck Anxiety Inventory
   - Hamilton's Depression Rating Scale
   - Conners Teacher Rating Scale (age 3–17 years)
   - Conners Parent Rating Scale (age 3–17 years)

3. Neuropsychological and Psychoeducational testing

   Cognitive and achievement profiles may suggest attention or information processing deficits. No single test or subtest should be used as the sole basis for a diagnostic decision. Acceptable documents include, but are not limited to:

   Aptitude/Cognitive Ability

   - Wechsler Adult Intelligence Scale–III (WAIS–III)
   - Woodcock-Johnson Psychoeducational Battery–Revised: Tests of Cognitive Ability
   - Kaufman Adolescent and Adult Intelligence Test

   Academic Achievement

   - Scholastic Abilities Test for Adults (SATA)

- Stanford Test of Academic Skills (TASK)
- Woodcock-Johnson Psychoeducational Battery–Revised: Tests of

Cognitive Achievement

- Wechsler Individual Achievement Test (WIAT) or specific achievement tests such as
- Nelson-Denny Reading Skills Test
- Stanford Diagnostic Mathematics Test
- Test of Written Language–3 (TOWL–3)
- Woodcock Reading Master Tests–Revised

Information Processing

- Detroit Tests of Learning Aptitude–3 (DTLA–3) or Detroit Tests of Learning Aptitude–Adult (DTLA–A).
- Information from subtests on WAIS–R or Woodcock-Johnson Psychoeducational Battery–Revised: Tests of Cognitive Ability,
- As well as other relevant instruments, may be useful when interpreted within the context of other diagnostic information.

4. Medical evaluation

Medical disorders may cause symptoms resembling AD(H)D. Therefore, it may be important to rule out the following:

- Neuroendocrine disorders (e.g., thyroid dysfunction)
- Neurologic disorders
- Impact of medication on attention if tried, and under what circumstances

5. Collateral information

Include third party sources that can be helpful to determine the presence or absence of AD(H)D in childhood:

- Description of current symptoms (e.g., by spouse, teachers, employer)
- Description of childhood symptoms (e.g., by parent)
- Information from old school and report cards and transcripts

Appendix D—Resources and Organizations

Association on Higher Education and Disability (AHEAD)

University of Massachusetts
100 Morrissey Boulevard
Boston, MA 02125-3393
617-287-3880
617-287-3881 FAX
www.AHEAD.org

An excellent organization to contact for individuals with disabilities who are planning to attend college and who will need accom-modations. Numerous training programs, workshops, publications, and conferences.

Children and Adults with Attention Deficit Disorders (CHADD)

8181 Professional Place, Suite 201
Landover, MD 20785
800-233-4050 toll free
301-306-7070
301-306-7090 FAX
www.chadd.org

CHADD is a national organiza-tion with over 32,000 members and more than 500 chapters nationwide that provides support and informa-tion for parents who have children with ADD and adults with ADD.

Council for Exceptional Children

1920 Association Drive
Reston, VA 22091-1589
888-CEC-SPED toll free
703-620-3660
703-264-9446 TTY
703-264-9494 FAX
www.cec.sped.org

The largest international professional organization committed to improving educational outcomes for individuals with disabilities.

HEALTH Resource Center

American Council on Education
One Dupont Circle NW, Suite 800
Washington, DC 20036-1193
800-544-3284 toll free
202-939-9300 TTY
202-833-4760 FAX
www.acenet.edu/About/programs/ Access&Equity/

HEATH/home.html

A clearinghouse of information on topics related to postsecondary education and disabilities. Publishes an annual resource directory.

International Dyslexia Association (IDA)

8600 LaSalle Road Chester Building, Suite 382
Baltimore, MD 21286-2044
410-296-0232
800-ABCD-123 messages
410-321-5069 FAX
www.interdys.org

The IDA is an international, nonprofit organization dedicated to the study and treatment of learning disabilities and dyslexia. For nearly 50 years, the IDA has been helping individuals with dyslexia, their families, teachers, physicians, and researchers to better understand dyslexia.

Learning Disabilities Association of America (LDA)

4156 Library Road
Pittsburgh, PA 15234-1349
412-344-0224 FAX
www.ldanatl.org

LDA is the largest nonprofit volunteer organization advocat-ing for individuals with learning disabilities. LDA has more than 600 local chapters and affiliates in 50 states, Washington, DC, and Puerto Rico. LDA seeks to educate individuals with learning disabilities and their parents about the nature of the disability and inform them of their rights.

Recording for the Blind & Dyslexic (RFB&D)

20 Roszel Road
Princeton, NJ 08540
609-452-0606 voice
800-221-4792 voice (book orders only)
609-520-7990 FAX
www.rfbd.org

RFB&D is recognized as the nation's leading educational lending library of academic and professional textbooks on audiotape from ele-mentary through post-graduate and professional levels. Students with print disabilities can request cassette or diskette versions of books and order 4-track tape players.

Guidelines for Documenting Learning Disabilities and Attention Deficit Disorder is printed with permission from Louise H. Russell, MA

Harvard University Division of Continuing Education
Harvard Extension School
Harvard Summer School
51 Brattle Street
Cambridge, Massachusetts 02138-3722
617-495-0977
617-495-9419 (TTY)

Students with Disabilities Preparing for Postsecondary Education: Know Your Rights and Responsibilities

U.S. Department of Education Office for Civil Rights, Washington, DC 20202
First published July 2002, Reprinted May 2004

More and more high school students with disabilities are planning to continue their education in postsecondary schools, including vocational and career schools, two- and four- year colleges, and universities. As a student with a disability, you need to be well informed about your rights and responsibilities as well as the responsibilities that postsecondary schools have toward you. Being well informed will help ensure that you have a full opportunity to enjoy the benefits of the postsecondary education experience without confusion or delay.

The Office for Civil Rights (OCR) in the U.S. Department of Education is providing this information to explain the rights and responsibilities of students with disabilities who are preparing to attend postsecondary schools. This also explains the obligations of a postsecondary school to provide academic adjustments, including auxiliary aids and services, to ensure that the school does not discriminate on the basis of disability.

OCR enforces Section 504 of the Rehabilitation Act of 1973 (Section 504) and Title II of the Americans with Disabilities Act of 1990 (Title II), which prohibit discrimination on the basis of disability. Practically every school district and postsecondary school in the United States is subject to one or both of these laws, which have similar requirements.

Because both school districts and postsecondary schools must comply with these same laws, you and your parents might believe that postsecondary schools and school districts have the same responsibilities. This is not true; the responsibilities of postsecondary schools are significantly different from those of school districts.

Moreover, you will have responsibilities as a postsecondary student that you do not have as a high school student. OCR strongly encourages you to know your responsibilities and those of postsecondary schools under Section 504 and Title II. Doing so will improve your opportunity to succeed as you enter postsecondary education.

The following questions and answers provide more specific information to help you succeed.

As a student with a disability leaving high school and entering postsecondary education, will I see differences in my rights and how they are addressed?

Yes. Section 504 and Title II protect elementary, secondary, and postsecondary students from discrimination. Nevertheless, several of the requirements that apply through high school are different from the requirements that apply beyond high school. For instance, Section 504 requires a school district to provide a free appropriate public education (FAPE) to each child with a disability in the district's jurisdiction. Whatever the disability, a school district must identify an individual's education needs and provide any regular or special education and related aids and services necessary to meet those needs as well as it is meeting the needs of students without disabilities.

Unlike your high school, your postsecondary school is not required to provide FAPE. Rather, your postsecondary school is required to provide appropriate academic adjustments as necessary to ensure that it does not discriminate on the basis of disability. In addition, if your postsecondary school provides housing to nondisabled students, it must provide comparable, convenient, and accessible housing to students with disabilities at the same cost.

Other important differences you need to know, even before you arrive at your postsecondary school, are addressed in the remaining questions.

May a postsecondary school deny my admission because I have a disability?

No. If you meet the essential requirements for admission, a postsecondary school may not deny your admission simply because you have a disability.

Do I have to inform a postsecondary school that I have a disability?

No. However, if you want the school to provide an academic adjustment, you must identify yourself as having a disability. Likewise, you should let the school know about your disability if you want to ensure that you are assigned to accessible facilities. In any event, your disclosure of a disability is always voluntary.

What academic adjustments must a postsecondary school provide?

The appropriate academic adjustment must be determined based on your disability and individual needs. Academic adjustments include modifications to academic requirements and auxiliary aids and services, for example, arranging for priority registration; reducing a course load; substituting one course for another; providing note-takers, recording devices, sign language interpreters, extended time for testing and, if telephones are provided in dorm rooms, a TTY in your dorm room; as well as equipping school computers with screen-reading, voice recognition, or other adaptive software or hardware.

In providing an academic adjustment, your postsecondary school is not required to lower or effect substantial modifications to essential requirements. For example, although your school may be required to provide extended testing time, it is not required to change the substantive content of the test. In addition, your postsecondary school does not have to make modifications that would fundamentally alter the nature of a service, program, or activity or would result in undue financial or administrative burdens. Finally, your postsecondary school does not have to provide personal attendants, individually prescribed devices, readers for personal use or study, or other devices or services of a personal nature, such as tutoring and typing.

If I want an academic adjustment, what must I do?

You must inform the school that you have a disability and need an academic adjustment. Unlike your school district, your postsecondary school is not required to identify you as having a disability or assess your needs.

Your postsecondary school may require you to follow reasonable procedures to request an academic adjustment. You are responsible for knowing and following these procedures. Postsecondary schools usually include, in their publications providing general information, information on the procedures and contacts for requesting an academic adjustment. Such publications include recruitment materials, catalogs, and student handbooks and are often available on school websites. Many schools also have staff whose purpose is to assist students with disabilities. If you are unable to locate the procedures, ask a school official, such as an admissions officer or counselor.

When should I request an academic adjustment?

Although you may request an academic adjustment from your postsecondary school at any time, you should request it as early as possible. Some academic adjustments may take more time to provide than others. You should follow your school's procedures to ensure that your school has enough time to review your request and provide an appropriate academic adjustment.

Do I have to prove that I have a disability to obtain an academic adjustment?

Generally, yes. Your school probably will require you to provide documentation that shows you have a current disability and need an academic adjustment.

What documentation should I provide?

Schools may set reasonable standards for documentation. Some schools require more documentation than others. They may require you to provide documentation prepared by an appropriate professional, such as a medical doctor, psychologist, or other qualified diagnostician. The required documentation may include one or more of the following: a diagnosis of your current disability; the date of the diagnosis; how the diagnosis was reached; the credentials of the professional; how your disability affects a major life activity; and how the disability affects your academic performance. The documentation should provide enough information for you and your school to decide what is an appropriate academic adjustment.

Although an individualized education program (IEP) or Section 504 plan, if you have one, may help identify services that have been effective for you, it generally is not sufficient documentation. This is because postsecondary education presents different demands than high school education, and what you need to meet these new demands may be different. Also in some cases, the nature of a disability may change.

If the documentation that you have does not meet the postsecondary school's requirements, a school official must tell you in a timely manner what additional documentation you need to provide. You may need a new evaluation in order to provide the required documentation.

Who has to pay for a new evaluation?

Neither your high school nor your postsecondary school is required to conduct or pay for a new evaluation to document your disability and need for an academic adjustment. This may mean that you have to pay or find funding to pay an appropriate professional to do it. If you are eligible for services through your state vocational rehabilitation agency, you may qualify for an evaluation at no cost to you. You may locate your state vocational rehabilitation agency through this Department of Education Web page: www.ed.gov/offices/OSERS/RSA/Resources/State/.

Once the school has received the necessary documentation from me, what should I expect?

The school will review your request in light of the essential requirements for the relevant program to help determine an appropriate academic adjustment. It is important to remember that the school is not required to lower or waive essential requirements. If you have requested a specific academic adjustment, the school may offer that academic adjustment or an alternative one if the alternative also would be effective. The school may also conduct its own evaluation of your disability and needs at its own expense.

You should expect your school to work with you in an interactive process to identify an appropriate academic adjustment. Unlike the experience you may have had in high school, however, do not expect your postsecondary school to invite your parents to participate in the process or to develop an IEP for you.

What if the academic adjustment we identified is not working?

Let the school know as soon as you become aware that the results are not what you expected. It may be too late to correct the problem if you wait until the course or activity is completed. You and your school should work together to resolve the problem.

May a postsecondary school charge me for providing an academic adjustment?

No. Furthermore, it may not charge students with disabilities more for participating in its programs or activities than it charges students who do not have disabilities.

What can I do if I believe the school is discriminating against me?

Practically every postsecondary school must have a person—frequently called the Section 504 Coordinator, ADA Coordinator, or Disability Services Coordinator—who coordinates the school's compliance with Section 504 or Title II or both laws. You may contact this person for information about how to address your concerns.

The school also must have grievance procedures. These procedures are not the same as the due process procedures with which you may be familiar from high school. However, the postsecondary school's grievance procedures must include steps to ensure that you may raise your concerns fully and fairly and must provide for the prompt and equitable resolution of complaints.

School publications, such as student handbooks and catalogs, usually describe the steps you must take to start the grievance process. Often, schools have both formal and informal processes. If you decide to use a grievance process, you should be prepared to present all the reasons that support your request.

If you are dissatisfied with the outcome from using the school's grievance procedures or you wish to pursue an alternative to using the grievance procedures, you may file a complaint against the school with OCR or in a court. You may learn more about the OCR complaint process from the brochure "How to File a Discrimination Complaint with the Office for Civil Rights," which you may obtain by contacting us at the addresses and phone numbers below, or at www.ed.gov/ocr/docs/howto.html.

If you would like more information about the responsibilities of postsecondary schools to students with disabilities, read the OCR brochure "Auxiliary Aids and Services for Postsecondary Students with Disabilities: Higher Education's Obligations Under Section 504 and Title II of the ADA." You may obtain a copy by contacting us at the address and phone numbers below, or at www.ed.gov/ocr/docs/auxaids.html.

Students with disabilities who know their rights and responsibilities are much better equipped to succeed in postsecondary school. We encourage you to work with the staff at your school because they, too, want you to succeed. Seek the support of family, friends, and fellow students, including those with disabilities. Know your talents and capitalize on them, and believe in yourself as you embrace new challenges in your education.

To receive more information about the civil rights of students with disabilities in education institutions, contact us at:

Customer Service Team
Office for Civil Rights
U.S. Department of Education
Washington, DC 20202-1100
Phone: 800-421-3481
TDD: 877-521-2172
Email: ocr@ed.gov
Internet home page: www.ed.gov/ocr/transition.html

This publication is in the public domain. Authorization to reproduce it in whole or in part is granted. The publication's citation should be: U.S. Department of Education, Office for Civil Rights, Students with Disabilities Preparing for Postsecondary Education: Know Your Rights and Responsibilities, Washington, DC, 2002.

GETTING READY

The purpose of *The K&W Guide* is to help students with learning disabilities acquire the basic knowledge necessary to begin the college exploration process and get ready to make appropriate college selections.

STUDENT PREPARATION CHECKLIST

- Understand their strengths and weaknesses.
- Articulate the nature of their learning disabilities.
- Understand the compensatory skills developed to accommodate the learning differences.
- Describe the services they received in high school.
- Identify short-term and long-term goals.
- Select appropriate college choices to match individual needs.

GUIDELINES FOR THE SEARCH AND SELECTION PROCESS

SELF ASSESSMENT

- What is the student's learning disability?
- When was the disability diagnosed?
- What is the student's level of performance in high school?
- Is the student enrolled in college-prep courses, modified courses, or individualized, special-education courses?
- What are the student's individual strengths and weaknesses?
- Is it easier for the student to learn from a lecture, reading the material, or having the material read to him/her?
- Does the student perform better on written assignments or oral presentations?
- Which subjects are easier, and which are more difficult?
- What are the student's favorite and least favorite courses and why?
- What are the student's short-term and long-term goals?
- Are these goals realistic?
- Is the student striving to improve in academic areas?
- What accommodations are being provided?
- Is the student actively utilizing resource assistance and learning compensatory strategies?
- What does the student plan to study in college?
- What skills and competencies are required for the career goals being pursued?
- When were the last diagnostic tests given?
- What level of services/accommodations are needed in college? Structured programs, comprehensive services, or basic services?

ARTICULATION

- Does the student understand the disability?
- Can the student describe the learning disability?
- Does the student comprehend how the disability impacts learning?
- Can the student explain the nature of the disability?
- Can the student explain the accommodations being utilized as well as any curriculum modifications received?
- Can the student explain necessary accommodations to teachers?

ACADEMIC ASSESSMENT

Does the student have difficulty with written language?

- Using appropriate words
- Organizing thoughts
- Writing lengthy compositions

- Using correct punctuation and sentence structure
- Expressing thoughts clearly

Does the student have trouble with verbal expression?
- Retrieving appropriate words
- Understanding what others are saying
- Using words in the correct context
- Carrying on conversations

Does the student have a problem with hand-eye coordination?
- Fnding certain information on a page
- Performing tasks that require fine motor coordination

Does the student get frustrated reading?
- Decoding unfamiliar words
- Understanding reading assignments
- Completing reading assignments within a time frame

Does the student often misspell words?
- Mix up the sequence of letters
- Become confused when spelling irregular words

Does the student experience difficulty performing mathematics?
- Multiplication table and fractions
- Sequencing of steps of various mathematical questions

Does the student have difficulty concentrating?
- Fidgets or squirms
- Distracted by noises
- Difficulty following intructions
- Difficulty finishing assignments

What are the student's study habits?
- Attentive in class for an extended period of time
- Easily distracted
- Needs extra time to respond to questions
- Note-taking skills
- Memory
- Time management
- Time orientation
- Organization

How is the student's handwriting ability?
- Assignments are difficult to read
- Appropriate capitalization used
- Stays within the lines when writing
- Leaves enough space between words

EXPLORATION AND TIMELINES

SOPHOMORE YEAR
- Explore options.
- Consider taking the PLAN (if available)—request appropriate testing accomodations.
- Meet with counselor and case manager.
- Review testing and documentation.
- Review course registration for junior year. Students considering four-year colleges should be enrolled in as many college prepatory courses as possible.

- Write to colleges or use college websites to explore schools.
- Contact the service providers on the college campus.

JUNIOR YEAR
- Consider taking the PSAT—request appropriate testing accomodations.
- Review achievement level.
- Review course registration for senior year. Students considering four-year colleges should be enrolled in as many college prepatory courses as possible.
- Review the level of services in high school.
- Identify the level of services needed in college.
- Visit colleges.
- Register for the ACT/SAT, standardized or nonstandardized.

- Request necessary updated psychoeducational testing (including the WAIS-R)

SENIOR YEAR
- Submit general applications.
- Submit special applications (if required).
- Schedule interviews (if appropriate).
- Write essays (if required).
- Disclose learning disability to college.
- Release current psychoeducational testing.*
- Release documentation of other health-related disabilities.*

   * Students under the age of 18 must have their parents' signature to release information to each of the colleges.

CAMPUS VISITS
- The student should call to make an arrangement for a visit.
- Visit while classes are in session.
- Meet with admissions and special support service providers.
- Take a guided tour.
- Attend a class.
- Eat a meal on campus.
- Drive around the boundaries of the campus.
- Take pictures, take notes, and talk to students on campus.
- Take parents or family members along (but not in the interview).
- Pick up college catalogue, view book, video, and support service brochures.
- Write thank you notes.

INTERVIEWS
To prepare for interviews, students should know the following:
- Strengths and weaknesses
- The accommodations needed
- How to describe learning disability

If an interview is required prior to an admission decision:
- View the interview as an opportunity.
- Prepare a list of questions.
- Know that interviews, if required, are either required of all applicants or required for a special program or special admission practice.

Questions the Director of Support Services may ask

- When was the learning disability first diagnosed?
- What type of assistance has the student been receiving in high school?

- What kind of accommodations will the student need in college?
- Can the student describe the learning difficulties?
- Can the student articulate strengths and weaknesses?
- How has the disability affected the student's learning?
- What high school courses were easy (or more difficult)?
- Is the student comfortable with the learning disability?
- Can the student self-advocate?
- What does the student plan to choose as a major?
- Is the student motivated?

Questions students and/or parents may ask
- What are the admission requirements?
- Is there any flexibility in admission policy? Course substitutions? GPA?
- What is the application procedure?
- Is a special application required?
- What auxiliary testing is required?
- Are there extra charges or fees for the special programs or services?
- Are there remedial or developmental courses?
- What is the procedure for requesting waivers or substitutions?
- Who is the contact person for learning disabilities?
- What are the academic qualifications of the individual who provides services to students with learning disabilities?
- What services and accommodations are available: Testing accommodations? Note takers? Books on tape? Skills classes? Support groups? Priority registration? Professional tutors? Peer tutors? Advising? Computer-aided technology? Scribes? Proctors? Oral tests? Use of computers and spell-checker in class? Use of calculators in class? Distraction-free environment for tests? Learning disability specialists? Advocacy with professors? Faculty in-services?
- How long has the program been in existence?
- How many students are receiving services?
- How long can students access services?
- What is the success rate of students receiving services?

For a successful interview
- Develop a list of questions.
- Know the accommodations needed.
- Provide new information.
- Practice interviewing.
- Be able to describe strengths and weaknesses.
- Talk about extracurricular activities.
- Take notes.
- Get the business card of the interviewer.
- Try to relax.
- Have fun!

LETTERS OF RECOMMENDATION
- Obtain descriptive letters from counselors, teachers, and case managers.
- Have recommenders address learning style, degree of motivation, level of achievement, abilities, attitudes, self-discipline, determination, creativity, mastery of subject matter, academic risks, and growth.
- Have a teacher describe the challenge in a difficult course.
- Advise recommenders when letters are due.

We have just highlighted some of the areas of importance. Now it is time to begin to use the information in this guide that describes the various programs and services at various colleges and universities in the United States.

How to Use This Guide

The school profiles in *The K&W Guide* include information on colleges and universities that offer services to students with learning disabilities. No two colleges are identical in the programs or services they provide, but there are some similarities.

In the School Profiles section of this book, the support programs at each school have been grouped according to one of the following three categories:

Structured Programs (SP)

Colleges with Structured Programs offer the most comprehensive services for students with learning disabilities. The director and/or staff are certified in learning disabilities or related areas. The director is actively involved in the admission decision, and often, the criteria for admission may be more flexible than general admission requirements. Services are highly structured and students are involved in developing plans to meet their particular learning styles and needs. Often students in Structured Programs sign a contract agreeing to actively participate in the program. There is usually an additional fee for the enhanced services. Students who have participated in a Structured Program or used Structured Services in high school such as the Learning Disabilities Resource Program, individualized or modified course work, tutorial assistance, academic monitoring, note-takers, test accommodations, or skill classes might benefit from exploring colleges with Structured Programs or Coordinated Services.

Coordinated Services (CS)

Coordinated Services differ from Structured Programs in that the services are not as comprehensive. These services are provided by at least one certified learning disability specialist. The staff is knowledgeable and trained to provide assistance to students in developing strategies for their individual needs. The director of the program or services may be involved in the admission decision, or be in a position to offer recommendations to the Admissions Office on the potential success of the applicant, or to assist the students with an appeal if denied admission to the college. Receiving these services generally requires specific documentation of the learning disability—students are encouraged to self-identify prior to entry. Students voluntarily request accommodations or services at schools in the Coordinated Services category, and there may be specific skills courses or remedial classes available or required for students with learning disabilities who are admitted probationally or conditionally. High school students who may have enrolled in some modified or remedial courses, utilized test accommodations, or required tutorial assistance, but who typically requested services only as needed, might benefit from exploring colleges with Coordinated Services or Services.

Services (S)

Services is the least comprehensive of the three categories. Colleges offering Services generally are complying with the federal mandate requiring reasonable accommodations to all students with appropriate and current documentation. These colleges routinely require documentation of the disability in order for the students with LD/ADD to receive accommodations. Staff and faculty actively support the students by providing basic services to meet the needs of the students. Services are requested on a voluntarily basis, and there may be some limitations as to what is reasonable and the degree of services available. Sometimes, just the small size of the student body allows for the necessary personal attention to help students with learning disabilities succeed in college. High school students who require minimum accommodations, but who would find comfort in knowing that services are available, knowing who the contact person is, and knowing that this person is sensitive to students with learning disabilities, might benefit from exploring colleges providing Services or Coordinated Services.

SOME COMMENTS REGARDING THE SCHOOL PROFILES

Each college in the book is covered on two pages, beginning with pertinent information describing the learning disability program or services. This is followed by LD/ADD admissions information, learning disability services, and finally general college information.

Please note the statement preceding the section on Learning Disability Services, which states "services and accommodations are determined individually for each student based on current and appropriate documentation." As discussed in previous sections of this book, the existence of a service or accommodation at a college does not mean that every student who wants it will receive it. The student must first disclose, then request services, and finally document. At that point, the college will determine the services and accommodations that are reasonable for the individual student.

For the most part, the availability of a particular service or accommodation at a college is clearly indicated with a "yes" and its unavailability is indicated with a "no." However, in some instances the availability of a service is a bit more complicated. In those cases, the following abbreviations are used:

- N/A (not applicable) when something in the profile does not apply to that particular college
- NR (not reported) when the college was unable to provide the information
- Y/N (Yes/No) when the answer is dependent on individual situations

The authors have made a conscientious effort to provide the most current information possible. However, names, costs, dates, policies, and other information are always subject to change. Therefore, colleges of particular interest or importance to the reader should be contacted directly for verification of the data.

DEFINITIONS OF TESTING INSTRUMENTS AND ASSESSMENTS

INTELLIGENCE TESTS

Stanford-Binet: Stanford-Binet Intelligence Scale, Fourth Edition

The Stanford-Binet Intelligence Scale assesses intelligence and cognitive abilities. Verbal responses are emphasized more than nonverbal responses. The Stanford-Binet is administered to individuals aged two through adult. Children tested at age two might score quite differently when tested on another IQ test several years later.

WISC–IV: Wechsler Intelligence Scale for Children IV

The structure of the WISC–IV has been updated to reflect current theory and practice of intellectual assessment in children, including increased attention to working memory and processing speed. There is no longer a Verbal IQ score or Performance IQ score. There is a Perceptual Reasoning Index (PRI) and a Working Memory Index (WMI). There are 5 new subtests. The Full IQ score is interpreted by adding the Verbal Comprehension Index (VCI), the Perceptual Reasoning Index (PRI), the Working Memory Index (WMI) and Processing Speed Index (PSI) together.

WAIS–III: Wechsler Adult Intelligence Scale, Third Edition

The Wechsler Adult Intelligence Scale assesses the intellectual ability of adults aged 16 through 89. The WAIS–III yields the three composite IQ scores: verbal, performance, and full-scale, as well as four index scores, in verbal comprehension, perceptual organization, working memory, and processing speed. This test is given to high school adolescents between the ages of 16 to 18. The WAIS–III identifies areas of learning strengths and weaknesses or disabilities.

ACHIEVEMENT TESTS

PIAT–R

The PIAT–R is an updated, revised, and re-standardized battery of the old PIAT, and includes a new written expression sub-test. This test is used to measure general academic achievement in reading mechanics and comprehension, spelling, math, and general knowledge. The PIAT–R is administered to individuals from grades K through 12, and aged 5 through 18.

SDAT: Stanford Diagnostic Achievement Tests

The SDAT measures performance in academic subjects such as spelling, grammar, arithmetic, and reading. This test also provides instructional objectives and suggestions for teaching.

TOWL: Test of Written Language

The TOWL identifies strengths and weaknesses in various writing abilities. It can be used to compare students to their peers, and determine performance levels in written expression.

WRAT–R: Wide Range Achievement Test–Revised

The WRAT–R evaluates oral reading, spelling, and arithmetic computation. This test is used from kindergarten through college, and scores are by grade level for each skill.

WJ-R: Woodcock-Johnson Psychoeducational Battery–Revised

The WJ–R is a battery of tests used from preschool through adult level to measure achievement in reading, math, written language, and general knowledge. These tests also assess the level of academic versus nonacademic accomplishments.

SAT/ACT CONVERSION CHART

SAT I to ACT		ACT to SAT I	
SAT I Verbal + Math Score	ACT Composite Score	ACT Composite Score	SAT I Verbal + Math Score
		36	1600
1570-1600	35	35	1580
1510-1560	34	34	1530
1450-1500	33	33	1460
1390-1440	32	32	1410
1350-1380	31	31	1360
1310-1340	30	30	1320
1270-1300	29	29	1280
1230-1260	28	28	1240
1200-1220	27	27	1210
1160-1190	26	26	1170
1120-1150	25	25	1140
1090-1110	24	24	1100
1050-1080	23	23	1060
1010-1040	22	22	1030
970-1000	21	21	990
930-960	20	20	950
890-920	19	19	910
840-880	18	18	860
800-830	17	17	820
750-790	16	16	770
700-740	15	15	720
630-690	14	14	670
570-620	13	13	600
510-560	12	12	540
450-500	11	11	480
410-440	10	10	430
400	9	1-9	400

SCHOOL PROFILES

JACKSONVILLE STATE UNIVERSITY

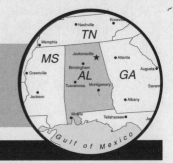

700 Pelham Road North, Jacksonville, AL 36265
Phone: 256-782-5268 • Fax: 256-782-5953
E-mail: info@jsu.edu • Web: www.jsu.edu
Support: CS • Institution type: 4-year public

LEARNING DISABILITY PROGRAM AND SERVICES

Under the Disability Support Services (DSS) the Academic Center for Excellence offers support for students with learning disabilities and ADD. It is an inclusive service community, promoting academic excellence and empowering students for success. Once a student has been admitted, DSS assists the qualified student with a documented disability in receiving academic support services. Accommodations are based solely on the supporting documentation. Required documents for a student with LD are current intelligence tests, current achievement tests, certified professional validation of the LD or high school records documenting prior identification and/or services as a student with LD. Students with IQs below 85 do not qualify for services. Each student with appropriate documentation identifying a learning disability will develop an individualized postsecondary plan (IPP). The IPP is prepared from the documentation received, input from the student (and parents, if appropriate) and the staff in support services. Copies of the IPP are given to the student, who is responsible for identifying him/herself and giving a copy to each instructor.

LD/ADD ADMISSIONS INFORMATION

College entrance tests required: Yes
Interview required: Recommended
Essay required: No
Documentation required for LD: Psychoeducational
evaluation
Documentation required for ADD: Yes
Submitted to: Disability Support Services
Special Ed. HS coursework accepted: Yes

Specific course requirements of all applicants: Yes
Separate application required for program servics: No
# of LD applications submitted each year: 100
# of LD applications accepted yearly: 100
Total # of students receiving LD services: 100
**Acceptance into program means acceptance into
college:** Student must be admitted and enrolled in the
university first and then request services.

ADMISSIONS

All applicants must meet the general entrance requirements. The middle 50 percent of the applicants have an ACT of 18–22. All students must have at least 3 years of English and no more than 4 of the 15 required courses in high school may be in vocational courses. Interviews are recommended but not required. Students with an ACT below 16 may enter through successful completion of a summer bridge program. The program, Experiencing Success in Education and Life, offers skill-building classes. Students with an ACT between 16 and 19 are conditionally admitted.

ADDITIONAL INFORMATION

DSS is funded to provide programming only for sensory impaired (blind/low vision and deaf/hard of hearing). However, they do provide services for all disabilities. Disability Support Services will provide services to any student with LD/ADD with appropriate documentation, and accommodations are based solely on the supporting documentation. DSS requires formal documentation (current within the last 3 years) and the academic accommodations needed are determined from this documentation. Services available may include note-takers, readers, scribes, priority registration, assistive technology, testing modifications, distraction-free environment for tests, and an individualized postsecondary plan. Academic Success Skills offers skills classes in time management, test strategies, organizational skills and other areas. These courses are offered for college credit. All students have access to tutoring, supplemental instruction, structured study sessions, and online tutorials. Students Involved with Disabilities is a support group for students with disabilities whose purpose is to spread disability awareness on campus and in the community.

Support Services Contact Information

Learning Disability Program/Services: Academic Center for Excellence: Disability Support Services
Director: Dan Miller
  E-mail: dmiller@jsucc.jsu.edu
  Telephone: 256-782-5093
  Fax: 256-782-5025

LEARNING DISABILITY SERVICES

Requests for the following/services accommodations will be evaluated individually based on appropriate and current documentation.

Allowed in exams	**Distraction-reduced environment:** Yes	**Added costs for services:** No
Calculator: Yes	**Tape recording in class:** Yes	**LD specialists:** Yes
Dictionary: Yes	**Books on tape from RFBD:** Yes	**Professional tutors:** No
Computer: Yes	**Taping of books not from RFBD:** Yes	**Peer tutors:** 40
Spellchecker: Yes	**Accommodations for students with**	**Max. hours/wk. for services:**
Extended test time: Yes	**ADD:** Yes	Unlimited
Scribes: Yes	**Reading machine:** Yes	**How professors are notified of**
Proctors: Yes	**Other assistive technology:** Yes	**LD/ADD:** By both student and director
Oral exams: Yes	**Priority registration:** Yes	
Note-takers: Yes		

GENERAL ADMISSIONS INFORMATION

Director of Admissions: Martha Mitchell
Telephone: 256-782-5268

ENTRANCE REQUIREMENTS

Academic units required: 2.0 GPA minimum. 4 English, 3 math, 3 science, 3 social studies, 1 foreign language (2 recommended), 2 academic electives. High school diploma is required and GED is accepted. TOEFL required of all international applicants, minimum paper TOEFL 500, minimum computer TOEFL 173.

Application deadline: Rolling	**Average SAT Math:** NR	**Graduated top 10% of class:** 3%
Notification: Rolling	**Average SAT Verbal:** NR	**Graduated top 25% of class:** 13%
Average GPA: 2.99	**Average ACT:** 20	**Graduated top 50% of class:** 34%

COLLEGE GRADUATION REQUIREMENTS

Course waivers allowed: Yes
Course substitutions allowed: Yes
In what course: Individual case by case decisions

ADDITIONAL INFORMATION

Environment: Located in a small town about 75 miles from Birmingham.

Student Body:	**Cost Information**	**Greek System**
Undergrad enrollment: 7,096	In-state tuition: $4,040	Fraternity: Yes
Women: 58%	Out-of-state tuition: $8,080	Sorority: Yes
Men: 42%	Room & board: $3,312	Athletics: NCAA Division I
Percent out-of-state: 12%	**Housing Information**	
	University housing: Yes	
	Percent living on campus: 15%	

U. OF ALABAMA—HUNTSVILLE

301 Sparkman Drive, Huntsville, AL 35899
Phone: 256-824-6070 • Fax: 256-824-6073
E-mail: admitme@email.uah.edu • Web: www.uah.edu
Support: S • Institution type: 4-year public

LEARNING DISABILITY PROGRAM AND SERVICES

The Office of Student Development Services offers a variety of services and accommodations to assist students with disabilities in eliminating barriers they encounter in pursuing higher education. The main objective is to provide access to academic, social, cultural, recreational, and housing opportunities at the university. The services offered encourage students to achieve and maintain autonomy.

LD/ADD ADMISSIONS INFORMATION

College entrance tests required: Yes
Interview required: No
Essay required: No
Documentation required for LD: Psychoeducational evaluation
Documentation required for ADD: Yes
Submitted to: Services for Students with Disabilities
Special Ed. HS coursework accepted: Yes

Specific course requirements of all applicants: Yes
Separate application required for program servics: Yes
# of LD applications submitted each year: NR
# of LD applications accepted yearly: NR
Total # of students receiving LD services: 167
Acceptance into program means acceptance into college: Student must be admitted and enrolled in the university first and then request services.

ADMISSIONS

Admission is based on grades and test scores. Additionally, applicants should have 4 years English, 3 years social studies, 3 years math, 2 years science, and a total of 20 Carnegie units.

ACT	SAT	GPA
17 or below	700 or below	3.25
18	740	3.00
19	790	2.75
20-21	860	2.50
22	920	2.25
23	970	2.00
24 or above	1010 or above	1.15

There is no special LD admission process. If a student becomes subject to academic suspension, the suspension is for a minimum of one term, and the student must petition the admissions committee for approval to re-enroll.

ADDITIONAL INFORMATION

Students should forward their documentation to Services for Students with Disabilities. Student Development Services provides the mandated services, including testing accommodations, distraction-free environments for tests, readers, proctors, scribes, note-takers, peer tutoring on an unlimited basis, specialized adaptive computers, and study skills classes that can be taken for credit. Math labs, chemistry labs, writing centers, and tutorial services are available for all students on campus. Additionally, all students have access to skills classes in time management, test-taking strategies, and study skills. Services and accommodations are available for undergraduate and graduate students.

Support Services Contact Information

Learning Disability Program/Services: Services for Students with Disabilities
Director: Delois H. Smith
  E-Mail: smithdh@email.uah.edu
  Telephone: 256-824-6203
  Fax: 256-824-6672
Contact Person: Rosemary Robinson
  E-Mail: robins@email.uah.edu
  Telephone: 256-824-6203
  Fax: 256-824-6672

LEARNING DISABILITY SERVICES

Requests for the following/services accommodations will be evaluated individually based on appropriate and current documentation.

Allowed in exams
  Calculator: Yes
  Dictionary: Yes
  Computer: Yes
  Spellchecker: Yes
Extended test time: Yes
Scribes: Yes
Proctors: Yes
Oral exams: Yes
Note-takers: Yes

Distraction-reduced environment: Yes
Tape recording in class: Yes
Books on tape from RFBD: Yes
Taping of books not from RFBD: Yes
Accommodations for students with
  ADD: Yes
Reading machine: Yes
Other assistive technology: Yes
Priority registration: Yes

Added costs for services: No
LD specialists: No
Professional tutors: 3
Peer tutors: 10
Max. hours/wk. for services:
  Unlimited
How professors are notified of
  LD/ADD: By both student and director

GENERAL ADMISSIONS INFORMATION

Director of Admissions: Ginger Reed
Telephone: 256-824-6070

ENTRANCE REQUIREMENTS

Academic units required: 4 English, 3 math, 3 science, 4 social studies, 6 academic electives. High school diploma is required and GED is accepted. ACT with or without Writing component accepted. TOEFL required of all international applicants, minimum paper TOEFL 500, minimum computer TOEFL 173.

Application deadline: 8/15
Notification: Rolling
Average GPA: 3.40

Average SAT Math: 583
Average SAT Verbal: 574
Average ACT: 25

Graduated top 10% of class: 25%
Graduated top 25% of class: 55%
Graduated top 50% of class: 85%

COLLEGE GRADUATION REQUIREMENTS

Course waivers allowed: Yes
Course substitutions allowed: Yes
In what course: Determined on a case-by-case basis

ADDITIONAL INFORMATION

Environment: The university is located on 337 acres 100 miles north of Birmingham and 100 miles south of Nashville.

Student Body:
  Undergrad enrollment: 5,125
  Women: 49%
  Men: 51%
  Percent out-of-state: 13%

Cost Information
  In-state tuition: $4,516
  Out-of-state tuition: $9,518
  Room & board: $5,200
Housing Information
  University housing: Yes
  Percent living on campus: 16%

Greek System
  Fraternity: Yes
  Sorority: Yes
Athletics: NCAA Division II

U. OF ALABAMA—TUSCALOOSA

Box 870132, Tuscaloosa, AL 35487-0132
Phone: 205-348-5666 • Fax: 205-348-9046
E-mail: admissions@ua.edu • Web: www.ua.edu
Support: S • Institution type: 4-year public

LEARNING DISABILITY PROGRAM AND SERVICES

The Office of Disability Services (ODS) serves as the central contact point for students with disabilities. The goal of ODS is to provide an environment that ensures an individual is viewed on the basis of ability, not disability. ODS works individually with students to determine appropriate and reasonable academic accommodations, and to ensure that students' academic performance is evaluated apart from the limiting effects of disability. Any student enrolled with a documented LD is eligible for services and accommodations. Students must provide documentation including a written report of an LD evaluation; a summary of areas of testing; actual test scores; overall summary and diagnosis; and recommendations and suggested strategies for student, professors, and academic advisors. The Office of Disability Services may request further testing.

LD/ADD ADMISSIONS INFORMATION

College entrance tests required: Yes
Interview required: No
Essay required: No
Documentation required for LD: Narrative report from appropriate professional including results of tests measuring aptitude, achievement, and information processing. Also, must include DSM–IV diagnosis
Documentation required for ADD: Narrative report from appropriate professional including results of tests measuring aptitude, achievement, and information processing. Also, must include DSM–IV diagnosis
Submitted to: Office of Disability Services
Special Ed. HS coursework accepted: Yes, if a teacher is certified in area

Specific course requirements of all applicants:
Separate application required for program servics: Yes
# of LD applications submitted each year: NR
# of LD applications accepted yearly: NR
Total # of students receiving LD services: 150–160
Acceptance into program means acceptance into college: Student must be admitted and enrolled in the university first and then request services.

ADMISSIONS

All students must meet regular entrance requirements. An interview with the Office of Disabilities is recommended. Students with an acceptable GPA but not test scores or vice versa may be considered for Summer Trial Admissions. Students who fall within this category are encouraged to submit teacher/counselor recommendations that could substantiate the student's potential for success. Students admitted through Summer Trial Admissions will be required to attend the summer session and enroll in an appropriate math class and either psychology or child development. Additionally, students will take a study skills lab, which will provide strategies and monitoring of the student's notes taken during the classes. The strategies are practical rather than theoretical. Students need a 2.0 GPA in the summer courses to be admitted for the fall.

ADDITIONAL INFORMATION

Accommodations are tailored to individual needs according to diagnostic testing. Accommodations include early registration; testing modifications; academic aids such as taping lectures, use of calculators, dictionaries, spellcheckers, note-takers, and taped materials; and reading assistance. The Center for Teaching and Learning (CTL) Independent Study Lab is available for all students at the university. Students can use videotapes, computer software, and other self-paced materials for review of math, chemistry, physics, biology, statistics, and other selected classes; study and reading skills; and graduate entrance exam preparation. Individual tutoring is offered for selected classes in math, chemistry, physics, statistics, economics, biology, accounting, and foreign languages. Math review and help sessions are available for students enrolled in selected math courses through small group review sessions. The CTL offers reading and reading comprehension workshops, as well as workshops in study skills and time management. The Writing Center is staffed by Instructors from the UA English department and provides individual assistance in developing the composition skills necessary to complete university coursework.

Support Services Contact Information

Learning Disability Program/Services: Office of Disability Services
Director: Judy Thorpe
  E-Mail: jthorpe@aalan.ua.edu
  Telephone: 205-348-4285
  Fax: 205-348-0804

LEARNING DISABILITY SERVICES

Requests for the following/services accommodations will be evaluated individually based on appropriate and current documentation.

Allowed in exams
  Calculator: Yes
  Dictionary: Yes
  Computer: Yes
  Spellchecker: Yes
Extended test time: Yes
Scribes: Yes
Proctors: Yes
Oral exams: Yes
Note-takers: Yes

Distraction-reduced environment: Yes
Tape recording in class: Yes
Books on tape from RFBD: Yes
Taping of books not from RFBD: No
Accommodations for students with ADD: Yes
Reading machine: Yes
Other assistive technology: Yes
Priority registration: Yes

Added costs for services: No
LD specialists: No
Professional tutors: No
Peer tutors: 20–25
Max. hours/wk. for services: Unlimited
How professors are notified of LD/ADD: By student

GENERAL ADMISSIONS INFORMATION

Director of Admissions: Mary K. Spiegel
Telephone: 205-348-8197

ENTRANCE REQUIREMENTS

Academic units required: 4 English, 3 math, 3 science (2 science lab), 1 foreign language, 3 social studies, 1 history, 5 academic electives. High school diploma is required and GED is accepted. ACT with or without Writing component accepted. TOEFL required of all international applicants, minimum paper TOEFL 500, minimum computer TOEFL 173.

Application deadline: 8/1
Notification: Rolling
Average GPA: 3.36

Average SAT Math: 561
Average SAT Verbal: 553
Average ACT: 24

Graduated top 10% of class: 22%
Graduated top 25% of class: 45%
Graduated top 50% of class: 76%

COLLEGE GRADUATION REQUIREMENTS

Course waivers allowed: Yes
Course substitutions allowed: Yes
In what course: Math and foreign language

ADDITIONAL INFORMATION

Environment: The university is located 55 miles from the city of Birmingham.

Student Body:
  Undergrad enrollment: 16,202
  Women: 53%
  Men: 47%
  Percent out-of-state: 20%

Cost Information
  In-state tuition: $4,630
  Out-of-state tuition: $12,664
  Room & board: $4,734
Housing Information
  University housing: Yes
  Percent living on campus: 24%

Greek System
  Fraternity: Yes
  Sorority: Yes
Athletics: NCAA Division I

UNIVERSITY OF ALASKA—ANCHORAGE

3211 Providence Drive, Anchorage, AK 99508-8046
Phone: 907-786-1480 • Fax: 907-786-4888
E-mail: enroll@uaa.alaska.edu • Web: www.uaa.alaska.edu
Support: S • Institution type: 4-year public

AK
Anchorage
★

Gulf of Alaska

LEARNING DISABILITY PROGRAM AND SERVICES

The University of Alaska—Anchorage provides equal opportunities for students who experience disabilities. Academic support services are available to students with learning disabilities. Staff trained to work with students with disabilities coordinate these services. To allow time for service coordination, students are encouraged to contact the Disability Support Services office several weeks before the beginning of each semester. Ongoing communication with the staff throughout the semester is encouraged.

LD/ADD ADMISSIONS INFORMATION

College entrance tests required: Yes
Interview required: No
Essay required: No
Documentation required for LD: Psychoeducational
   evaluation
Documentation required for ADD: Yes
Submitted to: Disability Support Services
Special Ed. HS coursework accepted: Yes, if regular level
   classes

Specific course requirements of all applicants: Yes
Separate application required for program servics: No
# of LD applications submitted each year: NR
# of LD applications accepted yearly: NR
Total # of students receiving LD services: 90 plus
**Acceptance into program means acceptance into
   college:** UAA has open enrollment; students are accepted to
   the university and then may request services.

ADMISSIONS

All students must meet the same admission requirements. The university has an open enrollment policy. However, admission to specific programs of study may have specific coursework or testing criteria that all students will have to meet. While formal admission is encouraged, the university has an open enrollment policy that allows students to register for courses in which they have the adequate background. Open enrollment does not guarantee subsequent formal admission to certificate or degree programs. Individuals with learning disabilities are admitted via the standard admissions procedures that apply to all students submitting applications for formal admission. Students with documentation of a learning disability are eligible to receive support services once they are enrolled in the university. LD students who self-disclose during the admission process are referred to DSS for information about services and accommodations.

ADDITIONAL INFORMATION

Slingerland Language Arts classes are available for all students in the areas of vocabulary building and study skills. There is no separate tutoring for students with learning disabilities. Tutorial help is available in the Reading and Writing Labs and the Learning Resource Center for all students. With appropriate documentation, students with LD or ADD may have access to accommodations such as: testing modifications; distraction-free environment for tests; scribes; proctors; note-takers; calculators, dictionary, and computers in exams; and assistive technology. Services and accommodations are available for undergraduate and graduate students.

Support Services Contact Information

Learning Disability Program/Services: Disability Support Services
Director: Kaela Parks
  E-Mail: ankmk4@uaa.alaska.edu
  Telephone: 907-786-4530
  Fax: 907-786-4531

LEARNING DISABILITY SERVICES

Requests for the following/services accommodations will be evaluated individually based on appropriate and current documentation.

Allowed in exams
  Calculator: Yes
  Dictionary: Yes
  Computer: Yes
  Spellchecker: Yes
Extended test time: Yes
Scribes: Yes
Proctors: Yes
Oral exams: Yes
Note-takers: Yes

Distraction-reduced environment: Yes
Tape recording in class: Yes
Books on tape from RFBD: Yes
Taping of books not from RFBD: Yes
Accommodations for students with ADD: Yes
Reading machine: Yes
Other assistive technology: Yes
Priority registration: Yes

Added costs for services: Yes
LD specialists: No
Professional tutors: No
Peer tutors: Yes
Max. hours/wk. for services: Unlimited
How professors are notified of LD/ADD: By student and director

GENERAL ADMISSIONS INFORMATION

Director of Admissions: Al Kastar
Telephone: 907-786-1480

ENTRANCE REQUIREMENTS

Academic units recommended: 4 English, 2 math, 3 science, 1 foreign language, 3 social studies, 1 history. High school diploma is required or GED is accepted. TOEFL required of all international applicants, minimum paper TOEFL 450, minimum computer TOEFL 133.

Application deadline: 7/1
Notification: Rolling
Average GPA: 3.05

Average SAT Math: 503
Average SAT Verbal: 502
Average ACT: 21

Graduated top 10% of class: 12%
Graduated top 25% of class: 32%
Graduated top 50% of class: 60%

COLLEGE GRADUATION REQUIREMENTS

Course waivers allowed: Yes
Course substitutions allowed: Yes
In what course: By petition, on case-by-case basis

ADDITIONAL INFORMATION

Environment: The University of Alaska—Anchorage is an urban campus on 350 acres 7 miles from downtown Anchorage.

Student Body:
  Undergrad enrollment: 9,861
  Women: 63%
  Men: 37%
  Percent out-of-state: 6%

Cost Information
  In-state tuition: $3,165
  Out-of-state tuition: $10,095
  Room & board: $6,430
Housing Information
  University housing: Yes
  Percent living on campus: 6%

Greek System
  Fraternity: Yes
  Sorority: Yes
Athletics: NCAA Division II

UNIVERSITY OF ALASKA—FAIRBANKS

PO Box 757480, Fairbanks, AK 99775-7480
Phone: 907-474-7500 • Fax: 907-474-5379
E-mail: admissions@uaf.edu • Web: www.uaf.edu
Support: S • Institution type: 4-year public

AK
★
Fairbanks

Gulf of Alaska

LEARNING DISABILITY PROGRAM AND SERVICES

The University of Alaska—Fairbanks is committed to providing equal opportunities to students with disabilities. Disability Services at UAF provides assistance to students with permanent or temporary disabilities. Campus Services include the Academic Advising Center, which is responsible for advising incoming freshmen and students with undeclared majors. It provides explanations of programs and requirements and assists students with choosing a major, electives, and classes consistent with their academic and career goals. Student Support Services provides academic and personal support including developmental classes and tutoring for students who are economically disadvantaged, are a first-generation college student, or have a documented disability. Disabled Students of UAF provides peer support groups for UAF students with disabilities. The Student Development and Learning Center provides tutoring, individual instruction in basic skills and counseling, career planning services, and assessment testing. Disability Services welcomes inquiries and seeks to make the college experience a success for students with disabilities.

LD/ADD ADMISSIONS INFORMATION

College entrance tests required: Yes
Interview required: No
Essay required: No
Documentation required for LD: Yes
Documentation required for ADD: Yes
Submitted to: Disability Services
Special Ed. HS coursework accepted: Yes

Specific course requirements of all applicants: Yes
Separate application required for program servics: No
# of LD applications submitted each year: NR
# of LD applications accepted yearly: NR
Total # of students receiving LD services: 30–40
Acceptance into program means acceptance into college: Student must be admitted and enrolled in the university first and then request services.

ADMISSIONS

The university has a liberal admissions policy. To qualify for admission, freshman students must meet one of the following: associate's degree program requires a high school diploma or GED, students must maintain a C average with 14 credits to enter a baccalaureate degree program; baccalaureate degree requires a high school diploma with a 2.0 GPA. Students must also complete a core curriculum including 4 years English, 3 years math, 3 years social sciences, and 3 years of natural or physical sciences with a minimum GPA of 2.5. Foreign language is recommended. Students can be provisionally accepted if they make up course deficiencies with a C or better in each of the developmental or university courses, and complete 9 credits of general degree requirements with a C or better. Being accepted to the university does not depend on minimum test scores; however these test scores are used to determine placement in English, math, and other freshman-level courses.

ADDITIONAL INFORMATION

Services include individual counseling to determine necessary accommodations; arrangements for special services such as readers, scribes, and note-takers; advocacy with faculty and staff; assistance to faculty and staff in determining appropriate accommodations; help in determining specific needs for students with learning disabilities; and referral to campus and community agencies for additional services. Basic study skill classes are offered for all students and may be taken for credit. Services and accommodations are provided for undergraduate and graduate students.

Support Services Contact Information

Learning Disability Program/Services: Disability Services
Director: Mary Matthews
  E-Mail: fydso@uaf.edu
  Telephone: 907-474-7043
  Fax: 907-474-5777

LEARNING DISABILITY SERVICES

Requests for the following/services accommodations will be evaluated individually based on appropriate and current documentation.

Allowed in exams
  Calculator: No
  Dictionary: Yes
  Computer: Yes
  Spellchecker: Yes
Extended test time: Yes
Scribes: Yes
Proctors: Yes
Oral exams: Yes
Note-takers: Yes

Distraction-reduced environment: Yes
Tape recording in class: Yes
Books on tape from RFBD: Yes
Taping of books not from RFBD: Yes
Accommodations for students with ADD: Yes
Reading machine: Yes
Other assistive technology: Yes
Priority registration: No

Added costs for services: No
LD specialists: No
Professional tutors: No
Peer tutors: No
Max. hours/wk. for services: N/A
How professors are notified of LD/ADD: By student

GENERAL ADMISSIONS INFORMATION

Director of Admissions: Claudia C. Clark
Telephone: 907-474-7500

ENTRANCE REQUIREMENTS
Academic units required: 4 English, 3 math, 3 science (1 science lab), 3 social studies, 3 academic electives.
Academic units recommended: 2 foreign language. High school diploma is required and GED is accepted. TOEFL required of all international applicants, minimum paper TOEFL 550, minimum computer TOEFL 213.

Application deadline: 8/1
Notification: Rolling
Average GPA: 3.11

Average SAT Math: 519
Average SAT Verbal: 532
Average ACT: 21

Graduated top 10% of class: 14%
Graduated top 25% of class: 32%
Graduated top 50% of class: 64%

COLLEGE GRADUATION REQUIREMENTS

Course waivers allowed: No
Course substitutions allowed: Yes
In what course: Depends on documentation

ADDITIONAL INFORMATION

Environment: The university is in a small town close to Fairbanks.

Student Body:
  Undergrad enrollment: 4,793
  Women: 57%
  Men: 43%
  Percent out-of-state: 14%

Cost Information
  In-state tuition: $3,480
  Out-of-state tuition: $11,100
  Room & board: $5,580
Housing Information
  University housing: Yes
  Percent living on campus: 29%

Greek System
  Fraternity: Yes
  Sorority: Yes
Athletics: NCAA Division II

ARIZONA STATE UNIVERSITY

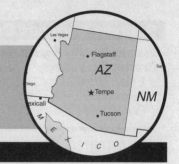

Box 870112, Tempe, AZ 85287-0112
Phone: 480-965-7788 • Fax: 480-965-3610
E-mail: ugradinq@asu.edu • Web: www.asu.edu
Support: CS • Institution type: 4-year public

LEARNING DISABILITY PROGRAM AND SERVICES

ASU's Disabled Student Resources (DSR) program strives to facilitate resources, services, and auxiliary aids to allow each qualified student with disabilities to equitably access educational, social, and career opportunities. Students utilizing the services through the DSR program are mainstreamed in all courses. Support is available but students need to be assertive and have a desire to succeed. The services are geared to the needs of the particular student and are individually based. Each student is encouraged to seek out methods for attaining the highest possible goals. All services and accommodations are provided upon request on an individual basis as appropriate for qualified/eligible individuals with learning disabilities. The goal of DSR is to assist the student in becoming academically and socially independent. The DSR staff includes professionals who facilitate a wide range of academic support services and accommodations. The center also provides consultation on disability issues to the surrounding community.

LD/ADD ADMISSIONS INFORMATION

College entrance tests required: Yes
Interview required: No
Essay required: No
Documentation required for LD: Psychoeducational
  evaluation
Documentation required for ADD: Yes
Submitted to: Disability Resource Center
Special Ed. HS coursework accepted: Yes

Specific course requirements of all applicants: Yes
Separate application required for program servics: No
# of LD applications submitted each year: 163
# of LD applications accepted yearly: 150
Total # of students receiving LD services: 359
**Acceptance into program means acceptance into
  college:** Student must be admitted and enrolled in the
  university first and then request services.

ADMISSIONS
Students with LD submit the regular ASU application. Students should self-disclose their LD and submit documentation. Courses required: 4 years English, 4 years math, 3 years science, 2 years social science, and 1 year fine arts. Arizona residents should rank in the top quarter or have a 22 ACT/930 SAT or a 3.0 GPA in core courses. Nonresidents should rank in the top quarter or have a 24 ACT/1010 SAT or a 3.0 GPA in core courses. Nonresidents who have a strong high school background and who rank in the top 50 percent or have a GPA of 2.5–2.9 will be considered individually. To appeal a denial an applicant should write a letter stating reasons for wanting to attend ASU and describing ability for success, send 3 recommendations showing motivation and perseverance and send a transcript showing gradual upward trend in courses and grades. Appeals are reviewed by admissions and disability support personnel. If applicant is ultimately denied after an appeal or 6 hours of credit or less is desired per semester, a non-degree seeking application is available. Transcripts are not required. Students can earn up to 15 non-degree hours to be applied toward a degree program. Non-degree candidates may live in residential housing at ASU and attend ASU and the local community college. After 24 credits and a GPA of 2.0 the student may apply for regular admission at ASU.

ADDITIONAL INFORMATION
Academic support accommodations include consultation, individualized program recommendations, registration information and advisement referrals, academic tutoring, Computer Technology Center, learning strategies instruction, library research assistance, supplemental readers in coordination with RFBD, mastery of Alternative Learning Techniques lab, in-class note taking, testing accommodations, and diagnostic testing referrals. DSR provides in-service training for faculty/staff. Services and accommodations are available for undergraduate and graduate students. DSR will accept current diagnosis of ADD that are based on appropriate diagnostic information given by a licensed/certified professional. The diagnosis must be written on professional letterhead and include a clinical history, instruments used for the diagnosis, narrative, DSM–IV diagnosis and recommendations for accommodations. All students have access to skills classes in time management, note taking strategies, test-taking and career awareness.

Support Services Contact Information

Learning Disability Program/Services: Disability Resource Center For Academic Access and Achievement
Director: Deb Taska
  E-Mail: woodel@asu.edu
  Telephone: 602-965-1234
  Fax: 602-965-0441
Contact Person: Susan DeFrank-Wingate
  E-Mail: swingate@asu.edu
  Telephone: 602-965-1234
  Fax: 602-965-0441

LEARNING DISABILITY SERVICES

Requests for the following/services accommodations will be evaluated individually based on appropriate and current documentation.

Allowed in exams
  Calculator: Yes
  Dictionary: Yes
  Computer: Yes
  Spellchecker: Yes
Extended test time: Yes
Scribes: Yes
Proctors: Yes
Oral exams: Yes
Note-takers: Yes

Distraction-reduced environment: Yes
Tape recording in class: Yes
Books on tape from RFBD: Yes
Taping of books not from RFBD: Yes
Accommodations for students with ADD: Yes
Reading machine: Yes
Other assistive technology: Yes
Priority registration: Yes

Added costs for services: No
LD specialists: Yes
Professional tutors: No
Peer tutors: No
Max. hours/wk. for services: 3
How professors are notified of LD/ADD: By student

GENERAL ADMISSIONS INFORMATION

Director of Admissions: Timothy Desch
Telephone: 480-965-7788

ENTRANCE REQUIREMENTS
Academic units required: 4 English, 4 math, 3 science (3 science lab), 2 foreign language, 1 social studies, 1 history, 1 fine arts. High school diploma is required and GED is accepted. ACT with or without Writing component accepted. TOEFL required of all international applicants, minimum paper TOEFL 500, minimum computer TOEFL 173.

Application deadline: Rolling
Notification: Rolling
Average GPA: 3.34

Average SAT Math: 559
Average SAT Verbal: 547
Average ACT: 23

Graduated top 10% of class: 27%
Graduated top 25% of class: 54%
Graduated top 50% of class: 83%

COLLEGE GRADUATION REQUIREMENTS

Course waivers allowed: No
Course substitutions allowed: Yes
In what course: Petitions for variance from degree requirements are evaluated on a case-by-case basis by the individual's college standards committee.

ADDITIONAL INFORMATION

Environment: Arizona State University is a city school about 5 miles from Phoenix.

Student Body:
  Undergrad enrollment: 38,117
  Women: 52%
  Men: 48%
  Percent out-of-state: 23%

Cost Information
  In-state tuition: $3,973
  Out-of-state tuition: $12,828
  Room & board: $6,574
Housing Information
  University housing: Yes
  Percent living on campus: 14%

Greek System
  Fraternity: Yes
  Sorority: Yes
Athletics: NCAA Division I

NORTHERN ARIZONA UNIVERSITY

PO Box 4084, Flagstaff, AZ 86011-4084
Phone: 928-523-5511 • Fax: 928-523-0226
E-mail: undergraduate.admissions@nau.edu • Web: www.nau.edu
Support: S • Institution type: 4-year public

LEARNING DISABILITY PROGRAM AND SERVICES

Disability Support Services promotes educational opportunities for students with disabilities at Northern Arizona University. DSS assists students with their determination to graduate and to realize their life goals by providing resources, services, and auxiliary aids. The goal is to assist students in achieving their academic goals while at the same time creating an environment conducive to learning and building self-esteem. The belief is that in providing supportive assistance the student will become an independent learner and self-advocate.

LD/ADD ADMISSIONS INFORMATION

College entrance tests required: Yes
Interview required: No
Essay required: No
Documentation required for LD: Psychoeducational evaluation
Documentation required for ADD: Yes
Submitted to: Disability Support Services
Special Ed. HS coursework accepted: Yes

Specific course requirements of all applicants: Yes
Separate application required for program servics: No
# of LD applications submitted each year: NR
# of LD applications accepted yearly: NR
Total # of students receiving LD services: 117
Acceptance into program means acceptance into college: Student must be admitted and enrolled in the university first and then request services.

ADMISSIONS

There are no special admissions criteria for students with learning disabilities. General admission requirements for unconditional admission include 4 years English, 4 years math, 2 years social science with 1 year being American history, 2–3 years lab science with additional requirements, 1 year fine arts, and 2 years foreign language. Students may be admitted conditionally with course deficiencies, but not in both math and science. 2.5 GPA or top 50 percent for in-state residents (3.0 GPA or the upper 25 percent of the graduating class for nonresidents) or SAT of 930 (1010 for nonresidents) or an ACT of 22 (24 for nonresidents). Conditional admissions is possible with a 2.5–2.99 GPA or top 50 percent of graduating class and ACT/ SAT scores. Exceptional admission may be offered to 10 percent of the new freshmen applicants or transfer applicants.

ADDITIONAL INFORMATION

Skills classes are available in note-taking; study techniques; reading, memory, and learning; overcoming math anxiety; speed reading; time management; and test-taking strategies. Specific workshops cover How to Make Math Easy; How to Get Started Writing; "How to Edit Writing;" and "How to Prepare for Final Exams." All services and accommodations are available for undergraduate and graduate students.

Support Services Contact Information

Learning Disability Program/Services: Disability Support Services
Director: Chad Loberger
  E-Mail: chad.loberger@nau.edu
  Telephone: 928-523-8773
  Fax: 928-523-8747
Contact Person: Terry Alban
  E-Mail: disability.support@nau.edu
  Telephone: 928-523-8773
  Fax: 928-523-8747

LEARNING DISABILITY SERVICES

Requests for the following/services accommodations will be evaluated individually based on appropriate and current documentation.

Allowed in exams
  Calculator: Yes
  Dictionary: Yes
  Computer: Yes
  Spellchecker: Yes
Extended test time: Yes
Scribes: Yes
Proctors: Yes
Oral exams: Yes
Note-takers: Yes

Distraction-reduced environment: Yes
Tape recording in class: Yes
Books on tape from RFBD: Yes
Taping of books not from RFBD: Yes
Accommodations for students with ADD: Yes
Reading machine: Yes
Other assistive technology: Yes
Priority registration: Yes

Added costs for services: No
LD specialists: No
Professional tutors: No
Peer tutors: 100
Max. hours/wk. for services: Unlimited
How professors are notified of LD/ADD: By student

GENERAL ADMISSIONS INFORMATION

Director of Admissions: David Bousquet
Telephone: 928-523-8483

ENTRANCE REQUIREMENTS

Academic units required: 4 English, 4 math, 3 science (1 science lab), 2 foreign language, 1 social studies, 1 history, 1 Fine Arts. **Academic units recommended:** 4 English, 4 math, 3 science (3 science lab). ACT with or without writing component accepted. High school diploma is required and GED is accepted. TOEFL required of all international applicants, minimum paper TOEFL 500, minimum computer TOEFL 173.

Application deadline: Rolling
Notification: Rolling
Average GPA: 3.40

Average SAT Math: 535
Average SAT Verbal: 451
Average ACT: 26

Graduated top 10% of class: 17%
Graduated top 25% of class: 47%
Graduated top 50% of class: 80%

COLLEGE GRADUATION REQUIREMENTS

Course waivers allowed: No
Course substitutions allowed: Yes
In what course: There is a math substitution (not waiver) program for individuals with a math learning disability. It only applies to the liberal studies math requirement.

ADDITIONAL INFORMATION

Environment: The university is located on 320 acres in an urban area 2 hours from Phoenix.

Student Body:
  Undergrad enrollment: 13,135
  Women: 60%
  Men: 40%
  Percent out-of-state: 14%

Cost Information
  In-state tuition: $3,983
  Out-of-state tuition: $12,503
  Room & board: $5,785
Housing Information
  University housing: Yes
  Percent living on campus: 38%

Greek System
  Fraternity: Yes
  Sorority: Yes
  Athletics: NCAA Division I

UNIVERSITY OF ARIZONA

PO Box 210040, Tucson, AZ 85721-0040
Phone: 520-621-3237 • Fax: 520-621-9799
E-mail: appinfo@arizona.edu • Web: www.arizona.edu
Support: SP • Institution type: 4-year public

LEARNING DISABILITY PROGRAM AND SERVICES

The Strategic Alternative Learning Techniques (SALT) Center challenges students with LD to succeed in their pursuit of higher education. Supporting the ideal of education for life, SALT encourages and provides experiences and opportunities to build confidence beyond the classroom. SALT encourages growth and independence, training individuals to improve learning, expression, and decision making. A major philosophy is to provide intensive service for the first year with the goal of increasing independence as the student learns the coping strategies to succeed in college. The following guidelines clarify the process of documenting LD at UA: Assessment and testing must be comprehensive and include a diagnostic interview and results of a neuropsychological or psychoeducational evaluation; a specific diagnosis and actual test scores; current evaluation by a qualified professional; recommended accommodations should include a rationale that correlates the accommodations to specific test results and clinical observations. Students providing documentation express a desire to qualify for consideration as an individual with a disability. Being identified as LD/ADD does not afford any individual automatic access to university accommodations or for privileges as an individual with disabilities. The university has established guidelines to meet diverse needs while maintaining the integrity of academic and non-academic programming.

LD/ADD ADMISSIONS INFORMATION

College entrance tests required: Yes
Interview required: No, but recommended
Essay required: No
Documentation required for LD: A complete diagnostic battery including measures of aptitude/intellectual functioning, cognitive/information processing, and academic achievement.
See http://drc.arizona.edu/drc/ldprotocol.shtml
Documentation required for ADD: A complete diagnostic battery including a complete clinical history including measures of attention, aptitude/intellectual functioning, cognitive/information processing, and academic achievement.
See http://drc.arizona.edu/drc/adhdprotocol.shtml

Submitted to: Both Admissions and Disability Resource Center
Special Ed. HS coursework accepted: No
Specific course requirements of all applicants: Yes
Separate application required for program servics: Yes, for SALT
# of LD applications submitted each year: 500 plus
# of LD applications accepted yearly: 180
Total # of students receiving LD services: 600
Acceptance into program means acceptance into college: Students are admitted to the university and then will be considered for SALT.

ADMISSIONS

The majority of students with disabilities seeking admission to UA meet the general admission requirements, which include either ACT 24 (22 in-state), or SAT 1010 (930 in-state); top 25 percent of class (top 50 percent in-state) or 3.0 GPA (2.5 in-state); and 4 years English, 4 years math, 3 years science, 2 years social studies, and 2 years foreign language, and 1 year fine arts. Candidates with disabilities, desiring special consideration, are expected to provide all documentation they feel necessary to represent the specific circumstances. If the candidate has a learning disability or attention deficit disorder and is requesting special consideration through admission to the SALT program, the student should submit all documentation of disability directly to UA admissions. Students may apply to SALT at any time beginning in August preceding their senior year of high school. A student may submit documentation with the SALT application as well, but one copy must accompany the UA application for admission in order to receive special consideration. Whenever possible, the SALT Center will announce its decision regarding a student's application for admission to SALT concurrently with the university's notification of acceptance. Incomplete records at SALT could delay a decision.

ADDITIONAL INFORMATION

Basic services include advocacy, auxiliary aids for classroom accommodations, and special testing; there is no charge for these services. Enhanced services provide a full-service program with academic monitoring, registration assistance, staff contact and trained learning specialists, tutoring, a writing enhancement program, a specially equipped computer learning laboratory, and personalized tutorial services. Each student works with a trained specialist to identify learning preferences, learning strategies, and appropriate compensatory, productive learning techniques. There is a fee for enhanced services. Support services include both academic programs and counseling components. Students receive assistance with academic planning and registration followed by regularly scheduled staff contact to monitor progress. A Drop-In Center is available for study, tutoring, and student/staff interaction. The SALT program is staffed by persons trained and experienced in working with students with LD.

Support Services Contact Information

Learning Disability Program/Services: Disability Resource Center
Director: Dr. Sue Kroeger
  E-Mail: uadrc@email.arizona.edu
  Telephone: 520-621-3268 V/TTY
  Fax: 520-621-9423
Contact Person: Christine Salvesen
  E-Mail: cls@email.arizona.edu
  Telephone: 520-626-9234
  Fax: 520-621-9423

LEARNING DISABILITY SERVICES

Requests for the following/services accommodations will be evaluated individually based on appropriate and current documentation.

Allowed in exams
  Calculator: Yes
  Dictionary: Yes
  Computer: Yes
  Spellchecker: Yes
Extended test time: Yes
Scribes: Yes
Proctors: Yes
Oral exams: Yes
Note-takers: Yes

Distraction-reduced environment: Yes
Tape recording in class: Yes
Books on tape from RFBD: Yes
Taping of books not from RFBD: Yes
Accommodations for students with ADD: Yes
Reading machine: Yes
Other assistive technology: Yes
Priority registration: Yes

Added costs for services: $900–$2,100 per semester
LD specialists: Yes
Professional tutors: No
Peer tutors: Yes
Max. hours/wk. for services: Unlimited
How professors are notified of LD/ADD: By student

GENERAL ADMISSIONS INFORMATION

Director of Admissions: Paul Kohn, Assistant VP for Admissions, Scholarship, and Financial Aid
Telephone: 520-621-3237

ENTRANCE REQUIREMENTS
Academic units required: 4 English, 4 math, 3 science (3 science lab), 2 foreign language, 1 social studies, 1 history, 1 Fine Arts. **Academic units recommended:** 22 ACT (24 out-of-state) or 930 SAT (1010 out-of-state) or top 50 percent (top 25 percent out-of-state) or 2.5 GPA (3.0 out-of-state). ACT with or without Writing component. High school diploma is required and GED is accepted, minimum paper TOEFL 500, minimum computer TOEFL 173.

Application deadline: 4/1
Notification: Rolling
Average GPA: 3.4

Average SAT Math: 563
Average SAT Verbal: 552
Average ACT: 23

Graduated top 10% of class: NR
Graduated top 25% of class: NR
Graduated top 50% of class: NR

COLLEGE GRADUATION REQUIREMENTS

Course waivers allowed: No
Course substitutions allowed: Yes
In what course: Course substitutions are typically in math or second language; approval must come from college/major department.

ADDITIONAL INFORMATION

Environment: Situated in downtown Tucson on 325 acres, the university is surrounded by the Santa Catalina Mountain range in the Sonora Desert.

Student Body:
  Undergrad enrollment: 27,853
  Women: 53%
  Men: 47%
  Percent out-of-state: 27%

Cost Information
  In-state tuition: $3,998
  Out-of-state tuition: $12,978
  Room & board: $7,108
Housing Information
  University housing: Yes
  Percent living on campus: 18%

Greek System
  Fraternity: Yes
  Sorority: Yes
Athletics: NCAA Division I

HARDING UNIVERSITY

PO Box 12255, Searcy, AR 72149
Phone: 501-279-4407 • Fax: 501-279-4129
E-mail: admissions@harding.edu • Web: www.harding.edu
Support: CS • Institution type: 4-year private

LEARNING DISABILITY PROGRAM AND SERVICES

The philosophy and goals of Student Support Services (SSS) are to foster an institutional climate supportive of the success of "high risk" students at Harding University. SSS strives to deliver a program of services that will result in increasing the college retention and graduation rates of these students. Each student in the program receives a high level of personal attention to and support for his/her needs throughout the school year. Students meet with an academic counselor concerning their specific needs. Students are given the opportunity to discuss their needs and goals with someone to help them better understand them. There are many workshops offered to provide students with hands-on learning. There is also a ropes course, which teaches a variety of skills including communication, trust, and working as a team.

LD/ADD ADMISSIONS INFORMATION

College entrance tests required: Yes
Interview required: No
Essay required: Yes
Documentation required for LD: Current psychological evaluation (preferred senior year in High School) by licensed professional.
Documentation required for ADD: Evaluation by medical doctor
Submitted to: Both Admissions and Student Support Services
Special Ed. HS coursework accepted: No

Specific course requirements of all applicants: Yes
Separate application required for program servics: No
# of LD applications submitted each year: 100
# of LD applications accepted yearly: 100
Total # of students receiving LD services: 78
Acceptance into program means acceptance into college: Student must be admitted and enrolled in the university first and then request services.

ADMISSIONS

Admission criteria for students with learning disabilities are the same as for regular applicants, except that scores made on special administrations of college entrance exams (ACT/SAT) are accepted. These scores, however, must meet accepted admissions criteria. Students who score 18 or below on the ACT (or equivalent SAT) are admitted into the Developmental Studies Program. Transfer students with low GPAs are accepted on probation. Course requirements include 4 years English, 3 years math, 3 years social studies, and 2 years science; 2 years of foreign language are recommended. The minimum GPA is a 2.0. The director of SSS makes admission decisions for the program and the director of admissions determines admissibility into the university. Students may self-disclose in the admission process and this information could be used as one component in making an admission decision.

ADDITIONAL INFORMATION

Testing accommodations are provided with documented evidence of a disability. These accommodations include extended time on exams, readers, taking the test in parts with breaks, use of a computer with spell-check, and providing a distraction-free environment. Classroom accommodations may include a computer with spell-check; extra time for proofreading and editing of written assignments; note-takers; books on tape; and taping outside reading assignments. Professors do not receive documentation or explanation unless the student signs a release form that would permit the release of such sensitive information. Each semester the student is asked to sign a permission form designating which professors should receive letters. Skills classes for college credit are offered in beginning algebra, basic English, college reading, and study skills. The CAPS (coaches and players) mentoring program targets primarily students with ADD/ADD.

Support Services Contact Information

Learning Disability Program/Services: Student Support Services (SSS)
Director: Linda Thompson, EdD
  E-Mail: lthompson@harding.edu
  Telephone: 501-279-4416
  Fax: 501-279-4217
Contact Person: Teresa McLeod, MEd
  E-Mail: tmcleod@harding.edu
  Telephone: 501-279-4019
  Fax: 501-279-4217

LEARNING DISABILITY SERVICES

Requests for the following/services accommodations will be evaluated individually based on appropriate and current documentation.

Allowed in exams
  Calculator: Yes
  Dictionary: Yes
  Computer: Yes
  Spellchecker: Yes
Extended test time: Yes
Scribes: Yes
Proctors: Yes
Oral exams: Yes
Note-takers: Yes

Distraction-reduced environment: Yes
Tape recording in class: Yes
Books on tape from RFBD: Yes
Taping of books not from RFBD: Yes
Accommodations for students with
  ADD: Yes
Reading machine: Yes
Other assistive technology: Yes
Priority registration: Yes

Added costs for services: No
LD specialists: Yes
Professional tutors: 1
Peer tutors: 15
Max. hours/wk. for services:
  Unlimited
How professors are notified of
  LD/ADD: By both student and director

GENERAL ADMISSIONS INFORMATION

Director of Admissions: Glenn Dillard
Telephone: 800-477-4407

ENTRANCE REQUIREMENTS
Academic units required: 4 English, 3 math, 2 science, 3 social studies, 3 academic electives. **Academic units recommended:** 4 English, 4 math, 4 science, 2 foreign language, 4 social studies, 2 academic electives. High school diploma is required and GED is accepted. ACT with or without Writing component accepted. TOEFL required of all international applicants, minimum paper TOEFL 500, minimum computer TOEFL 175.

Application deadline: 7/1
Notification: Rolling
Average GPA: 3.40

Average SAT Math: 548
Average SAT Verbal: 562
Average ACT: 23

Graduated top 10% of class: 26%
Graduated top 25% of class: 52%
Graduated top 50% of class: 80%

COLLEGE GRADUATION REQUIREMENTS

Course waivers allowed: No
Course substitutions allowed: No
In what course: N/A

ADDITIONAL INFORMATION

Environment: The university is located on 200 acres in a small town 50 miles northeast of Little Rock.

Student Body:
  Undergrad enrollment: 4,023
  Women: 54%
  Men: 46%
  Percent out-of-state: 70%

Cost Information
  Tuition: $10,380
  Room & board: $5,182
Housing Information
  University housing: Yes
  Percent living on campus: 73%

Greek System
  Fraternity: Yes
  Sorority: Yes
Athletics: NCAA Division II

UNIVERSITY OF THE OZARKS

415 College Avenue, Clarksville, AR 72830
Phone: 479-979-1227 • Fax: 479-979-1355
E-mail: jdecker@ozarks.edu • Web: www.ozarks.edu
Support: SP • Institution type: 4-year private

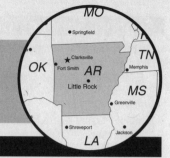

LEARNING DISABILITY PROGRAM AND SERVICES

The Jones Learning Center believes that students with specific learning disabilities are entitled to services that allow them to compete with other students. The Learning Center program emphasizes a total learning environment. Instruction is individualized and personalized. Enhanced services include individualized programming, a technology unit, centralized accessibility, and a supportive atmosphere with low student-to-staff ratio, which provides students even greater opportunity to realize their true academic potential. Ideas, instructional materials, and activities are presented on a variety of different levels commensurate with the educational needs of the individual student. This program is very comprehensive in every area. At the beginning of each semester the course load and needs of the student are assessed to determine what services will be needed.

LD/ADD ADMISSIONS INFORMATION

College entrance tests required: Yes
Interview required: Yes
Essay required: Yes
Documentation required for LD: Psychoeducational evaluation
Documentation required for ADD: Yes
Submitted to: Jones Learning Center
Special Ed. HS coursework accepted: Yes

Specific course requirements of all applicants: Yes
Separate application required for program servics: Yes
# of LD applications submitted each year: 50–60
# of LD applications accepted yearly: 25–30
Total # of students receiving LD services: 66
Acceptance into program means acceptance into college: Students admitted to the Learning Center are automatically accepted to the university.

ADMISSIONS

Students complete a special application. Applicants must be 18 or older, complete high school or obtain a GED, demonstrate average or above-average I.Q., have a learning disability or attention deficit disorder as a primary disability, provide diagnostic information from previous evaluations, complete the admissions packet, visit campus, and participate in a two-day psychoeducational evaluation that includes interviews. Applicants with some areas of concern for the admissions committee may be admitted on a one-year trial basis. This conditional admission is only available to students applying to the Jones Learning Center. There are no specific high school courses and no minimum ACT/SAT scores required for admission. Admission decisions are made by the admissions committee. Motivation is a key factor in the admission decision. Students are encouraged to begin the application to the Jones Learning Center during the spring semester of their junior year or early in the senior year. The JLC has a rolling admission policy.

ADDITIONAL INFORMATION

Students are assigned to a program coordinator who is responsible for the individualized planning of the student's program of study. The coordinator also acts as an advocate and monitors the student's progress. Students receive help understanding learning styles, utilizing strengths, circumventing deficits, building skills, and becoming independent learners and self-advocates. Skills classes are offered in study skills (for credit), writing (for credit), reading and math. Enhanced services include testing accommodations, one-to-one administration of a test with a reader and staff to take dictation if needed, assistive technology including Dragon Dictate and a Kurzweil Scanner/reader, peer tutoring, and note-takers. Developmental services include opportunities to improve basic skills in reading, writing and math. Students with ADD and/or LD may receive services from the Learning Center.

Support Services Contact Information

Learning Disability Program/Services: Jones Learning Center
Director: Julia Frost
  E-Mail: jfrost@ozarks.edu
  Telephone: 479-979-1401
  Fax: 479-979-1477
Contact Person: Debby Mooney
  E-Mail: dmooney@ozarks.edu
  Telephone: 479-979-1422
  Fax: 479-979-1477

LEARNING DISABILITY SERVICES

Requests for the following/services accommodations will be evaluated individually based on appropriate and current documentation.

Allowed in exams
  Calculator: Yes
  Dictionary: No
  Computer: Yes
  Spellchecker: Yes
Extended test time: Yes
Scribes: Yes
Proctors: Yes
Oral exams: Yes
Note-takers: Yes

Distraction-reduced environment: Yes
Tape recording in class: Yes
Books on tape from RFBD: No
Taping of books not from RFBD: Yes
Accommodations for students with ADD: Yes
Reading machine: Yes
Other assistive technology: Yes
Priority registration: No

Added costs for services: $6,800 per semester
LD specialists: Yes
Professional tutors: 15
Peer tutors: 100-125
Max. hours/wk. for services: Unlimited
How professors are notified of LD/ADD: By both student and director

GENERAL ADMISSIONS INFORMATION

Director of Admissions: Jana Hart
Telephone: 800-264-8600

ENTRANCE REQUIREMENTS

Academic units required: 4 English, 4 math, 3 science, (2 science lab), 2 foreign language, 1 social studies, 2 history. High school diploma is required and GED is accepted. TOEFL required of all international applicants, minimum paper TOEFL 500, minimum computer TOEFL 173.

Application deadline: Rolling
Notification: Rolling
Average GPA: 3.40

Average SAT Math: 510
Average SAT Verbal: 525
Average ACT: 22

Graduated top 10% of class: 23%
Graduated top 25% of class: 44%
Graduated top 50% of class: 77%

COLLEGE GRADUATION REQUIREMENTS

Course waivers allowed: No
Course substitutions allowed: Yes
In what course: College Algebra and foreign language

ADDITIONAL INFORMATION

Environment: The university is located on 56 acres, 100 miles northwest of Little Rock. Clarksville is a town of 5,000 residents in the Arkansas River Valley.

Student Body:
  Undergrad enrollment: 612
  Women: 53%
  Men: 47%
  Percent out-of-state: 42%

Cost Information
  Tuition: $13,312
  Room & board: $4,880
Housing Information
  University housing: Yes
  Percent living on campus: 64%

Greek System
  Fraternity: No
  Sorority: No
  Athletics: NCAA Division III

CAL POLYTECH. STATE U.—SAN LUIS OBISPO

Admissions Office, Cal Poly, San Luis Obispo, CA 93407
Phone: 805-756-2311 • Fax: 805-756-5400
E-mail: admissions@calpoly.edu • Web: www.calpoly.edu
Support: CS • Institution type: 4-year public

LEARNING DISABILITY PROGRAM AND SERVICES

The goal of the program is to assist students with learning disabilities to use their learning strengths. The Disability Resources Center (DRC) assists students with disabilities in achieving access to higher education, promotes personal and educational success, and increases the awareness and responsiveness of the campus community. DRC is actively involved with students and faculty and provides a newsletter and open house to keep the college population aware of who it is and what it does. Incoming students are encouraged to meet with DRC staff to receive assistance in the planning of class schedules. This allows for the selection of appropriate classes to fit particular needs and personal goals. It is the responsibility of each student seeking accommodations and services to provide a written, comprehensive psychological and/or medical evaluation verifying the diagnosis. The Cal Poly Student Learning Outcomes model promotes student personal growth and the development of self-advocacy for full inclusion of qualified students with verified disabilities. The promotion of student self-reliance and responsibility are necessary adjuncts to educational development. For learning disabilities, the assessments must be done by a licensed educational psychologist, psychologist, neurologist, or LD specialist. The diagnosis of ADD must be done by a licensed therapist, educational psychologist, psychologist, psychiatrist, neurologist, or physician.

LD/ADD ADMISSIONS INFORMATION

College entrance tests required: Yes
Interview required: No
Essay required: No
Documentation required for LD: Psychoeducational evaluation
Documentation required for ADD: Yes
Submitted to: Disability Resource Center
Special Ed. HS coursework accepted: Yes

Specific course requirements of all applicants: Yes
Separate application required for program servics: No
# of LD applications submitted each year: 100–150
# of LD applications accepted yearly: 50–70
Total # of students receiving LD services: 250–325
Acceptance into program means acceptance into college: Student must be admitted and enrolled in the university first and then request services.

ADMISSIONS

Students with LD must meet the same admission criteria as all applicants, and should submit a general admission application to the admissions office. General requirements include 4 years English, 3 years math, 1 year U.S. history or government, 1 year lab science, 2 years foreign language, 1 year fine arts, and 3 years electives. On a case-by-case basis, foreign language substitutions may be allowed. Some courses taken in the Special Education Department may be accepted. All documentation should be sent directly to the Support Program, and students who self-disclose will receive information. Admission decisions are made by the admissions office.

ADDITIONAL INFORMATION

Incoming students are strongly urged to schedule an appointment with DRC to receive assistance in the planning of classes. Academic accommodations are designed to meet a student's disabiity-related needs without fundamentally altering the nature of the instructional program, and are not intended to provide remediation. Supportive services may include academic advising, alternative format materials, assistive listening devices, note-taking, taped textbooks, test accommodations, tutorial services, and writing assistance. DRC may recommend the services of the Academic Skills Center of Student Academic Services and enrollment in English and math classes offering additional support. There is also a Peer Mentoring program and Partners for Success, and a career mentoring program available to all students. Students requesting accommodations, which include using a computer, dictionary, or spellcheck during an exam, will need the professor's permission. The university can provide some free psychoeducational assessment services, but there is a lengthy waiting period for these limited services. Services and accommodations are available to undergraduate and graduate students.

Support Services Contact Information

Learning Disability Program/Services: Disability Resource Center (DRC)
Director: William Bailey
  E-Mail: wbailey@calpoly.edu
  Telephone: 805-756-1395
  Fax: 805-756-5451
Contact Person: Dr. Steven Kane
  E-Mail: skane@calpoly.edu
  Telephone: 805-756-1395
  Fax: 805-756-5451

LEARNING DISABILITY SERVICES

Requests for the following/services accommodations will be evaluated individually based on appropriate and current documentation.

Allowed in exams
  Calculator: Yes
  Dictionary: Yes
  Computer: Yes
  Spellchecker: Yes
Extended test time: Yes
Scribes: Yes
Proctors: Yes
Oral exams: Yes
Note-takers: Yes

Distraction-reduced environment: Yes
Tape recording in class: Yes
Books on tape from RFBD: Yes
Taping of books not from RFBD: Yes
Accommodations for students with ADD: Yes
Reading machine: No
Other assistive technology: Yes
Priority registration: Varies

Added costs for services: No
LD specialists: Yes
Professional tutors: No
Peer tutors: No
Max. hours/wk. for services: Depends on service
How professors are notified of LD/ADD: By student

GENERAL ADMISSIONS INFORMATION

Director of Admissions: James Maraviglia
Telephone: 805-756-2311

ENTRANCE REQUIREMENTS

Academic units required: 4 English, 3 math, 3 science (1 science lab), 2 foreign language. High school diploma is required and GED is accepted. ACT with or without Writing component accepted. TOEFL required of all international applicants, minimum paper TOEFL 550, minimum computer TOEFL 213.

Application deadline: 11/30
Notification: Rolling
Average GPA: 3.70

Average SAT Math: 639
Average SAT Verbal: 594
Average ACT: 28

Graduated top 10% of class: 42%
Graduated top 25% of class: 79%
Graduated top 50% of class: 97%

COLLEGE GRADUATION REQUIREMENTS

Course waivers allowed: No
Course substitutions allowed: No
In what course: N/A

ADDITIONAL INFORMATION

Environment: The campus is located 100 miles north of Santa Barbara.

Student Body:
  Undergrad enrollment: 16,565
  Women: 43%
  Men: 57%
  Percent out-of-state: 7%

Cost Information
  In-state tuition: $3,804
  Out-of-state tuition: $10,284
  Room & board: $7,801
Housing Information
  University housing: Yes
  Percent living on campus: 22%

Greek System
  Fraternity: Yes
  Sorority: Yes
Athletics: NCAA Division I

CAL. STATE POLYTECH. U.—POMONA

3801 West Temple Avenue, Pomona, CA 91768
Phone: 909-869-3210 • Fax: 909-869-4529
E-mail: admissions@csupomona.edu • Web: www.csupomona.edu
Support: CS • Institution type: 4-year public

LEARNING DISABILITY PROGRAM AND SERVICES

The mission of the Office of Disabled Student Services is to help students with disabilities compete on an equal basis with their nondisabled peers by providing reasonable accommodations. This will allow them access to any academic program or to facilitate participation in any university activity that is offered to fellow students. The major purposes of DSS are: To determine reasonable accommodations based on disability as assessed by knowledgeable professionals; to emphasize self-advocacy; to maximize learning experience and to continuously assess students' needs; to actively recruit and increase retention and graduation rates of students with disabilities and provide greater educational equity; to facilitate the university in meeting requirements of the Americans with Disabilities Act; and to prepare students with disabilities for life, leadership, and careers in a changing world.

LD/ADD ADMISSIONS INFORMATION

College entrance tests required: Yes
Interview required: No
Essay required: No
Documentation required for LD: Report with scores for aptitude and achievement testing.
Documentation required for ADD: Any testing performed or history should be summarized in a report. Will also accept a 6th from diagnostician indicating the diagnostic functional limitation history and current problems, and recommendations of an academic setting
Submitted to: Disabled Student Services
Special Ed. HS coursework accepted: Yes

Specific course requirements of all applicants: Yes
Separate application required for program servics: No
# of LD applications submitted each year: NR
# of LD applications accepted yearly: NR
Total # of students receiving LD services: 400-plus
Acceptance into program means acceptance into college: Student must be admitted and enrolled in the university first and then request services.

ADMISSIONS

Students must meet the university's regular entrance requirements, including C or better in the subject requirements of 4 years English, 3 years math, 1 year U.S. history, 1 year lab science, 2 years foreign language, 1 year visual or performing arts, and 3 years electives, and a qualifiable eligibility index based on high school GPA and scores on either ACT or SAT. Special admits are very limited. Applicants with LD are encouraged to complete college-prep courses. However, if students are unable to fulfill a specific course requirement because of a learning disability, alternative college-prep courses may be substituted. Substitutions may be granted in foreign language, lab science, and math. Substitutions may be authorized on an individual basis after review and recommendation by applicant's guidance counselor in consultation with the director of DSS. Course substitutions could limit access to some majors. Students are encouraged to self-disclose a learning disability if it would help to explain lower grades. Students who self-disclose are reviewed by DSS, which provides a recommendation to admissions.

ADDITIONAL INFORMATION

Support services include counseling, advocacy services, registration, note-takers, readers, tutors, testing accommodations, and specialized equipment. Skills classes are not offered through DSS, but are available in other departments in the areas of reading skills, test preparation, test-taking strategies, and study skills. Services and accommodations are available to undergraduate and graduate students. Cal Poly offers a summer program for any high school student.

Support Services Contact Information

Learning Disability Program/Services: Disabled Student Services (DSS)
Director: Fred Henderson
  E-mail: fdhenderson@csupomona.edu
  Telephone: 909-869-3005
  Fax: 909-869-3271

LEARNING DISABILITY SERVICES

Requests for the following/services accommodations will be evaluated individually based on appropriate and current documentation.

Allowed in exams	**Distraction-reduced environment:** Yes	**Added costs for services:** No
Calculator: Yes	**Tape recording in class:** Yes	**LD specialists:** Yes
Dictionary: Yes	**Books on tape from RFBD:** Yes	**Professional tutors:** No
Computer: Yes	**Taping of books not from RFBD:** Yes	**Peer tutors:** Yes
Spellchecker: Yes	**Accommodations for students with**	**Max. hours/wk. for services:** 2
Extended test time: Yes	**ADD:** Yes	**How professors are notified of**
Scribes: Yes	**Reading machine:** Yes	**LD/ADD:** By student
Proctors: Yes	**Other assistive technology:** Yes	
Oral exams: Yes	**Priority registration:** Yes	
Note-takers: Yes		

GENERAL ADMISSIONS INFORMATION

Director of Admissions: Dr. George R. Bradshaw, Director, Admissions and Outreach
Telephone: 909-869-3427

ENTRANCE REQUIREMENTS

Academic units required: 4 English, 3 math, 2 science (2 science lab), 2 foreign language, 1 social studies, 1 history, 1 academic elective, 1 visual/performing arts. **Academic units recommended:** 4 math. High school diploma is required and GED is accepted. ACT without Writing component accepted. TOEFL required of all international applicants, minimum paper TOEFL 525, minimum computer TOEFL 195.

Application deadline: 11/30	**Average SAT Math:** 518	**Graduated top 10% of class:** NR
Notification: Rolling	**Average SAT Verbal:** 485	**Graduated top 25% of class:** NR
Average GPA: 3.30	**Average ACT:** 20	**Graduated top 50% of class:** NR

COLLEGE GRADUATION REQUIREMENTS

Course waivers allowed: No
Course substitutions allowed: No
In what course: N/A

ADDITIONAL INFORMATION

Environment: The university is located on 1,437 acres in a suburban area 30 miles east of Los Angeles.

Student Body:	**Cost Information**	**Greek System**
Undergrad enrollment: 16,484	**In-state tuition:** $2,046	**Fraternity:** Yes
Women: 43%	**Out-of-state tuition:** $10,506	**Sorority:** Yes
Men: 57%	**Room & board:** $6,747	**Athletics:** NCAA Division II
Percent out-of-state: 1%	**Housing Information**	
	University housing: Yes	
	Percent living on campus: 9%	

CALIFORNIA STATE U.—CHICO

400 West First Street, Chico, CA 95929-0722
Phone: 530-898-4428 • Fax: 530-898-6456
E-mail: info@csuchico.edu • Web: www.csuchico.edu
Support: CS • Institution type: 4-year public

LEARNING DISABILITY PROGRAM AND SERVICES

The goal of Disability Support Services (DSS) is to facilitate accommodation requests and provide the support services necessary to ensure equal access to university programs for students with disabilities. This goal is consistent with university policy and with federal and state laws. DSS provides a variety of services to university students at no charge. DSS advisers who specialize in various disabilities are available to assist students with individual accommodations. It is the student's responsibility to initiate accommodation requests early to ensure proper coordination of services. Students must provide current and appropriate documentation to support their requests for services/accommodations.

LD/ADD ADMISSIONS INFORMATION

College entrance tests required: Yes
Interview required: No
Essay required: No
Documentation required for LD: Psychoeducational evaluation
Documentation required for ADD: Yes
Submitted to: Disability Support Services
Special Ed. HS coursework accepted: Yes

Specific course requirements of all applicants: Yes
Separate application required for program servics: No
# of LD applications submitted each year: NR
# of LD applications accepted yearly: NR
Total # of students receiving LD services: 300
Acceptance into program means acceptance into college: Student must be admitted and enrolled in the university first and then request services.

ADMISSIONS

There are no special admission procedures for students with learning disabilities. Applicants must meet the general admission requirements that are based on GPA, test scores, and subject requirements. Course requirements include: 4 years English, 3 years math, 1 year U.S. history, 1 year science, 2 years foreign language, and 1 year visual and performing arts. Applicants with disabilities are encouraged to complete college-prep courses. If the applicant is judged unable to fulfill a specific course requirement because of a verified disability, alternate college-prep courses may be substituted for specific subject requirements. Substitutions may be authorized on an individual basis after review and recommendation by the high school counselor or academic advisor in consultation with the director of a CSU Disability Support Services program.

ADDITIONAL INFORMATION

General accommodations may include priority registration, note-takers, readers, scribes, test accommodations, computer access assistance, LD assessment, and liaison with faculty and administration. Students are also eligible for certain Retention Services programs, including the Academic Learning Forum and tutoring at the Student Learning Center. Advisors are available to discuss all accommodation requests. There is a math lab, a writing center, a tutoring center, and a Student Learning Center available to all students. The university is committed to making electronic information available to all students. Designated computer stations throughout campus have adaptive hardware and software installed. Software, hardware, and equipment include: Open Book Unbound Reading System, Kurzweil Reading System, DeckTalk PC, Couble Talk LT, Vocal/Window Eyes, Jaws for Windows, Ducksberry Software, and ZoomText Plus; most computers are networked for library and Internet access.

Support Services Contact Information

Learning Disability Program/Services: Disability Support Services
Director: Billie Jackson
  E-Mail: bfjackson@csuchico.edu
  Telephone: 530-898-5959
  Fax: 530-898-4411
Contact Person: Van Alexander
  E-Mail: valexander@csuchico.edu
  Telephone: 530-898-5959
  Fax: 530-898-4411

LEARNING DISABILITY SERVICES

Requests for the following/services accommodations will be evaluated individually based on appropriate and current documentation.

Allowed in exams
  Calculator: Yes
  Dictionary: Yes
  Computer: Yes
  Spellchecker: Yes
Extended test time: Yes
Scribes: Yes
Proctors: Yes
Oral exams: Yes
Note-takers: Yes

Distraction-reduced environment: Yes
Tape recording in class: Yes
Books on tape from RFBD: Yes
Taping of books not from RFBD: Yes
Accommodations for students with ADD: Yes
Reading machine: Yes
Other assistive technology: Yes
Priority registration: Yes

Added costs for services: No
LD specialists: Yes
Professional tutors: 25
Peer tutors: 25
Max. hours/wk. for services: Varies
How professors are notified of LD/ADD: By student

GENERAL ADMISSIONS INFORMATION

Director of Admissions: John Swiney
Telephone: 530-898-4428

ENTRANCE REQUIREMENTS

Academic units required: 4 English, 3 math, 2 science (2 science lab), 2 foreign language, 2 social studies, 1 academic elective, 1 visual and performing arts. High school diploma is required and GED is accepted. TOEFL required of all international applicants, minimum paper TOEFL 500, minimum computer TOEFL 173.

Application deadline: 11/30
Notification: 3/1
Average GPA: 3.28

Average SAT Math: 487
Average SAT Verbal: 486
Average ACT: 20

Graduated top 10% of class: 35%
Graduated top 25% of class: 76%
Graduated top 50% of class: 100%

COLLEGE GRADUATION REQUIREMENTS

Course waivers allowed: No
Course substitutions allowed: No
In what course: N/A

ADDITIONAL INFORMATION

Environment: The university is located in a small town 100 miles from Sacramento.

Student Body:
  Undergrad enrollment: 14,279
  Women: 54%
  Men: 46%
  Percent out-of-state: 1%

Cost Information
  In-state tuition: $2,520
  Out-of-state tuition: $12,609
  Room & board: $7,493
Housing Information
  University housing: Yes
  Percent living on campus: 12%

Greek System
  Fraternity: Yes
  Sorority: Yes
Athletics: NCAA Division II

California State University—Chico

CALIFORNIA STATE U.—FULLERTON

800 North State College Boulevard, Fullerton, CA 92834-6900
Phone: 714-773-2370 • Fax: 714-278-2356
E-mail: admissions@fullerton.edu • Web: www.fullerton.edu
Support: S • Institution type: 4-year public

LEARNING DISABILITY PROGRAM AND SERVICES

The Student Support Services Program is a wide network of support services that help ensure academic and personal success in college. The program is designed to increase retention and graduation rates for underrepresented students. Students are encouraged to fulfill their academic and career potential by participating in an exceptional support environment. Each participant is teamed with an academic counselor for one-on-one mentoring and advisement. The emphasis is on providing students with personal attention and access to support services that include: academic advisement; tutoring (referrals for individual and group tutoring including review sessions in select courses and development of study group); co-curricular events; peer mentoring for first-time freshmen; and workshops and study skills courses in reading, writing, math, and other subjects, as well as study skills and time management, counseling, and an introduction to campus resources.

LD/ADD ADMISSIONS INFORMATION

College entrance tests required: Yes
Interview required: No
Essay required: No
Documentation required for LD: Psychoeducational
  evaluation
Documentation required for ADD: Yes
Submitted to: Disabled Student Services
Special Ed. HS coursework accepted: No

Specific course requirements of all applicants: Yes
Separate application required for program servics: No
# of LD applications submitted each year: NR
# of LD applications accepted yearly: NR
Total # of students receiving LD services: NR
Acceptance into program means acceptance into
  college: Student must be accepted and enrolled and then
  request services.

ADMISSIONS

Students are admitted on an eligibility index based on high school GPA for a full complement of college prep courses and scores on either the ACT or SAT. Lower GPA requires higher scores on the test. Other factors such as impaction and residency status are also considered. The foreign language requirement for admission may be waived in rare cases when supported by the testing data supporting a relevant learning disability. All students must submit either the ACT or SAT. These tests should be taken no later than December so that the results are available in January.

All applicants must have the following: 2 years social science; 4 years English; 3 years math; 2 years science (science with a lab—1 year of biological and 1 year physical); 2 years foreign language. The GPA is calculated based on the college preparatory pattern only completed in grades 10, 11, and if available 12. College preparatory courses can only be counted toward the required units if you have earned at least a C in the course. Grades of D or less cannot be validated by a higher second semester grade in any of the following disciplines: social science/history, English, laboratory science, visual and performing arts, and electives. Students must have earned at least grades of C or higher in all semesters of English, other lab sciences than chemistry, social sciences/history, and visual and performing arts to have the course counted toward the required preparatory units. Applicants within the local area will be required to meet the minimum eligibility requirement of 2900 based on GPA and SAT result or a 694 based on GPA and ACT result. Students outside of the local area should not anticipate receiving an admissions decision until late January or February.

ADDITIONAL INFORMATION

The Intensive Learning Experience (ILE) program is designed not only to monitor the progress of any students in fulfilling remedial compliance requirements, but to also to help students make successful progress in fulfilling the requirements for graduation via intensive counseling and academic advising. They advise and inform students on class planning, study skills, transfer work, campus resources, time management, and campus organizations. Their goal is to give the student the essential skills to not only survive academically and socially, but to be successful at CSUF.

Support Services Contact Information

Learning Disability Program/Services: Disabled Student Services
Director: Paul K. Miller
 E-Mail: pmiller@fullerton.edu
 Telephone: 714-278-3112
 Fax: 714-278-2408
Contact Person: Doug Liverpool or Debra Fletcher
 E-Mail: dliverpool@fullerton.edu or dfletcher@fullerton.edu
 Telephone: 714-278-3112
 Fax: 714-278-2408

LEARNING DISABILITY SERVICES

Requests for the following/services accommodations will be evaluated individually based on appropriate and current documentation.

Allowed in exams
 Calculator: Yes
 Dictionary: Yes
 Computer: Yes
 Spellchecker: Yes
Extended test time: Yes
Scribes: Yes
Proctors: Yes
Oral exams: Yes
Note-takers: Yes

Distraction-reduced environment: Yes
Tape recording in class: Yes
Books on tape from RFBD: Yes
Taping of books not from RFBD: Yes
**Accommodations for students with
 ADD:** Yes
Reading machine: Yes
Other assistive technology: Yes
Priority registration: Yes

Added costs for services: No
LD specialists: No
Professional tutors: No
Peer tutors: No
Max. hours/wk. for services: Varies
**How professors are notified of
 LD/ADD:** By student

GENERAL ADMISSIONS INFORMATION

Director of Admissions: Nancy Dority
Telephone: 714-773-2370

ENTRANCE REQUIREMENTS
Academic units required: 2 science (2 science lab), 2 history, 1 academic elective, 1 visual/performing arts.   High school diploma is required and GED is accepted. TOEFL required of all international applicants, minimum paper TOEFL 500, minimum computer TOEFL 173.

Application deadline: 4/15
Notification: Rolling
Average GPA: 3.20

Average SAT Math: 502
Average SAT Verbal: 476
Average ACT: 20

Graduated top 10% of class: 15%
Graduated top 25% of class: 45%
Graduated top 50% of class: 81%

COLLEGE GRADUATION REQUIREMENTS

Course waivers allowed: No
Course substitutions allowed: Yes
In what course: Those students with a documented severe math disbility may be allowed a substitution for the math general education requirement.

ADDITIONAL INFORMATION

Environment: Located 35 miles from Los Angeles

Student Body:
 Undergrad enrollment: 25,261
 Women: 60%
 Men: 40%
 Percent out-of-state: 1%

Cost Information
 In-state tuition: $2,516
 Out-of-state tuition: $10,976
 Room & board: $3,953 (No food)
Housing Information
 University housing: Yes
 Percent living on campus: 2%

Greek System
 Fraternity: Yes
 Sorority: Yes
Athletics: NCAA Division I

CALIFORNIA STATE U.—NORTHRIDGE

PO Box 1286, Northridge, CA 91328-1286
Phone: 818-677-3773 • Fax: 818-677-4665
E-mail: lorraine.newlon@csun.edu • Web: www.csun.edu
Support: CS • Institution type: 4-year public

LEARNING DISABILITY PROGRAM AND SERVICES

The Office of Disabled Student Services recognizes that students with learning disabilities can be quite successful in a university setting if appropriate educational support services are offered to them. In an effort to assist students with learning disabilities in reaching their full potential, the program offers a comprehensive and well-coordinated system of educational support services that allow students to be judged on the basis of their ability rather than disability. The professional staff includes LD specialists trained in the diagnosis of learning disabilities and the provision of educational support services. Additionally, the program employs graduate students (Educational Support Specialists) who work under the direction of the professional staff and assist students with study skills, time management procedures, test-taking techniques, and other individualized programs.

LD/ADD ADMISSIONS INFORMATION

College entrance tests required: Yes
Interview required: Yes
Essay required: No
Documentation required for LD: Current documentation
Documentation required for ADD: Neuropsychological assessment
Submitted to: Students with Disabilities Resources
Special Ed. HS coursework accepted: Yes

Specific course requirements of all applicants: Yes
Separate application required for program servics: No
# of LD applications submitted each year: NR
# of LD applications accepted yearly: NR
Total # of students receiving LD services: 400
Acceptance into program means acceptance into college: Student must be admitted and enrolled in the university first and then request services.

ADMISSIONS

There is no special admission process. However, the Special Admission Committee of Students with Disabilities Resources makes recommendations to the Admissions Office. Students must get a C or better in 4 years English, 3 years math, 1 year U.S. history, 1 year science, 2 years foreign language, 1 year visual/performing arts, and 3 years of electives. Students with LD may request course substitutions. An eligibility index combining GPA and ACT or SATs used, and grades used are from 10th through 12th grade (bonus points for honor courses). Index is calculated by multiplying GPA by 800 and adding SAT, or multiplying GPA by 200 and adding 10 times the ACT. California residents need an index of 2900 using SAT or 694 using ACT. Nonresidents must have a minimum index of 3502 (SAT) or 842 (ACT). No test scores needed if GPA is a 3.0 plus for residents or 3.61 for nonresidents.

ADDITIONAL INFORMATION

The following services and accommodations are available for students presenting appropriate documentation: the use of calculators, dictionary, computer and spell checker for tests; extended testing time; scribes; proctors; oral exams; note-takers; distraction-free testing environments; tape recorder in class; books on tape; and priority registration. Testing accommodations may be arranged through the program without the integrity of the test being sacrificed. The Computer Access Lab provides computers along with professional assistance. The program and the CSUN Career Center work cooperatively to assist students with LD in planning and attaining their career goals. Diagnostic testing is available for students who suspect they may have a learning disability. Counselors are available to assist students in meeting their social/emotional needs as well as their academic requirements. Assistance in developing appropriate learning strategies is provided on an individual basis. Additionally, a support group for students with learning disabilities meets regularly. There are also workshops, a reader service, and note-takers. Services and accommodations are available for undergraduate and graduate students.

Support Services Contact Information

Learning Disability Program/Services: Students with Disabilities Resources
Director: Dr. Mary Ann Cummins Prager
  E-Mail: mary.ann.cummins.prager@csun.edu
  Telephone: 818-677-2684
  Fax: 818-677-4932
Contact Person: Dr. Jennifer Zvi
  Telephone: 818-677-2684
  Fax: 818-677-4932

LEARNING DISABILITY SERVICES

Requests for the following/services accommodations will be evaluated individually based on appropriate and current documentation.

Allowed in exams
  Calculator: Yes
  Dictionary: Yes
  Computer: Yes
  Spellchecker: Yes
Extended test time: Yes
Scribes: Yes
Proctors: Yes
Oral exams: Yes
Note-takers: Yes

Distraction-reduced environment: Yes
Tape recording in class: Yes
Books on tape from RFBD: Yes
Taping of books not from RFBD: Yes
Accommodations for students with ADD: Yes
Reading machine: Yes
Other assistive technology: Yes
Priority registration: Yes

Added costs for services: No
LD specialists: Yes
Professional tutors: No
Peer tutors: No
Max. hours/wk. for services: 2
How professors are notified of LD/ADD: By student

GENERAL ADMISSIONS INFORMATION

Director of Admissions: Lorraine Newlon
Telephone: 818-677-3773

ENTRANCE REQUIREMENTS

Academic units required: 4 English, 3 math, 1 science (2 science lab), 2 foreign language, 2 history, 1 academic elective, 1 visual/performing arts. High school diploma is required and GED is accepted. TOEFL required of all international applicants, minimum paper TOEFL 500, minimum computer TOEFL 173.

Application deadline: 11/30
Notification: Rolling
Average GPA: 3.1

Average SAT Math: NR
Average SAT Verbal: NR
Average ACT: NR

Graduated top 10% of class: NR
Graduated top 25% of class: 33%
Graduated top 50% of class: 33%

COLLEGE GRADUATION REQUIREMENTS

Course waivers allowed: Yes
Course substitutions allowed: Yes
In what course: Individual basis

ADDITIONAL INFORMATION

Environment: The university has a large suburban campus in the San Fernando Valley northwest of Los Angeles.

Student Body:
  Undergrad enrollment: 20.955
  Women: 59%
  Men: 41%
  Percent out-of-state: 1%

Cost Information
  In-state tuition: $2,770 (Fees)
  Out-of-state tuition: $12,948
  Room & board: $5,801
Housing Information
  University housing: Yes
  Percent living on campus: 8%

Greek System
  Fraternity: Yes
  Sorority: Yes
  Athletics: NCAA Division I

CAL. STATE U.—SAN BERNARDINO

5500 University Parkway, San Bernardino, CA 92407-2397
Phone: 909-880-5188 • Fax: 909-880-7034
E-mail: moreinfo@mail.csusb.edu • Web: www.csusb.edu
Support: CS • Institution type: 4-year public

LEARNING DISABILITY PROGRAM AND SERVICES

The Learning Disability Program is dedicated to assuring each student an opportunity to experience equity in education. Each student must complete an assessment and then the staff helps to develop compensatory methods for handling assignments and classroom projects. Careful attention is paid to helping the student acquire learning skills and formulating and implementing specific strategies for note-taking and management of written materials. Recommendations are designed for each student as a result of a psychometric assessment, personal interview, and academic requirements. The emphasis of the plan is to assist the students with a learning disability in finding techniques to deal with it in college and in the job market.

LD/ADD ADMISSIONS INFORMATION

College entrance tests required: Yes
Interview required: Yes
Essay required: No
Documentation required for LD: Yes
Documentation required for ADD: Yes
Submitted to: Services to Students with Disabilities
Special Ed. HS coursework accepted: No

Specific course requirements of all applicants: Yes
Separate application required for program servics: Yes
# of LD applications submitted each year: 75–101
# of LD applications accepted yearly: 45–66
Total # of students receiving LD services: 140–156
Acceptance into program means acceptance into college: Student must be admitted and enrolled in the university first and then request services.

ADMISSIONS

Applicants with learning disabilities must follow the same application procedure as all students. Entrance requirements include a minimum GPA of 2.0; 4 years English, 3 years math, 1 year U.S. history, 1 year science, 2 foreign language, 1 year visual or performing arts, and 3 years electives from any of the previous areas (including agriculture). The mid 50 percent have an ACT of 15–19 and SAT of 800–1020. Special admission may be requested through the Learning Disability Program if the student has a deficiency in course entrance requirements. The Director of the LD Program provides recommendations on the admissibility of those students who do not meet regular admissions requirements. Occasionally the special admit will consider students who are below the required GPA or test scores. These requirements can be substituted and the student can make up the deficiency on campus once enrolled.

ADDITIONAL INFORMATION

Services and accommodations for students with appropriate documentation could include the following: the use of calculators, dictionary, computer, or spellchecker in exams; extended time on tests; distraction-free testing environment; oral exams; note-taker; proctors; scribes; tape recorder in class; books on tape; assisting technology; and priority registration. Specific services include assessment counseling and testing accommodations. Students on academic probation have two quarters to raise their GPA to a 2.0. The LD Program provides continual academic support.

Support Services Contact Information

Learning Disability Program/Services: Services to Students with Disabilities
Director: Laurie Flynn
  E-Mail: lflynn@csusb.edu
  Telephone: 909-880-5238
  Fax: 909-880-7090
Contact Person: Doron A. Dula
  E-Mail: ddula@csusb.edu
  Telephone: 909-880-5238
  Fax: 909-880-7090

LEARNING DISABILITY SERVICES

Requests for the following/services accommodations will be evaluated individually based on appropriate and current documentation.

Allowed in exams
  Calculator: Yes
  Dictionary: Yes
  Computer: Yes
  Spellchecker: Yes
Extended test time: Yes
Scribes: Yes
Proctors: Yes
Oral exams: Yes
Note-takers: Yes

Distraction-reduced environment: Yes
Tape recording in class: Yes
Books on tape from RFBD: Yes
Taping of books not from RFBD: Yes
Accommodations for students with ADD: Yes
Reading machine: Yes
Other assistive technology: Yes
Priority registration: Yes

Added costs for services: No
LD specialists: Yes
Professional tutors: No
Peer tutors: No
Max. hours/wk. for services: N/A
How professors are notified of LD/ADD: By student

GENERAL ADMISSIONS INFORMATION

Director of Admissions: Dr. Milton Clark
Telephone: 909-880-5032

ENTRANCE REQUIREMENTS

Academic units required: 4 English, 3 math, 2 science (2 science lab), 2 foreign language, 1 social studies, 1 history, 1 academic elective, 1 visual & performing arts. High school diploma is required and GED is accepted. TOEFL required of all international applicants, minimum paper TOEFL 500, minimum computer TOEFL 173.

Application deadline: Rolling
Notification: Rolling
Average GPA: 3.22

Average SAT Math: 452
Average SAT Verbal: 410
Average ACT: 16

Graduated top 10% of class: NR
Graduated top 25% of class: NR
Graduated top 50% of class: NR

COLLEGE GRADUATION REQUIREMENTS

Course waivers allowed: Yes
In what course: Evaluated individually based on appropiate and current documentation
Course substitutions allowed: Yes
In what course: General education math

ADDITIONAL INFORMATION

Environment: The university is located in suburban area in the foothills of the San Bernadino Mountains.

Student Body:
  Undergrad enrollment: 12,109
  Women: 66%
  Men: 34%
  Percent out-of-state: 2%

Cost Information
  In-state tuition: $2,580 (fees)
  Out-of-state tuition: $7,302
  Room & board: $7,756
Housing Information
  University housing: Yes
  Percent living on campus: 11%

Greek System
  Fraternity: Yes
  Sorority: Yes
Athletics: NCAA Division II

COLLEGE OF THE SISKIYOUS

800 College Avenue, Weed, CA 96094
Phone: 530-938-4461 • Fax: 530-938-5367
E-mail: registration@siskiyous.edu • Web: www.siskiyous.edu
Support: CS • Institution type: 2-year public

LEARNING DISABILITY PROGRAM AND SERVICES

The Disabled Student Services Programs and Services Office are dedicated to meeting the needs of students with disabilities. The goal of DSP&S is to assist students to overcome barriers to allow access to the college's regular programs and activities. Support services are provided for students with a wide variety of disabilities. Any student who has a documented disability and demonstrates a need for a service that is directly related to the educational limitation is eligible for support services.

LD/ADD ADMISSIONS INFORMATION

College entrance tests required: Yes
Interview required: No
Essay required: No
Documentation required for LD: Testing results within the last 3 years
Documentation required for ADD: Yes
Submitted to: Disabled Student Services
Special Ed. HS coursework accepted: Yes

Specific course requirements of all applicants: No
Separate application required for program servics: Yes
# of LD applications submitted each year: 90–100
# of LD applications accepted yearly: 100
Total # of students receiving LD services: 100
Acceptance into program means acceptance into college: Student must be admitted and enrolled in the college first and then request services.

ADMISSIONS

Students with LD/ADD who self-disclose during the admission process may receive advice from DSP&S during the admission process. This advice provides descriptions of appropriate courses the students may take and the services and accommodations they may be eligible to receive. There are not any minimum admission requirements for a specific class rank, GPA, or ACT/SAT score. Applicants must have a high school diploma or equivalent certification.

ADDITIONAL INFORMATION

There is a LD specialist available in the Disability Support Services Office. There are support services available for students who have a documented disability and demonstrate a need for a service that is directly related to their educational limitations. They may include academic advising, registration assistance, and the development of an individualized educational plan, LD assessment, tutoring, readers, note-takers, testing accommodations, and adaptive educational equipment. The COS High Tech Center is designed to provide computer access and technology to students with disabilities to educate and prepare them for academic success and today's work force. In addition, all students have access to skills classes in areas such as time management, organization, study strategies, and test taking strategies.

Support Services Contact Information

Learning Disability Program/Services: Disabled Student Services
Director: Karen Zeigler
  Telephone: 530-938-5297
  Fax: 530-938-5379
  E-Mail: zeigler@siskiyous.edu

LEARNING DISABILITY SERVICES

Requests for the following/services accommodations will be evaluated individually based on appropriate and current documentation.

Allowed in exams
  Calculator: Yes
  Dictionary: Yes
  Computer: Yes
  Spellchecker: Yes
Extended test time: Yes
Scribes: Yes
Proctors: Yes
Oral exams: Yes
Note-takers: Yes

Distraction-reduced environment: Yes
Tape recording in class: Yes
Books on tape from RFBD: Yes
Taping of books not from RFBD: Yes
Accommodations for students with ADD: Yes
Reading machine: Yes
Other assistive technology: Yes
Priority registration: No

Added costs for services: No
LD specialists: Yes
Professional tutors: 2
Peer tutors: 70
Max. hours/wk. for services: Unlimited
How professors are notified of LD/ADD: By student

GENERAL ADMISSIONS INFORMATION

Director of Admissions: Theresa Winkelman
Telephone: 530-938-4461

ENTRANCE REQUIREMENTS

High school diploma or GED equivalent is required. TOEFL required of all international applicants, minimum paper TOEFL 470, minimum computer TOEFL 150.

Application deadline: Rolling
Notification: Rolling
Average GPA: NR

Average SAT Math: NR
Average SAT Verbal: NR
Average ACT: NR

Graduated top 10% of class: NR
Graduated top 25% of class: NR
Graduated top 50% of class: NR

COLLEGE GRADUATION REQUIREMENTS

Course waivers allowed: No
Course substitutions allowed: Yes
In what course: Students can petition for a substitute course.

ADDITIONAL INFORMATION

Environment: The college is located at the base of Mt. Shasta.

Student Body:
  Undergrad enrollment: 1,153
  Women: 57%
  Men: 43%
  Percent out-of-state: 10%

Cost Information
  In-state tuition: $805
  Out-of-state tuition: $5,514
  Room & board: $5,506
Housing Information
  University housing: Yes
  Percent living on campus: 9%

Greek System
  Fraternity: No
  Sorority: No
Athletics: Intercollegiate

LOYOLA MARYMOUNT UNIVERSITY

One LMU Drive, Suite 100, Los Angeles, CA 90045
Phone: 310-338-2750 • Fax: 310-338-2797
E-mail: admissions@lmu.edu • Web: www.lmu.edu
Support: S • Institution type: 4-year private

LEARNING DISABILITY PROGRAM AND SERVICES

The Office of Disability Support Services (DSS) provides specialized assistance and resources that enable students with physical, perceptual, emotional, and learning disabilities to achieve maximum independence while they pursue their educational goals. Assisted by staff specialists from all areas of the University, the DSS Office works to eliminate physical and attitudinal barriers. To be eligible for services, students must provide documentation of the disability from a licensed professional. At the Learning Resource Center students can receive tutoring in over 250 LMU classes, attend workshops, and access assistance in writing, reading, and math with LRC specialists.

LD/ADD ADMISSIONS INFORMATION

College entrance tests required: Yes
Interview required: No
Essay required: Yes
Documentation required for LD: Current psychoeducational evaluation
Documentation required for ADD: Yes
Submitted to: Disability Support Services
Special Ed. HS coursework accepted: No

Specific course requirements of all applicants: Yes (Recommended)
Separate application required for program servics: No
# of LD applications submitted each year: NR
# of LD applications accepted yearly: NR
Total # of students receiving LD services: 200
Acceptance into program means acceptance into college: Student must be admitted and enrolled in the university first and then request services.

ADMISSIONS

There is no special admissions process for students with LD or ADD. The admission decision will be based upon the student's grade point average, SAT/ACT scores, strength of curriculum, the application essay, letters of recommendation, and extracurricular activities. Enrolled students have an average GPA of 3.3, 25 ACT, and 1130 SAT Reasoning. Students are encouraged to have completed 4 years English, 3 years social sciences, 3 years foreign language, 3 years math (4 years for engineering and science), and 1 year elective.

ADDITIONAL INFORMATION

There is a Learning Resource Center where all students can find specialists and tutors. There are course-specific tutoring and study skills programs (which include learning time management, overcoming test anxiety, conquering math word problems, mastering the textbook, preparing for exams, and studying efficiently), and other academic support programs with full time professional staff members prepared to assist with writing, reading, math, ESL, and disability support services. Assistive technology includes equipment that enlarges print, Window Bridge 21000, screen-reading program, Kurzweil Reader, and Dragon Dictate. Specific accommodations for LD students with appropriate documentation could include priority registration, note-takers, readers, transcribers, alternate testing conditions, taped books, and advocacy.

Support Services Contact Information

Learning Disability Program/Services: Office of Disability Support Services (DSS)
Director: Robert Scholz MA, NCC
  E-mail: rscholz@lmu.edu
  Telephone: 310-338-4535
  Fax: 310-338-7657

LEARNING DISABILITY SERVICES

Requests for the following/services accommodations will be evaluated individually based on appropriate and current documentation.

Allowed in exams
  Calculator: Yes
  Dictionary: Yes
  Computer: Yes
  Spellchecker: Yes
Extended test time: Yes
Scribes: Yes
Proctors: Yes
Oral exams: Yes
Note-takers: Yes

Distraction-reduced environment: Yes
Tape recording in class: Yes
Books on tape from RFBD: Yes
Taping of books not from RFBD: No
Accommodations for students with
  ADD: Yes
Reading machine: Yes
Other assistive technology: Yes
Priority registration: Yes

Added costs for services: No
LD specialists: No
Professional tutors: No
Peer tutors: 60–80
Max. hours/wk. for services: 1
How professors are notified of
  LD/ADD: By student

GENERAL ADMISSIONS INFORMATION

Director of Admissions: Matt Fissinger
Telephone: 310-338-2750

ENTRANCE REQUIREMENTS

Academic units recommended: 4 English, 3 math, 2 science (2 science lab), 3 foreign language, 3 social studies, 1 academic elective. High school diploma is required and GED is accepted. TOEFL required of all international applicants, minimum paper TOEFL 550, minimum computer TOEFL 173.

Application deadline: Rolling
Notification: Beginning 1/1
Average GPA: 3.35

Average SAT Math: 583
Average SAT Verbal: 573
Average ACT: 24

Graduated top 10% of class: 30%
Graduated top 25% of class: 95%
Graduated top 50% of class: 99%

COLLEGE GRADUATION REQUIREMENTS

Course waivers allowed: No
Course substitutions allowed: No
In what course: N/A

ADDITIONAL INFORMATION

Environment: The university is located on 125 acres in a suburban setting close to Los Angeles.

Student Body:
  Undergrad enrollment: 5,465
  Women: 60%
  Men: 40%
  Percent out-of-state: 23%

Cost Information
  Tuition: $25,266
  Room & board: $7,966
Housing Information
  University housing: Yes
  Percent living on campus: 54%

Greek System
  Fraternity: Yes
  Sorority: Yes
Athletics: NCAA Division I

REEDLEY COLLEGE

995 North, Reed Avenue, Reedley, CA 93654
Phone: 559-638-3641 • Fax: 559-638-5040
E-mail: emerzian@scccd.org • Web: www.reedleycollege.com
Support: CS • Institution type: 2-year public

LEARNING DISABILITY PROGRAM AND SERVICES

The Disabled Student Program & Services (DSP&S) focuses on abilities, not disabilities. DSP&S offers services to students with learning disabilities beyond those provided by conventional programs at the college and enables students to successfully pursue their individual educational, vocational, and personal goals. The Learning Disabilities Program assesses the needs and skill levels of each student, tailoring a specific educational course of study designed to bring out the best in an individual at a college level. The instructional program in reading, writing, math, and other academics prepares students to function in the classroom, in their vocation, and throughout life. The LD Program provides special instruction and attention for students with specific educational needs not available in mainstream classes.

LD/ADD ADMISSIONS INFORMATION

College entrance tests required: No
Interview required: Yes
Essay required: No
Documentation required for LD: Psychoeducational evaluation
Documentation required for ADD: Yes
Submitted to: DSP & S
Special Ed. HS coursework accepted: Yes

Specific course requirements of all applicants: No
Separate application required for program servics: No
# of LD applications submitted each year: NR
# of LD applications accepted yearly: NR
Total # of students receiving LD services: 200
Acceptance into program means acceptance into college: Student must be admitted and enrolled in the college first and then request services.

ADMISSIONS

Reedley is an open-door admission college. Students present a high school diploma, certificate of high school completion equivalent or LD/special education test results. There is no minimum GPA or required courses required for admission. ACT/SAT tests are not required for admission. There is a separate application to access services for students with learning disabilities. This application is submitted after admission.

ADDITIONAL INFORMATION

The LD Program offers the following services: LD assessments, learning strategies instruction from LD specialist, small class sessions, adaptive instruction, matriculation and integration with mainstream classes, individualized student contact, and specialized educational counseling. In addition, students can access the following accommodations if they provide appropriate documentation: the use of calculators, dictionary, computer, or spell check in exams; extended time on tests; scribes; proctors; oral exams; note-takers; tape recorder in class; books on tape; assistive technology; and priority registration. American Sign Language may be substituted for foreign language and students are responsible for providing information about their disability to their professors.

Support Services Contact Information

Learning Disability Program/Services: Disabled Students Program & Services (DSP & S)
Director: Dr. Janice Emerzian
  E-mail: janice.emerzian@sccd.com
  Telephone: 559-638-0332
  Fax: 559-638-0382

LEARNING DISABILITY SERVICES

Requests for the following/services accommodations will be evaluated individually based on appropriate and current documentation.

Allowed in exams	**Distraction-reduced environment:** Yes	**Added costs for services:** No
Calculator: Yes	**Tape recording in class:** Yes	**LD specialists:** Yes
Dictionary: Yes	**Books on tape from RFBD:** Yes	**Professional tutors:** No
Computer: Yes	**Taping of books not from RFBD:** Yes	**Peer tutors:** Yes
Spellchecker: Yes	**Accommodations for students with**	**Max. hours/wk. for services:**
Extended test time: Yes	**ADD:** Yes	Unlimited
Scribes: Yes	**Reading machine:** Yes	**How professors are notified of**
Proctors: Yes	**Other assistive technology:** Yes	**LD/ADD:** By student
Oral exams: Yes	**Priority registration:** Yes	
Note-takers: Yes		

GENERAL ADMISSIONS INFORMATION

Director of Admissions: Letty Alvarez
Telephone: 559-638-3641

ENTRANCE REQUIREMENTS

High school diploma is required and GED is accepted. Open door admission. TOEFL required of all international applicants, minimum computer TOEFL 500, minimum computer TOEFL 173

Application deadline: Rolling	**Average SAT Math:** NR	**Graduated top 10% of class:** NR
Notification: Continuous	**Average SAT Verbal:** NR	**Graduated top 25% of class:** NR
Average GPA: NR	**Average ACT:** NR	**Graduated top 50% of class:** NR

COLLEGE GRADUATION REQUIREMENTS

Course waivers allowed: N/A
Course substitutions allowed: No
In what course: N/A

ADDITIONAL INFORMATION

Environment: The college is located 30 miles southeast of Fresno.

Student Body:	**Cost Information**	**Greek System**
Undergrad enrollment: 7434	**In-state tuition:** $1,400 (Fees only)	**Fraternity:** No
Women: 62%	**Out-of-state tuition:** $5,000	**Sorority:** No
Men: 38%	**Room & board:** $4,200	**Athletics:** NJCAA
Percent out-of-state: 1%	**Housing Information**	
	University housing: Yes	
	Percent living on campus: 18%	

SAN DIEGO STATE UNIVERSITY

5500 Campanile Drive, San Diego, CA 92182-7455
Phone: 619-594-7800 • Fax: 619-594-1250
E-mail: admissions@sdsu.edu • Web: www.sdsu.edu
Support: CS • Institution type: 4-year public

LEARNING DISABILITY PROGRAM AND SERVICES

The Learning Disability Program at San Diego State is under the umbrella of Disabled Student Services. The LD Program is designed to provide assessment, accommodations, and advocacy. Students must provide documentation prior to receiving services. Students with learning disabilities may be assessed using nationally standardized batteries. The university believes that students with learning disabilities can be successful at San Diego State and will try to provide the appropriate services to foster their success.

LD/ADD ADMISSIONS INFORMATION

College entrance tests required: Yes
Interview required: No
Essay required: No
Documentation required for LD: WAIS–III; WJ–III
Documentation required for ADD: Yes
Submitted to: Disability Student Services
Special Ed. HS coursework accepted: No

Specific course requirements of all applicants: Yes
Separate application required for program servics: Yes
# of LD applications submitted each year: NR
# of LD applications accepted yearly: 28 (Enrolled)
Total # of students receiving LD services: 275
Acceptance into program means acceptance into college: Student must be admitted and enrolled in the university first and then request services.

ADMISSIONS

Students with learning disabilities who are not admissible by the general admission criteria or who are denied admission may request a review through special admission. Students need to write a letter to the director of the LD Program explaining why they feel they should be admitted. Three recommendations are required for special admit. No student will be admitted with a GPA below 2.0. Students must provide documentation verifying the disability and demonstrate that they meet the California state definition of a learning disability. The director of Disabled Student Services reviews documentation and makes a recommendation to the Admissions Office.

ADDITIONAL INFORMATION

Students are encouraged to get volunteer note-takers from among other students enrolled in the class. Students with learning disabilities may request permission to tape a lecture. Students will also need permission from the professor to use a calculator, dictionary, computer, or spellchecker in exams. Tutoring services are provided at no charge. High Tech Center is a learning center available for all students with disabilities. Services and accommodations are available for undergraduates and graduate students.

Support Services Contact Information

Learning Disability Program/Services: Disabled Student Services
Director: Mary Shojai
  E-mail: mshojai@mail.sdsu.edu
  Telephone: 619-594-6473
  Fax: 619-594-4315

LEARNING DISABILITY SERVICES

Requests for the following/services accommodations will be evaluated individually based on appropriate and current documentation.

Allowed in exams
  Calculator: Yes
  Dictionary: Y/N
  Computer: Yes
  Spellchecker: Y/N
Extended test time: Yes
Scribes: No
Proctors: Yes
Oral exams: No
Note-takers: Yes

Distraction-reduced environment: Yes
Tape recording in class: Yes
Books on tape from RFBD: Yes
Taping of books not from RFBD: Yes
Accommodations for students with ADD: Yes
Reading machine: No
Other assistive technology: Yes
Priority registration: Yes

Added costs for services: No
LD specialists: Yes
Professional tutors: No
Peer tutors: 1–20
Max. hours/wk. for services: Depends on need
How professors are notified of LD/ADD: By student

GENERAL ADMISSIONS INFORMATION

Director of Admissions: Beverly Arata
Telephone: 619-594-7800

ENTRANCE REQUIREMENTS

Academic units required: 4 English, 3 math, 2 science (2 science lab), 2 foreign language, 1 social studies, 1 history, 1 academic elective, 1 visual and/or performing art, 1 biology, 1 physical science. **Academic units recommended:** 4 math, high school diploma is required and GED is accepted. TOEFL required of all international applicants, minimum paper TOEFL 550, minimum computer TOEFL 213.

Application deadline: 11/30
Notification: 3/1
Average GPA: 3.52

Average SAT Math: 550
Average SAT Verbal: 529
Average ACT: 22

Graduated top 10% of class: NR
Graduated top 25% of class: NR
Graduated top 50% of class: NR

COLLEGE GRADUATION REQUIREMENTS

Course waivers allowed: No
Course substitutions allowed: Yes
In what course: Varies; must be directly related to disability

ADDITIONAL INFORMATION

Environment: San Diego State is located on 300 acres 12 miles from the ocean.

Student Body:
  Undergrad enrollment: 27,345
  Women: 58%
  Men: 42%
  Percent out-of-state: 7%

Cost Information
  In-state tuition: $2,936
  Out-of-state tuition: $8,714
  Room & board: $9,391
Housing Information
  University housing: Yes
  Percent living on campus: 11%

Greek System
  Fraternity: Yes
  Sorority: Yes
Athletics: NCAA Division I

SAN FRANCISCO STATE UNIVERSITY

1600 Holloway Avenue, San Francisco, CA 94132
Phone: 415-338-6486 • Fax: 415-338-7196
E-mail: ugadmit@sfsu.edu • Web: www.sfsu.edu
Support: CS • Institution type: 4-year public

LEARNING DISABILITY PROGRAM AND SERVICES

The Disability Resource Center (DRC) is available to promote and provide equal access to the classroom and to campus-related activities. A full range of support services is provided so that students may define and achieve personal autonomy at SFSU. The staff is sensitive to the diversity of disabilities, including those only recently recognized as disabilities requiring reasonable accommodations. Confidential support services are available. All students registered with DRC are eligible for disability management advising. This consists of helping students access services from DRC; manage DRC services and school in general; problem solve conflicts/concerns that are disability-related with individuals, programs, and services on campus; and understand reasonable accommodation under the law. Generally the campus community is sensitive, but if an oversight occurs, students do have protection under Section 504 and ADA. Students are encouraged to contact DRC for guidance in pursuing a grievance. Resolution of a violation can often be achieved informally without completing the formal grievance procedure.

LD/ADD ADMISSIONS INFORMATION

College entrance tests required: Yes
Interview required: Yes
Essay required: No
Documentation required for LD: Psychoeducational evaluation
Documentation required for ADD: Yes
Submitted to: Disabilities Programs & Resource Center
Special Ed. HS coursework accepted: Yes

Specific course requirements of all applicants: Yes
Separate application required for program servics: Yes
# of LD applications submitted each year: NR
# of LD applications accepted yearly: NR
Total # of students receiving LD services: 250
Acceptance into program means acceptance into college: Student must be admitted and enrolled in the university first and then request services.

ADMISSIONS
Students with LDs apply to the university using the regular application process. If the student is not eligible for regular admission for a disability-related reason, DRC can provide special admissions assistance. To obtain special admissions assistance, students need to register with the DRC office, provide verification of the disability, and notify the admissions office that the DRC has the appropriate verification. When these steps have been taken, the admissions office will consult with DRC before making a decision. The admissions contact person can request substitutions of high school courses in math, foreign language, and science. Students with LD who are judged unable to fulfill specific requirements may take course substitutions. Substitutions are authorized on an individual basis after review and recommendation by the high school or community college counselor. Students taking substitutions must have 15 units of college-prep study. High school case managers may write summaries and provide a clinical judgment. DRC wants information about achievement deficits and may require the student to attend an admissions interview.

ADDITIONAL INFORMATION
The DRC offers a drop-in center with available tutorial services. DRC can also arrange for test accommodations and note-takers and will advocate for the student. The staff is very involved and offers comprehensive services through a team approach. There are no developmental courses offered at the university. However, there are skills classes. Students with documented LD may request assistance in locating tutors. Other services may include registration assistance, campus orientation, note-takers, readers, test-taking assistance, tutoring, disability-related counseling, and referral information.

Support Services Contact Information

Learning Disability Program/Services: Disability Programs & Resource Center
Director: Gene Chelberg
  E-Mail: chelberg@sfsu.edu
  Telephone: 415-405-3728
  Fax: 415-338-1041
Contact Person: Deidre Defreese, Associate Director
  E-Mail: defreese@sfsu.edu
  Telephone: 415-338-6356
  Fax: 415-338-1041

LEARNING DISABILITY SERVICES

Requests for the following/services accommodations will be evaluated individually based on appropriate and current documentation.

Allowed in exams
  Calculator: Yes
  Dictionary: Yes
  Computer: Yes
  Spellchecker: Yes
Extended test time: Yes
Scribes: Yes
Proctors: Yes
Oral exams: Yes
Note-takers: Yes

Distraction-reduced environment: Yes
Tape recording in class: Yes
Books on tape from RFBD: Yes
Taping of books not from RFBD: Yes
Accommodations for students with
  ADD: Yes
Reading machine: Yes
Other assistive technology: Yes
Priority registration: Yes

Added costs for services: No
LD specialists: Yes
Professional tutors: No
Peer tutors: Yes
Max. hours/wk. for services: Limited
How professors are notified of
  LD/ADD: By student

GENERAL ADMISSIONS INFORMATION

Director of Admissions: Valerie Perry
Telephone: 415-338-2037

ENTRANCE REQUIREMENTS

Academic units required: 4 English, 3 math, 2 science (2 science lab), 2 foreign language, 1 social studies, 1 history. **Academic units recommended:** 1 academic elective. High school diploma is required and GED is accepted. ACT with or without Writing component accepted. TOEFL required of all international applicants, minimum paper TOEFL 550, minimum computer TOEFL 173.

Application deadline: Rolling
Notification: Rolling
Average GPA: 3.17

Average SAT Math: 500
Average SAT Verbal: 488
Average ACT: 19

Graduated top 10% of class: 0%
Graduated top 25% of class: 0%
Graduated top 50% of class: 0%

COLLEGE GRADUATION REQUIREMENTS

Course waivers allowed: Yes
Course substitutions allowed: Yes
In what course: Subjects where impact of disability is evident; decisions are made on a case-by-case basis.

ADDITIONAL INFORMATION

Environment: The school is located in downtown San Francisco on a 130-acre campus.

Student Body:
  Undergrad enrollment: 22,291
  Women: 59%
  Men: 41%
  Percent out-of-state: 1%

Cost Information
  In-state tuition: $2,520
  Out-of-state tuition: $10,958
  Room & board: $7,810
Housing Information
  University housing: Yes
  Percent living on campus: NR

Greek System
  Fraternity: Yes
  Sorority: Yes
  Athletics: NCAA Division II

SAN JOSE STATE UNIVERSITY

1 Washington Square, San Jose, CA 95112-0001
Phone: 408-283-7500 • Fax: 408-924-2050
E-mail: contact@sjsu.edu • Web: www.sjsu.edu
Support: CS • Institution type: 4-year public

LEARNING DISABILITY PROGRAM AND SERVICES

The goal of the Disability Resource Center is to provide appropriate academic adjustments and support services to students with disabilities while training them to become self-advocates and to develop maximum independence. The Disability Resource Center provides services to students and consultation to faculty to educate every department so that they best serve students with disabilities. In order to request services, students must self identify and meet with a DRC counselor to create a student file. Documention of the disability should verify a disabiity and support the requests for accommodations or academic adjustments.

LD/ADD ADMISSIONS INFORMATION

College entrance tests required: Yes
Interview required: No
Essay required: No
Documentation required for LD: WJ–R III, Parts 1–2; WAIS and WJ–R, Part 2, and other skills test will be accepted to support LD
Documentation required for ADD: Yes
Submitted to: Disability Resource Center
Special Ed. HS coursework accepted: No

Specific course requirements of all applicants: Yes
Separate application required for program servics: No
# of LD applications submitted each year: NR
# of LD applications accepted yearly: NR
Total # of students receiving LD services: 450
Acceptance into program means acceptance into college: Student must be admitted and enrolled in the university first and then request services.

ADMISSIONS

Students with Learning Disabilities apply directly to the admissions office, there is no special handling of the student's applications through the DRC. All assessments and disability verifications go direct to DRC for establishment of a confidential file. (The assessment should include the WJ–R Parts 1 & 2 or the WAIS–III and WJ–R Part 2, and other skills tests.) Students must have at least a 2.0 GPA, and a sliding scale is used combining GPA and test scores. Only courses from grades 10–12 are used to compute GPA. High school courses required are 4 years English, 3 years math, 1 year lab science, 1 year U.S. history, 2 years foreign language, 1 year visual and/or performing arts, and 3 years electives. Foreign language admission requirements can be waived for students with learning disabilities if their high school sends a letter stating that other college-prep courses have been substituted for the foreign language. Those students not meeting general entrance criteria can petition the exceptional admissions committee of the admissions office. These students must submit a personal statement and two letters of recommendation, plus disclosure of their learning disability, to be eligible for special consideration.

ADDITIONAL INFORMATION

No skills courses are offered by DRC, nor is tutoring offered by DRC. Referral for skills courses and tutoring is made to regular University services. Recent changes in CSU policy requires that any remediation needed in math and English be cleared during the student's first year if they enter as a freshman. Transfer students must have completed oral communication, English 1A equivalent, critical thinking, and math higher than intermediate algebra. Books on tape are provided through Recording For the Blind and Dyslexic (RFBD). Students who request the use of a calculator in an exam will need to secure permission from the professor, as well as have appropriate documentation identifying that this is a necessary accommodation to compensate for the disability. Some accommodations include note-taking, priority registration, test accommodations, adaptive technology, disability management, learning disability assessment, readers, academic counseling, and faculty and staff consultation to assist with access and to recommend accommodations. Students who are transferring to San Jose State University from another campus in California do not need to provide new documentation of the learning disability.

Support Services Contact Information

Learning Disability Program/Services: Disability Resource Center (DRC)
Director: Martin Schulter
  E-Mail: mschulter@drc.sjsu.edu
  Telephone: 408-924-6000
  Fax: 408-924-5999
Contact Person: Cindy Marota
  E-Mail: cindy@drc.sjsu.edu
  Telephone: 408-924-6000
  Fax: 408-924-5999

LEARNING DISABILITY SERVICES

Requests for the following/services accommodations will be evaluated individually based on appropriate and current documentation.

Allowed in exams
  Calculator: Y/N
  Dictionary: Y/N
  Computer: Yes
  Spellchecker: Yes
Extended test time: Yes
Scribes: Yes
Proctors: Yes
Oral exams: Yes
Note-takers: Yes

Distraction-reduced environment: Yes
Tape recording in class: Yes
Books on tape from RFBD: Yes
Taping of books not from RFBD: Yes
Accommodations for students with ADD: Yes
Reading machine: Yes
Other assistive technology: Yes
Priority registration: Yes

Added costs for services: No
LD specialists: Yes
Professional tutors: No
Peer tutors: No
Max. hours/wk. for services: Case-by-case basis
How professors are notified of LD/ADD: By student

GENERAL ADMISSIONS INFORMATION

Director of Admissions: John Loera
Telephone: 408-283-7500

ENTRANCE REQUIREMENTS
Academic units required: 4 English, 3 math, 2 science (2 science lab), 2 foreign language, 1 social studies, 1 history, 1 academic elective, 1 visual & performing arts. High school diploma is required and GED is accepted. ACT with Writing component required or SAT Reasoning Test. TOEFL required of all international applicants, minimum paper TOEFL 550, minimum computer TOEFL 213.

Application deadline: 2/1
Notification: Rolling
Average GPA: 3.17

Average SAT Math: 502
Average SAT Verbal: 468
Average ACT: 19

Graduated top 10% of class: NR
Graduated top 25% of class: NR
Graduated top 50% of class: 50%

COLLEGE GRADUATION REQUIREMENTS

Course waivers allowed: Yes
Course substitutions allowed: Yes
In what course: General education quantitative reasoning substitutions made on case-by-case basis.

ADDITIONAL INFORMATION

Environment: The university is located on 117 acres in an urban area in the center of San Jose.

Student Body:
  Undergrad enrollment: 21,663
  Women: 51%
  Men: 49%
  Percent out-of-state: 1%

Cost Information
  In-state tuition: $2,944
  Out-of-state tuition: $12,520
Housing Information
  University housing: Yes
  Percent living on campus: 7%

Greek System
  Fraternity: Yes
  Sorority: Yes
  Athletics: NCAA Division I

Santa Clara University

500 El Camino Real, Santa Clara, CA 95053
Phone: 408-554-4700 • Fax: 408-554-5255
E-mail: ugadmissions@scu.edu • Web: www.scu.edu
Support: CS • Institution type: 4-year private

LEARNING DISABILITY PROGRAM AND SERVICES

The primary mission of Disabilities Resources is to enhance academic progress, promote social involvement, and build bridges connecting the various services of the university for all students. This goal is met by providing: academic intervention programs, opportunities to increase students' personal understanding of their disability, role models, and community outreach. Disabilities Resources is a resource area within the Drahmann Center that helps to ensure equal access to all academic and programmatic activities for students with disabilities. This goal is met through the provision of Academic Support Services, contact with other university offices, educational programming on disability issues for the university, and most importantly, assistance in teaching students effective self-advocacy skills under the student development model. Students with disabilities must have documentation of their disability from a qualified professional.

LD/ADD ADMISSIONS INFORMATION

College entrance tests required: Yes
Interview required: Yes
Essay required: Yes
Documentation required for LD: Psychoeducational evaluation
Documentation required for ADD: Yes
Submitted to: Disability Resources
Special Ed. HS coursework accepted: No

Specific course requirements of all applicants: Yes
Separate application required for program servics: No
# of LD applications submitted each year: NR
# of LD applications accepted yearly: NR
Total # of students receiving LD services: 125
Acceptance into program means acceptance into college: Student must be admitted and enrolled in the university first and then request services.

Admissions

All students submit the same general application. Santa Clara takes pride in the personal nature of its admission process. All applicants are carefully reviewed. Freshman applicants are offered admission based upon (1) high school record, (2) ACT/SAT (will mix and match the best Math and Verbal scores from multiple SAT tests), (3) one letter of recommendation, and (4) personal factors. Applicants submitting a nonstandardized ACT/SAT are encouraged to write a personal statement to assist the admission committee in evaluating the application. Recommended course requirements include 4 years English, 3 years math, 3 years social studies, 2 years lab science, and 3 years foreign language (4 years recommended).

Additional Information

The Disabilities Resources staff meets individually with students. Some of the academic accommodations provided by DR include note-taking, library assistance, proofreading, and test accommodations. Other support services include priority registration, tutoring or academic counseling, and workshops on legal issues and self-advocacy. The DR is in the process of purchasing computer-aided technology to assist the students. Graduate students with learning disabilities are offered the same services and accommodations as those provided for undergraduate students. Students can be better served if the professional documentation they submit specifically identifies the accommodations needed for the student to be successful in college. This should include the student's strengths and weaknesses and any required modifications. All students have access to peer tutoring, drop-in math lab, and a drop-in writing center.

Support Services Contact Information

Learning Disability Program/Services: Disability Resources (DR)
Director: Ann Ravenscroft, Coordinator
 E-Mail: eravenscroft@scu.edu
 Telephone: 408-554-4111
 Fax: 408-554-2709

LEARNING DISABILITY SERVICES

Requests for the following/services accommodations will be evaluated individually based on appropriate and current documentation.

Allowed in exams
 Calculator: Yes
 Dictionary: Yes
 Computer: Yes
 Spellchecker: Yes
Extended test time: Yes
Scribes: Yes
Proctors: Yes
Oral exams: Yes
Note-takers: Yes

Distraction-reduced environment: Yes
Tape recording in class: Yes
Books on tape from RFBD: Yes
Taping of books not from RFBD: No
Accommodations for students with
 ADD: Yes
Reading machine: No
Other assistive technology: Yes
Priority registration: Yes

Added costs for services: No
LD specialists: Yes
Professional tutors: No
Peer tutors: 50
Max. hours/wk. for services: 1
How professors are notified of
 LD/ADD: By both student and director

GENERAL ADMISSIONS INFORMATION

Director of Admissions: Sandra Hayes
Telephone: 408)554-525

ENTRANCE REQUIREMENTS

Academic units required: 4 English, 4 math, 3 science (2 science lab), 3 foreign language, 1 social studies, 1 history, 2 academic electives. **Academic units recommended:** 4 English, 4 math, 4 science (2 science lab), 4 foreign language, 2 social studies, 1 history, 2 academic electives, 1 visual & performing arts. High school diploma is required and GED is not accepted. ACT with or without Writing component accepted. TOEFL required of all international applicants, minimum paper TOEFL 550, minimum computer TOEFL 213.

Application deadline: 1/15
Notification: 4/1
Average GPA: 3.60

Average SAT Math: 613
Average SAT Verbal: 592
Average ACT: 26

Graduated top 10% of class: 37%
Graduated top 25% of class: 72%
Graduated top 50% of class: 100%

COLLEGE GRADUATION REQUIREMENTS

Course waivers allowed: No
Course substitutions allowed: Yes
In what course: Foreign language

ADDITIONAL INFORMATION

Environment: The university is located 1 hour south of San Francisco in "Silicon Valley," 3 miles from San Jose airport and 4 hours from Lake Tahoe.

Student Body:
 Undergrad enrollment: 4391
 Women: 55%
 Men: 45%
 Percent out-of-state: 32%

Cost Information
 Tuition: $28,899
 Room & board: $10,032
Housing Information
 University housing: Yes
 Percent living on campus: 44%

Greek System
 Fraternity: No
 Sorority: No
 Athletics: NCAA Division I

Santa Clara University

SANTA MONICA COLLEGE

1900 Pico Blvd, Santa Monica, CA 90405
Phone: 310-434-4000 • Fax: 310-434-3645
E-mail: admission@smc.edu • Web: www.smc.edu
Support: CS • Institution type: 2-year public

LEARNING DISABILITY PROGRAM AND SERVICES

The Santa Monica College Learning Disabilities Program is designed to provide support services to students with learning disabilities who are enrolled in regular college classes. The college is dedicated to helping students with learning disabilities achieve their goals by identifying those eligible for special services according to state-mandated guidelines, and by assisting them in becoming independent, optimally functioning college students. These goals are met by the following: screening, testing, and certification of learning disabilities according to state guidelines; developing individual plans and recommending appropriate academic accommodations to provide academic equity for LD students; teaching compensatory learning strategies; and fostering self-awareness of learning strengths and weaknesses. Before a student can receive these support services, the student must be evaluated to determine eligibility for the program. This evaluation is achieved in an eight-week Assessment Workshop. During this time, students discover their learning strengths and weaknesses through a series of tasks. Both academic and thinking skills are assessed. Test results will be compared to guidelines provided by the State of California, in accordance with federal mandates, to determine whether a student qualifies for on-going support services as a learning disabled student. The LD specialist will interpret test results and will make individual recommendations on how to improve learning and study strategies. Orientations explaining the assessment process are offered regularly throughout the year.

LD/ADD ADMISSIONS INFORMATION

College entrance tests required: No
Interview required: No
Essay required: No
Documentation required for LD: Yes
Documentation required for ADD: MD letter
Submitted to: Disability Student Services
Special Ed. HS coursework accepted: Yes

Specific course requirements of all applicants: No
Separate application required for program servics: No
# of LD applications submitted each year: 120
# of LD applications accepted yearly: 100
Total # of students receiving LD services: 300
Acceptance into program means acceptance into college: Student must be admitted and enrolled in the college first and then request services.

ADMISSIONS

Students may enroll at Santa Monica College if they have graduated from high school, or are 18 years of age or older, or are 16 years or age or older and submit a "Student Score Report" for passing the California high school proficiency examination. Students taking courses leading to degrees or certificates, or wish to transfer to a four-year college or university should file an application for admissions and schedule time for assessments. Assessment tests are required to enroll in English or math courses unless the student meets the exemption criteria. Students should arrange for transcripts from the high school and/or previous college work be sent to the college. Students must complete orientation. Orientation can be completed in person or online. After the orientation, the student will be able to proceed with enrollment. Printed applications are processed at a lower priority than the online applications therefore submission of the printed application will result in a significantly lower priority date for enrollment.

ADDITIONAL INFORMATION

After the assessment process, an individual education plan is developed with recommendations for needed skills training and appropriate accommodations. The following is a list of services that the student may be eligible for as indicated in the personal plan: study strategies workshops; drop-in tutoring appointments that are available for "short term" help; and tutoring. Students should see their contact instructor to discuss needs. The LD program has help available in math and English. There are many options available for tutoring campus wide. Additional accommodations or services could include test proctoring; a quiet, distraction-free environment; priority registration for fall and spring only; volunteer note-takers for students who have difficulty listening and taking notes at the same time; tape recording lectures, also possible to request the assistance of a student in the class who is a good note-taker and is willing to volunteer; books on tape is an excellent resource for students who have severe reading diffuclties; High Tech Training Center including assistive technology training, word processing classes, computer-assisted instruction, introduction to the internet, and "open lab times" to get help or work on an assignment; academic advisement; and on/off campus referrals.

Support Services Contact Information

Learning Disability Program/Services: Disabled Student Services
Director: Mary Jane Weil
  E-Mail: weil_Mary-Jane@smc.edu
  Telephone: 310-434-4265
  Fax: 310-434-4272
Contact Person: George Marcopulos
  E-Mail: marcopulos_george@smc.edu
  Telephone: 310-434-4684
  Fax: 310-434-4272

LEARNING DISABILITY SERVICES

Requests for the following/services accommodations will be evaluated individually based on appropriate and current documentation.

Allowed in exams
  Calculator: Yes
  Dictionary: Yes
  Computer: Yes
  Spellchecker: Yes
Extended test time: Yes
Scribes: No
Proctors: Yes
Oral exams: Yes
Note-takers: Yes

Distraction-reduced environment: Yes
Tape recording in class: Yes
Books on tape from RFBD: Yes
Taping of books not from RFBD: No
Accommodations for students with ADD: Yes
Reading machine: Yes
Other assistive technology: Yes
Priority registration: Yes

Added costs for services: No
LD specialists: Yes
Professional tutors: No
Peer tutors: No
Max. hours/wk. for services: N/A
How professors are notified of LD/ADD: By student

GENERAL ADMISSIONS INFORMATION

Director of Admissions: Brenda Simmons
Telephone: 310-434-4000

ENTRANCE REQUIREMENTS

Academic units required: No ACT/SAT required. High school diploma or GED accepted. **Academic units recommended:** 16 total (4 years English, 3 years math, 3 years science, 4 years social studies, 2 years foreign language). TOEFL required of all international applicants, minimum paper TOEFL 450, minimum computer TOEFL 133

Application deadline: Rolling
Notification: Rolling
Average GPA: NR

Average SAT Math: NR
Average SAT Verbal: NR
Average ACT: NR

Graduated top 10% of class: NR
Graduated top 25% of class: NR
Graduated top 50% of class: NR

COLLEGE GRADUATION REQUIREMENTS

Course waivers allowed: Yes
Course substitutions allowed: Yes
In what course: Math proficiency exam

ADDITIONAL INFORMATION

Environment: Santa Monica College is located in West Los Angeles.

Student Body:
  Undergrad enrollment: 13,160
  Women: 76%
  Men: 24%
  Percent out-of-state: NR

Cost Information
  In-state tuition: $26 per unit
  Out-of-state tuition: $155 per unit
  Fees: $624
Housing Information
  University housing: Yes, off campus
  Percent living on campus: NR

Greek System
  Fraternity: No
  Sorority: No
Athletics: NJCAA

SANTA ROSA JUNIOR COLLEGE

1501 Mendocino Avenue, Santa Rosa, CA 95401
Phone: 707-527-4685 • Fax: 707-527-4798
E-mail: admininfo@santarosa.edu • Web: www.santarosa.edu
Support: CS • Institution type: 2-year public

LEARNING DISABILITY PROGRAM AND SERVICES

The Disability Resources Department provides students with disabilities equal access to a community college education through specialized instruction, disability-related support services, and advocacy activities. Santa Rosa Junior College is a state-supported school that accepts all students with learning disabilities who apply and meet the mandatory state eligibility requirements that verify their learning disability. If a student is eligible for the program, an individualized educational plan is developed and implemented. Students may participate in a combination of special and mainstream college classes with appropriate support services as needed. The college encourages and fosters autonomy, independence, and responsibility in students with disabilities and challenges them to become self-advocates. The college also creates a campus climate in which diverse learning styles are respected and equal access for students with disabilities can be realized.

LD/ADD ADMISSIONS INFORMATION

College entrance tests required: Yes
Interview required: No
Essay required: No
Documentation required for LD: WAIS–III, Woodcock-Johnson
Documentation required for ADD: Yes
Submitted to: Disability Resources
Special Ed. HS coursework accepted: Yes

Specific course requirements of all applicants: No
Separate application required for program servics: No
# of LD applications submitted each year: 150–200
# of LD applications accepted yearly: 125–175
Total # of students receiving LD services: 500
Acceptance into program means acceptance into college: Student must be admitted and enrolled in the college first and then request services.

ADMISSIONS

Admission to Santa Rosa is open to students with a high school diploma or a GED. There are no specific requirements for admission. Students with learning disabilities must meet state eligibility requirements verifying a learning disability to qualify to receive services. Students must demonstrate average to above-average intellectual ability, adequate measured achievement in at least one academic area or employment setting, a severe processing deficit in one or more areas, a severe discrepancy between aptitude and achievement in one or more academic areas, and adaptive behavior appropriate to a college setting. Students may also qualify on the basis of a communicative disorder and head injuries. All students must demonstrate appropriate behavior and an ability to benefit from the instructional program.

ADDITIONAL INFORMATION

The Learning Skills Program offers small specialized classes in the following areas for non-transferable credit: basic academic skills, guidance/independent living, sensory-motor integration, and speech and language. Support services include assessment for learning disabilities, counseling, tutoring, speech/language skills development, and liaison. Skills classes are offered in spelling, writing, math, study strategies, computers, and art process. All of these courses may be taken for college credit.

Support Services Contact Information

Learning Disability Program/Services: Disability Resources Dept.
Director: Patie Wegman
  E-Mail: pwegman@santarosa.edu
  Telephone: 707-527-4278
  Fax: 707-524-1768
Contact Person: Marcy Stinnett
  Telephone: 707-527-4278
  Fax: 707-524-1768

LEARNING DISABILITY SERVICES

Requests for the following/services accommodations will be evaluated individually based on appropriate and current documentation.

Allowed in exams
  Calculator: Yes
  Dictionary: Yes
  Computer: Yes
  Spellchecker: Yes
Extended test time: Yes
Scribes: Yes
Proctors: Yes
Oral exams: Yes
Note-takers: Yes

Distraction-reduced environment: Yes
Tape recording in class: Yes
Books on tape from RFBD: Yes
Taping of books not from RFBD: Yes
Accommodations for students with
  ADD: Yes
Reading machine: Yes
Other assistive technology: Yes
Priority registration: Yes

Added costs for services: No
LD specialists: Yes
Professional tutors: 10
Peer tutors: No
Max. hours/wk. for services: N/A
How professors are notified of
  LD/ADD: By student

GENERAL ADMISSIONS INFORMATION

Director of Admissions: Ricardo Navarrette
Telephone: 707-527-4685

ENTRANCE REQUIREMENTS

Open door admissions policy. **Academic units required:** GED or high school diploma required. **Academic units recommended:** 16 total (4 years English, 3 years math, 3 years science, 4 years social studies, 2 years foreign language.) TOEFL required of all international applicants, minimum paper TOEFL 475, minimum computer TOEFL 153

Application deadline: Rolling
Notification: Rolling
Average GPA: NR

Average SAT Math: NR
Average SAT Verbal: NR
Average ACT: NR

Graduated top 10% of class: NR
Graduated top 25% of class: NR
Graduated top 50% of class: NR

COLLEGE GRADUATION REQUIREMENTS

Course waivers allowed: Yes
Course substitutions allowed: No
In what course: Math after attempting regular math courses

ADDITIONAL INFORMATION

Environment: The college is located on 93 acres with easy access to San Francisco.

Student Body:
  Undergrad enrollment: 28,233
  Women: 59%
  Men: 41%
  Percent out-of-state: 2%

Cost Information
  In-state tuition: $26 per unit
  Out-of-state tuition: $177 per unit
  Room & board: $2,100
  Fees: $264
Housing Information
  University housing: Yes
  Percent living on campus: 22%

Greek System
  Fraternity: Yes
  Sorority: Yes
Athletics: Intercollegiate

SIERRA COLLEGE

5000 Rocklin Road, Rocklin, CA 95677
Phone: 916-781-0430 • Fax: 916-789-2878
E-mail: jradford@sierracollege.edu • Web: www.sierracollege.edu
Support: CS • Institution type: 2-year public

LEARNING DISABILITY PROGRAM AND SERVICES

The goals of the program are to assist students with learning disabilities in reaching their academic/vocational goals, to help the students strengthen and develop their perceptual skills and to provide the support needed to maximize student success. Sierra College subscribes to the psychometric-evaluation model established by the California Community College System. This six-step process includes (1) intake screening, (2) measured achievement, (3) ability level, (4) processing deficit, (5) aptitude-achievement discrepancy, and (6) eligibility recommendation. Students are evaluated individually through the Learning Disabilities Orientation course. This is a mainstreamed program with no special classes, but it does provide support and accommodations for students with learning disabilities.

LD/ADD ADMISSIONS INFORMATION

College entrance tests required: No
Interview required: No
Essay required: No
Documentation required for LD: WAIS–III; WJ
Documentation required for ADD: Yes
Submitted to: Learning Opportunities Center
Special Ed. HS coursework accepted: Yes

Specific course requirements of all applicants: No
Separate application required for program servics: No
# of LD applications submitted each year: NR
# of LD applications accepted yearly: NR
Total # of students receiving LD services: 400
Acceptance into program means acceptance into
   college: Student must be admitted and enrolled in the
   college first and then request services.

ADMISSIONS

Sierra College has an open admissions policy for those students who meet the regular entrance requirements and who have completed testing and evaluation by a learning disabilities specialist. ACT/SAT are not required and there are no cut-offs for GPA, class rank, or test scores. Additionally, no specific courses are required for admission. Any student who holds a high school diploma or GED is admitted. Services are provided to all enrolled students with appropriate documentation.

ADDITIONAL INFORMATION

In order to receive services and accommodations, students must meet the eligibility requirements set forth by the state of California for students with learning disabilities. Skills courses are available in reading, math, writing, study strategies, English as a Second Language, and spelling. These skills classes are offered for college credit. In addition, students can get assistance in test-taking techniques, priority registration, and peer tutoring. Other services include assessment and evaluation of learning disabilities, individual education plans, identification of students' learning styles and modalities, perceptual training programs, test-taking facilitation, compensatory learning strategies/techniques, computer-assisted instruction, and classroom accommodations.

Support Services Contact Information

Learning Disability Program/Services: Learning Opportunities Center
Director: Delecia J. Nunnally
  E-Mail: dnunnally@sierracollege.edu
  Telephone: 916-781-2598
  Fax: 916-789-2936
Contact Person: Denise Stone
  E-Mail: dstone@sierracollege.edu
  Telephone: 916-789-2697
  Fax: 916-789-2967

LEARNING DISABILITY SERVICES

Requests for the following/services accommodations will be evaluated individually based on appropriate and current documentation.

Allowed in exams
  Calculator: Yes
  Dictionary: Yes
  Computer: Yes
  Spellchecker: Yes
Extended test time: Yes
Scribes: No
Proctors: Yes
Oral exams: Yes
Note-takers: Yes

Distraction-reduced environment: Yes
Tape recording in class: Yes
Books on tape from RFBD: Yes
Taping of books not from RFBD: Yes
Accommodations for students with ADD: Yes
Reading machine: No
Other assistive technology: Yes
Priority registration: Yes

Added costs for services: No
LD specialists: Yes
Professional tutors: No
Peer tutors: 100
Max. hours/wk. for services: Unlimited
How professors are notified of LD/ADD: By both student and director

GENERAL ADMISSIONS INFORMATION

Director of Admissions: Carla Epting-Davis
Telephone: 916-781-0430

ENTRANCE REQUIREMENTS
Open door admissions policy. High school diploma or GED is accepted. ACT/SAT not required for admission.

Application deadline: Rolling
Notification: Rolling
Average GPA: NR

Average SAT Math: NR
Average SAT Verbal: NR
Average ACT: NR

Graduated top 10% of class: NR
Graduated top 25% of class: NR
Graduated top 50% of class: NR

COLLEGE GRADUATION REQUIREMENTS

Course waivers allowed: Yes
Course substitutions allowed: Yes
In what course: Waivers or substitutions are provided on an individual basis.

ADDITIONAL INFORMATION

Environment: The school is located on a 327 acre campus in a rural setting with easy access to Sacramento.

Student Body:
  Undergrad enrollment: 20,173
  Women: 56%
  Men: 44%
  Percent out-of-state: NR

Cost Information
  In-state tuition: $26 per unit
  Out-of-state tuition: $149 per unit
  Room & board: $6,250
Housing Information
  University housing: Yes
  Percent living on campus: 1%

Greek System
  Fraternity: No
  Sorority: No
Athletics: Intercollegiate

SONOMA STATE UNIVERSITY

1801 East Cotati Avenue, Rohnert Park, CA 94928
Phone: 707-664-2778 • Fax: 707-664-2060
E-mail: admitme.@sonoma.edu • Web: www.sonoma.edu
Support: S • Institution type: 4-year public

LEARNING DISABILITY PROGRAM AND SERVICES

The goal of Disabled Student Services (DSS) is to provide reasonable accommodations and equal access to the educational process while helping students with disabilities become self-advocates. Services at Sonoma State University are provided primarily through two offices on campus. DSS offers support services and advocacy, and Learning Skills Services provides academic support and skill development. One-to-one sessions and workshops are given by specialists in various subject areas. In addition, a campus tutorial program offers individual peer tutoring. Appropriate documentation for LD/ADD students is required and must be completed by a qualified professional. The documentation should be submitted to DSS.

LD/ADD ADMISSIONS INFORMATION

College entrance tests required: Yes
Interview required: No
Essay required: Yes
Documentation required for LD: WAIS R, WAIS–III, WS–R, TAPS, TVPS, TOMAL
Documentation required for ADD: Yes
Submitted to: Disability Student Services
Special Ed. HS coursework accepted: No

Specific course requirements of all applicants: Yes
Separate application required for program servics: Yes
# of LD applications submitted each year: 40–50
# of LD applications accepted yearly: 20–25
Total # of students receiving LD services: 200
Acceptance into program means acceptance into college: Student must be admitted and enrolled in the university first and then request services.

ADMISSIONS

Admission is based on a combination of high school GPA, test scores, and college-preparatory classes. Courses include 4 years English, 3 years math, 1 year social studies, 1 year science, 2 years foreign language, 1 year visual or performing arts, and 3 electives. SAT/ACT score requirements depend on the GPA. However, a 2.0 GPA is the absolute minimum. Students with learning disabilities must submit a general application. If a limited number of required courses are missing, students can be granted a conditional admission and these courses must be made up in college. Students not meeting either regular or conditional admissions may initiate a request for special admissions by writing a letter to the DSS director providing information about strengths, weaknesses, and why special admission is needed. LD diagnostic evaluation and 2 letters of recommendations are also required for conditional admission. All special admission applicants are interviewed in person or by phone. Special admission is only available to designated groups of students. Special Admissions applicants need to submit a letter describing what subject areas are missing or if the GPA or SAT/ACT are low. The staff of DSS makes recommendations, but the final decision is made by the Office of Admission.

ADDITIONAL INFORMATION

DSS does not offer skills classes or tutoring. Reading, writing, and math are offered through the Learning Skills Services. Tutorial assistance is available in the Tutorial Center. There are no LD specialists in the DSS; however, there are disability management advisors who authorize accommodations. With appropriate documentation, some of the services or accommodations offered include the use of calculators, dictionaries, computers or spellcheckers in exams; extended time on tests; scribes; proctors; oral exams; note-takers; distraction-free testing environments; tape recorder in class; taped text; and priority registration.

Support Services Contact Information

Learning Disability Program/Services: Disabled Student Services (DSS)
Director: Linda Lipps
  E-mail: Linda.Lipp@sonoma.edu
  Telephone: 707-664-2677
  Fax: 707-644-3330
Contact Person: Aurelia Melgar
  Telephone: 707-664-2677
  Fax: 707-644-3330

LEARNING DISABILITY SERVICES

Requests for the following/services accommodations will be evaluated individually based on appropriate and current documentation.

Allowed in exams
  Calculator: Yes
  Dictionary: Yes
  Computer: Yes
  Spellchecker: Yes
Extended test time: Yes
Scribes: Yes
Proctors: No
Oral exams: Yes
Note-takers: Yes

Distraction-reduced environment: Yes
Tape recording in class: Yes
Books on tape from RFBD: Yes
Taping of books not from RFBD: Yes
Accommodations for students with ADD: Yes
Reading machine: Yes
Other assistive technology: Yes
Priority registration: Yes

Added costs for services: No
LD specialists: No
Professional tutors: No
Peer tutors: 40–45
Max. hours/wk. for services: 4
How professors are notified of LD/ADD: By student

GENERAL ADMISSIONS INFORMATION

Director of Admissions: Gustavo Flores
Telephone: 707-664-2778

ENTRANCE REQUIREMENTS

Academic units required: 4 English, 3 math, 2 science (1 science lab), 2 foreign language, 1 history, 3 academic electives, 1 visual/performing arts, 1 U.S. government. High school diploma is required and GED is accepted. TOEFL required of all international applicants, minimum paper TOEFL 500, minimum computer TOEFL 173.

Application deadline: 1/31
Notification: Rolling
Average GPA: 3.23

Average SAT Math: 520
Average SAT Verbal: 548
Average ACT: 21

Graduated top 10% of class: NR
Graduated top 25% of class: NR
Graduated top 50% of class: NR

COLLEGE GRADUATION REQUIREMENTS

Course waivers allowed: No
Course substitutions allowed: Yes
In what course: Allowed sometimes in math by petition; the university offers an alternative math class to fulfill the general education requirements. May substitute foreign language only.

ADDITIONAL INFORMATION

Environment: The school is located on 220 acres with easy access to San Francisco.

Student Body:
  Undergrad enrollment: 6,677
  Women: 63%
  Men: 37%
  Percent out-of-state: 4%

Cost Information
  In-state tuition: $3,010
  Out-of-state tuition: $11,470
  Room & board: $8,805
Housing Information
  University housing: Yes
  Percent living on campus: 35%

Greek System
  Fraternity: Yes
  Sorority: Yes
  Athletics: NCAA Division II

STANFORD UNIVERSITY

Old Union 232, Stanford, CA 94305-3005
Phone: 650-723-2091 • Fax: 650-723-6050
E-mail: admissions@stanford.edu • Web: www.stanford.edu
Support: CS • Institution type: 4-year private

LEARNING DISABILITY PROGRAM AND SERVICES

Since its creation in 1983, the Disability Resource Center has provided direct academic services for students with learning disabilities. It also serves as an advocacy group to assist students who encounter accessibility problems and to facilitate special arrangements for housing and campus activities.

LD/ADD ADMISSIONS INFORMATION

College entrance tests required: Yes
Interview required: No
Essay required: No
Documentation required for LD: Psychoeducational evaluation
Documentation required for ADD: Yes
Submitted to: Disability Resource Center
Special Ed. HS coursework accepted: No

Specific course requirements of all applicants: Yes
Separate application required for program servics: No
# of LD applications submitted each year: NR
# of LD applications accepted yearly: NR
Total # of students receiving LD services: NR
Acceptance into program means acceptance into college: Students must be admitted and enrolled in the university and then request services.

ADMISSIONS

Stanford seeks to enroll students with excellent academic records, who show evidence of personal achievement outside the classroom, and who have used the resources available to them to their fullest potential. The policy on the admissions of students with learning disabilities makes clear there is no separate academic program. Students should take a strong college-preparatory curriculum, including honors and Advanced Placement courses. The university will look at ACT/SAT test scores in context of the learning disability. Typically, applicants to Stanford rank in the top 10 percent from a public high school or the top 20–30 percent in a private high school.

ADDITIONAL INFORMATION

Students seeking services or accommodations for specific learning disabilities or attention deficit disorders must submit psychoeducational evaluations that are recent enough to reflect current levels of functioning. There are no skill courses offered. Tutoring is available on campus through the Center for Teaching and Learning. A peer support group is available. Services and accommodations are offered to undergraduate and graduate students.

Support Services Contact Information

Learning Disability Program/Services: Disability Resource Center
Director: Joan Bisagno, PhD
  E-Mail: joan.bisagno@stanford.edu
  Telephone: 650-723-1066
  Fax: 650-725-5301

LEARNING DISABILITY SERVICES

Requests for the following/services accommodations will be evaluated individually based on appropriate and current documentation.

Allowed in exams
  Calculator: Y/N
  Dictionary: Y/N
  Computer: Y/N
  Spellchecker: Y/N
Extended test time: Yes
Scribes: Yes
Proctors: Yes
Oral exams: Yes
Note-takers: Yes

Distraction-reduced environment: Yes
Tape recording in class: Yes
Books on tape from RFBD: Yes
Taping of books not from RFBD: Yes
Accommodations for students with
  ADD: Yes
Reading machine: Yes
Other assistive technology: Yes
Priority registration: Yes

Added costs for services: No
LD specialists: Yes
Professional tutors: No
Peer tutors: Yes
Max. hours/wk. for services: Varies
How professors are notified of
  LD/ADD: By student

GENERAL ADMISSIONS INFORMATION

Director of Admissions: Anna Marie Porras
Telephone: 650-723-2091

ENTRANCE REQUIREMENTS

Academic units recommended: 4 English, 4 math, 3 science (3 science lab), 3 foreign language, 2 social studies, 1 history. High school diploma is required and GED is accepted. ACT with Writing component required or SAT Reasoning and 3 SAT Subject Tests.

Application deadline: 12/15
Notification: 4/1
Average GPA: 3.9

Average SAT Math: 600–800
Average SAT Verbal: 600–800
Average ACT: 32–36

Graduated top 10% of class: 87%
Graduated top 25% of class: 97%
Graduated top 50% of class: 100%

COLLEGE GRADUATION REQUIREMENTS

Course waivers allowed: No
Course substitutions allowed: No
In what course: N/A

ADDITIONAL INFORMATION

Environment: Stanford University is located about 30 minutes south of San Francisco.

Student Body:
  Undergrad enrollment: 6,500
  Women: 48%
  Men: 52%
  Percent out-of-state: 53%

Cost Information
  Tuition: $29,847
  Room & board: $9,503
Housing Information
  University housing: Yes
  Percent living on campus: 91%

Greek System
  Fraternity: Yes
  Sorority: Yes
Athletics: NCAA Division I

U. OF CALIFORNIA—BERKELEY

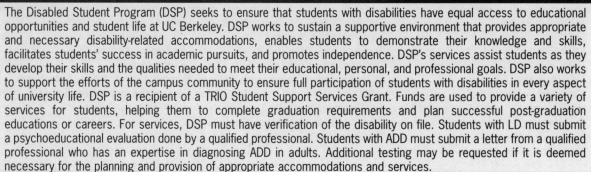

110 Sproul Hall #5800, Berkeley, CA 94720-5800
Phone: 510-642-3175 • Fax: 510-642-7333
E-mail: ouars@uclink.berkeley.edu • Web: www.berkeley.edu
Support: CS • Institution type: 4-year public

LEARNING DISABILITY PROGRAM AND SERVICES

The Disabled Student Program (DSP) seeks to ensure that students with disabilities have equal access to educational opportunities and student life at UC Berkeley. DSP works to sustain a supportive environment that provides appropriate and necessary disability-related accommodations, enables students to demonstrate their knowledge and skills, facilitates students' success in academic pursuits, and promotes independence. DSP's services assist students as they develop their skills and the qualities needed to meet their educational, personal, and professional goals. DSP also works to support the efforts of the campus community to ensure full participation of students with disabilities in every aspect of university life. DSP is a recipient of a TRIO Student Support Services Grant. Funds are used to provide a variety of services for students, helping them to complete graduation requirements and plan successful post-graduation educations or careers. For services, DSP must have verification of the disability on file. Students with LD must submit a psychoeducational evaluation done by a qualified professional. Students with ADD must submit a letter from a qualified professional who has an expertise in diagnosing ADD in adults. Additional testing may be requested if it is deemed necessary for the planning and provision of appropriate accommodations and services.

LD/ADD ADMISSIONS INFORMATION

College entrance tests required: Yes
Interview required: No
Essay required: Yes
Documentation required for LD: Current WAIS–III and WJ
Documentation required for ADD: Yes
Submitted to: Disabled Student Services
Special Ed. HS coursework accepted: No

Specific course requirements of all applicants: Yes
Separate application required for program servics: No
# of LD applications submitted each year: NR
# of LD applications accepted yearly: NR
Total # of students receiving LD services: 242
Acceptance into program means acceptance into
college: Student must be admitted and enrolled in the
university first and then request services.

ADMISSIONS

An LD specialist and admission specialist are available to meet with students with LD interested in applying to UC—Berkeley. These specialists will review the applicant's high school or college transcript and give advice on how to proceed with the application. DSP works closely with the Office of Admissions and Records. There are two tiers for admission: Tier I is an automatic admission; Tier II applicants may need other criteria to be admitted. The impact of a disability could be a factor in an admission for a Tier II applicant. When an applicant indicates on the application that there is a disability, DSP contacts the applicant to request information, documentation of the disability, and a statement from the applicant about the impact of the disability on his/her life and academic achievement. DSP uses this information to answer questions about the applicant from Admissions. UC—Berkeley seeks to identify students with disabilities who have a high potential for success if provided with appropriate accommodation and support services.

ADDITIONAL INFORMATION

DSP staff provide the following services: recommending and ensuring the provision of academic accommodations; consulting with instructors about accommodations; authorizing auxiliary services, teaching academic strategies and study skills; promoting on-campus awareness; academic advising; adaptive technology; support groups; a special section of the course "Facilitating Success" for students with LD and ADD that centers on understanding learning differences; maximizing strengths; academic planning; research, writing, exam preparation, and using university resources; priority registration; specialist to help in developing problem-solving strategies and solutions to difficult problems; a series of informational workshops on topics like understanding disabilities and individual learning styles, improving reading, writing, research efficiency, and memory strategies; self-advocacy; computer applications that facilitate learning; and career or graduate school planning. Specialists may recommend a reduced course load.

Support Services Contact Information

Learning Disability Program/Services: Disabled Students' Program (DSP)
Director: Ed Rogers
  E-Mail: erogers@berkeley.edu
  Telephone: 510-642-0518
  Fax: 510-643-9686
Contact Person: Connie Chiba
  E-Mail: cchiba@uclink4.berkeley.edu
  Telephone: 510-642-0518
  Fax: 510-643-9686

LEARNING DISABILITY SERVICES

Requests for the following/services accommodations will be evaluated individually based on appropriate and current documentation.

Allowed in exams
  Calculator: Yes
  Dictionary: Y/N
  Computer: Y/N
  Spellchecker: Yes
Extended test time: Yes
Scribes: Yes
Proctors: Yes
Oral exams: Yes

Note-takers: Yes
Distraction-reduced environment: Yes
Tape recording in class: Yes
Books on tape from RFBD: Yes
Taping of books not from RFBD: Yes
Accommodations for students with ADD: Yes
Reading machine: Yes
Other assistive technology: Yes

Priority registration: Yes
Added costs for services: No
LD specialists: Yes
Professional tutors: No
Peer tutors: Student Learning Center
Max. hours/wk. for services: NR
How professors are notified of LD/ADD: By student

GENERAL ADMISSIONS INFORMATION

Director of Admissions: Camila Hicks
Telephone: 510-642-3175

ENTRANCE REQUIREMENTS

Academic units required: 4 English, 3 math, 2 science (2 science lab), 2 foreign language, 2 social studies, 2 history, 1 academic elective, 1 visual or performing arts. **Academic units recommended:** 4 English, 4 math, 3 science (3 science lab), 3 foreign language, 2 social studies, 2 history, 1 academic elective, 1 visual or performing arts. High school diploma is required and GED is accepted. ACT with Writing component required. Students submitting the SAT Reasoning Test must also submit 2 SAT Subject Tests. TOEFL required of all international applicants, minimum paper TOEFL 550, minimum computer TOEFL 213.

Application deadline: 11/30
Notification: 3/31
Average GPA: 3.93

Average SAT Math: 671
Average SAT Verbal: 629
Average ACT: NR

Graduated top 10% of class: 98%
Graduated top 25% of class: 100%
Graduated top 50% of class: 100%

COLLEGE GRADUATION REQUIREMENTS

Course waivers allowed: Yes
In what course: Math waivers are considered on a case-by-case basis.
Course substitutions allowed: Yes, limited
In what course: Foreign language requirement can be substituted with cultural courses on a case-by-case basis.

ADDITIONAL INFORMATION

Environment: The 1,232-acre campus is in an urban area, 10 miles east of San Francisco.

Student Body:
  Undergrad enrollment: 22,880
  Women: 54%
  Men: 46%
  Percent out-of-state: 6%

Cost Information
  In-state tuition: $6,730 (Fees)
  Out-of-state tuition: $23,686
  Room & board: $11,630
Housing Information
  University housing: Yes
  Percent living on campus: 35%

Greek System
  Fraternity: Yes
  Sorority: Yes
Athletics: NCAA Division I

University of California—Berkeley

U. OF CALIFORNIA—LOS ANGELES

405 Hilgard Avenue, Box 951436, Los Angeles, CA 90095-1436
Phone: 310-825-3101 • Fax: 310-206-1206
E-mail: ugadm@saonet.ucla.edu • Web: www.ucla.edu
Support: CS • Institution type: 4-year public

LEARNING DISABILITY PROGRAM AND SERVICES

UCLA complies with state, federal, and university guidelines that mandate full access for students with disabilities, including learning disabilities. UCLA complies with the requirement to provide reasonable accommodations for documented students to allow them to participate in their academic program to the greatest extent possible. Students with other documented types of learning disabilities, including attention deficit (hyperactive) disorder and traumatic brain injury, are also served by the Learning Disabilities program. The UCLA Learning Disabilities Program is coordinated by a full-time learning disabilities specialist, and offers a full range of accommodations and services. Services are individually designed, and include counseling, special test arrangements, note-taker services, readers, priority enrollment, adaptive technology, and individual tutoring. An active support group provides opportunities for students to discuss mutual concerns and enhance learning strategies. Workshops and speakers address skill development and topics of interest. In the peer-mentor program, continuing students with learning disabilities serve as resources to entering students.

LD/ADD ADMISSIONS INFORMATION

College entrance tests required: Yes
Interview required: No
Essay required: Yes
Documentation required for LD: Psychoeducational evaluation
Documentation required for ADD: Yes
Submitted to: Office for Students with Disabilities
Special Ed. HS coursework accepted: No

Specific course requirements of all applicants: Yes
Separate application required for program servics: No
# of LD applications submitted each year: NR
# of LD applications accepted yearly: NR
Total # of students receiving LD services: 225–300
Acceptance into program means acceptance into college: Student must be admitted and enrolled in the university first and then request services.

ADMISSIONS

There are no special admissions criteria for students with learning disabilities. In an academic review the university will assess and balance a variety of academic factors to determine the overall scholastic strength of each applicant. UCLA does not use a formula. The comprehensive review includes the remainder of the freshman applicants after the academic review. While commitment to intellectual development and academic progress continues to be of primary importance, the personal statement also forms an integral part of this review. All applicants are required to submit the SAT or ACT and SAT Subject Tests (including Mathematics–Level 1 or 2, and either English Literature, Foreign Language, Science, or Social Studies). To be competitive students usually score in the high 20s on the ACT or high 1100s on the SAT, and between 500–600 on each of the SAT Subject Tests. High school courses required are 4 years English, 2 years history/social science, 3 years math, 2 years foreign language (3 years recommended), 2 years lab science (3 years recommended), and 2 years electives. Additional criteria are based on an eligibility index using test scores and class rank. Selected students are admitted for winter. Admissions readers pay attention to significant obstacles and challenges related in personal statements. The LD specialists provide disability-related information to admissions staff.

ADDITIONAL INFORMATION

LD Program includes tutors for individual classes; peer mentors; support group meetings; learning skills workshops; advocacy; referrals to campus resources; priority enrollment; orientation program; LD screening; and disability management counseling by four LD specialist including disability awareness, learning and time-management strategies, self-advocacy skills, and interpretation of evaluation reports. Compensations could include alternatives in (1) printed materials: taped textbooks, computerized voice synthesizer, RFBD; (2) test-taking procedures: extended time, proctor to assist with reading and writing, distraction-free test area, computer for essay exams, alternative test formats including essay-type rather than multiple choice-type or taped exams rather than written exams, use of calculator or spellchecker; (3) note taking: note-takers, taped lecture; (4) writing essays and papers: word processors with voice synthesizers, composition tutors; (5) reduced course load; and (6) extended time to complete a program and (7) tutors for individual classes.

Support Services Contact Information

Learning Disability Program/Services: Office for Students with Disabilities
Director: Kathy Molini
E-Mail: kmolini@saonet.ucla.edu
Telephone: 310-825-1501
Fax: 310-825-9656

LEARNING DISABILITY SERVICES

Requests for the following/services accommodations will be evaluated individually based on appropriate and current documentation.

Allowed in exams
Calculator: Yes
Dictionary: Yes
Computer: Yes
Spellchecker: Yes
Extended test time: Yes
Scribes: Yes
Proctors: Yes
Oral exams: No
Note-takers: Yes

Distraction-reduced environment: Yes
Tape recording in class: Yes
Books on tape from RFBD: Yes
Taping of books not from RFBD: Yes
Accommodations for students with ADD: Yes
Reading machine: Yes
Other assistive technology: Yes
Priority registration: Yes

Added costs for services: No
LD specialists: Yes
Professional tutors: No
Peer tutors: Yes
Max. hours/wk. for services: Unlimited
How professors are notified of LD/ADD: By both student and director

GENERAL ADMISSIONS INFORMATION

Director of Admissions: Dr. Vu T. Tran, Director
Telephone: 310-825-3101

ENTRANCE REQUIREMENTS

Academic units required: 4 English, 3 math, 2 science (2 science lab), 2 foreign language, 2 history, 1 academic elective, 1 visual and performing arts. **Academic units recommended:** 4 math, 3 science (3 science lab), 3 foreign language. High school diploma is required and GED is accepted. ACT with Writing component required or SAT Reasoning Test plus 2 SAT Subject Tests. TOEFL required of all international applicants, minimum paper TOEFL 550, minimum computer TOEFL 220.

Application deadline: 11/30
Notification: Rolling
Average GPA: 4.12

Average SAT Math: 660
Average SAT Verbal: 629
Average ACT: 27

Graduated top 10% of class: 97%
Graduated top 25% of class: NR
Graduated top 50% of class: 100%

COLLEGE GRADUATION REQUIREMENTS

Course waivers allowed: No
Course substitutions allowed: Yes
In what course: Foreign language, history, and math as appropriate based on documentation.

ADDITIONAL INFORMATION

Environment: The university is located on 419 acres in an urban area of Los Angeles.

Student Body:
Undergrad enrollment: 24,946
Women: 57%
Men: 43%
Percent out-of-state: 5%

Cost Information
In-state tuition: $6,575 (Fees)
Out-of-state tuition: $23,531
Room & board: $11,187
Housing Information
University housing: Yes
Percent living on campus: 35%

Greek System
Fraternity: Yes
Sorority: Yes
Athletics: NCAA Division I

University of California—Los Angeles

U. OF CALIFORNIA—SAN DIEGO

9500 Gilman Drive, 0021, La Jolla, CA 92093-0021
Phone: 858-534-4831 • Fax: 858-534-5723
E-mail: admissionsinfo@ucsd.edu • Web: www.ucsd.edu
Support: CS • Institution type: 4-year public

LEARNING DISABILITY PROGRAM AND SERVICES

The primary objective of the Office for Students with Disabilities (OSD) is to integrate mainstream students with learning disabilities into campus programs, services, and activities. Academic accommodations are designed to meet disability-related needs without fundamentally altering the program; are not remedial; and may include part-time enrollment, exception to minimum academic progress requirements, substitution of coursework required for graduation, and alternative test formats. This program is not intended to provide remediation. Students seeking accommodations must provide a comprehensive written evaluation that meets the following requirements: assessment must be comprehensive and include aptitude (WAIS–R with subtest scores and/or WJ–R); achievement (WJ–R); information processing (WAIS–R subtests or WJ–R-cognitive portions) within 3 years; diagnostic report with written summary of educational, medical, and family histories and behavioral observation; test scores, testing procedures followed, interpretation, dates, evaluator; specified intracognitive and/or cognitive-achievement discrepancies; statement of how the LD substantially interferes with the student's educational progress; and recommendations for academic accommodations. OSD's peer mentoring program is designed to match new students who have disabilities (mentees) with continuing students (mentors) who have the same major, interests, and/or disabilities. Mentors and mentees meet as a group once a week throughout the academic year. The group provides for informal meetings and serve as a place to receive emotional support from several students who understand and have something in common. The group also gives students a place where they can feel comfortable discussing issues. Topics covered in the past include: problem-solving techniques, study strategies, test-taking problems, and social issues.

LD/ADD ADMISSIONS INFORMATION

College entrance tests required: Yes
Interview required: No
Essay required: Yes
Documentation required for LD: Psychoeducational
   evaluation, WAIS, WJ–R
Documentation required for ADD: Documentation from the
   student's doctor
Submitted to: Office for Students with Disabilities
Special Ed. HS coursework accepted: N/A

Specific course requirements of all applicants: Yes
Separate application required for program servics: Yes
# of LD applications submitted each year: 40–50
# of LD applications accepted yearly: 50
Total # of students receiving LD services: 150
**Acceptance into program means acceptance into
   college:** Student must be admitted and enrolled in the
   university first and then reviewed for LD services.

ADMISSIONS
There is no special admissions process for students with learning disabilities. All applicants must meet the same admission criteria. Students need to check the disability information on the application if they wish to receive information about university resources and services available. There is an Eligibility Index based on ACT/SAT and GPA such as 2.82 GPA and 36 ACT/1590–1600 SAT up to 3.29 GPA and 12 ACT/490–570 SAT. Meeting the eligibility index requirements does not guarantee admission. The minimum GPA for a California resident is 2.8 and for a nonresident a 3.4. Students must submit 2 SAT Subject Tests. There is a Summer Bridge Program for conditional admits that is available to a specific group of students.

ADDITIONAL INFORMATION
Depending upon the nature of the disability and level of functional limitation coordination may include the following: note-takers; readers; peer mentoring; priority registration; typists; problem resolution assistance; peer mentoring; extended time for tests; distraction-free testing environment; calculators, dictionary, computer or spellchecker in exams; scribes; proctors; tape recorder in class; peer tutoring; and priority registration. Course substitutions are dependent on the college and major requirements. Skills classes are offered for all students in study and time management, and skill building.

Support Services Contact Information

Learning Disability Program/Services: Office for Students with Disabilities (OSD)
Director: Roberta J. Gimblett
E-Mail: rgimblett@ucsd.edu
Telephone: 858-534-4382
Fax: 858-534-4650

LEARNING DISABILITY SERVICES

Requests for the following/services accommodations will be evaluated individually based on appropriate and current documentation.

Allowed in exams
 Calculator: Yes
 Dictionary: Yes
 Computer: Yes
 Spellchecker: Yes
Extended test time: Yes
Scribes: Yes
Proctors: Yes
Oral exams: Yes
Note-takers: Yes

Distraction-reduced environment: Yes
Tape recording in class: Yes
Books on tape from RFBD: Yes
Taping of books not from RFBD: Yes
Accommodations for students with ADD: Yes
Reading machine: Yes
Other assistive technology: Yes
Priority registration: Yes

Added costs for services: No
LD specialists: Yes
Professional tutors: No
Peer tutors: 200–300
Max. hours/wk. for services: Unlimited
How professors are notified of LD/ADD: By student

GENERAL ADMISSIONS INFORMATION

Director of Admissions: Ms. Mae Brown
Telephone: 858-534-4831

ENTRANCE REQUIREMENTS

Academic units required: 4 English, 3 math, 2 science lab, 2 foreign language, 2 history, 1 academic elective, 1 visual and performing arts. **Academic units recommended:** 4 English, 4 math, 3 science lab, 3 foreign language, 2 history, 1 academic elective, 1 visual and performing arts. ACT with Writing component or SAT with 2 SAT Subject Tests required. High school diploma is required and GED is accepted. TOEFL required of all international applicants, minimum paper TOEFL 550, minimum computer TOEFL 213.

Application deadline: 11/30
Notification: Rolling
Average GPA: 3.98

Average SAT Math: 646
Average SAT Verbal: 593
Average ACT: 25

Graduated top 10% of class: 99%
Graduated top 25% of class: 100%
Graduated top 50% of class: 100%

COLLEGE GRADUATION REQUIREMENTS

Course waivers allowed: Yes
Course substitutions allowed: Yes
In what course: Course substitution is dependent on college and major requirements.

ADDITIONAL INFORMATION

Environment: The university has a suburban campus north of downtown San Diego.

Student Body:
 Undergrad enrollment: 20,339
 Women: 52%
 Men: 48%
 Percent out-of-state: 2%

Cost Information
 In-state tuition: $4,629
 Out-of-state tuition: $18,109
 Room & board: $8,622
Housing Information
 University housing: Yes
 Percent living on campus: 33%

Greek System
 Fraternity: Yes
 Sorority: Yes
Athletics: NCAA Division II

University of California—San Diego

U. OF CALIFORNIA—SANTA BARBARA

Office of Admissions, 1210 Cheadle Hall, Santa Barbara, CA 93106-2014
Phone: 805-893-2881 • Fax: 805-893-2676
E-mail: appinfo@sa.ucsb.edu • Web: www.ucsb.edu
Support: CS • Institution type: 4-year public

LEARNING DISABILITY PROGRAM AND SERVICES

The Disabled Student Program (DSP) is a department within the NCAA Division of Student Affairs that works to increase the retention and graduation ratio of students with temporary and permanent disabilities, assure equal access to all educational and academic programs, and foster student independence. The university is strongly committed to maintaining an environment that guarantees students with disabilities full access to educational programs and activities. The DSP office serves as campus liaison regarding issues and regulations related to students with disabilities. DSP provides reasonable accommodations to students with learning disabilities; specific accommodations are determined on an individual basis. Admitted students should send LD documentation to DSP and schedule an appointment with the LD specialist. Accommodations and academically related services are not designed to provide remediation, but to accommodate a perceptual disorder that impairs the student's ability to acquire, process, or communicate information. Each accommodation will be made available to the extent that it does not compromise the academic integrity of the student's program. In all cases, it is the student's responsibility to communicate special needs to the professor and/or DSP.

LD/ADD ADMISSIONS INFORMATION

College entrance tests required: Yes
Interview required: No
Essay required: Yes
Documentation required for LD: WAIS–III; Woodcock
   Johnson; Achievement R or III (preferred), NDRT
Documentation required for ADD: Yes
Submitted to: Disabled Student Program
Special Ed. HS coursework accepted: No

Specific course requirements of all applicants: Yes
Separate application required for program servics: No
# of LD applications submitted each year: NR
# of LD applications accepted yearly: NR
Total # of students receiving LD services: 300
Acceptance into program means acceptance into
   college: Student must be admitted and enrolled in the
   university first and then request services.

ADMISSIONS

There is no special application for students with learning disabilities. All students must meet the same admission criteria. However, students may self-disclose the existence of a learning disability. Students should use their autobiographical statement to address their disability and how they have coped with it in high school. All documentation is submitted to the Office of Admissions, including tests and letters that could be helpful in determining the student's ability to succeed in college. Special circumstances qualifying students for special action admissions is viewed on a case-by-case basis, such as waiving foreign language, math, and science. General admission requirements include 4 years English, 3 years math, 1 year world history, 1 year U.S. history, 2 years lab science, 2 years foreign language, 2 years electives. The ACT or SATs required as well as 2 SAT Subject Tests in English composition, math, or one other additional subject. DSP does not admit students but may consult with Admissions. Admission decisions are made by admissions officers and consultation from an LD specialist regarding documentation submitted.

ADDITIONAL INFORMATION

Academic accommodations may include substitution of courses required for graduation, non-remedial individualized tutoring, and instruction in reading and writing strategies and in compensatory study skills. Academic support services include priority registration; aids with reading, writing; note-takers; test-taking; proofreading; and liaison with faculty. Skills classes and tutoring are provided through CLASS, the Campus Learning Assistance Program. These classes are available for all students on campus. DSP Office does not have the space to provide areas for testing accommodations, but individual professors assist by securing space. Students are not required to attend a summer program or special orientation. However, DSP orientation is highly recommended prior to the fall quarter. Services and accommodations are available for undergraduate and graduate students.

Support Services Contact Information

Learning Disability Program/Services: Disabled Student Program (DSP)
Director: Diane Glenn
  E-Mail: Glenn-d@ucsb.edu
  Telephone: 805-893-2182
  Fax: 805-893-7127
Contact Person: Claudia Batty
  E-Mail: Batty-c@ucsb.edu
  Telephone: 805-893-8897
  Fax: 805-893-7127

LEARNING DISABILITY SERVICES

Requests for the following/services accommodations will be evaluated individually based on appropriate and current documentation.

Allowed in exams
  Calculator: Yes
  Dictionary: No
  Computer: Yes
  Spellchecker: Yes
Extended test time: Yes
Scribes: Yes
Proctors: Yes
Oral exams: No
Note-takers: Yes

Distraction-reduced environment: Yes
Tape recording in class: Yes
Books on tape from RFBD: Yes
Taping of books not from RFBD: Yes
Accommodations for students with ADD: Yes
Reading machine: Yes
Other assistive technology: Yes
Priority registration: Yes

Added costs for services: No
LD specialists: Yes
Professional tutors: No
Peer tutors: NR
Max. hours/wk. for services: 1
How professors are notified of LD/ADD: By student

GENERAL ADMISSIONS INFORMATION

Director of Admissions: Christine Van Gieson
Telephone: 805-893-3641

ENTRANCE REQUIREMENTS

Academic units required: 4 English, 3 math, 2 science (2 science lab), 2 foreign language, 2 social studies, 2 history, 2 academic electives. **Academic units recommended:** 4 math, 3 science (3 science lab), 3 foreign language. ACT plus optional writing or SAT reasoning test and 2 SAT subject tests required. High school diploma is required and GED is accepted. TOEFL required of all international applicants, minimum paper TOEFL 550, minimum computer TOEFL 213.

Application deadline: 11/30
Notification: 3/15
Average GPA: 3.76

Average SAT Math: 603
Average SAT Verbal: 579
Average ACT: 25

Graduated top 10% of class: 95%
Graduated top 25% of class: 100%
Graduated top 50% of class: 100%

COLLEGE GRADUATION REQUIREMENTS

Course waivers allowed: No
Course substitutions allowed: Yes
In what course: Substitutions depend on documentation and an attempt by the student to take the course. Typically the requests for substitutions are in math and foreign language. Requests for substitutions of course work are reviewed by a committee.

ADDITIONAL INFORMATION

Environment: The university is located on 813 acres in a small city 10 miles west of Santa Barbara.

Student Body:
  Undergrad enrollment: 18,114
  Women: 55%
  Men: 45%
  Percent out-of-state: 5%

Cost Information
  In-state tuition: $6,137 (fees)
  Out-of-state tuition: $23,093
  Room & board: $10,183
Housing Information
  University housing: Yes
  Percent living on campus: 26%

Greek System
  Fraternity: Yes
  Sorority: Yes
Athletics: NCAA Division I

University of California—Santa Barbara

UNIVERSITY OF REDLANDS

1200 East Colton Avenue, Redlands, CA 92373
Phone: 909-335-4074 • Fax: 909-335-4089
E-mail: admissions@redlands.edu • Web: www.redlands.edu
Support: S • Institution type: 4-year private

LEARNING DISABILITY PROGRAM AND SERVICES

Students identified as learning disabled are eligible for tutoring and individual assistance from Academic Support Services. While the university does not have a formal program for students with learning disabilities, the goal is to help students succeed in college once they are enrolled. Although the services and accommodations offered are minimal, they do comply with the mandates of Section 504 of the Rehabilitation Act of 1973. Academic Support Services is sensitive to the needs of students with disabilities, and strives to provide the services and accommodations that are identified in the professional documentation.

LD/ADD ADMISSIONS INFORMATION

College entrance tests required: Yes
Interview required: No
Essay required: Yes
Documentation required for LD: Psychoeducational
  evaluation
Documentation required for ADD: Yes
Submitted to: Academic Support Services
Special Ed. HS coursework accepted: No

Specific course requirements of all applicants: Yes
Separate application required for program servics: No
# of LD applications submitted each year: NR
# of LD applications accepted yearly: 50–70
Total # of students receiving LD services: 200
**Acceptance into program means acceptance into
  college:** Student must be admitted and enrolled in the
  university first and then request services.

ADMISSIONS
Students with learning disabilities are required to submit the general application form and meet the same admission standards as all applicants. Redlands strongly recommends a college preparatory program that includes four years of English and two or three years each of foreign language, lab sciences, and social studies. Three years of math up to and including Algebra II is required. The middle 50 percent of the class has between 1060 and 1240 SAT Reasoning Test and between 22 and 27 ACT. Faculty admits are for those students whose GPAs or SAT/ACT scores do not meet admissions standards, but who show promise of success in college. The director of Academic Support Services is involved in the admission decision for students with learning disabilities.

ADDITIONAL INFORMATION
Each service provided by Academic Support Services encourages students to take personal responsibility for their academic success. Study skills courses are available as well as basic skills classes in math, writing, and learning strategies. Students have access to tutoring on a one-to-one basis. The peer tutoring program provides friendly, supportive assistance for most academic subjects. Peer tutors must have faculty recommendations in the subjects they wish to tutor and at least a 3.0 GPA in the area they tutor. The director of Academic Support Services will work with students to assist them in identifying their needs and securing appropriate accommodations. Additionally, students may make individual appointments for assistance with time management and study skills. However, it is the students' responsibility to seek out help and request assistance.

Support Services Contact Information

Learning Disability Program/Services: Academic Support Services
Director: Judy Bowman
  E-Mail: judy_bowman@redland.edu
  Telephone: 909-335-4079
  Fax: 909-335-5297

LEARNING DISABILITY SERVICES

Requests for the following/services accommodations will be evaluated individually based on appropriate and current documentation.

Allowed in exams
  Calculator: Yes
  Dictionary: Yes
  Computer: Yes
  Spellchecker: Yes
Extended test time: Yes
Scribes: Yes
Proctors: Yes
Oral exams: Yes
Note-takers: Yes

Distraction-reduced environment: Yes
Tape recording in class: Yes
Books on tape from RFBD: Yes
Taping of books not from RFBD: No
Accommodations for students with ADD: Yes
Reading machine: No
Other assistive technology: No
Priority registration: N/A

Added costs for services: No
LD specialists: No
Professional tutors: No
Peer tutors: 80–100
Max. hours/wk. for services: Unlimited
How professors are notified of LD/ADD: By both student and director

GENERAL ADMISSIONS INFORMATION

Director of Admissions: Paul Driscoll
Telephone: 909-335-4074

ENTRANCE REQUIREMENTS
Academic units required: 4 English, 3 math, 2 science, 2 foreign language, 2 social studies. High school diploma is required and GED is accepted. ACT with or without Writing component accepted. TOEFL required of all international applicants, minimum paper TOEFL 550, minimum computer TOEFL 213.

Application deadline: 6/1
Notification: Rolling
Average GPA: 3.54

Average SAT Math: 580
Average SAT Verbal: 584
Average ACT: 24

Graduated top 10% of class: 32%
Graduated top 25% of class: 66%
Graduated top 50% of class: 93%

COLLEGE GRADUATION REQUIREMENTS

Course waivers allowed: No
Course substitutions allowed: Yes
In what course: Math, foreign language

ADDITIONAL INFORMATION

Environment: The university is located on 130 acres in a small town 60 miles east of Los Angeles.

Student Body:
  Undergrad enrollment: 2,345
  Women: 59%
  Men: 41%
  Percent out-of-state: 28%

Cost Information
  Tuition: $25,224
  Room & board: $8,696
Housing Information
  University housing: Yes
  Percent living on campus: 73%

Greek System
  Fraternity: Yes
  Sorority: Yes
Athletics: NCAA Division III

University of Redlands

UNIVERSITY OF SAN FRANCISCO

2130 Fulton Street, San Francisco, CA 94117
Phone: 415-422-6563 • Fax: 415-422-2217
E-mail: admission@usfca.edu • Web: www.usfca.edu
Support: CS • Institution type: 4-year private

LEARNING DISABILITY PROGRAM AND SERVICES

The University of San Francisco believes that students with learning disabilities are capable of succeeding and becoming contributing members of the university community and society. To this end, USF provides educational support and assistance to those students whose goals are successful completion of college and who take an active participatory role in their own education. Services provided enable students to achieve grades that accurately reflect their ability, promote healthy self-images, remediate deficit areas, and promote USF's LD program by conducting in-services for faculty, admissions, and other staff; providing brochures; advertising services; and working closely with faculty to provide accommodations to students with learning disabilities.

LD/ADD ADMISSIONS INFORMATION

College entrance tests required: Yes
Interview required: No
Essay required: No
Documentation required for LD: Current pychoeducational asessment report by a qualified professional verifying the presence of a specific learning disability
Documentation required for ADD: Comprehensive neuropsychological or psychoeducational assessment report by a qualified professional clearly stating the presence of ADD which includes evidence of early impairment, current impairment, and rules out alternative diagnoses
Submitted to: Both Admissions and Student Disability Services
Special Ed. HS coursework accepted: Yes

Specific course requirements of all applicants: Yes
Separate application required for program servics: No
# of LD applications submitted each year: 100
# of LD applications accepted yearly: 80
Total # of students receiving LD services: 100
Acceptance into program means acceptance into college: Students must be admitted and enrolled in the university and then may request services.

ADMISSIONS

If a student who is a borderline admit self-discloses on the regular application form, the director of USF Services reviews the documentation and gives an evaluation before an admission decision is made. The final decision is made jointly between the director of the program and the office of admissions. Students who are accepted to the university under conditional status are encouraged to participate in the Summer Forward program. This voluntary program focuses on the academic needs of the students and prepares them for the demands of college life.

ADDITIONAL INFORMATION

Services include trained tutors, instruction in study skills and coping strategies, academic advising, maintaining regular contact with the LD coordinator, diagnostic testing, individual or small group instruction for educational skills building, and helping students improve their understanding of their learning disability. Assistive technology includes Dragon Naturally Speaking. Services and accommodations are available for undergraduate and graduate students. Students with attention deficit disorder request services through Disability Related Services. A comprehensive neuropsychological or psycho educational assessment report by a qualified professional clearly stating the presence of this disorder is required.

Support Services Contact Information

Learning Disability Program/Services: Student Disability Services
Director: Tom Merrell
   E-Mail: merrellt@usfca.edu
   Telephone: 415-422-6876
   Fax: 415-422-5906
Contact Person: Teresa Ong
   E-Mail: ongt@usfca.edu
   Telephone: 415-422-6876
   Fax: 415-422-5906

LEARNING DISABILITY SERVICES

Requests for the following/services accommodations will be evaluated individually based on appropriate and current documentation.

Allowed in exams
  Calculator: Yes
  Dictionary: Yes
  Computer: Yes
  Spellchecker: Yes
Extended test time: Yes
Scribes: Yes
Proctors: Yes
Oral exams: Yes
Note-takers: Yes

Distraction-reduced environment: Yes
Tape recording in class: Yes
Books on tape from RFBD: Yes
Taping of books not from RFBD: Yes
Accommodations for students with
  ADD: Yes
Reading machine: Yes
Other assistive technology: Yes
Priority registration: Yes

Added costs for services: No
LD specialists: Yes
Professional tutors: 20
Peer tutors: 100
Max. hours/wk. for services: 3
How professors are notified of
  LD/ADD: By student

GENERAL ADMISSIONS INFORMATION

Director of Admissions: William Henley
Telephone: 415-422-6563

ENTRANCE REQUIREMENTS

Academic units recommended: 4 English, 3 math, 2 science (2 science lab), 2 foreign language, 3 social studies, 6 academic electives, 1 chemistry and 1 biology or physics is required of nursing and science applicants. High school diploma is required and GED is accepted. ACT with Writing component required or SAT Reasoning Test. TOEFL required of all international applicants, minimum paper TOEFL 550, minimum computer TOEFL 213.

Application deadline: 2/1 Priority
Notification: Rolling
Average GPA: 3.45

Average SAT Math: NR
Average SAT Verbal: NR
Average ACT: NR

Graduated top 10% of class: 25%
Graduated top 25% of class: 57%
Graduated top 50% of class: 90%

COLLEGE GRADUATION REQUIREMENTS

Course waivers allowed: Yes
Course substitutions allowed: Yes
In what course: Foreign language, statistical reasoning/math

ADDITIONAL INFORMATION

Environment: The University of San Francisco is located on 52 acres in the heart of the city.

Student Body:
  Undergrad enrollment: 4,274
  Women: 65%
  Men: 35%
  Percent out-of-state: 38%

Cost Information
  Tuition: $26,680
  Room & board: $10,240
Housing Information
  University housing: Yes
  Percent living on campus: 54%

Greek System
  Fraternity: Yes
  Sorority: Yes
Athletics: NCAA Division I

UNIVERSITY OF SOUTHERN CALIFORNIA

700 Childs Way, Los Angeles, CA 90089-0911
Phone: 213-740-1111 • Fax: 213-740-6364
E-mail: admitusc@usc.edu • Web: www.usc.edu
Support: CS • Institution type: 4-year private

LEARNING DISABILITY PROGRAM AND SERVICES

Disability Services and Programs is responsible for delivery of services to students with learning disabilities. It offers a comprehensive support program in the areas of educational therapy, content area tutoring, study skills instruction, special exam administration, liaison with textbook taping services, advocacy, and network referral system. The learning specialists, graduate assistants, and learning assistants are available to students for academic therapy. A computer lab is available for computer-assisted learning and for word processing when working with a staff person. After admission, students with LD are counseled by advisors who dialogue with the learning specialist, and who are sensitive to special needs. Educational counseling is done by the learning specialist. Off-campus referrals are made to students desiring comprehensive diagnostic testing. The support structure for students with documented learning disabilities is one that is totally individualized. There is no special program per se. Support is given at the request of the student. The Learning disabilities specialist and/or grad assistants at USC are prepared to act as advocates when appropriate for any student experiencing academic problems that are related to the learning disability. USC aims to assure close, personal attention to its students even though it is a large campus.

LD/ADD ADMISSIONS INFORMATION

College entrance tests required: Yes
Interview required: No
Essay required: Yes
Documentation required for LD: WAIS–III; WJ; Achievement
Documentation required for ADD: Yes
Submitted to: Disability Services and Programs
Special Ed. HS coursework accepted: Yes

Specific course requirements of all applicants: Yes
Separate application required for program servics: NR
# of LD applications submitted each year: NR
# of LD applications accepted yearly: NR
Total # of students receiving LD services: 350
Acceptance into program means acceptance into college: Student must be admitted and enrolled in the university first and then request services.

ADMISSIONS

There are no special admissions for students with learning disabilities. Course requirements include 4 years English, 3 years math, 2 years natural science, 2 years social studies, 2 years foreign language, and 4 year-long electives. (The foreign language requirement is not waived in the admission process). Transfer students are admitted on the basis of their college coursework as well as the high school record. It is the student's responsibility to provide recent educational evaluations for documentation as part of the admissions application process. Testing must be current within 3 years, or 5 years for transfer or returning students.

ADDITIONAL INFORMATION

The services provided are modifications that are determined to be appropriate for students with LD. During the first three weeks of each semester, students are seen on a walk-in basis by the staff in the LD Support Services. Students requesting assistance must have a planning appointment with an LD specialist or grad assistant; provide a copy of the current class schedule; and be sure that eligibility has been determined by documentation of specific learning disabilities. Learning assistance most often involves one-to-one attention for academic planning, scheduling, organization, and methods of compensation. Students may have standing appointments with learning assistants and subject tutors. Course accommodations could include taping of lectures, note-taking, extended time for tests, use of word processor, proofreader, limiting scheduling of consecutive exams, and advocacy. Other services include support groups, counseling, and coaching.

Support Services Contact Information

Learning Disability Program/Services: Disability Services and Programs
Director: Edward Roth, PhD
  E-Mail: eroth@usc.edu
  Telephone: 213-740-0776
  Fax: 213-740-8216
Contact Person: Dr. Patricia Tobey
  E-Mail: tobey@usc.edu
  Telephone: 213-740-0776
  Fax: 213-740-8216

LEARNING DISABILITY SERVICES

Requests for the following/services accommodations will be evaluated individually based on appropriate and current documentation.

Allowed in exams
  Calculator: NR
  Dictionary: NR
  Computer: Yes
  Spellchecker: Yes
Extended test time: Yes
Scribes: Yes
Proctors: Yes
Oral exams: No
Note-takers: Yes

Distraction-reduced environment: Yes
Tape recording in class: Yes
Books on tape from RFBD: Yes
Taping of books not from RFBD: Yes
Accommodations for students with ADD: Yes
Reading machine: Yes
Other assistive technology: Yes
Priority registration: No

Added costs for services: No
LD specialists: Yes
Professional tutors: Yes
Peer tutors: 15
Max. hours/wk. for services: 2
How professors are notified of LD/ADD: By both student and director

GENERAL ADMISSIONS INFORMATION

Director of Admissions: J. Michael Thompson
Telephone: 213-740-1111

ENTRANCE REQUIREMENTS

Academic units required: 4 English, 3 math, 3 science (2 science lab), 2 foreign language, 2 social studies.
Academic units recommended: 4 math, 4 science (3 science lab), 3 foreign language, 3 social studies. High school diploma is required and GED is not accepted. ACT with Writing component required or SAT Reasoning Test.

Application deadline: 1/10
Notification: 4/1
Average GPA: NR

Average SAT Math: 685
Average SAT Verbal: 665
Average ACT: 29

Graduated top 10% of class: 84%
Graduated top 25% of class: 94%
Graduated top 50% of class: 100%

COLLEGE GRADUATION REQUIREMENTS

Course waivers allowed: No
Course substitutions allowed: Yes
In what course: May petition for substitution for foreign language. LD specialtist decides if appeal is valid and writes a letter recommending course substitutions. Course valid for substitutions include literature in translation, linguistics, and classics.

ADDITIONAL INFORMATION

Environment: The university is located on 150 acres in an urban area, 2 miles south of downtown Los Angeles.

Student Body:
  Undergrad enrollment: 16,271
  Women: 51%
  Men: 49%
  Percent out-of-state: 32%

Cost Information
  Tuition: $29,988
  Room & board: $8,998
Housing Information
  University housing: Yes
  Percent living on campus: 36%

Greek System
  Fraternity: Yes
  Sorority: Yes
Athletics: NCAA Division I

UNIVERSITY OF THE PACIFIC

3601 Pacific Avenue, Stockton, CA 95211
Phone: 209-946-2211 • Fax: 209-946-2413
E-mail: admissions@pacific.edu • Web: www.pacific.edu
Support: S • Institution type: 4-year private

LEARNING DISABILITY PROGRAM AND SERVICES

There is no special program for students with learning disabilities, but the university does have a Learning Disabilities Support program. This program offers assistance through tutoring, study skills classes, support groups, and testing accommodations. Documentation for LD must include psychoeducational evaluations from a professional. The documentation for ADD must be from a medical doctor. Documentation should be sent to the director of the Educational Resource Center. Students register for services after admission by contacting the Educational Resource Center. Student confidentiality is protected. The ultimate goal is for the student to earn a degree that is unmodified and unflagged. Faculty and staff are dedicated to providing students with learning disabilities all reasonable accommodations, so that they may enjoy academic success. The LD Support program helps keep UOP in compliance with the Americans with Disabilities Act and Section 504 of the Rehabilitation Act. Compliance is accomplished without compromising UOP standards, placing undue financial or administrative burden on the university, fundamentally altering the nature of programs, or extending unreasonable accommodations.

LD/ADD ADMISSIONS INFORMATION

College entrance tests required: Yes
Interview required: No
Essay required: Yes
Documentation required for LD: Psychoeducational evaluation(no more than 3–5 years old)
Documentation required for ADD: Yes (no more than 3 years old)
Submitted to: Services for Students with Disabilities
Special Ed. HS coursework accepted: Yes

Specific course requirements of all applicants: Yes
Separate application required for program servics: Yes
# of LD applications submitted each year: NR
# of LD applications accepted yearly: NR
Total # of students receiving LD services: 140–160
Acceptance into program means acceptance into college: Student must be admitted and enrolled in the university first and then request services.

ADMISSIONS

UOP welcomes students with learning disabilities. Although there is no special admission procedure, students are given special consideration. There is no minimum ACT/SAT requirement. There are two alternative methods for admissions: (1) Probationary Admissions for the marginal student: C/D average with no special requirements, but the university advisor is notified of status, no required test score, and no quota regarding the number of students admitted; and (2) Special Admissions: students who begin college courses in the summer prior to freshman year and receive at least a C average in 2 courses and 1 study skills class (can take those courses at any local community college).

ADDITIONAL INFORMATION

All admitted students are eligible for LD services with the appropriate assessment documentation. Academic Support Services offers services to improve learning opportunities for students with LD and are provided within reasonable limits. These services could include diagnostic assessment, accommodations for academic needs, taped texts, readers, tutorials for academic courses and referrals to appropriate resources. Other related services include career development and guidance, counseling, and LD support groups. The Educational Resource Center is open to all students on campus. Skills courses for credit are available in reading, study skills, writing, and math. Services and accommodations are available for undergraduate and graduate students. The university offers a special summer program for pre-college freshmen students with learning disabilities.

Support Services Contact Information

Learning Disability Program/Services: Office of Services for Students with Disabilities
Director: Dr. Vivian Snyder (Educational Resource Center)
  E-Mail: vsnyder@uop.edu
  Telephone: 209-946-2458
  Fax: 209-946-2278
Contact Person: Lisa Cooper, Coordinator
  E-Mail: ssd@uop.edu
  Telephone: 209-946-2879
  Fax: 209-946-2278

LEARNING DISABILITY SERVICES

Requests for the following/services accommodations will be evaluated individually based on appropriate and current documentation.

Allowed in exams
  Calculator: Yes
  Dictionary: Yes
  Computer: Yes
  Spellchecker: Yes
Extended test time: Yes
Scribes: Yes
Proctors: Yes
Oral exams: Yes
Note-takers: Yes

Distraction-reduced environment: Yes
Tape recording in class: Yes
Books on tape from RFBD: Yes
Taping of books not from RFBD: Yes
Accommodations for students with ADD: Yes
Reading machine: Yes
Other assistive technology: Yes
Priority registration: Yes

Added costs for services: No
LD specialists: No
Professional tutors: No
Peer tutors: 80
Max. hours/wk. for services: n/a
How professors are notified of LD/ADD: By Director

GENERAL ADMISSIONS INFORMATION

Director of Admissions: Marc McGee
Telephone: 209-946-2211

ENTRANCE REQUIREMENTS

Academic units recommended: 4 English, 3 math, 2 science (2 science lab), 2 foreign language, 1 history, 3 academic electives, 1 fine arts/performing arts. High school diploma is required and GED is accepted. TOEFL required of all international applicants, minimum paper TOEFL 475, minimum computer TOEFL 150.

Application deadline: 1/15
Notification: Rolling
Average GPA: 3.47

Average SAT Math: 600
Average SAT Verbal: 574
Average ACT: 25

Graduated top 10% of class: 37%
Graduated top 25% of class: 72%
Graduated top 50% of class: 92%

COLLEGE GRADUATION REQUIREMENTS

Course waivers allowed: Yes
Course substitutions allowed: Yes
In what course: NR

ADDITIONAL INFORMATION

Environment: The university is located on 150 acres 90 miles east of San Francisco.

Student Body:
  Undergrad enrollment: 3,446
  Women: 57%
  Men: 43%
  Percent out-of-state: 13%

Cost Information
  Tuition: $24,320
  Room & board: $7,858
Housing Information
  University housing: Yes
  Percent living on campus: 58%

Greek System
  Fraternity: Yes
  Sorority: Yes
Athletics: NCAA Division I

University of the Pacific

WHITTIER COLLEGE

13406 Philadelphia Street, PO Box 634, Whittier, CA 90608
Phone: 562-907-4238 • Fax: 562-907-4870
E-mail: admission@whittier.edu • Web: www.whittier.edu
Support: S • Institution type: 4-year private

LEARNING DISABILITY PROGRAM AND SERVICES

The director of Disability Services provides assistance to students with documented disabilities. Accommodation requests are made through the director's office. Students with disabilities must make their needs known to the director of Learning Support Services (LSS) in order to receive accommodations. To arrange for services students must self-disclose the disability, and make an individual appointment to discuss their accommodation requests with the director. LSS offers the following additional services: peer tutoring, workshops on study skills, and basic English and math skills assistance. These services are provided at no cost.

LD/ADD ADMISSIONS INFORMATION

College entrance tests required: Yes
Interview required: No
Essay required: Yes
Documentation required for LD: Psychoeducational evaluation
Documentation required for ADD: Yes
Submitted to: Disability Services
Special Ed. HS coursework accepted: N/A

Specific course requirements of all applicants: Yes
Separate application required for program servics: No
# of LD applications submitted each year: 25–30
# of LD applications accepted yearly: NR
Total # of students receiving LD services: 130
Acceptance into program means acceptance into college: Student must be admitted and enrolled in the College first and then reviewed for LD services.

ADMISSIONS

There is no special admissions process for students with disabilities. All applicants are expected to meet the same admission criteria. Students must submit the ACT or SAT and have a minimum of a 2.0 GPA; the recommended courses include 4 years English, 3–4 years math, 2–3 years foreign language, 2–3 years social studies, and 2–3 years lab science.

ADDITIONAL INFORMATION

The use of calculators, dictionary, computer, or spellchecker in exams would be considered on a case-by-case basis depending on appropriate documentation and student needs. Students with appropriate documentation will have access to note-takers, readers, extended exam time, alternative exam locations, proctors, scribes, oral exams, books on tape, and priority registration. All students have access to Math Lab, Writing Center, Leaning Lab, and academic counseling.

Support Services Contact Information

Learning Disability Program/Services: Disability Services
Director: Joan Smith, MA
  E-Mail: jsmith@whittier.edu
  Telephone: 562-907-4825
  Fax: 562-907-4827

LEARNING DISABILITY SERVICES

Requests for the following/services accommodations will be evaluated individually based on appropriate and current documentation.

Allowed in exams
  Calculator: Yes
  Dictionary: Yes
  Computer: Yes
  Spellchecker: Yes
Extended test time: Yes
Scribes: Yes
Proctors: Yes
Oral exams: Yes
Note-takers: Yes

Distraction-reduced environment: Yes
Tape recording in class: Yes
Books on tape from RFBD: Yes
Taping of books not from RFBD: Yes
Accommodations for students with ADD: Yes
Reading machine: Yes
Other assistive technology: Yes
Priority registration: No

Added costs for services: No
LD specialists: No
Professional tutors: No
Peer tutors: 15–30
Max. hours/wk. for services: Unlimited
How professors are notified of LD/ADD: By Director

GENERAL ADMISSIONS INFORMATION

Director of Admissions: Lisa Meyer, Vice President of Enrollment
Telephone: 562-907-4238

ENTRANCE REQUIREMENTS
Academic units required: 4 English, 3 math, 1 science, 2 foreign language, 1 social studies. **Academic units recommended:** 3 science (2 science lab), 3 foreign language, 2 social studies, 3 history. High school diploma is required and GED is accepted. ACT with Writing component required or SAT Reasoning Test. TOEFL required of all international applicants, minimum paper TOEFL 550, minimum computer TOEFL 230.

Application deadline: 2/1
Notification: Rolling
Average GPA: 3.40

Average SAT Math: 553
Average SAT Verbal: 547
Average ACT: 23

Graduated top 10% of class: 20%
Graduated top 25% of class: 39%
Graduated top 50% of class: 78%

COLLEGE GRADUATION REQUIREMENTS

Course waivers allowed: No
Course substitutions allowed: Yes
In what course: Foreign Language as an admissions requirement.

ADDITIONAL INFORMATION

Environment: The college is on a suburban campus 20 miles southeast of Los Angeles.

Student Body:
  Undergrad enrollment: 1,304
  Women: 57%
  Men: 43%
  Percent out-of-state: 33%

Cost Information
  Tuition: $25,838
  Room & board: $8,000
Housing Information
  University housing: Yes
  Percent living on campus: 68%

Greek System
  Fraternity: Yes
  Sorority: Yes
Athletics: NCAA Division III

Whittier College

COLORADO STATE U.—PUEBLO

Admissions, 2200 Bonforte Blvd, Pueblo, CO 81001
Phone: 719-549-2461 • Fax: 719-549-2419
E-mail: info@colostate-pueblo.edu • Web: www.colostate-pueblo.edu
Support: S • Institution type: 4-year public

LEARNING DISABILITY PROGRAM AND SERVICES

The Disabilities Services Office, an affiliate of the Learning Assistance Center, strives to provide optimal services to students who have disabilities in order to enhance learning and increase retention. Students with LD or ADD are encouraged to submit additional documentation, as well as letters of recommendation from counselors, teachers, or special education specialists. Documentation must include a comprehensive psychological evaluation with diagnostic and description of the disability to the learning environment with recommendations for specific accommodations.

LD/ADD ADMISSIONS INFORMATION

College entrance tests required: Yes
Interview required: No
Essay required: No
Documentation required for LD: Psychoeducational evaluation
Documentation required for ADD: Yes
Submitted to: Disability Resource Office
Special Ed. HS coursework accepted: NR

Specific course requirements of all applicants: No
Separate application required for program servics: No
# of LD applications submitted each year: NR
# of LD applications accepted yearly: NR
Total # of students receiving LD services: NR
Acceptance into program means acceptance into college: Student must be admitted and enrolled in the university first and then request services.

ADMISSIONS

All first-time freshmen must submit their high school transcripts with GPA and ACT/SAT scores along with the general application. There is no special admission procedure for students with disabilities, but all information submitted will be considered in making an admission decision. Twenty percent of the freshmen applicants are eligible for admission based on criteria in addition to GPA and test scores. Students who do not meet the general admission criteria should submit letters of recommendation with information describing their ability to be successful in the university curriculum. Since there are no course requirements for admission, only recommendations, waivers are not necessary.

ADDITIONAL INFORMATION

Skills classes are offered in note-taking strategies, study skills, and textbook-reading strategies. The request for the use of a dictionary, computer, or spellchecker during exams will depend on the student's documented needs and permission from the professor. Students with specific needs are encouraged to provide documentation that specifically identifies the disability and the accommodations identified to compensate for it. Services and accommodations are available for undergraduate and graduate students

Support Services Contact Information

Learning Disability Program/Services: Disability Resource Office
Director: Pam Chambers
  E-Mail: chambersp@uscolo.edu
  Telephone: 719-549-2584
  Fax: 719-549-2195

LEARNING DISABILITY SERVICES

Requests for the following/services accommodations will be evaluated individually based on appropriate and current documentation.

Allowed in exams
  Calculator: Yes
  Dictionary: Yes
  Computer: Yes
  Spellchecker: Yes
Extended test time: Yes
Scribes: Yes
Proctors: Yes
Oral exams: Yes
Note-takers: Yes

Distraction-reduced environment: Yes
Tape recording in class: Yes
Books on tape from RFBD: Yes
Taping of books not from RFBD: Yes
Accommodations for students with ADD: Yes
Reading machine: Yes
Other assistive technology: Yes
Priority registration: No

Added costs for services: No
LD specialists: No
Professional tutors: No
Peer tutors: No
Max. hours/wk. for services: As needed
How professors are notified of LD/ADD: By student

GENERAL ADMISSIONS INFORMATION

Director of Admissions: Mr. Joseph Marshall, Director
Telephone: 719-549-2461

ENTRANCE REQUIREMENTS

Academic units recommended: 4 English, 3 math, 2 science (1 science lab), 2 foreign language, 2 social studies, 1 history. High school diploma is required and GED is accepted. ACT with or without Writing component accepted. TOEFL required of all international applicants, minimum paper TOEFL 500, minimum computer TOEFL 173.

Application deadline: 8/1
Notification: Rolling
Average GPA: 3.00

Average SAT Math: 477
Average SAT Verbal: 470
Average ACT: 20

Graduated top 10% of class: 2%
Graduated top 25% of class: 10%
Graduated top 50% of class: 41%

COLLEGE GRADUATION REQUIREMENTS

Course waivers allowed: No
Course substitutions allowed: Yes
In what course: Possibly math with appropriate documentation

ADDITIONAL INFORMATION

Environment: The university is located 100 miles south of Denver in an urban area.

Student Body:
  Undergrad enrollment: 4,457
  Women: 59%
  Men: 41%
  Percent out-of-state: 8%

Cost Information
  In-state tuition: $2,524
  Out-of-state tuition: $13,543
  Room & board: $5,912
Housing Information
  University housing: Yes
  Percent living on campus: 2%

Greek System
  Fraternity: Yes
  Sorority: Yes
Athletics: NCAA Division II

REGIS UNIVERSITY

3333 Regis Boulevard, Denver, CO 80221-1099
Phone: 303-458-4900 • Fax: 303-964-5534
E-mail: regisadm@regis.edu/college.asp • Web: www.regis.edu
Support: CS • Institution type: 4-year private

LEARNING DISABILITY PROGRAM AND SERVICES

Regis University does not have a specific structured program for students with LD/ADD. Regis is committed to providing equal opportunities for students with disabilities to succeed by providing equal access. Disability Services provides services to all students with documented disabilities on an individualized basis. The Freshman Commitment Program is not specifically for students with LD/ADD, although students with disabilities may be in the program. This program is not connected with disability services. Recommendations from high school teachers and evidence of extracurricular activities, as well as all other information a student provides, are considered for inclusion in this program. The goals of the Commitment Program are to provide a means for underachieving students to enter college; to provide the support needed to be a successful learner; and to help students develop the analytical processes that lead to high achievement. Students remain in the program for two semesters. To be successful, students must attend and pass all required Commitment courses with a C or better; cannot fall below a 2.0 GPA in non-commitment courses; may not participate in varsity sports, forensics, or other activities that could interfere with class attendance; and must limit outside work, events, or other extracurricular activities that could impact their scholastic success.

LD/ADD ADMISSIONS INFORMATION

College entrance tests required: Yes
Interview required: No
Essay required: Yes
Documentation required for LD: Psychoeducational evaluation
Documentation required for ADD: Yes
Submitted to: Disability Services
Special Ed. HS coursework accepted: N/A

Specific course requirements of all applicants: Yes
Separate application required for program servics: No
# of LD applications submitted each year: 90
# of LD applications accepted yearly: 20
Total # of students receiving LD services: 1–150
Acceptance into program means acceptance into college: Students are reviewed by Freshman Commitment and a recommendation is provided to the Admissions Committee for a final decision.

ADMISSIONS

There is no special admission procedure for students with learning disabilities. Although an interview is not required, the college would prefer that the student visit the school and have a minimum GPA of 2.56, an SAT of 930, or ACT of 20 and 15 academic units. Students may be considered with 17 ACT or 810 SAT and 2.3 GPA. Students need to show sufficient evidence of motivation and ability to succeed in college, even though they may not have the required GPA or test scores. Recommendations from counselors and evidence of extracurricular activities will be used in their decision-making process. Students admitted on probation are typically students with stronger test scores and lower GPAs. These students are admitted into the college's degree program on one semester probation. They must have a 2.0 GPA to return the second semester. Other students may be admitted into the freshman Commitment Program. These students usually have lower test scores, C+ average and the probationary admission is for 2 semesters.

ADDITIONAL INFORMATION

Disability Services provides the following services for students with appropriate documentation: self-advocacy training, test-taking and learning strategies assistance; mentoring program; note-takers; readers; scribes; extended testing time; course substitutions; and priority registration. Students in the Commitment Program remain for one year and, with successful completion, are officially admitted to the college. There are learning support courses, study groups, and tutorials as needed. Three study rooms are staffed by tutors during the daytime and in the evening. All students must pass 3 hours of math, but there is a math learning support course or a remedial math class available for students to take prior to taking the regular college algebra class. The program offers learning support classes in reading skills, writing skills, and study skills, which apply toward elective credit. Special advising, tutoring, diagnostic academic testing, and study and testing assistance are other services offered.

Support Services Contact Information

Learning Disability Program/Services: Disability Services
Director: Marijo (Joie) Williams
  E-Mail: disability@regis.edu
  Telephone: 303-458-4941
  Fax: 303-964-3647

LEARNING DISABILITY SERVICES

Requests for the following/services accommodations will be evaluated individually based on appropriate and current documentation.

Allowed in exams
  Calculator: Yes
  Dictionary: Yes
  Computer: Yes
  Spellchecker: Yes
Extended test time: Yes
Scribes: Yes
Proctors: Yes
Oral exams: Yes
Note-takers: Yes

Distraction-reduced environment: Yes
Tape recording in class: Yes
Books on tape from RFBD: Yes
Taping of books not from RFBD: Yes
Accommodations for students with ADD: Yes
Reading machine: Yes
Other assistive technology: Yes
Priority registration: Yes

Added costs for services: $2,000 for Commitment Program
LD specialists: Yes
Professional tutors: No
Peer tutors: 22
Max. hours/wk. for services: Unlimited
How professors are notified of LD/ADD: By student

GENERAL ADMISSIONS INFORMATION

Director of Admissions: Vic Davolt
Telephone: 303-458-4900

ENTRANCE REQUIREMENTS

Academic units recommended: 4 English, 2 math, 2 science, 2 foreign language, 2 social studies, 1 history. High school diploma is required and GED is accepted. TOEFL required of all international applicants, minimum paper TOEFL 550, minimum computer TOEFL 213.

Application deadline: Rolling
Notification: Rolling
Average GPA: 3.24

Average SAT Math: 543
Average SAT Verbal: 546
Average ACT: 23

Graduated top 10% of class: 21%
Graduated top 25% of class: 47%
Graduated top 50% of class: 79%

COLLEGE GRADUATION REQUIREMENTS

Course waivers allowed: Yes
Course substitutions allowed: Yes
In what course: All students must take 3 hours of math. Foreign culture courses are substituted for foreign language if the documentation verifies a disability.

ADDITIONAL INFORMATION

Environment: The university is on a 90-acre campus in a suburban area of Denver.

Student Body:
  Undergrad enrollment: 5,430
  Women: 62%
  Men: 38%
  Percent out-of-state: 53%

Cost Information
  Tuition: $22,400
  Room & board: $7,870
Housing Information
  University housing: Yes
  Percent living on campus: 8%

Greek System
  Fraternity: No
  Sorority: No
  Athletics: NCAA Division II

UNIVERSITY OF COLORADO—BOULDER

552 UCB, Boulder, CO 80309-0552
Phone: 303-492-6301 • Fax: 303-492-7115
E-mail: apply@colorado.edu • Web: www.colorado.edu
Support: CS • Institution type: 4-year public

LEARNING DISABILITY PROGRAM AND SERVICES

The Academic Access and Resource Program (AAR) is a component of Disability Services. The Academic Access and Resource Program provides services to students with non-visible disabilities such as learning disabilities, attention deficit disorder, head injuries, and psychiatric disabilities. The philosophy is that a student with a disability can be successful in a competitive post secondary environment given self-acknowledgment of the disability and appropriate support services. Inherent in this philosophy is the importance of the student understanding his/her diagnostic profile so that relevant learning strategies can be learned and applied. The goal is for the student to become an independent learner who takes ownership and responsibility for the learning process. This process begins with the student understanding his/her areas of strengths and weaknesses and then building both awareness of needs and the development of appropriate compensatory strategies. In this process it is imperative that students take ownership for their own learning process and self-acknowledge the disability. The student develops compensatory strategies and builds a network of resources. A profile of individual strengths and weaknesses is developed between the student and the diagnostician. This information enables the student to understand how learning occurs and how strategies may be developed. Students need to be aware that there are no waivers or substitutions provided at the university. The goal of the program is to help students be successful within this academic community and provide them with skills and tools to be productive members of society. Disability Services has established documentation guidelines for LD and ADD. Students should request information from Disability Services or can access it directly off the website.

LD/ADD ADMISSIONS INFORMATION

College entrance tests required: Yes
Interview required: No
Essay required: No
Documentation required for LD: Psychoeducational
  evaluation
Documentation required for ADD: Yes
Submitted to: Disability Services
Special Ed. HS coursework accepted: NR

Specific course requirements of all applicants: Yes
Separate application required for program services: No
# of LD applications submitted each year: NR
# of LD applications accepted yearly: NR
Total # of students receiving LD services: 200–250
Acceptance into program means acceptance into
  college: Student must be admitted and enrolled in the
  university first and then reviewed for LD services.

ADMISSIONS

There is not a special admission process for students with LD. All students are considered under the same competitive admissions criteria. All application information should be submitted to admissions by 2/15, but documentation should be submitted directly to Disability Services. For the College of Arts and Sciences minimum academic requirements include 4 years English, 3 years math, 3 years natural science (must include chemistry or physics, and include 2 years of lab science), 3 years social science (including geography) and 3 years foreign language. UC—Boulder is a competitive institution and admitted students must meet the same requirements as all other students. Graduation requirements are never waived. Students with documented LD/ADD who struggle with foreign language learning may qualify for enrollment in the modified foreign language. Students who struggle with math need to speak with a Disability Specialist about options for satisfying this requirement.

ADDITIONAL INFORMATION

Services are provided through Disability Services, of which AAR is a component. The Academic Access and Resources Program provides an opportunity to meet with a disability specialist to work on academic strategies. If tutoring is needed, the disability specialist can refer the student to the appropriate resources, but the student pays for the service. Other services include advocacy and support, evening writing lab, assistive technology lab and a career program for students with disabilities. Lectures may be taped with the professor's permission. Priority registration is provided only if it directly responds to the disability. Support services and accommodations are available to undergraduate and graduate students who provide documentation of a disability. Students may seek an assessment to determine the possibility of the existence of a learning disability. The AAR will respond to all students with appropriate documentation who request services.

Support Services Contact Information

Learning Disability Program/Services: Disability Services
Director: Cindy Donahue
  E-Mail: dsinfo@colorado.edu
  Telephone: 303-492-8671
  Fax: 303-492-5601
Contact Person: Jayne MacArthur, Coordinator of Academic Access and Resources Program
  E-Mail: Jayne.MacArthur@colorado.edu
  Telephone: 303-492-8671
  Fax: 303-492-5601

LEARNING DISABILITY SERVICES

Requests for the following/services accommodations will be evaluated individually based on appropriate and current documentation.

Allowed in exams
  Calculator: Yes
  Dictionary: No
  Computer: Yes
  Spellchecker: Yes
Extended test time: Yes
Scribes: Yes
Proctors: Yes
Oral exams: No
Note-takers: Yes

Distraction-reduced environment: Yes
Tape recording in class: Yes
Books on tape from RFBD: Yes
Taping of books not from RFBD: Yes
Accommodations for students with ADD: Yes
Reading machine: No
Other assistive technology: Yes
Priority registration: Yes

Added costs for services: No
LD specialists: Yes
Professional tutors: No
Peer tutors: No
Max. hours/wk. for services: Varies
How professors are notified of LD/ADD: By student

GENERAL ADMISSIONS INFORMATION

Director of Admissions: Kevin Maclennan
Telephone: 303-492-6301

ENTRANCE REQUIREMENTS

Academic units required: 4 English, 3 math, 3 science (2 science lab), 3 foreign language, 1 social studies, 1 history, 1 geography. High school diploma is required and GED is accepted. ACT without Writing component accepted. TOEFL required of all international applicants, minimum paper TOEFL 500, minimum computer TOEFL 173.

Application deadline: 1/15
Notification: Rolling
Average GPA: 3.53

Average SAT Math: 596
Average SAT Verbal: 579
Average ACT: 25

Graduated top 10% of class: 25%
Graduated top 25% of class: 58%
Graduated top 50% of class: 92%

COLLEGE GRADUATION REQUIREMENTS

Course waivers allowed: Yes
Course substitutions allowed: Yes
In what course: Decisions on academic requirements are within the domain of the academic deans. Decisions are made on an individualized basis. There are no waivers/substitutions for entrance to College of Arts & Science.

ADDITIONAL INFORMATION

Environment: The school is located at the base of the Rocky Mountains 45 minutes from Denver.

Student Body:
  Undergrad enrollment: 25,607
  Women: 47%
  Men: 53%
  Percent out-of-state: 32%

Cost Information
  In-state tuition: $4,500
  Out-of-state tuition: $21,460
  Room & board: $7,564
Housing Information
  University housing: Yes
  Percent living on campus: 22%

Greek System
  Fraternity: Yes
  Sorority: Yes
Athletics: NCAA Division I

University of Colorado—Boulder

U. OF COLORADO—CO. SPRINGS

Admissions Office, PO Box 7150, Colorado Springs, CO 80933-7150
Phone: 719-262-3383 • Fax: 719-262-3116
E-mail: admrec@uccs.edu • Web: www.uccs.edu
Support: CS • Institution type: 4-year public

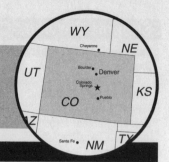

LEARNING DISABILITY PROGRAM AND SERVICES

University of Colorado-Colorado Springs is committed to providing equal educational opportunity for all students who meet the academic admission requirements. The purpose of Disability Services is to provide comprehensive support to meet the individual needs of students with disabilities.

LD/ADD ADMISSIONS INFORMATION

College entrance tests required: Yes
Interview required: No
Essay required: No
Documentation required for LD: WAIS-II; WJ
Documentation required for ADD: Yes
Submitted to: Disability Services
Special Ed. HS coursework accepted: No

Specific course requirements of all applicants: Yes
Separate application required for program servics: No
# of LD applications submitted each year: NR
# of LD applications accepted yearly: NR
Total # of students receiving LD services: 40
Acceptance into program means acceptance into college: Student must be admitted and enrolled in the university first and then reviewed for LD services.

ADMISSIONS

An applicant's learning disability is not considered in an admission decision. All applicants are required to meet the Minimum Academic Preparation Standards (MAPS), including 4 years English, 3 years math (4 years for engineering and business), 3 years natural science, 2 years social science, 2 years foreign language, and 1 year elective; fine and performing arts are encouraged. Courses taken before 9th grade are accepted as long as the documentation provided shows that the courses were completed. American Sign Language is a qualified substitute for a foreign language. Successfully completing 2 years of foreign language will satisfy the foreign language requirement regardless of whether the courses were taken before the 9th grade. Students with deficiencies may be admitted to the university provided they meet the other admission standards of test scores, rank in class, and GPA (minimum of 2.8), and provided they make up any deficiencies in the MAPS prior to graduation.

ADDITIONAL INFORMATION

Students with learning disabilities receive information in their acceptance letter about contacting Disability Services if they wish to request accommodations or services. Strategy development is offered in study skills, reading, test performance, stress reduction, time management, and writing skills. Disability Services offers the use of volunteers who use carbonless paper provided by the support services. Services and accommodations are available for undergraduate and graduate students with learning disabilities. Tutors are available for all university students in labs; tutors are also provided for students with disabilities.

Support Services Contact Information

Learning Disability Program/Services: Disability Services
Director: Kaye Simonton
  E-mail: disbserv@mail.uccs.edu
  Telephone: 719-262-3354
  Fax: 719-262-3195

LEARNING DISABILITY SERVICES

Requests for the following/services accommodations will be evaluated individually based on appropriate and current documentation.

Allowed in exams
  Calculator: Y/N
  Dictionary: Yes
  Computer: Yes
  Spellchecker: Yes
Extended test time: Yes
Scribes: Yes
Proctors: Yes
Oral exams: Yes
Note-takers: No

Distraction-reduced environment: Yes
Tape recording in class: Yes
Books on tape from RFBD: Yes
Taping of books not from RFBD: Yes
Accommodations for students with ADD: Yes
Reading machine: Yes
Other assistive technology: Yes
Priority registration: No

Added costs for services: No
LD specialists: Yes
Professional tutors: No
Peer tutors: No
Max. hours/wk. for services: N/A
How professors are notified of LD/ADD: By student

GENERAL ADMISSIONS INFORMATION

Director of Admissions: Steve Ellis
Telephone: 719-262-3383

ENTRANCE REQUIREMENTS

Academic units required: 4 English, 3 math, 3 science (2 science lab), 2 foreign language, 2 social studies, 1 academic elective. **Academic units recommended:** 4 math. High school diploma is required and GED is accepted. TOEFL required of all international applicants, minimum paper TOEFL 550, minimum computer TOEFL 213.

Application deadline: 7/1
Notification: Rolling
Average GPA: 3.36

Average SAT Math: 532
Average SAT Verbal: 526
Average ACT: 23

Graduated top 10% of class: 13%
Graduated top 25% of class: 48%
Graduated top 50% of class: 74%

COLLEGE GRADUATION REQUIREMENTS

Course waivers allowed: No
Course substitutions allowed: Yes
In what course: American Sign Language is accepted as a foreign language.

ADDITIONAL INFORMATION

Environment: The university has an urban campus 70 miles south of Denver.

Student Body:
  Undergrad enrollment: 5,886
  Women: 61%
  Men: 39%
  Percent out-of-state: 11%

Cost Information
  In-state tuition: $4,229
  Out-of-state tuition: $16,310
  Room & board: $6,785
Housing Information
  University housing: Yes
  Percent living on campus: 10%

Greek System
  Fraternity: No
  Sorority: Yes
  Athletics: NCAA Division II

UNIVERSITY OF DENVER

University Hall, Room 110, 2197 S. University Blvd., Denver, CO 80208
Phone: 303-871-2036 • Fax: 303-871-3301
E-mail: admission@du.edu • Web: www.du.edu/admission
Support: SP • Institution type: 4-year private

LEARNING DISABILITY PROGRAM AND SERVICES

Learning Effectiveness Program (LEP) is a comprehensive program structured to provide students with individualized support. LEP counselors work one-on-one with students to determine their learning strengths and to develop skills that will make them successful University students. Three crucial areas of skill development are encouraged: self-advocacy, articulation of strengths and weaknesses, and independent learning strategies. Cognitive strategy development is a basic part of individual sessions with a learning specialist. Students participate in regular coursework and do not take special classes. One major focus of the LEP is reducing anxiety about learning in a college environment. Students learn how to focus on higher-level thought processes in order to compensate for lower-level processing deficits. They are also taught non-traditional study skills designed to increase reading, writing, and memory. Students are treated as responsible adults and are expected to participate in the program willingly.

LD/ADD ADMISSIONS INFORMATION

College entrance tests required: Yes
Interview required: Yes (For all applicants)
Essay required: Yes
Documentation required for LD: Psychoeducational evaluation
Documentation required for ADD: Yes
Submitted to: Learning Effectiveness Program
Special Ed. HS coursework accepted: No

Specific course requirements of all applicants: Yes
Separate application required for program servics: Yes
# of LD applications submitted each year: 300
# of LD applications accepted yearly: 95
Total # of students receiving LD services: NR
Acceptance into program means acceptance into college: Student must be admitted first to the university to enroll in the LEP.

ADMISSIONS

Admission to the university and LEP are two distinct processes. All potential candidates with LD/ADD must submit a general admissions application, essay, recommendations, activity sheet, high school transcript, and ACT/SAT scores. Students applying to LEP must also provide documentation of LD/ADD; recent diagnostic tests; the completed LEP Intake Form provided upon disclosure of an LD; and a letter from a counselor, teacher, or LD specialist. The verification form from an appropriate specialist is critical and should describe the students' learning deficit and the support services necessary for success. Strengths, weaknesses, maturity level, ability to handle frustration, and feelings about limitations should also be included in documentation sent to the LEP. A successful background in college-prep classes is desirable. The minimum GPA is 3.1. A campus visit and interview are recommended after submission of all documentation and testing. Interviews should be scheduled as far in advance as possible.

ADDITIONAL INFORMATION

LEP services are only available to students who are enrolled in the program. The LEP is a fee for service program that provides services beyond the mandated services provided under Section 504. There is a $2,550 fee per year for this program. The Director and Associate Director are LD specialists, and the staff is composed of professionals in a variety of academic disciplines. Professional tutoring is also available to students enrolled in this program. Students who feel that they need only basic accommodations and do not wish to participate in the comprehensive program should contact Disability Services Program at 303-871-2455 to make those arrangements. The use of a calculator, dictionary, computer, and/or spellchecker require the professor's permission. Services and accommodations are available for undergraduate and graduate students. Learning disability assessments are available on campus.

Support Services Contact Information

Learning Disability Program/Services: Learning Effectiveness Program / Disability Services Program
Director: Ted F. May Director, LEP/DSP
  E-Mail: tmay@du.edu
  Telephone: 303-871-2372
  Fax: 303-871-3939
Contact Person: David Luker, Associate Director, Learning Effectiveness Program
  E-Mail: dluker@du.edu
  Telephone: 303-871-2372
  Fax: 303-871-3939

LEARNING DISABILITY SERVICES

Requests for the following/services accommodations will be evaluated individually based on appropriate and current documentation.

Allowed in exams
  Calculator: Y/N
  Dictionary: Y/N
  Computer: Y/N
  Spellchecker: No
Extended test time: Yes
Scribes: Yes
Proctors: Yes
Oral exams: Yes
Note-takers: Yes

Distraction-reduced environment: Yes
Tape recording in class: Yes
Books on tape from RFBD: Y/N
Taping of books not from RFBD: Yes
Accommodations for students with
  ADD: Yes
Reading machine: Yes
Other assistive technology: Yes
Priority registration: Yes

Added costs for services: Yes
LD specialists: Yes
Professional tutors: 15
Peer tutors: 20
Max. hours/wk. for services:
  Unlimited
How professors are notified of
  LD/ADD: By student

GENERAL ADMISSIONS INFORMATION

Director of Admissions: Tom Willoughby, Vice Chancellor for Enrollment
Telephone: 303-871-3383

ENTRANCE REQUIREMENTS

Academic units recommended: All applicants must have an interview (may be done by telephone). 4 English, 4 math, 4 science (2 science lab), 3 foreign language, 2 social studies, 2 history. High school diploma is required and GED is accepted. ACT with Writing component required or SAT Reasoning Test. TOEFL required of all international applicants, minimum paper TOEFL 500, minimum computer TOEFL 173

Application deadline: 1/15
Notification: 1/5
Average GPA: 3.48

Average SAT Math: 576
Average SAT Verbal: 570
Average ACT: 25

Graduated top 10% of class: 33%
Graduated top 25% of class: 59%
Graduated top 50% of class: 85%

COLLEGE GRADUATION REQUIREMENTS

Course waivers allowed: Yes
In what course: In the area of foreign language
Course substitutions allowed: No

ADDITIONAL INFORMATION

Environment: The university has a 230-acre campus 7 miles southeast of Denver.

Student Body:
  Undergrad enrollment: 4,643
  Women: 55%
  Men: 45%
  Percent out-of-state: 50%

Cost Information
  Tuition: $27,756
  Room & board: $8,000
Housing Information
  University housing: Yes
  Percent living on campus: 45%

Greek System
  Fraternity: Yes
  Sorority: Yes
Athletics: NCAA Division I

UNIVERSITY OF NORTHERN COLORADO

UNC Admissions Office, Greeley, CO 80639
Phone: 970-351-2881 • Fax: 970-351-2984
E-mail: unc@mail.unco.edu • Web: www.unco.edu
Support: S • Institution type: 4-year public

LEARNING DISABILITY PROGRAM AND SERVICES

Although the university does not offer a formal LD program, individual assistance is provided whenever possible. The Disability Access Center (DAC) provides access, accommodations, and advocacy for UNC students who have documented disabilities. Academic needs are determined by the documentation and a student interview. Students with disabilities have an equal opportunity to pursue their educational goals. DAC provides test accommodations, adaptive hardware and software, learning strategies, organizational skills, and a reader program. Students requesting accommodations at UNC must provide test instruments from a certified professional that measures general intellect, aptitude, and more specific information processing tests; academic and vocational measures of achievement; and a clinical interview, which is the primary measure of previous educational and psychological functioning. Suggestions of reasonable accommodations which might be appropriate at the post-secondary level are encouraged. These recommendations should be supported by the diagnosis. Students with ADD must provide a medical or clinical diagnosis from a developmental pediatrician, neurologist, psychiatrist, licensed clinical or educational psychologist, family physician, or a combination of such professionals.

LD/ADD ADMISSIONS INFORMATION

College entrance tests required: Yes
Interview required: Yes
Essay required: No
Documentation required for LD: Current psychological evaluation, including aptitude and achievement
Documentation required for ADD: Yes
Submitted to: Disability Support Services
Special Ed. HS coursework accepted: Yes

Specific course requirements of all applicants: Yes
Separate application required for program servics: No
# of LD applications submitted each year: 100–120
# of LD applications accepted yearly: NR
Total # of students receiving LD services: 160
Acceptance into program means acceptance into college: Student must be admitted and enrolled in the university first and then request services.

ADMISSIONS

There is no special admission process for students with learning disabilities. All students with disabilities are admitted to UNC under the standard admission requirements of the university. The university uses class rank, GPA and test scores to determine a selection index. UNC requires three years of math and the classes must be college prep. Pre-algebra does not count. UNC recommends four years of English, three of history/social sciences, and three years of natural science. When UNC evaluates a transcript for admissions, they only look at the math.The UNC has a special window for admitting students who do not meet UNC's freshman admission requirements but want to earn full admission into a degree program. Students wishing to participate in this program need to call the Admissions Office. Each applicant is judged on an individual basis. Students do not need to be LD to apply for this DAC program, but must have a documented disability. To assist in determining eligibility for the program, current medical/clinical information is necessary. In order to receive services students must request accommodations upon arrival at UNC. Students enrolled in the Challenge Program must take 12 hours of college credit and earn a GPA of 2.0 after 1 or 2 semesters in order to remain at UNC.

ADDITIONAL INFORMATION

Services for individuals with LD/ADD includes learning strategies/organizational skills/advocacy skills; reader program; test accommodations; assistance in arranging for note-takers; assistive technology, including voice synthesizers, screen readers, screen enlargers, scanners, voice-recognition computer systems, large monitors, and word processing with spell check. Workshops are offered in student skills, organizational skills, study strategies, and time management. These workshops are electives and are not for credit. There is a support group for students with LD/ADD, facilitated by DAC staff, which assists students in developing a support network. Services and accommodations are available for undergraduate and graduate students.

Support Services Contact Information

Learning Disability Program/Services: Disability Support Services (DSS)
Director: Nancy Kauffman
  E-mail: nancy.kauffman@unco.edu
  Telephone: 970-351-2289
Fax: 970-351-4166

LEARNING DISABILITY SERVICES

Requests for the following/services accommodations will be evaluated individually based on appropriate and current documentation.

Allowed in exams
  Calculator: Yes
  Dictionary: Yes
  Computer: Yes
  Spellchecker: Yes
Extended test time: Yes
Scribes: Yes
Proctors: Yes
Oral exams: Yes
Note-takers: Yes

Distraction-reduced environment: Yes
Tape recording in class: Yes
Books on tape from RFBD: Yes
Taping of books not from RFBD: Yes
Accommodations for students with
  ADD: Yes
Reading machine: Yes
Other assistive technology: Yes
Priority registration: Yes

Added costs for services: No
LD specialists: No
Professional tutors: No
Peer tutors: 20
Max. hours/wk. for services: Varies
How professors are notified of
  LD/ADD: By student

GENERAL ADMISSIONS INFORMATION

Director of Admissions: Gary Gullickson
Telephone: 970-351-2281

ENTRANCE REQUIREMENTS

Academic units required: 3 math, **Academic units recommended:** 4 English, 2 science (1 science lab), 2 social studies. High school diploma is required and GED is accepted. ACT with or without Writing component accepted. TOEFL required of all international applicants, minimum paper TOEFL 520, minimum computer TOEFL 156.

Application deadline: 8/1
Notification: rolling
Average GPA: 3.2

Average SAT Math: 516
Average SAT Verbal: 519
Average ACT: 22

Graduated top 10% of class: 10%
Graduated top 25% of class: 29%
Graduated top 50% of class: 67%

COLLEGE GRADUATION REQUIREMENTS

Course waivers allowed: No
Course substitutions allowed: Yes
In what course: N/A

ADDITIONAL INFORMATION

Environment: The university is located on 240 acres in a small town 50 miles north of Denver.

Student Body:
  Undergrad enrollment: 9,921
  Women: 61%
  Men: 39%
  Percent out-of-state: 11%

Cost Information
  In-state tuition: $2,850
  Out-of-state tuition: $11,740
  Room & board: $5,954
Housing Information
  University housing: Yes
  Percent living on campus: 31%

Greek System
  Fraternity: Yes
  Sorority: Yes
Athletics: NCAA Division I

University of Northern Colorado

WESTERN STATE COLLEGE OF CO

600 North Adams Street, Gunnison, CO 81231
Phone: 970-943-2119 • Fax: 970-943-2212
E-mail: discover@western.edu • Web: www.western.edu
Support: S • Institution type: 4-year public

LEARNING DISABILITY PROGRAM AND SERVICES

Disability Services, located in Western's Learning Assistance Center, coordinates support services for all qualified students with disabilities. We offer a variety of resources and accommodations to assist students as they pursue their academic and career goals. While providing a supportive environment, we encourage students to develop independence and to take responsibility for their academic experiences. Personal consultation and workshops are available to help students improve learning, problem-solving, and self-advocacy skills.

LD/ADD ADMISSIONS INFORMATION

College entrance tests required: Yes
Interview required: No
Essay required: No
Documentation required for LD: Psychoeducational evaluation
Documentation required for ADD: Yes
Submitted to: Disability Services
Special Ed. HS coursework accepted: Yes

Specific course requirements of all applicants: Yes
Separate application required for program servics: No
# of LD applications submitted each year: NR
# of LD applications accepted yearly: NR
Total # of students receiving LD services: NR
Acceptance into program means acceptance into college: Students must be admitted and enrolled and then request services.

ADMISSIONS

Admission to Western depends on academic performance and background, standardized test scores, and personal attributes. In addition to general admissions requirements, Western State recommends a personal essay and recommendations from teachers, counselors, or others who know the student's academic ability. The college tries to admit those students who have demonstrated their ability to succeed. Normally, students are admitted if they meet the following criteria: graduation from an accredited high school; a cumulative grade point average of 2.5 or better (on a 4.0 scale of college-prep courses) and/or rank in the upper two-thirds of the student's graduating class; and a score of 20 or higher on the ACT or 950 on the SAT. Western recommends four years of English, three years of mathematics to include Algebra II, two years of natural science, and two years of social science. Modern language and computer science units are also important.

ADDITIONAL INFORMATION

Students who choose to register for disability support services typically do so soon after acceptance to Western. A Disability Services registration packet will be sent to accepted students who contact our office. We encourage students to meet with our staff during a campus visit or new-student orientation and to attend our Disability Services welcome and information session, which is offered at the beginning of each semester to help students become familiar with policies, procedures, and resources.

Support Services Contact Information

Learning Disability Program/Services: Disability Services
Director: Jan Edwards
  E-Mail: jedwards@western.edu
  Telephone: 970-943-7056
  Fax: 970-943-3409

LEARNING DISABILITY SERVICES

Requests for the following/services accommodations will be evaluated individually based on appropriate and current documentation.

Allowed in exams
  Calculator: Yes
  Dictionary: No
  Computer: Yes
  Spellchecker: Yes
Extended test time: Yes
Scribes: Yes
Proctors: Yes
Oral exams: Yes
Note-takers: Yes

Distraction-reduced environment: Yes
Tape recording in class: Yes
Books on tape from RFBD: Yes
Taping of books not from RFBD: Yes
Accommodations for students with
  ADD: Yes
Reading machine: Yes
Other assistive technology: No
Priority registration: Yes

Added costs for services: No
LD specialists: No
Professional tutors: No
Peer tutors: NR
Max. hours/wk. for services: Varies
How professors are notified of
  LD/ADD: By student

GENERAL ADMISSIONS INFORMATION

Director of Admissions: Tim Albers, Asst. VP
Telephone: 970-943-2119

ENTRANCE REQUIREMENTS

Academic units required: 4 English, 3 math, 2 science (2 science lab), 2 social studies, 2 history, 3 academic electives. **Academic units recommended:** 4 English, 4 math, 3 science, 2 foreign language, 3 social studies, 3 history. High school diploma is required and GED is accepted. ACT with or without Writing component accepted. TOEFL required of all international applicants, minimum paper TOEFL 550, minimum computer TOEFL 213.

Application deadline: 8/1
Notification: Rolling
Average GPA: 2.99

Average SAT Math: 482
Average SAT Verbal: 500
Average ACT: 21

Graduated top 10% of class: 5%
Graduated top 25% of class: 21%
Graduated top 50% of class: 52%

COLLEGE GRADUATION REQUIREMENTS

Course waivers allowed: No
Course substitutions allowed: Yes
In what course: Math substitutions may be approved for students with documented math learning disabilities, when appropriate.

ADDITIONAL INFORMATION

Environment: Western State College of Colorado is located in the heart of the Rocky Mountains.

Student Body:
  Undergrad enrollment: 2,152
  Women: 40%
  Men: 60%
  Percent out-of-state: 25%

Cost Information
  In-state tuition: $1,980
  Out-of-state tuition: $9,966
  Room & board: $7,200
Housing Information
  University housing: Yes
  Percent living on campus: 38%

Greek System
  Fraternity: Yes
  Sorority: Yes
Athletics: NCAA Division II

FAIRFIELD UNIVERSITY

1073 North Benson Road, Fairfield, CT 06824-5195
Phone: 203-254-4100 • Fax: 203-254-4199
E-mail: admis@mail.fairfield.edu • Web: www.fairfield.edu
Support: CS • Institution type: 4-year private

LEARNING DISABILITY PROGRAM AND SERVICES

The university provides services for students with disabilities through Student Support Services. There is no learning disability program, only services that are available for all students with disabilities. These services are designed to provide equal access to the learning environment. Students are supported while being encouraged to be self-advocates. Students with learning disabilities must provide documentation from an appropriate testing agent. For students with learning disabilities, cognitive and academic achievement tests and information processing must be administered. Students with ADD must have documentation from appropriate professionals who can provide behavior rating scales, ruling out other disabilities and showing the onset of the ADD between ages 7-12. All documentation should be submitted to Student Support Services.

LD/ADD ADMISSIONS INFORMATION

College entrance tests required: Yes
Interview required: No
Essay required: No
Documentation required for LD: Psychoeducational
    evaluation
Documentation required for ADD: Yes
Submitted to: Student Support Services
Special Ed. HS coursework accepted: Yes

Specific course requirements of all applicants: Yes
Separate application required for program servics: No
# of LD applications submitted each year: NR
# of LD applications accepted yearly: NR
Total # of students receiving LD services: 150
**Acceptance into program means acceptance into
    college:** Student must be admitted and enrolled in the
    university first and then request services.

ADMISSIONS
There is no special admissions process for students with learning disabilities. Admission criteria include: status in top 40 percent of graduating class or better; B average; 25 ACT; counselor recommendations; and college-prep courses including 4 years English, 3–4 years math, 2–4 years foreign language, 1–3 years lab science, and 2–3 years history. Courses taken in the Special Education department may be acceptable. The mid 50 percent SAT scores are 1120–1270. Once students have been admitted and have enrolled they may initiate a contact for services.

ADDITIONAL INFORMATION
Skills courses are offered in study skills, note-taking strategies, time management skills, and strategies for success. These skills courses are not for credit. Students are offered meetings with a professional who has a background in teaching students with disabilities. Letters are sent to professors upon students' request. All students have access to content tutoring and a writing center. Services and accommodations are available for undergraduate and graduate students.

Support Services Contact Information

Learning Disability Program/Services: Office of Student Support Services
Director: Rev. W. Laurence O'Neil, S.J.
  E-Mail: WLONEIL@mail.fairfield.edu
  Telephone: 203-254-4000
  Fax: 203-254-5542
Contact Person: David Ryan-Soderlund
  E-Mail: drsoderlund@mail.fairfield.edu
  Telephone: 203-254-4000 ext. 2445
  Fax: 203-254-5542

LEARNING DISABILITY SERVICES

Requests for the following/services accommodations will be evaluated individually based on appropriate and current documentation.

Allowed in exams
  Calculator: Yes
  Dictionary: Yes
  Computer: Yes
  Spellchecker: Yes
Extended test time: Yes
Scribes: Yes
Proctors: Yes
Oral exams: Yes
Note-takers: Yes

Distraction-reduced environment: Yes
Tape recording in class: Yes
Books on tape from RFBD: Yes
Taping of books not from RFBD: Yes
Accommodations for students with ADD: Yes
Reading machine: Yes
Other assistive technology: Yes
Priority registration: No

Added costs for services: No
LD specialists: Yes
Professional tutors: No
Peer tutors: 90–120
Max. hours/wk. for services: Unlimited
How professors are notified of LD/ADD: By student

GENERAL ADMISSIONS INFORMATION

Director of Admissions: Karen Pelligrino-Director
Telephone: 203-254-4100

ENTRANCE REQUIREMENTS
Academic units required: 4 English, 3 math, 3 science (3 science lab), 2 foreign language, 3 social studies.
Academic units recommended: 4 English, 4 math, 4 science (3 science lab), 4 foreign language, 4 social studies, 1 history. Highly recommended: portfolio for music majors, resume for theatre majors. High school diploma is required and GED is not accepted. ACT without Writing component accepted. TOEFL required of all international applicants, minimum paper TOEFL 550, minimum computer TOEFL 213.

Application deadline: 1/15
Notification: 4/1
Average GPA: 3.00

Average SAT Math: 607
Average SAT Verbal: 590
Average ACT: 26

Graduated top 10% of class: 32%
Graduated top 25% of class: 73%
Graduated top 50% of class: 99%

COLLEGE GRADUATION REQUIREMENTS

Course waivers allowed: Yes
Course substitutions allowed: Yes
In what course: Math, foreign language (must have severe impairment).

ADDITIONAL INFORMATION

Environment: The university is located on 200 acres in a suburban area 60 miles northeast of New York City.

Student Body:
  Undergrad enrollment: 3,552
  Women: 57%
  Men: 43%
  Percent out-of-state: 75%

Cost Information
  Tuition: $27,450
  Room & board: $9,270
Housing Information
  University housing: Yes
  Percent living on campus: 80%

Greek System
  Fraternity: No
  Sorority: No
Athletics: NCAA Division I

MITCHELL COLLEGE

437 Pequot Avenue, New London, CT 06320
Phone: 800-701-5037 • Fax: 860-444-1209
E-mail: admissions@mitchell.edu • Web: www.mitchell.edu
Support: SP • Institution type: 2-year and 4-year private

LEARNING DISABILITY PROGRAM AND SERVICES

Mitchell College is dedicated to providing a student-centered supportive learning environment that addresses the educational needs of all students, including those with learning disabilities, through associate and baccalaureate degree programs. The Academic Support Center offers the Learning Resource Center whose mission is to provide a spectrum of academic support services to students with disabilities at three levels of support. A Tutoring Center provides tutoring across the content areas to all students enrolled at the college on the basis of individual appointments and walk-in accommodations, and a soon to be implemented Testing Center will serve to monitor, proctor, and administer professors' tests and exams.   The Learning Resource Center's three levels of support include a Level I fee-based program that is the most comprehensive (a team of specialists); to a non-fee based Level II standard support services, including weekly consultation and review sessions, accommodations and modifications; to Level III accommodations and modifications. The fundamental components that characterize the Level I Enhanced Support are individual appointments or small group; guided reading and structured study sessions; regularly scheduled skills mini-workshops; collaboration with academic advisor to assist in planning a program of study; collaboration with other C.A.R.E.S. staff as necessary; review and modification of course selections or credit loads if necessary; ensuring documented modifications and/or accommodations. The staff is comprised of specialists with specific training in working with students who have difficulties with reading, mathematics, writing and organization. Generally, students who are successful at Mitchell College have a college-prep curriculum in high school. Additionally, these students must have a solid level of skills in reading, writing and math, plus determination, persistence, and motivation to achieve personal goals.

LD/ADD ADMISSIONS INFORMATION

College entrance tests required: Yes
Interview required: No
Essay required: Yes
Documentation required for LD: Both an aptitude and an achievement test reflecting reading, writing, and math standard scores
Documentation required for ADD: The documentation that was appropriate for the student's school/school district is acceptable
Submitted to: Admissions

Special Ed. HS coursework accepted: N/A
Specific course requirements of all applicants: No
Separate application required for program servics: No
# of LD applications submitted each year: 400
# of LD applications accepted yearly: 300
Total # of students receiving LD services: 215
Acceptance into program means acceptance into college: Students are reviewed by both the program and the Office of Admissions, but the final decision is with Admissions. Once admitted, students may request services.

ADMISSIONS

Students with identified specific learning disabilities may apply for admission through the LRC program. Students must complete an application process that includes the submission of a high school transcript; documentation of a learning disability and/or attention deficit disorder; current assessment information; and aptitude and achievement test scores (reading, writing, and math) reflecting all subtest and summative scores in the form of standard scores and/or percentile ranks, college board test scores (ACT/SAT), and written letters of comment and recommendation from LD teacher(s) and guidance counselors. In addition, each applicant is required to submit a writing sample that is part of the formal application itself. Often, an interview with the LRC staff is requested following a review of the completed application. The applicant's academic program of study in high school should be within a mainstream and/or inclusion framework, with a consistent C or better performance reflected in the core academic subjects. Evidence of commitment, motivation, and preparedness for college-level study is desired. While they do require the SAT/ACT, the admission is dependent more on potential and the student's desire to be successful than what he/she has necessarily done in the past. The Director and Learning Specialists of the LRC review all LRC applicant information and make a recommendation to the Dean of Admissions. Mitchell operates on a rolling admission basis and notifies of a decision as soon as all of the credentials are received and reviewed.

ADDITIONAL INFORMATION

During the first year students accepted into the LRC program are expected to work with their assigned Learning Specialists at least four hours per week divided between individual and small group sessions. These training sessions focus on developing and/or strengthening skills in a variety of learning-study strategies, as well as other ancillary skills and strategies that are designed to promote academic success. The LRC students are expected to fulfill all degree requirements for their chosen major program of study, and to follow all college requirements and procedures in the Student Catalog.

Support Services Contact Information

Learning Disability Program/Services: Learning Resource Center (LRC)
Director: Peter F. Troiano, PhD
  E-Mail: troiano_p@mitchell.edu
  Telephone: 860-701-5141
  Fax: 860-701-5090
Contact Person: Joanne Carnevale
  E-Mail: carnevale_j@mitchell.edu
  Telephone: 860-701-5071
  Fax: 860-701-5090

LEARNING DISABILITY SERVICES

Requests for the following/services accommodations will be evaluated individually based on appropriate and current documentation.

Allowed in exams
  Calculator: Yes
  Dictionary: Yes
  Computer: Yes
  Spellchecker: Yes
Extended test time: Yes
Scribes: Yes
Proctors: Yes
Oral exams: Yes
Note-takers: Yes

Distraction-reduced environment: Yes
Tape recording in class: Yes
Books on tape from RFBD: Yes
Taping of books not from RFBD: Yes
Accommodations for students with
  ADD: Yes
Reading machine: Yes
Other assistive technology: Yes
Priority registration: N/A

Added costs for services: Yes
LD specialists: Yes
Professional tutors: 10–12
Peer tutors: No
Max. hours/wk. for services: 4
How professors are notified of
  LD/ADD: By student

GENERAL ADMISSIONS INFORMATION

Director of Admissions: Kim Hodges
Telephone: 800-701-5037

ENTRANCE REQUIREMENTS

Academic units recommended: 4 English, 3 math, 3 science, 2 social studies, 2 history, 2 academic electives. High school diploma is required and GED is accepted. TOEFL required of all international applicants, minimum paper TOEFL 500, minimum computer TOEFL 173.

Application deadline: 3/31
Notification: Rolling
Average GPA: 2.70

Average SAT Math: 440
Average SAT Verbal: 470
Average ACT: 22

Graduated top 10% of class: 3%
Graduated top 25% of class: 15%
Graduated top 50% of class: 35%

COLLEGE GRADUATION REQUIREMENTS

Course waivers allowed: No
Course substitutions allowed: Yes
In what course: Varies based on the student's history with the subject area and the school policies and procedures.

ADDITIONAL INFORMATION

Environment: 65-acre campus on a former estate, located in a safe and quiet residential area of historic New London.

Student Body:
  Undergrad enrollment: 508
  Women: 50%
  Men: 50%
  Percent out-of-state: 36%

Cost Information
  Tuition: $18,058
  Room & board: $8,680
Housing Information
  University housing: Yes
  Percent living on campus: 85%

Greek System
  Fraternity: No
  Sorority: No
Athletics: NCAA Division III

SOUTHERN CONNECTICUT STATE U.

131 Farnham Avenue, New Haven, CT 06515-1202
Phone: 203-392-5656 • Fax: 203-392-5727
E-mail: adminfo@scsu.ctstateu.edu • Web: www.southernct.edu
Support: CS • Institution type: 4-year public

LEARNING DISABILITY PROGRAM AND SERVICES

The purpose of the Disability Resource Office (DRO) is to ensure educational equity for students with disabilities. The DRO works to provide access to full participation in all aspects of campus life. The DRO assists students in arranging for individualized accommodations and support services. The DRO is a resource to students, faculty, and the university at large. Use of DRO services is voluntary and confidential. The DRO provides academic, career, and personal support for all university students with disabilities, including students with specific learning disabilities and attention deficit disorders. The DRO is a component of Student Supportive Services.

LD/ADD ADMISSIONS INFORMATION

College entrance tests required: Yes
Interview required: No
Essay required: Yes
Documentation required for LD: Pyschoeducational
Documentation required for ADD: Yes
Submitted to: Disability Resource Office
Special Ed. HS coursework accepted: Yes

Specific course requirements of all applicants: Yes
Separate application required for program servics: No
# of LD applications submitted each year: NR
# of LD applications accepted yearly: NR
Total # of students receiving LD services: 400
Acceptance into program means acceptance into college: Student must be admitted and enrolled in the university first and then request services.

ADMISSIONS

There is no special admissions process for students with learning disabilities. All applicants must meet the same criteria. Course requirements include 4 years English, 3 years math, 2 years science, 2 years foreign language, 2 years social studies, and 2 years history. Conditional Admission is considered and based on the following: WAIS scores and sub scores, achievement tests, SAT/ACT scores, and transcript. Applicants who wish DRO to be involved in the admission decision should note disability on the application, which goes to admissions. They should also submit current psychoeducational testing information to DRO.

ADDITIONAL INFORMATION

The DRO assists students in arranging for individualized accommodations and support services. Services are available to both prospective and current students as follows: prospective students should attend one of the several workshops offered each fall for prospective students and their parents seeking information regarding the program and should obtain an application to the university. Current students should make an appointment with the office and bring educational documentation including achievement testing and psychoeducational evaluation or medical documentation. Services include course selection and registration; course and testing accommodations; support from learning specialists in developing time management and study skills, in identifying strengths and weaknesses, and in acquiring compensatory strategies; liaison with faculty and university departments; and advocacy and self-advocacy information and training. Services and accommodations are available for undergraduate and graduate students.

Support Services Contact Information

Learning Disability Program/Services: Disability Resource Office (DRO)
Director: Suzanne Tucker
  E-Mail: tucker@southernct.edu
  Telephone: 203-392-6828
  Fax: 203-392-6829
Contact Person: Above and Debbie Fairchild

LEARNING DISABILITY SERVICES

Requests for the following/services accommodations will be evaluated individually based on appropriate and current documentation.

Allowed in exams
  Calculator: Yes
  Dictionary: Yes
  Computer: Yes
  Spellchecker: Yes
Extended test time: Yes
Scribes: Yes
Proctors: Yes
Oral exams: Yes
Note-takers: Yes

Distraction-reduced environment: Yes
Tape recording in class: Yes
Books on tape from RFBD: Yes
Taping of books not from RFBD: Yes
Accommodations for students with ADD: Yes
Reading machine: Yes
Other assistive technology: Yes
Priority registration: Y/N

Added costs for services: No
LD specialists: Yes
Professional tutors: No
Peer tutors: Yes
Max. hours/wk. for services: .5
How professors are notified of LD/ADD: By student

GENERAL ADMISSIONS INFORMATION

Director of Admissions: Sharon Brenner
Telephone: 203-392-5656

ENTRANCE REQUIREMENTS

Academic units required: 4 English, 3 math, 2 science, 2 foreign language, 2 social studies, 2 history.   High school diploma is required and GED is accepted. TOEFL required of all international applicants, minimum paper TOEFL 525, minimum computer TOEFL 193.

Application deadline: 5/1
Notification: Rolling
Average GPA: NR

Average SAT Math: 451
Average SAT Verbal: 466
Average ACT: NR

Graduated top 10% of class: 5%
Graduated top 25% of class: 22%
Graduated top 50% of class: 57%

COLLEGE GRADUATION REQUIREMENTS

Course waivers allowed: Yes
Course substitutions allowed: Yes
In what course: Foreign Language

ADDITIONAL INFORMATION

Environment: The university is located on 168 acres in an urban area 35 miles south of Hartford, and 90 miles from New York City.

Student Body:
  Undergrad enrollment: 7,624
  Women: 59%
  Men: 41%
  Percent out-of-state: 5%

Cost Information
  In-state tuition: $2,124
  Out-of-state tuition: $6,874
  Room & board: $5,934
Housing Information
  University housing: Yes
  Percent living on campus: 24%

Greek System
  Fraternity: Yes
  Sorority: Yes
Athletics: NCAA Division II

UNIVERSITY OF CONNECTICUT

2131 Hillside Road, Unit 3088, Storrs, CT 06268-3088
Phone: 860-486-3137 • Fax: 860-486-1476
E-mail: beahusky@uconn.edu • Web: www.uconn.edu
Support: CS • Institution type: 4-year public

LEARNING DISABILITY PROGRAM AND SERVICES

The major goal of the University Program for College Students with LD (UPLD) is to assist qualified students with LD to become independent and successful learners within the regular university curriculum. The program is designed to complement and support, but not to duplicate, the university's existing campus services and programs. Three types of program services are offered along a continuum leading to independence: (1) direct instruction, in which students meet with learning specialists weekly to learn compensatory skills to strengthen learning strategies; (2) monitoring for students who need periodic contact; and (3) consultation with UPLD staff on a student-initiated basis. Most students find that it is beneficial to access services at the Direct Instruction Level, and to progress at an individual rate through the UPLD Continuum as they experience increasing confidence and competence. UPLD staff is available to help student's access additional campus resources. Staff of UPLD is not qualified to serve as academic advisors. In cases where the disability does not include a specific LD, such as ADD/ADD, students can receive support services from the Center for Students with Disabilities (CSD). Students diagnosed with LD and ADD have services coordinated through UPLD and CSD. Students are fully integrated within programs at the university.

LD/ADD ADMISSIONS INFORMATION

College entrance tests required: Yes
Interview required: No
Essay required: No
Documentation required for LD: Psychoeducational evaluation
Documentation required for ADD: Yes
Submitted to: UPLD
Special Ed. HS coursework accepted: No

Specific course requirements of all applicants: Yes
Separate application required for program servics: Yes
# of LD applications submitted each year: NR
# of LD applications accepted yearly: NR
Total # of students receiving LD services: 160
Acceptance into program means acceptance into college: Student must be admitted and enrolled in the university first and then request services.

ADMISSIONS

There is no separate application or application process for students with LD, and they must be qualified for admission according to regular admissions criteria. The typical academic profile is rank in top one-third of graduating class, academic GPA of 3.2 in college-prep courses, and SAT Reasoning Test of 1100 and above. Transfer students need a cumulative GPA of at least a 2.5 and be in good standing at their current institution. To access services, students must refer themselves to UPLD and submit documentation that meets the criteria of the university's guidelines for documentation of a specific LD. Documentation must verify eligibility and support requests for reasonable accommodations, academic adjustments, and/or auxiliary aids. Testing must be comprehensive. Minimally, domains to be addressed include aptitude; achievement (current levels of functioning in reading, math, and written language); and information processing. Testing must be current, usually within 3 years, and there must be clear and specific evidence and identification of a LD. Individual learning styles and learning differences in and of themselves do not constitute a LD. Actual test scores must be provided including interpretation of the results. The assessments must be conducted by qualified professionals. A written summary about relevant educational, medical, and family histories that relate to LD must be included. Recommendations for accommodations should be based on objective evidence of a current substantial limitation to learning, and descriptions of any accommodation and/or auxiliary aid used in high school or college should be discussed. IEPs and Section 504 plans alone are useful but are not sufficient to establish the rationale for services.

ADDITIONAL INFORMATION

Trained staff work with students on developing learning strategies and offer individual structured sessions. Students are encouraged to plan their coursework to ensure success, including a reduced course load and extending their time for graduation. Learning specialists help students in self-advocacy, identify and monitor needs, and develop individualized goals. Reasonable accommodations are determined on a case-by-case basis. Other services include counseling and career planning, math and writing centers, and mental health services. The CSD coordinates requests for proctors or scribes and provides services to students with ADD without a diagnosed LD. The university has a formal course substitution policy for students with LD which requires current, valid diagnostic evidence that the nature and severity of the LD precludes completion of courses in foreign language or math despite the provision of accommodations. A waiver of a subject in high school does not guarantee a substitution at the university.

Support Services Contact Information

Learning Disability Program/Services: University Program for College Students with LD (UPLD)
Director: David R. Parker, PhD
  E-Mail: David.Parker@uconn.edu
  Telephone: 860-486-0178
  Fax: 860-486-5799

LEARNING DISABILITY SERVICES

Requests for the following/services accommodations will be evaluated individually based on appropriate and current documentation.

Allowed in exams
  Calculator: Yes
  Dictionary: Yes
  Computer: Yes
  Spellchecker: Yes
Extended test time: Yes
Scribes: Yes
Proctors: Yes
Oral exams: Yes
Note-takers: Yes

Distraction-reduced environment: Yes
Tape recording in class: Yes
Books on tape from RFBD: Yes
Taping of books not from RFBD: Yes
Accommodations for students with
  ADD: No
Reading machine: No
Other assistive technology: No
Priority registration: No

Added costs for services: No
LD specialists: Yes
Professional tutors: No
Peer tutors: No
Max. hours/wk. for services: 2
How professors are notified of
  LD/ADD: By student

GENERAL ADMISSIONS INFORMATION

Director of Admissions: Lee H. Melvin
Telephone: 860-486-3137

ENTRANCE REQUIREMENTS

Academic units required: 4 English, 3 math, 2 science (2 science lab), 2 foreign language, 2 social studies, 3 academic electives. **Academic units recommended:** 3 foreign language. High school diploma is required and GED is accepted. ACT with Writing component required or SAT Reasoning Test. TOEFL required of all international applicants, minimum paper TOEFL 550, minimum computer TOEFL 213.

Application deadline: 2/1
Notification: Rolling
Average GPA: NR

Average SAT Math: 646
Average SAT Verbal: 481
Average ACT: NR

Graduated top 10% of class: 35%
Graduated top 25% of class: 79%
Graduated top 50% of class: 98%

COLLEGE GRADUATION REQUIREMENTS

Course waivers allowed: No
Course substitutions allowed: Yes
In what course: Based on documented evidence, some students qualify for course substitutions in foreign language or math courses.

ADDITIONAL INFORMATION

Environment: University of Connecticut is located 30 miles northeast of Hartford.

Student Body:
  Undergrad enrollment: 15,260
  Women: 52%
  Men: 48%
  Percent out-of-state: 24%

Cost Information
  In-state tuition: $6,096
  Out-of-state tuition: $18,600
  Room & board: $7,848
Housing Information
  University housing: Yes
  Percent living on campus: 72%

Greek System
  Fraternity: Yes
  Sorority: Yes
Athletics: NCAA Division I

UNIVERSITY OF HARTFORD

200 Bloomfield Avenue, West Hartford, CT 06117
Phone: 860-768-4296 • Fax: 860-768-4961
E-mail: admissions@mail.hartford.edu • Web: www.hartford.edu
Support: CS • Institution type: 4-year private

LEARNING DISABILITY PROGRAM AND SERVICES

The Learning Plus program facilitates equal opportunity for academic achievement and is available to any student diagnosed with LD. Program objectives include help to understand strengths and weaknesses provide learning strategies; develop self-advocacy skills; connect with campus resources; develop decision-making skills; facilitate appropriate testing modifications; provide information to faculty and students regarding LD; classroom accommodations and testing modifications; legal rights and responsibilities; and protect the confidentiality of student records. Learning Plus services include Direct Strategies, in which students are assigned to an LP tutor and meet weekly for instruction in metacognitive skills such as information processing or organizational strategies; Check-In, where students meet every other week with tutor for monitoring and organizational strategies; and Drop-In, for as needed assistance. Service determination depends on semester standing, GPA, and course curricula. Freshmen are assigned to Direct Strategies Instruction. Students with documentation are advised to contact the director of LP during the first week of classes. The director will discuss the disability, appropriate services, and classroom accommodations. Students are encouraged to discuss effective accommodations with professors. To receive services and accommodations from Learning Plus, students should submit comprehensive documentation to the Director of Learning Plus, not admissions, after being accepted to the university.

LD/ADD ADMISSIONS INFORMATION

College entrance tests required: Yes
Interview required: No
Essay required: No
Documentation required for LD: WAIS and achievement testing.
Documentation required for ADD: Yes
Submitted to: Learning Plus
Special Ed. HS coursework accepted: Sometimes

Specific course requirements of all applicants: Yes
Separate application required for program servics: No
# of LD applications submitted each year: NR
# of LD applications accepted yearly: NR
Total # of students receiving LD services: 100–300
Acceptance into program means acceptance into college: Student must be admitted and enrolled in the university first and then request services.

ADMISSIONS
Students with LD do not apply to the Learning Plus Program, but do apply directly to one of the nine colleges within the university. If admitted, students with LD may then elect to receive the support services offered. The Admissions Committee pays particular attention to the student's individual talents and aspirations, especially as they relate to programs available at the university. Some borderline applicants may be admitted as a summer admission. Course requirements include 4 years English, 3–3.5 years of math, 2 years science, 2 years social studies, plus electives. Substitutions are allowed on rare occasions and depend on disability and major. Students may also apply to Hillyer College, which is a 2-year program with more flexible admission criteria. This is a developmental program, with flexible admission standards, offering many services. Hillyer provides students with the opportunity to be in a college atmosphere and, if successful, transfer into the 4-year program. Hillyer is not necessarily for students with LD, although some students with LD are enrolled.

ADDITIONAL INFORMATION
Learning Plus is voluntary and students are required to seek assistance and to maintain contact. All modifications are determined on a case-by-case, course-by-course basis. Students are responsible for disclosing their LD to their professors. Skills classes are offered in study skills and math. Students can also receive one individual appointment weekly consisting of learning strategies from masters-level professionals. Instruction focuses on time management, organization strategies, reading, writing, mathematics, and course-specific study techniques. Some students with LD choose not to avail themselves of Learning Plus services. That is their privilege. The director of Learning Plus maintains confidential files of all documentation, should students request services at any time during their college career.

Support Services Contact Information

Learning Disability Program/Services: Learning Plus
Director: Lynne Golden
  E-Mail: golden@hartford.edu
  Telephone: 860-768-5129
  Fax: 860-768-4183

LEARNING DISABILITY SERVICES

Requests for the following/services accommodations will be evaluated individually based on appropriate and current documentation.

Allowed in exams
  Calculator: Yes
  Dictionary: No
  Computer: Yes
  Spellchecker: Yes
Extended test time: Yes
Scribes: No
Proctors: Yes
Oral exams: No
Note-takers: Yes

Distraction-reduced environment: Yes
Tape recording in class: Yes
Books on tape from RFBD: Yes
Taping of books not from RFBD: No
Accommodations for students with
  ADD: Yes
Reading machine: No
Other assistive technology: No
Priority registration: No

Added costs for services: No
LD specialists: Yes
Professional tutors: No
Peer tutors: No
Max. hours/wk. for services: NR
How professors are notified of
  LD/ADD: By student

GENERAL ADMISSIONS INFORMATION

Director of Admissions: Richard Zeiser
Telephone: 860-768-4296

ENTRANCE REQUIREMENTS

Academic units required: 4 English, 2 math, 2 science, 2 social studies, 2 history, 4 academic electives.
Academic units recommended: 3 math, 3 science, 2 foreign language, 3 social studies. High school diploma is required and GED is accepted. TOEFL required of all international applicants, minimum paper TOEFL 550, minimum computer TOEFL 213.

Application deadline: Rolling
Notification: Rolling
Average GPA: NR

Average SAT Math: 520
Average SAT Verbal: 520
Average ACT: 22

Graduated top 10% of class: NR
Graduated top 25% of class: NR
Graduated top 50% of class: NR

COLLEGE GRADUATION REQUIREMENTS

Course waivers allowed: Yes
In what course: On rare occasions; depends on disabilities and major.
Course substitutions allowed: Yes
In what course: Math and foreign language

ADDITIONAL INFORMATION

Environment: The university is located on a 320-acre campus in a residential section of West Hartford, 90 minutes from Boston.

Student Body:
  Undergrad enrollment: 5,254
  Women: 51%
  Men: 49%
  Percent out-of-state: 64%

Cost Information
  Tuition: $23,480
  Room & board: $8,996
Housing Information
  University housing: Yes
  Percent living on campus: 66%

Greek System
  Fraternity: Yes
  Sorority: Yes
  Athletics: NCAA Division I

UNIVERSITY OF NEW HAVEN

300 Orange Avenue, West Haven, CT 06516
Phone: 203-932-7319 • Fax: 203-931-6093
E-mail: adminfo@newhaven.edu • Web: www.newhaven.edu
Support: S • Institution type: 4-year private

LEARNING DISABILITY PROGRAM AND SERVICES

The primary responsibility of the Disability Services and Resource Office (DSR) is to provide services and support that promote access to the university's educational programs and services for students with disabilities. Students must self identify and submit documentation of a disability and the need for accommodations. Documentation should be submitted once the student is accepted to the university along with a signed DSR Intake form requesting accommodations. Students must also follow the established policies and procedures for making arrangements for accommodations each semester. Staff members act as advocates, liaisons, planners, and troubleshooters. The staff is responsible for assuring access, but at the same time they avoid creating an artificial atmosphere of dependence on services that cannot reasonably be expected after graduation. The Center for Learning Resources offers free tutoring for all students including students with disabilities. The Office of Academic Services offers academic assistance to all students. Academic Skills Counselors work one-on-one with students to strengthen abilities and develop individualized study strategies, which focus on reading, note taking, time management, learning/memory and test taking skills.

LD/ADD ADMISSIONS INFORMATION

College entrance tests required: Yes
Interview required: No
Essay required: No
Documentation required for LD: Intelligence
test/Achievement test including information processing
Documentation required for ADD: Diagnosis by qualified
examiner including data from any tests performed, functional
limitations relative to learning, and information regarding
medications and side effects.
Submitted to: Disability Services and Resources
Special Ed. HS coursework accepted: Yes

Specific course requirements of all applicants: Yes
Separate application required for program servics: No
# of LD applications submitted each year: NR
# of LD applications accepted yearly: NR
Total # of students receiving LD services: NR
**Acceptance into program means acceptance into
college:** Student must be admitted and enrolled in the
university first and then request services.

ADMISSIONS

All applicants must meet the same admission requirements. Foreign language is not required for admission. Students with learning disabilities may self disclose if they feel that it would positively affect the admissions decision. Students admitted as a conditional admit are limited to four classes for the first semester.

ADDITIONAL INFORMATION

DSR provides services that include the coordination of classroom accommodations such as extended time for exams; use of a tape recorder, calculator, note-takers; readers, scribes or books on tape; assistance during the course registration process; proctoring of tests when accommodations cannot be arranged for in the classroom; proctoring of English course post-tests and the Writing Proficiency Exam. DSR also provides training in time management, organizational skills and test anxiety management. The office includes testing rooms and a mini computer lab with some adaptive software. The Center for Learning Resources (CLR) has a math lab, writing lab and computer lab. The CLR presents free workshops on preparing resumes and preparing for the Writing Proficiency Exam. The Office of Academic Services presents free workshops on improving study skills such as how to get organized, textbook and lecture note-taking techniques, and test preparation and strategies.

Support Services Contact Information

Learning Disability Program/Services: Disability Services and Resources
Director: Linda Copney-Okeke
  E-Mail: lcokeke@newhaven.edu
  Telephone: 203-932-7331
  Fax: 203-931-6082

LEARNING DISABILITY SERVICES

Requests for the following/services accommodations will be evaluated individually based on appropriate and current documentation.

Allowed in exams
  Calculator: Yes
  Dictionary: Yes
  Computer: Yes
  Spellchecker: Yes
Extended test time: Yes
Scribes: Yes
Proctors: Yes
Oral exams: Yes
Note-takers: Yes

Distraction-reduced environment: Yes
Tape recording in class: Yes
Books on tape from RFBD: Yes
Taping of books not from RFBD: Yes
Accommodations for students with
  ADD: Yes
Reading machine: No
Other assistive technology: Yes
Priority registration: No

Added costs for services: No
LD specialists: No
Professional tutors: NR
Peer tutors: NR
Max. hours/wk. for services:
  Unlimited
How professors are notified of
  LD/ADD: By student

GENERAL ADMISSIONS INFORMATION

Director of Admissions: Jane Sangeloty
Telephone: 203-932-7319

ENTRANCE REQUIREMENTS

Academic units required: 4 English, 3 math, 2 science, 2 history, 3 academic electives. **Academic units recommended:** 2 foreign language, 2 social studies. High school diploma is required and GED is accepted. TOEFL required of all international applicants, minimum paper TOEFL 520, minimum computer TOEFL 190.

Application deadline: NR
Notification: Rolling
Average GPA: 3.00

Average SAT Math: 519
Average SAT Verbal: 520
Average ACT: NR

Graduated top 10% of class: 14%
Graduated top 25% of class: 35%
Graduated top 50% of class: 67%

COLLEGE GRADUATION REQUIREMENTS

Course waivers allowed: No
Course substitutions allowed: Yes
In what course: Courses which are not essential to the students program of study.

ADDITIONAL INFORMATION

Environment: Located close to New Haven and 75 miles from New York City.
Student Body:
  Undergrad enrollment: 2,627
  Women: 45%
  Men: 55%
  Percent out-of-state: 38%

Cost Information
  Tuition: $20,130
  Room & board: $8,040
Housing Information
  University housing: Yes
  Percent living on campus: 60%

Greek System
  Fraternity: Yes
  Sorority: Yes
Athletics: NCAA Division II

University of New Haven

WESTERN CONNECTICUT STATE U.

Undergraduate Admissions Office, 181 White Street,
Danbury, CT 06810-6855 • Phone: 203-837-9000 • Fax: 203-837-8338
E-mail: admissions@wcsu.edu • Web: www.wcsu.edu
Support: CS • Institution type: 4-year public

LEARNING DISABILITY PROGRAM AND SERVICES

There are two primary purposes of the Department of Students with Disabilities Services: to provide the educational development of disabled students, and to improve understanding and support in the campus environment. Students with learning disabilities will receive the services necessary to achieve their goals.

LD/ADD ADMISSIONS INFORMATION

College entrance tests required: Yes
Interview required: No
Essay required: No
Documentation required for LD: Psychoeducational
   evaluation
Documentation required for ADD: Yes
Submitted to: Disability Services
Special Ed. HS coursework accepted: Yes

Specific course requirements of all applicants: Yes
Separate application required for program servics: No
# of LD applications submitted each year: NR
# of LD applications accepted yearly: NR
Total # of students receiving LD services: 190
**Acceptance into program means acceptance into
   college:** Student must be admitted and enrolled in the
   university first and then request services.

ADMISSIONS

Students with learning disabilities submit the general application form. No alternative admission policies are offered. Students should have a 2.5 GPA (C+ or better) and the average SAT 894 (ACT may be substituted). Courses required include 4 years English, 3 years math, 2 years science, 2 science labs, 2 years foreign language (3 years foreign language recommended), 1 year social studies, 1 year history, and 3 years of electives. Students are encouraged to self-disclose their disability on the application, and submit documentation to be used after admission to determine services and accommodations.

ADDITIONAL INFORMATION

Services include priority registration, tutoring, testing accommodations, and advocacy and counseling. The university does not offers any skills classes. The university offers a special summer program for pre-college freshmen with learning disabilities. Services and accommodations are available for undergraduate and graduate students.

Support Services Contact Information

Learning Disability Program/Services: Disability Services
Director: Barbara Barnwell
 E-mail: bbarnwell@wcsu.edu
 Telephone: 203-837-8277
 Fax: 203-837-9337

LEARNING DISABILITY SERVICES

Requests for the following/services accommodations will be evaluated individually based on appropriate and current documentation.

Allowed in exams
 Calculator: Yes
 Dictionary: No
 Computer: NR
 Spellchecker: NR
Extended test time: Yes
Scribes: Yes
Proctors: Yes
Oral exams: Yes
Note-takers: Yes

Distraction-reduced environment: Yes
Tape recording in class: Yes
Books on tape from RFBD: Yes
Taping of books not from RFBD: Yes
Accommodations for students with
 ADD: Yes
Reading machine: No
Other assistive technology: No
Priority registration: Yes

Added costs for services: Yes
LD specialists: Yes
Professional tutors: Yes
Peer tutors: Yes
Max. hours/wk. for services:
 Unlimited
How professors are notified of
 LD/ADD: By both student and director

GENERAL ADMISSIONS INFORMATION

Director of Admissions: William Hawkins, Enrollment Management Officer
Telephone: 203-837-9000

ENTRANCE REQUIREMENTS
Academic units required: 4 English, 3 math, 2 science (2 science lab), 2 foreign language, 1 social studies, 1 history. **Academic units recommended:** 3 foreign language. High school diploma is required and GED is accepted. TOEFL required of all international applicants, minimum paper TOEFL 550, minimum computer TOEFL 213.

Application deadline: May 1
Notification: Rolling
Average GPA: NR

Average SAT Math: 487
Average SAT Verbal: 491
Average ACT: NR

Graduated top 10% of class: 4%
Graduated top 25% of class: 18%
Graduated top 50% of class: 62%

COLLEGE GRADUATION REQUIREMENTS

Course waivers allowed: Yes
Course substitutions allowed: Yes
In what course: As required by the student's disability.

ADDITIONAL INFORMATION

Environment: The university is located on 315 acres, 60 miles from New York City.

Student Body:
 Undergrad enrollment: 4,587
 Women: 56%
 Men: 44%
 Percent out-of-state: 12%

Cost Information
 In-state tuition: $3,010
 Out-of-state tuition: $9,744
 Room & board: $7,085
Housing Information
 University housing: Yes
 Percent living on campus: 37%

Greek System
 Fraternity: Yes
 Sorority: Yes
Athletics: NCAA Division III

UNIVERSITY OF DELAWARE

Admissions Office, 116 Hullihen Hall, Newark, DE 19716-6210
Phone: 302-831-8123 • Fax: 302-831-6905
E-mail: admissions@udel.edu • Web: www.udel.edu
Support: CS• Institution type: 4-year public

LEARNING DISABILITY PROGRAM AND SERVICES

The University of Delaware is committed to providing reasonable and timely academic accommodations for students with disabilities. The Academic Services Center (ASC) focuses primarily on serving students with learning disabilities and ADD. ASC is not a program but rather a center that provides services and accommodations to help students. ASC works jointly with other offices. The staff has been trained to understand LD and ADD and is available to assist faculty in providing accommodations for students whose documentation is complete. Independent, highly motivated students will do well at the university.

LD/ADD ADMISSIONS INFORMATION

College entrance tests required: Yes
Interview recommended: No
Essay recommended: Yes
Documentation required for LD: Yes
Documentation required for ADD: Yes
Submitted to: Academic Services
Special Ed. HS coursework accepted: Yes

Specific course requirements of all applicants: Yes
Separate application required for program services: NR
# of LD applications submitted each year: NR
# of LD applications accepted yearly: NR
Total # of students receiving LD services: 450–550
Acceptance into program means acceptance into college: Student must be admitted and enrolled in the university first and then reviewed for LD services.

ADMISSIONS

Students must be otherwise qualified for university admissions, which means they must meet university and college admissions criteria. In other words, students are admitted on the basis of their abilities. General admission requirements include essays, letters of recommendation, 4 years English, 2 years math (4 recommended), 3 years science, 2 years social studies (4 recommended), 2 years foreign language (4 recommended) and 2 electives. Once admitted, students are encouraged to self-disclose their individual disability by returning a form they receive during orientation, or by making an appointment to discuss their needs with an ASC staff member. Documentation sent as part of the admissions application does not constitute official notification to the university that the student is seeking services. The admissions office requests documentation sent directly from the psychologist or medical doctor.

ADDITIONAL INFORMATION

With appropriate documentation, students with LD could be eligible for some of the following services: the use of calculators, computer, and spell check in exams; extended time on tests; proctors; oral exams; note-takers; distraction-free environment for tests; tape recorder in class; books on tape; and priority registration. There are one-credit courses offered through the School of Education that assist students in their study skills, critical thinking, and problem Solving. In addition the ASC offers College Intensive Literacy for students who need additional assistance. Students with ADD are provided assistance jointly by the ASC and the Center for Counseling and Student Development. All students have access to a Writing Center, Math Center and tutoring and study skills workshops in the Academic Services Center.

Support Services Contact Information

Learning Disability Program/Services: Academic Services Center/LD/ADD Services
Director: Lysbet J. Murray
  E-Mail: lysbet@udel.edu
  Telephone: 302-831-1639
  Fax: 302-831-4128

LEARNING DISABILITY SERVICES

Requests for the following services/accommodations will be evaluated individually based on appropriate and current documentation.

Allowed in exams
  Calculator: Yes
  Dictionary: No
  Computer: Yes
  Spellchecker: Yes
Extended test time: Yes
Scribes: No
Proctors: Yes
Oral exams: Yes
Note-takers: Yes

Distraction reduced environment: Yes
Tape recording in class: Yes
Books on tape from RFBD: Yes
Taping of books not from RFBD: Yes
Accommodations for students with
  ADD: Yes
Reading machine: Yes
Other assistive technology: Yes
Priority registration: Yes

Added costs for services: No
LD specialists: Yes
Professional tutors: No
Peer tutors: 40
Max. hours/wk. for services: Varies, students make appointments
How professors are notified of
  LD/ADD: By both student and director

GENERAL ADMISSIONS INFORMATION

Director of Admissions: Lou Hirsh
Telephone: 302-831-8123

ENTRANCE REQUIREMENTS

Academic units required: 4 English, 3 math, 3 science (2 science lab), 2 foreign language, 2 social studies, 2 history. **Academic units recommended:** 4 English, 4 math, 4 science (3 science lab), 4 foreign language, 2 social studies, 2 history, 2 academic electives. High school diploma is required and GED is accepted. ACT with Writing component required or SAT Reasoning test. TOEFL required of all international applicants, minimum paper TOEFL 550, minimum computer TOEFL 213.

Application deadline: 1/15
Notification: 3/15
Average GPA: 3.50

Average SAT Math: NR
Average SAT Verbal: NR
Average ACT: NR

Graduated top 10% of class: 38%
Graduated top 25% of class: 76%
Graduated top 50% of class: 97%

COLLEGE GRADUATION REQUIREMENTS

Course waivers allowed: No
Course substitutions allowed: Yes
In what course: Foreign language; the Educational Affairs Committee of the College of Arts and Sciences makes decisions on a case-by-case basis. Students are asked to attempt the class and work closely with a tutor before submitting a petition for a substitution.

ADDITIONAL INFORMATION

Environment: The 1,100-acre campus is in a small town 12 miles southwest of Wilmington and midway between Philadelphia and Baltimore.

Student Body:
  Undergrad enrollment: 16,023
  Women: 58%
  Men: 42%
  Percent out-of-state: 58%

Cost Information
  In-state tuition: $6,304
  Out-of-state tuition: $15,990
  Room & board: $6,458
Housing Information
  University housing: Yes
  Percent living on campus: 45%

Greek System
  Fraternity: Yes
  Sorority: Yes
Athletics: NCAA Division I

AMERICAN UNIVERSITY

4400 Massachusetts Avenue, NW, Washington, DC 20016-8001
Phone: 202-885-6000 • Fax: 202-885-1025
E-mail: admissions@american.edu • Web: www.american.edu
Support: SP• Institution type: 4-year private

LEARNING DISABILITY PROGRAM AND SERVICES

The focus of the Learning Services Program is to assist students with their transition from high school to college during their freshman year. The Learning Services Program is a mainstream program offering additional support in college writing and finite math. The Academic Support Center (ASC) provides services for students with learning disabilities. These services are provided to promote full participation in academic programs and other campus activities. Disability Support Services and the Academic Support Center have the specific responsibility for reviewing professionally prepared documentation of a disability, determining effective and reasonable modification for a disability, verifying a disability for faculty and other persons, and recommending course and learning accommodations on behalf of the university. Support continues to be available until graduation.

LD/ADD ADMISSIONS INFORMATION

College entrance tests required: Yes
Interview recommended: No
Essay recommended: Yes
Documentation required for LD: Psychoeducational
  evaluation, WAIS–III, WJ–III
Documentation required for ADD: A complete
  psychoeducational report
Submitted to: Academic Support Center
Special Ed. HS coursework accepted: N/A

Specific course requirements of all applicants: Yes
Separate application required for program services: Yes
# of LD applications submitted each year: 85–180
# of LD applications accepted yearly: 40–50
Total # of students receiving LD services: 300–350
**Acceptance into program means acceptance into
  college:** Student must be admitted and enrolled in the
  university first and then reviewed for LD services.

ADMISSIONS

Students with LD must be admitted to the university and then to the Learning Services Program. Students who wish to have program staff consult with admissions about their LD during the admissions process must submit a Supplemental Application to the Learning Services program that requires documentation of the LD. Students using a Common Application should indicate interest in the Program on their application. Special education courses taken in high school may be accepted if they meet the criteria for the Carnegie Units. The academic credentials of successful applicants with LD fall within the range of regular admissions criteria; the mean GPA is 2.9 for LD admits and 3.2 for regularly admitted students; ACT ranges from 24–29 for regular admits and 24–28 for LD admits; SAT ranges from 1110–1270 for regular admits and 1131 for LD admits. American Sign Language is an acceptable substitution for foreign language. The admissions decision is made by a special admissions committee and is based on the high school record, recommendations, and all pertinent diagnostic reports. For selected students, admission to the university will be contingent upon enrollment in the Learning Services Program; for others, the program will be optional though strongly recommended. Conditional admission is offered to some students through the Excell Program.

ADDITIONAL INFORMATION

Students have an academic advisor experienced in advising students with LD. All entering freshmen have the same requirements, including college writing (a section is reserved for students in the program) and college reading. Students meet weekly with a learning specialist for individual tutorial sessions that help them further develop college-level reading, writing, and study strategies. Peer tutors assist with course content tutoring. Individual and group counseling is offered through Psychological Services. The staff of the program will consult professors with students' written permission. All modifications are based upon diagnostic testing and educational recommendations, and students are held to the same academic standards but may meet these standards through non-traditional means. As sophomores, basic skills tutorial sessions are offered on an as-needed basis.

Support Services Contact Information

Learning Disability Program/Services: Academic Support Center
Director: Kathy Schwartz
 E-Mail: kschwar@american.edu
 Telephone: 202-885-3360
 Fax: 202-885-1042

LEARNING DISABILITY SERVICES

Requests for the following services/accommodations will be evaluated individually based on appropriate and current documentation.

Allowed in exams
 Calculator: Yes
 Dictionary: Yes
 Computer: Yes
 Spellchecker: Yes
Extended test time: Yes
Scribes: Yes
Proctors: Yes
Oral exams: Yes
Note-takers: Yes

Distraction reduced environment: Yes
Tape recording in class: Yes
Books on tape from RFBD: Yes
Taping of books not from RFBD: Yes
**Accommodations for students with
 ADD:** Yes
Reading machine: Yes
Other assistive technology: Yes
Priority registration: Yes

Added costs for services: Yes
LD specialists: Yes
Professional tutors: No
Peer tutors: 20–40
Max. hours/wk. for services:
 Unlimited
**How professors are notified of
 LD/ADD:** By both student and director

GENERAL ADMISSIONS INFORMATION

Director of Admissions: Dr. Sharon M. Alston (Director, Undergraduate Admissions)
Telephone: 202-885-6000

ENTRANCE REQUIREMENTS

Academic units required: 4 English, 3 math, 2 science (2 science lab), 2 foreign language, 2 social studies, 3 academic electives. **Academic units recommended:** 4 English, 4 math, 4 science, 3 foreign language, 4 social studies, 1 academic elective. High school diploma is required and GED is accepted. ACT with Writing component required or SAT Reasoning test. TOEFL required of all international applicants, minimum paper TOEFL 550, minimum computer TOEFL 213.

Application deadline: 1/15
Notification: 4/1
Average GPA: 3.47

Average SAT Math: 603
Average SAT Verbal: 620
Average ACT: 27

Graduated top 10% of class: 44%
Graduated top 25% of class: 82%
Graduated top 50% of class: 97%

COLLEGE GRADUATION REQUIREMENTS

Course waivers allowed: No
Course substitutions allowed: No
In what course: N/A

ADDITIONAL INFORMATION

Environment: The university is located on 77 acres, close to the Capitol in Washington, DC.

Student Body:
 Undergrad enrollment: 5,731
 Women: 62%
 Men: 38%
 Percent out-of-state: 95%

Cost Information
 Tuition: $27,552
 Room & board: $10,700
Housing Information
 University housing: Yes
 Percent living on campus: 68%

Greek System
 Fraternity: Yes
 Sorority: Yes
Athletics: NCAA Division I

American University

THE CATHOLIC U. OF AMERICA

620 Michigan Avenue, Northeast, Washington, DC 20064
Phone: 202-319-5305 • Fax: 202-319-6533
E-mail: cua-admissions@cua.edu • Web: www.cua.edu
Support: CS • Institution type: 4-year private

LEARNING DISABILITY PROGRAM AND SERVICES

The university does not have a specially designated program for students with learning disabilities, but offers comprehensive support services and accommodations. The university has an advisory committee on students with LD composed of faculty members and administrators with expertise in a variety of specialized areas. The committee assists students with an LD that might preclude their full participation in university academic activities. The goals of the services are to facilitate academic success, support personal growth, and encourage self-advocacy. Students with LD are required to meet the same academic standards as other students at the university. Students must submit current diagnostic verification of the LD. To initiate services and accommodations students make an appointment with an advisor to students with LD as soon as possible after arrival on campus. A disabilities advisor will consult with students to determine appropriate accommodations and coordinate services. Students with LD/ADD that impairs their ability to acquire a foreign language may apply to substitute for the requirement. The decision to grant a substitution is based on an individual's learning history, documentation of a disability that impairs foreign language acquisition, and future educational goals.

LD/ADD ADMISSIONS INFORMATION

College entrance tests required: Yes
Interview recommended: No
Essay recommended: Yes
Documentation required for LD: Psychoeducational evaluation
Documentation required for ADD: Yes
Submitted to: Disability Support Services and Admissions
Special Ed. HS coursework accepted: Yes

Specific course requirements of all applicants: Yes
Separate application required for program services: Yes
# of LD applications submitted each year: No
# of LD applications accepted yearly: No
Total # of students receiving LD services: 140
Acceptance into program means acceptance into college: Student must be admitted and enrolled in the university first and then request services.

ADMISSIONS

Students with LD may apply for admission through the regular admission procedures or may request a special admissions review. If an otherwise intellectually qualified applicant feels that there are weaknesses in admissions material due to a preexisting learning disability and voluntarily informs the Office of Admissions, the application will be referred to a Special Admissions Committee for review. The review process will be used to provide a fuller assessment of the total student than regular admissions material might provide. Applicants wishing to be considered under the special admissions policy for students with LD/ADD should submit the following along with regular admissions requirements: diagnostic reports certifying the LD and the ability to do college work; three teacher evaluations from the most recent teachers of math, English, and one other subject; a supervised handwritten writing sample, on a topic of the applicant's choice; and an optional interview. These optional procedures are intended to enhance each applicant's opportunity for admission to the university and will not be used to discriminate against the individual.

ADDITIONAL INFORMATION

Services include advocacy; advising and referral to tutoring or study skills; faculty consultation and support; assistance in arranging note-takers and recorded texts; support and positive feedback; tape recording; extended time on tests; priority registration; and reasonable extension of deadlines on written papers. The department of Academic Tutoring and Learning Assistance Services offers individual and group tutoring, "study strategies," writing skills assistance, counseling, and an ADD/LD support group. Students with LD that impairs the ability to learn a foreign language (two semesters required for graduation) may apply for a substitution by providing LD documentation; completing basic language testing; writing a letter formally requesting the substitution; and meeting with an LD advisor. If granted a foreign language substitution, students meet with the Associate Dean of Arts and Sciences to determine alternate courses.

Support Services Contact Information

Learning Disability Program/Services: Disability Support Services
Director: Bonnie McClellan
  E-Mail: disabilityservices@cua.edu
  Telephone: 202-319-5211 tty 202-299-2899
  Fax: 202-319-5126

LEARNING DISABILITY SERVICES

Requests for the following services/accommodations will be evaluated individually based on appropriate and current documentation.

Allowed in exams
  Calculator: Yes
  Dictionary: Yes
  Computer: Yes
  Spellchecker: Yes
Extended test time: Yes
Scribes: Yes
Proctors: Yes
Oral exams: Yes
Note-takers: Yes

Distraction reduced environment: Yes
Tape recording in class: Yes
Books on tape from RFBD: Yes
Taping of books not from RFBD: Yes
Accommodations for students with
  ADD: Yes
Reading machine: Yes
Other assistive technology: Yes
Priority registration: Yes

Added costs for services: No
LD specialists: Yes
Professional tutors: 1
Peer tutors: 55–100
Max. hours/wk. for services: 3
How professors are notified of
  LD/ADD: By student

GENERAL ADMISSIONS INFORMATION

Director of Admissions: Christine Mica
Telephone: 202-319-5305

ENTRANCE REQUIREMENTS

Academic units recommended: 4 English, 3 math, 3 science (1 science lab), 2 foreign language, 4 social studies, 1 history. High school diploma is required and GED is not accepted. ACT with Writing component required. TOEFL required of all international applicants, minimum paper TOEFL 560, minimum computer TOEFL 220.

Application deadline: 2/1
Notification: 3/1
Average GPA: 3.37

Average SAT Math: 569
Average SAT Verbal: 583
Average ACT: 24

Graduated top 10% of class: 22%
Graduated top 25% of class: 57%
Graduated top 50% of class: 88%

COLLEGE GRADUATION REQUIREMENTS

Course waivers allowed: N/A
Course substitutions allowed: Yes
In what course: Foreign language

ADDITIONAL INFORMATION

Environment: The university is situated in northeast Washington, DC, within minutes of the capitol.

Student Body:
  Undergrad enrollment: 2,871
  Women: 56%
  Men: 44%
  Percent out-of-state: 93%

Cost Information
  Tuition: $24,800
  Room & board: $9,838
Housing Information
  University housing: Yes
  Percent living on campus: 68%

Greek System
  Fraternity: Yes
  Sorority: Yes
Athletics: NCAA Division III

The Catholic University of America

GEORGE WASHINGTON UNIVERSITY

2121 I Street NW, Suite 201, Washington, DC 20052
Phone: 202-994-6040 • Fax: 202-994-0325
E-mail: gwadm@gwu.edu • Web: www.gwu.edu
Support: CS• Institution type: 4-year private

LEARNING DISABILITY PROGRAM AND SERVICES

Disability Support Services (DSS) was established to provide support to disabled students so that they might participate fully in university life, derive the greatest benefit from their educational experiences, and achieve maximum personal success. There is no LD program at GW with a fee for service. Students with LD/ADD are served through DSS. Services are designed to eliminate competitive disadvantages in an academic environment while preserving academic integrity. The staff is committed to providing student-centered services that meet the individual needs of each student. The ultimate goal of DSS is to assist students with disabilities as they gain knowledge to recognize strengths, accommodate differences, and become strong self-advocates. Staff are available to discuss issues such as courseload, learning strategies, academic accommodations, and petitions for course waivers or substitutions. DSS offers individual assistance in addressing needs not provided through routine services. Students with LD must provide the following: documentation, including a comprehensive diagnostic interview, psychoeducational evaluation, and a treatment plan; include test scores and an interpretation of overall intelligence, information processing, executive functioning, spatial ability, memory, motor ability, achievement skills, reading, writing and math; and a specific diagnosis and description of the student's functional limitations in an educational setting.

LD/ADD ADMISSIONS INFORMATION

College entrance tests required: Yes
Interview recommended: No
Essay recommended: Yes
Documentation required for LD: Psychoeducational evaluation, Eligibility guidelines available on our website, www.gwu.edu/~dss
Documentation required for ADD: Yes
Special Ed. HS coursework accepted: No

Specific course requirements of all applicants: Yes
Separate application required for program services: No
# of LD applications submitted each year: NR
# of LD applications accepted yearly: NR
Total # of students receiving LD services: 301
Acceptance into program means acceptance into college: Student must be admitted and enrolled in the university and then reviewed for services with Disability Support Services.

ADMISSIONS

GWU does not discriminate on the basis of disability in the recruitment and admission of students. There are no separate admissions procedures or criteria for disabled students. The minimal course requirements include 2 years math (prefer 4), 4 years English, 2 years foreign language (prefer 4), 2–3 years social sciences (prefer 4), and 2–3 years science (prefer 4). The score range for the ACT is 25–30 or SAT 1160–1320. SAT Subject tests are optional. Since there is no automatic referral from Admissions or other campus offices, students are encouraged to contact DSS directly prior to or upon admission.

ADDITIONAL INFORMATION

Students need to make a specific request for services or accommodations. Based upon the documentation, the director of DSS authorizes the needed academic adjustments. DSS provides services without charge, including advocacy, readers, scribes, test proctors, LD advising, and assistance with registration and note-taking. Students may be referred for additional services, including diagnostic testing, tutors, and specialized non-credit courses that are available on a fee basis. There is a learning disabilities support group that meets twice throughout the academic year. This group focuses on issues important to students with LD and/or ADD. In addition to providing an opportunity for peer support, the group discusses topics ranging from study strategies, note-taking, and the planning of papers, to social issues facing the GW student with LD/ADD. Also, there is a Disability Resource Association, which is a student organization that has a Speakers Bureau and offers support groups.

Support Services Contact Information

Learning Disability Program/Services: LD Program/Services: Disability Support Services
Director: Christy Willis
 E-Mail: cwillis@gwu.edu
 Telephone: 202-994-8250
 Fax: 202-994-7610

LEARNING DISABILITY SERVICES

Requests for the following services/accommodations will be evaluated individually based on appropriate and current documentation.

Allowed in exams
 Calculator: Yes
 Dictionary: Yes
 Computer: Yes
 Spellchecker: Yes
 Extended test time: Yes
 Scribes: Yes
 Proctors: Yes
 Oral exams: No
 Note-takers: Yes

Distraction reduced environment: Yes
Tape recording in class: Yes
Books on tape from RFBD: Yes
Taping of books not from RFBD: Yes
Accommodations for students with
 ADD: Yes
Reading machine: Yes
Other assistive technology: Yes
Priority registration: Yes

Added costs for services: No
LD specialists: Yes
Professional tutors: Yes
Peer tutors: Yes
Max. hours/wk. for services:
 Unlimited
How professors are notified of
 LD/ADD: By both student and director

GENERAL ADMISSIONS INFORMATION

Director of Admissions: Kathryn Napper
Telephone: 202-994-6040

ENTRANCE REQUIREMENTS
Academic units required: 4 English, 2 math, 2 science (1 science lab), 2 foreign language, 2 social studies.
Academic units recommended: 4 English, 4 math, 4 science, 4 foreign language, 4 social studies. High school diploma is required and GED is not accepted. TOEFL required of all international applicants, minimum paper TOEFL 550, minimum computer TOEFL 300.

Application deadline: 1/15
Notification: 3/15
Average GPA: A–/B+

Average SAT Math: 620
Average SAT Verbal: 620
Average ACT: 26

Graduated top 10% of class: 58%
Graduated top 25% of class: 87%
Graduated top 50% of class: 99%

COLLEGE GRADUATION REQUIREMENTS

Course waivers allowed: No
Course substitutions allowed: Yes
In what course: Determination is made on a case by case basis primarily in the areas of math and foreign language

ADDITIONAL INFORMATION

Environment: The university has an urban campus 3 blocks from the White House.
Student Body:
 Undergrad enrollment: 9,953
 Women: 57%
 Men: 43%
 Percent out-of-state: 98%

Cost Information
 Tuition: $30,790
 Room & board: $10,210
Housing Information
 University housing: Yes
 Percent living on campus: 68%

Greek System
 Fraternity: Yes
 Sorority: Yes
 Athletics: NCAA Division I

GEORGETOWN UNIVERSITY

37th and O Streets, NW, 103 White-Gravenor, Washington, DC 20057
Phone: 202-687-3600 • Fax: 202-687-5084
E-mail: guadmiss@georgetown.edu • Web: www.georgetown.edu
Support: CS • Institution: 4-year private

LEARNING DISABILITY PROGRAM AND SERVICES

Georgetown University will not discriminate against or deny access to any otherwise qualified student with a disability. Learning Services requires that all students with learning disabilities provide documentation. Once the disability is on record the university will provide reasonable accommodations. Learning Services will advise students about their college coursework and provide study skill assistance on the basis of availability.

LD/ADD ADMISSIONS INFORMATION

College entrance tests required: Yes
Interview recommended: No
Essay recommended: No
Documentation required for LD: Pyschoeducational evaluation
Documentation required for ADD: Yes
Special Ed. HS coursework accepted: No

Specific course requirements of all applicants: Yes
Separate application required for program services: No
# of LD applications submitted each year: NR
# of LD applications accepted yearly: NR
Total # of students receiving LD services: NR
Acceptance into program means acceptance into college: There is no program. Student must be admitted and enrolled in the university first and then reviewed for LD services.

ADMISSIONS

Students with learning disabilities are admitted under the same competitive standards used for all students. Services are offered to enrolled students. While the Committee on Admissions is most interested in the quality of a student's work, general promise, and seriousness of purpose, it is recommended that students take 4 years English, 4 years math, 4 years science (1 science lab recommended) , 4 years foreign language and 4 social studies. Georgetown accepts the ACT in lieu of the SAT. Students who submit scores from the ACT need not take the optional writing section for admissions consideration at Georgetown. However, all applicants, whether they submit scores from the SAT or ACT, should submit scores from 3 SAT Subject Tests.

ADDITIONAL INFORMATION

Georgetown uses AHEAD (Association for Higher Education and Disability) guidelines for documentation of LD/ADD. Testing must be comprehensive and address the following areas: aptitude; achievement, including current levels of functioning in reading, math, and written language; and information processing. Testing must be current within the last three years. There must be clear and specific evidence and identification of a LD. Actual test scores must be provided including interpretation of results. Professionals conducting assessment and rendering diagnoses of LD must be qualified. Test used to document eligibility must be technically sound and standardized for use with an adult population. A written summary of the student's relevant educational, medical, and family histories that relate to the LD must be included. Recommendations for accommodations should be based on objective evidence of a substantial limitation to learning and should establish rationale for any accommodation recommended.

Support Services Contact Information

Learning Disability Program/Services: Disability Support Services/Learning Services
Director: Marcia Fulk
  Telephone: 202-687-6985
  Fax: 202-687-6158

LEARNING DISABILITY SERVICES

Requests for the following services/accommodations will be evaluated individually based on appropriate and current documentation.

Allowed in exams
  Calculator: Yes
  Dictionary: Y/N
  Computer: Yes
  Spellchecker: Yes
Extended test time: Yes
Scribes: Yes
Proctors: Yes
Oral exams: Yes
Note-takers: Yes

Distraction reduced environment: Yes
Tape recording in class: Yes
Books on tape from RFBD: Yes
Taping of books not from RFBD: Yes
Accommodations for students with
  ADD: Yes
Reading machine: No
Other assistive technology: Yes
Priority registration: Yes

Added costs for services: No
LD specialists: Yes
Professional tutors: No
Peer tutors: No
Max. hours/wk. for services: N/A
How professors are notified of
  LD/ADD: By both student and director

GENERAL ADMISSIONS INFORMATION

Director of Admissions: Charles A. Deacon
Telephone: 202-687-3600

ENTRANCE REQUIREMENTS

Academic units required: 4 English, 2 math, 2 science, 2 foreign language, 2 social studies, 2 history. **Academic units recommended:** 4 English, 4 math, 4 science (1 science lab), 4 foreign language, 4 social studies. High school diploma is required and GED is accepted. ACT without Writing component accepted. 3 SAT Subject Tests required with ACT or SAT. TOEFL required of all international applicants, minimum paper TOEFL 600, minimum computer TOEFL 250.

Application deadline: 1/10
Notification: 4/1
Average GPA: NR

Average SAT Math: NR
Average SAT Verbal: NR
Average ACT: NR

Graduated top 10% of class: 90%
Graduated top 25% of class: 98%
Graduated top 50% of class: 100%

COLLEGE GRADUATION REQUIREMENTS

Course waivers allowed: No
Course substitutions allowed: Yes
In what course: Foreign language can be substituted if not required for major.

ADDITIONAL INFORMATION

Environment: The university is located on 110 acres, 1.5 miles north of downtown Washington, DC.

Student Body:
  Undergrad enrollment: 6,282
  Women: 54%
  Men: 46%
  Percent out-of-state: 98%

Cost Information
  Tuition: $29,808
  Room & board: $10,554
Housing Information
  University housing: Yes
  Percent living on campus: 78%

Greek System
  Fraternity: No
  Sorority: No
Athletics: NCAA Division I

BARRY UNIVERSITY

11300 North East Second Avenue, Miami Shores, FL 33161-6695
Phone: 305-899-3100 • Fax: 305-899-2971
E-mail: Des-forms@mail.barry.edu • Web: www.barry.edu
Support: SP• Institution type: 4-year private

LEARNING DISABILITY PROGRAM AND SERVICES

Barry University offers a special program for students with LD. The Clinical Center for Advanced Learning Program (CCAL) is a comprehensive, intensive, highly structured, and individualized approach to assisting students with LD throughout their college careers. It is designed to move students gradually toward increasing self-direction in academic, personal, and career activities. This program affirms Barry University's commitment to expand college opportunities to students with LD and to provide the specialized services that can enhance college success. To apply to the CCAL Program students must complete and return to CCAL the general Barry application for admission and the CCAL Application; write a 1–2 page personal statement on how the student would benefit from the CCAL Program; have a personal interview at the CCAL; sign the Informed Consent Form and present this form to their high school in order for documentation to be released; forward Psychoeducational Evaluation Report including the WAIS–R, achievement tests, and Information processing testing; and provide a copy of the most recent IEP, high school transcript, and a letter of recommendation from a school counselor or LD specialist. It is important for students with LD to understand the need for a commitment to working with the CCAL Program to achieve success at college.

LD/ADD ADMISSIONS INFORMATION

College entrance tests required: Yes
Interview recommended: Yes
Essay recommended: Yes
Documentation required for LD: Psychoeducational evaluation
Documentation required for ADD: Yes
Submitted to: Center for Advanced Learning
Special Ed. HS coursework accepted: Yes

Specific course requirements of all applicants: Yes
Separate application required for program services: No
# of LD applications submitted each year: 125
# of LD applications accepted yearly: 25
Total # of students receiving LD services: 45
Acceptance into program means acceptance into college: Student must be admitted and enrolled in the university first and then request services from CCAL.

ADMISSIONS

Students with learning disabilities must meet the regular admission criteria for the university: 2.0 GPA; ACT of 17 or above or SAT of 800 or above; 4 years English, 3–4 years math, 3 years natural science, and 3–4 years social science. However, there is a process of individual review by learning disability professionals for those students who have a diagnosed disability and who do not meet the general admission criteria. These students must have an interview and provide appropriate and current LD documentation. An essay is required for admission into the LD Program. Students admitted to the CCAL Program will be expected to meet all requirements established for them and those of the specific university program in which they enroll.

ADDITIONAL INFORMATION

The Clinical Center for Advanced Learning (CCAL) Program includes a full range of professionally managed and intensive support services that includes the following: individual diagnostic evaluation allowing for development of a personalized educational plan; intensive scheduled classes to improve math, reading, and written and oral communication skills; individual and small-group, subject-area tutoring; instruction in learning and study strategies based on individual needs; academic advising; assistance in developing interpersonal skills; individual and small-group personal, academic, and career counseling; assistance in obtaining study aids; computer access; special test administration services; advocacy with faculty; and optional summer college transition program. Additionally, all students have access to math labs, writing centers, reading clinics, and educational seminars. All instructional staff hold advanced degrees in their area of specialization. Services are available for both undergraduate and graduate students.

Support Services Contact Information

Learning Disability Program/Services: Clinical Center for Advanced Learning
Director: Vivian Castro
Telephone: 305-899-3461
Fax: 305-899-3778

LEARNING DISABILITY SERVICES

Requests for the following services/accommodations will be evaluated individually based on appropriate and current documentation.

Allowed in exams
  Calculator: Yes
  Dictionary: Yes
  Computer: Yes
  Spellchecker: Yes
Extended test time: Yes
Scribes: Yes
Proctors: Yes
Oral exams: Yes
Note-takers: Yes

Distraction reduced environment: Yes
Tape recording in class: Yes
Books on tape from RFBD: Yes
Taping of books not from RFBD: Yes
Accommodations for students with
  ADD: Yes
Reading machine: Yes
Other assistive technology: Yes
Priority registration: No

Added costs for services: Yes
LD specialists: Yes
Professional tutors: 13
Peer tutors: No
Max. hours/wk. for services:
  Unlimited
How professors are notified of
  LD/ADD: By both student and director

GENERAL ADMISSIONS INFORMATION

Director of Admissions: Marcia Nance
Telephone: 305-899-3100

ENTRANCE REQUIREMENTS

Academic units recommended: 4 English, 3 math, 3 science, 3 social studies. High school diploma is required and GED is accepted. ACT with or without Writing component accepted. TOEFL required of all international applicants, minimum paper TOEFL 550, minimum computer TOEFL 213.

Application deadline: Rolling
Notification: Rolling
Average GPA: 2.97

Average SAT Math: NR
Average SAT Verbal: NR
Average ACT: NR

Graduated top 10% of class: NR
Graduated top 25% of class: NR
Graduated top 50% of class: 100%

COLLEGE GRADUATION REQUIREMENTS

Course waivers allowed: No
Course substitutions allowed: No
In what course: N/A

ADDITIONAL INFORMATION

Environment: The university is located 7 miles from Miami.

Student Body:
  Undergrad enrollment: 5,652
  Women: 68%
  Men: 32%
  Percent out-of-state: 15%

Cost Information
  Tuition: $21,350
  Room & board: $7,400
Housing Information
  University housing: Yes
  Percent living on campus: 17%

Greek System
  Fraternity: Yes
  Sorority: Yes
Athletics: NCAA Division II

BEACON COLLEGE

105 East Main Street, Leesburg, FL 34748
Phone: 352-787-7249 • Fax: 352-787-0721
E-mail: admissions@beaconcollege.edu • Web: www.beaconcollege.edu
Support: SP • Institution: 4-year private

LEARNING DISABILITY PROGRAM AND SERVICES

The philosophy of Beacon College is to offer LD/ADD students academic programs supplemented by appropriate accommodations and support services that will help them prepare for meaningful participation in society. The purpose of Beacon College is to create a campus community that facilitates academic and personal success. The mission of Beacon College is to offer academic degree programs to students with learning disabilities. To accomplish this, the College provides associate of arts (AA) and bachelor of arts (BA) programs in Human Services and Liberal Studies. The Human Services programs provide a practical experience in the professional fields associated with public and community services. The Liberal Studies program provides a broad-based liberal arts education for students seeking intellectual growth and personal change. Liberal Studies exposes students to a variety of subjects designed to establish a basis for effective lifelong learning and attainment of personal goals. Beacon serves students with language-based learning disabilities, math disabilities, ADD/ADD, auditory and visual processing differences, expressive/receptive language deficits, and reading/writing disabilities.

LD/ADD ADMISSIONS INFORMATION

College entrance tests required: No
Interview recommended: Yes
Essay recommended: Yes
Documentation required for LD: Psychoeduactional evaluation, WAIS–R
Documentation required for ADD: Yes
Submitted to: Admissions
Special Ed. HS coursework accepted: Yes

Specific course requirements of all applicants: Yes
Separate application required for program services: No
# of LD applications submitted each year: 87
# of LD applications accepted yearly: 47
Total # of students receiving LD services: 97
Acceptance into program means acceptance into
  college: Students admitted directly into the college and the program simultaneously.

ADMISSIONS

Applicants must submit current (within two years) academic reports and test scores, recent psychoeducational evaluations documenting a learning disability, and records that may help clarify learning problems. Students must also submit a high school transcript, personal statements, and three recommendation forms. All applicants must have a high school diploma or the GED. Each applicant must have an interview prior to an admission decision being made. There are no specific high school courses required for admission, and courses taken in a special education curriculum are accepted. The college does not require either the ACT or SAT. The admission decision is made by Admissions Committee. Beacon may admit students on a provisional basis.

ADDITIONAL INFORMATION

Beacon College is a growing program that serves college students with documented learning disabilities who each have the ability, desire, and perseverance to earn either an AA or BA degree. Some students are recent high school graduates, while others are older students who transfer from other colleges or who meet after being in the workforce. Beacon serves a culturally diverse group of men and women from 22 different states. Small class size, at an average of 10 students per class, helps to meet the needs of individual students. Beacon's Academic Mentoring Program guides students with a focus on self-awareness, time management/organization skills and strategies for academic success. The field placement program assists students with goal setting, career exploration and work experience. Students gain life skills through living within the Leesburg community in apartments leased by the college. Beacon students graduate with a college academic degree and the life skills to live independently. In addition to the ability to set personal goals, graduates are also prepared to seek gainful employment or explore additional academic or vocational training.

Support Services Contact Information

Learning Disability Program/Services: Beacon College
Director: Deborah Brodbeck, President
  E-Mail: admissions@beaconcollege.edu
  Telephone: 352-787-7660
  Fax: 352-787-0721
Contact Person: Carolyn A. Scott, Director of Admissions
  E-Mail: cscott@beaconcollege.edu
  Telephone: 352-315-9269
  Fax: 352-787-0721

LEARNING DISABILITY SERVICES

Requests for the following services/accommodations will be evaluated individually based on appropriate and current documentation.

Allowed in exams
  Calculator: Yes
  Dictionary: Yes
  Computer: Yes
  Spellchecker: Yes
Extended test time: Yes
Scribes: Yes
Proctors: Yes
Oral exams: Yes
Note-takers: Yes

Distraction reduced environment: Yes
Tape recording in class: Yes
Books on tape from RFBD: Yes
Taping of books not from RFBD: Yes
**Accommodations for students with
  ADD:** Yes
Reading machine: Yes
Other assistive technology: Yes
Priority registration: N/A

Added costs for services: No
LD specialists: Yes
Professional tutors: 5–6
Peer tutors: NR
Max. hours/wk. for services:
  Unlimited
**How professors are notified of
  LD/ADD:** By both student and director

GENERAL ADMISSIONS INFORMATION

Director of Admissions: Carolyn A. Scott
Telephone: 352-315-92

ENTRANCE REQUIREMENTS

Academic units required: 4 English, 1 math, 1 science, 1 social studies, 2 history, 3 academic electives,   High school diploma is required and GED is accepted. ACT with or without Writing component accepted.

Application deadline: 8/20
Notification: Rolling
Average GPA: NR

Average SAT Math: NR
Average SAT Verbal: NR
Average ACT: NR

Graduated top 10% of class: NR
Graduated top 25% of class: NR
Graduated top 50% of class: NR

COLLEGE GRADUATION REQUIREMENTS

Course waivers allowed: Yes
Course substitutions allowed: Yes
In what course: Math

ADDITIONAL INFORMATION

Environment: The college is located in the city of Leesburg, 1 hour from Orlando.

Student Body:
  Undergrad enrollment: 97
  Women: 41%
  Men: 59%
  Percent out-of-state: 85%

Cost Information
  Tuition: $21,700
  Room & board: $6,860
Housing Information
  University housing: Yes
  Percent living on campus: 98%

Greek System
  Fraternity: No
  Sorority: No
Athletics: Individual Sports

FLORIDA A&M UNIVERSITY

Suite G-9, Foote-Hilyer Administration Center, Tallahassee, FL 32307
Phone: 850-599-3796 • Fax: 850-599-3069
E-mail: adm@famu.edu • Web: www.famu.edu
Support: SP • Institution: 4-year public

LEARNING DISABILITY PROGRAM AND SERVICES

Florida A&M offers an education for students with LD, and meets the challenge consistent with the objective indicated by the Learning Development and Evaluation Center (LDEC) club name, "Excellence Through Caring." The goals of the LDEC are threefold: first, students with specific learning disabilities can successfully pursue college level studies with a reasonable level of expectation for degree success; second, preparation for college level studies for students with specific learning disabilities should begin early; and third, postsecondary students should actively engage in developmental learning. The need for life-long learning is evident in the ever-changing society and for the learning disabled person is mandatory for continued success. Tutoring for developmental learning is a major component. The program does not offer "blanket" accommodations, but services offered are very comprehensive, such as preparation classes for tests, adapted courses, opportunities for test retakes, alternative courses, and academic activities structured according to students' diagnostic evaluation. A reduced course load is considered a viable option to maintaining an acceptable GPA. The LDEC is a multifaceted program providing psychoeducational evaluation, personalized prescription, and comprehensive support services.

LD/ADD ADMISSIONS INFORMATION

College entrance tests required: Yes
Interview recommended: Yes
Essay recommended: Yes
Documentation required for LD: Psychoeducational evaluation no more than 3 years old
Documentation required for ADD: Yes
Submitted to: LDEC
Special Ed. HS coursework accepted: No

Specific course requirements of all applicants: Yes
Separate application required for program services: Yes
# of LD applications submitted each year: 40-50
# of LD applications accepted yearly: 20-25
Total # of students receiving LD services: 275
Acceptance into program means acceptance into college: Students are admitted directly into LDEC and attend the summer LD program as part of special admissions to the university.

ADMISSIONS

Acceptance into the LDEC does not ensure admission to the university. If students with learning disabilities apply and are rejected, they may ask for special admission consideration and send verifying information of a learning disability. The Office of Admissions gives all information to the LDEC director for a recommendation for admission to the university based upon acceptance into the LDEC program. Applicants must have a regular high school diploma, take the ACT/SAT, have a recent psychoeducational evaluation, and attend a summer program. Most students who have learning disabilities and who seek admission through the LDEC enter Florida A&M through the special admission process. ACT scores should be 12 or higher. The required GPA is 1.7 or above.

ADDITIONAL INFORMATION

Specific course offerings in reading, study skills, English, and math; additional class meetings and assignments to meet the individual needs of the students are available. Students must register for reading and student life-skills courses each semester until the student and program staff feel that optimal learning development skills have been reached. When appropriate, students may have a peer tutor attend classes and take notes (student and tutor will exchange notes in the LDEC) or the peer tutor may only need to help the student organize notes from a taped lecture. LDEC offers a 2-week Summer Transition Program (required for incoming students with LD) to students entering 11th or 12th grade or recent graduates from high school. This program provides students a chance to focus on certain skills such as memory, technology, or a particular academic area. Mastery of the College Study Skills Institute provides a firm foundation for students with learning disabilities to enhance success in college and their future employment.

Support Services Contact Information

Learning Disability Program/Services: Learning Development and Evaluation Center (LDEC)
Director: Dr. Sharon M. Wooten
  E-Mail: sharon.wooten@famu.edu
  Telephone: 850-599-8474
  Fax: 850-561-2513
Contact Person: Ms. Donna C. Shell/Ms. LaCoadia Harrell
  Telephone: 850-599-3180

LEARNING DISABILITY SERVICES

Requests for the following services/accommodations will be evaluated individually based on appropriate and current documentation.

Allowed in exams
  Calculator: Yes
  Dictionary: Yes
  Computer: Yes
  Spellchecker: Yes
Extended test time: Yes
Scribes: Yes
Proctors: Yes
Oral exams: Yes
Note-takers: Yes

Distraction reduced environment: Yes
Tape recording in class: Yes
Books on tape from RFBD: Yes
Taping of books not from RFBD: Yes
**Accommodations for students with
  ADD:** Yes
Reading machine: Yes
Other assistive technology: Yes
Priority registration: No

Added costs for services: Yes
LD specialists: Yes
Professional tutors: Yes
Peer tutors: 10
Max. hours/wk. for services: 45
**How professors are notified of
  LD/ADD:** By both student and director

GENERAL ADMISSIONS INFORMATION

Director of Admissions: Mitchie Stewart
Telephone: 850-599-3888

ENTRANCE REQUIREMENTS

Academic units required: 4 English, 3 math, 3 science (1 science lab), 2 foreign language, 3 social studies, 4 academic electives. **Academic units recommended:** 4 English, 3 math, 3 science, 2 foreign language, 3 social studies, 4 academic electives. High school diploma is required and GED is accepted. TOEFL required of all international applicants, minimum paper TOEFL 500, minimum computer TOEFL 173.

Application deadline: 5/9
Notification: rolling
Average GPA: 3.18

Average SAT Math: NR
Average SAT Verbal: NR
Average ACT: 21

Graduated top 10% of class: 10%
Graduated top 25% of class: 30%
Graduated top 50% of class: 55%

COLLEGE GRADUATION REQUIREMENTS

Course waivers allowed: No
Course substitutions allowed: Yes
In what course: NR

ADDITIONAL INFORMATION

Environment: The university is located on 419 acres 169 miles west of Jackson.

Student Body:
  Undergrad enrollment: 10,592
  Women: 57%
  Men: 43%
  Percent out-of-state: 20%

Cost Information
  In-state tuition: $2,702
  Out-of-state tuition: $11,765
  Room & board: $5,492
Housing Information
  University housing: Yes
  Percent living on campus: 77%

Greek System
  Fraternity: Yes
  Sorority: Yes
Athletics: NCAA Division I

FLORIDA ATLANTIC UNIVERSITY

777 Glades Road, PO Box 3091, Boca Raton, FL 33431-0991
Phone: 561-297-3040 • Fax: 561-297-2758
E-mail: admisweb@fau.edu • Web: www.fau.edu
Support: CS • Institution: 4-year public

LEARNING DISABILITY PROGRAM AND SERVICES

The Office for Students with Disabilities (OSD) offers equal access to a quality education by providing reasonable accommodations to qualified students. Students who have a documented LD may receive strategy tutoring from the LD specialist by appointment. Students are expected to be self-sufficient and strong self-advocates. There is a Counseling Center with professionally trained staff to help students with interpersonal conflicts and concerns, test anxiety, poor concentration, and guidance services.

LD/ADD ADMISSIONS INFORMATION

College entrance tests required: Yes
Interview recommended: No
Essay recommended: No
Documentation required for LD: Test of aptitude (WAIS preferred), achievement battery, tests of information processing, performed on adult scale
Documentation required for ADD: Diagnostician's report
Submitted to: Students with Disabilities
Special Ed. HS coursework accepted: Yes

Specific course requirements of all applicants: Yes
Separate application required for program services: Yes
# of LD applications submitted each year: NR
# of LD applications accepted yearly: NR
Total # of students receiving LD services: NR
Acceptance into program means acceptance into college: Student must be admitted and enrolled in the university first (they can appeal a denial) and then request services.

ADMISSIONS

There is no special application process for students with LD. However, students with LD may be eligible to substitute for certain admission requirements. Students not meeting admission criteria may be admitted by a faculty admission committee, if they possess the potential to succeed in university studies or will enhance the university. Supporting documentation explaining circumstances that adversely affected the student's past academic performances will be required. An admissions counselor will assess each applicant in developing supporting materials to be presented to the committee by the Director of Admissions. Students are expected to have a minimum ACT of 20 or SAT of 860. A sliding scale is used with GPA and test scores. Students who self-disclose and are admitted are then reviewed for services. In some cases, these students are reviewed by the OSD, which provides a recommendation to admissions. Typical courses required for admission include 4 years English, 3 years math (algebra I and higher), 3 years science, 2 years foreign language, 3 years social studies, and 4 electives.

ADDITIONAL INFORMATION

Students must provide documentation including aptitude (WAIS preferred) and achievement battery. The diagnostician's report must indicate standardized assessment measures on attention, reported history and corroboration of current symptoms using two rating scales. With appropriate documenation students may receive the following accommodations or services: the use of calculators, dictionary, computer or spell check in exams; extended time on tests; distraction free environment for tests; oral exams; proctors; scribes; tape recorder in class; textbooks on tape; note-takers; and course substitutions. Skills classes are offered in study skill techniques and organizational strategies. There are occasionally instances where a student is unable to master a particular course because of a disability. In those cases, course substitutions may be permitted if the course in question is not essential to the degree program or related to a licensing requirement. If a student feels he/she may be eligible for a course substitution, the student must first contact OSD for information regarding the substitution process.

Support Services Contact Information

Learning Disability Program/Services: Office for Students with Disabilities (OSD)
Director: Nicole Rokos, M.Ed.
  E-Mail: nrokos@fau.edu
  Telephone: 561-297-3880
  Fax: 561-297-2184

LEARNING DISABILITY SERVICES

Requests for the following services/accommodations will be evaluated individually based on appropriate and current documentation.

Allowed in exams
  Calculator: Yes
  Dictionary: No
  Computer: Yes
  Spellchecker: Yes
Extended test time: Yes
Scribes: Yes
Proctors: Yes
Oral exams: Yes
Note-takers: Yes

Distraction reduced environment: Yes
Tape recording in class: Yes
Books on tape from RFBD: Yes
Taping of books not from RFBD: Yes
Accommodations for students with ADD: Yes
Reading machine: Yes
Other assistive technology: Yes
Priority registration: No

Added costs for services: No
LD specialists: Yes
Professional tutors: No
Peer tutors: 1–10
Max. hours/wk. for services: Unlimited
How professors are notified of LD/ADD: By both student and director

GENERAL ADMISSIONS INFORMATION

Director of Admissions: Albert Colom
Telephone: 561-297-3040

ENTRANCE REQUIREMENTS

Academic units required: 4 English, 3 math, 3 science (2 science lab), 2 foreign language, 3 social studies, 3 academic electives. High school diploma is required and GED is accepted. TOEFL required of all international applicants, minimum paper TOEFL 550, minimum computer TOEFL 300.

Application deadline: 6/3
Notification: Rolling
Average GPA: 3.40

Average SAT Math: 530
Average SAT Verbal: 520
Average ACT: 21

Graduated top 10% of class: NR
Graduated top 25% of class: NR
Graduated top 50% of class: NR

COLLEGE GRADUATION REQUIREMENTS

Course waivers allowed: Yes
Course substitutions allowed: Yes
In what course: Varies, depending on the major elective requirements and the disability. Substitutions used rather than waivers when possible.

ADDITIONAL INFORMATION

Environment: The university is located on 1,000 acres, 1 1/2 miles from the ocean and in proximity to Miami and Ft. Lauderdale.

Student Body:
  Undergrad enrollment: 19,081
  Women: 61%
  Men: 39%
  Percent out-of-state: 6%

Cost Information
  In-state tuition: $2,943
  Out-of-state tuition: $13,955
  Room & board: $6,134
Housing Information
  University housing: Yes
  Percent living on campus: 8%

Greek System
  Fraternity: Yes
  Sorority: Yes
Athletics: NCAA Division I

FLORIDA STATE UNIVERSITY

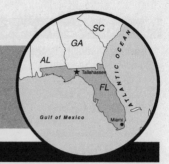

2500 University Center, Tallahassee, FL 32306-2400
Phone: 850-644-6200 • Fax: 850-644-0197
E-mail: admissions@admin.fsu.edu • Web: www.fsu.edu
Support: CS • Institution: 4-year public

LEARNING DISABILITY PROGRAM AND SERVICES

The Student Disability Resource Center at FSU is the primary advocate on campus for students with disabilities. The center works with faculty and staff to provide accommodations for the unique needs of students both in and out of the classroom. Learning specialists can meet individually, on a regular or occasional basis, with students who have LD, Attention Deficit Disorder or other impairments. FSU is noted for its sensitivity to students with disabilities. By providing support services at no cost to students with disabilities, the Student Disability Resource Center offers an opportunity for students with disabilities to achieve their academic and personal goals. Students who self disclose their disability must complete a Request for Services form in order to receive accommodations. LD documentation must be no more than three years old and submitted from a licensed psychologist.

LD/ADD ADMISSIONS INFORMATION

College entrance tests required: Yes
Interview recommended: No
Essay recommended: Yes
Documentation required for LD: Psychoeducational
   evaluation
Documentation required for ADD: Yes
Submitted to: Both Admissions and Student Disability
   Resource Center
Special Ed. HS coursework accepted: Yes

Specific course requirements of all applicants: Yes
Separate application required for program services: Yes
# of LD applications submitted each year: NR
# of LD applications accepted yearly: NR
Total # of students receiving LD services: 300
**Acceptance into program means acceptance into
   college:** Student must be admitted and enrolled in the
   university first and then request services.

ADMISSIONS
Students with LD or ADD who are borderline candidates for admission are encouraged to self-disclose in the admission process. These students can choose to apply for special consideration based on a disability. Special consideration is specifically designed for students who do not meet general admissions requirements. A disability sub-committee reviews the documentation, personal statement, recommendations, transcripts, and standardized test scores to determine eligibility for admissions. Under certain circumstances students may be offered summer admission.

ADDITIONAL INFORMATION
Students who choose to disclose their disability to receive accommodations must complete a Request for Services form available from the Student Disability Resource Center. For a LD, documentation less than three years old is required from a licensed psychologist. Staff members assist students in exploring their needs and determining the necessary services and accommodations. Academic accommodations include alternative testing/extended time, editing, note-takers, registration assistance, test writing, tutors, and study partners. Learning specialists meet individually with students with LD/ADD. Services include teaching study skills, memory enhancement techniques, organizational skills, test-taking strategies, stress management techniques, ways to structure tutoring for best results, skills for negotiating accommodations with instructors, and supportive counseling. Advocates for Disability Awareness act as a support group for students with disabilities. Through their participation, students and others in the university community involved develop skills in leadership, self-advocacy, and career development.

Support Services Contact Information

Learning Disability Program/Services: Student Disability Resource Center
Director: Lauren Miller
E-Mail: sdrc@admin.fsu.edu
Telephone: 850-644-9566
Fax: 850-644-7164

LEARNING DISABILITY SERVICES

Requests for the following services/accommodations will be evaluated individually based on appropriate and current documentation.

Allowed in exams
Calculator: Yes
Dictionary: Yes
Computer: Yes
Spellchecker: Yes
Extended test time: Yes
Scribes: Yes
Proctors: Yes
Oral exams: Yes
Note-takers: Yes

Distraction reduced environment: Yes
Tape recording in class: Yes
Books on tape from RFBD: Yes
Taping of books not from RFBD: Yes
Accommodations for students with
ADD: Yes
Reading machine: Yes
Other assistive technology: Yes
Priority registration: Yes

Added costs for services: No
LD specialists: Yes
Professional tutors: NR
Peer tutors: NR
Max. hours/wk. for services: N/A
How professors are notified of
LD/ADD: By student

GENERAL ADMISSIONS INFORMATION

Director of Admissions: Janice Finney
Telephone: 850-644-6200

ENTRANCE REQUIREMENTS

Academic units required: 4 English, 3 math, 3 science (2 science lab), 2 foreign language, 2 social studies, 1 history, 4 academic electives. **Academic units recommended:** 4 English, 4 math, 4 science (2 science lab), 2 foreign language, 2 social studies, 1 history, 4 academic electives. High school diploma is required and GED is accepted. ACT with Writing component required or SAT Reasoning test. TOEFL required of all international applicants, minimum paper TOEFL 550, minimum computer TOEFL 213.

Application deadline: 3/1
Notification: Rolling Beginning 11/1
Average GPA: 3.73
Average SAT Math: 584

Average SAT Verbal: 580
Average ACT: 25

Graduated top 10% of class: 55%
Graduated top 25% of class: 93%
Graduated top 50% of class: 100%

COLLEGE GRADUATION REQUIREMENTS

Course waivers allowed: No
Course substitutions allowed: Yes
In what course: Math, foreign language

ADDITIONAL INFORMATION

Environment: The university is a suburban campus in Tallahassee, 160 miles from Jacksonville.

Student Body:
Undergrad enrollment: 29,820
Women: 57%
Men: 43%
Percent out-of-state: 15%

Cost Information
In-state tuition: $2,290
Out-of-state tuition: $14,796
Room & board: $6,488
Housing Information
University housing: Yes
Percent living on campus: 14%

Greek System
Fraternity: Yes
Sorority: Yes
Athletics: NCAA Division I

LYNN UNIVERSITY

3601 North Military Trail, Boca Raton, FL 33431-5598
Phone: 561-237-7000 • Fax: 561-237-7100
E-mail: admission@lynn.edu • Web: www.lynn.edu
Support: SP • Institution: 4-year private

LEARNING DISABILITY PROGRAM AND SERVICES

The Academic Resource Center (ARC) Academic support services provide assistance to help students remain in college. is available to all students. The Advancement Program is designed for a limited number of students with LD who have the motivation and intellectual capacity for college level work, yet whose skill and performance levels indicate that without support they would be at risk. In The Advancement Program (TAP), students enroll in regular college courses and, concurrently, in elective credit courses designed for this program. One 3-credit specialized course is offered in the first semester. This course, Language and Learning, is diagnostic and offers an opportunity for students to explore their strengths, learning styles, and college skills. A research-based text, *Frames of Mind*, is required reading. Programs are scheduled for each individual with special consideration, usually resulting in a reduced academic courseload. Tutorials, both individual and group, and study groups are facilitated by TAP personnel. Currently, 24 tutors holding MEds and PhDs provide support to students.

LD/ADD ADMISSIONS INFORMATION

College entrance tests required: Yes
Interview recommended: No
Essay recommended: Yes
Documentation required for LD: Psychoeducational evaluations
Documentation required for ADD: DSM–IV diagnosis or documentation from a physcian
Submitted to: Admissions
Special Ed. HS coursework accepted: Yes

Specific course requirements of all applicants: Yes
Separate application required for program services: No
# of LD applications submitted each year: 500
# of LD applications accepted yearly: 300
Total # of students receiving LD services: 300
Acceptance into program means acceptance into college: Student must be admitted and enrolled in the university first and then offered services through ACA.

ADMISSIONS

Students should submit the general application to Lynn University. Admissions criteria are dependent on the level of services required. Students needing the least restrictive services should have taken college-prep high school courses. Some students may be admitted provisionally after submitting official information. Other students may be admitted conditionally into the Frontiers Program. Typically, these students have an ACT of 18 or lower or an SAT of 850 or lower and 2.0 GPA. Students admitted conditionally take a reduced courseload, no science for the first semester, and 1 1/2 hours of scheduled tutoring. The program director and staff make a final recommendation on status to the admission committee regarding the admission of students to TAP. Interviews are strongly encouraged.

ADDITIONAL INFORMATION

All tests are monitored by TAP personnel, and advocacy work with faculty is provided by the director. TAP students may choose any major as they work toward degree completion in subsequent years. Students who continue to need support services after one year will continue in the program for specific tutoring, untimed tests, and program guidance as needed. Skills classes are offered for credit in Language and Learning Development. There is also one-to-one tutoring with professional tutors.

Support Services Contact Information

Learning Disability Program/Services: Institute for Achievement and Learning
Director: Dr. Marsha A. Glines
  E-Mail: admission@lynn.edu
  Telephone: 561-237-7881
  Fax: 561-237-7100
Contact Person: Admissions
  Telephone: 561-237-7900
  Fax: 561-237-7100

LEARNING DISABILITY SERVICES

Requests for the following services/accommodations will be evaluated individually based on appropriate and current documentation.

Allowed in exams
  Calculator: Yes
  Dictionary: Yes
  Computer: Yes
  Spellchecker: Yes
Extended test time: Yes
Scribes: Yes
Proctors: Yes
Oral exams: Yes
Note-takers: No

Distraction reduced environment: Yes
Tape recording in class: Yes
Books on tape from RFBD: No
Taping of books not from RFBD: No
**Accommodations for students with
  ADD:** Yes
Reading machine: Yes
Other assistive technology: Yes
Priority registration: No

Added costs for services: Yes
LD specialists: Yes
Professional tutors: 30
Peer tutors: No
Max. hours/wk. for services:
  Unlimited
**How professors are notified of
  LD/ADD:** By student

GENERAL ADMISSIONS INFORMATION

Director of Admissions: Alejandra Carvajal, Associate Director of Admissions
Telephone: 561-237-7000

ENTRANCE REQUIREMENTS

Academic units required: 4 English, 4 math, 4 science, 2 social studies, 2 history. High school diploma is required and GED is accepted. TOEFL required of all international applicants, minimum paper TOEFL 500, minimum computer TOEFL 173.

Application deadline: Rolling
Notification: Rolling
Average GPA: 2.55

Average SAT Math: 482
Average SAT Verbal: 471
Average ACT: 21

Graduated top 10% of class: 10%
Graduated top 25% of class: 24%
Graduated top 50% of class: 54%

COLLEGE GRADUATION REQUIREMENTS

Course waivers allowed: No
Course substitutions allowed: Yes
In what course: Foreign language

ADDITIONAL INFORMATION

Environment: The university is located on 123 acres in a suburban area on Florida's Gold Coast.

Student Body:
  Undergrad enrollment: 1,903
  Women: 51%
  Men: 49%
  Percent out-of-state: 45%

Cost Information
  Tuition: $22,000
  Room & board: $8,000
Housing Information
  University housing: Yes
  Percent living on campus: 65%

Greek System
  Fraternity: Yes
  Sorority: Yes
Athletics: NCAA Division II

UNIVERSITY OF CENTRAL FLORIDA

PO Box 160111, Orlando, FL 32816-0111
Phone: 407-823-3000 • Fax: 407-823-5625
E-mail: admission@mail.ucf.edu • Web: www.ucf.edu
Support: CS • Institution: 4-year public

LEARNING DISABILITY PROGRAM AND SERVICES

The Office of Student Disability Services provides information and individualized services consistent with the student's documented disability. To be eligible for disability-related services, individuals must have a documented disability as defined by applicable federal and state laws. Individuals seeking services are required to provide recent documentation from an appropriate health care provider or professional. See www.sds.ucf.edu for specific documentation required.

LD/ADD ADMISSIONS INFORMATION

College entrance tests required: Yes
Interview recommended: No
Essay recommended: No
Documentation required for LD: Psychoeducational evaluation
Documentation required for ADD: Yes
Submitted to: Admissions
Special Ed. HS coursework accepted: No

Specific course requirements of all applicants: Yes
Separate application required for program services: No
# of LD applications submitted each year: NR
# of LD applications accepted yearly: NR
Total # of students receiving LD services: NR
Acceptance into program means acceptance into college: Students must be admitted and enrolled in the university and then request services.

ADMISSIONS

Admission to the University of Central Florida requires graduation from an accredited high school with certain high school academic units, a cumulative high school grade point average in those academic units, and SAT or ACT test scores. Course requirements include 4 years of English (at least 3 with substantial writing requirements); 3 years of mathematics (Algebra I and above); 3 years of natural science (at least 2 with laboratory); 3 years of social science; 2 sequential years of the same foreign language; 3 elective years, preferably from English, mathematics, natural science, social science, or foreign language areas. Students with disabilities who have not taken high school foreign language must submit, along with appropriate documentation, a letter from a school official verifying that not taking a foreign language was an accommodation for the disability. If a student needs special admission consideration based on a disability, the student should send the requested appropriate documentation to the undergraduate admissions office. Satisfying minimum requirements does not guarantee admission to UCF, since preference will be given to those students whose credentials indicate the greatest promise of academic success.

ADDITIONAL INFORMATION

The University Writing Center (UWC) provides free writing support to all undergraduates and graduates at the University of Central Florida. The Student Academic Resource Center (SARC) provides high-quality academic support programs, including tutoring and supplemental instruction, retention programs, academic advising programs, and various other academic programs and services. The Math Lab provides tutoring for students enrolled in mathematics courses.

Support Services Contact Information

Learning Disability Program/Services: Student Disibility Services
Director: Dr. Philip Kalfin
  E-Mail: sds@mail.ucf.edu
  Telephone: 407-823-2371
  Fax: 407-823-2372

LEARNING DISABILITY SERVICES

Requests for the following services/accommodations will be evaluated individually based on appropriate and current documentation.

Allowed in exams
  Calculator: Yes
  Dictionary: Yes
  Computer: Yes
  Spellchecker: Yes
Extended test time: Yes
Scribes: Yes
Proctors: Yes
Oral exams: No
Note-takers: Yes

Distraction reduced environment: Yes
Tape recording in class: Yes
Books on tape from RFBD: Yes
Taping of books not from RFBD: Yes
Accommodations for students with ADD: Yes
Reading machine: Yes
Other assistive technology: Yes
Priority registration: Yes

Added costs for services: No
LD specialists: Yes
Professional tutors: No
Peer tutors: N/A
Max. hours/wk. for services: Varies
How professors are notified of LD/ADD: By student

GENERAL ADMISSIONS INFORMATION

Director of Admissions: Dr. Gordon Chavis
Telephone: 407-823-3000

ENTRANCE REQUIREMENTS

Academic units required: 4 English, 3 math, 3 science (2 science lab), 2 foreign language, 3 social studies, 4 academic electives. High school diploma is required and GED is accepted. ACT with Writing component required or SAT Reasoning. TOEFL required of all international applicants, minimum paper TOEFL 500, minimum computer TOEFL 220.

Application deadline: 5/1
Notification: Rolling
Average GPA: 3.80

Average SAT Math: 597
Average SAT Verbal: 589
Average ACT: 26

Graduated top 10% of class: 35%
Graduated top 25% of class: 75%
Graduated top 50% of class: 91%

COLLEGE GRADUATION REQUIREMENTS

Course waivers allowed: No
Course substitutions allowed: Yes
In what course: With appropriate documentation, math and foreign language may be substituted with selected other courses.

ADDITIONAL INFORMATION

Environment: The main campus of UCF is located 13 miles east of the city of Orlando, 45 miles from the Atlantic Ocean and Cape Canaveral, and 100 miles from Tampa and the Gulf of Mexico.

Student Body:
  Undergrad enrollment: 34,940
  Women: 55%
  Men: 45%
  Percent out-of-state: 3%

Cost Information
  In-state tuition: $2,982
  Out-of-state tuition: $15,488
  Room & board: $7,132
Housing Information
  University housing: Yes
  Percent living on campus: 20%

Greek System
  Fraternity: Yes
  Sorority: Yes
Athletics: NCAA Division I

UNIVERSITY OF FLORIDA

201 Criser Hall, Box 114000, Gainesville, FL 32611-4000
Phone: 352-392-1365 • Fax: 904-392-3987
E-mail: accessf@ufl.edu • Web: www.ufl.edu
Support: CS • Institution: 4-year public

LEARNING DISABILITY PROGRAM AND SERVICES

The University of Florida offers a full range of support services designed to assist students with learning disabilities. Support services are individually tailored to each student's needs and those supports may be modified to meet the specific demands and requirements of individual courses. Advisement and support services are available to students on an as-needed basis. Assistance can be provided regarding registration, learning strategies, classroom accommodations, and the University of Florida petition process.

LD/ADD ADMISSIONS INFORMATION

College entrance tests required: Yes
Interview recommended: No
Essay recommended: No
Documentation required for LD: Psychoeducational
  evaluation
Documentation required for ADD: Yes
Submitted to: Admissions
Special Ed. HS coursework accepted: Yes

Specific course requirements of all applicants: Yes
Separate application required for program services: No
# of LD applications submitted each year: NR
# of LD applications accepted yearly: NR
Total # of students receiving LD services: 350
**Acceptance into program means acceptance into
  college:** Students must be admitted and enrolled in the
  university first (they can appeal a denial) and then request
  services.

ADMISSIONS
The student with learning disabilities applies to the university under the same guidelines as all other students. However, students with learning disabilities may request a separate review. Students should check the box on the general application to request information and submit a personal statement describing how their learning disabilities may have had an impact or an effect on their grade point average or standardized test scores, if applicable. The required SAT or ACT varies according to the student's GPA. Students denied admission may petition for a review of their application. This review process petition should be directed to the director of the Office of Student Services (OSS).

ADDITIONAL INFORMATION
Skills workshops are offered in reading, note-taking, memory, and time management. OSS sponsors "Preview," an early registration and orientation program. Assistance can be provided regarding learning strategies, classroom accommodations, and petitions. Services are available to focus on strategic learning strategies and success strategies.

Support Services Contact Information

Learning Disability Program/Services: Disability Resources
Director: John Denny
  E-Mail: johnpd@dso.ufl.edu
  Telephone: 352-392-1261 ext. 222
  Fax: 352-392-1430

LEARNING DISABILITY SERVICES

Requests for the following services/accommodations will be evaluated individually based on appropriate and current documentation.

Allowed in exams
  Calculator: Yes
  Dictionary: No
  Computer: Yes
  Spellchecker: Yes
Extended test time: Yes
Scribes: Yes
Proctors: Yes
Oral exams: Yes
Note-takers: Yes

Distraction reduced environment: Yes
Tape recording in class: Yes
Books on tape from RFBD: Yes
Taping of books not from RFBD: Yes
**Accommodations for students with
  ADD:** Yes
Reading machine: Yes
Other assistive technology: Yes
Priority registration: Yes

Added costs for services: No
LD specialists: Yes
Professional tutors: No
Peer tutors: No
Max. hours/wk. for services: As
  needed
**How professors are notified of
  LD/ADD:** By student

GENERAL ADMISSIONS INFORMATION

Director of Admissions: William Kolb, Associate University Registrar
Telephone: 352-392-1365

ENTRANCE REQUIREMENTS

Academic units required: 4 English, 3 math, 3 science (2 science lab), 2 foreign language, 3 social studies. High school diploma is required and GED is accepted. TOEFL required of all international applicants, minimum paper TOEFL 550, minimum computer TOEFL 213

Application deadline: 1/12
Notification: March
Average GPA: 3.9

Average SAT Math: 680
Average SAT Verbal: 660
Average ACT: 29

Graduated top 10% of class: 79%
Graduated top 25% of class: 90%
Graduated top 50% of class: 97%

COLLEGE GRADUATION REQUIREMENTS

Course waivers allowed: Yes
Course substitutions allowed: Yes
In what course: Students may petition for substitutions in foreign language and math courses. These cases are individually decided on a case-by-case basis.

ADDITIONAL INFORMATION

Environment: The university is located on 2,000 acres in a small city 115 miles north of Orlando, Florida, and 20 minutes from the Gainesville airport.

Student Body:
  Undergrad enrollment: 33,094
  Women: 53%
  Men: 47%
  Percent out-of-state: 4%

Cost Information
  In-state tuition: $2,780
  Out-of-state tuition: $13,808
  Room & board: $5,800
Housing Information
  University housing: Yes
  Percent living on campus: 22%

Greek System
  Fraternity: Yes
  Sorority: Yes
Athletics: NCAA Division I

University of Florida

BRENAU UNIVERSITY

500 Washington Street SE, Gainesville, GA 30501
Phone: 770-534-6100 • Fax: 770-538-4306
E-mail: wcadmissions@lib.brenau.edu • Web: www.brenau.edu
Support: SP • Institution: 4-year private

LEARNING DISABILITY PROGRAM AND SERVICES

The Brenau Learning Center is a program for students with a diagnosed learning disability or attention deficit disorder. Students must also have average to above average academic aptitude with an adequate high school preparation for college studies. The program is designed to provide support services for students as they attend regular college courses. It also offers a more structured learning environment as well as the freedom associated with college living. Full-time students enroll in four or five courses per semester. Learning Center students receive academic advising from the college, as well as the director of the program. Students have the opportunity to register early, which allows them to take required courses at the appropriate time in their college career. Many students become inactive in the program as they experience success and require less assistance. They may re-enter the program at any time. Brenau University attempts to offer a more personalized, caring approach to college education. The faculty is very supportive of students who request extra help. In addition to receiving special services from the Learning Center, staff, and tutors, the student is educated in an environment conducive to learning.

LD/ADD ADMISSIONS INFORMATION

College entrance tests required: Yes
Interview recommended: Yes
Essay recommended: Yes
Documentation required for LD: Psychological report
Documentation required for ADD: Physician's report or psychological report
Submitted to: Admissions and Learning Center
Special Ed. HS coursework accepted: Yes

Specific course requirements of all applicants: Yes
Separate application required for program services: No
# of LD applications submitted each year: 15–20
# of LD applications accepted yearly: 15
Total # of students receiving LD services: 40–50
Acceptance into program means acceptance into college: Students can be reviewed by the LD Program Director, but must be admitted and enrolled in the university first and then request services.

ADMISSIONS

Regular admission criteria include an SAT of 900+ or ACT of 18+, and a GPA of 2.5+. Applicants with an LD not meeting regular admission criteria may be admitted through a "Learning Center Admission" and must participate in the LD program. These students should be "college-able," motivated, and have appropriate high school preparation. Students must have the intellectual potential and academic foundation to be successful. Applicants must provide documentation. Not all students with a diagnosed LD are eligible for the program; the learning differences must not be the primary result of emotional problems. Both the director of the LC and the Director of Admissions make a decision after reviewing SAT/ACT scores, academic performance and preparation, counselor's recommendation and other letters of reference, test results contained in the psychological evaluation, and a campus interview.

ADDITIONAL INFORMATION

Learning Center students can register early and receive regular academic advising from the director of the program. Study skills, including word processing, reading, and math skills classes are offered for credit. At all service levels students may take tests in an extended-time format where oral assistance is available. Learning Center students begin tutoring with professional tutors during the first week of the term and contract to regularly attend tutoring sessions throughout the semester. All LC students may receive one hour of educational support per week in addition to scheduled tutoring. Students may be tutored in one to four academic classes per semester. Skills classes in word processing, time management, study skills, and research may be taken for credit. LD services and accommodations are available for undergraduate and graduate students. Courses are offered in the summer and entering freshman are encouraged to attend. Summer school allows students to get ahead with courses and take a reduced course load the first year.

Support Services Contact Information

Learning Disability Program/Services: Learning Center (LC)
Director: Vincent Yamilkoski, EdD
  E-Mail: vyamilkoski@lib.brenau.edu
  Telephone: 770-534-6134
  Fax: 770-534-6221
Contact Person: Evelyn Asher
  E-Mail: easher@ub.brenau.edu
  Telephone: 770-534-6133
  Fax: 770-297-5883

LEARNING DISABILITY SERVICES

Requests for the following services/accommodations will be evaluated individually based on appropriate and current documentation.

Allowed in exams
  Calculator: Yes
  Dictionary: Yes
  Computer: Yes
  Spellchecker: Yes
Extended test time: Yes
Scribes: Yes
Proctors: Yes
Oral exams: Yes
Note-takers: Yes

Distraction reduced environment: Yes
Tape recording in class: Yes
Books on tape from RFBD: Yes
Taping of books not from RFBD: No
Accommodations for students with
  ADD: Yes
Reading machine: Yes
Other assistive technology: Yes
Priority registration: Yes

Added costs for services: Yes
LD specialists: Yes
Professional tutors: 15–20
Peer tutors: No
Max. hours/wk. for services: 9
How professors are notified of
  LD/ADD: By both student and director

GENERAL ADMISSIONS INFORMATION

Director of Admissions: Scott Briell
Telephone: 770-538-4704

ENTRANCE REQUIREMENTS

High school diploma is required and GED is accepted. ACT with or without Writing component accepted. TOEFL required of all international applicants, minimum paper TOEFL 500, minimum computer TOEFL 173.

Application deadline: Rolling
Notification: As Received/Rolling
Average GPA: 3.2

Average SAT Math: 494
Average SAT Verbal: 516
Average ACT: NR

Graduated top 10% of class: NR
Graduated top 25% of class: NR
Graduated top 50% of class: NR

COLLEGE GRADUATION REQUIREMENTS

Course waivers allowed: No
Course substitutions allowed: No
In what course: N/A

ADDITIONAL INFORMATION

Environment: Brenau University is in a small city setting 50 miles northeast of Atlanta in the foothills of the Blue Ridge Mountains.

Student Body:
  Undergrad enrollment: 663
  Women: 100%
  Men: 0%
  Percent out-of-state: 8%

Cost Information
  Tuition: $15,450
  Room & board: $8,350
Housing Information
  University housing: Yes
  Percent living on campus: 55%

Greek System
  Fraternity: No
  Sorority: Yes
Athletics: NAIA

EMORY UNIVERSITY

Boisfeuillet Jones Center, Atlanta, GA 30322
Phone: 404-727-6036 • Fax: 404-727-4303
E-mail: admiss@emory.edu • Web: www.emory.edu
Support: CS • Institution: 4-year private

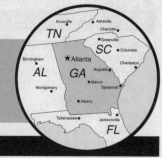

LEARNING DISABILITY PROGRAM AND SERVICES

Emory University ensures that all services/accommodations are accessible to students with disabilities. Accommodations are made on an individualized basis. Students are responsible for seeking available assistance and establishing their needs. The goals of Disability Services (DS) include coordinating services to provide equal access to programs, services, and activities; reducing competitive disadvantage in academic work; providing individual counseling and referral; serving as an advocate for student needs; providing a variety of support services; and serving as a liaison between students and university officers or community agencies. Documentation for LD must include intelligence tests; specific cognitive processing, oral language assessment, social-emotional assessment, significant specific achievement deficits relative to potential, assessment instruments appropriate for adult population, and recommendations regarding accommodations for the student in an academic setting. ADD documentation must include reported history of symptoms by age 7; self-report of 3 major behaviors from DSM–IV items; observations from 2 professionals; mandatory corroboration of behaviors by another adult (parent, relative, guardian); documentation on 2 rating scales of ADD behaviors; and recommendations regarding suggested accommodations.

LD/ADD ADMISSIONS INFORMATION

College entrance tests required: Yes
Interview recommended: No
Essay recommended: No
Documentation required for LD: Specific documentation criteria available upon request
Documentation required for ADD: Yes
Submitted to: Office of Disability Services
Special Ed. HS coursework accepted: No

Specific course requirements of all applicants: Yes
Separate application required for program services: No
# of LD applications submitted each year: NR
# of LD applications accepted yearly: NR
Total # of students receiving LD services: 100–150
Acceptance into program means acceptance into college: Student must be admitted and enrolled in the university first and then request services.

ADMISSIONS

Students with learning disabilities are required to submit everything requested by the Office of Admission for regular admissions. Teacher and/or counselor recommendations may be weighted more heavily in the admissions process. A professional diagnosis of the learning disability with recommended accommodations is helpful. Essentially, each student with a disability is evaluated individually, and admitted based on potential for success in the Emory environment, taking into consideration the necessary accommodations requested. Documentation is required for services, not admissions. Once admitted, the admissions office sends a self-Identification form in the acceptance packet to each student who discloses a learning disability.

ADDITIONAL INFORMATION

The needs of students with LD are met through counseling and referral advocacy, and a variety of support services. Deans are notified by a report each semester of students who have self-identified as having LD. Tutoring is offered on a one-to-one basis or in small groups in most subjects. Students also are eligible for priority registration. Skills classes are offered, and the coordinator can monitor and track students to follow their progress. The coordinator meets with students to assess needs and develop an individualized service plan. The coordinator is also an advocate for students and provides information to faculty to help with their understanding of providing accommodations to students with LD. DS sends memos to professors to support student accommodation requests. DS acknowledges they have sufficient verification to support the request and will provide the professor with the identified accommodations necessary. The Emory Students Enabling Association provides a support network for students with disabilities.

Support Services Contact Information

Learning Disability Program/Services: Office of Disablility Services
Director: Gloria Weaver
  E-Mail: gloria.weaver@emory.edu
  Telephone: 404-727-6016
  Fax: 404-727-1126
Contact Person: Jessalyn Smiley
  E-Mail: jessalyn.p.smiley@emory.edu
  Telephone: 404-727-6016
  Fax: 404-727-1126

LEARNING DISABILITY SERVICES

Requests for the following services/accommodations will be evaluated individually based on appropriate and current documentation.

Allowed in exams	**Distraction reduced environment:** Yes	**Added costs for services:** No
Calculator: Yes	**Tape recording in class:** Yes	**LD specialists:** Yes
Dictionary: Yes	**Books on tape from RFBD:** Yes	**Professional tutors:** Yes
Computer: Yes	**Taping of books not from RFBD:** Yes	**Peer tutors:** Yes
Spellchecker: Yes	**Accommodations for students with**	**Max. hours/wk. for services:** NR
Extended test time: Yes	**ADD:** Yes	**How professors are notified of**
Scribes: Yes	**Reading machine:** No	**LD/ADD:** By student
Proctors: Yes	**Other assistive technology:** Yes	
Oral exams: Yes	**Priority registration:** Yes	
Note-takers: Yes		

GENERAL ADMISSIONS INFORMATION

Director of Admissions: Daniel C. Walls
Telephone: 800 727-6036

ENTRANCE REQUIREMENTS

Academic units required: 4 English, 3 math, 2 science (2 science lab), 2 foreign language, 2 social studies, 2 history, 3 academic electives. High school diploma is required and GED is not accepted. ACT with or without Writing component accepted. TOEFL required of all international applicants, minimum paper TOEFL 560, minimum computer TOEFL 220

Application deadline: 1/15	**Average SAT Math:** 700	**Graduated top 10% of class:** 90%
Notification: 4/1	**Average SAT Verbal:** 680	**Graduated top 25% of class:** 99%
Average GPA: 3.8	**Average ACT:** 31	**Graduated top 50% of class:** 100%

COLLEGE GRADUATION REQUIREMENTS

Course waivers allowed: No
Course substitutions allowed: No
In what course: N/A

ADDITIONAL INFORMATION

Environment: The 631-acre campus is in a suburban section 5 miles northeast of Atlanta.

Student Body:	**Cost Information**	**Greek System**
Undergrad enrollment: 6,260	**Tuition:** $28,940	**Fraternity:** Yes
Women: 57%	**Room & board:** $9,650	**Sorority:** Yes
Men: 43%	**Housing Information**	**Athletics:** NCAA Division III
Percent out-of-state: 69%	**University housing:** Yes	
	Percent living on campus: 66%	

GEORGIA SOUTHERN UNIVERSITY

PO Box 8024, Statesboro, GA 30460
Phone: 912-681-5391 • Fax: 912-486-7240
E-mail: admissions@georgiasouthern.edu • Web: www.georgiasouthern.edu
Support: CS • Institution: 4-year public

LEARNING DISABILITY PROGRAM AND SERVICES

Georgia Southern University wants all students to have a rewarding and pleasant college experience. The university offers a variety of services specifically tailored to afford students with learning disabilities an equal opportunity for success. These services are in addition to those provided to all students and to the access provided by campus facilities. Opportunities available through the Disabled Student Services program include special registration, which allows students to complete the course registration process without going through the standard procedure, and academic/personal assistance for students who are having difficulty with passing a class and need help with time management, note-taking skills, study strategies, and self-confidence. The university has a support group designed to help students with disabilities deal with personal and academic problems related to their disability.

LD/ADD ADMISSIONS INFORMATION

College entrance tests required: Yes
Interview recommended: No
Essay recommended: No
Documentation required for LD: Psychoeducational evaluation
Documentation required for ADD: Yes
Submitted to: Support Program/Services
Special Ed. HS coursework accepted: Yes

Specific course requirements of all applicants: Yes
Separate application required for program services: No
# of LD applications submitted each year: NR
# of LD applications accepted yearly: NR
Total # of students receiving LD services: 236
Acceptance into program means acceptance into college: Student must be admitted and enrolled in the university first and then request services.

ADMISSIONS

There is no special admissions procedure for students with learning disabilities. The university system feels that all applicants must meet the same minimum requirements. Courses required for admission include 4 years English, 3 years math, 3 years science, 2 years foreign language, and 3 years social studies. The minimum SAT Verbal score is 480 and math is 440. The minimum GPA is 2.0.

ADDITIONAL INFORMATION

To ensure the provision of services, the Disabled Student Services office requests that any student with learning disabilities who will need accommodations and/or assistance identify him/herself as a student with a disability as soon as possible by either returning the voluntary declaration of disability form found in the admissions acceptance packet or by contacting the Disabled Student Services office directly.

Support Services Contact Information

Learning Disability Program/Services: Disabled Student Services
Director: Wayne Akins
  E-Mail: cwatkins@gsix2.cc.gasou.edu
  Telephone: 912-871-1566
  Fax: 912-871-1419

LEARNING DISABILITY SERVICES

Requests for the following services/accommodations will be evaluated individually based on appropriate and current documentation.

Allowed in exams
  Calculator: Yes
  Dictionary: Yes
  Computer: Yes
  Spellchecker: Yes
Extended test time: Yes
Scribes: Yes
Proctors: Yes
Oral exams: Yes
Note-takers: Yes

Distraction reduced environment: Yes
Tape recording in class: Yes
Books on tape from RFBD: Yes
Taping of books not from RFBD: Yes
Accommodations for students with
  ADD: Yes
Reading machine: No
Other assistive technology: No
Priority registration: Yes

Added costs for services: No
LD specialists: Yes
Professional tutors: No
Peer tutors: Yes
Max. hours/wk. for services:
  Unlimited
How professors are notified of
  LD/ADD: By student

GENERAL ADMISSIONS INFORMATION

Director of Admissions: Dr. Teresa Thompson
Telephone: 912-681-5391

ENTRANCE REQUIREMENTS

Academic units required: 4 English, 4 math, 3 science (2 science lab), 2 foreign language, 3 social studies. High school diploma is required and GED is not accepted. ACT with Writing component required or SAT Reasoning. TOEFL required of all international applicants, minimum paper TOEFL 500, minimum computer TOEFL 173.

Application deadline: 8/1
Notification: Rolling
Average GPA: 3.08

Average SAT Math: 527
Average SAT Verbal: 525
Average ACT: 21

Graduated top 10% of class: NR
Graduated top 25% of class: NR
Graduated top 50% of class: NR

COLLEGE GRADUATION REQUIREMENTS

Course waivers allowed: No
Course substitutions allowed: Yes
In what course: Substitutions have only been granted in foreign language and a deficit area.

ADDITIONAL INFORMATION

Environment: The campus is in a small town close to Savannah.

Student Body:
  Undergrad enrollment: 13,526
  Women: 49%
  Men: 51%
  Percent out-of-state: 4%

Cost Information
  In-state tuition: $2,322
  Out-of-state tuition: $9,290
  Room & board: $6,000
Housing Information
  University housing: Yes
  Percent living on campus: 23%

Greek System
  Fraternity: Yes
  Sorority: Yes
Athletics: NCAA Division I

GEORGIA STATE UNIVERSITY

PO Box 4009, Atlanta, GA 30302-4009
Phone: 404-651-2365 • Fax: 404-651-4811
E-mail: admissions@gsu.edu • Web: www.gsu.edu
Support: CS • Institution: 4-year public

LEARNING DISABILITY PROGRAM AND SERVICES

Georgia State University is committed to helping each student—including those students with disabilities—realize their full potential. This commitment is fulfilled through the provision of reasonable accommodations to ensure equitable access to its programs and services for all qualified students with disabilities. In general, the university will provide accommodations for students with disabilities on an individualized and flexible basis. It is the student's responsibility to seek available assistance and to make their needs known. All students are encouraged to contact the Office of Disability Services and/or Student Support Services in the early stages of their college planning. The pre-admission services include information regarding admission requirements and academic support services. Students should register with both services before classes begin. This will assure that appropriate services are in place prior to the first day of classes. As a rule, the university does not waive academic requirements because of any disability. Therefore, the student should carefully evaluate degree requirements early in their studies. The only exception to this policy is if there is a documented learning disability that would hinder the learning of a foreign language, in which case a student may petition for a substitution in the foreign language requirement.

LD/ADD ADMISSIONS INFORMATION

College entrance tests required: Yes
Interview recommended: No
Essay recommended: No
Documentation required for LD: WAIS–III, Stanford-Binet, KBIT, WJ–R, WRAT–R, all less than 3 years old
Documentation required for ADD: Yes
Submitted to: Office of Disability Services
Special Ed. HS coursework accepted: No

Specific course requirements of all applicants: Yes
Separate application required for program services: No
# of LD applications submitted each year: NR
# of LD applications accepted yearly: NR
Total # of students receiving LD services: 149
Acceptance into program means acceptance into college: Student must be admitted and enrolled in the university first and then request services.

ADMISSIONS

Students with LD must meet the same admission criteria as all other applicants. The university uses a predicted GPA of 2.1 for admission to a degree program or a GPA of 1.8 for admission to Learning Support Systems. This is determined by the ACT/SAT score and the high school GPA. The higher the GPA, the lower the ACT/SAT can be and vice versa. Course requirements include 4 years English, 3 years science, 3 years math, 3 years social science, and 2 years foreign language. (Substitutions are allowed for foreign language if the student has documentation that supports the substitution). Students may appeal an admissions decision if they are denied, and could be offered a probationary admission. If a student contacts the Office of Disability Services and provides documentation of a LD, the office will write the Admissions Office and verify the existence of the LD.

ADDITIONAL INFORMATION

To receive LD services students must submit documentation that evaluates intelligence; academic achievement in reading, math, and written language; auditory/phonological processing; language; visual-perceptual-spatial-constructural capabilities; attention; memory; executive function; motor skills; and social emotional skills. Student Support Services provides individual and group counseling, tutoring, advocacy, taped texts, advising, readers, learning lab, computer training, and referral for diagnosis of LD. The University Counseling Center provides study skills training, test-taking strategies, note-taking skills, textbook reading skills, test anxiety and stress management, time management,organizational techniques, thesis and dissertation writing, and personal counseling. Passport is a special section of the Personal and Academic Development Seminar Class offered through Learning Support Program, and is specifically designed for students with LD. The Office of Disability Services offers advisement, study lab, readers, and testing accommodations.

Support Services Contact Information

Learning Disability Program/Services: Margaret A. Staton Office of Disability Services
Director: Rodney E. Pennamon
  E-Mail: dismail@langate.gsu.edu
  Telephone: 404-463-9044
  Fax: 404-463-9049
Contact Person: Louise Bedrossian
  E-Mail: lbedrossian@gsu.edu
  Telephone: 404-463-9044
  Fax: 404-463-9049

LEARNING DISABILITY SERVICES

Requests for the following services/accommodations will be evaluated individually based on appropriate and current documentation.

Allowed in exams
  Calculator: Yes
  Dictionary: Yes
  Computer: Yes
  Spellchecker: Yes
Extended test time: Yes
Scribes: Yes
Proctors: Yes
Oral exams: Yes
Note-takers: Yes

Distraction reduced environment: Yes
Tape recording in class: Yes
Books on tape from RFBD: Yes
Taping of books not from RFBD: Yes
Accommodations for students with ADD: Yes
Reading machine: Yes
Other assistive technology: Yes
Priority registration: Yes

Added costs for services: No
LD specialists: Yes
Professional tutors: No
Peer tutors: Yes
Max. hours/wk. for services: Based on need and availability of space and staff
How professors are notified of LD/ADD: By student

GENERAL ADMISSIONS INFORMATION

Director of Admissions: Diane Weber
Telephone: 404-651-2365

ENTRANCE REQUIREMENTS

Academic units required: 4 English, 4 math, 3 science, 2 foreign language, 2 social studies, 1 history. **Academic units recommended:** 4 English, 4 math, 3 science, 2 foreign language, 2 social studies, 1 history. High school diploma is required and GED is not accepted. ACT with Writing component required or SAT Reasoning test. TOEFL required of all international applicants, minimum paper TOEFL 525, minimum computer TOEFL 193.

Application deadline: 3/1
Notification: Rolling
Average GPA: 3.31

Average SAT Math: 521
Average SAT Verbal: 525
Average ACT: 22

Graduated top 10% of class: NR
Graduated top 25% of class: NR
Graduated top 50% of class: NR

COLLEGE GRADUATION REQUIREMENTS

Course waivers allowed: No
Course substitutions allowed: Yes
In what course: Foreign language course substitutions to a very limited number of students with significant language-based learning disabilites, by appeal.

ADDITIONAL INFORMATION

Environment: The university's campus is in an urban area in Atlanta.

Student Body:
  Undergrad enrollment: 19,239
  Women: 61%
  Men: 39%
  Percent out-of-state: 2%

Cost Information
  In-state tuition: $3,705
  Out-of-state tuition: $14,821
  Room & board: $6,730
Housing Information
  University housing: Yes
  Percent living on campus: 10%

Greek System
  Fraternity: Yes
  Sorority: Yes
Athletics: NCAA Division I

Georgia State University

REINHARDT COLLEGE

7300 Reinhardt College Circle, Waleska, GA 30183
Phone: 770-720-5526 • Fax: 770-720-5899
E-mail: admissions@reinhardt.edu • Web: www.reinhardt.edu
Support: SP • Institution: 4-year private

LEARNING DISABILITY PROGRAM AND SERVICES

The Academic Support Office (ASO) provides assistance to students with specific learning abilities or attention deficit disorders. Students are enrolled in regular college courses. The program focuses on compensatory skills and provides special services in academic advising and counseling, individual and group tutoring, assistance in writing assignments, note-taking, testing accommodations, and taped texts. The ASO was established in 1982 to provide assistance to students with learning disabilities who meet regular college entrance requirements, have a diagnosed LD, and may or may not have received any LD services in the past due to ineligibility for high school services, or a recent diagnosis.

LD/ADD ADMISSIONS INFORMATION

College entrance tests required: Yes
Interview recommended: Yes
Essay recommended: Yes
Documentation required for LD: WISC–R, WAIS–III, WJ or WRAT, all less than 3 years old
Documentation required for ADD: Yes
Submitted to: Admissions
Special Ed. HS coursework accepted: No

Specific course requirements of all applicants: Yes
Separate application required for program services: Yes
# of LD applications submitted each year: 70
# of LD applications accepted yearly: 30
Total # of students receiving LD services: 70
Acceptance into program means acceptance into college: Students are admitted jointly by the college and ASO.

ADMISSIONS

Applicants with learning disabilities should request an ASO admission packet from Admissions. They should complete the regular application, and check the ASO admission box, and fill out the supplemental form from ASO. Students must provide IEPs from as many years of high school as possible; psychological evaluations documenting the disability; and three references addressing aptitude, motivation, ability to set realistic goals, interpersonal skills, and readiness for college. Students applying to the ASO program must submit SAT/ACT scores, and may be asked to interview with the ASO staff. Admission decisions are made by the admissions office with recommendations from the program director.

ADDITIONAL INFORMATION

The ASO is staffed by four full-time faculty members. Additional tuition is required for students enrolled in ASO tutorials. A generous financial aid program is available to all qualified students. Academic Support Services include faculty-led tutorials (for a fee); academic advisement and counseling; accommodative services for students with documented LD/ADD, such as individualized testing, note-takers, and the coordination of taped texts. All students admitted and enrolled in the ASO Program attend a regular student orientation program plus have an interview and orientation with the staff from the ASO Program.

Support Services Contact Information

Learning Disability Program/Services: Academic Support Office (ASO)
Director: Sylvia Robertson
  E-Mail: srr@reinhardt.edu
  Telephone: 770-720-5567
  Fax: 770-720-5602

LEARNING DISABILITY SERVICES

Requests for the following services/accommodations will be evaluated individually based on appropriate and current documentation.

Allowed in exams
  Calculator: Yes
  Dictionary: No
  Computer: Yes
  Spellchecker: Yes
Extended test time: Yes
Scribes: Yes
Proctors: Yes
Oral exams: Yes
Note-takers: Yes

Distraction reduced environment: Yes
Tape recording in class: Yes
Books on tape from RFBD: Yes
Taping of books not from RFBD: No
Accommodations for students with ADD: Yes
Reading machine: Yes
Other assistive technology: Yes
Priority registration: Yes

Added costs for services: Yes
LD specialists: Yes
Professional tutors: 4
Peer tutors: 0
Max. hours/wk. for services: Unlimited
How professors are notified of LD/ADD: By both student and director

GENERAL ADMISSIONS INFORMATION

Director of Admissions: Julie Cook
Telephone: 770-720-5524

ENTRANCE REQUIREMENTS
Academic units required: 4 English, 4 math, 3 science, 3 social studies. **Academic units recommended:** 2 foreign language. High school diploma is required and GED is accepted. TOEFL required of all international applicants, minimum paper TOEFL 500, minimum computer TOEFL 150.

Application deadline: No deadline
Notification: Rolling beginning 8/1
Average GPA: 2.95

Average SAT Math: 470
Average SAT Verbal: 485
Average ACT: 20

Graduated top 10% of class: NR
Graduated top 25% of class: NR
Graduated top 50% of class: 35%

COLLEGE GRADUATION REQUIREMENTS

Course waivers allowed: No
Course substitutions allowed: No
In what course: N/A

ADDITIONAL INFORMATION

Environment: The college is located on a 600-acre campus in a small town 40 miles from Atlanta.

Student Body:
  Undergrad enrollment: 1,054
  Women: 59%
  Men: 41%
  Percent out-of-state: 12%

Cost Information
  Tuition: $12,000
  Room & board: $5,270
Housing Information
  University housing: Yes
  Percent living on campus: 61%

Greek System
  Fraternity: No
  Sorority: No
Athletics: NAIA

UNIVERSITY OF GEORGIA

Terrell Hall, Athens, GA 30602
Phone: 706-542-8776 • Fax: 706-542-1466
E-mail: undergrad@admissions.uga.edu • Web: www.uga.edu
Support: CS • Institution: 4-year public

LEARNING DISABILITY PROGRAM AND SERVICES

The purpose of the Learning Disabilities Center (LDC) is to provide support and direct services to students who demonstrate a specific LD so that they may function as independently as possible while at the university. The objectives of the program are to (1) assist students in understanding their disability, (2) coordinate information about other support services, (3) recommend modifications for the Regents Exam (required to graduate) and program of study where appropriate, and (4) consult with faculty. All UGA students whose LD have been confirmed by the LCD are eligible for support services. Students must meet the Learning Disability Criteria accepted by the Georgia Board of Regents, including documentation within three years; average broad cognitive functioning; specific cognitive processing deficits; social-emotional assessment that doesn't suggest primary emotional basis for results; oral language assessment; significant specific achievement deficits relative to potential documented in the areas of written language, reading, and math; utilization of assessment instruments with appropriate age norms; and all standardized measures must be represented by standard score or percentile ranks based on published norms.

LD/ADD ADMISSIONS INFORMATION

College entrance tests required: Yes
Interview recommended: No
Essay recommended: No
Documentation required for LD: Psychoeducational evaluation See www.coe.uga.edu for Board of Regents criteria for LD & ADD.
Documentation required for ADD: Yes
Submitted to: Disability Services
Special Ed. HS coursework accepted: No

Specific course requirements of all applicants: Yes
Separate application required for program services: Yes
# of LD applications submitted each year: NR
# of LD applications accepted yearly: NR
Total # of students receiving LD services: 225–275
Acceptance into program means acceptance into college: Student must be admitted and enrolled in the university first and then request services.

ADMISSIONS

Students with LD are encouraged to self-disclose on the general application form. This disclosure sets the process in motion, and the admissions office notifies the LDC. LDC contacts the applicant and offers to discuss services available, and then refers the student's name back to admissions. LDC provides the admissions office with a diagnosis to assist with an admissions decision. Students must submit documentation of their disability to be considered for special admission. Admissions may be flexible with GPA and test scores, but students should take college-prep courses in high school. GPA is the most important criterion and the sub score on the verbal section of the ACT/SATs weighted more heavily than math. Required SAT and GPA are adjusted in relation to general admission averages. The final decision is made by the admissions office.

ADDITIONAL INFORMATION

Specialists help with learning strategies for courses. Students meet with LD specialists to register quarterly and design a schedule that considers their LD along with curriculum requirements. Students are assisted in communicating their disabilities and learning needs with their instructors. Course substitutions for foreign language may be approved with appropriate documentation. Modifications for assignments and tests are designed to meet students' specific needs. Skills classes for college credit are offered to all students at UGA in study techniques, time management, problem-solving, research paper writing, and career selection. Students with ADD are serviced by Disability Services.

Support Services Contact Information

Learning Disability Program/Services: Disability Services
Director: Dr. Karen Kalivoda
  E-Mail: voda@uga.edu
  Telephone: 706-542-8719
  Fax: 706-542-7719

LEARNING DISABILITY SERVICES

Requests for the following services/accommodations will be evaluated individually based on appropriate and current documentation.

Allowed in exams
  Calculator: Yes
  Dictionary: Yes
  Computer: Yes
  Spellchecker: Yes
Extended test time: Yes
Scribes: Yes
Proctors: Yes
Oral exams: Yes
Note-takers: Yes

Distraction reduced environment: Yes
Tape recording in class: Yes
Books on tape from RFBD: Yes
Taping of books not from RFBD: Yes
Accommodations for students with
  ADD: Yes
Reading machine: Yes
Other assistive technology: Yes
Priority registration: Yes

Added costs for services: No
LD specialists: Yes
Professional tutors: Yes
Peer tutors: No
Max. hours/wk. for services: N/A
How professors are notified of
  LD/ADD: By student

GENERAL ADMISSIONS INFORMATION

Director of Admissions: Nancy McDuff
Telephone: 706-542-8776

ENTRANCE REQUIREMENTS

Academic units required: 4 English, 4 math, 3 science (2 science lab), 2 foreign language, 3 social studies. High school diploma is required and GED is accepted. ACT with Writing component required or SAT Reasoning. TOEFL required of all international applicants, minimum paper TOEFL 550, minimum computer TOEFL 213.

Application deadline: 2/1
Notification: 4/1
Average GPA: 3.71

Average SAT Math: 609
Average SAT Verbal: 604
Average ACT: 26

Graduated top 10% of class: 50%
Graduated top 25% of class: 85%
Graduated top 50% of class: 98%

COLLEGE GRADUATION REQUIREMENTS

Course waivers allowed: No
Course substitutions allowed: Yes
In what course: Foreign language

ADDITIONAL INFORMATION

Environment: The university is located on a large campus 80 miles from Atlanta.

Student Body:
  Undergrad enrollment: 24,615
  Women: 57%
  Men: 43%
  Percent out-of-state: 11%

Cost Information
  In-state tuition: $3,368
  Out-of-state tuition: $14,684
  Room & board: $5,756
Housing Information
  University housing: Yes
  Percent living on campus: 27%

Greek System
  Fraternity: Yes
  Sorority: Yes
Athletics: NCAA Division I

UNIVERSITY OF IDAHO

Admissions Office, PO Box 444264, Moscow, ID 83844-4264
Phone: 208-885-6326 • Fax: 208-885-9119
E-mail: admappl@uidaho.edu • Web: www.uidaho.edu
Support: S • Institution: 4-year public

LEARNING DISABILITY PROGRAM AND SERVICES

Student Support Services (SSS) is an Educational Assistance Program that offers participating students academic and personal support services necessary to reach their educational goals. Designed to complement existing resources on campus, this federally funded program offers students opportunities to identify and pursue educational and career goals, establish and improve academic performance, and balance the challenges of university and personal life. SSS provides highly individualized assistance, which often makes the difference in a student's persistence with his/her educational plan. Tutoring is available from one to three hours per week, per class. One hour per week is with a professional counselor, the rest with peer tutors. A math specialist is available. Enrollment is limited to the first 200 students on a first-come-first-served basis. To qualify for services a student must be a United States citizen; accepted for enrollment or currently enrolled; and be either first generation, financially limited or physically or learning disabled; in addition, a student must show a need for and a potential to benefit from the SSS Program.

LD/ADD ADMISSIONS INFORMATION

College entrance tests required: Yes
Interview recommended: No
Essay recommended: No
Documentation required for LD: Psychoeducational evaluation
Documentation required for ADD: Yes
Submitted to: Student Disability Services
Special Ed. HS coursework accepted: NR

Specific course requirements of all applicants: Yes
Separate application required for program services: No
# of LD applications submitted each year: NR
# of LD applications accepted yearly: NR
Total # of students receiving LD services: 100
Acceptance into program means acceptance into college: Student must be admitted and enrolled in the university first and then reviewed for LD services.

ADMISSIONS
Students must meet the general admission requirements. The following index is used for general admission: GPA 3.0 and no ACT/SAT required; GPA 2.6–2.99 and ACT 15+ or SAT 790+; GPA 2.5–2.59 and ACT 17+ or SAT 870+; GPA 2.4-2.49 and ACT 19+ or SAT 930+; GPA 2.30-2.39 and ACT 21+ or SAT 1000+; GPA 2.20-2.29 and ACT 23+ or SAT 1070+; plus 2.0 GPA in 4 years English, 3 years math, 1 year humanities or foreign language, 2 1/2 years social science, 3 years natural science, plus electives. A freshman applicant who does not qualify for regular admission may be considered for provisional admission. A student seeking provisional admission must submit a written statement and 3 letters of recommendation. The student statement should include the student's goals, educational and/or professional objectives, an explanation of past academic performance, information and/or documentation regarding any extenuating circumstances, and anything else which may be pertinent to the applicant's request. The file is reviewed by the Admission Committee. A staff person from SSS is part of the special admissions committee for students with disabilities who do not meet regular admissions criteria. Students admitted specially or on probation must successfully complete 14 credits in 4 core areas over 3 semesters.

ADDITIONAL INFORMATION
Students with LD who participate in the SSS Program receive assistance with learning strategies, organization and time management, career advisory and employment readiness, advocacy, academic advisory, and instruction in unprepared areas in reading, writing, and math. An academic plan is mutually developed and students take an active role in their education. Students with LD who exhibit a need for and the potential to benefit from the SSS program are eligible to participate. Currently, there are 125 students with LD and 15–20 students with ADD receiving services. There are no LD specialists, but the director and Senior Program Counselor of SSS have had extensive training. The office of Student Disability Services serves as a clearinghouse to direct students with disabilities to various services on campus. The SSS Computer Lab has software programs that are useful for students with LD. All students have access to the Tutoring and Academic Assistance Center, Math and Statistics Center, and the Writing Center.

Support Services Contact Information

Learning Disability Program/Services: Student Disability Services (SDS)
Director: Gloria R. Jensen
  E-Mail: dss@uidaho.edu
  Telephone: 208-885-7200
  Fax: 208-885-9404

LEARNING DISABILITY SERVICES

Requests for the following services/accommodations will be evaluated individually based on appropriate and current documentation.

Allowed in exams
  Calculator: Yes
  Dictionary: Yes
  Computer: Yes
  Spellchecker: Yes
Extended test time: Yes
Scribes: Yes
Proctors: Yes
Oral exams: Yes
Note-takers: Yes

Distraction reduced environment: Yes
Tape recording in class: Yes
Books on tape from RFBD: Yes
Taping of books not from RFBD: Yes
Accommodations for students with
  ADD: Yes
Reading machine: No
Other assistive technology: Yes
Priority registration: Yes

Added costs for services: No
LD specialists: No
Professional tutors: No
Peer tutors: Yes
Max. hours/wk. for services: No
How professors are notified of
  LD/ADD: By student

GENERAL ADMISSIONS INFORMATION

Director of Admissions: Dan Davenport
Telephone: 208-885-6326

ENTRANCE REQUIREMENTS

Academic units required: 4 English, 3 math, 3 science (1 science lab), 1 foreign language, 3 social studies, 2 academic electives. High school diploma is required and GED is accepted. TOEFL required of all international applicants, minimum paper TOEFL 525, minimum computer TOEFL 193.

Application deadline: 8/1
Notification: Rolling basis
Average GPA: 3.4

Average SAT Math: 559
Average SAT Verbal: 549
Average ACT: 23

Graduated top 10% of class: 20%
Graduated top 25% of class: 47%
Graduated top 50% of class: 78%

COLLEGE GRADUATION REQUIREMENTS

Course waivers allowed: No
Course substitutions allowed: Yes
In what course: Math and foreign language: students must request by petition.

ADDITIONAL INFORMATION

Environment: The university is located on a 800-acre campus in a small town 90 miles south of Spokane, Washington.

Student Body:
  Undergrad enrollment: 9,047
  Women: 45%
  Men: 55%
  Percent out-of-state: 22%

Cost Information
  In-state tuition: $3,348
  Out-of-state tuition: $10,740
  Room & board: $4,868
Housing Information
  University housing: Yes
  Percent living on campus: 90%

Greek System
  Fraternity: Yes
  Sorority: Yes
Athletics: NCAA Division I

DePaul University

1 East Jackson Boulevard, Chicago, IL 60604-2287
Phone: 312-362-8300 • Fax: 312-362-5749
E-mail: admitdpu@depaul.edu • Web: www.depaul.edu
Support: CS • Institution: 4-year private

LEARNING DISABILITY PROGRAM AND SERVICES

Productive Learning Strategies (PLuS) is designed to service students with learning disabilities and/or attention deficit disorder who are motivated to succeed in college. The immediate goals are to provide learning strategies, based on the strengths and weaknesses of the individual, to assist students in the completion of coursework. The ultimate goal is to impart academic and study skills that will enable the students to function independently in the academic environment and competitive job market. PLuS provides intensive help on a one-to-one basis. It is designed to assist with regular college courses, improve learning deficits, and help the student learn compensatory skills. Students can choose to work with learning disability specialists whom they can meet for up to two hours per week.

LD/ADD ADMISSIONS INFORMATION

College entrance tests required: Yes
Interview recommended: Yes
Essay recommended: No
Documentation required for LD: WAIS–III academics achievement and information processing, measures (could include Woodcock-Johnson psychoeducational battery
Documentation required for ADD: Report with background information, DSM—II criteria, symptoms that met diagnosis recommendations for academic accomodations
Submitted to: Plus Program
Special Ed. HS coursework accepted: Yes

Specific course requirements of all applicants: Yes
Separate application required for program services: Yes
# of LD applications submitted each year: 50–75
# of LD applications accepted yearly: 50–75
Total # of students receiving LD services: 176
Acceptance into program means acceptance into college: Student must be admitted and enrolled in the university first and then request services.

ADMISSIONS

There is no separate admission process for students with learning disabilities. Students with learning disabilities must be accepted to DePaul University before they can be accepted to PLuS. The diagnostic testing that is required, if done within the last 3–5 years, will be used in the evaluation. General admission criteria include a GPA of 2.5, top 40 percent of class, and ACT 21 or SAT 1000. Students should have 4 years of English, 3 years of math, 2 years of science, and 2 years of social studies (1 history). Students with appropriate documentation may request substitutions in entrance requirements. Students may elect to self-disclose the disability during the admission process and submit their application to the attention of the PLuS Program. If the student does not have the required testing, PLuS will administer the appropriate assessments. Some students who are considered "high potential" but who have borderline admission criteria may qualify for admissions through the Bridge Program. This is an enhancement program for incoming freshmen. Bridge students may have an ACT of 18–20 or SAT of 850–880. (This program is not for students with learning disabilities although some students are learning disabled.) Bridge students must begin in a summer program prior to freshman year. Some students can be admitted on a probationary basis as Special Students. Adult students (over 24) can be admitted through the Adult Admissions Program.

ADDITIONAL INFORMATION

PLuS is housed in the Reading and Learning Lab and the program is only available to students with learning disabilities and/or attention deficit disorder. Some accommodations are offered through the Office for Students with Disabilities. Students who do the best at DePaul and the PLuS program are students who are highly motivated and who have received LD resource support in grade school and high school but were enrolled in mainstream classes. Accommodations include extended time of exams, separate and distraction-free space to take exams, and books on tape. Services provided by PLUS include advocacy with professors 2 hours per week with a learning disabilities specialist to receive direct instruction in learning strategies, coping strategies, and mentoring. Students can choose to participate in this "fee-for-service" component of the program. Services and accommodations are available for undergraduate and graduate students.

Support Services Contact Information

Learning Disability Program/Services: Productive Learning Strategies Program (PLUS)
Director: Coordinator: Karen Meyer
  E-Mail: kmeyer@depaul.edu
  Telephone: 773-325-7290
  Fax: 773-325-7396

LEARNING DISABILITY SERVICES

Requests for the following services/accommodations will be evaluated individually based on appropriate and current documentation.

Allowed in exams
  Calculator: Yes
  Dictionary: Yes
  Computer: Yes
  Spellchecker: Yes
Extended test time: Yes
Scribes: Yes
Proctors: Yes
Oral exams: Yes
Note-takers: Yes

Distraction reduced environment: Yes
Tape recording in class: Yes
Books on tape from RFBD: Yes
Taping of books not from RFBD: No
**Accommodations for students with
  ADD:** Yes
Reading machine: No
Other assistive technology: Yes
Priority registration: Yes

Added costs for services: Yes
LD specialists: Yes
Professional tutors: No
Peer tutors: No
Max. hours/wk. for services: 2
**How professors are notified of
  LD/ADD:** By student

GENERAL ADMISSIONS INFORMATION

Director of Admissions: Carlene Klass
Telephone: 312-362-8146

ENTRANCE REQUIREMENTS
Academic units required: 4 English, 2 math, 2 science (2 science lab), 2 social studies, 4 academic electives. High school diploma is required and GED is accepted. TOEFL required of all international applicants, minimum paper TOEFL 550, minimum computer TOEFL 213.

Application deadline: Rolling
Notification: Rolling
Average GPA: 3.3

Average SAT Math: 570
Average SAT Verbal: 560
Average ACT: 24

Graduated top 10% of class: 19%
Graduated top 25% of class: 43%
Graduated top 50% of class: 75%

COLLEGE GRADUATION REQUIREMENTS

Course waivers allowed: No
Course substitutions allowed: Yes
In what course: Foreign language requirement can be substituted.

ADDITIONAL INFORMATION

Environment: DePaul has a 3-acre urban campus located in Chicago's Lincoln Park area 3 miles north of the downtown area.

Student Body:
  Undergrad enrollment: 14,239
  Women: 58%
  Men: 42%
  Percent out-of-state: 13%

Cost Information
  Tuition: $19,700
  Room & board: $9,307
Housing Information
  University housing: Yes
  Percent living on campus: 18%

Greek System
  Fraternity: Yes
  Sorority: Yes
  Athletics: NCAA Division I

EASTERN ILLINOIS UNIVERSITY

600 Lincoln Avenue, Charleston, IL 61920
Phone: 217-581-2223 • Fax: 217-581-7060
E-mail: admissns@www.eiu.edu • Web: www.eiu.edu
Support: S • Institution: 4-year public

LEARNING DISABILITY PROGRAM AND SERVICES

EIU will provide services as deemed effective and reasonable to assist students with LD to obtain access to the proper university programs. Students applying to the university who are requesting support services and/or accommodations from the Office of Disability Services are required to submit documentation to verify eligibility under Section 504. The assessment and diagnosis of specific LD must be conducted by a qualified professional. The written diagnostic evaluation report should include the following information: diagnostic report clearly stating the LD and the rationale for the diagnosis; the tests administered and the specific scores including grade level scores, standard scores, and percentile scores; descriptive written text beyond that which is provided on a typical IEP and including qualitative information about the student's abilities; recommendations for accommodations that include specific suggestions based on the diagnostic evaluation results and supported by the diagnosis; and identifying information about the evaluator/diagnostician. The diagnostic tests should be current within the last three years, should be comprehensive, and include a battery of more than one test and/or subtest. They should also include at least one instrument to measure aptitude or cognitive ability; and should include at least one measurement in reading, written language, and math.

LD/ADD ADMISSIONS INFORMATION

College entrance tests required: Yes
Interview recommended: No
Essay recommended: No
Documentation required for LD: Psychoeducational evaluation
Documentation required for ADD: Yes
Submitted to: Disability Services
Special Ed. HS coursework accepted: Yes

Specific course requirements of all applicants: Yes
Separate application required for program services: No
# of LD applications submitted each year: 80–90
# of LD applications accepted yearly: NR
Total # of students receiving LD services: 80–90
Acceptance into program means acceptance into college: Student must be admitted and enrolled in the university first and then request services.

ADMISSIONS

All applicants must meet the same admission criteria. General admission requires students to (1) rank in the top half of the class and have a minimum ACT of 18 or SAT of 860 or (2) rank in the top three-quarters of the class and have a minimum ACT of 22 or SAT of 1020. Additionally, all students must have 4 years of English, 3 years math, 3 years social science, 3 years laboratory science, and 2 years electives. Once admitted, students with LD or ADD must provide appropriate documentation in order to access services and accommodations.

ADDITIONAL INFORMATION

Students should meet with the Office of Disability Services to discuss accommodations or make further arrangements as needed. Some services provided include priority registration, alternate format for classroom materials, note-takers, assistance locating tutors and liaison with tutors to develop effective study strategies, proctors, and liaison with instructors. Skills classes can be arranged in time management, note taking, test-taking, and study strategies.

Support Services Contact Information

Learning Disability Program/Services: Office of Disability Services
Director: Kathy Waggoner
  E-Mail: cfkw@eiu.edu
  Telephone: 217-581-6583
  Fax: 217-581-7208

LEARNING DISABILITY SERVICES

Requests for the following services/accommodations will be evaluated individually based on appropriate and current documentation.

Allowed in exams
  Calculator: Yes
  Dictionary: Y/N
  Computer: Y/N
  Spellchecker: Yes
Extended test time: Yes
Scribes: Yes
Proctors: Yes
Oral exams: Yes
Note-takers: Yes

Distraction reduced environment: Yes
Tape recording in class: Yes
Books on tape from RFBD: Yes
Taping of books not from RFBD: Yes
Accommodations for students with
  ADD: Yes
Reading machine: Yes
Other assistive technology: Yes
Priority registration: Yes

Added costs for services: Yes
LD specialists: No
Professional tutors: NR
Peer tutors: No
Max. hours/wk. for services: N/A
How professors are notified of
  LD/ADD: By student and director

GENERAL ADMISSIONS INFORMATION

Director of Admissions: Dale Wolf
Telephone: 217-581-2223

ENTRANCE REQUIREMENTS
Academic units required: 4 English, 3 math, 3 science (3 science lab), 3 social studies, 2 academic electives. High school diploma is required and GED is accepted ACT or SAT required but no writing component. TOEFL required of all international applicants, minimum paper TOEFL 500, minimum computer TOEFL 173.

Application deadline: Rolling
Notification: Rolling
Average GPA: NR

Average SAT Math: NR
Average SAT Verbal: NR
Average ACT: 22

Graduated top 10% of class: 7%
Graduated top 25% of class: 27%
Graduated top 50% of class: 65%

COLLEGE GRADUATION REQUIREMENTS

Course waivers allowed: No
Course substitutions allowed: No
In what course: N/A

ADDITIONAL INFORMATION

Environment: The university is in a small town 50 miles south of the University of Illinois.

Student Body:
  Undergrad enrollment: 9,714
  Women: 58%
  Men: 42%
  Percent out-of-state: 3%

Cost Information
  In-state tuition: $3,563
  Out-of-state tuition: $10,688
  Room & board: $6,210
Housing Information
  University housing: Yes
  Percent living on campus: 46%

Greek System
  Fraternity: Yes
  Sorority: Yes
Athletics: NCAA Division I

ILLINOIS STATE UNIVERSITY

Admissions Office, Campus Box 2200, Normal, IL 61790-2200
Phone: 309-438-2181 • Fax: 309-438-3932
E-mail: admissions@ilstu.edu • Web: www.ilstu.edu
Support: CS • Institution: 4-year public

LEARNING DISABILITY PROGRAM AND SERVICES

The mission of the Disability Concerns office is to ensure the full and equal participation for persons with disabilities in the university community through empowering individuals, promoting equal access, encouraging self-advocacy, reducing attitudinal and communication barriers, and providing appropriate accommodation. The Disability Concerns program is designed to work with students who have learning disabilities on becoming academically and socially successful while attending Illinois State University. After a review of the appropriate documentation by the coordinator of the learning disability services and a consultation, accommodations can then be determined based on the needs of the individual. A psychoeducational evaluation consisting of the adult assessment scale is required. It should include test scores and the following: the diagnosis, including specific areas of the disability; the impact the disability has on the academic performance of the student; and the accommodations suggested in view of the impact of the disability on learning.

LD/ADD ADMISSIONS INFORMATION

College entrance tests required: Yes
Interview recommended: No
Essay recommended: No
Documentation required for LD: The student must provide a complete psychoeducational evaluation and a report that includes the following adult assessment measurement of apptitude.
Documentation required for ADD: The student must provide a complete psychoeducational evalution and a report that includes the following adult assessment measurements of aptitude.
Submitted to: Disability Concerns
Special Ed. HS coursework accepted: Yes

Specific course requirements of all applicants: Yes
Separate application required for program services: No
# of LD applications submitted each year: NR
# of LD applications accepted yearly: NR
Total # of students receiving LD services: 150
Acceptance into program means acceptance into college: Students must be admitted and enrolled in the university first and then request services.

ADMISSIONS

Admissions criteria for students with learning disabilities are the same as for other students at this time. Applicants with questions should contact the Disability Concerns Office. In general, students are admissible if they are in the top three-fourths of their high school class and have an ACT of 23 or better. High school courses required include 4 years English, 3 years math, 2 years social science, 2 years science, 2 years electives. Students with learning disabilities who are borderline admits or who are denied admission may self-disclose and ask to be reviewed by Disability Concerns. The director will review the documentation and make a recommendation to admissions.

ADDITIONAL INFORMATION

The following are options for accommodations based on appropriate documentation and needs: note-takers, peer tutors, readers, scribes, taped textbooks, computers, testing accommodations, conference with LD specialist, and quiet study rooms. Learning through Mini Sessions (LMS) are designed to help students make college academics and college life a little less stressful. Sessions could include stress management, self advocacy, test anxiety, communication skills, and organizational skills.

Support Services Contact Information

Learning Disability Program/Services: Disability Concerns
Director: Ann M. Caldwell
  E-Mail: ableisu@ilstu.edu
  Telephone: 309-438-5853
  Fax: 309-438-7713
Contact Person: Sheryl Hogan
  E-Mail: ableisu@ilstu.edu
  Telephone: 309-438-5853
  Fax: 309-438-7713

LEARNING DISABILITY SERVICES

Requests for the following services/accommodations will be evaluated individually based on appropriate and current documentation.

Allowed in exams
  Calculator: Yes
  Dictionary: No
  Computer: Yes
  Spellchecker: Yes
Extended test time: Yes
Scribes: Yes
Proctors: Yes
Oral exams: Yes
Note-takers: Yes

Distraction reduced environment: Yes
Tape recording in class: Yes
Books on tape from RFBD: Yes
Taping of books not from RFBD: Yes
Accommodations for students with ADD: Yes
Reading machine: Yes
Other assistive technology: Yes
Priority registration: No

Added costs for services: No
LD specialists: Yes
Professional tutors: No
Peer tutors: As needed
Max. hours/wk. for services: Unlimited
How professors are notified of LD/ADD: By both student and director

GENERAL ADMISSIONS INFORMATION

Director of Admissions: Molly Arnold
Telephone: 309-438-2181

ENTRANCE REQUIREMENTS

Academic units required: 4 English, 3 math, 2 science (2 science lab), 2 foreign language, 2 social studies, 2 academic electives. High school diploma is required and GED is accepted. ACT with or without Writing component accepted. TOEFL required of all international applicants, minimum paper TOEFL 550, minimum computer TOEFL 213.

Application deadline: 3/1
Notification: Rolling
Average GPA: NR

Average SAT Math: NR
Average SAT Verbal: NR
Average ACT: 23

Graduated top 10% of class: 11%
Graduated top 25% of class: 38%
Graduated top 50% of class: 81%

COLLEGE GRADUATION REQUIREMENTS

Course waivers allowed: No
Course substitutions allowed: Yes
In what course: Determined on individual basis.

ADDITIONAL INFORMATION

Environment: The university is located on 850 acres in a small town 125 miles south of Chicago, and 180 miles north of St. Louis.

Student Body:
  Undergrad enrollment: 17,806
  Women: 57%
  Men: 43%
  Percent out-of-state: 1%

Cost Information
  In-state tuition: $4,800
  Out-of-state tuition: $10,020
  Room & board: $5,576
Housing Information
  University housing: Yes
  Percent living on campus: 35%

Greek System
  Fraternity: Yes
  Sorority: Yes
Athletics: NCAA Division I

LINCOLN COLLEGE

300 Keokuk Street, Lincoln, IL 62656
Phone: 800-569-0556 • Fax: 217-732-7715
E-mail: admission@lincolncollege.com • Web: www.lincolncollege.edu
Support: S • Institution: 4-year private

LEARNING DISABILITY PROGRAM AND SERVICES

Lincoln College is committed to enhancing student achievement through supportive service community efforts in combination with parental involvement. The college offers personal attention and a number of supportive services to assist students. The Academic Enrichment Program meets every day to improve fundamental learning skills in writing, reading, mathematics, and oral communication. Study skills and study habits are also emphasized. Tutoring is assigned and each student's course schedule is strictly regulated. The Breakfast Club is for students who are failing 2 or more classes. These students meet with the college president and the academic dean to discuss ways to change direction and achieve academic success. Class attendance is monitored and faculty members inform the dean weekly if a student has missed class. Advisors help students to change counterproductive behaviors regarding attendance. C.A.S.P. (Concerned about Student Progress) warnings are sent the fifth week of each semester to provide an early indicator of below average performance, and allow students time to recover and change behaviors. The Connection Program targets incoming freshmen who may benefit from an established peer group. These groups of 8–10 meet with professors and foster awareness and build relationships.

LD/ADD ADMISSIONS INFORMATION

College entrance tests required: Yes
Interview recommended: Yes
Essay recommended: No
Documentation required for LD: Psychoeducational evaluation
Documentation required for ADD: Yes
Submitted to: Admissions
Special Ed. HS coursework accepted: Yes

Specific course requirements of all applicants: No
Separate application required for program services: No
# of LD applications submitted each year: NR
# of LD applications accepted yearly: NR
Total # of students receiving LD services: NR
Acceptance into program means acceptance into college: Students are admitted and enrolled at the college and then reviewed for supportive services.

ADMISSIONS

There is no special admissions process for students with learning disabilities. Students must submit the general application, a high school transcript, and counselor recommendation. Students with sub-17 ACT scores are required to attend the one week Academic Development Seminar prior to the fall semester. Upon completing the Academic Development Seminar, a student's probationary status is removed. Students may be admitted and placed into a split semester, which means the student will take two courses per nine weeks if this is recommended by the Academic Development Seminar.

ADDITIONAL INFORMATION

Lincoln College offers the Academic Development Seminar for students the week before fall semester starts. Students learn writing and speaking skills, effective library skills, and science lab orientation. They develop effective student techniques; lab and field orientation; methods to evaluate social science graphs, charts, and maps; and concepts and values in the humanities. The Academic Writing Seminar is also offered for one week in the summer to cover crucial college skills such as writing skill development, note-taking techniques, exam tips, speaking skills, writing to define and classify; college expectations, analytical thinking and writing, and writing to understand and evaluate.

Support Services Contact Information

Learning Disability Program/Services: Supportive Educational Services
Director: Tony Schilling
   E-Mail: tschilling@lincolncollege.edu
   Telephone: 800-569-0556
   Fax: 217-732-7715

LEARNING DISABILITY SERVICES

Requests for the following services/accommodations will be evaluated individually based on appropriate and current documentation.

Allowed in exams
   Calculator: Yes
   Dictionary: Yes
   Computer: Yes
   Spellchecker: Yes
Extended test time: Yes
Scribes: No
Proctors: No
Oral exams: No
Note-takers: No

Distraction reduced environment: Yes
Tape recording in class: Yes
Books on tape from RFBD: Yes
Taping of books not from RFBD: No
Accommodations for students with
   ADD: Yes
Reading machine: No
Other assistive technology: No
Priority registration: Yes

Added costs for services: No
LD specialists: No
Professional tutors: 15
Peer tutors: 20–30
Max. hours/wk. for services: Unlimited
How professors are notified of LD/ADD: By student

GENERAL ADMISSIONS INFORMATION

Director of Admissions: Tony Schilling, Executive Director of Enrollment Management
Telephone: 800-569-0556

ENTRANCE REQUIREMENTS

16 total recommendations, including 4 English, 3 math, 3 science, 3 social studies, and 2 foreign language. ACT of 16 or higher admitted without restriction. Those with an ACT of 15 or lower may be admitted upon review by the Admission Committee. These students must complete and pass the academic development seminar. TOEFL required of all international applicants, minimum paper TOEFL 480, minimum computer TOEFL 157.

Application deadline: Rolling
Notification: Rolling
Average GPA: NR

Average SAT Math: NR
Average SAT Verbal: NR
Average ACT: 18

Graduated top 10% of class: NR
Graduated top 25% of class: NR
Graduated top 50% of class: NR

COLLEGE GRADUATION REQUIREMENTS

Course waivers allowed: No
Course substitutions allowed: No

ADDITIONAL INFORMATION

Environment: The college has a suburban campus in Normal, Illinois, and a small town campus in Lincoln.

Student Body:
   Undergrad enrollment: 700
   Women: 40%
   Men: 60%
   Percent out-of-state: 10%

Cost Information
   Tuition: 14,300
   Room & board: $5,600
Housing Information
   University housing: Yes
   Percent living on campus: 83%

Greek System
   Fraternity: No
   Sorority: No
Athletics: NJCAA

LOYOLA UNIVERSITY—CHICAGO

820 North Michigan Avenue, Chicago, IL 60611
Phone: 312-915-6500 • Fax: 312-915-7216
E-mail: admission@luc.edu • Web: www.luc.edu
Support: CS • Institution type: 4-year private

LEARNING DISABILITY PROGRAM AND SERVICES

Every student with a disability is unique and her or his requests for services will be considered on a case-by-case basis. Services for Students with Disabilities work closely with several Loyola departments and outside agencies to ensure that educational needs are met. The goal of Services for Students with Disabilities is to maximize each student's potential in assisting him or her to develop and maintain independence. Our philosophy encourages self-awareness, self-determination, self-advocacy and independence in an accessible learning environment. Encouragement is given to all students to visit the Learning Assistance Center and Services for Students with Disabilities to explore the services available. The Office of Services for Students with Disabilities is part of the Learning Assistance Center.

LD/ADD ADMISSIONS INFORMATION

College entrance tests required: Yes
Interview recommended: No
Essay recommended: No
Documentation required for LD: Psychoeducational
   evaluation
Documentation required for ADD: Yes
Submitted to: Services for Students with Disabilities
Special Ed. HS coursework accepted: Yes

Specific course requirements of all applicants: Yes
Separate application required for program services: No
# of LD applications submitted each year: NR
# of LD applications accepted yearly: NR
Total # of students receiving LD services: NR
Acceptance into program means acceptance into
   college: Students must be admitted and enrolled in the
   university and then may request services.

ADMISSIONS

There is not a special admissions procedure for students with disabilities. All admission applications are handled on a case-by-case basis by the Office for Undergraduate Admissions. The following units or courses are suggested for admission to Loyola University Chicago: 4 years of English (required), 3–4 years of math; 3 years of social science, 2 or more years of foreign language, and 3–4 years of natural or physical science. Each application is reviewed individually and thoroughly. The writing sample, counselor recommendation, student activities, grades and standardized test scores are all considered to determine if Loyola will be a good academic match for the strengths and abilities of the applicant. Loyola does not require or use the new written sections on the SAT and ACT for admission or placement.

ADDITIONAL INFORMATION

The Office of Services for Students with Disabilities is part of the Learning Assistance Center, which offers individual and group sessions for improving learning, tutorial services, and in-class workshops. Many students with disabilities work closely with both the coordinator and a learning assistance counselor. Students are encouraged to meet with the coordinator of services for students with Disabilities during the first two weeks of each semester to determine accommodations and services for the current semester. Documentation should provide a clear description of the recommended accommodations, connect these to the impact of the condition, provide possible alternatives to the recommended accommodations, and include a statement of the level of need (or consequences of not receiving) the accommodations. The Learning Enrichment for Academic Progress (LEAP) Program takes otherwise strong freshman students with low ACT/SAT scores, and offers them an intensive, 2-week seminar each August to shape study skills and habits. This program is not specifically for students with LD. The Academic Success Program is offered during the school year and is for all students who could benefit from intensive work on study strategies and college survival skills.

Support Services Contact Information

Learning Disability Program/Services: Services for Students with Disabilities
Director: Maggie Rogers
  E-Mail: mrogers@luc.edu
  Telephone: 773-508-2741
  Fax: 773-508-3123

LEARNING DISABILITY SERVICES

Requests for the following services/accommodations will be evaluated individually based on appropriate and current documentation.

Allowed in exams
  Calculator: Yes
  Dictionary: Yes
  Computer: Yes
  Spellchecker: Yes
Extended test time: Yes
Scribes: Yes
Proctors: Yes
Oral exams: Yes
Note-takers: Yes

Distraction reduced environment: Yes
Tape recording in class: Yes
Books on tape from RFBD: Yes
Taping of books not from RFBD: Yes
**Accommodations for students with
  ADD:** Yes
Reading machine: Yes
Other assistive technology: Yes
Priority registration: Yes

Added costs for services: N/A
LD specialists: Yes
Professional tutors: No
Peer tutors: 20
Max. hours/wk. for services: NR
**How professors are notified of
  LD/ADD:** By both student and director

GENERAL ADMISSIONS INFORMATION

Director of Admissions: April Hansen
Telephone: 312-915-6500

ENTRANCE REQUIREMENTS

Academic units required: 4 English, 2 math, 2 science, 2 social studies, 1 history. **Academic units recommended:** 4 English, 4 math, 3 science, 2 foreign language, 3 social studies, 2 history, 1 academic elective, High school diploma is required and GED is accepted. TOEFL required of all international applicants, minimum paper TOEFL 550, minimum computer TOEFL 213.

Application deadline: Rolling
Notification: Rolling
Average GPA: 3.53

Average SAT Math: 570
Average SAT Verbal: 583
Average ACT: 25

Graduated top 10% of class: 28%
Graduated top 25% of class: 66%
Graduated top 50% of class: 93%

COLLEGE GRADUATION REQUIREMENTS

Course waivers allowed: N/A
Course substitutions allowed: Yes
In what course: Substitution and/or waiver for math and foreign language if documentation supports the request.

ADDITIONAL INFORMATION

Environment: Located in downtown Chicago just east of Lake Michigan.

Student Body:
  Undergrad enrollment: 7,320
  Women: 66%
  Men: 34%
  Percent out-of-state: 34%

Cost Information
  Tuition: $21,780
    Room & board: $8,824
  Housing Information
    University housing: Yes
    Percent living on campus: 29%

Greek System
  Fraternity: Yes
  Sorority: Yes
  Athletics: NCAA Division I

NATIONAL-LOUIS UNIVERSITY

2840 Sheridan Road, Evanston, IL 60201
Phone: 847-465-0575 • Fax: 847-465-0594
E-mail: nlnuinfo@wheeling1.nl.edu • Web: www.nl.edu
Support: CS• Institution type: 4-year private

LEARNING DISABILITY PROGRAM AND SERVICES

The Center for Academic Development is designed to assist students with learning disabilities to pursue and complete a college education. It is a supportive program for students admitted by the university and enrolled in regular and developmental college courses. While the total services furnished in this program are provided by the university to all students who might experience difficulty with a regular college curriculum, emphasis is placed on individual program planning, tutoring, monitoring, arranged counseling, and special testing for the learning disabled. The center provides peer tutoring, a liaison with faculty, academic advising, and career/emotional counseling for students who make reasonable progress toward a degree in one of the college programs.

LD/ADD ADMISSIONS INFORMATION

College entrance tests required: Yes
Interview recommended: No
Essay recommended: No
Documentation required for LD: At least WAIS–III; WJ
Documentation required for ADD: Yes
Submitted to: Support Program/Services
Special Ed. HS coursework accepted: No

Specific course requirements of all applicants: Yes
Separate application required for program services: No
# of LD applications submitted each year: NR
# of LD applications accepted yearly: NR
Total # of students receiving LD services: 25
Acceptance into program means acceptance into college: Student must be admitted and enrolled in the university first and then request services.

ADMISSIONS

Students must meet regular admission requirements of a 2.0 GPA in non-remedial academic courses. Interested students should indicate on the supplemental application form the nature of their learning disability and return the form to the admissions office. An informal assessment session is held with the applicants by a learning specialist. Students forward all requested reports to admissions with authorization for release of information. Students should submit a statement from a diagnostician that they can function at college level. Social service or psychiatric reports should also be submitted. The learning specialist evaluates reports and admits 10 students each fall and they must participate in the Summer Bridge Program and LD counseling group. Alternative admission for all students is offered through Provisional Admission and/or Summer Admission.

ADDITIONAL INFORMATION

The Center for Academic Development is staffed by specialists. Special services provided include Summer Bridge Program; developmental reading, writing, and math courses; special advising and orientation; assistance in registration; individualized tutoring and monitoring; organizational and student skill training; academic and career counseling; and an arrangement with faculty for modification of course presentation and examination. Support services and accommodations are offered to undergraduate and graduate students. The PACE Program is housed on this campus. This is a non-credit transition program for students with low I.Q. scores who want to experience residential living and develop life skills. These students have the opportunity to get work experience as Teacher Aides or in Human Resources. (Contact Dr. Robert Harth at 847-256-5150.)

Support Services Contact Information

Learning Disability Program/Services: Center for Academic Development
Director: Jady Piper
  E-Mail: jpiper@nl.edu
  Telephone: 312-261-3300
  Fax: 312-261-3057
Contact Person: Margaret Wong
  E-Mail: mwong@nl.edu
  Telephone: 312-261-3367
  Fax: 312-261-3289

LEARNING DISABILITY SERVICES

Requests for the following services/accommodations will be evaluated individually based on appropriate and current documentation.

Allowed in exams
  Calculator: Yes
  Dictionary: Yes
  Computer: Yes
  Spellchecker: Yes
Extended test time: Yes
Scribes: Yes
Proctors: Yes
Oral exams: No
Note-takers: Yes

Distraction reduced environment: Yes
Tape recording in class: Yes
Books on tape from RFBD: Yes
Taping of books not from RFBD: No
Accommodations for students with
  ADD: Yes
Reading machine: No
Other assistive technology: Yes
Priority registration: No

Added costs for services: No
LD specialists: Yes
Professional tutors: 5
Peer tutors: 5
Max. hours/wk. for services: 2
How professors are notified of
  LD/ADD: By student

GENERAL ADMISSIONS INFORMATION

Director of Admissions: Pat Patillo
Telephone: 847-465-0575

ENTRANCE REQUIREMENTS
Academic units recommended: 4 English, 3 math, 2 science (1 science lab), 2 foreign language, 3 social studies. High school diploma is required and GED is accepted. TOEFL required of all international applicants, minimum paper TOEFL 500, minimum computer TOEFL 173

Application deadline: Rolling
Notification: Rolling
Average GPA: NR

Average SAT Math: NR
Average SAT Verbal: NR
Average ACT: 18

Graduated top 10% of class: 0%
Graduated top 25% of class: 29%
Graduated top 50% of class: 89%

COLLEGE GRADUATION REQUIREMENTS

Course waivers allowed: No
Course substitutions allowed: No
In what course: N/A

ADDITIONAL INFORMATION

Environment: Formerly known as National College of Education, the school is located in Evanston. NLU sits on 12 acres in a suburban neighborhood 12 miles north of Chicago.

Student Body:
  Undergrad enrollment: 3,545
  Women: 72%
  Men: 28%
  Percent out-of-state: 1%

Cost Information
  Tuition: $13,095
  Room & board: $6,336
Housing Information
  University housing: Yes
  Percent living on campus: 5%

Greek System
  Fraternity: No
  Sorority: No
Athletics: NCAA NCAA Division I

NORTHERN ILLINOIS UNIVERSITY

Office of Admissions, Williston Hall 101, NIU, DeKalb, IL 60115-2857
Phone: 815-753-0446 • Fax: 815-753-1783
E-mail: admissions-info@niu.edu • Web: www.niu.edu
Support: CS • Institution type: 4-year public

LEARNING DISABILITY PROGRAM AND SERVICES

The main goal of the Center for Access Ability Resources (CAAR) is to create and maintain a supportive atmosphere to assist students with LD develop self-esteem, self-advocacy skills, and effective strategies for college success. CAAR is staffed by personnel who are supportive and sensitive to students. CAAR provides a comprehensive range of support services that are integrated within university resources. Assistance must be requested by the student. The LD Coordinator assists students in identifying appropriate accommodations, compensatory, and remediation strategies, and in the utilization of both on- and off-campus resources. Not all students are eligible for services. It is the responsibility of CAAR to see that qualified students who request services are provided appropriate accommodations. Instructors can also verify student accommodation requests through CAAR. The goal is to enhance student success through an individualized program of support services. To request and initiate services, students must submit to CAAR the necessary and appropriate official documentation verifying the disability.

LD/ADD ADMISSIONS INFORMATION

College entrance tests required: Yes
Interview recommended: No
Essay recommended: No
Documentation required for LD: Psychoeducational
  evaluation less than 3 years old
Documentation required for ADD: Yes
Submitted to: CAAR
Special Ed. HS coursework accepted: No

Specific course requirements of all applicants: Yes
Separate application required for program services: No
# of LD applications submitted each year: NR
# of LD applications accepted yearly: NR
Total # of students receiving LD services: 125–150
Acceptance into program means acceptance into
  college: Students admitted may request services. Students denied admission may appeal the decision and once admitted may request services.

ADMISSIONS

Regular admission requires: 50–99 percent class rank and 19 ACT or 34–49 percent class rank and 23 ACT. Course requirements include 4 years English, 2–3 math, 2–3 sciences, 3 social studies, and 1–2 years of foreign language, art or music. Substitutions may be allowed with appropriate documentation. Students with LD apply through regular admissions, but can disclose the LD and request that their application be given special consideration if they feel that their entrance tests scores or high school performance was adversely affected by special circumstances related to a documented disability. Special admission consideration for students with disabilities applies only to freshman applicants who do not meet standard admission criteria and/or have already been denied admission. The special admission process involves (1) completing the standard NIU application, and (2) attaching a "special consideration" letter asking that the application be given special consideration based on a diagnosed disability. This helps to describe the disability. This alerts Admissions to forward the application to CAAR. CAAR will need the following: (1) documentation of the disability with a personal statement explaining your interest in attending NIU, your academic and career goals, and any other information you would like to share (2) three letters of recommendation from persons who have worked with you in an academic setting, and (3) any additional information about the disability that is pertinent. The admission process begins when all requested information has been received. Students may be contacted for an on-campus interview with a CAAR coordinator. CAAR staff make a recommendation to Admissions, who will notify students of the admission decision.

ADDITIONAL INFORMATION

Academic resources include priority registration, exam accommodations, limited tutoring, individualized study skill learning strategy advisement and instruction by LD specialists, reading and study techniques course taught by an LD specialist, foreign language course substitution with documentation; and taped texts. Other requests for course substitutions will be reviewed individually. Advocacy services include orientation, self-advocacy training, and liaison with faculty, information on LD/ADD-related events, and in-service training for faculty. Advisement resources include academic advising, referrals to University Counseling, and support and consultation by staff. Diagnostic evaluation for LD and ADD are offered through referral to private diagnostician. Not all students are eligible for all services.

Support Services Contact Information

Learning Disability Program/Services: Center for Access-Ability Resources
Director: Nancy Kasinski
  E-Mail: nancyk@niu.edu
  Telephone: 815-753-9734
  Fax: 815-753-9570
Contact Person: Garth Rubin
  E-Mail: grubin@niu.edu
  Telephone: 815-753-9750
  Fax: 815-753-9570

LEARNING DISABILITY SERVICES

Requests for the following services/accommodations will be evaluated individually based on appropriate and current documentation.

Allowed in exams
  Calculator: Yes
  Dictionary: Yes
  Computer: Yes
  Spellchecker: Yes
Extended test time: Yes
Scribes: Yes
Proctors: Yes
Oral exams: Yes
Note-takers: Yes

Distraction reduced environment: Yes
Tape recording in class: Yes
Books on tape from RFBD: Yes
Taping of books not from RFBD: Yes
Accommodations for students with ADD: Yes
Reading machine: Yes
Other assistive technology: Yes
Priority registration: Yes

Added costs for services: No
LD specialists: Yes
Professional tutors: No
Peer tutors: No
Max. hours/wk. for services: Unlimited
How professors are notified of LD/ADD: By student

GENERAL ADMISSIONS INFORMATION

Director of Admissions: Robert Burk
Telephone: 815-753-0446

ENTRANCE REQUIREMENTS
Academic units required: 4 English, 2 math, 2 science (1 science lab), 1 foreign language, 2 social studies, 1 history. **Academic units recommended:** 4 math, 4 science (2 science lab), 2 foreign language, 3 social studies, High school diploma is required and GED is accepted. TOEFL required of all international applicants, minimum paper TOEFL 525, minimum computer TOEFL 193.

Application deadline: 8/1
Notification: Rolling
Average GPA: NR

Average SAT Math: NR
Average SAT Verbal: NR
Average ACT: 22

Graduated top 10% of class: 9%
Graduated top 25% of class: 34%
Graduated top 50% of class: 74%

COLLEGE GRADUATION REQUIREMENTS

Course waivers allowed: No
Course substitutions allowed: Yes
In what course: Primarily for foreign language if disability severely impacts the learning of foreign language.

ADDITIONAL INFORMATION

Environment: The school is located on 460 acres in a small town 65 miles from Chicago.

Student Body:
  Undergrad enrollment: 18,025
  Women: 53%
  Men: 47%
  Percent out-of-state: 4%

Cost Information
  In-state tuition: $4,347
  Room & board: $5,010
Housing Information
  University housing: Yes
  Percent living on campus: 33%

Greek System
  Fraternity: Yes
  Sorority: Yes
Athletics: NCAA Division I

NORTHWESTERN UNIVERSITY

PO Box 3060, 1801 Hinman Avenue, Evanston, IL 60204-3060
Phone: 847-491-7271 • Fax: 555-555-5555
E-mail: ug-admission@northwestern.edu • Web: www.northwestern.edu
Support: CS• Institution type: 4-year private

LEARNING DISABILITY PROGRAM AND SERVICES

It is the policy at Northwestern University to ensure that no qualified student with a disability is denied the benefit of, excluded from participation in, or subjected to discrimination in any university program or activity.

LD/ADD ADMISSIONS INFORMATION

College entrance tests required: Yes
Interview recommended: No
Essay recommended: Yes
Documentation required for LD: WAIS–III
Documentation required for ADD: Yes
Submitted to: Services for Studens with Disabilities
Special Ed. HS coursework accepted: No

Specific course requirements of all applicants: Yes
Separate application required for program services: No
# of LD applications submitted each year: NR
# of LD applications accepted yearly: NR
Total # of students receiving LD services: 120–175
Acceptance into program means acceptance into college: Students must be admitted and enrolled in the university first and then request services.

ADMISSIONS

There is no special admissions procedure for students with learning disabilities. All applicants must meet the general admission criteria. Most students have taken AP and Honors courses in high school and been very successful in these competitive college-prep courses. ACT/SAT tests are required and SAT Subject tests are recommended.

ADDITIONAL INFORMATION

Services are available for all students with disabilities and include the Writing Center, comprehensive assistive technology, support groups, and individualized counseling. There are LD specialists on staff and all of the staff has knowledge in all disability categories. Students with learning disabilities must provide current psychoeducational evaluations normed on an adult population. Students with ADD must provide a letter from an appropriate professional including a diagnosis, functional limitations, and recommendations. This documentation should be submitted to Services for Students with Disabilities.

Support Services Contact Information

Learning Disability Program/Services: Services for Students with Disabilities
Director: Margie Roe
  E-Mail: m-roc@northwestern.edu
  Telephone: 847-467-5530
  Fax: 847-467-5531

LEARNING DISABILITY SERVICES

Requests for the following services/accommodations will be evaluated individually based on appropriate and current documentation.

Allowed in exams	**Distraction reduced environment:** Yes	**Added costs for services:** No
Calculator: Yes	**Tape recording in class:** Yes	**LD specialists:** Yes
Dictionary: Yes	**Books on tape from RFBD:** Yes	**Professional tutors:** No
Computer: Yes	**Taping of books not from RFBD:** Yes	**Peer tutors:** No
Spellchecker: Yes	**Accommodations for students with**	**Max. hours/wk. for services:**
Extended test time: Yes	**ADD:** Yes	Unlimited
Scribes: Yes	**Reading machine:** Yes	**How professors are notified of**
Proctors: Yes	**Other assistive technology:** Yes	**LD/ADD:** By both student and director
Oral exams: Yes	**Priority registration:** Yes	
Note-takers: Yes		

GENERAL ADMISSIONS INFORMATION

Director of Admissions: Keith Todd
Telephone: 847-491-7271

ENTRANCE REQUIREMENTS

Academic units recommended: 4 English, 3 math, 2 science (2 science lab), 2 foreign language, 2 social studies, 1 academic elective. High school diploma or equivalent is not required. ACT with Writing component or SAT. SAT Subject Tests are recommended. TOEFL required of all international applicants, minimum paper TOEFL 600, minimum computer TOEFL 250.

Application deadline: 1/1	**Average SAT Math:** 702	**Graduated top 10% of class:** 83%
Notification: 4/15	**Average SAT Verbal:** 687	**Graduated top 25% of class:** 97%
Average GPA: NR	**Average ACT:** 30	**Graduated top 50% of class:** 99%

COLLEGE GRADUATION REQUIREMENTS

Course waivers allowed: No
Course substitutions allowed: Yes
In what course: On case-by-case basis

ADDITIONAL INFORMATION

Environment: The Evanston campus, which houses the undergraduate schools, is located approximately 15 miles from downtown Chicago.

Student Body:	**Cost Information**	**Greek System**
Undergrad enrollment: 7,988	**Tuition:** $29,940	**Fraternity:** Yes
Women: 53%	**Room & board:** $9,393	**Sorority:** Yes
Men: 47%	**Housing Information**	**Athletics:** NCAA Division I
Percent out-of-state: 75%	**University housing:** Yes	
	Percent living on campus: 65%	

ROOSEVELT UNIVERSITY

430 South Michigan Avenue, Chicago, IL 60605
Phone: 312-341-3515 • Fax: 312-341-3523
E-mail: applyRU@roosevelt.edu • Web: www.roosevelt.edu
Support: CS• Institution type: 4-year private

LEARNING DISABILITY PROGRAM AND SERVICES

The goal of the Learning and Support Services Program (LSSP) is to provide a highly individualized support system that will help students discover their learning style. The staff works with each student individually on reading comprehension, writing skills, note-taking, study skills, time management skills, and test-taking skills. Roosevelt's small class size provides an opportunity for students to get to know their professors, and the faculty has been very responsive to the needs of LSSP students. The program is for students who would otherwise experience difficulty with a regular college curriculum. Emphasis is placed on individual program planning, tutoring, arranged counseling, and modified test-taking. The program helps students to define their strengths so that they can overcome their weaknesses and become independent, successful college students.

LD/ADD ADMISSIONS INFORMATION

College entrance tests required: No
Interview recommended: Yes
Essay recommended: NR
Documentation required for LD: Psychoeducational evaluation by licensed psychologist
Documentation required for ADD: Diagnostic work-up from psychologist
Submitted to: Disability Services
Special Ed. HS coursework accepted: No

Specific course requirements of all applicants: Yes
Separate application required for program services: Yes
# of LD applications submitted each year: 3–5
# of LD applications accepted yearly: 2–4
Total # of students receiving LD services: 15–20
Acceptance into program means acceptance into college: Students must be separately admitted through the regular university admissions process and once enrolled may request services.

ADMISSIONS

There is a special admissions process through LSSP. Students write a letter to the LSSP director to request services and state the purpose and reason for seeking help. After reviewing the letter, LSSP staff holds an informal interview assessment with the student. Applicants send reports to the LSSP with authorization for release of information. These reports should include the following: (1) most recent transcript and confidential records, (2) health and academic history, (3) test results and reports, including achievement, individual I.Q. or other measurements of academic performance, and (4) the latest IEP. The LSSP staff will evaluate the reports and an admission meeting will be held to determine eligibility and possible enrollment. Students may be admitted during the summer with probationary status.

ADDITIONAL INFORMATION

The Learning and Support Services Program is only available to students with learning disabilities. Assistance is available in course selection, required course readings, assignments, and more. A major department advisor is assigned to each student. Depending on individual needs, tutoring assistance may include course-related training, reading, writing, and spelling. Help is offered in specific problem areas such as note-taking, basic skills improvement, time management, and organization. Qualified counseling psychologists help students cope with personal concerns and advise them on career goals. Students are encouraged to use Roosevelt's Learning Resource Center and Writing Laboratory. Services and accommodations are available to undergraduate and graduate students. Students with learning disabilities are not required to take the Roosevelt University Assessment Test.

Support Services Contact Information

Learning Disability Program/Services: Disability Services
Director: Nancy Litke
  E-Mail: nlitke@roosevelt.edu
  Telephone: 312-341-3810
  Fax: 312-341-2471

LEARNING DISABILITY SERVICES

Requests for the following services/accommodations will be evaluated individually based on appropriate and current documentation.

Allowed in exams	**Distraction reduced environment:** Yes	**Added costs for services:** Yes
Calculator: Yes	**Tape recording in class:** Yes	**LD specialists:** Yes
Dictionary: Yes	**Books on tape from RFBD:** Yes	**Professional tutors:** 3
Computer: Yes	**Taping of books not from RFBD:** Yes	**Peer tutors:** Yes
Spellchecker: Yes	**Accommodations for students with**	**Max. hours/wk. for services:** NR
Extended test time: Yes	**ADD:** Yes	**How professors are notified of**
Scribes: Yes	**Reading machine:** No	**LD/ADD:** By student
Proctors: Yes	**Other assistive technology:** Yes	
Oral exams: Yes	**Priority registration:** No	
Note-takers: Yes		

GENERAL ADMISSIONS INFORMATION

Director of Admissions: Gwen Kanelos
Telephone: 312-341-3515

ENTRANCE REQUIREMENTS

Academic units required: 4 English, 3 math, 3 science (2 science lab), 2 social studies, 1 history, 2 academic electives.**Academic units recommended:** 4 English, 4 math, 3 science (2 science lab), 2 foreign language, 2 social studies, 2 history, 2 academic electives. High school diploma is required and GED is accepted. ACT with or without Writing component accepted. TOEFL required of all international applicants, minimum paper TOEFL 525, minimum computer TOEFL 197.

Application deadline: 8/21	**Average SAT Math:** NR	**Graduated top 10% of class:** 3%
Notification: Rolling	**Average SAT Verbal:** NR	**Graduated top 25% of class:** 9%
Average GPA: 3.03	**Average ACT:** 21	**Graduated top 50% of class:** 39%

COLLEGE GRADUATION REQUIREMENTS

Course waivers allowed: Yes
Course substitutions allowed: Yes
In what course: Each request considered individually and subject to department approval.

ADDITIONAL INFORMATION

Environment: Roosevelt University is located in an urban area in downtown Chicago.

Student Body:	**Cost Information**	**Greek System**
Undergrad enrollment: 3,863	Tuition: $16,080	Fraternity: Yes
Women: 68%	Room & board: $7,700	Sorority: Yes
Men: 32%	**Housing Information**	Athletics: NR
Percent out-of-state: 6%	University housing: Yes	
	Percent living on campus: 9%	

SHIMER COLLEGE

PO Box 500, Waukegan, IL 60079-0500
Phone: 847-249-7174 • Fax: 847-249-8798
E-mail: wdapp@shimer.edu • Web: www.shimer.edu
Support: S• Institution type: 4-year private

LEARNING DISABILITY PROGRAM AND SERVICES

Shimer has no specific program for students with learning disabilities. Some students with relatively mild learning disabilities who have been unsuccessful in other settings have been successful at Shimer because of the unusual approach to education. Shimer offers an integrated curriculum where students read original sources and not textbooks. Students gather to discuss the books in small groups. Shimer has been able to meet the needs of students with learning disabilities who are motivated to seek this kind of education. Students are responsible for seeking the supportive help they want. The class size varies from 8 to 12 students, and a great deal of individual attention is available to all students.

LD/ADD ADMISSIONS INFORMATION

College entrance tests required: No
Interview recommended: Yes
Essay recommended: Yes
Documentation required for LD: Psychoeducational evaluation
Documentation required for ADD: Yes
Submitted to: Disability Services
Special Ed. HS coursework accepted: Yes

Specific course requirements of all applicants: Yes
Separate application required for program services: No
# of LD applications submitted each year: NR
# of LD applications accepted yearly: NR
Total # of students receiving LD services: NR
Acceptance into program means acceptance into college: Student must be admitted and enrolled in the university first and then request services.

ADMISSIONS

The goal of Shimer is to select students who will benefit from and contribute to its intellectual community. Each applicant is considered on an individual basis. Motivation, intellectual curiosity, and commitment to a rigorous and integrative educational program are important qualifications. Shimer will consider the application of any individual who has the potential to perform well. Admissions standards are the same for all students. Admission is based on whether or not the college feels it can provide the services necessary for successful learning. Students are encouraged to have a personal interview, which can be conducted by telephone, write a personal essay, submit ACT/SAT scores, submit letters of recommendation, and have the psychoeducational reports sent to the admissions office. There is no minimum GPA or specific high school courses required. ACT/SAT scores are considered in the admission decision, but are not required. Writing samples and other personal contact will be used by the admissions committee to make an evaluation. A visit to campus is encouraged and an interview is highly recommended and, in some cases, required. The essay portion of the application asks the applicant to provide an analysis of academic experience and offers the opportunity to demonstrate creative talent. These essays are major criteria in determining candidacy for admission. Shimer will accept a limited number of students on a threshold basis. These students often lack specific evidence of academic achievement, but are able to convince the admissions committee of their commitment and potential. These students receive special guidance. Continuation after 1 semester is dependent upon academic achievement.

ADDITIONAL INFORMATION

Skills courses are offered to all students for credit in writing, reading, math, study strategies, and learning strategies. The skills developed in these courses do not depend upon earlier study in the core curriculum, so that most do not have prerequisites. Classes are never larger than 12 students. All courses are conducted through discussion and all course reading is from original sources. Extraordinary support is available to all students by faculty, staff, and other students.

Support Services Contact Information

Learning Disability Program/Services: Disability Services
Director: Alan Solid
  E-Mail: a.solid@shimer.edu
  Telephone: 847-249-7174
  Fax: 847-249-8798
Contact Person: David B. Buchanan
  Telephone: 847-249-7174
  Fax: 847-249-8798

LEARNING DISABILITY SERVICES

Requests for the following services/accommodations will be evaluated individually based on appropriate and current documentation.

Allowed in exams	**Distraction reduced environment:** Yes	**Added costs for services:** No
Calculator: Yes	**Tape recording in class:** No	**LD specialists:** No
Dictionary: Yes	**Books on tape from RFBD:** Yes	**Professional tutors:** Yes
Computer: Yes	**Taping of books not from RFBD:** Yes	**Peer tutors:** Yes
Spellchecker: Yes	**Accommodations for students with**	**Max. hours/wk. for services:**
Extended test time: Yes	**ADD:** Yes	Unlimited
Scribes: No	**Reading machine:** No	**How professors are notified of**
Proctors: No	**Other assistive technology:** No	**LD/ADD:** By student
Oral exams: Yes	**Priority registration:** No	
Note-takers: No		

GENERAL ADMISSIONS INFORMATION

Director of Admissions: Alan Solid
Telephone: 847-249-7174

ENTRANCE REQUIREMENTS

High school diploma or equivalent is not required. TOEFL required of all international applicants. One letter of recommendation required. Admission requirements are highly personalized. Interview required. ACT/SAT recommended but not required. Writing samples used for admissions.

Application deadline: Rolling	**Average SAT Math:** Not required	**Graduated top 10% of class:** NR
Notification: Rolling	**Average SAT Verbal:** Not required	**Graduated top 25% of class:** NR
Average GPA: NR	**Average ACT:** Not required	**Graduated top 50% of class:** NR

COLLEGE GRADUATION REQUIREMENTS

Course waivers allowed: No
Course substitutions allowed: No
In what course: N/A

ADDITIONAL INFORMATION

Environment: The school is located in a city setting 40 miles north of Chicago and 40 miles south of Milwaukee.

Student Body:	**Cost Information**	**Greek System**
Undergrad enrollment: 126	**Tuition:** $17,760	**Fraternity:** No
Women: 33%	**Room & board:** $2,900	**Sorority:** No
Men: 67%	**Housing Information**	**Athletics:** Intramural
Percent out-of-state: 60%	**University housing:** Yes	
	Percent living on campus: 60%	

SOUTHERN ILLINOIS U.—CARBONDALE

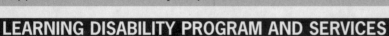

MC 4710, Carbondale, IL 62901
Phone: 618-536-4405 • Fax: 618-453-3250
E-mail: joinsiuc@siu.edu • Web: www.siuc.edu
Support: SP • Institution: 4-year public

LEARNING DISABILITY PROGRAM AND SERVICES

The Achieve Program is an academic support program for students with learning disabilities. The program provides comprehensive academic support services to meet the needs of students with previously diagnosed learning disabilities. Students interested in Achieve must make an application to the program and provide supporting documentation. All appropriate applicants must complete a two-day battery of diagnostic tests prior to entering the program. There are fees for application, diagnostic testing, and support services offered by Achieve. Students are accepted on a first come, first served basis providing they qualify for the program. Students are enrolled in regular college courses and are never restricted from any course offerings. Freshman year students are enrolled as full-time students but are restricted to 12 semester hours. As students become more successful they may enroll in more semester hours

LD/ADD ADMISSIONS INFORMATION

College entrance tests required: Yes
Interview recommended: Yes
Essay recommended: No
Documentation required for LD: Psychoeducational testing given by professional within 3 years
Documentation required for ADD: Yes
Submitted to: Project Achieve
Special Ed. HS coursework accepted: No

Specific course requirements of all applicants: Yes
Separate application required for program services: Yes
# of LD applications submitted each year: 200
# of LD applications accepted yearly: 50
Total # of students receiving LD services: 120
Acceptance into program means acceptance into college: Students are offered admission to the university and admission to Project Achieve.

ADMISSIONS

Application to the university and the program are separate. University application requires a general application form, ACT scores, and transcript. Students with an ACT of 21 and 4 years of English, 3 years of math, 3 years of science and 3 years of social studies and electives are automatically admissible to the university. Applicants to the Achieve Program are required to provide an Achieve application, $50 application fee, recent photo, and documentation of the LD. There is a fee of $1,000 for diagnostic testing (some fee waivers available), which is required before admissions. The Achieve application can be submitted any time during high school (the earlier the better). Students who self-disclose on their applications will be reviewed by the program, which provides a recommendation to Admissions. The required 21 ACT can be reviewed for Achieve Program applicants. For students not automatically admitted, Southern offers selected admissions through the Center for Basic Skills. In addition, a two-year associates program will consider admitting students not meeting minimum standards for regular admission.

ADDITIONAL INFORMATION

Students take tests in five subject areas and are assigned specific classes within those course areas. Peer tutors are assigned to assist students with understanding course material, studying and preparing for exams, homework assignments, projects, written work, and time management. Note-takers are hired to go into classes and take notes for students who demonstrate difficulty with visual-motor, auditory-memory-to-motor, and auditory comprehension tasks. Students must attend classes even if they are receiving note-taking support. Students may take exams and quizzes in the Achieve office, and may receive extended time, as well as a reader or writer if needed. Students may have textbooks and other written material taped. Some students will benefit from remediation of reading, spelling, math, and/or organizational deficits. Achieve students may take a developmental writing course before attempting the required English course. Graduate assistants work with students on a one-to-one basis so that the students have individual attention. Students have access to individualized tutoring, taped texts, test accommodations, remedial classes, developmental writing courses, test proctoring, and advocacy service.

Support Services Contact Information

Learning Disability Program/Services: Disability Support Services
Director: Kathleen Plesko
  E-Mail: kplesko@siu.edu
  Telephone: 618-453-5738
  Fax: 618-453-7000

LEARNING DISABILITY SERVICES

Requests for the following services/accommodations will be evaluated individually based on appropriate and current documentation.

Allowed in exams
  Calculator: Yes
  Dictionary: Yes
  Computer: Yes
  Spellchecker: Yes
Extended test time: Yes
Scribes: Yes
Proctors: Yes
Oral exams: Yes
Note-takers: Yes

Distraction reduced environment: Yes
Tape recording in class: Yes
Books on tape from RFBD: Yes
Taping of books not from RFBD: Yes
Accommodations for students with
  ADD: Yes
Reading machine: Yes
Other assistive technology: Yes
Priority registration: Yes

Added costs for services: Yes
LD specialists: Yes
Professional tutors: 20–40
Peer tutors: 50–80
Max. hours/wk. for services:
  Unlimited
How professors are notified of
  LD/ADD: By both student and director

GENERAL ADMISSIONS INFORMATION

Director of Admissions: Anne DeLuca, Asst. Vice Chancellor Student Affairs & Enrollment Management and Dir. of Admissions
Telephone: 618-536-4405

ENTRANCE REQUIREMENTS

Academic units required: 4 English, 3 math, 3 science (3 science lab), 3 social studies, 2 academic electives. High school diploma is required and GED is accepted. ACT with or without Writing component accepted. TOEFL required of all international applicants, minimum paper TOEFL 520, minimum computer TOEFL 190.

Application deadline: Rolling
Notification: Rolling
Average GPA: NR

Average SAT Math: NR
Average SAT Verbal: NR
Average ACT: 22

Graduated top 10% of class: 9%
Graduated top 25% of class: 32%
Graduated top 50% of class: 66%

COLLEGE GRADUATION REQUIREMENTS

Course waivers allowed: Yes
Course substitutions allowed: Yes
In what course: Foreign language and math

ADDITIONAL INFORMATION

Environment: The campus lies at the edge of the Shawnee National Forest, 6 hours south of Chicago.

Student Body:
  Undergrad enrollment: 16,786
  Women: 43%
  Men: 57%
  Percent out-of-state: 15%

Cost Information
  In-state tuition: $4,245
  Out-of-state tuition: $8,490
  Room & board: $4,886
Housing Information
  University housing: Yes
  Percent living on campus: 31%

Greek System
  Fraternity: Yes
  Sorority: Yes
Athletics: NCAA Division I

SOUTHERN ILLINOIS U.—EDWARDSVILLE

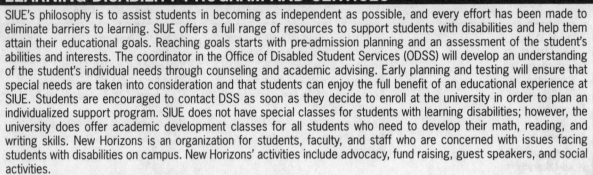

PO Box 1600, Edwardsville, IL 62026-1080
Phone: 618-650-3705 • Fax: 618-650-5013
E-mail: admissions@siue.edu • Web: www.siue.edu
Support: CS • Institution type: 4-year public

LEARNING DISABILITY PROGRAM AND SERVICES

SIUE's philosophy is to assist students in becoming as independent as possible, and every effort has been made to eliminate barriers to learning. SIUE offers a full range of resources to support students with disabilities and help them attain their educational goals. Reaching goals starts with pre-admission planning and an assessment of the student's abilities and interests. The coordinator in the Office of Disabled Student Services (ODSS) will develop an understanding of the student's individual needs through counseling and academic advising. Early planning and testing will ensure that special needs are taken into consideration and that students can enjoy the full benefit of an educational experience at SIUE. Students are encouraged to contact DSS as soon as they decide to enroll at the university in order to plan an individualized support program. SIUE does not have special classes for students with learning disabilities; however, the university does offer academic development classes for all students who need to develop their math, reading, and writing skills. New Horizons is an organization for students, faculty, and staff who are concerned with issues facing students with disabilities on campus. New Horizons' activities include advocacy, fund raising, guest speakers, and social activities.

LD/ADD ADMISSIONS INFORMATION

College entrance tests required: Yes
Interview recommended: No
Essay recommended: No
Documentation required for LD: Psychoeducational
   evaluation
Documentation required for ADD: Yes
Submitted to: Disability Support Services
Special Ed. HS coursework accepted: Y/N

Specific course requirements of all applicants: Yes
Separate application required for program services: No
# of LD applications submitted each year: NR
# of LD applications accepted yearly: NR
Total # of students receiving LD services: 91
Acceptance into program means acceptance into
   college: Student must be admitted and enrolled in the
   university first and then reviewed for LD services.

ADMISSIONS
Students with learning disabilities are required to submit the same general application form as all other students. Students should submit documentation of their learning disability in order to receive services once enrolled. This documentation should be sent to ODSS. Regular admissions criteria recommend 4 years English, 3 years math, 3 years science, 3 years social science, 2 years foreign language or electives (students with deficiencies need to check with the Office of Admission); a class rank in the top two-thirds; and an ACT minimum of 17 (average is 21) or SAT of 640–680. Students denied admission may appeal the decision.

ADDITIONAL INFORMATION
The advisers of ODSS will assist students with learning disabilities with pre-admission planning, including an assessment of abilities and interests. Counseling and academic advisement provides assistance in developing an understanding of individual needs. Skills classes are available in math, writing, and reading. Current resources include testing accommodations, assistance in writing/reading exams, assistance with library research, tutoring, and volunteer note-takers. In addition, the coordinator of ODSS acts as a liaison with faculty and staff regarding learning disabilities and accommodations needed by students. Services and accommodations are available for undergraduate and graduate students.

Support Services Contact Information

Learning Disability Program/Services: Disability Support Services
Director: Jane Floyd-Hendey
  E-Mail: jfloydh@siue.edu
  Telephone: 618-650-3782
  Fax: 618-650-5691

LEARNING DISABILITY SERVICES

Requests for the following services/accommodations will be evaluated individually based on appropriate and current documentation.

Allowed in exams
  Calculator: Yes
  Dictionary: Yes
  Computer: Yes
  Spellchecker: Yes
Extended test time: Yes
Scribes: Yes
Proctors: Yes
Oral exams: Yes
Note-takers: Yes

Distraction reduced environment: Yes
Tape recording in class: Yes
Books on tape from RFBD: NR
Taping of books not from RFBD: No
Accommodations for students with
  ADD: Yes
Reading machine: Yes
Other assistive technology: Yes
Priority registration: Yes

Added costs for services: No
LD specialists: Yes
Professional tutors: No
Peer tutors: Yes
Max. hours/wk. for services: 47
How professors are notified of
  LD/ADD: By student

GENERAL ADMISSIONS INFORMATION

Director of Admissions: Todd Burrell
Telephone: 618-650-3705

ENTRANCE REQUIREMENTS

Academic units required: 4 English, 3 math, 3 science (3 science lab), 3 social studies, 2 academic electives.
Academic units recommended: 2 foreign language. High school diploma is required and GED is accepted. TOEFL required of all international applicants, minimum paper TOEFL 550, minimum computer TOEFL 213.

Application deadline: 5/31
Notification: Rolling
Average GPA: NR

Average SAT Math: NR
Average SAT Verbal: NR
Average ACT: 22

Graduated top 10% of class: 14%
Graduated top 25% of class: 41%
Graduated top 50% of class: 78%

COLLEGE GRADUATION REQUIREMENTS

Course waivers allowed: No
Course substitutions allowed: Yes
In what course: Math, foreign language

ADDITIONAL INFORMATION

Environment: The university is located on 2,664 acres 18 miles northeast of St. Louis.

Student Body:
  Undergrad enrollment: 10,709
  Women: 58%
  Men: 42%
  Percent out-of-state: 13%

Cost Information
  In-state tuition: $4,320
  Out-of-state tuition: $10,800
  Room & board: $5,819
Housing Information
  University housing: Yes
  Percent living on campus: 27%

Greek System
  Fraternity: Yes
  Sorority: Yes
Athletics: NCAA Division II

U. OF ILLINOIS—URBANA-CHAMPAIGN

901 West Illinois Street, Urbana, IL 61801
Phone: 217-333-0302 • Fax: 217-244-0903
E-mail: ugradadmissions@uiuc.edu • Web: www.uiuc.edu
Support: CS • Institution type: 4-year public

LEARNING DISABILITY PROGRAM AND SERVICES

The Division of Rehabilitation Education Services (DRES) assists qualified students with disabilities in the pursuit of their higher education objectives. DRES assists students with disabilities in gaining access to and benefiting from all the related experiences that are an integral part of a University of Illinois education. Professional staff are also available at DRES to assist university students in the following areas: planning and implementing academic accommodations, compensatory strategies, academic coaching, obtaining additional aids (e.g., interpreters, readers/writer), obtaining modified test accommodations, counseling, and priority registration/scheduling assistance.

LD/ADD ADMISSIONS INFORMATION

College entrance tests required: Yes
Interview recommended: No
Essay recommended: No
Documentation required for LD: LD documentation should include diagnostic interviews (developmental, medical, family histories), WAIS–III, Woodcock-Johnson test of Cognitive Ability, Academic Achievement Battery, and a specific LD diagnosis by a qualified professional.
Documentation required for ADD: ADD documentation should include evidence of early impairment; an extensive interview, developmental history, consideration of alternative causes, all appropriate neuropsych tests, extensive clinical summary, and specific DSM–IV diagnosis
Submitted to: Disability Resources and Educational Services
Special Ed. HS coursework accepted: Yes

Specific course requirements of all applicants: Yes
Separate application required for program services: Yes
# of LD applications submitted each year: NR
# of LD applications accepted yearly: NR
Total # of students receiving LD services: 175–225
Acceptance into program means acceptance into college: Student must be admitted and enrolled in the university first and then request services.

ADMISSIONS

Applicants with LD are expected to meet the same admission criteria as all other applicants. Any tests for undergraduate and graduate admissions taken with accommodations are considered as competitive. Applicants whose qualifications are slightly below a college's admission guidelines are encouraged to use the "Background Statement" section on the application to provide additional information that could be useful in understanding the student's academic history. Students are encouraged to provide diagnostic evidence from a licensed clinical examiner. The university admits students to particular colleges on the basis of class rank, GPA, ACT/SAT scores, extracurricular activities, personal statements, achievements and challenge of curriculum. Prospective students should contact the appropriate college for complete course requirements. Required courses include 4 years English, 3 years math, 2 years foreign language, 2 years social science, and 2 years lab science.

ADDITIONAL INFORMATION

Accommodations are individually student centered. The student is expected to declare and document all concurrent disabilities for which services are expected. The design and implementation of accommodations depend on the student's perspective of his/her functional limitations relative to the academic requirements of each course. Timely communication to the learning disability specialist of any situations that are projected to need accommodations during the semester is essential. Individual inquiries and early contacts prior to campus residency strengthen the process of accommodation. Students with LD/ADD can work with a specialist to develop compensatory strategies. Reading and study skills workshops and writer's workshops are available for all students. Skills classes are offered in time management, test anxiety, stress management, and study strategies.

Support Services Contact Information

Learning Disability Program/Services: Division of Disability Resources and Educational Services (DRES)
Director: Brad Hedrick
  E-Mail: bhedrick@uiuc.edu
  Telephone: 217-333-4600
  Fax: 217-333-0248
Contact Person: Kim Collins, PhD
  E-Mail: kdcollin@uiuc.edu
  Telephone: 217-333-4603
  Fax: 217-333-0248

LEARNING DISABILITY SERVICES

Requests for the following services/accommodations will be evaluated individually based on appropriate and current documentation.

Allowed in exams
  Calculator: Yes
  Dictionary: Yes
  Computer: Yes
  Spellchecker: Yes
Extended test time: Yes
Scribes: Yes
Proctors: Yes
Oral exams: Yes
Note-takers: Yes

Distraction reduced environment: Yes
Tape recording in class: Yes
Books on tape from RFBD: Yes
Taping of books not from RFBD: Yes
**Accommodations for students with
  ADD:** Yes
Reading machine: Yes
Other assistive technology: Yes
Priority registration: Yes

Added costs for services: No
LD specialists: Yes
Professional tutors: No
Peer tutors: No
Max. hours/wk. for services:
  Unlimited
**How professors are notified of
  LD/ADD:** By student

GENERAL ADMISSIONS INFORMATION

Director of Admissions: Stacy Kostell
Telephone: 217-333-2034

ENTRANCE REQUIREMENTS

Academic units required: 4 English, 3 math, 2 science (2 science lab), 2 foreign language, 2 social studies, 2 academic electives. High school diploma is required and GED is accepted. ACT with or without Writing component accepted. TOEFL required of all international applicants, minimum paper TOEFL 550, minimum computer TOEFL 213.

Application deadline: 12/15
Notification: December to March
Average GPA: NR

Average SAT Math: 674
Average SAT Verbal: 614
Average ACT: 28

Graduated top 10% of class: 50%
Graduated top 25% of class: 86%
Graduated top 50% of class: 99%

COLLEGE GRADUATION REQUIREMENTS

Course waivers allowed: No
Course substitutions allowed: Yes
In what course: Course substitutions for foreign language and math through a petition process through the student's college.

ADDITIONAL INFORMATION

Environment: The university has an urban campus 130 miles south of Chicago.

Student Body:
  Undergrad enrollment: 28,931
  Women: 47%
  Men: 53%
  Percent out-of-state: 12%

Cost Information
  In-state tuition: $6,460
  Out-of-state tuition: $19,380
  Room & board: $7,176
Housing Information
  University housing: Yes
  Percent living on campus: 30%

Greek System
  Fraternity: Yes
  Sorority: Yes
Athletics: NCAA Division I

WESTERN ILLINOIS UNIVERSITY

1 University Circle, 115 Sherman Hall, Macomb, IL 61455-1390
Phone: 309-298-3157 • Fax: 309-298-3111
E-mail: wiuadm@wiu.edu • Web: www.wiu.edu
Support: CS• Institution type: 4-year public

LEARNING DISABILITY PROGRAM AND SERVICES

Western Illinois University is committed to justice, equity, and diversity. Academically qualified students who have disabilities are an important part of our student body. Providing equal opportunities for students with disabilities is a campus-wide responsibility and commitment. University personnel work with students to modify campus facilities and programs to meet individual needs. Disability Support Services is responsible for coordinating support services for Western Illinois University students who have disabilities. It is important to note that while services are available, there is no formal program for students with learning disabilities. WIU does not provide any remedial programs or offer any specialized curriculum. Students requesting accommodations must provide documentation verifying the specific learning disability. P.R.I.D.E. (Promoting the Rights of Individuals with Disabilities Everywhere) is an organization composed of students with and without disabilities. Members work together to remove attitudinal barriers within the university community. The group sponsors awareness-raising activities and serves as a resource for faculty, staff, and students who are interested in disability issues.

LD/ADD ADMISSIONS INFORMATION

College entrance tests required: Yes
Interview recommended: No
Essay recommended: No
Documentation required for LD: Psychoeducational
   assessment within 3 years
Documentation required for ADD: Yes
Submitted to: Disability Support Services
Special Ed. HS coursework accepted: No

Specific course requirements of all applicants: Yes
Separate application required for program services: Yes
# of LD applications submitted each year: NR
# of LD applications accepted yearly: NR
Total # of students receiving LD services: 114–129
Acceptance into program means acceptance into
   college: Student must be admitted and enrolled in the
   university first and then request services.

ADMISSIONS

Students with learning disabilities must meet the same admission criteria as all applicants, which includes 4 years English, 3 years social studies, 3 years math, 3 years science, and 2 years of electives. Applicants must also have an ACT 22/SAT 1010 and a 2.2 GPA or ACT 18/SAT 850 and rank in the top 40 percent of their class, and have a 2.2 GPA. Students not meeting these standards may be considered for alternative admission. The application should be supported by a letter of recommendation from the counselor and a letter of appeal from the student. The Academic Services Program provides an opportunity for admission to a limited number of students yearly who do not meet the regular WIU admissions. Students considered for alternative admissions must have an ACT of 15 and a high school cumulative GPA of 2.2. Students admitted in the Academic Services Program are chosen on the basis of demonstrated academic potential for success. Several criteria are considered including, but not limited to high school academic GPA, grade patterns, references, and student letter expressing interest in the program.

ADDITIONAL INFORMATION

There are tutoring support services available to all WIU students through laboratories for writing and math, which are staffed by the English and mathematics departments. Students can receive one-to-one help with study skills including time management, note-taking skills, and exam preparation. There is tutoring available in some subjects, but there is no guarantee for tutoring in all subjects. Some tutors charge $4 to $7 per hour, and some tutorials offered through the Office of Academic Services are free. Academic advisors in the Academic Services Program monitor student progress during each semester for students admitted in the program. These students are provided with tutorial support throughout freshman year. These students enroll in appropriate general education curriculum courses and introductory courses in their majors. The goal of the program is to promote the development of skills necessary for students to achieve academic success at WIU.

Support Services Contact Information

Learning Disability Program/Services: Disability Support Services
Director: Joan Green
  E-Mail: JE-Green1@wiu.edu
  Telephone: 309-298-2512
  Fax: 309-298-2361
Contact Person: Robin Hyman
  E-Mail: RR-Hyman@wiu.edu
  Telephone: 309-298-2512
  Fax: 309-298-2361

LEARNING DISABILITY SERVICES

Requests for the following services/accommodations will be evaluated individually based on appropriate and current documentation.

Allowed in exams
  Calculator: Yes
  Dictionary: Yes
  Computer: Yes
  Spellchecker: Yes
Extended test time: Yes
Scribes: Yes
Proctors: Yes
Oral exams: Yes
Note-takers: Yes

Distraction reduced environment: Yes
Tape recording in class: Yes
Books on tape from RFBD: No
Taping of books not from RFBD: No
Accommodations for students with
  ADD: Yes
Reading machine: No
Other assistive technology: Yes
Priority registration: Yes

Added costs for services: No
LD specialists: Yes
Professional tutors: 1–3
Peer tutors: Yes
Max. hours/wk. for services:
  Unlimited
How professors are notified of
  LD/ADD: By student

GENERAL ADMISSIONS INFORMATION

Director of Admissions: David Garcia
Telephone: 309-298-1968

ENTRANCE REQUIREMENTS

Academic units recommended: 4 English, 3 math, 3 science, 3 social studies, and 2 years electives. High school diploma is required and GED is accepted. ACT without Writing component accepted. TOEFL required of all international applicants, minimum paper TOEFL 550, minimum computer TOEFL 213.

Application deadline: 5/15
Notification: Within 24-48 hours after receiving application.
Average GPA: NR

Average SAT Math: NR
Average SAT Verbal: NR
Average ACT: 22

Graduated top 10% of class: 6%
Graduated top 25% of class: 22%
Graduated top 50% of class: 59%

COLLEGE GRADUATION REQUIREMENTS

Course waivers allowed: Yes
Course substitutions allowed: Yes
In what course: Students may submit a request for course subsitutions to the council on admission, graduation, and academic standards for review.

ADDITIONAL INFORMATION

Environment: The university is located in a rural area 75 miles from Peoria.

Student Body:
  Undergrad enrollment: 11,297
  Women: 53%
  Men: 47%
  Percent out-of-state: 6%

Cost Information
  In-state: 5,485
  Out-of-state: 9,400
  Room & board: $5,366
Housing Information
  University housing: Yes
  Percent living on campus: 52%

Greek System
  Fraternity: Yes
  Sorority: Yes
Athletics: NCAA Division I

ANDERSON UNIVERSITY

1100 East Fifth Street, Anderson, IN 46012
Phone: 765-641-4080 • Fax: 765-641-4091
E-mail: info@anderson.edu • Web: www.anderson.edu
Support: SP• Institution type: 4-year private

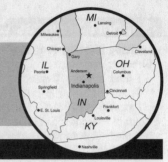

LEARNING DISABILITY PROGRAM AND SERVICES

It is the philosophy of Anderson University that those students who are qualified and have a sincere motivation to complete a college education should be given every opportunity to work towards that goal. Students with specific learning disabilities may be integrated into any of the many existing services at the Kissinger Learning Center, or more individual programming may be designed. Students receive extensive personal contact through the program. The director of the program schedules time with each student to evaluate personal learning style in order to assist in planning for the most appropriate learning environment. One of the most successful programs is individual or small group tutorial assistance. Social and emotional support is also provided. The college strives to provide the maximum amount of services necessary to assist students with learning disabilities in their academic endeavors, while being careful not to create an over-dependency.

LD/ADD ADMISSIONS INFORMATION

College entrance tests required: Yes
Interview recommended: Yes
Essay recommended: Yes
Documentation required for LD: WISC–R or WAIS–R (within 3 years)
Documentation required for ADD: TOVA
Submitted to: Kissinger Learning Center
Special Ed. HS coursework accepted: Y/N will consult on individual basic

Specific course requirements of all applicants: Yes
Separate application required for program services: No
# of LD applications submitted each year: 15–25
# of LD applications accepted yearly: 20
Total # of students receiving LD services: 48
Acceptance into program means acceptance into college: It is a joint decision between Admissions and the program.

ADMISSIONS

Students with specific learning disabilities who apply to Anderson do so through the regular admission channels. The university recommends that students have the following courses in their high school background: 4 years of English, 3 years of mathematics, 2 years of a foreign language, 3 years of science, and 3 years of social studies. Also considered in the evaluation of each application is the student's seriousness of purpose, personality and character, expressed willingness to live within the standards of the Anderson University community, and service to school, church and community. Documentation of a specific learning disability must be included with the application. We encourage students to self-disclose because they may qualify for special consideration and be admitted through the LD program. Failure to disclose could result in non-acceptance based on standardized test scores, GPA, and other criteria. Upon request for consideration for the program, prospective students are expected to make an on-campus visit, at which time a personal interview is arranged with the program director. All applicants are considered on an individual basis.

ADDITIONAL INFORMATION

Freshmen enrolled in the program are typically limited to 12–13 credit hours of coursework during the first semester, including a two-hour study skills class. As students become more independent and demonstrate the ability to deal with increased hours, an additional course load may be considered. There are currently 42 students with LD and 41 students with ADD receiving accommodations or services. Depending upon the specific needs of the student, all or a selected number of services may be provided, including assistance with advising, study skills instruction, time management, career counseling, alternative testing situations, and advocacy/liaison. The Kissinger Learning Center offers a variety of services, including a Writing Assistance Program directed by a faculty member of the English department. Individuals needing further assistance receive a diagnostic evaluation, which enables staff to work more efficiently with school personnel in creating programs to fit the needs of students with learning disabilities. Students are fully integrated into the university and are expected to meet the same academic standards as all other students.

Support Services Contact Information

Learning Disability Program/Services: Kissinger Learning Center
Director: Rinda Vogelgesang
  E-Mail: rsvogel@anderson.edu
  Telephone: 765-641-4226
  Fax: 765-641-3851

LEARNING DISABILITY SERVICES

Requests for the following services/accommodations will be evaluated individually based on appropriate and current documentation.

Allowed in exams
  Calculator: Yes
  Dictionary: Yes
  Computer: Yes
  Spellchecker: Yes
Extended test time: Yes
Scribes: Yes
Proctors: Yes
Oral exams: Yes
Note-takers: Yes

Distraction reduced environment: Yes
Tape recording in class: Yes
Books on tape from RFBD: Yes
Taping of books not from RFBD: No
Accommodations for students with
  ADD: Yes
Reading machine: No
Other assistive technology: Yes
Priority registration: No

Added costs for services: No
LD specialists: Yes
Professional tutors: 1
Peer tutors: 25
Max. hours/wk. for services:
  Unlimited
How professors are notified of
  LD/ADD: By both student and director

GENERAL ADMISSIONS INFORMATION

Director of Admissions: Jim King
Telephone: 765-641-4080

ENTRANCE REQUIREMENTS

Academic units required: 4 English, 3 math, 2 science (2 science lab), 2 social studies, 2 history. **Academic units recommended:** 3 science (3 science lab), 2 foreign language, 3 social studies, 5 academic electives, High school diploma is required and GED is accepted. TOEFL required of all international applicants, minimum paper TOEFL 677, minimum computer TOEFL 300.

Application deadline: 8/1
Notification: Rolling
Average GPA: 3.40

Average SAT Math: 538
Average SAT Verbal: 533
Average ACT: 24

Graduated top 10% of class: 23%
Graduated top 25% of class: 53%
Graduated top 50% of class: 85%

COLLEGE GRADUATION REQUIREMENTS

Course waivers allowed: No
Course substitutions allowed: No
In what course: Not usually, but will be considered on an individual basis.

ADDITIONAL INFORMATION

Environment: Anderson University is located on 100 acres 40 miles northeast of Indianapolis.

Student Body:
  Undergrad enrollment: 1,965
  Women: 60%
  Men: 40%
  Percent out-of-state: 36%

Cost Information
  Tuition: $16,140
  Room & board: $5,260
Housing Information
  University housing: Yes
  Percent living on campus: 60%

Greek System
  Fraternity: Yes
  Sorority: NR
Athletics: NCAA Division III

INDIANA UNIVERSITY

300 North Jordan Avenue, Bloomington, IN 47405-1106
Phone: 812-855-0661 • Fax: 812-855-5102
E-mail: iuadmit@indiana.edu • Web: www.iub.edu
Support: CS• Institution type: 4-year public

LEARNING DISABILITY PROGRAM AND SERVICES

The goal of the Office of Disabled Student Services is to provide services that enable students with disabilities to participate in, and benefit from all university programs and activities. There is no specific program for students with LD. However there is a learning disabilities coordinator who provides supportive services necessary to help students pursue their academic objectives. The Briscoe Academic Support Center offers free assistance to all IU students, night and day. Daily it is used for study groups, meetings, and advising. In the evenings it provides free tutoring, advising, and academic support to assist with course assignments and studying. No appointments are necessary. Students with LD must provide current and appropriate psychoeducational evaluations that address aptitude, achievement, information processing, and clear and specific evidence and identification of a LD. Test scores/data must be included, and evaluations must be done by a qualified professional. Current IEPs are helpful. Students with ADD must provide documentation that includes a clear statement of ADD with a current diagnosis, including a description of supporting symptoms; current testing, preferably within three years; a summary of assessment procedures and evaluations used; a summary supporting diagnosis; medical history; suggestions of reasonable accommodations; and current IEP is helpful.

LD/ADD ADMISSIONS INFORMATION

College entrance tests required: Yes
Interview recommended: No
Essay recommended: No
Documentation required for LD: A comprehensive psychoeducational evaluation that meets our documentation guidelines.
Documentation required for ADD: A comprehensive evaluation that meets our documentation guidelines.
Submitted to: Disability Services for Students
Special Ed. HS coursework accepted: No

Specific course requirements of all applicants: Yes
Separate application required for program services: Yes
# of LD applications submitted each year: NR
# of LD applications accepted yearly: NR
Total # of students receiving LD services: NR
Acceptance into program means acceptance into college: Student must be admitted and enrolled in the university first and then request services.

ADMISSIONS

There is no special admission process for students with learning disabilities. Each applicant is reviewed individually. IU is concerned with the strength of the college-prep program, including senior year, grade trends, and the student's class rank. Students falling below the minimum standards may receive serious consideration for admission if their grades have been steadily improving in a challenging college-prep program. Conversely, declining grades and/or a program of less demanding courses are often reasons to deny admission. The minimum admission standards include 4 years English, 3 years math, 1 year science, 2 years social science, plus additional courses in math, science, social science and/or foreign language to be competitive for admission. Indiana residents must complete Core 40 which includes a minimum of 28 semesters of college-prep courses. Nonresidents must complete a minimum of 32 semesters of college-prep classes. All students should be enrolled in at least 3-4 college-prep courses each semester. Students usually rank in the top one-third out-of-state and top half in-state. Students must submit either the ACT with Writing components or the SAT.

ADDITIONAL INFORMATION

The LD specialist assists students with LD on an individual basis. Accommodations can be made to provide test modifications, referrals to tutors, peer note-takers, books on tape, adaptive technology, and priority registration for students needing books on tape. Students must provide appropriate documentation. Students need to request a letter from DSS to give to their professors. Two years of foreign language are required for a degree from the College of Arts and Sciences. Students with a disability that impacts their ability to learn a foreign language must attempt taking one and the dean will monitor the student's sincere effort to succeed. If the student is unsuccessful, there will be a discussion of alternatives. There are special math courses and one is a remedial course for credit. Currently, there are approximately 400 students with LD/ADD receiving services.

Support Services Contact Information

Learning Disability Program/Services: Disability Services for Students (DSS)
Director: Martha P. Jacques
  E-Mail: iubdss@indiana.edu
  Telephone: 812-855-7578
  Fax: 812-855-7650
Contact Person: Jody K. Ferguson
  E-Mail: iubdss@indiana.edu
  Telephone: 812-855-3508
  Fax: 812-855-7650

LEARNING DISABILITY SERVICES

Requests for the following services/accommodations will be evaluated individually based on appropriate and current documentation.

Allowed in exams
  Calculator: Yes
  Dictionary: Yes
  Computer: Yes
  Spellchecker: Yes
Extended test time: Yes
Scribes: Yes
Proctors: Yes
Oral exams: Yes
Note-takers: Yes

Distraction reduced environment: Yes
Tape recording in class: Yes
Books on tape from RFBD: Yes
Taping of books not from RFBD: Yes
Accommodations for students with
  ADD: Yes
Reading machine: Yes
Other assistive technology: Yes
Priority registration: Yes

Added costs for services: No
LD specialists: Yes
Professional tutors: No
Peer tutors: Varies
Max. hours/wk. for services: Varies
How professors are notified of
  LD/ADD: By student

GENERAL ADMISSIONS INFORMATION

Director of Admissions: Mary Ellen Anderson
Telephone: 812-855-0661

ENTRANCE REQUIREMENTS
Academic units required: 4 English, 3 math, 1 science (1 science lab), 2 social studies, 4 academic electives. ACT with Writing components or SAT Reasoning test required.
Academic units recommended: 4 math, 3 science, 3 foreign language, 3 social studies. High school diploma is required and GED is accepted. TOEFL required of all international applicants, minimum paper TOEFL 560, minimum computer TOEFL 223

Application deadline: 2/1
Notification: Rolling
Average GPA: NR

Average SAT Math: 556
Average SAT Verbal: 543
Average ACT: 24

Graduated top 10% of class: 23%
Graduated top 25% of class: 56%
Graduated top 50% of class: 95%

COLLEGE GRADUATION REQUIREMENTS

Course waivers allowed: No
Course substitutions allowed: Yes
In what course: There are processes to request accommodations and substitutions regarding math and foreign language for eligible students with LD. Students are required to attempt the course.

ADDITIONAL INFORMATION

Environment: The university is located in a small town 45 minutes from Indianapolis.

Student Body:
  Undergrad enrollment: 29,062
  Women: 52%
  Men: 48%
  Percent out-of-state: 29%

Cost Information
  In-state tuition: $5,800
  Out-of-state tuition: $16,739
  Room & board: $6,006
Housing Information
  University housing: Yes
  Percent living on campus: 42%

Greek System
  Fraternity: Yes
  Sorority: Yes
Athletics: NCAA Division I

Indiana University

INDIANA WESLEYAN UNIVERSITY

4201 South Washington Street, Marion, IN 46953-4974
Phone: 800-332-6901 • Fax: 317-677-2333
E-mail: admissions@indwes.edu • Web: www.indwes.edu
Support: S• Institution type: 4-year private

LEARNING DISABILITY PROGRAM AND SERVICES

The services offered at IWU are designed to assist students who have documented learning disabilities through advocacy and provision of appropriate accommodations. Student Support Services (SSS) provides tutoring, counseling, note-takers, and test accommodations. The Learning Center is available to all students who seek assistance with raising the quality of their academic work. Developmental educational courses are offered in reading improvement, fundamentals of communication, and skills for academic success.

LD/ADD ADMISSIONS INFORMATION

College entrance tests required: Yes
Interview recommended: No
Essay recommended: No
Documentation required for LD: Standardized intelligence or psychometric testing or other documentation related to disability.
Documentation required for ADD: Yes
Submitted to: Center for Student Support Services
Special Ed. HS coursework accepted: No

Specific course requirements of all applicants: Yes
Separate application required for program services: No
# of LD applications submitted each year: 30–40
# of LD applications accepted yearly: 30–40
Total # of students receiving LD services: 101
Acceptance into program means acceptance into college: Students are admitted to the university and to the program simultaneously.

ADMISSIONS

The Office of Admissions seeks students with at least a 2.6 GPA and an ACT of 18 or SAT of 880. Students not meeting these requirements may be accepted on a conditional status and are required to enroll in a student success program designed to enhance their academic skills. Students with learning disabilities may self-disclose their LD or ADD through a personal statement attached to the application for admission. There is a separate application for requesting services/accommodations for disabilities that is submitted after a student has been accepted and enrolled.

ADDITIONAL INFORMATION

All admitted students are given the Compass English Proficiency Test. If they score below 10.7, they are required to take developmental reading, writing, and study skills classes. An SAT verbal score below 350 or ACT English below 14 will also be indicators that the student should take developmental reading and fundamentals of communication classes. With appropriate documentation students with LD/ADD may be eligible for some of the following services or accommodations: the use of a calculator, dictionary, computer or spell check in exams; extended time on tests; scribes; proctors; oral exams; note-takers; distraction-free environment; tape recorder in class; books on tape; assistive technology; priority registration; and workshops for all students in time management, test taking skills, reading, and stress management.

Support Services Contact Information

Learning Disability Program/Services: Center for Student Support Services (CSSS)
Director: Todd Ream, PhD
  E-Mail: Todd.Ream@indwes.edu
  Telephone: 765-677-2257
  Fax: 765-677-2140
Contact Person: Nathan Herring, MA
  E-Mail: Nathan.Herring@indwes.edu
  Telephone: 765-677-2257
  Fax: 765-677-2140

LEARNING DISABILITY SERVICES

Requests for the following services/accommodations will be evaluated individually based on appropriate and current documentation.

Allowed in exams
  Calculator: Yes
  Dictionary: Yes
  Computer: Yes
  Spellchecker: Yes
Extended test time: Yes
Scribes: Yes
Proctors: Yes
Oral exams: Yes
Note-takers: Yes

Distraction reduced environment: Yes
Tape recording in class: Yes
Books on tape from RFBD: Yes
Taping of books not from RFBD: Yes
Accommodations for students with ADD: Yes
Reading machine: Yes
Other assistive technology: Yes
Priority registration: Yes

Added costs for services: No
LD specialists: No
Professional tutors: No
Peer tutors: 40
Max. hours/wk. for services: 1 hour per week per course
How professors are notified of LD/ADD: By student

GENERAL ADMISSIONS INFORMATION

Director of Admissions: Dr. John Gredy (VP)
Telephone: 800-332-6901

ENTRANCE REQUIREMENTS

High school diploma is required and GED is accepted. TOEFL required of all international applicants, minimum paper TOEFL 550, minimum computer TOEFL 213.

Application deadline: 7/1
Notification: Rolling
Average GPA: 3.47

Average SAT Math: 540
Average SAT Verbal: 545
Average ACT: 24

Graduated top 10% of class: 31%
Graduated top 25% of class: 59%
Graduated top 50% of class: 83%

COLLEGE GRADUATION REQUIREMENTS

Course waivers allowed: Yes
Course substitutions allowed: Yes
In what course: Dependent upon course of study and specific disability, assessed on an individual basis.

ADDITIONAL INFORMATION

Environment: The university is located on a 50-acre campus in a rural city 65 miles from Indianapolis and 50 miles south of Fort Wayne.
Student Body:
  Undergrad enrollment: 6,554
  Women: 64%
  Men: 36%
  Percent out-of-state: 56%

Cost Information
  Tuition: $16,184
  Room & board: $5,890
Housing Information
  University housing: Yes
  Percent living on campus: 76%

Greek System
  Fraternity: No
  Sorority: No
Athletics: NAIA

MANCHESTER COLLEGE

604 East College Avenue, North Manchester, IN 46962
Phone: 260-982-5055 • Fax: 260-982-5239
E-mail: admitinfo@manchester.edu • Web: www.manchester.edu
Support: CS• Institution type: 4-year private

LEARNING DISABILITY PROGRAM AND SERVICES

Manchester College does not have a specific program for students with learning disabilities. The college is, however, very sensitive to all students. The key word at Manchester College is "success," which means graduating in four years. The college wants all students to be able to complete their degree in four years. The college does provide support services to students identified as disabled to allow them to be successful. The goal is to assist students in their individual needs.

LD/ADD ADMISSIONS INFORMATION

College entrance tests required: Yes
Interview recommended: Yes
Essay recommended: No
Documentation required for LD: Psychoeducational evaluation
Documentation required for ADD: Yes
Submitted to: Services for Students with Disabilities
Special Ed. HS coursework accepted: Yes

Specific course requirements of all applicants: Yes
Separate application required for program services: No
# of LD applications submitted each year: NR
# of LD applications accepted yearly: NR
Total # of students receiving LD services: 20–30
Acceptance into program means acceptance into college: Students must be admitted and enrolled in the university first and then request services.

ADMISSIONS

Students with learning disabilities submit the regular application form, and are required to meet the same admission criteria as all other applicants. Required courses include 4 years English, 2 years math, 2 years science (2 years science lab), 2 years foreign language, 2 years social studies, 1 year history, 1 year elective. Recommended courses 3 years math, 3 years science (3 years science lab), 2 years history, 2 years electives. Students are admitted to the college and use the support services as they choose. If special consideration for admission is requested, it is done individually, based on potential for graduation from the college. Manchester considers a wide range of information in making individual admission decisions. Students are encouraged to provide information beyond what is required on the application form if they believe it will strengthen their application or help the college to understand the student's performance or potential. Students who self-disclose the existence of a learning disability and are denied can ask to appeal the decision and have their application reviewed in an alternative way. The key question that will be asked is if the student can graduate in four years, or at the most, five years.

ADDITIONAL INFORMATION

College Study Skills is offered for one credit. A support group meets biweekly. No developmental or remedial courses are offered. A learning center provides tutoring for all students at the college. The college is in the process of developing a handbook that will describe services for students with disabilities. Services and accommodations are offered to undergraduate and graduate students.

Support Services Contact Information

Learning Disability Program/Services: Services for Students with Disabilities
Director: Denise L.S. Howe, EdS
E-Mail: dshow@manchester.edu
Telephone: 260-982-5076
Fax: 260-982-5043

LEARNING DISABILITY SERVICES

Requests for the following services/accommodations will be evaluated individually based on appropriate and current documentation.

Allowed in exams
Calculator: No
Dictionary: No
Computer: Yes
Spellchecker: Yes
Extended test time: Yes
Scribes: Yes
Proctors: Yes
Oral exams: Yes
Note-takers: Yes

Distraction reduced environment: Yes
Tape recording in class: Yes
Books on tape from RFBD: No
Taping of books not from RFBD: No
Accommodations for students with ADD: Yes
Reading machine: No
Other assistive technology: No
Priority registration: No

Added costs for services: No
LD specialists: Yes
Professional tutors: No
Peer tutors: Yes
Max. hours/wk. for services: Unlimited
How professors are notified of LD/ADD: By both student and director

GENERAL ADMISSIONS INFORMATION

Director of Admissions: Jolane Rohr
Telephone: 260-982-5055

ENTRANCE REQUIREMENTS

Academic units required: 4 English, 2 math, 2 science (2 science lab), 2 foreign language, 2 social studies, 1 history, 1 academic elective, **Academic units recommended:** 4 English, 3 math, 3 science (3 science lab), 2 foreign language, 2 social studies, 2 history, 2 academic electives. High school diploma is required and GED is accepted. TOEFL required of all international applicants, minimum paper TOEFL 550, minimum computer TOEFL 213.

Application deadline: Rolling
Notification: Rolling
Average GPA: NR

Average SAT Math: 511
Average SAT Verbal: 504
Average ACT: 22

Graduated top 10% of class: 18%
Graduated top 25% of class: 46%
Graduated top 50% of class: 79%

COLLEGE GRADUATION REQUIREMENTS

Course waivers allowed: No
Course substitutions allowed: No
In what course: N/A

ADDITIONAL INFORMATION

Environment: The college is located in North Manchester, 35 miles west of Fort Wayne.

Student Body:
Undergrad enrollment: 1,113
Women: 55%
Men: 45%
Percent out-of-state: 10%

Cost Information
Tuition: $17,950
Room & board: $6,710
Housing Information
University housing: Yes
Percent living on campus: 74%

Greek System
Fraternity: No
Sorority: No
Athletics: NCAA Division III

UNIVERSITY OF INDIANAPOLIS

1400 East Hanna Avenue, Indianapolis, IN 46227-3697
Phone: 317-788-3216 • Fax: 317-788-3300
E-mail: admissions@uindy.edu • Web: admissions.uindy.edu
Support: SP• Institution type: 4-year private

LEARNING DISABILITY PROGRAM AND SERVICES

The University of Indianapolis offers a full support system for students with learning disabilities called B.U.I.L.D. (Baccalaureate for University of Indianapolis Learning Disabled). The goal of this program is to help students with learning disabilities reach their academic potential. Helen Keller expressed this goal best: "Although the world is full of suffering, it is also full of the overcoming of it." All students with LD at the university have reasonable modifications available to them at no extra charge. The B.U.I.L.D. program offers accommodations significantly more in depth than just the minimal requirements. Services are extensive and the staff is very supportive and knowledgeable about learning disabilities.

LD/ADD ADMISSIONS INFORMATION

College entrance tests required: Yes
Interview recommended: Yes
Essay recommended: No
Documentation required for LD: Current IQ tests and reading and math achievement tests less than 3 years old
Documentation required for ADD: Appropriate testing results and recommendations by a qualified professional
Submitted to: B.U.I.L.D
Special Ed. HS coursework accepted: No

Specific course requirements of all applicants: Yes
Separate application required for program services: Yes
# of LD applications submitted each year: 50
# of LD applications accepted yearly: 25
Total # of students receiving LD services: 35
Acceptance into program means acceptance into college: Students must be admitted by the university and then admitted to B.U.I.L.D. If not accepted by Admissions, a committee confers.

ADMISSIONS

Admission to the B.U.I.L.D. program occurs after a student has been accepted to the university, and students with LD must meet the university admissions requirements. Recommended courses for general admission include 4 years English, 3 years math, 3 years science, 2 years lab science, 2 years foreign language, and 3 years social studies. However, flexibility is allowed to consider individual strengths. Students are encouraged to self-disclose their learning disability. It is important for the university to know the circumstances of a student's learning, but self-disclosing also allows the student to learn how the university views disabilities. To seek admission to the university and to B.U.I.L.D., students must submit the following: regular application for admission; B.U.I.L.D. application; high school transcript; current documentation regarding I.Q. scores, reading and math proficiency levels, primary learning style, and major learning difficulty; recommendations from an LD teacher discussing the applicant's main areas of strength and weakness, and a mainstream teacher or guidance counselor; and an optional letter from an employer. After the directors of B.U.I.L.D. review the information, interviews will be arranged for those applicants being considered for final selection. Acceptance into the B.U.I.L.D. Program is determined by the program director.

ADDITIONAL INFORMATION

The tutorial coordinator assigns tutors to each student in B.U.I.L.D. All students must have at least two hours per week of individualized tutoring. Books on tape, test modifications, and group study are also provided. Course substitution is a possibility. B.U.I.L.D. offers three special courses to meet university requirements for English and math proficiency, all other classes are regular classes. Students are limited to 12 hours each semester until they can demonstrate academic success indicating they can handle the demands of a heavier courseload. Other services include specialized study skills course; specialized note-taking paper; test-taking arrangements; private study area; advice with course selection and career planning; possible course substitution; diagnostic testing referrals; and other aids such as books on tape, compresses-time tape recorder, and computers.

Support Services Contact Information

Learning Disability Program/Services: Baccalaureate for University of Indianapolis Learning Disabled (B.U.I.L.D.)
Director: Deborah L. Spinney
  E-Mail: dspinney@uindy.edu
  Telephone: 317-788-3536
  Fax: 317-788-3300
Contact Person: Vicki Buzash
  E-Mail: vbuzash@uindy.edu
  Telephone: 317-788-3536
  Fax: 317-788-3300

LEARNING DISABILITY SERVICES

Requests for the following services/accommodations will be evaluated individually based on appropriate and current documentation.

Allowed in exams
  Calculator: Yes
  Dictionary: Yes
  Computer: Yes
  Spellchecker: Yes
Extended test time: Yes
Scribes: Yes
Proctors: Yes
Oral exams: Yes
Note-takers: No

Distraction reduced environment: Yes
Tape recording in class: Yes
Books on tape from RFBD: Yes
Taping of books not from RFBD: No
Accommodations for students with ADD: Yes
Reading machine: Yes
Other assistive technology: Yes
Priority registration: Yes

Added costs for services: Yes
LD specialists: Yes
Professional tutors: 16
Peer tutors: 2
Max. hours/wk. for services: Unlimited
How professors are notified of LD/ADD: By both student and director

GENERAL ADMISSIONS INFORMATION

Director of Admissions: Ron Wilks
Telephone: 317-788-3216

ENTRANCE REQUIREMENTS

Academic units recommended: 4 English, 3 math, 3 science (2 science lab), 2 foreign language, 3 social studies. High school diploma is required and GED is accepted. TOEFL required of all international applicants, minimum paper TOEFL 500, minimum computer TOEFL 173.

Application deadline: Rolling
Notification: Rolling
Average GPA: 3.05

Average SAT Math: 512
Average SAT Verbal: 503
Average ACT: 25

Graduated top 10% of class: 21%
Graduated top 25% of class: 51%
Graduated top 50% of class: 84%

COLLEGE GRADUATION REQUIREMENTS

Course waivers allowed: No
Course substitutions allowed: Yes
In what course: Modern language requirements

ADDITIONAL INFORMATION

Environment: The 60-acre campus in a suburban neighborhood is located 10 miles south of downtown Indianapolis.

Student Body:
  Undergrad enrollment: 3,100
  Women: 67%
  Men: 33%
  Percent out-of-state: 8%

Cost Information
  Tuition: $17,200
  Room & board: $6,150
Housing Information
  University housing: Yes
  Percent living on campus: 52%

Greek System
  Fraternity: No
  Sorority: No
  Athletics: NCAA Division II

University of Indianapolis

UNIVERSITY OF NOTRE DAME

220 Main Building, Notre Dame, IN 46556
Phone: 574-631-7505 • Fax: 574-631-8865
E-mail: admissio.1@nd.edu • Web: www.nd.edu
Support: S • Institution type: 4-year private

LEARNING DISABILITY PROGRAM AND SERVICES

It is the mission of the Office for Students with Disabilities (OSD) to ensure that Notre Dame students with disabilities have access to the programs and facilities of the university. OSD is committed to forming partnerships with students to share the responsibility of meeting individual needs. At the University of Notre Dame, students with disabilities may use a variety of services intended to reduce the effects that a disability may have on their educational experience. Services do not lower course standards or alter essential degree requirements, but instead give students an equal opportunity to demonstrate their academic abilities. Students can initiate a request for services by registering with the Office for Students with Disabilities and providing information that documents the disability. Individual assistance is provided in selecting the services that will provide access to the academic programs and facilities of the university.

LD/ADD ADMISSIONS INFORMATION

College entrance tests required: Yes
Interview recommended: No
Essay recommended: No
Documentation required for LD: Psychoeducational evaluation
Documentation required for ADD: Yes
Submitted to: Office for Students with Disabilities
Special Ed. HS coursework accepted: N/A

Specific course requirements of all applicants: Yes
Separate application required for program services: No
# of LD applications submitted each year: NR
# of LD applications accepted yearly: NR
Total # of students receiving LD services: 75
Acceptance into program means acceptance into college: Student must be admitted and enrolled in the university first and then request services.

ADMISSIONS

The university does not have a special admission process for students with learning disabilities. All students submit the same application and are expected to meet the same admission criteria. Admission to the university is highly competitive. The university seeks to enroll an exceptionally distinguished student body from among its broadly diverse and richly talented applicant pool. The admissions office prides itself on reviewing each application individually and with care. Students are expected to have 4 years English, 4 years math, 4 years science, 2 years foreign language, 2 years social studies, and 3 years of additional courses from these areas mentioned.

ADDITIONAL INFORMATION

Services for students with learning disabilities or attention deficit disorder include taped textbooks, note-takers, assistance with developing time management skills and learning strategies, and screening and referral for diagnostic testing. All students with disabilities are given assistance in developing a positive working relationship with faculty, facilitation of classroom accommodations, liaison with Vocational Rehabilitation and other state and local agencies, informal academic, personal and vocational counseling, and referral to other university resources. Currently 20 students with LD and 29 students with ADD are receiving services/accommodations. Undergraduates and graduates with appropriate documentation are eligible to request services and accommodations.

Support Services Contact Information

Learning Disability Program/Services: Office for Students with Disabilities
Director: Scott Howland
  E-Mail: showland@nd.edu
  Telephone: 219-631-7141
  Fax: 219-631-7939

LEARNING DISABILITY SERVICES

Requests for the following services/accommodations will be evaluated individually based on appropriate and current documentation.

Allowed in exams	Distraction reduced environment: Yes	Added costs for services: No
Calculator: Yes	Tape recording in class: Yes	LD specialists: No
Dictionary: Yes	Books on tape from RFBD: Yes	Professional tutors: No
Computer: Yes	Taping of books not from RFBD: No	Peer tutors: No
Spellchecker: Yes	Accommodations for students with	Max. hours/wk. for services:
Extended test time: Yes	ADD: Yes	Unlimited
Scribes: Yes	Reading machine: No	How professors are notified of
Proctors: Yes	Other assistive technology: Yes	LD/ADD: By both student and director
Oral exams: Yes	Priority registration: Yes	
Note-takers: Yes		

GENERAL ADMISSIONS INFORMATION

Director of Admissions: Dan Saracino
Telephone: 574-631-7505

ENTRANCE REQUIREMENTS

Academic units required: 4 English, 3 math, 2 science (1 science lab), 2 foreign language, 2 history, 3 academic electives. **Academic units recommended:** 4 English, 4 math, 4 science, 4 foreign language, 4 history. High school diploma is required and GED is not accepted. ACT with or without Writing component accepted. TOEFL required of all international applicants, minimum paper TOEFL 600, minimum computer TOEFL 250.
Application deadline: 12/31

Notification: 4/1	Average SAT Verbal: 676	Graduated top 25% of class: 95%
Average GPA: NR	Average ACT: 31	Graduated top 50% of class: 100%
Average SAT Math: 693	Graduated top 10% of class: 85%	

COLLEGE GRADUATION REQUIREMENTS

Course waivers allowed: No
Course substitutions allowed: Yes
In what course: Foreign language

ADDITIONAL INFORMATION

Environment: The university is located in a suburban area about 1 1/2 hours from Chicago.

Student Body:	Cost Information	Greek System
Undergrad enrollment: 8,322	Tuition: 31,540	Fraternity: No
Women: 47%	Room & board: $8,180	Sorority: No
Men: 53%	Housing Information	Athletics: NCAA Division I
Percent out-of-state: 87%	University housing: Yes	
	Percent living on campus: 76%	

University of Notre Dame

UNIVERSITY OF SAINT FRANCIS (IN)

2701 Spring Street, Fort Wayne, IN 46808
Phone: 260-434-3279 • Fax: 260-434-7590
E-mail: admis@sf.edu • Web: www.sf.edu
Support: CS • Institution type: 4-year private

LEARNING DISABILITY PROGRAM AND SERVICES

The Student Learning Center assists and acts as an advocte for students with disabilities. Students are encouraged to be self-advocates, and to develop skills to become independent learners. The Learning Center strives to provide students with disabilities with special services and acadmic support needed to achieve success in the college environment. Students with disabilities are encouraged to meet with the Learning Center director, prior to the start of the school year, to discuss the types of accommodations necessary to provide the best opportunity for academic success.

LD/ADD ADMISSIONS INFORMATION

College entrance tests required: Yes
Interview recommended: No
Essay recommended: No
Documentation required for LD: The most recent psychological evaluation and the student's last individual education plan (within 3 years)
Documentation required for ADD: Yes
Submitted to: Both Admissions and Student Learning Center
Special Ed. HS coursework accepted: No

Specific course requirements of all applicants: Yes
Separate application required for program services: No
# of LD applications submitted each year: NR
# of LD applications accepted yearly: NR
Total # of students receiving LD services:
Acceptance into program means acceptance into college: Students must be admitted and enrolled in the university first and then request services.

ADMISSIONS

There is no special admission process for students with learning disabilities. Entrance is based on an overall evaluation of the student's high school transcript, recommendations, and tests. The minimum ACT is 19 or SATs 800. Automatic admission is given to students with a 920 SAT. College-prep course requirements include 4 years English, 3 years math, 2 years lab science, 2 years social studies, and 2 years foreign language. The minimum GPA is 2.2. Some students may be asked to come to campus for an interview and/or to write a personal statement or essay. Students may be admitted "on warning," on a 13-hour limit or a part-time basis.

ADDITIONAL INFORMATION

Incoming freshmen may be asked to take placement exams in reading, writing, and math to determine appropriate beginning level courses. Curriculum consideration is given to applicants whose test scores show that a limited number of credit hours would be helpful. Skills classes are offered in reading, writing, and math. The writing consultant helps students with all phases of the research paper or essay writing process including forming and refining ideas, planning a rough draft, revising, editing, and proofreading. Specialized services provided by the Student Learning Center are accommodations on admission placement exams, alternative exam site, extended exam time, reading of exams or reading directions, carbonless paper for note-taking, assistance in ordering taped texts, altered exam procedures, large print, LD specialist for individuial assistance, peer tutors, academic progress monitoring with two reports per semester,letter to professors regarding accommodations, assistance with study and organizational skills, and assistance in facilitating a positive relationship with faculty and staff. Help is also available in the areas of time management, efficient study reading, memory techniques, concentration and motivation, test-taking strategies, and note-taking techniques.

Support Services Contact Information

Learning Disability Program/Services: Student Learning Center
Director: Michelle Kruyer
  E-Mail: mkruyer@sf.edu
  Telephone: 219-434-7677
  Fax: 219-434-3183

LEARNING DISABILITY SERVICES

Requests for the following services/accommodations will be evaluated individually based on appropriate and current documentation.

Allowed in exams
  Calculator: Yes
  Dictionary: Yes
  Computer: Yes
  Spellchecker: Yes
Extended test time: Yes
Scribes: Yes
Proctors: Yes
Oral exams: Yes
Note-takers: Yes

Distraction reduced environment: Yes
Tape recording in class: Yes
Books on tape from RFBD: Yes
Taping of books not from RFBD: No
Accommodations for students with
  ADD: Yes
Reading machine: Yes
Other assistive technology: Yes
Priority registration: No

Added costs for services: No
LD specialists: Yes
Professional tutors: Yes
Peer tutors: Yes
Max. hours/wk. for services:
  Unlimited
How professors are notified of
  LD/ADD: By both student and director

GENERAL ADMISSIONS INFORMATION

Director of Admissions: Matthew P. Nettleton
Telephone: 260-434-3279

ENTRANCE REQUIREMENTS

Academic units recommended: 4 English, 3 math, 2 science, 2 foreign language, 2 social studies. High school diploma is required and GED is accepted. TOEFL required of all international applicants, minimum paper TOEFL 500, minimum computer TOEFL 173.

Application deadline: NR
Notification: Rolling
Average GPA: 2.90

Average SAT Math: 481
Average SAT Verbal: 479
Average ACT: 20

Graduated top 10% of class: 12%
Graduated top 25% of class: 32%
Graduated top 50% of class: 73%

COLLEGE GRADUATION REQUIREMENTS

Course waivers allowed: Yes
Course substitutions allowed: Yes
In what course: N/A

ADDITIONAL INFORMATION

Environment: The 70-acre campus is located west of Fort Wayne.

Student Body:
  Undergrad enrollment: 1,413
  Women: 66%
  Men: 34%
  Percent out-of-state: 8%

Cost Information
  Tuition: $14,900
  Room & board: $5,450
Housing Information
  University housing: Yes
  Percent living on campus: 16%

Greek System
  Fraternity: No
  Sorority: No
Athletics: NAIA

UNIVERSITY OF SOUTHERN INDIANA

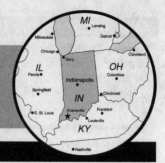

8600 University Boulevard, Evansville, IN 47712
Phone: 812-464-1765 • Fax: 812-465-7154
E-mail: enroll@usi.edu • Web: www.usi.edu
Support: S• Institution type: 4-year public

LEARNING DISABILITY PROGRAM AND SERVICES

Staff provide support to assist students with disabilities so they can participate in educational programming. This mission is accomplished by offering student support and advocacy, being available for student and faculty consultation, coordinating accommodation services, and serving as a centralizing service for disabilty information for the university. Students must have a professionally diagnosed disabilty to qualify for disability support.

LD/ADD ADMISSIONS INFORMATION

College entrance tests required: Yes
Interview recommended: No
Essay recommended: No
Documentation required for LD: complete diagnostic report including test scores, diagnosis and recommendations for accommodations.
Documentation required for ADD: Yes
Submitted to: Counseling Center
Special Ed. HS coursework accepted: Yes

Specific course requirements of all applicants: Yes
Separate application required for program services: No
# of LD applications submitted each year: NR
# of LD applications accepted yearly: NR
Total # of students receiving LD services: 74
Acceptance into program means acceptance into college: Student must be admitted and enrolled in the university first and then request services.

ADMISSIONS

Admissions criteria are the same for all students; however, the admissions office will always work with students on an individual basis if needed. In general, students with a 3.6 GPA or higher are admitted with honors. Students with a 2.0-3.5 GPA are admitted in good standing, and students with a GPA below a 2.0 are accepted conditionally. The conditional admissions procedure is for new freshmen who earned below a 2.0 in English, math, science, and social studies. The following are required for those admitted conditionally: freshman seminar; 2.0 GPA; registration through the university division rather than a specific major; and enrollment in no more than 12 credit hours. ACT/SAT scores are used for placement purposes. The college accepts courses taken through the special education department of the high school.

ADDITIONAL INFORMATION

In order to receive support services, documentation of a LD must be provided by the student. Skills classes are offered in basic grammar, algebra review, reading, and study skills. Credit is given for the hours, but the grades are Pass/No Pass. There are no note-takers, but special supplies are provided to allow the students to get other students to carbon their notes in class. Other services include readers/taping services, test accommodations, tutor referral, advocacy and counseling, and career planning. Services and accommodations are available for undergraduate and graduate students.

Support Services Contact Information

Learning Disability Program/Services: Counseling Center
Director: James Browning
  E-Mail: jbrowning@usi.edu
  Telephone: 812-464-1867
  Fax: 812-461-5288
  Contact Person: Leslie Smith
  E-Mail: lmsmith@usi.edu

LEARNING DISABILITY SERVICES

Requests for the following services/accommodations will be evaluated individually based on appropriate and current documentation.

Allowed in exams
  Calculator: Yes
  Dictionary: Yes
  Computer: Yes
  Spellchecker: Yes
Extended test time: Yes
Scribes: Yes
Proctors: Yes
Oral exams: Yes
Note-takers: Yes

Distraction reduced environment: Yes
Tape recording in class: Yes
Books on tape from RFBD: Yes
Taping of books not from RFBD: Yes
Accommodations for students with ADD: Yes
Reading machine: Yes
Other assistive technology: Yes
Priority registration: Yes

Added costs for services: No
LD specialists: No
Professional tutors: NR
Peer tutors: 56
Max. hours/wk. for services: Unlimited
How professors are notified of LD/ADD: By student

GENERAL ADMISSIONS INFORMATION

Director of Admissions: Mr. Eric H. Otto
Telephone: 812-464-1765

ENTRANCE REQUIREMENTS

Academic units recommended: 4 English, 4 math, 3 science, 2 foreign language, 2 social studies, 2 history, 2 academic electives. High school diploma is required and GED is accepted. ACT with Writing component required or SAT Reasoning. TOEFL required of all international applicants, minimum paper TOEFL 525, minimum computer TOEFL 197.

Application deadline: 8/15
Notification: Rolling
Average GPA: 2.91

Average SAT Math: 476
Average SAT Verbal: 473
Average ACT: 19

Graduated top 10% of class: 9%
Graduated top 25% of class: 26%
Graduated top 50% of class: 59%

COLLEGE GRADUATION REQUIREMENTS

Course waivers allowed: Not recommended
Course substitutions allowed: Yes
In what course: Math, physical education

ADDITIONAL INFORMATION

Environment: The university is located on 300 acres in a suburban area 150 miles south of Indianapolis.

Student Body:
  Undergrad enrollment: 8,925
  Women: 60%
  Men: 40%
  Percent out-of-state: 9%

Cost Information
  In-state tuition: $4,017
  Out-of-state tuition: $9,582
  Room & board: $5,480
Housing Information
  University housing: Yes
  Percent living on campus: 31%

Greek System
  Fraternity: Yes
  Sorority: Yes
Athletics: NCAA Division II

VINCENNES UNIVERSITY

1002 North First Street, Vincennes, IN 47591
Phone: 800-742-9198 • Fax: 812-888-8888
E-mail: vuadmit@vinu.edu • Web: www.vinu.edu
Support: SP • Institution type: 2-year public

LEARNING DISABILITY PROGRAM AND SERVICES

Students Transition into Education Program (STEP) is an LD support program for students in the mainstream. Students' strengths rather than deficits are the emphasis; compensatory techniques rather than remediation are the thrust. STEP is designed to give students the opportunity to develop their own unique abilities, achieve their highest academic potential, and develop a sense of self-worth and the skills needed to function and learn independently in college. STEP students take four semesters in Coping in College I–IV: the course teaches requisite social, study, and self-awareness skills and serves as a support group. The curriculum is practical and emphasizes active thinking, independent learning, student accountability, and the acquisition of specific strategies proven to improve academic performance. Coping in College I addresses self-advocacy, compensatory techniques, coping, adaptation, stress, and socialization; II emphasizes socialization and metacognitive skills; III further develops social skills and solidifies study skills; IV emphasizes career planning, job-search, and social skills, and includes the STEP retreat. Cope Student Support Services is a program designed to help students with all aspects of the college experience. This is a Trio Program, requiring that the student meet one of three requirements: first generation college student, low income, or disabled.

LD/ADD ADMISSIONS INFORMATION

College entrance tests required: Yes
Interview recommended: N/A
Essay recommended: No
Documentation required for LD: Psychoeducational evaluation
Documentation required for ADD: Yes
Submitted to: Step Program
Special Ed. HS coursework accepted: Yes

Specific course requirements of all applicants: Yes
Separate application required for program services: Yes
# of LD applications submitted each year: 400
# of LD applications accepted yearly: 60
Total # of students receiving LD services: 100–120
Acceptance into program means acceptance into college: Students must apply separately to the university and STEP or Cope. Students will be accepted to the university first and then to the STEP or Cope.

ADMISSIONS

Students with learning disabilities must submit the general application form to Vincennes University. Vincennes offers open-door admissions to any student with a high school diploma or the GED. SAT or ACT scores are required for all Health Occupations majors. SAT and ACT scores are not required for other majors, however they are used for placement in course levels appropriate to your academic preparation. If students have not taken the SAT or ACT, they will be required to take a placement test before they can register for classes. Students with learning disabilities must apply separately to STEP by sending the follwing: STEP application; psychological evaluation; and letters of recommendation from LD specialists, counselors, or teachers. The transcript is of less importance and the recommendations are more important. Once accepted, students reserve a spot with a deposit of $110 to STEP. Deposits are refundable if students do not matriculate to Vincennes. Admission to the program is based on completion of the application process, determination of student eligibility, available funding, and space remaining. Space in the program is limited. Early application is important and the deadline date is 2/1. Students applying to Cope should apply separately to the university prior to applying to STEP.

ADDITIONAL INFORMATION

STEP benefits include LD specialists for individualized tutoring/remediation, professional/peer tutoring, specialized remedial and/or support classes, weekly academic monitoring, coordinated referral to Counseling/Career Center, special classes, note-taking paper, reduced class load, audit class before taking test modifications, papers rather than tests, and alternative ways to demonstrate competency. STEP does not exempt students from classes, class requirements, or provide taped books and note-takers. Cope provides individual counselor to assist with needs; tutoring; progress reports; academic advising; appropriate accommodations; academic support groups; workshops on study skills, test anxiety, self-esteem, and interview skills. The Study Skills Center is open to all students and offers free tutoring; study skills classes in spelling, study skills, success strategies, and learning strategies; individualized materials to help improve performance in problem areas; assessment center; and study skills lab.

Support Services Contact Information

Learning Disability Program/Services: Students Transition into Education Program (STEP)
Director: Jane Kavanaugh
  E-Mail: jkavanaugh@vinu.edu
  Telephone: 812-888-4485
  Fax: 812-888-5531
Contact Person: Robin Draeger, Director of Cope
  E-Mail: rdraeger@vinu.edu
  Telephone: 812-888-4214 or 812-888-4212
  Fax: 812-888-5531

LEARNING DISABILITY SERVICES

Requests for the following services/accommodations will be evaluated individually based on appropriate and current documentation.

Allowed in exams
  Calculator: Yes
  Dictionary: Yes
  Computer: Yes
  Spellchecker: Yes
Extended test time: Yes
Scribes: No
Proctors: Yes
Oral exams: Yes
Note-takers: No

Distraction reduced environment: Yes
Tape recording in class: Yes
Books on tape from RFBD: Yes
Taping of books not from RFBD: Yes
**Accommodations for students with
  ADD:** Yes
Reading machine: Yes
Other assistive technology: Yes
Priority registration: Yes

Added costs for services: Yes
LD specialists: Yes
Professional tutors: 10–20
Peer tutors: 25–45
Max. hours/wk. for services:
  Unlimited
**How professors are notified of
  LD/ADD:** By student

GENERAL ADMISSIONS INFORMATION

Director of Admissions: Phyllis Carling
Telephone: 800-742-9198

ENTRANCE REQUIREMENTS

Open door admissions. High school diploma or GED required. No ACT/SAT required. Courses recommended: 4 English, 3 math, 3 science, 4 social studies, 2 foreign language (16 total). TOEFL required of all international applicants, minimum paper TOEFL 528, minimum computer TOEFL 197

Application deadline: Rolling
Notification: Rolling
Average GPA: NR

Average SAT Math: NR
Average SAT Verbal: NR
Average ACT: NR

Graduated top 10% of class: NR
Graduated top 25% of class: NR
Graduated top 50% of class: NR

COLLEGE GRADUATION REQUIREMENTS

Course waivers allowed: Yes
Course substitutions allowed: Yes
In what course: Each case handled on an individual basis.

ADDITIONAL INFORMATION

Environment: The school is located on 95 acres 45 minutes south of Terre Haute.

Student Body:
  Undergrad enrollment: 6,000
  Women: 43%
  Men: 57%
  Percent out-of-state: 9%

Cost Information
  In-state: $3,000
  Out-of-state: $7,000
  Room & board: $5,500
Housing Information
  University housing: Yes
  Percent living on campus: 60%

Greek System
  Fraternity: Yes
  Sorority: Yes
Athletics: NJCAA

DRAKE UNIVERSITY

2507 University Avenue, Des Moines, IA 50311-4505
Phone: 515-271-3181 • Fax: 515-271-2831
E-mail: admission@drake.edu • Web: www.choose.drake.edu
Support: S• Institution type: 4-year private

LEARNING DISABILITY PROGRAM AND SERVICES

The purpose of the Disability Resource Center (DRC) is to facilitate and enhance the opportunity for students with any type of disability to successfully complete their post-secondary education. The DRC is committed to enriching the academic experience of Drake students with disabilities through individualized assessment of accommodations and resource needs. To initiate a request for services, students should contact the DRC. An appointment will be made with a staff member to begin the registration process. Students are encouraged to meet with a DRC counselor each semester to identify accommodations that are needed. It is the students' responsibility to self-identify that they have a learning disability, to provide professional documentation of their disability, and to request the accommodations that they need. The DRC office maintains a collection of information on disabilities, and there are many sources on the instruction and evaluation of students with disabilities. DRC encourages faculty, staff, and students to contact the office if they are interested in this type of information.

LD/ADD ADMISSIONS INFORMATION

College entrance tests required: Yes
Interview recommended: No
Essay recommended: No
Documentation required for LD: Psychoeducational
evaluation
Documentation required for ADD: Yes
Submitted to: Student Disabilities Services
Special Ed. HS coursework accepted: Yes

Specific course requirements of all applicants: Yes
Separate application required for program services: No
# of LD applications submitted each year: NR
# of LD applications accepted yearly: NR
Total # of students receiving LD services: NR
**Acceptance into program means acceptance into
college:** Student must be admitted and enrolled in the
university first and then reviewed for LD services.

ADMISSIONS
There is no special admission process for students with learning disabilities. All applicants are expected to meet the same admission criteria, including 16 academic college-prep courses with a minimum of 4 years English, 2 years math, 2 years science, 2 years social studies, 1 year history, and 2 years foreign language; 21 ACT or 970 SAT; and a minimum of a 2.0 GPA. Students must be admitted and enrolled in the university prior to seeking accommodations or services for a learning disability.

ADDITIONAL INFORMATION
The DRC can offer students appointments at the pre-admission and pre-enrollment stages; review of Drake's policies and procedures regarding students with disabilities; identification and coordination of classroom accommodations; assessment of service needs; note-takers, scribes, and readers; referral to appropriate campus resources; advocacy and liaison with the university community; and training on the use of assistive technology. Services provided by the DRC do not lower any course standards or change any requirements of a particular degree. The services are intended to allow equal access and provide an opportunity for students with disabilities to demonstrate their abilities.

Support Services Contact Information

Learning Disability Program/Services: Student Disability Services
Director: Chrystal Stanley
   E-Mail: chrystal.stanley@drake.edu
   Telephone: 515-271-1835
   Fax: 515-271-1855

LEARNING DISABILITY SERVICES

Requests for the following services/accommodations will be evaluated individually based on appropriate and current documentation.

Allowed in exams
   Calculator: Yes
   Dictionary: Yes
   Computer: Yes
   Spellchecker: Yes
Extended test time: Yes
Scribes: Yes
Proctors: Yes
Oral exams: Yes
Note-takers: Yes

Distraction reduced environment: Yes
Tape recording in class: Yes
Books on tape from RFBD: Yes
Taping of books not from RFBD: Yes
Accommodations for students with ADD: Yes
Reading machine: Yes
Other assistive technology: Yes
Priority registration: No

Added costs for services: No
LD specialists: No
Professional tutors: No
Peer tutors: 30–40
Max. hours/wk. for services: Unlimited
How professors are notified of LD/ADD: By student

GENERAL ADMISSIONS INFORMATION

Director of Admissions: Tom Delahunt, VP for Admission of Financial Aid
Telephone: 515-271-3181

ENTRANCE REQUIREMENTS

Academic units recommended: 4 English, 3 math, 2 science, 2 foreign language, 4 social studies. High school diploma is required and GED is accepted. ACT with or without Writing component accepted. TOEFL required of all international applicants, minimum paper TOEFL 530, minimum computer TOEFL 197.

Application deadline: 3/1
Notification: Rolling
Average GPA: 3.66

Average SAT Math: 584
Average SAT Verbal: 570
Average ACT: 25

Graduated top 10% of class: 38%
Graduated top 25% of class: 72%
Graduated top 50% of class: 96%

COLLEGE GRADUATION REQUIREMENTS

Course waivers allowed: No
Course substitutions allowed: Yes
In what course: Documentation must be provided and is considered on a case by case basis.

ADDITIONAL INFORMATION

Environment: The campus is located in the suburbs of Des Moines.

Student Body:
   Undergrad enrollment: 3,118
   Women: 58%
   Men: 42%
   Percent out-of-state: 61%

Cost Information
   Tuition: $21,100
   Room & board: $6,170
Housing Information
   University housing: Yes
   Percent living on campus: 34%

Greek System
   Fraternity: Yes
   Sorority: Yes
Athletics: NCAA Division I

GRAND VIEW COLLEGE

1200 Grandview Avenue, Des Moines, IA 50316-1599
Phone: 515-263-2810 • Fax: 515-263-2974
E-mail: admissions@gvc.edu • Web: www.gvc.edu
Support: CS• Institution type: 4-year private

LEARNING DISABILITY PROGRAM AND SERVICES

The Academic Success Program is available for all students on campus. The objective of the program is to provide a variety of learning environments and teaching techniques. Academic Success provides academic support programs, services and courses designed to optimize student performance. Students who participate in the Center for Academic and Career Success Program make a smoother transition to Grand View, develop social and academic networks essential to their success, and benefit from informal student/faculty/staff interactions. Grand View is committed to enriching the academic experience of every qualified student with LD and endorses reasonable accommodations for participation in all programs and activities. Students are encouraged to make an appointment in the Academic Success Center to review college policies and procedures, request accommodations, develop an accommodation plan, or discuss personal advocacy issues.

LD/ADD ADMISSIONS INFORMATION

College entrance tests required: Yes
Interview recommended: No
Essay recommended: No
Documentation required for LD: Verification of learning disabilities by licensed psychologist required.
Documentation required for ADD: Yes
Submitted to: Academic Success
Special Ed. HS coursework accepted: Yes

Specific course requirements of all applicants: Yes
Separate application required for program services: No
# of LD applications submitted each year: NR
# of LD applications accepted yearly: NR
Total # of students receiving LD services: 15
Acceptance into program means acceptance into college: Student must be admitted and enrolled at the college and then request services

ADMISSIONS

There is no special admissions process for students with LD and ADD. There is a probationary admit for students with an 18 ACT and a 2.0 high school GPA and below. This is offered to students who show that they are committed and have the potential for success at college.

ADDITIONAL INFORMATION

The Academic Success Center provides resources which complement classroom instruction enabling students to optimize their academic experience. Students can receive help with reading rate and reading comprehension, study skills, organizational skills, developing a personal management plan, test taking strategies, writing skills, personalized instruction in math, and peer tutoring. The Career Center provides services, resources, and educational opportunities by assisting students in developing, evaluating, initiating, and implementing personal career and life plans. Faculty members serve as academic advisors. Core courses can have substitution options. Other services or accommodations offered for students with appropriate documentation include the use of calculators, computers or spell checkers; extended testing time; scribes; proctors; oral exams; note-takers; distraction-free environment for taking tests; tape recording of lectures; and services for students with ADD. There is one professional staff member who is certified in LD.

Support Services Contact Information

Learning Disability Program/Services: Academic Success
Director: Carolyn Wassenaar
  E-Mail: cwassenaar@gve.edu
  Telephone: 515-263-2971
  Fax: 515-263-2840

LEARNING DISABILITY SERVICES

Requests for the following services/accommodations will be evaluated individually based on appropriate and current documentation.

Allowed in exams
  Calculator: Yes
  Dictionary: Yes
  Computer: Yes
  Spellchecker: Yes
Extended test time: Yes
Scribes: Yes
Proctors: Yes
Oral exams: Yes
Note-takers: Yes

Distraction reduced environment: Yes
Tape recording in class: Yes
Books on tape from RFBD: Yes
Taping of books not from RFBD: Yes
Accommodations for students with ADD: Yes
Reading machine: No
Other assistive technology: No
Priority registration: Yes

Added costs for services: No
LD specialists: Yes
Professional tutors: 1
Peer tutors: No
Max. hours/wk. for services: Unlimited
How professors are notified of LD/ADD: By both student and director

GENERAL ADMISSIONS INFORMATION

Director of Admissions: Diane Schafer Johnson
Telephone: 515-263-2810

ENTRANCE REQUIREMENTS

Academic units recommended: 4 English, 3 math, 3 science, 2 foreign language, 3 social studies. High school diploma is required and GED is accepted. TOEFL required of all international applicants, minimum paper TOEFL 550, minimum computer TOEFL 210.

Application deadline: 8/15
Notification: Rolling
Average GPA: 3.13

Average SAT Math: NR
Average SAT Verbal: NR
Average ACT: 21

Graduated top 10% of class: 13%
Graduated top 25% of class: 32%
Graduated top 50% of class: 68%

COLLEGE GRADUATION REQUIREMENTS

Course waivers allowed: No
Course substitutions allowed: Yes
In what course: We have included acceptable substitions/options within our core.

ADDITIONAL INFORMATION

Environment: Located in Des Moines

Student Body:
  Undergrad enrollment: 1,697
  Women: 69%
  Men: 31%
  Percent out-of-state: 8%

Cost Information
  Tuition: $15,052
  Room & board: $5,436
Housing Information
  University housing: Yes
  Percent living on campus: 32%

Greek System
  Fraternity: NR
  Sorority: NR
Athletics: NAIA

GRINNELL COLLEGE

1103 Park Street, Grinnell, IA 50112-1690
Phone: 641-269-3600 • Fax: 641-269-4800
E-mail: askgrin@grinnell.edu • Web: www.grinnell.edu
Support: S• Institution type: 4-year private

LEARNING DISABILITY PROGRAM AND SERVICES

Grinnell College is dedicated to educating young people whose achievements show a high level of intellectual capacity, initiative, and maturity. Every year, this highly qualified group of students includes people with learning disabilities. Grinnell is committed to providing academic adjustments and reasonable accommodations for students with disabilities who are otherwise qualified for admission. Many of Grinnell's characteristics make it a positive educational environment for all students: an open curriculum, small classes, easy access to professors, and openness to diversity. The director of academic advising coordinates services for students with LD, arranges for academic accommodations, acts as a liaison to the faculty, and offers personal, individual assistance. Once students are admitted and they accept the offer of admission, Grinnell likes to plan with them for any reasonable accommodation they will need in order to enjoy a successful experience. Students have the responsibility to make their needs known. The most important factors for college success are seeking help early and learning to be self-advocates. Students are encouraged to notify the director of academic advising about their needs before they arrive for the first semester. For planning purposes, sooner is always better.

LD/ADD ADMISSIONS INFORMATION

College entrance tests required: Yes
Interview recommended: No
Essay recommended: No
Documentation required for LD: Current written evaluation from a psychologist, LD specialist or M.D. indicating results from testing, a specific diagnosis, a clinical summary, and recommendations for academic accommodation
Documentation required for ADD: Yes
Submitted to: Academic Advising
Special Ed. HS coursework accepted: N/A

Specific course requirements of all applicants: Yes
Separate application required for program services: No
# of LD applications submitted each year: NR
# of LD applications accepted yearly: NR
Total # of students receiving LD services: 25
Acceptance into program means acceptance into college: Student must be admitted and enrolled in the university first and then request services.

ADMISSIONS

Grinnell welcomes applications from students with learning disabilities. While the same admissions standards apply to all students, the college does accept nonstandardized test scores. Students are advised to document their needs in the application for admission and how learning disabilities may have affected their secondary school performance. Interviews are encouraged. Grinnell is looking for a strong scholastic record from high school, recommendations, satisfactory results on the ACT/SAT, and specific units of high school coursework, including 4 years English, 3 years math, 3 years social studies, 3 years science, and 3 years foreign language. Applicants with appropriate documentation may substitute for some entrance requirements such as foreign language. The mid 50 percent range for the ACT is 28-31 and 1238–1433 for the SAT. Over 85 percent of the admitted students are from the top 20 percent of the class. The minimum GPA is a 2.5. Students are encouraged to have an interview either on or off campus.

ADDITIONAL INFORMATION

Students need to meet with professors and the director of academic advising to plan for their individual needs. The Office of Academic Advising coordinates services for students and arranges for academic accommodations. The ADA Task Force ensures compliance with the Americans with Disabilities Act. The Reading Lab helps students improve reading speed, vocabulary, and reading comprehension. The director of academic advising assists students with LD in identifying effective academic strategies. The Science and Math Learning Center provides instruction in math and science courses for students who want to strengthen their background in these areas. Student tutoring will help students make arrangements for tutoring at no charge. Additional resources include referral for LD testing, reduced course loads, untimed exams, personal counseling, and volunteers who are willing to read to students with learning disabilities. Skills classes for credit are offered in reading, writing, and math.

Support Services Contact Information

Learning Disability Program/Services: Academic Advising Office
Director: Joyce M. Stern
  E-Mail: sternjm@grinnell.edu
  Telephone: 641-269-3702
  Fax: 641-269-3710
Contact Person: Same

LEARNING DISABILITY SERVICES

Requests for the following services/accommodations will be evaluated individually based on appropriate and current documentation.

Allowed in exams
  Calculator: Yes
  Dictionary: Yes
  Computer: Yes
  Spellchecker: Yes
Extended test time: Yes
Scribes: Yes
Proctors: Yes
Oral exams: Yes
Note-takers: Yes

Distraction reduced environment: Yes
Tape recording in class: Yes
Books on tape from RFBD: Yes
Taping of books not from RFBD: Yes
**Accommodations for students with
  ADD:** Yes
Reading machine: Yes
Other assistive technology: Yes
Priority registration: No

Added costs for services: No
LD specialists: No
Professional tutors: 7
Peer tutors: 50
Max. hours/wk. for services:
  Unlimited
**How professors are notified of
  LD/ADD:** By both student and director

GENERAL ADMISSIONS INFORMATION

Director of Admissions: James Sumner
Telephone: 641-269-3600

ENTRANCE REQUIREMENTS

Academic units recommended: 4 English, 4 math, 4 science (3 science lab), 4 foreign language, 4 social studies. High school diploma is required and GED is accepted. ACT with or without Writing component accepted. TOEFL required of all international applicants, minimum paper TOEFL 550, minimum computer TOEFL 220.

Application deadline: 1/20
Notification: 4/1
Average GPA: NR

Average SAT Math: 683
Average SAT Verbal: 684
Average ACT: 30

Graduated top 10% of class: 67%
Graduated top 25% of class: 94%
Graduated top 50% of class: 100%

COLLEGE GRADUATION REQUIREMENTS

Course waivers allowed: No
Course substitutions allowed: No
In what course: N/A

ADDITIONAL INFORMATION

Environment: The college is located on 95 acres in a small town 55 miles east of Des Moines.

Student Body:
  Undergrad enrollment: 1,518
  Women: 54%
  Men: 46%
  Percent out-of-state: 75%

Cost Information
  Tuition: $27,504
  Room & board: $7,310
Housing Information
  University housing: Yes
  Percent living on campus: 88%

Greek System
  Fraternity: No
  Sorority: No
Athletics: NCAA Division III

INDIAN HILLS COMMUNITY COLLEGE

525 Grandview, Ottumwa, IA 52501
Phone: 800-726-2585
E-mail: bhenderso@ihcc.cc.ia.us • Web: www.ihcc.cc.ia.us
Support: CS• Institution type: 2-year public

LEARNING DISABILITY PROGRAM AND SERVICES

The Success Center provides academic and physical accommodations and services for students with disabilities based upon documented needs. Students with a documented learning disability or attention deficit disorder must provide current documentation which has been completed by a qualified professional.

LD/ADD ADMISSIONS INFORMATION

College entrance tests required: Yes
Interview recommended: No
Essay recommended: No
Documentation required for LD: WAIS–III; WJ
Documentation required for ADD: Yes
Submitted to: Success Center
Special Ed. HS coursework accepted: Yes

Specific course requirements of all applicants: No
Separate application required for program services: Yes
# of LD applications submitted each year: 20–45
# of LD applications accepted yearly: 45
Total # of students receiving LD services: 45
Acceptance into program means acceptance into college: Student must be admitted and enrolled in the university first and then request services.

ADMISSIONS

Indian Hills Community College is an "open door" institution. All students must present a high school diploma or GED or must earn one while enrolled in order to receive a college degree. ACT/SAT are not required, and there are no specific high school courses required for admission. Although an interview is not required, it is highly recommended. Students enroll with widely varying levels of achievement and differing goals, and some discover that they can move ahead more quickly. Applicants are required to submit a portfolio, which is reviewed by a selection committee. Many eventually enter one or more of the Indian Hills credit courses. A decision to move into college credit courses is made by staff members, parents, and the student involved.

ADDITIONAL INFORMATION

All students have access to skills classes in study skills and specialized vocabulary skills. These credits earn college credit. There are currently approximately 35 students with learning disabilities and 10 with attention deficit disorder receiving accommodations or services.

Support Services Contact Information

Learning Disability Program/Services: Success Center
Director: Mary Stewart
  E-Mail: mstewart@ihcc.cc.ia.us
  Telephone: 641-683-5238
  Fax: 641-683-5184
Contact Person: Marva Philipsen
  E-Mail: mphilip@ihcc.cc.ia.us
  Telephone: 641-683-5238
  Fax: 641-683-5184

LEARNING DISABILITY SERVICES

Requests for the following services/accommodations will be evaluated individually based on appropriate and current documentation.

Allowed in exams
  Calculator: Yes
  Dictionary: Yes
  Computer: Yes
  Spellchecker: Yes
Extended test time: Yes
Scribes: Yes
Proctors: Yes
Oral exams: Yes
Note-takers: Yes

Distraction reduced environment: Yes
Tape recording in class: Yes
Books on tape from RFBD: Yes
Taping of books not from RFBD: Yes
Accommodations for students with
  ADD: Yes
Reading machine: No
Other assistive technology: No
Priority registration: No

Added costs for services: No
LD specialists: Yes
Professional tutors: 9
Peer tutors: 20–30
Max. hours/wk. for services:
  Unlimited
How professors are notified of
  LD/ADD: By both student and director

GENERAL ADMISSIONS INFORMATION

Director of Admissions: Sally Harris
Telephone: 800-726-2585

ENTRANCE REQUIREMENTS

Recommended courses: 4 English, 3 math, 3 science, 4 social studies, 2 foreign language (16 total). Open door admissions. High school diploma or GED accepted. Students can complete requirements in college. Some majors require specific math courses.

Application deadline: Rolling
Notification: Rolling
Average GPA: NR

Average SAT Math: NR
Average SAT Verbal: NR
Average ACT: NR

Graduated top 10% of class: NR
Graduated top 25% of class: NR
Graduated top 50% of class: NR

COLLEGE GRADUATION REQUIREMENTS

Course waivers allowed: No
Course substitutions allowed: No
In what course: N/A

ADDITIONAL INFORMATION

Environment: The college is located on 400 acres about 2 hours east of Iowa City or west of Des Moines.

Student Body:
  Undergrad enrollment: 3,700
  Women: 50%
  Men: 50%
  Percent out-of-state: 9%

Cost Information
  In-state tuition: $2,200
  Out-of-state tuition: $135 per credit
  Room & board: $3,000
Housing Information
  University housing: Yes
  Percent living on campus: 15%

Greek System
  Fraternity: No
  Sorority: No
Athletics: NJCAA

IOWA STATE UNIVERSITY

100 Alumni Hall, Ames, IA 50011-2011
Phone: 515-294-5836 • Fax: 515-294-2592
E-mail: admissions@iastate.edu • Web: www.iastate.edu
Support: CS• Institution type: 4-year public

LEARNING DISABILITY PROGRAM AND SERVICES

ISU is committed to providing equal opportunities and facilitating the personal growth and development of all students. Several departments and organizations cooperate to accomplish these goals. The LD specialist assists students with issues relating to LD and helps them adjust to the university setting, provides a review of students' most current LD evaluation and documentation to determine the accommodations needed, offers assistance in articulating needs to faculty and staff, and may serve as a liaison in student/staff negotiations.

LD/ADD ADMISSIONS INFORMATION

College entrance tests required: Yes
Interview recommended: No
Essay recommended: No
Documentation required for LD: WAIS–III; or WISC–R (Part II) less than 3 years old
Documentation required for ADD: Yes
Submitted to: Disability Services
Special Ed. HS coursework accepted: Yes

Specific course requirements of all applicants: Yes
Separate application required for program services: No
# of LD applications submitted each year: NR
# of LD applications accepted yearly: NR
Total # of students receiving LD services: 265
Acceptance into program means acceptance into college: Student must be admitted and enrolled in the university first and then request services.

ADMISSIONS

Documentation should include demographic data about the student and examiner's qualifications; behavioral observation of the way students present themselves, manner of dress, verbal and nonverbal communication, interpersonal skills and behavior during testing; a narrative describing developmental and educational history; a description of the effect of the LD on academic learning; a report of the results of an assessment of intellectual functioning (including WAIS–R or WISC–R); a report of the results of academic testing including Woodcock—Johnson; testing for foreign language substitute; and specific recommendations concerning academic compensatory strategies and whether the student qualifies for specific academic accommodations. If a student is learning disabled and does not meet minimum requirements, the student can request a review. However, this is not a program for students with extreme deficits. Iowa State is looking for students who can succeed, have good verbal skills, and have an upward trend in grades. Students not meeting high school course requirements, but otherwise qualified, may be admitted after an individual review. The pattern on the ACT, not just the score, will be considered. There is a Summer Trial Program for students not regularly admissible through test scores or class rank. Students take six credits and are required to achieve grade C or better; these students are often in the top 75 percent of their class but may not have a 25 ACT.

ADDITIONAL INFORMATION

The Academic Learning Lab is a "learning-how-to-learn" center designed to help all students; counselors work one-to-one to evaluate and identify problem study habits and devise strategies to improve them. The Learning Lab, Tutoring, and Student Support Services are in one area called the Academic Success Center. ASC coordinates services including counseling, teaching reading, and study skills, and provides a list of tutors. The Writing Center, available for all students, helps students to write papers. The English department has a list of approved proofreaders. The LD specialist provides information about readers, note-takers, and scribes. SI is an academic assistance program attached to very difficult courses. Peer SI leaders attend classes and conduct biweekly sessions to help students learn and study the course material. Student Support Services is a federally funded program for students with LD and others qualified to receive academic support in the form of free tutoring and skill-building workshops.

Support Services Contact Information

Learning Disability Program/Services: Disability Resources
Director: Bea Awoniyi
  E-Mail: awoniyib@iastate.edu
  Telephone: 515-294-6644
  Fax: 515-294-5670

LEARNING DISABILITY SERVICES

Requests for the following services/accommodations will be evaluated individually based on appropriate and current documentation.

Allowed in exams
  Calculator: Yes
  Dictionary: Yes
  Computer: Yes
  Spellchecker: Yes
Extended test time: Yes
Scribes: Yes
Proctors: Yes
Oral exams: No
Note-takers: Yes

Distraction reduced environment: Yes
Tape recording in class: Yes
Books on tape from RFBD: Yes
Taping of books not from RFBD: Yes
**Accommodations for students with
  ADD:** Yes
Reading machine: Yes
Other assistive technology: Yes
Priority registration: No

Added costs for services: No
LD specialists: Yes
Professional tutors: No
Peer tutors: Varies
Max. hours/wk. for services: 5
**How professors are notified of
  LD/ADD:** By student

GENERAL ADMISSIONS INFORMATION

Director of Admissions: Mark Harding
Telephone: 515-294-0815

ENTRANCE REQUIREMENTS

Academic units required: 4 English, 3 math, 3 science (2 science lab), 2 foreign language, 2 social studies.
Academic units recommended: 4 math, 4 science (3 science lab), 4 foreign language, 4 social studies. High school diploma is required and GED is accepted. ACT with or without Writing component accepted. TOEFL required of all international applicants, minimum paper TOEFL 500, minimum computer TOEFL 173.

Application deadline: 7/1
Notification: Rolling
Average GPA: 3.49

Average SAT Math: 620
Average SAT Verbal: 590
Average ACT: 24

Graduated top 10% of class: 24%
Graduated top 25% of class: 56%
Graduated top 50% of class: 92%

COLLEGE GRADUATION REQUIREMENTS

Course waivers allowed: Yes
Course substitutions allowed: Yes
In what course: Foreign language

ADDITIONAL INFORMATION

Environment: Iowa State University is located on a 1,000-acre campus about 30 miles north of Des Moines.

Student Body:
  Undergrad enrollment: 20,993
  Women: 44%
  Men: 56%
  Percent out-of-state: 20%

Cost Information
  In-state tuition: $4,702
  Out-of-state tuition: $14,404
  Room & board: $5,958
Housing Information
  University housing: Yes
  Percent living on campus: 36%

Greek System
  Fraternity: Yes
  Sorority: Yes
Athletics: NCAA Division I

LORAS COLLEGE

1450 Alta Vista, Dubuque, IA 52004-0178
Phone: 800-245-6727 • Fax: 563-588-7119
E-mail: admissions@loras.edu • Web: www.loras.edu
Support: SP• Institution type: 4-year private

LEARNING DISABILITY PROGRAM AND SERVICES

Loras College provides a supportive, comprehensive program for the motivated individual with a learning disability. Students can be successful in Loras' competitive environment if they have had adequate preparation, are willing to work with program staff, and take responsibility for their own learning. The LD Program staff has two full-time specialists to serve as guides and advocates, encouraging and supporting students to become independent learners. Students with LD who are enrolled in college-preparatory courses in high school are the most appropriate candidates for the Loras program. Often high school students who previously were in LD programs, but are not currently receiving services, are appropriate candidates for the program if they have taken college-prep classes.

LD/ADD ADMISSIONS INFORMATION

College entrance tests required: Yes
Interview recommended: Yes
Essay recommended: Yes
Documentation required for LD: Diagnostic evaluation, including IQ and achievement testing, completed within the last 3 years
Documentation required for ADD: Yes
Submitted to: Both Admissions and Learning Disabilities Program
Special Ed. HS coursework accepted: Yes

Specific course requirements of all applicants: Yes
Separate application required for program services: Yes
# of LD applications submitted each year: 50
# of LD applications accepted yearly: 30
Total # of students receiving LD services: 125
Acceptance into program means acceptance into college: Students are admitted into the LD Program and the college simultaneously. The decision is made by the LD Program director.

ADMISSIONS

Students may contact program staff in their junior year and request an early assessment of their chances for admission; the admission process will be explained and students will receive an application. Students should arrange for an evaluation documenting the learning disability if the evaluation is more than two years old. Include the WAIS—R, as well as achievement/diagnostic tests of reading, written expression, and math and send the evaluation when completed. Transcript with 4 years English, 3 years math, 3 years social studies, 2–3 years science; ACT/SAT; and 3 letters of recommendation should be submitted by November 1 if students are applying for the Enhanced Program. Criteria for admission include strong average intelligence, class rank close to or above 50 percent, 2.0 GPA (minimum), 16+ ACT or 750 SAT. Students must be able to present their needs, strengths, and interests in a required interview with the LD Program director that is scheduled for those who are invited to visit after all materials have been received. An admission decision is made by the director of the LD Program.

ADDITIONAL INFORMATION

The Loras LD Program provides 2 levels of service: Enhanced and Mandated. The Enhanced Program for the first year students includes a 2-credit class, Learning Strategies, both semesters of the first year, an individual meeting with program staff each week, and tutors, as needed. Upper-classmen, continuing students and transfer students receive the same support with the exception of the class. The students in the Enhanced Program are also eligible to receive Mandated Services, which include note-takers, taped textbooks, and a place to take extended time tests in a quiet room. Students in the Enhanced Program are charged a fee for services; those receiving only Mandated Services are not. Students who want Mandated Services are not required to self-disclose their need for services until after they are accepted to Loras. However, those who want the more comprehensive Enhanced Program should make their intention known on the application and submit all materials before the deadline of 11/1 of senior year.

Support Services Contact Information

Learning Disability Program/Services: Learning Disabilities Program
Director: Dianne Gibson
   E-Mail: dianne.gibson@loras.edu
   Telephone: 563-588-7134
   Fax: 563-588-7147
Contact Person: Rochelle Fury
   E-Mail: rochelle.fury@loras.edu
   Telephone: 563-588-7134
   Fax: 563-588-7147

LEARNING DISABILITY SERVICES

Requests for the following services/accommodations will be evaluated individually based on appropriate and current documentation.

Allowed in exams
   Calculator: Yes
   Dictionary: Yes
   Computer: Yes
   Spellchecker: Yes
Extended test time: Yes
Scribes: Yes
Proctors: Yes
Oral exams: Yes
Note-takers: Yes

Distraction reduced environment: Yes
Tape recording in class: Yes
Books on tape from RFBD: Yes
Taping of books not from RFBD: Yes
Accommodations for students with ADD: Yes
Reading machine: Yes
Other assistive technology: Yes
Priority registration: Yes

Added costs for services: Yes
LD specialists: Yes
Professional tutors: No
Peer tutors: 5–15
Max. hours/wk. for services: Unlimited
How professors are notified of LD/ADD: By student

GENERAL ADMISSIONS INFORMATION

Director of Admissions: Tim Hauber
Telephone: 800-245-6727

ENTRANCE REQUIREMENTS

Academic units recommended: 4 English, 3 math, 3 science, 3 social studies, 3 history. High school diploma is required and GED is accepted. TOEFL required of all international applicants, minimum paper TOEFL 500, minimum computer TOEFL 173.

Application deadline: Rolling
Notification: Rolling
Average GPA: 3.22

Average SAT Math: NR
Average SAT Verbal: NR
Average ACT: 23

Graduated top 10% of class: 11%
Graduated top 25% of class: 30%
Graduated top 50% of class: 61%

COLLEGE GRADUATION REQUIREMENTS

Course waivers allowed: Yes
In what course: Possible for math after attempting math coursework; no foreign language waivers necessary because there is no foreign language requirement.
Course substitutions allowed: No

ADDITIONAL INFORMATION

Environment: The college is located on 66 hilltop acres in northeast Iowa overlooking the Mississippi River.

Student Body:
   Undergrad enrollment: 1,615
   Women: 51%
   Men: 49%
   Percent out-of-state: 44%

Cost Information
   Tuition: $18,670
   Room & board: $5,845
Housing Information
   University housing: Yes
   Percent living on campus: 64%

Greek System
   Fraternity: Yes
   Sorority: NR
   Athletics: NCAA Division III

ST. AMBROSE UNIVERSITY

518 West Locust Street, Davenport, IA 52803-2898
Phone: 563-333-6300 • Fax: 563-333-6297
E-mail: admit@sau.edu • Web: www.sau.edu
Support: CS• Institution type: 4-year private

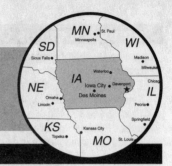

LEARNING DISABILITY PROGRAM AND SERVICES

St. Ambrose University's Services for Students with Disabilities is two dimensional. The first dimension is the education of the faculty to the specific needs of students. The second dimension is the development of services that allow programmatic access to students with disabilities. The key to both dimensions is the coordinator of Services for Students with Disabilities. It is the responsibility of this individual to prepare seminars for the faculty and staff, to advise students, and to be the conscience of the St. Ambrose University community in regard to students with disabilities. Students with learning disabilities are provided with an individual program of services. Services do not lower academic standards, but rather help "level the playing field" for individuals with disabilities. The coordinator works with students to develop skills and select accommodations to compensate for their learning disabilities and become their own advocates. Students with disabilities at St. Ambrose University may use a variety of services or reasonable accommodations intended to reduce the effects that a disability may have on their performance in a traditional academic setting.

LD/ADD ADMISSIONS INFORMATION

College entrance tests required: Yes
Interview recommended: No
Essay recommended: No
Documentation required for LD: Ability Test (WAIS–III, Stanford-Binct–IV); Achievement Test (eg. Woodcock Johnson, WIAT); Information Processing Test (eg. Woodcock Johnson, Detroit Tests, WMS–III)
Documentation required for ADD: DSM diagnosis by a licensed clinical professional
Submitted to: Services for Students with Disabilities

Specific course requirements of all applicants: Yes
Special Ed. HS coursework accepted: Yes
Separate application required for program services: No
# of LD applications submitted each year: NR
# of LD applications accepted yearly: NR
Total # of students receiving LD services: 155–165
Acceptance into program means acceptance into college: Student must be admitted and enrolled in the university first and then request services.

ADMISSIONS

Students meeting minimum admission requirements are not required to send additional information for admission purposes, but it is helpful in providing effective services. The general admission criteria include minimum ACT 20 or minimum 950 SAT, 2.5 GPA, and no specific courses are required. Students not meeting minimum requirements for admission may request special consideration by (1) submitting a regular application accompanied by a letter directed to the Dean of Admissions including a description of the LD, how the student has compensated for academic deficits, what resources were utilized in high school, and whether the student has independently requested accommodations; (2) submitting written assessment of learning problems (including all test scores) done by a certified professional, clearly stating that the student is LD and/or ADD; (3) submitting recommendations from teachers who have first-hand knowledge of the student's academic abilities; and (4) scheduling a meeting with the coordinator of services. Students who have completed junior year may also attend the Summer Transition Program to assess their ability for regular admission. Students who do not meet the criteria are encouraged to contact the coordinator for additional consideration

ADDITIONAL INFORMATION

Through the Office of Services for Students with Disabilities, students may have access to the following services: academic advising; advocacy; alternate exam arrangements including extended time, large print, separate testing room, readers, scribes, or use of a computer; books on tape; assistive technology; equipment loans; LD specialist to provide one-to-one learning skills instruction; liaison with outside agencies; screening and referral for diagnosis of learning disabilities; and other accommodations to meet appropriate needs. A 4-week Summer Transition Program is available for college-bound students with learning disabilities who have completed junior year in high school. Students do not have to be admitted to St. Ambrose to participate in this program, and completion of the program does not guarantee admission to the college. Students take intro to psychology; tutoring and study skills sessions, where they receive instruction on study skills, note-taking, textbook reading, memorization strategies, and test preparation; LD Seminar, an informal discussion group on topics such as rights and responsibilities of LD, selecting accommodations, understanding LD, and self-advocacy; Socializing in College, which relates to making new friends, dealing with stress, and communication skills.

SUPPORT SERVICES CONTACT INFORMATION

Services for Students with Disabilities
Director: Ryan C. Saddler
　E-Mail: SaddlerRyanC@sau.edu
　Telephone: 563-333-6275
　Fax: 563-333-6248

LEARNING DISABILITY SERVICES

Requests for the following services/accommodations will be evaluated individually based on appropriate and current documentation.

Allowed in exams
　Calculator: Yes
　Dictionary: Yes
　Computer: Yes
　Spellchecker: Yes
Extended test time: Yes
Scribes: Yes
Proctors: Yes
Oral exams: Yes
Note-takers: Yes

Distraction reduced environment: Yes
Tape recording in class: Yes
Books on tape from RFBD: Yes
Taping of books not from RFBD: Yes
Accommodations for students with ADD: Yes
Reading machine: Yes
Other assistive technology: Yes
Priority registration: No

Added costs for services: No
LD specialists: Yes
Professional tutors: No
Peer tutors: 36
Max. hours/wk. for services: Unlimited
How professors are notified of LD/ADD: By student

GENERAL ADMISSIONS INFORMATION

Director of Admissions: Meg Higgins
Telephone: 563-333-6300

ENTRANCE REQUIREMENTS

Academic units recommended: 4 English, 3 math, 2 science (2 science lab), 1 foreign language, 1 social studies, 1 history, 4 academic electives. High school diploma is required and GED is accepted. TOEFL required of all international applicants, minimum paper TOEFL 500, minimum computer TOEFL 213.

Application deadline: Rolling
Notification: Rolling
Average GPA: 3.08

Average SAT Math: NR
Average SAT Verbal: NR
Average ACT: 22

Graduated top 10% of class: 13%
Graduated top 25% of class: 32%
Graduated top 50% of class: 65%

COLLEGE GRADUATION REQUIREMENTS

Course waivers allowed: Yes
Course substitutions allowed: Yes
In what course: Foreign language, phyiscal education

ADDITIONAL INFORMATION

Environment: The campus is located in an urban area 180 miles west of Chicago.

Student Body:
　Undergrad enrollment: 2,394
　Women: 59%
　Men: 41%
　Percent out-of-state: 38%

Cost Information
　Tuition: $17,565
　Room & board: $6,635
Housing Information
　University housing: Yes
　Percent living on campus: 45%

Greek System
　Fraternity: No
　Sorority: No
Athletics: NAIA

UNIVERSITY OF DUBUQUE

2000 University Avenue, Dubuque, IA 52001-5050
Phone: 319-589-3200 • Fax: 319-589-3690
E-mail: admssns@dbq.edu • Web: www.dbq.edu
Support: CS• Institution type: 4-year private

LEARNING DISABILITY PROGRAM AND SERVICES

The University of Dubuque meets the requirements of the American Disability Act and provides reasonable accommodations for qualified students. The goal of the Academic Support Center is to assist all students to achieve success in college. Those wishing to receive accommodations need to meet with the director of the Academic Support Center. A written formal request must be submitted. Documentation regarding the disability must be provided.

LD/ADD ADMISSIONS INFORMATION

College entrance tests required: Yes
Interview recommended: No
Essay recommended: Yes
Documentation required for LD: Psychoeducational
Documentation required for ADD: Yes
Submitted to: Support Program/Services
Special Ed. HS coursework accepted: Yes

Specific course requirements of all applicants: Yes
Separate application required for program services: Yes
# of LD applications submitted each year: NR
# of LD applications accepted yearly: NR
Total # of students receiving LD services: NR
Acceptance into program means acceptance into college: Students must be admitted and enrolled in the university and then may request services.

ADMISSIONS

An applicant for admission to the University of Dubuque should be a graduate of a high school or have an equivalent (GED). Applicants should have a minimum of 15 high school units of which 10 should be from academic fields (English, social studies, natural science, mathematics, foreign language). Preference is given to students in the upper one-half of their graduating class and who have an ACT score of 18 or higher. A limited number of students may be granted provisional admittance based on counselor recommendations and evidence of potential for college success. These students are admitted to the University of Dubuque Opportunity Program. The Opportunity Program provides consistent tutoring and grade monitoring in a welcoming environment.

ADDITIONAL INFORMATION

The Academic Support Center provides help for all University of Dubuque students and seminary students needing one-on-one assistance with coursework, writing, study skills, and other academic matters. Students can improve their grades and study habits with the assistance of tutors, who help with a variety of subjects. The Academic Support Center's professional tutors and peer tutors have expertise in almost all academic areas taught. Specific accommodations for students with learning disabilities include textbooks on tape and numerous resource materials, duplicate note pads for students who need class notes taken for them, test monitoring for students who are overly anxious about time constraints of regular class room testing, tests read aloud to students when necessary, monitoring of progress by the Director of the Academic Support Center, and advocacy for students with academic disabilities. The Academic Support Center is dedicated to helping students get the most out of college. They offer free supplemental and supportive assistance for students in all majors and at all grade-point levels.

Support Services Contact Information

Learning Disability Program/Services: Academic Support Center
Director: Susanna Robey
  E-Mail: srobey@dbq.edu
  Telephone: 563-589-3218
  Fax: 563-589-3722

LEARNING DISABILITY SERVICES

Requests for the following services/accommodations will be evaluated individually based on appropriate and current documentation.

Allowed in exams	**Distraction reduced environment:** Yes	**Added costs for services:** No
Calculator: Yes	**Tape recording in class:** Yes	**LD specialists:** Yes
Dictionary: Yes	**Books on tape from RFBD:** Yes	**Professional tutors:** 6
Computer: Yes	**Taping of books not from RFBD:** No	**Peer tutors:** 12
Spellchecker: Yes	**Accommodations for students with**	**Max. hours/wk. for services:**
Extended test time: Yes	**ADD:** Yes	Unlimited
Scribes: Yes	**Reading machine:** No	**How professors are notified of**
Proctors: Yes	**Other assistive technology:** Y/N	**LD/ADD:** By student
Oral exams: Yes	**Priority registration:** N/A	
Note-takers: Yes		

GENERAL ADMISSIONS INFORMATION

Director of Admissions: Jesse James
Telephone: 563-589-3214

ENTRANCE REQUIREMENTS

Academic units required: 4 English, 3 math, 3 science, 3 social studies, 3 academic electives. High school diploma is required and GED is accepted. ACT with or without Writing component accepted. TOEFL required of all international applicants, minimum paper TOEFL 500, minimum computer TOEFL 275.

Application deadline: NR	**Average SAT Math:** NR	**Graduated top 10% of class:** 7%
Notification: rolling	**Average SAT Verbal:** NR	**Graduated top 25% of class:** 21%
Average GPA: 3.00	**Average ACT:** 22	**Graduated top 50% of class:** 51%

COLLEGE GRADUATION REQUIREMENTS

Course waivers allowed: No
Course substitutions allowed: No
In what course: N/A

ADDITIONAL INFORMATION

Environment: The University of Dubuque is located in Dubuque, Iowa on the Mississippi River.

Student Body:	**Cost Information**	**Greek System**
Undergrad enrollment: 1,101	**Tuition:** $16,660	**Fraternity:** Yes
Women: 36%	**Room & board:** $5,700	**Sorority:** Yes
Men: 64%	**Housing Information**	**Athletics:** NCAA Division III
Percent out-of-state: 57%	**University housing:** Yes	
	Percent living on campus: 85%	

UNIVERSITY OF IOWA

107 Calvin Hall, Iowa City, IA 52242
Phone: 319-335-3847 • Fax: 319-333-1535
E-mail: admissions@uiowa.edu • Web: www.uiowa.edu
Support: CS• Institution type: 4-year public

LEARNING DISABILITY PROGRAM AND SERVICES

The mission of LD/ADD Services in the University of Iowa's Student Disability Services (SDS) is to facilitate individualized academic accommodations for eligible students. Each student has an assigned staff adviser who assists the student in identifying appropriate course accommodations, communicating classroom needs to faculty, accessing other related services and resources. Students with LD/ADD who believe they will need disability services in order to have an equal educational opportunity are encouraged to self-disclose their disability to SDS as soon as possible. Students who self-disclose when applying for admission will be contacted by SDS with information about LD/ADD services at Iowa. They are encouraged to schedule an on-campus interview with the LD/ADD coordinator in order to learn more about disability services for students with LD/ADD and about the university.

LD/ADD ADMISSIONS INFORMATION

College entrance tests required: Yes
Interview recommended: No
Essay recommended: No
Documentation required for LD: Psychoeducational
Documentation required for ADD: Yes
Submitted to: Student Disability Services
Special Ed. HS coursework accepted: Yes

Specific course requirements of all applicants: Yes
Separate application required for program services: No
# of LD applications submitted each year: NR
# of LD applications accepted yearly: NR
Total # of students receiving LD services: 180–300
Acceptance into program means acceptance into college: Student must be admitted and enrolled in the university first and then request services.

ADMISSIONS

In-state residents must rank in top 50 percent of class or present an admission index score of 90. Nonresidents must rank in the top 30 percent or present an admission index of 100 (students with scores between 90–100 will be considered). The College of Engineering requires an ACT of 25 with a math score of 25+. There is a "special considerations" procedure for students not meeting general admission requirements who do not believe their academic record accurately reflects their ability to do college work. Students must submit a general application, transcript, and test scores; a letter disclosing the disability and requesting "special consideration," describing how the disability affected academic performance and what accommodations and compensation strategies are used to strengthen performance in deficit areas; a description of resources used and a statement explaining why the student may not have completed high school requirements, if applicable; letters from 2 people, not related, who can attest to the applicant's ability to be successful; and a diagnostic report verifying the disability and providing information about both the process and findings of the diagnostic assessment. The report should contain specific recommendations concerning the eligible academic accommodations, including whether the student qualifies for foreign language or math substitutions, and be signed by a licensed professional with the license number.

ADDITIONAL INFORMATION

Students requesting services and resources from Student Disability Services must self-disclose and provide satisfactory evidence of their disability-related eligibility for services. It is the responsibility of each student to determine whether or not to utilize services for which he or she is eligible. Services available through SDS for which students may be eligible on a case-by-case basis include pre-admission information, new student orientation, assistance in communicating with faculty and administrators, note-taking assistance, alternative examination services, obtaining audio-tapes of required reading materials, referrals to other university resources for counseling, tutoring, study skills development, and time management training. SDS notes that due to the high demand for tutoring at the university, tutors are not always available for all courses.

Support Services Contact Information

Learning Disability Program/Services: Student Disability Services (SDS)
Director: Dau-shen Ju, PhD
  E-Mail: daushen-ju@uiowa.edu
  Telephone: 319-335-1462
  Fax: 319-335-3973

LEARNING DISABILITY SERVICES

Requests for the following services/accommodations will be evaluated individually based on appropriate and current documentation.

Allowed in exams
  Calculator: Yes
  Dictionary: Yes
  Computer: Yes
  Spellchecker: Yes
Extended test time: Yes
Scribes: Yes
Proctors: Yes
Oral exams: No
Note-takers: Yes

Distraction reduced environment: Yes
Tape recording in class: Yes
Books on tape from RFBD: Yes
Taping of books not from RFBD: Yes
Accommodations for students with ADD: Yes
Reading machine: Yes
Other assistive technology: Yes
Priority registration: Yes

Added costs for services: No
LD specialists: Yes
Professional tutors: No
Peer tutors: 50–60
Max. hours/wk. for services: 1
How professors are notified of LD/ADD: By both student and director

GENERAL ADMISSIONS INFORMATION

Director of Admissions: Michael Barron
Telephone: 319-335-3847

ENTRANCE REQUIREMENTS

Academic units required: 4 English, 3 math, 3 science, 2 foreign language, 3 social studies. **Academic units recommended:** 4 foreign language. High school diploma is required and GED is accepted. ACT with or without Writing component accepted. TOEFL required of all international applicants, minimum paper TOEFL 530, minimum computer TOEFL 197.

Application deadline: 4/1
Notification: Rolling
Average GPA: 3.54

Average SAT Math: NR
Average SAT Verbal: NR
Average ACT: NR

Graduated top 10% of class: 21%
Graduated top 25% of class: 48%
Graduated top 50% of class: 92%

COLLEGE GRADUATION REQUIREMENTS

Course waivers allowed: No
Course substitutions allowed: Yes
In what course: Math, foreign language, or both

ADDITIONAL INFORMATION

Environment: The university is on a 1,900-acre campus in a small city 180 miles east of Des Moines.

Student Body:
  Undergrad enrollment: 19,401
  Women: 54%
  Men: 46%
  Percent out-of-state: 31%

Cost Information
  In-state tuition: $4,702
  Out-of-state tuition: $15,354
  Room & board: $6,350
Housing Information
  University housing: Yes
  Percent living on campus: 27%

Greek System
  Fraternity: Yes
  Sorority: Yes
Athletics: NCAA Division I

University of Iowa

UNIVERSITY OF NORTHERN IOWA

1227 West 27th Street, Cedar Falls, IA 50614-0018
Phone: 319-273-2281 • Fax: 319-273-2885
E-mail: admissions@uni.edu • Web: www.uni.edu
Support: S• Institution type: 4-year public

LEARNING DISABILITY PROGRAM AND SERVICES

The Office of Disability Services is dedicated to serving the special needs of students at the University of Northern Iowa. The Office of Disability Services works with students to ensure that all persons with disabilities have access to university activities, programs, and services. Specialized services are provided to enhance the overall academic, career, and personal development of each person with a physical, psychological, or learning disability. Services are available to currently enrolled students, who must apply for services, and provide appropriate documentation to substantiate the claimed disability. RUN (Restrict Us Not) is a recognized student organization, sponsored by the Office of Disability Services.

LD/ADD ADMISSIONS INFORMATION

College entrance tests required: Yes
Interview recommended: N/A
Essay recommended: No
Documentation required for LD: Psychoeducational evaluation
Documentation required for ADD: Yes
Submitted to: Disability Services
Special Ed. HS coursework accepted: Yes

Specific course requirements of all applicants: Yes
Separate application required for program services: No
# of LD applications submitted each year: NR
# of LD applications accepted yearly: NR
Total # of students receiving LD services: 75
Acceptance into program means acceptance into college: Student must be admitted and enrolled in the university first and then request services.

ADMISSIONS

There is no special admission process for students with learning disabilities. Students with disabilities are considered for admission on the same basis as all other applicants, and must meet the same academic standards. Students must have 4 years English, 3 years math, 3 years science, 3 years social studies, and 2 years academic elective (can be foreign language). The university will accept college-preparatory courses taken through the special education department of the high school. Students must rank in the top half of their class, and submit either the ACT or the SAT.

ADDITIONAL INFORMATION

Services available include individualized pre-enrollment interview and orientation to disability services, preferred registration, list of students interested in serving as academic aides, alternative testing arrangements, and auxiliary aides. The Center for Academic Achievement services all students at UNI who wish to receive additional academic support outside of the classroom. The center provides students with a variety of supportive services that will enhance academic achievement and success. Students may access help in Writing Assistance in any of their classes. Students may schedule a single appointment to work on a specific assignment or a regular appointment to work on a variety of assignments. Assistance with math skills is also available in the Math Lab. Services include one-to-one and small group instruction, individual instruction and practice through a variety of self-instructional modes, and review lessons to support the development and practice of concepts/skills taught in math courses. Drop-in hours are available.

Support Services Contact Information

Learning Disability Program/Services: Disability Services
Director: David Towle, PhD
  E-Mail: david.towle@uni.edu
  Telephone: 319-273-2676
  Fax: 319-273-6884
Contact Person: Jane Slykhuis, Coordinator
  E-Mail: jane.slykhuis@uni.edu
  Telephone: 319-273-2676
  Fax: 319-273-6884

LEARNING DISABILITY SERVICES

Requests for the following services/accommodations will be evaluated individually based on appropriate and current documentation.

Allowed in exams
  Calculator: Yes
  Dictionary: No
  Computer: Yes
  Spellchecker: Yes
Extended test time: Yes
Scribes: Yes
Proctors: No
Oral exams: Yes
Note-takers: Yes

Distraction reduced environment: Yes
Tape recording in class: Yes
Books on tape from RFBD: Yes
Taping of books not from RFBD: Yes
Accommodations for students with ADD: Yes
Reading machine: Yes
Other assistive technology: No
Priority registration: Yes

Added costs for services: No
LD specialists: No
Professional tutors: No
Peer tutors: Yes
Max. hours/wk. for services: 1
How professors are notified of LD/ADD: By both student and director

GENERAL ADMISSIONS INFORMATION

Director of Admissions: Roland Carrillo
Telephone: 319-273-2701

ENTRANCE REQUIREMENTS

Academic units required: 4 English, 3 math, 3 science, 3 social studies, 2 academic electives. **Academic units recommended:** 1 science lab, 2 foreign language, High school diploma is required and GED is accepted. ACT with or without Writing component accepted. TOEFL required of all international applicants, minimum paper TOEFL 550, minimum computer TOEFL 213.

Application deadline: 8/15
Notification: Rolling
Average GPA: NR

Average SAT Math: 524
Average SAT Verbal: 505
Average ACT: 23

Graduated top 10% of class: 19%
Graduated top 25% of class: 54%
Graduated top 50% of class: 90%

COLLEGE GRADUATION REQUIREMENTS

Course waivers allowed: Yes
In what course: The university is in the process of establishing guidelines for waiver/substitutions in math and foreign language.
Course substitutions allowed: Yes
In what course: Case-by-case basis for math and foreign language.

ADDITIONAL INFORMATION

Environment: The campus is in a small town about 1-1/2 hours from Des Moines.

Student Body:
  Undergrad enrollment: 11,032
  Women: 57%
  Men: 43%
  Percent out-of-state: 5%

Cost Information
  In-state tuition: $4,702
  Out-of-state tuition: $12,020
  Room & board: $5,261
Housing Information
  University housing: Yes
  Percent living on campus: 34%

Greek System
  Fraternity: Yes
  Sorority: Yes
Athletics: NCAA Division I

University of Northern University

WALDORF COLLEGE

106 South 6th Street, Forest City, IA 50436
Phone: 641-585-8112 • Fax: 641-585-8125
E-mail: admissions@waldorf.edu • Web: www.waldorf.edu
Support: SP • Institution type: 4-year private

LEARNING DISABILITY PROGRAM AND SERVICES

The Learning Disabilities Program (LDP) fully integrates students with learning disabilities into mainstream courses. The program features a special orientation session, academic advising, tutoring, specialized services, and developmental courses. The LDP takes a holistic approach to address the social, emotional, and academic needs of the person with a learning disability. The LDP is learning strategies-based. Students are accepted as individuals with the potential to succeed in college. The students have the opportunity to participate fully in college life and to experience academic success. Students benefit from a 12 to 1 student to instructor ratio, with each student having a laptop computer to use while a student is here. To be eligible for the Waldorf LDP, students must meet the following criteria: students must have psychological and achievement test results, preferably no more than two years old; students must have been involved with intervention on some level during high school; and students must exhibit a positive attitude and potential for good college success when appropriate learning strategies and coping skills are used.

LD/ADD ADMISSIONS INFORMATION

College entrance tests required: Yes
Interview required: Yes
Essay required: No
Documentation required for LD: Psychoeducational
    evaluation
Documentation required for ADD: Yes
Submitted to: LDP
Special Ed. HS coursework accepted: Yes

Specific course requirements of all applicants: Yes
Separate application required for program services: No
# of LD applications submitted each year: NR
# of LD applications accepted yearly: NR
Total # of students receiving LD services: 30
Acceptance into program means acceptance into
    college: Students are either admitted directly into the
    college and then must request LDP or are reviewed by LDP
    and a joint decision is made.

ADMISSIONS

There is no special admissions process for students with learning disabilities. LDP students go through the regular admission procedures. General admission requirements include 4 years English, 2 years math, and science; ACT 18+ and a 2.0 GPA. There is a probationary admission for students not meeting the regular criteria. Students will be asked to participate in a special interview, either by phone or in person, in order to be considered for LDP. The number of spaces in LDP is limited. The stronger candidates are reviewed and admitted by the Office of Admission; the students with weaker records, who have a documented learning disability, are reviewed by the LDP director and the Office of Admission and they make a joint decision on admission.

ADDITIONAL INFORMATION

Services in the LDP include the following: specialized academic advising regarding schedules and academic classes; priority time and scheduling with the learning specialist; counseling services available upon referral or request; special orientation for LDP students at the beginning of the academic year, prior to the arrival of the other students; tutor time above and beyond the regular services available to all students; specialized materials and/or technology for LD students; priority assignment for developmental and study skills classes; as-needed academic and psychological testing with a learning style emphasis; instructor notification of learning disability; and academic progress monitoring that will be shared with the student, and parents if permission is given. There are skills classes for credit in study skills, math/pre-algebra, reading, and writing. There is a one-day LD orientation prior to the beginning of the regular freshman orientation in the fall.

Support Services Contact Information

Director: Michelle Murray
Telephone: 641-584-8207
Fax: 641-584-8194
E-Mail: murraym@waldorf.edu

LEARNING DISABILITY SERVICES

Requests for the following services/accommodations will be evaluated individually based on appropriate and current documentation.

Allowed in exams
  Calculator: Yes
  Dictionary: Yes
  Computer: Yes
  Spellchecker: Yes
Extended test time: Yes
Scribes: No
Proctors: Yes
Oral exams: Yes
Note-takers: Yes

Distraction reduced environment: Yes
Tape recording in class: Yes
Books on tape from RFBD: Yes
Taping of books not from RFBD: No
Accommodations for students with
  ADD: Yes
Reading machine: No
Other assistive technology: No
Priority registration: Yes

Added costs for services: Yes
LD specialists: Yes
Professional tutors: 2
Peer tutors: 25
Max. hours/wk. for services:
  Unlimited
How professors are notified of
  LD/ADD: By director

GENERAL ADMISSIONS INFORMATION

Director of Admissions: Steve Lovik
Telephone: 641-585-8112

ENTRANCE REQUIREMENTS

Academic units recommended: 4 English, 3 math, 3 science, 2 foreign language, 4 history. High school diploma is required and GED is accepted. TOEFL required of all international applicants, minimum paper TOEFL 500, minimum computer TOEFL 173.

Application deadline: Rolling
Notification: Rolling
Average GPA: NR

Average SAT Math: NR
Average SAT Verbal: NR
Average ACT: 21

Graduated top 10% of class: NR
Graduated top 25% of class: NR
Graduated top 50% of class: NR

COLLEGE GRADUATION REQUIREMENTS

Course waivers allowed: No
Course substitutions allowed: Yes
In what course: NR

ADDITIONAL INFORMATION

Environment: The campus is in a small town.

Student Body:
  Undergrad enrollment: 573
  Women: 53%
  Men: 47%
  Percent out-of-state: 25%

Cost Information
  Tuition: $14,599
  Room & board: $5,670
Housing Information
  University housing: Yes
  Percent living on campus: 71%

Greek System
  Fraternity: Yes
  Sorority: Yes
Athletics: NAIA

KANSAS STATE UNIVERSITY

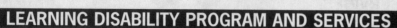

119 Anderson Hall, Manhattan, KS 66506
Phone: 785-532-6250 • Fax: 785-532-6393
E-mail: kstate@ksu.edu • Web: www.consider.k-state.edu
Support: CS • Institution type: 4-year public

LEARNING DISABILITY PROGRAM AND SERVICES

Kansas State provides a broad range of support services to students with learning disabilities through Disabled Student Services (DSS), as well as through numerous other university departments. Under DSS the Services for Learning Disabled Students serves as a liaison between students and instructors. The goals of the program are to recommend and provide accommodations and assistance tailored to the students' needs. Faculty and staff are sensitive to the special needs of the students and will work with them in their pursuit of educational goals. DSS works with students to plan accommodations that best aid the students to overcome areas of difficulty. DSS does not modify or reduce the content of courses. Rather, DSS helps to set up ways for students to demonstrate academic knowledge without interference from the disability. To qualify for services students must provide DSS with documentation of a learning disability that includes a complete record of all testing administered, a signed statement from a professional documenting LD, and information about strengths and weaknesses to help plan accommodations best suited to the student's needs. Many of the services provided take time to arrange. Consequently, students are encouraged to apply for services early in the process of planning for college.

LD/ADD ADMISSIONS INFORMATION

College entrance tests required: Yes
Interview required: No
Essay required: No
Documentation required for LD: WAIS–III, Woodcock-Johnson, less than 3 years old
Documentation required for ADD: Yes
Submitted to: Disability Support Services
Special Ed. HS coursework accepted: Yes

Specific course requirements of all applicants: Yes
Separate application required for program services: No
# of LD applications submitted each year: 268
# of LD applications accepted yearly: NR
Total # of students receiving LD services: 380–421
Acceptance into program means acceptance into college: Student must be admitted and enrolled in the university first and then request services.

ADMISSIONS

There is no special admissions process for students with learning disabilities. Kansas State has open admissions for state residents. Out-of-state students must either meet the basic course requirements for general admissions to the university including 4 years English, 3 years math, 3 years science, 3 years social studies, and 1 semester of computer technology or be in the top one-third of their high school graduating class. High schools may recommend approval of course substitutions to the Regents. Special consideration may be given when requested. The director of Support Services may be asked to consult with admissions on individual applicants.

ADDITIONAL INFORMATION

To access support services students must provide DSS with verification of LD. A signed statement documenting LD qualifies students for services. Specific information about strengths and weaknesses help DSS plan accommodations best suited to students' needs. Students contact Services for LD Students for assistance. Many services take time to arrange so early applications are encouraged. Students with LD are eligible for services, such as test-taking accommodations, readers, assistance in obtaining taped texts, note-takers, taped lectures, and priority registration. Tutoring is offered in some freshman/sophomore classes. All students may attend an orientation meeting prior to registration freshman year. Special courses are offered in Enhanced University Experience to learn note-taking, textbook reading, and test-taking skills; math review for students experiencing difficulty with arithmetic computations; intermediate algebra; and college algebra. Services are available for undergrads and graduate students.

Support Services Contact Information

Learning Disability Program/Services: Disability Support Services (DSS)
Director: Gretchen Holden
  E-Mail: gretch@ksu.edu
  Telephone: 785-532-6441
  Fax: 785-532-6457
Contact Person: Andrea Blair
  E-Mail: andreab@ksu.edu
  Telephone: 785-532-6441
  Fax: 785-532-6457

LEARNING DISABILITY SERVICES

Requests for the following services/accommodations will be evaluated individually based on appropriate and current documentation.

Allowed in exams
  Calculator: Yes
  Dictionary: Yes
  Computer: Yes
  Spellchecker: Yes
Extended test time: Yes
Scribes: Yes
Proctors: Yes
Oral exams: Yes
Note-takers: Yes

Distraction reduced environment: Yes
Tape recording in class: Yes
Books on tape from RFBD: Yes
Taping of books not from RFBD: Yes
Accommodations for students with ADD: Yes
Reading machine: Yes
Other assistive technology: Yes
Priority registration: Yes

Added costs for services: No
LD specialists: Yes
Professional tutors: No
Peer tutors: Yes
Max. hours/wk. for services: 3
How professors are notified of LD/ADD: By both student and director

GENERAL ADMISSIONS INFORMATION

Director of Admissions: Larry Moeder
Telephone: 785-532-6250

ENTRANCE REQUIREMENTS

Academic units recommended: 4 English, 3 math, 3 science, 3 social studies, 1 computer technology. High school diploma is required and GED is accepted. ACT with or without Writing component accepted. TOEFL required of all international applicants, minimum paper TOEFL 550, minimum computer TOEFL 213

Application deadline: 8/1
Notification: Rolling
Average GPA: 3.4

Average SAT Math: NR
Average SAT Verbal: NR
Average ACT: 24

Graduated top 10% of class: 32%
Graduated top 25% of class: 54%
Graduated top 50% of class: 80%

COLLEGE GRADUATION REQUIREMENTS

Course waivers allowed: No
Course substitutions allowed: Yes
In what course: Substitutions only, no waivers; math and foreign language are most frequently requested.

ADDITIONAL INFORMATION

Environment: The university is located on 664 acres in a suburban area 125 miles west of Kansas City.

Student Body:
  Undergrad enrollment: 18,893
  Women: 49%
  Men: 51%
  Percent out-of-state: 11%

Cost Information
  In-state tuition: $4,110
  Out-of-state tuition: $12,870
  Room & board: $5,738
Housing Information
  University housing: Yes
  Percent living on campus: 37%

Greek System
  Fraternity: Yes
  Sorority: Yes
Athletics: NCAA Division I

PITTSBURG STATE UNIVERSITY

1701 South Broadway, Pittsburg, KS 66762-5880
Phone: 620-235-4251 • Fax: 620-235-6003
E-mail: psuadmit@pittstate.edu • Web: www.pittstate.edu
Support: CS • Institution type: 4-year public

LEARNING DISABILITY PROGRAM AND SERVICES

The Learning Center at Pittsburgh State University is committed to providing appropriate educational and related services to students with LD. PSU works hard to help meet the transition needs of new students with identified LD. The specific type of assistance is determined on an individual basis. Previous records and an interview determine the type and degree of assistance appropriate for the student. The main purpose of the LD Assistance Team is to assist students in understanding and preparing assignments and completing tests. They provide a minimum amount of tutoring, but look to respective departments to provide these services. The key to their services is assistance. They do not provide content, information, or answers that do not reflect knowledge obtained by the student. Bright, highly motivated students with LD who are confident that they can succeed with hard work and supervision are welcomed to explore the educational possibilities at PSU.

LD/ADD ADMISSIONS INFORMATION

College entrance tests required: Yes
Interview required: No
Essay required: No
Documentation required for LD: A recent IEP or a current diagnosis
Documentation required for ADD: A recent 504 Plan or a current diagnosis
Submitted to: Learning Center
Special Ed. HS coursework accepted: Yes

Specific course requirements of all applicants: Yes
Separate application required for program services: Yes
# of LD applications submitted each year: NR
# of LD applications accepted yearly: NR
Total # of students receiving LD services: 15–20
Acceptance into program means acceptance into college: Student must be admitted and enrolled in the university first and then request services.

ADMISSIONS

Students must meet the regular admissions criteria to the university. Upon acceptance, they should visit the campus in the spring, request to visit with a member of the Learning Disabilities Assistance team, attend a summer orientation program on campus, and forward a copy of the most recent individualized education plan or documentation from the high school or doctor stating the nature of the LD. Once on campus, contact the team for an appointment to plan your study schedule at the Learning Center.

ADDITIONAL INFORMATION

Specific assistance is determined on an individual basis based on documentation and an interview. Services provided by the Learning Disabilities Assistance team include academic advising and planning; study skills strategies; testing modifications include extended time for tests, reading multiple choice and true-false tests verbatim, reading and defining words on a test (if the definition of that word does not give the student an unfair advantage in answering questions), reading and explaining what is being asked on short answer and essay tests; reading and helping the student understand the notes they took in class or the notes they took from their tape recorded lectures; writing or typing a tape recorded assignment prepared by the student; and reading and explaining the assignment to the student. They will also monitor student's class attendance, study schedule, and free time schedule.

Support Services Contact Information

Learning Disability Program/Services: Learning Center
Director: Dr. Jamie Wood
  E-Mail: jwood@pittstate.edu
  Telephone: 620-235-4193
  Fax: 620-235-6102

LEARNING DISABILITY SERVICES

Requests for the following services/accommodations will be evaluated individually based on appropriate and current documentation.

Allowed in exams
  Calculator: Yes
  Dictionary: Yes
  Computer: Yes
  Spellchecker: Yes
Extended test time: Yes
Scribes: No
Proctors: Yes
Oral exams: Yes
Note-takers: No

Distraction reduced environment: Yes
Tape recording in class: Yes
Books on tape from RFBD: No
Taping of books not from RFBD: No
Accommodations for students with ADD: Yes
Reading machine: No
Other assistive technology: No
Priority registration: No

Added costs for services: No
LD specialists: Yes
Professional tutors: 5
Peer tutors: 2
Max. hours/wk. for services: 40
How professors are notified of LD/ADD: By director

GENERAL ADMISSIONS INFORMATION

Director of Admissions: Ange Peterson
Telephone: 620-235-4251

ENTRANCE REQUIREMENTS
Academic units recommended: 4 English, 3 math, 3 science, 2 social studies, 1 history, 1 computer technology. High school diploma is required and GED is accepted. Out-of-state applicants must rank in top 50 percent of their class and have a 2.0 GPA. TOEFL required of all international applicants, minimum paper TOEFL 520, minimum computer TOEFL 190.

Application deadline: Rolling
Notification: Rolling
Average GPA: 3.30

Average SAT Math: NR
Average SAT Verbal: NR
Average ACT: 21

Graduated top 10% of class: 17%
Graduated top 25% of class: 41%
Graduated top 50% of class: 75%

COLLEGE GRADUATION REQUIREMENTS

Course waivers allowed: No
Course substitutions allowed: No
In what course: N/A

ADDITIONAL INFORMATION

Environment: 120 miles from Kansas City and Tulsa

Student Body:
  Undergrad enrollment: 5,422
  Women: 50%
  Men: 50%
  Percent out-of-state: 22%

Cost Information
  In-state tuition: 2,400
  Out-of-state tuition: 9,000
  Room & board: $4,500
Housing Information
  University housing: Yes
  Percent living on campus: 17%

Greek System
  Fraternity: Yes
  Sorority: Yes
Athletics: NCAA Division II

UNIVERSITY OF KANSAS

Office of Admissions, 1502 Iowa Street, Lawrence, KS 66045
Phone: 785-864-3911 • Fax: 785-864-5017
E-mail: adm@ku.edu • Web: www.ku.edu
Support: S • Institution type: 4-year public

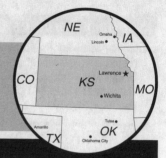

LEARNING DISABILITY PROGRAM AND SERVICES

The university accommodates the student with LD by understanding the student's ability and individualizing the services as much as possible. KU's philosophy is one of mainstreaming students with disabilities, including LD. Thus, there are no special classes, resource rooms, tutoring services, or other services specifically for the student with a LD. Course requirements and academic standards are not reduced. Rather, once the LD is adequately documented, the student receives classroom accommodations to meet specific individual needs. The Services for Students with Disabilities (SSD) also serves as a referral agent to other resources at the university and in the Lawrence community. Integration and mainstreaming, decentralized services with appropriate accommodations centrally coordinated, and student involvement and responsibility are critical aspects of the university's philosophy. Documentation is necessary and should include a recent diagnostic report of LD, and LD programs and progress will need to be identified. Students are encouraged to begin planning early so that programs are in place at the beginning of the semester to facilitate studies. The goal of SSD is to facilitate independence in preparation for needs after graduation.

LD/ADD ADMISSIONS INFORMATION

College entrance tests required: Yes
Interview required: No
Essay required: No
Documentation required for LD: WAIS–III; WJ
Documentation required for ADD: Yes
Submitted to: Disability Services
Special Ed. HS coursework accepted: Yes

Specific course requirements of all applicants: Yes
Separate application required for program services: No
# of LD applications submitted each year: NR
# of LD applications accepted yearly: NR
Total # of students receiving LD services: 256
Acceptance into program means acceptance into college: Student must be admitted and enrolled in the university first (they can appeal a denial) and then request services.

ADMISSIONS

All applicants are admitted using the same criteria. Students unable to meet admission criteria because of LD should submit a personal statement providing additional information, such as no foreign language taken in high school because of LD. Applicants should contact SSD for information and an early assessment of needs. It is important to include recent documentation or diagnosis, and samples of student's work and parent and student statements regarding educational history. Regular admission requires (1) 2.5 GPA in Board of Regent courses including 4 years English, 3 years of college-prep math, 3 years natural science, 3 years social science, 1 year computer technology or (2) an ACT of 24 and a 2.0 GPA or (3) a 3.0 GPA and no cut-off on the ACT. The university is very concerned that a student with LD be competitive in this academic environment. If admission criteria are not met because of LD, the applicant should submit documentation and counselor recommendation, and the director of SSD will review and make a recommendation to admissions to waive requirements.

ADDITIONAL INFORMATION

Skill workshops are available in study skills, time management, listening, note-taking, calculus, speed and reading comprehension, learning a foreign language, and preparing for exams. SSD also serves as an advocate or liaison for students. Tutoring services for students who meet qualifications are available through Supportive Educational Services at no cost. Private tutors can also be hired by the student for specific subjects. In neither instance is the tutor specifically trained regarding learning disabilities. SSD does not offer a reduced standard for academic performance, special classes, supplemental instruction, a learning center, special tutorial program, or exemption to graduation requirements. Services and accommodations are available for undergraduate and graduate students.

Support Services Contact Information

Learning Disability Program/Services: Disability Resources
Director: Mary Ann Rasnak
  E-Mail: mnasnak@ku.edu
  Telephone: 785-864-2620
  Fax: 785-864-2817

LEARNING DISABILITY SERVICES

Requests for the following services/accommodations will be evaluated individually based on appropriate and current documentation.

Allowed in exams
  Calculator: Yes
  Dictionary: Yes
  Computer: Yes
  Spellchecker: Yes
Extended test time: Yes
Scribes: Yes
Proctors: Yes
Oral exams: Yes
Note-takers: Yes

Distraction reduced environment: Yes
Tape recording in class: Yes
Books on tape from RFBD: Yes
Taping of books not from RFBD: Yes
Accommodations for students with
  ADD: Yes
Reading machine: Yes
Other assistive technology: Yes
Priority registration: No

Added costs for services: No
LD specialists: No
Professional tutors: Yes
Peer tutors: 55
Max. hours/wk. for services:
  Unlimited
How professors are notified of
  LD/ADD: By both student and director

GENERAL ADMISSIONS INFORMATION

Director of Admissions: Lisa Pinamonti-Kress
Telephone: 785-864-3911

ENTRANCE REQUIREMENTS

Academic units required: 4 English, 3 math, 3 science, 3 social studies, and 1 computer technology or proficiency. **Academic units recommended:** 4 English, 4 math, 3 science, 2 foreign language, 3 social studies, and 1 computer technology or proficiency. High school diploma is required and GED is accepted. ACT without Writing component accepted. 24 ACT and 2.0 GPA are granted automatic admission within 48 hours of application (liberal arts only). TOEFL required of all international applicants, minimum paper TOEFL 600, minimum computer TOEFL 250

Application deadline: 4/1
Notification: Rolling
Average GPA: 3.44

Average SAT Math: NR
Average SAT Verbal: NR
Average ACT: 24

Graduated top 10% of class: 28%
Graduated top 25% of class: 56%
Graduated top 50% of class: 87%

COLLEGE GRADUATION REQUIREMENTS

Course waivers allowed: No
Course substitutions allowed: Yes
In what course: Math, foreign language

ADDITIONAL INFORMATION

Environment: The 1,000-acre campus is located in a small city 40 miles west of Kansas City.

Student Body:
  Undergrad enrollment: 21,037
  Women: 51%
  Men: 49%
  Percent out-of-state: 24%

Cost Information
  In-state tuition: $4,163
  Out-of-state tuition: $12,117
  Room & board: $5,126
Housing Information
  University housing: Yes
  Percent living on campus: 23%

Greek System
  Fraternity: Yes
  Sorority: Yes
Athletics: NCAA Division I

University of Kansas

EASTERN KENTUCKY UNIVERSITY

Coates Box 2A, Richmond, KY 40475
Phone: 859-622-2106 • Fax: 606-622-8024
E-mail: stephen.byrn@eku.edu • Web: www.eku.edu
Support: CS • Institution type: 4-year public

LEARNING DISABILITY PROGRAM AND SERVICES

The mission of Project SUCCESS is to respond effectively and efficiently to the individual educational needs of eligible university students with learning disabilities through a cost-effective, flexible program of peer tutors, workshops, group support, and program referral. Upon admittance, Project SUCCESS develops an individualized program of services that serve to enhance the academic success of each student. The services a student uses will be determined in a conference between the student and the program director. All services are offered free of charge to the student. EKU also offers a summer transition program for students with learning disabilities. The program is designed to smooth the transition between high school and college. To apply for participation in Project SUCCESS, students are encouraged to visit both the campus and the Office of Services for Students with Disabilities. The student will be asked to fill out an application and provide appropriate, current documentation of the disability. The application for services through Project SUCCESS is in no way connected to admission to EKU.

LD/ADD ADMISSIONS INFORMATION

College entrance tests required: Yes
Interview required: Yes
Essay required: No
Documentation required for LD: Achievement and aptitude, less than 3 years old
Documentation required for ADD: Yes
Submitted to: Services for Individuals with Disabilities
Special Ed. HS coursework accepted: Yes
Specific course requirements of all applicants: Yes

Specific course requirements of all applicants: Yes
Separate application required for program services: Yes
# of LD applications submitted each year: 55
# of LD applications accepted yearly: 50
Total # of students receiving LD services: 226
Acceptance into program means acceptance into college: Students must be in the process of admittance to apply to project SUCCESS.

ADMISSIONS

There are no special admissions criteria for students with learning disabilities. Students must be admitted and enrolled in the university in order to be eligible for entrance into Project SUCCESS. Full admission includes a 2.0 GPA and high school diploma, or GED or distance-learning degree; ACT 18 (with no score below 18 in English, Math and Reading); and meet the Kentucky pre-college curriculum or its equivalent ACT scores of 21 in English, 20 in Math, 22 in Reading and 21 in Science Reasoning. Students not meeting probationary admission (2.0 GPA, or GED or distance-learning diploma, ACT 15–17) may apply to EKU through a retention support program by applying for special admission. Collaborating retention support programs include Project SUCCESS.

ADDITIONAL INFORMATION

Project SUCCESS services provided include one-on-one tutoring, note-taking services, books on tape, test accommodations, advocacy, weekly seminars. Skills classes are offered in study skills, reading skills, weekly workshops in transition, time management, learning and study strategies, test-taking skills, developmental math, developmental reading, and developmental writing. A special summer program for pre-college freshmen with learning disabilities is offered. All services and accommodations are available for undergraduate and graduate students.

Support Services Contact Information

Learning Disability Program/Services: Office of Services for Individuals with Disabilities
Director: Teresa Belluscio
  E-Mail: disbellu@acseku.edu
  Telephone: 859-622-2933
  Fax: 859-622-6395

LEARNING DISABILITY SERVICES

Requests for the following services/accommodations will be evaluated individually based on appropriate and current documentation.

Allowed in exams
  Calculator: Yes
  Dictionary: Yes
  Computer: Yes
  Spellchecker: Yes
Extended test time: Yes
Scribes: Yes
Proctors: Yes
Oral exams: Yes
Note-takers: Yes

Distraction reduced environment: Yes
Tape recording in class: Yes
Books on tape from RFBD: Yes
Taping of books not from RFBD: Yes
Accommodations for students with ADD: Yes
Reading machine: Yes
Other assistive technology: Yes
Priority registration: Yes

Added costs for services: No
LD specialists: Yes
Professional tutors: No
Peer tutors: 20
Max. hours/wk. for services: Unlimited
How professors are notified of LD/ADD: By student

GENERAL ADMISSIONS INFORMATION

Director of Admissions: Stephen Byrn
Telephone: 859-622-2106

ENTRANCE REQUIREMENTS
Academic units required: 4 English, 3 math, 3 science (1 science lab), 3 social studies, 1 history, 7 academic electives, 1 health & physical education. High school diploma is required and GED is accepted. TOEFL required of all international applicants, minimum paper TOEFL 500, minimum computer TOEFL 173.

Application deadline: 8/1
Notification: Rolling
Average GPA: 3.12

Average SAT Math: NR
Average SAT Verbal: NR
Average ACT: 20

Graduated top 10% of class: 13%
Graduated top 25% of class: 35%
Graduated top 50% of class: 66%

COLLEGE GRADUATION REQUIREMENTS

Course waivers allowed: Yes
Course substitutions allowed: Yes
In what course: Waivers and substitutions are determined on a case-by-case basis.

ADDITIONAL INFORMATION

Environment: The university is located on 350 acres in a small town 20 miles south of Lexington.

Student Body:
  Undergrad enrollment: 12,944
  Women: 62%
  Men: 38%
  Percent out-of-state: 11%

Cost Information
  In-state tuition: $3,332
  Out-of-state tuition: $10,004
  Room & board: $4,658
Housing Information
  University housing: Yes
  Percent living on campus: 31%

Greek System
  Fraternity: Yes
  Sorority: Yes
Athletics: NCAA Division I

LEXINGTON COMMUNITY COLLEGE*

208 Oswald Building, Cooper Drive, Lexington, KY 40506
Phone: 859-257-4872 • Fax: 859-257-2634
E-mail: eabel10@uky.edu • Web: www.uky.edu/LCC
Support: S • Institution type: 2-year public

LEARNING DISABILITY PROGRAM AND SERVICES

Lexington Community College has made a firm commitment to providing high quality post-secondary education to persons with disabilities. The Office of Services for Students with Disabilities seeks to ensure equal access and full participation for persons with disabilities in post-secondary education, and empower students to obtain the life skills necessary for a fulfilling, productive lifestyle after leaving LCC. Students can request services by visiting Disability Support Services (DSS). Full participation in the DSS program is encouraged from initial admission contact throughout the student's academic career. Positive peer contacts as well as guidance from the DSS coordinator and other faculty and staff also play a major role in encouraging participation in the DSS program.

LD/ADD ADMISSIONS INFORMATION

College entrance tests required: No
Interview required: No
Essay required: No
Documentation required for LD: Psychoeducational evaluation
Documentation required for ADD: Yes
Submitted to: Disability Support Services
Special Ed. HS coursework accepted: Yes

Specific course requirements of all applicants: Yes
Separate application required for program services: No
# of LD applications submitted each year: NR
# of LD applications accepted yearly: NR
Total # of students receiving LD services: NR
Acceptance into program means acceptance into college: Students must be admitted and enrolled at LCC and then may request services.

ADMISSIONS

LCC offers an "open door" admission to all applicants who meet the following requirements: proof of a high school diploma or the GED; ACT for placement not admission; 4 years English, algebra I & II, biology, chemistry or physics, U.S. history, and geometry; any areas of deficiency can be made up at LCC before enrolling in college courses; there is no required GPA or class rank. Students may live in the residence halls at the University of Kentucky and attend classes at LCC, which is located on the same campus as the university. There is an articulation agreement between LCC and the University of Kentucky. Students wishing to apply to Project Success must submit a separate application, call for an appointment, and bring supporting materials.

ADDITIONAL INFORMATION

DSS provides a full range of services, including academic advising, career counseling, supportive counseling, specialized computer software, recorded textbooks, note-takers, readers, writers/scribes, tutors, and testing accommodation. The DSS coordinator serves as student liaison with college faculty, staff and administrators, vocational rehabilitational counselors, and various other social service agencies. A case management approach is used to ensure continuity of services between agencies. LD assessments are available on campus for $175–200. Study Strategies is offered for college credit. The Athena Club is a student organization created to assume an advocacy role on behalf of students with disabilities at LCC through education, recruiting, support groups, and social opportunities.

Now called Bluegrass Community and Technical College

Support Services Contact Information

Learning Disability Program/Services: Disability Support Services
Director: Veronica Miller
  E-Mail: vimill1@email.uky.edu
  Telephone: 859-257-4872
  Fax: 859-323-7136

LEARNING DISABILITY SERVICES

Requests for the following services/accommodations will be evaluated individually based on appropriate and current documentation.

Allowed in exams
  Calculator: Yes
  Dictionary: No
  Computer: Yes
  Spellchecker: Yes
Extended test time: Yes
Scribes: Yes
Proctors: Yes
Oral exams: Yes
Note-takers: Yes

Distraction reduced environment: Yes
Tape recording in class: Yes
Books on tape from RFBD: Yes
Taping of books not from RFBD: Yes
**Accommodations for students with
  ADD:** Yes
Reading machine: Yes
Other assistive technology: Yes
Priority registration: No

Added costs for services: No
LD specialists: No
Professional tutors: Yes
Peer tutors: Yes
Max. hours/wk. for services: 2
**How professors are notified of
  LD/ADD:** By director

GENERAL ADMISSIONS INFORMATION

Director of Admissions: Shelblie Hugle
Telephone: 859-257-4872

ENTRANCE REQUIREMENTS

Open door admissions (not including health technology program). High school diploma or GED accepted. ACT/SAT used for placement. TOEFL required of all international applicants, minimum paper TOEFL 500, minimum computer TOEFL 173.

Application deadline: Rolling
Notification: Rolling
Average GPA: NR

Average SAT Math: NR
Average SAT Verbal: NR
Average ACT: NR

Graduated top 10% of class: NR
Graduated top 25% of class: NR
Graduated top 50% of class: NR

COLLEGE GRADUATION REQUIREMENTS

Course waivers allowed: No
Course substitutions allowed: Yes
In what course: Students may request subsitutions for courses with the approriate documentation.

ADDITIONAL INFORMATION

Environment: The college is located on the campus of the University of Kentucky.

Student Body:
  Undergrad enrollment: 7,000
  Women: 58%
  Men: 42%
  Percent out-of-state: 4%

Cost Information
  In-state tuition: $3,002
  Out-of-state tuition: $7,706
Housing Information
  University housing: Yes
  Percent living on campus: 1%

Greek System
  Fraternity: Yes
  Sorority: No
Athletics: Intermural

THOMAS MORE COLLEGE

333 Thomas More Parkway, Crestview Hill, KY 41017-3495
Phone: 859-344-3332 • Fax: 859-344-3444
E-mail: admissions@thomasmore.edu • Web: www.thomasmore.edu
Support: S • Institution type: 4-year private

LEARNING DISABILITY PROGRAM AND SERVICES

Thomas More College's Student Support Services program is committed to the individual academic, personal, cultural, social, and financial needs of the student. It is committed to promoting sensitivity and cultural awareness of the population served and to promoting varied on- and off-campus services and events that enhance the student's educational opportunities. A variety of support services are offered, including developmental courses, peer tutoring, and individual counseling. Students with deficits in speech/language, study skills, written expression, ongoing additional skills, perceptual skills, reading, speaking, math, fine motor, and ADD/ADD with or without LD are admissible. Students may need five years to graduate. The college offers small classes, excellent faculty, and solid preparation for the future.

LD/ADD ADMISSIONS INFORMATION

College entrance tests required: Yes
Interview required: No
Essay required: No
Documentation required for LD: Psychoeducational
  evaluation
Documentation required for ADD: Yes
Submitted to: Student Support Services
Special Ed. HS coursework accepted: Yes

Specific course requirements of all applicants: Yes
Separate application required for program services: No
# of LD applications submitted each year: NR
# of LD applications accepted yearly: NR
Total # of students receiving LD services: 10
Acceptance into program means acceptance into
  college: Student must be admitted and enrolled in the
  university first and then request services.

ADMISSIONS

There is no separate application required for an applicant with learning disabilities. All students must submit the general application for admission. A Student Support Services staff person is part of the Admissions Committee. Students with learning disabilities may be conditionally admitted so that they can receive extra support. General admission criteria include a recommendation for 4 years English, 2 years math, 2 years science, 2 years social studies, and 2 years foreign language. Foreign language, and possibly math requirements, may be substituted. ACT 19–23 or 950 SAT; rank in top half of class; and a B-minus average. The college can waive ACT/SAT scores after considering the student's LD status. A WAIS–R is not required, but diagnostic testing is encouraged before enrolling, as it is required to be on file before students can access services.

ADDITIONAL INFORMATION

Students with learning disabilities could be limited to 12–13 hours the first semester. Student progress will be monitored. Some students may be required to take developmental courses based on the college's assessment of reading, writing, and math skills. Skills classes are paired with world history and there is college credit for classes in study skills, reading skills, and math skills. Some students are admitted on a conditional status and are given additional support through Student Support Services.

Support Services Contact Information

Learning Disability Program/Services: Student Support Services
Director: Barbara S. Davis
 E-Mail: barb.davis@thomasmore.edu
 Telephone: 606-344-3521
 Fax: 606-433-3638

LEARNING DISABILITY SERVICES

Requests for the following services/accommodations will be evaluated individually based on appropriate and current documentation.

Allowed in exams	**Distraction reduced environment:** Yes	**Added costs for services:** No
Calculator: No	**Tape recording in class:** Yes	**LD specialists:** No
Dictionary: Y/N	**Books on tape from RFBD:** Y/N	**Professional tutors:** 2
Computer: No	**Taping of books not from RFBD:** Yes	**Peer tutors:** 15
Spellchecker: No	**Accommodations for students with**	**Max. hours/wk. for services:**
Extended test time: Yes	**ADD:** Yes	Unlimited
Scribes: Yes	**Reading machine:** No	**How professors are notified of**
Proctors: Yes	**Other assistive technology:** No	**LD/ADD:** By student
Oral exams: Yes	**Priority registration:** No	
Note-takers: Yes		

GENERAL ADMISSIONS INFORMATION

Director of Admissions: Angela Griffin-Jones
Telephone: 859-344-3332

ENTRANCE REQUIREMENTS

Academic units required: 4 English, 3 math, 3 science (1 science lab), 2 foreign language, 3 social studies.
Academic units recommended: 2 arts appreciation, 1 computer literacy. High school diploma is required and GED is accepted. TOEFL required of all international applicants, minimum paper TOEFL 515, minimum computer TOEFL 187.

Application deadline: 8/15	**Average SAT Math:** 530	**Graduated top 10% of class:** 7%
Notification: Rolling	**Average SAT Verbal:** 527	**Graduated top 25% of class:** 31%
Average GPA: 2.88	**Average ACT:** 21	**Graduated top 50% of class:** 85%

COLLEGE GRADUATION REQUIREMENTS

Course waivers allowed: No
Course substitutions allowed: Yes
In what course: Foreign language and math

ADDITIONAL INFORMATION

Environment: The college is located on a 160-acre campus 8 miles from Cincinnati.

Student Body:	**Cost Information**	**Greek System**
Undergrad enrollment: 1,371	**Tuition:** $17,600	**Fraternity:** Yes
Women: 51%	**Room & board:** $5,900	**Sorority:** No
Men: 49%	**Housing Information**	**Athletics:** NCAA Division III
Percent out-of-state: 66%	**University housing:** Yes	
	Percent living on campus: 20%	

WESTERN KENTUCKY UNIVERSITY

Potter Hall 117, 1 Big Red Way, Bowling Green, KY 42101-3576
Phone: 270-745-2551 • Fax: 270-745-6133
E-mail: admission@wku.edu • Web: www.wku.edu
Support: S • Institution type: 4-year public

LEARNING DISABILITY PROGRAM AND SERVICES

The goal of the Office of Affirmative Action is to foster the full and self-directed participation of persons with disabilities attending the university. The service is established to facilitate the participation of students at Western Kentucky University by providing information on services, acting as liaison with faculty and staff for reasonable accommodation, and providing learning disability services. Office for Disability Services (ODS) coordinates support services so that students can be self-sufficient and can develop to their maximum academic potential. To be eligible for these services, documentation from a licensed professional must be provided. This documentation must be no more than 3 years old, state the nature of the disability, and clearly describe the kinds of accommodations recommended. Once accepted students should provide the documentation; discuss the disability and ways to accommodate special needs; arrange to take placement tests and register for classes early; contact instructors to learn what each instructor will require in terms of grading criteria, amount of weekly reading, and number and types of homework assignments and tests; order books on tape; and request alternative testing conditions, note-takers, and readers. Students needing specialized help beyond that offered by the university may need to seek financial assistance.

LD/ADD ADMISSIONS INFORMATION

College entrance tests required: Yes
Interview required: No
Essay required: No
Documentation required for LD: Psychoeducational
    evaluation or Completed Student Disability Verification Form
    (providing by SDS)
Documentation required for ADD: Yes
Submitted to: Student Disability Services
Special Ed. HS coursework accepted: Yes

Specific course requirements of all applicants: Yes
Separate application required for program services: No
# of LD applications submitted each year: 50
# of LD applications accepted yearly: 50
Total # of students receiving LD services: 127
Acceptance into program means acceptance into
    college: Student must be admitted and enrolled in the
    university first and then request services.

ADMISSIONS

There is no special admissions process for students with learning disabilities. All applicants must meet the same admission criteria. High school courses required include 4 years English, 3 years math, 2 years social science, and 2 years lab science (biology, physics, and chemistry). In-state residents must have a minimum 2.3 GPA or 18 ACT; out-of-state students must have a minimum 2.3 GPA and 18 ACT or 990 SAT. Factors considered for admission are ACT/SAT, high school performance, any post-secondary record, recommendations, personal qualifications and conduct, interview, and complete and accurate information listed on the application for admission. Students can be admitted by exception through the director of admissions. Western Kentucky University's Community College will admit students who do not meet high school course requirements.

ADDITIONAL INFORMATION

The program for students with LD offers students adapted test administrations; taped textbooks; short-term loan of special equipment; reading referral services; faculty liaison; peer tutoring; academic, personal, and career counseling; and assistance with the Reading and Learning Labs. Academic advisors assist students in course selection. The university combines intensive academic advisement with special seminars to provide support during the freshman year. The University Counseling Services Center provides assistance in personal, social, emotional, and intellectual development. Skills classes are offered in math, reading, vocabulary, study skills, and English through the Community College. College credit is given for these classes. Services and accommodations are available for undergraduate and graduate students.

Support Services Contact Information

Learning Disability Program/Services: Office for Student Disability Services
Director: Matt Davis, Coordinator
  E-Mail: matt.davis@wky.edu
  Telephone: 502-745-5004
  Fax: 502-745-3623

LEARNING DISABILITY SERVICES

Requests for the following services/accommodations will be evaluated individually based on appropriate and current documentation.

Allowed in exams
  Calculator: Yes
  Dictionary: No
  Computer: Yes
  Spellchecker: Yes
Extended test time: Yes
Scribes: Yes
Proctors: Yes
Oral exams: Yes
Note-takers: Yes

Distraction reduced environment: Yes
Tape recording in class: Yes
Books on tape from RFBD: Yes
Taping of books not from RFBD: Yes
**Accommodations for students with
  ADD:** Yes
Reading machine: No
Other assistive technology: No
Priority registration: Yes

Added costs for services: No
LD specialists: No
Professional tutors: 15
Peer tutors: 20
Max. hours/wk. for services:
  Unlimited
**How professors are notified of
  LD/ADD:** By both student and director

GENERAL ADMISSIONS INFORMATION

Director of Admissions: Dr. Dean R. Kahler
Telephone: 270-745-2551

ENTRANCE REQUIREMENTS

Academic units required: 4 English, 3 math, 3 science (1 science lab), 2 foreign language, 3 social studies, 1 1/2 phyiscal education, 1/2 art history/appreciation. **Academic units recommended:** 4 math, 4 science, 3 foreign language, 4 social studies, 1 1/2 phyiscal education, 1/2 art history/appreciation. High school diploma is required and GED is accepted. ACT with or without Writing component accepted. TOEFL required of all international applicants, minimum paper TOEFL 525, minimum computer TOEFL 197.

Application deadline: 8/1
Notification: Immediately
Average GPA: 3.10

Average SAT Math: 499
Average SAT Verbal: 498
Average ACT: 21

Graduated top 10% of class: 17%
Graduated top 25% of class: 39%
Graduated top 50% of class: 68%

COLLEGE GRADUATION REQUIREMENTS

Course waivers allowed: No
Course substitutions allowed: No
In what course: N/A

ADDITIONAL INFORMATION

Environment: The university is located on 200 acres in a suburban area 65 miles north of Nashville.

Student Body:
  Undergrad enrollment: 15,211
  Women: 59%
  Men: 41%
  Percent out-of-state: 17%

Cost Information
  In-state tuition: $4,596
  Out-of-state tuition: $11,184
  Room & board: $4,728
Housing Information
  University housing: Yes
  Percent living on campus: 31%

Greek System
  Fraternity: Yes
  Sorority: Yes
Athletics: NCAA Division I

LOUISIANA COLLEGE

1140 College Drive, PO Box 560, Pineville, LA 71359-0560
Phone: 318-487-7259 • Fax: 318-487-7550
E-mail: admissions@lacollege.edu • Web: www.lacollege.edu
Support: SP • Institution type: 4-year private

LEARNING DISABILITY PROGRAM AND SERVICES

The goal of the Program to Assist Student Success (PASS) is to facilitate the academic success of students with disabilities and to serve as an advocate for the students. This highly individualized, limited enrollment program provides support services and personal attention to students who need special academic counseling, tutoring, or classroom assistance. Three levels of services are provided. Level I students are required to attend weekly individual counseling and tutoring sessions; the emphasis at this level is to provide individualized help to ensure the student's successful transition to college and to compensate for any identifiable disability. Level II students have, at a minimum, completed 24 hours of college credit at Louisiana College with at least a 2.5 grade point average; regularly scheduled individual counseling sessions continue to be provided, all other services continue to be available to the student as needed. Level III students have learned to compensate for their disability and are independently achieving college success; these students will have their progress monitored by the staff and tutoring will continue to be available. Any student not maintaining a 2.5 GPA must remain in or return to Level I.

LD/ADD ADMISSIONS INFORMATION

College entrance tests required: Yes
Interview required: Yes
Essay required: Yes
Documentation required for LD: Current professional evaluation
Documentation required for ADD: Current medical evaluation
Submitted to: Program to Assist Student Success
Special Ed. HS coursework accepted: Yes

Specific course requirements of all applicants: Yes
Separate application required for program services: Yes
# of LD applications submitted each year: 15–20
# of LD applications accepted yearly: 8–13
Total # of students receiving LD services: 44
Acceptance into program means acceptance into college: Student must be admitted and enrolled in the university first and then request admission to PASS.

ADMISSIONS

All qualified applicants must submit the regular application, meet the general criteria for admission to Louisiana College, and have a diagnosed learning or physical disability. Successful applicants must have the intellectual potential (average to superior), the appropriate academic foundation (class standing and/or ACT/SAT scores), and the personal desire and motivation to succeed. The PASS director and staff make the final decision about admission to the program after reviewing the following: 20 or above on ACT or 930 or above on SAT; 4 years English, 3 years science, 3 years social studies, and 3 years math; 2.0 GPA; counselor's recommendation and other letters of reference; psychological or medical reports; and an essay outlining why the student feels they can succeed in college. At least one personal interview with student and parent(s) is required. Students are encouraged to apply early and will be advised of admission on or after May 31. There is an application evaluation fee of $25. Students may appeal to the Appeals Board if they are denied admission.

ADDITIONAL INFORMATION

Tutoring sessions are conducted in most subjects taken by Level I students. Additional tutorial help is available at the higher levels as needed. The PASS staff will carefully work with individual professors and the student's academic advisor to coordinate and accommodate the student's learning needs. Students admitted to PASS will remain in the program as long as they are at Louisiana College. Noncompliance with any component of the program may result in a student's dismissal from the program. Skills classes are offered in study techniques, test-taking strategies, and time management through orientation, and private tutoring from a PASS staff member. Incoming freshmen are encouraged to attend one summer session (five weeks) to become familiar with the campus and college life.

Support Services Contact Information

Learning Disability Program/Services: Program to Assist Student Success (PASS)
Director: Betty P. Matthews
  E-Mail: pass@lacollege.edu
  Telephone: 318-487-7629
  Fax: 318-487-7285

LEARNING DISABILITY SERVICES

Requests for the following services/accommodations will be evaluated individually based on appropriate and current documentation.

Allowed in exams
  Calculator: Yes
  Dictionary: Yes
  Computer: Yes
  Spellchecker: Yes
Extended test time: Yes
Scribes: Yes
Proctors: Yes
Oral exams: Yes
Note-takers: Yes

Distraction reduced environment: Yes
Tape recording in class: Yes
Books on tape from RFBD: Yes
Taping of books not from RFBD: Yes
Accommodations for students with
  ADD: Yes
Reading machine: No
Other assistive technology: No
Priority registration: No

Added costs for services: Yes
LD specialists: Yes
Professional tutors: 3
Peer tutors: 50–60
Max. hours/wk. for services: 10
How professors are notified of
  LD/ADD: By both student and director

GENERAL ADMISSIONS INFORMATION

Director of Admissions: Scarlett Pourciau
Telephone: 318-487-7259

ENTRANCE REQUIREMENTS
Academic units required: 4 English, 3 math, 3 science (2 science lab), 2 social studies, 1 history, 4 academic electives. **Academic units recommended:** 2 foreign language. High school diploma is required and GED is accepted. TOEFL required of all international applicants, minimum paper TOEFL 550, minimum computer TOEFL 213.

Application deadline: 8/15
Notification: Rolling
Average GPA: 3.40

Average SAT Math: NR
Average SAT Verbal: NR
Average ACT: 23

Graduated top 10% of class: 23%
Graduated top 25% of class: 47%
Graduated top 50% of class: 78%

COLLEGE GRADUATION REQUIREMENTS

Course waivers allowed: No
Course substitutions allowed: Yes
In what course: Appeals for substitutions must be made to special committee. However, the director of PASS rarely makes a recommendation.

ADDITIONAL INFORMATION

Environment: The college is located on 81 acres in a small town, 1 mile northeast of Alexandria.

Student Body:
  Undergrad enrollment: 1,014
  Women: 56%
  Men: 44%
  Percent out-of-state: 9%

Cost Information
  Tuition: $8,850
  Room & board: $3,740
Housing Information
  University housing: Yes
  Percent living on campus: 56%

Greek System
  Fraternity: Yes
  Sorority: Yes
Athletics: NCAA Division III

LOUISIANA STATE U.—BATON ROUGE

110 Thomas Boyd Hall, Baton Rouge, LA 70803
Phone: 225-578-1175 • Fax: 225-578-4433
E-mail: admissions@lsu.edu • Web: www.lsu.edu
Support: CS • Institution type: 4-year public

LEARNING DISABILITY PROGRAM AND SERVICES

The purpose of the Office of Disability Services (ODS) is to assist any student who finds his or her disability to be a barrier to achieving educational and/or personal goals. The office provides support services to students with learning disabilities. These services are provided to encourage students with LD/ADD to achieve success in college. The consequences of a disability may include specialized requirements, therefore, the particular needs of each student are considered on an individual basis. ODS dedicates its efforts to meeting both the needs of students with disabilities and the interests of faculty, staff, and the university as a whole. It is the practice of ODS that issues concerning accommodations of students with disabilities in academic and other programs and activities be resolved between the student requesting the accommodation and the university employee representing the specific academic department. After intervention, if the student does not find the provision of an accommodation satisfactory, the student may file a formal grievance.

LD/ADD ADMISSIONS INFORMATION

College entrance tests required: Yes
Interview required: No
Essay required: No
Documentation required for LD: WAIS–III; WJ
Documentation required for ADD: Yes
Submitted to: Office of Disability Services
Special Ed. HS coursework accepted: No

Specific course requirements of all applicants: Yes
Separate application required for program services: Yes
# of LD applications submitted each year: NR
# of LD applications accepted yearly: NR
Total # of students receiving LD services: 600
Acceptance into program means acceptance into
   college: Student must be admitted and enrolled in the university first and then request services.

ADMISSIONS
There is no special admissions process for students with learning disabilities. All applicants must meet the general admission requirements, including 4 years English, 3 years math (including algebra I and II and an advanced math), biology, chemistry and physics, American and world history or world geography or history of western civilization and 1 additional social studies, foreign language, 1/2 year of computers, and 2 academic electives; ACT 20 or above or SAT 910 or above, but the exact scores are dependent on an individual student record; 2.3 GPA. If an applicant does not meet the general admission criteria but is borderline, the student can be admitted through the Access Program.

ADDITIONAL INFORMATION
Specialized support services are based on individual disability-based needs. Services available include disability management counseling; adaptive equipment loan; note-takers; referral for tutoring; assistance with enrollment and registration; liaison assistance and referral to on- and off-campus resources; supplemental orientation to the campus; and advocacy on behalf of students with campus faculty, staff, and students. The Learning Assistance Center is open to all students on campus. Computer labs, science tutoring, math lab, learning skills assistance, supplemental instruction, and skills classes in time management, test-taking strategies, note-taking skills, reading skills, and study skills are available. The decision to provide accommodations and services is made by the SSD after reviewing documentation. Currently there are 175 students with LD and 300 students with ADD receiving services and accommodations.

Support Services Contact Information

Learning Disability Program/Services: Office of Disability Services (ODS)
Director: Ben Cornwell
  E-Mail: bjcornw@lsu.edu
  Telephone: 225-578-4401
  Fax: 225-578-4560
Contact Person: Wendy Devall
  Telephone: 225-578-4310
  Fax: 225-578-4560

LEARNING DISABILITY SERVICES

Requests for the following services/accommodations will be evaluated individually based on appropriate and current documentation.

Allowed in exams
  Calculator: Yes
  Dictionary: Yes
  Computer: Yes
  Spellchecker: Yes
Extended test time: Yes
Scribes: Yes
Proctors: Yes
Oral exams: Yes
Note-takers: Yes

Distraction reduced environment: Yes
Tape recording in class: Yes
Books on tape from RFBD: Yes
Taping of books not from RFBD: Yes
Accommodations for students with
  ADD: Yes
Reading machine: Yes
Other assistive technology: Yes
Priority registration: Yes

Added costs for services: No
LD specialists: Yes
Professional tutors: No
Peer tutors: No
Max. hours/wk. for services:
  Unlimited
How professors are notified of
  LD/ADD: By student

GENERAL ADMISSIONS INFORMATION

Director of Admissions: Cleve Brooks
Telephone: 225-578-1175

ENTRANCE REQUIREMENTS

Academic units required: 4 English, 3 math, 3 science, 2 foreign language, 3 social studies, 2 academic electives. High school diploma is required and GED is accepted. ACT with Writing component required or SAT Reasoning Test. TOEFL required of all international applicants, minimum paper TOEFL 550, minimum computer TOEFL 213.

Application deadline: 4/15
Notification: Rolling
Average GPA: 3.42

Average SAT Math: NR
Average SAT Verbal: NR
Average ACT: 24

Graduated top 10% of class: 23%
Graduated top 25% of class: 50%
Graduated top 50% of class: 80%

COLLEGE GRADUATION REQUIREMENTS

Course waivers allowed: No
Course substitutions allowed: No
In what course: N/A

ADDITIONAL INFORMATION

Environment: The campus is in an urban area in Baton Rouge.

Student Body:
  Undergrad enrollment: 25,849
  Women: 52%
  Men: 48%
  Percent out-of-state: 12%

Cost Information
  In-state tuition: $4,400
  Out-of-state tuition: $12,600
  Room & board: $5,882
Housing Information
  University housing: Yes
  Percent living on campus: 23%

Greek System
  Fraternity: Yes
  Sorority: Yes
Athletics: NCAA Division I

NICHOLLS STATE UNIVERSITY

PO Box 2004, Thibodaux, LA 70310
Phone: 985-448-4507 • Fax: 985-448-4929
E-mail: nicholls@nicholls.edu • Web: www.nicholls.edu
Support: S • Institution type: 4-year public

LEARNING DISABILITY PROGRAM AND SERVICES

The Center for the Study of Dyslexia offers assistance to serious, capable, students with learning disabilities at Nicholls State University who seek to earn an undergraduate degree. They believe that everyone has the right and the obligation to pursue the fulfillment of their learning potential. The center's programs are data driven, goal oriented, and committed to change. The center is committed to continually questioning and evaluating its own practices. It has its own research program and has close ties with leading scholars and researchers in dyslexia. The center is impressed with multisensory, linguistic, and direct instructional approaches, but to maintain its own integrity, it projects an orientation that is objective, open-minded, and directed toward the future. The goals of the center are focused on the need to increase the understanding of dyslexia and to upgrade and improve the accessibility and quality of the services that individuals with dyslexia depend upon to help them to become self-sufficient, well-adjusted, and contributing members of society.

LD/ADD ADMISSIONS INFORMATION

College entrance tests required: Yes
Interview required: Yes
Essay required: No
Documentation required for LD: Psychoeducational evaluation
Documentation required for ADD: Yes
Submitted to: Office of Disability Services
Special Ed. HS coursework accepted: Yes

Specific course requirements of all applicants: Yes
Separate application required for program services: Yes
# of LD applications submitted each year: 0-60
# of LD applications accepted yearly: 0-50
Total # of students receiving LD services: 0-100
Acceptance into program means acceptance into college: Student must be admitted and enrolled in the university first and then request to be reviewed for services.

ADMISSIONS

There is no special admissions process for students with learning disabilities. The college has an open admissions policy for all graduates of high school or a GED. The college recommends that students have 4 years English, 3 years math, 3 years science, 3 years social studies, and 2 years foreign language. ACT/SAT are not required for admission. The average high school GPA is 2.7 and the average ACT is 20. There are a limited number of openings in the center and students should apply early to ensure space. The program seeks highly motivated students who have been diagnosed as having a learning disability. Admission decisions are made after careful review of all submitted documentation. The final decision is based upon selecting the option best suited to providing a successful experience at NSU for the student.

ADDITIONAL INFORMATION

The dyslexia center provides a support system, equipment, remediation, academic planning, resources, and assistance. With the student's permission, letters requesting appropriate classroom and testing accommodations are written to professors. Typical accommodations may include but are not limited to extended time, use of an electronic dictionary, oral reader, or use of a computer. Students meet weekly with an identified program coordinator and are enrolled in regular college classes. Other campus services for students with disabilities include the Office for Students with Disabilities; the Testing Center for special testing accommodations such as extended time or a quiet room; the Tutorial Learning Center for tutoring assistance; the University Counseling Center, which provides counseling directed at self-encouragement, self-esteem, assertiveness, stress management, and test anxiety; and the Computer Lab for assistance with written assignments. Assessment is available for a fee for students applying to the university.

Support Services Contact Information

Learning Disability Program/Services: Office of Disability Services
Director: Gerald Sanders
E-Mail: stsv-jws@nicholls.edu
Telephone: 504-448-4429
Fax: 985-449-7009

LEARNING DISABILITY SERVICES

Requests for the following services/accommodations will be evaluated individually based on appropriate and current documentation.

Allowed in exams
 Calculator: Yes
 Dictionary: Yes
 Computer: Yes
 Spellchecker: Yes
Extended test time: Yes
Scribes: Yes
Proctors: Yes
Oral exams: Yes
Note-takers: No

Distraction reduced environment: Yes
Tape recording in class: Yes
Books on tape from RFBD: Yes
Taping of books not from RFBD: No
Accommodations for students with ADD: Yes
Reading machine: No
Other assistive technology: Yes
Priority registration: No

Added costs for services: No
LD specialists: No
Professional tutors: 3
Peer tutors: No
Max. hours/wk. for services: NR
How professors are notified of LD/ADD: By student

GENERAL ADMISSIONS INFORMATION

Director of Admissions: Becky Durocher
Telephone: 985-448-4507

ENTRANCE REQUIREMENTS

Academic units recommended: 4 English, 3 math, 3 science, 2 foreign language, 1 social studies, 2 history, 7 academic electives, 2 health and phyiscal education. High school diploma is required and GED is accepted. TOEFL required of all international applicants, minimum paper TOEFL 500, minimum computer TOEFL 173.

Application deadline: Rolling
Notification: Rolling
Average GPA: 2.91

Average SAT Math: NR
Average SAT Verbal: NR
Average ACT: 19

Graduated top 10% of class: 11%
Graduated top 25% of class: 30%
Graduated top 50% of class: 61%

COLLEGE GRADUATION REQUIREMENTS

Course waivers allowed: No
Course substitutions allowed: No
In what course: N/A

ADDITIONAL INFORMATION

Environment: The university is in a small town 1 hour from New Orleans.

Student Body:
 Undergrad enrollment: 6,490
 Women: 62%
 Men: 38%
 Percent out-of-state: 3%

Cost Information
 In-state tuition: $2,115
 Out-of-state tuition: $7,563
 Room & board: $3,402
Housing Information
 University housing: Yes
 Percent living on campus: 15%

Greek System
 Fraternity: Yes
 Sorority: Yes
Athletics: NCAA Division I

UNIVERSITY OF NEW ORLEANS

AD 103, Lakefront, New Orleans, LA 70148
Phone: 504-280-6595 • Fax: 504-280-5522
E-mail: admissions@uno.edu • Web: www.uno.edu
Support: S • Institution type: 4-year public

LEARNING DISABILITY PROGRAM AND SERVICES

The University of New Orleans is committed to providing all students with equal opportunities for academic and extra-curricular success. The Disabled Student Services (DSS) office coordinates all services and programs. In addition to serving its primary function as a liaison between the student and the university, the office provides a limited number of direct services to students with all kinds of permanent and temporary disabilities. Services begin when a student registered with the university contacts the DSS office, provides documentation of the disability, and requests assistance. DSS encourages student independence, program accessibility, and a psychologically supportive environment, so students may achieve their educational objectives. DSS also seeks to educate the campus community about disability issues.

LD/ADD ADMISSIONS INFORMATION

College entrance tests required: Yes
Interview required: No
Essay required: No
Documentation required for LD: Psychoeducational evaluation
Documentation required for ADD: Yes
Submitted to: Support Program/Services
Special Ed. HS coursework accepted: Yes

Specific course requirements of all applicants: Yes
Separate application required for program services: Yes
# of LD applications submitted each year: NR
# of LD applications accepted yearly: NR
Total # of students receiving LD services: NR
Acceptance into program means acceptance into college: Student must be admitted and enrolled in the university first and then request services.

ADMISSIONS

University of New Orleans does not have any special admissions process for students with learning disabilities. Students with learning disabilities should submit the general application form and are expected to meet the same admission standards as all other applicants. Any student who is denied admission may apply to the College Life Program, which is designed as an alternative admission for "high risk" students (not only students with learning disabilities). This program is for students who need assistance in one or more academic areas. The students remain with this program until they are able to remediate their deficits and then transfer into the appropriate college.

ADDITIONAL INFORMATION

DSS provides regular support services to all UNO students. Drop-in tutoring for math and writing is available. Audio tapes are available in math and English courses. Tutors are available in the Learning Resource Center and Testing Centers in the Library for test-taking, adaptive technology, and/or test administration. Developmental courses are offered in math and English and skills classes are available for assistance in study techniques. PREP START is a special summer outreach program for recent high school graduates to gain admission to the university.

Support Services Contact Information

Learning Disability Program/Services: Office of Disability Services (ODS)
Director: Janice G. Lyn,PhD
  E-Mail: jlyn@uno.edu
  Telephone: 504-280-6222
  Fax: 504-280-3975
Contact Person: Amy King
  E-Mail: aaking@uno.edu
  Telephone: 504-280-7284
  Fax: 504-280-3998

LEARNING DISABILITY SERVICES

Requests for the following services/accommodations will be evaluated individually based on appropriate and current documentation.

Allowed in exams
  Calculator: Yes
  Dictionary: Yes
  Computer: Yes
  Spellchecker: Yes
Extended test time: Yes
Scribes: Yes
Proctors: Yes
Oral exams: Yes
Note-takers: Yes

Distraction reduced environment: Yes
Tape recording in class: Yes
Books on tape from RFBD: Yes
Taping of books not from RFBD: Yes
Accommodations for students with
  ADD: Yes
Reading machine: Yes
Other assistive technology: Yes
Priority registration: No

Added costs for services: No
LD specialists: No
Professional tutors: No
Peer tutors: No
Max. hours/wk. for services: Referred
  to Learning Resource Center
How professors are notified of
  LD/ADD: By both student and director

GENERAL ADMISSIONS INFORMATION

Director of Admissions: Ms. Roslyn Sheley
Telephone: 504-280-6595

ENTRANCE REQUIREMENTS

Academic units required: 4 English, 3 math, 3 science, 2 foreign language, 3 history, 1 academic elective. High school diploma is required and GED is accepted. ACT with or without Writing component accepted. TOEFL required of all international applicants, minimum paper TOEFL 550, minimum computer TOEFL 213.

Application deadline: 8/30
Notification: Rolling
Average GPA: 2.94

Average SAT Math: 517
Average SAT Verbal: 524
Average ACT: 21

Graduated top 10% of class: 11%
Graduated top 25% of class: 32%
Graduated top 50% of class: 60%

COLLEGE GRADUATION REQUIREMENTS

Course waivers allowed: No
Course substitutions allowed: Yes
In what course: Foreign language and math with appropriate documentation

ADDITIONAL INFORMATION

Environment: The university is located on 345 acres in downtown New Orleans.

Student Body:
  Undergrad enrollment: 13,225
  Women: 56%
  Men: 44%
  Percent out-of-state: 4%

Cost Information
  In-state tuition: $3,184
  Out-of-state tuition: $10,228
  Room & board: $4,590
Housing Information
  University housing: Yes
  Percent living on campus: 9%

Greek System
  Fraternity: Yes
  Sorority: Yes
Athletics: NCAA Division I

SOUTHERN MAINE COMM. COLLEGE

Fort Road, South Portland, ME 04106
Phone: 207)741-5800 • Fax: 207)741-5760
E-mail: adms@smtc.edu • Web: www.smccme.edu
Support: S • Institution type: 2-year public

LEARNING DISABILITY PROGRAM AND SERVICES

The Disability Services program is designed to offer academic support to students through various individualized services. Students can get professional faculty tutoring in their most difficult courses; learn about their specific learning style; improve concentration and memory; study more efficiently for tests; learn how to manage their time better; learn the basic skills that are the foundation of their specific technology; and use a computer toward processing, internet research, and other computer application. The NoveNET Learning Lab at SMTC uses a specially designed set of lessons and offers an alternative to adult education or other classes to complete high school level math, s283cience, and English. The Learning Lab is a good place to become reacquainted with oneself as a learner. Students can start using it anytime during the school year and work at their own pace, study only the lessons that they need, and work at home on their own personal computer. There is an instructor available during regular lab hours; the instruction meets SMTC's prerequisite admissions requirements, it has day and evening hours, and it allows students to earn credit for work in math courses in the lab by credit-by-examination.

LD/ADD ADMISSIONS INFORMATION

College entrance tests required: Yes
Interview required: No
Essay required: No
Documentation required for LD: Psychoeducational
  evaluation
Documentation required for ADD: Yes
Submitted to: Disability Services
Special Ed. HS coursework accepted: Yes

Specific course requirements of all applicants: Yes
Separate application required for program services: No
# of LD applications submitted each year: NR
# of LD applications accepted yearly: NR
Total # of students receiving LD services: 75
Acceptance into program means acceptance into
  college: Student must be admitted and enrolled in the
  college first and then request services.

ADMISSIONS

All students must meet the same admission criteria. There is no special admissions process for students with learning disabilities. All students have access to disability services, including those with a diagnosed learning disability. Applicants must submit a high school transcript, essay, and recommendation. Interviews are required. Students must have two years algebra, and one year biology, physics, or chemistry for most programs. The SATs required for applicants to the associate degree programs who have been out of high school two years or less. The ACT is not required. Students are expected to have a C average with at least a C in prerequisite courses. Assessment tests sometimes are required as well.

ADDITIONAL INFORMATION

Students with diagnosed LD, as well as any students with academic needs, are provided with tutoring by faculty and students; access to NoveNET; access to resources in study skills, in the form of personal advising/counseling, skill inventories, and study guides; and for LD, access to academic accommodations such as untimed exams, testing in a quiet area, and note-takers or readers. Other services are learning assessments; faculty consulting; curriculum development; preparation of materials to assist students in all courses; study skills counseling; academic advising; counseling and support for students with learning disabilities; access to multimedia self-teaching materials including computer-assisted instruction, videotapes, and audio cassettes; and microcomputers, and tape recorder. The college administers the ASSET test to any student who has not provided scores from the ACT or SAT.

Support Services Contact Information

Learning Disability Program/Services: Disability Services
Director: Mark Krogman
  E-Mail: mkrogman@smccme.edu
  Telephone: 207-741-5629
  Fax: 207-741-5653
Contact Person: Joyce Leslie, Learning Assistance Center
  E-Mail: jleslie@smccme.edu
  Telephone: 207-7415534
  Fax: 207-741-5752

LEARNING DISABILITY SERVICES

Requests for the following services/accommodations will be evaluated individually based on appropriate and current documentation.

Allowed in exams
  Calculator: Yes
  Dictionary: Yes
  Computer: Yes
  Spellchecker: Yes
Extended test time: Yes
Scribes: Yes
Proctors: Yes
Oral exams: Yes
Note-takers: Yes

Distraction reduced environment: Yes
Tape recording in class: Yes
Books on tape from RFBD: Yes
Taping of books not from RFBD: Yes
Accommodations for students with ADD: Yes
Reading machine: Yes
Other assistive technology: Yes
Priority registration: Yes

Added costs for services: No
LD specialists: No
Professional tutors: 3
Peer tutors: 3
Max. hours/wk. for services: 3
How professors are notified of LD/ADD: By both student and director

GENERAL ADMISSIONS INFORMATION

Director of Admissions: Robert Weimont
Telephone: 207-741-5800

ENTRANCE REQUIREMENTS

Academic units recommended: 4 English, 3 math, 1 science (1 science lab). High school diploma is required and GED is accepted. TOEFL required of all international applicants, minimum paper TOEFL 500, minimum computer TOEFL 173.

Application deadline: Rolling
Notification: Rolling
Average GPA: 2.2 minimum

Average SAT Math: NR
Average SAT Verbal: NR
Average ACT: NR

Graduated top 10% of class: NR
Graduated top 25% of class: NR
Graduated top 50% of class: NR

COLLEGE GRADUATION REQUIREMENTS

Course waivers allowed: No
Course substitutions allowed: No
In what course: N/A

ADDITIONAL INFORMATION

Environment: The college, part of the Maine Technical College System, is located on a 50-acre campus.

Student Body:
  Undergrad enrollment: 3,816
  Women: 51%
  Men: 49%
  Percent out-of-state: 3%

Cost Information
  In-state tuition: $2,040
  Out-of-state tuition: $4,470
  Room & board: $5,728
Housing Information
  University housing: Yes
  Percent living on campus: 10%

Greek System
  Fraternity: No
  Sorority: No
Athletics: NJCAA

UNITY COLLEGE

PO Box 532, Unity, ME 04988-0532
Phone: 207-948-3131 • Fax: 207-948-6277
E-mail: admissions@unity.edu • Web: www.unity.edu
Support: CS • Institution type: 4-year private

LEARNING DISABILITY PROGRAM AND SERVICES

Unity College offers services for students with learning disabilities and encourages them to begin their studies in the summer prior to freshman year in the Summer Institute. The institute provides an opportunity for students to become familiar with the college, and is an effective way to prepare for college coursework. The Learning Resource Center (LRC) provides a program for bright, highly motivated students. Once admitted, students with learning disabilities follow a carefully coordinated program that combines regular coursework, supportive services, and intensive individual work on academic course support. The LD specialist meets regularly with students, monitoring progress and ensuring personal contact. The LRC's staff is composed of faculty members, a learning disabilities specialist, and peer tutors. The staff is available to help students develop effective learning strategies, with special emphasis placed on individual student needs. Most importantly, the LRC gives necessary attention to each student's academic and personal growth. With the support of the LRC, students can gain confidence, knowledge, and skills to complete a high-quality college education.

LD/ADD ADMISSIONS INFORMATION

College entrance tests required: Yes
Interview required: Yes
Essay required: Yes
Documentation required for LD: WAIS–III
Documentation required for ADD: Yes
Submitted to: Learning Resources Center
Special Ed. HS coursework accepted: Yes

Specific course requirements of all applicants: Yes
Separate application required for program services: No
# of LD applications submitted each year: NR
# of LD applications accepted yearly: NR
Total # of students receiving LD services: 60–75
Acceptance into program means acceptance into college: Student must be admitted and enrolled in the college prior to requesting services from the Learning Resource Center.

ADMISSIONS

To apply for admission students with learning disabilities should submit the general college application and the results of recent diagnostic testing, including a WAIS–R. Students should submit other diagnostic materials that indicate their level of functioning. SAT and ACT scores are not required but should be submitted if available. Students also must send 2 letters of recommendation and their official high school transcript. The Office of Admissions may require an on-campus interview, on-campus testing, or submission of additional supporting materials. Students with learning disabilities may request an interview with the director of Student Support Services. Other students may be admitted with the stipulation that they attend the Summer Institute and be successful prior to being admitted as a student for the fall semester. Other factors used in the admission decision include special talents, leadership, activities, and personality. Students not regularly admissible are reviewed by the LD specialist, who provides a recommendation to admissions, and a joint decision is made.

ADDITIONAL INFORMATION

The Summer Institute ($1,495), required of some incoming freshmen, is a 4-week pre-college program offering basic academic skills in writing, math, study strategies, computers, Unity College orientation, as well as the natural environment of Maine. The institute includes credit and non-credit courses and individual tutorial assistance. Students meet with academic advisors and pre-register for fall courses. A learning disability specialist is on staff and services during the school year include specialized academic advising, support groups, taped texts, tutoring on a one-to-one basis or in small groups, and skills remediation in reading, math, spelling, written language, and learning techniques. Special courses, mostly for credit, are offered in composition, math, reading, college survival skills, and study skills. This program is curriculum based, designed to foster independence and allow students to achieve maximum academic goals and maximum potential.

Support Services Contact Information

Learning Disability Program/Services: Learning Resource Center (LRC)
Director: James Horan
  E-Mail: jreed@unity.edu
  Telephone: 207-948-3131 ext. 241
Contact Person: Ann Dailey
  Telephone: 207-948-3131 ext. 236

LEARNING DISABILITY SERVICES

Requests for the following services/accommodations will be evaluated individually based on appropriate and current documentation.

Allowed in exams
  Calculator: Yes
  Dictionary: Yes
  Computer: Yes
  Spellchecker: Yes
Extended test time: Yes
Scribes: Yes
Proctors: Yes
Oral exams: Yes
Note-takers: Yes

Distraction reduced environment: NR
Tape recording in class: Yes
Books on tape from RFBD: Yes
Taping of books not from RFBD: NR
Accommodations for students with ADD: Yes
Reading machine: No
Other assistive technology: No
Priority registration: Yes

Added costs for services: No
LD specialists: Yes
Professional tutors: Yes
Peer tutors: Yes
Max. hours/wk. for services: Unlimited
How professors are notified of LD/ADD: By both student and director

GENERAL ADMISSIONS INFORMATION

Director of Admissions: John Craig
Telephone: 207-948-3131

ENTRANCE REQUIREMENTS

Academic units required: 4 English, 2 science. **Academic units recommended:** 4 math, 2 foreign language, 4 social studies. High school diploma is required and GED is accepted. TOEFL required of all international applicants, minimum paper TOEFL 500, minimum computer TOEFL 173.

Application deadline: Rolling
Notification: Rolling
Average GPA: 2.70

Average SAT Math: 480
Average SAT Verbal: 510
Average ACT: NR

Graduated top 10% of class: 3%
Graduated top 25% of class: 13%
Graduated top 50% of class: 48%

COLLEGE GRADUATION REQUIREMENTS

Course waivers allowed: Yes
Course substitutions allowed: Yes
In what course: Waivers and substitutions are handled on an individual basis for each student.

ADDITIONAL INFORMATION

Environment: The college is located on 185-acres in a rural community about 20 miles from Waterville.

Student Body:
  Undergrad enrollment: 512
  Women: 31%
  Men: 69%
  Percent out-of-state: 64%

Cost Information
  Tuition: $16,190
  Room & board: $6,250
Housing Information
  University housing: Yes
  Percent living on campus: 80%

Greek System
  Fraternity: Yes
  Sorority: Yes
  Athletics: NAIA

UNIVERSITY OF MAINE—MACHIAS

Office of Admissions, 9 O'Brien Avenue, Machias, ME 04654
Phone: 207-255-1318 • Fax: 207-255-1363
E-mail: ummadmissions@maine.edu • Web: www.umm.maine.edu
Support: S • Institution type: 4-year public

LEARNING DISABILITY PROGRAM AND SERVICES

The University of Maine at Machias offers a personal approach to education. Students with documented disabilities may request modifications, accommodations, or auxiliary aids that will enable them to participate in and benefit from all postsecondary educational programs and activities. Students must provide current documentation completed within the last 3 years. This documentation should be submitted to the student resources coordinator. The student resources coordinator works one-on-one with any student who needs academic support. This support takes the form of working with methods specific to the LD. All accommodation requests must be processed through the student resources coordinator.

LD/ADD ADMISSIONS INFORMATION

College entrance tests required: Yes
Interview required: No
Essay required: No
Documentation required for LD: Woodcock Johnson Full Battery or WISC within last 3 years
Documentation required for ADD: Doctor's letter explaining degree of the problem
Submitted to: Both Admissions and Student Resources
Special Ed. HS coursework accepted: Yes

Specific course requirements of all applicants: Yes
Separate application required for program services: No
# of LD applications submitted each year: NR
# of LD applications accepted yearly: NR
Total # of students receiving LD services: NR
Acceptance into program means acceptance into college: Student must be admitted and enrolled in the university first and then request services.

ADMISSIONS

There is no special admissions process for students with LD and ADD. An interview is strongly suggested. Applicants in general have a 1000 on the SAT, rank in the top 50 percent of their senior class and have a 3.0 GPA. Students seeking admission to an associate degree program should have a C average and rank in the top two-thirds of their senior class.

ADDITIONAL INFORMATION

One-on-one services are available upon request. One-on-one assistance is offered in the following areas: learning style and learning strategies, time management, organizing and writing papers, basic skills and study skills, anxiety management, major and career focus, assistance using the library, information and/or referral, advocacy, and peer tutoring. In order for a student to have a waiver or substitution of a course a disabilities committee meets to evaluate the documentation and make a recommendation to the vice president of academic affairs.

Support Services Contact Information

Learning Disability Program/Services: Student Resources
Director: Jean Schild
  E-Mail: schild@maine.edu
  Telephone: 207-255-1228
  Fax: 208-255-4864
Contact Person: Same

LEARNING DISABILITY SERVICES

Requests for the following services/accommodations will be evaluated individually based on appropriate and current documentation.

Allowed in exams
  Calculator: Yes
  Dictionary: Yes
  Computer: Yes
  Spellchecker: Yes
Extended test time: Yes
Scribes: Yes
Proctors: Yes
Oral exams: Yes
Note-takers: Yes

Distraction reduced environment: Yes
Tape recording in class: Yes
Books on tape from RFBD: Yes
Taping of books not from RFBD: No
**Accommodations for students with
  ADD:** Yes
Reading machine: No
Other assistive technology: Yes
Priority registration: Yes

Added costs for services: No
LD specialists: No
Professional tutors: No
Peer tutors: 14
Max. hours/wk. for services:
  Unlimited
**How professors are notified of
  LD/ADD:** By director

GENERAL ADMISSIONS INFORMATION

Director of Admissions: Stewart Bennett
Telephone: 207-255-1318

ENTRANCE REQUIREMENTS

Academic units required: 4 English, 3 math, 2 science (2 science lab), 2 social studies. **Academic units recommended:** 2 foreign language, 3 academic electives. High school diploma is required and GED is accepted. ACT with or without Writing component accepted. TOEFL required of all international applicants, minimum paper TOEFL 500, minimum computer TOEFL 173.

Application deadline: 8/15
Notification: Rolling
Average GPA: 2.80

Average SAT Math: 463
Average SAT Verbal: 470
Average ACT: 20

Graduated top 10% of class: 15%
Graduated top 25% of class: 31%
Graduated top 50% of class: 69%

COLLEGE GRADUATION REQUIREMENTS

Course waivers allowed: Yes
Course substitutions allowed: Yes
In what course: Disabilities committee makes recommendation to the vice president of academic affairs for final determination.

ADDITIONAL INFORMATION

Environment: Rural campus 85 miles east of Bangor.

Student Body:
  Undergrad enrollment: 625
  Women: 67%
  Men: 33%
  Percent out-of-state: 24%

Cost Information
  In-state tuition: $3,960
  Out-of-state tuition: $10,320
  Room & board: $5,408
Housing Information
  University housing: Yes
  Percent living on campus: 43%

Greek System
  Fraternity: Yes
  Sorority: Yes
  Athletics: NAIA

University of Maine—Machias

UNIVERSITY OF NEW ENGLAND

Hills Beach Road, Biddeford, ME 04005
Phone: 207-283-0171 • Fax: 207-294-5900
E-mail: jshea@mailbox.une.edu • Web: www.une.edu
Support: S • Institution type: 4-year private

LEARNING DISABILITY PROGRAM AND SERVICES

The University of New England's Disability Services Program exists to ensure that the university fulfills the part of its mission that seeks to promote respect for individual differences and to ensure that no one person who meets the academic and technical standards requisite for admission to, and the continued enrollment at, the university is denied benefits or subjected to discrimination at UNE solely by reason of the disability. Toward this end, and in conjunction with federal and state laws, the university both accepts and provides reasonable accommodations for qualified students. Students with learning disabilities or attention deficit disorder must provide current documentation that identifies the specific disability. All documentation should be submitted to Disability Services.

LD/ADD ADMISSIONS INFORMATION

College entrance tests required: Yes
Interview required: No
Essay required: N/A
Documentation required for LD:
  Psychoeducational/neuropsychological evaluation
Documentation required for ADD: Yes
Submitted to: Disability Services
Special Ed. HS coursework accepted: Yes

Specific course requirements of all applicants: Yes
Separate application required for program services: No
# of LD applications submitted each year: NR
# of LD applications accepted yearly: NR
Total # of students receiving LD services: 25
Acceptance into program means acceptance into college: Student must be admitted and enrolled in the university first and then request services.

ADMISSIONS

All applicants must meet the same admission criteria. There is no separate process for students with LD/ADD. General admission criteria include 4 years English, 2–4 years math, 2–4 years social studies, 2–4 years science, and 2–4 years foreign language. It is recommended that students submit an essay and have an interview. Interviews are especially helpful for borderline applicants. After being admitted, students may submit documentation to Disability Services in order to request accommodations and services.

ADDITIONAL INFORMATION

Documentation requirements have been established by the Disability Services. Students with learning disabilities should submit psychoeducational assessment reports based on adult-normed tests of ability and achievement. Students with ADD must also submit appropriate documentation from a qualified professional. Services could include priority registration, note-takers, scribes, proctors, and books on tape through the Recordings for the Blind and Dyslexic. Accommodations could include the use of a calculator, dictionary, computer, or spellchecker in exams; reduced-distraction site for exams; extended time on tests; oral exams; and assistive technology. All students have access to tutoring.

Support Services Contact Information

Learning Disability Program/Services: Disability Services
Director: Susan Church, Coordinator
  E-Mail: schurch@une.edu
  Telephone: 207-283-0170
  Fax: 207-294-5971

LEARNING DISABILITY SERVICES

Requests for the following services/accommodations will be evaluated individually based on appropriate and current documentation.

Allowed in exams
  Calculator: Yes
  Dictionary: Yes
  Computer: Yes
  Spellchecker: Yes
Extended test time: Yes
Scribes: Yes
Proctors: Yes
Oral exams: Yes
Note-takers: No

Distraction reduced environment: Yes
Tape recording in class: Yes
Books on tape from RFBD: Yes
Taping of books not from RFBD: Yes
Accommodations for students with
  ADD: Yes
Reading machine: Yes
Other assistive technology: Yes
Priority registration: Yes

Added costs for services: No
LD specialists: No
Professional tutors: 1
Peer tutors: 15
Max. hours/wk. for services:
  Unlimited
How professors are notified of
  LD/ADD: By student

GENERAL ADMISSIONS INFORMATION

Director of Admissions: Alan Liebrecht
Telephone: 207-283-0171

ENTRANCE REQUIREMENTS

Academic units required: 4 English, 3 math, 3 science (2 science lab), 2 social studies, 2 history. **Academic units recommended:** 4 math, 4 science (3 science lab), 2 foreign language, 4 social studies, 4 history, 4 academic electives. High school diploma is required and GED is accepted. TOEFL required of all international applicants, minimum paper TOEFL 550, minimum computer TOEFL 213.

Application deadline: Rolling
Notification: Rolling
Average GPA: 3.2

Average SAT Math: 509
Average SAT Verbal: 511
Average ACT: NR

Graduated top 10% of class: 17%
Graduated top 25% of class: 46%
Graduated top 50% of class: 80%

COLLEGE GRADUATION REQUIREMENTS

Course waivers allowed: No
Course substitutions allowed: No
In what course: N/A

ADDITIONAL INFORMATION

Environment: The 121-acre campus is in a rural area 16 miles east of Portland.

Student Body:
  Undergrad enrollment: 1,660
  Women: 81%
  Men: 19%
  Percent out-of-state: 50%

Cost Information
  Tuition: $21,540
  Room & board: $8,730
Housing Information
  University housing: Yes
  Percent living on campus: 45%

Greek System
  Fraternity: No
  Sorority: No
Athletics: NCAA Division III

University of New England

FROSTBURG STATE UNIVERSITY

FSU, 101 Braddock Road, Frostburg, MD 21532
Phone: 301-687-4201 • Fax: 301-687-7074
E-mail: fsuadmissions@frostburg.edu • Web: www.frostburg.edu
Support: S • Institution type: 4-year public

LEARNING DISABILITY PROGRAM AND SERVICES

Frostburg State provides comprehensive support services for students with learning disabilities to assist them in achieving their potential. To be eligible for the Frostburg State University support services, admitted students must provide records of evaluation not more than three years old. Services include advising and counseling by a qualified counselor familiar with each student's needs; assistance in course selection; guaranteed schedules; liaison with faculty; representation at academic standards committee meetings; tutoring; and study skills workshops. The goal of the programs is to provide appropriate support services to enhance learning, and to strive for student self-advocacy and understanding of and independence in learning style.

LD/ADD ADMISSIONS INFORMATION

College entrance tests required: Yes
Interview required: No
Essay required: No
Documentation required for LD: Psychoeducational evaluation
Documentation required for ADD: Yes
Submitted to: Disability Support Services
Special Ed. HS coursework accepted: Yes

Specific course requirements of all applicants: Yes
Separate application required for program services: No
# of LD applications submitted each year: NR
# of LD applications accepted yearly: NR
Total # of students receiving LD services: 300
Acceptance into program means acceptance into college: Student must be admitted and enrolled in the university first and then request services. There is an equal appeal procedure for students who are denied admission.

ADMISSIONS

There is no special admission procedure for students with learning disabilities. All students must complete the mainstream program in high school and meet all requirements for the university and the state. There is a Student Support Services/Disabled Student Services information form that must be completed by students to enroll in these programs. Admission to FSU is determined by the admissions office, which assesses an applicant's likelihood of success in a regular college program with Support Service assistance.

ADDITIONAL INFORMATION

Basic skills courses are available in time management, study techniques, organizational skills, and test-taking strategies. Other services include note-takers, dictation services, and readers. There is an orientation course to the university taught by an LD specialist. Students with LD or ADD must provide current and appropriate documentation in order to receive services. Students who believe they may have a learning disability, but who have not been tested, may request testing and assessment for no fee.

Support Services Contact Information

Learning Disability Program/Services: Disability Support Services
Director: Leroy Pullen
  E-Mail: lpullen@frostburg.edu
  Telephone: 301-687-4483
  Fax: 301-687-4671

LEARNING DISABILITY SERVICES

Requests for the following services/accommodations will be evaluated individually based on appropriate and current documentation.

Allowed in exams
  Calculator: Yes
  Dictionary: Yes
  Computer: Yes
  Spellchecker: Yes
Extended test time: Yes
Scribes: Yes
Proctors: Yes
Oral exams: Yes
Note-takers: Yes

Distraction reduced environment: Yes
Tape recording in class: Yes
Books on tape from RFBD: Yes
Taping of books not from RFBD: Yes
Accommodations for students with
  ADD: Yes
Reading machine: NR
Other assistive technology: No
Priority registration: NR

Added costs for services: No
LD specialists: No
Professional tutors: 7
Peer tutors: Yes
Max. hours/wk. for services: Varies
How professors are notified of
  LD/ADD: By student

GENERAL ADMISSIONS INFORMATION

Director of Admissions: James Antonio
Telephone: 301-687-4305

ENTRANCE REQUIREMENTS

Academic units required: 4 English, 3 math, 3 science (2 science lab), 2 foreign language, 3 social studies. High school diploma is required and GED is accepted. TOEFL required of all international applicants, minimum paper TOEFL 550, minimum computer TOEFL 213.

Application deadline: Rolling
Notification: Rolling
Average GPA: 3.02

Average SAT Math: NR
Average SAT Verbal: NR
Average ACT: NR

Graduated top 10% of class: 10%
Graduated top 25% of class: 29%
Graduated top 50% of class: 65%

COLLEGE GRADUATION REQUIREMENTS

Course waivers allowed: No
Course substitutions allowed: Yes
In what course: Students may appeal for any course to be substituted; appeals are determined on a case-by-case basis.

ADDITIONAL INFORMATION

Environment: The university in located on 260 acres in the Appalachian Highlands in a small town 150 miles northwest of Baltimore.

Student Body:
  Undergrad enrollment: 4,453
  Women: 49%
  Men: 51%
  Percent out-of-state: 10%

Cost Information
  In-state tuition: $5,000
  Out-of-state tuition: $13,250
  Room & board: $6,148
Housing Information
  University housing: Yes
  Percent living on campus: 35%

Greek System
  Fraternity: Yes
  Sorority: Yes
Athletics: NCAA Division III

MCDANIEL COLLEGE

2 College Hill, Westminster, MD 21157
Phone: 410-857-2230 • Fax: 410-857-2757
E-mail: admissions@mcdaniel.edu • Web: www.mcdaniel.edu
Support: CS • Institution type: 4-year private

LEARNING DISABILITY PROGRAM AND SERVICES

The goal of the Academic Skills Center (ASC) is to assist students with learning disabilities. More time is given to freshmen and transfer students to help with the transition into Mc Daniel. The Academic Skills Center provides three levels of services: Level I (no fee) students receive appropriate accommodations, tutoring, monthly support groups, and 2 hours a semester advising with ASC coordinator; Level II ($1,000 fee) provides Level I services and pre-scheduling of courses, consulting with ASC coordinator, Study Lab, 5 hours per week of study skills tutoring, and assignment to an ASC mentor; Level III ($1,500 fee) provides services from Level I and Level II and diagnostic testing, planning, developmental implementation, and evaluation of a yearly individualized academic program.

LD/ADD ADMISSIONS INFORMATION

College entrance tests required: Yes
Interview required: No
Essay required: Yes
Documentation required for LD: WAIS–III, psychoeducational testing: within three years
Documentation required for ADD: Yes
Submitted to: Academic Skills Center
Special Ed. HS coursework accepted: No

Specific course requirements of all applicants: Yes
Separate application required for program services: Yes
# of LD applications submitted each year: 100
# of LD applications accepted yearly: 55
Total # of students receiving LD services: 150
Acceptance into program means acceptance into college: Student must be admitted and enrolled in the university first and then request services.

ADMISSIONS

The admission process is the same for all applicants. General admission criteria include a minimum 2.75 GPA in core academic courses including 4 years English, 3 years math, 3 years science, 3 years social studies, and 3 years foreign language (substitutions allowed in foreign language if appropriate). Any LD or ADD documentation should be sent to ASC to be used after a student is admitted and enrolled.

ADDITIONAL INFORMATION

Enrolled new students must attend one guidance day during the summer prior to freshman year to select classes. Students with learning disabilities should attend an orientation meeting before college begins and schedule individual appointments with the ASC coordinator. All students must pass one math course. There is a basic math class and two math review courses for students needing more math foundation prior to taking the required course. One skills class is offered and students have access to unlimited tutoring.

Support Services Contact Information

Learning Disability Program/Services: Student Acedemic Support Services–SASS
Director: Kevin Selby, Acting Director
E-Mail: kselby@umdc.edu
Telephone: 410-857-2504
Fax: 410-386-4617

LEARNING DISABILITY SERVICES

Requests for the following services/accommodations will be evaluated individually based on appropriate and current documentation.

Allowed in exams
  Calculator: Yes
  Dictionary: Yes
  Computer: Yes
  Spellchecker: Yes
Extended test time: Yes
Scribes: Yes
Proctors: Yes
Oral exams: Yes
Note-takers: Yes

Distraction reduced environment: Yes
Tape recording in class: Yes
Books on tape from RFBD: Yes
Taping of books not from RFBD: Yes
Accommodations for students with ADD: Yes
Reading machine: Yes
Other assistive technology: Yes
Priority registration: Yes

Added costs for services: Yes
LD specialists: Yes
Professional tutors: Yes
Peer tutors: 10
Max. hours/wk. for services: Unlimited
How professors are notified of LD/ADD: By student

GENERAL ADMISSIONS INFORMATION

Director of Admissions: M. Martha O'Connell
Telephone: 410-857-2230

ENTRANCE REQUIREMENTS
Academic units required: 4 English, 3 math, 3 science (2 science lab), 3 foreign language, 2 social studies, 2 history. **Academic units recommended:** 4 math, 4 science, 4 foreign language, 3 social studies, 3 history. High school diploma is required and GED is accepted. TOEFL required of all international applicants, minimum paper TOEFL 550, minimum computer TOEFL 213.

Application deadline: 2/1
Notification: 3/15
Average GPA: 3.40

Average SAT Math: 556
Average SAT Verbal: 554
Average ACT: NR

Graduated top 10% of class: 25%
Graduated top 25% of class: 52%
Graduated top 50% of class: 87%

COLLEGE GRADUATION REQUIREMENTS

Course waivers allowed: Yes
Course substitutions allowed: Yes
In what course: Foreign language

ADDITIONAL INFORMATION

Environment: The college is located on 160 acres in a small town 30 miles northwest of Baltimore.

Student Body:
  Undergrad enrollment: 1,581
  Women: 58%
  Men: 42%
  Percent out-of-state: 27%

Cost Information
  Tuition: $24,500
  Room & board: $5,600
Housing Information
  University housing: Yes
  Percent living on campus: 80%

Greek System
  Fraternity: Yes
  Sorority: Yes
Athletics: NCAA Division III

TOWSON UNIVERSITY

8000 York Road, Towson, MD 21252-0001
Phone: 410-704-2113 • Fax: 410-704-3030
E-mail: admissions@towson.edu • Web: www.towson.edu
Support: CS • Institution type: 4-year public

LEARNING DISABILITY PROGRAM AND SERVICES

Towson University does not have a separate program for students with learning disabilities and/or attention deficit disorder. The university policy is to ask students what their needs are rather than to present them with a plan to which they must adapt. There is involvement in class selection. Professors are notified of students' disabilities, which eliminates the need for students to explain or prove their disability. Towson University also offers all students tutorial services, a Reading Center, and a Writing Lab. All students requesting services and/or accommodations must have an interview with the director of support services in order to establish what is necessary. Towson University's program for students with learning disabilities is individualistic, as the compensating skills of the students are unique.

LD/ADD ADMISSIONS INFORMATION

College entrance tests required: Yes
Interview required: No
Essay required: No
Documentation required for LD: Current psychoeducational evaluation
Documentation required for ADD: Current psychiatrist or psychologist report
Submitted to: Disability Support Services
Special Ed. HS coursework accepted: Yes

Specific course requirements of all applicants: Yes
Separate application required for program services: N/A
# of LD applications submitted each year: NR
# of LD applications accepted yearly: NR
Total # of students receiving LD services: 400
Acceptance into program means acceptance into college: Student must be admitted and enrolled in the university first and then request services.

ADMISSIONS

There is no question on the application that inquires about a learning disability. Students with learning disabilities who want special consideration and/or services should provide documentation and information about their learning disability. Exceptions to published entrance requirements are made by a committee for students with documented learning disabilities. Credentials are reviewed by a committee that has some flexibility in interpreting scores. Students submitting documentation should send copies to admissions and DSS. Interviews are recommended. The mid 50 percent SAT range for applicants is 1020–1180. Priority admission is granted to applicants with a GPA of 3.0 and 4 years English, 3 years social science, 3 years lab science, 3 years math, 2 years foreign language (waived with appropriate documentation) and an 1100 SAT. Courses taken in special education may be considered. Applicants with lower GPA and test scores will be considered after 7th semester grades on a space-available basis, with priority given to those with the highest GPA.

ADDITIONAL INFORMATION

Towson University provides students with learning disabilities the necessary accommodations based on recent psychoeducational evaluations. These accommodations are based on recommendations from the evaluation. The Learning Center provides reading and study skills development services. The Writing Lab provides assistance for students who need improvement in writing skills. A quiet study area is available. Additionally, Disability Support Services provides note-takers; a resource room to be used for a quiet place to take a test; use of the services of a reader; extended testing time and other testing arrangements; student advocacy; interpretation of documentation; authorization of accommodations; assistance with implementation of reasonable accommodations; scribes and readers; short-term instructional support in time management, study and test taking strategies, and reading and writing assistance; assistive technology; and referrals for other services. Students must be registered with RFB to get taped textbooks. Those textbooks not available through RFB may be requested from Disability Support Service.

Support Services Contact Information

Learning Disability Program/Services: Disability Support Services
Director: Ronni Uhland
  E-Mail: ruhland@towson.edu
  Telephone: 410-704-2638
  Fax: 410-704-4247
Contact Person: Susan Willemin-Learning Disabilities Specialist
  E-Mail: swillemin@towson.edu
  Telephone: 410-704-2638
  Fax: 410-704-4247

LEARNING DISABILITY SERVICES

Requests for the following services/accommodations will be evaluated individually based on appropriate and current documentation.

Allowed in exams
  Calculator: Yes
  Dictionary: No
  Computer: Yes
  Spellchecker: Yes
Extended test time: Yes
Scribes: Yes
Proctors: Yes
Oral exams: Yes
Note-takers: Yes

Distraction reduced environment: Yes
Tape recording in class: Yes
Books on tape from RFBD: Yes
Taping of books not from RFBD: Yes
Accommodations for students with ADD: Yes
Reading machine: Yes
Other assistive technology: Yes
Priority registration: Yes

Added costs for services: No
LD specialists: Yes
Professional tutors: No
Peer tutors: Yes
Max. hours/wk. for services: Varies
How professors are notified of LD/ADD: By student

GENERAL ADMISSIONS INFORMATION

Director of Admissions: Louise Shulack
Telephone: 410-704-2113

ENTRANCE REQUIREMENTS

Academic units required: 4 English, 3 math, 3 science (3 science lab), 2 foreign language, 3 social studies, 6 academic electives. **Academic units recommended:** 4 English, 4 math, 3 science (3 science lab), 4 foreign language, 4 social studies.High school diploma is required and GED is accepted. ACT with Writing component required or SAT Reasoning Test. TOEFL required of all international applicants, minimum paper TOEFL 500, minimum computer TOEFL 173.

Application deadline: 2/15
Notification: Rolling
Average GPA: 3.46

Average SAT Math: NR
Average SAT Verbal: NR
Average ACT: NR

Graduated top 10% of class: 17%
Graduated top 25% of class: 48%
Graduated top 50% of class: 90%

COLLEGE GRADUATION REQUIREMENTS

Course waivers allowed: NR
Course substitutions allowed: Yes
In what course: Course substitutions are based on individual need and current documentation.

ADDITIONAL INFORMATION

Environment: The school is located on 306 landscaped and wooded acres minutes from downtown Baltimore.

Student Body:
  Undergrad enrollment: 13,627
  Women: 61%
  Men: 39%
  Percent out-of-state: 19%

Cost Information
  In-state tuition: $5,180
  Out-of-state tuition: $14,114
  Room & board: $6,828
Housing Information
  University housing: Yes
  Percent living on campus: 24%

Greek System
  Fraternity: Yes
  Sorority: Yes
Athletics: NCAA Division I

U. OF MARYLAND—COLLEGE PARK

Mitchell Building, College Park, MD 20742-5235
Phone: 301-314-8385 • Fax: 301-314-9693
E-mail: um-admit@uga.umd.edu • Web: www.maryland.edu
Support: CS • Institution type: 4-year public

LEARNING DISABILITY PROGRAM AND SERVICES

The goal of the Disability Support Services is to coordinate accommodations and services for students with learning disabilities and physical disabilities. Services are offered through the Learning Assistance Service as well through accommodations as provided by the Disability Support Services. Students are expected to facilitate contact with instructors and negotiate any special accommodations. Students may request assistance from the Service Office in handling interactions with instructors. Commonly used services include testing assistance, note-takers, readers, and priority registration. Besides the standard accommodations, students receive support through special study skills course workshops, mentoring, and support groups.

LD/ADD ADMISSIONS INFORMATION

College entrance tests required: Yes
Interview required: No
Essay required: NR
Documentation required for LD: Apititude and achievement
Documentation required for ADD: Yes
Submitted to: Both Admissions and Disability Support Services
Special Ed. HS coursework accepted: Yes

Specific course requirements of all applicants: Yes
Separate application required for program services: No
# of LD applications submitted each year: NR
# of LD applications accepted yearly: NR
Total # of students receiving LD services: 450
Acceptance into program means acceptance into college: Student must be admitted and enrolled in the university first and then request services.

ADMISSIONS

There is no special admissions or alternative admissions process for students with learning disabilities. Applicants with learning disabilities must meet general admissions criteria. The admission decision is based on courses taken in high school, which include 4 years English, 3 years social studies, 2 years lab science, 3 years math, and 2 years foreign language; GPA; SAT/ACT; class rank; personal statement; recommendations; and the psychoeducational evaluation. All freshmen applicants must submit a personal statement for admissions. The student may submit supporting documentation, which will be considered during the decision-making process. The learning disabilities coordinator may review the documentation and make a recommendation to the admissions office. The final decision rests with the Office of Admissions.

ADDITIONAL INFORMATION

There is a math lab and writing center available for all students. There is no centralized tutoring service. However, limited free tutoring is available through departments. For most tutoring needs students need to hire their own tutors. There are approximately 500 students with either LD or ADD currently receiving services or accommodations on campus. Note-takers are volunteers and could be students enrolled in the course. There is a mentoring program and support programs for students with disabilities. Priority registration is available. Services and accommodations are available to undergraduate and graduate students. There is a summer program for high school students. While it is not specifically for those with learning disabilities, these students could benefit from the program. The university is currently working on developing a special summer program for students with learning disabilities.

Support Services Contact Information

Learning Disability Program/Services: Disability Support Service (DSS)
Director: Jo Ann Hutchinson, RhD, CRC, LCPC
  E-Mail: jahutch@umd.edu
  Telephone: 301-314-7682
  Fax: 301-405-0813
Contact Person: Same

LEARNING DISABILITY SERVICES

Requests for the following services/accommodations will be evaluated individually based on appropriate and current documentation.

Allowed in exams
  Calculator: Yes
  Dictionary: No
  Computer: Yes
  Spellchecker: Yes
Extended test time: Yes
Scribes: Yes
Proctors: Yes
Oral exams: Yes
Note-takers: Yes

Distraction reduced environment: Yes
Tape recording in class: Yes
Books on tape from RFBD: Yes
Taping of books not from RFBD: Yes
Accommodations for students with ADD: Yes
Reading machine: Yes
Other assistive technology: Yes
Priority registration: Yes

Added costs for services: No
LD specialists: Yes
Professional tutors: No
Peer tutors: No
Max. hours/wk. for services: Unlimited
How professors are notified of LD/ADD: By student

GENERAL ADMISSIONS INFORMATION

Director of Admissions: Barbara Gill
Telephone: 301-314-8350

ENTRANCE REQUIREMENTS

Academic units required: 4 English, 3 math, 3 science (2 science lab), 2 foreign language, 3 social studies.
Academic units recommended: 4 math. High school diploma is required and GED is accepted. ACT with Writing component required or SAT Reasoning Test. TOEFL required of all international applicants, minimum paper TOEFL 575, minimum computer TOEFL 233.

Application deadline: 1/20
Notification: 4/1
Average GPA: 3.85

Average SAT Math: NR
Average SAT Verbal: NR
Average ACT: NR

Graduated top 10% of class: 53%
Graduated top 25% of class: 87%
Graduated top 50% of class: 99%

COLLEGE GRADUATION REQUIREMENTS

Course waivers allowed: No
Course substitutions allowed: Yes
In what course: Math, foreign language

ADDITIONAL INFORMATION

Environment: The university is in a small town setting within proximity to Washington, DC, and Baltimore.

Student Body:
  Undergrad enrollment: 24,590
  Women: 49%
  Men: 51%
  Percent out-of-state: 24%

Cost Information
  In-state tuition: $6,200
  Out-of-state tuition: $17,500
  Room & board: $7,791
Housing Information
  University housing: Yes
  Percent living on campus: 33%

Greek System
  Fraternity: Yes
  Sorority: Yes
Athletics: NCAA Division I

U. OF MARYLAND—EASTERN SHORE

Office of Admissions, Backbone Road, Princess Anne, MD 21853
Phone: 410-651-6410 • Fax: 410-651-7922
E-mail: ccmills@mail.umes.edu • Web: www.umes.edu
Support: CS • Institution type: 4-year public

LEARNING DISABILITY PROGRAM AND SERVICES

Disabled Student Services assures the commitment of the university to provide access and equal opportunity to students with disabilities admitted to the university. The Office of Services for Students with Disabilities (OSSD) assures the commitment of the University of Maryland—Eastern Shore to provide access and equal opportunity to the students with disabilities that are admitted to the university. Although there is no special curriculum for students with disabilities, OSSD is designed to assist students in maximizing the academic potential. OSSD maintains a comprehensive support network for students with disabilities. The office provides consultation with university staff, faculty, administrators, and student body to increase awareness of the needs of students with disabilities and to eliminate accessibility barriers. The OSSD focus is on supporting the positive development of students with disabilities.

LD/ADD ADMISSIONS INFORMATION

College entrance tests required: Yes
Interview required: No
Essay required: Yes
Documentation required for LD: Psychoeducational evaluation
Documentation required for ADD: Yes
Submitted to: Department of Rehabilitation/Student Development
Special Ed. HS coursework accepted: Yes

Specific course requirements of all applicants: Yes
Separate application required for program services: No
# of LD applications submitted each year: 30–40
# of LD applications accepted yearly: NR
Total # of students receiving LD services: 25–35
Acceptance into program means acceptance into college: Student must be admitted and enrolled in the university first and then request services.

ADMISSIONS

There is no special admission. All applicants must meet the same criteria. General admission requirements include 4 years English, 3 years math, 2 years foreign language, 3 years social studies; minimum SAT of 750; and minimum GPA of 2.5 are recommended. In-state students who have a high school diploma and minimum C average may be admitted on the basis on the predictive index weighting SAT scores and GPA. The PACE Summer Program is a 6-week residential program designed to provide basic skills enhancement and college orientation for any applicant whose high school grade-point averages and/or SAT scores do not meet the criteria for admission to the university. For those who do not meet regular admission standards, participation and success in the program is required as a preliminary step to admission to the university. The program offers students an opportunity to enhance their proficiency in the following fundamental skills areas: math, science, reading/study skills, writing, and college orientation. In addition, students learn to use the library to conduct research, go on cultural and scientific field trips, receive tutoring, attend seminars with key university personnel, and receive group counseling and basic skills testing. Upon successful completion of the summer program, students may be admitted. Evaluation of student performance in the program will include the successful completion of math, writing, and science components, as well as social development and adjustment to university life.

ADDITIONAL INFORMATION

Tutoring is available in every subject for all students. Developmental Skills classes are extensions of the university's academic program. At some point in their educational careers, students may find themselves in need of planned instructional assistance in reading, study skills, math and writing skills. These tutorials are taught and directed by professional staff specialists. The emphasis will be on assisting students to master college level basic skills as required in their academic programs. As a result of the placement test, many students are required to successfully complete the fundamentals of reading/study skills, math or writing classes.

Support Services Contact Information

Learning Disability Program/Services: Department of Rehabilitation/Student Development
Director: Dorling K. Joseph
 E-Mail: djoseph@mail.umes.edu
 Telephone: 410-651-6262
 Fax: 410-651-6322

LEARNING DISABILITY SERVICES

Requests for the following services/accommodations will be evaluated individually based on appropriate and current documentation.

Allowed in exams
 Calculator: Yes
 Dictionary: Yes
 Computer: Yes
 Spellchecker: Yes
Extended test time: Yes
Scribes: Yes
Proctors: Yes
Oral exams: Yes
Note-takers: Yes

Distraction reduced environment: Yes
Tape recording in class: Yes
Books on tape from RFBD: NR
Taping of books not from RFBD: Yes
**Accommodations for students with
 ADD:** Yes
Reading machine: No
Other assistive technology: No
Priority registration: No

Added costs for services: No
LD specialists: Yes
Professional tutors: No
Peer tutors: No
Max. hours/wk. for services:
 Unlimited
**How professors are notified of
 LD/ADD:** By student

GENERAL ADMISSIONS INFORMATION

Director of Admissions: Barbara Gill
Telephone: 410-651-6410

ENTRANCE REQUIREMENTS

Academic units required: 4 English, 3 math, 2 science (2 science lab), 2 foreign language, 3 social studies, 6 academic electives. High school diploma is required and GED is accepted. TOEFL required of all international applicants, minimum paper TOEFL 500, minimum computer TOEFL 173.

Application deadline: 7/15
Notification: rolling
Average GPA: 2.68

Average SAT Math: 410
Average SAT Verbal: 430
Average ACT: NR

Graduated top 10% of class: NR
Graduated top 25% of class: NR
Graduated top 50% of class: NR

COLLEGE GRADUATION REQUIREMENTS

Course waivers allowed: Yes
Course substitutions allowed: Yes
In what course: Math and foreign language

ADDITIONAL INFORMATION

Environment: The university is located on a 600-acre campus in a rural area 15 miles south of Salisbury.

Student Body:
 Undergrad enrollment: 2,704
 Women: 57%
 Men: 43%
 Percent out-of-state: 26%

Cost Information
 In-state tuition: $3,994
 Out-of-state tuition: $9,800
 Room & board: $5,800
Housing Information
 University housing: Yes
 Percent living on campus: 56%

Greek System
 Fraternity: Yes
 Sorority: Yes
Athletics: NCAA Division I

University of Maryland—Eastern Shore

AMERICAN INTERNATIONAL COLLEGE

1000 State Street, Springfield, MA 01109-3184
Phone: 413-205-3201 • Fax: 413-205-3051
E-mail: inquiry@alc.edu • Web: www.aic.edu
Support: SP • Institution type: 4-year private

LEARNING DISABILITY PROGRAM AND SERVICES

AIC believes that individuals who have LD can compensate for their difficulties and meet with success in the college environment. AIC feels that the Supportive Learning Services Program (SLSP) has all the components necessary to allow for a successful college career for a student with LD. AIC models compensatory technique and teaching strategies to enable students to be effective in college and plan for their future. Students receiving Supportive Learning Services may elect to participate in the comprehensive services offered by the Curtis Blake Center. Metacognitive strategies are taught in order to help students use their intellect more efficiently. Students are mainstreamed and may receive a minimum of two hours of tutoring/studying strategies weekly. Students create an individual educational plan with their tutor freshman year and may take as few as four courses each semester. Students generally stay in the program for four years. In addition to comprehensive services AIC also offers a limited services component which allows students with LD to reserve 5-10 hours of professional tutoring to be used over the semester. Additional hours can also be arranged for a fee.

LD/ADD ADMISSIONS INFORMATION

College entrance tests required: Yes
Interview required: No
Essay required: No
Documentation required for LD: Wechsler Adult Intelligence Scale and accompanying diagnosis, relevant diagnostic results of achievement testing
Documentation required for ADD: Diagnosis of ADD or ADD and psychoeducational assessment
Submitted to: Supportive Learning Services Program
Special Ed. HS coursework accepted: No

Specific course requirements of all applicants: Yes
Separate application required for program services: No
# of LD applications submitted each year: 300
# of LD applications accepted yearly: 35
Total # of students receiving LD services: 95
Acceptance into program means acceptance into college: Simultaneous admission decisions are made by the program and admissions.

ADMISSIONS

In addition to submitting an application to admissions, students interested in applying for the support program must also contact the coordinator of SLSP. Applicants must schedule an on-campus interview with admissions and SLSP. Applicants must submit the results of the WAIS–R and accompanying report, relevant diagnostic material, and information about supportive assistance in the past. The college requires a high school transcript and ACT/SAT scores. There should be a strong indication of achievement and motivation in the fields of knowledge studied. The majority of applicants have a GPA of 2.0-3.0. Courses required include 16 academic units from English, math, science, and social studies. Foreign language is not required. The admission decision is made simultaneously between admissions and SLSP.

ADDITIONAL INFORMATION

At the heart of the services provided is a minimum of 2 hours of regularly scheduled direct, one-to-one assistance provided by a learning specialist. The specialist develops a tailored support program based on a student's needs. Priority is given to practical assistance to help students negotiate demands of the curriculum. Provisions can be made for more basic remediation of the student's learning difficulties. Specialists assist in course selection, organizing work and study schedules, and as a resource. Students have access to skills seminars in many areas. Classes in reading, spelling, math, study strategies, time management, written language, and handwriting are offered. The Supportive Learning Services Center is only open to students who are participating in the program. Services and accommodations are available to undergraduate and graduate students.

Support Services Contact Information

Learning Disability Program/Services: Supportive Learning Services Program
Director: Prof. Mary M. Saltus
  E-Mail: cbc2@aicstudent.com
  Telephone: 413-205-3426
  Fax: 413-205-3908
Contact Person: Anne Midura
  E-Mail: cbc2@aicstudent.com
  Telephone: 413-205-3426
  Fax: 413-205-3908

LEARNING DISABILITY SERVICES

Requests for the following services/accommodations will be evaluated individually based on appropriate and current documentation.

Allowed in exams
  Calculator: Yes
  Dictionary: No
  Computer: Yes
  Spellchecker: Yes
Extended test time: Yes
Scribes: Yes
Proctors: Yes
Oral exams: Yes
Note-takers: No

Distraction reduced environment: Yes
Tape recording in class: Yes
Books on tape from RFBD: Yes
Taping of books not from RFBD: Yes
**Accommodations for students with
  ADD:** Yes
Reading machine: Yes
Other assistive technology: Yes
Priority registration: No

Added costs for services: Yes
LD specialists: Yes
Professional tutors: 9
Peer tutors: No
Max. hours/wk. for services: 5
**How professors are notified of
  LD/ADD:** By both student and director

GENERAL ADMISSIONS INFORMATION

Director of Admissions: Peter Miller
Telephone: 413-205-3201

ENTRANCE REQUIREMENTS

Academic units required: 4 English, 2 math, 2 science (1 science lab), 1 social studies, 1 history, 5 academic electives. **Academic units recommended:** 4 English, 3 math, 2 science (1 science lab), 2 foreign language, 1 social studies, 1 history, 3 academic electives. High school diploma is required and GED is accepted. ACT with or without Writing component accepted. TOEFL required of all international applicants, minimum paper TOEFL 500, minimum computer TOEFL 173.

Application deadline: Rolling
Notification: Rolling
Average GPA: 2.9

Average SAT Math: 487
Average SAT Verbal: 456
Average ACT: NR

Graduated top 10% of class: 15%
Graduated top 25% of class: 25%
Graduated top 50% of class: 70%

COLLEGE GRADUATION REQUIREMENTS

Course waivers allowed: No
Course substitutions allowed: Yes
In what course: Foreign language not required for graduation. May use pass/fail option for math.

ADDITIONAL INFORMATION

Environment: The school is located on 58 acres in Springfield, 75 miles west of Boston and 30 miles north of Hartford.

Student Body:
  Undergrad enrollment: 1,227
  Women: 53%
  Men: 47%
  Percent out-of-state: 53%

Cost Information
  Tuition: $18,000
  Room & board: $8,390
Housing Information
  University housing: Yes
  Percent living on campus: 55%

Greek System
  Fraternity: Yes
  Sorority: Yes
Athletics: NCAA Division II

BOSTON COLLEGE

140 Commonwealth Ave., Devlin Hall 208, Chestnut Hill, MA 02467-3809
Phone: 617-552-3100 • Fax: 617-552-0798
E-mail: ugadmis@bc.edu • Web: www.bc.edu
Support: CS • Institution type: 4-year private

LEARNING DISABILITY PROGRAM AND SERVICES

There is no specific program at Boston College for students with LD. The Academic Development Center (ADC) offers instructional support to faculty and graduate students, special services to students with LD, and tutoring and skills workshops to all Boston College students. The ADC provides academic support to more that 250 BC students with LD. The ADC aims to help students with LD to become independent learners who understand their abilities and disabilities and can act effectively as self-advocates. The ADC also offers free tutoring to all students at BC. All tutors receive training and must be recommended or approved by the chair of the department for which the student will tutor. Students who are seeking support services are required to submit documentation to verify eligibility. Testing must be current, comprehensive, performed by a certified LD specialist or licensed psychologist, and there must be clear and specific evidence of a LD. Educational recommendations regarding the impact of the disability and accommodations recommended at the postsecondary level must be included. Documentation for ADD must include an in depth evaluation from the psychiatrist/psychologist/physician who made the diagnosis as well as specific educational recommendations.

LD/ADD ADMISSIONS INFORMATION

College entrance tests required: Yes

Interview required: No
Essay required: No
Documentation required for LD: Psychological evaluation no less than 3 years old
Documentation required for ADD: Yes
Submitted to: Admissions and then academic Development Center
Special Ed. HS coursework accepted: No

Specific course requirements of all applicants: Yes
Separate application required for program services: No
# of LD applications submitted each year: NR
# of LD applications accepted yearly: NR
Total # of students receiving LD services: 325
Acceptance into program means acceptance into college: Student must be admitted and enrolled in the college first and then request services.

ADMISSIONS

Students with LD, who self-disclose during the admission process, may receive a second review by the committee on learning disabilities. Some students may be given the option of a summer admit into a transition program the summer prior to freshman year. General admission requirements for BC are very competitive. The mid 50 percent for the SAT is 1230–1370. SATI Subject Tests are required in writing, math and one additional subject. It is recommended that students have 4 years of English, 4 years of foreign language, 4 years of math, 3 years of science and 3 years of social studies. All students must submit an essay and interviews are recommended. Students with LD who may be deficient in foreign language or math should provide documentation and request a substitution for these courses. Documentation of the LD should be sent to the Office of Admission. Students are encouraged to self-disclose during the admission process.

ADDITIONAL INFORMATION

Services offered by the Academic Development Center include a Summer Transition Program for entering freshmen students with LD, screening sessions for students who may have LD, individual consultations with a learning specialist, letters to faculty confirming and explaining the LD, reduced course load during the academic year combined with summer school, access to textbooks on tape, testing in a distraction-free room, workshops on study skills and time management, and small group seminars on learning strategies.

Support Services Contact Information

Learning Disability Program/Services: Academic Development Center
Director: Dr. Kathleen Duggan
  E-Mail: kathleen.duggan@bc.edu
  Telephone: 617-552-8055
  Fax: 617-552-6075

LEARNING DISABILITY SERVICES

Requests for the following services/accommodations will be evaluated individually based on appropriate and current documentation.

Allowed in exams	Distraction reduced environment: Yes	Added costs for services: No
Calculator: Y/N	Tape recording in class: Yes	LD specialists: Yes
Dictionary: Y/N	Books on tape from RFBD: Yes	Professional tutors: No
Computer: Yes	Taping of books not from RFBD: No	Peer tutors: Yes
Spellchecker: Yes	Accommodations for students with	Max. hours/wk. for services: N/A
Extended test time: Yes	ADD: Yes	How professors are notified of
Scribes: Yes	Reading machine: Yes	LD/ADD: By both student and director
Proctors: Yes	Other assistive technology: Yes	
Oral exams: No	Priority registration: Yes	
Note-takers: Yes		

GENERAL ADMISSIONS INFORMATION

Director of Admissions: John Mahoney
Telephone: 617-552-3100

ENTRANCE REQUIREMENTS

Academic units recommended: 4 English, 4 math, 4 science (4 science lab), 4 foreign language. High school diploma is required and GED is accepted. ACT with Writing component required OR SAT Reasoning Tests. TOEFL required of all international applicants, minimum paper TOEFL 600, minimum computer TOEFL 250.

Application deadline: 1/2	Average SAT Math: 670	Graduated top 10% of class: 74%
Notification: 4/15	Average SAT Verbal: 645	Graduated top 25% of class: 95%
Average GPA: NR	Average ACT: NR	Graduated top 50% of class: 99%

COLLEGE GRADUATION REQUIREMENTS

Course waivers allowed: No
Course substitutions allowed: Yes
In what course: Foreign language

ADDITIONAL INFORMATION

Environment: Located six miles from downtown Boston.

Student Body:	Cost Information	Greek System
Undergrad enrollment: 9,059	Tuition: $28,940	Fraternity: No
Women: 53%	Room & board: $10,580	Sorority: No
Men: 47%	Housing Information	Athletics: NCAA Division I
Percent out-of-state: 72%	University housing: Yes	
	Percent living on campus: 78%	

BOSTON UNIVERSITY

121 Bay State Road, Boston, MA 02215
Phone: 617-353-2300 • Fax: 617-353-9695
E-mail: admissions@bu.edu • Web: www.bu.edu
Support: CS • Institution type: 4-year private

LEARNING DISABILITY PROGRAM AND SERVICES

Boston University recognizes that many students with a learning disability, attention disorder, or a mental disability can succeed in a university if they are provided with support services and appropriate accommodations. The Office of Disability Services, including its division of Learning Disability Support Services (LDSS), is committed to assisting individuals with disabilities in achieving fulfillment and success in all aspects of university life. As part of the Office of the Vice President and Dean of Students, the primary objective of LDSS is to foster academic excellence, personal responsibility and leadership growth in students with disabilities through vigorous programming and the provision of reasonable accommodation services. LDSS seeks to further this commitment through the promotion of independence and self-advocacy in students with LD, ADD, or other cognitive disabilities. The university does not waive program requirements or permit substitutions for required courses. Several degree programs have foreign language or mathematics requirements. The university considers these degree requirements essential to its programs.

LD/ADD ADMISSIONS INFORMATION

College entrance tests required: Yes
Interview required: No
Essay required: No
Documentation required for LD: Psychoeducational
  evaluation less than 3 years old
Documentation required for ADD: Yes
Submitted to: Office of Disabitility Services
Special Ed. HS coursework accepted: No

Specific course requirements of all applicants: Yes
Separate application required for program services: No
# of LD applications submitted each year: NR
# of LD applications accepted yearly: NR
Total # of students receiving LD services: 550
**Acceptance into program means acceptance into
  college:** Student must be admitted and enrolled in the
  university first and then request to be considered for
  services.

ADMISSIONS

All admissions decisions are made on an individualized basis by the Office of Undergraduate Admissions. Because requirements may vary substantially depending upon the college or program within the university, students are encouraged to contact BU for information regarding admissions requirements. BU expects that students with disabilities, including those with LD, will meet the same competitive admissions criteria as their peers without disabilities. Thus, there are no special admissions procedures for applicants with LD. The Office of Disability Services does not participate in any way in the application process or in admissions decisions. Admissions is based on the strength of a student's secondary school record. Teacher and counselor recommendations and other personal qualifications as demonstrated by extracurricular activities are evaluated and weighed before admission decisions are made. The essay is considered a significant part of the application process. In school or out of school activities are important, and it is helpful if there is a match between the student's experiences or academic interests and the opportunities available at Boston University.

ADDITIONAL INFORMATION

LDSS offers support services to students with LD/ADD including access to academic accommodations for which the student is eligible, counseling and support in self-advocacy, assistive technology, and LDSS skills workshops for academic and study strategies, note-taking, time management, and self-advocacy. Students are active in the accommodation process, and notify faculty about the implementation of approved accommodations. Students needing more extensive support may enroll in Comprehensive Services, a fee-based program offering one-to-one strategy tutoring with a professional learning specialist. Tutoring includes writing development, critical reading, note-taking, study skills, testing strategies, time management, and organization. Tutoring is tailored to an individual learning profile of strengths and weaknesses, academic program, other resources, and personal goals. The Enhanced Services strategy plan is designed in collaboration with the student, the learning specialist, and LDSS professional staff. In order to be considered for LDS services, admitted students must submit the results of a comprehensive evaluation done within the past three years, including (but not limited to) level intelligence and achievement testing.

Support Services Contact Information

Learning Disability Program/Services: Office of Disability Services
Director: Allan Macurdy
  E-Mail: amacurdy@bu.edu
  Telephone: 617-353-3658
  Fax: 617-353-9646
Contact Person: Dr. Lorraine Wolf, Clinical Director
  E-Mail: lwolf@bu.edu
  Telephone: 617-353-3658
  Fax: 617-353-9446

LEARNING DISABILITY SERVICES

Requests for the following services/accommodations will be evaluated individually based on appropriate and current documentation.

Allowed in exams
  Calculator: Yes
  Dictionary: No
  Computer: Yes
  Spellchecker: Yes
Extended test time: Yes
Scribes: Yes
Proctors: Yes
Oral exams: Yes
Note-takers: Yes

Distraction reduced environment: Yes
Tape recording in class: Yes
Books on tape from RFBD: Yes
Taping of books not from RFBD: Yes
Accommodations for students with
  ADD: Yes
Reading machine: Yes
Other assistive technology: Yes
Priority registration: No

Added costs for services: Yes
LD specialists: Yes
Professional tutors: 8
Peer tutors: No
Max. hours/wk. for services: 4
How professors are notified of
  LD/ADD: By student

GENERAL ADMISSIONS INFORMATION

Director of Admissions: Ms. Kelly A. Walter
  Telephone: 617-353-2300

ENTRANCE REQUIREMENTS
Academic units required: 4 English, 3 math, 3 science (3 science lab), 2 foreign language, 3 social studies.
Academic units recommended: 4 English, 4 math, 4 science (4 science lab), 4 foreign language, 4 social studies.
High school diploma is required and GED is accepted. ACT with Writing component required or SAT Reasoning Test.
TOEFL required of all international applicants, minimum paper TOEFL 550, minimum computer TOEFL 215.

Application deadline: 1/1
Notification: 3/15–4/15
Average GPA: 3.50

Average SAT Math: 656
Average SAT Verbal: 643
Average ACT: 28

Graduated top 10% of class: 60%
Graduated top 25% of class: 92%
Graduated top 50% of class: 100%

COLLEGE GRADUATION REQUIREMENTS

Course waivers allowed: No
Course substitutions allowed: No
In what course: N/A

ADDITIONAL INFORMATION

Environment: The university is located on a 131-acre campus in an urban area.

Student Body:
  Undergrad enrollment: 15,953
  Women: 60%
  Men: 40%
  Percent out-of-state: 77%

Cost Information
  Tuition: $29,988
  Room & board: $9,680
Housing Information
  University housing: Yes
  Percent living on campus: 74%

Greek System
  Fraternity: Yes
  Sorority: Yes
Athletics: NCAA Division I

CLARK UNIVERSITY

950 Main Street, Worcester, MA 01610-1477
Phone: 508-793-7431 • Fax: 508-793-8821
E-mail: admissions@clarku.edu • Web: www.clarku.edu
Support: CS • Institution type: 4-year private

LEARNING DISABILITY PROGRAM AND SERVICES

The learning disabilities services at Clark University, based within the Academic Advising Center, was developed to advocate and support the needs of the student with learning disabilities in a college environment. Strategies are developed to help the student with learning disabilities cope with the increased demands of the college curriculum. Resources are available to students who experience difficulties, and who may require some support or wish to learn more about their own learning styles. Support services in the AAC are coordinated with services offered by the university's Writing Center, Math Clinic, and dean of students. The most successful students are the ones who accept their disability, develop good self-advocacy skills, and are capable of good time management. The ultimate goal of Special Services is to help students improve their self-awareness and self-advocacy skills, and to assist them in being successful and independent in college.

LD/ADD ADMISSIONS INFORMATION

College entrance tests required: Yes
Interview required: No
Essay required: No
Documentation required for LD: An evaluation completed within the last 3 years by a qualified diagnostician; must include the WAIS–III with subtest scores and achievement tests reflecting scores in the area of the student's learning disability
Documentation required for ADD: Documentation diagnosing the disability by a relevantly trained physician and or other relevantly trained professionals
Submitted to: Disability Services

Specific course requirements of all applicants: Yes
Special Ed. HS coursework accepted: Yes
Separate application required for program services: No
# of LD applications submitted each year: NR
# of LD applications accepted yearly: NR
Total # of students receiving LD services: NR
Acceptance into program means acceptance into college: Student must be admitted and enrolled in the university first and then request services.

ADMISSIONS

Special Services and the Office of Undergraduate Admissions work together in considering students for admission. Admission is based on ability, rather than disability. Applicants must meet standard admissions requirements. An interview with Clark's Special Services Office is highly recommended. If a student requires any classroom accommodations or support services, a diagnostic assessment completed within the last two years must be submitted, documenting the learning disability. This documentation is needed to evaluate the applicant's needs and determine what services the university can provide. The university looks at a student's upward trend in high school, as well as the challenge of the curriculum and the number of mainstream courses. Some special education courses in freshman year may be allowed if they have been followed by a college-prep curriculum during the rest of high school. The director of Special Services makes a recommendation to admissions about the applicant, but the final decision rests with the Office of Admission. The university feels that successful candidates for admission should have a strong senior year course load (at least four, preferably five, solid academic courses).

ADDITIONAL INFORMATION

An early orientation program two days prior to general orientation is designed to meet the needs of entering students with LD. This program is highly recommended as it provides intensive exposure to academic services on campus. Students take a reading comprehension and writing exam, and results are used to match students to the most appropriate academic program. Graduate students work with students on time management and organizational skills. Although note-takers are available, Special Services supplements with taping of lectures, and highly recommends that students use a cassette recorder with a count. It is also recommended that freshmen students take only three courses for the first semester. All students must complete one math course in basic algebra prior to graduating. The overall GPA of freshmen receiving services from Special Services is a 2.7. Clark offers space to an outside LD specialist who will provide tutoring and services for a fee. Services and accommodations are available to undergraduates and graduates.

Support Services Contact Information

Learning Disability Program/Services: Disability Services
Director: Sharon de Klerk
  E-Mail: sdeklerk@clarku.edu
  Telephone: 508-793-7468
  Fax: 508-421-3700
Contact Person: Danielle Early
  E-Mail: dearly@clarku.edu
  Telephone: 508-793-7431

LEARNING DISABILITY SERVICES

Requests for the following services/accommodations will be evaluated individually based on appropriate and current documentation.

Allowed in exams
  Calculator: Yes
  Dictionary: Yes
  Computer: Yes
  Spellchecker: Yes
Extended test time: Yes
Scribes: No
Proctors: Yes
Oral exams: No
Note-takers: Yes

Distraction reduced environment: Yes
Tape recording in class: Yes
Books on tape from RFBD: Yes
Taping of books not from RFBD: No
Accommodations for students with
  ADD: Yes
Reading machine: No
Other assistive technology: Yes
Priority registration: Yes

Added costs for services: No
LD specialists: Yes
Professional tutors: No
Peer tutors: No
Max. hours/wk. for services: N/A
How professors are notified of
  LD/ADD: By both student and director

GENERAL ADMISSIONS INFORMATION

Director of Admissions: Harold Wingood
Telephone: 508-793-7431

ENTRANCE REQUIREMENTS

Academic units recommended: 4 English, 3 math, 3 science (2 science lab), 2 foreign language, 2 social studies, 2 history. High school diploma is required and GED is accepted. ACT with or without Writing component accepted. TOEFL required of all international applicants, minimum paper TOEFL 550, minimum computer TOEFL 213.

Application deadline: 2/1
Notification: 4/1
Average GPA: 3.40

Average SAT Math: 588
Average SAT Verbal: 593
Average ACT: 25

Graduated top 10% of class: 31%
Graduated top 25% of class: 72%
Graduated top 50% of class: 99%

COLLEGE GRADUATION REQUIREMENTS

Course waivers allowed: No
Course substitutions allowed: Yes
In what course: Foreign language with documentation

ADDITIONAL INFORMATION

Environment: The university is located on 45 acres in a small city 38 miles west of Boston.

Student Body:
  Undergrad enrollment: 2,082
  Women: 61%
  Men: 39%
  Percent out-of-state: 60%

Cost Information
  Tuition: $29,300
  Room & board: $5,400
Housing Information
  University housing: Yes
  Percent living on campus: 77%

Greek System
  Fraternity: No
  Sorority: No
Athletics: NCAA Division III

CURRY COLLEGE

1071 Blue Hill Avenue, Milton, MA 02186
Phone: 617-333-2210 • Fax: 617-333-2114
E-mail: curryadm@curry.edu • Web: www.curry.edu
Support: SP • Institution type: 4-year private

LEARNING DISABILITY PROGRAM AND SERVICES

The Program for Advancement of Learning (PAL) at Curry College is a comprehensive individualized program for students with specific learning disabilities. Students in PAL participate fully in Curry College coursework and extracurricular activities. The goal of PAL is to facilitate students' understanding of their individual learning styles and to help them achieve independence as learners. Students' empowerment is developed via intensive study of their own strengths, needs, and learning styles. PAL is a place where students are honored for the strengths and talents they bring to the learning process and are given the chance to demonstrate their abilities. PAL students are leaders on campus. PAL summer program is a three-week course that is strongly recommended for new students to ease the transition and provide excellent preparation.

LD/ADD ADMISSIONS INFORMATION

College entrance tests required: Yes
Interview required: No
Essay required: Yes
Documentation required for LD: Psychoeducational evaluation
Documentation required for ADD: Yes
Submitted to: Program for Advancement of Learning
Special Ed. HS coursework accepted: Yes

Specific course requirements of all applicants: Yes
Separate application required for program services: Yes
# of LD applications submitted each year: 700
# of LD applications accepted yearly: 175
Total # of students receiving LD services: 400
Acceptance into program means acceptance into college: Student must be admitted and enrolled in the college first and then request services.

ADMISSIONS

Applicants must submit the regular application, fee, official transcript, SAT or ACT (recommended), and counselor or teacher recommendation. Courses required for general admission include: 4 English, 3 math, 2 science, 2 science lab, 1 social studies, 1 history, and 5 electives. For admission into the Program for Advancement in Learning the following needs to be submitted: diagnostic evaluations and other material which describe a specific learning disability; testing that includes the WAIS—III or WAIS—R accompanied by a narrative report, administered within two years of application; achievement testing indicating current levels in areas such as reading, written language and math. An IEP (individualized educational plan) or its equivalent is requested, if available. Interviews on campus are strongly recommended, and may be required of some applicants. Space is limited for the program. Students applying to PAL are not required to submit SAT or ACT scores. Admission decisions are made jointly by PAL and the Office of Admissions.

ADDITIONAL INFORMATION

PAL students must committ to the program for at least one year, and have the option to continue with full or partial support beyond the first year. A three-week, three-credit summer PAL orientation session is strongly recommended. Students meet regularly with their own PAL instructor who is a learning specialist. The focus is on using strengths to improve skills in areas such as listening, speaking, reading, writing, organization and time management, note-taking, and test-taking skills. Students also receive help with readings, papers, and assignments for classes as the basis for learning about their unique learning style. The specialist reviews diagnostic testing to help the student understand the profile of strengths and needs. Students earn three credits toward graduation for the first year. Skills classes, for credit, are offered through the Essential Skills Center in developmental reading, writing, and math. Diagnostic testing is available through the Educational Diagnostic Center at PAL.

Support Services Contact Information

Learning Disability Program/Services: Program for Advancement of Learning (PAL)
Director: Dr. Lisa Ijiri
  E-Mail: curryadm@curry.edu
  Telephone: 617-333-2250
  Fax: 617-333-2018
Contact Person: Dr. Susan Pratt, Coordinator
  E-Mail: curryadm@curry.edu
  Telephone: 617-333-2250
  Fax: 617-333-2018

LEARNING DISABILITY SERVICES

Requests for the following services/accommodations will be evaluated individually based on appropriate and current documentation.

Allowed in exams
  Calculator: Yes
  Dictionary: Yes
  Computer: Yes
  Spellchecker: Yes
Extended test time: Yes
Scribes: No
Proctors: Yes
Oral exams: Y/N
Note-takers: Y/N

Distraction reduced environment: Yes
Tape recording in class: Yes
Books on tape from RFBD: Yes
Taping of books not from RFBD: Yes
Accommodations for students with
  ADD: Yes
Reading machine: Y/N
Other assistive technology: Yes
Priority registration: No

Added costs for services: Yes
LD specialists: Yes
Professional tutors: Yes
Peer tutors: No
Max. hours/wk. for services: 2.5
How professors are notified of
  LD/ADD: By student

GENERAL ADMISSIONS INFORMATION

Director of Admissions: Burt Batty
Telephone: 617-333-2210

ENTRANCE REQUIREMENTS
Academic units required: 4 English, 3 math, 2 science (2 science lab), 1 social studies, 1 history, 5 academic electives. High school diploma is required and GED is accepted. TOEFL required of all international applicants, minimum paper TOEFL 500, minimum computer TOEFL 173.

Application deadline: 3/1
Notification: Rolling
Average GPA: 2.3

Average SAT Math: 420
Average SAT Verbal: 440
Average ACT: NR

Graduated top 10% of class: 5%
Graduated top 25% of class: 22%
Graduated top 50% of class: 65%

COLLEGE GRADUATION REQUIREMENTS

Course waivers allowed: No
Course substitutions allowed: Yes
In what course: Varies

ADDITIONAL INFORMATION

Environment: Curry's 120-acre campus is minutes from metropolitan Boston.

Student Body:
  Undergrad enrollment: 1,709
  Women: 53%
  Men: 47%
  Percent out-of-state: 40%

Cost Information
  Tuition: $21,530
  Room & board: $8,700
Housing Information
  University housing: Yes
  Percent living on campus: 60%

Greek System
  Fraternity: Yes
  Sorority: Yes
Athletics: NCAA Division III

DEAN COLLEGE

Office of Admission, 99 Main Street, Franklin, MA 02038-1994
Phone: 508-541-1508
E-mail: admissions@dean.edu • Web: www.dean.edu
Support: SP • Institution type: 2-year private

LEARNING DISABILITY PROGRAM AND SERVICES

Dean College faculty and staff are committed to maintaining a caring and nurturing environment. While much of this support comes in the form of informal, face-to-face interactions, students will find that a number of programs have been developed specifically to provide students with structured guidance in both academics and student life. The Learning Center offers student academic support and assistance through the Berenson Writing Center, the Math Tutoring Program, Disability Support Services, and course-specific tutoring. Personalized Learning Services offers a comprehensive system of support for students with documented learning disabilities. Learning specialists work with students to develop customized programs that address both short-term goals and the skills and knowledge that create a foundation for success in future academic and professional settings. The goal of PLS is to assist students in becoming confident, successful, independent learners. This program is designed to help all students achieve their academic goals. The FACTS Advising Center (Financial, Academic, Career, Transfer, and Student life) provides comprehensive assistance and information to students. Students are assigned a personal advising team to guide them as they move through the academic year.

LD/ADD ADMISSIONS INFORMATION

College entrance tests required: Yes
Interview required: No
Essay required: Yes
Documentation required for LD: WAIS–III; WJ
Documentation required for ADD: Yes
Submitted to: Disability Support Services
Special Ed. HS coursework accepted: Yes

Specific course requirements of all applicants: No
Separate application required for program services: No
# of LD applications submitted each year: 50
# of LD applications accepted yearly: 25
Total # of students receiving LD services: 70
Acceptance into program means acceptance into college: Student must be admitted and enrolled in the college first and then reviewed for LD services.

ADMISSIONS

There is no special admission process for students with learning disabilities. All students submit the same general application. Every application is carefully reviewed by admissions, and students are selected based on their academic performance in high school, recommendations, and personal accomplishments. Students who self-disclose and submit documentation may have their materials reviewed by the LD specialist, who will make a recommendation to admissions. There is no simple formula applied to an application. The dean strives to make the best match between what it offers as an institution and each student's skills, interests, and abilities. Interviews are highly recommended. Students should have college-prep, including 4 years English and 3 years math. Interviews are not required but students must submit a counselor recommendation. SAT/ACT are required, but viewed as less important than school records. Students who do not meet the general admission requirements may be considered for conditional admission through successful completion of the Summer Bridge Program.

ADDITIONAL INFORMATION

Accommodations may include, but are not limited to, taped texts, access to computers, scribes and note-takers, alternative testing modes, and extended time for testing. The Learning Center provides free academic assistance and support services for all students through tutoring, workshops, and study groups. Professional and peer tutors are available throughout the day to assist students in developing writing, math, and study skills, and to provide course-specific tutoring. Personalized Learning Services offers tutorial support to students with documented LD, unique learning styles or other diagnosed learning needs. Students meet weekly with LD specialists one-to-one or in small groups. Learning and study strategies taught by specialists include test-taking, test preparation, note-taking skills, time management, academic organization, reading comprehension, research and writing skills, and self-awareness and advocacy. The fee is $700 to $3,500 per semester.

Support Services Contact Information

Learning Disability Program/Services: Disability Support Services
Director: Anne Smith, Ph.D.
  E-Mail: asmith@dean.edu
  Telephone: 508-541-1764
  Fax: 508-541-1829
Contact Person: Kendra Slatkavitz
  E-Mail: kslatkavitz@dean.edu
  Telephone: 508-541-1768
  Fax: 508-541-1829

LEARNING DISABILITY SERVICES

Requests for the following services/accommodations will be evaluated individually based on appropriate and current documentation.

Allowed in exams
  Calculator: Yes
  Dictionary: Yes
  Computer: Yes
  Spellchecker: Yes
Extended test time: Yes
Scribes: Yes
Proctors: Yes
Oral exams: Yes
Note-takers: Yes

Distraction reduced environment: Yes
Tape recording in class: Yes
Books on tape from RFBD: Yes
Taping of books not from RFBD: Yes
**Accommodations for students with
  ADD:** Yes
Reading machine: Yes
Other assistive technology: Yes
Priority registration: No

Added costs for services: Yes
LD specialists: Yes
Professional tutors: 15
Peer tutors: 12-18
Max. hours/wk. for services: 5
**How professors are notified of
  LD/ADD:** By both student and director

GENERAL ADMISSIONS INFORMATION

Director of Admissions: Kathleen Lynch
Telephone: 508-541-1508

ENTRANCE REQUIREMENTS

16 total recommended: 4 English, 3 math, 3 science, 2 foreign language, 4 social studies.

Application deadline: Rolling
Notification: Rolling
Average GPA: 2.0

Average SAT Math: 450
Average SAT Verbal: 450
Average ACT: NR

Graduated top 10% of class: NR
Graduated top 25% of class: NR
Graduated top 50% of class: NR

COLLEGE GRADUATION REQUIREMENTS

Course waivers allowed: No
Course substitutions allowed: No
In what course: N/A

ADDITIONAL INFORMATION

Environment: The campus is in a small town near Boston.

Student Body:
  Undergrad enrollment: 850
  Women: 45%
  Men: 55%
  Percent out-of-state: 57%

Cost Information
  Tuition: $22,650
  Room & board: $9,700
Housing Information
  University housing: Yes
  Percent living on campus: 90%

Greek System
  Fraternity: NoR
  Sorority: No
  Athletics: NJCAA

EMERSON COLLEGE

120 Boylston Street, Boston, MA 02116-4624
Phone: 617-824-8600 • Fax: 617-824-8609
E-mail: admission@emerson.edu • Web: www.emerson.edu
Support: CS • Institution type: 4-year private

LEARNING DISABILITY PROGRAM AND SERVICES

Emerson College is committed to providing equal access to its academic, residential, and social activities to all qualified students. The college makes every effort to accommodate individuals with disabilities according to ADA and Section 504 of the Rehabilitation Act. Emerson offers services through the Disabilities Services Office (DSO) to students with documented physical, visual, hearing, learning, or psychiatric disabilities. The Disabilities Service Coordinator is the primary contact person for all students with disabilities. Emerson does not require students with disabilities to register with the DSO; however, students with accommodation needs will need to register to take advantage of the services. Students must register in a timely manner in order to have accommodations or services in place when needed. Students must also provide appropriate documentation of the disability. This documentation must be prepared by qualified professionals, and will serve as a basis for determining appropriate accommodations.

LD/ADD ADMISSIONS INFORMATION

College entrance tests required: Yes
Interview required: No
Essay required: No
Documentation required for LD: Students typically supply documentation recommended by ETS (Educational Testing Service) such as the Wechsler Adult Intelligence Scale, Woodcock-Johnson, Kaufman Adolescent and Adult Intelligence Test, or Stanford-Binet
Documentation required for ADD: Yes
Submitted to: Disability Services
Special Ed. HS coursework accepted: N/A

Specific course requirements of all applicants: Yes
Separate application required for program services: No
# of LD applications submitted each year: NR
# of LD applications accepted yearly: NR
Total # of students receiving LD services: NR
Acceptance into program means acceptance into college: Student must be admitted and enrolled in college and then may request services

ADMISSIONS

Admission is competitive. In choosing candidates for the entering class, Emerson looks for students who present academic promise in their secondary school record, recommendations, and writing competency, as well as personal qualities as seen in extracurricular activities, community involvement, and demonstrated leadership. There is no separate application for students with learning disabilities. A complete application includes the Emerson application form and application fee, application essay, an official secondary school transcript, 2 letters of recommendation (one from a guidance counselor/college advisor and the other from a teacher of an academic subject), and official SAT or ACT test results. The academic preparation of successful candidates should include 4 years of English and 3 years each of mathematics, science, social science, and a single foreign language.

ADDITIONAL INFORMATION

Emerson offers services through its Disability Services Office to students with documented disabilities. Services are determined on an individual basis with appropriate documentation. The college's Learning Assistance Center offers reading tutorials, writing assistance, and seminars on such topics as strengthening study skills, improving time management, and conducting library searches. Course-specific tutorials can also be arranged.

Support Services Contact Information

Learning Disability Program/Services: Disability Services Office
Director: Dr. Anthony Bashir
  E-Mail: dso@emerson.edu
  Telephone: 617-824-8415
  Fax: 617-824-8941

LEARNING DISABILITY SERVICES

Requests for the following services/accommodations will be evaluated individually based on appropriate and current documentation.

Allowed in exams
  Calculator: Yes
  Dictionary: Yes
  Computer: Yes
  Spellchecker: Yes
Extended test time: Yes
Scribes: Yes
Proctors: Yes
Oral exams: Yes
Note-takers: Yes

Distraction reduced environment: Yes
Tape recording in class: Yes
Books on tape from RFBD: No
Taping of books not from RFBD: No
Accommodations for students with
  ADD: Yes
Reading machine: Yes
Other assistive technology: Yes
Priority registration: N/A

Added costs for services: No
LD specialists: Yes
Professional tutors: No
Peer tutors: 14
Max. hours/wk. for services: 4
How professors are notified of
  LD/ADD: By both student and director

GENERAL ADMISSIONS INFORMATION

Director of Admissions: Sara S. Ramirez
Telephone: 617-824-8600

ENTRANCE REQUIREMENTS

Academic units required: 4 English, 3 math, 3 science, 3 foreign language, 3 social studies. **Academic units recommended:** 4 English, 3 math, 3 science, 3 foreign language, 3 social studies, 4 academic electives. High school diploma is required and GED is accepted. ACT with Writing component required or SAT Reasoning test. TOEFL required of all international applicants, minimum paper TOEFL 550, minimum computer TOEFL 213.

Application deadline: 1/15
Notification: 4/1
Average GPA: 3.53

Average SAT Math: 591
Average SAT Verbal: 628
Average ACT: 26

Graduated top 10% of class: 32%
Graduated top 25% of class: 77%
Graduated top 50% of class: 99%

COLLEGE GRADUATION REQUIREMENTS

Course waivers allowed: Yes
Course substitutions allowed: Yes
In what course: Documentation-specific

ADDITIONAL INFORMATION

Environment: Emerson's campus is located on Boston Common in the heart of the city's theater district.

Student Body:
  Undergrad enrollment: 3,076
  Women: 58%
  Men: 42%
  Percent out-of-state: 63%

Cost Information
  Tuition: $22,976
  Room & board: $10,118
Housing Information
  University housing: Yes
  Percent living on campus: 42%

Greek System
  Fraternity: Yes
  Sorority: Yes
Athletics: NCAA Division III

FITCHBURG STATE UNIVERSITY

160 Pearl Street, Fitchburg, MA 01420-2697
Phone: 978-665-3144 • Fax: 978-665-4540
E-mail: admissions@fsc.edu • Web: www.fsc.edu
Support: S • Institution type: 4-year public

LEARNING DISABILITY PROGRAM AND SERVICES

The Disability Services Office provides individually tailored support services and programs for students with disabilities. Disability Services empowers eligible students to succeed by striving to assure equal access and opportunity of curricular and extra-curricular activities. Student autonomy is encouraged through the provision of reasonable accommodations, services, training in the use of assistive technology, self advocacy, and leadership.

LD/ADD ADMISSIONS INFORMATION

College entrance tests required: Yes
Interview required: No
Essay required: No
Documentation required for LD: IEP, psychological
   evaluation, Warsle, Johnson
Documentation required for ADD: Yes
Submitted to: Admissions and Disability Services
Special Ed. HS coursework accepted: No

Specific course requirements of all applicants: Yes
Separate application required for program services: No
# of LD applications submitted each year: NR
# of LD applications accepted yearly: NR
Total # of students receiving LD services: 80
**Acceptance into program means acceptance into
   college:** Student must be remitted and enrolled in the
   university and then request services.

ADMISSIONS

The admissions office forwards folders for students with documented disabilities, who have waived the SAT or foreign language entrance requirement, or have requested evaluation by the admissions advocacy committee for students with disabilities. Students may opt to come in for an interview with staff from the Office of Disability Services. Review by the Admissions Advocacy Committee can be requested by the candidate. General admission requirements include 16 Carnegie units (college-prep classes). GPA is based on all college-prep courses and weights Honors and Advanced Placement courses. The college looks for a minimum weighted GPA of 3.0. However, the Admissions Committee will consider applicants with GPAs between 2.0 and 2.99 if they submit SAT/ACT scores meeting the sliding scale requirements. Applicants who do not meet the sliding scale requirements will be considered on an individual basis for a limited number of admission exceptions. Meeting the minimum GPA and SAT/ACT requirements does not guarantee admission to the college. Applicants who meet the 3.0 GPA requirements do not have to use the sliding scale for admission, but still must submit competitive SAT/ACT scores if they are applying within three years of high school graduation.

ADDITIONAL INFORMATION

Students with disabilities needing testing accommodations for placement exams or other standardized tests must submit requests for accommodations to the Office of Disability Services at least one week prior to the test date. Extended-time, out-of-classroom testing, oral exams, and other alternative testing are options offered to students with disabilities.

Support Services Contact Information

Learning Disability Program/Services: Disability Services
Director: Willa Peterson
  E-Mail: wpeterson@fsc.edu
  Telephone: 978-665-3427
  Fax: 978-665-3021

LEARNING DISABILITY SERVICES

Requests for the following services/accommodations will be evaluated individually based on appropriate and current documentation.

Allowed in exams
  Calculator: Yes
  Dictionary: Yes
  Computer: Yes
  Spellchecker: Yes
Extended test time: Yes
Scribes: Yes
Proctors: Yes
Oral exams: Yes
Note-takers: Yes

Distraction reduced environment: Yes
Tape recording in class: Yes
Books on tape from RFBD: Yes
Taping of books not from RFBD: No
Accommodations for students with ADD: Yes
Reading machine: Yes
Other assistive technology: Yes
Priority registration: Yes

Added costs for services: No
LD specialists: No
Professional tutors: 2–5
Peer tutors: 15–30
Max. hours/wk. for services: Unlimited
How professors are notified of LD/ADD: By student

GENERAL ADMISSIONS INFORMATION

Director of Admissions: Lynn Petrillo
Telephone: 978-665-3144

ENTRANCE REQUIREMENTS

Academic units required: 4 English, 3 math, 3 science (2 science lab), 2 foreign language, 1 social studies, 1 history, 2 academic electives. **Academic units recommended:** 4 math. High school diploma is required and GED is accepted. TOEFL required of all international applicants, minimum paper TOEFL 550, minimum computer TOEFL 213.

Application deadline: Rolling
Notification: Rolling
Average GPA: 2.95

Average SAT Math: 506
Average SAT Verbal: 511
Average ACT: 19

Graduated top 10% of class: NR
Graduated top 25% of class: NR
Graduated top 50% of class: NR

COLLEGE GRADUATION REQUIREMENTS

Course waivers allowed: Yes
Course substitutions allowed: Yes
In what course: Determined by documentation and student performance with accommodation

ADDITIONAL INFORMATION

Environment: 45-acre campus is located 50 miles from Boston

Student Body:
  Undergrad enrollment: 3,157
  Women: 57%
  Men: 43%
  Percent out-of-state: 5%

Cost Information
  In-state tuition: $970
  Out-of-state tuition: $7,050
  Room & board: $5,120
Housing Information
  University housing: Yes
  Percent living on campus: 41%

Greek System
  Fraternity: Yes
  Sorority: Yes
Athletics: NCAA Division III

MOUNT IDA COLLEGE

777 Dedham Street, Newton, MA 02459
Phone: 617-928-4553 • Fax: 617-928-4507
E-mail: admissions@mountida.edu • Web: www.mountida.edu
Support: SP • Institution type: 2 year/4-year private

LEARNING DISABILITY PROGRAM AND SERVICES

Learning Opportunities Program (LOP) provides additional academic support for students with LD. The program focuses on developing and strengthening individual learning styles that create successful, independent learning. Students are mainstreamed in a regular degree curriculum. Mount Ida goes the extra mile for all its students and the LOP is a natural extension of this philosophy. Students discover a supportive environment where a positive, successful experience is the goal. An important component of the LOP is the mentoring relationship with individual learning specialists. Mount Ida also has the Horizon Program to serve the needs of students not accepted into the LOP but who still demonstrate some academic promise and the ability to contribute to the college community. Horizon is a non-degree, transitional program; students take a reduced number of academic classes bolstered by non-academic support classes and tutorials. Students achieving a minimum 2.0 GPA are eligible to transfer into LOP after their first year. Academic performance is not the only measure of success; the goal of Horizon is to improve the quality of the college experience by providing a support network so students can better understand themselves, exchanging feelings and personal learning histories, and discovering a commonality that they are not alone in dealing with LD.

LD/ADD ADMISSIONS INFORMATION

College entrance tests required: Yes
Interview required: No
Essay required: Yes
Documentation required for LD: WAIS–III
Documentation required for ADD: Yes
Submitted to: Admissions and LOP
Special Ed. HS coursework accepted: Yes

Specific course requirements of all applicants: Yes
Separate application required for program services: Yes
# of LD applications submitted each year: 100
# of LD applications accepted yearly: 70–90
Total # of students receiving LD services: 60–90
Acceptance into program means acceptance into college: Students are admitted first to the college and then to the LOP.

ADMISSIONS

There is no special admissions process for students with learning disabilities. Open admission is available. ACT/SAT are not required for admission. An interview is strongly recommended. Students with disabilities should submit the WAIS–R, a test indicating appropriate reading grade level, and evaluative documentation of the learning disability. Some students may be admitted into a pilot program called Horizon, which is a special admit program. It is a transition program prior to entering LOPS that reduces academic challenge and increases support.

ADDITIONAL INFORMATION

In the Learning Skills Laboratory students have an opportunity to work with Mount Ida faculty and students to improve study skills. Tutoring provided by professional tutors who are learning specialists is available two times per week. Each tutoring session is private and strategy based. These meetings focus on developing self-advocacy skills and independent learning skills. Other services include reduced course load, enrollment in basic English extended time testing, note-taking, diagnostic testing, course substitutions, and counseling. Study skills courses in math and English are available. Additional support and content tutoring are offered in the Academic Success Center. The college also runs a Freshman Experience course specifically for students who may be under prepared for college that focuses on building the skills necessary to facilitate student success. Students work to identify and strengthen their individual learning styles.

Support Services Contact Information

Learning Disability Program/Services: Learning Opportunities Program (LOP)
Director: Jill Mehler
  E-Mail: jmehler@mountida.edu
  Telephone: 617-928-4648
  Fax: 617-928-4648

LEARNING DISABILITY SERVICES

Requests for the following services/accommodations will be evaluated individually based on appropriate and current documentation.

Allowed in exams
  Calculator: Yes
  Dictionary: Yes
  Computer: No
  Spellchecker: Yes
Extended test time: Yes
Scribes: No
Proctors: No
Oral exams: Yes
Note-takers: No

Distraction reduced environment: Yes
Tape recording in class: Yes
Books on tape from RFBD: Yes
Taping of books not from RFBD: Yes
Accommodations for students with
  ADD: Yes
Reading machine: Yes
Other assistive technology: Yes
Priority registration: Yes

Added costs for services: Yes
LD specialists: Yes
Professional tutors: Yes
Peer tutors: Yes
Max. hours/wk. for services: 2
How professors are notified of
  LD/ADD: By both student and director

GENERAL ADMISSIONS INFORMATION

Director of Admissions: Elizabeth Storinge
Telephone: 617-928-4553

ENTRANCE REQUIREMENTS
Academic units required: 4 English. **Academic units recommended:** 3 math, 3 science, 2 foreign language, 2 social studies, 2 history. High school diploma is required and GED is accepted. TOEFL required of all international applicants, minimum paper TOEFL 525, minimum computer TOEFL 195.

Application deadline: Rolling
Notification: Rolling
Average GPA: 2.0-2.9

Average SAT Math: NR
Average SAT Verbal: NR
Average ACT: NR

Graduated top 10% of class: NR
Graduated top 25% of class: NR
Graduated top 50% of class: NR

COLLEGE GRADUATION REQUIREMENTS

Course waivers allowed: Yes
Course substitutions allowed: Yes
In what course: Depends on the major and the learning style issues.

ADDITIONAL INFORMATION

Environment: Mount Ida's 85-acre campus is in a suburban neighborhood 8 miles west of Boston.

Student Body:
  Undergrad enrollment: 2,009
  Women: 51%
  Men: 49%
  Percent out-of-state: 39%

Cost Information
  Tuition: $17,075
  Room & board: $9,400
Housing Information
  University housing: Yes
  Percent living on campus: 72%

Greek System
  Fraternity: No
  Sorority: No
  Athletics: NCAA Division III

NORTHEASTERN UNIVERSITY

360 Huntington Avenue, 150 Richards Hall, Boston, MA 02115
Phone: 617-373-2200 • Fax: 617-373-8780
E-mail: admissions@neu.edu • Web: www.northeastern.edu
Support: SP • Institution type: 4-year private

LEARNING DISABILITY PROGRAM AND SERVICES

The Disability Resource Center (DRC) offers ongoing support and counseling services, academic advising, student advocacy, and help with course and exam modifications for students with LD. Students who apply must have the LD documented through a recent evaluation and the willingness to use the resources and services of the program. Students work on a one-to-one basis and in small groups with a learning disabilities specialist. There is no charge for basic support services. Persons with LD who need intensive support may be interested in the independent highly structured LD Program. Students meet with a psychologist and LD specialist who act as primary advisors to explore learning strengths and weaknesses and develop specific goals for each quarter. On the basis of individual need, each student receives three-5 hours of one-on-one tutoring weekly. This privately sponsored program, only for students with LD, has an additional cost of $2,100 per quarter. The LD Program best serves students who can use individualized support to take action toward their goals.

LD/ADD ADMISSIONS INFORMATION

College entrance tests required: Yes
Interview required: Yes
Essay required: Yes
Documentation required for LD: Extensive psychoeducational evaluations performed within 3 years
Documentation required for ADD: Yes
Submitted to: Disability Resources Center
Special Ed. HS coursework accepted: Decided by the director of the program

Specific course requirements of all applicants: Yes
Separate application required for program services: N/A
# of LD applications submitted each year: 50
# of LD applications accepted yearly: 12
Total # of students receiving LD services: 300
Acceptance into program means acceptance into college: Student must be admitted and enrolled in the university first and then request LD services from DRC or admission to the LD program.

ADMISSIONS

There are two separate application processes involved in admission to Northeastern. Admission requirements to the university are the same for all students and any student may be eligible for help in the Disability Resource Center. General applicants have a 3.0 GPA and an average SAT of 1150. Depending on the program, courses, and diagnosis of the student's learning disability, courses may be substituted for admission. Students apply to the program after admission to the university. There is a separate application and interview needed for The Learning Disability Program, which is the independent program. Students must take a full 6-10 hour battery of tests for this program, and must also submit previous diagnostic tests. These students must have an interview. Notification of acceptance is sent from the Office of Admissions.

ADDITIONAL INFORMATION

DRC services include note-taking; readers and scribes; liaison and advocacy services; counseling and referral services; support groups; and basic skills courses taught by LD specialists in time management, learning strategies, study strategies, social skills, and perceptual skills. There are currently 35 students enrolled in the program and their are always students waiting to be admitted. Documentation must address attention, perception, motor abilities, language, memory, processing speed, organization, emotional factors, and general intellectual and academic functioning. Services and accommodations are available for undergraduate and graduate students.

Support Services Contact Information

Learning Disability Program/Services: Disability Resource Program (DRC)
Director: Dean G. Ruth Kukiela Bork
  E-Mail: r.bork@neu.edu
  Telephone: 617-373-2675
  Fax: 617-373-7800
Contact Person: Debbie Auerbach
  E-Mail: d.auerbach@neu.edu
  Telephone: 617-373-4428
  Fax: 617-373-7800

LEARNING DISABILITY SERVICES

Requests for the following services/accommodations will be evaluated individually based on appropriate and current documentation.

Allowed in exams
  Calculator: Yes
  Dictionary: Yes
  Computer: Yes
  Spellchecker: Yes
Extended test time: Yes
Scribes: Yes
Proctors: Yes
Oral exams: Yes
Note-takers: Yes

Distraction reduced environment: Yes
Tape recording in class: Yes
Books on tape from RFBD: Yes
Taping of books not from RFBD: No
Accommodations for students with
  ADD: Yes
Reading machine: Yes
Other assistive technology: Yes
Priority registration: N/A

Added costs for services: Yes
LD specialists: Yes
Professional tutors: 1–8
Peer tutors: Yes
Max. hours/wk. for services:
  Unlimited
How professors are notified of
  LD/ADD: By student

GENERAL ADMISSIONS INFORMATION

Director of Admissions: Ronne Patrick Turner
Telephone: 617-373-2200

ENTRANCE REQUIREMENTS

Academic units required: 4 English, 3 math, 3 science (2 science lab), 2 foreign language, 3 social studies, 2 history. **Academic units recommended:** 4 math, 4 science (4 science lab), 4 foreign language. High school diploma is required and GED is accepted. ACT with Writing component required or SAT Reasoning Test. TOEFL required of all international applicants, minimum paper TOEFL 550, minimum computer TOEFL 213.

Application deadline: 2/1
Notification: Between 3/1 and 4/1
Average GPA: NR

Average SAT Math: 615
Average SAT Verbal: 596
Average ACT: NR

Graduated top 10% of class: 36%
Graduated top 25% of class: 67%
Graduated top 50% of class: 93%

COLLEGE GRADUATION REQUIREMENTS

Course waivers allowed: No
Course substitutions allowed: Yes
In what course: Foreign language substitutes as well as a math class specifically for students with dyscalculea are available with approval from the DRC counselor.

ADDITIONAL INFORMATION

Environment: The school is located on 55 acres in the city of Boston.

Student Body:
  Undergrad enrollment: 14618
  Women: 50%
  Men: 50%
  Percent out-of-state: 65%

Cost Information
  Tuition: $26,750
  Room & board: $10,180
Housing Information
  University housing: Yes
  Percent living on campus: 65%

Greek System
  Fraternity: Yes
  Sorority: Yes
Athletics: NCAA Division I

PINE MANOR COLLEGE

400 Heath Street, Chestnut Hill, MA 02467-2332
Phone: 617-731-7104 • Fax: 617-731-7102
E-mail: admission@pmc.edu • Web: www.pmc.edu
Support: CS • Institution type: 2-year private

LEARNING DISABILITY PROGRAM AND SERVICES

The Learning Resource Center (LRC) is an expression of the college's strong commitment to the individual learning experience. The LRC supports and challenges students to realize their maximum academic potential in the way that best suits their individual learning styles. There are several professional tutors: writing and math tutors, learning specialists, and the director, who provides tutoring that is individually tailored to the learning style and needs of the student. The tutoring is not content-oriented, but rather strategy-based and process-oriented. The LRC hopes that students with learning disabilities enter college with some compensatory techniques and study skills. The learning specialists furnish guidance and academic skills assistance to students whose learning disabilities create a gap between their true capacity and daily performance. The LRC serves the whole college population free of charge, whether or not a student has a documented learning disability.

LD/ADD ADMISSIONS INFORMATION

College entrance tests required: Yes
Interview required: No-Recommended
Essay required: Yes
Documentation required for LD: WAIS–R or WISC–R with all subscores reported, achievement, and/or Woodcock Johnson
Documentation required for ADD: Yes
Submitted to: Learning Resources Center
Special Ed. HS coursework accepted: Yes

Specific course requirements of all applicants: Yes
Separate application required for program services: No
# of LD applications submitted each year: NR
# of LD applications accepted yearly: NR
Total # of students receiving LD services: 35–50
Acceptance into program means acceptance into college: Students must be admitted and enrolled at the College prior to requesting services from the LRC.

ADMISSIONS

All applicants submit the same general application. Although not required, an interview is highly recommended. The average ACT is 19 or SAT 870. Courses required are 4 years English, 3 years math, 2 years science, 4 years social studies. Courses taken in special education are accepted. Admissions decisions are made by the Office of Admissions. However, the director of the LRC assists in interpreting testing and documentation and makes a recommendation to the Office of Admissions. Students are encouraged to self-disclose during the admissions process. There is a special Optional Response Form that is used by the LRC after the student is accepted.

ADDITIONAL INFORMATION

LRC staff works with students on a once or twice a week basis, or on a drop-in basis. Students also work closely with their academic advisors. LRC tutors offer diagnosis and remediation for students in academic difficulty; enrichment for successful students; and assistance to faculty and staff. The LRC can also obtain recorded textbooks and arrange for tutors and diagnostic testing. In addition, the following accommodations have proved useful: reduced course load each semester; additional time to complete exams, quizzes, or written assignments; and a separate room for examinations. Basic skills classes are offered in reading, math, learning strategies, written language, study strategies, and time management.

Support Services Contact Information

Learning Disability Program/Services: Learning Resource Center (LRC)
Director: Mary Walsh
   E-Mail: walshmar@pmc.edu
   Telephone: 617-731-7181
   Fax: 617-731-7638

LEARNING DISABILITY SERVICES

Requests for the following services/accommodations will be evaluated individually based on appropriate and current documentation.

Allowed in exams
  Calculator: Yes
  Dictionary: Yes
  Computer: Yes
  Spellchecker: Yes
Extended test time: Yes
Scribes: Yes
Proctors: Yes
Oral exams: Yes
Note-takers: Yes

Distraction reduced environment: Yes
Tape recording in class: Yes
Books on tape from RFBD: Yes
Taping of books not from RFBD: No
Accommodations for students with
  ADD: Yes
Reading machine: No
Other assistive technology: Yes
Priority registration: No

Added costs for services: No
LD specialists: Yes
Professional tutors: 5
Peer tutors: No
Max. hours/wk. for services: 3
How professors are notified of
  LD/ADD: By both student and director

GENERAL ADMISSIONS INFORMATION

Director of Admissions: Bill Nichols
Telephone: 617-731-7167

ENTRANCE REQUIREMENTS

Academic units recommended: 4 English, 3 math, 3 science, 2 foreign language, 2 social studies. High school diploma is required and GED is accepted. ACT with or without Writing component accepted. TOEFL required of all international applicants, minimum paper TOEFL 475, minimum computer TOEFL 150.

Application deadline: Rolling
Notification: Rolling
Average GPA: 2.4

Average SAT Math: 400
Average SAT Verbal: 420
Average ACT: 17

Graduated top 10% of class: 0%
Graduated top 25% of class: 23%
Graduated top 50% of class: 49%

COLLEGE GRADUATION REQUIREMENTS

Course waivers allowed: Yes
Course substitutions allowed: Yes
In what course: Mathematics

ADDITIONAL INFORMATION

Environment: Pine Manor is located on a 79-acre campus in Chestnut Hill, 5 miles west of Boston.

Student Body:
  Undergrad enrollment: 477
  Women: 100%
  Men: 0%
  Percent out-of-state: 24%

Cost Information
  Tuition: $14,544
  Room & board: $9,500
Housing Information
  University housing: Yes
  Percent living on campus: 74%

Greek System
  Fraternity: No
  Sorority: No
Athletics: NCAA Division III

SMITH COLLEGE

7 College Lane, Northampton, MA 01063
Phone: 413-585-2500 • Fax: 413-585-2527
E-mail: admission@smith.edu • Web: www.smith.edu
Support: S • Institution type: 4-year private

LEARNING DISABILITY PROGRAM AND SERVICES

Smith College does not have a formal LD program. However, the college is both philosophically committed and legally required to enable students with documented disabilities to participate in college programs by providing reasonable accommodations for them. The Office of Disabilities Services (ODS) facilitates the provision of services and offers services aimed to eliminate barriers through modification of the program where necessary. A student may voluntarily register with ODS by completing a disability identification form and providing documentation of the disability, after which proper accommodations will be determined. Students with disabilities who need academic services are asked to make their needs known and to file timely request forms each semester with ODS for accommodations in coursework. The college cannot make retroactive accommodations. Students are encouraged to tell professors about the accommodations needed. The college is responsible for providing that, within certain limits, students are not denied the opportunity to participate in college programs on the basis of a disability. The college will provide support services to students with appropriate evaluations and documentation. Students should contact the ODS for consultation and advice.

LD/ADD ADMISSIONS INFORMATION

College entrance tests required: Yes
Interview required: Yes
Essay required: Yes
Documentation required for LD: WAIS–III, WRAT, psychoeducational evaluation
Documentation required for ADD: Yes
Submitted to: Office of Disability Services
Special Ed. HS coursework accepted: No

Specific course requirements of all applicants: Yes
Separate application required for program services: Yes
# of LD applications submitted each year: NR
# of LD applications accepted yearly: NR
Total # of students receiving LD services: 80
Acceptance into program means acceptance into college: Student must be admitted and enrolled in the college first and then request services.

ADMISSIONS

There is no special admissions procedure for students with learning disabilities. Tests that evaluate cognitive ability, achievement, and information processing should be included with the regular application. It is also helpful to have a letter from a diagnostician documenting services that will be needed in college. SAT and 2 SAT Subject Tests are required, or the ACT with optional essay without SAT Subject Tests. Leniency may be granted in regard to a high school's waiving of foreign language requirements due to a learning disability. High school courses recommended are 4 years English composition and literature, 3 years foreign language (or 2 years in each of 2 languages), 3 years math, 2 years science, and 2 years history.

ADDITIONAL INFORMATION

Because college and departmental requirements are implemented for sound academic reasons, Smith College does not provide waivers for required courses for students with LD. The support services assist students to meet their requirements through modifications to programs when necessary. Courses are available in quantitative skills, study skills, and time management skills. The Special Needs Action Group for Support is a cross-disability, student-led group that meets regularly to provide support and peer mentoring and to plan activities. Support services include readers, note-takers, scribes, assistive listening devices, typists, computing software and hardware, books on tape, writing counseling (more and/or longer appointments), peer tutoring, and time management/study skills training. If peer tutors are not available, other tutorial services may be sought. The college will not provide services that create an undue burden for the college.

Support Services Contact Information

Learning Disability Program/Services: Office of Disability Services (ODS)
Director: Laura Rauscher Coordinator
   E-Mail: lrausche@smith.edu
   Telephone: 413-585-2071
   Fax: 413-585-2206

LEARNING DISABILITY SERVICES

Requests for the following services/accommodations will be evaluated individually based on appropriate and current documentation.

Allowed in exams
   Calculator: Yes
   Dictionary: No
   Computer: Yes
   Spellchecker: Yes
Extended test time: Yes
Scribes: Yes
Proctors: No
Oral exams: Yes
Note-takers: Yes

Distraction reduced environment: Yes
Tape recording in class: Yes
Books on tape from RFBD: Yes
Taping of books not from RFBD: Yes
Accommodations for students with ADD: Yes
Reading machine: Yes
Other assistive technology: Yes
Priority registration: Yes

Added costs for services: No
LD specialists: No
Professional tutors: 2
Peer tutors: Yes
Max. hours/wk. for services: Unlimited
How professors are notified of LD/ADD: By both student and director

GENERAL ADMISSIONS INFORMATION

Director of Admissions: Debra Shaver
Telephone: 413-585-2500

ENTRANCE REQUIREMENTS

Academic units recommended: 4 English, 3 math, 3 science (3 science lab), 3 foreign language, 2 history. High school diploma or equivalent is not recommended. ACT with optional essay or SAT Reasoning and 2 SAT Subject tests. TOEFL required of all international applicants, minimum paper TOEFL 600, minimum computer TOEFL 250.

Application deadline: 1/15
Notification: 4/1
Average GPA: 3.80

Average SAT Math: 620
Average SAT Verbal: 640
Average ACT: 27

Graduated top 10% of class: 59%
Graduated top 25% of class: 88%
Graduated top 50% of class: 99%

COLLEGE GRADUATION REQUIREMENTS

Course waivers allowed: No
Course substitutions allowed: Yes
In what course: Foreign language

ADDITIONAL INFORMATION

Environment: The 204-acre campus is located in a small city 85 miles west of Boston and 15 minutes from Amherst.

Student Body:
   Undergrad enrollment: 2682
   Women: 100%
   Men: 0%
   Percent out-of-state: 76%

Cost Information
   Tuition: $27,330
   Room & board: $9,490
Housing Information
   University housing: Yes
   Percent living on campus: 88%

Greek System
   Fraternity: No
   Sorority: No
Athletics: NCAA Division III

SPRINGFIELD COLLEGE

263 Alden Street, Springfield, MA 01109
Phone: 413-748-3136 • Fax: 413-748-3694
E-mail: admissions@spfldcol.edu • Web: www.spfldcol.edu
Support: CS • Institution type: 4-year private

LEARNING DISABILITY PROGRAM AND SERVICES

Springfield College is committed to providing an equal educational opportunity and full participation in college activities for persons with disabilities. The Office of Student Support Services provides services that ensure that students with disabilities are given an equal educational opportunity and the opportunity for full participation in all college programs and activities. In addition to supporting students with disabilities, Student Support Services works with students who are having academic difficulty. Students can receive services by meeting with the director of Student Support Services to verify eligibility for services, identify student needs, and determine appropriate services and accommodations. To receive services students must provide documentation of their learning disability which is current and comprehensive with specific evidence and identification of a learning disability. Documentation should be no older than three years.

LD/ADD ADMISSIONS INFORMATION

College entrance tests required: Yes
Interview required: No-Recommended
Essay required: Yes
Documentation required for LD: Any psychoeducational testing, must be less than 3 years old
Documentation required for ADD: Yes
Submitted to: Student Support Services
Special Ed. HS coursework accepted: No

Specific course requirements of all applicants: Yes
Separate application required for program services: No
# of LD applications submitted each year: NR
# of LD applications accepted yearly: NR
Total # of students receiving LD services: 150–160
Acceptance into program means acceptance into college: Student must be admitted and enrolled in the college first and then request services.

ADMISSIONS

There is no special admissions process for students with learning disabilities. All applicants must submit the same general application and meet the same admission criteria. Students may submit ACT or SAT. There is no minimum GPA required, although the average GPA is a 3.0. Courses required include 4 years English, 3 years math, 2 years history, and 2–3 years science. All applicants must submit a personal essay and a personal reference from a teacher, counselor, or employer. Admissions decisions are made by the Office of Admissions.

ADDITIONAL INFORMATION

Services provided through the Office of Student Support Services include taped textbooks, taped lectures, readers, alternative testing, note-takers, tutors, computers with spell-check, Reading Edge, reduced course loads, study skills and time management, course accommodations, and course selection.

Support Services Contact Information

Learning Disability Program/Services: Student Support Services
Director: Deb Dickens
   E-Mail: ddickens@spfldcol.edu
   Telephone: 413-748-3768
   Fax: 413-748-3937

LEARNING DISABILITY SERVICES

Requests for the following services/accommodations will be evaluated individually based on appropriate and current documentation.

Allowed in exams
   Calculator: Yes
   Dictionary: Yes
   Computer: Yes
   Spellchecker: Yes
Extended test time: Yes
Scribes: Yes
Proctors: Yes
Oral exams: Yes
Note-takers: Yes

Distraction reduced environment: Yes
Tape recording in class: Yes
Books on tape from RFBD: Yes
Taping of books not from RFBD: Yes
Accommodations for students with ADD: Yes
Reading machine: Yes
Other assistive technology: Yes
Priority registration: No

Added costs for services: No
LD specialists: Yes
Professional tutors: No
Peer tutors: No
Max. hours/wk. for services: Unlimited
How professors are notified of LD/ADD: By both student and director

GENERAL ADMISSIONS INFORMATION

Director of Admissions: Mary D'Angelo
Telephone: 413-748-3136

ENTRANCE REQUIREMENTS

Academic units recommended: 4 English, 2 math, 2 science, 2 foreign language, 2 social studies, 4 academic electives. High school diploma is required and GED is accepted. TOEFL required of all international applicants, minimum paper TOEFL 525, minimum computer TOEFL 195.

Application deadline: 4/11
Notification: Rolling
Average GPA: NR

Average SAT Math: 510
Average SAT Verbal: 500
Average ACT: NR

Graduated top 10% of class: 14%
Graduated top 25% of class: 35%
Graduated top 50% of class: 76%

COLLEGE GRADUATION REQUIREMENTS

Course waivers allowed: Yes
Course substitutions allowed: Yes
In what course: Foreign language

ADDITIONAL INFORMATION

Environment: The campus is in a suburban area about 30 minutes north of Hartford.

Student Body:
   Undergrad enrollment: 12,046
   Women: 51%
   Men: 49%
   Percent out-of-state: 66%

Cost Information
   Tuition: $21,000
   Room & board: $7,350
Housing Information
   University housing: Yes
   Percent living on campus: 85%

Greek System
   Fraternity: Yes
   Sorority: Yes
Athletics: NCAA Division III

U. OF MASSACHUSETTS—AMHERST

University Admissions Center, Amherst, MA 01003-9291
Phone: 413-545-0222 • Fax: 413-545-4312
E-mail: mail@admissions.umass.edu • Web: www.umass.edu
Support: CS • Institution type: 4-year public

LEARNING DISABILITY PROGRAM AND SERVICES

Learning Disabilities Support Services (LDSS) is a support service for all students with documented LD. Students are eligible for services if they can document their LD with the appropriate diagnostic evidence. To be eligible, all students must provide one or more of the following types of documentation: an individualized educational plan indicating LD from elementary or secondary school, a report from a state-certified assessment center indicating LD, psychoeducational test results to be interpreted in the LDSS. Not all students with learning problems have learning disabilities. Only students with disabilities may be served by LDSS. Students whose predominate disability is a form of ADD/ADD are served by the Program for Students with Medical Disabilities and not LDSS. Each student enrolled in LDSS is assigned a case manager who is a graduate student in education, counseling, or a related field. Case Managers have prior relevant professional experience and are supervised by professional staff. Students work with the same case manager for the entire academic year on three objectives: understanding and obtaining accommodations needed, identifying and utilizing resources, and identifying and implementing learning strategies to compensate for the disability. The goal of LDSS is for students to become independent self-advocates by the time they graduate.

LD/ADD ADMISSIONS INFORMATION

College entrance tests required: Yes
Interview required: N/A
Essay required: Yes
Documentation required for LD: Formal psychoeducational evaluation completed within the past 5 years. See http://www.umass.edu/ldss/policies.html for more information
Documentation required for ADD: Yes
Submitted to: Learning Disability Support Services

Specific course requirements of all applicants: Yes
Special Ed. HS coursework accepted: No
Separate application required for program services: Yes
# of LD applications submitted each year: NR
# of LD applications accepted yearly: NR
Total # of students receiving LD services: 700–800
Acceptance into program means acceptance into college: Student must be admitted and enrolled in the university first and then request services.

ADMISSIONS

There are no special admissions criteria for students with learning disabilities. General admission requirements recommend that students be in the top 35 percent of their class with 3.0 GPA, SAT 1140 or ACT 24. Course requirements include 4 years English, 3 years math, 3 years social studies, 2 years science and 2 years foreign language (this can be waived if it is part of the disability). Massachusetts students with learning disabilities do not need to submit ACT/SAT. All admissions and support documents go through the admissions office. All applicants who check the learning disabilities box are reviewed individually by learning disabilities specialists. If any information is missing, the applicant will be notified. There is no quota on the number of students with LD who can be admitted to the university. Students who are otherwise qualified and have taken college-preparatory courses in high school should submit a recent individual educational plan and documentation.

ADDITIONAL INFORMATION

Students and case managers prepare learning style sheets for professors that request various accommodations, such as untimed exams, extended time on assignments, alternate form of tests, and note-taking. At mid-semester each professor who received an accommodation sheet receives a request from LDSS asking for the student's grades, attendance, and performance. There is individual tutoring weekly for most introductory level courses as well as in math skills, study skills, language arts, written expression, time management, learning strategies, and organizational skills. Tutors are graduate students trained to work with LD. Students with LD can request to substitute foreign language with cultural courses. Disability Student Network is an organization designed to support the needs of students with disabilities. Faculty Friends is a group of instructors nominated by Disability Student Network as outstanding in teaching and meeting the needs of students with disabilities.

Support Services Contact Information

Learning Disability Program/Services: Learning Disabilities Support Services
Director: Susan Bronstein
  E-Mail: sbronstein@acad.vmass.edu
  Telephone: 413-545-5334
  Fax: 413-577-0691

LEARNING DISABILITY SERVICES

Requests for the following services/accommodations will be evaluated individually based on appropriate and current documentation.

Allowed in exams	Distraction reduced environment: Yes	Added costs for services: No
Calculator: Yes	Tape recording in class: Yes	LD specialists: Yes
Dictionary: Yes	Books on tape from RFBD: Yes	Professional tutors: Yes
Computer: Yes	Taping of books not from RFBD: Yes	Peer tutors: Varies
Spellchecker: Yes	Accommodations for students with	Max. hours/wk. for services: 1
Extended test time: Yes	ADD: Yes	How professors are notified of
Scribes: Yes	Reading machine: Yes	LD/ADD: By both student and director
Proctors: Yes	Other assistive technology: Yes	
Oral exams: Yes	Priority registration: No	
Note-takers: Yes		

GENERAL ADMISSIONS INFORMATION

Director of Admissions: Michael Gargano
Telephone: 413-545-0222

ENTRANCE REQUIREMENTS
Academic units required: 4 English, 3 math, 3 science (2 science lab), 2 foreign language, 2 social studies, 2 academic electives. High school diploma is required and GED is accepted. ACT with Writing component required or SAT Reasoning test. TOEFL required of all international applicants, minimum paper TOEFL 550, minimum computer TOEFL 213.

Application deadline: 1/15	Average SAT Math: 576	Graduated top 10% of class: 15%
Notification: Rolling	Average SAT Verbal: 561	Graduated top 25% of class: 45%
Average GPA: 3.29	Average ACT: NR	Graduated top 50% of class: 84%

COLLEGE GRADUATION REQUIREMENTS

Course waivers allowed: No
Course substitutions allowed: Yes
In what course: The College of Arts and Sciences requires foreign language. This requirement is never waived; however, if documented disabilities prevent a student from learning a foreign language, a student can petition for a foreign language modification.

ADDITIONAL INFORMATION

Environment: The university is located on 1,405 acres in a small town 90 miles west of Boston.

Student Body:	Cost Information	Greek System
Undergrad enrollment: 18,378	In-state tuition: $10,000	Fraternity: Yes
Women: 50%	Out-of-state tuition: $9,008	Sorority: Yes
Men: 50%	Room & board: $6,189	Athletics: NCAA Division I
Percent out-of-state: 15%	Housing Information	
	University housing: Yes	
	Percent living on campus: 61%	

WHEATON COLLEGE (MA)

Office of Admission, Norton, MA 02766
Phone: 508-286-8251 • Fax: 508-286-8271
E-mail: admission@wheatoncollege.edu • Web: www.wheatoncollege.edu
Support: S • Institution type: 4-year private

LEARNING DISABILITY PROGRAM AND SERVICES

Wheaton College encourages life-long learning by assisting students to become self-advocates and independent learners. The college does not have a special program for students with LD. The assistant dean for college skills serves as the 504/ADA coordinator. Students with LD can access services through the dean. The Academic Advising Center houses the dean of academic advising who holds drop-in office hours and assists students with petitions to the committee on admissions and academic standing on such issues as orientation, probation, general advising and incomplete grade resolution. The advising staff can assist with pressing advising questions. Students also have access to tutors, peer advisors and preceptors who offer assistance with study strategies. All students have access to these services.

LD/ADD ADMISSIONS INFORMATION

College entrance tests required: No
Interview required: No
Essay required: Yes
Documentation required for LD: WAIS–III, WJR, Wexler Memory Scales, aptitude testing, achievement testing, diagnostic interview, clinical summary, explanation of accommodations with rationale
Documentation required for ADD: The tests mentioned above and tests for attention and distractability
Submitted to: Admissions and Academic Support Services
Special Ed. HS coursework accepted: Yes

Specific course requirements of all applicants: Yes
Separate application required for program services: No
# of LD applications submitted each year: NR
# of LD applications accepted yearly: NR
Total # of students receiving LD services: 91
Acceptance into program means acceptance into college: Student must be admitted and enrolled in the college first and then request services.

ADMISSIONS

All applicants must meet the same admission standards. Students with LD may choose to meet with the assistant dean for college skills. Wheaton College does not require the ACT/SAT for admission. It is strongly suggested that students take 4 years of English, 3–4 years math, 3–4 years foreign language, 2 years social studies, 3–4 years science. Students are encouraged to take AP and honors courses and to also take courses in visual and performing arts. Wheaton will accept courses taken in the special education department. Students with LD are encouraged to self-disclose and provide current documentation. All LD testing information should be sent to both admissions and support services.

ADDITIONAL INFORMATION

Services for students with LD can include classroom accommodations, college skills workshops, course tutor program, general advising, and study strategy tutors as well as strategy workshops. Reasonable accommodations are available for students with appropriate documentation. There is a summer program available for students who wish to participate. Proctors are not offered because Wheaton has an honor code for exams.

Support Services Contact Information

Learning Disability Program/Services: Academic Support Services
Director: Marty Bledsoe, Assistant Dean for College Skills
  E-Mail: mbledsoe@wheatonma.edu
  Telephone: 508-286-8215
  Fax: 508-286-8276

LEARNING DISABILITY SERVICES

Requests for the following services/accommodations will be evaluated individually based on appropriate and current documentation.

Allowed in exams
  Calculator: Yes
  Dictionary: Yes
  Computer: Yes
  Spellchecker: Yes
Extended test time: Yes
Scribes: Yes
Proctors: No
Oral exams: Yes
Note-takers: Yes

Distraction reduced environment: Yes
Tape recording in class: Yes
Books on tape from RFBD: Yes
Taping of books not from RFBD: Yes
Accommodations for students with
  ADD: Yes
Reading machine: Yes
Other assistive technology: Yes
Priority registration: Yes

Added costs for services: No
LD specialists: No
Professional tutors: 7
Peer tutors: N/A
Max. hours/wk. for services:
  Unlimited
How professors are notified of
  LD/ADD: By both student and director

GENERAL ADMISSIONS INFORMATION

Director of Admissions: Gail Berson
Telephone: 508-286-8251

ENTRANCE REQUIREMENTS

Academic units recommended: 4 English, 4 math, 3 science (2 science lab), 4 foreign language, 2 social studies. High school diploma is required and GED is accepted. TOEFL required of all international applicants, minimum paper TOEFL 550, minimum computer TOEFL 213.

Application deadline: 1/15
Notification: 4/1
Average GPA: 3.45

Average SAT Math: 610
Average SAT Verbal: 620
Average ACT: 27

Graduated top 10% of class: 42%
Graduated top 25% of class: 76%
Graduated top 50% of class: 93%

COLLEGE GRADUATION REQUIREMENTS

Course waivers allowed: Yes
Course substitutions allowed: Yes
In what course: Foreign language, by petition

ADDITIONAL INFORMATION

Environment: The college is located 35 miles from Boston, and 15 miles from Providence, Rhode Island

Student Body:
  Undergrad enrollment: 1,524
  Women: 63%
  Men: 37%
  Percent out-of-state: 65%

Cost Information
  Tuition: $30,355
  Room & board: $7,580
Housing Information
  University housing: Yes
  Percent living on campus: 97%

Greek System
  Fraternity: No
  Sorority: No
Athletics: NCAA Division III

WHEELOCK COLLEGE

200 The Riverway, Boston, MA 02215
Phone: 617-879-2206 • Fax: 617-566-4453
E-mail: undergrad@wheelock.edu • Web: www.wheelock.edu
Support: CS • Institution type: 4-year private

LEARNING DISABILITY PROGRAM AND SERVICES

The Disability Services Program in the Office of Academic Advising and Assistance (OAAA) at Wheelock College ensures that students with disabilities can actively participate in all facets of college life. They also provide and coordinate support services and programs that will enable students to maximize their educational potential. Students are encouraged to be independent individuals who know their strengths and develop compensatory skills for academic success. When working with students, the two major goals are to help with becoming independent and assisting in developing self-advocacy skills. Students with LD are encouraged to self-disclose to OAAA. Students are required to provide documentation from a qualified professional. Disability Services will assist in identifying appropriate accommodations based on the documentation provided.

LD/ADD ADMISSIONS INFORMATION

College entrance tests required: Yes
Interview required: N/A
Essay required: NR
Documentation required for LD: Cognitive/achievement
Documentation required for ADD: Medical diagnosis/treatment plan (M.D. Psychologist)
Submitted to: Office of Disability Support Services
Special Ed. HS coursework accepted: Yes

Specific course requirements of all applicants: Yes
Separate application required for program services: N/A
# of LD applications submitted each year: NR
# of LD applications accepted yearly: NR
Total # of students receiving LD services: 67
Acceptance into program means acceptance into college: Student must be admitted and enrolled in the college first and then request services.

ADMISSIONS

There is no special admissions process for students with LD and ADD. All applicants are expected to meet the general admission criteria. All students should have 4 years English, 1 year U.S. history and additional social studies, 3 years of college-prep math, and at least 1 lab science. Substitutions are not allowed for entrance requirements. Wheelock will accept courses in high school that were taken in the special education department. Students should feel free to self-disclose the disability in the application process.

ADDITIONAL INFORMATION

With appropriate documentation students may be eligible for the following services or accommodations: priority registration, letters informing the instructors of the disability and what reasonable accommodations the student will need, individual sessions with a learning specialist to help with time management, academic and organizational skills support. The writing center is available for all students interested in assistance with writing skills and peer tutors work one-on-one. Students may request referrals for peer tutors and study groups are available. In addition, workshops on the following topics are offered throughout the academic year: academic survival skills, reading skills, and "evaluation of your learning style." Other academic supports include academic advising, note-takers, textbooks on tape, testing modifications, readers, scribes and referrals for diagnostic testing.

Support Services Contact Information

Learning Disability Program/Services: Office Disability and Support Services
Director: Paul Hastings
  E-Mail: phastings@wheelock.edu
  Telephone: 617-879-2304
  Fax: 617-879- 2395

LEARNING DISABILITY SERVICES

Requests for the following services/accommodations will be evaluated individually based on appropriate and current documentation.

Allowed in exams
  Calculator: Yes
  Dictionary: Yes
  Computer: Yes
  Spellchecker: Yes
Extended test time: Yes
Scribes: Yes
Proctors: Yes
Oral exams: Yes
Note-takers: Yes

Distraction reduced environment: Yes
Tape recording in class: Yes
Books on tape from RFBD: Yes
Taping of books not from RFBD: Yes
Accommodations for students with ADD: Yes
Reading machine: Yes
Other assistive technology: Yes
Priority registration: Yes

Added costs for services: No
LD specialists: Yes
Professional tutors: No
Peer tutors: 25
Max. hours/wk. for services: Unlimited
How professors are notified of LD/ADD: By student

GENERAL ADMISSIONS INFORMATION

Director of Admissions: NR
Telephone: 617-879-2206

ENTRANCE REQUIREMENTS

Academic units required: 4 English, 3 math, 2 science (1 science lab), 2 social studies. High school diploma is required and GED is accepted. TOEFL required of all international applicants, minimum paper TOEFL 500, minimum computer TOEFL 173.

Application deadline: 3/1
Notification: Rolling
Average GPA: 2.90

Average SAT Math: 505
Average SAT Verbal: 516
Average ACT: NR

Graduated top 10% of class: 8%
Graduated top 25% of class: 35%
Graduated top 50% of class: 70%

COLLEGE GRADUATION REQUIREMENTS

Course waivers allowed: No
Course substitutions allowed: No
In what course: N/A

ADDITIONAL INFORMATION

Environment: Wheelock College is located in the Fenway area of Boston, 2 miles from downtown.

Student Body:
  Undergrad enrollment: 616
  Women: 94%
  Men: 6%
  Percent out-of-state: 48%

Cost Information
  Tuition: $27,500
  Room & board: $9,000
Housing Information
  University housing: Yes
  Percent living on campus: 70%

Greek System
  Fraternity: No
  Sorority: No
  Athletics: NCAA Division III

ADRIAN COLLEGE

110 South Madison Street, Adrian, MI 49221
Phone: 517-265-5161 • Fax: 517-264-3331
E-mail: admissions@adrian.edu • Web: www.adrian.edu
Support: CS • Institution type: 4-year private

LEARNING DISABILITY PROGRAM AND SERVICES

Adrian College has extensive academic support services for all students with disabilities. The more the students are mainstreamed in high school, the greater their chances of success at Adrian in their mainstream program. There is no special or separate curriculum for students with learning disabilities. Project EXCEL is the umbrella program for all services at Adrian.

LD/ADD ADMISSIONS INFORMATION

College entrance tests required: Yes
Interview required: No
Essay required: No
Documentation required for LD: Current psychoeducational evaluation
Documentation required for ADD: Current evaluation
Submitted to: Access
Special Ed. HS coursework accepted: Yes

Specific course requirements of all applicants: Yes
Separate application required for program services: Yes
# of LD applications submitted each year: 10
# of LD applications accepted yearly: NR
Total # of students receiving LD services: 23
Acceptance into program means acceptance into college: Student must be admitted and enrolled in the college first and then request services.

ADMISSIONS

Students with learning disabilities must meet regular admission criteria. Students should demonstrate the ability to do college-level work through an acceptable GPA in college-preparatory classes such as 4 years English, 2 years math, social studies, science, and foreign language, ACT (17+) or SAT, and a psychological report. Furthermore, by their senior year in high school, students should, for the most part, be mainstreamed. Courses taken in special education will be considered for admission. The applications of students who self-disclose are reviewed by academic services staff, not to determine admissions, but to start a documentation file. There is a special admissions program designed for students who demonstrate academic potential. This Special Admissions Support Program (SASP) requires students to sign a contract and maintain a certain GPA each of the first 2 semesters.

ADDITIONAL INFORMATION

Course adaptations help to make courses more understandable. Skills classes are available in reading, math, study skills and research paper writing, and students are granted credit toward their GPA. Support services and accommodations are available if appropriate in the following areas: extended time on tests; distraction-free testing environment; scribes; note-takers; proctors; use of calculators, dictionary, spellchecker and computers in exams; taped textbooks; and reading machines. Tutorial assistance is available for all students and there are three LD specialists on staff.

Support Services Contact Information

Learning Disability Program/Services: ACCESS, Academic Services
Director: Jane McCloskey
　E-Mail: jmccloskey@adrian.edu
　Telephone: 517-265-5161
　Fax: 517-264-3181
Contact Person: Carol Tapp
　E-Mail: ctapp@adrian.edu
　Telephone: 517-265-5161
　Fax: 517-264-3181

LEARNING DISABILITY SERVICES

Requests for the following services/accommodations will be evaluated individually based on appropriate and current documentation.

Allowed in exams
　Calculator: Yes
　Dictionary: No
　Computer: Yes
　Spellchecker: Yes
Extended test time: Yes
Scribes: Yes
Proctors: Yes
Oral exams: Yes
Note-takers: Yes

Distraction reduced environment: Yes
Tape recording in class: Yes
Books on tape from RFBD: Yes
Taping of books not from RFBD: Yes
**Accommodations for students with
　ADD:** Yes
Reading machine: Yes
Other assistive technology: No
Priority registration: No

Added costs for services: No
LD specialists: Yes
Professional tutors: No
Peer tutors: 30–40
Max. hours/wk. for services:
　Unlimited
**How professors are notified of
　LD/ADD:** By both student and director

GENERAL ADMISSIONS INFORMATION

Director of Admissions: Ms. Janel A. Sutkus
Telephone: 517-265-5161

ENTRANCE REQUIREMENTS

Academic units recommended: 4 English, 2 math, 2 science (1 science lab), 2 foreign language, 1 social studies, 1 history, 3 academic electives. High school diploma is required and GED is accepted. ACT with or without Writing component accepted. TOEFL required of all international applicants, minimum paper TOEFL 500, minimum computer TOEFL 173.

Application deadline: 8/15
Notification: Rolling
Average GPA: 3.1

Average SAT Math: NR
Average SAT Verbal: NR
Average ACT: 22

Graduated top 10% of class: 13%
Graduated top 25% of class: 32%
Graduated top 50% of class: 61%

COLLEGE GRADUATION REQUIREMENTS

Course waivers allowed: No
Course substitutions allowed: No
In what course: N/A

ADDITIONAL INFORMATION

Environment: The school is located on 100 acres in a residential section of Michigan, 35 miles northeast of Ann Arbor.

Student Body:
　Undergrad enrollment: 1,010
　Women: 54%
　Men: 46%
　Percent out-of-state: 20%

Cost Information
　Tuition: $12,200
　Room & board: $5,800
Housing Information
　University housing: Yes
　Percent living on campus: 77%

Greek System
　Fraternity: Yes
　Sorority: Yes
Athletics: NCAA Division III

CALVIN COLLEGE

3201 Burton Street Southeast, Grand Rapids, MI 49546
Phone: 616-526-6106 • Fax: 616-526-6777
E-mail: admissions@calvin.edu • Web: www.calvin.edu
Support: CS • Institution type: 4-year private

LEARNING DISABILITY PROGRAM AND SERVICES

The mission of Student Academic Services is to ensure that otherwise qualified students are able to benefit from a distinctly Christian education based on liberal arts. The Calvin community responds appropriately in a way that avoids handicapping the student with a disability. The coaching program is for students with learning disabilities, attention deficit disorders and other students who specifically need help with time management and study skills. The coaches give suggestions and feedback as well as encouragement on how to manage academics with other areas of life. First year students are encouraged to apply for the Coaching Program at the beginning of the fall semester.

LD/ADD ADMISSIONS INFORMATION

College entrance tests required: Yes
Interview required: No
Essay required: No
Documentation required for LD: Psychoeducation Evaluation
Documentation required for ADD: Clear statement of DSM–IV diagnosis. Description of assessment procedures including behavior rating scales, vigilance and sustained attention tasks, neuropsychological tests and statement of medical treatment
Submitted to: Student Academic Services
Special Ed. HS coursework accepted: No

Specific course requirements of all applicants: Yes
Separate application required for program services: No
# of LD applications submitted each year: NR
# of LD applications accepted yearly: NR
Total # of students receiving LD services: 106
Acceptance into program means acceptance into college: Student must be admitted and enrolled in the college first and then request services.

ADMISSIONS

There are no special admissions for students with learning disabilities. Applicants are expected to have an ACT of 20 (19 English and 20 math) or SAT of 810 (390 verbal and 420 math). Courses required include 3 years English, 1 year algebra, 1 year geometry, and minimum of 2 years in any 2 of the following fields: social science, language, or natural science; 1 of the fields from math, foreign language, social science, and natural science must include at least 3 years of study. The Access Program is a conditional admission program for all students who do not meet admission requirements, but show promise of developing into successful college students.

ADDITIONAL INFORMATION

The Office of Student Academic Services is a learning center that is open to all students on campus. Skill classes are available in English, math, and study skills. These classes may be taken for college credit. The Coaching Program is an interactive relationship with another student who learns about the student's disability and learning style and then provides direction and strategies for the student. The program provides support in the areas of education and self-advocacy, time management, procrastination, note-taking, environment for studying, taking tests, and general organizational skills. Services and accommodations are offered to undergraduate and graduate students. Students who self-disclose and are admitted to the college are than reviewed for services.

Support Services Contact Information

Learning Disability Program/Services: Student Academic Services
Director: James Mackenzie , PhD
  E-Mail: jmackenz@calvin.edu
  Telephone: 616-957-6113
  Fax: 616-957-8551
Contact Person: June DeBoer
  E-Mail: jed4@calvin.edu
  Telephone: 616-957-6937
  Fax: 616-957-7066

LEARNING DISABILITY SERVICES

Requests for the following services/accommodations will be evaluated individually based on appropriate and current documentation.

Allowed in exams
  Calculator: Yes
  Dictionary: No
  Computer: Yes
  Spellchecker: Yes
Extended test time: Yes
Scribes: Yes
Proctors: Yes
Oral exams: No
Note-takers: Yes

Distraction reduced environment: Yes
Tape recording in class: Yes
Books on tape from RFBD: Yes
Taping of books not from RFBD: Yes
Accommodations for students with
  ADD: Yes
Reading machine: No
Other assistive technology: Yes
Priority registration: Yes

Added costs for services: No
LD specialists: Yes
Professional tutors: 2
Peer tutors: 65–70
Max. hours/wk. for services:
  Unlimited
How professors are notified of
  LD/ADD: By student

GENERAL ADMISSIONS INFORMATION

Director of Admissions: Dale Kuiper
Telephone: 616-526-6110

ENTRANCE REQUIREMENTS

Academic units required: 3 English, 3 math, 2 science, 2 social studies, 3 academic electives. **Academic units recommended:** 4 English, 3 math, 2 science (1 science lab), 2 foreign language, 3 social studies, 3 academic electives. High school diploma is required and GED is accepted. ACT with or without Writing component accepted. TOEFL required of all international applicants, minimum paper TOEFL 550, minimum computer TOEFL 213.

Application deadline: 8/15
Notification: Rolling
Average GPA: 3.56

Average SAT Math: 605
Average SAT Verbal: 599
Average ACT: 26

Graduated top 10% of class: 28%
Graduated top 25% of class: 57%
Graduated top 50% of class: 81%

COLLEGE GRADUATION REQUIREMENTS

Course waivers allowed: No
Course substitutions allowed: Yes
In what course: Foreign language with documentation

ADDITIONAL INFORMATION

Environment: The college is located on a 370-acre campus in a suburban area 7 miles southeast of Grand Rapids.

Student Body:
  Undergrad enrollment: 4,028
  Women: 55%
  Men: 45%
  Percent out-of-state: 39%

Cost Information
  Tuition: $17,770
  Room & board: $6,185
Housing Information
  University housing: Yes
  Percent living on campus: 56%

Greek System
  Fraternity: No
  Sorority: No
  Athletics: NCAA Division III

FERRIS STATE UNIVERSITY

1201 South State Street, Center for Student Services, Big Rapids, MI 49307
Phone: 231-591-2100 • Fax: 231-591-3944
E-mail: admissions@ferris.edu • Web: www.ferris.edu
Support: CS • Institution type: 4-year public

LEARNING DISABILITY PROGRAM AND SERVICES

Ferris State is committed to a policy of equal opportunity for qualified students. The mission of Disabilities Services is to serve and advocate for students with disabilities, empowering them for self-reliance and independence. Ferris State does not have a program for students with learning disabilities, but does provide a variety of support services and accommodations for students with documented learning disabilities that interfere with the learning process. Ferris State does not, however, attempt to rehabilitate learning disabilities. To obtain support services, students need to meet with the special needs counselor in the Academic Support Center. Students will complete a request for services application and a release form allowing the university to obtain a copy of the documentation of the disability. Documentation for LD/ADD must be current and be submitted by a qualified professional. Professional development is offered to faculty and staff.

LD/ADD ADMISSIONS INFORMATION

College entrance tests required: Yes
Interview required: No
Essay required: No
Documentation required for LD: Psychoeducational report: WAIS and KTEA or WRAT or WIAT or Woodcock-Johnson Battery
Documentation required for ADD: ADD Behavior Checklist Report must contain a diagnosis, scores and/or results of behavior ratings, and the evaluator's credentials
Submitted to: Disability Services
Special Ed. HS coursework accepted: Yes

Specific course requirements of all applicants: Yes
Separate application required for program services: Yes
# of LD applications submitted each year: 60–75
# of LD applications accepted yearly: 60–75
Total # of students receiving LD services: NR
Acceptance into program means acceptance into college: Student must be admitted and enrolled in the university first and then request services.

ADMISSIONS

Students with learning disabilities submit the general application form and should meet the same entrance criteria as all students. Qualified persons with disabilities may not be denied or subjected to discrimination in admission. There is no limit on the number of students admitted with disabilities. ACT scores are used for placement only and may not have an adverse effect on applicants with disabilities. No pre-admission inquiry regarding a possible disability can be made. Therefore, students with LD/ADD are encouraged to self-disclose and provide information as to the extent of the disability. Sometimes a pre-admission interview is required if the GPA is questionable. In general students should have a 2.0 GPA, but some programs require a higher GPA in specific courses. Diverse curricula offerings and a flexible admissions policy allow for the admission of most high school graduates and transfer students. Some programs are selective in nature and require the completion of specific courses and/or a minimum GPA. The special needs counselor is involved in the admissions decision when there is a question about academic preparedness.

ADDITIONAL INFORMATION

Student Development Services offers tutoring for most courses. Flex tutoring is designed for in-depth clarification and review of subject material, and workshop tutoring is designed for short-term, walk-in assistance. The Collegiate Skills Program is designed to help academically underprepared students succeed in college by offering assistance in reading, writing, and study skills. Students also have an opportunity to develop skills in goal-setting, decision-making, and time management. The Academic Skills Center offers special instruction to assist students in improving their academic performance. Additionally, the following are offered: admission assistance; early registration; counseling/career awareness; academic assistance; campus advocacy; case conferences with referring agencies; and referrals to appropriate university and community agencies. There are currently 38 students with LD and 6 students with ADD receiving services on campus.

Support Services Contact Information

Learning Disability Program/Services: Disabilities Services
Director: Eunice Merwin
  E-Mail: EuniceMerwin@ferris.edu
  Telephone: 231-591-3772
  Fax: 231-591-3686
Contact Person: Ceytru Josephson
  E-Mail: CeytruJosephson@ferris.edu
  Telephone: 231-591-5039

LEARNING DISABILITY SERVICES

Requests for the following services/accommodations will be evaluated individually based on appropriate and current documentation.

Allowed in exams
  Calculator: Yes
  Dictionary: Yes
  Computer: Yes
  Spellchecker: Yes
Extended test time: Yes
Scribes: Yes
Proctors: Yes
Oral exams: Yes
Note-takers: Yes

Distraction reduced environment: Yes
Tape recording in class: Yes
Books on tape from RFBD: Yes
Taping of books not from RFBD: Yes
Accommodations for students with ADD: Yes
Reading machine: Yes
Other assistive technology: Yes
Priority registration: No
Added costs for services: No

LD specialists: Yes
Professional tutors: 5
Peer tutors: 100
Max. hours/wk. for services: 2
  Subjects per week
How professors are notified of LD/ADD: By director

GENERAL ADMISSIONS INFORMATION

Director of Admissions: Craig Westman
Telephone: 231-591-2100

ENTRANCE REQUIREMENTS

Academic units recommended: 4 English, 4 math, 3 science, 2 foreign language, 3 social studies, 2 fine arts & computer literacy. High school diploma is required and GED is accepted. ACT with or without Writing component accepted. TOEFL required of all international applicants, minimum paper TOEFL 500, minimum computer TOEFL 173.

Application deadline: 8/1
Notification: Rolling
Average GPA: 3.14

Average SAT Math: NR
Average SAT Verbal: NR
Average ACT: 20

Graduated top 10% of class: NR
Graduated top 25% of class: NR
Graduated top 50% of class: NR

COLLEGE GRADUATION REQUIREMENTS

Course waivers allowed: No
Course substitutions allowed: No
In what course: N/A

ADDITIONAL INFORMATION

Environment: The university is located on 600 acres, 50 miles north of Grand Rapids.

Student Body:
  Undergrad enrollment: 10,300
  Women: 46%
  Men: 54%
  Percent out-of-state: 5%

Cost Information
  In-state tuition: $6,190
  Out-of-state tuition: $12,380
  Room & board: $6,522
Housing Information
  University housing: Yes
  Percent living on campus: 38%

Greek System
  Fraternity: Yes
  Sorority: Yes
Athletics: NCAA Division II

FINLANDIA UNIVERSITY

601 Quincy Street, Hancock, MI 49930
Phone: 906-487-7274 • Fax: 906-487-7383
E-mail: admissions@finlandia.edu • Web: www.finlandia.edu
Support: SP • Institution type: 4-year private

LEARNING DISABILITY PROGRAM AND SERVICES

Through Finlandia's Learning Disabilities Program, students will receive individual counseling, tutoring, academic advising, career counseling, and lots of support and encouragement. The LD Program is designed for students needing personalized attention and additional education before entering a liberal arts or career program. Careful academic planning is performed by the LD director to ensure that students carry a reasonable credit load that is sequential and well-balanced with attention to reading, written assignments, and other course requirements. The faculty is supportive and written and verbal communication between the LD director and faculty is frequent. Student performance is monitored and there are weekly scheduled meetings. The director is the advisor and support person overseeing and coordinating each individual's program. Self-advocacy and compensatory skills are goals, rather than remediation. There is a seven-day orientation prior to freshman year. Advisors work with students during orientation to plan the best course of study, provide advice and assurance that the student will get what is needed in the program, provide encouragement, and may even be able to match the student with professors whose style of teaching best complements the student's style of learning.

LD/ADD ADMISSIONS INFORMATION

College entrance tests required: No
Interview required: No
Essay required: No
Documentation required for LD: WAIS–III, WJ
Documentation required for ADD: Yes
Submitted to: Learning Disabilities Program
Special Ed. HS coursework accepted: No

Specific course requirements of all applicants: No
Separate application required for program services: No
# of LD applications submitted each year: 15–20
# of LD applications accepted yearly: 15–20
Total # of students receiving LD services: 50
Acceptance into program means acceptance into college: The students are reviewed jointly by the LD Program and the Office of Admission to reach an admission decision.

ADMISSIONS

General admission requirements must be met by all applicants. In addition, students with learning disabilities should submit an evaluation, within the last three years, documenting the learning disability; an IEP; and a handwritten essay by the student describing the learning disability. Sometimes a telephone interview or visitation is requested to help determine eligibility for the program. An applicant must have the academic ability and background for work on a college level. Each applicant is evaluated individually by the director of the LD Program and the admissions staff. Depending on the high school information provided, some students will be given the dual designation of LD/Pro-College if the director of the program feels the student may be "at risk."

ADDITIONAL INFORMATION

The program director provides professors with a disability data sheet to request accommodations and also meets individually with faculty regarding student needs. Special services offered include alternative testing, individual counseling, career counseling, auxiliary aids and services, academic advising, computer-based instruction, group and individualized courses, support from the Teaching/Learning Center, and support from Student Support Services. The Director of the program is certified to teach students with learning disabilities, and will help them set up a plan for growth and strength in areas that are challenging. Students will meet with their advisor once a week for as much or as little time as is needed. Students may take skills classes, for non-college credit, in reading and study strategies. There is a one-week required summer orientation program for incoming freshmen.

Support Services Contact Information

Learning Disability Program/Services: Learning Disabilities Program
Contact Person: Kirsti Arko
  E-Mail: kirsti.arko@finlandia.edu
  Telephone: 906-487-7276
  Fax: 906-487-7535

LEARNING DISABILITY SERVICES

Requests for the following services/accommodations will be evaluated individually based on appropriate and current documentation.

Allowed in exams	Distraction reduced environment: Yes	Added costs for services: No
Calculator: Yes	Tape recording in class: Yes	LD specialists: Yes
Dictionary: Y/N	Books on tape from RFBD: Yes	Professional tutors: 6
Computer: Yes	Taping of books not from RFBD: Yes	Peer tutors: 5
Spellchecker: Yes	Accommodations for students with ADD: Yes	Max. hours/wk. for services: Unlimited
Extended test time: Yes	Reading machine: Yes	How professors are notified of LD/ADD: By student and director
Scribes: Yes	Other assistive technology: Yes	
Proctors: Yes	Priority registration: Yes	
Oral exams: Yes		
Note-takers: Yes		

GENERAL ADMISSIONS INFORMATION

Director of Admissions: Ben Larson
Telephone: 877-202-5491

ENTRANCE REQUIREMENTS

High school diploma or GED accepted. Applicants must have the academic ability and background to work on a college level. TOEFL required of all international applicants, minimum computer TOEFL 400, minimum computer TOEFL 97.

Application deadline: Rolling	Average SAT Math: NR	Graduated top 10% of class: 15%
Notification: Rolling	Average SAT Verbal: NR	Graduated top 25% of class: 33%
Average GPA: 2.8	Average ACT: 19	Graduated top 50% of class: 70%

COLLEGE GRADUATION REQUIREMENTS

Course waivers allowed: No
Course substitutions allowed: No
In what course: N/A

ADDITIONAL INFORMATION

Environment: The school is located in a beautiful and rugged area of the Upper Peninsula of Michigan.

Student Body:	Cost Information	Greek System
Undergrad enrollment: 515	Tuition: $15,434	Fraternity: No
Women: 69%	Room & board: $5,274	Sorority: No
Men: 31%	Housing Information	Athletics: Intramural and Varsity Sports
Percent out-of-state: 24%	University housing: Yes	
	Percent living on campus: 45%	

GRAND VALLEY STATE UNIVERSITY

1 Campus Drive, Allendale, MI 49401
Phone: 616-331-2025 • Fax: 616-331-2000
E-mail: go2gvsu@gvsu.edu • Web: www.gvsu.edu
Support: S • Institution type: 4-year public

LEARNING DISABILITY PROGRAM AND SERVICES

The Office of Academic Support at Grand Valley State University provides academic support services and accommodations that enhance the learning environment for students with disabilities and helps educate the university community on disability issues. In addition to the regular services, the university offers student skill assessment, academic and career advising, specialized tutoring, textbooks on tape, note-taking assistance, alternative test-taking assistance, peer mentoring and counseling. OAS provides students with memoranda documenting their disability. The documentation will contain information on the nature of the disability and what academic accommodations the student may need.

LD/ADD ADMISSIONS INFORMATION

College entrance tests required: Yes
Interview required: No
Essay required: No
Documentation required for LD: Psychoeducational
  evaluation
Documentation required for ADD: Yes
Submitted to: Academic Support and Admissions
Special Ed. HS coursework accepted: Yes

Specific course requirements of all applicants: Yes
Separate application required for program services: Yes
# of LD applications submitted each year: 20–55
# of LD applications accepted yearly: 11
Total # of students receiving LD services: 263
**Acceptance into program means acceptance into
  college:** Student must be admitted and enrolled in the
  university first and then request services.

ADMISSIONS

Students are given the opportunity to provide documentation of their LD or ADD. Information is reviewed by the Office of Academic Support and Admissions. Students interested in special accommodations need to submit both the regular admissions application and a separate application for the program. An evaluation report should include the summary of a comprehensive diagnostic interview. Standardized tests are required for admission. General admission requirements include 4 years English, 3 years math, 3 years social science, and 2 years science. The average ACT score is 23.

ADDITIONAL INFORMATION

Once admitted into the program students may request that an Instructor Progress Report be sent to each of their professors. The purpose of this report is to inform students of their current academic standing in a class. Academic Support staff provide the following services: work with students to help them improve their academic weaknesses and increase their areas of strength; academic and career advising; specialized tutoring in addition to the general tutoring available for all students; seminars on reading textbooks, note-taking, time management, test-taking strategies; tape recording of texts not available through RFBD; alternative test-taking; peer mentoring; counseling; and a student organization to advance the educational and career goals of students with disabilities, Organization for the Achievement of Disabled Students.

Support Services Contact Information

Learning Disability Program/Services: Academic Support (OAS)
Director: Kathleen Vanderveen
  E-Mail: vandervk@gvsu.edu
  Telephone: 616-331-2490
  Fax: 616-331-3440
Contact Person: Sandy Sall/Pat DeJoug
  E-Mail: salls@gvsu.edu
  Telephone: 616-331-2490
  Fax: 616-331-3440

LEARNING DISABILITY SERVICES

Requests for the following services/accommodations will be evaluated individually based on appropriate and current documentation.

Allowed in exams
  Calculator: Yes
  Dictionary: Yes
  Computer: Yes
  Spellchecker: Yes
Extended test time: Yes
Scribes: Yes
Proctors: Yes
Oral exams: Yes
Note-takers: Yes

Distraction reduced environment: Yes
Tape recording in class: Yes
Books on tape from RFBD: Yes
Taping of books not from RFBD: No
Accommodations for students with
  ADD: Yes
Reading machine: No
Other assistive technology: Yes
Priority registration: Yes

Added costs for services: No
LD specialists: No
Professional tutors: No
Peer tutors: 140
Max. hours/wk. for services: 4
How professors are notified of
  LD/ADD: By student

GENERAL ADMISSIONS INFORMATION

Director of Admissions: Jodi Chycinski
Telephone: 616-331-2025

ENTRANCE REQUIREMENTS

Academic units recommended: 4 English, 4 math, 4 science (2 science lab), 2 foreign language, 3 social studies, 1 computer science. 1 fine arts. High school diploma is required and GED is accepted. TOEFL required of all international applicants, minimum paper TOEFL 550, minimum computer TOEFL 213.

Application deadline: 5/1
Notification: Rolling
Average GPA: 3.50

Average SAT Math: NR
Average SAT Verbal: NR
Average ACT: 24

Graduated top 10% of class: 18%
Graduated top 25% of class: 53%
Graduated top 50% of class: 90%

COLLEGE GRADUATION REQUIREMENTS

Course waivers allowed: No
Course substitutions allowed: No
In what course: N/A

ADDITIONAL INFORMATION

Environment: Located 12 miles from Grand Rapids, Michigan

Student Body:
  Undergrad enrollment: 18,160
  Women: 61%
  Men: 39%
  Percent out-of-state: 4%

Cost Information
  In-state tuition: $5,782
  Out-of-state tuition: $12,510
  Room & board: $6,160
Housing Information
  University housing: Yes
  Percent living on campus: 29%

Greek System
  Fraternity: Yes
  Sorority: Yes
Athletics: NCAA Division II

MICHIGAN STATE UNIVERSITY

250 Administration Building, East Lansing, MI 48824-1046
Phone: 517-355-8332 • Fax: 517-353-1647
E-mail: admis@msu.edu • Web: www.msu.edu
Support: CS • Institution type: 4-year public

LEARNING DISABILITY PROGRAM AND SERVICES

MSU is serious in its commitment to helping students no matter what the disability. Their mission is to be an advocate for the inclusion of students with disabilities into the total university experience. The purpose of RCPD (Resource Center for persons with disabilities) is to respond to the needs of students by providing resources that equalize their chances for success, support their full participation in all university programs, and act as a resource for the university community and the community at large. RCPD will facilitate reasonable accommodations for persons with disabilities, coordinate the identification of students with disabilities, and provide referrals. Students must provide recent documentation and history in the form of a school report, psychologist's assessment, or certification by another recognized authority and must contain a clearly stated diagnosis. RCPD will help facilitate reasonable accommodations for students.

LD/ADD ADMISSIONS INFORMATION

College entrance tests required: Yes
Interview required: No
Essay required: No
Documentation required for LD: Psychoeducational evaluation
Documentation required for ADD: Yes
Submitted to: Both Admissions and Center for Persons with Disabilities
Special Ed. HS coursework accepted: No

Specific course requirements of all applicants: Yes
Separate application required for program services: No
# of LD applications submitted each year: NR
# of LD applications accepted yearly: NR
Total # of students receiving LD services: 540
Acceptance into program means acceptance into college: Student must be admitted and enrolled in the university first and then request services.

ADMISSIONS

Admission for students with learning disabilities to the university is based on the same criteria used for all other students. Courses required include 4 years of English, including instruction and practice in writing; 3 years of mathematics, including a calculus preparatory class; 3 years of social science with at least 1 year of history and 1 year in such areas as sociology, anthropology, economics, geography, government, political science, and psychology; 2 years of college preparatory science from the disciplines of biology, chemistry, physics, and earth science; and 2 years of a single foreign language. College Achievement Admissions Program (CAAP) is an alternative admissions procedure for students who have academic potential but who would be unable to realize that potential without special support services due to their economic, cultural, or educational background. Students with learning disabilities should not send any documentation to the Office of Admissions. All documentation should be sent to RCPD.

ADDITIONAL INFORMATION

Specialists are available by appointment to provide information to students. Accommodations include priority registration; study skills and tutoring; assistive technology and training; taped texts; voice output computers; taping of lectures; extended time, reader or scribe, quiet room, and word processing for tests; advocacy assistance from specialists and letters to professors; support groups through RCPD; and consultation with service providers. Various other resources on campus include the Learning Resource Center; the Office of Supportive Services; the MSU Counseling Center; and the Undergraduate University Division of Academic Advising. The Learning Resource Center works with students with learning disabilities on an individual basis to help the student learn to utilize appropriate learning strategies and to mediate their learning environment.

Support Services Contact Information

Learning Disability Program/Services: Resource Center for Persons with Disabilities
Director: Michael Hudson
   E-Mail: mjh@msu.edu
   Telephone: 517-353-9642
   Fax: 517-438-3191
Contact Person: Elaine High
   E-Mail: high@msu.edu
   Telephone: 517-432-4266
   Fax: 517-432-3191

LEARNING DISABILITY SERVICES

Requests for the following services/accommodations will be evaluated individually based on appropriate and current documentation.

Allowed in exams
   Calculator: Yes
   Dictionary: Yes
   Computer: Yes
   Spellchecker: Yes
Extended test time: Yes
Scribes: Yes
Proctors: Yes
Oral exams: Yes
Note-takers: Yes

Distraction reduced environment: Yes
Tape recording in class: Yes
Books on tape from RFBD: Yes
Taping of books not from RFBD: Yes
Accommodations for students with ADD: Yes
Reading machine: Yes
Other assistive technology: Yes
Priority registration: Yes

Added costs for services: No
LD specialists: Yes
Professional tutors: 2
Peer tutors: 10
Max. hours/wk. for services: Unlimited
How professors are notified of LD/ADD: By student

GENERAL ADMISSIONS INFORMATION

Director of Admissions: Pamela Horne
Telephone: 517-355-8332

ENTRANCE REQUIREMENTS

Academic units required: 4 English, 3 math, 2 science, 2 foreign language, 3 social studies. High school diploma is required and GED is accepted. SAT Reasoning or ACT with Writing component required. TOEFL required of all international applicants, minimum paper TOEFL 550, minimum computer TOEFL 213.

Application deadline: 8/1
Notification: 9/1
Average GPA: 3.55

Average SAT Math: 579
Average SAT Verbal: 556
Average ACT: 24

Graduated top 10% of class: 24%
Graduated top 25% of class: 61%
Graduated top 50% of class: 93%

COLLEGE GRADUATION REQUIREMENTS

Course waivers allowed: No
Course substitutions allowed: Yes
In what course: Individual consideration

ADDITIONAL INFORMATION

Environment: Michigan State is located 1 hour from Ann Arbor and 1 1/2 hours from Detroit.

Student Body:
   Undergrad enrollment: 35,107
   Women: 53%
   Men: 47%
   Percent out-of-state: 10%

Cost Information
   In-state tuition: $6,893
   Out-of-state tuition: $17,640
   Room & board: $5,458
Housing Information
   University housing: Yes
   Percent living on campus: 42%

Greek System
   Fraternity: Yes
   Sorority: Yes
Athletics: NCAA Division I

Michigan State University

NORTHERN MICHIGAN UNIVERSITY

1401 Presque Isle Avenue, 304 Cohodas, Marquette, MI 49855
Phone: 906-227-2650 • Fax: 906-227-1747
E-mail: admiss@nmu.edu • Web: www.nmu.edu
Support: S • Institution type: 4-year public

LEARNING DISABILITY PROGRAM AND SERVICES

Disability Services provides services and accommodations to all students with disabilities. The goal of Disability Services is to meet the individual needs of students. Student Support Services is a multifaceted educational support project designed to assist students in completing their academic programs at Northern Michigan University. The Student Support Services professional staff, peer tutors, mentors, and peer advisors provide program participants with the individualized attention needed to successfully complete a college degree. This program is funded through the U.S. Department of Education. Federal regulations require that all participants meet at least one of the following eligibility criteria: come from a low-income background; be a first generation college student; or have a physical or a learning disability.

LD/ADD ADMISSIONS INFORMATION

College entrance tests required: Yes
Interview required: No
Essay required: No
Documentation required for LD: WAIS–III; achievement
Documentation required for ADD: Yes, SB–1
Submitted to: Disability Services
Special Ed. HS coursework accepted: Yes

Specific course requirements of all applicants: Yes
Separate application required for program services: Yes
# of LD applications submitted each year: NR
# of LD applications accepted yearly: 150
Total # of students receiving LD services: 150
Acceptance into program means acceptance into college: Student must be admitted and enrolled in the university first and then request services.

ADMISSIONS

There are no special admissions for students with learning disabilities. All students submit the same general application, and are expected to have an ACT of 19 or higher and a high school GPA of at least 2.25. There are no specific high school courses required for admissions, although the university recommends 4 years English, 4 years math, 3 years history/social studies, 3 years science, 3 years foreign language, 2 years fine or performing arts, and 1 year computer instruction.

ADDITIONAL INFORMATION

The director of Disability Services works on a one-to-one basis with students as needed, and will also meet with students who do not have specific documentation if they request assistance. Skill classes are offered in reading, writing, math, study skills, socio-cultural development, and interpersonal growth. No course waivers are granted for graduation requirements from NMU because the university views waivers as an institutional failure to educate its students with disabilities. Substitutions, however, are granted when appropriate. Services and accommodations are available for undergraduate and graduate students. Student Support Services provides each student with an individual program of educational support services including academic advising; basic skill building in reading, math, and writing; counseling; career advisement; developmental skill building; mentoring; support groups and study groups; tutoring from paraprofessionals; specialized tutors; group tutoring or supplemental instruction; and workshops on personal development and study skills improvement.

Support Services Contact Information

Learning Disability Program/Services: Disability Services
Director: Lynn Walden, Coordinator
 E-Mail: lwalden@nmu.edu
 Telephone: 906-227-1737
 Fax: 906-227-1714

LEARNING DISABILITY SERVICES

Requests for the following services/accommodations will be evaluated individually based on appropriate and current documentation.

Allowed in exams
 Calculator: Yes
 Dictionary: Yes
 Computer: Yes
 Spellchecker: Yes
 Extended test time: Yes
 Scribes: Yes
 Proctors: Yes
 Oral exams: No
 Note-takers: Yes

Distraction reduced environment: Yes
Tape recording in class: Yes
Books on tape from RFBD: No
Taping of books not from RFBD: Yes
Accommodations for students with
 ADD: Yes
Reading machine: No
Other assistive technology: Yes
Priority registration: Yes

Added costs for services: No
LD specialists: No
Professional tutors: No
Peer tutors: Yes
Max. hours/wk. for services: 2–4
How professors are notified of
 LD/ADD: By director

GENERAL ADMISSIONS INFORMATION

Director of Admissions: Gerri Daniels
Telephone: 800-682-9797

ENTRANCE REQUIREMENTS

 Academic units recommended: 4 English, 3 math, 2 science, 3 foreign language, 1 social studies, 1 history, 2 fine arts, and 1 computer literacy. High school diploma is required and GED is accepted. TOEFL required of all international applicants, minimum paper TOEFL 500, minimum computer TOEFL 173.

Application deadline: Rolling
Notification: Rolling
Average GPA: 3.05

Average SAT Math: NR
Average SAT Verbal: NR
Average ACT: 23

Graduated top 10% of class: NR
Graduated top 25% of class: NR
Graduated top 50% of class: NR

COLLEGE GRADUATION REQUIREMENTS

Course waivers allowed: No
Course substitutions allowed: Yes
In what course: Substitutions permitted to fulfill graduation requirements with appropriate documentation.

ADDITIONAL INFORMATION

Environment: The campus is located in an urban area about 300 miles north of Milwaukee, Wisconsin.

Student Body:
 Undergrad enrollment: 8,312
 Women: 52%
 Men: 48%
 Percent out-of-state: 18%

Cost Information
 In-state tuition: $5,334
 Out-of-state tuition: $8,742
 Room & board: $6,182
Housing Information
 University housing: Yes
 Percent living on campus: 30%

Greek System
 Fraternity: Yes
 Sorority: Yes
Athletics: NCAA Division II

UNIVERSITY OF MICHIGAN

1220 Student Activities Building, Ann Arbor, MI 48109-1316
Phone: 734-764-7433 • Fax: 734-936-0740
E-mail: ugadmiss@umich.edu • Web: www.admissions.umich.edu
Support: CS • Institution type: 4-year public

LEARNING DISABILITY PROGRAM AND SERVICES

The philosophy of Services for Students with Disabilities (SSD) is based on the legal actions described in Section 504 of the Rehabilitation Act of 1973. SSD services are dependent on self-advocacy of the students and are "non-intrusive," giving the students the responsibility to seek out assistance. SSD offers selected student services that are not provided by other University of Michigan offices or outside organizations. SSD assists students in negotiating disability-related barriers to the pursuit of their education; strives to improve access to university programs, activities, and facilities; and promotes increased awareness of disability issues on campus. SSD encourages inquiries for information and will confidentially discuss concerns relating to a potential or recognized disability and, if requested, provide appropriate referrals for further assistance.

LD/ADD ADMISSIONS INFORMATION

College entrance tests required: Yes
Interview required: Yes
Essay required: NR
Documentation required for LD: Psychoeducational
  evaluation
Documentation required for ADD: Yes
Submitted to: Services for Students with Disabilities
Special Ed. HS coursework accepted: No

Specific course requirements of all applicants: Yes
Separate application required for program services: No
# of LD applications submitted each year: NR
# of LD applications accepted yearly: NR
Total # of students receiving LD services: 300–350
Acceptance into program means acceptance into
  college: Students must be admitted and enrolled in the
  university first and then request services.

ADMISSIONS

Students with learning disabilities are expected to meet the same admission requirements as their peers. Courses required include 4 years English, 2 years foreign language (4 years recommended), 3 years math (4 years recommended including algebra, trigonometry, and geometry), 2 years biological and physical sciences (3 years recommended), are 3 years history and the social sciences (2 years history recommended, including 1 year of U.S. history). One year hands-on computer study is also strongly recommended, as is 1 year in the fine or performing arts, or equivalent preparation. Mid 50 percent for the ACT 26–30, SAT 1200–1410. There is no set minimum GPA, as it is contingent on several other factors. For students with learning disabilities, the admissions office will accept letters of recommendation from LD specialists. When applying for admission to the University of Michigan, students with learning disabilities are encouraged to self-identify on the application form or by writing a cover letter.

ADDITIONAL INFORMATION

All accommodations are based on documented needs by the student. Services for students with learning disabilities include volunteer readers, volunteer tutors, referral for psychoeducational assessments, selected course book loans for taping, Franklin Spellers, free cassette tapes, APH 4-track recorders, advocacy and referral, advocacy letters to professors, limited scholarships, newsletters, volunteer note-takers, carbonized notepaper, free photocopying of class notes, free course notes service for some classes, assisted earlier registration, adaptive technology, and library reading rooms. SSD also provides appropriate services for students with other health related disabilities such as ADD. There is a special summer program at the university for high school students with learning disabilities. Services and accommodations are available for undergraduates and graduates.

Support Services Contact Information

Learning Disability Program/Services: Services for Students with Disabilities (SSD)
Director: Stuart Segal,PhD and Virginia Grubaugh
  E-Mail: ssegal@umich.edu
  Telephone: 734-763-3000
  Fax: 734-936-3947

LEARNING DISABILITY SERVICES

Requests for the following services/accommodations will be evaluated individually based on appropriate and current documentation.

Allowed in exams
  Calculator: Yes
  Dictionary: Yes
  Computer: Yes
  Spellchecker: Yes
Extended test time: Yes
Scribes: Yes
Proctors: No
Oral exams: No
Note-takers: Yes

Distraction reduced environment: Yes
Tape recording in class: Yes
Books on tape from RFBD: NR
Taping of books not from RFBD: Yes
**Accommodations for students with
  ADD:** Yes
Reading machine: Yes
Other assistive technology: Yes
Priority registration: Yes

Added costs for services: No
LD specialists: Yes
Professional tutors: No
Peer tutors: No
Max. hours/wk. for services: Varies
**How professors are notified of
  LD/ADD:** By student

GENERAL ADMISSIONS INFORMATION

Director of Admissions: Theodore L. Spencer
Telephone: 734-764-7433

ENTRANCE REQUIREMENTS

Academic units required: 4 English, 3 math, 2 science, 2 foreign language, 3 social studies. **Academic units recommended:** 4 English, 4 math, 3 science, (1 science lab), 4 foreign language, 3 social studies, 2 history, 2 academic electives. High school diploma is required and GED is accepted. ACT with Writing component required or SAT Reasoning tests. TOEFL required of all international applicants, minimum paper TOEFL 570, minimum computer TOEFL 230.

Application deadline: 2/1
Notification: Rolling
Average GPA: 3.72

Average SAT Math: NR
Average SAT Verbal: NR
Average ACT: NR

Graduated top 10% of class: 90%
Graduated top 25% of class: 99%
Graduated top 50% of class: 100%

COLLEGE GRADUATION REQUIREMENTS

Course waivers allowed: No
Course substitutions allowed: No
In what course: N/A

ADDITIONAL INFORMATION

Environment: The campus is located in a suburban area about 30 minutes west of Detroit.

Student Body:
  Undergrad enrollment: 24,677
  Women: 51%
  Men: 49%
  Percent out-of-state: 31%

Cost Information
  In-state tuition: $8,535
  Out-of-state tuition: $26,754
  Room & board: $7,030
Housing Information
  University housing: Yes
  Percent living on campus: 37%

Greek System
  Fraternity: Yes
  Sorority: Yes
Athletics: NCAA Division I

AUGSBURG COLLEGE

2211 Riverside Avenue South, Minneapolis, MN 55454
Phone: 612-330-1001 • Fax: 612-330-1590
E-mail: admissions@augsburg.edu • Web: www.augsburg.edu
Support: SP • Institution type: 4-year private

LEARNING DISABILITY PROGRAM AND SERVICES

The Center for Learning and Adaptive Student Services (CLASS) affirms Augsburg College's commitment to provide a high-quality liberal arts education by assisting students in developing self-confidence, independence, and self-advocacy skills in an academic setting. Augsburg has a commitment to recruit, retain, and graduate students with learning disabilities who demonstrate the willingness and ability to participate in college-level learning. Typically, the program provides a very intensive level of support to students during the early phases of their college career, while at the same time teaching them self-advocacy and independence skills. As students master these skills, they gradually assume an increasing degree of responsibility. It is expected that over time, CLASS students will develop the ability to advocate for themselves, gain working knowledge of the accommodations they need, and acquire the skills to access those accommodations independently.

LD/ADD ADMISSIONS INFORMATION

College entrance tests required: Yes
Interview required: Yes
Essay required: Yes
Documentation required for LD: Cognitive (e.g. WAIS–III); achievement (e.g. Woodcok–Johnson); Measures of information processing and memory; within 3 years
Documentation required for ADD: As above with addition of measures of attention and concentration
Submitted to: CLASS
Special Ed. HS coursework accepted: N/A

Specific course requirements of all applicants: Yes
Separate application required for program services: Yes
# of LD applications submitted each year: 140–160
# of LD applications accepted yearly: 70–90
Total # of students receiving LD services: 135–195
Acceptance into program means acceptance into college: Students must be admitted and enrolled in the college first and then request services.

ADMISSIONS

Applicants with learning disabilities must first complete the Augsburg application form. Students with a 2.5 GPA, a rank in the top half of the class, or a 20 ACT score are automatically admissible. Courses required include 4 years English, 3 years math, 3 years science, 2 years foreign language, and 3 years social studies (4 recommended). Students complete a brief application form and submit LD documentation directly to CLASS. The written diagnostic report must contain a definite statement that a LD is present. Specific recommendations about accommodations and academic strengths and weaknesses are valuable. A formal interview will be scheduled to allow the student to provide information and receive more details about accommodations at Augsburg. Students admitted on probation or as high-risk students must take a study skills class and earn a 2.0 GPA for the first year.

ADDITIONAL INFORMATION

Students admitted into CLASS are given individual assistance, from application through graduation, by learning specialists. Academic support includes assistance with registration and advising, guidance with coursework, assistance with writing, instruction in learning strategies and compensatory techniques, help with improving basic skills, and advocacy. Accommodations include testing arrangements, access to computers and training, taped texts, the use of Kurzweil software, assistance in securing note-takers, assistance in obtaining tutors, and foreign language alternatives. There are also many community resources available. Currently there are 190 students with learning disabilities receiving services and accommodations. Undergraduates and graduates can access support services.

Support Services Contact Information

Learning Disability Program/Services: Center for Learning and Adaptive Student Services (CLASS)
Director: James M. Hodgson
  E-Mail: class@augsburg.edu
  Telephone: 612-330-1053
  Fax: 612-330-1137

LEARNING DISABILITY SERVICES

Requests for the following services/accommodations will be evaluated individually based on appropriate and current documentation.

Allowed in exams
  Calculator: Yes
  Dictionary: Yes
  Computer: Yes
  Spellchecker: Yes
Extended test time: Yes
Scribes: Yes
Proctors: Yes
Oral exams: Yes
Note-takers: Yes

Distraction reduced environment: Yes
Tape recording in class: Yes
Books on tape from RFBD: Yes
Taping of books not from RFBD: No
Accommodations for students with ADD: Yes
Reading machine: No
Other assistive technology: Yes
Priority registration: No

Added costs for services: No
LD specialists: Yes
Professional tutors: No
Peer tutors: 80
Max. hours/wk. for services: As needed
How professors are notified of LD/ADD: By student

GENERAL ADMISSIONS INFORMATION

Director of Admissions: Sally Daniels
Telephone: 612-330-1001

ENTRANCE REQUIREMENTS

Academic units required: 4 English, 3 math, 3 science, 2 foreign language, 3 social studies. **Academic units recommended:** 4 social studies, 2 history, high school diploma is required and GED is accepted. TOEFL required of all international applicants, minimum paper TOEFL 550, minimum computer TOEFL 213.

Application deadline: 8/15
Notification: Rolling
Average GPA: 3.26

Average SAT Math: 548
Average SAT Verbal: 559
Average ACT: 23

Graduated top 10% of class: 16%
Graduated top 25% of class: 36%
Graduated top 50% of class: 68%

COLLEGE GRADUATION REQUIREMENTS

Course waivers allowed: Yes
Course substitutions allowed: Yes
In what course: Foreign language

ADDITIONAL INFORMATION

Environment: The college is located on 25 acres near downtown Minneapolis.

Student Body:
  Undergrad enrollment: 2,720
  Women: 57%
  Men: 43%
  Percent out-of-state: 10%

Cost Information
  Tuition: $20,260
  Room & board: $6,080
Housing Information
  University housing: Yes
  Percent living on campus: 33%

Greek System
  Fraternity: No
  Sorority: No
Athletics: NCAA Division III

THE COLLEGE OF ST. CATHERINE

2004 Randolph Avenue, St. Paul, MN 55105
Phone: 651-690-8850 • Fax: 651-690-8824
E-mail: admissions@stkate.edu • Web: www.stkate.edu
Support: CS • Institution type: 4-year private

LEARNING DISABILITY PROGRAM AND SERVICES

The O'Neill Learning Center houses the special learning programs for students with learning disabilities. Accommodations are made on an individual basis. The center's staff works with students and departments to provide reasonable and appropriate accommodations for access to and fair treatment in college programs and activities. The Learning Center and Counseling Center offer staff in-services to help them accommodate students with learning disabilities. A reduced course load is strongly suggested for the student's first semester. Services include information sessions to access services, faculty consultations, and early registration. While the college does not have all of the resources that students with learning disabilities may need, it is committed to responding in flexible manner to individual needs.

LD/ADD ADMISSIONS INFORMATION

College entrance tests required: Yes
Interview required: No
Essay required: Yes
Documentation required for LD: Psychoeducational evaluation within the past three years
Documentation required for ADD: A diagnosis from a physician along with a psychoeducational assessment to measure the impact of the condition
Submitted to: Resouces for Disabilities
Special Ed. HS coursework accepted: Yes

Specific course requirements of all applicants: Yes
Separate application required for program services: No
# of LD applications submitted each year: NR
# of LD applications accepted yearly: NR
Total # of students receiving LD services: 35–40
Acceptance into program means acceptance into college: Students must be admitted and enrolled in the college first and then request services.

ADMISSIONS

There is no special admission procedure for students with learning disabilities, although the college tends to give special consideration if students self-disclose this information. The director of Services for Students with Disabilities serves on the admissions committee. The College of St. Catherine does not discriminate on the basis of disability in admission. A student may enter as a LEAP student-a program which provides special advising, limited course load and a course in strategies for success.

ADDITIONAL INFORMATION

Drop-in help is available on a one-to-one basis from student assistants in writing, study skills, and time management. Students with learning disabilities also have access to support groups and practice in self-advocacy. Tutoring is free for all students. Only students with proper documentation can use the Testing Center to take exams. Accommodations depend on particular student needs. Each semester, students and the supportive services coordinator develop an accommodation plan.

Support Services Contact Information

Learning Disability Program/Services: Resources for Disabilities/O'Neil L Sarning Center
Director: Susan Pauly
   E-Mail: smpaulyl@stkate.edu
   Telephone: 651-590-6563
   Fax: 651-690-6718

LEARNING DISABILITY SERVICES

Requests for the following services/accommodations will be evaluated individually based on appropriate and current documentation.

Allowed in exams
   Calculator: Yes
   Dictionary: Yes
   Computer: Yes
   Spellchecker: Yes
Extended test time: Yes
Scribes: Yes
Proctors: Yes
Oral exams: Yes
Note-takers: Yes

Distraction reduced environment: Yes
Tape recording in class: Yes
Books on tape from RFBD: Yes
Taping of books not from RFBD: Yes
Accommodations for students with
   ADD: Yes
Reading machine: Yes
Other assistive technology: Yes
Priority registration: Yes

Added costs for services: No
LD specialists: Yes
Professional tutors: No
Peer tutors: 25-35
Max. hours/wk. for services:
   Unlimited
How professors are notified of
   LD/ADD: By student

GENERAL ADMISSIONS INFORMATION

Director of Admissions: Cal Mosley
Telephone: 651-690-8850

ENTRANCE REQUIREMENTS

 Academic units recommended: 4 English, 3 math, 2 science, 4 foreign language, 2 social studies, 1 history, 3 academic electives. High school diploma is required and GED is accepted. TOEFL required of all international applicants, minimum paper TOEFL 500, minimum computer TOEFL 173.

Application deadline: NR
Notification: rolling
Average GPA: 3.60

Average SAT Math: 552
Average SAT Verbal: 580
Average ACT: 23

Graduated top 10% of class: 31%
Graduated top 25% of class: 64%
Graduated top 50% of class: 93%

COLLEGE GRADUATION REQUIREMENTS

Course waivers allowed: No
Course substitutions allowed: Yes
In what course: Math, foreign language

ADDITIONAL INFORMATION

Environment: The college is located on 110 acres in an urban area in central St. Paul.

Student Body:
   Undergrad enrollment: 3,593
   Women: 97%
   Men: 3%
   Percent out-of-state: 10%

Cost Information
   Tuition: $19,750
   Room & board: $5,800
Housing Information
   University housing: Yes
   Percent living on campus: 36%
Greek System

Fraternity: No
Sorority: Yes
Athletics: NCAA Division III

The College of St. Catherine

MINNESOTA STATE U.—MOORHEAD

Owens Hall, Moorhead, MN 56563
Phone: 218-477-2161 • Fax: 218-477-4374
E-mail: dragon@mnstate.edu • Web: www.mnstate.edu
Support: S • Institution type: 4-year public

LEARNING DISABILITY PROGRAM AND SERVICES

The university is committed to ensuring that all students have equal access to programs and services. The office of Services to Students with Disabilities addresses the needs of students who have disabilities. The purpose of Disability Services (DS) is to provide services and accommodations to students with disabilities and to work closely with faculty and staff in an advisory capacity. DS will also assist in the development of reasonable accommodations for students, and provide equal access for otherwise qualified individuals with disabilities. Any Moorhead State student with a documented learning disability is eligible for services. This documentation should identify the nature and extent of the disability and provide information on the functional limitations as related to the academic environment. The documentation should provide recommended reasonable accommodations. Requests that would alter the academic standards are not granted. Students are responsible for monitoring their progress with faculty, requesting assistance, and meeting university standards.

LD/ADD ADMISSIONS INFORMATION

College entrance tests required: Yes
Interview required: No
Essay required: No
Documentation required for LD: Completion of a disability verification form
Documentation required for ADD: Yes
Submitted to: Disabilities Services
Special Ed. HS coursework accepted: Yes

Specific course requirements of all applicants: Yes
Separate application required for program services: No
# of LD applications submitted each year: NR
# of LD applications accepted yearly: NR
Total # of students receiving LD services: 25–50
Acceptance into program means acceptance into college: Student must be admitted and enrolled in the university first and then request services.

ADMISSIONS

There are no special admissions for students with learning disabilities. All students must meet the same criteria, including a rank in the top half of class or the following scores on standardized college admission tests: ACT 21+, PSAT 90+, or SAT 900+. They must also have 4 years English, 3 years math (2 algebra and 1 geometry), 3 years science (1 biological, 1 physical science, and at least 1 course must include significant laboratory experience), 3 years social studies (including American history and at least 1 course that includes significant emphasis on geography), 3 electives chosen from at least 2 of the following: world language, world culture, visual and performing arts. The New Center offers an alternative way to begin university studies to students who reside within the MSU service region. If a student does not meet the above admission requirements the application will be reviewed on the basis of strength of college preparation coursework, grade point average, probability of success, academic progression as well as class rank and test scores. Supplemental information may be requested before an admission decision can be made. The New Center offers small, interdisciplinary courses, which meet MSUM's liberal studies requirement for graduation. Enrollment is limited. Students who do not meet New Center admission criteria will be admitted to the Gateway program—a partnership offered by MSUM and Minnesota State Community and Technical College, with courses taught on the MSUM campus.

ADDITIONAL INFORMATION

Examples of general accommodations or services include the following: extended testing time, distraction-free testing environment, taped texts, note-taking, assistive technology, scribe, reader, extra time for assignment completion, tape recording lectures, faculty liaison, strategy development; priority registration, and individual support. Courses are offered in study skills and test anxiety, and students may earn credit for these courses. Services and accommodations are available for undergraduate and graduate students.

Support Services Contact Information

Learning Disability Program/Services: Disability Services
Director: toutges@mnstate.edu
  E-Mail: class@augsburg.edu
  Telephone: 218-477-2652
  Fax: 218-477-5050

LEARNING DISABILITY SERVICES

Requests for the following services/accommodations will be evaluated individually based on appropriate and current documentation.

Allowed in exams
  Calculator: Yes
  Dictionary: Yes
  Computer: Yes
  Spellchecker: Yes
Extended test time: Yes
Scribes: Yes
Proctors: Yes
Oral exams: Yes
Note-takers: Yes

Distraction reduced environment: Yes
Tape recording in class: Yes
Books on tape from RFBD: Yes
Taping of books not from RFBD: Yes
Accommodations for students with
  ADD: Yes
Reading machine: Yes
Other assistive technology: Yes
Priority registration: Yes

Added costs for services: No
LD specialists: No
Professional tutors: No
Peer tutors: Yes
Max. hours/wk. for services: 1
How professors are notified of
  LD/ADD: By director

GENERAL ADMISSIONS INFORMATION

Director of Admissions: Regina Monson
Telephone: 218-477-2161

ENTRANCE REQUIREMENTS

Academic units required: 4 English, 3 math, 3 science (1 science lab), 3 social studies, 3 academic electives. High school diploma is required and GED is accepted. TOEFL required of all international applicants, minimum paper TOEFL 500, minimum computer TOEFL 173.

Application deadline: 8/1
Notification: Rolling
Average GPA: NR

Average SAT Math: NR
Average SAT Verbal: NR
Average ACT: 22

Graduated top 10% of class: 9%
Graduated top 25% of class: 28%
Graduated top 50% of class: 65%

COLLEGE GRADUATION REQUIREMENTS

Course waivers allowed: Yes
Course substitutions allowed: Yes
In what course: Varies based on disability and requirements of major.

ADDITIONAL INFORMATION

Environment: The university has a suburban campus 240 miles northwest of Minneapolis.

Student Body:
  Undergrad enrollment: 7,045
  Women: 61%
  Men: 39%
  Percent out-of-state: 43%

Cost Information
  Tuition: $4,896
  Out-of-state tuition: $4,896
  Room & board: $4,530
Housing Information
  University housing: Yes
  Percent living on campus: 24%

Greek System
  Fraternity: Yes
  Sorority: Yes
Athletics: NCAA Division II

ST. OLAF COLLEGE

1520 St. Olaf Avenue, Northfield, MN 55057
Phone: 507-646-3025 • Fax: 507-646-3832
E-mail: admissions@stolaf.edu • Web: www.stolaf.edu
Support: S • Institution type: 4-year private

LEARNING DISABILITY PROGRAM AND SERVICES

The goal of disability services at St. Olaf is to provide equal access to a St. Olaf education for all students with disabilities. Because it is a small institution, we are able to work individually with students to reach this goal. Its purpose is to create and maintain an environment in which students may achieve their fullest potential, limited to the least extent possible by individual disabilities. All faculty, staff, and students of the college are expected to adhere to this philosophy of equal access to educational opportunity and to assume broad responsibility for its implementation.

LD/ADD ADMISSIONS INFORMATION

College entrance tests required: Yes
Interview required: N/A
Essay required: N/A
Documentation required for LD: Statement (within 3 years) on letterhead of professional noting the history of the disability, testing done for diagnosis, effects of disability on academics and possible recommendations.
Documentation required for ADD: Yes
Submitted to: Academic Support Center
Special Ed. HS coursework accepted: No

Specific course requirements of all applicants: Yes
Separate application required for program services: No
# of LD applications submitted each year: NR
# of LD applications accepted yearly: NR
Total # of students receiving LD services: 25
Acceptance into program means acceptance into college: Students must be admitted and enrolled in the college first and then request services.

ADMISSIONS

All applicants must meet the standard competitive admission criteria. There is no separate application process for students with learning disabilities or attention deficit disorder. Students are encouraged to self-disclose the disability in a personal statement. The mid 50 percent score range for the ACT is 25–30 and for the SAT 1170–1380. It is recommended that students have a strong academic curriculum with 4 years English, 3–4 years math, 3–4 years social studies, 3–4 years science, and 2–4 years foreign language. High school diploma is required and the GED is accepted. The TOEFL is required of all international applicants with a minimum score of 550. Once admitted, students with documented disabilities should have their current documentation sent to the Academic Support Center.

ADDITIONAL INFORMATION

All students have access to tutoring, math clinics, writing centers, study skills assistance, and weekly meetings, if necessary. Other accommodations and services are available with appropriate documentation, including extended testing time; distraction-free testing environment; use of a calculator, spellchecker or computer in exams; scribes; readers; note-takers; and taped texts.

Support Services Contact Information

Learning Disability Program/Services: Academic Support Center
Director: Linne Jensen
  E-Mail: jensenl@stolaf.edu
  Telephone: 507-646-3288
  Fax: 507-646-3786
Contact Person: Ruth Bolstad
  E-Mail: bolstadr@stolaf.edu
  Telephone: 507-646-3288
  Fax: 507-646-3786

LEARNING DISABILITY SERVICES

Requests for the following services/accommodations will be evaluated individually based on appropriate and current documentation.

Allowed in exams	**Distraction reduced environment:** Yes	**Added costs for services:** No
Calculator: Yes	**Tape recording in class:** Yes	**LD specialists:** No
Dictionary: No	**Books on tape from RFBD:** Yes	**Professional tutors:** No
Computer: Yes	**Taping of books not from RFBD:** Yes	**Peer tutors:** 200–250
Spellchecker: Yes	**Accommodations for students with**	**Max. hours/wk. for services:** 3
Extended test time: Yes	**ADD:** Yes	**How professors are notified of**
Scribes: Yes	**Reading machine:** No	**LD/ADD:** By student
Proctors: Yes	**Other assistive technology:** Yes	
Oral exams: Yes	**Priority registration:** Yes	
Note-takers: Yes		

GENERAL ADMISSIONS INFORMATION

Director of Admissions: Jennifer Krengel Olsen, Acting Director of Admissions
Telephone: 800-800-3025

ENTRANCE REQUIREMENTS

Academic units required: 4 English, 2 math, 2 science (1 science lab), 2 foreign language, 1 social studies, 1 history, 2 academic electives. **Academic units recommended:** 4 English, 4 math, 4 science (2 science lab), 4 foreign language, 2 social studies, 2 history, 4 academic electives. High school diploma is required and GED is accepted. ACT with or without Writing component accepted. TOEFL required of all international applicants, minimum paper TOEFL 550, minimum computer TOEFL 213.

Application deadline: NR	**Average SAT Math:** 640	**Graduated top 10% of class:** 48%
Notification: 3/1	**Average SAT Verbal:** 650	**Graduated top 25% of class:** 79%
Average GPA: 3.65	**Average ACT:** 27	**Graduated top 50% of class:** 98%

COLLEGE GRADUATION REQUIREMENTS

Course waivers allowed: 2/1
Course substitutions allowed: Yes
In what course: Alternatives are rarely considered. A subcommittee must recommend substitutions and a faculty committee makes the decision. Most often a student is required to try a language with support from department, tutors, labs and study groups first.

ADDITIONAL INFORMATION

Environment: The college is located on 350 acres in a small town near Minneapolis.

Student Body:	**Cost Information**	**Greek System**
Undergrad enrollment: 2,976	**Tuition:** $26,500	**Fraternity:** No
Women: 58%	**Room & board:** $6,300	**Sorority:** No
Men: 42%	**Housing Information**	**Athletics:** NCAA Division III
Percent out-of-state: 45%	**University housing:** Yes	
	Percent living on campus: 96%	

St. Olaf College

UNIVERSITY OF ST. THOMAS(MN)

2115 Summit Avenue, Mail #32-F1, St. Paul, MN 55105-1096
Phone: 651-962-6150 • Fax: 651-962-6160
E-mail: admissions@stthomas.edu • Web: www.stthomas.edu
Support: S • Institution type: 4-year private

LEARNING DISABILITY PROGRAM AND SERVICES

The mission of the Enhancement program and Specialized Services is to ensure that all students with disabilities achieve their educational, career and personal goals. Comprehensive support services and accommodations are offered that will allow the student equal access to all the university programs and facilities. Students qualify for services through the Enhancement program upon self-disclosure and presentation of appropriate documentation of a LD/ADD. Qualified students, along with the Enhancement program staff, work to realize their potential for academic success. The staff acknowledges that individuals with documented disabilities have unique learning needs. Reasonable accommodations are arranged on an individual basis based on the disability and with the requirements of a particular course. To be eligible for these services, documentation from a licensed professional is required. The documentation should state the nature of the disability and the types of accommodations recommended by the licensed professional. The Enhancement program represents an institutional commitment to individual guidance for students to develop the skills necessary to become independent life-long learners.

LD/ADD ADMISSIONS INFORMATION

College entrance tests required: Yes
Interview required: No
Essay required: Yes
Documentation required for LD: A psychoeduactional assessment completed within the last 3 years, Woodcock-Johnson Test of Achievement, Weschler Adult Intelligence Scale
Documentation required for ADD: Assessment completed within the last 3 years, letter outlining DSM–IV diagnosis, symptoms, methods used to diagnose
Submitted to: Enhancement
Special Ed. HS coursework accepted: Yes

Specific course requirements of all applicants: Yes
Separate application required for program services: No
# of LD applications submitted each year: 35–41
# of LD applications accepted yearly: NR
Total # of students receiving LD services: 145
Acceptance into program means acceptance into college: Students must be admitted to and enrolled in the university and then request services.

ADMISSIONS

There are general requirements for admission, however, some exceptions are made on a case-by-case basis. The general requirements include an ACT score of 20–21, GPA of 3.0 or 35–40 percent of a student's class, recommendations, and an essay. If it is known that a student has a disability, the Office of Admissions may ask the director of the Enrichment Program to assess the documentation. The Office of Admissions has the final decision, but the director of the Enhancement Program may be asked to provide information and recommendations. Students can be admitted on a probationary status. They will be required to develop an academic contract with a counselor and meet with that person regularly throughout the semester. Students cannot get an F in any of their classes. They must maintain this for 2 semesters, and if they do, they are admitted regularly.

ADDITIONAL INFORMATION

Comprehensive services are available through a collaborative effort of the Enhancement Program counselors, the accommodations coordinator, and student employees. Academic and personal counseling is offered pertaining to the student's specific disability. Reasonable accommodations such as note-takers, readers, scribes, books on tape, alternate testing arrangements, and course/program modifications are offered if appropriate. The student's skills are assessed through a pre-screening interview to see if further testing is necessary, and the staff will collaborate with outside agencies for complete diagnostic services. The Enhancement Program offers a "testing, tutoring, and technology" center which houses adaptive technology. Additionally, they offer one-on-one tutoring that emphasizes strategies to improve course content and retention.

Support Services Contact Information

Learning Disability Program/Services: Enhancement Program—Disability Services
Director: Kimberly Schumann
  E-Mail: kjschumann@stthomas.edu
  Telephone: 651-962-6315
  Fax: 651-962-5965
Contact Person: Same

LEARNING DISABILITY SERVICES

Requests for the following services/accommodations will be evaluated individually based on appropriate and current documentation.

Allowed in exams
  Calculator: Yes
  Dictionary: Yes
  Computer: Yes
  Spellchecker: Yes
Extended test time: Yes
Scribes: Yes
Proctors: Yes
Oral exams: Yes
Note-takers: Yes

Distraction reduced environment: Yes
Tape recording in class: Yes
Books on tape from RFBD: Yes
Taping of books not from RFBD: Yes
Accommodations for students with ADD: Yes
Reading machine: Yes
Other assistive technology: Yes
Priority registration: Yes

Added costs for services: No
LD specialists: No
Professional tutors: No
Peer tutors: Yes
Max. hours/wk. for services: Unlimited
How professors are notified of LD/ADD: By both student and director

GENERAL ADMISSIONS INFORMATION

Director of Admissions: Marla Friederichs
Telephone: 651-962-6151

ENTRANCE REQUIREMENTS

Academic units required: 3 math. **Academic units recommended:** 4 English, 4 math, 2 science, 4 foreign language, 2 social science/history. High school diploma is required and GED is accepted. ACT without Writing component accepted. TOEFL required of all international applicants, minimum paper TOEFL 550, minimum computer TOEFL 213.

Application deadline: NR
Notification: Rolling
Average GPA: 3.54

Average SAT Math: 584
Average SAT Verbal: 575
Average ACT: 25

Graduated top 10% of class: 22%
Graduated top 25% of class: 53%
Graduated top 50% of class: 86%

COLLEGE GRADUATION REQUIREMENTS

Course waivers allowed: Yes
Course substitutions allowed: Yes
In what course: Math and foreign language; with assistance, students must petition the Committee on Studies.

ADDITIONAL INFORMATION

Environment: University of St. Thomas is located 5 miles from downtown St. Paul.

Student Body:
  Undergrad enrollment: 5,292
  Women: 51%
  Men: 49%
  Percent out-of-state: 16%

Cost Information
  Tuition: $22,880
  Room & board: $6,706
Housing Information
  University housing: Yes
  Percent living on campus: 39%

Greek System
  Fraternity: NR
  Sorority: NR
  Athletics: NCAA Division III

University of Saint Thomas (MN)

WINONA STATE UNIVERSITY

Office of Admissions, Winona State University, Winona, MN 55987
Phone: 507-457-5100 • Fax: 507-457-5620
E-mail: admissions@winona.edu • Web: www.winona.edu
Support: S • Institution type: 4-year public

LEARNING DISABILITY PROGRAM AND SERVICES

The Disability Resource Center serves Winona State University students and faculty by providing a complex of advising and academic support services and programs that enhance student success, student identification with and commitment to the university, and student persistence to graduation. If a student has been diagnosed with a disability, the student should bring the documentation to the DRC. The coordinator will assist the student in determining which services would be most beneficial, and how to obtain them.

LD/ADD ADMISSIONS INFORMATION

College entrance tests required: Yes
Interview required: No
Essay required: No
Documentation required for LD: Psychoeducational
  evaluation
Documentation required for ADD: Yes
Submitted to: Disability Resource Center

Specific course requirements of all applicants: Yes
Special Ed. HS coursework accepted: N/A
Separate application required for program services: Yes
# of LD applications submitted each year: NR
# of LD applications accepted yearly: NR
Total # of students receiving LD services: 50–100

ADMISSIONS

There is no special admission process for students with learning disabilities. Winona State University admissions requirements include: ACT 21+ or top 50 percent of graduating class with an ACT of 18. Academic transcripts will be reviewed to see that the Minnesota State University preparation requirements have been completed. Admissions decisions are processed in 15 to 20 days.

ADDITIONAL INFORMATION

The Winona State University Disability Resource Center has many services to help students with disabilities. Some of these services include advising (academic, career, and personal), readers, auditory textbooks, testing accommodations, study skills seminars, and academic tutoring days.

Support Services Contact Information

Learning Disability Program/Services: Disability Resource Center
Director: Nancy Dumke
  E-Mail: ndumke@winona.edu
  Telephone: 507-457-2391
  Fax: 507-457-2427

LEARNING DISABILITY SERVICES

Requests for the following services/accommodations will be evaluated individually based on appropriate and current documentation.

Allowed in exams
  Calculator: Yes
  Dictionary: Yes
  Computer: Yes
  Spellchecker: Yes
Extended test time: Yes
Scribes: Yes
Proctors: Yes
Oral exams: Yes
Note-takers: Yes

Distraction reduced environment: Yes
Tape recording in class: Yes
Books on tape from RFBD: Yes
Taping of books not from RFBD: Yes
Accommodations for students with
  ADD: Yes
Reading machine: Yes
Other assistive technology: Yes
Priority registration: Yes

Added costs for services: No
LD specialists: No
Professional tutors: 1-4
Peer tutors: 5–13
Max. hours/wk. for services: Varies
How professors are notified of
  LD/ADD: By both student and director

GENERAL ADMISSIONS INFORMATION

Director of Admissions: Carl Stange
Telephone: 507-457-5100

ENTRANCE REQUIREMENTS

Academic units required: 4 English, 3 math, 3 science (3 science lab), 2 foreign language, 2 social studies, 1 history, 1 academic elective. High school diploma is required and GED is accepted. TOEFL required of all international applicants, minimum paper TOEFL 550, minimum computer TOEFL 213.

Application deadline: Rolling
Notification: Rolling
Average GPA: 3.30

Average SAT Math: 560
Average SAT Verbal: 540
Average ACT: 23

Graduated top 10% of class: 15%
Graduated top 25% of class: 50%
Graduated top 50% of class: 96%

COLLEGE GRADUATION REQUIREMENTS

Course waivers allowed: No
Course substitutions allowed: Yes
In what course: Decisions are made on a case by case basis.

ADDITIONAL INFORMATION

Environment: Located 90 miles south of Minneapolis.

Student Body:
  Undergrad enrollment: 6,996
  Women: 60%
  Men: 40%
  Percent out-of-state: 40%

Cost Information
  In-state tuition: $4,007
  Out-of-state tuition: $7,960
  Room & board: $5,060
Housing Information
  University housing: Yes
  Percent living on campus: 35%

Greek System
  Fraternity: Yes
  Sorority: Yes
Athletics: NCAA Division II

UNIVERSITY OF SOUTHERN MISSISSIPPI

118 College Drive #5166, Hattiesburg, MS 39406
Phone: 601-266-5000 • Fax: 601-266-5148
E-mail: admissions@usm.edu • Web: www.usm.edu
Support: S • Institution type: 4-year public

LEARNING DISABILITY PROGRAM AND SERVICES

The philosophy of USM is to provide services to students with learning disabilities to give them the maximum opportunity to complete a college education. The Office for Disability Accommodations (ODA) is USM's designated office to verify eligibility for accommodations under the Americans with Disabilities Act, and to develop and coordinate plans for the provision of such accommodations. After receiving documentation of the disability, ODA works with students to develop a plan for the provision of reasonable accommodations that are specific to their disabilities.

LD/ADD ADMISSIONS INFORMATION

College entrance tests required: Yes
Interview required: No
Essay required: No
Documentation required for LD: Psychoeducational evaluation
Documentation required for ADD: Yes
Submitted to: Office for Disabilities Accommodations

Specific course requirements of all applicants: Yes
Special Ed. HS coursework accepted: NR
Separate application required for program services: No
# of LD applications submitted each year: NR
# of LD applications accepted yearly: NR
Total # of students receiving LD services: NR
Acceptance into program means acceptance into college: Students must be admitted and enrolled in the university and then request services

ADMISSIONS

There is no special application for students with learning disabilities. Freshmen have specific curriculum, GPA and test score requirements. The mean ACT is 18 and 850 SAT and the minimum GPA is 2.0. Course requirements include 4 years of English, 3 years of math, 3 years of social studies, 3 years of science and 2 electives. An interview is not required, but is preferred. The university offers a pre-admission summer program.

ADDITIONAL INFORMATION

In order to receive reasonable accommodations for a disability, students must file an application with ODA and provide current documentation of a disability. After an application is filed, students schedule an appointment with the ODA coordinator, complete an intake form, and establish a plan for reasonable accommodations and services. The ODA helps students locate tutors, note-takers, and other ancillary aids for their classwork. The office works with vocational rehabilitation in order to pay for these services. The office staff works with students on a one-to-one basis in order to determine how they learn best. There are remedial programs in math, writing, and reading.

Support Services Contact Information

Learning Disability Program/Services: Office for Disability Accommodations
Director: Suzy B. Hebert, Coordinator
  E-Mail: suzanne.hebert@usm.edu
  Telephone: 601-266-5024
  Fax: 601-266-6035
Contact Person: Same

LEARNING DISABILITY SERVICES

Requests for the following services/accommodations will be evaluated individually based on appropriate and current documentation.

Allowed in exams
  Calculator: Y/N
  Dictionary: Y/N
  Computer: Y/N
  Spellchecker: Y/N
Extended test time: Yes
Scribes: Yes
Proctors: Yes
Oral exams: Yes
Note-takers: Yes

Distraction reduced environment: Yes
Tape recording in class: Yes
Books on tape from RFBD: Yes
Taping of books not from RFBD: Yes
Accommodations for students with
  ADD: Yes
Reading machine: Yes
Other assistive technology: Yes
Priority registration: Yes

Added costs for services: No
LD specialists: No
Professional tutors: No
Peer tutors: No
Max. hours/wk. for services: Varies
How professors are notified of
  LD/ADD: By student

GENERAL ADMISSIONS INFORMATION

Director of Admissions: NR
Telephone: 601-266-5000

ENTRANCE REQUIREMENTS

Academic units required: 4 English, 3 math, 3 science, 1 foreign language, 1 social studies, 2 history, 1 academic elective. High school diploma is required and GED is accepted. ACT with or without Writing component accepted. TOEFL required of all international applicants, minimum paper TOEFL 525, minimum computer TOEFL 193.

Application deadline: Rolling
Notification: Rolling
Average GPA: 3.02

Average SAT Math: NR
Average SAT Verbal: NR
Average ACT: 22

Graduated top 10% of class: 23%
Graduated top 25% of class: 52%
Graduated top 50% of class: 82%

COLLEGE GRADUATION REQUIREMENTS

Course waivers allowed: No
Course substitutions allowed: Yes
In what course: N/A

ADDITIONAL INFORMATION

Environment: The university is located on 840 acres in a small city 90 miles southeast of Jackson.

Student Body:
  Undergrad enrollment: 12,520
  Women: 60%
  Men: 40%
  Percent out-of-state: 10%

Cost Information
  In-state tuition: $4,106
  Out-of-state tuition: $9,276
  Room & board: $4,190
Housing Information
  University housing: Yes
  Percent living on campus: 31%

Greek System
  Fraternity: Yes
  Sorority: Yes
Athletics: NCAA Division I

EVANGEL UNIVERSITY

111 North Glenstone, Springfield, MO 65802
Phone: 417-865-2811 • Fax: 417-520-0545
E-mail: admissions@evangel.edu • Web: www.evangel.edu
Support: CS • Institution type: 4-year private

LEARNING DISABILITY PROGRAM AND SERVICES

The Academic Support Center supports the needs of all students at Evangel University. The center focuses on assisting students with improving academic skills so that they remain successful in college. The center offers study skills assistance, tutorial services, and individual college planning. Group and individual support counseling is also available. Study skills are offered for credit. Checkpoint was established in response to the freshman progress reports and offers resources to at-risk students.

LD/ADD ADMISSIONS INFORMATION

College entrance tests required: Yes
Interview required: No
Essay required: No
Documentation required for LD: Psychoeducational
    diagnostic evaluation
Documentation required for ADD: Yes
Submitted to: Academic Development Center
Special Ed. HS coursework accepted: Yes

Specific course requirements of all applicants: Yes
Separate application required for program services: No
# of LD applications submitted each year: NR
# of LD applications accepted yearly: NR
Total # of students receiving LD services: 27
**Acceptance into program means acceptance into
    college:** Student must be admitted and enrolled in the
    university first and then request services.

ADMISSIONS

There is no special application for students with learning disabilities. All students must meet the same admission criteria. Evangel University looks at the completed application, ACT test is required, 2.0 GPA, pastor's recommendation, and high school recommendation. Course requirements include 3 years English, 2 years math, 2 years social science, and 1 year science. Students with documented LD can request a substitute for specific courses if their disability impacts their ability to learn that particular subject. Special admission to the SOAR Program is offered to students with ACT scores between 14 and 17. These students will be enrolled in study skills as well as other proficiency classes.

ADDITIONAL INFORMATION

Some study skills classes are required for students who are admitted conditionally. The Academic Support Center offers tutoring, at no cost, in a variety of courses. The center offers resources in such topics as personal growth, goal setting, self-concept enrichment; stress management, memory and concentration, test-taking, underlining, note-taking, outlining, reading a textbook, research, writing term papers, time scheduling, reading efficiency, and vocabulary. Additional resources include the design and implementation of individualized programs with an instructor, personal professional counseling at no charge, career counseling with the director of Career Development Services, reading labs for increased reading speed, and tutoring in other classes at no charge. Checkpoint offers the following resources to students: performance assessments of text reading and note-taking, assessment of study and time management skills; personal interviews to help address academic difficulties, information about tutoring, and academic advising. SOAR is designed to assist selected provisionally admitted students during the first 2 semesters of college. SOAR courses focus on specific modules such as assessment and skills review in reading, math, and writing; study skills application; and career planning.

Support Services Contact Information

Learning Disability Program/Services: Academic Development Center
Director: Sheri Phillips
 E-Mail: phillipss@evangel.edu
 Telephone: 417-865-2811
 Fax: 417-520-0545

LEARNING DISABILITY SERVICES

Requests for the following services/accommodations will be evaluated individually based on appropriate and current documentation.

Allowed in exams
 Calculator: Yes
 Dictionary: Yes
 Computer: Yes
 Spellchecker: Yes
Extended test time: Yes
Scribes: Yes
Proctors: Yes
Oral exams: Yes
Note-takers: Yes

Distraction reduced environment: Yes
Tape recording in class: Yes
Books on tape from RFBD: Yes
Taping of books not from RFBD: Yes
**Accommodations for students with
 ADD:** Yes
Reading machine: Yes
Other assistive technology: Yes
Priority registration: No

Added costs for services: No
LD specialists: Yes
Professional tutors: 1
Peer tutors: 8
Max. hours/wk. for services:
 Unlimited
**How professors are notified of
 LD/ADD:** By both student and director

GENERAL ADMISSIONS INFORMATION

Director of Admissions: Charity Waltner
Telephone: 417-865-2811

ENTRANCE REQUIREMENTS

Academic units recommended: 3 English, 2 math, 1 science (1 science lab), 2 foreign language, 2 social studies, 3 academic electives. High school diploma is required and GED is accepted. TOEFL required of all international applicants, minimum paper TOEFL 490, minimum computer TOEFL 163.

Application deadline: 8/15
Notification: Rolling
Average GPA: NR

Average SAT Math: NR
Average SAT Verbal: NR
Average ACT: 23

Graduated top 10% of class: NR
Graduated top 25% of class: NR
Graduated top 50% of class: NR

COLLEGE GRADUATION REQUIREMENTS

Course waivers allowed: No
Course substitutions allowed: Yes
In what course: Math

ADDITIONAL INFORMATION

Environment: The college is located on 80 acres in an urban area 225 miles west of St. Louis.

Student Body:
 Undergrad enrollment: 1,616
 Women: 56%
 Men: 44%
 Percent out-of-state: 60%

Cost Information
 Tuition: $12,040
 Room & board: $4,620
Housing Information
 University housing: Yes
 Percent living on campus: 82%

Greek System
 Fraternity: Yes
 Sorority: Yes
Athletics: NCAA Division II

KANSAS CITY ART INSTITUTE

4415 Warwick Boulevard, Kansas City, MO 64111-1762
Phone: 816-474-5225 • Fax: 816-802-3309
E-mail: admiss@kcai.edu • Web: www.kcai.edu
Support: CS • Institution type: 4-year private

LEARNING DISABILITY PROGRAM AND SERVICES

The Academic Resource Center is committed to the educational development of students at Kansas City Art Institute. A recognition of the individual cognitive and creative styles of students of art and design is reflected in the comprehensive support service offered. The goal is to foster independent thinking and problem solving, resourcefulness, and personal responsibility. All KCAI students are invited to take advantage of the services provided by the ARC. Services are aimed at enhancing a student's experience throughout their academic career. The staff takes a holistic approach, and is committed to the educational, personal, and professional development of all students. Students with formal documentation of a disability are encouraged to contact the ARC for assistance in arranging accommodations or developing self-advocacy strategies.

LD/ADD ADMISSIONS INFORMATION

College entrance tests required: Yes
Interview required: No Recommended
Essay required: No
Documentation required for LD: Psychoeducational evaluation
Documentation required for ADD: Yes
Submitted to: Both Admissions and Academic Resource Center
Special Ed. HS coursework accepted: Yes

Specific course requirements of all applicants: Yes
Separate application required for program services: No
# of LD applications submitted each year: NR
# of LD applications accepted yearly: NR
Total # of students receiving LD services: 15–20
Acceptance into program means acceptance into college: Student must be admitted and enrolled in the institute first and then request services.

ADMISSIONS

Students with learning disabilities must demonstrate art ability through a portfolio review and meet a combination of academic criteria, like all applicants, but with a more specialized evaluation. Admitted students should have a minimum ACT of 20 or SAT of 950 and a 2.5 GPA. Students must have had at least 4 years of high school English. If the criteria are not met, applicants are considered in depth via an admissions committee. An interview is recommended.

ADDITIONAL INFORMATION

Students are given assistance in the ARC on an individual basis. Students will consult with their academic advisor each semester about progress in their academic degree program. Advisors help assess progress toward a degree and provide guidance in course selection. Peer advisors are also available. The learning specialist helps students gain a more complete understanding of their individual learning styles, skills, strengths, and weaknesses to cope with the great demands of college courses. Assistance is available through study groups and one-on-one tutoring sessions to improve reading, writing, study, testing, and time management skills.

Support Services Contact Information

Learning Disability Program/Services: Academic Resource Center (ARC)
Director: Bambi Burgard, PhD
  E-Mail: bburgard@kcai.edu
  Telephone: 816-802-3376
  Fax: 816-802-3480

LEARNING DISABILITY SERVICES

Requests for the following services/accommodations will be evaluated individually based on appropriate and current documentation.

Allowed in exams
  Calculator: Yes
  Dictionary: Yes
  Computer: Yes
  Spellchecker: Yes
Extended test time: Yes
Scribes: No
Proctors: Yes
Oral exams: Yes
Note-takers: Yes

Distraction reduced environment: Yes
Tape recording in class: Yes
Books on tape from RFBD: Yes
Taping of books not from RFBD: Yes
Accommodations for students with
  ADD: Yes
Reading machine: No
Other assistive technology: Yes
Priority registration: No

Added costs for services: No
LD specialists: Yes
Professional tutors: 1
Peer tutors: 2
Max. hours/wk. for services:
  Unlimited
How professors are notified of
  LD/ADD: By both student and director

GENERAL ADMISSIONS INFORMATION

Director of Admissions: Larry Stone
  Telephone: 816-802-3304

ENTRANCE REQUIREMENTS

Academic units recommended: 4 English, 3 math, 3 science, 3 social studies, 3 academic electives, 4 fine art. High school diploma is required and GED is accepted. TOEFL required of all international applicants, minimum paper TOEFL 550, minimum computer TOEFL 213.

Application deadline: NR
Notification: Rolling
Average GPA: 3.3

Average SAT Math: 540
Average SAT Verbal: 559
Average ACT: 23

Graduated top 10% of class: 10%
Graduated top 25% of class: 35%
Graduated top 50% of class: 68%

COLLEGE GRADUATION REQUIREMENTS

Course waivers allowed: No
Course substitutions allowed: No
In what course: N/A

ADDITIONAL INFORMATION

Environment: The campus is located in an urban area in Kansas City.

Student Body:
  Undergrad enrollment: 579
  Women: 56%
  Men: 44%
  Percent out-of-state: 69%

Cost Information
  Tuition: $21,446
  Room & board: $7,150
Housing Information
  University housing: Yes
  Percent living on campus: 20%

Greek System
  Fraternity: Yes
  Sorority: Yes
Athletics: None

SOUTHWEST MISSOURI STATE U.

901 South National, Springfield, MO 65804
Phone: 417-836-5517 • Fax: 417-836-6334
E-mail: smsuinf@smsu.edu • Web: www.smsu.edu
Support: SP • Institution type: 4-year public

LEARNING DISABILITY PROGRAM AND SERVICES

The Learning Diagnostic Clinic (LDC) is an academic support facility to assist students with learning disabilities. The staff includes psychologists and learning specialists. LDC provides two levels of academic support to qualified individuals: one level of services includes those services that comprise basic accommodations guaranteed to the qualified students with disabilities under the law; these services are offered at no cost. The next level is called Project Success, an academic support program for college students with learning disabilities who desire more comprehensive services. This program provides academic and emotional support that will help to ease the transition to higher learning and the opportunity to function independently. Students applying to the Project Success program are required to have a psychoeducational evaluation by the LDC staff to ensure that the program is suitable for their needs and to provide appropriate accommodations. The fee for testing is $500. If background and documentation do not support a diagnosis of LD, alternatives and suggestions are discussed with the student. If the student wishes to appeal a decision not to provide services, he/she is referred to the ADA/504 compliance officer.

LD/ADD ADMISSIONS INFORMATION

College entrance tests required: Yes
Interview required: Yes
Essay required: No
Documentation required for LD: Pyschoeducational evaluation
Documentation required for ADD: Yes
Submitted to: Learning Disabilities Clinic
Special Ed. HS coursework accepted: No

Specific course requirements of all applicants: Yes
Separate application required for program services: No
# of LD applications submitted each year: NR
# of LD applications accepted yearly: NR
Total # of students receiving LD services: 200
Acceptance into program means acceptance into college: Students must be admitted and enrolled at the university first and then may request an application to LDC or Project Success.

ADMISSIONS

Students must be admitted to the university to be eligible for the services, and students with learning disabilities must meet the same requirements for admission to the university as all other applicants. There is a special application to be completed as well as a required evaluation fee for students requesting special services. Eligibility for admissions is based on a sliding scale determined by ACT scores and class rank. To apply for project success, students must gain acceptance to by the university self-identify and request application at LDC, submit an application and the requested information. A personal interview and testing is then scheduled, once interview and testing is completed the test data and information are evaluated by staff. The student is accepted or offered alternative suggestions.

ADDITIONAL INFORMATION

Students must self-identify as having a learning disability in order to request accommodations from LDC. Early referral permits the LDC more time to gather information and evaluate documentation. Appropriate accommodations are determined by the director and the student. The student is assigned to a graduate assistant who maintains contact, monitors progress, and assesses the effectiveness of accommodations. Project Success staff provides intensive remediation, focusing upon written language and mathematics strategies; caseworkers provide assistance/advocacy skills; tutors, trained by the LDC, are available to students enrolled in the Project Success program. The fee for this level of accommodations is $1,000 per semester. Basic services from LDC may include assistance in obtaining recorded textbooks, testing accommodations, counseling, advisement, and note-taking assistance; there is no fee for basic services.

Support Services Contact Information

Learning Disability Program/Services: Learning Diagnostic Clinic (LDC)
Director: Steve Capps, PhD
  E-Mail: stevencapps@msu.edu
  Telephone: 417-836-4787
  Fax: 417-836-5475
Contact Person: Candi Vincent, PsyD
  E-Mail: candivincent@smsu.edu
  Telephone: 417-836-6631

LEARNING DISABILITY SERVICES

Requests for the following services/accommodations will be evaluated individually based on appropriate and current documentation.

Allowed in exams
  Calculator: Yes
  Dictionary: Yes
  Computer: Y/N
  Spellchecker: Yes
Extended test time: Yes
Scribes: Yes
Proctors: Yes
Oral exams: Yes
Note-takers: Yes

Distraction reduced environment: Yes
Tape recording in class: Yes
Books on tape from RFBD: Yes
Taping of books not from RFBD: Yes
Accommodations for students with
  ADD: Yes
Reading machine: Yes
Other assistive technology: Yes
Priority registration: Yes

Added costs for services: Yes for
  project success
LD specialists: Yes
Professional tutors: No
Peer tutors: Yes
Max. hours/wk. for services: N/A
How professors are notified of
  LD/ADD: By both student and director

GENERAL ADMISSIONS INFORMATION

Director of Admissions: Mr. Don Simpson
  Telephone: 417-836-5521

ENTRANCE REQUIREMENTS

Academic units required: 4 English, 3 math, 2 science (1 science lab), 3 social studies, 3 academic electives. High school diploma is required and GED is accepted. TOEFL required of all international applicants, minimum paper TOEFL 500, minimum computer TOEFL 173.

Application deadline: 7/20
Notification: Rolling
Average GPA: 3.50

Average SAT Math: NR
Average SAT Verbal: NR
Average ACT: 24

Graduated top 10% of class: 20%
Graduated top 25% of class: 47%
Graduated top 50% of class: 79%

COLLEGE GRADUATION REQUIREMENTS

Course waivers allowed: No
Course substitutions allowed: Yes
In what course: In special circumstances

ADDITIONAL INFORMATION

Environment: The 200-acre rural campus is located 170 miles from Kansas City and 120 miles from St. Louis.

Student Body:
  Undergrad enrollment: 14,565
  Women: 56%
  Men: 44%
  Percent out-of-state: 7%

Cost Information
  In-state tuition: $4,620
  Out-of-state tuition: $9,240
  Room & board: $4,660
Housing Information
  University housing: Yes
  Percent living on campus: 24%

Greek System
  Fraternity: Yes
  Sorority: Yes
Athletics: NCAA Division I

UNIVERSITY OF MISSOURI—COLUMBIA

230 Jesse Hall, Columbia, MO 65211
Phone: 573-882-7786 • Fax: 573-882-7887
E-mail: MU4U@missouri.edu • Web: www.missouri.edu
Support: CS • Institution type: 4-year public

LEARNING DISABILITY PROGRAM AND SERVICES

The mission of Disability Support Services is to encourage the educational development of students with disabilities, and to improve the understanding and support of the campus environment by providing assistance to students with a documented disability and encouraging independence, serving as a liaison and advocate, and working with students to ensure equal access to all programs and services. The Office for Disability Services (ODS) provides accommodations and support services within the resources of the university. The goal of the program is to promote independence and self-advocacy. In addition, ODS assists other college departments in providing access to services and programs in the most integrated setting possible. In order to access services or accommodations, students with LD must provide the most recent documentation indicating both ability, achievement, and I.Q. testing, performed by a qualified professional. Students with ADD must have written documentation from a qualified professional stating client history, tests given, diagnosis, and accommodations recommended.

LD/ADD ADMISSIONS INFORMATION

College entrance tests required: Yes
Interview required: No
Essay required: No
Documentation required for LD: Students with LD must provide the most recent documentation indicating both ability, achievement, and I.Q. testing, performed by a qualified professional
Documentation required for ADD: Students with ADD must have written documentation from a qualified professional stating client history, tests given, diagnosis, and accommodations recommended
Submitted to: Office of Disabilities Services
Special Ed. HS coursework accepted: Yes

Specific course requirements of all applicants: Yes
Separate application required for program services: No
# of LD applications submitted each year: NR
# of LD applications accepted yearly: NR
Total # of students receiving LD services: 610
Acceptance into program means acceptance into college: Students must be admitted and enrolled in the university first and then request services.

ADMISSIONS

There are no special admissions for students with learning disabilities. General admission is based upon high school curriculum and ACT and class rank. Applicants must have 4 years English, 4 years math, 3 years social studies, 3 years science, 2 years foreign language, and 1 unit of fine arts. Math, science, and foreign language requirements may be satisfied by completion of courses in middle school, junior high, or senior high. Any student with an ACT of 24 with the required courses is automatically admissible. Students with 23 ACT or 1050–1090 SAT need class rank of 48 percent; 22 ACT or 1010–1040 SAT need 54 percent; 21 ACT or 970–1000 SAT need 62 percent; 20 ACT or 930–960 SAT need 69 percent; 19 ACT or 890–920 SAT need 78 percent; 18 ACT or 840–880 SAT need 86 percent; 17 ACT or 800–830 SAT need 94 percent; ACT below 17 or SAT below 800 does not meet regular admission standards. Graduates of Missouri high schools who do not meet the standards for regular admission may be admitted on a conditional basis through summer session.

ADDITIONAL INFORMATION

Auxiliary aids and classroom accommodations include note-takers, lab assistants, readers, and specialized equipment. Testing accommodations include time extensions, quiet rooms, readers, scribes, or adaptive equipment. The learning disabilities specialist offers support and counseling in the areas of time management, study skills, learning styles and other academic and social issues. Group support is also available. Disabilities Services offers a mentoring program to provide first year students the opportunity to meet with upperclassmen with disabilities. The Learning Center works cooperatively with DSO to provide individual tutoring free of charge. Other services include writing assistance, math assistance, test reviews, help with reading comprehension and study skills.

Support Services Contact Information

Learning Disability Program/Services: Office of Disability Services (ODS)
Director: Sarah Colby Weaver, PhD
  E-Mail: weavers@missouri.edu
  Telephone: 573-882-4696
  Fax: 573-884-9272

LEARNING DISABILITY SERVICES

Requests for the following services/accommodations will be evaluated individually based on appropriate and current documentation.

Allowed in exams
  Calculator: Yes
  Dictionary: Yes
  Computer: Yes
  Spellchecker: Yes
Extended test time: Yes
Scribes: Yes
Proctors: Yes
Oral exams: Yes
Note-takers: Yes

Distraction reduced environment: Yes
Tape recording in class: Yes
Books on tape from RFBD: Yes
Taping of books not from RFBD: Yes
Accommodations for students with
  ADD: Yes
Reading machine: Yes
Other assistive technology: Yes
Priority registration: Yes

Added costs for services: No
LD specialists: Yes
Professional tutors: 7
Peer tutors: 120
Max. hours/wk. for services:
  Unlimited
How professors are notified of
  LD/ADD: By student

GENERAL ADMISSIONS INFORMATION

Director of Admissions: Barbara Rupp
Telephone: 573-882-7786

ENTRANCE REQUIREMENTS
Academic units required: 4 English, 4 math, 3 science (1 science lab), 2 foreign language, 3 social studies, 1 fine arts. High school diploma is required and GED is accepted. ACT with or without Writing component accepted. Minimum paper TOEFL 500, minimum computer TOEFL 173.

Application deadline: Rolling
Notification: Rolling
Average GPA: NR

Average SAT Math: NR
Average SAT Verbal: NR
Average ACT: 25

Graduated top 10% of class: 29%
Graduated top 25% of class: 60%
Graduated top 50% of class: 95%

COLLEGE GRADUATION REQUIREMENTS

Course waivers allowed: No
Course substitutions allowed: N/A
In what course: N/A

ADDITIONAL INFORMATION

Environment: The university is located on 1,350 acres in a small town.

Student Body:
  Undergrad enrollment: 20,541
  Women: 51%
  Men: 49%
  Percent out-of-state: 12%

Cost Information
  In-state tuition: $7,100
  Out-of-state tuition: $16,547
  Room & board: $6,220
Housing Information
  University housing: Yes
  Percent living on campus: 39%

Greek System
  Fraternity: Yes
  Sorority: Yes
Athletics: NCAA Division I

WASHINGTON U. IN ST. LOUIS

Campus Box 1089, One Brookings Drive, St. Louis, MO 63130-4899
Phone: 314-935-6000 • Fax: 314-935-4290
E-mail: admissions@wustl.edu • Web: wustl.edu
Support: CS • Institution type: 4-year private

LEARNING DISABILITY PROGRAM AND SERVICES

The Disability Resource Center recognizes that there are many types of disabilities that can hinder a student in showing his or her true academic ability. It is the goal of Disability Support Services (DSS) to treat students with disabilities as individuals with specific needs and to provide services responsive to those needs. DSS provides a wide range of services and accommodations to help remove barriers posed by the students' disabilities. Students are encouraged to be their own advocates and have the major responsibility for securing services and accommodations. Reasonable accommodations will be made to assist students in meeting their individual needs. It is the goal of DSS to incorporate students with disabilities into the mainstream of the university community. Any student who has a permanent or temporary psychological or physical disability is eligible for services. Students must self-identify and provide current documentation. The director of DSS will work with the student to identify appropriate accommodations and services based upon documentation and previous experiences. Most accommodations result from communication and agreements between the students and the classroom instructors.

LD/ADD ADMISSIONS INFORMATION

College entrance tests required: Yes
Interview required: Recommended
Essay required: Yes
Documentation required for LD: Psychoeducational
   evaluation: adult-based
Documentation required for ADD: Yes
Submitted to: Disability Resources
Special Ed. HS coursework accepted: Yes

Specific course requirements of all applicants: Yes
Separate application required for program services: Yes
# of LD applications submitted each year: NR
# of LD applications accepted yearly: NR
Total # of students receiving LD services: 114
Acceptance into program means acceptance into
   college: Student must be admitted and enrolled in the
   university first and then request services.

ADMISSIONS

Washington University gives full consideration to all applicants for admission. There is no special admissions process for students with learning disabilities. Students may choose to voluntarily identify themselves as learning disabled in the admissions process. If they chose to self-identify, details of the history and treatment of the disability, how the individual has met different academic requirements in light of the disability, and the relationship between the disability and academic record help the university to understand more fully the applicant profile. This information can be helpful in the application process to explain, for example, lower grades in certain subjects. Washington University is a competitive school and looks for students with rigorous academic preparation, including 4 years English, 3 or 4 years math, 3 or 4 years science, 3 or 4 years social studies, and 2 years foreign language preferred but not required. ACT with or without Writing component or SAT required.

ADDITIONAL INFORMATION

The Learning Center services focus on reading, writing, vocabulary, time management, and study techniques. Skills classes are offered in time management, rapid reading, and self-advocacy, but they are not for credit. Common services and accommodations include, but are not limited to, readers or scribes, note-takers, campus orientation, assistnace in obtaining accommodations for professional exams, referral for disability evaluation, audiotaping class lectures, extra time to complete exams, alternative exam formats, and distraction-free exam sites. Services and accommodations are available for undergraduate and graduate students.

Support Services Contact Information

Learning Disability Program/Services: Disability Resources
Director: Robert Koff, PhD
  E-Mail: drc@dosa.wustl.edu
  Telephone: 314-935-4062
  Fax: 314-935-8272
Contact Person: Zachary McBee
  Telephone: 314-935-4062
  Fax: 314-935-8272

LEARNING DISABILITY SERVICES

Requests for the following services/accommodations will be evaluated individually based on appropriate and current documentation.

Allowed in exams
  Calculator: Yes
  Dictionary: Yes
  Computer: Yes
  Spellchecker: Yes
Extended test time: Yes
Scribes: Yes
Proctors: Yes
Oral exams: Yes
Note-takers: Yes

Distraction reduced environment: Yes
Tape recording in class: Yes
Books on tape from RFBD: Yes
Taping of books not from RFBD: Yes
**Accommodations for students with
  ADD:** Yes
Reading machine: Yes
Other assistive technology: Yes
Priority registration: No

Added costs for services: No
LD specialists: Yes
Professional tutors: No
Peer tutors: No
Max. hours/wk. for services:
  Unlimited
**How professors are notified of
  LD/ADD:** By both student and director

GENERAL ADMISSIONS INFORMATION

Director of Admissions: Nanette Tarrouni
Telephone: 314-935-6000

ENTRANCE REQUIREMENTS

 Academic units recommended: 4 English, 4 math, 4 science (4 science lab), 2 foreign language, 4 social studies, 4 history. High school diploma or equivalent is not required. ACT with or without Writing component accepted. TOEFL required of all international applicants, minimum paper TOEFL 550, minimum computer TOEFL 213.

Application deadline: 1/15
Notification: 4/1
Average GPA: NR

Average SAT Math: NR
Average SAT Verbal: NR
Average ACT: NR

Graduated top 10% of class: 93%
Graduated top 25% of class: 99%
Graduated top 50% of class: 100%

COLLEGE GRADUATION REQUIREMENTS

Course waivers allowed: No
Course substitutions allowed: Yes
In what course: No foreign language required

ADDITIONAL INFORMATION

Environment: The Washington University campus is located 7 miles west of St. Louis on 169 acres.

Student Body:
  Undergrad enrollment: 6,355
  Women: 51%
  Men: 49%
  Percent out-of-state: 88%

Cost Information
  Tuition: $31,100
  Room & board: $10,064
Housing Information
  University housing: Yes
  Percent living on campus: 75%

Greek System
  Fraternity: Yes
  Sorority: Yes
  Athletics: NCAA Division III

WESTMINSTER COLLEGE

501 Westminster Avenue, Fulton, MO 65251-1299
Phone: 573-592-5251 • Fax: 573-592-5255
E-mail: admissions@westminster-mo.edu • Web: www.westminster-mo.edu
Support: SP • Institution type: 4-year private

LEARNING DISABILITY PROGRAM AND SERVICES

The goal of the Learning Disabilities Program is to give students with learning disabilities the special attention they need to succeed in basically the same academic program as that pursued by regularly admitted students. Westminster offers the students a supportive environment, small classes, and professors who are readily accessible. The LD staff offers intensive instruction in reading, writing, and study skills. Much of the instruction is conducted on a one-to-one basis, and is directed to the student's specific problem. Close supervision of the curriculum is essential in the freshman year, and the student's progress is monitored for any difficulties that may arise. The staff is LD certified and faculty members have the specific role of providing LD support.

LD/ADD ADMISSIONS INFORMATION

College entrance tests required: Yes
Interview required: Yes
Essay required: Yes
Documentation required for LD: WAIS–R; (WISC–III) and written evaluation no less than 2 years old, Woodcock-Johnson
Documentation required for ADD: Yes
Submitted to: Both Admissions and Learning Disability Program
Special Ed. HS coursework accepted: No

Specific course requirements of all applicants: Yes
Separate application required for program services: Yes
# of LD applications submitted each year: 40–60
# of LD applications accepted yearly: 14–17
Total # of students receiving LD services: 15–20
Acceptance into program means acceptance into college: Students are admitted jointly to the LD program and the college.

ADMISSIONS
There is a special application and admissions procedure for students with learning disabilities. Students submit a completed Westminster College application form and a separate application form for the LD Program; results of an eye and hearing exam; WAIS–R; WJ; achievement tests; SAT score of 900+ or ACT score of 19+ (untimed); 2 copies of the high school transcript; recent reports from school counselors, learning specialists, psychologists, or physicians who have diagnosed the applicant's disability; 4 recommendations from counselors or teachers familiar with the student's performance; and an evaluation from an educational specialist. An on-campus interview is required. Following the interview and a review of the file, the director and assistant director of the program confer and reach an admission decision usually within one week after the visit. Students are either admitted directly into the college and then reviewed for LD services or admitted into the LD Program, which results in an admission to the college.

ADDITIONAL INFORMATION
Students are mainstreamed and need a solid college-prep background in high school. There is a fee of $1,800 for the first year of the program and $900 each year thereafter. Students have access to unlimited tutoring. Learning resources include audio tapes of textbooks; self-instructional materials; special classes in study, reading and listening skills, test-taking strategies, time management, and English composition; and word processors to assist in writing instruction. The Student Development Center is a learning center that is open to all students.

Support Services Contact Information

Learning Disability Program/Services: Learning Disabilities Program
Director: Hank Ottinger
  E-Mail: ottingh@jwestminster-mo.edu
  Telephone: 573-592-5304
  Fax: 573-592-5191

LEARNING DISABILITY SERVICES

Requests for the following services/accommodations will be evaluated individually based on appropriate and current documentation.

Allowed in exams
  Calculator: Yes
  Dictionary: No
  Computer: Yes
  Spellchecker: Yes
Extended test time: Yes
Scribes: Yes
Proctors: Yes
Oral exams: Yes
Note-takers: Yes

Distraction reduced environment: Yes
Tape recording in class: Yes
Books on tape from RFBD: Yes
Taping of books not from RFBD: Yes
Accommodations for students with
  ADD: Yes
Reading machine: No
Other assistive technology: No
Priority registration: No
Added costs for services: Yes

LD specialists: Yes
Professional tutors: 2.5
Peer tutors: 20
Max. hours/wk. for services:
  Unlimited
How professors are notified of
  LD/ADD: By director

GENERAL ADMISSIONS INFORMATION

Director of Admissions: Patrick T. Kirby
Telephone: 800-475-3361

ENTRANCE REQUIREMENTS

Academic units required: 4 English, 3 math, 2 science (2 science lab), **Academic units recommended:** 2 foreign language, 2 social studies, 2 academic electives. High school diploma is required and GED is accepted. ACT with or without Writing component accepted. TOEFL required of all international applicants, minimum paper TOEFL 550, minimum computer TOEFL 213.

Application deadline: Rolling
Notification: Rolling
Average GPA: 3.47

Average SAT Math: 528
Average SAT Verbal: 544
Average ACT: 24

Graduated top 10% of class: 18%
Graduated top 25% of class: 40%
Graduated top 50% of class: 68%

COLLEGE GRADUATION REQUIREMENTS

Course waivers allowed: No
Course substitutions allowed: Yes
In what course: Students can petition the faculty.

ADDITIONAL INFORMATION

Environment: The 250-acre college campus is located in a small town 20 miles east of Columbia, Missouri.

Student Body:
  Undergrad enrollment: 843
  Women: 42%
  Men: 58%
  Percent out-of-state: 30%

Cost Information
  Tuition: $18,020
  Room & board: $5,870
Housing Information
  University housing: Yes
  Percent living on campus: 85%

Greek System
  Fraternity: Yes
  Sorority: Yes
Athletics: NCAA Division III

MONTANA STATE U.—BILLINGS

1500 University Drive, Billings, MT 59101
Phone: 406-657-2158 • Fax: 406-657-2051
E-mail: cjohannes@msubillings.edu • Web: www.msubillings.edu
Support: S • Institution type: 4-year public

LEARNING DISABILITY PROGRAM AND SERVICES

The mission of Disability Support Services (DDS) is to encourage the educational development of students with disabilities and improve the understanding and support of the campus environment by providing assistance to students with disabilities, encouraging independence, and providing a supportive emotional atmosphere. DSS also serves serving as a liaison and advocate and works with students to ensure equal access to all programs and services. MSU—Billings has a policy of providing reasonable accommodations, to qualified students with a documented disability. Students requiring accommodations such as exam accessibility or reader services, are encouraged to contact DSS at least 4 weeks before services are required. The guidelines used for providing services to students with LD are as follows: (1) the student must meet the definition of LD set forth by the National Joint Committee on LD, (2) the student must have a LD diagnosed by a qualified professional, and a statement of the disability and a summary of academic strengths and weaknesses must be included, (3) quantitative data acceptable for documentation must include standardized and informal measures including case histories, interviews, and previous records that confirm the learning problem. DSS reserves the right to determine whether a student qualifies for services that clearly states a learning disability.

LD/ADD ADMISSIONS INFORMATION

College entrance tests required: Yes
Interview required: No
Essay required: No
Documentation required for LD: Psychoeducational evacuation
Documentation required for ADD: Yes
Submitted to: Disability Support Services

Specific course requirements of all applicants: Yes
Special Ed. HS coursework accepted: Yes
Separate application required for program services: No
# of LD applications submitted each year: NR
# of LD applications accepted yearly: NR
Total # of students receiving LD services: 59
Acceptance into program means acceptance into college: Student must be admitted and enrolled in the university first and then request services.

ADMISSIONS

There is no special admission process for students with learning disabilities. All students must meet the same admission criteria. Freshmen applicants must meet one of the following conditions: (1) ACT of 22 or SAT 920, (2) 2.5 GPA, (3) rank Their the top half of the class. Students must have 4 years English, 3 years math (students are encouraged to take math in senior year), 3 years social studies, 2 years laboratory science (1 year must be earth science, biology, chemistry, or physics), 2 years chosen from foreign language, computer science, visual and performing arts, or vocational education that meet the Office of Public Instruction guidelines. Students not meeting the college-preparatory requirements have four options: (1) apply for an exemption by writing a letter and addressing special needs, talents, or other reasons, (2) enroll part-time in a summer session, (3) enroll as a part-time student with 7 or fewer credits the first semester, (4) attend a community college or other college and attempt at least 12 credits or make up any deficiency.

ADDITIONAL INFORMATION

Students must request services, provide documentation specifying a learning disability or ADD, make an appointment for an intake with DSS, meet with professors at the beginning of each semester, and work closely with DSS. DSS must keep documentation and intake on file, make a determination of accommodations, issue identification cards to qualified students, and serve as a resource and a support system. Services include course and testing accommodations; alternative testing; priority scheduling; technical assistance; liaison and referral services; taped textbooks; and career, academic, and counseling referrals. The use of computer, calculator, dictionary, or spell checker is at the discretion of the individual professor, and based on the documented needs of the student. Services and accommodations are available for undergraduate and graduate students.

Support Services Contact Information

Learning Disability Program/Services: Disability Support Services (DSS)
Director: Trudy Carey
  E-Mail: tcarey@msubillings.edu
  Telephone: 406-657-2283
  Fax: 406-657-2187

LEARNING DISABILITY SERVICES

Requests for the following services/accommodations will be evaluated individually based on appropriate and current documentation.

Allowed in exams
  Calculator: Yes
  Dictionary: No
  Computer: Yes
  Spellchecker: Yes
Extended test time: Yes
Scribes: Yes
Proctors: Yes
Oral exams: No
Note-takers: Yes

Distraction reduced environment: Yes
Tape recording in class: Yes
Books on tape from RFBD: Yes
Taping of books not from RFBD: Yes
Accommodations for students with ADD: Yes
Reading machine: Yes
Other assistive technology: Yes
Priority registration: Yes

Added costs for services: No
LD specialists: No
Professional tutors: 1
Peer tutors: 10–20
Max. hours/wk. for services: Unlimited
How professors are notified of LD/ADD: By student

GENERAL ADMISSIONS INFORMATION

Director of Admissions: Curt Kochner
Telephone: 406-657-2307

ENTRANCE REQUIREMENTS

Academic units required: 4 English, 3 math, 2 science (2 science lab), 3 social studies, 2 foreign language, 1 visual arts, 1 computer science. High school diploma is required and GED is accepted. ACT with or without Writing component accepted. TOEFL required of all international applicants, minimum paper TOEFL 500, minimum computer TOEFL 173.

Application deadline: 7/1
Notification: Rolling
Average GPA: 3.13

Average SAT Math: 497
Average SAT Verbal: 507
Average ACT: 21

Graduated top 10% of class: 11%
Graduated top 25% of class: 30%
Graduated top 50% of class: 62%

COLLEGE GRADUATION REQUIREMENTS

Course waivers allowed: Yes
Course substitutions allowed: Yes
In what course: In foreign language and math under strict guidelines.

ADDITIONAL INFORMATION

Environment: The campus is in an urban area.

Student Body:
  Undergrad enrollment: 4,166
  Women: 65%
  Men: 35%
  Percent out-of-state: 8%

Cost Information
  In-state tuition: $4,550
  Out-of-state tuition: $12,831
  Room & board: $5,500
Housing Information
  University housing: Yes
  Percent living on campus: 11%

Greek System
  Fraternity: No
  Sorority: No
Athletics: NCAA Division II

Montana Tech of the U. of MT

1300 West Park Street, Butte, MT 59701
Phone: 406-496-4178 • Fax: 406-496-4710
E-mail: admissions@mtech.edu • Web: www.mtech.edu
Support: CS • Institution type: 2-year public

LEARNING DISABILITY PROGRAM AND SERVICES

All persons with disabilities have the right to participate fully and equally in the programs and services of Montana Tech. Tech is committed to making the appropriate accommodations. The primary contact and resource person for students with disabilities is the dean of students. The dean serves as a general resource for all students who might need assistance. Availability of services from Disability Services is subject to a student's eligibility for these and any services. Students must provide appropriate and current documentation prior to requesting and receiving services or accommodations. All faculty and staff at the college are responsible for assuring access by providing reasonable accommodations. The Montana Tech Learning Center offers a variety of services to help students achieve their full academic potential. Tutors are available to help all students with course work in an assortment of subject areas. The TLC addresses the importance of developing basic college success skills.

LD/ADD ADMISSIONS INFORMATION

College entrance tests required: Yes
Interview required: No
Essay required: No
Documentation required for LD: Accommodation recommendations from a certified professional
Documentation required for ADD: Yes
Submitted to: Disability Services
Special Ed. HS coursework accepted: No

Specific course requirements of all applicants: Yes
Separate application required for program services: No
# of LD applications submitted each year: NR
# of LD applications accepted yearly: NR
Total # of students receiving LD services: NR
Acceptance into program means acceptance into college: students must be admitted and enrolled at the university and then request services.

ADMISSIONS

There is no special admission process for students with LD or ADD. Applicants must have a 22 ACT or 920 SAT or be in the upper 50 percent of their high school class or have a 2.5 GPA. The GED is accepted. Students must have 14 academic high school credits including 4 years of English, 2 years of science, 3 years of math, 3 years of social studies, and 2 years from other academic areas, including foreign language, computer science, visual and performing arts, and vocational education. Interviews are not required and special education courses in high school are not accepted. Students who do not meet any of the general admission criteria may ask to be evaluated considering other factors. Students with LD/ADD are encouraged to self-disclose in the admission process.

ADDITIONAL INFORMATION

The following types of services are offered to students with disabilities: responding to requests for accommodation; assistance in working with faculty members, text accommodation in concert with instructors, assistive technology, note taking, disability evaluation and testing, and career services. Documentation to receive services should be sent directly to Disability Services. The Learning Center houses computer stations for students. In addition Montana Tech offers compensatory classes for students with LD in both math and English. Services and accommodations are available for undergraduate and graduate students.

Support Services Contact Information

Learning Disability Program/Services: Disability Services
Director: Lee Barnett
  E-Mail: emaillbarnett@mtech.edu
  Telephone: 406-496-3730
  Fax: 406-496-3710

LEARNING DISABILITY SERVICES

Requests for the following services/accommodations will be evaluated individually based on appropriate and current documentation.

Allowed in exams
  Calculator: No
  Dictionary: No
  Computer: Yes
  Spellchecker: No
Extended test time: Yes
Scribes: Yes
Proctors: Yes
Oral exams: Yes
Note-takers: Yes

Distraction reduced environment: Yes
Tape recording in class: Yes
Books on tape from RFBD: Yes
Taping of books not from RFBD: Yes
Accommodations for students with ADD: No
Reading machine: Yes
Other assistive technology: Yes
Priority registration: No

Added costs for services: No
LD specialists: Yes
Professional tutors: 2
Peer tutors: 0–12
Max. hours/wk. for services: Unlimited
How professors are notified of LD/ADD: By both student and director

GENERAL ADMISSIONS INFORMATION

Director of Admissions: Tony Campeau
Telephone: 406-469-4632

ENTRANCE REQUIREMENTS

Academic units required: 4 English, 3 math, 2 science, 3 social studies, 2 years of foreign language, visual & performing arts, computer science, or vocational education units. **Academic units recommended:** 4 English, 4 math, 4 science (2 science lab), 2 foreign language. High school diploma is required and GED is accepted. ACT with or without Writing component accepted. TOEFL required of all international applicants, minimum paper TOEFL 525, minimum computer TOEFL 195.

Application deadline: Rolling
Notification: Rolling
Average GPA: 3.20

Average SAT Math: 539
Average SAT Verbal: 530
Average ACT: 22

Graduated top 10% of class: 11%
Graduated top 25% of class: 44%
Graduated top 50% of class: 67%

COLLEGE GRADUATION REQUIREMENTS

Course waivers allowed: No
Course substitutions allowed: No
In what course: N/A

ADDITIONAL INFORMATION

Environment: Located 65 miles from Helena.

Student Body:
  Undergrad enrollment: 1,913
  Women: 44%
  Men: 56%
  Percent out-of-state: 10%

Cost Information
  In-state tuition: $4,600
  Out-of-state tuition: $13,400
  Room & board: $5,128
Housing Information
  University housing: Yes
  Percent living on campus: 15%

Greek System
  Fraternity: No
  Sorority: No
Athletics: NAIA

ROCKY MOUNTAIN COLLEGE

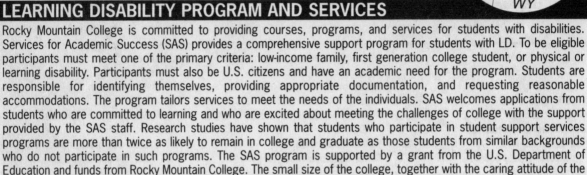

1511 Poly Drive, Billings, MT 59102-1796
Phone: 406-657-1026 • Fax: 406-657-1189
E-mail: admissions@rocky.edu • Web: www.rocky.edu
Support: CS • Institution type: 4-year private

LEARNING DISABILITY PROGRAM AND SERVICES

Rocky Mountain College is committed to providing courses, programs, and services for students with disabilities. Services for Academic Success (SAS) provides a comprehensive support program for students with LD. To be eligible participants must meet one of the primary criteria: low-income family, first generation college student, or physical or learning disability. Participants must also be U.S. citizens and have an academic need for the program. Students are responsible for identifying themselves, providing appropriate documentation, and requesting reasonable accommodations. The program tailors services to meet the needs of the individuals. SAS welcomes applications from students who are committed to learning and who are excited about meeting the challenges of college with the support provided by the SAS staff. Research studies have shown that students who participate in student support services programs are more than twice as likely to remain in college and graduate as those students from similar backgrounds who do not participate in such programs. The SAS program is supported by a grant from the U.S. Department of Education and funds from Rocky Mountain College. The small size of the college, together with the caring attitude of the faculty and an excellent support program, make Rocky a learning disability-friendly college.

LD/ADD ADMISSIONS INFORMATION

College entrance tests required: Yes
Interview required: No
Essay required: No
Documentation required for LD: Psychoeducational
   evaluation
Documentation required for ADD: Yes
Submitted to: Services for Academic Success
Special Ed. HS coursework accepted: No

Specific course requirements of all applicants: Yes
Separate application required for program services: Yes
# of LD applications submitted each year: 10–20
# of LD applications accepted yearly: 10–20
Total # of students receiving LD services: 30–40
**Acceptance into program means acceptance into
   college:** Student must be admitted and enrolled in the
   university first and then request services.

ADMISSIONS

There is no special admissions application for students with learning disabilities. All applicants must meet the same criteria which include an ACT of 21 or SAT of 1000, GPA of 2.5, and courses in English, math, science, and social studies. There is the opportunity to be considered for a conditional admission if scores or grades are below standards. However, to identify and provide necessary support services as soon as possible, students with disabilities are encouraged to complete a Services for Academic Success application form at the same time they apply for admission to Rocky Mountain College. Recommended courses for admissions include 4 years English, 3 years math, 3 years social science, 2 years lab science, and 2 years foreign language. Students who do not meet the normal admission requirements may be admitted conditionally.

ADDITIONAL INFORMATION

SAS provides a variety of services tailored to meet a student's individual needs. Services are free to participants and include developmental coursework in reading, writing, and mathematics; study skills classes; tutoring in all subjects; academic, career, and personal counseling; graduate school counseling; accommodations for students with learning disabilities; alternative testing arrangements; taping of lectures or textbooks; cultural and academic enrichment opportunities; and advocacy. SAS staff meet with each student to talk about the supportive services the student needs, and then develop a semester plan. Skills classes for college credit are offered in math, English, and study skills.

Support Services Contact Information

Learning Disability Program/Services: Services for Academic Success (SAS)
Director: Dr. Jane Van Dyk
  E-Mail: vandykj@rocky.edu
  Telephone: 406-657-1128
  Fax: 406-259-9751

LEARNING DISABILITY SERVICES

Requests for the following services/accommodations will be evaluated individually based on appropriate and current documentation.

Allowed in exams
  Calculator: Yes
  Dictionary: Yes
  Computer: Yes
  Spellchecker: Yes
Extended test time: Yes
Scribes: Yes
Proctors: Yes
Oral exams: Yes
Note-takers: Yes

Distraction reduced environment: Yes
Tape recording in class: Yes
Books on tape from RFBD: Yes
Taping of books not from RFBD: Yes
**Accommodations for students with
  ADD:** Yes
Reading machine: No
Other assistive technology: Yes
Priority registration: Yes

Added costs for services: No
LD specialists: Yes
Professional tutors: 2
Peer tutors: 30
Max. hours/wk. for services:
  Unlimited
**How professors are notified of
  LD/ADD:** By both student and director

GENERAL ADMISSIONS INFORMATION

Director of Admissions: Bonnie Knapp
Telephone: 406-657-1026

ENTRANCE REQUIREMENTS

Academic units required: 4 English, 2 math, 2 science (1 science lab), 1 foreign language, 2 social studies, 2 history. **Academic units recommended:** 4 English, 3 math, 2 science (1 science lab), 2 foreign language, 2 social studies, 2 history. High school diploma is required and GED is accepted. ACT with or without Writing component accepted. TOEFL required of all international applicants, minimum paper TOEFL 525, minimum computer TOEFL 197.

Application deadline: Rolling
Notification: Rolling
Average GPA: 3.31

Average SAT Math: 531
Average SAT Verbal: 510
Average ACT: 22

Graduated top 10% of class: 17%
Graduated top 25% of class: 41%
Graduated top 50% of class: 69%

COLLEGE GRADUATION REQUIREMENTS

Course waivers allowed: Y/N
Course substitutions allowed: Y/N
In what course: Substitutions and waivers are provided on a limited basis.

ADDITIONAL INFORMATION

Environment: The campus is located in a small town over 500 miles north of Denver, Colorado.

Student Body:
  Undergrad enrollment: 920
  Women: 55%
  Men: 45%
  Percent out-of-state: 29%

Cost Information
  Tuition: $14,500
  Room & board: $5,480
Housing Information
  University housing: Yes
  Percent living on campus: 43%

Greek System
  Fraternity: No
  Sorority: No
Athletics: NAIA

UNIVERSITY OF MONTANA

Lommasson Center 103, Missoula, MT 59812
Phone: 406-243-6266 • Fax: 406-243-5711
E-mail: admiss@umontana.edu • Web: www.umt.edu
Support: S • Institution type: 4-year public

LEARNING DISABILITY PROGRAM AND SERVICES

Disability Services for Students (DSS) ensures equal access to the university by students with disabilities. DSS is a stand-alone student affairs office at the university. It is staffed by more than 10 full-time professionals. Students with learning disabilities have the same set of rights and responsibilities and the same set of services and accommodations offered to other students with disabilities. Written documentation from a qualified diagnostician containing the diagnosis and functional limitation of the LD must be provided to DSS. It should be noted that DSS does not operate the same way many special education programs in secondary schools do. At the university, students have a right to access education, not a right to education. This means that DSS treats students as adults who succeed or fail on their own merits. Students should determine their needs, initiate requests for accommodations, and follow up with the delivery of those rights. DSS refrains from seeking out individuals for interventionist actions. Once a student makes the disability and needs known to DSS, DSS will provide the accommodations that will grant the student the right of equal access. Transitioning from high school to college is enhanced when students grasp and apply the principles of self-advocacy.

LD/ADD ADMISSIONS INFORMATION

College entrance tests required: Yes
Interview required: No
Essay required: No
Documentation required for LD: WAIS–III, 1 achievement battery unless ADD considered, no less than 3 years old
Documentation required for ADD: Yes
Submitted to: Disability Services for students
Special Ed. HS coursework accepted: N/A

Specific course requirements of all applicants: Yes
Separate application required for program services: Yes
# of LD applications submitted each year: NR
# of LD applications accepted yearly: NR
Total # of students receiving LD services: 190
Acceptance into program means acceptance into college: Student must be admitted and enrolled in the university first and then request services.

ADMISSIONS

Admissions criteria are the same for all applicants. However, consideration will be given to students who do not meet the general admissions criteria. General admission criteria include, 22 ACT/1030 SAT, rank in the upper half of the class and, 2.5 GPA. DSS will act as an advocate for students with learning disabilities during the admission process. Applicants not meeting admission criteria may request and receive a review of their eligibility by an admissions committee. Students should send documentation verifying the disability directly to the DSS office. Documentation should include a complete and current (3–5 years), psychological evaluation written by a qualified professional stating the diagnosis. Additional in the report should be the list of standardized tests, relevant history, functional limitations and recommend ed accommodations.

ADDITIONAL INFORMATION

Students with LD can expect reasonable accommodations to suit their individual needs. Accommodations may include a direct service or academic adjustment, but will not reduce the academic standards of the institution. Academic assistants at the university provide auxiliary aids such as reading textbooks and other instructional materials,scribing assignments or tests, assisting in library research, and proofreading materials. Services may include academic adjustments, admissions assistance, assistive technology, auxiliary aids, consultation with faculty, counseling, course waiver assistance, letter of verification, note-taking, orientation, priority registration, scribes, study skills course, test accommodations services, and tutoring services. Academic adjustments may include extended testing time, substitute course requirements; or lecture notes from instructors.

Support Services Contact Information

Learning Disability Program/Services: Disability Services for Students (DSS)
Director: James Marks
  E-Mail: jim.marks@umontana.edu
  Telephone: 406-243-2243
  Fax: 406-243-5330

LEARNING DISABILITY SERVICES

Requests for the following services/accommodations will be evaluated individually based on appropriate and current documentation.

Allowed in exams
  Calculator: Yes
  Dictionary: Yes
  Computer: Yes
  Spellchecker: Yes
Extended test time: Yes
Scribes: Yes
Proctors: Yes
Oral exams: Yes
Note-takers: Yes

Distraction reduced environment: Yes
Tape recording in class: Yes
Books on tape from RFBD: Yes
Taping of books not from RFBD: Yes
Accommodations for students with ADD: Yes
Reading machine: Yes
Other assistive technology: Yes
Priority registration: Yes

Added costs for services: Yes
LD specialists: No
Professional tutors: No
Peer tutors: 0
Max. hours/wk. for services: N/A
How professors are notified of LD/ADD: By student

GENERAL ADMISSIONS INFORMATION

Director of Admissions: Jed Liston
Telephone: 406-243-2362

ENTRANCE REQUIREMENTS
Academic units required: 4 English, 3 math, 2 science (2 science lab), 3 social studies, 2 history, 2 academic electives, 2 units in foreign language, computer science, visual/performing arts, or vocational education.   High school diploma is required and GED is accepted. TOEFL required of all international applicants, minimum paper TOEFL 500, minimum computer TOEFL 173.

Application deadline: Rolling
Notification: Rolling
Average GPA: 3.18

Average SAT Math: NR
Average SAT Verbal: NR
Average ACT: NR

Graduated top 10% of class: 14%
Graduated top 25% of class: 33%
Graduated top 50% of class: 66%

COLLEGE GRADUATION REQUIREMENTS

Course waivers allowed: Yes
Course substitutions allowed: Yes
In what course: Varies by need and department.

ADDITIONAL INFORMATION

Environment: The university's urban campus is 200 miles from Spokane.

Student Body:
  Undergrad enrollment: 10,943
  Women: 53%
  Men: 47%
  Percent out-of-state: 21%

Cost Information
  In-state tuition: $4,900
  Out-of-state tuition: $13,800
  Room & board: $9,000
Housing Information
  University housing: Yes
  Percent living on campus: 22%

Greek System
  Fraternity: Yes
  Sorority: Yes
Athletics: NCAA Division I

UNIVERSITY OF MONTANA—WESTERN

710 South Atlantic, Dillon, MT 59725
Phone: 406-683-7331 • Fax: 406-683-7493
E-mail: admissions@umwestern.edu • Web: www.umwestern.edu
Support: S • Institution type: 4-year public

LEARNING DISABILITY PROGRAM AND SERVICES

Western Montana College strives to accommodate all students with special needs. These needs may be physical, social, or academic. Almost all services are free to the student. The associate dean of students is in charge of making special accommodations available to students with learning disabilities. If an applicant has a documented learning disability and requests special accommodations for a class, they must contact the associate dean of students so that arrangements can be made. The professor of the class, the Associate Dean, and the student will meet to set up an individualized educational plan for that class and documentation will be kept on file in the Student Life Office.

LD/ADD ADMISSIONS INFORMATION

College entrance tests required: Yes
Interview required: No
Essay required: No
Documentation required for LD: Psychoeducational evaluation
Documentation required for ADD: Yes
Submitted to: Disability Services
Special Ed. HS coursework accepted: Yes

Specific course requirements of all applicants: Yes
Separate application required for program services: No
# of LD applications submitted each year: NR
# of LD applications accepted yearly: NR
Total # of students receiving LD services: 21
Acceptance into program means acceptance into college: Student must be admitted and enrolled in the university first and then request services.

ADMISSIONS

The college has no special requirements other than those outlined by the state Board of Regents (a valid high school diploma or GED). Admission criteria for general admission include 4 years English, 3 years math, 3 years science, 3 years social studies, and 2 years from foreign language, computer science, visual or performing arts, or vocational education; 2.5 GPA (minimum 2.0 for students with learning disabilities); 20 ACT or 960 SAT; top 50 percent of class. Students with documented learning disabilities may request waivers or substitutions in courses affected by the disability. Because Western Montana is a small college, each individual can set up an admissions plan. There is a 15 percent window of exemption for some students who do not meet admission requirments. These students can be admitted provisionally if they provide satisfactory evidence that they are prepared to pursue successfully the special courses required.

ADDITIONAL INFORMATION

Students who present appropriate documentation may be eligible for some of the following services or accommodations: the use of calculators, dictionary, computer or spell checker for tests; extended time on tests; distraction-free environment for tests; proctors; scribes; oral exams; note-takers; tape recorder in class; books on tape; and priority registration. The Learning Center offers skill-building classes in reading, writing, and math. These classes don't count toward a student's GPA, but do for athletic eligibility. Students whose ACT or entrance tests show that they would profit from such instruction will be placed in courses that will best meet their needs and ensure a successful college career. Free tutoring is available in most areas on a drop-in basis or at prescribed times. Services and accommodations are available for undergraduate and graduate students.

Support Services Contact Information

Learning Disability Program/Services: Disability Services
Director: Dr. Eric Murray, Dean of Students
  E-Mail: e_murray@umwestern.edu
  Telephone: 406-683-7565
  Fax: 406-683-7570

LEARNING DISABILITY SERVICES

Requests for the following services/accommodations will be evaluated individually based on appropriate and current documentation.

Allowed in exams
  Calculator: Yes
  Dictionary: Yes
  Computer: Yes
  Spellchecker: Yes
Extended test time: Yes
Scribes: Yes
Proctors: Yes
Oral exams: Yes
Note-takers: Yes

Distraction reduced environment: Yes
Tape recording in class: Yes
Books on tape from RFBD: Yes
Taping of books not from RFBD: Yes
Accommodations for students with
  ADD: Yes
Reading machine: No
Other assistive technology: No
Priority registration: Yes

Added costs for services: No
LD specialists: No
Professional tutors: 3
Peer tutors: 6
Max. hours/wk. for services:
  Unlimited
How professors are notified of
  LD/ADD: By both student and director

GENERAL ADMISSIONS INFORMATION

Director of Admissions: Arlene Williams
Telephone: 406-683-7331

ENTRANCE REQUIREMENTS

Academic units required: 4 English, 3 math, 2 science (2 science lab), 3 social studies, 4 academic electives. High school diploma is required and GED is accepted. TOEFL required of all international applicants, minimum paper TOEFL 500, minimum computer TOEFL 173.

Application deadline: 7/1
Notification: Rolling
Average GPA: 2.99

Average SAT Math: 466
Average SAT Verbal: 457
Average ACT: 18

Graduated top 10% of class: 5%
Graduated top 25% of class: 17%
Graduated top 50% of class: 44%

COLLEGE GRADUATION REQUIREMENTS

Course waivers allowed: Yes
Course substitutions allowed: Yes
In what course: General education courses

ADDITIONAL INFORMATION

Environment: The college is located on 20 acres in a small town about 60 miles south of Butte.

Student Body:
  Undergrad enrollment: 1046
  Women: 57%
  Men: 43%
  Percent out-of-state: 14%

Cost Information
  In-state tuition: $4,000
  Out-of-state tuition: $11,600
  Room & board: $4,600
Housing Information
  University housing: Yes
  Percent living on campus: 22%

Greek System
  Fraternity: No
  Sorority: No
Athletics: NAIA

University of Montana—Western

UNION COLLEGE (NE)

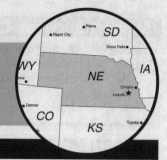

3800 South 48th Street, Lincoln, NE 68506-4300
Phone: 402-486-2504 • Fax: 402-486-2566
E-mail: ucenroll@ucollege.edu • Web: www.ucollege.edu
Support: SP • Institution type: 4-year private

LEARNING DISABILITY PROGRAM AND SERVICES

The Teaching Learning Center is a specialized program serving the Union College student with learning disabilities/dyslexia and all students with disabilities. The Teaching Learning Center offers assistance to the serious, capable student with learning disabilities who seeks to earn an undergraduate degree in a Christian environment. In order to qualify for accommodations a student must have an I.Q. commensurate with college achievement; have a diagnosis based on current data, which will be reviewed by the Teaching Leaning Center staff; complete admission procedures to Union College; take an untimed ACT; apply to the Teaching Learning Center and provide needed information; and arrange for a two-day visit to campus to complete diagnostic/prescriptive testing to determine needed accommodations and remediation. Students with LD in the program enroll in regular college classes, although a light load is initially recommended.

LD/ADD ADMISSIONS INFORMATION

College entrance tests required: Yes
Interview required: No
Essay required: No
Documentation required for LD: Psychoeducational, preferably WAIS–III, Woodcock-Johnson
Documentation required for ADD: Yes
Submitted to: Teaching Learning Center
Special Ed. HS coursework accepted: Yes

Specific course requirements of all applicants: Yes
Separate application required for program services: Yes
# of LD applications submitted each year: 60–70
# of LD applications accepted yearly: NR
Total # of students receiving LD services: 80–90
Acceptance into program means acceptance into college: Students are admitted to the TLC program and the college jointly.

ADMISSIONS

There is no special admission process for students with learning disabilities. All applicants are expected to meet the same admission criteria, including a GPA of 2.5; ACT of 16+; 3 years English, 2 years natural science, 2 years history, 2 years algebra, and 3 years selected from English, math, natural science, social studies, religion, modern foreign language, or vocational courses. Students with course deficiencies can be admitted and make up the deficiencies in college. The staff from the Teaching Learning Center may review documentation from some applicants and provide a recommendation to the Office of Admissions regarding an admission decision. The final decision for admission into the program is made by TLC. Special Admission status is for students with no immediate plans to graduate. Temporary Admission status is valid on a semester by semester basis allowing students to secure official transcripts from high school or other colleges. This status is limited to 3 semesters. Conditional admission status is for students who lack certain entrance requirements such as math, English, history, or science which must be satisfied within the first year of attendance. A three-semester-hour course taken in college to remove an entrance deficiency is equivalent to one full year of a high school course.

ADDITIONAL INFORMATION

Reasonable accommodation is an individualized matter determined in consultation between the student, parents, project staff, and appropriate faculty members. Accommodations may include texts on tape, oral testing, individual testing; extended time/alternate assignments, note-takers, remediation, academic tutoring (additional fee), counseling, instruction in word processing, and assistance with term papers. Skills classes for college credit are offered in reading, spelling, math, and writing. The Technology Resource Center for learning disabilities provides information on available technology such as: Four-Track tape player (fits in your hand); Personal Voice Organizer; Language Master 600 (voice powered, had-held dictionary, thesaurus, and word games); Calcu-Talk (scientific and financial talking calculator; plus laser printer, character recognition scanner and two personal computers with screen filters. Software includes: Arkenstone (reads written page); Dragon Dictate (control computer by voice); Grammatik (analyzes and corrects grammar); Kurzweil (combines with scanner to convert written test to spoken word); Inspiration (allows the visual person to organize thoughts in outline and cluster form); and Telepathic II (word prediction engine).

Support Services Contact Information

Learning Disability Program/Services: Teaching Learning Center (TLC)
Director: Jennifer Forbes
  E-Mail: jeforbes@ucollege.edu
  Telephone: 402-486-2506
  Fax: 402-486-2895
Contact Person: Terri Ingram
  E-Mail: tlc@ucollege.edu
  Telephone: 402-486-2506
  Fax: 402-486-2895

LEARNING DISABILITY SERVICES

Requests for the following/services accommodations will be evaluated individually based on appropriate and current documentation.

Allowed in exams
  Calculator: Yes
  Dictionary: Yes
  Computer: Yes
  Spellchecker: Yes
Extended test time: Yes
Scribes: Yes
Proctors: Yes
Oral exams: Yes
Note-takers: Yes

Distraction reduced environment: Yes
Tape recording in class: Yes
Books on tape from RFBD: Yes
Taping of books not from RFBD: Yes
Accommodations for students with ADD: Yes
Reading machine: Yes
Other assistive technology: Yes
Priority registration: No

Added costs for services: Yes
LD specialists: Yes
Professional tutors: 3
Peer tutors: 15-25
Max. hours/wk. for services: 5
How professors are notified of LD/ADD: By both student and director

GENERAL ADMISSIONS INFORMATION

Director of Admissions: Huda McClelland
Telephone: 402-486-2051

ENTRANCE REQUIREMENTS

Academic units required: 3 English, 2 math, 2 science (1 science lab), 1 social studies, 1 history, 3 academic electives. **Academic units recommended:** 4 English, 3 math, 3 science, 1 foreign language. High school diploma is required and GED is accepted. ACT with or without Writing component accepted. TOEFL required of all international applicants, minimum paper TOEFL 550, minimum computer TOEFL 213.

Application deadline: 8/1
Notification: Rolling
Average GPA: NR

Average SAT Math: NR
Average SAT Verbal: NR
Average ACT: 22

Graduated top 10% of class: 22%
Graduated top 25% of class: 27%
Graduated top 50% of class: 37%

COLLEGE GRADUATION REQUIREMENTS

Course waivers allowed: No
Course substitutions allowed: No
In what course: N/A

ADDITIONAL INFORMATION

Environment: The college has a suburban campus near Lincoln.

Student Body:
  Undergrad enrollment: 883
  Women: 56%
  Men: 44%
  Percent out-of-state: 79%

Cost Information
  Tuition: $13,990
  Room & board: $3,950
Housing Information
  University housing: Yes
  Percent living on campus: 58%

Greek System
  Fraternity: No
  Sorority: No
Athletics: NCAA Division III

UNIVERSITY OF NEBRASKA—LINCOLN

313 North 13th Street, Van Brunt Visitors Center, Lincoln, NE 68588-0256
Phone: 402-472-2023 • Fax: 402-472-0670
E-mail: nuhusker@unl.edu • Web: www.unl.edu
Support: S • Institution type: 4-year public

LEARNING DISABILITY PROGRAM AND SERVICES

Services for Students with Disabilities (SSD) provide special assistance to students with disabilities through individualized help and counseling. Because adjustment to college life and its academic demands is a new experience and there are special challenges confronting disabled students, SSD is committed to providing students with the support that will help them to reach their academic goals. SSD coordinates and delivers the services required to accommodate a disability. All accommodation requests are initiated at the SSD office with appropriate documentation. Once the accommodations are approved the individual student is responsible for requesting services each semester from the SSD office

LD/ADD ADMISSIONS INFORMATION

College entrance tests required: Yes
Interview required: No
Essay required: No
Documentation required for LD: Psychoeducational
  evaluation
Documentation required for ADD: Yes
Submitted to: Services for students with disabilities
Special Ed. HS coursework accepted: N/A

Specific course requirements of all applicants: Yes
Separate application required for program services: No
# of LD applications submitted each year: NR
# of LD applications accepted yearly: NR
Total # of students receiving LD services: NR
**Acceptance into program means acceptance into
  college:** Students must be admitted and enrolled in the
  university and then request services.

ADMISSIONS

There is no special admission process for students with disabilities. All applicants are expected to meet the same admission criteria, including an ACT of 20 or higher, or an SAT of 950 or higher, or rank in the top half of their graduating class along with meeting the course requirements of 4 units of math, 4 units of English, 3 units of social sciences, 3 units of natural sciences, and 2 units of foreign language. There is an appeals process for deferred students.

ADDITIONAL INFORMATION

Accommodations are provided in an individualized manner for all students. Reasonable accommodations include extended time on exams, a separate testing area, a reader, a scribe, an interpreter, taped exams, Braille or large print exams, spelling assistance, the use of computer of other adaptive equipment for exams, classroom note-taker, a tape recorder in the classroom, C Print captioning for classes, and alternative formats which include Braille, e-text and taped textbooks. Other services provided include intercampus transportation coordination, priority registration and assistance with advocacy.

Support Services Contact Information

Learning Disability Program/Services: Services for Students with Disabilities
Director: Veva Cheney
  E-Mail: vcheney2@unl.edu
  Telephone: 402-472-3787
  Fax: 402-472-0080

LEARNING DISABILITY SERVICES

Requests for the following/services accommodations will be evaluated individually based on appropriate and current documentation.

Allowed in exams
  Calculator: Yes
  Dictionary: No
  Computer: Yes
  Spellchecker: Yes
Extended test time: Yes
Scribes: Yes
Proctors: Yes
Oral exams: Yes
Note-takers: Yes

Distraction reduced environment: Yes
Tape recording in class: Yes
Books on tape from RFBD: Yes
Taping of books not from RFBD: Yes
Accommodations for students with ADD: Yes
Reading machine: Yes
Other assistive technology: Yes
Priority registration: Yes

Added costs for services: No
LD specialists: No
Professional tutors: No
Peer tutors: No
Max. hours/wk. for services: Varies
How professors are notified of LD/ADD: By both student and director

GENERAL ADMISSIONS INFORMATION

Director of Admissions: Alan Cerveny
Telephone: 402-472-2023

ENTRANCE REQUIREMENTS

Academic units required: 4 English, 4 math, 3 science (1 science lab), 2 foreign language, 3 social studies.
Academic units recommended: 1 history, High school diploma is required and GED is accepted. ACT with or without Writing component accepted. TOEFL required of all international applicants, minimum paper TOEFL 525, minimum computer TOEFL 193.

Application deadline: 6/30
Notification: Rolling
Average GPA: NR

Average SAT Math: 596
Average SAT Verbal: 576
Average ACT: 25

Graduated top 10% of class: 28%
Graduated top 25% of class: 54%
Graduated top 50% of class: 85%

COLLEGE GRADUATION REQUIREMENTS

Course waivers allowed: No
Course substitutions allowed: Yes
In what course: Foreign language

ADDITIONAL INFORMATION

Environment: UNL is located in Lincoln, NE, which is the capital and the second largest city in the state.

Student Body:
  Undergrad enrollment: 17,137
  Women: 47%
  Men: 53%
  Percent out-of-state: 20%

Cost Information
  In-state tuition: $5,268
  Out-of-state tuition: $13,759
  Room & board: $6,008
Housing Information
  University housing: Yes
  Percent living on campus: 24%

Greek System
  Fraternity: Yes
  Sorority: Yes
Athletics: NCAA Division I

WAYNE STATE COLLEGE

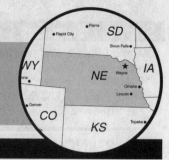

1111 Main Street, Wayne, NE 68787
Phone: 402-375-7234 • Fax: 402-375-7204
E-mail: admit1@wsc.edu • Web: www.wsc.edu
Support: S • Institution type: 4-year public

LEARNING DISABILITY PROGRAM AND SERVICES

Students with LD and ADD are provided an individualized, cooperatively planned program of accommodations and services that are structured yet integrated within existing college services and programs. Accommodations and services are matched to the individual student's needs and are provided free of charge. STRIDE (Students Taking Responsibility In Development and Education) is a program of student support services that includes individual attention, academic and personal support, and disability services. STRIDE services help new students adjust more quickly and fully to college life. Students with disabilities are one of the populations eligible for STRIDE. STRIDE expects students to place a high priority on academic performance, invest the time and effort needed for college level learning, and take advantage of the services and programs available. Students with LD or ADD must complete a special application for STRIDE and submit written information that verifies the disability diagnosis.

LD/ADD ADMISSIONS INFORMATION

College entrance tests required: Yes
Interview required: No
Essay required: No
Documentation required for LD: Psychoeducational evaluation
Documentation required for ADD: Yes
Submitted to: Disability Services Office
Special Ed. HS coursework accepted: Yes

Specific course requirements of all applicants: Yes
Separate application required for program services: No
# of LD applications submitted each year: NR
# of LD applications accepted yearly: NR
Total # of students receiving LD services: NR
Acceptance into program means acceptance into college: Student must be admitted and enrolled in the university first and then request services.

ADMISSIONS

Admission to Wayne State College is open to all high school graduates or students with a GED or equivalent. The college recommends that students take 4 years of English, 3 years of math, 3 years of social studies, and 2 years of science. Foreign language is not an entrance or graduation requirement. High school special education courses are accepted.

ADDITIONAL INFORMATION

Through the STRIDE Program students have access to the following personal support services: a summer STRIDE pre-college experience, STRIDE peer mentor program, academic, personal, and career counseling. Academic support services include academic advising and course selection guidance, a "Succeeding in College" course, one-on-one peer tutoring, writing skills, professional tutoring, individual study skills assistance in time management and organization, note taking, study techniques and test taking strategies. STRIDE provides a cooperatively planned program of disability-related services and accommodations, which include assistance in arranging accommodations, tape recorded textbooks and materials, and alternative exam arrangements.

Support Services Contact Information

Learning Disability Program/Services: Disability Services Office
Director: Dr. Jeff Carstens
  E-Mail: jecarst1@wsc.edu
  Telephone: 402-375-7213
  Fax: 402-375-7079

LEARNING DISABILITY SERVICES

Requests for the following/services accommodations will be evaluated individually based on appropriate and current documentation.

Allowed in exams
  Calculator: Yes
  Dictionary: Yes
  Computer: Yes
  Spellchecker: Yes
Extended test time: Yes
Scribes: Yes
Proctors: Yes
Oral exams: Yes
Note-takers: Yes

Distraction reduced environment: Yes
Tape recording in class: Yes
Books on tape from RFBD: Yes
Taping of books not from RFBD: Yes
Accommodations for students with ADD: Yes
Reading machine: Yes
Other assistive technology: No
Priority registration: Yes

Added costs for services: No
LD specialists: No
Professional tutors: No
Peer tutors: 35
Max. hours/wk. for services: Unlimited
How professors are notified of LD/ADD: By student

GENERAL ADMISSIONS INFORMATION

Director of Admissions: R. Lincoln Morris
Telephone: 402 375-7234

ENTRANCE REQUIREMENTS

Academic units recommended: 4 English, 3 math, 3 science (3 science lab), 2 foreign language, 3 social studies, 2 academic electives. High school diploma is required and GED is accepted. TOEFL required of all international applicants, minimum paper TOEFL 550, minimum computer TOEFL 213.

Application deadline: 8/1
Notification: Rolling
Average GPA: 3.18

Average SAT Math: NR
Average SAT Verbal: NR
Average ACT: 21

Graduated top 10% of class: 10%
Graduated top 25% of class: 27%
Graduated top 50% of class: 59%

COLLEGE GRADUATION REQUIREMENTS

Course waivers allowed: No
Course substitutions allowed: Yes
In what course: N/A

ADDITIONAL INFORMATION

Environment: The college is located in a rural area 45 miles southwest of Sioux City, Iowa.

Student Body:
  Undergrad enrollment: 2,750
  Women: 55%
  Men: 45%
  Percent out-of-state: 15%

Cost Information
  In-state tuition: $2,850
  Out-of-state tuition: $5,700
  Room & board: $4,120
Housing Information
  University housing: Yes
  Percent living on campus: 42%

Greek System
  Fraternity: Yes
  Sorority: Yes
Athletics: NCAA Division II

UNIVERSITY OF NEVADA—LAS VEGAS

4505 Maryland Parkway, Box 451021, Las Vegas, NV 89154-1021
Phone: 702-774-8658 • Fax: 702-774-8008
E-mail: gounlv@ccmail.nevada.edu • Web: www.unlv.edu
Support: S • Institution type: 4-year public

LEARNING DISABILITY PROGRAM AND SERVICES

The Disability Resource Center (DRC) provides academic accommodations for students with documented disabilities who are otherwise qualified for university programs. Compliance with Section 504 requires that reasonable academic accommodations be made for students with disabilities. These accommodations might include note-taking, testing accommodations, books on tape, readers, tutoring, priority registration, transition training, assistance with course registration and class monitoring, counseling, and information of the laws pertaining to disabilities. The center also serves as a resource area for all disability issues affecting students, faculty, and staff. To establish services, students will need to provide the DRC with appropriate documentation of their disability. Each semester a student wishes to receive assistance, a review of current documentation and assessment of the course needs will be made to determine the appropriate academic accommodations. On some occasions decisions are based on input from the students, faculty, and the designated DRC staff.

LD/ADD ADMISSIONS INFORMATION

College entrance tests required: Yes
Interview required: No
Essay required: No
Documentation required for LD: Psychoeducational
  evaluation (no more than 3 years old)
Documentation required for ADD: Yes
Submitted to: Disability Resources Center
Special Ed. HS coursework accepted: N/A

Specific course requirements of all applicants: Yes
Separate application required for program services: No
# of LD applications submitted each year: NR
# of LD applications accepted yearly: NR
Total # of students receiving LD services: 450
**Acceptance into program means acceptance into
  college:** Any student attending classes at UNLV who has a
  documented disability may apply for accommodations
  through the Learning Enhancement Services.

ADMISSIONS

All applicants are expected to meet the same admission criteria, which include a 2.5 GPA and 13 1/2 college-prep courses or a 3.0 GPA and no specific high school courses. ACT/SAT are not required for admission, but are used for placement. Students are encouraged to self-disclose their learning disability and request information about services. DRC will assess the student's documentation and write a recommendation to the Office of Admission based on the director's opinion of the student's chance for success. Students denied admission may request assistance for an appeal through the director of the Disability Resource Center. This requires a special application with an explanation of the circumstances of previous academic performance. Students, not parents, should call DRC to inquire about initiating an appeal of the denial. Some of these students may be offered admission by alternative criteria. If admitted on probation the students must maintain a 2.0 GPA for the first semester. Others can enter on special status as a part-time student, take 15 credits, and then transfer into the university.

ADDITIONAL INFORMATION

The Disabilities Resource Center offers help to all students on campus who have a diagnosed disability. Following the evaluation, students meet with DRC director and staff to develop a plan for services. Students are encouraged to only enroll in 12 credit hours the first semester, including courses in abilities or skill development. Psychological services are available through the counseling office. Workshops are offered in time management, organization, test-taking strategies, and note-taking skills. DRC offers workshops to teach classroom success techniques and self-advocacy skills. Assistance is provided year round to active students. Students remain active by signing a new contract for service before each semester. DRC hires enrolled students to be note-takers, readers, scribes, and proctors. Services are available to undergraduate and graduate students.

Support Services Contact Information

Learning Disability Program/Services: Disability Resource Center (DRC)
Director: Anita Stockbauer
  Telephone: 702-895-0866
  Fax: 702-895-0651
Contact Person: Phillip Pownall
  E-Mail: LES@ccmail.nevada.edu

LEARNING DISABILITY SERVICES

Requests for the following/services accommodations will be evaluated individually based on appropriate and current documentation.

Allowed in exams
  Calculator: Yes
  Dictionary: Yes
  Computer: Yes
  Spellchecker: Yes
Extended test time: Yes
Scribes: Yes
Proctors: Yes
Oral exams: Yes
Note-takers: Yes

Distraction reduced environment: Yes
Tape recording in class: Yes
Books on tape from RFBD: Yes
Taping of books not from RFBD: Yes
Accommodations for students with ADD: Yes
Reading machine: Yes
Other assistive technology: Yes
Priority registration: Yes

Added costs for services: No
LD specialists: No
Professional tutors: No
Peer tutors: Yes
Max. hours/wk. for services: 2
How professors are notified of LD/ADD: By both student and director

GENERAL ADMISSIONS INFORMATION

Director of Admissions: Pamela Hicks, Director of Undergraduate Recruitment
Telephone: 702-774-8658

ENTRANCE REQUIREMENTS
Academic units required: 4 English, 3 math, 3 science (2 science lab), 3 social studies. **Academic units recommended:** 4 English, 3 math, 3 science (2 science lab), 3 social studies. High school diploma is required and GED is accepted. ACT with or without Writing component accepted. TOEFL required of all international applicants, minimum paper TOEFL 500, minimum computer TOEFL 173.

Application deadline: 4/1
Notification: Rolling
Average GPA: 3.34

Average SAT Math: 515
Average SAT Verbal: 505
Average ACT: 21

Graduated top 10% of class: 18%
Graduated top 25% of class: 47%
Graduated top 50% of class: 82%

COLLEGE GRADUATION REQUIREMENTS

Course waivers allowed: No
Course substitutions allowed: Yes
In what course: Foreign language is only required for English majors; substitutions are available. Math is required for graduation. All requests go to Academic Standards Committee after initial approval from the college advisor, chair of the department, and dean.

ADDITIONAL INFORMATION

Environment: The university is located on 355 acres in an urban area, minutes from downtown Las Vegas.

Student Body:
  Undergrad enrollment: 20,607
  Women: 56%
  Men: 44%
  Percent out-of-state: 22%

Cost Information
  In-state tuition: $3,060
  Out-of-state tuition: $12,527
  Room & board: $8,326
Housing Information
  University housing: Yes
  Percent living on campus: 7%

Greek System
  Fraternity: Yes
  Sorority: Yes
Athletics: NCAA Division I

UNIVERSITY OF NEVADA—RENO

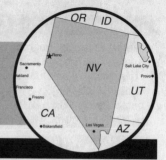

Mail Stop 120, Reno, NV 89557
Phone: 775-784-4700 • Fax: 775-784-4283
E-mail: asknevada@unr.edu • Web: www.unr.edu
Support: CS • Institution type: 4-year public

LEARNING DISABILITY PROGRAM AND SERVICES

The Disability Resource Center (DRC) was created to meet the unique educational needs of students with disabilities. The purpose of the DRC is to ensure that students with disabilities have equal access to participate in, contribute to, and benefit from all university programs. Their goal is to act as a catalyst for elimination of barriers and to increase awareness of students with disabilities attending the university. The DRC staff is available to provide students with sensitive and individualized assistance at the student's request. Students who wish to request academic accommodations must provide the DRC with documentation of a verified disability. Appropriate services are determined and provided based upon the student's specific disability and the academic requirements of the appropriate department. Students need to request their desired accommodations at least four weeks prior to their actual need for accommodations. Students requesting accommodations must sign a release of information form giving DRC permission to discuss the student's educational situation with other professionals with a legitimate need to know. Students requesting accommodations will also be required to sign a student contract defining the student's responsibilities in receiving services.

LD/ADD ADMISSIONS INFORMATION

College entrance tests required: No
Interview required: Yes
Essay required: No
Documentation required for LD: Psychoeducational evaluation
Documentation required for ADD: Yes
Submitted to: Disability Resource Center
Special Ed. HS coursework accepted: No

Specific course requirements of all applicants: Yes
Separate application required for program services: Yes
# of LD applications submitted each year: NR
# of LD applications accepted yearly: 153
Total # of students receiving LD services: 352
Acceptance into program means acceptance into college: Student must be admitted and enrolled in the university first and then request services.

ADMISSIONS

There is no special admission process for students with LD or attention deficit disorders. However, students with LD/ADD are encouraged to self-disclose if they do not meet general admission requirements and provide documentation. Admissions will consult with the DRC director during the admission process. General admission criteria include a 2.5 GPA; ACT of 20 in English and Math or SAT Verbal or Math of 500; 4 years of English, 3 years of math, 3 years of social studies, 3 years of natural science and one-half year of computer literacy. Students may appeal to use a substitute course for one of the required courses for admission. Students who do not meet the general admission criteria may appeal. Some students may be admitted on appeal and brought in under a special admit.

ADDITIONAL INFORMATION

DRC provides accommodations and services tailored to the individual needs of each student. When appropriate, reasonable accommodations can include the following: reader services/books on tape, note-taking services, alternative testing accommodations/proctors/scribes, adaptive computer equipment access, accommodations counseling; registration assistance, faculty liaisons, learning strategies instruction, course substitutions, Math 019/119 (a 2 semester course equivalent to Math 120), referrals to campus and community services, and other appropriate services as necessary. There is also a Writing Center, Tutorial Program, Math Lab, Counseling Center, and Women's Resource Center.

Support Services Contact Information

Learning Disability Program/Services: Disability Resource Center
Director: Mary Zabel
  E-Mail: mzabel@unr.edu
  Telephone: 775-784-6000
  Fax: 775-784-6955
Contact Person: Mary Anne Christensen
 E-Mail: maryac@unr.edu
  Telephone: 775-784-6000
  Fax: 775-784-6955

LEARNING DISABILITY SERVICES

Requests for the following/services accommodations will be evaluated individually based on appropriate and current documentation.

Allowed in exams
  Calculator: Yes
  Dictionary: Yes
  Computer: Yes
  Spellchecker: Yes
Extended test time: Yes
Scribes: Yes
Proctors: Yes
Oral exams: Yes
Note-takers: Yes

Distraction reduced environment: Yes
Tape recording in class: Yes
Books on tape from RFBD: Yes
Taping of books not from RFBD: Yes
**Accommodations for students with
  ADD:** Yes
Reading machine: Yes
Other assistive technology: Yes
Priority registration: No

Added costs for services: No
LD specialists: Yes
Professional tutors: No
Peer tutors: 50
Max. hours/wk. for services: NR
**How professors are notified of
  LD/ADD:** By student

GENERAL ADMISSIONS INFORMATION

Director of Admissions: Melissa Choroszy
Telephone: 775-784-4700

ENTRANCE REQUIREMENTS

Academic units required: 4 English, 3 math, 3 science (2 science lab), 3 social studies. High school diploma is required and GED is not accepted. TOEFL required of all international applicants, minimum paper TOEFL 500, minimum computer TOEFL 173.

Application deadline: Rolling
Notification: Rolling
Average GPA: 3.36

Average SAT Math: 489
Average SAT Verbal: 435
Average ACT: 22

Graduated top 10% of class: NR
Graduated top 25% of class: NR
Graduated top 50% of class: NR

COLLEGE GRADUATION REQUIREMENTS

Course waivers allowed: No
Course substitutions allowed: Yes
In what course: Foreign language (depending on declared major)

ADDITIONAL INFORMATION

Environment: The campus is located in Reno, Nevada.

Student Body:
  Undergrad enrollment: 11,605
  Women: 55%
  Men: 45%
  Percent out-of-state: 18%

Cost Information
  In-state tuition: $3,040
  Out-of-state tuition: $11,404
  Room & board: $7,745
Housing Information
  University housing: Yes
  Percent living on campus: 14%

Greek System
  Fraternity: Yes
  Sorority: Yes
Athletics: NCAA Division I

University of Nevada—Reno

COLBY-SAWYER COLLEGE

541 Main Street, New London, NH 03257-7835
Phone: 603-526-3700 • Fax: 603-526-3452
E-mail: csadmiss@colbysawyer.edu • Web: www.colby-sawyer.edu
Support: CS • Institution type: 4-year private

LEARNING DISABILITY PROGRAM AND SERVICES

The goal of the Academic Development Center is to offer students with LD the same opportunities that the college extends to other students. This includes providing individualized, free of charge academic support services designed to enable Colby-Sawyer College students to realize their full academic potential. By way of implementation, the Academic Development Center staff are trained to meet the academic needs of the entire student body by providing supplemental assistance to those who need help in specific courses or development of basic study skills, seek academic achievement beyond their already strong level, and have learning styles with diagnosed differences.

LD/ADD ADMISSIONS INFORMATION

College entrance tests required: Yes
Interview required: No
Essay required: N/A
Documentation required for LD: Psychoeducational evaluation—aptitude and achievement results
Documentation required for ADD: Yes
Submitted to: Support Program/Services
Special Ed. HS coursework accepted: Yes

Specific course requirements of all applicants: Yes
Separate application required for program services: No
# of LD applications submitted each year: NR
# of LD applications accepted yearly: NR
Total # of students receiving LD services: NR
Acceptance into program means acceptance into college: Student must be admitted and enrolled in the university first and then request services.

ADMISSIONS
There is no special admissions process for students with learning disabilities. Students must submit one recommendation from their counselor and one from a teacher. An essay is also required. It is recommended that students have at least 15 units of college-preparatory courses. Students with documented learning disabilities may substitute courses for math or foreign language if those are the areas of deficit. GPA is evaluated in terms of factors that may have affected GPA, as well as a subjective assessment of students' chances of succeeding in college.

ADDITIONAL INFORMATION
Essential to the success of the Academic Development Center is the informal, individualized, non-judgmental nature of the learning that occurs during tutoring sessions. Tutors must qualify for their jobs by presenting a GPA of 3.3 with no less than an A– in every course they designate as part of their area of expertise. Other services provided include (1) classroom modifications—students meet with a learning specialist to develop a profile, which includes the student's learning style, learning strengths and weaknesses, and recommendations to professors for accommodations, (2) special help—learning specialists assist students in improving study skills, and /or developing writing skills, and (3) academic advising—each student has a faculty advisor, interested in student progress, who confers with students at regular intervals to set and achieve goals and select courses. There are currently 50 students with LD and 25 students with ADD receiving services.

Support Services Contact Information

Learning Disability Program/Services: Academic Development Center
Director: Jennifer Zotalis, MA
  E-Mail: jzotalis@colby-sawyer.edu
  Telephone: 603-526-3714
  Fax: 603-526-3452

LEARNING DISABILITY SERVICES

Requests for the following/services accommodations will be evaluated individually based on appropriate and current documentation.

Allowed in exams
  Calculator: Yes
  Dictionary: Yes
  Computer: Yes
  Spellchecker: Yes
  Extended test time: Yes
  Scribes: Yes
  Proctors: Yes
  Oral exams: Yes
  Note-takers: Yes

Distraction reduced environment: Yes
Tape recording in class: Yes
Books on tape from RFBD: Yes
Taping of books not from RFBD: No
Accommodations for students with ADD: Yes
Reading machine: No
Other assistive technology: No
Priority registration: No

Added costs for services: No
LD specialists: Yes
Professional tutors: 2
Peer tutors: 12–15
Max. hours/wk. for services: 5
How professors are notified of LD/ADD: By student

GENERAL ADMISSIONS INFORMATION

Director of Admissions: Wendy Beckemeyer
Telephone: 603-526-3700

ENTRANCE REQUIREMENTS

Academic units required: 4 English, 3 math, 2 science (2 science lab), 2 foreign language, 3 social studies. High school diploma is required and GED is accepted. TOEFL required of all international applicants, minimum paper TOEFL 500, minimum computer TOEFL 173.

Application deadline: Rolling
Notification: Rolling
Average GPA: 2.90

Average SAT Math: 498
Average SAT Verbal: 513
Average ACT: 20

Graduated top 10% of class: NR
Graduated top 25% of class: NR
Graduated top 50% of class: NR

COLLEGE GRADUATION REQUIREMENTS

Course waivers allowed: No
Course substitutions allowed: Yes
In what course: Substitutions are usually unnecessary but could be made under special circumstances.

ADDITIONAL INFORMATION

Environment: The college has an 80-acre campus in a small town.

Student Body:
  Undergrad enrollment: 954
  Women: 65%
  Men: 35%
  Percent out-of-state: 70%

Cost Information
  Tuition: $23,310
  Room & board: $8,950
Housing Information
  University housing: Yes
  Percent living on campus: 87%

Greek System
  Fraternity: No
  Sorority: No
Athletics: NCAA Division III

NEW ENGLAND COLLEGE

26 Bridge Street, Henniker, NH 03242
Phone: 603-428-2223 • Fax: 603-428-3155
E-mail: admission@nec.edu • Web: www.nec.edu
Support: CS • Institution type: 4-year private

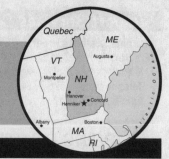

LEARNING DISABILITY PROGRAM AND SERVICES

The Academic Advising & Support Center provides services for all students in a welcoming and supportive environment. Students come to the center with a variety of academic needs; some want help writing term papers some feel they read too slowly. Others are confused and anxious about their ability to perform as college students and may have learning disabilities. The center provides individual or small group tutoring, academic counseling, and referral services. Tutoring is available in most subject areas. The center focuses primarily on helping students make a successful transition to New England College while supporting all students in their effort to become independent and successful learners. The support services meet the needs of students who do not require a formal, structured program, but who can find success when offered support and advocacy by a trained and experienced staff in conjunction with small classes and personal attention by faculty. Typically these students have done well in mainstream programs in high school when given assistance. Students with learning disabilities are encouraged to visit NEC and the Pathways Center to determine whether the support services will adequately meet their academic needs.

LD/ADD ADMISSIONS INFORMATION

College entrance tests required: Yes
Interview required: No
Essay required: No
Documentation required for LD: WAIS (to include the subtest scores), Woodcock-Johnson, Reading, Writing
Documentation required for ADD: WAIS (to include the subtest scores), Woodcock–Johnson, Reading, and Writing. Physician's diagnosis alone does not meet the requirement
Submitted to: Pathway Center
Special Ed. HS coursework accepted: N/A

Specific course requirements of all applicants: Yes
Separate application required for program services: No
# of LD applications submitted each year: NR
# of LD applications accepted yearly: NR
Total # of students receiving LD services: NR
Acceptance into program means acceptance into college: Student must be admitted and enrolled in the college first and then request services.

ADMISSIONS

Students with learning disabilities submit the general New England College application. Students should have a 2.0 GPA. SAT/ACT are optional. Course requirements include 4 years English, 2 years math, 2 years science, and 2 years social studies. Documentation of the learning disability should be submitted along with counselor and teacher recommendations. An interview is recommended. Successful applicants have typically done well in mainstream programs in high school when given tutorial and study skills assistance.

ADDITIONAL INFORMATION

Students may elect to use the Pathways Center services with regular appointments or only occasionally in response to particular or difficult assignments. The center provides tutoring in content areas; computer facilities; study skills instruction; time management strategies; writing support in planning, editing, and proofreading; referrals to other college services; and one-on-one writing support for first year students taking WR 101–102. Students are encouraged to use the word processors to generate writing assignments, and to use the tutors to help plan and revise papers. The writing faculty works closely with the center to provide coordinated and supportive learning for all students. The Skills Center has its own building and the director is a LD specialist. Professional tutors work with students individually and in small groups. These services are provided in a secure and accepting atmosphere. Currently 20 percent of the student body has diagnosed LD and 10 percent have a diagnosed ADD.

Support Services Contact Information

Learning Disability Program/Services: There is no LD program, but services offerred in Pathways Center
Director: Anna Carlson or Mary Lou Pashko
  E-Mail: acarslon@nec.edu
  Telephone: 603-428-2218
  Fax: 603-428-2433
Contact Person: Mary Lou Pashko

LEARNING DISABILITY SERVICES

Requests for the following/services accommodations will be evaluated individually based on appropriate and current documentation.

Allowed in exams	**Distraction reduced environment:** Yes	**Added costs for services:** No
Calculator: Yes	**Tape recording in class:** Yes	**LD specialists:** Yes
Dictionary: No	**Books on tape from RFBD:** Yes	**Professional tutors:** 7–10
Computer: Yes	**Taping of books not from RFBD:** No	**Peer tutors:** 2–5
Spellchecker: Yes	**Accommodations for students with**	**Max. hours/wk. for services:** 4
Extended test time: Yes	**ADD:** Yes	**How professors are notified of**
Scribes: Yes	**Reading machine:** No	**LD/ADD:** By student
Proctors: Yes	**Other assistive technology:** No	
Oral exams: Yes	**Priority registration:** No	
Note-takers: No		

GENERAL ADMISSIONS INFORMATION

Director of Admissions: Paul Miller
Telephone: 603-428-2223

ENTRANCE REQUIREMENTS

Academic units recommended: 4 English, 3 math, 3 science (1 science lab), 2 foreign language, 3 social studies. High school diploma is required and GED is accepted. TOEFL required of all international applicants, minimum paper TOEFL 550, minimum computer TOEFL 213.

Application deadline: Rolling	**Average SAT Math:** 450	**Graduated top 10% of class:** 4%
Notification: Rolling	**Average SAT Verbal:** 460	**Graduated top 25% of class:** 13%
Average GPA: 2.62	**Average ACT:** NR	**Graduated top 50% of class:** 42%

COLLEGE GRADUATION REQUIREMENTS

Course waivers allowed: No
Course substitutions allowed: No
In what course: The college prefers to try other accommodations first. Waivers or substitutions are rarely given. No foreign language requirements for graduation.

ADDITIONAL INFORMATION

Environment: The college is located in the town of Henniker on 212 acres 17 miles west of Concord.

Student Body:	**Cost Information**	**Greek System**
Undergrad enrollment: 919	**Tuition:** $21,300	**Fraternity:** Yes
Women: 51%	**Room & board:** $8,052	**Sorority:** Yes
Men: 49%	**Housing Information**	**Athletics:** NCAA Division III
Percent out-of-state: 29%	**University housing:** Yes	
	Percent living on campus: 68%	

RIVIER COLLEGE

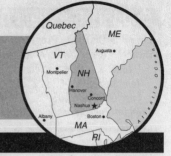

420 Main Street, Nashua, NH 03060
Phone: 603-897-8507 • Fax: 603-891-1799
E-mail: rivadmit@rivier.edu • Web: www.rivier.edu
Support: S • Institution type: 4-year private

LEARNING DISABILITY PROGRAM AND SERVICES

Rivier College recognizes that learning styles differ from person to person. The college is committed to providing support that allows all otherwise qualified individuals with disabilities an equal educational opportunity. Special Needs Services provides the opportunity for all individuals who meet academic requirements to be provided auxiliary services, facilitating their earning of a college education. To be eligible for support services, students are required to provide appropriate documentation of their disabilities to the coordinator of Special Needs Services. This documentation shall be provided from a professional in the field of psychoeducational testing or a physician and shall be current (within 3–5 years). This information will be confidential and is kept in the coordinator's office for the purpose of planning appropriate support services. To access services students must contact the coordinator of Special Needs Services before the start of each semester to schedule an appointment and provide documentation; together the coordinator and the student will discuss and arrange for support services specifically related to the disability.

LD/ADD ADMISSIONS INFORMATION

College entrance tests required: Yes
Interview required: No
Essay required: Yes
Documentation required for LD: Psychoeducational evaluation
Documentation required for ADD: Yes
Submitted to: Special Needs Services
Special Ed. HS coursework accepted: Yes

Specific course requirements of all applicants: Yes
Separate application required for program services: No
# of LD applications submitted each year: NR
# of LD applications accepted yearly: NR
Total # of students receiving LD services: 25
Acceptance into program means acceptance into college: Student must be admitted and enrolled in the college first and then request services.

ADMISSIONS

There is no special admissions process for students with LD. All applicants must meet the same criteria. Students should have a combined SAT of 820, GPA in the top 80 percent, and take college-prep courses in high school. Courses required include 4 years English, 2 years foreign language*, 1 year science, 3 years math, 2 years social science, 4 years academic electives (*equals substitution). Applicants not meeting the general admission requirements may inquire about alternative admissions. The college has a probational admit that requires students to maintain a minimum 2.0 GPA their first semester.

ADDITIONAL INFORMATION

Services available include academic, career, and personal counseling; preferential registration; classroom accommodations including tape recording of lectures, extended time for test completion, testing free from distractions, and note-takers; student advocacy; Writing Center for individualized instruction in writing and individualized accommodations as developed by the coordinator of Special Needs Services with the student. Skills classes are offered in English and math and students may take these classes for college credit. Services and accommodations are available for undergraduate and graduate students.

Support Services Contact Information

Learning Disability Program/Services: Special Services
Director: Dina DiGregorio Karlon
 E-Mail: dkarlon@rivier.edu
 Telephone: 603-897-8497
 Fax: 603-897-8887

LEARNING DISABILITY SERVICES

Requests for the following/services accommodations will be evaluated individually based on appropriate and current documentation.

Allowed in exams
 Calculator: Yes
 Dictionary: Yes
 Computer: Yes
 Spellchecker: Yes
Extended test time: Yes
Scribes: Yes
Proctors: Yes
Oral exams: Yes
Note-takers: Yes

Distraction reduced environment: Yes
Tape recording in class: Yes
Books on tape from RFBD: Yes
Taping of books not from RFBD: No
Accommodations for students with ADD: Yes
Reading machine: No
Other assistive technology: Yes
Priority registration: Yes

Added costs for services: No
LD specialists: No
Professional tutors: No
Peer tutors: No
Max. hours/wk. for services: N/A
How professors are notified of LD/ADD: By both student and director

GENERAL ADMISSIONS INFORMATION

Director of Admissions: David A. Boisvert
Telephone: 603-897-8507

ENTRANCE REQUIREMENTS

Academic units recommended: 4 English, 3 math, 1 science (1 science lab), 2 foreign language, 2 social studies, 1 history, 3 academic electives. High school diploma is required and GED is accepted. TOEFL required of all international applicants, minimum paper TOEFL 500, minimum computer TOEFL 173.

Application deadline: 8/30
Notification: Rolling
Average GPA: 2.87

Average SAT Math: 480
Average SAT Verbal: 490
Average ACT: NR

Graduated top 10% of class: 0%
Graduated top 25% of class: 0%
Graduated top 50% of class: 80%

COLLEGE GRADUATION REQUIREMENTS

Course waivers allowed: No
Course substitutions allowed: Yes
In what course: Each course subtitution is looked at individually

ADDITIONAL INFORMATION

Environment: The college is located on 60 acres in a suburban area 40 miles north of Boston.

Student Body:
 Undergrad enrollment: 1,447
 Women: 80%
 Men: 20%
 Percent out-of-state: 51%

Cost Information
 Tuition: $19,200
 Room & board: $7,274
Housing Information
 University housing: Yes
 Percent living on campus: 62%

Greek System
 Fraternity: No
 Sorority: No
Athletics: NCAA Division III

UNIVERSITY OF NEW HAMPSHIRE

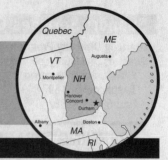

4 Garrison Avenue, Durham, NH 03824
Phone: 603-862-1360 • Fax: 603-862-0077
E-mail: admissions@unh.edu • Web: www.unh.edu
Support: CS • Institution type: 4-year public

LEARNING DISABILITY PROGRAM AND SERVICES

UNH encourages students to self-disclose within the admissions procedure. There is no LD program. Rather services/accommodations are based on student self-disclosure and obtaining the proper guidelines for documentation of LD/ADD. ACCESS Office: Support for Students with Disabilities is where students with documented disabilities can receive those accommodations and academic services which enable students to have equal access to the classroom. Additionally, students can learn and further develop their self-advocacy skills and increase their knowledge about communicating regarding their disability. Students need to be aware that having been tested for a learning disability, having old documentation (more than 3 years old), or being previously coded in secondary education in and of itself, does not necessarily mean that the student will be currently qualified with a disability under federal laws in college. UNH does not offer a program for subject area tutorial, nor are LD specialists on-staff. Services and accommodations at UNH can be defined as those generic activities offered to ensure educational opportunity for any student with a documented disability. All students with LD/ADD must provide current and appropriate documentation to qualify for services.

LD/ADD ADMISSIONS INFORMATION

College entrance tests required: Yes
Interview required: No
Essay required: No
Documentation required for LD: Psychoeducational evaluation
Documentation required for ADD: Yes
Submitted to: Access Office
Special Ed. HS coursework accepted: Yes

Specific course requirements of all applicants: Yes
Separate application required for program services: No
# of LD applications submitted each year: NR
# of LD applications accepted yearly: NR
Total # of students receiving LD services: 253
Acceptance into program means acceptance into college: Student must be admitted and enrolled in the university first and then request services.

ADMISSIONS
Admissions criteria are the same for all applicants. Typically, students who are admitted to the university are in the top 30 percent of their class, have a B average in college-preparatory courses, and have taken 4 years of college-prep math, 3–4 years of a lab science, and 3–4 years of a foreign language; SAT average range is 1050–1225 but there are no cut offs (or equivalent ACT). There are no alternative options for admissions. Access has no involvement in any admissions decision. However, there is a member of the admissions staff with a background in special education.

ADDITIONAL INFORMATION
Academic accommodations provided, based on documentation, include the following: individually scheduled meetings with ACCESS coordinator for guidance, advising, and referrals; mediation and advocacy; note-takers; scribes; proctors; readers; taped texts; extended exam time; distraction-free rooms for exams; alternative methods for exam administration; pre-registration priority scheduling; reduced course load; and faculty support letters. UNH does not provide a university-wide service or program for subject area tutoring; it is the student's responsibility to secure subject area tutoring. However, the Center for Academic Resources provides all students with drop-in tutoring in selected courses; referrals to free academic assistance opportunities and to private pay tutors; individualized study skills assistance; and peer support for academic and personal concerns. There is a federally funded grant that allows some students to receive free peer tutoring and reading/writing assistance with a specialist.

Support Services Contact Information

Learning Disability Program/Services: ACCESS Office: Support for Students with Disabilities
Director: Maxine Little
  E-Mail: Maxine.Little@unh.edu
  Telephone: 603-862-2607
  Fax: 603-862-4043

LEARNING DISABILITY SERVICES

Requests for the following/services accommodations will be evaluated individually based on appropriate and current documentation.

Allowed in exams	**Distraction reduced environment:** Yes	**Added costs for services:** No
Calculator: Yes	**Tape recording in class:** Yes	**LD specialists:** Yes
Dictionary: Yes	**Books on tape from RFBD:** Yes	**Professional tutors:** No
Computer: Yes	**Taping of books not from RFBD:** Yes	**Peer tutors:** No
Spellchecker: Yes	**Accommodations for students with**	**Max. hours/wk. for services:** Varies
Extended test time: Yes	**ADD:** Yes	**How professors are notified of**
Scribes: Yes	**Reading machine:** Yes	**LD/ADD:** By student
Proctors: Yes	**Other assistive technology:** Yes	
Oral exams: Yes	**Priority registration:** Yes	
Note-takers: Yes		

GENERAL ADMISSIONS INFORMATION

Director of Admissions: Robert McGann
Telephone: 603-862-1360

ENTRANCE REQUIREMENTS

Academic units recommended: 4 English, 4 math, 4 science (4 science lab), 3 foreign language, 3 social studies. High school diploma is required and GED is accepted. TOEFL required of all international applicants, minimum paper TOEFL 550, minimum computer TOEFL 213.

Application deadline: 2/1	**Average SAT Math:** 561	**Graduated top 10% of class:** 22%
Notification: 4/15	**Average SAT Verbal:** 550	**Graduated top 25% of class:** 63%
Average GPA: 3.0	**Average ACT:** NR	**Graduated top 50% of class:** 97%

COLLEGE GRADUATION REQUIREMENTS

Course waivers allowed: Yes
Course substitutions allowed: Yes
In what course: Only in foreign language on a case-by-case basis by a petition process.

ADDITIONAL INFORMATION

Environment: The university is located in a rural area about one hour north of Boston.

Student Body:	**Cost Information**	**Greek System**
Undergrad enrollment: 10,942	**In-state tuition:** $9,226	**Fraternity:** Yes
Women: 57%	**Out-of-state tuition:** $20,256	**Sorority:** Yes
Men: 43%	**Room & board:** $6,612	**Athletics:** NCAA Division I
Percent out-of-state: 41%	**Housing Information**	
	University housing: Yes	
	Percent living on campus: 56%	

CALDWELL COLLEGE

9 Ryerson Avenue, Caldwell, NJ 07006-6195
Phone: 973-618-3500 • Fax: 973-618-3600
E-mail: admissions@caldwell.edu • Web: www.caldwell.edu
Support: CS • Institution type: 4-year private

LEARNING DISABILITY PROGRAM AND SERVICES

Caldwell College offers students with disabilities a support program through the Learning Center and the Office of Disability Services. Students with documentation of a LD are fully integrated into college degree programs of study and, in addition, are offered support services. The Office of Disability Services functions as a service coordinator for students with disabilities, advocating with faculty for reasonable accommodations in accordance with the Americans with Disabilities Act.

LD/ADD ADMISSIONS INFORMATION

College entrance tests required: Yes
Interview required: No
Essay required: No
Documentation required for LD: WAIS and Woodcock–Johnson psychoeducational battery. Revised (WJPB–J)
Documentation required for ADD: Letter from physician
Submitted to: Both Admissions and Office of Disability Services
Special Ed. HS coursework accepted: Yes

Specific course requirements of all applicants: Yes
Separate application required for program services: No
# of LD applications submitted each year: NR
# of LD applications accepted yearly: NR
Total # of students receiving LD services: NR
Acceptance into program means acceptance into college: Student must be admitted and enrolled in the college first and then request services.

ADMISSIONS
There is no special admissions process for students with LD and ADD. There is a pre-freshman summer program for students considered at risk for success in the fall. The decision to advise a student for this program may be based on low SAT/ACT scores or a borderline (1.9) GPA. This conditional admission program is available to all applicants regardless of a disability. The mid 50 percent SAT range for general admissions is 900. Additionally, students generally have a minimum GPA of 2.0, and have 16 high school academic units including 4 English, 2 years of foreign language, and 2 years of math, 2 years science and 1 year of history. With appropriate documentation applicants with LD may request to substitute some of the required courses with other high school courses.

ADDITIONAL INFORMATION
There is 1 LD specialist on staff and no fee charged for tutoring or other services. Individual tutoring sessions with a professional learning specialist are offered to help students improve organizational skills and promote self-advocacy. Meetings are also scheduled to facilitate advocacy in the form of accommodation letters to faculty and to coordinate peer tutoring. There is a Writing Center, Learning Center, supplemental instruction, and peer tutoring for all students. The library is equipped with various programs to assist students with disabilities.

Support Services Contact Information

Learning Disability Program/Services: Office of Disability Services
Director: Abbe Benowitz, Coordinator
  E-Mail: abenowitz@caldwell.edu
  Telephone: 973-618-3645
  Fax: 973-618-3488

LEARNING DISABILITY SERVICES

Requests for the following/services accommodations will be evaluated individually based on appropriate and current documentation.

Allowed in exams
  Calculator: Yes
  Dictionary: Yes
  Computer: Yes
  Spellchecker: Yes
Extended test time: Yes
Scribes: Yes
Proctors: Yes
Oral exams: Yes
Note-takers: Yes

Distraction reduced environment: Yes
Tape recording in class: Yes
Books on tape from RFBD: Yes
Taping of books not from RFBD: Yes
Accommodations for students with ADD: Yes
Reading machine: Yes
Other assistive technology: Yes
Priority registration: No

Added costs for services: No
LD specialists: Yes
Professional tutors: 5
Peer tutors: 30–40
Max. hours/wk. for services: Unlimited
How professors are notified of LD/ADD: By both student and director

GENERAL ADMISSIONS INFORMATION

Director of Admissions: Dr. Richard Ott
Telephone: 973-618-3500

ENTRANCE REQUIREMENTS

Academic units required: 4 English, 2 math, 2 science (1 science lab), 2 foreign language, 1 history, 5 academic electives. High school diploma is required and GED is accepted. TOEFL required of all international applicants, minimum paper TOEFL 500, minimum computer TOEFL 173.

Application deadline: Rolling
Notification: Rolling
Average GPA: 3.01

Average SAT Math: 462
Average SAT Verbal: 458
Average ACT: NR

Graduated top 10% of class: 5%
Graduated top 25% of class: 22%
Graduated top 50% of class: 54%

COLLEGE GRADUATION REQUIREMENTS

Course waivers allowed: Yes
Course substitutions allowed: Yes
In what course: Students may receive substitutions in foreign language if documentation supports the need for it.

ADDITIONAL INFORMATION

Environment: Located 10 miles from Newark, New Jersey, and 20 miles from New York City.

Student Body:
  Undergrad enrollment: 1,687
  Women: 67%
  Men: 33%
  Percent out-of-state: 7%

Cost Information
  Tuition: $16,960
  Room & board: $7,000
Housing Information
  University housing: Yes
  Percent living on campus: 23%

Greek System
  Fraternity: No
  Sorority: No
  Athletics: NCAA Division II

FAIRLEIGH DICKINSON U.—METROPOLITAN CAMPUS

1000 River Road, Teaneck, NJ 07666-1966
Phone: 201-692-2553 • Fax: 201-692-7319
E-mail: globaleducation@fdu.edu • Web: www.fdu.edu
Support: SP • Institution type: 4-year private

LEARNING DISABILITY PROGRAM AND SERVICES

The Regional Center for College Students with LD offers a structured plan of intensive advisement, academic support, and counseling services that is tailored to the unique needs of students with LD. The goal is to provide a framework within which college students with LD will develop the confidence to succeed in their studies and the independence to do their best. Planning, learning strategies, professional tutors, counseling, and accommodations are the cornerstones of the Regional Center. Staffed by professionals with services at both the Teaneck and the Madison campus, the LD program and special services are free of charge. Assistance to students is intensive and the program is fully integrated into the coursework. Students are in touch with faculty on a regular basis. The program encourages involvement in the community, particularly service-type activities relevant to the students with LD. Performance data are routinely reviewed to identify students in need of more intensive help. Upon admission, students are invited to attend a summer orientation session. During this time, students meet with center staff to develop an individual education plan in order to develop a class schedule with the right balance.

LD/ADD ADMISSIONS INFORMATION

College entrance tests required: Yes
Interview required: No
Essay required: No
Documentation required for LD: WAIS–III; WJPEB or must be primary diagnosis LD.
Documentation required for ADD: Yes
Submitted to: Regional Center for College Students with LD
Special Ed. HS coursework accepted: No

Specific course requirements of all applicants: Yes
Separate application required for program services: Yes
# of LD applications submitted each year: 260
# of LD applications accepted yearly: 50
Total # of students receiving LD services: 150
Acceptance into program means acceptance into college: Students are accepted jointly by the Regional Center for College Students with Learning Disabilities and the Office of Admissions.

ADMISSIONS

Admissions decisions are made jointly by admissions and the LD Program director. Criteria include documentation of LD made by licensed professionals dated within 24 months of the application, I.Q. in average to above average range, evidence of adequate performance in mainstream college-prep high school courses, and evidence of motivation as reflected in recommendations. Students enrolled in all special education high school classes are usually not admissible. Lower level mainstream classes are acceptable from high schools offering different levels in the same subjects. ACT/SAT are required but do not carry much weight. Grades are viewed as the best predictors for success. Students with a 2.5 GPA and 850 SAT can be accepted. General admissions require top 2/5 of class or B average and 850 SAT. If applicants are below a 2.5 GPA and 850 SAT they may be referred to Edward Williams College, a two-year college located on the Teaneck campus that requires an 18 ACT or 600 SAT. Admission decisions are made after careful review.

ADDITIONAL INFORMATION

Edward Williams College, a two-year liberal arts college on the campus, offers services and accommodations to students with learning disabilities who are not admissible to Fairleigh Dickinson. FDU students already enrolled in the university may request LD assessments on campus for no charge. Skills class for no college credit are offered in math and writing. Tutorial sessions incorporate a variety of teaching techniques. There is a 13:1 ratio between student and LD specialists. Support sessions are small, individualized, and flexible. In their sophomore year students can request tutoring for 3 courses. Students have priority registration. Most students are seen by 3–4 different LD specialists who regularly exchange views on academic and counseling issues. Services include recorded textbooks, extended testing time and other class support, technological support, and supervised study to meet with specialists in study rooms.

Support Services Contact Information

Learning Disability Program/Services: Regional Center for College Students with Learning Disabilities
Director: Dr. Mary Farrell
  E-Mail: farrell@fdu.edu
  Telephone: 201-692-2087
  Fax: 201-692-2813
Contact Person: Grace Hottinger or Vincent J. Varrassi

LEARNING DISABILITY SERVICES

Requests for the following/services accommodations will be evaluated individually based on appropriate and current documentation.

Allowed in exams
  Calculator: Yes
  Dictionary: No
  Computer: Yes
  Spellchecker: Yes
Extended test time: Yes
Scribes: No
Proctors: Yes
Oral exams: Yes
Note-takers: No

Distraction reduced environment: Yes
Tape recording in class: Yes
Books on tape from RFBD: Yes
Taping of books not from RFBD: No
Accommodations for students with ADD: Yes
Reading machine: No
Other assistive technology: No
Priority registration: Yes

Added costs for services: No
LD specialists: Yes
Professional tutors: 10
Peer tutors: No
Max. hours/wk. for services: 8 hrs. freshman; 3 hrs. sophmores; 2 hrs. juniors; 1 hr. seniors
How professors are notified of LD/ADD: By the student and director

GENERAL ADMISSIONS INFORMATION

Director of Admissions: Bernetta Millonde
Telephone: 201-692-2553

ENTRANCE REQUIREMENTS

Academic units required: 4 English, 3 math, 2 science (2 science lab), 2 foreign language, 2 history, 4 academic electives. High school diploma is required and GED is accepted. ACT with or without Writing component accepted. TOEFL required of all international applicants, minimum paper TOEFL 550, minimum computer TOEFL 213.

Application deadline: Rolling
Notification: Rolling
Average GPA: NR

Average SAT Math: NR
Average SAT Verbal: NR
Average ACT: NR

Graduated top 10% of class: 10%
Graduated top 25% of class: 34%
Graduated top 50% of class: 69%

COLLEGE GRADUATION REQUIREMENTS

Course waivers allowed: No
Course substitutions allowed: Yes
In what course: Math and foreign language.

ADDITIONAL INFORMATION

Environment: The Teaneck campus is located on the banks of the Hackensack River. It is within walking distance of Edward Williams Junior College.

Student Body:
  Undergrad enrollment: 3,114
  Women: 58%
  Men: 42%
  Percent out-of-state: 13%

Cost Information
  Tuition: $22,000
  Room & board: $5,100
Housing Information
  University housing: Yes
  Percent living on campus: 26%

Greek System
  Fraternity: Yes
  Sorority: Yes
Athletics: NCAA Division I

GEORGIAN COURT UNIVERSITY

900 Lakewood Avenue, Lakewood, NJ 08701-2697
Phone: 732-364-2200 • Fax: 732-987-2000
E-mail: admissions@georgian.edu • Web: www.georgian.edu
Support: SP • Institution type: 4-year private

LEARNING DISABILITY PROGRAM AND SERVICES

The Learning Center (TLC) is an assistance program designed to provide an environment for students with mild to moderate learning disabilities who desire a college education. The program is not one of remediation, but is an individualized support program to assist candidates in becoming successful college students. Emphasis is placed on developing self-help strategies and study techniques. To be eligible for the TLC program all applicants must submit the following: documentation for learning disability by a certified professional within a school system or state certified agency (documentation must be current within 3 years and must include identification and description of the learning disability, including the student's level of academic performance and effect upon learning), a recent individualized education plan, other evaluations or recommendations from professionals who have recently provided services to the student, and additional documentation upon request. All applicants must have a personal interview.

LD/ADD ADMISSIONS INFORMATION

College entrance tests required: Yes
Interview required: No
Essay required: No
Documentation required for LD: Psychoeducational
  evaluation
Documentation required for ADD: Yes
Submitted to: Both Admissions and the Learning Center
Special Ed. HS coursework accepted: No

Specific course requirements of all applicants: Yes
Separate application required for program services: No
# of LD applications submitted each year: 120
# of LD applications accepted yearly: 40
Total # of students receiving LD services: 45
**Acceptance into program means acceptance into
  college:** Students are admitted into The Learning Center and
  Georgian Court College.

ADMISSIONS

Applicants must meet the following: 16 academic units that include 4 years English, 2 years foreign language, 2 years math, 1 year lab science, 1 year history, and electives. The class rank and transcript should give evidence of the ability to succeed in college. Students must submit SAT scores. Conditional admission may be offered to some applicants. The associate director of admissions is the liaison person between the admissions staff and the TLC.

ADDITIONAL INFORMATION

College graduation requirements are not waived for TLC students. Reduced course load is recommended for students with learning disabilities, and program completion may take longer than 4 years. A social worker and counselor are on the staff of the TLC to help students as well. TLC offers the following: an individualized support program; scheduled tutorial sessions with a learning disabilities specialist; faculty liaison; academic counseling; priority registration; organizational skills including time management, test-taking, note-taking, and outlining; study techniques; memory and concentration techniques; techniques for planning and writing research papers; and content tutoring if needed.

Support Services Contact Information

Learning Disability Program/Services: The Learning Center (TLC)
Director: Patricia A. Cohen
  E-Mail: cohenp@georgian.edu
  Telephone: 732-364-2200,2650
  Fax: 732-987-2026

LEARNING DISABILITY SERVICES

Requests for the following/services accommodations will be evaluated individually based on appropriate and current documentation.

Allowed in exams
  Calculator: Yes
  Dictionary: Yes
  Computer: Yes
  Spellchecker: Yes
Extended test time: Yes
Scribes: Yes
Proctors: Yes
Oral exams: Yes
Note-takers: Yes

Distraction reduced environment: Yes
Tape recording in class: Yes
Books on tape from RFBD: Yes
Taping of books not from RFBD: No
Accommodations for students with ADD: Yes
Reading machine: No
Other assistive technology: No
Priority registration: Yes

Added costs for services: Yes
LD specialists: Yes
Professional tutors: 6
Peer tutors: No
Max. hours/wk. for services: Varies
How professors are notified of LD/ADD: By both student and director

GENERAL ADMISSIONS INFORMATION

Director of Admissions: Ann Diehl
Telephone: 732-364-2200

ENTRANCE REQUIREMENTS

Academic units required: 4 English, 2 math, 1 science (1 science lab), 2 foreign language, 1 history, 6 academic electives. High school diploma is required and GED is accepted. ACT with or without Writing component accepted. TOEFL required of all international applicants, minimum paper TOEFL 550, minimum computer TOEFL 213.

Application deadline: 8/1
Notification: Rolling
Average GPA: 3.16

Average SAT Math: 455
Average SAT Verbal: 465
Average ACT: NR

Graduated top 10% of class: 9%
Graduated top 25% of class: 30%
Graduated top 50% of class: 73%

COLLEGE GRADUATION REQUIREMENTS

Course waivers allowed: No
Course substitutions allowed: Yes
In what course: Foreign language, if applicable.

ADDITIONAL INFORMATION

Environment: Georgian Court College is a small private institution centrally located in New Jersey.

Student Body:
  Undergrad enrollment: 1,805
  Women: 92%
  Men: 8%
  Percent out-of-state: 1%

Cost Information
  Tuition: $17,224
  Room & board: $7,200
Housing Information
  University housing: Yes
  Percent living on campus: 15%

Greek System
  Fraternity: Yes
  Sorority: Yes
Athletics: NCAA Division II

KEAN UNIVERSITY

1000 Morris Avenue, Union, NJ 07083-0411
Phone: 908-737-7100 • Fax: 908-737-7105
E-mail: admitme@kean.edu • Web: www.kean.edu
Support: CS • Institution type: 4-year public

LEARNING DISABILITY PROGRAM AND SERVICES

Kean University believes qualified students with difficulties processing oral and written material have the potential to earn a college degree if they are provided with certain individualized support services. These services are designed to help students develop skills to be independent, involved, responsible learners, and use their own assets to become successful learners. Students with LD attend the same classes and meet the same academic requirements as their peers. Once admitted to Kean University, students who choose to register with Project Excel may do so by providing complete documentation of a diagnosed disability. Students are asked to complete a Project Excel application after admission to Kean. In the application, students are asked to describe their least and most successful academic areas, how the LD affects their work, what support services are needed for success, any past services received, what high school mainstream courses they have taken, and when their LD was diagnosed.

LD/ADD ADMISSIONS INFORMATION

College entrance tests required: Yes
Interview required: No
Essay required: Yes
Documentation required for LD: Psychoeducational battery within 3 years, test scores, diagnosis of LD and professional summary.
Documentation required for ADD: Full written evaluation and diagnosis of ADD performed by a qualified practioner.
Submitted to: Project Excel

Specific course requirements of all applicants: Yes
Special Ed. HS coursework accepted: No
Separate application required for program services: No
# of LD applications submitted each year: 15–20
# of LD applications accepted yearly: NR
Total # of students receiving LD services: 110–120
Acceptance into program means acceptance into college: Student must be admitted and enrolled in the university first and then may request services through Project Excel.

ADMISSIONS

There is no special admissions process for students with LD. It is recommended that students self-disclose in the admission process. All applicants must meet the same admission criteria, which include 4 years English, 3 years math, 2 years social studies, 2 years science, and 5 elective credits. Courses taken in special education may be considered. SAT/ACT is required and the average SAT range is 950–1020. The minimum GPA is 2.8. The student must be highly motivated, able to do college work, be of at least average intelligence, have a documented learning disability, have areas of academic strength, and make a commitment to work responsibly and attend classes, tutoring, workshops, and counseling sessions. Students are encouraged to apply by early March.

ADDITIONAL INFORMATION

Project Excel does not provide remedial or developmental instruction. A number of services are available through Project Excel: diagnostic assessments; academic, career, and personal advisement/counseling; development of a college education plan (CEP) for the individual student; student advocacy with faculty; referral to other college services as appropriate, such as tutoring in basic skills and course materials. All information about the student's LD is held in strict confidence. Information shared on- or off-campus is only done with the student's signed consent. LD assessments are available for a fee of $250 for a professional assessment and $150 for an assessment from a student intern. All students in Project Excel select from the same schedule of classes and attend with all other students in the college.

Support Services Contact Information

Learning Disability Program/Services: Project Excel
Director: Marie Segal, EdD
  E-Mail: pexcel@kean.edu
  Telephone: 908-737-5400
  Fax: 908-737-5405
Contact Person: Ellen Gottdenker, LDT-C: Mentor

LEARNING DISABILITY SERVICES

Requests for the following/services accommodations will be evaluated individually based on appropriate and current documentation.

Allowed in exams
  Calculator: Yes
  Dictionary: Yes
  Computer: Yes
  Spellchecker: Yes
Extended test time: Yes
Scribes: No
Proctors: Yes
Oral exams: Yes
Note-takers: No

Distraction reduced environment: Yes
Tape recording in class: Yes
Books on tape from RFBD: Yes
Taping of books not from RFBD: No
Accommodations for students with
  ADD: Yes
Reading machine: Yes
Other assistive technology: Yes
Priority registration: Yes

Added costs for services: No
LD specialists: Yes
Professional tutors: Yes
Peer tutors: Yes
Max. hours/wk. for services:
  Unlimited
How professors are notified of
  LD/ADD: By student

GENERAL ADMISSIONS INFORMATION

Director of Admissions: Audley Bridges
Telephone: 908-737-7100

ENTRANCE REQUIREMENTS

Academic units required: 4 English, 3 math, 2 science (2 science lab), 2 social studies, 5 academic electives. High school diploma is required and GED is accepted. ACT with or without Writing component accepted.

Application deadline: 5/31
Notification: Rolling
Average GPA: 2.80

Average SAT Math: 511
Average SAT Verbal: 500
Average ACT: NR

Graduated top 10% of class: 8%
Graduated top 25% of class: 24%
Graduated top 50% of class: 60%

COLLEGE GRADUATION REQUIREMENTS

Course waivers allowed: No
Course substitutions allowed: No
In what course: N/A

ADDITIONAL INFORMATION

Environment: The college is located on 151 acres in a suburban area 20 miles west of New York City.

Student Body:
  Undergrad enrollment: 9,469
  Women: 64%
  Men: 36%
  Percent out-of-state: 1%

Cost Information
  In-state tuition: $7,149
  Out-of-state tuition: $9,654
  Room & board: $7,953
Housing Information
  University housing: Yes
  Percent living on campus: 14%

Greek System
  Fraternity: Yes
  Sorority: Yes
Athletics: NCAA Division III

MONMOUTH UNIVERSITY

400 Cedar Avenue, West Long Branch, NJ 07764-1898
Phone: 732-571-3456 • Fax: 732-263-5166
E-mail: admission@monmouth.edu • Web: www.monmouth.edu
Support: CS • Institution type: 4-year private

LEARNING DISABILITY PROGRAM AND SERVICES

Monmouth University recognizes the special needs of students with disabilities who are capable, with appropriate assistance, of excelling in a demanding college environment. Comprehensive support services and a nurturing environment contribute to their success. Monmouth's commitment is to provide a learning process and atmosphere that allows students to pursue their educational goals, realize their full potential, contribute actively to their community and society, and determine the direction of their lives. Students are enrolled in regular courses and are not isolated from the rest of the student body in any manner. Students with documented disabilities may request reasonable modifications, accommodations, or auxiliary aids. It is important that students disclose their disability and provide the required learning accommodations to DSS. Much of their success has to do with individual recognition of their specific learning needs combined with supportive faculty. Monmouth is very proud of the many important contributions of students with learning disabilities to life at the university.

LD/ADD ADMISSIONS INFORMATION

College entrance tests required: Yes
Interview required: No
Essay required: No
Documentation required for LD: Psychoeducational evaluation
Documentation required for ADD: Yes
Submitted to: Disability Services
Special Ed. HS coursework accepted: No

Specific course requirements of all applicants: Yes
Separate application required for program services: No
# of LD applications submitted each year: NR
# of LD applications accepted yearly: NR
Total # of students receiving LD services: 208
Acceptance into program means acceptance into college: Students are accepted jointly into the university and the learning disabilities program.

ADMISSIONS
There is no special admissions process for students with diagnosed learning disabilities. General admission requirements include 4 years of English, 3 years of math, 2 years of social science, 2 years of science and 5 electives from English, math, science, social studies and/or foreign language. Courses taken in the special education department may be accepted. The minimum GPA is 2.5. Students are encouraged to self-disclose if they believe that their high school performance needs an explanation.

ADDITIONAL INFORMATION
Students with documented disabilities may request reasonable modifications, accommodations, or auxiliary aids that will enable them to participate in and benefit from post secondary educational programs and activities. These may include extended time, reader assistance, and note-takers. Monmouth University also offers a summer transition session during the university's freshman orientation, assistance with advocacy such as serving as liaison between the student and the professors.

Support Services Contact Information

Learning Disability Program/Services: Department of Disability Services for Students
Director: Stacey Harris
  E-Mail: Sharris@monmouth.edu
  Telephone: 732-571-3460
  Fax: 732-263-5126
Contact Person: Arthea Watson
  E-Mail: awatson@monmouth.edu
  Telephone: 732-571-3456
  Fax: 732-263-5166

LEARNING DISABILITY SERVICES

Requests for the following/services accommodations will be evaluated individually based on appropriate and current documentation.

Allowed in exams
  Calculator: Yes
  Dictionary: Yes
  Computer: Yes
  Spellchecker: Yes
Extended test time: Yes
Scribes: Yes
Proctors: Yes
Oral exams: Yes
Note-takers: Yes

Distraction reduced environment: Yes
Tape recording in class: Yes
Books on tape from RFBD: Yes
Taping of books not from RFBD: No
Accommodations for students with
  ADD: Yes
Reading machine: Yes
Other assistive technology: Yes
Priority registration: Yes

Added costs for services: Yes
LD specialists: Yes
Professional tutors: No
Peer tutors: No
Max. hours/wk. for services:
  Unlimited
How professors are notified of
  LD/ADD: By both student and director

GENERAL ADMISSIONS INFORMATION

Director of Admissions: Lauren Vento Cifelli
Telephone: 732-571-3456

ENTRANCE REQUIREMENTS

Academic units required: 4 English, 3 math, 2 science (1 science lab), 2 history, 5 academic electives. **Academic units recommended:** 2 foreign language, 2 social studies. High school diploma is required and GED is accepted. TOEFL required of all international applicants, minimum paper TOEFL 525, minimum computer TOEFL 197.

Application deadline: 3/1
Notification: prior to 04/01
Average GPA: 3.00

Average SAT Math: 534
Average SAT Verbal: 525
Average ACT: NR

Graduated top 10% of class: 9%
Graduated top 25% of class: 30%
Graduated top 50% of class: 60%

COLLEGE GRADUATION REQUIREMENTS

Course waivers allowed: Yes
Course substitutions allowed: Yes
In what course: Case by case determination (most majors do not require foreign languages).

ADDITIONAL INFORMATION

Environment: The college is located on 125 acres in a suburb 60 miles south of New York City.

Student Body:
  Undergrad enrollment: 4,448
  Women: 59%
  Men: 41%
  Percent out-of-state: 8%

Cost Information
  Tuition: $19,108
  Room & board: $7,911
Housing Information
  University housing: Yes
  Percent living on campus: 43%

Greek System
  Fraternity: Yes
  Sorority: Yes
Athletics: NCAA Division I

NEW JERSEY CITY UNIVERSITY

2039 Kennedy Boulevard, Jersey City, NJ 07305
Phone: 888-441-6528 • Fax: 201-200-2044
E-mail: admissions@njcu.edu • Web: www.njcu.edu
Support: SP • Institution type: 4-year public

LEARNING DISABILITY PROGRAM AND SERVICES

Project Mentor is a support program that "opens the door" to higher education for students with learning disabilities by providing them with a faculty mentor—a teacher, advisor, and facilitator—for their entire college career. A low-cost four week pre-college summer orientation program prepares freshmen students for success in the academic setting. (Residential students pay for food and housing). In addition to the traditional university admissions process there is an alternate admissions pathway through Project Mentor. Faculty mentors, advisement, priority registration, special tutorials, compensatory strategy development, counseling, and advocacy are among the many services that are available to student participants throughout the academic year.

LD/ADD ADMISSIONS INFORMATION

College entrance tests required: Yes
Interview required: Yes
Essay required: Yes
Documentation required for LD: Educational, psychological
   (current—within the past 3 years)
Documentation required for ADD: Yes
Submitted to: Project Mentor
Special Ed. HS coursework accepted: No

Specific course requirements of all applicants: Yes
Separate application required for program services: Yes
# of LD applications submitted each year: 30–50
# of LD applications accepted yearly: 20–25
Total # of students receiving LD services: 75–100
Acceptance into program means acceptance into
   college: Admission is given to the College and Project
   Mentor at the same time.

ADMISSIONS

Students with LD may gain admission through one of two procedures: (1) the traditional university admissions process: and (2) Project Mentor's alternate admissions process. These two procedures operate concurrently and their outcomes are independent of one another. A student who is admitted traditionally may receive all of the support and advocacy services available by providing LD documentation. To be considered for alternate admissions, students must submit recent documentation of the LD, evidence of motivation, and successful academic performance. The Project Mentor admissions committee analyzes the documentation to gain a better understanding of the student's academic strengths and how the disability may impact academic performance. Admitted students into Project Mentor must attend a summer program. All applicants to Project Mentor are requested to schedule an interview, submit recommendations or telephone calls from a high school counselor and/or teacher, and have a recent child study team evaluation. The admissions process involves a review of the psychoeducational report. Project Mentor is looking for students with the intellectual potential to achieve in a 4-year college setting who were mostly in mainstream college-prep classes in high school. Although SAT scores are required, they are not used for admission purposes. All applications from students with learning disabilities are referred to Project Mentor. Project faculty review applications and make recommendations to the Admissions Office for acceptance, rejection, or trial status for a pre-college summer orientation program. The staff considers each candidate individually.

ADDITIONAL INFORMATION

Students meet once a week with mentors. Sessions might include instruction, counseling, and/or referral to services available to all students at the college. Exclusive tutorials for Project Mentor students are staffed by highly trained professionals. Mentors help the students to negotiate accommodations with their professors. Extending the limits on examinations, providing tutorial assistance, and permitting tape recording of lectures are among the types of accommodations provided. Professors try to provide for the special needs of students with learning differences/disabilities while maintaining appropriate academic standards.

Support Services Contact Information

Learning Disability Program/Services: Project Mentor
Director: Sharon Jackson
  E-Mail: Sjackson@njcu.edu
  Telephone: 201-200-2557
  Fax: 201-200-2575

LEARNING DISABILITY SERVICES

Requests for the following/services accommodations will be evaluated individually based on appropriate and current documentation.

Allowed in exams
  Calculator: Yes
  Dictionary: Yes
  Computer: Yes
  Spellchecker: Yes
Extended test time: Yes
Scribes: Yes
Proctors: Yes
Oral exams: Yes
Note-takers: No

Distraction reduced environment: Yes
Tape recording in class: Yes
Books on tape from RFBD: Yes
Taping of books not from RFBD: Yes
Accommodations for students with ADD: Yes
Reading machine: No
Other assistive technology: Yes
Priority registration: Yes

Added costs for services: No
LD specialists: Yes
Professional tutors: 7
Peer tutors: 2–4
Max. hours/wk. for services: Unlimited
How professors are notified of LD/ADD: By both student and director

GENERAL ADMISSIONS INFORMATION

Director of Admissions: Jason Hand, Acting Director of Admissions
Telephone: 888-441-6528

ENTRANCE REQUIREMENTS

Academic units required: 4 English, 4 math, 4 science (2 science lab), 4 social studies. **Academic units recommended:** 4 English, 4 math, 4 science (3 science lab), 2 foreign language, 4 social studies. High school diploma is required and GED is accepted. TOEFL required of all international applicants, minimum paper TOEFL 500, minimum computer TOEFL 173.

Application deadline: 4/1
Notification: Rolling
Average GPA: 2.7

Average SAT Math: NR
Average SAT Verbal: NR
Average ACT: NR

Graduated top 10% of class: 16%
Graduated top 25% of class: 23%
Graduated top 50% of class: 36%

COLLEGE GRADUATION REQUIREMENTS

Course waivers allowed: NR
Course substitutions allowed: Yes
In what course: Each case is reviewed on an individual basis.

ADDITIONAL INFORMATION

Environment: The college is located on 150 acres in a suburban area 20 miles west of New York City.

Student Body:
  Undergrad enrollment: 5,838
  Women: 63%
  Men: 37%
  Percent out-of-state: 2%

Cost Information
  In-state tuition: $6,550
  Out-of-state tuition: $11,230
  Room & board: $6,958
Housing Information
  University housing: Yes
  Percent living on campus: 5%

Greek System
  Fraternity: Yes
  Sorority: Yes
Athletics: NCAA Division III

RIDER UNIVERSITY

2083 Lawrenceville Road, Lawrenceville, NJ 08648-3099
Phone: 609-896-5042 • Fax: 609-895-6645
E-mail: admissions@rider.edu • Web: www.rider.edu
Support: CS • Institution type: 4-year private

LEARNING DISABILITY PROGRAM AND SERVICES

The Education Enhancement Program offers a range of services to help students with documented LD obtain appropriate accommodations. These services include screening and referral, supplementary assessment, and instructional services. The goal of the program is to assist students in becoming more independent and efficient learners. A learning disability specialist meets individually with students who have learning disabilities and/or attention deficit disorder. Students must initiate the request for this meeting and must supply documentation of the disability. These learning disability specialists conduct an intake interview and, based on the information resulting from this interview, refer students to appropriate support services. They also determine the appropriate academic adjustments.

LD/ADD ADMISSIONS INFORMATION

College entrance tests required: Yes
Interview required: No
Essay required: Yes
Documentation required for LD: Educational and
   psychological tests: within three years. Please see website
   for complete documentation guidelines.
Documentation required for ADD: Please see website for
   complete documentation guidelines.
Submitted to: Support Program/Services
Special Ed. HS coursework accepted: No

Specific course requirements of all applicants: Yes
Separate application required for program services: No
# of LD applications submitted each year: NR
# of LD applications accepted yearly: NR
Total # of students receiving LD services: NR
**Acceptance into program means acceptance into
   college:** Student must be admitted and enrolled in the
   university first and then request services.

ADMISSIONS

There is no special admissions process for students with learning disabilities. All students must submit the general university application. Admissions criteria are based on the following: high school academic record and GPA of 2.0 or better, SAT or ACT test results, and a college writing sample (essay). Courses required include 16 acceptable units from a college-prep curriculum: 4 years English; 2 years math, sciences, foreign language, social science, and humanities. For students with a learning disability, proper documentation recognizing the differing abilities of the student is requested. The Rider Achievement Program is for academically admissible students who are just below the admissions criteria for the regularly admitted student. The Educational Opportunity Fund Program is the state-funded program for academically disadvantaged or economically disadvantaged students.

ADDITIONAL INFORMATION

The Rider Learning Center provides individual and small group tutoring in writing, reading comprehension, and study strategies. The staff offers study strategy workshops and students have access to computers. The Mathematics Skill Lab provides a math course for students who do not meet the placement criteria for college level math. The course is taught via individual tutoring, structured workshops, and computer-assisted instruction. The MSL staff offers weekly tutorial sessions for Finite Math, helps students prepare for the Algebra & Trig Qualifying Exam, and provides tutoring for other courses. Tutoring Services provide a peer tutoring program for students needing extra help. The Education Enhancement Program offers a course in college reading and Introduction to Academic Reading.

Support Services Contact Information

Learning Disability Program/Services: Education Enhancement Program/Services for Students with Disabilities
Director: Jacqueline Simon, EdD
  E-Mail: serv4dstu@rider.edu
  Telephone: 609-895-5492
  Fax: 609-895-5507

LEARNING DISABILITY SERVICES

Requests for the following/services accommodations will be evaluated individually based on appropriate and current documentation.

Allowed in exams
  Calculator: Yes
  Dictionary: Yes
  Computer: Yes
  Spellchecker: Yes
Extended test time: Yes
Scribes: Yes
Proctors: Yes
Oral exams: Yes
Note-takers: Yes

Distraction reduced environment: Yes
Tape recording in class: Yes
Books on tape from RFBD: Yes
Taping of books not from RFBD: Yes
Accommodations for students with ADD: Yes
Reading machine: No
Other assistive technology: Yes
Priority registration: Yes

Added costs for services: No
LD specialists: Yes
Professional tutors: 5
Peer tutors: 50
Max. hours/wk. for services: 3
How professors are notified of LD/ADD: By both student and director

GENERAL ADMISSIONS INFORMATION

Director of Admissions: Susan C. Christian, Dean of Enrollment
Telephone: 609-895-5768

ENTRANCE REQUIREMENTS

Academic units required: 4 English, 2 math. **Academic units recommended:** 3 math, 3 science, 3 foreign language, 2 social studies, 2 history. High school diploma is required and GED is accepted. ACT with or without Writing component accepted. TOEFL required of all international applicants, minimum paper TOEFL 550, minimum computer TOEFL 213.

Application deadline: Rolling
Notification: Rolling
Average GPA: 3.12

Average SAT Math: 529
Average SAT Verbal: 530
Average ACT: NR

Graduated top 10% of class: 13%
Graduated top 25% of class: 36%
Graduated top 50% of class: 70%

COLLEGE GRADUATION REQUIREMENTS

Course waivers allowed: No
Course substitutions allowed: Yes
In what course: Substitutions are considered on a case-by-case basis only and may be considered for foreign language and math. The more common practice is for students to accomplish the courses with academic support.

ADDITIONAL INFORMATION

Environment: The college is located on a 353-acre campus between Princeton and Trenton, New Jersey.

Student Body:
  Undergrad enrollment: 4,038
  Women: 60%
  Men: 40%
  Percent out-of-state: 24%

Cost Information
  Tuition: $22,300
  Room & board: $8,400
Housing Information
  University housing: Yes
  Percent living on campus: 56%

Greek System
  Fraternity: Yes
  Sorority: Yes
  Athletics: NCAA Division I

SETON HALL UNIVERSITY

Enrollment Services, 400 South Orange Avenue, South Orange, NJ 07079
Phone: 973-761-9332 • Fax: 973-275-2040
E-mail: thehall@shu.edu • Web: www.shu.edu
Support: CS • Institution type: 4-year private

LEARNING DISABILITY PROGRAM AND SERVICES

Student Support Services is an academic program that addresses the needs of all eligible undergraduates. The program provides individual and group tutoring in many disciplines. Academic, career, and other counseling services are also available. The program provides individual and group tutoring in many disciplines. Special emphasis is placed on mathematics, laboratory sciences, and business. Student Support Services is especially attentive to the needs of students who can provide professional documentation of specific disabilities. Every effort is made to accommodate the special academic needs of these students by recommending extended test time and a distraction-free testing environment.

LD/ADD ADMISSIONS INFORMATION

College entrance tests required: Yes
Interview required: No
Essay required: No
Documentation required for LD: Psychoeducational evaluation
Documentation required for ADD: Yes
Submitted to: Support Program/Services
Special Ed. HS coursework accepted: No

Specific course requirements of all applicants: Yes
Separate application required for program services: No
# of LD applications submitted each year: NR
# of LD applications accepted yearly: NR
Total # of students receiving LD services: 140
Acceptance into program means acceptance into college: Student must be admitted and enrolled in the university first and then request services.

ADMISSIONS

There is no special admission process for students with learning disabilities, and all applicants must meet the same admission criteria. Courses required include 4 years English, 3 years math, 1 year lab science, 2 years foreign language, 2 years social studies, and 4 electives. If students have been waived from a world language via his or her IEP, the requirement would be waived if it is not a core requirement of a particular program. The minimum SAT is 900. Students need to rank in the top two-fifths of their class and a minimum 2.5 GPA is recommended.

ADDITIONAL INFORMATION

In coordinating its activities with other departments of the university (such as Residence Life and Academic Services), Student Support Services works to assure that the university remains in compliance with all federal laws and regulations. Students must self-identify and submit the Self-Identification Form with appropriate documentation. The DSS office provides the following services: development of accommodation plans, assistance with self-advocacy, coordination of tutoring, testing accommodations, student support groups, note-takers, student workshops and strategy training, individual assistance with organizational skills, and coursework management.

Support Services Contact Information

Learning Disability Program/Services: Disability Support Services
Director: Linda Raye Walter
  E-Mail: walter@shu.edu
  Telephone: 973-313-6003
  Fax: 973-761-9185

LEARNING DISABILITY SERVICES

Requests for the following/services accommodations will be evaluated individually based on appropriate and current documentation.

Allowed in exams	Distraction reduced environment: Yes	Added costs for services: No
Calculator: Yes	Tape recording in class: Yes	LD specialists: Yes
Dictionary: Yes	Books on tape from RFBD: No	Professional tutors: Yes
Computer: Yes	Taping of books not from RFBD: Yes	Peer tutors: Yes
Spellchecker: Yes	Accommodations for students with	Max. hours/wk. for services:
Extended test time: Yes	ADD: Yes	Unlimited
Scribes: Yes	Reading machine: Yes	How professors are notified of
Proctors: Yes	Other assistive technology: Yes	LD/ADD: By both student and director
Oral exams: Yes	Priority registration: No	
Note-takers: Yes		

GENERAL ADMISSIONS INFORMATION

Director of Admissions: Darryl Jones
Telephone: 973-761-9332

ENTRANCE REQUIREMENTS

Academic units required: 4 English, 3 math, 1 science, 2 foreign language, 2 social studies, 4 academic electives. High school diploma is required and GED is accepted. TOEFL required of all international applicants, minimum paper TOEFL 550, minimum computer TOEFL 213.

Application deadline: 3/1	Average SAT Math: 553	Graduated top 10% of class: 26%
Notification: Rolling	Average SAT Verbal: 549	Graduated top 25% of class: 54%
Average GPA: 3.3	Average ACT: NR	Graduated top 50% of class: 85%

COLLEGE GRADUATION REQUIREMENTS

Course waivers allowed: Yes
In what course: No core courses are waived.
Course substitutions allowed: Yes
In what course: Students may request course substitutions which are approved by the dean of each school or college upon recommendation of the DSS office.

ADDITIONAL INFORMATION

Environment: The university is located on 58 acres in a suburban area 14 miles west of New York City.

Student Body:	Cost Information	Greek System
Undergrad enrollment: 5,009	Tuition: $22,944	Fraternity: Yes
Women: 52%	Room & board: $9,000	Sorority: Yes
Men: 48%	Housing Information	Athletics: NCAA Division I
Percent out-of-state: 25%	University housing: Yes	
	Percent living on campus: 42%	

COLLEGE OF SANTA FE

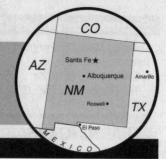

1600 St. Michaels Drive, Santa Fe, NM 87505-7634
Phone: 505-473-6133 • Fax: 505-473-6129
E-mail: admissions@csf.edu • Web: www.csf.edu
Support: S • Institution type: 4-year private

LEARNING DISABILITY PROGRAM AND SERVICES

The Center for Academic Excellence is a federally funded Title IV Support Services Program designed to assist eligible students to graduate from CSF. There is no formal disabilities program at the college, but the students do have access to many services and accommodations. Students may receive services in basic skills instruction of reading, study strategies, writing, math, humanities, and science. Students work with the professional staff to set up a support program that meets their specific needs. The initial meeting is during registration. In order to be eligible for services students with learning disabilities must provide a current psychoeducational evaluation that identifies the learning disability. Once this documentation is on file with the Center for Academic Excellence, students may meet with staff to identify the necessary accommodations and services needed to be successful in college.

LD/ADD ADMISSIONS INFORMATION

College entrance tests required: Yes
Interview required: Yes
Essay required: Yes
Documentation required for LD: Psychiatrist, psychologist, educational diagnostician or medical physician report based on testing less than three years old, (submit what you have even if it is older.
Documentation required for ADD: Letter from counselor or psychiartrist stating diagnosis and medications.
Submitted to: Center for Academics Excellence
Special Ed. HS coursework accepted: Yes

Specific course requirements of all applicants: Yes
Separate application required for program services: No
# of LD applications submitted each year: NR
# of LD applications accepted yearly: NR
Total # of students receiving LD services: 75–100
Acceptance into program means acceptance into college: Students are admitted to the college and to the Center for Academic Excellence after applying for services.

ADMISSIONS

There is no separate admission process for students with learning disabilities/ADD. Students with learning disabilities/ADD are required to meet the general admission criteria. This includes course requirements of 3 years English, 2 years math, 2 years science, 2 years social science, and a recommended of 2 years foreign language. All applicants are required to interview either in person or by telephone. Each applicant is evaluated individually. If admitted, students with a GPA inconsistent with their level of ability arrange for academic support from the Center for Academic Excellence. Copies of diagnostic examinations not more than three years old must document the student's leaning disability or ADD. The results of these tests are sent to the Center for Academic Excellence after the student is admitted.

ADDITIONAL INFORMATION

Throughout the academic year, the Disabilities Service Office works to support the needs of students with disabilities by providing an initial interview, assessment of accommodation needs, and ongoing support. Services provided by the college could include but are not limited to the following: alternative testing, specialized tutoring, academic advisement, career planning, note-takers, interpreters for the hearing impaired, screen reader software, other assistive technology, peer tutoring, and resource information and referrals. Accommodations are provided on an individual basis.

Support Services Contact Information

Learning Disability Program/Services: Disability Service Office/Center for Academic Excellence
Director: Donna Collins
  E-Mail: dcollins@csf.edu
  Telephone: 505-473-6552
  Fax: 505-473-6124

LEARNING DISABILITY SERVICES

Requests for the following/services accommodations will be evaluated individually based on appropriate and current documentation.

Allowed in exams
  Calculator: Yes
  Dictionary: Yes
  Computer: Yes
  Spellchecker: Yes
Extended test time: Yes
Scribes: Yes
Proctors: Yes
Oral exams: Yes
Note-takers: Yes

Distraction reduced environment: Yes
Tape recording in class: Yes
Books on tape from RFBD: Yes
Taping of books not from RFBD: No
Accommodations for students with ADD: Yes
Reading machine: Yes
Other assistive technology: Yes
Priority registration: No

Added costs for services: No
LD specialists: No
Professional tutors: 2
Peer tutors: 25–40
Max. hours/wk. for services: 3
How professors are notified of LD/ADD: By director

GENERAL ADMISSIONS INFORMATION

Director of Admissions: Jeff Miller
Telephone: 505-473-6133

ENTRANCE REQUIREMENTS

Academic units required: 4 English, 2 math, 2 science (2 science lab), 2 social studies, 6 academic electives.
Academic units recommended: 4 English, 3 math, 3 science (2 science lab), 2 foreign language, 2 social studies, 2 history, 4 academic electives. High school diploma is required and GED is accepted. ACT with Writing component required. TOEFL required of all international applicants, minimum paper TOEFL 550, minimum computer TOEFL 213.

Application deadline: Rolling
Notification: Rolling
Average GPA: 3.32

Average SAT Math: 543
Average SAT Verbal: 581
Average ACT: 23

Graduated top 10% of class: 18%
Graduated top 25% of class: 43%
Graduated top 50% of class: 80%

COLLEGE GRADUATION REQUIREMENTS

Course waivers allowed: Yes
In what course: This is done on an individual basis, depending on the experience of the individual student.
Course substitutions allowed: Yes
In what course: It is done on a case by case basis, but substitution is common for all students here.

ADDITIONAL INFORMATION

Environment: The college is located on 118 acres in a suburban area of Santa Fe.

Student Body:
  Undergrad enrollment: 1,279
  Women: 59%
  Men: 41%
  Percent out-of-state: 78%

Cost Information
  Tuition: $20,214
  Room & board: $6,340
Housing Information
  University housing: Yes
  Percent living on campus: 62%

Greek System
  Fraternity: No
  Sorority: No
  Athletics: NAIA

New Mexico Inst. of Mining & Tech.

Campus Station, 801 Leroy Place, Socorro, NM 87801
Phone: 505-835-5424 • Fax: 505-835-5989
E-mail: admission@admin.nmt.edu • Web: www.nmt.edu
Support: S • Institution type: 4-year public

LEARNING DISABILITY PROGRAM AND SERVICES

New Mexico Tech does not have a specific program for students with LD. Services for students with disabilities are available in the Counseling and Student Health Center. Students must present documentation within the previous three years. The documentation should be sent to Services for Students with Disabilities. New Mexico Tech sends a letter to all admitted students asking those with disabilities to contact the Services for Students with Disabilities. There is a special application required after admission and enrollment in order to receive services or accommodations. The counseling staff works with students with disabilities on an individual basis to accommodate their special needs. Students may also use the counseling service to reduce their stress, think through problems or difficulties, clarify options, and express and explore feelings.

LD/ADD ADMISSIONS INFORMATION

College entrance tests required: Yes
Interview required: No
Essay required: No
Documentation required for LD: Psychoeducational evaluation
Documentation required for ADD: Yes
Submitted to: Services for students with disabilities
Special Ed. HS coursework accepted: N/A

Specific course requirements of all applicants: No
Separate application required for program services: Yes
# of LD applications submitted each year: NR
# of LD applications accepted yearly: NR
Total # of students receiving LD services: 24
Acceptance into program means acceptance into college: Student must be admitted and enrolled in the college first and then request services.

ADMISSIONS

There is no special admission process for students with LD. The minimum GPA is a 2.5, ACT composite score of 21 or higher or SAT of 970 or higher. The college will accept the SAT but prefers the ACT. The GED is accepted with a score of 50 or higher. High school course requirements include 4 years of English; 2 years of science among biology, physics, chemistry and earth science; 3 years of math; and 3 years of social science, one of which must be history. Students are encouraged to self-disclose their disability during the admission process.

ADDITIONAL INFORMATION

Students will work with staff to determine appropriate accommodations or services. These services may include coordinating academic accommodations, extended time for tests, calculators in exams, skills classes in study strategies and time management, and tutorial services are available for all students on campus.

Support Services Contact Information

Learning Disability Program/Services: Services for Students with Disabilities
Director: Dr. Judith Raymond
  E-Mail: jraymond@admin-nmt.edu
  Telephone: 505-835-5443
  Fax: 505-835-5223

LEARNING DISABILITY SERVICES

Requests for the following/services accommodations will be evaluated individually based on appropriate and current documentation.

Allowed in exams
  Calculator: Yes
  Dictionary: No
  Computer: Yes
  Spellchecker: Yes
Extended test time: Yes
Scribes: Yes
Proctors: Yes
Oral exams: Yes
Note-takers: Yes

Distraction reduced environment: Yes
Tape recording in class: Yes
Books on tape from RFBD: Yes
Taping of books not from RFBD: Yes
Accommodations for students with
  ADD: Yes
Reading machine: No
Other assistive technology: Yes
Priority registration: Yes

Added costs for services: No
LD specialists: No
Professional tutors: No
Peer tutors: 50
Max. hours/wk. for services:
  Unlimited
How professors are notified of
  LD/ADD: By both student and director

GENERAL ADMISSIONS INFORMATION

Director of Admissions: Melissa Jaramillo-Fleming
Telephone: 505-835-5424

ENTRANCE REQUIREMENTS

Academic units required: 4 English, 3 math, 2 science (2 science lab), 2 social studies, 1 history, 3 academic electives. **Academic units recommended:** 4 English, 4 math, 4 science (3 science lab), 2 foreign language, 3 social studies, 1 history. High school diploma is required and GED is accepted. TOEFL required of all international applicants, minimum paper TOEFL 540, minimum computer TOEFL 207.

Application deadline: 8/1
Notification: Rolling
Average GPA: 3.6

Average SAT Math: 612
Average SAT Verbal: 596
Average ACT: 26

Graduated top 10% of class: 37%
Graduated top 25% of class: 59%
Graduated top 50% of class: 88%

COLLEGE GRADUATION REQUIREMENTS

Course waivers allowed: No
Course substitutions allowed: No
In what course: N/A

ADDITIONAL INFORMATION

Environment: Located 75 miles from Albuquerque

Student Body:
  Undergrad enrollment: 1,148
  Women: 25%
  Men: 75%
  Percent out-of-state: 15%

Cost Information
  In-state tuition: $3,280
  Out-of-state tuition: $9,911
  Room & board: $4,470
Housing Information
  University housing: Yes
  Percent living on campus: 59%

Greek System
  Fraternity: No
  Sorority: No
Athletics: Intramural

NEW MEXICO STATE UNIVERSITY

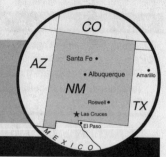

Box 30001, MSC 3A, Las Cruces, NM 88003-8001
Phone: 505-646-3121 • Fax: 505-646-6330
E-mail: admissions@nmsu.edu • Web: www.nmsu.edu
Support: S • Institution type: 4-year public

LEARNING DISABILITY PROGRAM AND SERVICES

Services for Students with Disabilities is a component of the Office of Student Development. The staff is committed to providing information and services that assist students with disabilities in personal and academic adjustment to the university community. Services for Students with Disabilities provides assistance with procuring auxiliary aids, coordinating services and resources, discussing special needs and accommodations, and consultants students regarding questions about various accommodations. They work with students to ensure that they have access to all programs and services that will effect their full participation in the campus community. Students are encouraged to contact Services for Students with Disabilities to discuss needs and to register for the program. Students should complete the Petition for Services for Students with Disabilities and return it with the appropriate documentation for evaluation and review. A review committee will determine eligibility and the specific services and accommodations to be provided, and the student will be notified by a coordinator. This process takes time and students are encouraged to start the process as soon as possible.

LD/ADD ADMISSIONS INFORMATION

College entrance tests required: Yes
Interview required: No
Essay required: No
Documentation required for LD: Psychoeducational evaluation
Documentation required for ADD: Yes
Submitted to: Services with students with disabilities
Special Ed. HS coursework accepted: Yes

Specific course requirements of all applicants: Yes
Separate application required for program services: No
# of LD applications submitted each year: NR
# of LD applications accepted yearly: NR
Total # of students receiving LD services: 90
Acceptance into program means acceptance into college: Student must be admitted and enrolled in the university first and then request services.

ADMISSIONS

Admission criteria are the same for all students. Admissions can be granted on a regular status or provisional status. Regular admission requires high school GPA of 2.5 and 21 ACT or 970 SAT. Course requirements include 4 years English, 2 years science, 3 years math, and 3 years social studies (1 must be history). Provisional status is possible for students who have a high school GPA of 2.1 and 18 ACT. Students admitted provisionally must take at least 6 but not more than 12 credits in a regular semester and at least 3, but not more than 6, in a summer session.

ADDITIONAL INFORMATION

The Center for Learning Assistance offers students the skills they need to excel in college. Students work with learning facilitators to develop or maximize the skills needed for college success. Assistance is offered in time management, concentration, memory, test preparation, test taking, listening/note-taking, textbook reading techniques, math/science study skills, reasoning skills, writing, spelling, and grammar. Student Support Services is a program of academic and personal support with the goal of improving the retention and graduation of undergraduate students with disabilities. A mentor is provided for all participants to help motivate them and tutors help with study skills in specific subjects. Students may have tutors in two subjects and can meet weekly. Other services available are early registration; note-taking services; readers; and test accommodations including extended time, a quiet location, scribes, readers, or other assistance with exams. All services are free.

Support Services Contact Information

Learning Disability Program/Services: Services for Students with Disabilities (SSD)
Director: Michael Armendariz
  E-Mail: ssd@nmsu.edu
  Telephone: 505-646-6840
  Fax: 505-646-5222

LEARNING DISABILITY SERVICES

Requests for the following/services accommodations will be evaluated individually based on appropriate and current documentation.

Allowed in exams
  Calculator: Yes
  Dictionary: No
  Computer: Yes
  Spellchecker: Yes
Extended test time: Yes
Scribes: Yes
Proctors: Yes
Oral exams: Yes
Note-takers: Yes

Distraction reduced environment: Yes
Tape recording in class: Yes
Books on tape from RFBD: Yes
Taping of books not from RFBD: Yes
Accommodations for students with ADD: Yes
Reading machine: Yes
Other assistive technology: Yes
Priority registration: Yes

Added costs for services: No
LD specialists: No
Professional tutors: No
Peer tutors: 50
Max. hours/wk. for services: Unlimited
How professors are notified of LD/ADD: By both student and director

GENERAL ADMISSIONS INFORMATION

Director of Admissions: Angela Mora-Riley
Telephone: 505-646-3121

ENTRANCE REQUIREMENTS
Academic units required: 4 English, 3 math, 2 science, (2 science lab), 1 foreign language. High school diploma is required and GED is accepted. TOEFL required of all international applicants, minimum paper TOEFL 500, minimum computer TOEFL 173.

Application deadline: Rolling
Notification: rolling basis
Average GPA: 3.4

Average SAT Math: NR
Average SAT Verbal: NR
Average ACT: 21

Graduated top 10% of class: 20%
Graduated top 25% of class: 49%
Graduated top 50% of class: 82%

COLLEGE GRADUATION REQUIREMENTS

Course waivers allowed: Yes
Course substitutions allowed: Yes
In what course: Students need to negotiate with the college in which they are majoring.

ADDITIONAL INFORMATION

Environment: The university is located on 5,800 acres in a suburban area 40 miles north of El Paso, Texas.

Student Body:
  Undergrad enrollment: 12,145
  Women: 55%
  Men: 45%
  Percent out-of-state: 17%

Cost Information
  In-state tuition: $3,666
  Out-of-state tuition: $12,210
  Room & board: $5,000
Housing Information
  University housing: Yes
  Percent living on campus: 16%

Greek System
  Fraternity: Yes
  Sorority: Yes
Athletics: NCAA Division I

ADELPHI UNIVERSITY

Levermore Hall 114, 1 South Avenue, Garden City, NY 11530
Phone: 516-877-3050 • Fax: 516-877-3039
E-mail: admissions@adelphi.edu • Web: www.adelphi.edu
Support: SP • Institution type: 4-year private

LEARNING DISABILITY PROGRAM AND SERVICES

The approach of the Learning Disabilities Program at Adelphi is to provide an atmosphere where students with LD/ADD can realize their potential. The program is specially designed for students unable to process oral and written materials in conventional ways, but who excel in other ways. Each student is provided with the support of an interdisciplinary team of experienced professionals in tutoring and counseling. All instruction, counseling, and assessment are provided by more than 15 professionals with advanced degrees in special education and social work. Students meet individually with an educator and a counselor who work as a team. There is a mandatory 5-week summer program prior to freshman year. Students must attend tutoring sessions two times a week, participate in all the program's services, and sign an agreement acknowledging their academic commitment. Students attend classes in their chosen major, and meet standard academic requirements. The goal is independence in the academic and the real world.

LD/ADD ADMISSIONS INFORMATION

College entrance tests required: Yes
Interview required: Yes
Essay required: Yes
Documentation required for LD: WAIS–III, WJ–R, Specific LD diagnosis with psychoeducational evaluation.
Documentation required for ADD: Comprehensive evaluation with written interpretive report.
Submitted to: Learning Disabilities Program
Special Ed. HS coursework accepted: No

Specific course requirements of all applicants: No
Separate application required for program services: Yes
# of LD applications submitted each year: 350–400
# of LD applications accepted yearly: 75–100
Total # of students receiving LD services: 125–137
Acceptance into program means acceptance into college: Yes.

ADMISSIONS

The Admissions Committee reviews all submitted materials for a total picture of strengths and disabilities. Applicants with LD who show an ability to succeed academically are invited to interview. They must submit a high school transcript, documentation of LD, ACT/SAT scores and a recent testing. The director of the program is actively involved in the admissions decision, and conducts a highly individualized assessment of each applicant and the documentation. Motivation, college-prep courses, average or higher I.Q. (WAIS–III), interview, documentation, and a recommendation from an LD specialist are other factors that are used in making an admission decision. Prior to applying applicants should attend an information session conducted by the program. The program seeks highly motivated and socially mature individuals with average to superior intelligence that are capable of handling full academic schedules. Judgment of the professional staff will determine eligibility for the program.

ADDITIONAL INFORMATION

Students receive intensive academic tutoring and individual counseling, which begins in the summer program. Course content and requirements are never compromised for students with learning disabilities, but program procedures do help to ease the way in the classroom. For example, in individual tutorials professional special educators teach how to get the most of studies; instructors are privately notified in writing and by phone if program students are in their classes; students may tape record class lectures if note-taking is difficult; and individual counseling enables students to understand their behavior, reduce anxiety, and grow emotionally. Approximately 25 percent of these students make the dean's list. There are currently 105 students with LD/ADD receiving services.

Support Services Contact Information

Learning Disability Program/Services: Learning Disabilities Program
Director: Susan Spencer
  E-Mail: LDProgram@adelphi.edu
  Telephone: 516-877-4710
  Fax: 516-877-4711

LEARNING DISABILITY SERVICES

Requests for the following/services accommodations will be evaluated individually based on appropriate and current documentation.

Allowed in exams
  Calculator: No
  Dictionary: No
  Computer: No
  Spellchecker: No
Extended test time: Yes
Scribes: Yes
Proctors: Yes
Oral exams: Yes
Note-takers: Yes

Distraction reduced environment: Yes
Tape recording in class: Yes
Books on tape from RFBD: Yes
Taping of books not from RFBD: No
Accommodations for students with
  ADD: Yes
Reading machine: Yes
Other assistive technology: Yes
Priority registration: Yes

Added costs for services: Yes
LD specialists: Yes
Professional tutors: Yes
Peer tutors: No
Max. hours/wk. for services: 3
How professors are notified of
  LD/ADD: By both student and director

GENERAL ADMISSIONS INFORMATION

Director of Admissions: Christine Murphy
Telephone: 516-877-3050

ENTRANCE REQUIREMENTS

Academic units recommended: 4 English, 3 math, 3 science, 2 foreign language, 4 social studies. High school diploma is required and GED is accepted. ACT with Writing component required or SAT Reasoning. TOEFL required of all international applicants, minimum paper TOEFL 550, minimum computer TOEFL 213.

Application deadline: NR
Notification: Rolling
Average GPA: 3.3

Average SAT Math: 558
Average SAT Verbal: 548
Average ACT: 24

Graduated top 10% of class: 22%
Graduated top 25% of class: 55%
Graduated top 50% of class: 90%

COLLEGE GRADUATION REQUIREMENTS

Course waivers allowed: No
Course substitutions allowed: No
In what course: N/A

ADDITIONAL INFORMATION

Environment: The university is located on a 75-acre campus 20 miles from New York City.

Student Body:
  Undergrad enrollment: 4,413
  Women: 71%
  Men: 29%
  Percent out-of-state: 8%

Cost Information
  Tuition: $17,700
  Room & board: $8,900
Housing Information
  University housing: Yes
  Percent living on campus: 24%

Greek System
  Fraternity: Yes
  Sorority: Yes
Athletics: NCAA Division II

COLGATE UNIVERSITY

13 Oak Drive, Hamilton, NY 13346
Phone: 315-228-7401 • Fax: 315-228-7544
E-mail: admission@mail.colgate.edu • Web: www.colgate.edu
Support: CS • Institution type: 4-year private

LEARNING DISABILITY PROGRAM AND SERVICES

Colgate provides for a small student body a liberal arts education that will expand individual potential and ability to participate effectively in society's affairs. There are many resources available for all students. Colgate's goal is to offer resources and services within the campus-wide support system that are responsive to the various talents, needs, and preferences of students with disabilities. In order for the university to understand and prepare for the accommodations that may be requested, students are asked to complete a confidential self-assessment questionnaire and provide appropriate documentation about their disability. The director of academic support works with students and faculty to assure that the needs of students with disabilities are met serves as clearinghouse for information about disabilities, provides training and individual consultation for all members of the Colgate community, and provides academic counseling and individualized instruction. Students should contact the director of academic support in order to make the university aware of the existence of their learning disability. Seeking help early and learning to be a self-advocate are essential to college success.

LD/ADD ADMISSIONS INFORMATION

College entrance tests required: Yes
Interview required: No
Essay required: Yes
Documentation required for LD: Psychoeducational evaluation
Documentation required for ADD: Yes
Submitted to: Academic Support
Special Ed. HS coursework accepted: No

Specific course requirements of all applicants: Yes
Separate application required for program services: No
# of LD applications submitted each year: NR
# of LD applications accepted yearly: NR
Total # of students receiving LD services: NR
Acceptance into program means acceptance into college: Student must be admitted and enrolled in the university first and then request services.

ADMISSIONS

There is no special admission process for students with learning disabilities. The Office of Admissions reviews the applications of all candidates for admission. The admissions staff looks for evidence of substantial achievement in a rigorous secondary school curriculum, one counselor recommendation, standardized testing, personalized essay, and extracurricular involvement. Also valued are qualities such as curiosity, originality, thoughtfulness, and persistence. Admission is very competitive. ACT average is 29 or SAT Reasoning Test average is 1348. Two SAT Subject Tests are required of student choice if the applicant submits the SAT Reasoning Test. However, SAT Subject Tests are not required if the applicant submits the ACT.

ADDITIONAL INFORMATION

Students are encouraged to seek help early; meet with professors at the beginning of each semester to discuss approaches and accommodations that will meet their needs; and seek assistance from the director of Academic Support and Disability Services, administrative adviser, and faculty adviser. Modifications in the curriculum are made on an individual basis. Colgate provides services in support of academic work on as-needed basis, such as note-takers tape-recorded lectures, tutors, readers, and assistive technology. There is a Writing Center, Math Clinic, and Departmental Tutoring. Skills help is available in writing, reading, and study strategies. Services and accommodations are available for undergraduate and graduate students.

Support Services Contact Information

Learning Disability Program/Services: Academic Program Support and Disability Services
Director: Lynn Waldman
  E-Mail: lwaldman@mailcolgate.edu
  Telephone: 315-228-7225
  Fax: 315-228-7831

LEARNING DISABILITY SERVICES

Requests for the following/services accommodations will be evaluated individually based on appropriate and current documentation.

Allowed in exams
  Calculator: Yes
  Dictionary: Yes
  Computer: Yes
  Spellchecker: Yes
Extended test time: Yes
Scribes: Yes
Proctors: Yes
Oral exams: Yes
Note-takers: Yes

Distraction reduced environment: Yes
Tape recording in class: Yes
Books on tape from RFBD: Yes
Taping of books not from RFBD: Yes
Accommodations for students with ADD: Yes
Reading machine: Yes
Other assistive technology: Yes
Priority registration: Yes

Added costs for services: No
LD specialists: Yes
Professional tutors: No
Peer tutors: Yes
Max. hours/wk. for services: Unlimited
How professors are notified of LD/ADD: By student

GENERAL ADMISSIONS INFORMATION

Director of Admissions: Gary L. Ross
Telephone: 315-228-7401

ENTRANCE REQUIREMENTS

Academic units required: 4 English, 3 math, 3 science (2 science lab), 3 foreign language, 2 social studies, 1 history. **Academic units recommended:** 4 English, 4 math, 4 science, (3 science lab), 4 foreign language, 2 social studies, 3 history. High school diploma is required and GED is accepted. ACT with or without Writing component accepted. TOEFL required of all international applicants, minimum paper TOEFL 600, minimum computer TOEFL 250.

Application deadline: 1/15
Notification: 4/1
Average GPA: 3.60

Average SAT Math: 676
Average SAT Verbal: 659
Average ACT: 30

Graduated top 10% of class: 73%
Graduated top 25% of class: 95%
Graduated top 50% of class: 100%

COLLEGE GRADUATION REQUIREMENTS

Course waivers allowed: NR
Course substitutions allowed: Yes
In what course: Foreign language. All requests are considered case-by-case.

ADDITIONAL INFORMATION

Environment: The university is located in a small town about 45 miles from Syracuse.

Student Body:
  Undergrad enrollment: 2,800
  Women: 52%
  Men: 48%
  Percent out-of-state: 65%

Cost Information
  Tuition: $31,230
  Room & board: $7,620
Housing Information
  University housing: Yes
  Percent living on campus: 90%

Greek System
  Fraternity: Yes
  Sorority: Yes
  Athletics: NCAA Division I

CONCORDIA COLLEGE (NY)

171 White Plains Road, Bronxville, NY 10708
Phone: 914-337-9300 • Fax: 914-395-4636
E-mail: admission@concordia-ny.edu • Web: www.concordia-ny.edu
Support: SP • Institution type: 4-year private

LEARNING DISABILITY PROGRAM AND SERVICES

Concordia Connection is a program for students with LD who have demonstrated the potential to earn a college degree. Their commitment is to provide an intimate, supportive, and caring environment where students with special learning needs can experience college as a successful and rewarding endeavor. This is a mainstream program. Students are fully integrated into the college. During the fall and spring semesters students are registered for four or five classes. Additionally, students are registered for a one credit independent study, which incorporates a weekly, one hour group session with the director and staff that focuses on the development of individualized learning strategies. Progress is monitored and assessment of learning potential and academic levels is provided. The program's assistant director serves as the freshman advisor and coordinates support services. Enrollment is limited to 15 students. A three day summer orientation and academic seminar is required for all new Concordia Connection students.

LD/ADD ADMISSIONS INFORMATION

College entrance tests required: Yes
Interview required: No
Essay required: Yes
Documentation required for LD: WAIS–R or Woodcock Johnson-III. IEP Recommendations from teacher/counselor
Documentation required for ADD: WAIS–R or Woodcock Johnson–III. Psychoeducational report documenting ADD/ADD
Submitted to: Admissions/Concordia Connections
Special Ed. HS coursework accepted: No

Specific course requirements of all applicants: Yes
Separate application required for program services: No
# of LD applications submitted each year: 30–45
# of LD applications accepted yearly: 10–16
Total # of students receiving LD services: 15–25
Acceptance into program means acceptance into college: Student must be admitted and enrolled in the college first and then request services. Some are reviewed by the LD program, which provides a recommendation to the Admissions Office.

ADMISSIONS

Students wishing to apply should submit the following documents to the admissions office: a Concordia application; current transcript; SAT/ACT scores; documentation of LD, which must minimally include a WAIS–R profile with subtest scores within the past year and the most recent IEP; recommendations from LD specialist and guidance counselor; and an essay describing the nature of the LD and the effect on learning patterns and reason for pursuing college. Visits are encouraged. Applicants must be high school graduates, have a diagnosed LD, have college-prep courses, and be emotionally stable and committed to being successful. General admissions criteria include a B average; ACT/SAT, used to assess strengths and weaknesses rather than for acceptance or denial; college-preparatory courses in high school (foreign language is recommended but not required). Students with LD who self-disclose and provide documentation will be reviewed by the admissions office and the director of Concordia Connection.

ADDITIONAL INFORMATION

The Concordia Connection provides services to all students. These include test-taking modifications, taped text books, computer access, and tutoring. Although there are no charges for students requesting peer tutoring, there is a $2,500 per semester charge for program services. Skills courses for credit are offered in time management, organizational skills, and study skills. The three-day summer orientation helps students get acquainted with support services, get exposure to academic expectations, review components and requirements of the freshman year, develop group cohesion, and explore individualized needs and strategies for seeking assistance.

Support Services Contact Information

Learning Disability Program/Services: The Concordia Connection Program
Director: George Groth, PsyD
  E-Mail: ghg@concordia-ny.edu
  Telephone: 914-337-9300 x 2361
  Fax: 914-395-4500

LEARNING DISABILITY SERVICES

Requests for the following/services accommodations will be evaluated individually based on appropriate and current documentation.

Allowed in exams
  Calculator: Yes
  Dictionary: Yes
  Computer: Yes
  Spellchecker: Yes
Extended test time: Yes
Scribes: Yes
Proctors: Yes
Oral exams: Yes
Note-takers: Yes

Distraction reduced environment: Yes
Tape recording in class: Yes
Books on tape from RFBD: Yes
Taping of books not from RFBD: No
**Accommodations for students with
  ADD:** Yes
Reading machine: No
Other assistive technology: No
Priority registration: Yes

Added costs for services: Yes
LD specialists: Yes
Professional tutors: 3–6
Peer tutors: 10–20
Max. hours/wk. for services: 10
**How professors are notified of
  LD/ADD:** By both student and director

GENERAL ADMISSIONS INFORMATION

Director of Admissions: Amy Becher
Telephone: 914-337-9300

ENTRANCE REQUIREMENTS
Academic units required: 4 English, 3 math, 2 science, 2 social studies. **Academic units recommended:** 2 foreign language. High school diploma is required and GED is accepted. TOEFL required of all international applicants, minimum paper TOEFL 550, minimum computer TOEFL 213.

Application deadline: 6/1
Notification: Rolling
Average GPA: 2.70

Average SAT Math: 500
Average SAT Verbal: 500
Average ACT: 23

Graduated top 10% of class: 5%
Graduated top 25% of class: 14%
Graduated top 50% of class: 44%

COLLEGE GRADUATION REQUIREMENTS

Course waivers allowed: No
Course substitutions allowed: Yes
In what course: Substitution of American Sign Language for foreign language.

ADDITIONAL INFORMATION

Environment: The college is in a suburban area approximately 15 miles north of New York City.

Student Body:
  Undergrad enrollment: 540
  Women: 59%
  Men: 41%
  Percent out-of-state: 21%

Cost Information
  Tuition: $18,700
  Room & board: $7,600
Housing Information
  University housing: Yes
  Percent living on campus: 68%

Greek System
  Fraternity: No
  Sorority: No
Athletics: NCAA Division II

CORNELL UNIVERSITY

Undergraduate Admissions, 410 Thurston Avenue, Ithaca, NY 14850
Phone: 607-255-5241 • Fax: 607-255-0659
E-mail: admissions@cornell.edu • Web: www.cornell.edu
Support: CS • Institution type: 4-year private

LEARNING DISABILITY PROGRAM AND SERVICES

Cornell University is committed to ensuring that students with disabilities have equal access to all university programs and activities. Policy and procedures have been developed to provide students with as much independence as possible, to preserve confidentiality, and to provide students with disabilities the same exceptional opportunities available to all Cornell students. Student Disability Services (SDS), in concert with the Center for Learning and Teaching, provides a unique, integrated model to serve the needs of students with disabilities. A major goal of SDS is to develop self-advocacy skills for students with disabilities. This consists of having a clear understanding of the disability, an understanding of how the disability affects functioning within the university community, and the ability to communicate this information.

LD/ADD ADMISSIONS INFORMATION

College entrance tests required: Yes
Interview required: No
Essay required: No
Documentation required for LD: Current comprehensive psychoeducational evaluation based on adult norms
Documentation required for ADD: Yes
Submitted to: Student Disabililty Services
Special Ed. HS coursework accepted: Yes

Specific course requirements of all applicants: Yes
Separate application required for program services: No
# of LD applications submitted each year: NR
# of LD applications accepted yearly: NR
Total # of students receiving LD services: 135–160
Acceptance into program means acceptance into college: Student must be admitted and enrolled in the university first and then request services.

ADMISSIONS

Cornell does not have a special admissions process for students with learning disabilities. All students applying to Cornell are expected to meet admissions criteria. General admission requirements include 16 units of English, math, science, social studies, and foreign language. Each of the seven undergraduate colleges has its own specific requirements. Admission is very competitive and most of the admitted students rank in at least the top 20 percent of the class, and have taken AP and Honors courses in high school. Disability documentation should not be sent along with the admissions application, but should be sent directly to Student Disability Services after acceptance to Cornell.

ADDITIONAL INFORMATION

Students are encouraged to complete a disability self-identification form that is included in acceptance materials. Once Student Disability Services has received current and complete documentation of a disability, it will work with students to determine appropriate accommodations. Diagnostic testing, remedial courses, and tutors specifically selected to work with students with LD are not available at Cornell. The Learning Strategies Center provides general supportive services including classes and workshops in reading comprehension, organizational skills, note taking, and exam preparation. The Learning Strategies Center is open to all students.

Support Services Contact Information

Learning Disability Program/Services: Student Disability Services
Director: Matthew F. Tominey
  E-Mail: clt_sds@cornell.edu
  Telephone: 607-254-4545
  Fax: 607-255-1562
  Contact Person: Matthew Tominey/Michele Fish
  E-Mail: clt_sds@cornell.edu
  Telephone: 607-254-4545
  Fax: 607-255-1562

LEARNING DISABILITY SERVICES

Requests for the following/services accommodations will be evaluated individually based on appropriate and current documentation.

Allowed in exams
  Calculator: Yes
  Dictionary: Yes
  Computer: Yes
  Spellchecker: Yes
Extended test time: Yes
Scribes: Yes
Proctors: Yes
Oral exams: No
Note-takers: Yes

Distraction reduced environment: Yes
Tape recording in class: Yes
Books on tape from RFBD: Yes
Taping of books not from RFBD: Yes
Accommodations for students with ADD: Yes
Reading machine: Yes
Other assistive technology: Yes
Priority registration: No

Added costs for services: No
LD specialists: Yes
Professional tutors: No
Peer tutors: Yes
Max. hours/wk. for services: Unlimited
How professors are notified of LD/ADD: By student

GENERAL ADMISSIONS INFORMATION

Director of Admissions: Jason Locke
Telephone: 607-255-5241

ENTRANCE REQUIREMENTS

Academic units required: 4 English, 3 math, **Academic units recommended:** 3 science (3 science lab), 3 foreign language, 3 social studies, 3 history. High school diploma or equivalent is not required. ACT with Writing component required or SAT Reasoning and SAT Subject tests. TOEFL required of all international applicants, minimum paper TOEFL 550, minimum computer TOEFL 250.

Application deadline: 1/1
Notification: 4/1
Average GPA: NR

Average SAT Math: 700
Average SAT Verbal: 670
Average ACT: 29

Graduated top 10% of class: 85%
Graduated top 25% of class: 95%
Graduated top 50% of class: 99%

COLLEGE GRADUATION REQUIREMENTS

Course waivers allowed: No
Course substitutions allowed: Yes
In what course: Foreign language

ADDITIONAL INFORMATION

Environment: Cornell is located 45 minutes from Syracuse on the southern end of Lake Cayuga in the Finger Lakes Region.

Student Body:
  Undergrad enrollment: 13,577
  Women: 50%
  Men: 50%
  Percent out-of-state: 60%

Cost Information
  Tuition: $30,000
  Room & board: $9,882
Housing Information
  University housing: Yes
  Percent living on campus: 58%

Greek System
  Fraternity: Yes
  Sorority: Yes
Athletics: NCAA Division I

DOWLING COLLEGE

Idle Hour Boulevard, Oakdale, NY 11769-1999
Phone: 800-369-5464 • Fax: 631-563-3827
E-mail: admissions@dowling.edu • Web: www.dowling.edu
Support: SP • Institution type: 4-year private

LEARNING DISABILITY PROGRAM AND SERVICES

Dowling College's Program for College Students with Learning Disabilities is a small, individualized program that provides for cognitive development. The college is looking for students who are committed to lifelong learning who have taken academically demanding courses in high school. They seek students who are eager and willing to persevere to achieve goals. Additionally, students need to be interested and involved in community and extracurricular activities. There is a fee of $1,500 per semester for services from the LD Program. Students must submit a recent psychoevaluation and IEP in order to be eligible to receive services or accommodations. Students are encouraged to make sure that their IEP includes all of the necessary accommodations. Students sign a contract promising to attend tutoring sessions and to attend all classes. Services are available all four years.

LD/ADD ADMISSIONS INFORMATION

College entrance tests required: Yes	**Specific course requirements of all applicants:** Yes
Interview required: No	**Separate application required for program services:** Yes
Essay required: No	**# of LD applications submitted each year:** 20
Documentation required for LD: Psychological evauation; IEP	**# of LD applications accepted yearly:** 6–11
Documentation required for ADD: Yes	**Total # of students receiving LD services:** 25
Submitted to: Support Program/Services	**Acceptance into program means acceptance into**
Special Ed. HS coursework accepted: NR	**college:** Student must be admitted and enrolled in the university first and then request services.

ADMISSIONS

Students must be admitted to Dowling College first and then may request an application to the Program for College Students with LD. Applicants to Dowling college are encouraged to submit either the ACT or SAT. Students should have 16 academic courses in high school including 4 years of English. Students are encouraged to have an interview. Once a student with a LD has been admitted to the college, they may submit an application to the LD program. Both student and parent are required to complete an application. Students must submit their most recent IEP and psychoeducational evaluation. An interview is required, and the LD program director looks for students with tenacity and motivation. Approximately 25 students are admitted to the program each year.

ADDITIONAL INFORMATION

The Program for Students with Learning Disabilities offers support services in word processing and language development, a liaison between individual professors and students, weekly writing workshops, and a freshman college orientation for course requirements geared to the specific needs of students with LD. There is no learning resource center, but students have access to tutors who are available in the library. Tutors are trained to provide academic support. There is a Lab School at which students with learning disabilities may receive special tutoring two times a week in learning strategies. Students are eligible to receive all accommodations or services that are listed in their most recent IEP.

Support Services Contact Information

Learning Disability Program/Services: Program for College Students with Learning Disabilities
Director: Dr. Dorothy Stracher
  E-Mail: strached@dowling.edu
  Telephone: 631-244-3306
  Fax: 631-244-5036

LEARNING DISABILITY SERVICES

Requests for the following/services accommodations will be evaluated individually based on appropriate and current documentation.

Allowed in exams
  Calculator: Yes
  Dictionary: Yes
  Computer: Yes
  Spellchecker: Yes
Extended test time: Yes
Scribes: Yes
Proctors: Yes
Oral exams: Yes
Note-takers: Yes

Distraction reduced environment: Yes
Tape recording in class: Yes
Books on tape from RFBD: Yes
Taping of books not from RFBD: Yes
Accommodations for students with
  ADD: Yes
Reading machine: Yes
Other assistive technology: Yes
Priority registration: Yes
Added costs for services: Yes

LD specialists: Yes
Professional tutors: 25
Peer tutors: No
Max. hours/wk. for services:
  Unlimited
How professors are notified of
  LD/ADD: By director

GENERAL ADMISSIONS INFORMATION

Director of Admissions: Bridget Mastruzo
Telephone: 631-244-3436

ENTRANCE REQUIREMENTS

Academic units recommended: 4 English, 3 math, 2 science, 3 social studies. High school diploma is required and GED is accepted.

Application deadline: Rolling
Notification: Rolling
Average GPA: 2.60

Average SAT Math: 480
Average SAT Verbal: 470
Average ACT: 21

Graduated top 10% of class: 5%
Graduated top 25% of class: 19%
Graduated top 50% of class: NR

COLLEGE GRADUATION REQUIREMENTS

Course waivers allowed: Yes
Course substitutions allowed: Yes
In what course: Foreign language

ADDITIONAL INFORMATION

Environment: The University is located 50 miles from New York City.

Student Body:
  Undergrad enrollment: 3,357
  Women: 59%
  Men: 41%
  Percent out-of-state: 9%

Cost Information
  Tuition: $17,745
  Room & board: $8,300
Housing Information
  University housing: Yes
  Percent living on campus: 17%

Greek System
  Fraternity: No
  Sorority: No
Athletics: NCAA Division II

FARMINGDALE STATE UNIVERSITY

Admissions Office, 2350 Broadhollow Road, Farmingdale, NY 11735
Phone: 631-420-2200 • Fax: 631-420-2633
E-mail: admissions@farmingdale.edu • Web: www.farmingdale.edu
Support: CS • Institution type: 4-year public

LEARNING DISABILITY PROGRAM AND SERVICES

There is no learning disabilities program at the college, but the Office for Students with Disabilities is dedicated to the principle that equal opportunity to realize one's full potential should be available to all students. In keeping with this philosophy, the staff offers individualized services to students with disabilities in accordance with their needs. Students may meet individually with a learning disability specialist or in group meetings. Services include academic remediation with emphasis on compensatory strategies, study skills strategies training, test accommodations, time management instruction, tutoring, and self-understanding of disability. The services offered strive to instill independence, self-confidence, and self-advocacy skills.

LD/ADD ADMISSIONS INFORMATION

College entrance tests required: Yes
Interview required: Yes
Essay required: No
Documentation required for LD: WAIS–III; WJ
Documentation required for ADD: NR
Submitted to: Support Services for student with disabilities
Special Ed. HS coursework accepted: Yes

Specific course requirements of all applicants: Yes
Separate application required for program services: No
# of LD applications submitted each year: NR
# of LD applications accepted yearly: NR
Total # of students receiving LD services: 145–155
Acceptance into program means acceptance into college: Student must be admitted and enrolled in the university first (they can appeal a denial) and then request services.

ADMISSIONS
There is no special admissions procedure for applicants with learning disabilities. The pre-college Pathways Program has more flexible entrance requirements. Elementary algebra is the minimum requirement in math. Students should self-identify on the application. Admission decisions are made by the Office of Admission. Students should submit psychoeducational reports and letters of recommendation and request a personal interview. Students are required to take the SAT/ACT. The university has rolling admissions. Almost all of the programs accept students throughout the year.

ADDITIONAL INFORMATION
The university would like the high school individualized educational plan (IEP) and the WAIS–R to help identify the services necessary to help the student to be successful. Services and accommodations available with appropriate documentation include extended testing time; distraction-free environment; calculator, computer, spell-check, or dictionary in exams; note-takers; scribes; proctors; assistive technology; professional tutors; and tape recording in class. Students are responsible for arranging for accommodations with professors.

Support Services Contact Information

Learning Disability Program/Services: Support Services for Students with Disabilities
Director: Malka Edelman
E-Mail: edelmanp@farmingdale.edu
Telephone: 631-420-2411
Fax: 631-420-2163

LEARNING DISABILITY SERVICES

Requests for the following/services accommodations will be evaluated individually based on appropriate and current documentation.

Allowed in exams
  Calculator: Yes
  Dictionary: Yes
  Computer: Yes
  Spellchecker: Yes
Extended test time: Yes
Scribes: Yes
Proctors: Yes
Oral exams: Yes
Note-takers: Yes

Distraction reduced environment: Yes
Tape recording in class: Yes
Books on tape from RFBD: Yes
Taping of books not from RFBD: No
Accommodations for students with ADD: Yes
Reading machine: Yes
Other assistive technology: No
Priority registration: No

Added costs for services: No
LD specialists: Yes
Professional tutors: No
Peer tutors: Yes
Max. hours/wk. for services: Unlimited
How professors are notified of LD/ADD: By student

GENERAL ADMISSIONS INFORMATION

Director of Admissions: James Hall
Telephone: 631-420-2200

ENTRANCE REQUIREMENTS

Academic units required: 4 English, 2 math, 1 science (1 science lab), 4 social studies. **Academic units recommended:** 4 English, 4 math, 3 science (3 science lab), 4 social studies. High school diploma is required and GED is accepted. TOEFL required of all international applicants, minimum paper TOEFL 500, minimum computer TOEFL 173.

Application deadline: NR
Notification: Rolling
Average GPA: NR

Average SAT Math: 460
Average SAT Verbal: 445
Average ACT: Rolling

Graduated top 10% of class: NR
Graduated top 25% of class: NR
Graduated top 50% of class: NR

COLLEGE GRADUATION REQUIREMENTS

Course waivers allowed: Yes
Course substitutions allowed: Yes
In what course: Foreign language or math

ADDITIONAL INFORMATION

Environment: Farmingdale is a small town within easy access to New York City.

Student Body:
  Undergrad enrollment: 3,909
  Women: 47%
  Men: 53%
  Percent out-of-state: 2%

Cost Information
  In-state tuition: $24,350
  Out-of-state tuition: $10,300
  Room & board: $8,200
Housing Information
  University housing: Yes
  Percent living on campus: 10%

Greek System
  Fraternity: No
  Sorority: No
Athletics: NCAA Division III

HOFSTRA UNIVERSITY

Admissions Center, Bernon Hall, Hempstead, NY 11549
Phone: 516-463-6700 • Fax: 516-463-5100
E-mail: admitme@hofstra.edu • Web: www.hofstra.edu
Support: SP • Institution type: 4-year private

LEARNING DISABILITY PROGRAM AND SERVICES

The Program for Academic Learning Skills (PALS) seeks candidates who have been diagnosed with LD and show above-average intellectual ability and emotional stability. The program concentrates on identifying qualified applicants for entrance to the university, and on enhancing the skills that will help students achieve academic success. This program is part of the Division of Special Studies. Normally, candidates will be accepted into PALS for a period of one academic year. In the first semester students enroll in courses offered through DSS, and in the second semester they enroll in regular Hofstra classes.

LD/ADD ADMISSIONS INFORMATION

College entrance tests required: Yes
Interview required: Yes
Essay required: No
Documentation required for LD: WAIS–III, within one year; achievement testing; full psychoeducational report with a diagnostic statement
Documentation required for ADD: Yes
Submitted to: Admissions
Special Ed. HS coursework accepted: Yes

Specific course requirements of all applicants: Yes
Separate application required for program services: No
# of LD applications submitted each year: 175–200
# of LD applications accepted yearly: 45–60
Total # of students receiving LD services: 200
Acceptance into program means acceptance into college: Students who are admitted to PALS are automatically admitted to the University.

ADMISSIONS

Students with LD who are not admissible as regular students are invited to interview and may be offered admission to PALS. The Division of Special Studies, which administers PALS, has always conducted a highly individualized admissions process. Students with LD, who may be in the bottom 30 percent of their high school class and have an 800–850 SAT, may be eligible for the PALS program. The interview is very important and students may be asked to write an essay at this time. Only 18 of the 100 students accepted into the Division of Special Studies are learning disabled. PALS is looking for students who have self-knowledge and understanding of their strengths and weaknesses, as well as a willingness to work hard. There are no specific high school course requirements for PALS. In cooperation with the admissions office, candidates are encouraged to apply for admission for the fall semester. Admission decisions are made jointly by PALS and the Office of Admissions. Only in exceptional cases will applicants be admitted in midyear.

ADDITIONAL INFORMATION

There are course waivers available. However, the university prefers to substitute courses where possible. Once admitted the students meet with a specialist two times a week, and information regarding progress is shared with the family. Basic skills courses are offered in spelling, learning strategies, study strategies, time management, written language, and social skills. Students in the PALS program sign an agreement to attend all scheduled meetings and keep instructors informed of progress or lack thereof. Accommodations include extended testing time, quiet test-taking environment, readers for exams, note-takers, skills instruction and development (mandatory for first-year), individualized weekly meetings with PALS instructor.

Support Services Contact Information

Learning Disability Program/Services: Program for Academic Learning Skills (PALS)
Director: Linda De Motta
  E-Mail: pals@hofstra.edu
  Telephone: 516-463-5761
  Fax: 516-463-4049

LEARNING DISABILITY SERVICES

Requests for the following/services accommodations will be evaluated individually based on appropriate and current documentation.

Allowed in exams
  Calculator: Yes
  Dictionary: Yes
  Computer: Yes
  Spellchecker: Yes
Extended test time: Yes
Scribes: Yes
Proctors: Yes
Oral exams: Yes
Note-takers: No

Distraction reduced environment: Yes
Tape recording in class: No
Books on tape from RFBD: Yes
Taping of books not from RFBD: Yes
Accommodations for students with
  ADD: Yes
Reading machine: Yes
Other assistive technology: Yes
Priority registration: No

Added costs for services: Yes
LD specialists: Yes
Professional tutors: No
Peer tutors: No
Max. hours/wk. for services:
  Unlimited
How professors are notified of
  LD/ADD: By both student and director

GENERAL ADMISSIONS INFORMATION

Director of Admissions: Peter Farrell
Telephone: 516-463-6318

ENTRANCE REQUIREMENTS
 Academic units required: 4 English, 3 math, 3 science (1 science lab), 2 foreign language, 3 social studies.
Academic units recommended: 4 math, 4 science, 3 foreign language, 4 social studies. High school diploma is required and GED is accepted. ACT with Writing component required or SAT. TOEFL required of all international applicants, minimum paper TOEFL 550, minimum computer TOEFL 213.

Application deadline: NR
Notification: Rolling
Average GPA: 3.22

Average SAT Math: 577
Average SAT Verbal: 567
Average ACT: 24

Graduated top 10% of class: 22%
Graduated top 25% of class: 54%
Graduated top 50% of class: 84%

COLLEGE GRADUATION REQUIREMENTS

Course waivers allowed: No
Course substitutions allowed: Yes
In what course: Students requesting accommodations for foreign language requirements must meet with the PALS Director soon after beginning their first semester.

ADDITIONAL INFORMATION

Environment: Hempstead is a residential community in Long Island, just outside New York City.

Student Body:
  Undergrad enrollment: 8,869
  Women: 53%
  Men: 47%
  Percent out-of-state: 27%

Cost Information
  Tuition: $19,010
  Room & board: $9,000
Housing Information
  University housing: Yes
  Percent living on campus: 44%

Greek System
  Fraternity: Yes
  Sorority: Yes
Athletics: NCAA Division I

IONA COLLEGE

715 North Avenue, New Rochelle, NY 10801
Phone: 914-633-2502 • Fax: 914-633-2642
E-mail: icad@iona.edu • Web: www.iona.edu
Support: SP • Institution type: 4-year private

LEARNING DISABILITY PROGRAM AND SERVICES

The College Assistance Program (CAP) offers comprehensive support and services for students with LD/ADD. CAP is designed to encourage success by providing instruction tailored to individual strengths and needs. Students take standard full-time course requirements to ensure the level of quality education expected of all degree candidates. Professional tutors teach individually appropriate strategies that cross disciplines. CAP staff encourages students to become active, involved members of the college community. All CAP freshmen must participate in a three-week summer orientation. During the orientation, the staff instructs and guides students in intensive writing instruction and study, organizational, and time management skills; students are oriented to the college and services; individual learning styles are explored; opportunities are provided to practice self-advocacy; several workshops are offered in areas that meet the student's specific needs; and individual fall classes are developed. Semester servcies include supplementary advisement, counseling, regularly scheduled weekly skill-based tutoring with an LD professional, study-groups, skills workshops, and provision of appropriate documented accommodations.

LD/ADD ADMISSIONS INFORMATION

College entrance tests required: Yes
Interview required: Yes
Essay required: No
Documentation required for LD: WAIS–III; IEP: within 2 years
Documentation required for ADD: Yes
Submitted to: College Assistance Program
Special Ed. HS coursework accepted: No

Specific course requirements of all applicants: Yes
Separate application required for program services: No
# of LD applications submitted each year: 150–250
# of LD applications accepted yearly: 20
Total # of students receiving LD services: 65
Acceptance into program means acceptance into college: Students must be admitted and enrolled at the College first and then may request admission to CAP.

ADMISSIONS

All applicants must meet the same admission criteria, which include 4 years English, 1 year U.S. history, 1 year social studies, 2 years foreign language (waivers granted), 1 year natural science, and 3 years math. Students should send the following to the CAP office: a complete psychological evaluation conducted within the past 2 years including the WAIS–or WAIS–R subtest scores and a comprehensive report, a copy of the most recent individualized educational plan; and two letters of recommendation (one from the LD instructor). A personal interview is required. CAP is designed for students with LD and ADD who have been mainstreamed in their academic courses in high school. Students should be average or above average in intellectual ability, socially mature, emotionally stable, and motivated to work hard.

ADDITIONAL INFORMATION

CAP services include a freshman summer college transition program, suplementary academic advising and program planning based on each student's learning style, priority registration, 2 hours per week of scheduled skill-based individual tutoring with a professional learning specialist, (additional tutoring sessions are possible), small group tutoring and workshops, testing accommodations, alternative testing procedures, special equipment, self-advocacy training, referrals to additional services on campus, and counseling services. The CAP director works with faculty to help them understand the problems faced by students with LD, and to explore creative ways to support the learning process. The Samuel Rudin Academic Resource Center (ARC) offers free services to all students who wish to improve their learning skills or who want academic support. ARC provides free reasonable services to all students with documented LD/ADD.

Support Services Contact Information

Learning Disability Program/Services: College Assistance Program (CAP)
Director: Linda Robertello
  E-Mail: LRobertello@iona.edu
  Telephone: 914-633-2159
  Fax: 914-633-2011

LEARNING DISABILITY SERVICES

Requests for the following/services accommodations will be evaluated individually based on appropriate and current documentation.

Allowed in exams
  Calculator: Yes
  Dictionary: Yes
  Computer: Yes
  Spellchecker: Yes
Extended test time: Yes
Scribes: Yes
Proctors: Yes
Oral exams: No
Note-takers: Yes

Distraction reduced environment: Yes
Tape recording in class: Yes
Books on tape from RFBD: Yes
Taping of books not from RFBD: Yes
**Accommodations for students with
  ADD:** Yes
Reading machine: Yes
Other assistive technology: Yes
Priority registration: Yes

Added costs for services: Yes
LD specialists: Yes
Professional tutors: 10
Peer tutors: No
Max. hours/wk. for services:
  Unlimited
**How professors are notified of
  LD/ADD:** By both student and director

GENERAL ADMISSIONS INFORMATION

Director of Admissions: Thomas Weede
Telephone: 914-633-2120

ENTRANCE REQUIREMENTS

Academic units required: 4 English, 3 math, 2 science (2 science lab), 2 foreign language, 1 social studies, 1 history, 4 academic electives. **Academic units recommended:** 4 English, 4 math, 3 science (2 science lab), 2 foreign language, 1 social studies, 1 history, 3 academic electives. High school diploma is required and GED is accepted. TOEFL required of all international applicants, minimum paper TOEFL 550, minimum computer TOEFL 213.

Application deadline: 2/15
Notification: Rolling
Average GPA: 3.40

Average SAT Math: 541
Average SAT Verbal: 540
Average ACT: 23

Graduated top 10% of class: 29%
Graduated top 25% of class: 51%
Graduated top 50% of class: 94%

COLLEGE GRADUATION REQUIREMENTS

Course waivers allowed: No
Course substitutions allowed: Y/N
In what course: Foreign language

ADDITIONAL INFORMATION

Environment: The college is located on 56 acres 20 miles northeast of New York City.

Student Body:
  Undergrad enrollment: 3,413
  Women: 54%
  Men: 46%
  Percent out-of-state: 18%

Cost Information
  Tuition: $18,990
  Room & board: $9,698
Housing Information
  University housing: Yes
  Percent living on campus: 30%

Greek System
  Fraternity: Yes
  Sorority: Yes
Athletics: NCAA Division I

KEUKA COLLEGE

Office of Admissions, Keuka Park, NY 14478-0098
Phone: 315-279-5254 • Fax: 315-536-5386
E-mail: admissions@mail.keuka.edu • Web: www.keuka.edu
Support: CS • Institution type: 4-year private

LEARNING DISABILITY PROGRAM AND SERVICES

The Academic Support Program will assist students in becoming competent, independent learners able to achieve their maximum potential in academic endeavors. Students with documented disabilities who are admitted and enrolled are encouraged to request services either in advance of the new semester or immediately at the beginning of the semester. Every effort is made to provide services and accommodations as quickly and appropriately as possible. It is the student's responsibility to contact the Academic Support Program office. The coordinator will meet with the student and review the documentation to create a plan of services and accommodations. The provision of services will be based on the specific diagnoses and recommendations of the professional performing the assessments. Students are encouraged to ensure that the diagnoses and all recommendations for accommodations are clearly stated within the report. Students who are eligible for testing accommodations will be required to make these arrangements with the professor prior to every test of the semester, as well as signing up for each test with the Academic Support Program Office.

LD/ADD ADMISSIONS INFORMATION

College entrance tests required: Yes
Interview required: No
Essay required: Yes
Documentation required for LD: Psychoeducational evaluation
Documentation required for ADD: Yes
Submitted to: Academic Support Program
Special Ed. HS coursework accepted: NR

Specific course requirements of all applicants: Yes
Separate application required for program services: No
# of LD applications submitted each year: NR
# of LD applications accepted yearly: NR
Total # of students receiving LD services: 45
Acceptance into program means acceptance into college: Student must be admitted and enrolled in the college first and then request services.

ADMISSIONS

There is no special admissions process available and all students are expected to meet the general admission criteria. Students are expected to rank in the top 50 percent of their high school class and have a minimum 2.8 GPA. Course requirements include 4 years of English, 3 years of history a campus visit with an interview is recommended.

ADDITIONAL INFORMATION

The provision of support is based on the specific diagnosis and recommendations of the professional performing the assessments. Examples of some support services offered by the Academic Support Program are testing accommodations, tutors (group and individual), individual appointments with professional staff members, career counseling, and books on tape. Workshops for all students are offered in note taking strategies, testing strategies, time management and study skills. A coaching program for students with ADD is also offered.

Support Services Contact Information

Learning Disability Program/Services: Academic Support Program
Director: Dr. Joanne Desotelle
  E-Mail: jdesotel@mail.keuka.edu
  Telephone: 315-279-5615
  Fax: 315-279-5216
Contact Person: Beth Demay
  E-Mail: bdemay@mail.keuka.edu
  Telephone: 315-279-5636
  Fax: 315-279-5216

LEARNING DISABILITY SERVICES

Requests for the following/services accommodations will be evaluated individually based on appropriate and current documentation.

Allowed in exams
  Calculator: Yes
  Dictionary: Yes
  Computer: Yes
  Spellchecker: Yes
Extended test time: Yes
Scribes: Yes
Proctors: Yes
Oral exams: Yes
Note-takers: Yes

Distraction reduced environment: Yes
Tape recording in class: Yes
Books on tape from RFBD: Yes
Taping of books not from RFBD: Yes
Accommodations for students with
  ADD: Yes
Reading machine: Yes
Other assistive technology: Yes
Priority registration: No

Added costs for services: No
LD specialists: Yes
Professional tutors: 3
Peer tutors: 30–40
Max. hours/wk. for services: No
How professors are notified of
  LD/ADD: By student

GENERAL ADMISSIONS INFORMATION

Director of Admissions: Carolanne Marquis (VP of Keuka College)
Telephone: 315-279-5262

ENTRANCE REQUIREMENTS

Academic units recommended: 4 English, 3 math, 3 science (2 science lab), 3 foreign language, 3 social studies, 2 history. High school diploma is required and GED is accepted. TOEFL required of all international applicants, minimum paper TOEFL 500, minimum computer TOEFL 300.

Application deadline: NR
Notification: Rolling
Average GPA: 2.90

Average SAT Math: 492
Average SAT Verbal: 495
Average ACT: 21

Graduated top 10% of class: 9%
Graduated top 25% of class: 27%
Graduated top 50% of class: 57%

COLLEGE GRADUATION REQUIREMENTS

Course waivers allowed: Rolling
Course substitutions allowed: Yes
In what course: When appropriate and agreed upon by student, instructor, division chair, and registrar.

ADDITIONAL INFORMATION

Environment: The college is located 50 miles from Rochester.

Student Body:
  Undergrad enrollment: 1,154
  Women: 71%
  Men: 29%
  Percent out-of-state: 6%

Cost Information
  Tuition: $16,820
  Room & board: $7,790
Housing Information
  University housing: Yes
  Percent living on campus: 67%

Greek System
  Fraternity: No
  Sorority: No
Athletics: NCAA Division III

LONG ISLAND UNIVERSITY—C. W. POST

720 Northern Boulevard, Brookville, NY 11548
Phone: 516-299-2900 • Fax: 516-299-2137
E-mail: enroll@cwpost.liu.edu • Web: www.liu.edu
Support: SP • Institution type: 4-year private

LEARNING DISABILITY PROGRAM AND SERVICES

The Academic Resource Center (ARC) is a comprehensive support program designed for students with learning disabilities to help them achieve their academic potential in a university setting. The objective is to encourage students to become independent learners and self-advocates. Students participate in mainstream college courses and assume full responsibility for attendance in class and at the ARC. Students work with learning assistants on a one-to-one basis. graduate assistants are students enrolled in the School of Education who are pursuing master's degrees. The graduate assistants help students make the transition from high school to college. They assist students in time management, organizational skills, note- taking techniques, study skills, and other learning strategies. Students are responsible for attendance and participation in meetings with the learning assistants. ARC staff communicates with professors, and students are tutored by learning assistants. Students learn time management, reading, study and test-taking strategies, organizational skills, and note-taking techniques. The ARC provides an environment that helps students demonstrate positive attitudes toward themselves and learning.

LD/ADD ADMISSIONS INFORMATION

College entrance tests required: Yes
Interview required: Yes
Essay required: Yes
Documentation required for LD: WAIS–III within last 3 years, IEP, any other testing (Woodcock-Johnson, etc.)
Documentation required for ADD: Yes
Submitted to: Academic Resources Center
Special Ed. HS coursework accepted: Yes

Specific course requirements of all applicants: Yes
Separate application required for program services: Yes
# of LD applications submitted each year: 200
# of LD applications accepted yearly: 50–60
Total # of students receiving LD services: 85–125
Acceptance into program means acceptance into college: Student must be admitted and enrolled in the university first and then request services.

ADMISSIONS
The student must be admitted to the university first and then apply to the ARC. Acceptance into the university is separate and distinct from acceptance into the ARC. Students admitted to the university and who identify themselves as learning disabled are sent information and an application to apply to the ARC. Applications must include a Diagnostic Evaluation describing the specific LD, WAIS–R, and a handwritten essay indicating why the student is requesting admittance into the ARC. Once all of the information is on file the student will be invited to interview. This interview is an integral part of the admission process. Some students may be admitted through the General Studies Program if the GPA or tests are low. During an interview students must convince the admissions counselor that they have changed and are now willing to focus on studies. Motivation is very important. If students have a deficiency, the people responsible for testing must write letters stating what specifically in the test data indicates the students should be granted a waiver.

ADDITIONAL INFORMATION
Ancillary services include note-takers in individual course lectures, subject tutors, proctors, assistance securing books on tape, audio and video tapes to supplement learning, assistance with planning and scheduling classes, study and social skills workshops, and a mentor program. Other services include individualized learning strategies on a one-to-one basis two times a week, extended time and readers for exams, academic advisement and faculty liaison; and assistance in formulating an overall plan and structure when approaching an assignment. The program is a four-year program, but the majority of students opt to handle their own class work at the end of sophomore year. Freshmen are limited to 12 credits for their first semester, and all must enroll in a freshman seminar. There are no special or remedial classes.

Support Services Contact Information

Learning Disability Program/Services: Academic Resource Program
Director: Susan Rock
  E-Mail: susan.rock@liu.edu
  Telephone: 516-299-3057
  Fax: 516-299-2126

LEARNING DISABILITY SERVICES

Requests for the following/services accommodations will be evaluated individually based on appropriate and current documentation.

Allowed in exams
  Calculator: Yes
  Dictionary: Yes
  Computer: Yes
  Spellchecker: Yes
Extended test time: Yes
Scribes: Yes
Proctors: Yes
Oral exams: Y/N
Note-takers: Yes

Distraction reduced environment: Yes
Tape recording in class: Yes
Books on tape from RFBD: Yes
Taping of books not from RFBD: Yes
Accommodations for students with
  ADD: Yes
Reading machine: Yes
Other assistive technology: Yes
Priority registration: No

Added costs for services: Yes
LD specialists: Yes
Professional tutors: 15–20
Peer tutors: No
Max. hours/wk. for services:
  Unlimited
How professors are notified of
  LD/ADD: By both student and director

GENERAL ADMISSIONS INFORMATION

Director of Admissions: Beth Carson
Telephone: 516-299-2900

ENTRANCE REQUIREMENTS

Academic units required: 4 English, 2 math, 2 science (2 science lab), 2 foreign language, 3 social studies, 1 academic elective. **Academic units recommended:** 4 English, 4 math, 4 science (4 science lab), 4 foreign language, 4 social studies. High school diploma is required and GED is accepted. TOEFL required of all international applicants, minimum paper TOEFL 500, minimum computer TOEFL 173.

Application deadline: Rolling
Notification: Rolling
Average GPA: 3.00

Average SAT Math: 518
Average SAT Verbal: 517
Average ACT: NR

Graduated top 10% of class: 10%
Graduated top 25% of class: 26%
Graduated top 50% of class: 61%

COLLEGE GRADUATION REQUIREMENTS

Course waivers allowed: Yes
Course substitutions allowed: Yes
In what course: A specific computer course for core math requirement. English 7 & 8 (Anthology courses) for a foreign language. These are for core requirements only.

ADDITIONAL INFORMATION

Environment: The college is located in Long Island, about 30 minutes from New York City.

Student Body:
  Undergrad enrollment: 5,748
  Women: 57%
  Men: 43%
  Percent out-of-state: 6%

Cost Information
  Tuition: $21,890
  Room & board: $8,200
Housing Information
  University housing: Yes
  Percent living on campus: 37%

Greek System
  Fraternity: Yes
  Sorority: Yes
  Athletics: NCAA Division II

MANHATTANVILLE COLLEGE

2900 Purchase Street, Admissions Office, Purchase, NY 10577
Phone: 914-323-5124 • Fax: 914-694-1732
E-mail: admissions@mville.edu • Web: www.mville.edu
Support: SP • Institution type: 4-year private

LEARNING DISABILITY PROGRAM AND SERVICES

The Higher Education Learning Program (HELP) is designed to help motivated and committed students with learning disabilities successfully meet the academic challenge of the college experience. HELP offers a range of support services for students with learning disabilities throughout their years of college. HELP remains focused on instruction and applications of compensatory strategies to college content courses. The HELP Program offers a credit bearing writing course, specifically designed for students with learning disabilities that fulfills the college's writing requirement. Students in the HELP Program, as well as all students at the college, are entitled to reasonable accommodations and modifications. Students in the HELP Program are assisted by tutors in developing those advocacy skills needed to secure accommodations and modifications.

LD/ADD ADMISSIONS INFORMATION

College entrance tests required: Yes
Interview required: Yes
Essay required: No
Documentation required for LD: WAIS–III, achievement
Documentation required for ADD: Yes
Submitted to: Help Program
Special Ed. HS coursework accepted: N/A

Specific course requirements of all applicants: Yes
Separate application required for program services: No
# of LD applications submitted each year: NR
# of LD applications accepted yearly: NR
Total # of students receiving LD services: 30
Acceptance into program means acceptance into college: Joint decision but students are admitted to the college first then the program.

ADMISSIONS

Applicants must meet the requirements for general admission. These criteria include 3.0 GPA and 4 years English, 2 years math, 2 years science, 2 years foreign language, and 2 years history. The average ACT is 24 and SAT is 1015. Applicants must also submit diagnostic testing identifying the learning disability.

ADDITIONAL INFORMATION

The core of the program is one-to-one tutoring in learning strategies directly applicable to coursework. Services are individualized to accommodate the specific needs of each student and are coordinated and implemented by trained learning disabilities professionals.

Support Services Contact Information

Learning Disability Program/Services: Higher Education Learning Program
Director: Elenor Schwartz
  E-Mail: help@muille.edu
  Telephone: 914-323-3186
  Fax: 914-798-2764

LEARNING DISABILITY SERVICES

Requests for the following/services accommodations will be evaluated individually based on appropriate and current documentation.

Allowed in exams
  Calculator: Yes
  Dictionary: Y/N
  Computer: Yes
  Spellchecker: Y/N
Extended test time: Yes
Scribes: Yes
Proctors: Yes
Oral exams: Yes
Note-takers: Yes

Distraction reduced environment: Yes
Tape recording in class: Yes
Books on tape from RFBD: Yes
Taping of books not from RFBD: Yes
Accommodations for students with
  ADD: Yes
Reading machine: Yes
Other assistive technology: Yes
Priority registration: No

Added costs for services: $3,800
LD specialists: Yes
Professional tutors: 7–10
Peer tutors: Yes
Max. hours/wk. for services: 3
How professors are notified of
  LD/ADD: By both student and director

GENERAL ADMISSIONS INFORMATION

Director of Admissions: Jose Flores
Telephone: 914-323-5124

ENTRANCE REQUIREMENTS
Academic units required: 4 English, 3 math, 2 science, 2 social studies, 5 academic electives. High school diploma is required and GED is accepted. TOEFL required of all international applicants, minimum paper TOEFL 550, minimum computer TOEFL 217.

Application deadline: 3/1
Notification: Rolling
Average GPA: 3.00

Average SAT Math: 540
Average SAT Verbal: 550
Average ACT: 24

Graduated top 10% of class: NR
Graduated top 25% of class: NR
Graduated top 50% of class: NR

COLLEGE GRADUATION REQUIREMENTS

Course waivers allowed: No
Course substitutions allowed: No
In what course: N/A

ADDITIONAL INFORMATION

Environment: The college is located on a 100-acre campus in a suburban area 25 miles north of New York City.

Student Body:
  Undergrad enrollment: 1,606
  Women: 69%
  Men: 31%
  Percent out-of-state: 34%

Cost Information
  Tuition: $23,620
  Room & board: $10,130
Housing Information
  University housing: Yes
  Percent living on campus: 68%

Greek System
  Fraternity: No
  Sorority: No
Athletics: NCAA Division III

MARIST COLLEGE

3399 North Road, Poughkeepsie, NY 12601-1387
Phone: 845-575-3226 • Fax: 845-575-3215
E-mail: admissions@marist.edu • Web: www.marist.edu
Support: SP • Institution type: 4-year private

LEARNING DISABILITY PROGRAM AND SERVICES

Marist College believes that bright, motivated students with specific learning disabilities are more similar than different to other college students and can achieve a higher education. Marist offers a program of support for students with learning disabilities through the Learning Disabilities Program. Students receive a complement of academic services designed to meet individual needs. The program focuses on the development and use of strategies to promote independence and personal success. The philosophy of the program does not emphasize remediation, but rather the development of compensatory strategies. Each student is enrolled in credit-bearing courses and completes the same degree requirements as all students. Program staff work closely with faculty and administration and students are encouraged to discuss their learning disability with faculty. The goal is for each student to achieve the maximum level of independence possible and to become an effective self-advocate. Participation in the program is available on a continual basis for as long as the LD specialist and the student agree that is necessary.

LD/ADD ADMISSIONS INFORMATION

College entrance tests required: Yes
Interview required: Yes
Essay required: Yes
Documentation required for LD: Psychoeducational evaluation
Documentation required for ADD: Yes
Submitted to: LD Program or Services
Special Ed. HS coursework accepted: No

Specific course requirements of all applicants: Yes
Separate application required for program services: Yes
# of LD applications submitted each year: 200
# of LD applications accepted yearly: 50
Total # of students receiving LD services: 70
Acceptance into program means acceptance into college: Students are admitted jointly into the college and the LD Program.

ADMISSIONS

Students with LD must submit an application for admission and all required materials to the Office of Admissions. A supplementary application for the LD Support Program must also be completed and sent directly to the OSS. Additionally, students must submit to the OSS the results of the WAIS–R, including subtest scores; calculated I.Q. and narrative; achievement testing with current levels of functioning in reading, mathematics and written language; an unedited essay describing the impact of the LD on academic achievement; and a $20 fee. ACT/SAT scores are required of students with LD. After applications have been reviewed, those most qualified and suited to the program will be invited to interview. Students accepted into the program should have an acceptance and understanding of their LD; know their academic strengths and weaknesses; have college-prep courses; provide recommendations that communicate strengths, motivation to succeed, and willingness to accept and access supports; and have sound study skills and work habits. Admission to the program is competitive and students are encouraged to apply early. There is no early decision option.

ADDITIONAL INFORMATION

Upon enrollment students complete a comprehensive survey of abilities and attitudes toward academics. This survey is combined with diagnostic evaluations and the comprehensive record of students' performance to develop an Individual Support Service Plan. Students meet an LD specialist two times a week and typically concentrate on writing skills, note taking, organizational skills, study skills, and testing strategies. Accommodations may include adaptive testing procedures, note-takers/tape recorder, scribes, taped textbooks/personal readers, use of adaptive equipment. A program fee is charged only for the services of the learning specialist. Students in the program also have access to content tutors and a counselor who can address academic, career, and personal issues. Services and accommodations are available for undergraduate and graduate students.

Support Services Contact Information

Learning Disability Program/Services: Office of Special Services(OSS)/ Learning Disabilities Program
Director: Linda Cooper
  E-Mail: SpecServ@marist.edu
  Telephone: 845-575-3274
  Fax: 845-575-3011
Contact Person: Gale Canale
  E-Mail: SpecServ@marist.edu
  Telephone: same as above
  Fax: same as above

LEARNING DISABILITY SERVICES

Requests for the following/services accommodations will be evaluated individually based on appropriate and current documentation.

Allowed in exams
  Calculator: Yes
  Dictionary: Yes
  Computer: Yes
  Spellchecker: Yes
Extended test time: Yes
Scribes: Yes
Proctors: Yes
Oral exams: Yes
Note-takers: Yes

Distraction reduced environment: Yes
Tape recording in class: Yes
Books on tape from RFBD: Yes
Taping of books not from RFBD: Yes
Accommodations for students with
  ADD: Yes
Reading machine: Yes
Other assistive technology: Yes
Priority registration: Yes

Added costs for services: Yes
LD specialists: Yes
Professional tutors: 4
Peer tutors: 60
Max. hours/wk. for services: 1.5
How professors are notified of
  LD/ADD: By student

GENERAL ADMISSIONS INFORMATION

Director of Admissions: Sean P. Kaylor
Telephone: 845-575-3226

ENTRANCE REQUIREMENTS

Academic units required: 4 English, 3 math, 3 science (2 science lab), 2 social studies, 1 history, 2 academic elec-tives. **Academic units recommended:** 4 math, 4 science, (3 science lab), 2 foreign language. High school diploma is required and GED is accepted. ACT with Writing component required or SAT Reasoning test. TOEFL required of all international applicants, minimum paper TOEFL 550, minimum computer TOEFL 213.

Application deadline: 2/15
Notification: 3/15
Average GPA: 3.00

Average SAT Math: 589
Average SAT Verbal: 580
Average ACT: 26

Graduated top 10% of class: 24%
Graduated top 25% of class: 64%
Graduated top 50% of class: 94%

COLLEGE GRADUATION REQUIREMENTS

Course waivers allowed: Yes
Course substitutions allowed: Yes
In what course: Substitutions are made in math.

ADDITIONAL INFORMATION

Environment: The college is located on 120 acres in upstate New York, 75 miles from New York City.

Student Body:
  Undergrad enrollment: 4,686
  Women: 57%
  Men: 43%
  Percent out-of-state: 40%

Cost Information
  Tuition: $20,535
  Room & board: $9,218
Housing Information
  University housing: Yes
  Percent living on campus: 56%

Greek System
  Fraternity: Yes
  Sorority: Yes
Athletics: NCAA Division I

MARYMOUNT MANHATTAN COLLEGE

221 East 71st Street, New York, NY 10021
Phone: 212-517-0430 • Fax: 212-517-0465
E-mail: admissions@mmm.edu • Web: www.marymount.mmm.edu
Support: SP • Institution type: 4-year private

LEARNING DISABILITY PROGRAM AND SERVICES

Marymount Manhattan College's Program for Academic Access includes a full range of support services that center on academic and personal growth for students with learning disabilities. Students who have been admitted to the full-time program are required to demonstrate commitment to overcoming learning difficulties through regular attendance and tutoring. Academic advisement and counseling is provided to assist in developing a program plan suited to individual needs. The college is looking for highly motivated students with a commitment to compensate for their learning disabilities and to fully participate in the tutoring program. Once admitted into the program, students receive a program plan suited to their needs, based on a careful examination of the psychoeducational evaluations. Full time students sign a contract to regularly attend tutoring provided by professionals experienced within the field of LD. In addition to assisting students in the development of skills and strategies for their coursework, LD specialists coach participants in the attitudes and behavior necessary for college success. Professors assist learning specialists in carefully monitoring students' progress throughout the academic year and arranging for accommodations. Students must submit a current and complete psychoeducational evaluation that meets the documentation guidelines by giving clear and specific evidence of the disability and its limitations on academic functioning in the diagnosis summary statement. Students with ADD must have a licensed physician, psychiatrist, or psychologist provide a complete and current documentation of the disorder.

LD/ADD ADMISSIONS INFORMATION

College entrance tests required: Yes
Interview required: Yes
Essay required: Yes
Documentation required for LD: Psychoeducational evaluation
Documentation required for ADD: Yes
Submitted to: Both Admissions and Program for Academic Access
Special Ed. HS coursework accepted: Yes

Specific course requirements of all applicants: Yes
Separate application required for program services: No
# of LD applications submitted each year: 40
# of LD applications accepted yearly: 30
Total # of students receiving LD services: 30
Acceptance into program means acceptance into college: Students may be admitted to the college through the Program for Academic Access.

ADMISSIONS

Admission to Marymount Manhattan College's Program for Academic Access is based on a diagnosis of dyslexia, ADD, or other primary learning disability; intellectual potential within the average to superior range; and a serious commitment in attitude and work habits to meeting the program and college academic requirements. Prospective students are required to submit the following: high school transcript or GED. Students are expected to have college prep courses in high school but foreign language is not required for admission; ACT or SAT are preferred but not required; results of a recent complete psychoeducational evaluation (within one year); letters of recommendation from teachers, tutors, or counselors; and have a personal interview. Students may be admitted to the college through the Program for Academic Access. Students interested in being considered for admission through the program must self-disclose their LD/ADD in a personal statement with the application. There is no fixed deadline for the application, however there are a limited number of slots available. Priority is given to students who apply by January for fall admission.

ADDITIONAL INFORMATION

There are three LD professionals associated with the program. Students have access to two hours of tutoring per week plus drop-in tutoring. Skills classes are offered in study skills, reading, vocabulary development and workshops in overcoming procrastination. The following services are offered to students with appropriate documentation: the use of calculators, computer and spell checker in exams; extended time on tests; proctors; oral exams; distraction-free testing environment; tape recorder in class; books on tape; separate and alternative forms of testing; and priority registration. The program fee is $3,000 per academic year above tuition.

Support Services Contact Information

Learning Disability Program/Services: Program for Academic Access
Director: Dr. Ann Jablon
  E-Mail: aiablon@mmm.edu
  Telephone: 212-774-0725
  Fax: 212-517-0419
Contact Person: Dr. Jacquelyn Bonono
  E-Mail: jbonono@mmm.edu
  Telephone: 212-774-0724
  Fax: same as above

LEARNING DISABILITY SERVICES

Requests for the following/services accommodations will be evaluated individually based on appropriate and current documentation.

Allowed in exams
  Calculator: Yes
  Dictionary: No
  Computer: Yes
  Spellchecker: Yes
Extended test time: Yes
Scribes: No
Proctors: Yes
Oral exams: Yes
Note-takers: No

Distraction reduced environment: Yes
Tape recording in class: Yes
Books on tape from RFBD: Yes
Taping of books not from RFBD: No
Accommodations for students with ADD: Yes
Reading machine: No
Other assistive technology: Yes
Priority registration: Yes

Added costs for services: Yes
LD specialists: Yes
Professional tutors: 3
Peer tutors: No
Max. hours/wk. for services: 2
How professors are notified of LD/ADD: By student

GENERAL ADMISSIONS INFORMATION

Director of Admissions: Thomas Friebel
Telephone: 212-517-0430

ENTRANCE REQUIREMENTS

Academic units required: 4 English, 3 math, 1 science (1 science lab), 3 social studies, 4 academic electives.
Academic units recommended: 3 science, 3 foreign language. High school diploma is required and GED is accepted. TOEFL required of all international applicants, minimum paper TOEFL 500, minimum computer TOEFL 173.

Application deadline: 3/5 priority
Notification: Rolling
Average GPA: 3.40

Average SAT Math: 510
Average SAT Verbal: 540
Average ACT: 25

Graduated top 10% of class: 25%
Graduated top 25% of class: 75%
Graduated top 50% of class: 89%

COLLEGE GRADUATION REQUIREMENTS

Course waivers allowed: No
Course substitutions allowed: No
In what course: N/A

ADDITIONAL INFORMATION

Environment: Located on the upper east side of Manhattan.

Student Body:
  Undergrad enrollment: 2,244
  Women: 79%
  Men: 21%
  Percent out-of-state: 35%

Cost Information
  Tuition: $16,600
  Room & board: $9,000
Housing Information
  University housing: Yes
  Percent living on campus: 23%

Greek System
  Fraternity: No
  Sorority: No
Athletics: Intercollegiate

NEW YORK UNIVERSITY

22 Washington Square North, New York, NY 10011
Phone: 212-998-4500 • Fax: 212-995-4902
E-mail: admissions@nyu.edu/ • Web: www.nyu.edu
Support: CS • Institution type: 4-year private

LEARNING DISABILITY PROGRAM AND SERVICES

Success in college depends on such things as motivation, intelligence, talent, problem-solving abilities, and hard work. For students with learning disabilities these traits must be complemented by an understanding of their learning style and their ways of compensating for their disability. Access to Learning strives to help students capitalize on their strengths and minimize the impact of their learning disability. The goal of the Access to Learning program is to assist students with learning disabilities to achieve the highest level of academic independence and progress possible. Access to Learning provides support services and accommodations to all NYU students with learning disabilities. There is no fee. The program can assist students in coping with their learning disability while working towards independence, competence, and a college degree. Students with LD requesting accommodations or services must provide appropriate documentation that is clear and shows a specific diagnosis of LD, and evidence of a substantial limitation to academic functioning; must be recent and performed by a qualified professional. Students with ADD must provide documentation showing a clear and specific diagnosis of ADD. Documentation must be comprehensive, specify the criteria for the diagnosis and an interpretive summary, and be performed by a qualified professional.

LD/ADD ADMISSIONS INFORMATION

College entrance tests required: Yes
Interview required: No
Essay required: Yes
Documentation required for LD: Psychoeducational evaluation
Documentation required for ADD: NR
Submitted to: Access to Learning
Special Ed. HS coursework accepted: Yes

Specific course requirements of all applicants: Yes
Separate application required for program services: No
# of LD applications submitted each year: NR
# of LD applications accepted yearly: NR
Total # of students receiving LD services: 225
Acceptance into program means acceptance into college: Student must be admitted and enrolled in the university first and then request services.

ADMISSIONS

NYU is a competitive university that provides a challenging academic environment. Any student who applies—including students with learning disabilities—must demonstrate the potential to do well. As part of the admission decision, a learning disability specialist may be consulted for recommendations for students who self-disclose their learning disability. Students with learning disabilities typically have to work hard and manage their time well, but also find that they learn and accomplish a great deal at NYU. General admission criteria include 4 years English, 3 years math, 3 years science, 2 years foreign language, and 3 years social studies; SAT/ACT and SAT Subject tests for the BA/MD program.

ADDITIONAL INFORMATION

Students can meet with a learning specialist to help develop compensatory skills, work on testing strategies, time management, reading efficiency, organization, effective writing, proofreading, note-taking, and study skills. There are weekly support meetings with peers; test accommodations, which could include extended time, private test rooms, use of a computer or calculator, reader, scribe, and alternative formats for tests; assistance in arranging for taping of lectures and ordering books on tape; priority seating; and technology such as Franklin spellers, computers, and readers. Not all students need all of these services. An accommodation plan is made with each student based on individual needs, keeping in mind the goal of encouraging independence. It is possible for a student with LD to petition for a waiver of certain course requirements. The decision to allow for a waiver is made on a case-by-case basis by an academic standards committee.

Support Services Contact Information

Learning Disability Program/Services: Henry and Lucy Moses Center for Students with Disabilities/Access to Learning
Director: Yolanda Cacciolo
  E-Mail: yolanda.cacciolo@nyu.edu
  Telephone: 212-998-4975
  Fax: 212-995-4114

LEARNING DISABILITY SERVICES

Requests for the following/services accommodations will be evaluated individually based on appropriate and current documentation.

Allowed in exams
  Calculator: Yes
  Dictionary: Yes
  Computer: Yes
  Spellchecker: Yes
Extended test time: Yes
Scribes: Yes
Proctors: Yes
Oral exams: Yes
Note-takers: Yes

Distraction reduced environment: Yes
Tape recording in class: Yes
Books on tape from RFBD: Yes
Taping of books not from RFBD: Yes
Accommodations for students with ADD: Yes
Reading machine: Yes
Other assistive technology: Yes
Priority registration: No

Added costs for services: No
LD specialists: Yes
Professional tutors: No
Peer tutors: Yes
Max. hours/wk. for services: 2
How professors are notified of LD/ADD: By student

GENERAL ADMISSIONS INFORMATION

Director of Admissions: Barbara Hall
Telephone: 212-998-4500

ENTRANCE REQUIREMENTS

Academic units required: 4 English, 3 math, 3 science (2 science lab), 2 foreign language, 4 history. **Academic units recommended:** 4 math, 3 science lab. High school diploma is required and GED is accepted. ACT with Writing component required or SAT. TOEFL required of all international applicants, minimum paper TOEFL 600, minimum computer TOEFL 250.

Application deadline: 1/15
Notification: 4/1
Average GPA: 3.60

Average SAT Math: 676
Average SAT Verbal: 676
Average ACT: 29

Graduated top 10% of class: 63%
Graduated top 25% of class: 91%
Graduated top 50% of class: 99%

COLLEGE GRADUATION REQUIREMENTS

Course waivers allowed: Yes
Course substitutions allowed: Yes
In what course: Determined by an Academic Standards Committee on a case-by-case basis.

ADDITIONAL INFORMATION

Environment: The university has an urban campus in New York City.

Student Body:
  Undergrad enrollment: 19,826
  Women: 61%
  Men: 39%
  Percent out-of-state: 56%

Cost Information
  Tuition: $28,328
  Room & board: $11,210
  Housing Information
    University housing: Yes
    Percent living on campus: 54%

Greek System
  Fraternity: Yes
  Sorority: Yes
  Athletics: NCAA Division III

ROCHESTER INSTITUTE OF TECHNOLOGY

60 Lomb Memorial Drive, Rochester, NY 14623-5604
Phone: 585-475-6631 • Fax: 585-475-7424
E-mail: admissions@rit.edu • Web: www.rit.edu
Support: SP • Institution type: 4-year private

LEARNING DISABILITY PROGRAM AND SERVICES

The Learning Development Center offers a variety of services for students. Disability Services reviews requests for disability accommodations and approves accommodations and coordinates services. The Learning Support Services provides regularly scheduled check-ins with learning support a specialist who provides coaching in organizational skills, study strategies and advocacy. This service is intended for any student who anticipates difficulty navigating the college environment. Lunch 'n' Learning Workshops are a series of one-hour workshops dealing with specific study topics or strategies such as procrastination, test preparation, time management, and study skills. The Office of Special Services offers peer tutoring 2 hours per week to all RIT students.

LD/ADD ADMISSIONS INFORMATION

College entrance tests required: Yes
Interview required: No
Essay required: Yes
Documentation required for LD: Comprehensive psychological evaluation within three years. We follow AHEAD guidlines.
Documentation required for ADD: Diagnosis by qualified professional
Submitted to: Learning Support Services
Special Ed. HS coursework accepted: N/A

Specific course requirements of all applicants: Yes
Separate application required for program services: N/A
# of LD applications submitted each year: NR
# of LD applications accepted yearly: 125–150
Total # of students receiving LD services: 388
Acceptance into program means acceptance into college: Students must be admitted to the Institute and DSO/LSS seperately.

ADMISSIONS

There is no special admissions process for students with learning disabilities. However, students with learning disabilities may include a supporting essay. Although an interview is not required, it is recommended. The required scores on the SAT or ACT will depend on the college the student is applying to within RIT. It is also helpful to identify compensatory strategies used in high school and what will be needed for success in college. The admission decision is made jointly by the program chairperson and director of admission.

ADDITIONAL INFORMATION

RIT is currently serving over 600 students with disabilities of which 388 are currently students with learning disabilities or Attention Deficit Disorders. There are eight specialists on staff. Requests for accommodations and services are evaluated individually based on appropriate and current documentation. Services and accommodations which may be provided include calculator, dictionary, computer or spell checker on exams; extended test time; scribes, proctors, note-takers, distraction-free environment; books on tape; assistive technology; and priority registration. Disability information is confidential. Students distribute copies of letters to professors which lists approved accommodations only. Course substitutions are allowed depending on documentation. There are fees for Learning Support Services.

Support Services Contact Information

Learning Disability Program/Services: Disability Services/Learning Services
Director: Pamela Lloyd, Coordinator
  E-Mail: palldc@rit.edu
  Telephone: 585-475-7804 V/TTY
  Fax: 585-475-2215

LEARNING DISABILITY SERVICES

Requests for the following/services accommodations will be evaluated individually based on appropriate and current documentation.

Allowed in exams
  Calculator: Yes
  Dictionary: Yes
  Computer: Yes
  Spellchecker: Yes
Extended test time: Yes
Scribes: Yes
Proctors: Yes
Oral exams: Yes
Note-takers: Yes

Distraction reduced environment: Yes
Tape recording in class: Yes
Books on tape from RFBD: Yes
Taping of books not from RFBD: Yes
Accommodations for students with ADD: Yes
Reading machine: Yes
Other assistive technology: Yes
Priority registration: Yes

Added costs for services: Yes
LD specialists: Yes
Professional tutors: Yes
Peer tutors: Yes
Max. hours/wk. for services: 12
How professors are notified of LD/ADD: By student

GENERAL ADMISSIONS INFORMATION

Director of Admissions: Dr. Daniel Shelley
Telephone: 585-475-6631

ENTRANCE REQUIREMENTS
Academic units required: 4 English, 2 math, 2 science (1 science lab), 4 social studies, 10 academic electives.
Academic units recommended: 4 English, 3 math, 3 science (2 science lab), 3 foreign language, 4 social studies, 5 academic electives. High school diploma is required and GED is accepted. TOEFL required of all international applicants, minimum paper TOEFL 550, minimum computer TOEFL 215.

Application deadline: 2/1
Notification: Rolling
Average GPA: 3.7

Average SAT Math: NR
Average SAT Verbal: NR
Average ACT: NR

Graduated top 10% of class: 31%
Graduated top 25% of class: 66%
Graduated top 50% of class: 92%

COLLEGE GRADUATION REQUIREMENTS

Course waivers allowed: Yes
Course substitutions allowed: Yes
In what course: Courses may be substituted depending on documentation and for non-required courses only.

ADDITIONAL INFORMATION

Environment: RIT is located on a 1,300-acre campus 5 miles south of the city of Rochester, the third largest city in New York State.

Student Body:
  Undergrad enrollment: 11,750
  Women: 29%
  Men: 71%
  Percent out-of-state: 45%

Cost Information
  Tuition: $21,447
  Room & board: $8,136
Housing Information
  University housing: Yes
  Percent living on campus: 60%

Greek System
  Fraternity: Yes
  Sorority: Yes
Athletics: NCAA Division III

Rochester Institute of Technology

ST. BONAVENTURE UNIVERSITY

PO Box D, St. Bonaventure, NY 14778
Phone: 716-375-2400 • Fax: 716-375-4005
E-mail: admissions@sbu.edu • Web: www.sbu.edu
Support: CS • Institution type: 4-year private

LEARNING DISABILITY PROGRAM AND SERVICES

St. Bonaventure does not operate a specialized LD program but does provide services to students with identified disabilities. In the spirit of the federal mandates, reasonable accommodations are made for otherwise qualified students with disabilities. St. Bonaventure's Teaching and Learning Center is an intrinsic element of the university's goal of academic excellence. The credo is "to assist, not do." Once authentic, current documentation has been received, a careful review of the records will be conducted and an evaluation of appropriate accommodations will be made. Students who wait to identify themselves until after registration may find that some accommodations are not immediately available. Students with learning disabilities/attention deficit disorder who wish to request accommodations must meet with the Coordinator of Services for Students with Disabilities. It is the student's responsibility to deliver accommodation letters to professors after accommodations have been arranged. Accommodations are arranged each semester. Students are encouraged to discuss the disability with professors and arrange for specific accommodations for test-taking and other course requirements. Students must contact the coordinator of Services for Students with Disabilities to request a course substitution. The students need to accept responsibility for their own academic excellence and assistance will be provided.

LD/ADD ADMISSIONS INFORMATION

College entrance tests required: Yes
Interview required: No
Essay required: No
Documentation required for LD: WAIS–R or WAIS–III; IEP; some memory and/or perceptual test within three years
Documentation required for ADD: Yes
Submitted to: Disability Support Services
Special Ed. HS coursework accepted: Yes

Specific course requirements of all applicants: Yes
Separate application required for program services: No
# of LD applications submitted each year: NR
# of LD applications accepted yearly: NR
Total # of students receiving LD services: 50–100
Acceptance into program means acceptance into college: Student must be admitted and enrolled in the university first and then request services.

ADMISSIONS

Students with learning disabilities must meet regular admission standards and complete the same admissions process as all applicants. The mid 50 percent ACT score range is 23–24 and SAT 1070–1110; The minimum GPA is a 3.0. Course requirements include 4 years English, 4 years social studies, 3 years math, 3 years science, and 2 years foreign language (recommended). Special education courses may be considered. It is recommended that students self-disclose the disability in a personal statement. Once students are accepted and have enrolled they are encouraged to self-disclose their learning disability, if this has not already been done, and provide appropriate documentation to the Office of Services For Students with Disabilities. Documentation is reviewed and appropriate accommodations are arranged.

ADDITIONAL INFORMATION

Students with LD may obtain assistance with assessing learning strengths and weaknesses, and consult one-on-one or in groups to acquire a greater command of a subject, get help with a specific assignment, or discuss academic challenges. Services might include but are not limited to alternative testing arrangements, taped texts and classes, word processor/spell check, note-takers, tutors, peer mentors, time management and study skills training; and weekly individual appointments. To order books on tape from RFBD, students should allow three months to secure these books in time. Assistance can be offered in requesting books on tape. Tutoring services are available to all students and are not intended to be a substitute for independent study or preparation.

Support Services Contact Information

Learning Disability Program/Services: Disability Support Services
Director: Nancy A. Matthews
E-Mail: nmatthew@sbu.edu
Telephone: 716-375-2065
Fax: 716-375-2072

LEARNING DISABILITY SERVICES

Requests for the following/services accommodations will be evaluated individually based on appropriate and current documentation.

Allowed in exams
  Calculator: Yes
  Dictionary: Yes
  Computer: Yes
  Spellchecker: Yes
Extended test time: Yes
Scribes: Yes
Proctors: Yes
Oral exams: Yes
Note-takers: Yes

Distraction reduced environment: Yes
Tape recording in class: Yes
Books on tape from RFBD: Yes
Taping of books not from RFBD: Yes
Accommodations for students with ADD: Yes
Reading machine: No
Other assistive technology: Yes
Priority registration: No

Added costs for services: No
LD specialists: Yes
Professional tutors: 1
Peer tutors: 60–100
Max. hours/wk. for services: Unlimited
How professors are notified of LD/ADD: By both student and director

GENERAL ADMISSIONS INFORMATION

Director of Admissions: James M. DiRisio
Telephone: 716-375-2400

ENTRANCE REQUIREMENTS

Academic units required: 4 English, 3 math, 3 science, 2 foreign language, 4 social studies. **Academic units recommended:** 4 English, 3 math, 3 science (3 science lab), 2 foreign language, 4 social studies. High school diploma is required and GED is accepted. ACT with or without Writing component accepted. TOEFL required of all international applicants, minimum paper TOEFL 550, minimum computer TOEFL 213.

Application deadline: 4/15
Notification: Rolling
Average GPA: 3.1

Average SAT Math: 535
Average SAT Verbal: 524
Average ACT: 22

Graduated top 10% of class: 11%
Graduated top 25% of class: 36%
Graduated top 50% of class: 71%

COLLEGE GRADUATION REQUIREMENTS

Course waivers allowed: No
Course substitutions allowed: Yes
In what course: Math and foreign languages with appropriate documentation.

ADDITIONAL INFORMATION

Environment: The university is located on 600 acres in a rural area 70 miles southeast of Buffalo.

Student Body:
  Undergrad enrollment: 2,170
  Women: 50%
  Men: 50%
  Percent out-of-state: 24%

Cost Information
  Tuition: $18,650
  Room & board: $6,910
Housing Information
  University housing: Yes
  Percent living on campus: 79%

Greek System
  Fraternity: No
  Sorority: No
Athletics: NCAA Division I

ST. LAWRENCE UNIVERSITY

Payson Hall, Canton, NY 13617
Phone: 315-229-5261 • Fax: 315-229-5818
E-mail: admissions@stlawu.edu • Web: www.stlawu.edu
Support: CS Institution type: 4-year private

LEARNING DISABILITY PROGRAM AND SERVICES

The Office of Special Needs provides services to members of the university who either have identified themselves or believe they may have some type of learning disability. The office has several purposes: to serve students who are learning-challenged by documented disabilities; to help students get the academic help that they need; to put students in touch with other people on campus who can help; to advise and counsel students; to educate everyone on campus about special needs. The office works with students in developing Individual Educational Accommodations Plans for the purpose of receiving reasonable accommodations in their educational and residential life concerns. The service will also make referrals and advocate at several on-campus services, and if necessary, connect with state or regional support agencies. There is a Writing Center for help with writing assignments; peer tutors, for general assistance with academic work; and a Counseling Center and Health Center. As appropriate to the disability, documentation should include 1) A diagnostic statement identifying the disability, date of the current diagnostic evaluation, and the date of the original diagnosis; 2) A description of the diagnostic criteria and/or diagnostic test used; 3) A description of the current functional impact of the disability; 4) treatments, medications, assistive devices/services currently prescribed or in use; 5) A description of the expected progression or stability of the impact of the disability over time should be included and 6) The credentials of the diagnosing professional(s). Recommendations from professionals with a history of working with the individual provide valuable information for the review process. They will be included in the evaluation of requests for accommodation and/or auxiliary aids.

LD/ADD ADMISSIONS INFORMATION

College entrance tests required: Yes
Interview required: No
Essay required: No
Documentation required for LD: Psychoeducational evaluation
Documentation required for ADD: Yes
Submitted to: Services for Students with Special Needs
Special Ed. HS coursework accepted: Yes

Specific course requirements of all applicants: Yes
Separate application required for program services: No
# of LD applications submitted each year: NR
# of LD applications accepted yearly: NR
Total # of students receiving LD services: 130–141
Acceptance into program means acceptance into college: Student must be admitted and enrolled in the university first and then request services.

ADMISSIONS
There is no special admissions process for students with learning disabilities. All applicants must meet the same admission criteria, which include recommended courses of 4 years English, 3 years math, 3 years science, 3 years foreign language, 3 years social studies; SAT/ACT with the average SAT being 1130; an interview (recommended) which and can be done off campus with an alumni representative.

ADDITIONAL INFORMATION
Students need to be self-starters (to seek out the service early and follow through). They need to share as soon as possible the official documents that describe the learning disability so that the office can help develop the individual Education Plan (IEP). As soon as possible, students need to notify the professors and people in various offices about the learning disability. The director of services sends a memo to each professor that describes the student's IEP, discloses that the student is a documented and endorsed learning-challenged student on file with the Office of Special Needs, and lists the accommodations necessary for the student to be successful in the course. Services and accommodations are available for undergraduate and graduate students.

Support Services Contact Information

Learning Disability Program/Services: Office of Academic Services for Students with Special Needs
Director: John Meagher, Director
  E-Mail: jmeagher@stlawu.edu
  Telephone: 315-229-5104
  Fax: 315-229-7453

LEARNING DISABILITY SERVICES

Requests for the following/services accommodations will be evaluated individually based on appropriate and current documentation.

Allowed in exams
  Calculator: Yes
  Dictionary: Yes
  Computer: Yes
  Spellchecker: Yes
Extended test time: Yes
Scribes: Yes
Proctors: Yes
Oral exams: No
Note-takers: Yes

Distraction reduced environment: Yes
Tape recording in class: Yes
Books on tape from RFBD: Yes
Taping of books not from RFBD: No
Accommodations for students with ADD: Yes
Reading machine: Yes
Other assistive technology: Yes
Priority registration: Yes

Added costs for services: No
LD specialists: No
Professional tutors: Yes
Peer tutors: 75
Max. hours/wk. for services: Unlimited
How professors are notified of LD/ADD: By both student and director

GENERAL ADMISSIONS INFORMATION

Director of Admissions: Teresa Cowdrey
Telephone: 315-229-5261

ENTRANCE REQUIREMENTS

Academic units recommended: 4 English, 4 math, 4 science, 4 foreign language, 2 social studies, 2 history, High school diploma is required and GED is accepted. ACT with or without Writing component accepted. TOEFL required of all international applicants, minimum paper TOEFL 600, minimum computer TOEFL 250.

Application deadline: 2/15
Notification: 3/30
Average GPA: 3.43

Average SAT Math: 580
Average SAT Verbal: 583
Average ACT: 25

Graduated top 10% of class: 37%
Graduated top 25% of class: 73%
Graduated top 50% of class: 95%

COLLEGE GRADUATION REQUIREMENTS

Course waivers allowed: No
Course substitutions allowed: No
In what course: N/A

ADDITIONAL INFORMATION

Environment: The university is located on 1,000 acres in a rural area 80 miles south of Ottawa, Canada.

Student Body:
  Undergrad enrollment: 2,102
  Women: 52%
  Men: 48%
  Percent out-of-state: 50%

Cost Information
  Tuition: $30,270
  Room & board: $7,755
Housing Information
  University housing: Yes
  Percent living on campus: 95%

Greek System
  Fraternity: Yes
  Sorority: Yes
  Athletics: NCAA Division III

St. Thomas Aquinas College

125 Route 340, Sparkill, NY 10976
Phone: 845-398-4100 • Fax: 845-398-4224
E-mail: admissions@stac.edu • Web: www.stac.edu
Support: SP • Institution type: 4-year private

LEARNING DISABILITY PROGRAM AND SERVICES

St. Thomas Aquinas College (STAC) Exchange program services are comprehensive and specialized, based on research and actual experiences with bright college students with LD. The STAC Exchange has adapted to the increasing diversity of college students with LD/ADD, with a present emphasis on individualized services. STAC focuses on the development of effective learning strategies by critically evaluating and educating students about their specific needs and abilities. The aim is to break the pattern of dependency often created in students with learning deficits, foster a spirit of independent and active learning, teach students to maximize strengths to compensate for weaknesses, and inspire confidence in the student's own abilities. At the heart of the program are mentoring sessions. Students meet twice weekly with a professional mentor in one-to-one sessions tailored to meet specific needs. Mentors are not a tutors, but guides who help students develop learning strategies, improve organizational and editing skills, understand course concepts, and negotiate academic life. Study groups and workshops are also available, and incoming freshmen must attend a four-day residential summer program to help prepare them for college life.

LD/ADD ADMISSIONS INFORMATION

College entrance tests required: Yes
Interview required: Yes
Essay required: Yes
Documentation required for LD: Psychological report, including adult intelligence test (WAIS–III) and social/emotional functioning; educational evaluation (complete); IEP, if available
Documentation required for ADD: Same as LD, plus documentation of ADD, testing must be within 3 years
Submitted to: Stac Exchange

Specific course requirements of all applicants: Yes
Special Ed. HS coursework accepted: Yes
Separate application required for program services: Yes
# of LD applications submitted each year: 90–120
# of LD applications accepted yearly: 20–25
Total # of students receiving LD services: 65–75
Acceptance into program means acceptance into college: Students are admitted to the college and then to STAC.

ADMISSIONS

The STAC Exchange has a separate application and admissions process from the college itself. Admission to the program is limited to those students the program feels it can effectively serve, and is therefore extremely competitive. Students must be accepted by the college before their STAC Exchange application is evaluated. (SAT or ACT scores are required for regular college admission.) The following must be submitted to The STAC Exchange: a completed STAC application, high school transcripts (college transcripts for transfers), a letter of recommendation from a teacher, most recent IEP if available, and a comprehensive diagnostic assessment indicating a LD/ADD completed within the last 3 years. This diagnostic assessment must include an adult intelligence test (WAIS–III), measures of achievement, evaluation of social/emotional functioning, and the specific effects of the LD/ADD on the student's current academic performance. Reports are required; scores on an IEP are insufficient documentation. Students must also have a personal interview with STAC Exchange staff to be admitted into the program. Transfer applicatins are accepted

ADDITIONAL INFORMATION

STAC has a director, assistant director, and trained staff of mentors. Mentors are professionals with post-college education and experience in some aspect of teaching. The director and assistant director are hands-on administrators who also provide mentoring. Mentoring differs from traditional tutoring in that students come to sessions having already attended classes and prepared initial coursework. STAC Exchange students are required to attend regularly scheduled sessions with their own mentor and are encouraged to drop-in for additional help as needed. Workshops/seminars on organization and time management, note-taking, test taking, interview skills, resume writing, and self-advocacy are provided based on needs and interests. Study groups in specific areas are offered dependent upon student need and staff expertise. STAC Exchange students are also provided with academic counseling, course advisement, and priority registration. The required summer program for incoming STAC freshmen is designed to learn the specific needs of each student, to begin preparing them for academic rigors of higher education, and to build a sense of trust and community within the group. This summer program also integrates the first half of a three-credit academic course whose topic may vary from year to year.

Support Services Contact Information

Learning Disability Program/Services: The STAC Exchange
Director: Richard F. Heath, PhD
  E-Mail: pathways@stac.edu
  Telephone: 845-398-4230
  Fax: 845-398-4229

LEARNING DISABILITY SERVICES

Requests for the following/services accommodations will be evaluated individually based on appropriate and current documentation.

Allowed in exams
  Calculator: Yes
  Dictionary: Yes
  Computer: Yes
  Spellchecker: Yes
Extended test time: Yes
Scribes: Yes
Proctors: Yes
Oral exams: Yes
Note-takers: Yes

Distraction reduced environment: Yes
Tape recording in class: Yes
Books on tape from RFBD: Yes
Taping of books not from RFBD: No
Accommodations for students with
  ADD: Yes
Reading machine: No
Other assistive technology: Yes
Priority registration: Yes

Added costs for services: Yes
LD specialists: Yes
Professional tutors: 11
Peer tutors: N/A
Max. hours/wk. for services:
  Unlimited
How professors are notified of
  LD/ADD: By student

GENERAL ADMISSIONS INFORMATION

Director of Admissions: John G. Edel
Telephone: 845-398-4243

ENTRANCE REQUIREMENTS

Academic units required: 4 English, 3 math, 3 science (2 science lab), 3 foreign language, 4 social studies, 1 history. High school diploma is required and GED is accepted. ACT with or without Writing component accepted. TOEFL required of all international applicants, minimum paper TOEFL 530, minimum computer TOEFL 173.

Application deadline: NR
Notification: Rolling
Average GPA: 2.6

Average SAT Math: 469
Average SAT Verbal: 467
Average ACT: 18

Graduated top 10% of class: NR
Graduated top 25% of class: NR
Graduated top 50% of class: 50%

COLLEGE GRADUATION REQUIREMENTS

Course waivers allowed: No
Course substitutions allowed: Yes
In what course: Foreign language, only with appropriate documentation; two culture course substitutions from approved list are then required. Speech, only with appropriate documentation; one communications course substitution from approved list is then required.

ADDITIONAL INFORMATION

Environment: The school is located on 43 acres in a suburban area 15 miles from New York City.

Student Body:
  Undergrad enrollment: 1,451
  Women: 55%
  Men: 45%
  Percent out-of-state: 27%

Cost Information
  Tuition: $16,200
  Room & board: $8,850
Housing Information
  University housing: Yes
  Percent living on campus: 40%

Greek System
  Fraternity: Yes
  Sorority: Yes
Athletics: NAIA

STATE UNIVERSITY OF NY AT ALBANY

1400 Washington Avenue,
Albany, NY 12222 • Phone: 518-442-5435 • Fax: 518-442-5383
E-mail: ugadmissions@albany.edu • Web: www.albany.edu
Support: CS • Institution type: 4-year public

LEARNING DISABILITY PROGRAM AND SERVICES

The mission at SUNY at Albany is to provide a quality educational program to students with dyslexia/learning disabilities. The Learning Disabilities Resource Program is a division of Student Affairs that seeks to empower students with LD to become successful decision makers and problem solvers. It also promotes increased sensitivity to and appreciation for the uniqueness of students with LD. The goal is to provide general support for students as they attempt to gain access to services and accommodations necessary to their success. The program provides a writing center staffed by faculty, advocacy, assistance with recommended courses, tutoring assistance, and a willingness to explore innovative ways of providing the most efficient assistance possible. The Mentor Program provides extra academic assistance and support for students with LD/ADD. The mentor is a graduate student with a distinguished academic record who is paired with the mentee. They meet twice weekly and develop problem solving techniques. The mentor does not function as a content tutor, but does provide oversight and supervision for academic coursework. The cost for the Mentor Program is $675 per semester.

LD/ADD ADMISSIONS INFORMATION

College entrance tests required: Yes
Interview required: No
Essay required: No
Documentation required for LD: Current psychological educational evaluation less than 3 years old. Must state area of disability. Academic accommodations will be determined by the university
Documentation required for ADD: Medical documenation is sufficient for individual appointments. Educational psychological evalutation if academic accommodations are requested. The university will determine academic accommodations based on documentation
Submitted to: Disabled Students Services
Special Ed. HS coursework accepted: N/A

Specific course requirements of all applicants: Yes
Separate application required for program services: N/A
# of LD applications submitted each year: NR
# of LD applications accepted yearly: NR
Total # of students receiving LD services: 65–90
Acceptance into program means acceptance into college: Student must be admitted and enrolled in the university first and then request services.

ADMISSIONS

There is no special application for applicants with learning disabilities. Applicants who self-disclose may have their application files reviewed by the director of the LDRP and the Office of Admissions. Letters of recommendation, auxiliary testing, and a personal interview are helpful. Students must present 18 units from high school acceptable to the university, a 950 SAT score, a high school average of at least 85 percent, and class rank in the top one-third.

ADDITIONAL INFORMATION

Services include pre-admission review of the applicant's file in conjunction with admissions and individual counseling and advisement to applicants and their families; counseling and support; auxiliary aids and services such as testing accommodations, assistance in locating note-takers and tutors, reading services, and loan of tape recorder; information and referral to campus resources; and consultation and advocacy. Students diagnosed with ADD who have documented LD may receive support from the LDRP or, in some cases, from the Office of Disabled Student Services.

Support Services Contact Information

Learning Disability Program/Services: Disabled Student Services
Director: Nancy Belowich-Negron
  E-Mail: nbelowich@email.albany.edu
  Telephone: 518-442-5490
  Fax: 518-442-5589

LEARNING DISABILITY SERVICES

Requests for the following/services accommodations will be evaluated individually based on appropriate and current documentation.

Allowed in exams
  Calculator: Yes
  Dictionary: No
  Computer: Yes
  Spellchecker: Yes
Extended test time: Yes
Scribes: Yes
Proctors: Yes
Oral exams: Yes
Note-takers: Yes

Distraction reduced environment: Yes
Tape recording in class: Yes
Books on tape from RFBD: Yes
Taping of books not from RFBD: No
Accommodations for students with ADD: Yes
Reading machine: Yes
Other assistive technology: Yes
Priority registration: Yes

Added costs for services: No
LD specialists: Yes
Professional tutors: Yes
Peer tutors: Yes
Max. hours/wk. for services: Unlimited
How professors are notified of LD/ADD: By student

GENERAL ADMISSIONS INFORMATION

Director of Admissions: Robert Andrea
Telephone: 800-293-7869

ENTRANCE REQUIREMENTS

Academic units required: 4 English, 2 math, 2 science (2 science lab), 3 social studies, 2 history, 5 academic electives. **Academic units recommended:** 4 math, 3 science, (3 science lab), 3 foreign language. High school diploma is required and GED is accepted. TOEFL required of all international applicants, minimum paper TOEFL 550, minimum computer TOEFL 213.

Application deadline: 3/1
Notification: Rolling
Average GPA: 3.60

Average SAT Math: NR
Average SAT Verbal: NR
Average ACT: NR

Graduated top 10% of class: 16%
Graduated top 25% of class: 54%
Graduated top 50% of class: 92%

COLLEGE GRADUATION REQUIREMENTS

Course waivers allowed: No
Course substitutions allowed: Yes
In what course: Determined on a case-by-case basis with supporting documentation

ADDITIONAL INFORMATION

Environment: The university has an urban campus on 515 acres located on the fringe of the state capital.

Student Body:
  Undergrad enrollment: 11,309
  Women: 50%
  Men: 50%
  Percent out-of-state: 5%

Cost Information
  In-state tuition: $4,300
  Out-of-state tuition: $10,300
  Room & board: $7,181
Housing Information
  University housing: Yes
  Percent living on campus: 58%

Greek System
  Fraternity: Yes
  Sorority: Yes
Athletics: NCAA Division I

STATE UNIVERSITY OF NY AT BINGHAMTON

PO Box 6001, Binghamton, NY 13902-6001
Phone: 607-777-2171 • Fax: 607-777-4445
E-mail: admit@binghamton.edu • Web: www.binghamton.edu
Support: CS • Institution type: 4-year public

LEARNING DISABILITY PROGRAM AND SERVICES

The Services for Students with Disabilities office provides assistance to students with physical or learning disabilities. They operate on the philosophy that the individuals they serve are students first and that their disabilities are secondary. Support services assist students in taking advantage of the opportunities at Binghamton and in making their own contributions to the university community.

LD/ADD ADMISSIONS INFORMATION

College entrance tests required: Yes
Interview required: No
Essay required: Yes
Documentation required for LD: Psychoeducational
  evaluation
Documentation required for ADD: Yes
Submitted to: Services for Students with Disabilities
Special Ed. HS coursework accepted: No

Specific course requirements of all applicants: Yes
Separate application required for program services: No
# of LD applications submitted each year: NR
# of LD applications accepted yearly: NR
Total # of students receiving LD services: 81
**Acceptance into program means acceptance into
  college:** Student must be admitted and enrolled in the
  university first and then request services.

ADMISSIONS

Binghamton University welcomes applications from all qualified individuals. While there are no special admissions procedures or academic programs expressly for students with disabilities, the Services for Students with Disabilities office provides a wide range of support services to enrolled students. Diagnostic tests are not required for admissions, but students are encouraged to meet with the director of Services for Students with Disabilities and to provide documentation in order to determine appropriate accommodations. Through nonmatriculated enrollment, students can take courses but are not enrolled in a degree program. If they do well, they may then apply for matriculation, using credits earned toward their degree. General admission criteria includes 4 years of English, 2.5 years of math, 2 years of social science, 2 years of science, 2 years of two foreign languages or 3 years of one foreign language in the same language. The mid 50 percent score range on the SATs 1100–1330.

ADDITIONAL INFORMATION

Students with LD/ADD may use all campus wide services plus receive accommodations and services through SSD. Accommodations which are available for students with appropriate documentation include extended testing time; distraction-free environments for tests; scribes; proctors; use of calculators, dictionary, spellchecker, and computers in exams; assistive technology including voice recognition software, screen readers software, print enlargement, assistive listening devices, and variable speed tape recorder on loan. Tutorial services are provided to undergraduate students at no charge for 4 hours per week. However, SSD can arrange for more than 4 hours per week at the student's expense. The university's Center for Academic Excellence provides peer tutoring to any student at no cost. The university has offered courses in College Study and Coping Skills and Applying Study Skills to Career Research. Availability of these courses each year is dependent on staffing. Students are provided memos of reasonable accommodation written by the SSD Director or Learning Disabilities Specialist, to be given to their professors. Services and accommodations are available for undergraduate and graduate students.

Support Services Contact Information

Learning Disability Program/Services: Services for Students with Disabilities (SSD)
Director: B. Jean Fairbairn
 E-Mail: bjfairba@binghamton.edu
 Telephone: 607-777-2686
 Fax: 607-777-6893

LEARNING DISABILITY SERVICES

Requests for the following/services accommodations will be evaluated individually based on appropriate and current documentation.

Allowed in exams
 Calculator: Yes
 Dictionary: Yes
 Computer: Yes
 Spellchecker: Yes
Extended test time: Yes
Scribes: Yes
Proctors: Yes
Oral exams: Yes
Note-takers: Yes

Distraction reduced environment: Yes
Tape recording in class: Yes
Books on tape from RFBD: Yes
Taping of books not from RFBD: Yes
Accommodations for students with ADD: Yes
Reading machine: Yes
Other assistive technology: Yes
Priority registration: Yes

Added costs for services: No
LD specialists: Yes
Professional tutors: No
Peer tutors: Yes
Max. hours/wk. for services: 5
How professors are notified of LD/ADD: By student

GENERAL ADMISSIONS INFORMATION

Director of Admissions: Cheryl Brown, Director of Undergraduate Admissions
Telephone: 607-777-2171

ENTRANCE REQUIREMENTS

Academic units required: 4 English, 3 math, 2 science, 3 foreign language, 2 social studies. **Academic units recommended:** 4 math, 3 science, 3 foreign language, 3 history. High school diploma is required and GED is accepted. ACT with Writing component required or SAT. TOEFL required of all international applicants, minimum paper TOEFL 550, minimum computer TOEFL 213.

Application deadline: 2/15
Notification: Rolling
Average GPA: 3.6

Average SAT Math: 643
Average SAT Verbal: 607
Average ACT: 26

Graduated top 10% of class: NR
Graduated top 25% of class: 83%
Graduated top 50% of class: 99%

COLLEGE GRADUATION REQUIREMENTS

Course waivers allowed: Yes
In what course: Foreign language waivers or substitutions may be available when justified to the University Academic Standards Committee. Substitutions are recommended.
Course substitutions allowed: Yes
In what course: LD: Sometimes, depending upon nature and severity of disability, disability documentation and major of study. ADD: Rarely, depending upon nature and severity of disability, disability documentation and major of study.

ADDITIONAL INFORMATION

Environment: The university has a suburban campus near Binghamton.

Student Body:
 Undergrad enrollment: 10,898
 Women: 49%
 Men: 51%
 Percent out-of-state: 6%

Cost Information
 In-state tuition: $4,350
 Out-of-state tuition: $10,610
 Room & board: $7,710
Housing Information
 University housing: Yes
 Percent living on campus: 58%

Greek System
 Fraternity: Yes
 Sorority: Yes
Athletics: NCAA Division I

STATE UNIVERSITY OF NY AT STONY BROOK

Office of Admissions, Stony Brook, NY 11794-1901
Phone: 631-632-6868 • Fax: 631-632-9898
E-mail: enroll@stonybrook.edu • Web: www.stonybrook.edu
Support: CS • Institution type: 4-year public

LEARNING DISABILITY PROGRAM AND SERVICES

Disability Support Services (DSS) coordinates advocacy and support services for students with disabilities. These services assist integrating students' needs with the resources available at the university to eliminate physical or programmatic barriers and to ensure an accessible academic environment. All information and documentation of student disabilities is confidential. Students are responsible for identifying and documenting their disabilities through the DSS office. Students receive assistance with special housing and transportation, recruitment of readers, interpreters, note-takers, test accommodations and counseling. A LD specialist is available for referral for diagnostic testing and educational programming, to meet accommodation needs, and to provide in-service training to the university community. A supported education program offering individual counseling and group sessions is available for students with psychological disabilities. Students who anticipate requiring assistance should contact Disability Support Services as early as possible to allow time for implementing recommended services.

LD/ADD ADMISSIONS INFORMATION

College entrance tests required: Yes
Interview required: No
Essay required: Yes
Documentation required for LD: Psychoeducational evaluation; within 3 years
Documentation required for ADD: Yes
Submitted to: Disabilities Support Services
Special Ed. HS coursework accepted: No

Specific course requirements of all applicants: Yes
Separate application required for program services: No
# of LD applications submitted each year: NR
# of LD applications accepted yearly: NR
Total # of students receiving LD services: 145
Acceptance into program means acceptance into college: Student must be admitted and enrolled in the university first and then request services.

ADMISSIONS

Admission decisions are based on grades, GPA, and/or class rank and ACT/SAT. There is no separate or special admission because there are no developmental or remedial classes. However, each applicant who is identified at having a disability is given the special consideration of being reviewed by an Admissions counselor and a DSS staff member jointly. All special circumstances are taken into consideration. Students are encouraged to self-disclose the disability in the application process. The director of Disabilities Services will review documentation from students with learning disabilities and provide a recommendation to the Office of Admission.

ADDITIONAL INFORMATION

Types of services and accommodations available are pre-registration advisement, liaison with faculty and staff, taped texts, learning strategies and time management training, assistance in locating tutors, assistance in arranging for note-takers and/or readers, tutorial computer programs, proctoring and/or modified administration of exams, support group; referral to appropriate campus resources, peer advising, and aid in vocational decision making. Services and accommodations are available to undergraduate and graduate students. No skills classes are offered.

Support Services Contact Information

Learning Disability Program/Services: Disabilities Support Services
Director: Joanna Harris
  E-Mail: j.jharris@notes.cc.sunysb.edu
  Telephone: 631-632-6748
  Fax: 631-632-6747
Contact Person: Donna Molloy, Learning Disabilities Specialist

LEARNING DISABILITY SERVICES

Requests for the following/services accommodations will be evaluated individually based on appropriate and current documentation.

Allowed in exams
  Calculator: Y/N
  Dictionary: No
  Computer: Yes
  Spellchecker: Yes
Extended test time: Yes
Scribes: Yes
Proctors: Yes
Oral exams: No
Note-takers: Yes

Distraction reduced environment: Yes
Tape recording in class: Yes
Books on tape from RFBD: Yes
Taping of books not from RFBD: No
Accommodations for students with ADD: Yes
Reading machine: Yes
Other assistive technology: Yes
Priority registration: Yes

Added costs for services: No
LD specialists: Yes
Professional tutors: No
Peer tutors: Yes
Max. hours/wk. for services: 2
How professors are notified of LD/ADD: By student

GENERAL ADMISSIONS INFORMATION

Director of Admissions: Judith Burke-Berhannan
Telephone: 631-632-6868

ENTRANCE REQUIREMENTS

Academic units required: 4 English, 3 math, 3 science, 2 foreign language, 4 history. **Academic units recommended:** 4 English, 4 math, 4 science, 3 foreign language, 4 history. High school diploma is required and GED is accepted. ACT with Writing component required or SAT. TOEFL required of all international applicants, minimum paper TOEFL 550, minimum computer TOEFL 213.

Application deadline: 3/1
Notification: Rolling
Average GPA: 3.60

Average SAT Math: 611
Average SAT Verbal: 565
Average ACT: NR

Graduated top 10% of class: 33%
Graduated top 25% of class: 69%
Graduated top 50% of class: 97%

COLLEGE GRADUATION REQUIREMENTS

Course waivers allowed: No
Course substitutions allowed: Yes
In what course: Subsitutions possible for foreign language.

ADDITIONAL INFORMATION

Environment: The university is located on 1,100 acres in a suburban area on Long Island, 60 miles from New York City.

Student Body:
  Undergrad enrollment: 13,694
  Women: 49%
  Men: 51%
  Percent out-of-state: 4%

Cost Information
  In-state tuition: $5,340
  Out-of-state tuition: $11,300
  Room & board: $7,800
Housing Information
  University housing: Yes
  Percent living on campus: 59%

Greek System
  Fraternity: Yes
  Sorority: Yes
Athletics: NCAA Division I

STATE U. OF NY COLLEGE AT POTSDAM

44 Pierrepont Avenue, Potsdam, NY 13676
Phone: 315-267-2180 • Fax: 315-267-2163
E-mail: admissions@potsdam.edu • Web: www.potsdam.edu
Support: CS • Institution type: 4-year public

LEARNING DISABILITY PROGRAM AND SERVICES

The State University of New York College at Potsdam is committed to the full inclusion of al individuals who can benefit from educational opportunities. Accommodative Services provides academic accommodations for all qualified students who have documented learning, emotional, and/or physical disabilities and need for accommodation. The ultimate goal is to promote individuals' independence within the academic atmosphere of the university. Students are assisted in this process by the support services and programs available to all Potsdam students. Students must submit (written) documentation of the disability and the need for accommodations. After forwarding documentation, students are encouraged to make an appointment to meet with the coordinator to discuss accommodations. All accommodations are determined on an individual basis. Accommodative Services makes every effort to ensure access to academic accommodations.

LD/ADD ADMISSIONS INFORMATION

College entrance tests required: Yes
Interview required: No
Essay required: No
Documentation required for LD: Comprehensive assessment
  by a licensed profesional
Documentation required for ADD: Yes
Submitted to: Accommodative Services
Special Ed. HS coursework accepted: No

Specific course requirements of all applicants: Yes
Separate application required for program services: No
# of LD applications submitted each year: NR
# of LD applications accepted yearly: NR
Total # of students receiving LD services: 45–50
Acceptance into program means acceptance into
  college: Student must be admitted and enrolled in the
  university first and then request services.

ADMISSIONS

Students with learning disabilities must meet the same admission criteria as all applicants to the university. General admissions include an ACT of 20+ or SAT of 960, 80 percent GPA and 17 core courses including 3 years math, 2 years science, 4 years social studies, 4 years English, 3 years foreign language, and 1 year fine or performing arts. There is no conditional or probational admission plan. Students are encouraged to self-disclose the disability and provide appropriate documentation to Accommodative Services.

ADDITIONAL INFORMATION

Accommodations available through Accommodative Services include note-takers test readers/books on tape; alternative testing such as extended time and/or distraction-reduced environment, exam readers/scribes, and word processor with spell check; loan of some equipment; additional services can include special registration and academic advising. Accommodative Services will assist students requesting non-academic auxiliary aids or services in location the appropriate campus resources to address the request. The college Counseling Center provides psychological services. The Early Warning system asks each instructor to indicate at midpoint in each semester, if a student is making unsatisfactory academic progress. Results of this inquiry are sent to the student and advisor. Student Support Services provides academic support, peer mentoring, and counseling. Tutoring is available for all students on one-on-one or small group.

Support Services Contact Information

Learning Disability Program/Services: Accommodative Services
Director: Sharon House
  E-Mail: housese@potsdam.edu
  Telephone: 315-267-3267
  Fax: 315-267-3268

LEARNING DISABILITY SERVICES

Requests for the following/services accommodations will be evaluated individually based on appropriate and current documentation.

Allowed in exams	**Distraction reduced environment:** Yes	**Added costs for services:** No
Calculator: Yes	**Tape recording in class:** Yes	**LD specialists:** No
Dictionary: Yes	**Books on tape from RFBD:** Yes	**Professional tutors:** No
Computer: Yes	**Taping of books not from RFBD:** Yes	**Peer tutors:** 180
Spellchecker: Yes	**Accommodations for students with**	**Max. hours/wk. for services:** 3
Extended test time: Yes	**ADD:** Yes	**How professors are notified of**
Scribes: Yes	**Reading machine:** Yes	**LD/ADD:** By student
Proctors: Yes	**Other assistive technology:** Yes	
Oral exams: Yes	**Priority registration:** Yes	
Note-takers: Yes		

GENERAL ADMISSIONS INFORMATION

Director of Admissions: Thomas Nesbitt
Telephone: 315-267-2180

ENTRANCE REQUIREMENTS

Academic units required: 4 English, 3 math, 2 science (1 science lab), 3 foreign language, 4 social studies, 1 visual or performing arts. **Academic units recommended:** 4 English, 4 math, 3 science (2 science lab), 4 foreign language, 4 social studies, 1 visual or performing arts. High school diploma is required and GED is accepted. TOEFL required of all international applicants, minimum paper TOEFL 520, minimum computer TOEFL 190.

Application deadline: Open	**Average SAT Math:** 533	**Graduated top 10% of class:** 11%
Notification: Rolling	**Average SAT Verbal:** 534	**Graduated top 25% of class:** 37%
Average GPA: 85.00	**Average ACT:** 23	**Graduated top 50% of class:** 78%

COLLEGE GRADUATION REQUIREMENTS

Course waivers allowed: Yes
Course substitutions allowed: Yes
In what course: Substitutions only done on an individual basis

ADDITIONAL INFORMATION

Environment: The university is located on 240 acres in a rural area.

Student Body:	**Cost Information**	**Greek System**
Undergrad enrollment: 3,435	**In-state tuition:** $4,850	**Fraternity:** No
Women: 60%	**Out-of-state tuition:** $11,200	**Sorority:** No
Men: 40%	**Room & board:** $7,590	**Athletics:** NCAA Division III
Percent out-of-state: 3%	**Housing Information**	
	University housing: Yes	
	Percent living on campus: 49%	

SUNY COLLEGE OF TECH. AT ALFRED (ALFRED STATE UNIVERSITY)

Huntington Administration Building, Alfred, NY 14802
Phone: 800-425-3733 • Fax: 607-587-4299
E-mail: admissions@alfredstate.edu • Web: www.alfredstate.edu
Support: S • Institution type: 2-year public

LEARNING DISABILITY PROGRAM AND SERVICES

The goal of the Office of Services for Students with Disabilities (SSD) is to insure that students with disabilities, with appropriate documentation, have equal access to programs, activities, and services offered to other students. Once students present appropriate documentation, services are provided depending on individual needs. The Student Development Center has team of dedicated professionals committed to fostering personal and academic growth of all students. The centralized nature of the center allows for an important link among college supportive services dedicated to maximizing student growth and student success. The Alfred State Opportunity Program (ASOP) is a special admissions program designed to improve the student's opportunity to be academically successful. Reduced course loads and college-preparatory developmental courses assist students in meeting curricular prerequisites. Students should contact Learning Assistance and must provide adequate documentation before accommodations/services will be provided. The Services for Students with Disabilities counselor determines the extent of services provided.

LD/ADD ADMISSIONS INFORMATION

College entrance tests required: Yes
Interview required: No
Essay required: No
Documentation required for LD: Pyschoeducational evaluation
Documentation required for ADD: Yes
Submitted to: Services for Students with disabilities
Special Ed. HS coursework accepted: Yes

Specific course requirements of all applicants: Yes
Separate application required for program services: No
# of LD applications submitted each year: NR
# of LD applications accepted yearly: NR
Total # of students receiving LD services: 222
Acceptance into program means acceptance into college: Student must be admitted and enrolled in the college first and then request services.

ADMISSIONS
There is no special admission process for students with learning disabilities. All applicants must meet the same admission criteria. The minimum core courses that are preferred include 4 years English, 3 years math, 3 years science, 3 years social science, 2 years foreign language, and 1 year art. The minimum GPA is 74 percent. ASOP allows students to take 3 years to complete a 2-year program.

ADDITIONAL INFORMATION
Services available through SSD include individual academic skills development, note-takers and scribes, readers, peer tutors, taped texts, testing accommodations, extended curricular programs, referral to other offices and agencies, specialized equipment loan, advocacy, and registration. ASOP provides counseling, extensive advising, and tutoring. Peer and professional tutors are available by appointment and provide course-specific assistance such as answers to questions, clarification of information, and drill and/or review for exams. Academic skills assistance for reading improvement, student success, and study skills can be provided through individual appointments, small group seminars, classroom instruction, or computer tutorials.

Support Services Contact Information

Learning Disability Program/Services: Services for Students with Disabilities (SSD)
Director: Heather Meacham
  E-Mail: meachahm@alfredstate.edu
  Telephone: 607-587-4122
  Fax: 607-587-3210

LEARNING DISABILITY SERVICES

Requests for the following/services accommodations will be evaluated individually based on appropriate and current documentation.

Allowed in exams
  Calculator: Yes
  Dictionary: Yes
  Computer: Yes
  Spellchecker: Yes
Extended test time: Yes
Scribes: Yes
Proctors: Yes
Oral exams: No
Note-takers: Yes

Distraction reduced environment: Yes
Tape recording in class: Yes
Books on tape from RFBD: NR
Taping of books not from RFBD: Yes
Accommodations for students with ADD: Yes
Reading machine: Yes
Other assistive technology: Yes
Priority registration: Yes

Added costs for services: No
LD specialists: No
Professional tutors: 2
Peer tutors: 75
Max. hours/wk. for services: As needed
How professors are notified of LD/ADD: By director

GENERAL ADMISSIONS INFORMATION

Director of Admissions: Deborah Goodrich
Telephone: 800-425-3733

ENTRANCE REQUIREMENTS

Academic units recommended: 4 English, 4 math, 4 science, 4 social studies. High school diploma is required and GED is accepted. TOEFL required of all international applicants, minimum paper TOEFL 500, minimum computer TOEFL 173.

Application deadline: Rolling
Notification: Rolling
Average GPA: 2.70

Average SAT Math: 470
Average SAT Verbal: 470
Average ACT: 19

Graduated top 10% of class: NR
Graduated top 25% of class: NR
Graduated top 50% of class: NR

COLLEGE GRADUATION REQUIREMENTS

Course waivers allowed: No
Course substitutions allowed: No

ADDITIONAL INFORMATION

Environment: The university has a rural campus 70 miles from Rochester.

Student Body:
  Undergrad enrollment: 3,471
  Women: 35%
  Men: 65%
  Percent out-of-state: 7%

Cost Information
  In-state tuition: $4,350
  Out-of-state tuition: $7,000
  Room & board: $6,376
Housing Information
  University housing: Yes
  Percent living on campus: 70%

Greek System
  Fraternity: Yes
  Sorority: Yes
Athletics: NCAA Division III

State U. of NY College of Tech. at Canton

French Hall, SUNY Canton, Canton, NY 13617
Phone: 315-386-7123 • Fax: 315-386-7929
E-mail: admissions@canton.edu • Web: www.canton.edu
Support: S • Institution type: 2-year public

LEARNING DISABILITY PROGRAM AND SERVICES

At the State University of New York College of Technology at Canton, the Accommodative Services Program is equipped to help students with learning disabilities make a smooth transition to college, and receive the necessary accommodations to ensure their academic success. The mission of the Office of Accommodative Services is to create a comprehensively accessible environment where individuals are viewed on the basis of ability, not disability. This supports the mission of SUNY—Canton, a technical college, offering two- and four-year degrees to a diverse student body. Prospective students are welcome to contact the Accommodative Services office with any questions. Although students with learning disabilities may register at the office at any time during their stay at SUNY—Canton, they are encouraged to do so as early as possible. Students must register at the office in order to obtain the special resources and services. It is the students' responsibility to self-disclose, provide appropriate documentation, and request accommodations.

LD/ADD ADMISSIONS INFORMATION

College entrance tests required: No
Interview required: No
Essay required: No
Documentation required for LD: A current (three years) IEP and a psychological evaluation
Documentation required for ADD: Yes
Submitted to: Accommodation Services
Special Ed. HS coursework accepted: No

Specific course requirements of all applicants: No
Separate application required for program services: No
# of LD applications submitted each year: NR
# of LD applications accepted yearly: NR
Total # of students receiving LD services: 127
Acceptance into program means acceptance into college: Student must be admitted and enrolled in the college first and then request services.

ADMISSIONS

All students follow the same admissions procedure and are evaluated similarly for specific course placement. The Office of Accommodative Services is not directly involved in the admission process, but will usually meet with students (and families) during admission interviews. There are no specific course requirements as the requirements vary per curriculum, and foreign language is not required for admission. All students must have a high school diploma or the GED equivalent. No ACT/SAT tests are required for admission. Compass Tests are used for placement.

ADDITIONAL INFORMATION

A number of support services are offered on campus: academic advisement, Academic Computing Center; Canton Special Services Program, Counseling Center, Educational Opportunity Program, Learning Center, Math Lab, Writing Center, tutoring, and the Science Learning Center. Services or accommodations could include: testing accommodations; scribes, proctors; note-takers; books on tape; assistive technology; calculator, dictionary, computer or spell-check in exams; distraction-free environment for tests; and priority registration. Acceptance into the university ensures that students will receive the services they request when they provided appropriate documentation.

Support Services Contact Information

Learning Disability Program/Services: Accommodative Services (AS)
Director: Veigh Mehan Lee, Coordinator
  E-Mail: leev@canton.edu
  Telephone: 315-386-7392
  Fax: 315-379-3877

LEARNING DISABILITY SERVICES

Requests for the following/services accommodations will be evaluated individually based on appropriate and current documentation.

Allowed in exams
  Calculator: Yes
  Dictionary: Yes
  Computer: Yes
  Spellchecker: Yes
Extended test time: Yes
Scribes: Yes
Proctors: Yes
Oral exams: Yes
Note-takers: Yes

Distraction reduced environment: Yes
Tape recording in class: Yes
Books on tape from RFBD: Yes
Taping of books not from RFBD: Yes
Accommodations for students with ADD: Yes
Reading machine: Yes
Other assistive technology: Yes
Priority registration: Yes

Added costs for services: No
LD specialists: No
Professional tutors: 12–25
Peer tutors: 12
Max. hours/wk. for services: As needed
How professors are notified of LD/ADD: By director

GENERAL ADMISSIONS INFORMATION

Director of Admissions: Dave Gerlach
Telephone: 315-386-7123

ENTRANCE REQUIREMENTS

Academic units recommended: 4 English, 2 math, 2 science, 4 social studies. High school diploma is required and GED is accepted. TOEFL required of all international applicants, minimum paper TOEFL 550, minimum computer TOEFL 213.

Application deadline: Rolling
Notification: Rolling
Average GPA: NR

Average SAT Math: NR
Average SAT Verbal: NR
Average ACT: NR

Graduated top 10% of class: NR
Graduated top 25% of class: NR
Graduated top 50% of class: NR

COLLEGE GRADUATION REQUIREMENTS

Course waivers allowed: Yes
Course substitutions allowed: Yes
In what course: Depends upon disability

ADDITIONAL INFORMATION

Environment: The 550-acre campus is 135 miles northeast of Syracuse.

Student Body:
  Undergrad enrollment: 2,119
  Women: 48%
  Men: 52%
  Percent out-of-state: NR

Cost Information
  In-state tuition: $4,350
  Out-of-state tuition: $10,000
  Room & board: $7,820
Housing Information
  University housing: Yes
  Percent living on campus: 43%

Greek System
  Fraternity: Yes
  Sorority: Yes
Athletics: NCAA Division III

State U. of NY College of Tech. at Delhi

Bush Hall, 2 Main Street, Delhi, NY 13753
Phone: 607-746-4550 • Fax: 607-746-4104
E-mail: enroll@Delhi.edu • Web: www.delhi.edu
Support: CS • Institution type: 2-year public

LEARNING DISABILITY PROGRAM AND SERVICES

SUNY—Delhi provides students with learning disabilities with academic support services and equipment, including professional tutors; exams in a distraction-free environment; submission of exams on tape or dictating exams to an attendant; remedial courses in reading, math, English, and study skills; and enlarged video display computer terminals. The coordinator of services often confers with students regarding their unique learning, study, and time management needs.

LD/ADD ADMISSIONS INFORMATION

College entrance tests required: No
Interview required: No
Essay required: No
Documentation required for LD: Within three years of admission and using adult standards (norms). I.Q. achievment required
Documentation required for ADD: Same as above; if on medication, a doctor's statement
Submitted to: Center for Academic Services
Special Ed. HS coursework accepted: Yes

Specific course requirements of all applicants: No
Separate application required for program services: No
# of LD applications submitted each year: NR
# of LD applications accepted yearly: NR
Total # of students receiving LD services: NR
Acceptance into program means acceptance into college: Student must be admitted and enrolled in the university first and then request services.

ADMISSIONS

The admission requirements are the same for all students. It is always helpful if students with learning disabilities present themselves as confident, independent, goal-oriented, and self-directed learners. The minimum GPA is 2.0 and course requirements depend on the major. Courses taken in special education may be considered. Students are encouraged to self-disclose the disability in a personal statement. Admission counselors will refer students to the coordinator if the student provides information about a disability. To be eligible for services students must disclose information about their learning disability/attention deficit disorder and meet with the coordinator of Services for Students with Disabilities. ASSET scores are used for placement within courses.

ADDITIONAL INFORMATION

The coordinator of services for students with learning disabilities is available to answer any questions regarding academic and nonacademic matters. The coordinator also serves as a campus referral service. There is a Writing Lab, Tutoring Lab and Computer Lab available for all students. Skills classes are offered in test taking strategies, time management, and study skills. Services and accommodations available with appropriate documentation include extended testing time for exams; distraction-free environments; calculator, dictionary, computer, and spell-check in exams; scribes; proctors; note-takers; books on tape; assistive technology; and course substitutions for math or foreign language may be available in the Liberal Arts Program.

Support Services Contact Information

Learning Disability Program/Services: The Center For Academic Services
Director: Linda Weinberg, Coordinator
  E-Mail: weinbell@delhi.edu
  Telephone: 607-746-4593
  Fax: 607-746-4368

LEARNING DISABILITY SERVICES

Requests for the following/services accommodations will be evaluated individually based on appropriate and current documentation.

Allowed in exams
  Calculator: Yes
  Dictionary: Yes
  Computer: Yes
  Spellchecker: Yes
Extended test time: Yes
Scribes: Yes
Proctors: Yes
Oral exams: Yes
Note-takers: Yes

Distraction reduced environment: Yes
Tape recording in class: Yes
Books on tape from RFBD: Yes
Taping of books not from RFBD: No
Accommodations for students with
  ADD: No
Reading machine: Yes
Other assistive technology: Yes
Priority registration: No

Added costs for services: No
LD specialists: Yes
Professional tutors: 4
Peer tutors: 10
Max. hours/wk. for services: 2
How professors are notified of
  LD/ADD: By student

GENERAL ADMISSIONS INFORMATION

Director of Admissions: Lawrence Barratt
Telephone: 607-746-4550

ENTRANCE REQUIREMENTS

Academic units required: 4 English, 1 math, 1 science, 3 social studies, 1 history. **Academic units recommended:** 2 math, 2 science (1 science lab). High school diploma is required and GED is accepted. TOEFL required of all international applicants, minimum paper TOEFL 450, minimum computer TOEFL 133.

Application deadline: Rolling
Notification: Rolling
Average GPA: NR

Average SAT Math: NR
Average SAT Verbal: NR
Average ACT: NR

Graduated top 10% of class: NR
Graduated top 25% of class: NR
Graduated top 50% of class: NR

COLLEGE GRADUATION REQUIREMENTS

Course waivers allowed: Yes
Course substitutions allowed: Yes
In what course: Only in Liberal Arts programs

ADDITIONAL INFORMATION

Environment: The university is on 1,100 acres in a small town setting in upstate New York.

Student Body:
  Undergrad enrollment: 1,791
  Women: 44%
  Men: 56%
  Percent out-of-state: 4%

Cost Information
  In-state tuition: $4,350
  Room & board: $6,830
Housing Information
  University housing: Yes
  Percent living on campus: 70%

Greek System
  Fraternity: Yes
  Sorority: Yes
Athletics: NCAA Division III

SYRACUSE UNIVERSITY

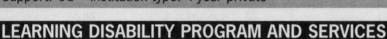

201 Tolley, Administration Building, Syracuse, NY 13244
Phone: 315-443-3611 • Fax: 315-443-4226
E-mail: orange@syr.edu • Web: www.syracuse.edu
Support: CS • Institution type: 4-year private

LEARNING DISABILITY PROGRAM AND SERVICES

The Center for Academic Achievement provides an integrated network of academic support, counseling, and advising services to meet the individual needs of students with diagnosed learning disabilities. Every student with learning disabilities who is accepted to the university is eligible for services, and must provide diagnostic information from which appropriate academic accommodations are determined. The staff is very supportive and sensitive to the needs of the students. Services are provided by a professional staff that sincerely care about the needs of every student. The program enables students to develop a sense of independence as they learn to advocate for themselves and become involved in their college education.

LD/ADD ADMISSIONS INFORMATION

College entrance tests required: Yes
Interview required: Yes
Essay required: Yes
Documentation required for LD: Psychoeducational evaluation
Documentation required for ADD: Yes
Submitted to: Learning Disability Services
Special Ed. HS coursework accepted: No

Specific course requirements of all applicants: Yes
Separate application required for program services: Yes
# of LD applications submitted each year: NR
# of LD applications accepted yearly: NR
Total # of students receiving LD services: 450
Acceptance into program means acceptance into college: Student must be admitted and enrolled in the university first and then request services.

ADMISSIONS

All students must meet regular admission standards and submit the general application form. General admission criteria include 4 years English, 3–4 years math, 3–4 years science, 3–4 years social studies, 2 years foreign language; 25 ACT or 1100+ SAT Reasoning test; B average or 80 percent or 3.0 GPA. However, consideration will be given to standardized testing scores in light of the disability. Students with learning disabilities may request substitutions for high school math or foreign language if documentation can substantiate a disability in any one of these areas. Students should include current testing and documentation. Student can write an accompanying letter describing the learning disability and their goals and the services needed. Students' grades should show an upward trend. In the event that an applicant is denied admission to a specific course of study, an alternative offer may be suggested.

ADDITIONAL INFORMATION

Students with identified learning disabilities are provided with an integrated network of academic and counseling services to meet their individual needs. Services include note-takers, proofreaders, readers for exams and textbooks, tutors, counseling, and advising. Accommodations include time extensions for exams, papers, or projects; alternative testing methods; and spelling waivers. The Center for Academic Achievement provides each student with an accommodation letter to be used when the students meet with instructors to verify their LD status. To take advantage of these support services, diagnosed students must submit recent documentation of their learning disability. The Summer Institute Program is a six-week program designed to enrich academic experience and ensure a smooth transition from high school to college with academic advising, orientation, tutoring, and career planning and counseling. Services are offered to undergraduate and graduate students.

Support Services Contact Information

Learning Disability Program/Services: Learning Disability Services (LDS)
Director: Stephen Simon
  E-Mail: shsimon@syu.edu
  Telephone: 315-443-4498
  Fax: 315-443-1312

LEARNING DISABILITY SERVICES

Requests for the following/services accommodations will be evaluated individually based on appropriate and current documentation.

Allowed in exams
  Calculator: Yes
  Dictionary: Y/N
  Computer: Yes
  Spellchecker: Yes
Extended test time: Yes
Scribes: Yes
Proctors: Yes
Oral exams: Yes
Note-takers: Yes

Distraction reduced environment: Yes
Tape recording in class: Yes
Books on tape from RFBD: Yes
Taping of books not from RFBD: Yes
**Accommodations for students with
  ADD:** Yes
Reading machine: Yes
Other assistive technology: Yes
Priority registration: No

Added costs for services: Yes
LD specialists: Yes
Professional tutors: 0
Peer tutors: Yes
Max. hours/wk. for services: 18
**How professors are notified of
  LD/ADD:** By student

GENERAL ADMISSIONS INFORMATION

Director of Admissions: Susan E. Donovan
Telephone: 315-443-3611

ENTRANCE REQUIREMENTS

 Academic units required: 4 English, 3 math, 3 science (3 science lab), 2 foreign language, 3 social studies, 5 academic electives. **Academic units recommended:** 4 English, 3 math, 3 science (3 science lab), 3 foreign language, 3 social studies, 5 academic electives. High school diploma is required and GED is accepted. ACT with Writing component required or SAT Reasoning test. TOEFL required of all international applicants, minimum paper TOEFL 550, minimum computer TOEFL 213.

Application deadline: 1/1
Notification: Rolling
Average GPA: 3.60

Average SAT Math: NR
Average SAT Verbal: NR
Average ACT: NR

Graduated top 10% of class: 44%
Graduated top 25% of class: 80%
Graduated top 50% of class: 98%

COLLEGE GRADUATION REQUIREMENTS

Course waivers allowed: No
Course substitutions allowed: Yes
In what course: Students can petition for substitutions for math or foreign language. Substitutions must be approved by each college.

ADDITIONAL INFORMATION

Environment: The school is located on 200 acres set on a hill overlooking the city of Syracuse.

Student Body:
  Undergrad enrollment: 10,750
  Women: 56%
  Men: 44%
  Percent out-of-state: 55%

Cost Information
  Tuition: $25,720
  Room & board: $9,970
Housing Information
  University housing: Yes
  Percent living on campus: 73%

Greek System
  Fraternity: Yes
  Sorority: Yes
Athletics: NCAA Division I

UTICA COLLEGE

1600 Burrstone Road, Utica, NY 13502-4892
Phone: 315-792-3006 • Fax: 315-792-3003
E-mail: admiss@utica.edu • Web: www.utica.edu
Support: CS • Institution type: 4-year private

LEARNING DISABILITY PROGRAM AND SERVICES

Utica College is dedicated to ensuring reasonable access to programs and continuously seeks to augment and improve their services. The Academic Support Services Center provides counseling and academic support to an increasing number of students who identify themselves as LD. Accommodations are determined as a result of a diagnostic evaluation. Students are responsible for initiating a request for accommodations, for verification of a disability, and for contacting the support office as early as possible upon admission. The coordinator of student services determines eligibility for services based on documentation, consults with students about appropriate accommodations, assists students in self-monitoring the effectiveness of the accommodations, coordinates auxiliary services, reviews disability documentation and development of a needs assessment, provides information regarding legal rights and responsibilities of students, provides personal and educational counseling, and serves as an advocate.

LD/ADD ADMISSIONS INFORMATION

College entrance tests required: NR
Interview required: No-Recommended
Essay required: Yes
Documentation required for LD: A written evaluation, including a discrepancy analysis, completed by a professional (i.e. medical doctor, licensed/certified psychologist, or other qualified diagnostician)
Documentation required for ADD: Yes
Submitted to: Academic Support Services and Admissions
Special Ed. HS coursework accepted: No

Specific course requirements of all applicants: Yes
Separate application required for program services: No
# of LD applications submitted each year: NR
# of LD applications accepted yearly: NR
Total # of students receiving LD services: NR
Acceptance into program means acceptance into college: Student must be admitted and enrolled in the college first and then request services.

ADMISSIONS

Utica College does not require standardized tests. Students are evaluated on an individual basis. Students should have 4 years of English, 3 years of social studies, 3 years of math, 3 years of science, and 2 years of foreign language. Special education courses are not accepted. Students with LD are encouraged to request an interview. Documentation of a LD should be sent to admissions and to support services. Students are encouraged to self-disclose the LD during the admission process.

ADDITIONAL INFORMATION

Student Services provides accommodations to students with LD based on appropriate and current documentation. Current documentation includes a written evaluation, including a discrepancy analysis, completed by a licensed psychologist or certified learning disability specialist, indicating the specific learning disability and the academic accommodations needed. Services could include priority registration, specific skill remediation, learning and study strategy development, referrals for diagnostic evaluation, time management strategies, individual peer tutoring, and other appropriate accommodations. Other accommodations could include such items as use of a tape recorder, time extensions for tests and/or alternative testing methods, note-takers, scribes, readers, tutors, and use of a proofreader to correct spelling on assignments outside of class. A disabilities form is provided stating what accommodations are appropriate in each individual case. It is the student's responsibility to notify instructors of the disability.

Support Services Contact Information

Learning Disability Program/Services: Learning Services/Academic Support Services Center
Director: Stephen Pattarini
  E-Mail: spattarini@utica.edu
  Telephone: 315-792-3032
  Fax: 315-223-2504
Contact Person: Kateri Teresa Henkel, Coordinator of Learning Services
  E-Mail: khenkel@utica.edu
  Telephone: 315-792-3032
  Fax: 315-223-2504

LEARNING DISABILITY SERVICES

Requests for the following/services accommodations will be evaluated individually based on appropriate and current documentation.

Allowed in exams
  Calculator: Yes
  Dictionary: Yes
  Computer: Yes
  Spellchecker: Yes
Extended test time: Yes
Scribes: No
Proctors: No
Oral exams: Yes
Note-takers: Yes

Distraction reduced environment: Yes
Tape recording in class: Yes
Books on tape from RFBD: No
Taping of books not from RFBD: Yes
Accommodations for students with
  ADD: Yes
Reading machine: No
Other assistive technology: Yes
Priority registration: Yes

Added costs for services: No
LD specialists: Yes
Professional tutors: 2
Peer tutors: Yes
Max. hours/wk. for services: Yes
How professors are notified of
  LD/ADD: By student

GENERAL ADMISSIONS INFORMATION

Director of Admissions: Patrick Quinn
Telephone: 315-792-3006

ENTRANCE REQUIREMENTS
Academic units required: 4 English, 3 math, 3 science, 2 foreign language, 3 social studies, 1 academic elective. High school diploma is required and GED is accepted. ACT with Writing component required. TOEFL required of all international applicants, minimum paper TOEFL 525, minimum computer TOEFL 195.

Application deadline: Open
Notification: Rolling
Average GPA: 3.2

Average SAT Math: 490
Average SAT Verbal: 483
Average ACT: 20

Graduated top 10% of class: 9%
Graduated top 25% of class: 29%
Graduated top 50% of class: 63%

COLLEGE GRADUATION REQUIREMENTS

Course waivers allowed: N/A
Course substitutions allowed: Yes
In what course: Foreign language substitutions are determined individually based on documentation, and only if the course is not an essential component of the major.

ADDITIONAL INFORMATION

Environment: The school has a suburban campus located 50 miles east of Syracuse

Student Body:
  Undergrad enrollment: 2,171
  Women: 57%
  Men: 43%
  Percent out-of-state: 11%

Cost Information
  Tuition: $20,980
  Room & board: $8,800
Housing Information
  University housing: Yes
  Percent living on campus: 48%

Greek System
  Fraternity: Yes
  Sorority: Yes
Athletics: NCAA Division III

APPALACHIAN STATE UNIVERSITY

Office of Admissions, PO Box 32004, Boone, NC 28608-2004
Phone: 828-262-2120 • Fax: 828-262-3296
E-mail: admissions@appstate.edu • Web: www.appstate.edu
Support: CS • Institution type: 4-year public

LEARNING DISABILITY PROGRAM AND SERVICES

The university Learning Disability Program is part of a larger academic support service called the Learning Assistance Program. The LD Program is designed to provide academic services for students who self-identify on a voluntary basis and attend regular classes. Students with learning disabilities are totally integrated throughout the university community. Students are expected to communicate with their instructors regarding their specific needs. The coordinator of services works with students and faculty to implement needed services and accommodations. The needs of each student are considered and treated individually in consultation with the student and are based on current documentation of the learning disability.

LD/ADD ADMISSIONS INFORMATION

College entrance tests required: Yes
Interview required: No
Essay required: No
Documentation required for LD: Psychoeducational
  evaluation
Documentation required for ADD: Yes
Submitted to: Office of Disability Services
Special Ed. HS coursework accepted: No

Specific course requirements of all applicants: Yes
Separate application required for program services: No
# of LD applications submitted each year: NR
# of LD applications accepted yearly: NR
Total # of students receiving LD services: 200-plus
Acceptance into program means acceptance into college: Students must be accepted and enrolled at the university first and then must identify and provide documentation to be eligible for assistance.

ADMISSIONS

Students with learning disabilities are admitted to the university through the regular admission procedure. The minimum admissions requirements include 4 years English, 3 years math, 3 years science (1 in biology and 1 in a physical science), 2 years social science, and recommended 2 years foreign language, including 1 course in math and foreign language in senior year. Applicants may self-disclose on their applications. This information would support their application for admission. Personal statement, letters of recommendations and school activities provide additional useful information. Once students have been accepted by the university, a form is provided in which the students can identify their disabilities. This identification process is necessary for the students to have access to the services of the LD Program. Students not regularly admissible may request a review of their application with additional or updated information.

ADDITIONAL INFORMATION

Tutoring is provided on a one-to-one basis for assistance with course content, as well as guidance in developing or improving learning skills. Tutors are trained in working with each student. Basic skills courses are available in memory skills, oral presentation, note taking strategies, reading textbooks, written language, math, time management, and study strategies. Skills courses for no credit are offered in English and math. Services and accommodations are available for undergraduates and graduates.

Support Services Contact Information

Learning Disability Program/Services: Office of Disability Services
Director: Suzanne T. Wehner
  E-Mail: wehnerst@appstate.edu
  Telephone: 828-262-2291
  Fax: 828-262-6834

LEARNING DISABILITY SERVICES

Requests for the following/services accommodations will be evaluated individually based on appropriate and current documentation.

Allowed in exams
  Calculator: Y/N
  Dictionary: Y/N
  Computer: Y/N
  Spellchecker: Y/N
Extended test time: Yes
Scribes: Yes
Proctors: Yes
Oral exams: Yes
Note-takers: Yes

Distraction reduced environment: Yes
Tape recording in class: Yes
Books on tape from RFBD: Yes
Taping of books not from RFBD: No
Accommodations for students with ADD: Yes
Reading machine: Yes
Other assistive technology: Yes
Priority registration: Yes

Added costs for services: No
LD specialists: Yes
Professional tutors: Yes
Peer tutors: Yes
Max. hours/wk. for services: Unlimited
How professors are notified of LD/ADD: By both student and director

GENERAL ADMISSIONS INFORMATION

Director of Admissions: Ms. Cindy Wallace, Acting Vice Chancellor for Enrollment
Telephone: 828-262-2120

ENTRANCE REQUIREMENTS

Academic units required: 4 English, 3 math, 3 science (1 science lab), 1 social studies, 1 history. **Academic units recommended:** 2 foreign language. High school diploma is required and GED is accepted. ACT with Writing component required. TOEFL required of all international applicants, minimum paper TOEFL 500, minimum computer TOEFL 173.

Application deadline: Rolling
Notification: Rolling
Average GPA: 3.65

Average SAT Math: 553
Average SAT Verbal: 548
Average ACT: 22

Graduated top 10% of class: 17%
Graduated top 25% of class: 52%
Graduated top 50% of class: 91%

COLLEGE GRADUATION REQUIREMENTS

Course waivers allowed: No
Course substitutions allowed: No
In what course: N/A

ADDITIONAL INFORMATION

Environment: The university has a 255-acre campus in a small town 90 miles northwest of Winston-Salem.

Student Body:
  Undergrad enrollment: 12,556
  Women: 50%
  Men: 50%
  Percent out-of-state: 11%

Cost Information
  In-state tuition: $1,820
  Out-of-state tuition: $11,260
  Room & board: $4,600
Housing Information
  University housing: Yes
  Percent living on campus: 38%

Greek System
  Fraternity: Yes
  Sorority: Yes
  Athletics: NCAA Division I

BREVARD COLLEGE

400 North Broad Street, Brevard, NC 28712
Phone: 828-884-8300 • Fax: 828-884-3790
E-mail: admissions@brevard.edu • Web: www.brevard.edu
Support: CS • Institution type: 4-year private

LEARNING DISABILITY PROGRAM AND SERVICES

Brevard College does not offer a special program or curriculum for students with learning disabilities. However, students with a documented learning disability or other disability can receive assistance from the Office for Students with Special Needs and Disabilities as they work toward their learning goals. The college has an excellent learning disabilities support service, as well as the Learning Enhancement Center where any student can receive such services as counseling on academic matters, tutoring in a specific subject, advice on organizing work and/or managing time, assistance with reading skills, study skills, test taking skills, and private note taking. Through private meetings with the director, students can review their documentation and identify academic accommodations, which are adjustments to course policies. The director of the Office for Students with Special Needs and Disabilities works with students to determine what accommodations would be good to use in a particular course, and what the student must do in order to obtain these accommodations. The director can also assist students with talking to their professors about the learning disability and accommodations.

LD/ADD ADMISSIONS INFORMATION

College entrance tests required: Yes
Interview required: No
Essay required: No
Documentation required for LD: A recent psychoeducational assessment
Documentation required for ADD: A recent psychoeducational assessment or a statement from the doctor currently treating the condition.
Submitted to: Office for Students with special needs

Specific course requirements of all applicants: Yes
Special Ed. HS coursework accepted: Yes
Separate application required for program services: No
# of LD applications submitted each year: NR
# of LD applications accepted yearly: NR
Total # of students receiving LD services: 63
Acceptance into program means acceptance into college: Student must be admitted and enrolled in the university first and then request services.

ADMISSIONS

There is no special admission process for students with learning disabilities. However, every applicant is unique and this is why Brevard College asks for quite a bit of information from applicants and from those who know the applicants and their learning style. If applicants are aware of a learning disability they are encouraged to provide as much information as possible, for example, counseling testing and reports, recommendations, and assessments. Applicants must provide official transcripts, letters of recommendation from college counselor or dean, a teacher of English, and one other teacher or adult who has worked with the student and knows the student well. An official SAT or ACT score is required. However, there is no cut-off point on these tests relative to admission. Brevard looks for strong verbal ability as represented in an applicant's writing sample(s) submitted with the application. Again, this is why Brevard feels speaking with an applicant is important. This gives the college a chance to know what the student struggles with, what the student feels confident about, what the student wants to achieve. The admission process changes only when the student does not meet the general admissions requirements and wants special consideration due to a disability. Students should enclose with their application (1) a statement that says he/she has a disability; (2) which admission requirements the student feels the disability impacts and how; (3) what alternative or additional info the student wants considered; (4) documentation of the disability. Special Admissions is available for students who are non-degree candidates. Special Admissions procedures require an on-campus interview.

ADDITIONAL INFORMATION

Brevard College has a variety of other achievement resources. Students have access to the Career Counseling Center, the Math Lab, and the Writing Center. The Learning Enhancement Center provides individualized and personalized assistance via such academic services such as academic counseling; course schedule advisement; tutor referrals; guidance with time management, project organization, study skills, textbook reading skills, concentration development, test anxiety reduction, and test taking skills; note-taking; limited textbook taping services, and distraction-reduced test sites. Brevard College also provides developmental courses in math, computers, and reading for students in need of a better academic foundation. Students placed in a developmental course will need to complete it successfully before certain college-level courses can be taken.

Support Services Contact Information

Learning Disability Program/Services: Office for Students with Special Needs and Disabilities
Director: Susan Kuehn
  E-Mail: skuehn@brevard.edu
  Telephone: 828-884-8131
  Fax: 828-884-8293

LEARNING DISABILITY SERVICES

Requests for the following/services accommodations will be evaluated individually based on appropriate and current documentation.

Allowed in exams
  Calculator: Yes
  Dictionary: Yes
  Computer: Yes
  Spellchecker: Yes
Extended test time: Yes
Scribes: Yes
Proctors: Yes
Oral exams: No
Note-takers: Yes

Distraction reduced environment: Yes
Tape recording in class: Yes
Books on tape from RFBD: Yes
Taping of books not from RFBD: Yes
Accommodations for students with ADD: Yes
Reading machine: Yes
Other assistive technology: Yes
Priority registration: Yes

Added costs for services: No
LD specialists: Yes
Professional tutors: 10–15
Peer tutors: 5–10
Max. hours/wk. for services: Unlimited
How professors are notified of LD/ADD: By student

GENERAL ADMISSIONS INFORMATION

Director of Admissions: Joretta Nelson
Telephone: 828-884-8313

ENTRANCE REQUIREMENTS

Academic units recommended: 4 English, 3 math, 3 science (1 science lab), 2 foreign language, 4 social studies, 1 history, 4 academic electives. High school diploma is required and GED is accepted. ACT with or without Writing component accepted. TOEFL required of all international applicants, minimum paper TOEFL 500, minimum computer TOEFL 203.

Application deadline: Rolling
Notification: Rolling
Average GPA: 3.03

Average SAT Math: 494
Average SAT Verbal: 514
Average ACT: 20

Graduated top 10% of class: 7%
Graduated top 25% of class: 23%
Graduated top 50% of class: 47%

COLLEGE GRADUATION REQUIREMENTS

Course waivers allowed: No
Course substitutions allowed: Yes
In what course: Math, foreign language, physical education

ADDITIONAL INFORMATION

Environment: Brevard College is a residential campus located in a small town 33 miles from Ashville, NC.

Student Body:
  Undergrad enrollment: 571
  Women: 46%
  Men: 54%
  Percent out-of-state: 51%

Cost Information
  Tuition: $14,450
  Room & board: $5,560
Housing Information
  University housing: Yes
  Percent living on campus: 70%

Greek System
  Fraternity: No
  Sorority: No
Athletics: NAIA

DAVIDSON COLLEGE

PO Box 7156, Davidson, NC 28035-5000
Phone: 704-894-2230 • Fax: 704-894-2016
E-mail: admission@davidson.edu • Web: www.davidson.edu
Support: CS • Institution type: 4-year private

LEARNING DISABILITY PROGRAM AND SERVICES

Students enroll in Davidson with a proven record of academic achievement and proven ability to utilize resources, perseverance and creativity to excel. The college provides services and accommodations to allow students an opportunity to continue to be successful. All students seeking accommodations on the basis of a LD must provide recent documentation. The evaluation should include recommendations for compensatory learning strategies used by the student and recommendations for accommodations and services to be provided by the college. The dean of students, with the student's permission, will notify professors of an individual student's need for adaptations. Accommodations are not universal in nature, but are designed to meet the specific need of the individual to offset a specific disability.

LD/ADD ADMISSIONS INFORMATION

College entrance tests required: Yes
Interview required: No
Essay required: Yes
Documentation required for LD: Psychoeducational evaluation
Documentation required for ADD: Yes
Submitted to: Dean of Students
Special Ed. HS coursework accepted: No

Specific course requirements of all applicants: Yes
Separate application required for program services: No
# of LD applications submitted each year: NR
# of LD applications accepted yearly: NR
Total # of students receiving LD services: 54
Acceptance into program means acceptance into college: Student must be admitted and enrolled in the college first and then request services.

ADMISSIONS

There is no special admission process for students with LD, although the Admissions office may seek comments from support staff knowledgeable about LD. Students are encouraged to self-disclose ADD. The admissions process is very competitive and the disclosure can help the admissions office more fairly evaluate the transcript. This disclosure could address any specific academic issues related to the LD such as no foreign language in high school because of the specific LD, or lower grades in math as a result of a math disability. The GPA is recalculated to reflect rigor with 97 percent of the accepted students having a recalculated GPA of 3.0. Students have completed at least 4 years of English, 3 years of math, 2 years of the same foreign language, 2 years of science and 2 years of history/social studies. Courses taken in special education are not accepted. The mid 50 percent of students have an ACT between 28-31 or SAT between 1240–1420. Interviews are not required but are recommended. Essays and recommendations are required.

ADDITIONAL INFORMATION

Support services and accommodations available include, but are not limited to referrals for appropriate diagnostic evaluation; individual coaching and instruction in compensatory strategies and study skills; consultation with faculty and staff; student support groups as requested; classroom accommodations such as extra test-taking time, taped texts, note-takers, use of tape recorder, use of computers with spell checkers, and individual space for study or test-taking; reduced course load; and course substitutions or waivers (rarely). There is a Math Center, Writing Lab, peer tutoring, and skill class in time management for all students. There are 1.5 LD specialists on staff and peer tutoring for all students as needed.

Support Services Contact Information

Learning Disability Program/Services: Dean of Students Office
Director: Associate Dean of Students Kathy Bray Merrell
  E-Mail: kamerrel@davidson.edu
  Telephone: 704-894-2225
  Fax: 704-894-2849

LEARNING DISABILITY SERVICES

Requests for the following/services accommodations will be evaluated individually based on appropriate and current documentation.

Allowed in exams
  Calculator: Yes
  Dictionary: Yes
  Computer: Yes
  Spellchecker: Yes
Extended test time: Yes
Scribes: Yes
Proctors: Yes
Oral exams: No
Note-takers: Yes

Distraction reduced environment: Yes
Tape recording in class: Yes
Books on tape from RFBD: Yes
Taping of books not from RFBD: No
Accommodations for students with ADD: Yes
Reading machine: No
Other assistive technology: No
Priority registration: No

Added costs for services: No
LD specialists: Yes
Professional tutors: No
Peer tutors: 100
Max. hours/wk. for services: Unlimited
How professors are notified of LD/ADD: By both student and director

GENERAL ADMISSIONS INFORMATION

Director of Admissions: Dr. Nancy Cable
Telephone: 704-894-2230

ENTRANCE REQUIREMENTS

Academic units required: 4 English, 3 math, 2 science, 1 foreign language, 2 social studies and history.
Academic units recommended: 4 math, 4 science, 4 foreign language, 4 social studies and hstory. High school diploma is required and GED is not accepted. ACT with or without Writing component accepted. TOEFL required of all international applicants, minimum paper TOEFL 600, minimum computer TOEFL 250.

Application deadline: 1/2
Notification: 4/1
Average GPA: 3.9

Average SAT Math: 656
Average SAT Verbal: 659
Average ACT: 28

Graduated top 10% of class: 71%
Graduated top 25% of class: 94%
Graduated top 50% of class: 100%

COLLEGE GRADUATION REQUIREMENTS

Course waivers allowed: No
Course substitutions allowed: Yes
In what course: Substitutions, yes waivers no in any appropriate course.

ADDITIONAL INFORMATION

Environment: Located 20 miles from Charlotte, NC.

Student Body:
  Undergrad enrollment: 1,702
  Women: 50%
  Men: 50%
  Percent out-of-state: 81%

Cost Information
  Tuition: $28,667
  Room & board: $8,158
Housing Information
  University housing: Yes
  Percent living on campus: 91%

Greek System
  Fraternity: Yes
  Sorority: No
Athletics: NCAA Division I

DUKE UNIVERSITY

2138 Campus Drive, Durham, NC 27708
Phone: 919-684-3214 • Fax: 919-681-8941
E-mail: undergrad-admissions@duke.edu • Web: www.duke.edu
Support: CS • Institution type: 4-year private

LEARNING DISABILITY PROGRAM AND SERVICES

Duke University does not provide a formal, highly structured program for students with LD. The university does provide, however, significant academic support services for students through the Academic Resource Center (ARC). Students who submit appropriate documentation of their learning disability to the ARC clinical director are eligible for assistance in obtaining reasonable academic adjustments and auxiliary aids. In addition, the ASC clinical director and instructors can provide individualized instruction in academic skills and learning strategies, academic support counseling, and referrals for other services. Students with learning disabilities voluntarily access and use the services of the ARC, just as they might access and use other campus resources. Student interactions with the ASC staff are confidential. The goals of the support services for students with learning disabilities are in keeping with the goals of all services provided through the ARC: to help students achieve their academic potential within the context of a competitive university setting; to promote a disciplined approach to study; and to foster active, independent learners.

LD/ADD ADMISSIONS INFORMATION

College entrance tests required: Yes
Interview required: No
Essay required: Yes
Documentation required for LD: Current psychoeducational testing: within 3 years
Documentation required for ADD: Yes
Submitted to: Student Disabilities Office
Special Ed. HS coursework accepted: No

Specific course requirements of all applicants: Yes
Separate application required for program services: No
# of LD applications submitted each year: NR
# of LD applications accepted yearly: NR
Total # of students receiving LD services: NR
Acceptance into program means acceptance into college: Student must be admitted and enrolled in the university first and then request services.

ADMISSIONS

There is no special admission process for students with learning disabilities. All applicants must meet the general Duke admissions criteria. Admission to Duke is highly competitive and most applicants are in the top 10 percent of their class. Most applicants have completed a demanding curriculum in high school including many Advanced Placement and Honors courses. Services and accommodations may be requested after enrollment in Duke.

ADDITIONAL INFORMATION

Assistance is available as needed from the student's academic dean and the clinical director of ARC. Students are encouraged to consult with their faculty advisor and the ARC, well in advance of registration, to determine the appropriate measures for particular courses. There is one staff member with special learning disability training, and three staff members who are writing/learning strategy instructors. Documentation and diagnostic tests are required for accommodations, not admissions. Students may also receive peer tutoring in introductory-level courses in several disciplines through the ARC Peer Tutoring Program. Up to 12 hours of tutoring in each course is offered at no additional charge. Students need to understand their LD, be able to self-advocate, and know what accommodations are necessary to assist them in being successful in college. Students are expected to work out reasonable accommodations with each of their professors. Outside testing referrals are made at the student's expense.

Support Services Contact Information

Learning Disability Program/Services: Student Disability Access Office
Director: Emma Swain
  E-Mail: eswain@duke.edu
  Telephone: 919-668-1267
  Fax: 919-668-3977
Contact Person: Jim Baker, Disability Specialist
  E-Mail: jbaker@duke.edu
  Telephone: 919-668-1267
  Fax: 919-668-3977

LEARNING DISABILITY SERVICES

Requests for the following/services accommodations will be evaluated individually based on appropriate and current documentation.

Allowed in exams
  Calculator: No
  Dictionary: Yes
  Computer: Yes
  Spellchecker: Yes
Extended test time: Yes
Scribes: Yes
Proctors: Yes
Oral exams: No
Note-takers: Yes

Distraction reduced environment: Yes
Tape recording in class: Yes
Books on tape from RFBD: Yes
Taping of books not from RFBD: Yes
Accommodations for students with
  ADD: Yes
Reading machine: Yes
Other assistive technology: Yes
Priority registration: No

Added costs for services: No
LD specialists: Yes
Professional tutors: Yes
Peer tutors: 80
Max. hours/wk. for services:
  Unlimited
How professors are notified of
  LD/ADD: By both student and director

GENERAL ADMISSIONS INFORMATION

Director of Admissions: Christoph Guttentag
Telephone: 919-684-3214

ENTRANCE REQUIREMENTS
Academic units recommended: 4 English, 3 math, 3 science, 3 foreign language, 3 social studies. High school diploma is required and GED is not accepted. ACT with writing or SAT Reasoning test and SAT Subject Tests. TOEFL required of all international applicants, minimum paper TOEFL 550, minimum computer TOEFL 213.

Application deadline: 1/2
Notification: 4/1
Average GPA: NR

Average SAT Math: NR
Average SAT Verbal: NR
Average ACT: 30

Graduated top 10% of class: 90%
Graduated top 25% of class: 98%
Graduated top 50% of class: 100%

COLLEGE GRADUATION REQUIREMENTS

Course waivers allowed: No
Course substitutions allowed: No
In what course: N/A

ADDITIONAL INFORMATION

Environment: The university is on 8,500 acres in a suburban area 285 miles southwest of Washington, DC.

Student Body:
  Undergrad enrollment: 6,066
  Women: 48%
  Men: 52%
  Percent out-of-state: 85%

Cost Information
  Tuition: $28,475
  Room & board: $8,205
Housing Information
  University housing: Yes
  Percent living on campus: 82%

Greek System
  Fraternity: Yes
  Sorority: Yes
Athletics: NCAA Division I

EAST CAROLINA UNIVERSITY

106 Whichard Building,
Greenville, NC 27858-4353 • Phone: 252-328-6640 • Fax: 252-328-6945
E-mail: admis@mail.ecu.edu • Web: www.ecu.edu
Support: CS • Institution type: 4-year public

LEARNING DISABILITY PROGRAM AND SERVICES

Through the Department for Disability Support Services, the university seeks to meet individual needs by coordinating and implementing internal policy regarding programs, services, and activities for individuals with disabilities. The department functions as a source of information and advice and as a communication link among individuals with disabilities, faculty and staff members, state rehab agencies, and the community at large. The overall purpose of the university's program for students with learning disabilities is to provide auxiliary support services, so they may derive equal benefits from all that East Carolina University has to offer. Individuals with learning disabilities and attention deficit disorder are required to provide the department with proper documentation of their disability. An acceptable psychoeducational evaluation administered within the past 3 years must be submitted to qualify for services. Students should schedule a meeting with the department well in advance of the beginning of their first semester to prevent delays in the planning of services. Students with LD or ADD will receive a letter describing the services required to give to their instructors. With the exception of tutorial services for personal use, academic support services are provided at no cost.

LD/ADD ADMISSIONS INFORMATION

College entrance tests required: Yes

Interview required: No
Essay required: No
Documentation required for LD: Current psychoeducational battery.
Documentation required for ADD: Diagnostic summary from qualified clinician
Submitted to: Disbility Support Services
Special Ed. HS coursework accepted: Yes

Specific course requirements of all applicants: Yes
Separate application required for program services: No
# of LD applications submitted each year: NR
# of LD applications accepted yearly: NR
Total # of students receiving LD services: 100–150
Acceptance into program means acceptance into college: Student must be admitted and enrolled in the university first and then request services.

ADMISSIONS

A student with a disability applies for admission and is considered for admission in the same manner as any other applicant. Neither the nature nor the severity of one's disability is used as a criterion for admission. Students with learning disabilities are admitted solely on academic qualifications. Out-of-state students must present slightly higher GPAs and test scores, but the minimum is 2.0 depending on the SAT score. Test scores vary but the minimum out-of-state ACT is 19, in-state is 17, and the average ACT is 21.The minimum SAT out-of-state is 1000 and in-state is 900 and the average SATs 1030. Students must have taken 4 years English, 2 years social science, 3 years science (1 year biology, 1 year physical science); 3 years math and 2 years foreign language is recommended.

ADDITIONAL INFORMATION

Once admitted to the university, students must self-identify and register with the Department for Disability Support Services. Students must show official verification of their disability. Students will be assigned to academic advisors from the department. Once students enter their major fields of study, the department will still be available to provide advising assistance but never to the exclusion of the individual's assigned academic advisor. Alternative testing accommodations may include extended time, a noise-free environment, reader-assisted test-taking, and other arrangements that satisfy the needs of the student. A maximum of double time can be allowed for students to complete a test or an exam. The university offers a modified language sequence for students enrolled in Spanish. There are several laboratories available, including the Writing Center, Reading Center, Mathematics Center, the Academic Support Center, and Computer Lab. Students pay for private tutoring. Skills classes for any student are available in time management, test taking/anxiety study strategies, and academic motivation.

Support Services Contact Information

Learning Disability Program/Services: Department for Disability Support Services
Director: Liz Johnston
  E-Mail: johnstone@mail.ecu.edu
  Telephone: 252-328-6799
  Fax: 252-328-4883
Contact Person: Diane Majewski
  E-Mail: majewskid@mail.ecu.edu
  Telephone: 252-328-6799
  Fax: 252-328-4883

LEARNING DISABILITY SERVICES

Requests for the following/services accommodations will be evaluated individually based on appropriate and current documentation.

Allowed in exams
  Calculator: Yes
  Dictionary: Yes
  Computer: Yes
  Spellchecker: Yes
Extended test time: Yes
Scribes: Yes
Proctors: Yes
Oral exams: Yes
Note-takers: Yes

Distraction reduced environment: Yes
Tape recording in class: Yes
Books on tape from RFBD: Yes
Taping of books not from RFBD: Yes
Accommodations for students with ADD: Yes
Reading machine: Yes
Other assistive technology: Yes
Priority registration: Yes

Added costs for services: No
LD specialists: Yes
Professional tutors: No
Peer tutors: 2
Max. hours/wk. for services: Unlimited
How professors are notified of LD/ADD: By student

GENERAL ADMISSIONS INFORMATION

Director of Admissions: Thomas E. Powell
Telephone: 252-328-6640

ENTRANCE REQUIREMENTS

Academic units required: 4 English, 3 math, 3 science (1 science lab), 2 foreign language, 2 social studies.
Academic units recommended: 1 unit fine arts, 1 unit of social studies (must be U.S. history). High school diploma is required and GED is accepted. TOEFL required of all international applicants, minimum paper TOEFL 550, minimum computer TOEFL 213.

Application deadline: 3/15
Notification: Rolling
Average GPA: 3.39

Average SAT Math: 530
Average SAT Verbal: 518
Average ACT: 20

Graduated top 10% of class: 15%
Graduated top 25% of class: 40%
Graduated top 50% of class: 83%

COLLEGE GRADUATION REQUIREMENTS

Course waivers allowed: No
Course substitutions allowed: No
In what course: N/A

ADDITIONAL INFORMATION

Environment: The school is located on over 370 acres within the city of Greenville, 85 miles from Raleigh.

Student Body:
  Undergrad enrollment: 17,406
  Women: 60%
  Men: 40%
  Percent out-of-state: 15%

Cost Information
  In-state tuition: $1,910
  Out-of-state tuition: $12,049
  Room & board: $5,540
Housing Information
  University housing: Yes
  Percent living on campus: 29%

Greek System
  Fraternity: Yes
  Sorority: Yes
Athletics: NCAA Division I

ELON UNIVERSITY

100 Campus Drive, Elon, NC 27244-2010
Phone: 336-278-3566 • Fax: 336-278-7699
E-mail: admissions@elon.edu • Web: www.elon.edu
Support: CS • Institution type: 4-year private

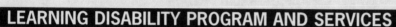

LEARNING DISABILITY PROGRAM AND SERVICES

Elon University is committed to the principle of equal opportunity. We assist students with disabilities in finding approaches and accommodations that provide them an opportunity to benefit from the many programs offered on campus. Faculty, staff, administrators and students work together to find approaches and accommodations that enable students to benefit from the wide variety of programs and activities on campus.

LD/ADD ADMISSIONS INFORMATION

College entrance tests required: Yes
Interview required: No
Essay required: Yes
Documentation required for LD: Psychoeducational evaluation
Documentation required for ADD: Yes
Submitted to: Disability Services

Specific course requirements of all applicants: Yes
Special Ed. HS coursework accepted: No
Separate application required for program services: No
# of LD applications submitted each year: NR
# of LD applications accepted yearly: NR
Total # of students receiving LD services: NR
Acceptance into program means acceptance into college: Students must be admitted and enrolled in the university and then may request services.

ADMISSIONS

Students with disabilities must meet the same admissions criteria as other students. There is no special disabilities admissions application. Minimum GPA is 2.4. Course requirements include 3 years Algebra, 4 years English, 2 years foreign language, 1 year history, and 1 year science. Students may be admitted with one deficiency.

ADDITIONAL INFORMATION

Though Elon does not have a formal disabilities program, we aim to make the campus, our academic programs, and activities accessible. Students must provide current documentation in order to request accommodations. Students with disabilities are encouraged to be proactive and to develop an on-going conversation with their professors and service providers. Elon has no foreign language requirement, though some majors do. Two years of foreign language are required for admission. However, if an admitted student has a deficiency in a foreign language because of a disability, a course substitution may be granted after reviewing documentation, demonstrating previous course failures in foreign language, and completing the Modern Language Aptitude Test with scores indicating a disability. Students with dyscalculia and a history of difficulty with math may be eligible for a math substitution. Alternative testing accommodations are available if appropriate. Students should make arrangements with professors. It is the student's responsibility to arrange for note-takers.

Support Services Contact Information

Learning Disability Program/Services: Disabilities Services
Director: Priscilla Lipe
  E-Mail: plipe@elon.edu
  Telephone: 336-278-6500
  Fax: 336-278-6514

LEARNING DISABILITY SERVICES

Requests for the following/services accommodations will be evaluated individually based on appropriate and current documentation.

Allowed in exams
  Calculator: Yes
  Dictionary: Yes
  Computer: Yes
  Spellchecker: Yes
Extended test time: Yes
Scribes: Yes
Proctors: Y/N
Oral exams: No
Note-takers: Yes

Distraction reduced environment: Yes
Tape recording in class: Yes
Books on tape from RFBD: Yes
Taping of books not from RFBD: No
Accommodations for students with
  ADD: Yes
Reading machine: Yes
Other assistive technology: No
Priority registration: Yes

Added costs for services: No
LD specialists: No
Professional tutors: No
Peer tutors: 25
Max. hours/wk. for services:
  Unlimited
How professors are notified of
  LD/ADD: By both student and director

GENERAL ADMISSIONS INFORMATION

Director of Admissions: Susan Klopman
Telephone: 336-278-3566

ENTRANCE REQUIREMENTS

Academic units required: 4 English, 3 math, 3 science (1 science lab), 2 foreign language, 1 social studies, 1 history, 1 academic elective. **Academic units recommended:** 4 math, 3 foreign language. High school diploma is required and GED is accepted. ACT with Writing component required or SAT Reasoning test. TOEFL required of all international applicants, minimum paper TOEFL 550, minimum computer TOEFL 213.

Application deadline: 1/10
Notification: 12/1
Average GPA: 3.63

Average SAT Math: 588
Average SAT Verbal: 581
Average ACT: 26

Graduated top 10% of class: 25%
Graduated top 25% of class: 59%
Graduated top 50% of class: 91%

COLLEGE GRADUATION REQUIREMENTS

Course waivers allowed: No
Course substitutions allowed: Yes
In what course: Not generally, but on a case-by-case basis. Rarely in foreign language or math unless required in major.

ADDITIONAL INFORMATION

Environment: The campus is on a 575-acres campus located in the Piedmont Triad area of North Carolina.

Student Body:
  Undergrad enrollment: 4,622
  Women: 61%
  Men: 39%
  Percent out-of-state: 69%

Cost Information
  Tuition: $18,698
  Room & board: $6,772
Housing Information
  University housing: Yes
  Percent living on campus: 59%

Greek System
  Fraternity: Yes
  Sorority: Yes
Athletics: NCAA Division I

GUILFORD COLLEGE

5800 West Friendly Avenue, Greensboro, NC 27410
Phone: 336-316-2100 • Fax: 336-316-2954
E-mail: admission@guilford.edu • Web: www.guilford.edu
Support: S • Institution type: 4-year private

LEARNING DISABILITY PROGRAM AND SERVICES

The Academic Skills Center serves the learning needs of a diverse campus by providing professional and peer tutoring, workshops, advocacy, and realistic encouragement. The focus is on self-advocacy and the articulation of both strengths and weaknesses. Faculty tutors work one-on-one with students in time management, study skills, test-taking, reading, math, science, and Spanish. A large Student Tutoring Service offers course-specific tutoring. The tutoring service also provides editors for students who need help checking final drafts. The center sponsors workshops and seminars on subjects pertaining to academic success. Faculty allow the usual accommodations requested by students, including extra time, permission to use a computer for in-class work, testing in a less distracting environment, and audio taping classes.

LD/ADD ADMISSIONS INFORMATION

College entrance tests required: Yes
Interview required: No
Essay required: Yes
Documentation required for LD: Psychoeducational
  evaluation
Documentation required for ADD: Yes
Submitted to: Academic Skills Center
Special Ed. HS coursework accepted: Yes

Specific course requirements of all applicants: Yes
Separate application required for program services: No
# of LD applications submitted each year: NR
# of LD applications accepted yearly: NR
Total # of students receiving LD services: 300–350
**Acceptance into program means acceptance into
  college:** Student must be admitted and enrolled in the
  college first and then request services.

ADMISSIONS

Students with LD must meet the same criteria as other students. The general admission criteria include the mid 50 percent range for the ACT 20–28 and the SAT 1030–1270 and GPA 2.8–3.4. Typically admitted students have 4 years English, 3 years math, 3–4 years natural science, 3 years social studies, 2 years foreign language. With appropriate documentation students with LD can substitute some high school courses in areas that impact their ability to learn. The ASC director reviews files to make certain that the college can provide appropriate support services.

ADDITIONAL INFORMATION

Guilford is writing intensive. The writing program is revision-driven and utilizes peer-editing and response groups. The Academic Skills Center (ASC) offers individualized professional tutoring in writing as well as work with trained student writing tutors. The ASC offers other services including faculty tutors to work one-on-one with students in time management, study skills, test-taking, reading, math, science, and Spanish. A large Student Tutoring Service offers course-specific tutoring. The center also sponsors workshops and seminars on subjects pertaining to academic success. Students are encouraged to speak with professors early concerning particular needs. Guilford waives the foreign language requirement if students submit appropriate documentation and petition through ASC.

Support Services Contact Information

Learning Disability Program/Services: Academic Skills Center
Director: Sue Keith
  E-Mail: skeith@guilford.edu
  Telephone: 336-316-2200
  Fax: 336-316-2950
Contact Person: Kimberly Garner
  E-Mail: kgarner@guilford.edu
  Telephone: 336 316-2451
  Fax: 336-316-2950

LEARNING DISABILITY SERVICES

Requests for the following/services accommodations will be evaluated individually based on appropriate and current documentation.

Allowed in exams	**Distraction reduced environment:** Yes	**Added costs for services:** No
Calculator: Yes	**Tape recording in class:** Yes	**LD specialists:** No
Dictionary: Yes	**Books on tape from RFBD:** Yes	**Professional tutors:** 4–7
Computer: Yes	**Taping of books not from RFBD:** Yes	**Peer tutors:** Yes
Spellchecker: Yes	**Accommodations for students with**	**Max. hours/wk. for services:**
Extended test time: Yes	**ADD:** Yes	Unlimited
Scribes: Yes	**Reading machine:** Yes	**How professors are notified of**
Proctors: Yes	**Other assistive technology:** Yes	**LD/ADD:** By student
Oral exams: Yes	**Priority registration:** Yes	
Note-takers: Yes		

GENERAL ADMISSIONS INFORMATION

Director of Admissions: B. Randy Doss
Telephone: 336-316-2100

ENTRANCE REQUIREMENTS

Academic units required: 4 English, 3 math, 2 science, 2 foreign language, 2 social studies, 1 history, 2 academic electives. **Academic units recommended:** 4 English, 3 math, 3 science, 2 foreign language, 1 social studies, 1 history, 2 academic electives. High school diploma is required and GED is accepted. TOEFL required of all international applicants, minimum paper TOEFL 550, minimum computer TOEFL 213.

Application deadline: 2/15	**Average SAT Math:** 550	**Graduated top 10% of class:** 14%
Notification: 4/1	**Average SAT Verbal:** 570	**Graduated top 25% of class:** 37%
Average GPA: 2.95	**Average ACT:** 25	**Graduated top 50% of class:** 77%

COLLEGE GRADUATION REQUIREMENTS

Course waivers allowed: No
Course substitutions allowed: Yes
In what course: Foreign language

ADDITIONAL INFORMATION

Environment: The College is located on a suburban campus in a small city.

Student Body:	**Cost Information**	**Greek System**
Undergrad enrollment: 2,101	**Tuition:** $19,940	**Fraternity:** No
Women: 61%	**Room & board:** $6,330	**Sorority:** No
Men: 39%	**Housing Information**	**Athletics:** NCAA Division III
Percent out-of-state: 34%	**University housing:** Yes	
	Percent living on campus: 73%	

LENOIR-RHYNE COLLEGE

Admissions Office, LRC Box 7227, Hickory, NC 28603
Phone: 828-328-7300 • Fax: 828-328-7378
E-mail: admission@lrc.edu • Web: www.lrc.edu
Support: CS • Institution type: 4-year private

LEARNING DISABILITY PROGRAM AND SERVICES

The Lenoir-Rhyne College Disability Services Office strives to provide the highest quality service to each student with a disability through appropriate modification of college policies, practices and procedures. It is the mission of the office to ensure that every student with a disability has an equal chance to benefit from college programs. Furthermore, the office emphasizes personal independence and responsibility, on the part of the student, in the provision of services. The office will also serve as a campus and community resource for information about people with disabilities and the issues that affect them.

LD/ADD ADMISSIONS INFORMATION

College entrance tests required: Yes
Interview required: No
Essay required: No
Documentation required for LD: Full psychoeducational evaluation with I.Q. scores listed
Documentation required for ADD: Yes
Submitted to: Disability Services
Special Ed. HS coursework accepted: N/A

Specific course requirements of all applicants: Yes
Separate application required for program services: No
# of LD applications submitted each year: 25
# of LD applications accepted yearly: 20
Total # of students receiving LD services: 40–50
Acceptance into program means acceptance into college: Students not admitted are reviewed by the LD program, which provides a recommendation to admissions. Once admitted they may request services.

ADMISSIONS

There is no special admissions process for students with learning disabilities. All students are reviewed on an individual case-by-case basis. Basic admissions criteria include 2.0 GPA, top 50 percent class rank, 850 SAT or 17 ACT, 4 years English, 3 years math, 1 year history, 2 years foreign language (substitution allowed).

ADDITIONAL INFORMATION

The Advising and Academic Services Center offers a variety of services to help students achieve academic success through group peer tutoring, advising and assessment, and academic skills counseling. With appropriate documentation students with LD/ADD may be appropriate for some of the following services/accommodations: the use of calculators, dictionary, computer or spell-check in exams; extended time on tests; distraction-free environment; scribe; proctor; oral exams; note-taker; tape recorder in class; books on tape; and substitution of the foreign language requirement. Students placed on academic probation by the college are monitored in the center. Also, the center provides access to supplementary computerized learning materials such as Learning Plus for prospective educators and computerized test preps for standardized tests (such as the GMAT).

Support Services Contact Information

Learning Disability Program/Services: Disability Services
Director: Dr. Janette L. Sims
  E-Mail: simsj@lrc.edu
  Telephone: 828-328-7296
  Fax: 828-267-3441

LEARNING DISABILITY SERVICES

Requests for the following/services accommodations will be evaluated individually based on appropriate and current documentation.

Allowed in exams	**Distraction reduced environment:** Yes	**Added costs for services:** No
Calculator: Yes	**Tape recording in class:** Yes	**LD specialists:** Yes
Dictionary: Yes	**Books on tape from RFBD:** Yes	**Professional tutors:** No
Computer: Yes	**Taping of books not from RFBD:** No	**Peer tutors:** 20–25
Spellchecker: Yes	**Accommodations for students with**	**Max. hours/wk. for services:**
Extended test time: Yes	**ADD:** Yes	Unlimited
Scribes: Yes	**Reading machine:** Yes	**How professors are notified of**
Proctors: Yes	**Other assistive technology:** No	**LD/ADD:** By both student and director
Oral exams: Yes	**Priority registration:** No	
Note-takers: Yes		

GENERAL ADMISSIONS INFORMATION

Director of Admissions: Rachel Nichols
Telephone: 828-328-7300

ENTRANCE REQUIREMENTS

Academic units required: 4 English, 3 math, 1 science (1 science lab), 2 foreign language, 1 social studies, 1 history. High school diploma is required and GED is accepted. TOEFL required of all international applicants, minimum paper TOEFL 500, minimum computer TOEFL 173.

Application deadline: NR	**Average SAT Math:** 519	**Graduated top 10% of class:** 18%
Notification: Rolling	**Average SAT Verbal:** 517	**Graduated top 25% of class:** 50%
Average GPA: 3.47	**Average ACT:** 22	**Graduated top 50% of class:** 82%

COLLEGE GRADUATION REQUIREMENTS

Course waivers allowed: Rolling
Course substitutions allowed: Yes
In what course: Substitution of foreign language is available.

ADDITIONAL INFORMATION

Environment: The college is located in a small town north of Charlotte.

Student Body:	**Cost Information**	**Greek System**
Undergrad enrollment: 1,358	**Tuition:** $17,550	**Fraternity:** Yes
Women: 64%	**Room & board:** $6,300	**Sorority:** Yes
Men: 36%	**Housing Information**	**Athletics:** NCAA Division II
Percent out-of-state: 29%	**University housing:** Yes	
	Percent living on campus: 60%	

NORTH CAROLINA STATE UNIVERSITY

Box 7103, Raleigh, NC 27695
Phone: 919-515-2434 • Fax: 919-515-5039
E-mail: undergrad_admissions@ncsu.edu • Web: www.ncsu.edu
Support: CS • Institution type: 4-year public

LEARNING DISABILITY PROGRAM AND SERVICES

Services for students with learning disabilities are handled by the LD Coordinator through Disability Services for Students. The functions of the coordinator include identifying students with learning disabilities, helping to accommodate and interpret the needs of these students to the faculty, and providing services to students according to their individual needs. Support groups meet periodically to provide workshops, mutual support, and awareness of handicapped issues to the university community. The purpose of the services is to ensure that students with documented learning disabilities receive appropriate accommodations in order to equalize their opportunities while studying at NCSU.

LD/ADD ADMISSIONS INFORMATION

College entrance tests required: Yes
Interview required: No
Essay required: No
Documentation required for LD: Full Psychoeducational evaluation with IQ scores listed
Documentation required for ADD: Yes
Submitted to: Admissions and Disability Services
Special Ed. HS coursework accepted: Yes

Specific course requirements of all applicants: Yes
Separate application required for program services: No
# of LD applications submitted each year: NR
# of LD applications accepted yearly: NR
Total # of students receiving LD services: 260–300
Acceptance into program means acceptance into college: Students not admitted are reviewed by the LD program, which provides a recommendation to admissions. Once admitted they may request services.

ADMISSIONS

Admission to the university for students with learning disabilities is determined on the basis of academic qualifications, and they are considered in the same manner as any other applicant. There is no pre-admission question regarding a learning disability. A cover letter from applicants, stating that a learning disability exists, alerts the admission staff to consider that there may be unusual circumstances. Self-disclosure of the learning disability could explain the high school record, such as late diagnosis and onset of LD accommodations or difficulty in particular subjects. General admission criteria include ACT 23–29 or SAT 1100–1300; over 75 percent of the students have a 3.5 GPA; course requirements include 4 years English, 3 years math, 3 years social studies, 3 years science, and 2 years foreign language.

ADDITIONAL INFORMATION

All enrolled students may receive services and accommodations through the coordinator of learning disabilities of the DSS if they present appropriate documentation. The documentation should include a written report with a statement specifying areas of learning disabilities. Services and accommodations available with appropriate documentation include extended testing time for exams; distraction-free testing environments; calculator, dictionary, computer or spell-check in exams; proctors; scribes; note-takers; books on tape; assistive technology; and priority registration. If new needs are identified, services are modified or developed to accommodate them.

Support Services Contact Information

Learning Disability Program/Services: Disability Services for Students (DSS)
Director: Cheryl Branker, EdD
  E-Mail: cheryl_branker@ncsu.edu
  Telephone: 919-515-7653
  Fax: 919-513-2840

LEARNING DISABILITY SERVICES

Requests for the following/services accommodations will be evaluated individually based on appropriate and current documentation.

Allowed in exams
  Calculator: Yes
  Dictionary: Yes
  Computer: Yes
  Spellchecker: Yes
Extended test time: Yes
Scribes: Yes
Proctors: Yes
Oral exams: Yes
Note-takers: Yes

Distraction reduced environment: Yes
Tape recording in class: Yes
Books on tape from RFBD: Yes
Taping of books not from RFBD: Yes
Accommodations for students with
  ADD: Yes
Reading machine: Yes
Other assistive technology: Yes
Priority registration: Yes

Added costs for services: No
LD specialists: Yes
Professional tutors: No
Peer tutors: 20–25
Max. hours/wk. for services:
  Unlimited
How professors are notified of
  LD/ADD: By both student and director

GENERAL ADMISSIONS INFORMATION

Director of Admissions: Thomas H. Griffin
Telephone: 919-515-2434

ENTRANCE REQUIREMENTS

Academic units required: 4 English, 3 math, 3 science (1 science lab), 2 foreign language, 1 social studies, 1 history, 1 academic elective. **Academic units recommended:** 4 English, 4 math, 4 science (1 science lab), 2 foreign language, 1 social studies, 1 history, 4 academic electives. High school diploma is required and GED is not accepted. ACT with Writing component required or SAT Reasoning test. TOEFL required of all international applicants, minimum paper TOEFL 550, minimum computer TOEFL 213.

Application deadline: 2/1
Notification: Rolling
Average GPA: 3.09

Average SAT Math: 613
Average SAT Verbal: 580
Average ACT: 25

Graduated top 10% of class: 43%
Graduated top 25% of class: 83%
Graduated top 50% of class: 98%

COLLEGE GRADUATION REQUIREMENTS

Course waivers allowed: No
Course substitutions allowed: Yes
In what course: Students may apply to substitute courses to satisfy the foreign lanuage proficiency requirement.

ADDITIONAL INFORMATION

Environment: The university sits on 623 acres in the central part of the state and has an adjacent 900-acre research campus.

Student Body:
  Undergrad enrollment: 20,302
  Women: 42%
  Men: 58%
  Percent out-of-state: 7%

Cost Information
  In-state tuition: $3,505
  Out-of-state tuition: $15,403
  Room & board: $6,851
Housing Information
  University housing: Yes
  Percent living on campus: 33%

Greek System
  Fraternity: Yes
  Sorority: Yes
Athletics: NCAA Division I

North Carolina State University

ST. ANDREWS PRESBYTERIAN COLLEGE

1700 Dogwood Mile, Laurinburg, NC 28352
Phone: 910-277-5555 • Fax: 910-277-5087
E-mail: admissions@sapc.edu • Web: www.sapc.edu
Support: S • Institution type: 4-year private

LEARNING DISABILITY PROGRAM AND SERVICES

St. Andrews Presbyterian College acknowledges its responsibility, both legally and educationally, to serve students with learning disabilities by providing reasonable accommodations. These services do not guarantee success, but endeavor to assist students in pursuing a quality post-secondary education. Disability and Academic Support Services provides a full range of learning disability support services. The services are meant to help students devise strategies for meeting college demands and to foster independence, responsibility, and self-advocacy. Disability and Academic Support Services is committed to ensuring that all information regarding a student is maintained as confidential.

LD/ADD ADMISSIONS INFORMATION

College entrance tests required: Yes
Interview required: No
Essay required: Yes
Documentation required for LD: Achievement and ability tests for adults
Documentation required for ADD: Achievement and ability for adults, and a DSM–IV diagnosis
Submitted to: Disability Services
Special Ed. HS coursework accepted: Yes

Specific course requirements of all applicants: Yes
Separate application required for program services: Yes
# of LD applications submitted each year: NR
# of LD applications accepted yearly: NR
Total # of students receiving LD services: 45
Acceptance into program means acceptance into college: Student must be admitted and enrolled in the college first and then request services.

ADMISSIONS

Each application is reviewed on an individual basis. Factors considered are SAT minimum of 700 or ACT minimum of 17; high school profile and courses attempted, as well as a minimum GPA of 2.0; essay and counselor and/or teacher recommendations are optional but strongly recommended. Courses recommended include 4 years English, 3 years math, 3 years science, 1 year social studies, 1 year history and 2 years foreign language. Prospective students are strongly encouraged to visit the campus. Students with learning disabilities complete the regular admissions application. Students with a diagnosis of attention deficit disorder are required to show achievement and ability testing (adult version), and that validates the DSM–IV diagnosis. Complete documentation guidelines available upon request. All students must meet the same admissions criteria. In order for the admissions committee to make the most informed decision, students are encouraged to self-disclose the existence of a learning disability in their personal statement. Any other personal information indicating the student's ability to succeed in college should also be included with the application. All documentation of a specific learning disability should be sent separately.

ADDITIONAL INFORMATION

All accommodations are based on the submitted, current documentation. Each case is reviewed individually. Disability Services reserves the right to determine eligibility for services based on the quality of the submitted documentation. The services and accommodations include note taking, extended time on tests, alternative test formats, separate location for tests, books on tape through Recordings for the Blind and Dyslexic or from readers, and content tutoring through individual departments. Franklin Language Masters and audiocassette equipment are available for loan. All computers in computer labs are equipped with spell-check. A Learning Resource Center is planned to open in the near future.

Support Services Contact Information

Learning Disability Program/Services: Disability Services
Director: Dorothy Wells
  E-Mail: ods@sapc.edu
  Telephone: 910-277-5331
  Fax: 910-277-5746

LEARNING DISABILITY SERVICES

Requests for the following/services accommodations will be evaluated individually based on appropriate and current documentation.

Allowed in exams
  Calculator: Yes
  Dictionary: Yes
  Computer: Yes
  Spellchecker: Yes
Extended test time: Yes
Scribes: Yes
Proctors: Yes
Oral exams: Yes
Note-takers: Yes

Distraction reduced environment: Yes
Tape recording in class: Yes
Books on tape from RFBD: Yes
Taping of books not from RFBD: Yes
Accommodations for students with ADD: Yes
Reading machine: Yes
Other assistive technology: Yes
Priority registration: No

Added costs for services: No
LD specialists: No
Professional tutors: No
Peer tutors: 5–15
Max. hours/wk. for services: Unlimited
How professors are notified of LD/ADD: By student

GENERAL ADMISSIONS INFORMATION

Director of Admissions: Cynthia Robinson
Telephone: 910-277-5555

ENTRANCE REQUIREMENTS

Academic units recommended: 4 English, 3 math, 2 science, 2 foreign language, 2 history. High school diploma is required and GED is accepted. TOEFL required of all international applicants, minimum paper TOEFL 500, minimum computer TOEFL 173.

Application deadline: Rolling
Notification: Rolling
Average GPA: NR

Average SAT Math: 488
Average SAT Verbal: 509
Average ACT: NR

Graduated top 10% of class: NR
Graduated top 25% of class: NR
Graduated top 50% of class: NR

COLLEGE GRADUATION REQUIREMENTS

Course waivers allowed: Yes
Course substitutions allowed: Yes
In what course: Foreign language

ADDITIONAL INFORMATION

Environment: The college is located on 600 acres in a small town 40 miles southwest of Fayetteville.

Student Body:
  Undergrad enrollment: 707
  Women: 62%
  Men: 38%
  Percent out-of-state: 47%

Cost Information
  Tuition: $15,125
  Room & board: $5,630
Housing Information
  University housing: Yes
  Percent living on campus: 76%

Greek System
  Fraternity: No
  Sorority: No
Athletics: NCAA Division II

U. OF NORTH CAROLINA—CHAPEL HILL

Jackson Hall 153A—Campus Box #2200, Chapel Hill, NC 27599
Phone: 919-966-3621 • Fax: 919-962-3045
E-mail: uadm@email.unc.edu • Web: www.unc.edu
Support: CS • Institution type: 4-year public

LEARNING DISABILITY PROGRAM AND SERVICES

Learning Disabilities Services (LDS) is one of seven units of Academic Support Services in the College of Arts and Sciences. The mission of LDS is to assist students in achieving their academic potential within the regular, academically competitive university curriculum. This is a comprehensive program with a team of LD specialists that meets both the letter and the spirit of the law. LDS works with students who are eligible for services and is the service provider to students with documented LD/ADD. LDS has developed innovative services for students with ADD and LD in college students. A student's documented disability becomes the foundation for accommodations; the student's desire to learn new ways to learn becomes the foundation for direct services. Accommodations are changes made by the university in how the students take in or express information. This is why the accommodations are determined case-by-case, based on each student's specific documented disability. Direct services focus on changes that students can make in how they learn. Services are offered in addition to the accommodations required by law. Students can meet as often as weekly in one-to-one sessions to learn more about their disability, develop self-advocacy skills, obtain referrals, and practice learning strategies.

LD/ADD ADMISSIONS INFORMATION

College entrance tests required: Yes
Interview required: No
Essay required: Yes
Documentation required for LD: Psychoeducational
   evaluation
Documentation required for ADD: Yes
Submitted to: Learning Disabilities Services
Special Ed. HS coursework accepted: Yes

Specific course requirements of all applicants: Yes
Separate application required for program services: No
# of LD applications submitted each year: NR
# of LD applications accepted yearly: NR
Total # of students receiving LD services: 350
Acceptance into program means acceptance into
   college: Student must be admitted and enrolled in the
   university first and then request services.

ADMISSIONS

In terms of admission criteria for students with LD, non-enrolled students can choose to voluntarily share documentation of their disability. If the student discloses a disability during admissions, his or her application is reviewed by subcommittee of the admissions committee. This subcommittee is made up of a number of campus professionals with expertise in disabilities, including the director of the Learning Disabilities Services. If a student who is reviewed by this subcommittee is admitted, the student is then automatically eligible to use LDS. Students with disabilities who apply for admissions have the right to refrain from disclosing. If, after being admitted, a student wishes to use LDS, that student would then submit documentation to be reviewed by the LD team.

ADDITIONAL INFORMATION

Accommodations provided include note-takers, taped textbooks, tutors in math or foreign language, extended time on tests, a distraction-free test environment, a reader during exams, a scribe to write dictated test answers, and a computer for writing test answers. Using the student's current coursework, LDS can teach a range of strategies, including how to plan, draft, and edit papers; how to take lecture notes and reading notes; how to read critically and efficiently; how to manage time; and how to prepare for and take exams. Group experiences are available to students each semester, based on their expressed interests. These can include support groups that promote understanding, acceptance, and pride; academic workshops that allow students to help each other learn specific skills; seminars that provide topical information from campus experts as well as other students; and panel discussions between students and university personnel. Currently there are 100 students with LD and 150 with ADD.

Support Services Contact Information

Learning Disability Program/Services: Learning Disabilities Services (LDS)
Director: Jane Byron
  E-Mail: jsbyron@email.unc.edu
  Telephone: 919-962-7227
  Fax: 919-962-3674
Contact Person: Kim Allison

LEARNING DISABILITY SERVICES

Requests for the following/services accommodations will be evaluated individually based on appropriate and current documentation.

Allowed in exams
  Calculator: Yes
  Dictionary: Yes
  Computer: Yes
  Spellchecker: Yes
Extended test time: Yes
Scribes: Yes
Proctors: Yes
Oral exams: Yes
Note-takers: Yes

Distraction reduced environment: Yes
Tape recording in class: Yes
Books on tape from RFBD: Yes
Taping of books not from RFBD: Yes
Accommodations for students with ADD: Yes
Reading machine: Yes
Other assistive technology: Yes
Priority registration: Yes

Added costs for services: No
LD specialists: Yes
Professional tutors: No
Peer tutors: Referral
Max. hours/wk. for services: 2
How professors are notified of LD/ADD: By Director

GENERAL ADMISSIONS INFORMATION

Director of Admissions: Stephen Farmer
Telephone: 919-966-3621

ENTRANCE REQUIREMENTS

Academic units required: 4 English, 4 math, 3 science (1 science lab), 2 foreign language, 2 social studies, 2 academic electives. **Academic units recommended:** 4 English, 4 math, 4 science (1 science lab), 4 foreign language, 3 social studies. High school diploma is required and GED is not accepted ACT with optional essay or SAT Reasoning test required. TOEFL required of all international applicants, minimum paper TOEFL 600, minimum computer TOEFL 250.

Application deadline: 1/15
Notification: January 31, March 31
Average GPA: 3.14

Average SAT Math: 649
Average SAT Verbal: 638
Average ACT: 27

Graduated top 10% of class: 70%
Graduated top 25% of class: 94%
Graduated top 50% of class: 99%

COLLEGE GRADUATION REQUIREMENTS

Course waivers allowed: No
Course substitutions allowed: No
In what course: N/A

ADDITIONAL INFORMATION

Environment: The university is located in a suburban town near Raleigh.

Student Body:
  Undergrad enrollment: 15,711
  Women: 59%
  Men: 41%
  Percent out-of-state: 18%

Cost Information
  In-state tuition: $3,205
  Out-of-state tuition: $16,303
  Room & board: $6,245
Housing Information
  University housing: Yes
  Percent living on campus: 44%

Greek System
  Fraternity: Yes
  Sorority: Yes
Athletics: NCAA Division I

U. OF NORTH CAROLINA—CHARLOTTE

9201 University City Boulevard, Charlotte, NC 28223-0001
Phone: 704-687-2213 • Fax: 704-687-6483
E-mail: unccadm@email.uncc.edu • Web: www.uncc.edu
Support: CS • Institution type: 4-year public

LEARNING DISABILITY PROGRAM AND SERVICES

The mission of Disability Services reflects the university's commitment to diversity by providing educational opportunities for persons with disabilities. This primary purpose is facilitated through ongoing research and development activities; development and presentation of educational seminars, workshops, and training designed to increase knowledge of disability-related issues; and a case management system approach to service delivery. The professional staff in Disability Services assists students with learning disabilities to meet their individual needs. In all possible cases, UNC Charlotte will use existing resources for educational auxiliary aids. Services could include registration assistance, orientation to available services, individualized educational plan, special testing arrangements, counseling, and peer support services.

LD/ADD ADMISSIONS INFORMATION

College entrance tests required: Yes
Interview required: Yes
Essay required: Yes
Documentation required for LD: Psychoeducational evaluation
Documentation required for ADD: Yes
Submitted to: Disability Services
Special Ed. HS coursework accepted: Yes

Specific course requirements of all applicants: Yes
Separate application required for program services: No
# of LD applications submitted each year: NR
# of LD applications accepted yearly: NR
Total # of students receiving LD services: 127
Acceptance into program means acceptance into college: Student must be admitted and enrolled in the university first and then request services.

ADMISSIONS

All applicants must meet the general admissions requirements and any special requirements for acceptance into a particular program of study. Students go through the regular application process. Courses required include 4 years English, 4 years math, 3 years science, 1 year science lab, 2 years foreign language, 2 years social studies, 1 year history recommended, and 2 years electives. Applicants with learning disabilities are encouraged to provide information about their learning disability at the time of application for admission. The university reserves the right to withhold the admission of any applicant who fails to meet any of the requirements for admission. Students who are not otherwise qualified, and who provide documentation of a learning disability, may be reviewed by the Disability Services, which will give a recommendation to the Office of Admissions. Once students have been admitted and enrolled they may request the necessary services.

ADDITIONAL INFORMATION

Services offered include academic advisement/priority registration, assistive technology, taped textbooks, special test administration, note-takers, broad-based case management activities to include orientation and assessment for services, individual consultation/counseling 30 minutes weekly, workshops, referral for tutorial services. There is a Tutoring Center and a Writing Center. Currently there are 127 students with LD and 91 students with ADD receiving services on campus. Students with ADD must provide documentation that includes a diagnosis and a verification of the diagnosis.

Support Services Contact Information

Learning Disability Program/Services: Disability Services
Director: Jo Ann A. Fernald
  E-Mail: jfermal@email.uncc.edu
  Telephone: 704-687-4355
  Fax: 704-687-3226

LEARNING DISABILITY SERVICES

Requests for the following/services accommodations will be evaluated individually based on appropriate and current documentation.

Allowed in exams
  Calculator: Yes
  Dictionary: No
  Computer: Yes
  Spellchecker: Yes
Extended test time: Yes
Scribes: Yes
Proctors: Yes
Oral exams: Yes
Note-takers: Yes

Distraction reduced environment: Yes
Tape recording in class: Yes
Books on tape from RFBD: Yes
Taping of books not from RFBD: Yes
Accommodations for students with
  ADD: Yes
Reading machine: Yes
Other assistive technology: Yes
Priority registration: Yes

Added costs for services: No
LD specialists: Yes
Professional tutors: No
Peer tutors: Yes
Max. hours/wk. for services: N/A
How professors are notified of
  LD/ADD: By both student and director

GENERAL ADMISSIONS INFORMATION

Director of Admissions: Craig Fulton
Telephone: 704-687-2213

ENTRANCE REQUIREMENTS

Academic units required: 4 English, 4 math, 3 science (1 science lab), 2 foreign language, 2 social studies, 2 academic electives. **Academic units recommended:** 1 history, 1 health education. High school diploma is required and GED is accepted. ACT with Writing component required or SAT Reasoning test. TOEFL required of all international applicants, minimum paper TOEFL 507, minimum computer TOEFL 180.

Application deadline: 7/1
Notification: Rolling
Average GPA: 3.5

Average SAT Math: 546
Average SAT Verbal: 530
Average ACT: 21

Graduated top 10% of class: 76%
Graduated top 25% of class: 47%
Graduated top 50% of class: 89%

COLLEGE GRADUATION REQUIREMENTS

Course waivers allowed: No
Course substitutions allowed: Yes
In what course: Foreign language substitution if supported by documentation and only done on a case-by-case basis

ADDITIONAL INFORMATION

Environment: The university is located on 1,000 acres 8 miles northeast of Charlotte.

Student Body:
  Undergrad enrollment: 15,472
  Women: 53%
  Men: 47%
  Percent out-of-state: 9%

Cost Information
  In-state tuition: $3,500
  Out-of-state tuition: $14,000
  Room & board: $5,984
Housing Information
  University housing: Yes
  Percent living on campus: 27%

Greek System
  Fraternity: Yes
  Sorority: Yes
Athletics: NCAA Division I

U. OF NORTH CAROLINA—GREENSBORO

123 Mossman Building, Greensboro, NC 27402-6170
Phone: 336-334-5243 • Fax: 336-334-4180
E-mail: undergrad_admissions@uncg.edu • Web: www.uncg.edu
Support: CS • Institution type: 4-year public

LEARNING DISABILITY PROGRAM AND SERVICES

The University of North Carolina—Greensboro is committed to equality of educational opportunities for qualified students with disabilities. The goal of Disabled Student Services is to provide a full range of academic accommodations. Students who need tests offered in a non-traditional format may request this service. Modifications may include extended time, private room, reader, scribe, or use of word processor for essay examinations. Documentation must verify the use of special accommodations. The Disability Services office provides a handbook for students to use as a helpful guide in making their experience at UNCG a positive one.

LD/ADD ADMISSIONS INFORMATION

College entrance tests required: Yes
Interview required: No
Essay required: No
Documentation required for LD: Psychoeducational
  evaluation
Documentation required for ADD: Yes
Submitted to: Disability Services
Special Ed. HS coursework accepted: No

Specific course requirements of all applicants: Yes
Separate application required for program services: No
# of LD applications submitted each year: NR
# of LD applications accepted yearly: NR
Total # of students receiving LD services: 200
Acceptance into program means acceptance into college: Student must be admitted and enrolled in the university first and then request services.

ADMISSIONS

There is no special admissions process for students with learning disabilities. Admission is competitive and based on academic qualifications. Students with learning disabilities must submit the regular application and are considered for admission in the same manner as any other applicant. No pre-admission inquiry regarding the learning disability is made. ACT with writing or SAT is required.

ADDITIONAL INFORMATION

Trained staff members are available for counseling to assist students with academic and/or personal problems. Voluntary note-takers are solicited through DSS, and photocopying is available. Students will meet with their faculty advisor to discuss courses that need to be taken, and DSS will stamp the students' registration cards to verify that they are registered with DSS and warrant priority registration. Assistance in securing taped textbooks through Recording for the Blind and Dyslexic is provided, and a file of available readers is available for instances when materials are not available through RFBD. Students are provided with information regarding campus tutorials and labs. Individual tutors are provided when it seems necessary. Students can receive help with study skills and time management techniques.

Support Services Contact Information

Learning Disability Program/Services: Disability Services
Director: Mary Culkin
  E-Mail: meculkin@uncc.edu
  Telephone: 336-334-5440
  Fax: 336-334-4412

LEARNING DISABILITY SERVICES

Requests for the following/services accommodations will be evaluated individually based on appropriate and current documentation.

Allowed in exams
  Calculator: Yes
  Dictionary: Yes
  Computer: Yes
  Spellchecker: Yes
Extended test time: Yes
Scribes: Yes
Proctors: Yes
Oral exams: Yes
Note-takers: Yes

Distraction reduced environment: Yes
Tape recording in class: Yes
Books on tape from RFBD: Yes
Taping of books not from RFBD: Yes
Accommodations for students with ADD: Yes
Reading machine: Yes
Other assistive technology: Yes
Priority registration: Yes

Added costs for services: No
LD specialists: Yes
Professional tutors: No
Peer tutors: Yes
Max. hours/wk. for services: Depends on needs
How professors are notified of LD/ADD: By both student and director

GENERAL ADMISSIONS INFORMATION

Director of Admissions: Jim Black
Telephone: 336-334-5243

ENTRANCE REQUIREMENTS

Academic units required: 4 English, 4 math, 3 science (1 science lab), 2 foreign language, 1 social studies, 1 history, 1 academic elective. High school diploma is required and GED is accepted ACT with writing or SAT required. TOEFL required of all international applicants, minimum paper TOEFL 550, minimum computer TOEFL 213.

Application deadline: 8/1
Notification: Rolling
Average GPA: 3.44

Average SAT Math: 523
Average SAT Verbal: 522
Average ACT: NR

Graduated top 10% of class: 13%
Graduated top 25% of class: 44%
Graduated top 50% of class: 85%

COLLEGE GRADUATION REQUIREMENTS

Course waivers allowed: No
Course substitutions allowed: Yes
In what course: Decided on a case-by-case basis in foreign language (extreme exception rather than the rule). All substitutions must be approved by faculty committee. Currently offer modified foreign language program.

ADDITIONAL INFORMATION

Environment: The university is located on 178 acres in an urban area in Greensboro, NC.

Student Body:
  Undergrad enrollment: 11,241
  Women: 68%
  Men: 32%
  Percent out-of-state: 8%

Cost Information
  In-state tuition: $4,056
  Out-of-state tuition: $26,000
  Room & board: $5,300
Housing Information
  University housing: Yes
  Percent living on campus: 32%

Greek System
  Fraternity: Yes
  Sorority: Yes
Athletics: NCAA Division I

U. OF NORTH CAROLINA—WILMINGTON

601 South College Road, Wilmington, NC 28403
Phone: 910-962-3243 • Fax: 910-962-3038
E-mail: admissions@uncw.edu • Web: www.uncw.edu
Support: CS • Institution type: 4-year public

LEARNING DISABILITY PROGRAM AND SERVICES

The university's goal is to provide access to all of its academic programs, support services, and extracurricular activities, and to enrich academic and vocational experience while in college. The coordinator of Disability Services (DS) meets with the student in order to appraise special needs, make referrals, and arrange for special accommodations. The university has devoted much time and energy to meeting the requirements of Section 504 and ADA. This effort is exemplified by the accommodating services offered through DS for students with learning disabilities and by special cooperation of the faculty. As the number of students with learning disabilities attending UNCW increases, so does the university's commitment to make facilities and programs more accessible.

LD/ADD ADMISSIONS INFORMATION

College entrance tests required: Yes
Interview required: No
Essay required: Yes
Documentation required for LD: Psychoeducational evaluation
Documentation required for ADD: Yes
Submitted to: Disability Services
Special Ed. HS coursework accepted: No

Specific course requirements of all applicants: Yes
Separate application required for program services: Yes
# of LD applications submitted each year: NR
# of LD applications accepted yearly: NR
Total # of students receiving LD services: 250
Acceptance into program means acceptance into college: Student must be admitted and enrolled in the university first and then request services.

ADMISSIONS

Students with learning disabilities must meet the same entrance requirements as all other applicants. Course requirements include 4 years English, 4 years math, 3 years science, 3 years social studies, and 2 years foreign language.

ADDITIONAL INFORMATION

Services are provided based on individual need as assessed through recent diagnostic information and personal interview. As new needs are identified, services may be modified or developed to accommodate them. Newly accepted students interested in services should complete and sign the disclosure form that is included with the letter of acceptance. This information should then be forwarded to the Student Development Center. Current documentation must be sent to the coordinator of DS after acceptance to the university. Diagnostic testing must be conducted by a licensed professional, and an adequate report must include specific educational recommendations. Priority registration is available to all returning students registered with DSS. Services and accommodations are offered to undergraduate and graduate students.

Support Services Contact Information

Learning Disability Program/Services: Disability Services (DS)
Director: Peggy Turner, PhD
  E-Mail: turnerm@uncw.edu
  Telephone: 910-962-3746
  Fax: 910-962-7124
Contact Person: Ginny Lundeen
  E-Mail: lundeenv@uncw.edu
  Telephone: 910-962-3746
  Fax: 910-962-7124

LEARNING DISABILITY SERVICES

Requests for the following/services accommodations will be evaluated individually based on appropriate and current documentation.

Allowed in exams
  Calculator: Yes
  Dictionary: Yes
  Computer: Yes
  Spellchecker: Yes
Extended test time: Yes
Scribes: Yes
Proctors: Yes
Oral exams: Yes
Note-takers: Yes

Distraction reduced environment: Yes
Tape recording in class: Yes
Books on tape from RFBD: Yes
Taping of books not from RFBD: Yes
Accommodations for students with ADD: Yes
Reading machine: Yes
Other assistive technology: Yes
Priority registration: Yes

Added costs for services: No
LD specialists: Yes
Professional tutors: No
Peer tutors: Yes
Max. hours/wk. for services: Depends on needs
How professors are notified of LD/ADD: By student

GENERAL ADMISSIONS INFORMATION

Director of Admissions: Roxie M. Shabazz, Asst VC for Admissions
Telephone: 910-962-4198

ENTRANCE REQUIREMENTS

Academic units required: 4 English, 3 math, 3 science (1 science lab), 2 foreign language, 2 social studies, 1 history, 5 academic electives. High school diploma is required and GED is accepted. Average SAT is 1150–1220 TOEFL required of all international applicants, minimum paper TOEFL 580, minimum computer TOEFL 213.

Application deadline: 2/1
Notification: ending date: 4/01
Average GPA: 3.62

Average SAT Math: 568
Average SAT Verbal: 558
Average ACT: NR

Graduated top 10% of class: 23%
Graduated top 25% of class: 62%
Graduated top 50% of class: 94%

COLLEGE GRADUATION REQUIREMENTS

Course waivers allowed: No
Course substitutions allowed: Yes
In what course: Foreign language

ADDITIONAL INFORMATION

Environment: The university is located on a 650-acre urban campus.

Student Body:
  Undergrad enrollment: 10,030
  Women: 59%
  Men: 41%
  Percent out-of-state: 13%

Cost Information
  In-state tuition: $1,928
  Out-of-state tuition: $11,638
  Room & board: $6,252
Housing Information
  University housing: Yes
  Percent living on campus: 23%

Greek System
  Fraternity: Yes
  Sorority: Yes
Athletics: NCAA Division I

University of North Carolina—Wilmington

WAKE FOREST UNIVERSITY

Box 7305, Reynolds Station, Winston-Salem, NC 27109
Phone: 336-758-5201 • Fax: 336-758-4324
E-mail: admissions@wfu.edu • Web: www.wfu.edu
Support: CS • Institution type: 4-year private

LEARNING DISABILITY PROGRAM AND SERVICES

The Learning Assistance Center (LAC) offers support for academic success. For students with documented disabilities, the program director will work with the student and members of the faculty to help implement any approved course accommodations. The students with learning disabilities have a series of conferences with staff members who specialize in academic skills and who help design an overall study plan to improve scholastic performance in those areas needing assistance. If special course accommodations are needed, the program director will serve as an advocate for the students with members of the faculty.

LD/ADD ADMISSIONS INFORMATION

College entrance tests required: Yes
Interview required: No
Essay required: Yes
Documentation required for LD: Psychoeducational
evaluation: within one year
Documentation required for ADD: Yes
Submitted to: Learning Assistance Center
Special Ed. HS coursework accepted: No

Specific course requirements of all applicants: Yes
Separate application required for program services: No
# of LD applications submitted each year: NR
# of LD applications accepted yearly: NR
Total # of students receiving LD services: 116
**Acceptance into program means acceptance into
college:** Student must be admitted and enrolled in the
university first and then request services.

ADMISSIONS

There are no special admissions. Students with learning disabilities submit the general Wake Forest University application and are expected to meet the same admission criteria as all applicants. Wake Forest does not accept the ACT. The mid 50 percent range for the SATs 1240–1360. Course requirements include 4 years English, 3 years math, 1 year science, 2 years social studies, and 2 years foreign language. Students should self-disclose to the Learning Assistance Center after admission. Services are available to all enrolled students with documentation on file. Students are encouraged to provide a recent psycho educational evaluation.

ADDITIONAL INFORMATION

The Learning Assistance Program staff will assist students with learning disabilities to learn new approaches to studying and methods for improving reading and comprehension, note-taking, time management, study organization, memory, motivation, and self-modification. The Learning Assistance Center offers peer tutoring services. In addition to one-on-one tutoring in most academic subjects, the LAC provides collaborative learning groups. Comprised of 2–5 students. The LAC also assists students who present special academic needs. Accommodations are determined based on appropriate documentation. Currently there are 30 students with LD and 23 with ADD receiving accommodations or services on campus. Applications are accepted for course substitutions. All students with or without learning disabilities are eligible for group or individual tutoring in basic academic subjects. The tutors are advanced undergraduates or graduate students who have demonstrated mastery of specific subject areas and are supervised by the LAC staff for their tutoring activities. The LAC also offers all students individual academic counseling to help develop study, organization, and time management strategies that are important for successful college-level learning.

Support Services Contact Information

Learning Disability Program/Services: Learning Assistance Center (LAC)
Director: Van D, Westervelt, PhD
  E-Mail: westerv@wfu.edu
  Telephone: 336-758-5929
  Fax: 336-758-1991

LEARNING DISABILITY SERVICES

Requests for the following/services accommodations will be evaluated individually based on appropriate and current documentation.

Allowed in exams
  Calculator: Yes
  Dictionary: Yes
  Computer: Yes
  Spellchecker: Yes
Extended test time: Yes
Scribes: No
Proctors: No
Oral exams: No
Note-takers: No

Distraction reduced environment: Yes
Tape recording in class: Yes
Books on tape from RFBD: No
Taping of books not from RFBD: No
Accommodations for students with ADD: Yes
Reading machine: No
Other assistive technology: No
Priority registration: No
Added costs for services: No

LD specialists: Yes
Professional tutors: No
Peer tutors: 90
Max. hours/wk. for services: 1 hr academic counseling; 3 hrs. of peer tutoring
How professors are notified of LD/ADD: By both student and director

GENERAL ADMISSIONS INFORMATION

Director of Admissions: Martha B. Allman
Telephone: 336-758-5201

ENTRANCE REQUIREMENTS

Academic units required: 4 English, 3 math, 1 science, 2 foreign language, 2 social studies. **Academic units recommended:** 4 English, 4 math, 4 science, 4 foreign language, 4 social studies. High school diploma is required and GED is accepted. TOEFL required of all international applicants, minimum paper TOEFL 600, minimum computer TOEFL 250.

Application deadline: 1/15
Notification: 4/1
Average GPA: NR

Average SAT Math: NR
Average SAT Verbal: NR
Average ACT: NR

Graduated top 10% of class: 65%
Graduated top 25% of class: 94%
Graduated top 50% of class: 99%

COLLEGE GRADUATION REQUIREMENTS

Course waivers allowed: No
Course substitutions allowed: Yes
In what course: Foreign language only. If there is a documented language-based LD and a "good faith effort" has been made to learn a foreign language without success, then two courses from an approved list of classics and humanities courses may be substituted.

ADDITIONAL INFORMATION

Environment: The 550-acre campus is located in the Piedmont region of North Carolina.

Student Body:
  Undergrad enrollment: 4,104
  Women: 51%
  Men: 49%
  Percent out-of-state: 71%

Cost Information
  Tuition: $30,110
  Room & board: $8,500
Housing Information
  University housing: Yes
  Percent living on campus: 78%

Greek System
  Fraternity: Yes
  Sorority: Yes
Athletics: NCAA Division I

WESTERN CAROLINA UNIVERSITY

242 HFR Administration, Cullowhee, NC 28723
Phone: 828-227-7317 • Fax: 828-227-7319
E-mail: admiss@email.wcu.edu • Web: www.wcu.edu
Support: CS • Institution type: 4-year public

LEARNING DISABILITY PROGRAM AND SERVICES

The Disabled Student Services Program attempts to respond to the needs of students with learning disabilities by making services and equipment available as needed, and by making judicious use of reading and tutoring services. Each student in the program is assigned a counselor/advisor. The students must meet with this counselor at least twice a month to discuss topics such as academic progress, study skills, adjustment to college life, career decision-making and personal concerns. In addition, students may take specially designed classes in English, reading, and study skills.

LD/ADD ADMISSIONS INFORMATION

College entrance tests required: Yes
Interview required: No
Essay required: No
Documentation required for LD: Psychoeducational
   evaluation: within three years
Documentation required for ADD: Yes
Submitted to: Student Support Services
Special Ed. HS coursework accepted: No

Specific course requirements of all applicants: Yes
Separate application required for program services: No
# of LD applications submitted each year: NR
# of LD applications accepted yearly: NR
Total # of students receiving LD services: 100–120
**Acceptance into program means acceptance into
   college:** Student must be admitted and enrolled in the
   university first and then request services.

ADMISSIONS

Students with learning disabilities are admitted under the same standards as students who have no learning disability. Minimum GPA is 2.0 plus 4 years English, 4 years math, 3 years science, 3 years social studies, and 2 years foreign language. Students who are admitted are encouraged to take the Summer Term Enrichment Program (STEP) in order to jump-start their introduction to college. Students not admissible through the regular admission process may be offered a probationary admission and may have to begin in the summer prior to freshman year. Applicants admitted on probation must demonstrate the aptitude and motivation to be successful in the first semester. These students will have additional tutoring and small classes. The admission decision is made by the admission office.

ADDITIONAL INFORMATION

To qualify for services students must be enrolled at the university, be evaluated within the last three years, be willing to participate in additional evaluations to confirm the disability, and be willing to participate in planning support services. The following services or accommodations are available for students with appropriate documementation: the use of calculators, dictionary, computer, or spell checker in exams; extended time on tests; distraction-free environment; scribe; proctor; oral exams; note-taker; tape recorder in class; taped texts; and priority registration. All students have access to tutoring, writing and math center, technology assistance center, and counseling and psychological services. Admitted students should maintain good class attendance, strive for good grades, cooperate with counselors and advisors, set realistic career goals, and meet with the LD team. Services and accommodations are available for undergraduate and graduate students.

Support Services Contact Information

Learning Disability Program/Services: Student Support Services
Director: Carol Mellen
 E-Mail: mellen@email.wcu.edu
 Telephone: 828-227-7127
 Fax: 828-227-7078

LEARNING DISABILITY SERVICES

Requests for the following/services accommodations will be evaluated individually based on appropriate and current documentation.

Allowed in exams
 Calculator: Yes
 Dictionary: Yes
 Computer: Yes
 Spellchecker: Yes
Extended test time: Yes
Scribes: Yes
Proctors: Yes
Oral exams: Yes
Note-takers: Yes

Distraction reduced environment: Yes
Tape recording in class: Yes
Books on tape from RFBD: Yes
Taping of books not from RFBD: Yes
Accommodations for students with ADD: Yes
Reading machine: Yes
Other assistive technology: Yes
Priority registration: Yes

Added costs for services: No
LD specialists: Yes
Professional tutors: At times
Peer tutors: 2–50
Max. hours/wk. for services: NR
How professors are notified of LD/ADD: By student

GENERAL ADMISSIONS INFORMATION

Director of Admissions: Phil Cauley
Telephone: 877-WCU-4YOU

ENTRANCE REQUIREMENTS
Academic units required: 4 English, 4 math, 3 science (3 science lab), 2 foreign language, 2 social studies, 1 history. **Academic units recommended:** 4 English, 4 math, 3 science (3 science lab), 2 foreign language, 2 social studies, 1 history, 7 academic electives. High school diploma is required and GED is accepted. ACT with Writing component required or SAT Reasoning test. TOEFL required of all international applicants, minimum paper TOEFL 550, minimum computer TOEFL 213.

Application deadline: 8/1
Notification: Rolling
Average GPA: 3.30

Average SAT Math: 517
Average SAT Verbal: 510
Average ACT: 20

Graduated top 10% of class: 10%
Graduated top 25% of class: 29%
Graduated top 50% of class: 64%

COLLEGE GRADUATION REQUIREMENTS

Course waivers allowed: Yes
Course substitutions allowed: Yes
In what course: Individually considered

ADDITIONAL INFORMATION

Environment: The university is located on 400 acres in a rural area, 50 miles southwest of Asheville.

Student Body:
 Undergrad enrollment: 6,650
 Women: 52%
 Men: 48%
 Percent out-of-state: 7%

Cost Information
 In-state tuition: $3,600
 Out-of-state tuition: $13,000
 Room & board: $4,400
Housing Information
 University housing: Yes
 Percent living on campus: 44%

Greek System
 Fraternity: Yes
 Sorority: Yes
 Athletics: NCAA Division I

WINGATE UNIVERSITY

Campus Box 3059, Wingate, NC 28174
Phone: 704-233-8200 • Fax: 704-233-8110
E-mail: admit@wingate.edu • Web: www.wingate.edu
Support: CS • Institution type: 4-year private

LEARNING DISABILITY PROGRAM AND SERVICES

Wingate University provides a program designed to assist students with diagnosed specific learning disabilities/dyslexia. Wingate University is aware that the students with learning disabilities may be successful in the college environment, provided that their special needs are recognized and proper services are made available to them. The coordinator works closely with each student in an effort to maximize the opportunity for a successful college experience. While each student will have specific needs, there are some modes of assistance available to assist each student with the maximum support necessary. This assistance will include identifying strengths and weaknesses, balancing course selections, pre-registration, access to word processing, oral testing, extra testing time, taped texts, and tutoring. Success will be determined by the motivation and initiative of the individual student in seeking available assistance.

LD/ADD ADMISSIONS INFORMATION

College entrance tests required: Yes
Interview required: Yes
Essay required: Yes
Documentation required for LD: Psychoeducational evaluation
Documentation required for ADD: Yes
Submitted to: Disability Services
Special Ed. HS coursework accepted: Yes

Specific course requirements of all applicants: Yes
Separate application required for program services: No
# of LD applications submitted each year: NR
# of LD applications accepted yearly: NR
Total # of students receiving LD services: 70–80
Acceptance into program means acceptance into college: Student must be admitted and enrolled in the university first and then request services.

ADMISSIONS

All applicants must submit the general application and meet the same admission requirements. There is no special process for students with learning disabilities. Applicants must submit either SAT/ACT, two letters of recommendation, 2.7 GPA, and a short self-statement or essay. Course requirements include 4 years English, 3 years math, 2 years history, 2 years science, 1 year social studies, and 2 years of foreign language are recommended. Once students are admitted and enrolled they should provide current documentation in order to receive appropriate accommodations and services.

ADDITIONAL INFORMATION

Services for enrolled students include developing a plan for study (including choice of major, proper class load, liaison with faculty, informing faculty, and regular evaluation sessions), and additional guidance through the college's counseling program. With appropriate documentation students may have accommodations such as extended testing time; distraction-free environment for tests; calculator, dictionary, computer, and spell-check in exams; scribes; proctors; note-takers; tape recording in class; books on tape; peer tutoring; and priority registration. There are no waivers or substitutions for college graduation requirements.

Support Services Contact Information

Learning Disability Program/Services: Disability Services
Director: Linda Stedje-Larsen
  E-Mail: stedje@wingate
  Telephone: 704-233-8269
  Fax: 704-233-8265

LEARNING DISABILITY SERVICES

Requests for the following/services accommodations will be evaluated individually based on appropriate and current documentation.

Allowed in exams
  Calculator: Yes
  Dictionary: Yes
  Computer: Yes
  Spellchecker: Yes
Extended test time: Y/N
Scribes: Y/N
Proctors: Y/N
Oral exams: Y/N
Note-takers: Y/N

Distraction reduced environment: Yes
Tape recording in class: Yes
Books on tape from RFBD: Yes
Taping of books not from RFBD: No
Accommodations for students with ADD: Yes
Reading machine: Yes
Other assistive technology: No
Priority registration: Yes

Added costs for services: No
LD specialists: Yes
Professional tutors: No
Peer tutors: Yes
Max. hours/wk. for services: Unlimited
How professors are notified of LD/ADD: By student

GENERAL ADMISSIONS INFORMATION

Director of Admissions: Walter Crutchfield
Telephone: 704-233-8200

ENTRANCE REQUIREMENTS

Academic units recommended: 4 English, 3 math, 2 science (1 science lab), 2 foreign language, 2 social studies. High school diploma is required and GED is accepted. TOEFL required of all international applicants, minimum paper TOEFL 550, minimum computer TOEFL 213.

Application deadline: Rolling
Notification: Rolling
Average GPA: 3.3

Average SAT Math: 523
Average SAT Verbal: 518
Average ACT: 23

Graduated top 10% of class: 22%
Graduated top 25% of class: 46%
Graduated top 50% of class: 74%

COLLEGE GRADUATION REQUIREMENTS

Course waivers allowed: No
Course substitutions allowed: No
In what course: N/A

ADDITIONAL INFORMATION

Environment: The university is located on 330 acres in a small town, 25 miles east of Charlotte.

Student Body:
  Undergrad enrollment: 1,277
  Women: 54%
  Men: 46%
  Percent out-of-state: 44%

Cost Information
  Tuition: $15,000
  Room & board: $6,200
Housing Information
  University housing: Yes
  Percent living on campus: 81%

Greek System
  Fraternity: Yes
  Sorority: Yes
Athletics: NCAA Division II

MINOT STATE U.—BOTTINEAU

105 Simrall Boulevard, Bottineau, ND 58318
Phone: 800-542-6866 • Fax: 701-288-5499
E-mail: groszk@misu.nodak.edu • Web: www.misu-b.nodak.edu
Support: CS • Institution type: 2-year public

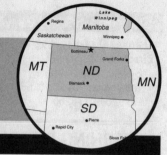

LEARNING DISABILITY PROGRAM AND SERVICES

The Learning Center provides a variety of academic support services to eligible students with LD. The Learning Center also provides individualized or small group instruction in English, algebra, biology, basic computer use, and other areas. Individuals are also provided with services that best meet their needs. In addition, study skills and reading improvement classes are offered for credit. A LD specialist/math instructor and an English/social studies instructor provide assistance in this program. Students planning to enroll at MSU—Bottineau should send documentation of the disability that is no more than three years old to the Learning Center. The documentation should include: an intelligence assessment (preferable the WAIS–R); achievement testing such as the Woodcock-Johnson Psychoeducational Battery; and education recommendations such as accommodations provided in high school and a recent IEP. Students should visit the Learning Center as soon as they arrive on campus. Students will be asked to complete an application and the Learning Center instructor will review the class schedule and arrange for tutoring if needed.

LD/ADD ADMISSIONS INFORMATION

College entrance tests required: No
Interview required: No
Essay required: No
Documentation required for LD: Documentation is needed only if the student requests accommodation. Psychological evaluation, recent IEP
Documentation required for ADD: Yes
Submitted to: Learning Center
Special Ed. HS coursework accepted: Yes

Specific course requirements of all applicants: Yes
Separate application required for program services: No
# of LD applications submitted each year: NR
# of LD applications accepted yearly: NR
Total # of students receiving LD services: 10–16
Acceptance into program means acceptance into college: Student must be admitted and enrolled in the university first and then request services.

ADMISSIONS

Minot State University has an open admission policy. Applicants must present a high school diploma or equivalent such as a GED. Standardized tests are not required. Students are encouraged to self-disclose the disability during the application process so that the university may provide information about accessing support once enrolled. All students who enroll are asked to complete a questionnaire that asks them to identify academic support services that they feel they may need once on campus.

ADDITIONAL INFORMATION

The Learning Center offers free tutoring and is open to all students. Sessions are adapted to fit a student's schedule. Individual tutoring is available. Students may receive accommodations that include class scheduling, although priority registration is not offered. Skills courses are offered in note taking strategies, test taking tips, and memory aids. There is a one credit reading improvement course that helps improve reading comprehension. Additional accommodations based on appropriate documentation could include extended testing time, note-takers, distraction-free testing environments, tape recorder in class, and auxiliary taping of books not available through RFBD. Partners Affiliated for Student Success is a consortium of educational institutions and businesses dedicated to assisting learners as they move from high school education to post-secondary education to work.

Support Services Contact Information

Learning Disability Program/Services: Learning Center
Director: Ms. Jan Nahinurk
 E-Mail: jan.nahinurk@misu.nodak.edu
 Telephone: 701-228-5479
 Fax: 701-228-5614

LEARNING DISABILITY SERVICES

Requests for the following/services accommodations will be evaluated individually based on appropriate and current documentation.

Allowed in exams
 Calculator: Y/N
 Dictionary: Y/N
 Computer: Y/N
 Spellchecker: Y/N
Extended test time: Yes
Scribes: Y/N
Proctors: Y/N
Oral exams: Y/N
Note-takers: Yes

Distraction reduced environment: Yes
Tape recording in class: Yes
Books on tape from RFBD: Yes
Taping of books not from RFBD: Yes
Accommodations for students with
 ADD: Yes
Reading machine: No
Other assistive technology: No
Priority registration: No

Added costs for services: No
LD specialists: Yes
Professional tutors: 2
Peer tutors: 2–5
Max. hours/wk. for services: Varies
How professors are notified of
 LD/ADD: By both student and director

GENERAL ADMISSIONS INFORMATION

Director of Admissions: Paula Berg
Telephone: 800-542-6866

ENTRANCE REQUIREMENTS

High school diploma is required and GED is accepted. Academic units required: 4 English, 3 math, 3 science, 3 social studies. Open admissions policy..

Application deadline: Rolling
Notification: Rolling
Average GPA: 3.1

Average SAT Math: NR
Average SAT Verbal: NR
Average ACT: 21

Graduated top 10% of class: NR
Graduated top 25% of class: NR
Graduated top 50% of class: NR

COLLEGE GRADUATION REQUIREMENTS

Course waivers allowed: No
Course substitutions allowed: No
In what course: N/A

ADDITIONAL INFORMATION

Environment: The campus is located in a small town 80 miles of Minot, ND.

Student Body:
 Undergrad enrollment: 450
 Women: 52%
 Men: 48%
 Percent out-of-state: 14%

Cost Information
 In-state tuition: $2,800
 Out-of-state tuition: $6,800
 Room & board: $3,000
Housing Information
 University housing: Yes
 Percent living on campus: 51%

Greek System
 Fraternity: No
 Sorority: No
Athletics: NAIA

Minot State University—Bottineau

NORTH DAKOTA STATE UNIVERSITY

Box 5454, Fargo, ND 58105
Phone: 701-231-8643 • Fax: 701-231-8802
E-mail: ndsu.admission@ndsu.nodak.edu • Web: www.ndsu.edu
Support: S • Institution type: 4-year public

LEARNING DISABILITY PROGRAM AND SERVICES

The mission of Disabilities Services is to assist students with disabilities in obtaining optimal access to educational programs, facilities, and employment at NDSU. Toward this end, the staff collaborates with other Counseling Center staff in providing consultation with students regarding accommodations that are therapeutic to their development as human beings and students. Disabilities Services works to provide equal access to academic programs, to promote self-awareness and advocacy, to educate the student body and faculty on disability-related issues, and to provide reasonable and appropriate accommodations. The staff educates faculty regarding the accommodation needs of students and works to ensure compliance with the Americans with Disabilities Act.

LD/ADD ADMISSIONS INFORMATION

College entrance tests required: Yes
Interview required: No
Essay required: No
Documentation required for LD: Psychoeducational evaluation
Documentation required for ADD: Yes
Submitted to: Disability Services
Special Ed. HS coursework accepted: Yes

Specific course requirements of all applicants: Yes
Separate application required for program services: No
# of LD applications submitted each year: NR
# of LD applications accepted yearly: NR
Total # of students receiving LD services: 80
Acceptance into program means acceptance into college: Student must be admitted and enrolled in the university first and then request services.

ADMISSIONS

Students with learning disabilities submit the general application form and are expected to meet the same admission standards as all applicants. The ACT range is 20–22 and the minimum GPA is 2.5. Applicants are expected to have high school courses in math, including algebra and above, English, lab sciences, and social studies. Students with learning disabilities may include a self-disclosure or information explaining or documenting the disability. When necessary, an admission decision is made jointly by the coordinator of the program and the admissions office. In this case Disabilities Services would review the documentation and provide a recommendation to admissions. Students can be admitted conditionally on probation and are required to take a study skills course.

ADDITIONAL INFORMATION

Skills courses are offered in study strategies, reading, computers, math, and science. A technology lab/resource room is available for student use. Assessment, counseling, and remedial support are coordinated through the Center for Student Counseling and Personal Growth. In addition, individual counseling, group support, career counseling, and personal/academic enrichment classes are offered. The NDSU Student Support Services Program provides tutoring and small group instruction. Students with appropriate documentation may request alternative testing accommodations. Skills classes are offered for credit for students with learning disabilities and ADD. Additionally, Disabilities Services offers support groups for students with ADD. Services and accommodations are available for undergraduate and graduate students.

Support Services Contact Information

Learning Disability Program/Services: Disability Services
Director: Bunnie Johnson-Messelt
  E-Mail: Bunnie.Johnson-Messelt@ndsu.nodak.edu
  Telephone: 701-231-7671
  Fax: 701-231-6318
Contact Person: Jennifer Erickson
  E-Mail: Jennifer.Erickson@ndsu.nodak.edu
  Telephone: 701-231-7671
  Fax: 701-231-6318

LEARNING DISABILITY SERVICES

Requests for the following/services accommodations will be evaluated individually based on appropriate and current documentation.

Allowed in exams
  Calculator: Yes
  Dictionary: Y/N
  Computer: Y/N
  Spellchecker: Y/N
Extended test time: Yes
Scribes: Yes
Proctors: Yes
Oral exams: Yes
Note-takers: Yes

Distraction reduced environment: Yes
Tape recording in class: Yes
Books on tape from RFBD: Yes
Taping of books not from RFBD: Yes
Accommodations for students with ADD: Yes
Reading machine: Yes
Other assistive technology: Yes
Priority registration: Yes

Added costs for services: No
LD specialists: No
Professional tutors: Yes
Peer tutors: 20–50
Max. hours/wk. for services: Unlimited
How professors are notified of LD/ADD: By student

GENERAL ADMISSIONS INFORMATION

Director of Admissions: Catherine Haugen
Telephone: 701-231-8643

ENTRANCE REQUIREMENTS

Academic units required: 4 English, 3 math, 3 science (3 science lab), 3 social studies. **Academic units recommended:** 2 foreign language. High school diploma is required and GED is accepted. ACT with or without Writing component accepted. TOEFL required of all international applicants, minimum paper TOEFL 525, minimum computer TOEFL 193.

Application deadline: 8/15
Notification: Rolling
Average GPA: 3.37

Average SAT Math: NR
Average SAT Verbal: NR
Average ACT: 23

Graduated top 10% of class: 18%
Graduated top 25% of class: 25%
Graduated top 50% of class: 75%

COLLEGE GRADUATION REQUIREMENTS

Course waivers allowed: No
Course substitutions allowed: N/A
In what course: N/A

ADDITIONAL INFORMATION

Environment: The university is located in a small city 250 miles from Minneapolis, Sioux Falls, and Winnipeg, Canada.

Student Body:
  Undergrad enrollment: 10,545
  Women: 45%
  Men: 55%
  Percent out-of-state: 46%

Cost Information
  In-state tuition: $3,981
  Out-of-state tuition: $10,629
  Room & board: $4,727
Housing Information
  University housing: Yes
  Percent living on campus: 29%

Greek System
  Fraternity: Yes
  Sorority: Yes
Athletics: NCAA Division I

North Dakota State University

BOWLING GREEN STATE UNIVERSITY

110 McFall Center, Bowling Green, OH 43403
Phone: 419-372-2478 • Fax: 419-372-6955
E-mail: admissions@bgnet.bgsu.edu • Web: www.bgsu.edu
Support: S • Institution type: 4-year public

LEARNING DISABILITY PROGRAM AND SERVICES

The philosophy of the university is to level the playing field for students with LD and/or ADD through the provision of appropriate accommodations and advocacy. The Office of Disability Services is evidence of BGSU's commitment to provide a support system that assists in conquering obstacles that persons with disabilities may encounter as they pursue their educational goals and activities. ODS provides services on an as-needed basis. The Study Skills Lab is open to all BGSU students, and the extent of participation is determined by the student. No grades are given in the lab, participation is voluntary, and the program is individualized. The lab is not a tutorial service, but students will be shown efficient techniques for studying, reading textbooks, taking notes, time management, and strategies for effective test-taking and test-preparation.

LD/ADD ADMISSIONS INFORMATION

College entrance tests required: Yes
Interview required: No
Essay required: No
Documentation required for LD: Psychoeducational evaluation within 3 years
Documentation required for ADD: Yes
Submitted to: Disability Services
Special Ed. HS coursework accepted: Yes

Specific course requirements of all applicants: Yes
Separate application required for program services: No
# of LD applications submitted each year: NR
# of LD applications accepted yearly: NR
Total # of students receiving LD services: 300–325
Acceptance into program means acceptance into college: Student must be admitted and enrolled in the university first and then request services.

ADMISSIONS

There is no special application or special admissions process. Core courses preferred include 4 years English, 3 years math, 3 years science, 3 years social studies, 2 years foreign language, 1 year art. Students with LD may substitute foreign language with another core course. The minimum GPA is approximately 2.0. Students with LD submit the regular application and are encouraged to self-disclose their LD and arrange an interview with ODS to allow staff to discuss any documentation they may require and any concerns of the students. Additional information such as school or medical history that describes specific strengths and weaknesses is helpful in determining services necessary, once the student is admitted. Information documenting the LD should be sent to ODS. Students should submit the results of a psychoeducational evaluation or other testing and documentation that establishes the presence of a specific LD. Students should indicate accommodations that have worked successfully in high school. There is a summer freshman program for freshmen applicants who do not meet the academic standards for fall admission.

ADDITIONAL INFORMATION

General services include priority registration; advising by sharing information on instructor's teaching and testing styles; Writing Lab for effective strategies; Study Skills Center for effective study skills, test-taking strategies, time management, and textbook reading skills; Math Lab, a walk-in lab for understanding basic and advanced concepts; computerized technology; note-takers, readers, and scribes; letters to professors explaining the disability and modifications needed; advocacy; and books on tape. To be eligible for test accommodations, students are required to provide documentation that provides a clear indication/recommendation for the need requested. Staff works with the student to reach consensus on the type of accommodation. Test accommodations may include extended time, oral exams, take-home exams, open-book exams, readers, scribes, computers and spell-check or grammar check, calculators, scratch paper, speller's dictionaries, question clarification, modification of test response format, and a quiet room.

Support Services Contact Information

Learning Disability Program/Services: Disability Services
Director: Rob Cunningham
  E-Mail: rcunnin@bgnct.bgsu.edu
  Telephone: 419-372-8495
  Fax: 419-372-8496

LEARNING DISABILITY SERVICES

Requests for the following/services accommodations will be evaluated individually based on appropriate and current documentation.

Allowed in exams
  Calculator: Yes
  Dictionary: Yes
  Computer: Yes
  Spellchecker: Yes
Extended test time: Yes
Scribes: Yes
Proctors: Yes
Oral exams: Yes
Note-takers: Yes

Distraction reduced environment: Yes
Tape recording in class: Yes
Books on tape from RFBD: Yes
Taping of books not from RFBD: Yes
Accommodations for students with ADD: Yes
Reading machine: Yes
Other assistive technology: Yes
Priority registration: Yes

Added costs for services: No
LD specialists: No
Professional tutors: Yes
Peer tutors: Yes
Max. hours/wk. for services: Unlimited
How professors are notified of LD/ADD: By student

GENERAL ADMISSIONS INFORMATION

Director of Admissions: Gary Swegan
Telephone: 419-372-2478

ENTRANCE REQUIREMENTS
Academic units required: 4 English, 3 math, 3 science (2 science lab), 2 foreign language, 3 social studies, 1 visual/performing arts. High school diploma is required and GED is accepted. TOEFL required of all international applicants, minimum paper TOEFL 500, minimum computer TOEFL 173.

Application deadline: 7/15
Notification: Rolling
Average GPA: 3.22

Average SAT Math: 508
Average SAT Verbal: 505
Average ACT: 22

Graduated top 10% of class: 13%
Graduated top 25% of class: 30%
Graduated top 50% of class: 71%

COLLEGE GRADUATION REQUIREMENTS

Course waivers allowed: Yes
Course substitutions allowed: Yes
In what course: Primarily foreign language; other requests will be considered.

ADDITIONAL INFORMATION

Environment: The 1,250-acre campus is in a small town 25 miles south of Toledo.

Student Body:
  Undergrad enrollment: 15,628
  Women: 55%
  Men: 45%
  Percent out-of-state: 7%

Cost Information
  In-state tuition: $6,818
  Out-of-state tuition: $14,126
  Room & board: $6,588
Housing Information
  University housing: Yes
  Percent living on campus: 45%

Greek System
  Fraternity: Yes
  Sorority: Yes
Athletics: NCAA Division I

CASE WESTERN RESERVE UNIVERSITY

103 Tomlinson Hall, 10900 Euclid Avenue, Cleveland, OH 44106-7055
Phone: 216-368-4450 • Fax: 216-368-5111
E-mail: admission@case.edu • Web: www.case.edu
Support: S • Institution type: 4-year private

LEARNING DISABILITY PROGRAM AND SERVICES

The goals of Educational Support Services (ESS) are to provide reasonable accommodations and serve as an advocate for individuals with diagnosed learning disabilities. ESS ensures that students with disabilities have access to services and accommodations needed to make the college experience a positive and successful one. ESS provides academic support, special accommodations, and personal encouragement.

LD/ADD ADMISSIONS INFORMATION

College entrance tests required: Yes
Interview required: No
Essay required: Yes
Documentation required for LD: Neuropsychological evaluation preferred.
Documentation required for ADD: Yes
Submitted to: Disability Services in Education Support Services
Special Ed. HS coursework accepted: No

Specific course requirements of all applicants: Yes
Separate application required for program services: No
# of LD applications submitted each year: NR
# of LD applications accepted yearly: NR
Total # of students receiving LD services: 40
Acceptance into program means acceptance into college: Student must be admitted and enrolled in the university first and then request services.

ADMISSIONS

Students with learning disabilities are encouraged to apply to CWRU. Admission is highly competitive, but all applicants are evaluated on an individual basis. Students who feel additional information would be helpful to the admission committee are encouraged to provide diagnostic information about their individual situation. General admission criteria include 4 years English, 3 years math, 3 years social science, 1 year science, and 2–4 years foreign language. Students must also submit a writing sample and are encouraged to have an interview. Most admitted students rank in the top 20 percent of their class and have an SAT of 1180–1380 or an ACT of 27–31.

ADDITIONAL INFORMATION

Skills courses are offered in study and learning strategies, time Management, and Reading. It is helpful for students to provide information regarding the nature of their disability so that services may be accommodated to their needs. High-performing students do well with the peer tutors available through ESS. These tutors are students who have successfully completed the appropriate coursework and have been approved by faculty. Special arrangements are made by ESS for students to have alternative testing such as additional time and proctored examinations in alternative settings. Students with LD are eligible for books on tape through RFBD. The ESS center has reading improvement software, word processing, and all network applications. A reading strategies tutorial program for one credit taught by a graduate student is also available for students with LD.

Support Services Contact Information

Learning Disability Program/Services: Disability Services in Educational Support Services (ESS)
Director: Susan Sampson, Coordinator
 E-Mail: sms170@po.cwru.edu
 Telephone: 216-368-5230

LEARNING DISABILITY SERVICES

Requests for the following/services accommodations will be evaluated individually based on appropriate and current documentation.

Allowed in exams
 Calculator: Y/N
 Dictionary: Yes
 Computer: Yes
 Spellchecker: Yes
Extended test time: Yes
Scribes: Yes
Proctors: Yes
Oral exams: Yes
Note-takers: Yes

Distraction reduced environment: Yes
Tape recording in class: Yes
Books on tape from RFBD: Yes
Taping of books not from RFBD: Yes
Accommodations for students with ADD: Yes
Reading machine: Yes
Other assistive technology: Yes
Priority registration: Yes

Added costs for services: No
LD specialists: No
Professional tutors: No
Peer tutors: Yes
Max. hours/wk. for services: Unlimited
How professors are notified of LD/ADD: By both student and director

GENERAL ADMISSIONS INFORMATION

Director of Admissions: Christopher Munoz
Telephone: 216-368-4450

ENTRANCE REQUIREMENTS
Academic units required: 4 English, 3 math, 3 science (1 science lab), 2 foreign language, 3 social studies.
Academic units recommended: 4 math, 2 science lab, 3 foreign language, 4 social studies. High school diploma is required and GED is accepted. ACT with Writing component required. TOEFL required of all international applicants, minimum paper TOEFL 550, minimum computer TOEFL 213.

Application deadline: 1/15
Notification: 3/1
Average GPA: NR

Average SAT Math: NR
Average SAT Verbal: NR
Average ACT: NR

Graduated top 10% of class: 68%
Graduated top 25% of class: 91%
Graduated top 50% of class: 99%

COLLEGE GRADUATION REQUIREMENTS

Course waivers allowed: No
Course substitutions allowed: No
In what course: Individual determination

ADDITIONAL INFORMATION

Environment: The university is located on 128 acres 4 miles east of downtown Cleveland.

Student Body:
 Undergrad enrollment: 3,424
 Women: 40%
 Men: 60%
 Percent out-of-state: 41%

Cost Information
 Tuition: $26,500
 Room & board: $8,202
Housing Information
 University housing: Yes
 Percent living on campus: 78%

Greek System
 Fraternity: Yes
 Sorority: Yes
 Athletics: NCAA Division III

Case Western Reserve University

CENTRAL OHIO TECHNICAL COLLEGE

1179 University Drive, Newark, OH 43055-1767
Phone: 740-366-9222 • Fax: 740-364-9531
E-mail: jmerrin@cotc.edu • Web: www.cotc.edu
Support: CS • Institution type: 4-year public

LEARNING DISABILITY PROGRAM AND SERVICES

The goals of Disability Services are to foster self-advocacy and independence. Disability Services provides diagnostic testing, counseling, and accommodations for students with learning disabilities. This is the only college in Ohio that provides free complete diagnostic testing. Placement tests are given after admissions. The Learning Assistance Center and Disability Services (LAC/DS) is the academic support unit. LAC/DS provides programs and services to any student desiring to strengthen academic skills. Students need to self-identify before scheduling classes. Early notice is needed for some services, such as alternate testing and recorded textbooks. The college advocates meeting the unique needs of students with disabilities, and accommodations provided allow for equal access to higher education.

LD/ADD ADMISSIONS INFORMATION

College entrance tests required: No
Interview required: No
Essay required: No
Documentation required for LD: Psychoeducational evaluation
Documentation required for ADD: Yes
Submitted to: Office of Disability Services
Special Ed. HS coursework accepted: No

Specific course requirements of all applicants: Yes
Separate application required for program services: No
# of LD applications submitted each year: NR
# of LD applications accepted yearly: NR
Total # of students receiving LD services: NR
Acceptance into program means acceptance into college: Students must be admitted and enrolled at the college and then reviewed for requests for supportive services.

ADMISSIONS

Admission is open to all applicants with a high school diploma or the GED except in health programs. There are no specific course requirements. ACT/SAT tests are not required. To receive accommodations, the student's diagnostic test results and diagnosis must be within the past three years.

ADDITIONAL INFORMATION

The Learning Assistance Center is a learning center for students with learning disabilities and ADD. Students who received learning disability services such as tutoring during their high school senior year are automatically eligible for services. The tutoring program includes peer tutoring in almost any course, scheduled at the student's convenience for two hours each week per course. The Academic Skills Lab has a Computer Lab; resources to improve reading, math, and language skills; word processing; and study aids for some courses and national tests. The Study Skills Workshop Series provides assistance in improving study skills and 50-minute workshops on time management, learning styles/memory, test preparing and taking, reading textbooks effectively, and note-taking. Students also have access to proctors, individualized instruction designed to meet special needs, advocacy assistance, diagnosis counseling, and assistance with accommodations.

Support Services Contact Information

Learning Disability Program/Services: Office for Disability Services
Director: Phyllis E. Thompson PhD
　E-Mail: thompson.33@osu.edu
　Telephone: 740-366-9246
　Fax: 740-364-9641

LEARNING DISABILITY SERVICES

Requests for the following/services accommodations will be evaluated individually based on appropriate and current documentation.

Allowed in exams
　Calculator: Yes
　Dictionary: Yes
　Computer: Yes
　Spellchecker: Yes
Extended test time: Yes
Scribes: Yes
Proctors: Yes
Oral exams: No
Note-takers: Yes

Distraction reduced environment: Yes
Tape recording in class: Yes
Books on tape from RFBD: Yes
Taping of books not from RFBD: Yes
Accommodations for students with ADD: Yes
Reading machine: Yes
Other assistive technology: Yes
Priority registration: Yes

Added costs for services: No
LD specialists: Yes
Professional tutors: No
Peer tutors: 25–40
Max. hours/wk. for services: Unlimited
How professors are notified of LD/ADD: By student

GENERAL ADMISSIONS INFORMATION

Director of Admissions: John Merrin
Telephone: 740-366-9222

ENTRANCE REQUIREMENTS

Open door admissions. No specific course requirements, no ACT/SAT required.

Application deadline: Rolling
Notification: Rolling
Average GPA: NR

Average SAT Math: NR
Average SAT Verbal: NR
Average ACT: NR

Graduated top 10% of class: NR
Graduated top 25% of class: NR
Graduated top 50% of class: NR

COLLEGE GRADUATION REQUIREMENTS

Course waivers allowed: N/A
Course substitutions allowed: Yes
In what course: Case by case

ADDITIONAL INFORMATION

Environment: The campus is located in a small town with easy access to Columbus.

Student Body:
　Undergrad enrollment: 1,988
　Women: 59%
　Men: 41%
　Percent out-of-state: 1%

Cost Information
　In-state tuition: $3,870
　Out-of-state tuition: $10,200
　Room & board: $5,283
Housing Information
　University housing: Yes
　Percent living on campus: 1%

Greek System
　Fraternity: No
　Sorority: No
Athletics: NJCAA

COLLEGE OF MOUNT ST. JOSEPH

5701 Delhi Road, Cincinnati, OH 45233
Phone: 513-244-4531 • Fax: 513-244-4629
E-mail: admission@mail.msj.edu • Web: www.msj.edu
Support: SP • Institution type: 4-year private

LEARNING DISABILITY PROGRAM AND SERVICES

Project EXCEL is a comprehensive academic support program for students with learning disabilities enrolled in the college. The program's goals are to assist students in the transition from a secondary program to a college curriculum and to promote the development of learning strategies and compensatory skills that will enable students to achieve success in a regular academic program. The structure of the program and supportive environment at the Mount give Project EXCEL its singular quality. Students admitted to the program must maintain a 2.25 overall GPA, and their progress is evaluated on an ongoing basis.

LD/ADD ADMISSIONS INFORMATION

College entrance tests required: Yes
Interview required: Yes
Essay required: Yes
Documentation required for LD: Psychoeducational evaluation within 3 years
Documentation required for ADD: Yes
Submitted to: Project Excel
Special Ed. HS coursework accepted: No

Specific course requirements of all applicants: Yes
Separate application required for program services: Yes
# of LD applications submitted each year: 50
# of LD applications accepted yearly: 30
Total # of students receiving LD services: 75
Acceptance into program means acceptance into college: Students are either admitted directly into EXCEL and the college; or EXCEL reviews applicants and recommends to admissions; or they are admitted to the College.

ADMISSIONS

Admission to Project EXCEL is multi-stepped, including an interview with the program director; completed general admission application completed Project EXCEL forms (general information, applicant goal and self-assessment, and educational data completed by high school), psychoeducational evaluation, transcript, ACT minimum of 15 or SAT of 700–740, and a recommendation. The application is reviewed by the Project EXCEL director and Project EXCEL admission committee. The diagnostic evaluation must indicate the presence of specific LD and provide reasonable evidence that the student can successfully meet college academic requirements. Academic performance problems that exist concomitantly with a diagnosed ADD/ADD will be considered in the review of the student's diagnostic profile. Students can be admitted to the college through Project EXCEL. Students not meeting all EXCEL admission requirements may be admitted part-time or on a probationary basis. Apply early. Other students not meeting admission requirements can take up to six hours per semester to a maximum of 13 hours. At that point, if they have a 2.0+ GPA they are admitted to the college.

ADDITIONAL INFORMATION

Project EXCEL students are assisted with course and major selection. Students are offered individualized attention and a variety of support services to meet specific needs, including supervised tutoring; monitoring of student progress; writing lab; note-takers; accommodated testing; instruction in learning strategies, time management, and coping skills; liaison with faculty; and academic advising with attention to specific learning needs. Students enroll in regular classes and must fulfill the same course requirements as all Mount students. The curriculum is closely supervised, and specialized instruction is offered in writing, reading, and study skills to fit the individual needs of the students. The program director serves as student advisor. The fees are $3,060 for freshman and sophomores in the Transition Program of Project EXCEL. The Structured Level of the Project EXCEL has a fee of $2,400 for juniors. The maintenance fee for seniors is $1,530.

Support Services Contact Information

Learning Disability Program/Services: Project Excel
Director: Jane Pohlman
  E-Mail: jane_pohlman@mail.msj.edu
  Telephone: 513-244-4623
  Fax: 513-244-4222

LEARNING DISABILITY SERVICES

Requests for the following/services accommodations will be evaluated individually based on appropriate and current documentation.

Allowed in exams
  Calculator: Yes
  Dictionary: Yes
  Computer: Yes
  Spellchecker: Yes
Extended test time: Yes
Scribes: Yes
Proctors: Yes
Oral exams: Yes
Note-takers: Yes

Distraction reduced environment: Yes
Tape recording in class: Yes
Books on tape from RFBD: Yes
Taping of books not from RFBD: Yes
**Accommodations for students with
  ADD:** Yes
Reading machine: No
Other assistive technology: No
Priority registration: No

Added costs for services: Yes
LD specialists: Yes
Professional tutors: 15
Peer tutors: No
Max. hours/wk. for services:
  Unlimited
**How professors are notified of
  LD/ADD:** By both student and director

GENERAL ADMISSIONS INFORMATION

Director of Admissions: Peggy Minnich
Telephone: 513-244-4531

ENTRANCE REQUIREMENTS

Academic units required: 4 English, 2 math, 2 science (1 science lab), 2 foreign language, 1 social studies, 1 history, 1 academic elective, 1 fine arts. **Academic units recommended:** 4 English, 4 math, 4 science (2 science lab), 4 foreign language, 2 social studies, 4 history, 4 academic electives, 4 fine arts. High school diploma is required and GED is accepted. TOEFL required of all international applicants, minimum paper TOEFL 500, minimum computer TOEFL 173.

Application deadline: 8/15
Notification: Rolling
Average GPA: 3.20

Average SAT Math: 510
Average SAT Verbal: 504
Average ACT: 21

Graduated top 10% of class: 13%
Graduated top 25% of class: 38%
Graduated top 50% of class: 70%

COLLEGE GRADUATION REQUIREMENTS

Course waivers allowed: No
Course substitutions allowed: Yes
In what course: Decisions made on a case-by-case basis.

ADDITIONAL INFORMATION

Environment: Mount St. Joseph is a Catholic, coeducational, liberal arts college located approximately 15 miles from downtown Cincinnati.

Student Body:
  Undergrad enrollment: 1,826
  Women: 69%
  Men: 31%
  Percent out-of-state: 12%

Cost Information
  Tuition: $17,200
  Room & board: $5,845
Housing Information
  University housing: Yes
  Percent living on campus: 23%

Greek System
  Fraternity: No
  Sorority: No
Athletics: NCAA Division III

HOCKING COLLEGE

3301 Hocking Parkway, Nelsonville, OH 45764
Phone: 740-753-3591 • Fax: 740-753-1452
E-mail: admissions@hocking.edu • Web: www.hocking.edu
Support: CS • Institution type: 4-year public

LEARNING DISABILITY PROGRAM AND SERVICES

The Access Center Office of Disability Support Services (ACODS) is dedicated to serving the various needs of individuals with disabilities and to promoting their full participation in college life. The Educational Coordinator for students with disabilities helps any student with a learning disability successfully adjust to college life by finding the right fit between the instructional offerings of Hocking College and his/her own individualized learning and personal needs. This is accomplished in part by working with assessment and counseling professionals to assist students in identifying individualized programs of study and means for success by more closely aligning interest and abilities with instructor and program effectiveness. The accommodation process is one of collaboration between students and instructors with support from ACODS. Eligibility is determined on the basis of the presence of a disability and a need for services and accommodations to support an equal educational opportunity. Information from the disability documentation, the student's stated experience with services and accommodations that have been effective in the past, and ACODS professional judgment will be drawn upon in making the eligibility determination.

LD/ADD ADMISSIONS INFORMATION

College entrance tests required: Yes
Interview required: No
Essay required: No
Documentation required for LD: Psychoeducational evaluation preferred.
Documentation required for ADD: Yes
Submitted to: Access Center
Special Ed. HS coursework accepted: N/A

Specific course requirements of all applicants: No
Separate application required for program services: Yes
# of LD applications submitted each year: All who apply
# of LD applications accepted yearly: NR
Total # of students receiving LD services: 171
Acceptance into program means acceptance into college: Student must be admitted and enrolled in the college first and then request services.

ADMISSIONS

The college has open enrollment for any student with a high school diploma or equivalent. Students are not required to take any specific courses or have any specific test score on the ACT/SAT. Students requesting accommodations or services for learning disabilities must be admitted and enrolled, and then they may request services. Current documentation should be submitted.

ADDITIONAL INFORMATION

ACODS staff and the student work together to identify individual needs and then determine which of the support services and accommodations would enable the student to achieve academic potential. Strategies used to assist students with disabilities include assistance with instructional and supportive needs; aligning interest and abilities with instructor and program effectiveness; to assuring individual program implementation consistent with the identified needs of the student; evaluating problematic situations regarding modes of presentation that affect student performance and potential for success; assist on course assignments, troubleshooting learning problems, and assisting in solutions to situations that inhibit success; help in obtaining tutoring services; priority scheduling; liaison with community agencies; and advocacy. Quest for Success is a program designed especially for new students to help them prepare to start technical classes in the fall. Additional services include professional tutors in some mathematics and communications courses, Compu-Lenz to enlarge type on a computer screen and reduce glare, academic advising, and an educational coordinator to act as a liaison with college instructors and community agencies.

Support Services Contact Information

Learning Disability Program/Services: Access Center
Director: Rosie Smith
  E-Mail: smith_r@hocking.edu
  Telephone: 740-753-3591
  Fax: 740-753-4495
Contact Person: Kim Forbes Powell
  E-Mail: forbes_k@hocking.edu
  Telephone: 740-753-3591
  Fax: 740-753-4097

LEARNING DISABILITY SERVICES

Requests for the following/services accommodations will be evaluated individually based on appropriate and current documentation.

Allowed in exams
  Calculator: Yes
  Dictionary: No
  Computer: Yes
  Spellchecker: Yes
Extended test time: Yes
Scribes: Yes
Proctors: Yes
Oral exams: Yes
Note-takers: Yes

Distraction reduced environment: Yes
Tape recording in class: Yes
Books on tape from RFBD: Yes
Taping of books not from RFBD: Yes
Accommodations for students with ADD: Yes
Reading machine: Yes
Other assistive technology: Yes
Priority registration: No
Added costs for services: No

LD specialists: Yes
Professional tutors: 3
Peer tutors: 25-40
Max. hours/wk. for services: Unlimited
How professors are notified of LD/ADD: By student and director

GENERAL ADMISSIONS INFORMATION

Director of Admissions: Lyn Hull
Telephone: 740-753-3591

ENTRANCE REQUIREMENTS

Academic units recommended: 4 English, 3 math, 3 science, 2 foreign language, 4 social studies. Open door admissions. No specific ACT/SAT score required.

Application deadline: Rolling
Notification: Rolling
Average GPA: NR

Average SAT Math: NR
Average SAT Verbal: NR
Average ACT: NR

Graduated top 10% of class: NR
Graduated top 25% of class: NR
Graduated top 50% of class: NR

COLLEGE GRADUATION REQUIREMENTS

Course waivers allowed: NR
Course substitutions allowed: Yes
In what course: Any with an appropriate substitution.

ADDITIONAL INFORMATION

Environment: The college is located on 150 acres in a rural area with easy access to Columbus.

Student Body:
  Undergrad enrollment: 5,070
  Women: 46%
  Men: 54%
  Percent out-of-state: 14%

Cost Information
  In-state tuition: $1,116
  Out-of-state tuition: $2,232
  Room & board: $3,000
Housing Information
  University housing: Yes
  Percent living on campus: 10%

Greek System
  Fraternity: Yes
  Sorority: Yes
Athletics: Intramural

KENT STATE UNIVERSITY

161 Michael Schwartz Center, Kent, OH 44242-0001
Phone: 330-672-2444 • Fax: 330-672-2499
E-mail: admissions@kent.edu • Web: www.kent.edu
Support: CS • Institution type: 4-year public

LEARNING DISABILITY PROGRAM AND SERVICES

The goals and philosophy of the Student Disability Services (SDS) program are to promote student independence and self-advocacy at the college level. The university believes that the ability to do college work is highly correlated with grades in high school. Students with learning disabilities who receive accommodations in high school and who are academically successful are most likely to be successful at KSU. If an LD support system has been available, and the student has been diligent and still has a low GPA in high school, lack of skills or disabilities may be too severe for that student to be successful at KSU. Students should meet with an SDS staff member six months before enrollment to discuss needs and accommodations.

LD/ADD ADMISSIONS INFORMATION

College entrance tests required: Yes
Interview required: Yes
Essay required: No
Documentation required for LD: Psychoeducational evaluation
Documentation required for ADD: Yes
Submitted to: Student Disability Services
Special Ed. HS coursework accepted: No

Specific course requirements of all applicants: Yes
Separate application required for program services: No
# of LD applications submitted each year: NR
# of LD applications accepted yearly: NR
Total # of students receiving LD services: 250
Acceptance into program means acceptance into college: Students must be admitted and enrolled in the university and then may request services.

ADMISSIONS

Students with LD must meet the same admission criteria as all other applicants. There is no special admissions procedure for students with LD. However, the high school may adjust GPA if the student was not diagnosed until late in high school. Documentation of disability is required. In addition to having completed standard college-preparatory courses, applicants should be able to type or use a computer and a calculator and have skills in performing addition, subtraction, multiplication, and division using natural numbers, integers, fractions, and decimals. Students should also have highly developed study skills based on their specific strengths. The minimum GPA for admission is a 2.2 and 21 ACT or 870 SAT. Students who have been in the upper 60 percent of their high school class and have an ACT score of 19+ or SAT of 900+ do very well at KSU.

ADDITIONAL INFORMATION

It is recommended that all documentation be submitted prior to enrolling, as services include academic assistance in selecting courses. All students with documentation of a learning disability may utilize the academic and counseling services, such as academic advising; developmental education courses for freshmen students with deficits in reading, writing, and math; individual and small group tutoring; support groups; and individual and group study-skills help through the Academic Success Center. Services and accommodations are available for undergraduate and graduate students.

Support Services Contact Information

Learning Disability Program/Services: Student Disability Services (SDS)
Director: Anne Jannarone
  E-Mail: ajannaro@kent.edu
  Telephone: 330-672-3391
  Fax: 330-672-3763

LEARNING DISABILITY SERVICES

Requests for the following/services accommodations will be evaluated individually based on appropriate and current documentation.

Allowed in exams
  Calculator: Yes
  Dictionary: Yes
  Computer: Yes
  Spellchecker: Yes
Extended test time: Yes
Scribes: Yes
Proctors: Yes
Oral exams: No
Note-takers: Yes

Distraction reduced environment: Yes
Tape recording in class: Yes
Books on tape from RFBD: Yes
Taping of books not from RFBD: Yes
Accommodations for students with
  ADD: Yes
Reading machine: No
Other assistive technology: Yes
Priority registration: Yes
Added costs for services: No

LD specialists: Yes
Professional tutors: 3
Peer tutors: 50
Max. hours/wk. for services: 4
How professors are notified of
  LD/ADD: By student

GENERAL ADMISSIONS INFORMATION

Director of Admissions: Paul J. Deutsch
Telephone: 330-672-2444

ENTRANCE REQUIREMENTS

Academic units recommended: 4 English, 3 math, 3 science (2 science lab), 2 foreign language, 3 social studies, 1 arts. High school diploma is required and GED is accepted. TOEFL required of all international applicants, minimum paper TOEFL 525, minimum computer TOEFL 197.

Application deadline: 5/1
Notification: Rolling
Average GPA: 3.15

Average SAT Math: 515
Average SAT Verbal: 513
Average ACT: 21

Graduated top 10% of class: 11%
Graduated top 25% of class: 33%
Graduated top 50% of class: 71%

COLLEGE GRADUATION REQUIREMENTS

Course waivers allowed: No
Course substitutions allowed: Y/N
In what course: Decisions are made by individual colleges, and they depend on the student's major.

ADDITIONAL INFORMATION

Environment: The university is a residential campus located on 1,200 acres 45 miles southeast of Cleveland.

Student Body:
  Undergrad enrollment: 19,061
  Women: 59%
  Men: 41%
  Percent out-of-state: 8%

Cost Information
  In-state tuition: $6,882
  Out-of-state tuition: $13,314
  Room & board: $7,920
Housing Information
  University housing: Yes
  Percent living on campus: 33%

Greek System
  Fraternity: Yes
  Sorority: Yes
Athletics: NCAA Division I

MIAMI UNIVERSITY

301 South Campus Avenue, Oxford, OH 45056
Phone: 513-529-2531 • Fax: 513-529-1550
E-mail: admissions@muohio.edu • Web: www.muohio.edu
Support: CS • Institution type: 4-year public

LEARNING DISABILITY PROGRAM AND SERVICES

The Learning Disabilities Program assists students in becoming independent and successful learners, preparing for meaningful careers, and achieving a positive college experience. The program staff coordinates university and community resources to meet the academic and personal needs of students with LD; assist faculty in understanding the characteristics and needs of these students; and provide services on an individual, confidential basis to students with appropriate documentation. All students with LD or ADD are ultimately responsible for their own academic adjustment, including class attendance, assignments, and all other course requirements. It is the student's responsibility to ask for assistance. Appropriate services and accommodations are determined through a flexible, interactive process that involves the student and the coordinator, and are arranged through dialogue with faculty and staff responsible for implementing many of these services or accommodations. Decisions about services and accommodations for students with LD are made on the basis of the disability documentation and the functional limitations caused by the disability, as well as the current needs of the student. Students with ADD must meet with the LD coordinator to initiate services after discussing disability-related needs and providing verification of the disability.

LD/ADD ADMISSIONS INFORMATION

College entrance tests required: Yes
Interview required: No
Essay required: Yes
Documentation required for LD: Psychoeducational
  evaluation
Documentation required for ADD: Yes
Submitted to: Learning Disability Services
Special Ed. HS coursework accepted: NR

Specific course requirements of all applicants: Yes
Separate application required for program services: No
# of LD applications submitted each year: NR
# of LD applications accepted yearly: NR
Total # of students receiving LD services: NR
**Acceptance into program means acceptance into
  college:** Student must be admitted and enrolled in the
  university first and then request services.

ADMISSIONS

Students with LD are admitted to Miami through the regular admission process; therefore, it is important to ensure that the information in the application accurately reflects a student's academic ability and potential. Students are expected to have 4 years English, 3 years math, 3 years science, 3 years social studies, 2 years foreign language, 1 year fine arts. Students with deficiencies may still be qualified for admission. Students may choose to indicate in their application the presence of an LD or ADD, either through a personal essay or the "extenuating circumstances" statement. Also, students may voluntarily choose to submit other information that may help the Office of Admission to understand their unique learning strengths and needs. Applicants with LD are encouraged to meet with the LD coordinator during the college search process to discuss the LD support services, the nature and extent of their disability, the types of accommodations that may be needed, and the program and course requirements in their field of study.

ADDITIONAL INFORMATION

Support services for students with learning disabilities include transition information; admission counseling; priority registration; classroom accommodations such as test modifications, extended exam time; academic assistance such as tutoring and study skills assistance; mentoring in learning strategies, time management, and coping strategies; liaison with faculty; campus advocacy; and counseling and career awareness. The Orton Student Association is a student organization that provides a support system—academically, socially, emotionally, and personally—to students with LD. The group encourages and promotes student and faculty awareness of these conditions through outreach efforts. The Terry A. Gould LD Fund is an endowed account providing funds for instructional materials, program expenses, and conference opportunities for students with LD. The Office of Learning Assistance works with students encountering academic difficulties. The Tutorial Assistance Program provides peer tutors.

Support Services Contact Information

Learning Disability Program/Services: Learning Disability Program/Services
Learning Disabilities Services
Director: Doug Green
 E-Mail: greendw@muohio.edu
 Telephone: 513-529-8741
 Fax: 513-529-8799

LEARNING DISABILITY SERVICES

Requests for the following/services accommodations will be evaluated individually based on appropriate and current documentation.

Allowed in exams
 Calculator: Yes
 Dictionary: Yes
 Computer: Yes
 Spellchecker: Yes
Extended test time: Yes
Scribes: Yes
Proctors: Yes
Oral exams: Yes
Note-takers: Yes

Distraction reduced environment: Yes
Tape recording in class: Yes
Books on tape from RFBD: Yes
Taping of books not from RFBD: Yes
**Accommodations for students with
 ADD:** Yes
Reading machine: Yes
Other assistive technology: Yes
Priority registration: Yes

Added costs for services: No
LD specialists: Yes
Professional tutors: No
Peer tutors: 100–220
Max. hours/wk. for services:
 Unlimited
**How professors are notified of
 LD/ADD:** By student

GENERAL ADMISSIONS INFORMATION

Director of Admissions: Michael Mills
Telephone: 513-529-2531

ENTRANCE REQUIREMENTS

Academic units recommended: 4 English, 3 math, 3 science, 2 foreign language, 3 social studies, 1 fine arts.
High school diploma is required and GED is accepted. ACT with Writing component required or SAT Reasoning test.
TOEFL required of all international applicants, minimum paper TOEFL 533, minimum computer TOEFL 200.

Application deadline: 1/31
Notification: 3/15
Average GPA: 3.70

Average SAT Math: 610
Average SAT Verbal: 590
Average ACT: 26

Graduated top 10% of class: 37%
Graduated top 25% of class: 75%
Graduated top 50% of class: 97%

COLLEGE GRADUATION REQUIREMENTS

Course waivers allowed: No
Course substitutions allowed: Yes
In what course: Foreign language and math—only if it is determined not to be an essential componant of the curriculum and/or major.

ADDITIONAL INFORMATION

Environment: The university is in a small town northwest of Cincinnati.

Student Body:
 Undergrad enrollment: 15,011
 Women: 54%
 Men: 46%
 Percent out-of-state: 28%

Cost Information
 In-state tuition: $11,410
 Out-of-state tuition: $21,410
 Room & board: $7,910
Housing Information
 University housing: Yes
 Percent living on campus: 45%

Greek System
 Fraternity: Yes
 Sorority: Yes
Athletics: NCAA Division I

MUSKINGUM COLLEGE

163 Stormont Drive, New Concord, OH 43762
Phone: 614-826-8137 • Fax: 614-826-8100
E-mail: adminfo@muskingum.edu • Web: www.muskingum.edu
Support: SP • Institution type: 4-year private

LEARNING DISABILITY PROGRAM AND SERVICES

The PLUS Program provides students who have disabilities with the opportunity to reach their academic potential while at Muskingum College. A learning-strategies instructional model administered by a professional staff is the basis for PLUS support. Students may revise full program participation to maintenance (reduced fee) or independence (no fee) based on academic achievement. A full range of accommodations in addition to a structured tutorial are provided through the Center for Advancement of Learning, the framework for academic support at Muskingum College. Program participants must maintain a minimum of one hour of individual tutoring time per week for each class. The program offers no remedial or developmental instruction, encourages individual responsibility for learning, and acknowledges successful individual efforts. The program offers qualified students individual or small group content-based learning strategies, instruction, and content tutorial support. Parent contact is made each semester for students participating in the PLUS Program.

LD/ADD ADMISSIONS INFORMATION

College entrance tests required: Yes
Interview required: Yes
Essay required: Yes
Documentation required for LD: Aptitude test, achievement test, diagnostic statement of functional limitations
Documentation required for ADD: Appropriate testing and diagnostic statement from a qualified professional
Submitted to: PLUS Program
Special Ed. HS coursework accepted: No

Specific course requirements of all applicants: Yes
Separate application required for program services: 150–160
# of LD applications submitted each year: NR
# of LD applications accepted yearly: 60–70
Total # of students receiving LD services: 130–160
Acceptance into program means acceptance into college: Admissions to the PLUS Program is an automatic admission to the College.

ADMISSIONS
Students may apply to the college and the PLUS program after completing their junior year of high school. Admission for students with LD is based on a careful evaluation of all the materials that are submitted with the application. Students must submit: a completed application for admission (check the box for PLUS Program); ACT/SAT; current psychoeducational evaluation documenting disability and administered by a licensed psychologist, or medical diagnosis of ADD; copy of current IEP and transition plan; and a detailed request for and description of auxiliary accommodations being requested. The student is evaluated for potential for academic success as a participant in the PLUS Program. Admission policies are flexible for students with LD, but a good distribution among college-prep courses is helpful. Students should submit recommendations from teachers or guidance counselor. Applicants are reviewed, and selected candidates are invited to interview. Space in the program is limited, and early application is encouraged. The admission decision is made jointly by the program director and admissions director. A summer transitions program is available to students who are admitted to the college and the PLUS Program. Some students admitted to the PLUS Program may be required to attend the transitions program.

ADDITIONAL INFORMATION
PLUS guides students toward increasing learning independence, assigns students to academic advisors and program advisors, and assists students in determining how to balance courses and create an appropriate load each semester. Professionals provide tutorial services and coordinate appropriate testing and instructional accommodations. Students are provided with a combination of individual and small group tutorial support. Students participating in the full program must maintain a minimum of one contact hour of tutoring per week for each course. PLUS maintenance is recommended for upperclassmen as they progress successfully in college. High school juniors and seniors with LD can participate in a comprehensive, two-week summer experience, "First Step," to help them make the transition to college. The primary emphasis is on the application of learning strategies within the context of a college-level expository course. The program focuses on social and emotional changes associated with the transition to college.

Support Services Contact Information

Learning Disability Program/Services: PLUS Program, Center for Advancement of Learning
Director: Dr. Eileen Henry, EdD, MBA
  E-Mail: ehenry@muskingum.edu
  Telephone: 740-826-8284
  Fax: 740-826-8285
Contact Person: Michelle Butler
  E-Mail: butler@muskingum.edu
  Telephone: 740-826-8280
  Fax: 740-826-8285

LEARNING DISABILITY SERVICES

Requests for the following/services accommodations will be evaluated individually based on appropriate and current documentation.

Allowed in exams
  Calculator: Yes
  Dictionary: Yes
  Computer: Yes
  Spellchecker: Yes
Extended test time: Yes
Scribes: Yes
Proctors: Yes
Oral exams: Yes
Note-takers: Yes

Distraction reduced environment: Yes
Tape recording in class: Yes
Books on tape from RFBD: Yes
Taping of books not from RFBD: Yes
Accommodations for students with ADD: Yes
Reading machine: Yes
Other assistive technology: Yes
Priority registration: Yes

Added costs for services: No
LD specialists: Yes
Professional tutors: 22
Peer tutors: No
Max. hours/wk. for services: 6.5
How professors are notified of LD/ADD: By both student and director

GENERAL ADMISSIONS INFORMATION

Director of Admissions: Beth Dalanzo
Telephone: 614-826-8137

ENTRANCE REQUIREMENTS

Academic units required: 4 English, 2 math, 2 science (1 science lab), 2 foreign language, 1 social studies, 2 history. **Academic units recommended:** 4 English, 3 math, 3 science (2 science lab), 2 foreign language, 1 social studies, 2 history. High school diploma is required and GED is accepted. TOEFL required of all international applicants, minimum paper TOEFL 550, minimum computer TOEFL 213.

Application deadline: 8/1
Notification: Rolling
Average GPA: 3.22

Average SAT Math: 520
Average SAT Verbal: 530
Average ACT: 22

Graduated top 10% of class: 22%
Graduated top 25% of class: 42%
Graduated top 50% of class: 74%

COLLEGE GRADUATION REQUIREMENTS

Course waivers allowed: No
Course substitutions allowed: No
In what course: N/A

ADDITIONAL INFORMATION

Environment: The college is located on 215 acres in a rural area 70 miles east of Columbus.

Student Body:
  Undergrad enrollment: 1,615
  Women: 48%
  Men: 52%
  Percent out-of-state: 9%

Cost Information
  Tuition: $14,920
  Room & board: $6,200
Housing Information
  University housing: Yes
  Percent living on campus: 85%

Greek System
  Fraternity: Yes
  Sorority: Yes
  Athletics: NCAA Division III

OBERLIN COLLEGE

101 North Professor Street, Oberlin College, Oberlin, OH 44074
Phone: 440-775-8411 • Fax: 440-775-6905
E-mail: college.admissions@oberlin.edu • Web: www.oberlin.edu
Support: S • Institution type: 4-year private

LEARNING DISABILITY PROGRAM AND SERVICES

Personnel from the Office of Services for Students with Disabilities (OSSD) understand that challenge and provide services, as well as coordinate accommodations, to meet the needs of students who have disabilities. The goal is to maximize the entire student's educational potential while helping him/her develop and maintain independence. The program philosophy is one that encourages self-advocacy. Students who are diagnosed by OSSD personnel as having a LD, as well as those who can provide documentation of a current diagnosis of a LD, are eligible for services. To verify a previously diagnosed LD, a student must provide a psychological assessment, educational test results, and a recent copy of an individualized education program that specifies placement in a learning disabilities program. These documents will be reviewed by personnel from OSSD to determine eligibility. Students requesting services are interviewed by a learning disability counselor before a service plan is developed or initiated.

LD/ADD ADMISSIONS INFORMATION

College entrance tests required: Yes
Interview required: No
Essay required: No
Documentation required for LD: A recent psychological evaluation.
Documentation required for ADD: Yes
Submitted to: Services for Students with Disabilities
Special Ed. HS coursework accepted: Yes

Specific course requirements of all applicants: Yes
Separate application required for program services: No
# of LD applications submitted each year: NR
# of LD applications accepted yearly: NR
Total # of students receiving LD services: 200
Acceptance into program means acceptance into college: Student must be admitted and enrolled in the university first and then request services.

ADMISSIONS

There is no special admissions procedure for students with LD. All applicants must meet the same admission requirements. Courses required include 4 years English and math and at least 3 years social science and science. GPA is typically a B average or better. ACT scores range between 25-30; SAT scores range between 1100–1320 and SAT Subject Test scores range between 560–680 on each Reasoning Test. Students who self-disclose and provide documentation may have their files read by OSSD personnel, who will provide a recommendation to the Office of Admissions. Students who can provide valid and recent documentation of a psycho educational diagnosis of a LD may receive services.

ADDITIONAL INFORMATION

A Learning Resource Center and an Adaptive Technology Center are available for all students. Skills classes are offered for college credit in reading, study skills, and writing. OSSD can arrange one or all of the following services for students with learning disabilities: quiet space for exams; extended examination time, up to twice the time typically allotted, based on diagnosis; oral exams; scribes; individual academic, personal, and vocational counseling; peer support groups for the development of academic strategies and psychosocial adjustments; computer resources for additional academic skill development and assistance; taped textbooks, based on careful planning and lead time; priority academic scheduling; peer tutoring; diagnostic testing; new student orientation assistance; and faculty/staff consultation. In addition, OSSD can provide information about other support services sponsored by the college.

Support Services Contact Information

Learning Disability Program/Services: Services for Students with Disabilities (OSSD)
Director: Jane Boomer
  E-Mail: jane.boomer@oberlin.edu
  Telephone: 440-775-8467
  Fax: 440-775-3010

LEARNING DISABILITY SERVICES

Requests for the following/services accommodations will be evaluated individually based on appropriate and current documentation.

Allowed in exams	**Distraction reduced environment:** Yes	**Added costs for services:** No
Calculator: Yes	**Tape recording in class:** Yes	**LD specialists:** No
Dictionary: Yes	**Books on tape from RFBD:** Yes	**Professional tutors:** No
Computer: Yes	**Taping of books not from RFBD:** Yes	**Peer tutors:** 38
Spellchecker: Yes	**Accommodations for students with**	**Max. hours/wk. for services:**
Extended test time: Yes	**ADD:** Yes	Unlimited
Scribes: Yes	**Reading machine:** Yes	**How professors are notified of**
Proctors: Yes	**Other assistive technology:** Yes	**LD/ADD:** By both student and director
Oral exams: Yes	**Priority registration:** Yes	
Note-takers: Yes		

GENERAL ADMISSIONS INFORMATION

Director of Admissions: Debra Chermonte
Telephone: 440.775.8411

ENTRANCE REQUIREMENTS

Academic units required: 4 English, 4 math, 3 science, 3 foreign language, 3 social studies. High school diploma is required and GED is accepted. ACT with Writing component required or SAT. TOEFL required of all international applicants, minimum paper TOEFL 600, minimum computer TOEFL 200.

Application deadline: 1/15	**Average SAT Math:** 656	**Graduated top 10% of class:** 67%
Notification: 4/1	**Average SAT Verbal:** 683	**Graduated top 25% of class:** 85%
Average GPA: 3.55	**Average ACT:** 30	**Graduated top 50% of class:** 96%

COLLEGE GRADUATION REQUIREMENTS

Course waivers allowed: No
Course substitutions allowed: Yes
In what course: Case by case

ADDITIONAL INFORMATION

Environment: The college is located on 440 acres in a small town, 35 miles southwest of Cleveland.

Student Body:	**Cost Information**	**Greek System**
Undergrad enrollment: 2,807	**Tuition:** $30,925	**Fraternity:** No
Women: 55%	**Room & board:** $7,643	**Sorority:** No
Men: 45%	**Housing Information**	**Athletics:** NCAA Division III
Percent out-of-state: 90%	**University housing:** Yes	
	Percent living on campus: 73%	

OHIO STATE UNIVERSITY—COLUMBUS

110 Emerson Hall, 154 West 12th Avenue, Columbus, OH 43210
Phone: 614-292-3980 • Fax: 614-292-4818
E-mail: askabuckeye@osu.edu • Web: www.osu.edu
Support: CS • Institution type: 4-year public

LEARNING DISABILITY PROGRAM AND SERVICES

The mission of the Office for Disability Services (ODS) is threefold: to seek to ensure that students can freely and actively participate in all facets of university life, to provide and coordinate support services and programs to maximize educational potential, and to increase the level of awareness among all members of the university community so that students with disabilities are able to perform at a level only by their abilities—not their disabilities. ODS helps students in their efforts to attain an excellent college education by promoting self-advocacy skills, self-understanding, and independence. Staff members are specialists in learning disabilities. Students are assigned to a counselor who understands their disability. Counselors assist and advise students about how to make the most of college life and, more importantly, will advise students on how to succeed academically. Disability Services matches services with students' needs. The staff recommends specific services, but students select the services that are suitable for them based upon recommendations.

LD/ADD ADMISSIONS INFORMATION

College entrance tests required: Yes
Interview required: No
Essay required: No
Documentation required for LD: Psychoeducational
evaluation administered within the last three years
Documentation required for ADD: Yes. Test results should
be no older than three years.
Submitted to: Office for Disability Services
Special Ed. HS coursework accepted: No

Specific course requirements of all applicants: Yes
Separate application required for program services: No
# of LD applications submitted each year: NR
# of LD applications accepted yearly: NR
Total # of students receiving LD services: 300
**Acceptance into program means acceptance into
college:** Student must be admitted and enrolled in the
university first and then request services.

ADMISSIONS

Students with LD are admitted under the same criteria as regular applicants. However, consideration can be given to students with LD with support from ODS in instances where the student's rank, GPA, or lack of courses, such as foreign language, have affected their performance in high school. Applicants interested in services should submit a general application for admission to the admissions office; complete the section on the application form under Optional Personal Statement that gives students the opportunity to provide information if they feel that their high school performance was adversely affected by special circumstances; and submit documentation of t he disability to ODS, including the latest IEP and the results of the last psychoeducational testing. ODS will review the application, look at coursework and deficiencies,review services received in high school and determine if the student's needs can be met at OSU if the student is not normally admissible; look at when a diagnosis was made and at the IEP; and make a recommendation to Admissions. ODS will send a letter acknowledging receipt of the documentation. The letter will indicate whether services needed can be provided and if additional information is necessary. Students exceeding the minimum curriculum in math, natural resources, or foreign language will be given additional consideration. Other factors considered include the competitiveness of the high school, accelerated courses taken, first-generation college student, or cultural, economic, racial, or geographic diversity, outstanding talents, extracurricular activities, significant work experiences, or leadership positions.

ADDITIONAL INFORMATION

ODS is staffed by many specialists, including learning disability specialists and 10 counselors. The LD specialists will meet with students once a week. ODS can arrange for services including quiet studio space for exams; extended exam time; readers and/or scribes; computers for essay exams; access to class notes; taped textbooks through RFBD; taping of textbooks not available through RFBD; peer support groups to help develop academic strategies and psychosocial adjustment; peer tutoring for assistance in learning specific class material; diagnostic testing for learning disabilities; orientation assistance, including scheduling and training to assist in accessing services; Computer Learning Center and assistance in computer usage; priority academic scheduling; faculty-staff consultation; and family consultation. Non-credit workshops are offered on academic effectiveness from the Counseling Center and the Reading/Study Skills Program.

Support Services Contact Information

Learning Disability Program/Services: Office for Disability Services (ODS)
Director: Patty Carlton
  E-Mail: carlton.1@osu.edu
  Telephone: 614-292-3307
  Fax: 614-292-4190
Contact Person: Lois Burke
  E-Mail: burke.4@osu.edu
  Telephone: 614-292-3307
  Fax: 614-292-4190

LEARNING DISABILITY SERVICES

Requests for the following/services accommodations will be evaluated individually based on appropriate and current documentation.

Allowed in exams
  Calculator: Yes
  Dictionary: Yes
  Computer: Yes
  Spellchecker: Yes
Extended test time: Yes
Scribes: Yes
Proctors: Yes
Oral exams: Yes
Note-takers: Yes

Distraction reduced environment: Yes
Tape recording in class: Yes
Books on tape from RFBD: Yes
Taping of books not from RFBD: Yes
Accommodations for students with ADD: Yes
Reading machine: Yes
Other assistive technology: Yes
Priority registration: Yes

Added costs for services: No
LD specialists: Yes
Professional tutors: No
Peer tutors: Yes
Max. hours/wk. for services: Varies
How professors are notified of LD/ADD: By student

GENERAL ADMISSIONS INFORMATION

Director of Admissions: Mabel Freeman
Telephone: 614-247-6281

ENTRANCE REQUIREMENTS

Academic units required: 4 English, 3 math, 2 science (2 science lab), 2 foreign language, 2 social studies, 1 academic elective, 1 visual and performing arts. **Academic units recommended:** 4 English, 4 math, 3 science (3 science lab), 3 foreign language, 3 social studies, 1 academic elective, 1 visual and performing arts. High school diploma is required and GED is accepted. ACT with Writing component required or SAT Reasoning test. TOEFL required of all international applicants, minimum paper TOEFL 527, minimum computer TOEFL 197.

Application deadline: 2/1
Notification: Rolling
Average GPA: NR
Average SAT Math: 601
Average SAT Verbal: 578
Average ACT: 25
Graduated top 10% of class: 34%
Graduated top 25% of class: 71%
Graduated top 50% of class: 96%

COLLEGE GRADUATION REQUIREMENTS

Course waivers allowed: No
Course substitutions allowed: Yes
In what course: On a case-by-case basis and with appropriate supporting disability documentation, some students can petition for a substitution of the foreign language if it is not essential for the major. Math substitutions are rare.

ADDITIONAL INFORMATION

Environment: The campus is in an urban area 4 miles from downtown Columbus.

Student Body:
  Undergrad enrollment: 36,097
  Women: 47%
  Men: 53%
  Percent out-of-state: 9%

Cost Information
  In-state tuition: $7,446
  Out-of-state tuition: $18,033
  Room & board: $6,792
Housing Information
  University housing: Yes
  Percent living on campus: 90%

Greek System
  Fraternity: Yes
  Sorority: Yes
Athletics: NCAA Division I

OHIO UNIVERSITY

120 Chubb Hall, Athens, OH 45701
Phone: 740-593-4100 • Fax: 740-593-0560
E-mail: admissions@ohiou.edu • Web: www.ohiou.edu
Support: S • Institution type: 4-year public

LEARNING DISABILITY PROGRAM AND SERVICES

The Office for Institutional Equity helps students with disabilities coordinate the services needed to enjoy full participation in academic programs and campus life. Students are heard, advised, and assisted in achieving goals. Students are urged to have confidence in their abilities and to feel comfortable talking with their professors about their disability. Accommodations are a result of collaborative efforts between the student, faculty, and staff of the Office for Institutional Equity. The goal is to identify and strategize a plan to assist the student in achieving success in his/her educational pursuits. Students should provide the Office for Institutional Equity with a course schedule the first week of the quarter in order for professors to be notified of the student's status in the class. Students also need to communicate with professors in advance of requesting accommodations. Extra time to complete assignments and take tests can be arranged. Students should also take advantage of the tutoring sessions that can be arranged. It is very important that students understand that the accommodations requested may not be the ones considered reasonable by the university.

LD/ADD ADMISSIONS INFORMATION

College entrance tests required: Yes
Interview required: No
Essay required: No
Documentation required for LD: Psychoeducational
  evaluations
Documentation required for ADD: Yes
Submitted to: Disability Student Services
Special Ed. HS coursework accepted: Yes

Specific course requirements of all applicants: Yes
Separate application required for program services: No
# of LD applications submitted each year: NR
# of LD applications accepted yearly: NR
Total # of students receiving LD services: 400
**Acceptance into program means acceptance into
  college:** Student must be admitted and enrolled in the
  university first and then request services.

ADMISSIONS

Applicants with learning disabilities are expected to meet the same admission criteria as all other applicants. General admission requires the applicant to be in the top 30 percent with 21 ACT or 990 SAT, or top 50% with 23 ACT or 1060 SAT. The mid 50 percent range for ACT is 22–26 and SAT 1030–1200. Students taking the ACT must must submit the optional writing section. Students can be admitted with deficiencies. Applicants with learning disabilities who meet the criteria should send documentation to special services after admission. Those students not meeting the admission criteria are encouraged to self-disclose by writing a narrative explaining the impact of the disability condition on the student's academic career as well as sending relevant documentation. This disclosure and accompanying documentation will be reviewed by admissions. Students, in general, must demonstrate the ability to perform in a mainstream academic setting where support is available when needed. Counselor recommendation is very helpful for students who do not meet the traditional criteria.

ADDITIONAL INFORMATION

General services provided include advising referral and liaison, academic adjustments and classroom accommodations, priority scheduling, free tutoring through the Academic Advancement Center (four hours per course per week), and tutoring in writing and reading skills. Skills classes are offered in learning strategies, college reading skills, reading, speed, and vocabulary. Services are available to undergraduate and graduate students.

Support Services Contact Information

Learning Disability Program/Services: Office for Institutional Equity/Disability Student Services
Director: Katherine Fahey
  E-Mail: fahey@oak.cats.ohiou.edu
  Telephone: 740-593-2620
  Fax: 740-593-0790

LEARNING DISABILITY SERVICES

Requests for the following/services accommodations will be evaluated individually based on appropriate and current documentation.

Allowed in exams	**Distraction reduced environment:** Yes	**Added costs for services:** No
Calculator: Yes	**Tape recording in class:** Yes	**LD specialists:** No
Dictionary: Yes	**Books on tape from RFBD:** Yes	**Professional tutors:** No
Computer: Yes	**Taping of books not from RFBD:** No	**Peer tutors:** 300
Spellchecker: Yes	**Accommodations for students with**	**Max. hours/wk. for services:** 4
Extended test time: Yes	**ADD:** Yes	**How professors are notified of**
Scribes: Yes	**Reading machine:** Yes	**LD/ADD:** By student
Proctors: No	**Other assistive technology:** Yes	
Oral exams: Yes	**Priority registration:** Yes	
Note-takers: No		

GENERAL ADMISSIONS INFORMATION

Director of Admissions: Jean Lewis, Interim Director
Telephone: 740-593-4100

ENTRANCE REQUIREMENTS

Academic units recommended: 4 English, 3 math, 3 science, 2 foreign language, 3 social studies, 1 visual or performing arts. High school diploma is required and GED is accepted. ACT with Writing component required.

Application deadline: 2/1	**Average SAT Math:** 550	**Graduated top 10% of class:** 17%
Notification: Rolling	**Average SAT Verbal:** 550	**Graduated top 25% of class:** 47%
Average GPA: 3.44	**Average ACT:** 23	**Graduated top 50% of class:** 86%

COLLEGE GRADUATION REQUIREMENTS

Course waivers allowed: No
Course substitutions allowed: Yes
In what course: Any substitution would be specific to each individual and his/her learning disability. This is not done as a general rule.

ADDITIONAL INFORMATION

Environment: The university is in a small town south of Ohio State University.

Student Body:	**Cost Information**	**Greek System**
Undergrad enrollment: 16,802	**In-state tuition:** $7,404	**Fraternity:** Yes
Women: 53%	**Out-of-state tuition:** $15,396	**Sorority:** Yes
Men: 47%	**Room & board:** $7,539	**Athletics:** NCAA Division I
Percent out-of-state: 8%	**Housing Information**	
	University housing: Yes	
	Percent living on campus: 43%	

UNIVERSITY OF CINCINNATI

P.O. Box 210091, Cincinnati, OH 45221-0091
Phone: 513-556-1100 • Fax: 513-556-1105
E-mail: admissions@uc.edu • Web: www.uc.edu
Support: S • Institution type: 4-year public

LEARNING DISABILITY PROGRAM AND SERVICES

The University of Cincinnati does not have a specific structured learning disability program. However, students with learning disabilities who use academic accommodations and support services available through the Disability Services and other resources of the university find they can be successful in achieving their academic objectives. The goal of Disability Services is to provide the necessary accommodations to students in order for them to become successful and independent learners. Remedial developmental courses are available along with campus wide tutoring. To receive support services students need to submit documentation from a licensed professional to the Disability Services Office. Service staff will work with students and faculty to arrange for special needs or accommodations.

LD/ADD ADMISSIONS INFORMATION

College entrance tests required: Yes
Interview required: No-Recommended
Essay required: No
Documentation required for LD: Psychoeducational evaluation
Documentation required for ADD: Yes
Submitted to: Disability Services
Special Ed. HS coursework accepted: No

Specific course requirements of all applicants: Yes
Separate application required for program services: No
# of LD applications submitted each year: NR
# of LD applications accepted yearly: NR
Total # of students receiving LD services: 250-plus
Acceptance into program means acceptance into college: Student must be admitted and enrolled in the university first and then request services.

ADMISSIONS

There is no special admissions procedure for students with learning disabilities. The admissions office looks at each individual situation; there is no set rule for admissions and waivers. All students submit the general university application form. Course requirements and waivers depend upon the college within the university. General course requirements include 4 years English, 3 years math (4 for engineering), 2 years science, 2 years social studies, and 2 years foreign language (not required in business) or can substitute American Sign Language. Some students who do not meet regular admissions standards may be admitted into the College Access Program (CAPS). Students may transfer to other majors after one year if they are doing well the four-year majors after receiving an associate degree. Students with learning disabilities are encouraged to request an interview with the Disability Services Office, which their parents may attend.

ADDITIONAL INFORMATION

Disabilities Services provides services and accommodations that are mandated under federal law. Support services include note taking, tutors, readers, taped textbooks, testing accommodations, scribes, loan of equipment, and library disability services. Peer tutoring is available as an accommodation at no cost. Students with appropriate documentation may request course substitutions in math or foreign language. Skills classes are offered for all students in time management, organizational skills, and study skills. Developmental courses in effective reading, English, and mathematics as well as a college study course are offered.

Support Services Contact Information

Learning Disability Program/Services: Disability Services
Director: Debra Merchant, JD
  E-Mail: debra.merchant@uc.edu
  Telephone: 513-556-6823
  Fax: 513-556-1383

LEARNING DISABILITY SERVICES

Requests for the following/services accommodations will be evaluated individually based on appropriate and current documentation.

Allowed in exams
  Calculator: Yes
  Dictionary: Yes
  Computer: Yes
  Spellchecker: Yes
Extended test time: Yes
Scribes: Yes
Proctors: Yes
Oral exams: Yes
Note-takers: Yes

Distraction reduced environment: Yes
Tape recording in class: Yes
Books on tape from RFBD: Yes
Taping of books not from RFBD: Yes
Accommodations for students with ADD: Yes
Reading machine: Yes
Other assistive technology: Yes
Priority registration: Yes
Added costs for services: No

LD specialists: Yes
Professional tutors: Grad Students
Peer tutors: 1–15
Max. hours/wk. for services: Unlimited
How professors are notified of LD/ADD: By student

GENERAL ADMISSIONS INFORMATION

Director of Admissions: Thomas Canepa
Telephone: 513-556-1082

ENTRANCE REQUIREMENTS

Academic units required: 4 English, 3 math, 2 science, 2 foreign language, 2 social studies, 2 academic electives.
Academic units recommended: 4 math, 3 science, 1 history. High school diploma is required and GED is accepted. Minimum paper TOEFL 515, minimum computer TOEFL 193.

Application deadline: 9/1
Notification: Rolling
Average GPA: 3.13

Average SAT Math: 556
Average SAT Verbal: 548
Average ACT: 22

Graduated top 10% of class: 16%
Graduated top 25% of class: 37%
Graduated top 50% of class: 67%

COLLEGE GRADUATION REQUIREMENTS

Course waivers allowed: No
Course substitutions allowed: Yes
In what course: Math, foreign lanuage

ADDITIONAL INFORMATION

Environment: The university is located on 392 acres in downtown Cincinnati.

Student Body:
  Undergrad enrollment: 18,993
  Women: 49%
  Men: 51%
  Percent out-of-state: 8%

Cost Information
  In-state tuition: $7,005
  Out-of-state tuition: $19,977
  Room & board: $7,425
Housing Information
  University housing: Yes
  Percent living on campus: 17%

Greek System
  Fraternity: Yes
  Sorority: Yes
Athletics: NCAA Division I

University of Cincinnati

University of Dayton

300 College Park, Dayton, OH 45469-1300
Phone: 937-229-4411 • Fax: 937-229-4729
E-mail: admission@udayton.edu • Web: www.udayton.edu
Support: CS • Institution type: 4-year private

LEARNING DISABILITY PROGRAM AND SERVICES

Every individual student with a disability is guaranteed equal access to all educational programs and activities at the University of Dayton. Qualified persons with disabilities who have been accepted at the University of Dayton are those who have met the University's standards. Students with disabilities must submit a copy of the results of a psychological/educational assessment or a physical and/or a psychological assessment by a qualified evaluator for the delivery of academic support and/or special services. Students who have provided appropriate documentation and have been interviewed by the Coordinator of the Office for Students with Disabilities are considered registered under the University policies. There is no obligation for any student to identify a disability; however, students who wish to receive special and/or reasonable accommodations must submit proper documentation, participate in an assessment interview with the Coordinator for Students with Disabilities, and request in writing the need for specific services.

LD/ADD ADMISSIONS INFORMATION

College entrance tests required: Yes
Interview required: No
Essay required: No
Documentation required for LD: Psychoeducational
    evaluation
Documentation required for ADD: Yes
Submitted to: LEAD: Disability Services
Special Ed. HS coursework accepted: N/A

Specific course requirements of all applicants: Yes
Separate application required for program services: No
# of LD applications submitted each year: NR
# of LD applications accepted yearly: NR
Total # of students receiving LD services: NR
**Acceptance into program means acceptance into
    college:** Students must be admitted and enrolled in the
    university and then request services

ADMISSIONS

Applications for admission are reviewed for specific academic majors or, when applicable, for undeclared status in an academic division. Five factors are considered when applications are assessed: your selection of courses in preparation for college, your grade record and pattern throughout high school, your class standing or ranking, results of either the SAT or ACT, and your character and record of leadership and service. Balanced consideration is given to all aspects of your college preparation. While no minimum grade point average, class rank or standardized test score is specified, these measures must provide evidence of your readiness for college studies in your chosen academic program.

ADDITIONAL INFORMATION

Because the university recognizes that students have individually unique academic and personal strengths and weaknesses, the office of Learning Enhancement and Academic Development (LEAD) provides support services to students such as drop-in tutoring (peer-facilitated), with additional support models (supplemental instruction) linked to specific classes, as well as tutor-supported English and math sections, and writing support across the curriculum. The Write Place tutors work with all students in their efforts to become better writers. LEAD offers a developmental math course designed to help students improve basic skills.

Support Services Contact Information

Learning Disability Program/Services: LEAD: Disability Services
Director: Timothy King, PhD
  E-Mail: Timothy.King@notes.udayton.edu
  Telephone: 937-229-2066
  Fax: 937-229-3270
Contact Person: Brenda D. Cooper, Program Coordinator
  E-Mail: Brenda.Cooper@notes.udayton.edu
  Telephone: 937-229-2066
  Fax: 937-229-3270

LEARNING DISABILITY SERVICES

Requests for the following/services accommodations will be evaluated individually based on appropriate and current documentation.

Allowed in exams
  Calculator: Yes
  Dictionary: Yes
  Computer: Yes
  Spellchecker: Yes
Extended test time: Yes
Scribes: Yes
Proctors: Yes
Oral exams: Yes
Note-takers: Yes

Distraction reduced environment: Yes
Tape recording in class: Yes
Books on tape from RFBD: Yes
Taping of books not from RFBD: No
Accommodations for students with ADD: Yes
Reading machine: No
Other assistive technology: Yes
Priority registration: Yes

Added costs for services: No
LD specialists: Yes
Professional tutors: No
Peer tutors: Yes
Max. hours/wk. for services: Varies
How professors are notified of LD/ADD: By student

GENERAL ADMISSIONS INFORMATION

Director of Admissions: Robert F. Durkle
Telephone: 937-229-4411

ENTRANCE REQUIREMENTS
Academic units required: 2 units of foreign language. **Academic units recommended:** 4 English, 3 math, 2 science, 3 social studies, 4 academic electives. High school diploma is required and GED is accepted. ACT with or without Writing component accepted. TOEFL required of all international applicants, minimum paper TOEFL 523, minimum computer TOEFL 193.

Application deadline: Rolling
Notification: Rolling
Average GPA: NR

Average SAT Math: 582
Average SAT Verbal: 568
Average ACT: 25

Graduated top 10% of class: 22%
Graduated top 25% of class: 46%
Graduated top 50% of class: 77%

COLLEGE GRADUATION REQUIREMENTS

Course waivers allowed: Yes
Course substitutions allowed: Yes
In what course: Each student's request would be reviewed on a case by case basis.

ADDITIONAL INFORMATION

Environment: The University of Dayton is an urban campus in Dayton.

Student Body:
  Undergrad enrollment: 7,008
  Women: 50%
  Men: 50%
  Percent out-of-state: 34%

Cost Information
  Tuition: $20,860
  Room & board: $6,700
Housing Information
  University housing: Yes
  Percent living on campus: 79%

Greek System
  Fraternity: Yes
  Sorority: Yes
Athletics: NCAA Division I

UNIVERSITY OF TOLEDO

2801 West Bancroft, Toledo, OH 43606
Phone: 419-530-8700 • Fax: 419-530-5713
E-mail: enroll@utnet.utoledo.edu • Web: www.utoledo.edu
Support: CS • Institution type: 4-year public

LEARNING DISABILITY PROGRAM AND SERVICES

The University of Toledo sees its students as people first. The university strives always to provide a nurturing environment that can help strengthen the student as a whole human being—mind, body, and spirit. The goal of the Office of Accessibility is to provide comprehensive academic support services to allow for equal opportunity in pursuing a post-secondary education. Students with learning disabilities should identify the nature of their disability and/or attention deficit disorder and provide this information to the Office of Accessibility along with current psychoeducational evaluation or medical diagnosis of ADD. Students should provide information about the support services received in high school. The Office of Accessibility respects the right to privacy for each student and maintains confidentiality. The support service personnel, faculty directly involved with the student's classes, academic advisers, and administrative staff members exchange information with the Office of Accessibility pertaining to the nature of the student's disability, accommodations requested, and academic status. Students must sign a form indicating their understanding of the release of information for the Office of Accessibility and giving permission to release the information.

LD/ADD ADMISSIONS INFORMATION

College entrance tests required: Yes
Interview required: No
Essay required: No
Documentation required for LD: Psychoeducational evaluation
Documentation required for ADD: Yes
Submitted to: Office of Accessibility
Special Ed. HS coursework accepted: Yes

Specific course requirements of all applicants: Yes
Separate application required for program services: No
# of LD applications submitted each year: NR
# of LD applications accepted yearly: 80–100
Total # of students receiving LD services: 300–375
Acceptance into program means acceptance into college: Student must be admitted and enrolled in the university first and then request services.

ADMISSIONS

There is no separate admissions process for students with learning disabilities. All students must meet the same admission criteria. Admissions standards include GPA of at least 2.0 or the equivalent of a C GPA; 18 ACT or higher for Ohio residents and 21 ACT or 1000 SAT score for non-Ohio residents; 4 years English, 3 years math, 3 years science, 3 years social studies, and 2 years foreign language; and high school graduation requirements fulfilled or successful passing score on the GED. Ohio residents not meeting these requirements are reviewed on an individual basis for admission consideration. Some programs, including engineering, nursing, physical therapy, pharmacy, premedical, pre-dentistry, and pre-veterinary, have higher requirements.

ADDITIONAL INFORMATION

The Office of Accessibility requests a program pnformation form giving background information and disability-related information. There are no limitations on the number of students who can receive services and accommodations. Students are automatically accepted into the program once they are admitted to the university and provide appropriate documentation. The following support services are provided if supported by documentation: note taking services; reader services, texts on tape, and a one-on-one reader; extension of time for quizzes and tests, and proctors to help with reading or/and writing; tutoring services; counseling for academic advising, social/interpersonal counseling, and disability advising; instructor contact, personal memos, and liaison between student and professor; registration assistance, advanced registration, and priority registration; scholarship funds; Challenged Individuals Association for students; and adaptive technology.

Support Services Contact Information

Learning Disability Program/Services: Office of Accessibility
Director: Kendra Johnson
  E-Mail: kjohnso3@utnet.utoledo.edu
  Telephone: 419-530-4981
  Fax: 419-530-6137

LEARNING DISABILITY SERVICES

Requests for the following/services accommodations will be evaluated individually based on appropriate and current documentation.

Allowed in exams
  Calculator: Yes
  Dictionary: Yes
  Computer: Yes
  Spellchecker: Yes
Extended test time: Yes
Scribes: Yes
Proctors: Yes
Oral exams: Yes
Note-takers: Yes

Distraction reduced environment: Yes
Tape recording in class: Yes
Books on tape from RFBD: No
Taping of books not from RFBD: No
Accommodations for students with
  ADD: Yes
Reading machine: No
Other assistive technology: Yes
Priority registration: Yes

Added costs for services: No
LD specialists: Yes
Professional tutors: No
Peer tutors: 75-80
Max. hours/wk. for services:
  Unlimited
How professors are notified of
  LD/ADD: By both student and director

GENERAL ADMISSIONS INFORMATION

Director of Admissions: Jennifer Kwiatkowski (Interim Director)
Telephone: 419-530-5737

ENTRANCE REQUIREMENTS

Academic units required: 4 English, 3 math, 3 science, 3 social studies. **Academic units recommended:** 4 English, 3 math, 3 science, (1 science lab), 2 foreign language, 3 social studies, 1 history. High school diploma is required and GED is accepted. ACT with Writing component required or SAT Reasoning test. TOEFL required of all international applicants, minimum paper TOEFL 500, minimum computer TOEFL 173.

Application deadline: Rolling
Notification: Rolling
Average GPA: 3.08

Average SAT Math: 517
Average SAT Verbal: 503
Average ACT: 21

Graduated top 10% of class: 16%
Graduated top 25% of class: 36%
Graduated top 50% of class: 63%

COLLEGE GRADUATION REQUIREMENTS

Course waivers allowed: No
Course substitutions allowed: Yes
In what course: Foreign language if considered appropriate. Each case is decided on an individualized basis.

ADDITIONAL INFORMATION

Environment: The University of Toledo is located on a 305-acre campus in Toledo, Ohio.

Student Body:
  Undergrad enrollment: 15,640
  Women: 50%
  Men: 50%
  Percent out-of-state: 3%

Cost Information
  In-state tuition: $5,988
  Out-of-state tuition: $14,800
  Room & board: $7,500
Housing Information
  University housing: Yes
  Percent living on campus: 20%

Greek System
  Fraternity: Yes
  Sorority: Yes
Athletics: NCAA Division I

URSULINE COLLEGE

2550 Lander Road, Pepper Pike, OH 44124-4398
Phone: 440-449-4203 • Fax: 440-684-6138
E-mail: admission@ursuline.edu • Web: www.ursuline.edu
Support: SP • Institution type: 4-year private

LEARNING DISABILITY PROGRAM AND SERVICES

Ursuline College is a small Catholic college committed to helping students with learning disabilities succeed in their courses and become independent learners. The Program for Students with Learning Disabilities (PSLD) is a voluntary, comprehensive fee-paid program. PSLD's goals include providing a smooth transition to college life, helping students learn to apply the most appropriate learning strategies in college courses, and teaching self-advocacy skills. To be eligible for PSLD, a student must present documentation of an LD, which consists of a WAIS–R, the Woodcock—Johnson, and any other standardized measures of achievement. The psychoeducational evaluation must clearly indicate that the student has a specific learning disability and should have been conducted within the last three years. Students must have average to above-average intellectual ability and an appropriate academic foundation to succeed in a four-year liberal arts college.

LD/ADD ADMISSIONS INFORMATION

College entrance tests required: Yes
Interview required: Yes
Essay required: No
Documentation required for LD: WAIS–R/Woodcock–Johnson
Documentation required for ADD: Testing—psychological/M.D.
Submitted to: Academic Support and Disabilities Services
Special Ed. HS coursework accepted: Yes

Specific course requirements of all applicants: Yes
Separate application required for program services: Yes
# of LD applications submitted each year: 6–11
# of LD applications accepted yearly: 10
Total # of students receiving LD services: 25
Acceptance into program means acceptance into college: Student must be admitted and enrolled in the college first and then request services.

ADMISSIONS

To participate in PSLD, students must first meet with the LD specialist to discuss whether the program is suitable for them. Students must then meet the requirements for clear or conditional admission to the college by applying to the Admissions Office and completing all regular admission procedures. Students with learning disabilities must meet the same requirements for admission to the college as all other students: 2.5 GPA and an ACT score of 17 or an SAT score of 850 for a clear admission. Courses recommended include 4 years English, 3 years social studies, 3 years math, 3 years science, and 2 years foreign language. A student may receive a conditional admission if the GPA and ACT are lower. Course deficiencies must be removed prior to graduation from college. Students with conditional admission are limited to 12 credit hours per semester for the first year. The final admission decision is made by the Office of Admissions.

ADDITIONAL INFORMATION

PSLD is a program that features an orientation that provides a smooth transition to the college, acquaints students with mentors and other students in PSLD, and introduces students to high-tech equipment and computers in the LRC. Individual, bi-weekly, one-hour sessions are offered with LD specialists to work on developing time management and organizational skills, design learning strategies for success in college, and learn note taking and test-taking skills. Also offered are individual weekly one-hour sessions with a writing specialist who provides assistance with writing assignments in specific courses and who helps with developing skills in writing effective sentences, paragraphs, and essays; weekly academic-skills support groups with LD specialist to learn coping skills, develop self-advocacy skills, and receive support for dealing with classroom issues; and academic advising for guidance on choosing appropriate courses and scheduling appropriate number of credits each semester.

Support Services Contact Information

Learning Disability Program/Services: Academic Support and Disabilities Services
Director: Eileen D. Kohut
  E-Mail: EKohut@ursuline.edu
  Telephone: 440-646-8123
  Fax: 440-644-6114
Contact Person: Jill Carroll
  E-Mail: jcarroll@ursuline.edu
  Telephone: 440-449-2049
  Fax: 440-684-6114

LEARNING DISABILITY SERVICES

Requests for the following/services accommodations will be evaluated individually based on appropriate and current documentation.

Allowed in exams
  Calculator: Yes
  Dictionary: Yes
  Computer: Yes
  Spellchecker: Yes
Extended test time: Yes
Scribes: Yes
Proctors: Yes
Oral exams: Yes
Note-takers: Yes

Distraction reduced environment: Yes
Tape recording in class: Yes
Books on tape from RFBD: Yes
Taping of books not from RFBD: Yes
**Accommodations for students with
  ADD:** Yes
Reading machine: Yes
Other assistive technology: Yes
Priority registration: Yes

Added costs for services: Yes
LD specialists: Yes
Professional tutors: 6
Peer tutors: No
Max. hours/wk. for services: 3
**How professors are notified of
  LD/ADD:** By student

GENERAL ADMISSIONS INFORMATION

Director of Admissions: Sarah Sundermeier, Director of Admission
Telephone: 440-449-4203

ENTRANCE REQUIREMENTS

Academic units recommended: 4 English, 3 math, 3 science (2 science lab), 2 foreign language, 3 social studies, 2 fine or performing arts, 1 physical education/heatlh. High school diploma is required and GED is accepted. ACT with or without Writing component accepted. TOEFL required of all international applicants, minimum paper TOEFL 500, minimum computer TOEFL 173.

Application deadline: Rolling
Notification: Rolling
Average GPA: 3.17

Average SAT Math: 470
Average SAT Verbal: 494
Average ACT: 20

Graduated top 10% of class: 34%
Graduated top 25% of class: 40%
Graduated top 50% of class: 81%

COLLEGE GRADUATION REQUIREMENTS

Course waivers allowed: N/A
Course substitutions allowed: N/A
In what course: N/A

ADDITIONAL INFORMATION

Environment: The college is located in a suburban area about 20 miles from Cleveland.

Student Body:
  Undergrad enrollment: 1,106
  Women: 92%
  Men: 8%
  Percent out-of-state: 10%

Cost Information
  Tuition: $20,160
  Room & board: $6,366
Housing Information
  University housing: Yes
  Percent living on campus: 14%

Greek System
  Fraternity: No
  Sorority: No
Athletics: NAIA

WRIGHT STATE UNIVERSITY

3640 Colonel Glenn Highway, Dayton, OH 45435
Phone: 937-775-5700 • Fax: 937-775-5795
E-mail: admissions@wright.edu • Web: www.wright.edu
Support: SP • Institution type: 4-year public

LEARNING DISABILITY PROGRAM AND SERVICES

The university is dedicated to the elimination of barriers that prevent intellectually qualified individuals with disabilities from attending colleges and universities across the country. Students with disabilities are encouraged to participate in all facets of university life according to their abilities and interests and to develop independence and responsibility to the fullest extent possible. The philosophy of the university is intended to stimulate students to pursue the career of study regardless of their learning disability. Through the Office of Disability Services, the university provides a comprehensive array of services on a campus with a long history of commitment to students with physical, visual, and/or learning disabilities. Students with learning disabilities may use a variety of services that will allow them to be equal and competitive in the classroom. A pre-service interview is required of all prospective students to discuss service needs. Eligibility for services is determined after documentation is received and the student has an individual interview.

LD/ADD ADMISSIONS INFORMATION

College entrance tests required: Yes
Interview required: Yes
Essay required: No
Documentation required for LD: WAIS–III, WRAT, WJ (within 3 years)
Documentation required for ADD: NR
Submitted to: Office of Disability Services
Special Ed. HS coursework accepted: No

Specific course requirements of all applicants: Yes
Separate application required for program services: Yes
# of LD applications submitted each year: 55–75
# of LD applications accepted yearly: All who are eligible
Total # of students receiving LD services: 175–200
Acceptance into program means acceptance into college: Student must be admitted and enrolled in the university first and then request services.

ADMISSIONS

The university has an open admission policy for in-state students. ACT/SATs used for placement, not admission. The mid 50 percent range for the ACT is 18–24 and SAT 990–1140. Students with LD must meet the identical criteria as all applicants and must be accepted prior to requesting service. However, out-of-state students are encouraged to self-disclose their learning disability and submit documentation to the Office of Disability Services prior to applying to the university if they would like to discuss eligibility for admission and services available on campus and determine if Wright State is a good fit for them. It is recommended that students self disclose the LD if GPA or test scores are low and the student feels that LD disclosure is important in explaining academic or testing information. Course requirements include 4 years English, 3 years math, 3 years science and social science, 2 years foreign language and 1 year fine arts. The director of Disability Services encourages students and their families to visit and interview. Admissions would ask ODS to review documentation, and transcripts and meet with the student to determine readiness for college. Students with a college-prep curriculum in high school have been more successful at Wright State than those who took a general curriculum. The final decision rests with admissions.

ADDITIONAL INFORMATION

Conditional admissions to the university is available to students who enter with a high school deficiency. They must remove it before graduating from the university or complete developmental education courses. All new students attend summer orientation. A separate orientation is held prior to the start of fall quarter for students with Learning Disabilities. To determine eligibility for support services after admission, the following are required: results of psychological testing, a Request for Support Services form completed by the student, and a transcript of high school classes completed, as well as of any post-secondary courses taken. Students must write a 100-word handwritten, uncorrected statement about why they are requesting support services through the Learning Disabilities Program. Application for services for ODS is separate and not connected to the application to the university. Interview and documentation are required.

Support Services Contact Information

Learning Disability Program/Services: Office of Disability Services
Director: Jeff Vernooy
  E-Mail: jeffrey.vernooy@wright.edu
  Telephone: 937-775-5680
  Fax: 937-775-5795
Contact Person: Cassandra Mitchell
  E-Mail: disability_services@wright.edu
  Telephone: 937-775-5680
  Fax: 937-775-5795

LEARNING DISABILITY SERVICES

Requests for the following/services accommodations will be evaluated individually based on appropriate and current documentation.

Allowed in exams
  Calculator: Yes
  Dictionary: Yes
  Computer: Yes
  Spellchecker: Yes
Extended test time: Yes
Scribes: Yes
Proctors: Yes
Oral exams: Yes
Note-takers: Yes

Distraction reduced environment: Yes
Tape recording in class: Yes
Books on tape from RFBD: Yes
Taping of books not from RFBD: Yes
Accommodations for students with
  ADD: Yes
Reading machine: Yes
Other assistive technology: Yes
Priority registration: No

Added costs for services: No
LD specialists: Yes
Professional tutors: No
Peer tutors: 40–50
Max. hours/wk. for services: 10
How professors are notified of
  LD/ADD: By student

GENERAL ADMISSIONS INFORMATION

Director of Admissions: Cathy Davis
Telephone: 937-775-5700

ENTRANCE REQUIREMENTS

Academic units required: 4 English, 3 math, 3 science (3 science lab), 2 foreign language, 3 social studies. High school diploma is required and GED is accepted. ACT with or without Writing component accepted. TOEFL required of all international applicants, minimum paper TOEFL 500, minimum computer TOEFL 173.

Application deadline: Rolling
Notification: Rolling
Average GPA: 2.99

Average SAT Math: 540
Average SAT Verbal: 425
Average ACT: 20

Graduated top 10% of class: 16%
Graduated top 25% of class: 36%
Graduated top 50% of class: 66%

COLLEGE GRADUATION REQUIREMENTS

Course waivers allowed: Yes
Course substitutions allowed: Yes
In what course: Foreign language and in a few cases, math

ADDITIONAL INFORMATION

Environment: The university is located on 645 acres eight miles northeast of Dayton.

Student Body:
  Undergrad enrollment: 11,691
  Women: 57%
  Men: 43%
  Percent out-of-state: 3%

Cost Information
  In-state tuition: $6,440
  Out-of-state tuition: $12,500
  Room & board: $6,300
Housing Information
  University housing: Yes
  Percent living on campus: 22%

Greek System
  Fraternity: Yes
  Sorority: Yes
Athletics: NCAA Division I

XAVIER UNIVERSITY (OH)

3800 Victory Parkway, Cincinnati, OH 45207-5311
Phone: 513-745-3301 • Fax: 513-745-4319
E-mail: xuadmit@xavier.edu • Web: www.xavier.edu
Support: CS • Institution type: 4-year private

LEARNING DISABILITY PROGRAM AND SERVICES

The Learning Assistance Center's mission is three-fold: to insure that all students with disabilities can freely and actively participate in every aspect of college life; to provide academic support services so that students with disabilities have equal educational access; and to seek to educate the community at large. The Learning Assistance Center provides support services to facilitate learning at Xavier. Our primary function is to serve students with disabilities. Second, we run various programs open to all Xavier students. These include tutoring, workshops, and study groups.

LD/ADD ADMISSIONS INFORMATION

College entrance tests required: Yes
Interview required: No
Essay required: Yes
Documentation required for LD: Psychoeducational evaluation
Documentation required for ADD: Yes
Submitted to: Learning Assistance Center
Special Ed. HS coursework accepted: Yes

Specific course requirements of all applicants: Yes
Separate application required for program services: No
# of LD applications submitted each year: NR
# of LD applications accepted yearly: NR
Total # of students receiving LD services: 240
Acceptance into program means acceptance into college: Student must be admitted and enrolled in the university first and then request services.

ADMISSIONS

There is no special admissions process for students with learning disabilities. However, there is a Freshman Success Program for some admitted students who would benefit from a reduced course load and more guidance and mentoring.

ADDITIONAL INFORMATION

The Xavier Learning Assistance Center (LAC) implements a co-active coaching program. Coaching is not counseling, but an on-going partnership between the coach and the student to help the student set and achieve goals in their academic lives. In the university setting, coaching focuses on the student's academic goals, emphasizing their grades and career decisions. It gives students who are struggling the opportunity to examine their own resources and strengths. With the guidance of a coach, these students will be able to implement the necessary changes to achieve their desired success. All students have access to the math lab, writing center, and tutoring center. Additionally, there are study skills classes offered in time management and test-taking strategies. Students with learning disabilities and/or ADD also have access to support groups, special testing, and mentoring. Accommodations and services are available for undergraduates and graduates.

Support Services Contact Information

Learning Disability Program/Services: Learning Assistance Center
Director: Ann Dinan, PhD
  E-Mail: dinan@xavier.edu
  Telephone: 513-745-3280
  Fax: 513-745-3387

LEARNING DISABILITY SERVICES

Requests for the following/services accommodations will be evaluated individually based on appropriate and current documentation.

Allowed in exams
  Calculator: Yes
  Dictionary: Yes
  Computer: Yes
  Spellchecker: Yes
Extended test time: Yes
Scribes: Yes
Proctors: Yes
Oral exams: Yes
Note-takers: Yes

Distraction reduced environment: Yes
Tape recording in class: Yes
Books on tape from RFBD: Yes
Taping of books not from RFBD: Yes
Accommodations for students with ADD: Yes
Reading machine: No
Other assistive technology: Yes
Priority registration: Yes

Added costs for services: No
LD specialists: Yes
Professional tutors: No
Peer tutors: 35
Max. hours/wk. for services: Unlimited
How professors are notified of LD/ADD: By Director

GENERAL ADMISSIONS INFORMATION

Director of Admissions: Marc Camille
Telephone: 513-745-2943

ENTRANCE REQUIREMENTS

Academic units recommended: 4 English, 3 math, 3 science, 2 foreign language, 3 social studies, 5 academic electives, 1 health/physical education. High school diploma is required and GED is accepted. ACT with or without Writing component accepted. TOEFL required of all international applicants, minimum paper TOEFL 500, minimum computer TOEFL 173.

Application deadline: 2/1
Notification: 3/15
Average GPA: 3.57

Average SAT Math: 588
Average SAT Verbal: 583
Average ACT: 26

Graduated top 10% of class: 29%
Graduated top 25% of class: 58%
Graduated top 50% of class: 89%

COLLEGE GRADUATION REQUIREMENTS

Course waivers allowed: Yes
Course substitutions allowed: Yes
In what course: Only substitutions are offered, usually in math and foreign language. Students are encouraged to petition the Deans Committee on Course Substitutions early in the Xavier careers. Documentation must support substitutions.

ADDITIONAL INFORMATION

Environment: The University is located five miles from downtown Cincinatti.

Student Body:
  Undergrad enrollment: 3,770
  Women: 56%
  Men: 44%
  Percent out-of-state: 37%

Cost Information
  Tuition: $21,000
  Room & board: $7,930
Housing Information
  University housing: Yes
  Percent living on campus: 48%

Greek System
  Fraternity: No
  Sorority: No
  Athletics: NCAA Division I

OKLAHOMA STATE UNIVERSITY

219 Student Union, Stillwater, OK 74078
Phone: 800-233-5019 • Fax: 405-744-5285
E-mail: admit@okstate.edu • Web: www.okstate.edu
Support: S • Institution type: 4-year public

LEARNING DISABILITY PROGRAM AND SERVICES

Oklahoma State University does not have a formal learning disabilities program but uses a service-based model to assist students in obtaining the necessary accommodations for specific learning disabilities. Students with learning disabilities may request priority enrollment and a campus orientation to assist in scheduling classes. Other services developed in coordination with special education work to minimize student difficulties in relation to coursework. These services could include test accommodations, course substitutions, and independent study. The underlying philosophy of this program is to provide assistance to students to facilitate their academic progress. Student Disability Services (SDS) also acts as a resource for faculty and staff.

LD/ADD ADMISSIONS INFORMATION

College entrance tests required: Yes
Interview required: No
Essay required: No
Documentation required for LD: Adult-normed evaluations of ability and achievement, WAIS–R (ability), Woodcock–Johnson–R (achievement) and clear diagnostic statement.
Documentation required for ADD: TOVA, Connor's checklist, clinical interiew and clear diagnostic statement
Submitted to: Student Disability Services
Special Ed. HS coursework accepted: No

Specific course requirements of all applicants: Yes
Separate application required for program services: No
# of LD applications submitted each year: NR
# of LD applications accepted yearly: NR
Total # of students receiving LD services: 180–190
Acceptance into program means acceptance into college: Student must be admitted and enrolled in the university first and then request services.

ADMISSIONS

There is no special admissions policy for students with learning disabilities. Applicants with learning disabilities must meet the same specific requirements of the program in which they wish to enroll. General admission requirements include ACT 22+ or SAT 1020+, 3.0 GPA, and courses in English, math, science, and history. Students with appropriate documentation may be allowed to substitute courses for math or foreign language. The alternative admission program allows students to present evidence of potential success. It is available to students whose high school achievement is slightly below the standards specified in the performance requirements and/or are deficient in no more than one curricular unit. Space is limited and only those applicants showing the best potential for academic success will be admitted. Eight percent of all students may be admitted on probation. Admitted students are encouraged to contact SDS to discuss special services or accommodations.

ADDITIONAL INFORMATION

There is a math lab and a writing center for all students. All students with LD/ADD requesting accommodations or services must provide appropriate and current documentation. All diagnostic testing and documentation should be sent to Student Disability Services. There are currently 180 students with learning disabilities and 60 with ADD receiving services on campus. The university also operates the Oklahoma City Technical Institute, which offers two-year, career-oriented programs.

Support Services Contact Information

Learning Disability Program/Services: Student Disability Services (SDS)
Director: Michael Shuttic
  E-Mail: shuttic@ okstate.edu
  Telephone: 405-744-7116
  Fax: 405-744-8380

LEARNING DISABILITY SERVICES

Requests for the following/services accommodations will be evaluated individually based on appropriate and current documentation.

Allowed in exams
  Calculator: Yes
  Dictionary: Yes
  Computer: Yes
  Spellchecker: Yes
Extended test time: Yes
Scribes: Yes
Proctors: Yes
Oral exams: Yes
Note-takers: Yes

Distraction reduced environment: Yes
Tape recording in class: Yes
Books on tape from RFBD: Yes
Taping of books not from RFBD: Yes
Accommodations for students with
  ADD: Yes
Reading machine: Yes
Other assistive technology: Yes
Priority registration: Yes

Added costs for services: No
LD specialists: No
Professional tutors: No
Peer tutors: No
Max. hours/wk. for services:
  Unlimited
How professors are notified of
  LD/ADD: By both student and director

GENERAL ADMISSIONS INFORMATION

Director of Admissions: Dr. Paul Carney
Telephone: 405-744-7275

ENTRANCE REQUIREMENTS

Academic units required: 4 English, 3 math, 2 science (2 science lab), 2 social studies, 1 history, 3 academic electives. **Academic units recommended:** 2 foreign language, 1 computer science. High school diploma is required and GED is accepted. ACT with or without Writing component accepted. TOEFL required of all international applicants, minimum paper TOEFL 500, minimum computer TOEFL 173.

Application deadline: Rolling
Notification: Rolling
Average GPA: 3.51

Average SAT Math: 569
Average SAT Verbal: 539
Average ACT: 24

Graduated top 10% of class: 24%
Graduated top 25% of class: 52%
Graduated top 50% of class: 84%

COLLEGE GRADUATION REQUIREMENTS

Course waivers allowed: Yes
Course substitutions allowed: Yes
In what course: Math, foreign language; based on degree requirements and major.

ADDITIONAL INFORMATION

Environment: The 415-acre campus is located in a small city, 65 miles north of Oklahoma City.

Student Body:
  Undergrad enrollment: 18,636
  Women: 49%
  Men: 51%
  Percent out-of-state: 14%

Cost Information
  In-state tuition: $2,910
  Out-of-state tuition: $10,200
  Room & board: $5,602
Housing Information
  University housing: Yes
  Percent living on campus: 40%

Greek System
  Fraternity: Yes
  Sorority: Yes
Athletics: NCAA Division I

UNIVERSITY OF OKLAHOMA

1000 Asp Aveune, Norman, OK 73019-4076
Phone: 405-325-2252 • Fax: 405-325-7124
E-mail: admrec@ou.edu • Web: www.ou.edu
Support: S • Institution type: 4-year public

LEARNING DISABILITY PROGRAM AND SERVICES

The Office of Disability Services provides support services and is committed to the goal of achieving equal educational opportunity and full participation for students with disabilities. In many cases, these services are developed in response to expressed student needs. There are no special LD or remedial classes. Students are encouraged to be self-advocates in making requests for reasonable academic accommodations. Assistance is to be used to support the accomplishment of educational goals. The coordinator of services sponsors the OU Association for Disabled Students, a student organization that provides a recognized forum for support, regular meetings, and social and recreational activities. Students must provide psychoeducational evaluations documenting learning disabilities in order to receive services. The evaluation should include full-scale, performance, and verbal I.Q. scores, scores from aptitude-achievement comparisons, and a summary and recommendations.

LD/ADD ADMISSIONS INFORMATION

College entrance tests required: Yes
Interview required: No
Essay required: No
Documentation required for LD: WAIS–II, WJR within three years prefered
Documentation required for ADD: DSM–IV, Narrative summary, description, medication needs and recommendation
Submitted to: Office of Disabilities Services
Special Ed. HS coursework accepted: No

Specific course requirements of all applicants: Yes
Separate application required for program services: No
# of LD applications submitted each year: NR
# of LD applications accepted yearly: NR
Total # of students receiving LD services: 225
Acceptance into program means acceptance into college: Student must be admitted and enrolled in the university first and then request services.

ADMISSIONS

Admission requirements for students with learning disabilities are the same as for all other students. Course requirements include 4 years English, 2 years science, 3 years math, 2 years social studies, 1 unit in economics, geography, government or non-western culture, and 3 additional subjects. The university strongly recommends additional course work in music, art, drama or speech. ACT score required is 22+ and/or SAT 1010+. The expected GPA is 3.0. and top 33 percent of the graduating class. Applicants who do not meet the general admission criteria but who believe they are prepared to be successful in college are encouraged to apply. Careful attention will be given to an applicant's written comments concerning background and educational goals, personal interviews, as well as letters of recommendation from counselors, teachers, principals, and employers attesting to the student's motivation and potential for academic success.

ADDITIONAL INFORMATION

After receiving academic advisement from the college, the student should make an appointment with Disabled Student Services. The office will also provide a personal campus orientation upon request. Services offered, based on individual needs, include alternative testing, readers, scribes, note-takers (who are volunteers), tutors, tape-recorded texts, and library assistance. Tutoring is provided on a one-to-one basis by peer tutors. Services are available for undergraduate and graduate students.

Support Services Contact Information

Learning Disability Program/Services: Office of Disability Services
Director: Suzette Dyer
  E-Mail: sdyer@ou.edu
  Telephone: 405-325-3852
  Fax: 405-325-4491

LEARNING DISABILITY SERVICES

Requests for the following/services accommodations will be evaluated individually based on appropriate and current documentation.

Allowed in exams
  Calculator: Yes
  Dictionary: Yes
  Computer: Yes
  Spellchecker: Yes
Extended test time: Yes
Scribes: Yes
Proctors: Yes
Oral exams: Yes
Note-takers: Yes

Distraction reduced environment: Yes
Tape recording in class: Yes
Books on tape from RFBD: Yes
Taping of books not from RFBD: Y/N
Accommodations for students with ADD: Yes
Reading machine: Yes
Other assistive technology: Yes
Priority registration: Yes

Added costs for services: No
LD specialists: No
Professional tutors: No
Peer tutors: 25–50
Max. hours/wk. for services: As needed
How professors are notified of LD/ADD: By Director

GENERAL ADMISSIONS INFORMATION

Director of Admissions: Patricia Lynch, Director
Telephone: 405)3252252

ENTRANCE REQUIREMENTS

Academic units required: 4 English, 3 math, 2 science (2 science lab), 2 social studies, 1 history, 3 academic electives. **Academic units recommended:** 3 foreign language, 1 computer science. High school diploma is required and GED is accepted. ACT with or without Writing component accepted. TOEFL required of all international applicants, minimum paper TOEFL 550, minimum computer TOEFL 213.

Application deadline: 4/1
Notification: Rolling
Average GPA: 3.59

Average SAT Math: 597
Average SAT Verbal: 589
Average ACT: 26

Graduated top 10% of class: 36%
Graduated top 25% of class: 71%
Graduated top 50% of class: 92%

COLLEGE GRADUATION REQUIREMENTS

Course waivers allowed: No
Course substitutions allowed: Yes
In what course: Students may petition for a substitution in foreign language.

ADDITIONAL INFORMATION

Environment: The 3,107-acre campus is located in a suburb 17 miles south of Oklahoma City.

Student Body:
  Undergrad enrollment: 20,843
  Women: 50%
  Men: 50%
  Percent out-of-state: 22%

Cost Information
  In-state tuition: $2,778
  Out-of-state tuition: $10,296
  Room & board: $5,814
Housing Information
  University housing: Yes
  Percent living on campus: 20%

Greek System
  Fraternity: Yes
  Sorority: Yes
Athletics: NCAA Division I

University of Oklahoma

UNIVERSITY OF TULSA

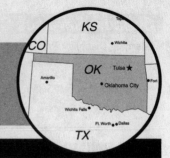

600 South College Avenue, Tulsa, OK 74104
Phone: 918-631-2307 • Fax: 918-631-5003
E-mail: admission@utulsa.edu • Web: www.utulsa.edu
Support: • Institution type: 4-year private

LEARNING DISABILITY PROGRAM AND SERVICES

The Center for Student Academic Support offers a comprehensive range of academic support services and accommodations to students with disabilities. The goal is to provide services which will, in combination with the resources and talents of the student, maximize student independence for full participation in the curriculum and provide an opportunity to achieve career goals. The policy of the University of Tulsa, in keeping with the Americans with Disabilities Act, is to provide reasonable accommodations for students with disabilities, including students with learning disabilities. Students who have specific disabilities that might impact their full access and participation in university programs are urged to provide the relevant documentation and make an appointment with the coordinator of the Center for Student Academic Support.

LD/ADD ADMISSIONS INFORMATION

College entrance tests required: Yes
Interview required: No
Essay required: Yes
Documentation required for LD: Psychoeducational
  evaluation
Documentation required for ADD: Yes
Submitted to: Center for Students Academic Support
Special Ed. HS coursework accepted: Yes

Specific course requirements of all applicants: Yes
Separate application required for program services: Yes
# of LD applications submitted each year: 80
# of LD applications accepted yearly: 74
Total # of students receiving LD services: 85
**Acceptance into program means acceptance into
  college:** Student must be admitted and enrolled in the
  university first and then request services.

ADMISSIONS

All students must meet the general admissions requirements. Students with disabilities are not required to disclose information about the disability, but may voluntarily disclose or request information from CSAS. The university does not consider disabilities in the decision-making process, even if there is knowledge of the disability, without a request and disclosure by the applicant. Students may provide verification of the disability which should be submitted directly to CSAS. General admission requirements include 4 years English, 3 years math, 4 years science, and 2 years foreign language. Students must have all required courses for admission. The average ACT is above 21 and for the SATs 1080–1140. Students applying to the nursing or athletic training programs must submit a special application. Conditional admission is available for freshmen and probational admission is an option for transfer students. The student with learning disabilities also needs to complete the application form and intake sheet. Also required is documentation presented from a doctor stating diagnostic material and diagnosis of the disorder.

ADDITIONAL INFORMATION

Accommodations students might qualify for, depending upon their documentation and needs, include extended time on tests, priority registration, testing in self-contained environment, use of spelling aids on written exams, texts on tape, note-takers, preferential seating, tests given orally, and enlarged print tests. Concerns regarding requests for a referral for evaluation of a learning disability should be directed to the coordinator of the Center for Student Academic Support. Students with LD must provide documentation that includes tests of intellect and of achievement administered by a professional. Students with documented ADD must provide behavior checklist (one completed by a doctor), a test of intellect, a test of attention, and a clinical interview that includes a history of the ADD.

Support Services Contact Information

Learning Disability Program/Services: Center for Student Academic Support
Director: Dr. Jane Corso
 E-Mail: jane-corso@utulsa.edu
 Telephone: 918-631-2315
 Fax: 918-631-3459

LEARNING DISABILITY SERVICES

Requests for the following/services accommodations will be evaluated individually based on appropriate and current documentation.

Allowed in exams
 Calculator: Yes
 Dictionary: Yes
 Computer: Yes
 Spellchecker: Yes
Extended test time: Yes
Scribes: Yes
Proctors: Yes
Oral exams: Yes
Note-takers: Yes

Distraction reduced environment: Yes
Tape recording in class: Yes
Books on tape from RFBD: Yes
Taping of books not from RFBD: Yes
Accommodations for students with ADD: Yes
Reading machine: Yes
Other assistive technology: Yes
Priority registration: Yes

Added costs for services: No
LD specialists: Yes
Professional tutors: 4
Peer tutors: 75
Max. hours/wk. for services: Unlimited
How professors are notified of LD/ADD: By both student and director

GENERAL ADMISSIONS INFORMATION

Director of Admissions: Mr. John C. Corso
Telephone: 918-631-2307

ENTRANCE REQUIREMENTS

Academic units recommended: 4 English, 3 math, 3 science (2 science lab), 2 foreign language, 1 social studies, 2 history, 1 academic elective. High school diploma is required and GED is accepted. ACT with or without Writing component accepted. TOEFL required of all international applicants, minimum paper TOEFL 500, minimum computer TOEFL 173.

Application deadline: NR
Notification: Rolling
Average GPA: 3.70

Average SAT Math: 610
Average SAT Verbal: 610
Average ACT: 26

Graduated top 10% of class: 56%
Graduated top 25% of class: 76%
Graduated top 50% of class: 94%

COLLEGE GRADUATION REQUIREMENTS

Course waivers allowed: Yes
Course substitutions allowed: Yes
In what course: N/A

ADDITIONAL INFORMATION

Environment: The campus is in an urban area.

Student Body:
 Undergrad enrollment: 2,699
 Women: 50%
 Men: 50%
 Percent out-of-state: 28%

Cost Information
 Tuition: $16,750
 Room & board: $5,896
Housing Information
 University housing: Yes
 Percent living on campus: 64%

Greek System
 Fraternity: Yes
 Sorority: Yes
Athletics: NCAA Division I

University of Tulsa

OREGON STATE UNIVERSITY

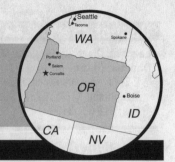

104 Kerr Administration Building, Corvallis, OR 97331-2106
Phone: 541-737-4411 • Fax: 541-737-2482
E-mail: osuadmit@orst.edu • Web: oregonstate.edu
Support: S • Institution type: 4-year public

LEARNING DISABILITY PROGRAM AND SERVICES

OSU is committed to providing equal opportunity for higher education to academically qualified students without regard to disability. Services for Students with Disabilities (SSD) strives to be sensitive to the individual needs of students by offering a variety of services. Services rendered are dependent on the type of learning disability. Services are provided to ensure an equal opportunity to succeed but do not guarantee success. Self-advocacy and independence are promoted. SSD is available for all students who need extra services. The Educational Opportunities Program (EOP) offers students who are learning disabled, economically disadvantaged, or first-generation college-bound a variety of remedial courses for credit. EOP tries to provide tutoring for any undergraduate class if tutors are available. To be recognized as a person with a learning disability, students are required to submit documentation from a qualified educational evaluator. Preferred diagnostic testing would include at least one test in each of the following categories: cognitive, achievement, and processing. Other documentation specifying a learning disability without testing in the three categories mentioned must include an in-depth valid assessment of the disability by a qualified professional.

LD/ADD ADMISSIONS INFORMATION

College entrance tests required: Yes
Interview required: No
Essay required: No-Recommended
Documentation required for LD: I.Q., Achievements, processing tests, less than 3 years old
Documentation required for ADD: Appropriate documentation from a psychologist/psychiatrist must include educational testing
Submitted to: Services for students with Disabilities
Special Ed. HS coursework accepted: No

Specific course requirements of all applicants: Yes
Separate application required for program services: No
# of LD applications submitted each year: NR
# of LD applications accepted yearly: NR
Total # of students receiving LD services: 150
Acceptance into program means acceptance into college: Student must be admitted and enrolled in the university first and then request services.

ADMISSIONS

All students must submit the general application for admission. If a student does not meet admissions requirements, admission will be denied. Enclosed with the notification, the student will receive information regarding petitioning for special admission. Students who want to petition their admission on the basis of a learning disability must submit all information required in the petition. Petitioning students must utilize the services of EOP. The director of SSD helps to make admission decisions and may recommend EOP for the student with LD. Regular admission requires a 3.0 GPA and special admit for students with 2.5. Students requesting services should self-identify; submit documentation of their LD, including educational history and diagnostic testing administered by professionals; and include information describing cognitive strengths and weaknesses, recommendations for accommodations or services, and any other additional information in the form of a family history. Students must also submit a handwritten one-two page statement outlining educational goals and explaining motivation to succeed at OSU. Students admitted through the EOP Program must start in the summer and attend a required SSD orientation in the beginning of fall. EOP admission decision is made jointly between admissions and EOP.

ADDITIONAL INFORMATION

Students with LD, whether admitted regularly or as special admits, are encouraged to apply for additional assistance from EOP, which can provide special counseling, tutoring, and intensive practice in study skills. Accommodations in instruction and related academic work may include alternative test methods, such as extended testing time, and use of resources, such as calculators and dictionaries. Accommodations are negotiated with instructors, academic departments, and the college as appropriate. Personal counseling is available through the Counseling Center. The director acts as a liaison between students and faculty.

Support Services Contact Information

Learning Disability Program/Services: Services for Students with Disabilities (SSD)
Director: Tracy Bentley-Townlin, PhD
  E-Mail: tracey.bentley@orst.edu
  Telephone: 541-737-4098
  Fax: 541-737-7354

LEARNING DISABILITY SERVICES

Requests for the following/services accommodations will be evaluated individually based on appropriate and current documentation.

Allowed in exams
  Calculator: Yes
  Dictionary: No
  Computer: Yes
  Spellchecker: Yes
Extended test time: Yes
Scribes: Yes
Proctors: Yes
Oral exams: Yes
Note-takers: Yes

Distraction reduced environment: Yes
Tape recording in class: Yes
Books on tape from RFBD: Yes
Taping of books not from RFBD: Yes
Accommodations for students with
  ADD: Yes
Reading machine: Yes
Other assistive technology: Yes
Priority registration: Yes

Added costs for services: No
LD specialists: No
Professional tutors: No
Peer tutors: Yes
Max. hours/wk. for services: Offered through EOP for all students as available
How professors are notified of LD/ADD: By both student and director

GENERAL ADMISSIONS INFORMATION

Director of Admissions: Robert Bontrager
Telephone: 541-737-4411

ENTRANCE REQUIREMENTS

Academic units required: 4 English, 3 math, 2 science, 2 foreign language, 3 social studies. **Academic units recommended:** 1 science lab. High school diploma is required and GED is accepted. TOEFL required of all international applicants, minimum paper TOEFL 550, minimum computer TOEFL 213.

Application deadline: Rolling
Notification: Rolling
Average GPA: 3.48

Average SAT Math: 548
Average SAT Verbal: 532
Average ACT: 23

Graduated top 10% of class: 19%
Graduated top 25% of class: 48%
Graduated top 50% of class: 83%

COLLEGE GRADUATION REQUIREMENTS

Course waivers allowed: No
Course substitutions allowed: Yes
In what course: On a case-by-case basis, dependent on the major selected, and documentation.

ADDITIONAL INFORMATION

Environment: The university is located on 530 acres in a small town 85 miles south of Portland.

Student Body:
  Undergrad enrollment: 15,137
  Women: 47%
  Men: 53%
  Percent out-of-state: 10%

Cost Information
  In-state tuition: $5,350
  Out-of-state tuition: $17,750
  Room & board: $6,786
Housing Information
  University housing: Yes
  Percent living on campus: 22%

Greek System
  Fraternity: Yes
  Sorority: Yes
Athletics: NCAA Division I

UNIVERSITY OF OREGON

1217 University of Oregon, Eugene, OR 97403-1217
Phone: 541-346-3201 • Fax: 541-346-5815
E-mail: uoadmit@oregon.uoregon.edu • Web: www.uoregon.edu
Support: CS • Institution type: 4-year public

LEARNING DISABILITY PROGRAM AND SERVICES

At the University of Oregon, Disability Services coordinates services and provides advocacy and support to students with documented learning disabilities. Eligibility for services must be supported by professional documentation of disability and need for services. Accommodations are determined on a case-by-case basis. Students who feel they are eligible for services should meet with the counselor for students with disabilities. At this meeting students will be able to discuss the documentation process, services available, and their educational goals. Disability Services will work with students and faculty members to best accommodate needs. A general letter explaining the particular disability and suggested accommodations will be written, by request, to share with faculty at the students' discretion. This letter is reissued each academic term to designated instructors. Students with learning disabilities should be motivated, hard-working, and willing to take responsibility for meeting their educational goals.

LD/ADD ADMISSIONS INFORMATION

College entrance tests required: Yes
Interview required: No
Essay required: Yes
Documentation required for LD: Psychoeducational
  evaluation
Documentation required for ADD: Yes
Submitted to: Disability Services
Special Ed. HS coursework accepted: Yes

Specific course requirements of all applicants: Yes
Separate application required for program services: No
# of LD applications submitted each year: NR
# of LD applications accepted yearly: NR
Total # of students receiving LD services: 350
**Acceptance into program means acceptance into
  college:** Student must be admitted and enrolled in the
  university first and then request services.

ADMISSIONS

Students with learning disabilities must meet the same admission criteria as all other applicants. Courses recommended for admission include 4 years English, 3 years math, 2 years science, 2 years foreign language, 3 years social studies, and 2 years electives. The average SATs 1140 and the average GPA is 3.3. Students not meeting the regular admission requirements who have extenuating circumstances due to a learning disability may request additional consideration of their application by a special committee. A completed application form, a writing sample, two letters of recommendation, and documentation of the disability with information about how it has influenced the student's ability to meet minimum admission requirements are required for special admission consideration based on disability.

ADDITIONAL INFORMATION

Students are encouraged to take an active role in using the services. Once admitted, students should meet with the counselor to discuss educational goals. Documentation will be put on file. Services available include note-takers; books on tape; modification of testing procedures, including additional testing time, audiotape answers, having someone write dictated answers, large print, or taking the exam in a distraction-free environment; Adaptive Technology Lab; and faculty liaison to assist in communicating needs to instructors and to help negotiate reasonable accommodations in courses and programs. The Office of Academic Advising provides counseling and assessment of progress toward graduation. There is a support group for unique learners. The university requires two writing classes for graduation. In addition, the BA & BS degree requires 1 year of college math, or 2 years of foreign language. Writing and math labs are available.

Support Services Contact Information

Learning Disability Program/Services: Disability Services
Director: Steve Pickett, MS, CRC
  E-Mail: spickett@uoregon.edu
  Telephone: 541-346-1155
  Fax: 541-346-6013

LEARNING DISABILITY SERVICES

Requests for the following/services accommodations will be evaluated individually based on appropriate and current documentation.

Allowed in exams	**Distraction reduced environment:** Yes	**LD specialists:** Yes
Calculator: Yes	**Tape recording in class:** Yes	**Professional tutors:** Yes
Dictionary: Yes	**Books on tape from RFBD:** Yes	**Peer tutors:** Yes
Computer: Yes	**Taping of books not from RFBD:** Yes	**Max. hours/wk. for services:** Varies
Spellchecker: Yes	**Accommodations for students with**	**How professors are notified of**
Extended test time: Yes	**ADD:** Yes	**LD/ADD:** By both student and director
Scribes: Yes	**Reading machine:** Yes	
Proctors: Yes	**Other assistive technology:** Yes	
Oral exams: Yes	**Priority registration:** Yes	
Note-takers: Yes	**Added costs for services:** Yes	

GENERAL ADMISSIONS INFORMATION

Director of Admissions: Martha Pitts, Assistant Vice President for Enrollment Management and Director of Admissions
Telephone: 541-346-3201

ENTRANCE REQUIREMENTS
Academic units required: 4 English, 3 math, 2 science, 2 foreign language, 3 social studies. **Academic units recommended:** 1 science lab, 2 college-prep courses. High school diploma is required and GED is accepted. ACT with Writing component required. TOEFL required of all international applicants, minimum paper TOEFL 500, minimum computer TOEFL 173.

Application deadline: 1/15	**Average SAT Math:** 559	**Graduated top 10% of class:** 21%
Notification: Rolling	**Average SAT Verbal:** 555	**Graduated top 25% of class:** 52%
Average GPA: 3.49	**Average ACT:** NR	**Graduated top 50% of class:** 87%

COLLEGE GRADUATION REQUIREMENTS

Course waivers allowed: No
Course substitutions allowed: Yes
In what course: In extreme cases with appropriate documentation.

ADDITIONAL INFORMATION

Environment: The university is located on 250 acres in an urban area of Eugene.

Student Body:	**Cost Information**	**Greek System**
Undergrad enrollment: 16,024	**In-state tuition:** $5,568	**Fraternity:** Yes
Women: 53%	**Out-of-state tuition:** $17,424	**Sorority:** Yes
Men: 47%	**Room & board:** $7,300	**Athletics:** NCAA Division I
Percent out-of-state: 22%	**Housing Information**	
	University housing: Yes	
	Percent living on campus: 21%	

WESTERN OREGON UNIVERSITY

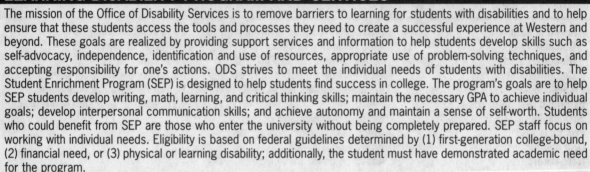

345 North Monmouth Avenue, Monmouth, OR 97361
Phone: 503-838-8211 • Fax: 503-838-8067
E-mail: wolfgram@wou.edu • Web: www.wou.edu
Support: S • Institution type: 4-year public

LEARNING DISABILITY PROGRAM AND SERVICES

The mission of the Office of Disability Services is to remove barriers to learning for students with disabilities and to help ensure that these students access the tools and processes they need to create a successful experience at Western and beyond. These goals are realized by providing support services and information to help students develop skills such as self-advocacy, independence, identification and use of resources, appropriate use of problem-solving techniques, and accepting responsibility for one's actions. ODS strives to meet the individual needs of students with disabilities. The Student Enrichment Program (SEP) is designed to help students find success in college. The program's goals are to help SEP students develop writing, math, learning, and critical thinking skills; maintain the necessary GPA to achieve individual goals; develop interpersonal communication skills; and achieve autonomy and maintain a sense of self-worth. Students who could benefit from SEP are those who enter the university without being completely prepared. SEP staff focus on working with individual needs. Eligibility is based on federal guidelines determined by (1) first-generation college-bound, (2) financial need, or (3) physical or learning disability; additionally, the student must have demonstrated academic need for the program.

LD/ADD ADMISSIONS INFORMATION

College entrance tests required: Yes
Interview required: No
Essay required: No
Documentation required for LD: Psychoeducational evaluation
Documentation required for ADD: Yes
Submitted to: Office of Disability Services
Special Ed. HS coursework accepted: No

Specific course requirements of all applicants: Yes
Separate application required for program services: Yes
# of LD applications submitted each year: NR
# of LD applications accepted yearly: NR
Total # of students receiving LD services: 60–70
Acceptance into program means acceptance into college: Student must be admitted and enrolled in the university first and then request services.

ADMISSIONS

General admission requires a 2.75 GPA and ACT/SAT scores, which are used only as alternatives to the required GPA. Course requirements include 4 years English, 3 years math, 2 years science, 3 years social science, and 2 years of the same foreign language. Alternatives to course requirements require either a score of 470 or above on 2 or ACT with essay SAT Subject Tests. A limited number of students who do not meet the regular admission requirements, alternatives, or exceptions may be admitted through special action of an admissions committee. These students must submit (by 1/1 for 1st session and 4/1 for the 2nd session a personal letter of petition stating why they don't meet the admission requirements and what they are doing to make up deficiencies and three letters of recommendation from school and community members.

ADDITIONAL INFORMATION

Skills classes are offered in academic survival strategies (no credit) and critical thinking (college credit). Other services include advocacy, computer stations, note-takers, readers and taping services, alternative testing, advisement, and assistance with registration. CEP offers counseling; basic math courses; advising; individualized instruction in reading, study skills, writing, and critical thinking; monitor programs; and workshops on study skills, research writing, math anxiety, rapid reading, note-taking, and time management. Services and accommodations are available for undergraduate and graduate students.

Support Services Contact Information

Learning Disability Program/Services: Office of Disability Services
Director: Mary Crawford, Esq.
  E-Mail: crawfor@wou.edu
  Telephone: 503-838-8250
  Fax: 503-838-8721

LEARNING DISABILITY SERVICES

Requests for the following/services accommodations will be evaluated individually based on appropriate and current documentation.

Allowed in exams
  Calculator: Yes
  Dictionary: Yes
  Computer: Yes
  Spellchecker: Yes
Extended test time: Yes
Scribes: Yes
Proctors: Yes
Oral exams: Yes
Note-takers: Yes

Distraction reduced environment: Yes
Tape recording in class: Yes
Books on tape from RFBD: Yes
Taping of books not from RFBD: Yes
**Accommodations for students with
  ADD:** Yes
Reading machine: Yes
Other assistive technology: Yes
Priority registration: No

Added costs for services: No
LD specialists: No
Professional tutors: No
Peer tutors: Yes
Max. hours/wk. for services: N/A
**How professors are notified of
  LD/ADD:** By both student and director

GENERAL ADMISSIONS INFORMATION

Director of Admissions: Rob Kvidt
Telephone: 503-838-8211

ENTRANCE REQUIREMENTS

Academic units required: 4 English, 3 math, 2 science, 2 foreign language, 2 social studies, 1 history. **Academic units recommended:** 1 science lab. High school diploma is required and GED is accepted. TOEFL required of all international applicants, minimum paper TOEFL 520, minimum computer TOEFL 190.

Application deadline: NR
Notification: rolling basis/no date
Average GPA: 3.26

Average SAT Math: 485
Average SAT Verbal: 495
Average ACT: 21

Graduated top 10% of class: 10%
Graduated top 25% of class: 36%
Graduated top 50% of class: 74%

COLLEGE GRADUATION REQUIREMENTS

Course waivers allowed: No
Course substitutions allowed: Yes
In what course: Decisions are made on a case-by-case basis.

ADDITIONAL INFORMATION

Environment: The university is located on 134 acres in a rural area 15 miles west of Salem.

Student Body:
  Undergrad enrollment: 4,366
  Women: 58%
  Men: 42%
  Percent out-of-state: 6%

Cost Information
  In-state tuition: $4,900
  Out-of-state tuition: $14,600
  Room & board: $6,300
Housing Information
  University housing: Yes
  Percent living on campus: 24%

Greek System
  Fraternity: No
  Sorority: No
Athletics: NCAA Division II

CLARION U. OF PENNSYLVANIA

Admissions Office, 840 Wood Street, Clarion, PA 16214
Phone: 814-393-2306 • Fax: 814-393-2030
E-mail: admissions@clarion.edu • Web: www.clarion.edu
Support: CS • Institution type: 4-year public

LEARNING DISABILITY PROGRAM AND SERVICES

Clarion does not have a special admissions policy for students with learning disabilities nor does it offer a structured LD Program. The Student Support Services Program works to ensure educational parity for students with learning disabilities within a mainstream setting. Academic accommodations and support focuses on minimizing the effects of the disability. The Special Services Program is the university's primary vehicle for providing a Tutoring Center and Academic Support Center, which are available to all students but are especially beneficial for students with learning disabilities. These services are free of charge and include extensive peer tutoring, study skills workshops, and individual learning to learn activities.

LD/ADD ADMISSIONS INFORMATION

College entrance tests required: Yes
Interview required: Yes
Essay required: No
Documentation required for LD: Psychoeducational evaluation
Documentation required for ADD: Yes
Submitted to: Disability Support Services
Special Ed. HS coursework accepted: Yes

Specific course requirements of all applicants: Yes
Separate application required for program services: No
# of LD applications submitted each year: NR
# of LD applications accepted yearly: NR
Total # of students receiving LD services: 75
Acceptance into program means acceptance into college: Student must be admitted and enrolled in the university first and then request services.

ADMISSIONS
Students with learning disabilities who wish to be admitted to the university must meet regular admission requirements. Course requirements include 4 years English, 2 years math (4 recommended), the avocate SAT is 980 and ACT is 21, 3 years science, 4 science recommended) 2 years foreign language recommended, and 4 years social studies. As part of the application process, students are encouraged to provide documentation of their learning disability in order to establish a clear need for individualized support services. Students should also include a copy of their individualized educational plan from high school. Students not meeting the general admission criteria may be admitted by either the Academic Support Acceptance (these students are referred to Student Support Services) or Summer Start (probationary admittance).

ADDITIONAL INFORMATION
The staff in Student Support Services serve as liaisons between students and faculty to provide special considerations when appropriate. The program also provides academic advising, special topic seminars, reading/study skills workshops, and referral to other campus resources such as the Tutoring and Writing Centers. Services and accommodations are available to undergraduate and graduate students.

Support Services Contact Information

Learning Disability Program/Services: Disability Support Services
Director: Jennifer May
  Telephone: 814-393-2095
  Fax: 814-393-2368
  E-mail: jmay@clarion.edu

LEARNING DISABILITY SERVICES

Requests for the following/services accommodations will be evaluated individually based on appropriate and current documentation.

Allowed in exams
  Calculator: Y/N
  Dictionary: Y/N
  Computer: Y/N
  Spellchecker: Y/N
Extended test time: Yes
Scribes: Yes
Proctors: Yes
Oral exams: Yes
Note-takers: Yes

Distraction reduced environment: Yes
Tape recording in class: Yes
Books on tape from RFBD: Yes
Taping of books not from RFBD: Yes
Accommodations for students with
  ADD: Yes
Reading machine: Yes
Other assistive technology: Yes
Priority registration: Yes

Added costs for services: No
LD specialists: Yes
Professional tutors: No
Peer tutors: 20
Max. hours/wk. for services: 1
How professors are notified of
  LD/ADD: By both student and director

GENERAL ADMISSIONS INFORMATION

Director of Admissions: Mr. William Bailey
Telephone: 814-393-2306

ENTRANCE REQUIREMENTS

Academic units required: 4 English, 2 math, 3 science, 4 social studies. **Academic units recommended:** 4 math, 4 science, 2 foreign language. High school diploma is required and GED is accepted. TOEFL required of all international applicants, minimum paper TOEFL 550, minimum computer TOEFL 213.

Application deadline: Rolling
Notification: Rolling
Average GPA: 3.00

Average SAT Math: 470
Average SAT Verbal: 480
Average ACT: NR

Graduated top 10% of class: 6%
Graduated top 25% of class: 24%
Graduated top 50% of class: 57%

COLLEGE GRADUATION REQUIREMENTS

Course waivers allowed: Yes
Course substitutions allowed: Yes
In what course: Determined case-by-case

ADDITIONAL INFORMATION

Environment: The university is located on 100 acres in a small town, 85 miles northeast of Pittsburgh.

Student Body:
  Undergrad enrollment: 5,855
  Women: 61%
  Men: 39%
  Percent out-of-state: 7%

Cost Information
  In-state tuition: $6,500
  Out-of-state tuition: $11,500
  Room & board: $5,688
Housing Information
  University housing: Yes
  Percent living on campus: 32%

Greek System
  Fraternity: Yes
  Sorority: Yes
Athletics: NCAA Division II

COLLEGE MISERICORDIA

301 Lake Street, Dallas, PA 18612
Phone: 570-674-6264 • Fax: 570-675-2441
E-mail: admiss@misericordia.edu • Web: www.misericordia.edu
Support: SP • Institution type: 4-year private

LEARNING DISABILITY PROGRAM AND SERVICES

All students who participate in the Alternate Learners Project (ALP) are enrolled in regular college classes. In most cases, they take a carefully selected, reduced credit load each semester. Students who participate in ALP are supported by an assortment of services delivered by a specially trained full-time staff. Services include Learning Strategies, which are designed to make students more efficient, and accommodations designed to work around student's disabilities whenever possible. Upon entry each student develops an individual education plan and signs a contract agreeing to weekly meetings with mentors. The ultimate goal of ALP is to help students with learning disabilities succeed in college.

LD/ADD ADMISSIONS INFORMATION

College entrance tests required: Yes
Interview required: Yes
Essay required: Yes
Documentation required for LD: Recent and complete psychological report
Documentation required for ADD: Psychological and medical report
Submitted to: Admissions and ALP Program
Special Ed. HS coursework accepted: No

Specific course requirements of all applicants: Yes
Separate application required for program services: No
# of LD applications submitted each year: 125
# of LD applications accepted yearly: 25
Total # of students receiving LD services: 50
Acceptance into program means acceptance into college: There is a joint acceptance between ALP and the Office of Admissions.

ADMISSIONS

College Misericordia's experience with students with learning disabilities is that students who are highly motivated and socially mature have an excellent chance to be successful. Each applicant has to secure a standard admissions form, enclose a written cover letter summarizing the learning disability, and indicate a desire to participate in the ALP. Additionally, a copy of the psychological report should be submitted along with the high school transcript and three letters of recommendation (one must be written by a special education professional). Class rank is usually above the top 60 percent. ACT/SAT are required but not used in any way for LD admissions. Students and their parents will be invited to interviews. This interview is very important. The program director reviews all information and recommends an action to the admissions department, which, after careful review, acts on the recommendation. The admission decision is made jointly by the program director and the director of admissions.

ADDITIONAL INFORMATION

All students served by ALP are asked to attend a summer program ($1,600) to learn strategies, understand needed accommodations, and learn about the college. The college, not ALP, offers several skills courses (non-credited) in basic areas such as reading, writing, and math. Services and accommodations are available for undergraduate and graduate students. College Misericordia offers a summer program for high school students with learning disabilities.

Support Services Contact Information

Learning Disability Program/Services: Alternative Learners Project (ALP)
Director: Dr. Joseph Rogan
E-Mail: Jrogan@misericordia.edu
  Telephone: 570-674-6347
  Fax: 570-675-2441

LEARNING DISABILITY SERVICES

Requests for the following/services accommodations will be evaluated individually based on appropriate and current documentation.

Allowed in exams
  Calculator: Yes
  Dictionary: Yes
  Computer: Yes
  Spellchecker: Yes
Extended test time: Yes
Scribes: Yes
Proctors: Yes
Oral exams: Yes
Note-takers: Yes

Distraction reduced environment: Yes
Tape recording in class: Yes
Books on tape from RFBD: Yes
Taping of books not from RFBD: No
Accommodations for students with ADD: No
Reading machine: Yes
Other assistive technology: Yes
Priority registration: Yes
Added costs for services: No

LD specialists: Yes
Professional tutors: 7
Peer tutors: 100
Max. hours/wk. for services: Unlimited
How professors are notified of LD/ADD: By director

GENERAL ADMISSIONS INFORMATION

Director of Admissions: Jane Dessoye
Telephone: 570-674-6168

ENTRANCE REQUIREMENTS

Academic units required: 4 English, 4 math, 4 science, 4 social studies. High school diploma is required and GED is accepted. ACT with or without Writing component accepted. TOEFL required of all international applicants, minimum paper TOEFL 500, minimum computer TOEFL 75.

Application deadline: Rolling
Notification: Rolling
Average GPA: 3.1

Average SAT Math: 502
Average SAT Verbal: 499
Average ACT: 23

Graduated top 10% of class: 15%
Graduated top 25% of class: 40%
Graduated top 50% of class: 71%

COLLEGE GRADUATION REQUIREMENTS

Course waivers allowed: Yes
Course substitutions allowed: Yes
In what course: Varies with curriculum program.

ADDITIONAL INFORMATION

Environment: The college is located on a 100-acre campus in a suburban small town nine miles south of Wilkes-Barre.

Student Body:
  Undergrad enrollment: 1,934
  Women: 74%
  Men: 26%
  Percent out-of-state: 16%

Cost Information
  Tuition: $17,850
  Room & board: $7,850
Housing Information
  University housing: Yes
  Percent living on campus: 39%

Greek System
  Fraternity: No
  Sorority: No
Athletics: NCAA Division III

DICKINSON COLLEGE

PO Box 1773, Carlisle, PA 17013-2896
Phone: 717-245-1231 • Fax: 717-245-1442
E-mail: admit@dickinson.edu • Web: www.dickinson.edu
Support: CS • Institution type: 4-year private

LEARNING DISABILITY PROGRAM AND SERVICES

Dickinson College is committed to providing reasonable accommodations to qualified individuals with disabilities. Students with disabilities will be integrated as completely as possible into the college community. Dickinson does not offer a specialized curriculum. Instead, a wide variety of ways to satisfy most requirements make it unnecessary for students to expect exemption form distribution requirements. Support is offered in designing an accommodations plan that identifies strengths, weaknesses and needs for reasonable accommodations. There are test accommodations, as appropriate, such as extended time, testing in a quiet location, readers, and tests in alternative formats. Also one-on-one assistance in developing study skills, time management, and compensatory learning strategies. In order to receive support services, students must submit documentation of the disability. Students with LD must send results of the most recent psychoeducational testing and IEP. Students with ADD must send the most recent psychoeducational testing with appropriate behavioral rating scales and diagnosis of ADD completed by a qualified physician.

LD/ADD ADMISSIONS INFORMATION

College entrance tests required: No
Interview required: No
Essay required: Yes
Documentation required for LD: A specific diagnosis of LD supported by an intellectual assessment (WAIS preferred) and achievement testing (Woodcock-Johnson). Results must include a summary of all test scores.
Documentation required for ADD: Structured interview identifying criteria for DSM–IV diagnosis supplemented by rating scales such as the Conners, ADD Rating Scale, or the Wender Utah Rating Scale.
Submitted to: Learning Support
Special Ed. HS coursework accepted: No

Specific course requirements of all applicants: Yes
Separate application required for program services: No
# of LD applications submitted each year: NR
# of LD applications accepted yearly: NR
Total # of students receiving LD services: 40–60
Acceptance into program means acceptance into college: Student must be admitted and enrolled in the university first and then request services.

ADMISSIONS
There is no special admissions process for students with learning disabilities. Students should include a separate statement concerning their interest in disability services. ACT/SAT tests are not required except for scholarships. Students should have 4 years English, 3 years math, 3 years science, 2 years social studies, and 2 years foreign language. The minimum GPA is a 2.0.

ADDITIONAL INFORMATION
Skills classes are available in time management, note-taking, test taking strategies, reading and writing. Substitutions may be requested in foreign language, but only after attempting a language and demonstrating effort to pass the course. Support services could include extended testing time; distraction-free environment; scribes; proctors; note-takers; books on tape; peer tutors; and the use of calculator, dictionary, computer, or spell checker in exams.

Support Services Contact Information

Learning Disability Program/Services: Learning Support
Director: Keith Jervis
E-Mail: jervis@dickinson.edu
  Telephone: 717-245-1080
  Fax: 717-245-1534

LEARNING DISABILITY SERVICES

Requests for the following/services accommodations will be evaluated individually based on appropriate and current documentation.

Allowed in exams	**Distraction reduced environment:** Yes	**Added costs for services:** No
Calculator: Yes	**Tape recording in class:** Yes	**LD specialists:** Yes
Dictionary: Yes	**Books on tape from RFBD:** Yes	**Professional tutors:** No
Computer: Yes	**Taping of books not from RFBD:** No	**Peer tutors:** 40-50
Spellchecker: Yes	**Accommodations for students with**	**Max. hours/wk. for services:**
Extended test time: Yes	**ADD:** Yes	Unlimited
Scribes: Yes	**Reading machine:** Yes	**How professors are notified of**
Proctors: Yes	**Other assistive technology:** No	**LD/ADD:** By student
Oral exams: Yes	**Priority registration:** No	
Note-takers: Yes		

GENERAL ADMISSIONS INFORMATION

Director of Admissions: Christopher Seth Allen, Dean of Admissions
Telephone: 800-644-1773

ENTRANCE REQUIREMENTS

Academic units required: 4 English, 3 math, 3 science (2 science lab), 2 foreign language, 2 social studies, 2 academic electives. **Academic units recommended:** 3 foreign language. High school diploma is required and GED is accepted. ACT with or without Writing component accepted. TOEFL required of all international applicants, minimum paper TOEFL 550, minimum computer TOEFL 250.

Application deadline: 2/1	**Average SAT Math:** 634	**Graduated top 10% of class:** 51%
Notification: 3/31	**Average SAT Verbal:** 640	**Graduated top 25% of class:** 82%
Average GPA: NR	**Average ACT:** 28	**Graduated top 50% of class:** 98%

COLLEGE GRADUATION REQUIREMENTS

Course waivers allowed: No
Course substitutions allowed: Yes
In what course: Foreign language courses, but only after attempting a language and demonstrating an effort to pass by attending class, requesting accommodations and use of a tutor.

ADDITIONAL INFORMATION

Environment: The college is located on a 103 acre suburban campus.

Student Body:	**Cost Information**	**Greek System**
Undergrad enrollment: 2,280	**Tuition:** $30,000	**Fraternity:** Yes
Women: 55%	**Room & board:** $7,600	**Sorority:** Yes
Men: 45%	**Housing Information**	**Athletics:** NCAA Division III
Percent out-of-state: 67%	**University housing:** Yes	
	Percent living on campus: 90%	

DREXEL UNIVERSITY

3141 Chestnut Street, Philadelphia, PA 19104
Phone: 215-895-2400 • Fax: 215-895-5939
E-mail: enroll@drexel.edu • Web: www.drexel.edu
Support: CS • Institution type: 4-year private

LEARNING DISABILITY PROGRAM AND SERVICES

Drexel University does not have a specific learning disability program, but services are provided through the Office of Disability Services. The professional staff works closely with the students who have special needs to ensure that they have the opportunity to participate fully in Drexel University's programs and activities and have access to facilities in accordance with sections 503 and 504 of the Rehabilitation Act of 1973 and the Americans with Disabilities Act of 1990.

LD/ADD ADMISSIONS INFORMATION

College entrance tests required: Yes
Interview required: No
Essay required: No
Documentation required for LD: Psychoeducational
evaluations and IEP
Documentation required for ADD: Yes
Submitted to: Office of Disability Services
Special Ed. HS coursework accepted: No

Specific course requirements of all applicants: Yes
Separate application required for program services: No
# of LD applications submitted each year: NR
# of LD applications accepted yearly: NR
Total # of students receiving LD services: 92
**Acceptance into program means acceptance into
college:** Student must be admitted and enrolled in the
university first and then request services.

ADMISSIONS

The regular admission requirements are the same for all students, and there is no special process for students with learning disabilities. Students are encouraged to self-disclose and provide current documentation of their learning disabilities. General admission criteria include recommended courses of 4 years English, 3 years math, 1 year science, 1 year social studies, 7 years electives (chosen from English, math, science, social studies, foreign language, history, or mechanical drawing); interview recommended; average SATs 1010, average GPA is 3.1, and 89 percent of the admitted students are in the top 60 percent of their high school graduating class.

ADDITIONAL INFORMATION

Services provided are tutors; readers; note-takers; proofreaders; LD specialists; personal academic and career counseling; liaison between student, faculty, and administration; priority scheduling; instructional modifications; augmented classes offered in math and English; and remedial services in study skills, writing, reading, math, time management, self-advocacy enhancement, as well as disability education for staff, faculty, and students. The Office of Disability Services also provides assistance with academic accommodations and learning strategies, and follows through on all Affirmative Action and ADA requirements.

Support Services Contact Information

Learning Disability Program/Services: Office of Disability Services (ODS)
Director: Robin Stokes
E-Mail: ras28@drexel.edu
  Telephone: 215-895-1401
  Fax: 215-895-1402

LEARNING DISABILITY SERVICES

Requests for the following/services accommodations will be evaluated individually based on appropriate and current documentation.

Allowed in exams	**Distraction reduced environment:** Yes	**Added costs for services:** No
Calculator: Yes	**Tape recording in class:** Yes	**LD specialists:** Yes
Dictionary: Yes	**Books on tape from RFBD:** Yes	**Professional tutors:** Yes
Computer: Yes	**Taping of books not from RFBD:** Yes	**Peer tutors:** Yes
Spellchecker: Yes	**Accommodations for students with**	**Max. hours/wk. for services:** 10
Extended test time: Yes	**ADD:** Yes	**How professors are notified of**
Scribes: Yes	**Reading machine:** Yes	**LD/ADD:** By student
Proctors: Yes	**Other assistive technology:** Yes	
Oral exams: Yes	**Priority registration:** Yes	
Note-takers: Yes		

GENERAL ADMISSIONS INFORMATION

Director of Admissions: Joan McDonald
Telephone: 215-895-2400

ENTRANCE REQUIREMENTS

 Academic units required: 3 math, 1 science (1 science lab). **Academic units recommended:** 1 foreign language. High school diploma is required and GED is accepted. ACT with or without Writing component accepted. TOEFL required of all international applicants, minimum paper TOEFL 550, minimum computer TOEFL 213.

Application deadline: 3/1	**Average SAT Math:** 600	**Graduated top 10% of class:** 34%
Notification: Rolling basis	**Average SAT Verbal:** 570	**Graduated top 25% of class:** 61%
Average GPA: 3.51	**Average ACT:** NR	**Graduated top 50% of class:** 91%

COLLEGE GRADUATION REQUIREMENTS

Course waivers allowed: Yes
Course substitutions allowed: Yes
In what course: Done on a case-by-case basis.

ADDITIONAL INFORMATION

Environment: The campus is located on 38 acres near the center of Philadelphia.

Student Body:	**Cost Information**	**Greek System**
Undergrad enrollment: 11,544	Tuition: $28,300	Fraternity: Yes
Women: 40%	Room & board: $10,515	Sorority: Yes
Men: 60%	**Housing Information**	Athletics: NCAA Division I
Percent out-of-state: 42%	University housing: Yes	
	Percent living on campus: 38%	

EAST STROUDSBURG U. OF PA

200 Prospect Street, East Stroudsburg, PA 18301-2999
Phone: 570-422-3542 • Fax: 570-422-3933
E-mail: undergrads@po-box.esu.edu • Web: www.esu.edu
Support: CS • Institution type: 4-year public

LEARNING DISABILITY PROGRAM AND SERVICES

There is no special program for students with learning disabilities at East Stroudsburg University. However, the university is committed to supporting otherwise qualified students with learning disabilities in their pursuit of an education. Disability Services offers students with LD academic and social support and acts as their advocate on campus. Students are encouraged to meet with the coordinator to schedule classes and to develop compensatory skills. Tutors are trained to be sensitive to individual learning styles. Students who request accommodations or academic adjustments are responsible for providing required documentation to the Office of Disability Services and for requesting those accommodations or academic adjustments. East Stroudsburg University will need documentation of the disability that consists of an evaluation by an appropriate professional and describes the current impact of the disability as it relates to the accommodation request. In order to receive services, students with disabilities must: identify that they have a disability, submit appropriate documentation, and request services.

LD/ADD ADMISSIONS INFORMATION

College entrance tests required: Yes
Interview required: No
Essay required: Yes
Documentation required for LD: Psychoeducational evaluation; most current.
Documentation required for ADD: Yes
Submitted to: Office of Disability Services
Special Ed. HS coursework accepted: Yes

Specific course requirements of all applicants: Yes
Separate application required for program services: No
# of LD applications submitted each year: 143
# of LD applications accepted yearly: 50
Total # of students receiving LD services: 130
Acceptance into program means acceptance into college: Student must be admitted and enrolled in the university first and then request services.

ADMISSIONS

Students with learning disabilities file the general application form and are encouraged to complete the section titled Disabilities Information and forward documentation of their disability to Disability Services. Notification of a learning disability is used as a part of the admissions process only if the student is denied admission. At this time the admissions office waits for a recommendation from the learning disability specialist. The Office of Academic Support may request that the admissions office reevaluate the student's application in light of information on the disability. For general admission, academic achievement is the primary factor considered in the selection process. While not specifically required for consideration, it is expected that successful applicants will have 4 years of English, algebra I and II, geometry, a senior year college-prep math course, 3 years of science (with at least 2 lab science courses), 3 years of social studies, and 2 years of a foreign language. ESU also looks for a good match between what each applicant can contribute to the university and how the university can meet each applicant's expectations. They refer to that process as a whole-person assessment. Tell them about your contributions to your school and community, your activities and achievements, your aspirations, and anything else that would help them evaluate your potential for success at ESU. Standardized test results—the SAT or ACT—are used as a common yardstick to help in the selection process. SAT Subject Tests are not required.

ADDITIONAL INFORMATION

There is a pre-admission summer program for Pennsylvania residents only called the Summer Intensive Study Program. All entering freshmen and their parents are invited to participate in a two-day summer orientation. Drop-in labs are offered in math and writing, as are study skills workshops. Students with learning disabilities may work individually with the Disability Services coordinator. All students enrolled in the university have the opportunity to take skills classes in reading, composition, and math. Other services include workshops in time management and test-taking strategies as well as support groups. The Learning Center provides individual and group tutoring by professional and peer tutors free of charge to ESU students in 100 and 200 level general education courses. Tutors are assigned on a first come, first served basis, and students must complete and submit a request form in order to receive tutoring. Although tutoring is not an accommodation for a disability, new peer and professional tutors participate in a tutor training program that includes strategies for tutoring students with disabilities. Services and accommodations are available for undergraduate and graduate students.

Support Services Contact Information

Learning Disability Program/Services: Office of Disability Services
Director: Edith F. Miller, EdD
E-Mail: emiller@PO-Box.esu.edu
  Telephone: 570-422-3954
  Fax: 717-422-3898

LEARNING DISABILITY SERVICES

Requests for the following/services accommodations will be evaluated individually based on appropriate and current documentation.

Allowed in exams
  Calculator: Yes
  Dictionary: Yes
  Computer: Yes
  Spellchecker: Yes
Extended test time: Yes
Scribes: Yes
Proctors: Yes
Oral exams: Yes
Note-takers: Yes

Distraction reduced environment: Yes
Tape recording in class: Yes
Books on tape from RFBD: Yes
Taping of books not from RFBD: Yes
Accommodations for students with ADD: Yes
Reading machine: Yes
Other assistive technology: Yes
Priority registration: NR

Added costs for services: No
LD specialists: Yes
Professional tutors: 70
Peer tutors: 50
Max. hours/wk. for services: 2
How professors are notified of LD/ADD: By student

GENERAL ADMISSIONS INFORMATION

Director of Admissions: Alan Chesterton
Telephone: 570-422-3542

ENTRANCE REQUIREMENTS

Academic units recommended: 4 English, 3 math, 3 science (1 science lab), 2 foreign language, 3 social studies. High school diploma is required and GED is accepted. ACT with or without Writing component accepted. TOEFL required of all international applicants, minimum paper TOEFL 500, minimum computer TOEFL 173.

Application deadline: 4/1
Notification: Rolling
Average GPA: 2.89

Average SAT Math: 493
Average SAT Verbal: 492
Average ACT: NR

Graduated top 10% of class: 5%
Graduated top 25% of class: 25%
Graduated top 50% of class: 70%

COLLEGE GRADUATION REQUIREMENTS

Course waivers allowed: No
Course substitutions allowed: Yes
In what course: Substitutions for math and foreign language

ADDITIONAL INFORMATION

Environment: The 813-acre campus is set in the foothills of the Pocono Mountains.

Student Body:
  Undergrad enrollment: 5,282
  Women: 59%
  Men: 41%
  Percent out-of-state: 20%

Cost Information
  In-state tuition: $4,810
  Out-of-state tuition: $12,026
  Room & board: $4,506
Housing Information
  University housing: Yes
  Percent living on campus: 43%

Greek System
  Fraternity: Yes
  Sorority: Yes
Athletics: NCAA Division II

Edinboro U. of Pennsylvania

Biggers House, Edinboro, PA 16412
Phone: 814-732-2761 • Fax: 814-732-2420
E-mail: eup_admissions@edinboro.edu • Web: www.edinboro.edu
Support: CS • Institution type: 4-year public

LEARNING DISABILITY PROGRAM AND SERVICES

Edinboro is actively involved in providing services for students with learning disabilities. The Office for Students with Disabilities (OSD) provides services that are individually directed by the program staff according to expressed needs. There are different levels of services offered depending on the student's needs. Level A offers supervised study sessions with trained mentors two hours per day, with additional hours based on academic progress; writing specialists 12 hours weekly; computer lab; study lab; required appointment every two weeks with professional staff to review progress; and all services in Level D. To be eligible for Level B, students must maintain a 2.5 GPA and complete two or more semesters at Level A. Level B offers supervised study sessions with peer mentor one hour per day, and two more hours based on progress; writing specialists one-two hours weekly; computer lab; study lab; a required appointment every two weeks with professional staff; and all services listed in Level D. Level C requires 2.5 GPA and one semester at Level B, and includes peer mentoring up to six hours weekly; writing specialists one-two hours weekly; computer lab; study lab; and all services in Level D. Level D provides assistance in arranging academic accommodations, including alternate test arrangements, priority scheduling, consultation with staff, and tape-recorded textbooks. Levels A, B, and C are fee-for-services levels.

LD/ADD ADMISSIONS INFORMATION

College entrance tests required: Yes
Interview required: No
Essay required: No
Documentation required for LD: WAIS–III and achievement testing within 3 years
Documentation required for ADD: Yes
Submitted to: Office for Students with Disabilities
Special Ed. HS coursework accepted: Yes

Specific course requirements of all applicants: Yes
Separate application required for program services: No
# of LD applications submitted each year: 40–100
# of LD applications accepted yearly: 40–60
Total # of students receiving LD services: 285
Acceptance into program means acceptance into college: Student must be admitted and enrolled in the university first and then request services.

ADMISSIONS

Students with LD submit the general application form. Upon receipt of the application from the admissions office, it is suggested that students identify any special services that may be required and contact the OSD so that a personal interview may be scheduled. Occasionally, OSD staff are asked for remarks on certain files, but it is not part of the admission decision. Students must provide a multifactored educational assessment; grade-level scores in reading, vocabulary and comprehension, math, and spelling; an individual intelligence test administered by a psychologist, including a list of the tests given; and a list of recommended accommodations. Evaluations submitted must have been completed recently (within three years). Evaluations submitted must have seen completed recently. The Trial Admissions Program (TAP) is a selective program for students whose academic credentials do not qualify them for direct admission. Students are reviewed for academic promise, motivation, and positive attitude.

ADDITIONAL INFORMATION

Students with LD are paired with peer mentors who help them with study skills, organizational skills, and time management skills. Students are recommended for different levels of services based on their needs. Students are not required to select a particular level, but OSD strongly recommends that students enroll for Level A if they have less than a 2.5 GPA. Specific academic scheduling needs may be complex, but students working through the OSD are given priority in academic scheduling. The Life Skills Center is a training area designed to enable students with disabilities to maximize their personal independence while completing their academic programs. Students enrolled in TAP must take a freshman orientation course, a developmental skill course, and nine semester hours in general education courses. Extensive tutoring is available for all students.

Support Services Contact Information

Learning Disability Program/Services: Office for Students with Disabilities (OSD)
Director: Robert McConnell, PhD
E-Mail: mcconnell@Edinboro.edu
 Telephone: 814-732-2462
 Fax: 814-732-2866
Contact Person: Kathleen Strosser
E-Mail: strosser@Edinboro.edu
 Telephone: 814-732-2462
 Fax: 814-732-2866

LEARNING DISABILITY SERVICES

Requests for the following/services accommodations will be evaluated individually based on appropriate and current documentation.

Allowed in exams
 Calculator: Yes
 Dictionary: Yes
 Computer: Yes
 Spellchecker: Yes
Extended test time: Yes
Scribes: Yes
Proctors: Yes
Oral exams: No
Note-takers: No

Distraction reduced environment: Yes
Tape recording in class: Yes
Books on tape from RFBD: Yes
Taping of books not from RFBD: Yes
Accommodations for students with
 ADD: Yes
Reading machine: Yes
Other assistive technology: Yes
Priority registration: Yes

Added costs for services: Yes
LD specialists: Yes
Professional tutors: 1
Peer tutors: 80-100
Max. hours/wk. for services: 12
How professors are notified of
 LD/ADD: By student

GENERAL ADMISSIONS INFORMATION

Director of Admissions: Terrence J. Carlin
Telephone: 888-8GO-BORO

ENTRANCE REQUIREMENTS

Academic units recommended: 4 English, 3 math, 3 science, 2 foreign language, 3 social studies, 4 academic electives, 1 keyboarding/computer. High school diploma is required and GED is accepted. TOEFL required of all international applicants, minimum paper TOEFL 500, minimum computer TOEFL 173.

Application deadline: Rolling
Notification: Rolling
Average GPA: 2.5

Average SAT Math: 465
Average SAT Verbal: 475
Average ACT: 18

Graduated top 10% of class: 6%
Graduated top 25% of class: 21%
Graduated top 50% of class: 53%

COLLEGE GRADUATION REQUIREMENTS

Course waivers allowed: No
Course substitutions allowed: Yes
In what course: Case by case basis; request reviewed by committee.

ADDITIONAL INFORMATION

Environment: Edinboro University is located on 600 acres in a small town, 20 miles south of Erie.

Student Body:
 Undergrad enrollment: 6,587
 Women: 58%
 Men: 42%
 Percent out-of-state: 11%

Cost Information
 In-state tuition: $4,810
 Out-of-state tuition: $9,620
 Room & board: $5,338
Housing Information
 University housing: Yes
 Percent living on campus: 27%

Greek System
 Fraternity: Yes
 Sorority: Yes
Athletics: NCAA Division II

GANNON UNIVERSITY

University Square, Erie, PA 16541
Phone: 814-871-7240 • Fax: 814-871-5803
E-mail: admissions@gannon.edu • Web: www.gannon.edu
Support: SP • Institution type: 4-year private

LEARNING DISABILITY PROGRAM AND SERVICES

Gannon's Program for Students with Learning Disabilities (PSLD) provides special support services for students who have been diagnosed with either LD or ADD who are highly motivated for academic achievement. PSLD faculty are committed to excellence and strive to offer each student individually designed instruction. Students in the program may select any academic major offered by the university. Freshman-year support includes weekly individual sessions with instructor-tutors and a writing specialist, and small group meetings with a reading specialist. They also provide an advocacy seminar course which includes participation in small group counseling. There is limited space in PSLD, and students should check the appropriate box on the admissions application if this service applies.

LD/ADD ADMISSIONS INFORMATION

College entrance tests required: Yes
Interview required: Yes
Essay required: Yes
Documentation required for LD: WAIS III
Documentation required for ADD: Official letter of documentation from a licensed professional.
Submitted to: Admissions and PSLD Program
Special Ed. HS coursework accepted: Yes

Specific course requirements of all applicants: Yes
Separate application required for program services: No
# of LD applications submitted each year: 45
# of LD applications accepted yearly: 15
Total # of students receiving LD services: 40
Acceptance into program means acceptance into college: The director of PSLD accepts students into the program and the university.

ADMISSIONS

Besides the regular application and interview there is a special admissions process for the student with LD. Students must check the box on the application indicating interest in the LD Program. Applicants must submit a psychoeducational evaluation, a high school transcript, two letters of recommendation, and a paragraph about why there is a need for support services. The program director and assistant director make an initial decision and advise admissions on their decision. Students who are admitted conditionally must enter as undeclared majors until they can achieve a 2.0 GPA. Special education high school courses are accepted in certain situations.

ADDITIONAL INFORMATION

Specific features of the program include twice-weekly tutoring sessions with the program instructors to review course material, learn study skills relevant to material from courses, and focus on specific needs; and weekly sessions with the writing specialist for reviewing, editing, and brainstorming. A one credit advocacy seminar course is part of the course load of first and second semester. This course covers self-advocacy, motivational techniques, college survival skills, the law and LD, and learning styles and strategies. Additional services available are computer access taped textbooks, taping of classes, extended time on exams, scribes, and oral exams. There is a $600 fee for support services.

Support Services Contact Information

Learning Disability Program/Services: Program for Students with Learning Disabilities
Director: Sister Joyce Lowrey, SSJ, MEd
E-Mail: lowrey@gannon.edu
  Telephone: 814-871-5326
  Fax: 814-871-7499
Contact Person: Jane Kanter
E-Mail: kanter@gannon.edu
  Telephone: 814-871-5360
  Fax: 814-871-7499

LEARNING DISABILITY SERVICES

Requests for the following/services accommodations will be evaluated individually based on appropriate and current documentation.

Allowed in exams
  Calculator: Yes
  Dictionary: No
  Computer: Yes
  Spellchecker: Yes
Extended test time: Yes
Scribes: Yes
Proctors: Yes
Oral exams: Yes
Note-takers: No

Distraction reduced environment: Yes
Tape recording in class: Yes
Books on tape from RFBD: Yes
Taping of books not from RFBD: Yes
Accommodations for students with
  ADD: Yes
Reading machine: Yes
Other assistive technology: No
Priority registration: N/A

Added costs for services: Yes
LD specialists: Yes
Professional tutors: 5
Peer tutors: 2
Max. hours/wk. for services: 3
How professors are notified of
  LD/ADD: By both student and director

GENERAL ADMISSIONS INFORMATION

Director of Admissions: Christopher Tremblay
Telephone: 814-871-5789

ENTRANCE REQUIREMENTS

Academic units required: 4 English, 12 combination of remaining academic units based on planned major. High school diploma is required and GED is accepted. ACT with or without Writing component accepted. TOEFL required of all international applicants, minimum paper TOEFL 500, minimum computer TOEFL 173.

Application deadline: Rolling
Notification: Rolling
Average GPA: 3.33

Average SAT Math: 532
Average SAT Verbal: 526
Average ACT: NR

Graduated top 10% of class: 22%
Graduated top 25% of class: 53%
Graduated top 50% of class: 80%

COLLEGE GRADUATION REQUIREMENTS

Course waivers allowed: Yes
Course substitutions allowed: Yes
In what course: Substitutions for foreign language in certain circumstances.

ADDITIONAL INFORMATION

Environment: The university is located on 13 acres in Erie, an urban area 135 miles north of Pittsburgh.

Student Body:
  Undergrad enrollment: 2,309
  Women: 60%
  Men: 40%
  Percent out-of-state: 21%

Cost Information
  Tuition: $18,220
  Room & board: $7,110
Housing Information
  University housing: Yes
  Percent living on campus: 49%

Greek System
  Fraternity: Yes
  Sorority: Yes
Athletics: NCAA Division II

KUTZTOWN U. OF PENNSYLVANIA

Admission Office, PO Box 730, Kutztown, PA 19530-0730
Phone: 610-683-4060 • Fax: 610-683-1375
E-mail: admission@kutztown.edu • Web: www.kutztown.edu
Support: CS • Institution type: 4-year public

LEARNING DISABILITY PROGRAM AND SERVICES

The philosophy of the university is to provide equal opportunity to all individuals. Services for Students with Disabilities provides all necessary and reasonable services while fostering independence in the students. The services provided are in accordance with the needs of the students and the academic integrity of the institution. The office acts as information and referral resource, provides direct services, coordinates services provided by other departments/agencies, and serves as a liaison between students with disabilities and university personnel working with students. Since information regarding a student's disability is not obtained through the admission process, it is the student's responsibility upon acceptance to the university to identify himself/herself to the program. Students are encouraged to do this as early as possible upon admission, or even when contemplating application. This will provide an opportunity to assess the university's capability of responding to special needs and provide the students with opportunity to assess the services available at the university. The ADA/504 coordinator works together with all university offices to help provide specific services as warranted by a diagnosis or clear need, as well as creative solutions to problems with which students with disabilities are confronted.

LD/ADD ADMISSIONS INFORMATION

College entrance tests required: Yes
Interview required: No
Essay required: No
Documentation required for LD: Pyschoeducational evaluation
Documentation required for ADD: Yes
Submitted to: Services for Students with Disabilities
Special Ed. HS coursework accepted: Yes

Specific course requirements of all applicants: Yes
Separate application required for program services: NR
# of LD applications submitted each year: NR
# of LD applications accepted yearly: NR
Total # of students receiving LD services: 278
Acceptance into program means acceptance into college: Student must be admitted and enrolled in the university first and then request services.

ADMISSIONS

There is no special admissions process for students with learning disabilities. All applicants are expected to meet the same admission criteria, which include college-prep courses and SAT of 900, with exceptions. Admission requirements are not so high that they impede access. An admissions exceptions committee considers applications that may warrant exceptions to the general admission standards. Students may enter through Extended Learning, and upon earning 21 credits, a student may be considered for regular matriculation. In-state residents who do not predict a 2.0 GPA may be considered for a five-week summer Developmental Studies Session.

ADDITIONAL INFORMATION

The coordinator of Human Diversity Programming is the initial resource person and record keeper who validates the existence of a disability and the need for any specific accommodations, and contacts faculty and other individuals who have reason to receive information. Academic assistance is provided through the Tutoring Center. Students with LD are eligible to receive services and accommodations prescribed in the psychoeducational evaluation, extended time on exams, use of tape recorder, use of calculator, testing in a separate location, readers, spell-check and grammar check on written assignments, scribes, tutorial assistance, early advisement and pre-registration, computer assistive technology, and referrals. Individualized study skills assessments are made, and tutorial assistance is provided. Skills classes are offered in study skills, stress management, and remedial math, English and reading, and ESL. Tutors are available to all students, and arrangements are made at no cost to the student.

Support Services Contact Information

Learning Disability Program/Services: Services for Students with Disabilities
Director: Patricia Richter
E-Mail: richter@kutztown.edu
Telephone: 610-683-4108
Fax: 610-683-1520

LEARNING DISABILITY SERVICES

Requests for the following/services accommodations will be evaluated individually based on appropriate and current documentation.

Allowed in exams
  Calculator: Yes
  Dictionary: Yes
  Computer: Yes
  Spellchecker: Yes
Extended test time: Yes
Scribes: Yes
Proctors: Yes
Oral exams: Yes
Note-takers: Yes

Distraction reduced environment: Yes
Tape recording in class: Yes
Books on tape from RFBD: Yes
Taping of books not from RFBD: Yes
Accommodations for students with
  ADD: Yes
Reading machine: Yes
Other assistive technology: Yes
Priority registration: Yes

Added costs for services: No
LD specialists: Yes
Professional tutors: No
Peer tutors: Yes
Max. hours/wk. for services:
  Unlimited
How professors are notified of
  LD/ADD: By both student and director

GENERAL ADMISSIONS INFORMATION

Director of Admissions: Dr. William Stahler
Telephone: 610-683-4060

Entrance Requirements

Academic units recommended: 4 English, 3 math, 3 science, 2 foreign language, 2 social studies. High school diploma is required and GED is accepted. ACT with or without Writing component accepted. TOEFL required of all international applicants, minimum paper TOEFL 500, minimum computer TOEFL 173.

Application deadline: Rolling
Notification: Rolling
Average GPA: 3.02

Average SAT Math: 491
Average SAT Verbal: 495
Average ACT: NR

Graduated top 10% of class: 6%
Graduated top 25% of class: 20%
Graduated top 50% of class: 64%

COLLEGE GRADUATION REQUIREMENTS

Course waivers allowed: No
Course substitutions allowed: Yes
In what course: Foreign language and math only with strong diagnostic recommendation through the undergraduate exceptions committee.

Additional Information

Environment: The university is located on 325 acres in a rural area 90 miles north of Philadelphia.

Student Body:
  Undergrad enrollment: 8,141
  Women: 58%
  Men: 42%
  Percent out-of-state: 9%

Cost Information
  In-state tuition: $4,810
  Out-of-state tuition: $12,026
  Room & board: $5,274
Housing Information
  University housing: Yes
  Percent living on campus: 42%

Greek System
  Fraternity: Yes
  Sorority: Yes
Athletics: NCAA Division II

MERCYHURST COLLEGE

Admissions, 501 East 38th Street, Erie, PA 16546
Phone: 814-824-2202 • Fax: 814-824-2071
E-mail: admissions@mercyhurst.edu • Web: www.mercyhurst.edu
Support: SP • Institution type: 4-year private

LEARNING DISABILITY PROGRAM AND SERVICES

The specialized program at Mercyhurst College is designed to assist students who have been identified as having LD. The emphasis is on students' individual strengths, abilities, and interests, as well as learning deficits. This program consists of a structured, individualized set of experiences designed to assist students with LD to get maximum value from their educational potential and earn a college degree. Students selecting the Structured Program for students with learning differences pay an additional fee for this service and must submit a recent psychological evaluation that includes the WAIS—III or WISC—R scores within two years; three letters of recommendation, one each from a math, English, and LD teacher or guidance counselor; SAT/ACT; and a written statement from a professional documenting the student's learning disability. Students choosing the Structured Program option must attend a summer session prior to entrance; classes may include learning strategies, basic writing, communications, career planning, and computer competency. The program lasts five weeks and costs approximately $1,600 (includes room, board, and tuition). Students with learning differences who feel that they do not require a structured program may opt to receive support services through the Academic Support Center at no additional charge.

LD/ADD ADMISSIONS INFORMATION

College entrance tests required: Yes
Interview required: Yes
Essay required: No
Documentation required for LD: Aptitude (eg. WAIS–R or WAIS–II with subtest scores), Achievement (eg. WAIT), information processing (eg. short- and long-term memory)
Documentation required for ADD: Updated medical evalution by licensed physician.
Submitted to: Admissions and Program for Students with Learing Differences
Special Ed. HS coursework accepted: No

Specific course requirements of all applicants: Yes
Separate application required for program services: No
# of LD applications submitted each year: 80
# of LD applications accepted yearly: 35
Total # of students receiving LD services: 75
Acceptance into program means acceptance into college: Student must be admitted and enrolled in the college first and then request services.

ADMISSIONS

To be eligible for any of the services at Mercyhurst, students with learning disabilities must adhere to the regular admission requirements and meet the regular admission criteria. General admission criteria include: 2.5 GPA; ACT 19+ or SAT 900+; and 4 years English, 2 years social science, 3 years math, 2 years science, and 2 years foreign language (waivers and substitutions are determined on an individual basis). Students who do not meet the regular admissions standards are referred to Mercyhurst—McAuley, or Mercyhurst—North East for consideration into the two-year division. Some students may be admitted on probation pending the completion of developmental course work. The college reserves the right to reject any student not meeting admission standards. The admission decisions are made jointly by the director of Programs for Students with Learning Differences and the Office of Admission. Upon acceptance to the college, if the student wishes special services, she/he must identify herself/himself to the admissions office and, at that time, choose to receive services in one of two options available to students with documented learning differences. These programs are a structured program and a basic service program.

ADDITIONAL INFORMATION

The Structured Program for Students with Learning Differences provides special services, including advisory board, advocacy, alternative testing, books on tape though RFBD, community skills, drop-in services, Kurzweil Personal Reader, midterm progress reports, note-takers, peer tutoring, professional advising/priority registration, special five-week Summer Orientation Program prior to freshman year, special section of basic writing, special section of math problem solving, study hall (required of all freshman), and a support group.

Support Services Contact Information

Learning Disability Program/Services: Program for Students with Learning Differences
Director: Dianne Rogers
E-Mail: drogers@mercyhurst.edu
  Telephone: 814-824-2450
  Fax: 814-824-2436

LEARNING DISABILITY SERVICES

Requests for the following/services accommodations will be evaluated individually based on appropriate and current documentation.

Allowed in exams
  Calculator: Yes
  Dictionary: Yes
  Computer: Yes
  Spellchecker: Yes
Extended test time: Yes
Scribes: Yes
Proctors: Yes
Oral exams: Yes
Note-takers: Yes

Distraction reduced environment: Yes
Tape recording in class: Yes
Books on tape from RFBD: Yes
Taping of books not from RFBD: No
Accommodations for students with ADD: Yes
Reading machine: Yes
Other assistive technology: Yes
Priority registration: Yes

Added costs for services: Yes
LD specialists: Yes
Professional tutors: No
Peer tutors: 30
Max. hours/wk. for services: Unlimited
How professors are notified of LD/ADD: By both student and director

GENERAL ADMISSIONS INFORMATION

Director of Admissions: Robin Engel
Telephone: 814-824-2202

ENTRANCE REQUIREMENTS

Academic units recommended: 4 English, 3 math, 3 science (1 science lab), 2 foreign language, 2 social studies, 2 history. High school diploma is required and GED is accepted. TOEFL required of all international applicants, minimum paper TOEFL 550, minimum computer TOEFL 300.

Application deadline: Rolling
Notification: Rolling
Average GPA: 3.20

Average SAT Math: 532
Average SAT Verbal: 549
Average ACT: 23

Graduated top 10% of class: 18%
Graduated top 25% of class: 45%
Graduated top 50% of class: 78%

COLLEGE GRADUATION REQUIREMENTS

Course waivers allowed: Yes
Course substitutions allowed: Yes
In what course: Foreign language

ADDITIONAL INFORMATION

Environment: The 80-acre campus of Mercyhurst overlooks Lake Erie.

Student Body:
  Undergrad enrollment: 3,537
  Women: 62%
  Men: 38%
  Percent out-of-state: 34%

Cost Information
  Tuition: $16,740
  Room & board: $6,798
Housing Information
  University housing: Yes
  Percent living on campus: 58%

Greek System
  Fraternity: No
  Sorority: No
Athletics: NCAA Division II

MESSIAH COLLEGE

PO Box 3005, One College Avenue, Grantham, PA 17027
Phone: 717-691-6000 • Fax: 717-796-5374
E-mail: admiss@messiah.edu • Web: www.messiah.edu
Support: S • Institution type: 4-year private

LEARNING DISABILITY PROGRAM AND SERVICES

Messiah College is committed to making reasonable accommodations for qualified students who present evidence of a disability. Documentation is reviewed, and, if adequate for determining eligibility, a plan of assistance is worked out with the student. The DS staff will assist the student in identifying accommodations needed in various classes and in communicating these needs to faculty. Students must make an appointment with DS to receive assistance in reviewing documentation and determining appropriate accommodations. DS may also require additional documentation or evaluations for determination of eligibility. Any costs incurred for evaluation are the responsibility of the student. Students who do not have documentation, but who think they may have a disability, may seek assistance from DS in locating screening services on campus. Students who are encouraged to pursue determination of eligibility or support services, but choose not to at the time, will be asked to sign a form indicating their preference in waiving their rights temporarily. Students may change their mind at a later date, as long as they are actively enrolled at Messiah College.

LD/ADD ADMISSIONS INFORMATION

College entrance tests required: Yes
Interview required: No
Essay required: No
Documentation required for LD: Complete psychoeducational report from a qualified examiner, to include all test details; IEP/504 service plan suggested to verify accommodations. Current reports are no more than 4 years old
Documentation required for ADD: Complete psychoeducational report from a qualified examiner, to include all test details; IEP/504 service plan suggested to verify accommodations, and additonal medical report with needed accommodations

Specific course requirements of all applicants: Yes
Submitted to: Disability Services
Special Ed. HS coursework accepted: Yes
Separate application required for program services: No
# of LD applications submitted each year: NR
# of LD applications accepted yearly: NR
Total # of students receiving LD services: 20–25
Acceptance into program means acceptance into college: Student must be admitted and enrolled in the college first and then request services.

ADMISSIONS

All applicants must meet the same admission criteria. There is an extensive application process including, letters of recommendation, ACT/SAT, high school transcript, essays, and a review by the admissions officer/committee. Admission requirements include a minimum of a 3.0 GPA, 20 ACT or 1000 SAT, and 4 English, 2 math, 2 natural sciences, 2 social studies, and 6 electives (prefer that 2 of these be in foreign language). Foreign language is recommended but alternatives are considered with appropriate documentation. Some applicants who are borderline candidates may be reviewed and admitted through a program called START. These students are required to attend a two-week orientation prior to the beginning of freshman year. Messiah College makes all efforts to avoid any possible prejudice in the admission process. Students with disabilities are encouraged to self disclose and request an interview with the DS director. The director can review the student's file and make a recommendation to the Office of Admission regarding a student's ability to succeed in college. Additionally, self-disclosure of a disability alerts the DS Office that the student has a potential disability that may make them eligible for accommodations.

ADDITIONAL INFORMATION

Commonly provided accommodations by the Disability Services include extended time for test-taking, proctored exams in an alternate location, assistance with getting notes, hard copies of transparencies, advocacy with instructors, taped textbooks for nonreaders, peer tutoring, referral source for other required services. Additionally, The Learning Center provides a range of tutorial services through trained peer tutors and the Writing Center provides peer tutors for written projects. Developmental Services offers assistance with time management, motivation, goal setting, reading skills, notetaking, learning theory, and taking exams.

Support Services Contact Information

Learning Disability Program/Services: Disability Services
Director: Keith W. Drahn, PhD
E-Mail: kdrahn@messiah.edu
Telephone: 717-796-5358
Fax: 717-796-5217

LEARNING DISABILITY SERVICES

Requests for the following/services accommodations will be evaluated individually based on appropriate and current documentation.

Allowed in exams
  Calculator: Yes
  Dictionary: Yes
  Computer: Yes
  Spellchecker: Yes
Extended test time: Yes
Scribes: Yes
Proctors: Yes
Oral exams: Yes
Note-takers: Yes

Distraction reduced environment: Yes
Tape recording in class: Yes
Books on tape from RFBD: Yes
Taping of books not from RFBD: Yes
Accommodations for students with ADD: Yes
Reading machine: No
Other assistive technology: Yes
Priority registration: Yes

Added costs for services: No
LD specialists: No
Professional tutors: No
Peer tutors: 16
Max. hours/wk. for services: Unlimited
How professors are notified of LD/ADD: By Director

GENERAL ADMISSIONS INFORMATION

Director of Admissions: William G. Strausbaugh
Telephone: 717-796-5374

ENTRANCE REQUIREMENTS
Academic units required: 4 English, 2 math, 2 science (2 science lab), 2 foreign language, 2 social studies, 4 academic electives. **Academic units recommended:** 4 English, 3 math, 3 science (3 science lab), 2 foreign language, 2 social studies, 2 history, 4 academic electives. High school diploma is required and GED is accepted. ACT with or without Writing component accepted. TOEFL required of all international applicants, minimum paper TOEFL 550, minimum computer TOEFL 213.

Application deadline: Rolling
Notification: Rolling
Average GPA: 3.73

Average SAT Math: 589
Average SAT Verbal: 602
Average ACT: 26

Graduated top 10% of class: 39%
Graduated top 25% of class: 69%
Graduated top 50% of class: 92%

COLLEGE GRADUATION REQUIREMENTS

Course waivers allowed: Yes
Course substitutions allowed: Yes
In what course: Foreign language substitutions from approved list of courses.

ADDITIONAL INFORMATION

Environment: The college is located on a hilly campus of 400 acres, within 15 minutes drive of Harrisburg.

Student Body:
  Undergrad enrollment: 2,887
  Women: 63%
  Men: 37%
  Percent out-of-state: 48%

Cost Information
  Tuition: $20,120
  Room & board: $6,560
Housing Information
  University housing: Yes
  Percent living on campus: 86%

Greek System
  Fraternity: No
  Sorority: No
  Athletics: NCAA Division III

PENN. STATE U.—UNIVERSITY PARK

201 Shields Building, Box 3000, University Park, PA 16802-3000
Phone: 814-865-5471 • Fax: 814-863-7590
E-mail: admissions@psu.edu • Web: www.psu.edu
Support: S • Institution type: 4-year public

LEARNING DISABILITY PROGRAM AND SERVICES

The goal of Penn State's academic support services for students with learning disabilities is to ensure that they receive appropriate accommodations so that they can function independently and meet the academic demands of a competitive university. Students with learning disabilities should be able to complete college-level courses with the help of support services and classroom accommodations. In order to receive any of the support services, students must submit documentation of their learning disability to the learning disability specialist in the Office for Disability Services. Documentation should be a psychoeducational report from a certified or licensed psychologist done within the past three years for students with learning disabilities. The report should include measures of intellectual functioning (WAIS–III preferred) and measures of achievement which describe current levels of functioning in reading, mathematics, and written language. Students with ADD/ADD should have the professional who diagnosed them complete the ADD Verification Form and submit it to the Office for Disability Services.

LD/ADD ADMISSIONS INFORMATION

College entrance tests required: Yes
Interview required: N/A
Essay required: No
Documentation required for LD: Psychoeducational evaluation
Documentation required for ADD: Yes
Submitted to: Office of Disability Services
Special Ed. HS coursework accepted: No

Specific course requirements of all applicants: Yes
Separate application required for program services: No
# of LD applications submitted each year: NR
# of LD applications accepted yearly: NR
Total # of students receiving LD services: 279
Acceptance into program means acceptance into college: Student must be admitted and enrolled in the university first and then request services.

ADMISSIONS

There is no special application process for students with learning disabilities or attention deficit disorder, and these students are considered for admission on the same basis as other applicants. The minimum 50 percent of admitted students have a GPA between 3.47–3.85 and an ACT between 26–30 or SAT between 1160–1340. Course requirements include 4 years English, 3 years math, 3 years science, 2 years foreign language and 3 years social studies. If the high school grades and the test scores are low, students may submit a letter explaining why their ability to succeed in college is higher than indicated by their academic records. The admissions office will consider this information as it is voluntarily provided. The acceptable ACT or SAT score will depend upon the high school grades and class rank of the student. Two-thirds of the evaluation is based on high school grades and one-third on test scores. Once admitted, students must submit documentation of their learning disability in order to receive support services. Students may seek admission as a provisional or non-degree student if they do not meet criteria required for admission as a degree candidate. Any student may enroll as a non-degree student.

ADDITIONAL INFORMATION

Students with LD are encouraged to participate in the Buddy Program; incoming students are matched with a senior buddy who is a current student with a disability and is available to share experiences with a junior buddy. Other services include audiotaped textbooks, arranging course substitutions with academic departments (when essential requirements are not involved), test accommodations, and individual counseling. Assistance with note-taking is offered through the ODS. Services are offered in a mainstream setting. The Learning Assistance Center operates a Math Center, Tutoring Center, Writing Center, and Computer Learning Center. Students may receive academic help either individually or in small groups for a number of different courses. One-to-one academic assistance is available through the Office of Disability Services. Graduate clinicians provide individual assistance with study skills, time management, and compensatory learning strategies. Currently 234 students with LD and 109 with ADD are receiving services or accommodations.

Support Services Contact Information

Learning Disability Program/Services: Office for Disability Services
Director: Bill Welsh
E-Mail: wjw9@psu.edu
  Telephone: 814-863-1807
  Fax: 814-863-3217

LEARNING DISABILITY SERVICES

Requests for the following/services accommodations will be evaluated individually based on appropriate and current documentation.

Allowed in exams
  Calculator: Yes
  Dictionary: No
  Computer: Yes
  Spellchecker: Yes
Extended test time: Yes
Scribes: Yes
Proctors: Yes
Oral exams: Yes
Note-takers: Yes

Distraction reduced environment: Yes
Tape recording in class: Yes
Books on tape from RFBD: Yes
Taping of books not from RFBD: Yes
Accommodations for students with
  ADD: Yes
Reading machine: Yes
Other assistive technology: Yes
Priority registration: Yes

Added costs for services: No
LD specialists: No
Professional tutors: No
Peer tutors: Yes
Max. hours/wk. for services:
  Unlimited
How professors are notified of
  LD/ADD: By student

GENERAL ADMISSIONS INFORMATION

Director of Admissions: Geoffrey Harford
 elephone: 814-865-5471

ENTRANCE REQUIREMENTS

Academic units required: 4 English, 3 math, 3 science, 2 foreign language, 3 social studies. High school diploma is required and GED is accepted. ACT with or without Writing component accepted. TOEFL required of all international applicants, minimum paper TOEFL 550, minimum computer TOEFL 213.

Application deadline: Rolling
Notification: Rolling
Average GPA: 3.56

Average SAT Math: 617
Average SAT Verbal: 593
Average ACT: NR

Graduated top 10% of class: 41%
Graduated top 25% of class: 80%
Graduated top 50% of class: 98%

COLLEGE GRADUATION REQUIREMENTS

Course waivers allowed: No
Course substitutions allowed: Yes
In what course: Foreign language, if a student's documentation supports the need for it.

ADDITIONAL INFORMATION

Environment: The school is located on over 5,000 acres in a small city 90 miles west of Harrisburg.

Student Body:
  Undergrad enrollment: 33,958
  Women: 47%
  Men: 53%
  Percent out-of-state: 23%

Cost Information
  In-state tuition: $9,374
  Out-of-state tuition: $19,286
  Room & board: $6,230
Housing Information
  University housing: Yes
  Percent living on campus: 38%

Greek System
  Fraternity: Yes
  Sorority: Yes
Athletics: NCAA Division I

SETON HILL UNIVERSITY

1 Seton Hill Drive, Greensburg, PA 15601
Phone: 724-838-4255 • Fax: 724-830-1294
E-mail: admit@setonhill.edu • Web: www.setonhill.edu
Support: S • Institution type: 4-year private

LEARNING DISABILITY PROGRAM AND SERVICES

Students who are eligible for, and are requesting, accommodations under the Americans with Disabilities Act are required to register with the coordinator of Disabled Student Services. Students work individually with the Disability Services coordinator to determine what learning or environmental supports are needed based on the documentation and recommendations for accommodations in the report. An individualized plan of accommodation will be developed with the student. It is the student's responsibility to implement the plan. The student should advise the coordinator of Disability Services if they experience any difficulties with their accommodation plan.

LD/ADD ADMISSIONS INFORMATION

College entrance tests required: Yes
Interview required: No
Essay required: No
Documentation required for LD: Psychoeducational evaluation
Documentation required for ADD: Yes
Submitted to: Disability Services
Special Ed. HS coursework accepted: NR

Specific course requirements of all applicants: Yes
Separate application required for program services: No
# of LD applications submitted each year: NR
# of LD applications accepted yearly: NR
Total # of students receiving LD services: 20
Acceptance into program means acceptance into college: Student must be admitted and enrolled in the university first and then request services.

ADMISSIONS

The admissions process is the same for all students. Those with documentation supporting a disability are given the option of meeting with the Disability Services coordinator. There is a summer program, which targets math, English, and study skills. These are required programs for students with weak transcripts or SAT/ACT scores who otherwise meet admissions standards. Students with documented learning disabilities may request course substitutions for deficiencies in entrance courses based on the LD. Pre-admission interviews are not required but are recommended.

ADDITIONAL INFORMATION

Accommodations may include but are not limited to priority registration, preferential seating, note-taking services, tape recorded lectures, extended time for projects, extended time for quizzes and tests, testing in distraction-free environments, alternative testing formats, tutoring, counseling, course substitutions, use of assisted technologies such as spell check, computer-based programs, and scribe services. Students are responsible for notifying professors about their disability and requesting accommodations. Course substitution requests are reviewed and considered on an individual basis. Skills classes for college credit are offered in time management, note-taking strategies, test taking strategies, and text reading.

Support Services Contact Information

Learning Disability Program/Services: Disability Services
Director: Teresa A. Bassi
E-Mail: bassi@setonhill.edu
  Telephone: 724-838-4295
  Fax: 724-830-4233

LEARNING DISABILITY SERVICES

Requests for the following/services accommodations will be evaluated individually based on appropriate and current documentation.

Allowed in exams
  Calculator: Yes
  Dictionary: Yes
  Computer: Yes
  Spellchecker: Yes
Extended test time: Yes
Scribes: Yes
Proctors: Yes
Oral exams: Yes
Note-takers: Yes

Distraction reduced environment: Yes
Tape recording in class: Yes
Books on tape from RFBD: Yes
Taping of books not from RFBD: Yes
Accommodations for students with ADD: Yes
Reading machine: Yes
Other assistive technology: Yes
Priority registration: Yes

Added costs for services: No
LD specialists: No
Professional tutors: No
Peer tutors: Yes
Max. hours/wk. for services: Unlimited
How professors are notified of LD/ADD: By student

GENERAL ADMISSIONS INFORMATION

Director of Admissions: Dr. Mary Kay Cooper
Telephone: 724-838-4255

ENTRANCE REQUIREMENTS

Academic units required: 4 English, 2 math, 1 science (1 science lab), 2 social studies, 4 academic electives.
Academic units recommended: 4 English, 2 math, 1 science (1 science lab), 2 foreign language, 2 social studies, 4 academic electives. High school diploma is required and GED is accepted. TOEFL required of all international applicants, minimum paper TOEFL 500, minimum computer TOEFL 173.

Application deadline: 8/15
Notification: Rolling
Average GPA: 3.2

Average SAT Math: NR
Average SAT Verbal: NR
Average ACT: NR

Graduated top 10% of class: 14%
Graduated top 25% of class: 38%
Graduated top 50% of class: 73%

COLLEGE GRADUATION REQUIREMENTS

Course waivers allowed: Yes
Course substitutions allowed: Yes
In what course: All appropriate substitutions are reviewed and considered

ADDITIONAL INFORMATION

Environment: Located 35 miles east of Pittsburgh

Student Body:
  Undergrad enrollment: 1,347
  Women: 70%
  Men: 30%
  Percent out-of-state: 17%

Cost Information
  Tuition: $21,870
  Room & board: $6,820-$8,790
Housing Information
  University housing: Yes
  Percent living on campus: 70%

Greek System
  Fraternity: No
  Sorority: No
Athletics: NAIA

TEMPLE UNIVERSITY

1801 North Broad Street, Philadelphia, PA 19122-6096
Phone: 215-204-7200 • Fax: 215-204-5694
E-mail: tuadm@mail.temple.edu • Web: www.temple.edu
Support: CS • Institution type: 4-year public

LEARNING DISABILITY PROGRAM AND SERVICES

Disability Resources and Services is the primary department for disability-related information and services. DRS arranges academic adjustments and accommodations for students. Students must meet with their DRS adviser and review recommended academic adjustments. Documentation should contain the specific diagnosis and indicate the source used to make this determination. Students may take a copy of an accommodation letter prepared by DRS staff to their professors at the start of each semester. Faculty members cannot retroactively provide academic adjustments for course requirements for students who have not previously presents a letter supporting such requests. Faculty may not alter the essential function of a course. Discussions of disability-related needs and ways to adjust course requirements can be developed. As changes occur, updated information describing new requests must be provided.

LD/ADD ADMISSIONS INFORMATION

College entrance tests required: Yes
Interview required: No
Essay required: No
Documentation required for LD: Psychoeducational test results and recommendations
Documentation required for ADD: Psychoeducational, neurological or other relevant medical assessment with educationally-based recommendations
Submitted to: Disability Resources and Services
Special Ed. HS coursework accepted: Yes

Specific course requirements of all applicants: Yes
Separate application required for program services: No
# of LD applications submitted each year: NR
# of LD applications accepted yearly: NR
Total # of students receiving LD services: 450
Acceptance into program means acceptance into college: Student must be admitted and enrolled in the university first and then request services.

ADMISSIONS

DRS staff encourage students with LD/ADD to use available accommodations/adjustments when taking standardized admissions examinations. In situations where standardized exams do not reflect academic potential because of a disability, applicants are encouraged to discuss anticipated strategies for success and explanations of past performance in a personal statement. General admission requirements include 4 years English, 3–4 years math, 2–3 years foreign language, 3 years social studies, 1 years science, 1 year arts, and 5 years other liberal arts/college-prep courses. Students may begin with a reduced load of courses. A six-week summer program is available for selected students (not specifically designed for students with LD).

ADDITIONAL INFORMATION

Making the Grade is a summer post-secondary transition program developed for high school graduates who have disabilities. Program goals include developing interpersonal skills; developing time management strategies, experience residential life, developing strategies for reading and writing, developing note-taking and organizational techniques, developing test taking proficiencies, articulating an understanding of personal strengths and goals, and practicing self-advocacy approaches. There is a math lab, writing lab, tutoring, and study skills program. Assistive technology available includes Dragon, Jaws, LDDeluxe, and Alphasmart. Skills classes are offered in time management, test strategies, and reading strategies. Career recruitment, peer coaching, and support counseling are also available. Students experiencing difficulty in areas such as foreign language or math, that are not essential to a specific major, should meet with DRS staff to discuss alternatives and procedures.

Support Services Contact Information

Learning Disability Program/Services: Disability Resources and Services
Director: Dorothy M. Cebula, PhD
E-Mail: drs@temple.edu
  Telephone: 215-204-1280
  Fax: 215-204-6794

LEARNING DISABILITY SERVICES

Requests for the following/services accommodations will be evaluated individually based on appropriate and current documentation.

Allowed in exams		
Calculator: Yes	**Distraction reduced environment:** Yes	**Added costs for services:** No
Dictionary: Yes	**Tape recording in class:** Yes	**LD specialists:** Yes
Computer: Yes	**Books on tape from RFBD:** Yes	**Professional tutors:** No
Spellchecker: Yes	**Taping of books not from RFBD:** Yes	**Peer tutors:** No
Extended test time: Yes	**Accommodations for students with ADD:** Yes	**Max. hours/wk. for services:** N/A
Scribes: Yes	**Reading machine:** Yes	**How professors are notified of LD/ADD:** By student
Proctors: Yes	**Other assistive technology:** Yes	
Oral exams: Yes	**Priority registration:** N/A	
Note-takers: Yes		

GENERAL ADMISSIONS INFORMATION

Director of Admissions: Dr. Timm Rinehart
Telephone: 215-204-8556

ENTRANCE REQUIREMENTS

Academic units required: 4 English, 3 math, 2 science (1 science lab), 2 foreign language, 2 social studies, 1 history, 1 academic elective. **Academic units recommended:** 4 English, 4 math, 3 science (2 science lab), 2 foreign language, 2 social studies, 2 history, 3 academic electives. High school diploma is required and GED is accepted. TOEFL required of all international applicants, minimum paper TOEFL 525.

Application deadline: 4/1	**Average SAT Math:** 547	**Graduated top 10% of class:** 17%
Notification: Rolling	**Average SAT Verbal:** 541	**Graduated top 25% of class:** 50%
Average GPA: 3.24	**Average ACT:** NR	**Graduated top 50% of class:** 90%

COLLEGE GRADUATION REQUIREMENTS

Course waivers allowed: No
Course substitutions allowed: Yes
In what course: Students can petition for substitutions for math or foreign language. Substitutions must be approved by each college's academic committee. Documentation that specifically recommends this as an accommodation must be on file in the LDSS.

ADDITIONAL INFORMATION

Environment: The university is located on a 76-acre urban campus.

Student Body:	Cost Information	Greek System
Undergrad enrollment: 22,780	**In-state tuition:** $8,622	**Fraternity:** Yes
Women: 57%	**Out-of-state tuition:** $15,788	**Sorority:** Yes
Men: 43%	**Room & board:** $7,522	**Athletics:** NCAA Division I
Percent out-of-state: 23%	**Housing Information**	
	University housing: Yes	
	Percent living on campus: 22%	

UNIVERSITY OF PITTSBURGH

4227 Fifth Avenue, First Floor Alumni Hall, Pittsburgh, PA 15260
Phone: 412-624-7488 • Fax: 412-648-8815
E-mail: oafa@pitt.edu • Web: www.pitt.edu
Support: CS • Institution type: 4-year public

LEARNING DISABILITY PROGRAM AND SERVICES

To access services, students must refer themselves to Disability Resource Services and submit documentation of their learning disability. Once eligibility is established, students meet regularly with a DRS learning specialist who will assist the student in accessing resources and developing an individualized, comprehensive educational plan. The objective of DRS is to work closely with students to empower them to plan and implement a successful academic experience. The Transition Program is a program designed to assist students with LD in their transition into the university through the exploration and development of self-awareness and self-advocacy skills, and to educate students in the use of learning strategies designed to compensate for limitations imposed by the disability. The objective of this program is to positively impact the retention, matriculation, and academic performance of students with LD through the provision of transferable skills necessary for academic work, and to foster self-reliance and independence. Participants attend one group session weekly to discuss self-advocacy, rights and responsibilities, and general skills and strategies. Students also met weekly with a DRS learning specialist to focus on individualized strategies and skills. There is no fee.

LD/ADD ADMISSIONS INFORMATION

College entrance tests required: Yes
Interview required: No
Essay required: No
Documentation required for LD: Full psychoeducational evaluation: within three years
Documentation required for ADD: Yes
Submitted to: Disability Resources and Services
Special Ed. HS coursework accepted: No

Specific course requirements of all applicants: Yes
Separate application required for program services: No
# of LD applications submitted each year: NR
# of LD applications accepted yearly: NR
Total # of students receiving LD services: 115
Acceptance into program means acceptance into college: Student must be admitted and enrolled in the university first and then request services.

ADMISSIONS

Students with Learning Disabilities must meet the admission criteria established for all applicants. These criteria include ACT 22 or SAT 1000, class rank in top two-fifths, and college-prep courses. Students may be admitted on probation for 1 term, and having met the continuation policy at a minimum GPA of 2.0, will be permitted to continue. This applies only in the College of General Studies.

ADDITIONAL INFORMATION

DRS individually designs and recommends services to enhance the skills and personal development of the student. Services available may include exam accommodations, use of calculators, dictionary, computer or spell checker in exams, scribes, proctors, distraction-free environments, taped textbooks, instructional strategy assistance, and adaptive computers. There are two LD specialists on staff.

Support Services Contact Information

Learning Disability Program/Services: Disability Resources & Services
Director: Lynnett Van Slyke
E-Mail: vanslyke@pitt.edu
  Telephone: 412-648-7890
  Fax: 412-624-3346
Contact Person: Noreen Mazzocca
E-Mail: njm974@pitt.edu
  Telephone: 412-648-7890
  Fax: 412-624-3346

LEARNING DISABILITY SERVICES

Requests for the following/services accommodations will be evaluated individually based on appropriate and current documentation.

Allowed in exams
  Calculator: Yes
  Dictionary: Yes
  Computer: Yes
  Spellchecker: Yes
Extended test time: Yes
Scribes: Yes
Proctors: Yes
Oral exams: Yes
Note-takers: No

Distraction reduced environment: Yes
Tape recording in class: Yes
Books on tape from RFBD: Yes
Taping of books not from RFBD: Yes
Accommodations for students with ADD: Yes
Reading machine: Yes
Other assistive technology: Yes
Priority registration: No

Added costs for services: No
LD specialists: Yes
Professional tutors: No
Peer tutors: No
Max. hours/wk. for services: Unlimited
How professors are notified of LD/ADD: By student

GENERAL ADMISSIONS INFORMATION

Director of Admissions: Betsy A. Porter
  Telephone: 412-624-7488

ENTRANCE REQUIREMENTS

Academic units required: 4 English, 3 math, 3 science (3 science lab), 1 social studies, 4 academic electives.
Academic units recommended: 3 foreign language, 3 social studies. High school diploma is required and GED is not accepted. ACT with Writing component required or SAT Reasoning test. TOEFL required of all international applicants, minimum paper TOEFL 550, minimum computer TOEFL 213.

Application deadline: Rolling
Notification: Rolling
Average GPA: NR

Average SAT Math: 621
Average SAT Verbal: 610
Average ACT: 26

Graduated top 10% of class: NR
Graduated top 25% of class: NR
Graduated top 50% of class: NR

COLLEGE GRADUATION REQUIREMENTS

Course waivers allowed: No
Course substitutions allowed: No
In what course: N/A

ADDITIONAL INFORMATION

Environment: The university is located on a 132 acre urban campus.

Student Body:
  Undergrad enrollment: 16,677
  Women: 52%
  Men: 48%
  Percent out-of-state: 6%

Cost Information
  In-state tuition: $10,130
  Out-of-state tuition: $19,500
  Room & board: $7,090
Housing Information
  University housing: Yes
  Percent living on campus: 36%

Greek System
  Fraternity: Yes
  Sorority: Yes
Athletics: NCAA Division I

University of Pittsburgh

WIDENER UNIVERSITY

One University Place, Chester, PA 19013
Phone: 610-499-4126 • Fax: 610-499-4676
E-mail: admissions.office@widener.edu • Web: www.widener.edu
Support: CS • Institution type: 4-year private

LEARNING DISABILITY PROGRAM AND SERVICES

Enable is a structured mainstream support service designed to assist students enrolled in one of Widener's standard academic programs. Students wishing to use Enable services must submit a copy of the psychological testing, including intelligence and achievement testing that describes the nature of the learning disability. Each student in Enable is provided each week with 2 private counseling sessions with a learning specialist. Typically these sessions focus on time management, study skills, social and emotional adjustment, and academic planning. Enable serves as a campus advocate for the needs of students with LD by making sure that accommodations are provided when appropriate. Participation in Enable is included in the basic tuition charge. Thus, there is no extra fee for the services offered through Enable.

LD/ADD ADMISSIONS INFORMATION

College entrance tests required: Yes
Interview required: No
Essay required: Yes
Documentation required for LD: WAIS–III; achievement within three years
Documentation required for ADD: Yes
Submitted to: Enable
Special Ed. HS coursework accepted: Yes

Specific course requirements of all applicants: Yes
Separate application required for program services: No
# of LD applications submitted each year: NR
# of LD applications accepted yearly: NR
Total # of students receiving LD services: 200
Acceptance into program means acceptance into college: Student must be admitted and enrolled in the university first and then request services.

ADMISSIONS

Students with learning disabilities submit the general application form. Admission decisions are made jointly by the Office of Admissions and the director of Enable. Students should submit documentation, essay, and recommendations. ACT scores range between 17–27 and SAT scores range between 750–1300. There are no specific course requirements for admissions. High school GPA range is 2.0-4.0.

ADDITIONAL INFORMATION

Enable is a personalized academic advising and counseling service designed to help students with learning disabilities who meet university entrance requirements cope with the rigors of academic life. Students are assigned counselors who help them understand and accept their disabilities; provide academic advice; individualize learning strategies; teach self-advocacy; and link the students with the Reading and Academic Skills Center, Math Lab, Writing Center, and tutoring services. This office assures that professors understand which accommodations are needed. The Writing Center provides assistance with writing assignments and is staffed by professors. The Math Center offers individualized and group tutoring and is staffed by professors and experienced tutors. The Reading Skills Center assists in improving reading comprehension and study skills. Skills classes are available in college reading, math, and English; only 3 credits are accepted for college credit. The Academic Skills Program assists students who receive less than a 2.0 GPA in the fall semester.

Support Services Contact Information

Learning Disability Program/Services: Enable
Director: Rebecca Corsey McKeogh, PsyD
E-Mail: rebecc.c.mckeogh@widener.edu
  Telephone: 610-499-4179
  Fax: 610-499-1192

LEARNING DISABILITY SERVICES

Requests for the following/services accommodations will be evaluated individually based on appropriate and current documentation.

Allowed in exams
  Calculator: Yes
  Dictionary: Yes
  Computer: Yes
  Spellchecker: Yes
Extended test time: Yes
Scribes: Yes
Proctors: Yes
Oral exams: Yes
Note-takers: Yes

Distraction reduced environment: Yes
Tape recording in class: Yes
Books on tape from RFBD: Yes
Taping of books not from RFBD: Yes
Accommodations for students with ADD: Yes
Reading machine: Yes
Other assistive technology: Yes
Priority registration: Yes

Added costs for services: No
LD specialists: Yes
Professional tutors: 1
Peer tutors: Yes
Max. hours/wk. for services: Unlimited
How professors are notified of LD/ADD: By student

GENERAL ADMISSIONS INFORMATION

Director of Admissions: Irina B. Capaldi
Telephone: 610-499-4126

ENTRANCE REQUIREMENTS

Academic units required: 4 English, 3 math, 3 science, 2 foreign language, 4 social studies, 3 academic electives.
Academic units recommended: 4 English, 4 math, 4 science (3 science lab), 2 foreign language, 4 social studies, 3 academic electives. High school diploma is required and GED is not accepted. ACT with or without Writing component accepted. TOEFL required of all international applicants, minimum paper TOEFL 500, minimum computer TOEFL 173.

Application deadline: Rolling
Notification: Rolling
Average GPA: NR

Average SAT Math: 515
Average SAT Verbal: 500
Average ACT: NR

Graduated top 10% of class: 13%
Graduated top 25% of class: 33%
Graduated top 50% of class: 62%

COLLEGE GRADUATION REQUIREMENTS

Course waivers allowed: No
Course substitutions allowed: No
In what course: N/A

ADDITIONAL INFORMATION

Environment: The university's 105-acre campus is located 15 miles south of Philadelphia.

Student Body:
  Undergrad enrollment: 2,472
  Women: 50%
  Men: 50%
  Percent out-of-state: 45%

Cost Information
  Tuition: $22,800
  Room & board: $8,100
Housing Information
  University housing: Yes
  Percent living on campus: 61%

Greek System
  Fraternity: Yes
  Sorority: Yes
Athletics: NCAA Division III

Widener University

BROWN UNIVERSITY

Box 1876, 45 Prospect Street, Providence, RI 02912
Phone: 401-863-2378 • Fax: 401-863-9300
E-mail: admission_undergraduate@brown.edu • Web: www.brown.edu
Support: CS • Institution type: 4-year private

LEARNING DISABILITY PROGRAM AND SERVICES

The Students with Alternative Learning Styles is a mainstreaming program providing accommodations and services to enable students with LD to succeed at Brown. Counseling is available, as well as the Writing Center, Computer Center, and Student-to-Student (a peer counseling group). Testing accommodations are available. Students may petition to take a reduced course load.

LD/ADD ADMISSIONS INFORMATION

College entrance tests required: Yes
Interview required: No
Essay required: No
Documentation required for LD: One of following: WAIS–R, Woodcock-Johnson–R Tests of cognitive ability: Kaufman Adolescent and Adult Intelligence Test
Documentation required for ADD: Yes
Submitted to: Disability Support Services
Special Ed. HS coursework accepted: No

Specific course requirements of all applicants: Yes
Separate application required for program services: N/A
# of LD applications submitted each year: N/A
# of LD applications accepted yearly: 0
Total # of students receiving LD services: 115
Acceptance into program means acceptance into college: Student must be admitted and enrolled in the university first and then request services.

ADMISSIONS

Admission is very competitive, and all students are required to submit the same application form and meet the same standards. Brown is a highly competitive university, and students have been enrolled in AP and honors courses in high school. If a student does disclose an area of disability, Brown admissions will carefully review any information submitted.

ADDITIONAL INFORMATION

Students requesting accommodations and/or support services must provide documentation of the existence of a LD. With appropriate documentation students may have access to the following services: extended testing time, note-takers, distraction-free testing environment, tape recorder, auxiliary taping of books, and other assistive technology. There is a writing center, an academic center and professional tutors (for a fee) available for all students. There are no specific graduation requirements and students determine what group of courses to take. Services and accommodations are available for undergraduate and graduate students.

Support Services Contact Information

Learning Disability Program/Services: Disability Support Services
Director: Catherine Axe, Director Disability Services
E-Mail: dss@brown.edu
  Telephone: 401-863-9588
  Fax: 401-863-1999
Contact Person: Admissions Office
E-Mail: dss@brown.edu
  Telephone: 401-863-2378

LEARNING DISABILITY SERVICES

Requests for the following/services accommodations will be evaluated individually based on appropriate and current documentation.

Allowed in exams
  Calculator: Yes
  Dictionary: Yes
  Computer: Yes
  Spellchecker: Yes
Extended test time: Yes
Scribes: Yes
Proctors: Yes
Oral exams: Yes
Note-takers: Yes

Distraction reduced environment: Yes
Tape recording in class: Yes
Books on tape from RFBD: Yes
Taping of books not from RFBD: Yes
**Accommodations for students with
  ADD:** Yes
Reading machine: Yes
Other assistive technology: Yes
Priority registration: No

Added costs for services: No
LD specialists: Yes
Professional tutors: For a fee
Peer tutors: 400
Max. hours/wk. for services:
  Unlimited
**How professors are notified of
  LD/ADD:** By both student and director

GENERAL ADMISSIONS INFORMATION

Director of Admissions: Annie Cappuccino (Acting Director)
Telephone: 401-863-2378

ENTRANCE REQUIREMENTS

Academic units required: 4 English, 3 math, 3 science (2 science lab), 3 foreign language, 2 history, 1 academic elective. **Academic units recommended:** 4 English, 4 math, 4 science (3 science lab), 4 foreign language, 2 history, 1 academic elective. High school diploma is required and GED is not accepted. ACT with Writing component required or SAT. All applications must be submit 2 SAT Subject Tests. TOEFL required of all international applicants, minimum paper TOEFL 600, minimum computer TOEFL 250.

Application deadline: 1/1
Notification: 4/1
Average GPA: NR

Average SAT Math: 700
Average SAT Verbal: 690
Average ACT: 29

Graduated top 10% of class: 90%
Graduated top 25% of class: 98%
Graduated top 50% of class: 100%

COLLEGE GRADUATION REQUIREMENTS

Course waivers allowed: No
Course substitutions allowed: Y/N
In what course: Case by case

ADDITIONAL INFORMATION

Environment: The university is located on 146 acres in the urban area of Providence, RI.

Student Body:
  Undergrad enrollment: 5,772
  Women: 54%
  Men: 46%
  Percent out-of-state: 96%

Cost Information
  Tuition: $30,672
  Room & board: $8,474
Housing Information
  University housing: Yes
  Percent living on campus: 85%

Greek System
  Fraternity: Yes
  Sorority: Yes
  Athletics: NCAA Division I

BRYANT UNIVERSITY

1150 Douglas Pike, Smithfield, RI 02917
Phone: 401-232-6100 • Fax: 401-232-6741
E-mail: admission@bryant.edu • Web: www.bryant.edu
Support: CS • Institution type: 4-year private

LEARNING DISABILITY PROGRAM AND SERVICES

The Academic Center for Excellence is dedicated to helping Bryant students achieve their goal of academic success. The center provides study skills training to help students become self-reliant, independent, and confident learners. This is achieved through this internationally accredited peer tutoring program and study skills instruction by professional staff. Group sessions as a mode of instruction are encouraged and the staff engages in a partnership with to students to help them achieve their goals. The Learning Specialist provides support for students with LD. Consideration is given for reasonable modifications, accommodations, or auxiliary aids which will enable qualified students to have access to, participate in, and benefit from the full range of their educational programs and activities offered to all students. As a liaison among students, faculty, and administration, ACE encourages students with LD requiring special accommodations to schedule an appointment with a learning specialist as soon as they register for courses each semester.

LD/ADD ADMISSIONS INFORMATION

College entrance tests required: Yes
Interview required: No-Recommended
Essay required: Yes
Documentation required for LD: Psychoeducational
 evaluation
Documentation required for ADD: Yes
Submitted to: Both Admissions and Academic Center for
 Excellence
Special Ed. HS coursework accepted: No

Specific course requirements of all applicants: Yes
Separate application required for program services: No
# of LD applications submitted each year: NR
# of LD applications accepted yearly: NR
Total # of students receiving LD services: 120
**Acceptance into program means acceptance into
 college:** Student must be admitted and enrolled in the
 university first and then request services.

ADMISSIONS

If students self-disclose during the admission process, the Office of Admissions will forward documentation to the Academic Center for Excellence. If students do not self-disclose, they must schedule an appointment at ACE to do so. Students may elect to self-disclose and provide current documentation which should be sent to admissions and to the ACE. General admission criteria include an average GPA of 3.0 and 4 years of English, 2 years of social studies, at least 1 year of lab science, and 3 years of college prep mathematics. Interviews are recommended. A probationary/conditional admission is available.

ADDITIONAL INFORMATION

Students with documented disabilities may receive accommodations and services based solely on the disability and appropriate services. Some of the accommodations could include extended testing time, readers, distraction-free environment, scribes, proctors, oral exams, note-takers, use of calculators, computers, spell checkers, and books on tape through the RFBD. ACE provides learning specialists to assist students in college level study skill development. Learning Specialists also help students find out what learning and study strategies work best for them. The College Reading and Learning Association certifies the Peer Tutoring Program and one-on-one tutoring is available in a variety of subjects. Students can drop in to work with a specialist or peer tutor in the Learning Labs. Study skills workshops are offered covering topics such as time management, note taking skills, test preparation, and combating procrastination. The ACE course is a seven-week, voluntary enrollment study strategies course designed to help students maintain superior GPAs. The Writing Center provides one-on-one conferencing in writing for all subjects. There are writing consultants, writing specialists, ESL writing specialists and writing workshops.

Support Services Contact Information

Learning Disability Program/Services: Academic Center for Excellence
Director: Laurie L. Hazard, EdD
E-Mail: lhazard@bryant.edu
  Telephone: 401-232-6746
  Fax: 401-232-6038
Contact Person: Selma (Sally) Riconscente
E-Mail: sriconsc@bryant.edu
  Telephone: 401-232-6532
  Fax: 401-232-6038

LEARNING DISABILITY SERVICES

Requests for the following/services accommodations will be evaluated individually based on appropriate and current documentation.

Allowed in exams	**Distraction reduced environment:** Yes	**Added costs for services:** No
Calculator: Yes	**Tape recording in class:** Yes	**LD specialists:** Yes
Dictionary: Yes	**Books on tape from RFBD:** Yes	**Professional tutors:** 6
Computer: Yes	**Taping of books not from RFBD:** No	**Peer tutors:** 50
Spellchecker: Yes	**Accommodations for students with**	**Max. hours/wk. for services:**
Extended test time: Yes	**ADD:** Yes	Unlimited
Scribes: Yes	**Reading machine:** No	**How professors are notified of**
Proctors: Yes	**Other assistive technology:** No	**LD/ADD:** By both student and director
Oral exams: Yes	**Priority registration:** No	
Note-takers: Yes		

GENERAL ADMISSIONS INFORMATION

Director of Admissions: Cynthia L. Bonn, Director of Admission
Telephone: 401-232-6100

ENTRANCE REQUIREMENTS

Academic units required: 4 English, 4 math, 3 science (2 science lab), 2 foreign language, 2 history/social sciences. **Academic units recommended:** 4 history/social sciences. High school diploma is required and GED is accepted. ACT with Writing component required or SAT Reasoning. TOEFL required of all international applicants, minimum paper TOEFL 550, minimum computer TOEFL 213.

Application deadline: 2/15	**Average SAT Math:** 569	**Graduated top 10% of class:** 13%
Notification: 3/15	**Average SAT Verbal:** 535	**Graduated top 25% of class:** 47%
Average GPA: 3.2	**Average ACT:** 24	**Graduated top 50% of class:** 88%

COLLEGE GRADUATION REQUIREMENTS

Course waivers allowed: No
Course substitutions allowed: No
In what course: N/A

ADDITIONAL INFORMATION

Environment: The campus is located in a suburban area 12 miles from Providence.		
Student Body:	**Cost Information**	**Greek System**
Undergrad enrollment: 3,030	**Tuition:** $24,762	**Fraternity:** Yes
Women: 40%	**Room & board:** $9,568	**Sorority:** Yes
Men: 60%	**Housing Information**	**Athletics:** NCAA Division II
Percent out-of-state: 78%	**University housing:** Yes	
	Percent living on campus: 78%	

JOHNSON AND WALES UNIVERSITY

8 Abbott Park Place, Providence, RI 02903-3703
Phone: 401-598-2310 • Fax: 401-598-2948
E-mail: admissions@jwu.edu • Web: www.jwu.edu
Support: CS • Institution type: 2-year and 4-year private

LEARNING DISABILITY PROGRAM AND SERVICES

Johnson and Wales University is dedicated to providing reasonable accommodations to allow students with learning disabilities to succeed in their academic pursuits. While maintaining the highest academic integrity, the university strives to balance scholarship with support services that will assist special needs students to function in the post-secondary learning process. It is important that these students identify themselves and present the appropriate neurological, medical, and/or psychoeducational documentation as soon as possible. Recommendations for specific accommodations will be based on the student's individual needs and learning style. The goal of the Student Success department is to support students in their efforts to develop their talents, empower them to direct their own learning, and lead them on the pathways of success.

LD/ADD ADMISSIONS INFORMATION

College entrance tests required: Yes
Interview required: No
Essay required: No
Documentation required for LD: Psychoeducational report
Documentation required for ADD: MD documentation
Submitted to: Center for Academic Support
Special Ed. HS coursework accepted: Yes

Specific course requirements of all applicants: Yes
Separate application required for program services: No
# of LD applications submitted each year: NR
# of LD applications accepted yearly: NR
Total # of students receiving LD services: 550
Acceptance into program means acceptance into college: Student must be admitted and enrolled in the university first and then request services.

ADMISSIONS

There is no special application process. Standardized tests are not required for admission, and foreign language is not required for admission. After the regular admissions process has been completed and the student is accepted, the student should self-identify and verify the learning disability with the appropriate neurological, medical, and/or psychoeducational documentation. This would include tests administered by the student's high school or private testing service within the past three years. Once admitted, a special needs advisor will meet with the student, and recommendations for specific accommodations will be based on the student's individual needs and learning styles. Any student admitted conditionally will be closely monitored by an academic counselor and must maintain a GPA of 2.0 (two terms below a 2.0 may result in dismissal).

ADDITIONAL INFORMATION

Academic counselors establish initial contact with probational, conditional, and special needs students. Counselors monitor and review grades and enforce academic policies. Accommodations could include decelerated course load, preferential scheduling, oral or extended time on exams, note-taker, use of tape recorder in class, LD support group, individualized tutoring, and a special needs advisor. Career counselors and personal counselors are also available. Program of Assisted Studies (PAS) provides a structured delivery of fundamental math, language, and major skills courses with a strong emphasis on learning strategy instruction and professional advising and tutoring. The Learning Center offers group and/or one-to-one tutoring, writing skills, culinary skills, grammar fundamentals, study groups, and supplemental instruction groups. Freshman requirements include a course in study and social adjustment skills and a course to teach effective job-search techniques, including career planning, personal development, resume writing, and interview techniques. Services and accommodations are available for undergraduate and graduate students.

Support Services Contact Information

Learning Disability Program/Services: Center for Academic Support
Director: Meryl Berstein
E-Mail: mberstein@jwu.edu
 Telephone: 401-598-4689
 Fax: 401-598-4657

LEARNING DISABILITY SERVICES

Requests for the following/services accommodations will be evaluated individually based on appropriate and current documentation.

Allowed in exams
 Calculator: Yes
 Dictionary: Yes
 Computer: Yes
 Spellchecker: Yes
Extended test time: Yes
Scribes: Yes
Proctors: Yes
Oral exams: Yes
Note-takers: Yes

Distraction reduced environment: Yes
Tape recording in class: Yes
Books on tape from RFBD: Yes
Taping of books not from RFBD: Yes
Accommodations for students with
 ADD: Yes
Reading machine: Yes
Other assistive technology: Yes
Priority registration: Yes

Added costs for services: No
LD specialists: Yes
Professional tutors: 18
Peer tutors: 18
Max. hours/wk. for services:
 Unlimited
How professors are notified of
 LD/ADD: By both student and director

GENERAL ADMISSIONS INFORMATION

Director of Admissions: Maureen Dumas
Telephone: 401-598-2310

ENTRANCE REQUIREMENTS

Academic units recommended: 4 English, 3 math, 3 science, 2 social studies. High school diploma is required and GED is accepted. ACT/SAT not required. TOEFL required of all international applicants, minimum paper TOEFL 550, minimum computer TOEFL 213.

Application deadline: Rolling
Notification: Rolling
Average GPA: 2.90

Average SAT Math: NR
Average SAT Verbal: NR
Average ACT: NR

Graduated top 10% of class: 4%
Graduated top 25% of class: 19%
Graduated top 50% of class: 58%

COLLEGE GRADUATION REQUIREMENTS

Course waivers allowed: Yes
Course substitutions allowed: Yes
In what course: Foreign language

ADDITIONAL INFORMATION

Environment: The university is located on 100 acres with easy access to Boston.

Student Body:
 Undergrad enrollment: 9,145
 Women: 50%
 Men: 50%
 Percent out-of-state: NR

Cost Information
 Tuition: $19,200
 Room & board: $7,545
Housing Information
 University housing: Yes
 Percent living on campus: 100%

Greek System
 Fraternity: Yes
 Sorority: Yes
Athletics: NCAA Division III

PROVIDENCE COLLEGE

River Avenue and Eaton Street, Providence, RI 02918
Phone: 401-865-2535 • Fax: 401-865-2826
E-mail: pcadmiss@providence.edu • Web: www.providence.edu
Support: CS • Institution type: 4-year private

LEARNING DISABILITY PROGRAM AND SERVICES

There is no formal program for students with LD. However, the director of the Office of Academic Services and the faculty of the college are very supportive and are diligent about providing comprehensive services. The goal of the college is to be available to assist students whenever help is requested. After admission, the Disability Support Services coordinator meets with the LD students during the summer, prior to entry, to help them select the appropriate courses for freshman year. Students are monitored for 4 years. The college makes every effort to provide "reasonable accommodations."

LD/ADD ADMISSIONS INFORMATION

College entrance tests required: Yes
Interview required: No
Essay required: Yes
Documentation required for LD: No Documentation is required for admission—Psychoeducational evaluation when enabled
Documentation required for ADD: NR
Submitted to: Support Program/Services
Special Ed. HS coursework accepted: N/A

Specific course requirements of all applicants: Yes
Separate application required for program services: No
# of LD applications submitted each year: NR
# of LD applications accepted yearly: NR
Total # of students receiving LD services: NR
Acceptance into program means acceptance into college: Student must be admitted and enrolled in the university first and then request services.

ADMISSIONS

There is no special admissions process for students with learning disabilities. However, an interview is highly recommended, during which individualized coursework is examined. General course requirements include 4 years English, 3 years math, 3 years foreign language, 2 years lab science, 2 years social studies, and 2 years electives. Students with learning disabilities who have lower test scores but a fairly good academic record may be accepted. The admission committee has the flexibility to overlook poor test scores for students with learning disabilities. Those who have higher test scores and reasonable grades in college-prep courses (C+/B) may also gain admission. Students should self-identify as learning disabled on their application. Also, with appropriate documentation, a student may substitute a required entrance course such as a foreign language with a college prep class.

ADDITIONAL INFORMATION

The following services and accommodations are available for students presenting appropriate documentation: the use of calculators, dictionary, computer and spell checker in exams; extended time on tests; distraction-free testing environment; scribes; proctors; oral exams; note-takers; tape recorder in class; assistive technology; and priority registration. Skills seminars, for no credit, are offered in study techniques and test-taking strategies. All students have access to the Tutorial Center and Writing Center. Services and accommodations are available for undergraduate and graduate students.

Support Services Contact Information

Learning Disability Program/Services: Office of Academic Services - Disabilty Support Services
Director: Nicole Kudarauskas, DSS Coordinator
E-Mail: nkudarau@providence.edu
  Telephone: 401-865-2494
  Fax: 401-865-1219

LEARNING DISABILITY SERVICES

Requests for the following/services accommodations will be evaluated individually based on appropriate and current documentation.

Allowed in exams
  Calculator: Yes
  Dictionary: Yes
  Computer: Yes
  Spellchecker: Yes
Extended test time: Yes
Scribes: Yes
Proctors: Yes
Oral exams: Yes
Note-takers: Yes

Distraction reduced environment: Yes
Tape recording in class: Yes
Books on tape from RFBD: No
Taping of books not from RFBD: Yes
Accommodations for students with ADD: Yes
Reading machine: Yes
Other assistive technology: Yes
Priority registration: Yes

Added costs for services: No
LD specialists: Yes
Professional tutors: Yes
Peer tutors: 30–35
Max. hours/wk. for services: Unlimited
How professors are notified of LD/ADD: By student

GENERAL ADMISSIONS INFORMATION

Director of Admissions: Christopher Lydon
Telephone: 401-865-2531

ENTRANCE REQUIREMENTS

Academic units required: 4 English, 4 math, 3 science (2 science lab), 3 foreign language, 2 social studies, 2 history. **Academic units recommended:** 4 English, 4 math, 4 science (3 science lab), 3 foreign language, 1 social studies, 2 history. High school diploma is required and GED is not accepted. ACT with Writing component required or SAT. TOEFL required of all international applicants, minimum paper TOEFL 550, minimum computer TOEFL 213.

Application deadline: 1/15
Notification: 4/1
Average GPA: 3.42

Average SAT Math: 604
Average SAT Verbal: 597
Average ACT: 25

Graduated top 10% of class: 42%
Graduated top 25% of class: 82%
Graduated top 50% of class: 98%

COLLEGE GRADUATION REQUIREMENTS

Course waivers allowed: Yes
Course substitutions allowed: Yes
In what course: Depends on student's disabilty

ADDITIONAL INFORMATION

Environment: Providence College has a 105-acre campus located in a small city, 50 miles south of Boston.

Student Body:
  Undergrad enrollment: 4,125
  Women: 57%
  Men: 43%
  Percent out-of-state: 81%

Cost Information
  Tuition: $23,180
  Room & board: $8,895
Housing Information
  University housing: Yes
  Percent living on campus: 75%

Greek System
  Fraternity: No
  Sorority: No
  Athletics: NCAA Division I

RHODE ISLAND COLLEGE

600 Mt. Pleasant Avenue, Providence, RI 02908
Phone: 401-456-8234 • Fax: 401-456-8817
E-mail: admissions@ric.edu • Web: www.ric.edu
Support: CS • Institution type: 4-year public

LEARNING DISABILITY PROGRAM AND SERVICES

Rhode Island College strives to create and promote an environment that is conducive to learning for all students. Necessary accommodations require that administration, faculty, and staff be consistent and use flexibility in making adaptations, and that the students be flexible in adapting to and using alternative modes of learning and instruction. Students with disabilities may self-identify at any point, but are encouraged to do so at admission. A registration card is sent to all new students. Filling out this card and returning it to the Office of Student Life starts the process. Faculty is responsible for stating at the beginning of each semester verbally or in writing that the instructor is available to meet individually with students who require accommodations. The college wants students to feel comfortable requesting assistance, and faculty and fellow students are encouraged to be friendly and supportive. The college feels that the presence of students with individual ways of learning and coping serves as a learning experience for the professor, the student, and the class.

LD/ADD ADMISSIONS INFORMATION

College entrance tests required: Yes
Interview required: No
Essay required: No
Documentation required for LD: Psychoeducational evaluation
Documentation required for ADD: Yes
Submitted to: Both Admissions and Disability Services
Special Ed. HS coursework accepted: No

Specific course requirements of all applicants: Yes
Separate application required for program services: Yes
# of LD applications submitted each year: NR
# of LD applications accepted yearly: NR
Total # of students receiving LD services: 177
Acceptance into program means acceptance into college: Student must be admitted and enrolled in the college first and then request services.

ADMISSIONS

Admission requirements are the same for all applicants. Students with LD/ADD should submit the general application for admission. If a student does not meet admission requirements and is considered as a conditional admit, this would be done regardless of having a LD or ADD. The majority of admitted students are ranked in the top 50 percent of their high school class.

ADDITIONAL INFORMATION

The Student Life Office provides the following services for students with appropriate documentation: one-to-one consultation; note taking arrangements, use of a tape recorder in class, readers/recorders, registration assistance, disability discussion groups, and assistive technology. The Office of Academic Support and Information Services provides the following for all students: academic advisement; Academic Development Center; Math Learning Center; tutorial services; and Writing Center. Students may request substitutions in courses not required by their major.

Support Services Contact Information

Learning Disability Program/Services: Disability Services, Student Life Office
Director: Mr. Scott Kane, Associate Dean of Student Life
E-Mail: skane@ric.edu
  Telephone: 401-456-8061
  Fax: 401-456-8702
Contact Person: Ann M. Roccio, Coordinator of Students with Disabilities
  Telephone: 401-456-8061
  Fax: 401-456-8702

LEARNING DISABILITY SERVICES

Requests for the following/services accommodations will be evaluated individually based on appropriate and current documentation.

Allowed in exams
  Calculator: Yes
  Dictionary: Yes
  Computer: Yes
  Spellchecker: Yes
Extended test time: Yes
Scribes: Yes
Proctors: No
Oral exams: Yes
Note-takers: Yes

Distraction reduced environment: Yes
Tape recording in class: Yes
Books on tape from RFBD: Yes
Taping of books not from RFBD: Yes
Accommodations for students with
  ADD: Yes
Reading machine: Yes
Other assistive technology: Yes
Priority registration: Yes

Added costs for services: No
LD specialists: Yes
Professional tutors: Yes
Peer tutors: Yes
Max. hours/wk. for services:
  Unlimited
How professors are notified of
  LD/ADD: By both student and director

GENERAL ADMISSIONS INFORMATION

Director of Admissions: Holly Shadoian
Telephone: 401-456-8234

ENTRANCE REQUIREMENTS
Academic units required: 4 English, 3 math, 2 science (2 science lab), 2 foreign language, 2 social studies, 4 academic electives, 1 art, 1/2 computer literacy. High school diploma is required and GED is accepted. TOEFL required of all international applicants, minimum paper TOEFL 550, minimum computer TOEFL 213.

Application deadline: 5/1
Notification: Rolling
Average GPA: NR

Average SAT Math: 484
Average SAT Verbal: 490
Average ACT: NR

Graduated top 10% of class: NR
Graduated top 25% of class: NR
Graduated top 50% of class: NR

COLLEGE GRADUATION REQUIREMENTS

Course waivers allowed: No
Course substitutions allowed: Yes
In what course: English and others if not required by student's major.

ADDITIONAL INFORMATION

Environment: Located a few miles from downtown Providence

Student Body:
  Undergrad enrollment: 6,531
  Women: 68%
  Men: 32%
  Percent out-of-state: 9%

Cost Information
  In-state tuition: $3,700
  Out-of-state tuition: $10,270
  Room & board: $6,650
Housing Information
  University housing: Yes
  Percent living on campus: 14%

Greek System
  Fraternity: Yes
  Sorority: Yes
Athletics: NCAA Division III

UNIVERSITY OF RHODE ISLAND

14 Upper College Road, Kingston, RI 02881
Phone: 401-874-7100 • Fax: 401-874-5523
E-mail: uriadmit@etal.uri.edu • Web: www.uri.edu
Support: CS • Institution type: 4-year public

LEARNING DISABILITY PROGRAM AND SERVICES

Disability Services for Students will assist students in arranging accommodations, facilitate communication between students and professors, and help them to develop effective coping skills in time management, study skills, and stress management. Accommodations are provided to meet the specific needs of individual students. Students are encouraged to have an on-going relationship with DSS and the professional staff is able to meet with students as often as desired. Students with LD/ADD who want to access services or accommodations must provide DSS with current documentation and communicate what needs are requested. Students are also expected to keep up with their requested accommodations (pick up, deliver, and return letters in timely manner) and be involved in the decision-making process when it comes to their needs. Students are encouraged to make accommodation requests as early as possible prior to the beginning of each semester.

LD/ADD ADMISSIONS INFORMATION

College entrance tests required: Yes
Interview required: No
Essay required: No
Documentation required for LD: Full psychoeducational testing including aptitude, achievement & information processing
Documentation required for ADD: Yes
Submitted to: Admissions/Disability Services
Special Ed. HS coursework accepted: N/A

Specific course requirements of all applicants: Yes
Separate application required for program services: No
# of LD applications submitted each year: NR
# of LD applications accepted yearly: 30–100
Total # of students receiving LD services: 500
Acceptance into program means acceptance into college: Student must be admitted and enrolled in the university first and then request services.

ADMISSIONS

All applicants are expected to meet the general admission criteria. There is not a special process for students with LD/ADD. General admission requirements expect students to rank in the upper 50 percent of their high school class and complete college preparatory courses including English, math, social studies, science, and foreign language. If there is current documentation of a language-based LD there is a waiver for the foreign language admissions requirement, but students must self-disclose during the admission process.

ADDITIONAL INFORMATION

Students need to provide the Disability Services for Students office with current documentation of their disability that includes: psychoeducational testing completed by a professional evaluator. DSS will assist students in arranging for accommodations, help to facilitate communication between students and professors, work with students to develop effective coping strategies, assist students with identifying appropriate resources and provide referrals, and offer support groups for students with ADD and a group working towards enhanced awareness of disability issues. Accommodations are based solely on documented disabilities and eligible students have access to services such as priority registration, extended time on exams, permission to tape record lectures, and access to a note-taker.

Support Services Contact Information

Learning Disability Program/Services: Disability Services for Students
Director: Pamela A. Rohland, Director
E-Mail: rohland@uri.edu
  Telephone: 401-874-2098
  Fax: 401-874-5574
Contact Person: Elizabeth A. Nee, Coordinator
E-Mail: bnee@uri.edu
  Telephone: 401-874-2098
  Fax: 401-874-5574

LEARNING DISABILITY SERVICES

Requests for the following/services accommodations will be evaluated individually based on appropriate and current documentation.

Allowed in exams
  Calculator: Yes
  Dictionary: Yes
  Computer: Yes
  Spellchecker: Yes
Extended test time: Yes
Scribes: Yes
Proctors: No
Oral exams: Yes
Note-takers: Yes

Distraction reduced environment: Yes
Tape recording in class: Yes
Books on tape from RFBD: Yes
Taping of books not from RFBD: Yes
Accommodations for students with ADD: Yes
Reading machine: Yes
Other assistive technology: Yes
Priority registration: Yes

Added costs for services: No
LD specialists: Yes
Professional tutors: By referral
Peer tutors: Yes
Max. hours/wk. for services: unlimited
How professors are notified of LD/ADD: By both student and director

GENERAL ADMISSIONS INFORMATION

Director of Admissions: Dave Taggart
Telephone: 401-874-7109

ENTRANCE REQUIREMENTS

Academic units required: 4 English, 3 math, 2 science (2 science lab), 2 foreign language, 2 social studies, 5 academic electives. **Academic units recommended:** 4 English, 4 math, 4 science, 4 foreign language, 4 social studies. High school diploma is required and GED is accepted. ACT with or without Writing component accepted. TOEFL required of all international applicants, minimum paper TOEFL 550, minimum computer TOEFL 213.

Application deadline: 2/1
Notification: Rolling
Average GPA: NR

Average SAT Math: 568
Average SAT Verbal: 556
Average ACT: 24

Graduated top 10% of class: 18%
Graduated top 25% of class: NR
Graduated top 50% of class: 89%

COLLEGE GRADUATION REQUIREMENTS

Course waivers allowed: No
Course substitutions allowed: Yes
In what course: Only substitutions are allowed in foreign language, and more rarely math.

ADDITIONAL INFORMATION

Environment: Located 30 miles from Providence.

Student Body:
  Undergrad enrollment: 10,957
  Women: 56%
  Men: 44%
  Percent out-of-state: 39%

Cost Information
  In-state tuition: $4,680
  Out-of-state tuition: $16,266
  Room & board: $7,810
Housing Information
  University housing: Yes
  Percent living on campus: 39%

Greek System
  Fraternity: Yes
  Sorority: Yes
Athletics: NCAA Division I

CLEMSON UNIVERSITY

105 Sikes Hall, Box 345124, Clemson, SC 29634-5124
Phone: 864-656-2287 • Fax: 864-656-2464
E-mail: cuadmissions@clemson.edu • Web: www.clemson.edu
Support: S • Institution type: 4-year public

LEARNING DISABILITY PROGRAM AND SERVICES

Student Disability Services coordinates the provision of reasonable accommodations for students with disabilities. All reasonable accommodations are individualized, flexible, and confidential based on the nature of the disability and the academic environment. Students requesting accommodations must provide current documentation of the disability from a physician or licensed professional. Reasonable accommodations will be made in the instructional process to ensure full educational opportunities. The objective is to provide appropriate services to accommodate the student's learning differences, not to lower scholastic requirements.

LD/ADD ADMISSIONS INFORMATION

College entrance tests required: Yes
Interview required: No
Essay required: No
Documentation required for LD: Psychoeducational
  evaluation: usually three to five years
Documentation required for ADD: Yes
Submitted to: Student Disability Services
Special Ed. HS coursework accepted: Yes

Specific course requirements of all applicants: Yes
Separate application required for program services: No
# of LD applications submitted each year: NR
# of LD applications accepted yearly: NR
Total # of students receiving LD services: 590
**Acceptance into program means acceptance into
  college:** Student must be admitted and enrolled in the
  university first and then request services.

ADMISSIONS

All students must have the same admission criteria for the university. There is no separate application process for students with learning disabilities. General admission requirements include ACT 22–27, SAT 1080–1260, 4 years English, 3 years math, 3 years lab science, 3 years foreign language, and 3 years social studies. Students may request a waiver of the foreign language by submitting a request to the exceptions committee. It is recommended that students self-disclose the learning disability it they need to explain the lack of a foreign language or other information which help to understand their challenges.

ADDITIONAL INFORMATION

Appropriate accommodations are discussed with each student individually and confidentially. Some of the accommodations offered are assistive technology; note-takers, readers, and transcribers; course substitutions; exam modifications (computer, extended time, private and quiet room, readers and scribes); priority registration; and taped lectures. All students have access to peer tutoring, writing lab, and departmental tutoring. Assistive technology available include screen readers, scanners, Dragon Dictate, and grammar check. Skills courses are offered in time management, test strategies, and study skills. Peer Academic Coaching is a collaborative process between students and a trained peer coach to improve academic and self-management skills through structure, support, and compensatory strategies. Any student is eligible to participate in Peer Academic Coaching. There are currently 230 students with learning disabilities and 310 students with ADD receiving services.

Support Services Contact Information

Learning Disability Program/Services: Student Disability Services
Director: Bonnie Martin
E-Mail: bmartin@clemson.edu
  Telephone: 864-656-6848
  Fax: 864-656-6849

LEARNING DISABILITY SERVICES

Requests for the following/services accommodations will be evaluated individually based on appropriate and current documentation.

Allowed in exams
  Calculator: Yes
  Dictionary: Yes
  Computer: Yes
  Spellchecker: Yes
Extended test time: Yes
Scribes: Yes
Proctors: Yes
Oral exams: Yes
Note-takers: Yes

Distraction reduced environment: Yes
Tape recording in class: Yes
Books on tape from RFBD: Yes
Taping of books not from RFBD: Yes
Accommodations for students with ADD: Yes
Reading machine: Yes
Other assistive technology: Yes
Priority registration: Yes

Added costs for services: No
LD specialists: No
Professional tutors: No
Peer tutors: Varies
Max. hours/wk. for services: Unlimited
How professors are notified of LD/ADD: By both student and director

GENERAL ADMISSIONS INFORMATION

Director of Admissions: Robert S. Barkley
Telephone: 864-656-2287

ENTRANCE REQUIREMENTS

Academic units required: 4 English, 3 math, 3 science (3 science lab), 3 foreign language, 3 social studies, 1 history, 2 academic electives, 1 PE or ROTC. **Academic units recommended:** 4 math, 4 science lab. High school diploma is required and GED is accepted. ACT with Writing component required or SAT Reasoning test. TOEFL required of all international applicants, minimum paper TOEFL 550, minimum computer TOEFL 213.

Application deadline: 5/1
Notification: Rolling
Average GPA: 3.90

Average SAT Math: 617
Average SAT Verbal: 587
Average ACT: 26

Graduated top 10% of class: 42%
Graduated top 25% of class: 72%
Graduated top 50% of class: 92%

COLLEGE GRADUATION REQUIREMENTS

Course waivers allowed: No
Course substitutions allowed: Yes
In what course: Math and foreign language, depending on program of study.

ADDITIONAL INFORMATION

Environment: The university is located on 1,400 acres in a small town.

Student Body:
  Undergrad enrollment: 13,808
  Women: 45%
  Men: 55%
  Percent out-of-state: 33%

Cost Information
  In-state tuition: $7,840
  Out-of-state tuition: $16,404
  Room & board: $5,292
Housing Information
  University housing: Yes
  Percent living on campus: 47%

Greek System
  Fraternity: Yes
  Sorority: Yes
Athletics: NCAA Division I

LIMESTONE COLLEGE

1115 College Drive, Gaffey, SC 29340-3799
Phone: 864-488-4549 • Fax: 864-487-8706
E-mail: admiss@limestone.edu • Web: www.limestone.edu
Support: CS • Institution type: 4-year private

LEARNING DISABILITY PROGRAM AND SERVICES

The Program for Alternative Learning Styles (PALS) was developed to service students with learning disabilities. Therefore, only students with documented learning disabilities are eligible to receive program services. For program purposes, LD refers to students with average to above average intelligence (above 90) who have a discrepancy between measured intelligence and achievement. PALS's biggest advantage is the follow-up system that is in place for the PALS students. Each student is very carefully monitored as to his/her progress in each course he or she takes. The students who are not successful are typically those students who do not take advantage of the system. With the follow-up system, the students in PALS are in no danger of falling between the cracks. The tracking system is specifically designed to keep the professors, the director, and the students informed about their progress toward a degree from Limestone College.

LD/ADD ADMISSIONS INFORMATION

College entrance tests required: Yes
Interview required: Yes
Essay required: No
Documentation required for LD: WAIS and Woodcock–Johnson
Documentation required for ADD: Yes
Submitted to: PALs Program
Special Ed. HS coursework accepted: Yes

Specific course requirements of all applicants: Yes
Separate application required for program services: Yes
# of LD applications submitted each year: 35
# of LD applications accepted yearly: 26
Total # of students receiving LD services: 14
Acceptance into program means acceptance into college: Students are admitted simultaneously into the College and to the PALS program.

ADMISSIONS

Students who self-disclose their LD and want the services of PALS must first be admitted to Limestone College either fully or conditionally. Students must submit a high school transcript with a diploma or GED certificate, SAT or ACT scores, and the general college application. The minimum GPA is a 2.0. To receive services through PALS students must submit the most recent psychological report (within three years) documenting the existence of the LD. Only evaluations by certified school psychologists will be accepted. In addition, only intelligence test scores from the Stanford Binet and/or Wechsler Scales will be acceptable. All available information is carefully reviewed prior to acceptance. Students may be admitted provisionally provided they are enrolled in PALS. Students interested in PALS must arrange for an interview with the director of PALS in order to learn what will be expected of the student and what the program will and will not do for the student. After the interview is completed students will be notified of their eligibility for the PALS and be given the opportunity to sign a statement indicating their wish to participate or not to participate.

ADDITIONAL INFORMATION

During the regular academic year, students will receive special instruction in the area of study skills. The director of PALS is in constant communication with students concerning grades, tutors, professors, accommodations, time management, and study habits. Tutorial services are provided on an individual basis so that all students can reach their maximum potential. Skills classes are offered in math and reading. Other services include counseling, time management skills, and screening for the best ways to make accommodations. All freshmen or new students are required to pay the full fee for the first year of services ($3,000). After the first two semesters, that fee will be reduced by 50 percent for all students who meet the following GPA requirements: 2.0 GPA after 2 semesters, 2.3 GPA after 4 semesters, and 2.5 GPA after 6 semesters.

Support Services Contact Information

Learning Disability Program/Services: Program for Alternative Learning Styles (PALS)
Director: Karen Kearse, MEd, Director
E-Mail: kkearse@limestone.edu
   Telephone: 864-488-8377
   Fax: 864-487-8706

LEARNING DISABILITY SERVICES

Requests for the following/services accommodations will be evaluated individually based on appropriate and current documentation.

Allowed in exams
   Calculator: Yes
   Dictionary: Yes
   Computer: Yes
   Spellchecker: Yes
Extended test time: Yes
Scribes: No
Proctors: No
Oral exams: Yes
Note-takers: No

Distraction reduced environment: Yes
Tape recording in class: Yes
Books on tape from RFBD: Yes
Taping of books not from RFBD: No
Accommodations for students with ADD: No
Reading machine: No
Other assistive technology: No
Priority registration: No

Added costs for services: Yes
LD specialists: $3,000 for first year
Professional tutors: No
Peer tutors: 16–24
Max. hours/wk. for services: Unlimited
How professors are notified of LD/ADD: By both student and director

GENERAL ADMISSIONS INFORMATION

Director of Admissions: Chris Phenicie (VP for Admissions)
Telephone: 864-488-4549

ENTRANCE REQUIREMENTS

Academic units required: 4 English, 3 math, 2 science (2 science lab), 3 foreign language. High school diploma is required and GED is accepted. ACT with Writing component required or SAT Reasoning test. TOEFL required of all international applicants, minimum paper TOEFL 500, minimum computer TOEFL 173.

Application deadline: 8/26
Notification: Rolling
Average GPA: 2.88

Average SAT Math: 489
Average SAT Verbal: 485
Average ACT: 19

Graduated top 10% of class: 3%
Graduated top 25% of class: 24%
Graduated top 50% of class: 56%

COLLEGE GRADUATION REQUIREMENTS

Course waivers allowed: No
Course substitutions allowed: No
In what course: N/A

ADDITIONAL INFORMATION

Environment: The campus is located in an urban area 45 miles south of Charlotte.

Student Body:
   Undergrad enrollment: 625
   Women: 45%
   Men: 55%
   Percent out-of-state: 37%

Cost Information
   Tuition: $14,040
   Room & board: $5,800
Housing Information
   University housing: Yes
   Percent living on campus: 49%

Greek System
   Fraternity: No
   Sorority: Yes
Athletics: NCAA Division II

SOUTHERN WESLEYAN UNIVERSITY

Wesleyan Drive, PO Box 1020, Central, SC 29630-1020
Phone: 864-644-5550 • Fax: 864-644-5972
E-mail: admissions@swu.edu • Web: www.swu.edu
Support: CS • Institution type: 4-year private

LEARNING DISABILITY PROGRAM AND SERVICES

Southern Wesleyan University provides the environment for success. In accepting students with learning disabilities, the university is committed to providing special services and assistance to these students. Services are provided after an assessment of the students' particular needs. The objectives of the SWU program are to help students with learning disabilities make a smooth transition from high school to college, provide faculty with methods to accommodate and help students succeed and become increasingly independent.

LD/ADD ADMISSIONS INFORMATION

College entrance tests required: Yes
Interview required: No
Essay required: No
Documentation required for LD: Psychoeducatioal evaluation
Documentation required for ADD: Yes
Special Ed. HS coursework accepted: Yes

Specific course requirements of all applicants: Yes
Separate application required for program services: No
# of LD applications submitted each year: NR
# of LD applications accepted yearly: NR
Total # of students receiving LD services: 20
Acceptance into program means acceptance into college: Students are admitted directly into the university and to special services for students with disabilities with appropriate documentation.

ADMISSIONS

Applicants with learning disabilities are reviewed on the basis of high school transcript, SAT or ACT, personal interview, recommendations, and psycho educational evaluation. Students may be conditionally admitted with less than a C average, an SAT lower than 740 or ACT lower than 19, or rank in the bottom 50 percent. High school courses should include 4 years English, 2 years math, 2 years science, 2 years social studies. Applicants not meeting these requirements may be admitted conditionally (on academic warning), on probation, or provisionally.

ADDITIONAL INFORMATION

There is a liaison person between faculty and students. Professors are available to students after class. Modifications can be made in test taking, which could include extended time and a quiet place to take exams. Additionally, students may receive assistance with note-taking. All services are offered in response to students' requests.

Support Services Contact Information

Learning Disability Program/Services: Learning Disabilities
Director: Carol Sinnamon
E-Mail: csinnamon@swu.edu
   Telephone: 864-644-5133

LEARNING DISABILITY SERVICES

Requests for the following/services accommodations will be evaluated individually based on appropriate and current documentation.

Allowed in exams
   Calculator: Yes
   Dictionary: Yes
   Computer: Yes
   Spellchecker: Yes
Extended test time: Yes
Scribes: Yes
Proctors: Yes
Oral exams: Yes
Note-takers: Yes

Distraction reduced environment: Yes
Tape recording in class: Yes
Books on tape from RFBD: Yes
Taping of books not from RFBD: Y/N
Accommodations for students with ADD: Yes
Reading machine: No
Other assistive technology: No
Priority registration: No

Added costs for services: No
LD specialists: Yes
Professional tutors: 1
Peer tutors: 4–6
Max. hours/wk. for services: 1 hour per week per course
How professors are notified of LD/ADD: By both student and director

GENERAL ADMISSIONS INFORMATION

Director of Admissions: Chad Peters
Telephone: 864-644-5558

ENTRANCE REQUIREMENTS

Academic units required: 4 English, 2 math, 2 science, 2 social studies. High school diploma is required and GED is accepted. ACT without Writing component accepted. TOEFL required of all international applicants, minimum paper TOEFL 500, minimum computer TOEFL 173.

Application deadline: 8/11
Notification: NR
Average GPA: 3.49

Average SAT Math: 508
Average SAT Verbal: 510
Average ACT: 20

Graduated top 10% of class: 11%
Graduated top 25% of class: 35%
Graduated top 50% of class: 73%

COLLEGE GRADUATION REQUIREMENTS

Course waivers allowed: No
Course substitutions allowed: No
In what course: N/A

ADDITIONAL INFORMATION

Environment: The college is located midway between Charlotte, NC, and Atlanta, GA, within sight of the Blue Ridge Mountains.

Student Body:
   Undergrad enrollment: 2,028
   Women: 64%
   Men: 36%
   Percent out-of-state: 21%

Cost Information
   Tuition: $14,100
   Room & board: $4,950
Housing Information
   University housing: Yes
   Percent living on campus: 19%

Greek System
   Fraternity: No
   Sorority: No
Athletics: NAIA

U. OF SOUTH CAROLINA—COLUMBIA

University of South Carolina, Columbia, SC 29208
Phone: 803-777-7700 • Fax: 803-777-0101
E-mail: admissions@sc.edu • Web: www.sc.edu
Support: CS • Institution type: 4-year public

LEARNING DISABILITY PROGRAM AND SERVICES

The University's Office of Disability Services provides educational support and assistance to students with LD who have the potential for success in a competitive university setting. The Office of Disability Services is specifically designed to empower them with the confidence to become self-advocates and to take an active role in their education. The university works with each student on an individualized basis to match needs with appropriate services. The services are tailored to provide educational support and assistance to students based on their specific needs. The Office of Disability Services recommends and coordinates support services with faculty, administrators, advisors, and deans' offices. The nature and severity of LD may vary considerably. All requests are based on documented diagnostic information regarding each student's specific learning disability. The first step in accessing services from the Office of Disability Services is to self-disclose the disability and arrange an interview. During the interview, staff members will discuss the student's educational background and determine which services best fit his/her needs.

LD/ADD ADMISSIONS INFORMATION

College entrance tests required: Yes
Interview required: Yes
Essay required: No
Documentation required for LD: Psychoeducational evaluation
Documentation required for ADD: MD letter and Psychoeducational evaluation
Submitted to: Student Disability Services
Special Ed. HS coursework accepted: No

Specific course requirements of all applicants: Yes
Separate application required for program services: No
# of LD applications submitted each year: NR
# of LD applications accepted yearly: NR
Total # of students receiving LD services: 300
Acceptance into program means acceptance into college: Student must be admitted and enrolled in the university first (they can appeal a denial) and then request services.

ADMISSIONS

There is no special application or admission process for students with LD. Required scores on the SAT and ACT vary with class rank. Applicants must have a cumulative C+ average on defined college-preparatory courses, including 4 years English, 3 years math, 3 years science, 2 years of the same foreign language, 4 years elective, and 1 year physical education, as well as a 1200 SAT or 27 ACT. If they are denied admission or feel they do not meet the required standards, students may petition the admissions committee for an exception to the regular admissions requirements. Once admitted, students should contact the Educational Support Services Center to arrange an interview to determine which services are necessary to accommodate their needs.

ADDITIONAL INFORMATION

Services are individually tailored to provide educational support and assistance. All requests are based on documented diagnostic information. The program is designed to provide educational support and assistance, including analysis of learning needs to determine appropriate interventions, consulting with the faculty about special academic needs, monitoring of progress by a staff member, study skills training, and tutorial referrals. Special program accommodations may include a reduced course load of 9–12 hours, waivers/substitutions for some courses, and expanded pass/fail options. Special classroom accommodations may include tape recorder, note-takers, and extended time on tests.

Support Services Contact Information

Learning Disability Program/Services: Office of Student Disability Services
Director: Deborah C. Haynes
E-Mail: debbie@gwm.sc.edu
 Telephone: 803-777-6142
 Fax: 803-777-6741

LEARNING DISABILITY SERVICES

Requests for the following/services accommodations will be evaluated individually based on appropriate and current documentation.

Allowed in exams	**Distraction reduced environment:** Yes	**Added costs for services:** No
Calculator: Yes	**Tape recording in class:** Yes	**LD specialists:** Yes
Dictionary: Yes	**Books on tape from RFBD:** Yes	**Professional tutors:** No
Computer: Yes	**Taping of books not from RFBD:** Yes	**Peer tutors:** No
Spellchecker: Yes	**Accommodations for students with**	**Max. hours/wk. for services:** 42.5
Extended test time: Yes	**ADD:** Yes	**How professors are notified of**
Scribes: Yes	**Reading machine:** Yes	**LD/ADD:** By student
Proctors: Yes	**Other assistive technology:** Yes	
Oral exams: No	**Priority registration:** Yes	
Note-takers: Yes		

GENERAL ADMISSIONS INFORMATION

Director of Admissions: R. Scott Verzyl
Telephone: 803-777-7700

ENTRANCE REQUIREMENTS

 Academic units required: 4 English, 3 math, 3 science (3 science lab), 2 foreign language, 2 social studies, 1 history, 4 academic electives, 1 PE or ROTC. High school diploma is required and GED is accepted. TOEFL required of all international applicants, minimum paper TOEFL 550, minimum computer TOEFL 210.

Application deadline: 2/15	**Average SAT Math:** 582	**Graduated top 10% of class:** 26%
Notification: Rolling	**Average SAT Verbal:** 569	**Graduated top 25% of class:** 58%
Average GPA: 3.80	**Average ACT:** 24	**Graduated top 50% of class:** 90%

COLLEGE GRADUATION REQUIREMENTS

Course waivers allowed: Yes
Course substitutions allowed: Yes
In what course: Students with learning disabilities may petition their college for substitution of the required foreign language if the requirement is not an intregal part of the degree program.

ADDITIONAL INFORMATION

Environment: The university is located on 242 acres in downtown Columbia.

Student Body:	**Cost Information**	**Greek System**
Undergrad enrollment: 17,016	**In-state tuition:** $5,548	**Fraternity:** Yes
Women: 54%	**Out-of-state tuition:** $14,886	**Sorority:** Yes
Men: 46%	**Room & board:** $5,590	**Athletics:** NCAA Division I
Percent out-of-state: 12%	**Housing Information**	
	University housing: Yes	
	Percent living on campus: 40%	

University of South Carolina—Columbia

BLACK HILLS STATE UNIVERSITY

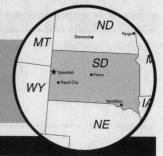

1200 University Street Unit 9502, Spearfish, SD 57799-9502
Phone: 605-642-6343 • Fax: 605-642-6254
E-mail: admissions@bhsu.edu • Web: www.bhsu.edu
Support: CS • Institution type: 4-year public

LEARNING DISABILITY PROGRAM AND SERVICES

Student Support Services ensures equal access and opportunities to educational programs for students with learning disabilities. Within the program, the Disabilities Services coordinator arranges accommodations, counseling services, and campus awareness activities for students with disabilities. The algebra advisor, language/learning skills instructor, and academic and career advisor provide tutoring and advising services to encourage students with disabilities to achieve academic success.

LD/ADD ADMISSIONS INFORMATION

College entrance tests required: Yes
Interview required: No
Essay required: No
Documentation required for LD: Psychoeducational
  evaluation
Documentation required for ADD: Yes
Submitted to: Student Support Services
Special Ed. HS coursework accepted: No

Specific course requirements of all applicants: Yes
Separate application required for program services: Yes
# of LD applications submitted each year: NR
# of LD applications accepted yearly: NR
Total # of students receiving LD services: 70
**Acceptance into program means acceptance into
  college:** Student must be admitted and enrolled in the
  university first and then request services.

ADMISSIONS

General admission requirements include a C average; an ACT of 20; or rank in the upper two-thirds for residents, or upper half for nonresidents. In addition, students must complete the following high school coursework: 4 years English, 2 years lab science, and 3 years math (or 2 years math and 2 years lab science), 3 years social studies, 1/2 year of fine arts, and 1/2 year of computer science. Students who do not meet the admission requirements for general admissions will be admitted to the Junior College at Black Hills State. Course deficiencies must be satisfied within two years of admittance. There is complete open enrollment for summer courses also. Transfer students who do not meet admission requirements will be admitted on probationary status.

ADDITIONAL INFORMATION

The Student Assistance Center offers peer tutoring to all students in most subject areas. Basic skills instruction is available in English and math, and a university learning skills course provides an introduction to college-level studies.

Support Services Contact Information

Learning Disability Program/Services: Student Support Services
Director: Sharon Hemmingson
E-Mail: sharonhemmingson@bhsu.edu
  Telephone: 605-642-6371
  Fax: 605-642-6598
Contact Person: Joan Wermers
  Telephone: 605-642-6099
  Fax: 605-642-6497

LEARNING DISABILITY SERVICES

Requests for the following/services accommodations will be evaluated individually based on appropriate and current documentation.

Allowed in exams
  Calculator: Yes
  Dictionary: Yes
  Computer: Yes
  Spellchecker: Yes
Extended test time: Yes
Scribes: Yes
Proctors: Yes
Oral exams: Yes
Note-takers: Yes

Distraction reduced environment: Yes
Tape recording in class: Yes
Books on tape from RFBD: Yes
Taping of books not from RFBD: Yes
Accommodations for students with
  ADD: Yes
Reading machine: Yes
Other assistive technology: Yes
Priority registration: No

Added costs for services: No
LD specialists: Yes
Professional tutors: Yes
Peer tutors: Yes
Max. hours/wk. for services: 40
How professors are notified of
  LD/ADD: By both student and director

GENERAL ADMISSIONS INFORMATION

Director of Admissions: Steve Ochsner
Telephone: 605-642-6343

ENTRANCE REQUIREMENTS
Academic units required: 4 English, 3 math, 3 science (3 science lab), 3 social studies, 1 fine arts.   High school diploma is required and GED is accepted. ACT with or without Writing component accepted. TOEFL required of all international applicants, minimum paper TOEFL 520, minimum computer TOEFL 190.

Application deadline: Rolling
Notification: Rolling
Average GPA: 3.0

Average SAT Math: NR
Average SAT Verbal: NR
Average ACT: 21

Graduated top 10% of class: 6%
Graduated top 25% of class: 23%
Graduated top 50% of class: 56%

COLLEGE GRADUATION REQUIREMENTS

Course waivers allowed: No
Course substitutions allowed: No
In what course: N/A

ADDITIONAL INFORMATION

Environment: The university is located on 123 acres in a small town, 45 miles northwest of Rapid City.

Student Body:
  Undergrad enrollment: 3,163
  Women: 62%
  Men: 38%
  Percent out-of-state: 18%

Cost Information
  In-state tuition: $2,308
  Out-of-state tuition: $7,333
  Room & board: $3,196
Housing Information
  University housing: Yes
  Percent living on campus: 25%

Greek System
  Fraternity: Yes
  Sorority: Yes
Athletics: NAIA

SOUTH DAKOTA STATE UNIVERSITY

Box 2201, ADM 200, Brookings, SD 57007-0649
Phone: 605-688-4121 • Fax: 605-688-6891
E-mail: sdsu_admissions@sdstate.edu • Web: www.sdstate.edu
Support: S • Institution type: 4-year public

LEARNING DISABILITY PROGRAM AND SERVICES

South Dakota State University is committed to providing equal opportunities for higher education to academically qualified students with LD who have a reasonable expectation of college success. The university does not offer a specialized curriculum, but it does share responsibility with students for modifying programs to meet individual needs. Students needing specialized tutoring service in reading and writing may have to seek assistance from Vocational Rehabilitation or personally pay for such help.

LD/ADD ADMISSIONS INFORMATION

College entrance tests required: Yes
Interview required: No
Essay required: No
Documentation required for LD: WAIS–III; WISC–R; WRAT
Documentation required for ADD: Yes
Submitted to: Disability Services
Special Ed. HS coursework accepted: No

Specific course requirements of all applicants: Yes
Separate application required for program services: Yes
# of LD applications submitted each year: 65
# of LD applications accepted yearly: NR
Total # of students receiving LD services: 87
Acceptance into program means acceptance into college: Student must be admitted and enrolled in the university first and then request services.

ADMISSIONS

Students with LD are required to submit the general application form. If they do not meet all of the course requirements, they may be admitted conditionally based on ACT scores or class rank. Courses required include 4 years English, 2–3 years math, 1/2 year computer science, 3 years social studies, 2–3 years science, and 1/2 year art or music. Students deficient in course requirements need an ACT of 22 (in-state or Minnesota) or 23 (out-of-state).

ADDITIONAL INFORMATION

A skills course is available entitled Mastering Lifelong Skills. Test proctoring for additional time, as well as reading or writing assistance with classroom exams, can be arranged. DSS will also assist students who are LD with finding readers or note-takers. The coordinator of disability services acts as a personal contact for any individual wishing to discuss university policies and procedures, as well as academic and personal concerns related to their disability. The coordinator provides information, accommodations, requests, referrals, support, and advice to students.

Support Services Contact Information

Learning Disability Program/Services: Disability Services (DS)
Director: Nancy Hartenhoff-Crooks, MS, Coordinator
E-Mail: nancy_harttenhoff@sdstate.edu
  Telephone: 605-688-4504
  Fax: 605-688-6450

LEARNING DISABILITY SERVICES

Requests for the following/services accommodations will be evaluated individually based on appropriate and current documentation.

Allowed in exams
  Calculator: Yes
  Dictionary: No
  Computer: Yes
  Spellchecker: Yes
Extended test time: Yes
Scribes: Yes
Proctors: Yes
Oral exams: Yes
Note-takers: No

Distraction reduced environment: Yes
Tape recording in class: Yes
Books on tape from RFBD: Yes
Taping of books not from RFBD: Yes
Accommodations for students with
  ADD: Yes
Reading machine: Yes
Other assistive technology: Yes
Priority registration: Yes

Added costs for services: No
LD specialists: No
Professional tutors: No
Peer tutors: Yes
Max. hours/wk. for services:
  Unlimited
How professors are notified of
  LD/ADD: By both student and director

GENERAL ADMISSIONS INFORMATION

Director of Admissions: Tracy Welsh
Telephone: 605-688-4121

ENTRANCE REQUIREMENTS

Academic units required: 4 English, 3 math, 3 science (3 science lab), 3 social studies, 1 fine arts.   High school diploma is required and GED is accepted. TOEFL required of all international applicants, minimum paper TOEFL 500, minimum computer TOEFL 173.

Application deadline: Rolling
Notification: Rolling
Average GPA: 3.28

Average SAT Math: NR
Average SAT Verbal: NR
Average ACT: 22

Graduated top 10% of class: 13%
Graduated top 25% of class: 36%
Graduated top 50% of class: 70%

COLLEGE GRADUATION REQUIREMENTS

Course waivers allowed: No
Course substitutions allowed: No
In what course: N/A

ADDITIONAL INFORMATION

Environment: The school is located on 220 acres in a rural area 50 miles north of Sioux Falls.

Student Body:
  Undergrad enrollment: 8,447
  Women: 52%
  Men: 48%
  Percent out-of-state: 27%

Cost Information
  In-state tuition: $4,500
  Out-of-state tuition: $9,400
  Room & board: $3,200
Housing Information
  University housing: Yes
  Percent living on campus: 50%

Greek System
  Fraternity: Yes
  Sorority: Yes
Athletics: NCAA Division I

UNIVERSITY OF SOUTH DAKOTA

414 East Clark, Vermillion, SD 57069
Phone: 605-677-5434 • Fax: 605-677-6323
E-mail: admiss@usd.edu • Web: www.usd.edu
Support: CS • Institution type: 4-year public

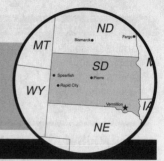

LEARNING DISABILITY PROGRAM AND SERVICES

The University of South Dakota Disability Services (USDDS) operates on the premise that students at the university are full participants in the process of obtaining appropriate accommodations for their disabilities. Students are encouraged to make their own decisions and become self-advocates for appropriate accommodations or services. The three main goals are to (1) help students become self-advocates (2) provide better transition services into and out of college and (3) to provide better instructional and support services. The university strives to ensure that all individuals with legally defined disabilities have access to the full range of the university's programs, services, and activities.

LD/ADD ADMISSIONS INFORMATION

College entrance tests required: Yes
Interview required: No
Essay required: No
Documentation required for LD: Psychoeducational
  evaluation
Documentation required for ADD: Yes
Submitted to: Disability Services
Special Ed. HS coursework accepted: Yes

Specific course requirements of all applicants: Yes
Separate application required for program services: Yes
# of LD applications submitted each year: NR
# of LD applications accepted yearly: NR
Total # of students receiving LD services: 187
**Acceptance into program means acceptance into
  college:** Student must be admitted and enrolled in the
  university first and then request services.

ADMISSIONS

The general admission requirements include standing in the top 60 percent of the class or an ACT score of 18 or above or GPA of 2.6 with a C or higher in the required high school courses. Course requirements include 4 years of English, or ACT English sub-test of 17 or above or AP English score of 2 or above; 3 years of math, or ACT math sub score of 17 or above, or AP Calculus score of 2 or above; 3 years of lab science, or ACT Science-Reasoning sub score of 17 or above or AP Science of 2 or above; 3 years of social studies, or ACT Reading sub score of 17 or above, or AP Social Studies score of 2 or above; and one half-year of fine arts, or AP fine arts score of 2 or above. Students are expected to be proficient in computer skills or they may be required to take specific computer skills courses at the university. Applicants to the associate degree program must meet the same criteria as general admissions or complete the General Equivalency Diploma with a combined score of at least 225 and a minimum score of 40 on each test. Applications submitted from students with deficiencies are reviewed on an individual basis. Non-traditional students (21 years or older) may be admitted at the university's discretion. There is an alternative option for the director of admissions to seek a recommendation from the director of disability services regarding admission questions for individuals with disabilities.

ADDITIONAL INFORMATION

Services are individualized for each student's learning needs. USDDS staff provides the following activities: planning, developing, delivering, and evaluating direct service programs; meeting individually with students for academic and related counseling and skill building; ensuring that students receive reasonable and appropriate accommodations that match their needs; consulting with faculty; and providing academic, career, and personal counseling referrals. Classroom accommodations include test modification, note-taking assistance, readers, books on tape, specialized computer facilities, and tutors.

Support Services Contact Information

Learning Disability Program/Services: USD Disability Services
E-Mail: epearson@usd.edu
Director: Elaine Pearson
Telephone: 605-677-6389
Fax: 605-677-3172

LEARNING DISABILITY SERVICES

Requests for the following/services accommodations will be evaluated individually based on appropriate and current documentation.

Allowed in exams
Calculator: Yes
Dictionary: Yes
Computer: Yes
Spellchecker: Yes
Extended test time: Yes
Scribes: Yes
Proctors: Yes
Oral exams: Yes
Note-takers: Yes

Distraction reduced environment: Yes
Tape recording in class: Yes
Books on tape from RFBD: Yes
Taping of books not from RFBD: Yes
Accommodations for students with ADD: Yes
Reading machine: Yes
Other assistive technology: Yes
Priority registration: No

Added costs for services: No
LD specialists: Yes
Professional tutors: No
Peer tutors: Yes
Max. hours/wk. for services: Unlimited
How professors are notified of LD/ADD: By student

GENERAL ADMISSIONS INFORMATION

Director of Admissions: Michelle Lavallee
Telephone: 605-677-5434

ENTRANCE REQUIREMENTS

Academic units required: 4 English, 3 math, 3 science (3 science lab), 3 social studies, 1 fine arts. **Academic units recommended:** 4 English, 4 math, 4 science (3 science lab), 2 foreign language, 3 social studies, 1 fine arts. High school diploma is required and GED is accepted. ACT with or without Writing component accepted. TOEFL required of all international applicants, minimum paper TOEFL 550, minimum computer TOEFL 213.

Application deadline: Rolling
Notification: Rolling
Average GPA: 3.27

Average SAT Math: NR
Average SAT Verbal: NR
Average ACT: 23

Graduated top 10% of class: 12%
Graduated top 25% of class: 34%
Graduated top 50% of class: 67%

COLLEGE GRADUATION REQUIREMENTS

Course waivers allowed: No
Course substitutions allowed: No
In what course: N/A

ADDITIONAL INFORMATION

Environment: The school is located 35 miles from Sioux City.

Student Body:
Undergrad enrollment: 5,315
Women: 62%
Men: 38%
Percent out-of-state: 27%

Cost Information
In-state tuition: $2,223
Out-of-state tuition: $7,067
Room & board: $3,741
Housing Information
University housing: Yes
Percent living on campus: 31%

Greek System
Fraternity: Yes
Sorority: Yes
Athletics: NCAA Division II

LEE UNIVERSITY

P.O. Box 3450, Cleveland, TN 37320-3450
Phone: 423-614-8500 • Fax: 423-614-8533
E-mail: admissions@leeuniversity.edu • Web: www.leeuniversity.edu
Support: CS • Institution type: 4-year private

LEARNING DISABILITY PROGRAM AND SERVICES

Lee University provides an Academic Support Program for students. This service is free to students. It is the goal of the Lee University Academic Support Program to empower students to actualize all the academic potential that they can. The college offers a Peer Tutorial Program, which hires the best students on campus to share their time, experience, and insight in the course or courses that are most difficult for the students who need tutoring. In addition, the college provides direct assistance for any student to verify a learning disability. For these students, Lee University provides support teams, testing adjustments, classroom adjustments, tutoring, and personal monitoring. Students must initiate the request for special accommodations by applying at the Academic Support Program office. Lee University is committed to the provision of reasonable accommodations for students with disabilities.

LD/ADD ADMISSIONS INFORMATION

College entrance tests required: Yes
Interview required: No
Essay required: No
Documentation required for LD: Psychoeducational
evaluation
Documentation required for ADD: Yes
Submitted to: Both Admissions and Academic Program
Special Ed. HS coursework accepted: Yes

Specific course requirements of all applicants: Yes
Separate application required for program services: No
# of LD applications submitted each year: 35%
# of LD applications accepted yearly: 80%
Total # of students receiving LD services: 15%
**Acceptance into program means acceptance into
college:** Student must be admitted and enrolled in the
university first and then request services.

ADMISSIONS

Each applicant is reviewed on a case-by-case basis. Each student must be able to perform successfully with limited support. ACT minimum is 17 or SAT 860. GPA required is 2.0. There are no specific course requirements. Students who do not meet the college policy for entrance are referred to a special committee for possible probational acceptance.

ADDITIONAL INFORMATION

The Academic Support Program is staffed by professional counselors, math and reading instructors, and a tutoring coordinator. The center has listening and study lab instructional materials, group study/discussion rooms, and tutoring services. The program provides readers and books on tape. Benefits included in the program are tutoring sessions with friendly and comfortable surroundings; 2 hours of tutoring per week per subject; tutoring in any subject, including biology, psychology, English, mathematics, religion, science, sociology, history, and foreign language. Freshmen are channeled into a gateway class, which provides study skills and time management skills.

Support Services Contact Information

Learning Disability Program/Services: Academic Support Program
Director: Gayle Gallaher
E-Mail: GGallaher@LeeUniversity.edu
  Telephone: 423-614-8181
  Fax: 423-614-8179

LEARNING DISABILITY SERVICES

Requests for the following/services accommodations will be evaluated individually based on appropriate and current documentation.

Allowed in exams
  Calculator: Y/N
  Dictionary: No
  Computer: No
  Spellchecker: No
Extended test time: Yes
Scribes: Yes
Proctors: Yes
Oral exams: Yes
Note-takers: Yes

Distraction reduced environment: Yes
Tape recording in class: Yes
Books on tape from RFBD: Yes
Taping of books not from RFBD: No
Accommodations for students with ADD: Yes
Reading machine: Yes
Other assistive technology: Yes
Priority registration: No

Added costs for services: No
LD specialists: Yes
Professional tutors: No
Peer tutors: 50
Max. hours/wk. for services: 2 hours per subject
How professors are notified of LD/ADD: By student

GENERAL ADMISSIONS INFORMATION

Director of Admissions: Phil Cook
Telephone: 423-614-8500

ENTRANCE REQUIREMENTS

Academic units required: 4 English, 3 math, 2 science, 1 foreign language, 2 social studies, 1 history. **Academic units recommended:** 4 English, 3 math, 2 science, 1 foreign language, 2 social studies, 1 history, 1 computer skills. High school diploma is required and GED is accepted. TOEFL required of all international applicants, minimum paper TOEFL 450, minimum computer TOEFL 133.

Application deadline: 9/1
Notification: Rolling
Average GPA: 3.42

Average SAT Math: 535
Average SAT Verbal: 515
Average ACT: 22

Graduated top 10% of class: 16%
Graduated top 25% of class: 39%
Graduated top 50% of class: 66%

COLLEGE GRADUATION REQUIREMENTS

Course waivers allowed: No
Course substitutions allowed: No
In what course: N/A

ADDITIONAL INFORMATION

Environment: The college is located on 40 acres in a small town 25 miles from Chattanooga.

Student Body:
  Undergrad enrollment: 3,479
  Women: 58%
  Men: 42%
  Percent out-of-state: 62%

Cost Information
  Tuition: $9,075
  Room & board: $5,020
Housing Information
  University housing: Yes
  Percent living on campus: 45%

Greek System
  Fraternity: No
  Sorority: No
Athletics: NAIA

MIDDLE TENNESSEE STATE U.

Office of Admissions, Murfreesboro, TN 37132
Phone: 800-433-6878 • Fax: 615-898-5478
E-mail: admissions@mtsu.edu • Web: www.mtsu.edu
Support: CS • Institution type: 4-year public

LEARNING DISABILITY PROGRAM AND SERVICES

The Learning Disabilities Program is a part of the Disabled Student Services office. The LD Program offers comprehensive support services for students diagnosed with LD and ADD. Eligibility for the program requires admission to MTSU and documentation of the disability. The LD Program is designed to ensure students have an equal opportunity to pursue an education. Students with LD are held to the same academic standards as all students; however, accommodations are available to assist meeting these requirements. Accommodations are determined on an individual basis considering the student's strengths, course requirements, and documentation. To register with the LD program, students schedule an appointment with the coordinator, complete the registration form, and provide the most current documentation of the disability.

LD/ADD ADMISSIONS INFORMATION

College entrance tests required: Yes
Interview required: No
Essay required: No
Documentation required for LD: Psychoeducational
evaluation
Documentation required for ADD: Physician statement
Submitted to: Disabled Students Services
Special Ed. HS coursework accepted: No

Specific course requirements of all applicants: Yes
Separate application required for program services: No
# of LD applications submitted each year: NR
# of LD applications accepted yearly: NR
Total # of students receiving LD services: 250–350
Acceptance into program means acceptance into
college: Student must be admitted and enrolled in the
university first and then request services.

ADMISSIONS

There is no special admission process for students with LD. All students must meet the same general admission requirements. The minimum GPA is a 2.3. Students should have 4 years of English, 2 years of math, 2 years of science, 2 years of social studies, 2 years of foreign language, and 1 year visual/performing arts. Course substitutions are not allowed. The average ACT is 21 or 970 SAT. Students are encouraged to self-disclose a disability in a personal statement during the admission process, although this is not required.

ADDITIONAL INFORMATION

Students are encouraged to initiate contact with the LD Program coordinator early in the semester to determine the necessary accommodations. Once enrolled in courses students schedule regular meetings with the coordinator in order to monitor progress and/or determine the need for adjustments to the accommodations. Services/resources provided include orientation to the LD Program; orientation to the Adaptive Technology Center; assistance with the admission process; advising and strategic scheduling of classes; early registration of classes; tutorial services; test accommodations; note-takers, readers, scribes, books on tape; exploration of time management/note taking strategies; career planning and employment strategies; and resume preparation. The Adaptive Technology Center provides training support for students, faculty and staff with disabilities in the use of adaptive/assistive technology application and devices. All disability documentation is conditional and is not released without the consent of the student.

Support Services Contact Information

Learning Disability Program/Services: Disabled Student Services
Director: John Harris
E-Mail: jharris@mtsu.edu
  Telephone: 615-898-2783
  Fax: 615-898-4893

LEARNING DISABILITY SERVICES

Requests for the following/services accommodations will be evaluated individually based on appropriate and current documentation.

Allowed in exams	Distraction reduced environment: Yes	Added costs for services: No
Calculator: Yes	Tape recording in class: Yes	LD specialists: Yes
Dictionary: Yes	Books on tape from RFBD: Yes	Professional tutors: No
Computer: Yes	Taping of books not from RFBD: Yes	Peer tutors: Yes
Spellchecker: Yes	Accommodations for students with	Max. hours/wk. for services:
Extended test time: Yes	ADD: Yes	Unlimited
Scribes: Yes	Reading machine: Yes	How professors are notified of
Proctors: Yes	Other assistive technology: Yes	LD/ADD: By both student and director
Oral exams: Yes	Priority registration: Yes	
Note-takers: Yes		

GENERAL ADMISSIONS INFORMATION

Director of Admissions: Lynn Palmer
Telephone: 800-433-6878

ENTRANCE REQUIREMENTS

Minimum GPA is 2.3. Course requirements include 4 years English, 2 years math, 2 years science, 2 social studies, 2 years foreign language, and fine arts ACT or SAT required. TOEFL required of all international applicants, minimum paper TOEFL 525, minimum computer TOEFL 300.

Application deadline: 7/1	Average SAT Math: NR	Graduated top 10% of class: 17%
Notification: rolling	Average SAT Verbal: NR	Graduated top 25% of class: 51%
Average GPA: 2.96	Average ACT: 22	Graduated top 50% of class: 64%

COLLEGE GRADUATION REQUIREMENTS

Course waivers allowed: Yes
Course substitutions allowed: Yes
In what course: On an individual basis

ADDITIONAL INFORMATION

Environment: The university is located 32 miles from Nashville.

Student Body:	Cost Information	Greek System
Undergrad enrollment: 19,050	In-state tuition: $4,130	Fraternity: Yes
Women: 54%	Out-of-state tuition: $12,600	Sorority: Yes
Men: 46%	Room & board: $4,889	Athletics: NCAA Division I
Percent out-of-state: 5%	Housing Information	
	University housing: Yes	
	Percent living on campus: 25%	

University of Memphis

229 Administration Building, Memphis, TN 38152
Phone: 901-678-2111 • Fax: 901-678-3053
E-mail: recruitment@memphis.edu • Web: www.memphis.edu
Support: CS • Institution type: 4-year public

LEARNING DISABILITY PROGRAM AND SERVICES

The university's LD/ADD program is designed to enhance academic strengths, provide support for areas of weakness, and build skills to help students with LD and ADD compete in the college environment. The program encourages development of life-long learning skills as well as personal responsibility for academic success. Training in college survival skills and regular meetings with the staff are emphasized during the first year to aid in the transition to college. Specific services are tailored to individual needs, considering one's strengths, weaknesses, course requirements, and learning styles. Students are integrated into regular classes and are held to the same academic standards as other students; however, academic accommodations are available to assist them in meeting requirements. The LD/ADD program places responsibility on students to initiate services and follow through with services once they are arranged. Most students who use the appropriate services are successful in their academic pursuits.

LD/ADD ADMISSIONS INFORMATION

College entrance tests required: Yes
Interview required: No
Essay required: No
Documentation required for LD: WAIS–III; WJ
Documentation required for ADD: Yes
Submitted to: LD Program
Special Ed. HS coursework accepted: Yes

Specific course requirements of all applicants: Yes
Separate application required for program services: No
# of LD applications submitted each year: 150–200
# of LD applications accepted yearly: 150–200
Total # of students receiving LD services: 250–325
Acceptance into program means acceptance into college: Student must be admitted and enrolled in the university first and then request services.

ADMISSIONS

If applicants with learning disabilities or ADD choose to disclose their disability and provide professional medical documentation, exceptions to the regular admissions criteria may be made on an individual basis. Course requirements include 4 years English, 2 years science, 2 years foreign language, 2 years social studies, and 1 year visual or performing arts. It is recommended that students self-disclose their LD during the admission process if they do not meet regular admission requirements. Exceptions are made only for applicants who have at least a 17 ACT composite, 2.0 GPA and no more than 3 high school curriculum deficiencies, only 1 of which can be math. Applicants who request admissions exceptions will be asked to provide 2 academic recommendations and a personal letter in addition to the documentation. Students requesting admissions exceptions based on learning disabilities or attention deficit disorders will have their documentation reviewed by the LD coordinator to determine if the documentation is sufficient to meet qualifying criteria.

ADDITIONAL INFORMATION

Transitional studies courses are available in basic math, algebra, and composition for credit; however, they do not apply toward a degree. One-on-one instruction is available in note-taking, time management, and organization skills. The university also offers orientation (highly advised for incoming students) for students with learning disabilities, early registration, use of computers and adaptive software, preferential classroom seating, and 2 special sections of Introduction to the university geared to the needs of students with LD and ADD. Services and accommodations are available for undergraduate and graduate students.

Support Services Contact Information

Learning Disability Program/Services: LD/ADD Program
Director: Susan Te Paske, Director
E-Mail: stepaske@memphis.edu
   Telephone: 901-678-2880
   Fax: 901-678-3070
Contact Person: Dr. Joey Ciavarella, Jr.
E-Mail: jciavrll@memphis.edu
   Telephone: 901-678-2880
   Fax: 901-678-3070

LEARNING DISABILITY SERVICES

Requests for the following/services accommodations will be evaluated individually based on appropriate and current documentation.

Allowed in exams
   Calculator: Yes
   Dictionary: Yes
   Computer: Yes
   Spellchecker: Yes
Extended test time: Yes
Scribes: Yes
Proctors: Yes
Oral exams: Yes
Note-takers: Yes

Distraction reduced environment: Yes
Tape recording in class: Yes
Books on tape from RFBD: Yes
Taping of books not from RFBD: Yes
Accommodations for students with ADD: Yes
Reading machine: Yes
Other assistive technology: Yes
Priority registration: Yes

Added costs for services: No
LD specialists: Yes
Professional tutors: 2
Peer tutors: 1-3
Max. hours/wk. for services: 6
How professors are notified of LD/ADD: By student

GENERAL ADMISSIONS INFORMATION

Director of Admissions: William Akey, Vice President for Enrollment Services
Telephone: 901-678-2111

ENTRANCE REQUIREMENTS

Academic units required: 3 math, 2 science, 2 foreign language. **Academic units recommended:** 4 math, 3 science, 2 social studies. High school diploma is required and GED is accepted. TOEFL required of all international applicants, minimum paper TOEFL 500, minimum computer TOEFL 173.

Application deadline: 8/1
Notification: Rolling
Average GPA: NR

Average SAT Math: NR
Average SAT Verbal: NR
Average ACT: 22

Graduated top 10% of class: NR
Graduated top 25% of class: NR
Graduated top 50% of class: NR

COLLEGE GRADUATION REQUIREMENTS

Course waivers allowed: Yes
Course substitutions allowed: Yes
In what course: Foreign language

ADDITIONAL INFORMATION

Environment: The university is located on 1,159 acres in an urban area.

Student Body:
   Undergrad enrollment: 15,485
   Women: 57%
   Men: 43%
   Percent out-of-state: 12%

Cost Information
   In-state tuition: $4,392
   Out-of-state tuition: $13,116
   Room & board: $5,700
Housing Information
   University housing: Yes
   Percent living on campus: 14%

Greek System
   Fraternity: Yes
   Sorority: Yes
Athletics: NCAA Division I

U. OF TENNESSEE AT CHATTANOOGA

615 McCallie Avenue, 131 Hooper Hall, Chattanooga, TN 37403
Phone: 423-425-4662 • Fax: 423-425-4157
E-mail: Yancy-Freeman@utc.edu • Web: www.utc.edu
Support: CS • Institution type: 4-year public

LEARNING DISABILITY PROGRAM AND SERVICES

The College Access Program (CAP) at the university provides academic, social, and emotional support for students with learning disabilities. CAP provides academic advisement, tutoring in all coursework, career planning, counseling, social skills development, survival skills, career advisement, word processing skills, extended time on tests, freshmen orientation, and psychological testing. Start Smart is a summer seminar for CAP students to prepare them for university coursework and general adjustment to the university.

LD/ADD ADMISSIONS INFORMATION

College entrance tests required: Yes
Interview required: No
Essay required: No
Documentation required for LD: WJ, WAIS–III, Achievement Battery within 3 years
Documentation required for ADD: NR
Submitted to: Admissions and College Access Program
Special Ed. HS coursework accepted: N/A

Specific course requirements of all applicants: Yes
Separate application required for program services: Yes
# of LD applications submitted each year: 20
# of LD applications accepted yearly: 20
Total # of students receiving LD services: 75
Acceptance into program means acceptance into college: Students must be admitted an enrolled at the university first in order to participate in CAP.

ADMISSIONS

Students with learning disabilities submit a general application to the admissions office and a special application to CAP. Applicants to CAP should also submit a LD evaluation, a transcript, and two letters of recommendation. Minimum admissions requirements are 2.0 GPA, 16 ACT or 760 SAT, and 4 years English, 3 years math, 2 years lab science, 1 year American history, 1 year European history or world history or world geography, 2 years foreign language, and 1 year fine arts. Students may be admitted conditionally if they fall below these guidelines and have only one unit deficiency. If the course deficiency is in the area of the LD, an appeals committee will sometimes allow a probationary admittance if CAP also accepts the student. Students admitted on condition must earn at least a 1.0 GPA their first semester or suspension will result. The dean of admissions or admission committee may recommend conditions for acceptance. Application to the Office for Students with Disabilities is a separate process and is not relevant to the admissions process.

ADDITIONAL INFORMATION

CAP does not, as a matter of policy, seek on a student's behalf a waiver of any coursework. Students admitted conditionally may be required to carry a reduced course load, take specific courses, have a specific advisor, and take specific programs of developmental study. Upper-class and graduate student tutors, trained to work with students with learning disabilities, hold regularly scheduled, individualized tutoring sessions. The coordinator matches tutors with CAP students according to learning styles. Social skills development activities may involve video and role-playing situations in group form as well as during informal gatherings. There is a monthly publication, The CAPsule, for CAP students and parents. UTC offers developmental math and English courses for institutional credit. Services and accommodations are available for undergraduate and graduate students.

Support Services Contact Information

Learning Disability Program/Services: College Access Program
Director: Debra Anderson
E-Mail: osd-cap@utc.edu
   Telephone: 423-425-4006
   Fax: 423-425-2288

LEARNING DISABILITY SERVICES

Requests for the following/services accommodations will be evaluated individually based on appropriate and current documentation.

Allowed in exams
   Calculator: Yes
   Dictionary: No
   Computer: Yes
   Spellchecker: Yes
Extended test time: Yes
Scribes: No
Proctors: No
Oral exams: Yes
Note-takers: Yes

Distraction reduced environment: Yes
Tape recording in class: Yes
Books on tape from RFBD: Yes
Taping of books not from RFBD: No
Accommodations for students with ADD: Yes
Reading machine: Yes
Other assistive technology: Yes
Priority registration: No

Added costs for services: Yes
LD specialists: Yes
Professional tutors: 3–5
Peer tutors: 3–5
Max. hours/wk. for services: Unlimited
How professors are notified of LD/ADD: By student

GENERAL ADMISSIONS INFORMATION

Director of Admissions: Yancy Freeman
Telephone: 423-425-4662

ENTRANCE REQUIREMENTS

 Academic units required: 4 English, 3 math, 2 science (2 science lab), 2 foreign language, 2 social studies, 1 history, 1 fine arts. High school diploma is required and GED is accepted. TOEFL required of all international applicants, minimum paper TOEFL 500, minimum computer TOEFL 200.

Application deadline: Rolling
Notification: Rolling
Average GPA: 3.1

Average SAT Math: NR
Average SAT Verbal: NR
Average ACT: 21

Graduated top 10% of class: NR
Graduated top 25% of class: NR
Graduated top 50% of class: NR

COLLEGE GRADUATION REQUIREMENTS

Course waivers allowed: N/A
Course substitutions allowed: N/A
In what course: N/A

ADDITIONAL INFORMATION

Environment: The university is located on 60 acres in an urban area in Chattanooga.

Student Body:
   Undergrad enrollment: 7,181
   Women: 57%
   Men: 43%
   Percent out-of-state: 6%

Cost Information
   In-state tuition: $4,128
   Out-of-state tuition: $12,350
   Room & board: $5,808
Housing Information
   University housing: Yes
   Percent living on campus: 28%

Greek System
   Fraternity: Yes
   Sorority: Yes
Athletics: NCAA Division I

UNIVERSITY OF TENNESSEE AT MARTIN

544 University Street, Martin, TN 38238
Phone: 731-587-7020 • Fax: 731-587-7029
E-mail: jrayburn@utm.edu • Web: www.utm.edu
Support: S • Institution type: 4-year public

LEARNING DISABILITY PROGRAM AND SERVICES

The university believes students with learning disabilities can achieve success in college without academic compromise and can become productive, self-sufficient members of society. A preliminary interview will include a review of previous assessments of the disability and the collection of background information. If the results of the PACE evaluation show that the academic and social needs of the student can be met by PACE services, the student will work with a learning disabilities specialist to develop an individually designed program. university staff who work with PACE students receive training in understanding learning disabilities and teaching strategies that meet the individual student's needs. Graduate supervisors coordinate support services. PACE is designed to complement and supplement existing university support services available for all students.

LD/ADD ADMISSIONS INFORMATION

College entrance tests required: Yes
Interview required: No
Essay required: No
Documentation required for LD: Psychoeducational
  evaluation
Documentation required for ADD: Yes
Submitted to: P.A.C.E
Special Ed. HS coursework accepted: No

Specific course requirements of all applicants: Yes
Separate application required for program services: No
# of LD applications submitted each year: NR
# of LD applications accepted yearly: NR
Total # of students receiving LD services: NR
Acceptance into program means acceptance into
  college: Students must be admitted and enrolled in the
  university and then request services.

ADMISSIONS

Applicants must meet regular admission criteria, including 16 ACT and 2.6 GPA or 19 ACT and 2.2 GPA. Some applicants are considered through qualified admission with a 14 ACT and 2.25 GPA. Course requirements include 4 years English, 3 years math, 2 years science, 2 years social studies, and 2 years foreign language. Each student is considered based on background, test scores, strengths/weaknesses, and motivation. Qualified students with learning disabilities should apply directly to both the PACE Center and the Office of Admissions. Students must complete all steps in both admission processes before an admission decision can be made. An interview in required for students applying to the PACE Program. Documentation should be sent to PACE. To be certain consideration is given to the learning disability, university decisions on acceptance are determined by both the PACE Center and the admissions office. Applicants are selected on the basis of intellectual potential (average to superior), motivation, academic preparation, and willingness to work hard.

ADDITIONAL INFORMATION

All freshmen students with LD selected to participate in PACE and admitted for fall semester must attend the second summer session program. Students take one selected university class in the mornings. In the afternoons, PACE staff teach learning strategies that can be applied to all future courses so that the students will have hands-on experience using the skills. The summer program will also address improvements in reading, spelling, written language, or math skills. Equally important are small group sessions to help students improve social skills. Students with ADD must have comprehensive documentation in order to receive accommodations and services. There is a math lab and an English Writing Center. Students with appropriate documentation may be eligible to receive the following services: extended testing time; distraction-free testing environment; calculators, dictionary, computer, and spellchecker in exams; proctors; oral exams; note-takers; taper recorders in class; books of tape; and tutoring. Services and accommodations are provided to undergraduate and graduate students.

Support Services Contact Information

Learning Disability Program/Services: Program Access for College Enhancement (P.A.C.E.)
Director: Michelle Arant
E-Mail: marant@utm.edu
  Telephone: 901-587-7195
  Fax: 901-587-7956
Contact Person: Beth Vise
E-Mail: bavise@utm.edu
  Telephone: 901-587-7195
  Fax: 901-587-7956

LEARNING DISABILITY SERVICES

Requests for the following/services accommodations will be evaluated individually based on appropriate and current documentation.

Allowed in exams
  Calculator: Y/N
  Dictionary: Y/N
  Computer: Y/N
  Spellchecker: Y/N
Extended test time: Yes
Scribes: Yes
Proctors: Yes
Oral exams: Yes
Note-takers: Yes

Distraction reduced environment: Yes
Tape recording in class: Yes
Books on tape from RFBD: Yes
Taping of books not from RFBD: Yes
**Accommodations for students with
  ADD:** Yes
Reading machine: Yes
Other assistive technology: Yes
Priority registration: NR

Added costs for services: No
LD specialists: No
Professional tutors: 2
Peer tutors: 20
Max. hours/wk. for services:
  Unlimited
**How professors are notified of
  LD/ADD:** By student

GENERAL ADMISSIONS INFORMATION

Director of Admissions: Judy Rayburn
Telephone: 731-587-7020

ENTRANCE REQUIREMENTS

Academic units required: 4 English, 3 math, 2 science (1 science lab), 2 foreign language, 2 history, 1 fine/performing arts. High school diploma is required and GED is accepted. TOEFL required of all international applicants, minimum paper TOEFL 500, minimum computer TOEFL 173.

Application deadline: 8/1
Notification: Rolling
Average GPA: 3.28

Average SAT Math: NR
Average SAT Verbal: NR
Average ACT: 21

Graduated top 10% of class: 21%
Graduated top 25% of class: 53%
Graduated top 50% of class: 87%

COLLEGE GRADUATION REQUIREMENTS

Course waivers allowed: No
Course substitutions allowed: No
In what course: N/A

ADDITIONAL INFORMATION

Environment: The university is located on a 200-acre campus in a small town 100 miles north of Memphis.

Student Body:
  Undergrad enrollment: 4,932
  Women: 57%
  Men: 43%
  Percent out-of-state: 5%

Cost Information
  In-state tuition: $5,682
  Out-of-state tuition: $12,400
  Room & board: $4,070
Housing Information
  University housing: Yes
  Percent living on campus: 33%

Greek System
  Fraternity: Yes
  Sorority: Yes
Athletics: NCAA Division I

U. OF TENNESSEE—KNOXVILLE

320 Student Service Building, Circle Park Drive, Knoxville, TN 37996-0230
Phone: 865-974-2184 • Fax: 865-974-6341
E-mail: admissions@tennessee.edu • Web: www.utk.edu
Support: CS • Institution type: 4-year public

LEARNING DISABILITY PROGRAM AND SERVICES

The mission of the Office of Disability Services is to provide each student with a disability an equal opportunity to participate in the university's programs and activities. Students who are requesting support services are required to submit documentation to verify eligibility under the ADA of 1990. The documentation must include medical or psychological information from a certified professional. It is each student's responsibility to meet the essential qualifications and institutional standards; disclose the disability in a timely manner to ODS; provide appropriate documentation; inform ODS of accommodation needs; talk with professors about accommodations in the classroom, as needed; inform ODS of barriers to a successful education; maintain and return borrowed equipment; keep all appointments with ODS staff members, or call to cancel or reschedule; be involved in your academic planning and course selection; and monitor your progress toward graduation.

LD/ADD ADMISSIONS INFORMATION

College entrance tests required: Yes
Interview required: No
Essay required: No
Documentation required for LD: Psychoeducational
   evaluation
Documentation required for ADD: Yes
Submitted to: Office of Disability Services
Special Ed. HS coursework accepted: N/A

Specific course requirements of all applicants: Yes
Separate application required for program services: Yes
# of LD applications submitted each year: NR
# of LD applications accepted yearly: NR
Total # of students receiving LD services: NR
Acceptance into program means acceptance into
   college: Students must be admitted and enrolled in the
   university and then request services.

ADMISSIONS

There is no special admission process for students with learning disabilities. The Office of Admissions makes every attempt to judge each application on its academic merits. The university does not ask if a prospective student has a disability prior to admission. If an applicant believes that their academic record does not accurately reflect their situation, then the student should self-identify. It is not recommended that the student include documentation with their admission materials. Documentation of a disability is not needed until the time of enrollment. Prospective students who include documentation with their application and are admitted are not guaranteed services. If more information is needed to compete at an equal level with others seeking admission, you may consider voluntarily self-identifying your disability and the circumstances to the admissions office. Qualified candidates with a disability will not be denied admissions solely on the basis of their disability. Applicants are required to have 4 years of English; 2 years of algebra; (1 year of geometry, trigonometry, advanced math, or calculus); 2 years of natural science, including at least 1 year of biology, chemistry, or physics; 1 year of American history; 1year of European history, world history, or world geography; 2 years of a single foreign language; and 1 year of visual or performing arts. A minimum high school GPA of 2.0 is required.

ADDITIONAL INFORMATION

The goals of ODS are to provide access to appropriate accommodations and support services; provide referrals and information for a variety of campus resources, including transportation and housing; encourage and assist students with disabilities to develop greater independence; increase faculty and staff understanding of the various needs of students with disabilities; and assist the university in interpreting legal mandates that address students with disabilities. Disability Services works with each student on a case-by-case basis to determine and implement appropriate accommodations based on documentation. Services could include note-takers, alternative testing arrangements such as extra time, books on tape, computer with speech input, separate testing room, tape recorder and foreign language substitution, content tutors are available on campus through different departments.

Support Services Contact Information

Learning Disability Program/Services: Office of Disability Services
Director: Emily Singer
E-Mail: esinger1@utk.edu
  Telephone: 865-974-6087
  Fax: 865-974-9552

LEARNING DISABILITY SERVICES

Requests for the following/services accommodations will be evaluated individually based on appropriate and current documentation.

Allowed in exams
  Calculator: Yes
  Dictionary: Yes
  Computer: Yes
  Spellchecker: Yes
Extended test time: Yes
Scribes: Yes
Proctors: Yes
Oral exams: Yes
Note-takers: Yes

Distraction reduced environment: Yes
Tape recording in class: Yes
Books on tape from RFBD: Yes
Taping of books not from RFBD: Yes
Accommodations for students with ADD: Yes
Reading machine: Yes
Other assistive technology: Yes
Priority registration: Yes

Added costs for services: No
LD specialists: Yes
Professional tutors: No
Peer tutors: Yes
Max. hours/wk. for services: Varies
How professors are notified of LD/ADD: By student

GENERAL ADMISSIONS INFORMATION

Director of Admissions: Marshall Rose
Telephone: 865-974-2184

ENTRANCE REQUIREMENTS

Academic units required: 4 English, 3 math, 2 science, (1 science lab), 2 foreign language, 1 social studies, 1 history, 1 visual or performing arts. Minimum GPA 2.0. High school diploma is required and GED is accepted. TOEFL required of all international applicants, minimum paper TOEFL 523, minimum computer TOEFL 193.

Application deadline: 2/1
Notification: Rolling
Average GPA: 3.38

Average SAT Math: 549
Average SAT Verbal: 551
Average ACT: 24

Graduated top 10% of class: 27%
Graduated top 25% of class: 54%
Graduated top 50% of class: 83%

COLLEGE GRADUATION REQUIREMENTS

Course waivers allowed: No
Course substitutions allowed: Yes
In what course: Foreign languages—if appropriate

ADDITIONAL INFORMATION

Environment: The university is located on a suburban campus in Knoxville.

Student Body:
  Undergrad enrollment: 19,580
  Women: 51%
  Men: 49%
  Percent out-of-state: 14%

Cost Information
  In-state tuition: $4,740
  Out-of-state tuition: $14,528
  Room & board: $4,912
Housing Information
  University housing: Yes
  Percent living on campus: 32%

Greek System
  Fraternity: Yes
  Sorority: Yes
Athletics: NCAA Division I

ABILENE CHRISTIAN UNIVERSITY

ACU Box 29000, Abilene, TX 79699
Phone: 325-674-2000 • Fax: 325-674-2130
E-mail: info@admissions.acu.edu • Web: www.acu.edu
Support: CS • Institution type: 4-year private

LEARNING DISABILITY PROGRAM AND SERVICES

Alpha Academic Services is a Student Support Service program funded under Title IV legislation governing TRIO programs. The program strives to assist students in programs that move them toward independence in learning and living. The staff is specially trained instructors, peer tutors, counselors, and administrators who focus on the problems encountered by college students. Staff members help qualifying students find and apply solutions to their problems. Students qualify for services if they are a first generation college student, economically disadvantaged, or a student with disabilities. Alpha means one-on-one help and the instruction and tutoring are tailored to the student's unique needs. Students with learning disabilities may receive special accommodation services to assist them in achieving success in their university studies. Documentation of the disability is required in order to receive disability accommodations. Students must make an appointment to determine if they qualify to receive services.

LD/ADD ADMISSIONS INFORMATION

College entrance tests required: Yes
Interview required: Yes
Essay required: Yes
Documentation required for LD: Psychological assesment for LD by a qualified professional. Recommended tests include WAIS–R and WJPB or other relevant tests
Documentation required for ADD: Psychological assessment for ADD such as Brown ADD Screening
Submitted to: Alpha Academic Services
Special Ed. HS coursework accepted: Yes

Specific course requirements of all applicants: Yes
Separate application required for program services: Yes
# of LD applications submitted each year: 30–40
# of LD applications accepted yearly: 25–30
Total # of students receiving LD services: 106
Acceptance into program means acceptance into college: Student must be admitted and enrolled in the university first and then request services.

ADMISSIONS

All students must be admitted to the university and meet the same criteria for admission. There is no special admission process for students with learning disabilities. Regular admissions criteria include 20 ACT or 930+ SAT; college-preparatory courses including 3 years math, 3 years science, 2 years foreign language, and 4 years English; and no specific GPA. Some students not meeting the admission criteria may be admitted conditionally. Students admitted conditionally must take specified courses in a summer term and demonstrate motivation and ability.

ADDITIONAL INFORMATION

Alpha Academic Services provides opportunities for individual instruction in basic skills areas such as writing, math, or study skills; assessment of learning preferences, strengths, and weaknesses; instruction and tutoring designed to fit the student's particular learning preferences strengths, and academic needs; classroom help if needed such as readers, note-takers, and alternative testing arrangements; personal, career, and academic counseling; and workshops on topics such as time management, resume writing, career placement, and study skills.

Support Services Contact Information

Learning Disability Program/Services: Alpha Academic Services
Director: Gloria Bradshaw
E-Mail: bradshawg@acu.edu
   Telephone: 325-674-2275
   Fax: 325-674-6847
Contact Person: Gloria Bradshaw, Ada Dodd, or Jamie Jimenez
   Telephone: 325-674-2667
   Fax: 325-674-6847

LEARNING DISABILITY SERVICES

Requests for the following/services accommodations will be evaluated individually based on appropriate and current documentation.

Allowed in exams
   Calculator: Yes
   Dictionary: Yes
   Computer: Yes
   Spellchecker: Yes
Extended test time: Yes
Scribes: Yes
Proctors: Yes
Oral exams: Yes
Note-takers: Yes

Distraction reduced environment: Yes
Tape recording in class: Yes
Books on tape from RFBD: Yes
Taping of books not from RFBD: Yes
Accommodations for students with ADD: Yes
Reading machine: Yes
Other assistive technology: Yes
Priority registration: No

Added costs for services: No
LD specialists: Yes
Professional tutors: 3
Peer tutors: 20–30
Max. hours/wk. for services: Unlimited
How professors are notified of LD/ADD: By both student and director

GENERAL ADMISSIONS INFORMATION

Director of Admissions: Robert Heil
Telephone: 325-674-2000

ENTRANCE REQUIREMENTS

Academic units recommended: 4 English, 3 math, 3 science (2 science lab), 2 foreign language. SAT or ACT with Writng required. High school diploma is required and GED is accepted. TOEFL required of all international applicants, minimum paper TOEFL 525, minimum computer TOEFL 193.

Application deadline: 8/1
Notification: Rolling
Average GPA: 3.48

Average SAT Math: 550
Average SAT Verbal: 547
Average ACT: 24

Graduated top 10% of class: 22%
Graduated top 25% of class: 50%
Graduated top 50% of class: 77%

COLLEGE GRADUATION REQUIREMENTS

Course waivers allowed: No
Course substitutions allowed: Yes
In what course: As appropriate with petition for reasonable substitute.

ADDITIONAL INFORMATION

Environment: The campus is in a suburban area 150 miles from Fort Worth.

Student Body:
   Undergrad enrollment: 4,166
   Women: 55%
   Men: 45%
   Percent out-of-state: 19%

Cost Information
   Tuition: $18,300
   Room & board: $5,200
Housing Information
   University housing: Yes
   Percent living on campus: 42%

Greek System
   Fraternity: Yes
   Sorority: Yes
Athletics: NCAA Division II

LAMAR UNIVERSITY

P.O. Box 10009, Beaumont, TX 77710
Phone: 409-880-8888 • Fax: 409-880-8463
E-mail: admissions@hal.lamar.edu • Web: www.lamar.edu
Support: S • Institution type: 4-year public

LEARNING DISABILITY PROGRAM AND SERVICES

Services are designed to help students become successful on the Lamar campus. Students with learning disabilities could qualify for registration assistance, tutoring, and other personalized services. Students are encouraged to notify the coordinator of services that specific disabilities exist, the modification needed, and preferably a conference prior to registration will allow the appropriate accommodations to be made. Prior to registration, students are requested to notify the coordinator of services for students with disabilities regarding assistance and/or accommodation they anticipate will be needed during the course of instruction for which they plan to register.

LD/ADD ADMISSIONS INFORMATION

College entrance tests required: Yes
Interview required: No
Essay required: No
Documentation required for LD: Psychoeducational evaluation, within three years
Documentation required for ADD: Diagnostic report, within three years
Submitted to: Services for Students with Disabilities
Special Ed. HS coursework accepted: No

Specific course requirements of all applicants: Yes
Separate application required for program services: Yes
# of LD applications submitted each year: NR
# of LD applications accepted yearly: NR
Total # of students receiving LD services: 66
Acceptance into program means acceptance into college: Student must be admitted and enrolled in the university first and then request services.

ADMISSIONS

Applicants with learning disabilities must meet the general admission requirements. Services will be offered to enrolled students who notify the coordinator of Services for Students with Disabilities (SSWD). Students must be in top half of their class and complete 14 solid credits to be admitted unconditionally, including 4 years English, 3 years math (algebra I-II and geometry or higher), 2 years science (physical science, biology, chemistry, physics, or geology), 2 1/2 years social science, and 2 1/2 years electives (foreign language is recommended). A very limited number of applicants not meeting the prerequisites may be admitted on individual approval. Those not in the top half must achieve a minimum composite score of 1000 SAT. Some students may be considered on an individual approval basis if they fail to meet unconditional admission. These students are subject to mandatory advisement, 6-credit limit in summer and 14 in fall term, and must successfully complete hours with 2.0 GPA. Students must meet these provisions or leave for one year.

ADDITIONAL INFORMATION

SSWD offers a variety of services designed to assist students in becoming full participating members of the university. Services or accommodations could include priority registration; alternative testing accommodations; copying of class notes; classroom accommodations; counseling for academic, personal, and vocational needs; note-takers; readers; textbooks on tape; and tutoring. Professional staff assists students with questions, problem solving, adjustment, decision making, goal planning, testing, and development of learning skills. Skills classes in study skills are offered, including developmental writing, reading, and math for credit. Students are referred to other offices and personnel in accord with the needs and intents of the individual. Services and accommodations are available for undergraduate and graduate students.

Support Services Contact Information

Learning Disability Program/Services: Services for Students with Disabilities (SSWD)
Director: Callie Trahan, Coordinator
E-Mail: trahancf@hal.lamar.edu
  Telephone: 409-880-8347
  Fax: 409-880-2225

LEARNING DISABILITY SERVICES

Requests for the following/services accommodations will be evaluated individually based on appropriate and current documentation.

Allowed in exams
  Calculator: Yes
  Dictionary: Yes
  Computer: Yes
  Spellchecker: Yes
Extended test time: Yes
Scribes: Yes
Proctors: Yes
Oral exams: Yes
Note-takers: Yes

Distraction reduced environment: Yes
Tape recording in class: Yes
Books on tape from RFBD: Yes
Taping of books not from RFBD: Yes
Accommodations for students with ADD: Yes
Reading machine: Yes
Other assistive technology: Yes
Priority registration: Yes

Added costs for services: No
LD specialists: No
Professional tutors: No
Peer tutors: Yes
Max. hours/wk. for services: 15
How professors are notified of LD/ADD: By student

GENERAL ADMISSIONS INFORMATION

Director of Admissions: Jim Rush
Telephone: 409-880-8888

ENTRANCE REQUIREMENTS

Academic units recommended: 4 English, 3 math, 2 science, 2 social studies, 2 academic electives. High school diploma is required and GED is accepted. TOEFL required of all international applicants, minimum paper TOEFL 500, minimum computer TOEFL 173.

Application deadline: 8/1
Notification: Rolling
Average GPA: NR

Average SAT Math: 459
Average SAT Verbal: 413
Average ACT: 20

Graduated top 10% of class: 10%
Graduated top 25% of class: 27%
Graduated top 50% of class: 90%

COLLEGE GRADUATION REQUIREMENTS

Course waivers allowed: No
Course substitutions allowed: Yes
In what course: Appropriateness of a substitution is determined by the academic department chair of the student's major; the dean of the college, and VP for academic affairs. The coordinator of SFSWD verfiies that the request is based on a qualifying disability.Must be documented.

ADDITIONAL INFORMATION

Environment: The university is located on 200 acres in an urban area, 90 miles east of Houston.

Student Body:
  Undergrad enrollment: 9,057
  Women: 55%
  Men: 45%
  Percent out-of-state: 1%

Cost Information
  In-state tuition: $2,800
  Out-of-state tuition: $10,700
  Room & board: $5,200
Housing Information
  University housing: Yes
  Percent living on campus: 11%

Greek System
  Fraternity: Yes
  Sorority: Yes
Athletics: NCAA Division I

MIDWESTERN STATE UNIVERSITY

3410 Taft Boulevard, Wichita Falls, TX 76308-2099
Phone: 940-397-4334 • Fax: 940-397-4672
E-mail: admissions@mwsu.edu • Web: www.mwsu.edu
Support: S • Institution type: 4-year public

LEARNING DISABILITY PROGRAM AND SERVICES

In accordance with Section 504 of the federal Rehabilitation Act of 1973 and the Americans with Disabilities Act of 1990, Midwestern State University endeavors to make reasonable adjustments in its policies, practices, services, and facilities to ensure equal opportunity for qualified persons with disabilities to participate in all educational programs and activities. Students requiring special accommodation or auxiliary aids must make application for such assistance through the Office of Disability Accommodations. The Office of Disability Accommodations focuses on helping students to negotiate all aspects of adapting to college life. These include academic, personal, career, and social concerns. To obtain services, students must be accepted for admissions at MSU, complete an application form from the Office of Disability Accommodations, and supply verification of the disability.

LD/ADD ADMISSIONS INFORMATION

College entrance tests required: Yes
Interview required: No
Essay required: No
Documentation required for LD: WAIS–III, WJ
Documentation required for ADD: Yes
Submitted to: Counseling and Disability Services
Special Ed. HS coursework accepted: Yes

Specific course requirements of all applicants: Yes
Separate application required for program services: Yes
# of LD applications submitted each year: NR
# of LD applications accepted yearly: NR
Total # of students receiving LD services: 30
Acceptance into program means acceptance into college: Student must be admitted and enrolled in the university first and then request services.

ADMISSIONS
Unconditional acceptance by the university is available to the student who graduates from an accredited high school with 4 years of English, 3 years math, 2 years science, 60 percent high school rank, an ACT of 20 or more, or SAT of 840 or more. Admission by review is an alternative admission with the same high school units as mentioned previously, but a high school rank between 40 percent and 60 percent, an ACT between 14 and 19, or an SAT of 560–839.

ADDITIONAL INFORMATION
The Office of Disability Accommodations arranges accommodations for the student with special needs. Help includes priority registration; testing arrangements; classroom accessibility; special equipment; and counseling for personal, academic, or vocational concerns. Skills courses for credit are offered in study skills and time management. Services and accommodations are available for undergraduate and graduate students.

Support Services Contact Information

Learning Disability Program/Services: Counseling & Disability Services
Director: Debra J. Higginbotham
E-Mail: fhiggnbo@nexus.mwsu.edu
Telephone: 940-397-4618
Fax: 940-397-4934

LEARNING DISABILITY SERVICES

Requests for the following/services accommodations will be evaluated individually based on appropriate and current documentation.

Allowed in exams
  Calculator: Yes
  Dictionary: Yes
  Computer: Yes
  Spellchecker: Yes
Extended test time: Yes
Scribes: Yes
Proctors: Yes
Oral exams: Yes
Note-takers: Yes

Distraction reduced environment: Yes
Tape recording in class: Yes
Books on tape from RFBD: Yes
Taping of books not from RFBD: No
Accommodations for students with ADD: Yes
Reading machine: Yes
Other assistive technology: Yes
Priority registration: Yes

Added costs for services: No
LD specialists: No
Professional tutors: No
Peer tutors: Yes
Max. hours/wk. for services: Yes
How professors are notified of LD/ADD: By both student and director

GENERAL ADMISSIONS INFORMATION

Director of Admissions: Barbara Merkle
Telephone: 940/397-4334

ENTRANCE REQUIREMENTS

Academic units required: 4 English, 3 math, 2 science, 6 academic electives. High school diploma is required and GED is accepted. ACT with Writing component required or SAT Reasoning test. TOEFL required of all international applicants, minimum paper TOEFL 530, minimum computer TOEFL 197.

Application deadline: NR
Notification: Rolling
Average GPA: 3.30

Average SAT Math: 489
Average SAT Verbal: 481
Average ACT: 20

Graduated top 10% of class: 6%
Graduated top 25% of class: 23%
Graduated top 50% of class: 62%

COLLEGE GRADUATION REQUIREMENTS

Course waivers allowed: Yes
Course substitutions allowed: Yes
In what course: Waivers and substitutions require an individual review by the Office of Disability Services, chair of the department, and vice president of academics.

ADDITIONAL INFORMATION

Environment: The campus is located 135 miles northwest of Dallas.

Student Body:
  Undergrad enrollment: 5,576
  Women: 57%
  Men: 43%
  Percent out-of-state: 5%

Cost Information
  In-state tuition: $1,440
  Out-of-state tuition: $9,180
  Room & board: $4,844
Housing Information
  University housing: Yes
  Percent living on campus: 15%

Greek System
  Fraternity: Yes
  Sorority: Yes
Athletics: NCAA Division II

Midwestern State University

SCHREINER UNIVERSITY

2100 Memorial Boulevard, Kerrville, TX 78028-5697
Phone: 830-792-7217 • Fax: 830-792-7226
E-mail: admissions@schreiner.edu • Web: www.schreiner.edu
Support: SP • Institution type: 2-year and 4-year private

LEARNING DISABILITY PROGRAM AND SERVICES

Extensive learning support is given to each student, and the ultimate goal is for students to be able to succeed without special help. The Learning Support Services (LSS) program is staffed by LD specialists and many tutors. Students with learning disabilities are enrolled in regular college courses and receive individual tutorial assistance in each subject. The goal of the service is to help students succeed in a rigorous academic environment. Students admitted to the Learning Support Services Program must be highly motivated, have the intellectual potential for success in a rigorous academic program, and have the ability to meet the demands of college life.

LD/ADD ADMISSIONS INFORMATION

College entrance tests required: Yes
Interview required: Yes
Essay required: NR
Documentation required for LD: WAIS–III; individually administered achievement test such as WIAT or Woodcock–Johnson
Documentation required for ADD: Letter from an MD or psychologist
Submitted to: Learning Student Services
Special Ed. HS coursework accepted: No

Specific course requirements of all applicants: Yes
Separate application required for program services: No
# of LD applications submitted each year: 60
# of LD applications accepted yearly: 30
Total # of students receiving LD services: 70–85
Acceptance into program means acceptance into college: Students admitted into the Learning Support Services program are automatically admitted into the college.

ADMISSIONS

Proof of high school diploma and all significant materials relevant to the specific learning disability must be submitted. Applicants should be enrolled in regular, mainstream English courses in high school. We recommend that students take a college preparatory curriculum. However, admission would not be denied to a qualified candidate if some coursework was not included. The Woodcock—Johnson Achievement Battery is preferred but other tests are accepted. An interview is required and is an important part of the admissions decision. Applicants are considered individually, and selected on the basis of their intellectual ability, motivation, academic preparation, and potential for success. LSS students are admitted contingent upon their participation in the program. Students admitted into LSS are automatically admitted into the college.

ADDITIONAL INFORMATION

The Learning Support Services Program is tailored to meet the needs of each student. Individualized services may include study skills development, regularly scheduled tutoring for all classes, alternative testing options (readers, scribes, extended time), note-takers, and a freshman seminar class addressing issues of specific concern to students with LD. Each semester, tutors prepare individual tutoring plans for students and review these plans each semester for effectiveness. Freshman progress in monitored and students are assisted in course selection.

Support Services Contact Information

Learning Disability Program/Services: Learning Support Services (LSS)
Director: Jude Gallik, PhD
E-Mail: jgallik@schreiner.edu
Telephone: 830-792-7256
Fax: 803-792-7448
Contact Person: Any Admission Counselor
E-Mail: admissions@schreiner.edu
Telephone: 800-343-4919
Fax: 830-792-7226

LEARNING DISABILITY SERVICES

Requests for the following/services accommodations will be evaluated individually based on appropriate and current documentation.

Allowed in exams
  Calculator: No
  Dictionary: No
  Computer: Yes
  Spellchecker: Yes
Extended test time: Yes
Scribes: Yes
Proctors: Yes
Oral exams: Yes
Note-takers: Yes

Distraction reduced environment: Yes
Tape recording in class: Yes
Books on tape from RFBD: No
Taping of books not from RFBD: Yes
Accommodations for students with ADD: Yes
Reading machine: Yes
Other assistive technology: No
Priority registration: No

Added costs for services: $7,250
LD specialists: Yes
Professional tutors: 15
Peer tutors: No
Max. hours/wk. for services: None
How professors are notified of LD/ADD: By both student and director

GENERAL ADMISSIONS INFORMATION

Director of Admissions: Todd Brown
Telephone: 830-792-7217

ENTRANCE REQUIREMENTS

Academic units recommended: 4 English, 3 math, 2 science (2 science lab), 2 social studies. High school diploma is required and GED is accepted. TOEFL required of all international applicants, minimum paper TOEFL 550, minimum computer TOEFL 213.

Application deadline: 8/1
Notification: Rolling
Average GPA: 3.50

Average SAT Math: 492
Average SAT Verbal: 492
Average ACT: 20

Graduated top 10% of class: 15%
Graduated top 25% of class: 46%
Graduated top 50% of class: 75%

COLLEGE GRADUATION REQUIREMENTS

Course waivers allowed: No
Course substitutions allowed: No
In what course: N/A

ADDITIONAL INFORMATION

Environment: The college is located on 175 acres in a rural wooded area 60 miles northwest of San Antonio.

Student Body:
  Undergrad enrollment: 730
  Women: 58%
  Men: 42%
  Percent out-of-state: 2%

Cost Information
  Tuition: $14,742
  Room & board: $6,800
Housing Information
  University housing: Yes
  Percent living on campus: 49%

Greek System
  Fraternity: Yes
  Sorority: Yes
Athletics: NCAA Division III

SOUTHERN METHODIST UNIVERSITY

PO Box 750181, Dallas, TX 75275-0181
Phone: 214-768-3417 • Fax: 214-768-4880
E-mail: enrol_serv@smu.edu • Web: www.smu.edu
Support: CS • Institution type: 4-year private

LEARNING DISABILITY PROGRAM AND SERVICES

The goal of Services for Students with Disabilities is to provide students with disabilities services or reasonable accommodations in order to reduce the effects that a disability may have on their performance in a traditional academic setting. The coordinator of Services for Students with Disabilities provides individual attention and support for students needing assistance with any aspect of their campus experience such as notifying professors, arranging accommodations, referrals, and accessibility. Students requesting LD assistance need to bring in their class schedules as soon as possible after receiving them to arrange accommodations in the desired classes. All students with LD who are requesting accommodations should have made their request with the Coordinator of Services for Students with Disabilities within 30 days after the first day of classes. A student with ADD must provide a report from either a physician or licensed psychologist that elaborates on how the student meets the diagnostic criteria for ADD, limitations the student is likely to experience in an academic environment which are directly related to the disability (substantial limitation), and suggested accommodations with explanation of why the accommodations are needed to mitigate impact of ADD on the student.

LD/ADD ADMISSIONS INFORMATION

College entrance tests required: Yes
Interview required: No
Essay required: No
Documentation required for LD: A full psychoeducational assessment conducted in the last three years, should follow the guidelines of AHEAD posted in its website.
Documentation required for ADD: Report from either a physician or licensed psychologist trained in diagnosing ADD. Must elaborate on how student meets the diagnostic criteria for ADD, limitations the student is likely to experience in an academic setting
Submitted to: Services for Students with Diabilities

Specific course requirements of all applicants: Yes
Special Ed. HS coursework accepted: N/A
Separate application required for program services: No
# of LD applications submitted each year: NR
# of LD applications accepted yearly: NR
Total # of students receiving LD services: 300
Acceptance into program means acceptance into college: Student must be admitted and enrolled in the university first and then request services.

ADMISSIONS

There is no special admissions process for students with LD. If their standardized tests were administered under non-standard conditions, this will not weigh unfavorably into the admission decision. Regular admission criteria include 4 years English, 3 years math, 3 years science, 3 years social studies, 2 years foreign language. Only foreign language may be waived with other appropriate and approved academic classes taken as substitutions. Candidates who exceed the minimum requirements are advantaged in the selection process.

ADDITIONAL INFORMATION

All students have access to tutoring, writing centers, study skills workshops, and classes to improve reading rate, comprehension, and vocabulary. Skills classes are offered in time management, test strategies, note-taking strategies, organizational skills, concentration, memory, and test anxiety. There are currently 170 students with learning disabilities and 146 students with ADD receiving services.

Support Services Contact Information

Learning Disability Program/Services: Services for Students with Disabilities
Director: Rebecca Marin, Coordinator
E-Mail: rmarin@smu.edu
  Telephone: 214-768-4557
  Fax: 214-768-1255

LEARNING DISABILITY SERVICES

Requests for the following/services accommodations will be evaluated individually based on appropriate and current documentation.

Allowed in exams
  Calculator: Yes
  Dictionary: Yes
  Computer: Yes
  Spellchecker: Yes
Extended test time: Yes
Scribes: Yes
Proctors: Yes
Oral exams: Yes
Note-takers: Yes

Distraction reduced environment: Yes
Tape recording in class: Yes
Books on tape from RFBD: Yes
Taping of books not from RFBD: Yes
Accommodations for students with ADD: Yes
Reading machine: Yes
Other assistive technology: Yes
Priority registration: Yes

Added costs for services: No
LD specialists: Yes
Professional tutors: No
Peer tutors: 50–60
Max. hours/wk. for services: Unlimited
How professors are notified of LD/ADD: By both student and director

GENERAL ADMISSIONS INFORMATION

Director of Admissions: Ron Moss
Telephone: 214-768-2058

ENTRANCE REQUIREMENTS

Academic units required: 4 English, 3 math, 3 science (2 science lab), 2 foreign language, 1 social studies, 2 history. **Academic units recommended:** 4 English, 4 math, 4 science (3 science lab), 3 foreign language, 2 social studies, 3 history. High school diploma is required and GED is not accepted. ACT with or without Writing component accepted. TOEFL required of all international applicants, minimum paper TOEFL 550, minimum computer TOEFL 213.

Application deadline: 3/15
Notification: Rolling
Average GPA: 3.46

Average SAT Math: NR
Average SAT Verbal: NR
Average ACT: NR

Graduated top 10% of class: 36%
Graduated top 25% of class: 67%
Graduated top 50% of class: 91%

COLLEGE GRADUATION REQUIREMENTS

Course waivers allowed: No
Course substitutions allowed: Yes
In what course: Foreign language and math

ADDITIONAL INFORMATION

Environment: The university is located on a 163-acre suburban campus.

Student Body:
  Undergrad enrollment: 6,090
  Women: 54%
  Men: 46%
  Percent out-of-state: 31%

Cost Information
  Tuition: $23,846
  Room & board: $9,208
Housing Information
  University housing: Yes
  Percent living on campus: 40%

Greek System
  Fraternity: Yes
  Sorority: Yes
Athletics: NCAA Division I

Southern Methodist University

TEXAS A&M U.—COLLEGE STATION

Admissions Counseling, College Station, TX 77843-1265
Phone: 979-845-3741 • Fax: 979-847-8737
E-mail: admissions@tamu.edu • Web: www.tamu.edu
Support: S • Institution type: 4-year public

LEARNING DISABILITY PROGRAM AND SERVICES

The Department of Student Life/Services with Disabilities (SSD) exits to provide an academic experience for all students that is fully inclusive and accessible. The philosophy of SSD is to empower students with the skills needed to act as their own advocate and succeed in the mainstream of the university environment. Services include testing, accommodations, note-takers, adaptive technology, interpreters, and registration assistance.

LD/ADD ADMISSIONS INFORMATION

College entrance tests required: Yes
Interview required: No
Essay required: No
Documentation required for LD: Comprehensive psychoeducational testing, intelligence and achievement scores, written report, WISC–III or WAIS–R with Woodcock Johnson Achievement Test
Documentation required for ADD: Psychoeducational testing along with documentation from qualified evaluator diagnosing the ADD. Documentation should match the DSM-W criteria.
Submitted to: Services for Students with Disabilities
Special Ed. HS coursework accepted: No

Specific course requirements of all applicants: Yes
Separate application required for program services: Yes
# of LD applications submitted each year: NR
# of LD applications accepted yearly: NR
Total # of students receiving LD services: 250–300
Acceptance into program means acceptance into college: Student must be admitted and enrolled in the university first and then request services.

ADMISSIONS

General application requirements require that students submit an essay, ACT (with optional essay) or new SAT, have at least 4 years English, 3.5 years math (algebra I and II, geometry and one half credit of advanced math), 3 years science (two must be in biology, chemistry or physics), and recommend 2 years of the same foreign language. Students ranked in the top 10 percent of the class are automatic with required courses. Students not in the top 10 percent but ranked in the top 25 percent must have 1300 SAT with a score of 600 or better in math and verbal or 29 ACT and have the course requirements. Applicants with learning disabilities submit the general application form and are considered under the same guidelines as all applicants. Students may have their application reviewed by requesting special consideration based on their disability and by providing letters of recommendation from their high school counselor stating what accommodations are needed in college to be successful. Admissions will be affected by the student's record indicating success with provided accommodations along with any activities and leadership skills. Students not meeting academic criteria for automatic admission may be offered admission to a Summer Provisional Program. These students must take 9–12 credits and receive a grade of C in each of the courses.

ADDITIONAL INFORMATION

Accommodations are provided on an individual basis as needs arise. SSD is a resource for information including, but not limited to, tutoring services, study skills and time management, community resources, disability awareness, and various university services. Skill classes in math, reading, and writing are offered to the entire student body though the Center for Academic Enhancement. Some of these classes may be taken for college credit. Services and accommodations are available for undergraduate and graduate students. Services include a new Adaptive Technology Laboratory equipped with state-of-the-art technology for students with disabilities, including text-to-speech scanning for personal computer use.

Support Services Contact Information

Learning Disability Program/Services: Services for Students with Disabilities
Director: Dr. Anne Reber
E-Mail: anne@studentlife.tamu.edu
 Telephone: 979-845-1637
 Fax: 979-458-1214

LEARNING DISABILITY SERVICES

Requests for the following/services accommodations will be evaluated individually based on appropriate and current documentation.

Allowed in exams
 Calculator: Yes
 Dictionary: Yes
 Computer: Yes
 Spellchecker: Yes
Extended test time: Yes
Scribes: Yes
Proctors: Yes
Oral exams: Yes
Note-takers: Yes

Distraction reduced environment: Yes
Tape recording in class: Yes
Books on tape from RFBD: Yes
Taping of books not from RFBD: Yes
**Accommodations for students with
 ADD:** Yes
Reading machine: Yes
Other assistive technology: Yes
Priority registration: Yes

Added costs for services: No
LD specialists: No
Professional tutors: No
Peer tutors: No
Max. hours/wk. for services:
 unlimited
**How professors are notified of
 LD/ADD:** By student

GENERAL ADMISSIONS INFORMATION

Director of Admissions: Dr. Kenneth Poenisch
Telephone: 979-458-0509

ENTRANCE REQUIREMENTS

 Academic units required: 4 English, 3 math, 3 science (2 science lab), 2 foreign language, 2 social studies, 1 history. **Academic units recommended:** 4 English, 3 math, 3 science (2 science lab), 2 foreign language, 2 social studies, 1 history, 1 computer course. High school diploma is required and GED is accepted. ACT with Writing component required or SAT Reasoning test. TOEFL required of all international applicants, minimum paper TOEFL 550, minimum computer TOEFL 213.

Application deadline: 2/15
Notification: Rolling
Average GPA: NR

Average SAT Math: 605
Average SAT Verbal: 578
Average ACT: 25

Graduated top 10% of class: 49%
Graduated top 25% of class: 78%
Graduated top 50% of class: 92%

COLLEGE GRADUATION REQUIREMENTS

Course waivers allowed: Yes
Course substitutions allowed: Yes
In what course: Math and foreign language courses are the only ones that have been requested. Courses are substituted, not waived.

ADDITIONAL INFORMATION

Environment: The school is located on over 5,000 acres in a college town of 100,000 about 90 miles from Houston.

Student Body:
 Undergrad enrollment: 35,605
 Women: 49%
 Men: 51%
 Percent out-of-state: 3%

Cost Information
 In-state tuition: $3,675
 Out-of-state tuition: $11,415
 Room & board: $6,887
Housing Information
 University housing: Yes
 Percent living on campus: 25%

Greek System
 Fraternity: Yes
 Sorority: Yes
Athletics: NCAA Division I

Texas A&M U.—Kingsville

MSC 105, Kingsville, TX 78363
Phone: 361-593-2315 • Fax: 361-593-2195
E-mail: ksossrx@tamuk.edu • Web: www.tamuk.edu
Support: S • Institution type: 4-year public

LEARNING DISABILITY PROGRAM AND SERVICES

The University is committed to providing an environment in which every student is encouraged to reach the highest level of personal and educational achievement. Students with disabilities may have special concerns and even special needs. Services vary according to the nature of the disability and are provided by the Center for Life Services and Wellness. Counseling services offer educational, vocational, and personal consultations, as well as tutoring, testing, and academic advising. Students with LD have access to note-takers, readers, writers, and other assistance that the university can provide. All students entering college as freshmen (or transfers with less than 30 hours) have the university's commitment to improve student achievement, retention, depth, and quality of instruction and services.

LD/ADD ADMISSIONS INFORMATION

College entrance tests required: Yes
Interview required: Yes
Essay required: No
Documentation required for LD: Psychoeducational evaluation
Documentation required for ADD: Yes
Submitted to: Services for Students with Disabilities
Special Ed. HS coursework accepted: Yes

Specific course requirements of all applicants: Yes
Separate application required for program services: No
# of LD applications submitted each year: NR
# of LD applications accepted yearly: NR
Total # of students receiving LD services: 190
Acceptance into program means acceptance into college: Student must be admitted and enrolled in the university first and then request services.

ADMISSIONS

All applicants must meet the same general admission criteria. Admission is very similar to open door admissions and thus most applicants are admitted either conditionally or unconditionally, or provisionally. ACT scores are 16+ or greater or SATs 610+ or greater. Unconditional admission requires a 2.0 GPA and 21+ ACT or 970 SAT. Conditional admission is granted when a student does not meet unconditional admission standards, but has a 17–20 ACT or 810–960 SAT. Students admitted conditionally must take one or more developmental courses. Students admitted on provisional admission are those with an ACT below 17 or SAT below 810. These students cannot take more than 15 credits the first semester, must pass 12 credits with a C or better, and earn an overall 2.0 GPA their first year. Provisional students must complete all assignments and meet with an advisor. There are no specific courses required for entrance; however, it is recommended that students take 4 years English, 3 years math, 3 years science, 4 years social studies, 3 years foreign language, 1/2 year health, 1 1/2 years physical education, 1 year computer, 1 year art/speech, and 3 years electives. Students with LD are encouraged to self-disclose during the application process.

ADDITIONAL INFORMATION

Developmental educational classes in writing, math, or reading (if necessary); tutoring or study groups; and academic rescue programs are offered for students in academic jeopardy. Skills classes are offered for no credit in stress management and test anxiety. Letters are sent to faculty each semester, hand delivered by the student. DSS provides tutoring on a limited basis. Testing accommodations are available, but students are responsible for scheduling the tests. Accommodations include extended testing time, private rooms, scribes, and readers. DSS will also proctor the exam and return the test to the instructor. DSS relies on a volunteer program for note-takers. Services and accommodations are available to undergraduate and graduate students.

Support Services Contact Information

Learning Disability Program/Services: Services for Students with Disabilities (SSD)
Director: Jeanie Alexander, MS
E-Mail: kacja01@tamuk.edu
Telephone: 361-593-3268
Fax: 361-593-2006

LEARNING DISABILITY SERVICES

Requests for the following/services accommodations will be evaluated individually based on appropriate and current documentation.

Allowed in exams
Calculator: Yes
Dictionary: Yes
Computer: Yes
Spellchecker: Yes
Extended test time: Yes
Scribes: Yes
Proctors: Yes
Oral exams: Yes
Note-takers: Yes

Distraction reduced environment: Yes
Tape recording in class: Yes
Books on tape from RFBD: Yes
Taping of books not from RFBD: Yes
Accommodations for students with ADD: Yes
Reading machine: No
Other assistive technology: Yes
Priority registration: No

Added costs for services: No
LD specialists: No
Professional tutors: No
Peer tutors: Yes
Max. hours/wk. for services: Case-by-case decision
How professors are notified of LD/ADD: By student and program director

GENERAL ADMISSIONS INFORMATION

Director of Admissions: Joe Estrada
Telephone: 361-593-2315

ENTRANCE REQUIREMENTS

Academic units recommended: 4 English, 3 math, 3 science, 3 foreign language, 4 social studies, 3 history, 3 academic electives. High school diploma is required and GED is accepted. TOEFL required of all international applicants, minimum paper TOEFL 500, minimum computer TOEFL 173.

Application deadline: Rolling
Notification: Rolling
Average GPA: NR

Average SAT Math: NR
Average SAT Verbal: NR
Average ACT: NR

Graduated top 10% of class: NR
Graduated top 25% of class: NR
Graduated top 50% of class: NR

COLLEGE GRADUATION REQUIREMENTS

Course waivers allowed: Yes
Course substitutions allowed: Yes
In what course: Case-by-case decision made by Provost.

ADDITIONAL INFORMATION

Environment: The 246-acre university campus is located 40 miles southwest of Corpus Christi.

Student Body:
Undergrad enrollment: 4,373
Women: 47%
Men: 52%
Percent out-of-state: 2%

Cost Information
In-state tuition: $5,000
Out-of-state tuition: $11,200
Room & board: $4,000
Housing Information
University housing: Yes
Percent living on campus: 30%

Greek System
Fraternity: Yes
Sorority: Yes
Athletics: NCAA Division I

Texas A&M University—Kingsville

Texas State U.—San Marcos

429 North Guadalupe Street, San Marcos, TX 78666
Phone: 512-245-2364 • Fax: 512-245-9020
E-mail: admissions@txstate.edu • Web: www.txstate.edu
Support: CS • Institution type: 4-year public

LEARNING DISABILITY PROGRAM AND SERVICES

The mission of the Office of Disability Services (ODS) is to assist students with disabilities to independently achieve their educational goals and enhance their leadership development by ensuring equal access to all programs, activities, and services. This is accomplished through a decentralizing approach in providing education and awareness so that programs, activities, and services are conducted in the most integrated setting appropriate. Students with learning disabilities are encouraged to self-identify and to submit documentation once admitted. By identifying and assessing student needs, ODS provides direct services and refers students to appropriate resources on and off campus. ODS also promotes awareness of the special needs and abilities of students with disabilities through educational events and outreach activities.

LD/ADD ADMISSIONS INFORMATION

College entrance tests required: Yes
Interview required: No
Essay required: No
Documentation required for LD: Psychoeducational evacuation
Documentation required for ADD: Yes
Submitted to: Office of Disability Services
Special Ed. HS coursework accepted: NR

Specific course requirements of all applicants: Yes
Separate application required for program services: Yes
# of LD applications submitted each year: NR
# of LD applications accepted yearly: NR
Total # of students receiving LD services: 357
Acceptance into program means acceptance into college: Student must be admitted and enrolled in the university first and then request services.

ADMISSIONS

Students with LD must meet the same admission requirements as other applicants. A student whose educational and/or personal goals for success have been negatively impacted due to disability-related reasons may provide a supplemental essay with their application for admission. This information may be considered by the admission office during the review process. General admission requirements include 4 years English, 3 years math, 2 years science, 3 years social studies, 1/2 year economics, and 2 years foreign language; 2.0 GPA or determined by class rank; 22 ACT is average and 850 SATs mid 50 percent. Students who are not accepted are free to write letters of appeal to the admissions office. All decisions are made by the admissions office. Probationary admission plans are available. Students not meeting the required rank in class may be admitted by review through Predicted Academic Success Option (PASO): students in top three-fourths may submit 7th semester transcript and a request that a PASO formula be attempted. (Students who rank in the fourth quarter are not eligible for PASO). The formula used is an individual's high school rank in combination with ACT or SAT scores. If admitted, these students are placed on a one-semester contract set by the director of admissions.

ADDITIONAL INFORMATION

Specialized support services are based on the individual student needs. Services available could include advance registration; books on tape; special testing accommodations; readers; note-takers; liaison and advocacy between students, faculty, and staff; assistance with tutoring; and an academic excellence seminar. Student Support Services provides one-on-one tutoring in limited subject areas. Remedial courses and an effective learning course are offered. An academic support group course covering various topics is offered for credit. Services and accommodations are available for undergraduate and graduate students. The following campus agencies provide students with special academic support services: ODS, Learning Resource Center, and Student Learning Assistance Center.

Support Services Contact Information

Learning Disability Program/Services: Office of Disability Services (ODS)
Director: Tina Schultz
E-Mail: ts12@txstate.edu
   Telephone: 512-245-3451
   Fax: 512-245-3452

LEARNING DISABILITY SERVICES

Requests for the following/services accommodations will be evaluated individually based on appropriate and current documentation.

Allowed in exams
   Calculator: Yes
   Dictionary: Yes
   Computer: Yes
   Spellchecker: Yes
Extended test time: Yes
Scribes: Yes
Proctors: Yes
Oral exams: Yes
Note-takers: Yes

Distraction reduced environment: Yes
Tape recording in class: Yes
Books on tape from RFBD: Yes
Taping of books not from RFBD: Yes
Accommodations for students with ADD: Yes
Reading machine: No
Other assistive technology: Yes
Priority registration: Yes

Added costs for services: No
LD specialists: Yes
Professional tutors: No
Peer tutors: No
Max. hours/wk. for services: Unlimited
How professors are notified of LD/ADD: By student

GENERAL ADMISSIONS INFORMATION

Director of Admissions: Christy Kangas
Telephone: 512-245-2364

ENTRANCE REQUIREMENTS

Academic units required: 4 English, 3 math, 3 science (2 science lab), 2 foreign language, 3 social studies, 1 comuter literacy. **Academic units recommended:** 4 English, 3 math, 3 science (2 science lab), 3 foreign language, 4 social studies, 2 academic electives, 2 comuter literacy. High school diploma is required and GED is accepted. TOEFL required of all international applicants, minimum paper TOEFL 550, minimum computer TOEFL 213.

Application deadline: 5/1
Notification: Rolling
Average GPA: NR

Average SAT Math: 534
Average SAT Verbal: 529
Average ACT: 22

Graduated top 10% of class: 12%
Graduated top 25% of class: 51%
Graduated top 50% of class: 94%

COLLEGE GRADUATION REQUIREMENTS

Course waivers allowed: No
Course substitutions allowed: Yes
In what course: Foreign language

ADDITIONAL INFORMATION

Environment: The 1,091-acre campus is located 30 miles south of Austin, and within easy access of San Antonio.

Student Body:
   Undergrad enrollment: 22,402
   Women: 55%
   Men: 45%
   Percent out-of-state: 1%

Cost Information
   In-state tuition: $2,760
   Out-of-state tuition: $9,840
   Room & board: $5,296
Housing Information
   University housing: Yes
   Percent living on campus: 23%

Greek System
   Fraternity: Yes
   Sorority: Yes
   Athletics: NCAA Division I

Texas State University—San Marcos

TEXAS TECH UNIVERSITY

PO Box 45005, Lubbock, TX 79409-5005
Phone: 806-742-1480 • Fax: 806-742-0062
E-mail: admissions@ttu.edu • Web: www.ttu.edu
Support: S • Institution type: 4-year public

LEARNING DISABILITY PROGRAM AND SERVICES

It is the philosophy of Texas Tech University to serve each student on a case-by-case basis. All services rendered are supported by adequate documentation. We firmly believe that all students should be and will become effective self-advocates. Students with disabilities attending Texas Tech will find numerous programs designed to provide services and to promote access to all phases of university activity. Such programming is coordinated through the dean of students' office with the assistance of an advisory committee of both disabled and non-disabled students, faculty, and staff. Services to disabled students are offered through a decentralized network of university and non-university resources. This means that many excellent services are available but that it is up to the student to initiate them. Each student is encouraged to act as his or her own advocate and take the major responsibility for securing services and accommodations. The Disabled Student Services team, dean of students office, faculty, and staff are supportive in this effort.

LD/ADD ADMISSIONS INFORMATION

College entrance tests required: Yes
Interview required: No
Essay required: No
Documentation required for LD: Psychoeducational evaluation
Documentation required for ADD: Yes
Submitted to: Student Disability Services
Special Ed. HS coursework accepted: Yes

Specific course requirements of all applicants: Yes
Separate application required for program services: Yes
# of LD applications submitted each year: NR
# of LD applications accepted yearly: NR
Total # of students receiving LD services: 600
Acceptance into program means acceptance into college: Student must be admitted and enrolled in the university first and then request services.

ADMISSIONS

There is no special admissions process for students with LD, and all applicants must meet the same criteria. All students must have 4 years English, 3 years math, 2 1/2 years social studies, 2 years science, and 3 1/2 years electives. Any applicant who scores a 1200 on the SAT or a 29 on the ACT is automatically admitted regardless of class rank. Some students are admissible who do not meet the stated requirements, but they must have a 2.0 GPA for a provisional admission. After a student is admitted, Disabled Student Services requires documentation that provides a diagnosis, provides an indication of the severity of the disability, and offers recommendations for accommodations, in order for students to receive services.

ADDITIONAL INFORMATION

Support services through Disabled Student Services include Academic Support Services, which can help students develop habits enabling them to get a good education. Students may receive academic support services in the PASS (Programs for Academic Support Services) Center, which is open to all students on campus. Services offered free of charge include tutor referral services (paid by student), study skills group, hour-long workshops that target a variety of subjects from "Overcoming Math Anxiety" to "Preparing for Finals", a self-help learning lab with videotapes, computer-assisted instruction, individual consultations assisting students with specific study problems, and setting study skills improvement goals. All students with LD are offered priority registration. Services and accommodations are available for undergraduate and graduate students.

Support Services Contact Information

Learning Disability Program/Services: Student Disability Services
Director: Frank Silvas
E-Mail: frank.silvas@ttu.edu
   Telephone: 806-742-2405
   Fax: 806-742-4837
Contact Person: Larry Phillippe, Assistant Director
E-Mail: larry.phillippe@ttu.edu
   Telephone: 806-742-2405
   Fax: 806-742-4837

LEARNING DISABILITY SERVICES

Requests for the following/services accommodations will be evaluated individually based on appropriate and current documentation.

Allowed in exams
   Calculator: Yes
   Dictionary: Y/N
   Computer: Yes
   Spellchecker: Yes
Extended test time: Yes
Scribes: Yes
Proctors: Yes
Oral exams: Yes
Note-takers: Yes

Distraction reduced environment: Yes
Tape recording in class: Yes
Books on tape from RFBD: Yes
Taping of books not from RFBD: No
**Accommodations for students with
   ADD:** Yes
Reading machine: Yes
Other assistive technology: Yes
Priority registration: Yes

Added costs for services: No
LD specialists: No
Professional tutors: Yes
Peer tutors: 25-35
Max. hours/wk. for services:
   Unlimited
**How professors are notified of
   LD/ADD:** By student

GENERAL ADMISSIONS INFORMATION

Director of Admissions: Djuana Young
Telephone: 806-742-1480

ENTRANCE REQUIREMENTS
Academic units required: 4 English, 3 math, 2 science (2 science lab), 2 foreign language. High school diploma is required and GED is accepted. ACT with or without Writing component accepted. TOEFL required of all international applicants, minimum paper TOEFL 550, minimum computer TOEFL 213.

Application deadline: Rolling
Notification: Rolling
Average GPA: NR

Average SAT Math: 573
Average SAT Verbal: 552
Average ACT: 24

Graduated top 10% of class: 23%
Graduated top 25% of class: 55%
Graduated top 50% of class: 87%

COLLEGE GRADUATION REQUIREMENTS

Course waivers allowed: Yes
Course substitutions allowed: Yes
In what course: Possible in math or foreign language.

ADDITIONAL INFORMATION

Environment: The university is located on 1,839 acres in an urban area in Lubbock.

Student Body:
   Undergrad enrollment: 23,329
   Women: 45%
   Men: 55%
   Percent out-of-state: 4%

Cost Information
   In-state tuition: $6,1400
   Out-of-state tuition: $13,880
   Room & board: $6,506
Housing Information
   University housing: Yes
   Percent living on campus: 22%

Greek System
   Fraternity: Yes
   Sorority: Yes
Athletics: NCAA Division I

UNIVERSITY OF HOUSTON

Office of Admissions, 122 E. Cullen Building, Houston, TX 77204-2023
Phone: 713-743-1010 • Fax: 713-743-9633
E-mail: admissions@uh.edu • Web: www.uh.edu
Support: CS • Institution type: 4-year public

LEARNING DISABILITY PROGRAM AND SERVICES

The Center for Students with Disabilities provides a wide variety of academic support services to students with all types of disabilities. Its goal is to help ensure that these otherwise qualified students are able to successfully compete with non-disabled students by receiving equal educational opportunities in college as mandated by law. Through advocacy efforts and a deliberate, ongoing, public education program, the staff strives to heighten the awareness of needs, legal rights, and abilities of persons with handicapping conditions.

LD/ADD ADMISSIONS INFORMATION

College entrance tests required: Yes
Interview required: Yes
Essay required: No
Documentation required for LD: WAIS–R; WJ; or a
  neuropsychological evaluation: within 3 years
Documentation required for ADD: Yes
Submitted to: Center for Students with Disabilities
Special Ed. HS coursework accepted: Yes

Specific course requirements of all applicants: Yes
Separate application required for program services: No
# of LD applications submitted each year: NR
# of LD applications accepted yearly: NR
Total # of students receiving LD services: 386
**Acceptance into program means acceptance into
  college:** Student must be admitted and enrolled in the
  university first and then request services.

ADMISSIONS

General admission requirements are top 10 percent, no minimum on SAT or ACT; 1st quarter, 920 SAT or 19 ACT; 2nd quarter 1010 SAT or 21 ACT; 3rd quarter, 1100 SAT or 24 ACT; or 4th quarter, 1180 SAT or 26 ACT. Courses required are 2 years English, 3 years math, 2 years science, and 3 years social studies. Applicants who do not qualify for admission may request a further review through the individual admission process. The review will be based on an overall assessment of each applicant's circumstances in respect to potential for academic success. If an applicant to a program with different requirements does not meet the stated standards, but does meet the general admission requirements, then that applicant may be admitted to the university with an undeclared status.

ADDITIONAL INFORMATION

Students who come from an educationally and/or economically disadvantaged background may be eligible to participate in the UH Challenger Program which is designed to provide intense support to students who face obstacles in their efforts to successfully complete college. Services to all students include tutoring, counseling, financial aid advisement, and social enrichment. Remedial reading, writing, and study skills courses for three hours of non-college credit are offered. There are also remedial courses for credit in English and college algebra. Other services include assistance with petitions for course substitutions, peer support groups, free carbonized paper for note-taking, textbooks, and class handouts put on tape by office staff or volunteer readers, and advocacy for student's legal rights to reasonable and necessary accommodations in their course work. Extended tutoring is available at the Learning Support Services and Math Lab.

Support Services Contact Information

Learning Disability Program/Services: Center for Students with Disabilities
Director: Cheryl Amoruso
E-Mail: camoruso@mail.uh.edu
  Telephone: 713-743-5400
  Fax: 713-743-5396
Contact Person: Molloy Donohue, Asst. Director
E-Mail: molly.donohue@mail.uh.edu
  Telephone: 713-743-5400
  Fax: 713-743-5396

LEARNING DISABILITY SERVICES

Requests for the following/services accommodations will be evaluated individually based on appropriate and current documentation.

Allowed in exams
  Calculator: Yes
  Dictionary: Yes
  Computer: Yes
  Spellchecker: Yes
Extended test time: Yes
Scribes: Yes
Proctors: Yes
Oral exams: Yes
Note-takers: Yes

Distraction reduced environment: Yes
Tape recording in class: Yes
Books on tape from RFBD: Yes
Taping of books not from RFBD: Yes
Accommodations for students with ADD: Yes
Reading machine: No
Other assistive technology: Yes
Priority registration: Yes

Added costs for services: No
LD specialists: Yes
Professional tutors: Yes
Peer tutors: Yes
Max. hours/wk. for services: 2–4
How professors are notified of LD/ADD: By student

GENERAL ADMISSIONS INFORMATION

Director of Admissions: Adriana Higgins
Telephone: 713-743-1010

ENTRANCE REQUIREMENTS

Academic units required: 4 English, 3 math, 2 science (2 science lab), 2 social studies, 2 history. **Academic units recommended:** 2 foreign language, High school diploma is required and GED is accepted. ACT with or without Writing component accepted. TOEFL required of all international applicants, minimum paper TOEFL 550, minimum computer TOEFL 213.

Application deadline: 4/1
Notification: Rolling
Average GPA: 3.20

Average SAT Math: 538
Average SAT Verbal: 516
Average ACT: 21

Graduated top 10% of class: 23%
Graduated top 25% of class: 52%
Graduated top 50% of class: 83%

COLLEGE GRADUATION REQUIREMENTS

Course waivers allowed: Yes
Course substitutions allowed: Yes
In what course: Foreign language course substitutions have been granted most recently.

ADDITIONAL INFORMATION

Environment: The university is located on 540 acres in an urban area 3 miles from Houston.

Student Body:
  Undergrad enrollment: 26,366
  Women: 52%
  Men: 48%
  Percent out-of-state: 2%

Cost Information
  In-state tuition: $1,440
  Out-of-state tuition: $9,180
  Room & board: $6,030
Housing Information
  University housing: Yes
  Percent living on campus: 10%

Greek System
  Fraternity: Yes
  Sorority: Yes
Athletics: NCAA Division I

University of Houston

UNIVERSITY OF NORTH TEXAS

PO Box 311277, Denton, TX 76203-1277
Phone: 940-565-2681 • Fax: 940-565-2408
E-mail: undergrad@unt.edu • Web: www.unt.edu
Support: CS • Institution type: 4-year public

LEARNING DISABILITY PROGRAM AND SERVICES

The goal of the Office of Disability Accommodations is to ensure that qualified students with disabilities have access to reasonable and appropriate services and learning resources needed to facilitate matriculation and successful completion of academic programs at the university. The office serves as a liaison to ensure that assistance and/or accommodation/adjustments are available for students with disabilities to enable them full access to the educational facilities and services at the university. The office provides consultation and assistance to academic and general service offices in making adaptations and adjustments for students with disabilities. It also provides alternative testing sites and proctors when the academic department is unable to provide assistance.

LD/ADD ADMISSIONS INFORMATION

College entrance tests required: Yes
Interview required: N/A
Essay required: No
Documentation required for LD: WAIS–III; WRAT–R; Nelson-Denny Reading test; Bender G
Documentation required for ADD: Yes
Submitted to: Office of Disability Accommodations
Special Ed. HS coursework accepted: No

Specific course requirements of all applicants: Yes
Separate application required for program services: No
# of LD applications submitted each year: NR
# of LD applications accepted yearly: NR
Total # of students receiving LD services: 225
Acceptance into program means acceptance into college: Students must be admitted and enrolled at the university first and then may request services. Students denied admission may appeal the decision.

ADMISSIONS

Students must apply directly to the admissions office and meet the current requirements. Course requirements include: 4 years English, 4 years math, 3 years science, 3 years foreign language, 4 years social studies, 3 years electives. When a student makes a written request for waivers for admission requirements, the request is sent to an individual approval review committee for consideration. Students in the top 10 percent of their high school class must submit ACT/SAT scores but no specific score is required; students in the remainder of top quarter need minimum 920 SAT or 19 ACT; the second quarter need a minimum 1010 SAT or 21 ACT; the third quarter need a minimum 1100 SAT or 24 ACT; and the fourth quarter need a minimum 1180 SAT or 27 ACT. If a student is not accepted, there is an appeal process on the basis of the learning disability. These students may need letters of support, a statement of commitment from the student, and an evaluation of the documentation by the disability office. Admission decisions are made by the Office of Admissions and the Office of Disability Accommodations.

ADDITIONAL INFORMATION

The Center for Development Studies provides tutoring to build academic knowledge and skills in various subject areas; academic counseling to plan class schedules and to evaluate areas of strengths and weaknesses; personal counseling to develop greater self-understanding and to learn ways to cope with adjustments to college and the pressures of life; and study skills assessment for evaluating and improving academic performance. Skills courses for credit are offered in time management, career choice, and study skills. Students requesting a distraction-free environment for tests must provide the appropriate documentation. Calculators, dictionaries, computers, and spellcheckers are allowed with instructor's approval. Services and accommodations are available for undergraduate and graduate students.

Support Services Contact Information

Learning Disability Program/Services: Office of Disability Accommodations
Director: Steve Pickett, MS, CRC
E-Mail: steve@dsa.admin.unt.edu
  Telephone: 940-565-4323
  Fax: 940-565-4376
Contact Person: Dee Wilson

LEARNING DISABILITY SERVICES

Requests for the following/services accommodations will be evaluated individually based on appropriate and current documentation.

Allowed in exams
  Calculator: Y/N
  Dictionary: Y/N
  Computer: Y/N
  Spellchecker: Y/N
Extended test time: Yes
Scribes: Yes
Proctors: Yes
Oral exams: Yes
Note-takers: Yes

Distraction reduced environment: Yes
Tape recording in class: Yes
Books on tape from RFBD: Yes
Taping of books not from RFBD: Yes
Accommodations for students with ADD: Yes
Reading machine: Yes
Other assistive technology: Yes
Priority registration: Yes

Added costs for services: No
LD specialists: Yes
Professional tutors: No
Peer tutors: Yes
Max. hours/wk. for services: Unlimited
How professors are notified of LD/ADD: By both student and director

GENERAL ADMISSIONS INFORMATION

Director of Admissions: Marcilla Collinsworth
Telephone: 940-565-2681

ENTRANCE REQUIREMENTS

Academic units required: 4 English, 3 math, 3 science, 2 foreign language, 2 social studies, 2 history. **Academic units recommended:** 4 English, 4 math, 3 science, 3 foreign language, 3 social studies, 2 history, 3 academic electives. High school diploma is required and GED is accepted. ACT without Writing component accepted. TOEFL required of all international applicants, minimum paper TOEFL 550, minimum computer TOEFL 213.

Application deadline: 8/19
Notification: Rolling
Average GPA: NR

Average SAT Math: 547
Average SAT Verbal: 547
Average ACT: 23

Graduated top 10% of class: 16%
Graduated top 25% of class: 38%
Graduated top 50% of class: 68%

COLLEGE GRADUATION REQUIREMENTS

Course waivers allowed: Yes
Course substitutions allowed: Yes
In what course: This is looked at on an approval basis by each department. Approval is not automatic, it is dependent on the student's situation.

ADDITIONAL INFORMATION

Environment: The university is located on 425 acres in an urban area 35 miles north of Dallas/Ft. Worth.

Student Body:
  Undergrad enrollment: 24,274
  Women: 55%
  Men: 45%
  Percent out-of-state: 3%

Cost Information
  In-state tuition: $6,000
  Out-of-state tuition: $14,100
  Room & board: $5,100
Housing Information
  University housing: Yes

Percent living on campus: 19%
Greek System
  Fraternity: Yes
  Sorority: Yes
Athletics: NCAA Division I

University of North Texas

UNIVERSITY OF TEXAS—EL PASO

500 West University Avenue, El Paso, TX 79968-0510
Phone: 915-747-5890 • Fax: 915-747-8893
E-mail: futureminer@utep.edu • Web: www.utep.edu
Support: S • Institution type: 4-year public

LEARNING DISABILITY PROGRAM AND SERVICES

The Disabled Student Services Office (DSSO) provides a program of support and advocacy for students with Learning Disabilities. Services offered include peer support group; assistance with learning strategies; note-takers for lectures; scribe/readers; extended time for in-class work; and altered format, such as oral exams. There is also a Tutoring and Learning Center whose free services include study skill assistance, subject-area tutoring, life management skills, exam reviews, peer mentoring, and distance tutoring.

LD/ADD ADMISSIONS INFORMATION

College entrance tests required: Yes
Interview required: No
Essay required: No
Documentation required for LD: Current diagnostic report from licensed psychologist/psychiatrist or educational diagnostician
Documentation required for ADD: Yes
Submitted to: Disability Student Services

Specific course requirements of all applicants: Yes
Special Ed. HS coursework accepted: Yes
Separate application required for program services: N/A
# of LD applications submitted each year: NR
# of LD applications accepted yearly: NR
Total # of students receiving LD services: 79
Acceptance into program means acceptance into college: Student must be admitted and enrolled in the university first and then request services.

ADMISSIONS

There is no special admissions process for students with learning disabilities. General admission criteria requires students to have a high school diploma, ACT/SAT, and they are not interested in class rank or GPA. Course requirements include 4 years English, 3 years math, 3 years science, 4 years social studies, 3 years foreign language, 1/2 year health, 1 year fine arts, 1 1/2 years PE, and 1 year computer science. For students not otherwise eligible to enter due to grades or scores, a study skills class is required plus other courses from a course list.

ADDITIONAL INFORMATION

In order to receive services, students must meet with the director of DSSO. Students need to provide current documentation from an appropriate licensed professional. Services offered to students, when appropriate, are diagnostic testing, peer support group, assistance with learning strategies, and priority registration. Classroom accommodations include note-takers, assistive technology, scribes, readers, extended testing time, and exam modifications. In the Tutoring and Learning Center, students can access study skills assistance, subject area tutoring, life management skills, and a special needs room with state of the art technology. Currently there are 60 students with LD and 17 with ADD receiving services.

Support Services Contact Information

Learning Disability Program/Services: Disabled Student Services Office
Director: Susan J. Lopez
E-Mail: slopez@utep.edu
  Telephone: 915-747-5148
  Fax: 915-747-8712
Contact Person: Hector E. Flores
E-Mail: dss@utep.edu
  Telephone: 915-747-5148
  Fax: 915-747-8712

LEARNING DISABILITY SERVICES

Requests for the following/services accommodations will be evaluated individually based on appropriate and current documentation.

Allowed in exams	**Distraction reduced environment:** Yes	**Added costs for services:** No
Calculator: Yes	**Tape recording in class:** Yes	**LD specialists:** No
Dictionary: Yes	**Books on tape from RFBD:** Yes	**Professional tutors:** Yes
Computer: Yes	**Taping of books not from RFBD:** Yes	**Peer tutors:** 75
Spellchecker: Yes	**Accommodations for students with**	**Max. hours/wk. for services:** 40
Extended test time: Yes	**ADD:** Yes	**How professors are notified of**
Scribes: Yes	**Reading machine:** Yes	**LD/ADD:** By student
Proctors: Yes	**Other assistive technology:** No	
Oral exams: Yes	**Priority registration:** Yes	
Note-takers: Yes		

GENERAL ADMISSIONS INFORMATION

Director of Admissions: Tammie Aragon-Campos
Telephone: 915-747-5890

ENTRANCE REQUIREMENTS

Academic units recommended: 4 English, 4 math, 3 science, 2 foreign language, 4 social studies, 1 computer science, 1 fine arts, 0.5 unit of health, and 1.5 of physical education. ACT or SAT required. High school diploma is required and GED is accepted. TOEFL required of all international applicants, minimum paper TOEFL 550, minimum computer TOEFL 213.

Application deadline: 7/31	**Average SAT Math:** 464	**Graduated top 10% of class:** 15%
Notification: Rolling	**Average SAT Verbal:** 457	**Graduated top 25% of class:** 40%
Average GPA: 3.48	**Average ACT:** 18	**Graduated top 50% of class:** 70%

COLLEGE GRADUATION REQUIREMENTS

Course waivers allowed: Yes
Course substitutions allowed: Yes
In what course: Math and foreign language

ADDITIONAL INFORMATION

Environment: The university is located on a 360-acre urban campus.

Student Body:	**Cost Information**	**Greek System**
Undergrad enrollment: 15,114	**In-state tuition:** $3,780	**Fraternity:** Yes
Women: 53%	**Out-of-state tuition:** $11,520	**Sorority:** Yes
Men: 47%	**Room & board:** $4,255	**Athletics:** NCAA Division I
Percent out-of-state: 2%	**Housing Information**	
	University housing: Yes	
	Percent living on campus: 3%	

U. OF TEXAS—PAN AMERICAN

1201 West University Drive, Edinburg, TX 78541
Phone: 956-381-2201 • Fax: 956-381-2212
E-mail: admissions@panam.edu • Web: www.panam.edu
Support: S • Institution type: 4-year public

LEARNING DISABILITY PROGRAM AND SERVICES

The Office of Services for Persons with Disabilities (OSPD) is a component of the Division of Enrollment and Student Services at the University of Texas—Pan American. It is designed and committed to providing support services to meet the educational, career, and personal needs of persons with disabilities attending, or planning to attend, the university. Students requesting accommodations must put their requests in writing must provide documentation from a professional who is qualified to diagnose and verify the particular disability; the testing and documentation must be current within three years. OSPD will use the documentation to properly prepare an assistance plan for the student to use while enrolled at the university. It typically takes at least 30 days to process requests for services or accommodations.

LD/ADD ADMISSIONS INFORMATION

College entrance tests required: Yes
Interview required: Yes
Essay required: No
Documentation required for LD: Psycoeducational evaluation
Documentation required for ADD: Yes
Submitted to: Office of Services for Students with Disabilities
Special Ed. HS coursework accepted: No

Specific course requirements of all applicants: Yes
Separate application required for program services: Yes
# of LD applications submitted each year: NR
# of LD applications accepted yearly: NR
Total # of students receiving LD services: 34
Acceptance into program means acceptance into college: Student must be admitted and enrolled in the university first and then request services.

ADMISSIONS

Students with learning disabilities must meet the same admission requirements as all other applicants. The criteria for entering freshmen are as follows: a high school diploma denoting graduation with Honors or Advanced or rank in the top 50 percent or 20+ ACT or 1200+ SAT; 4 years English, 4 years math, 3 years science, 4 years social studies, 3 years foreign language, 1 year fine arts, 1 1/2 years PE, 1/2 year health, 1/2 year computers, and 2 1/2 years electives. Students not meeting these criteria may enroll through the Provisional Enrollment Program (PEP). PEP students must attend orientation, be advised by counseling center, select classes prescribed, and participate in non-credit programs to develop study and academic skills. PEP students with a total of nine or more hours may fulfill criteria for regular admission by meeting specific requirements in GPA and completion of attempted hours. PEP students who do not have a 2.0 GPA after nine hours can take an additional semester if they have at least a 1.5 GPA and meet successful completion of attempted hours. Some students not eligible to continue may petition the admissions committee.

ADDITIONAL INFORMATION

OSPD provides the following services: assessment for special needs; note-takers; readers and writers; advisement, counseling, and guidance; assistance with admissions, orientation, registration; referral services to other university units; liaison between students, faculty, staff, and others; resolution of problems/concerns; computer hardware and software; reading machine. Skills classes for credit are offered in time management, test-taking strategies, note-taking skills, reading text, and stress management. OSPD assists students in preparing appeals and works with faculty/administrators to secure waivers. Services and accommodations are available for undergraduate and graduate students.

Support Services Contact Information

Learning Disability Program/Services: Office of Services for Persons with Disabilities (OSPD)
Director: Rick Gray (RN, MBA)
E-Mail: grayr@panam.edu
 Telephone: 956-316-7005
 Fax: 956-316-7034
Contact Person: Esperanza Cavazos, Associate Director
E-Mail: cavazose@panam.edu
 Telephone: 956-316-7005
 Fax: 956-316-7034

LEARNING DISABILITY SERVICES

Requests for the following/services accommodations will be evaluated individually based on appropriate and current documentation.

Allowed in exams
 Calculator: Yes
 Dictionary: Yes
 Computer: Yes
 Spellchecker: Yes
Extended test time: Yes
Scribes: Yes
Proctors: Yes
Oral exams: Yes
Note-takers: Yes

Distraction reduced environment: Yes
Tape recording in class: Yes
Books on tape from RFBD: Yes
Taping of books not from RFBD: Yes
Accommodations for students with ADD: Yes
Reading machine: Yes
Other assistive technology: Yes
Priority registration: Yes

Added costs for services: No
LD specialists: No
Professional tutors: Yes
Peer tutors: 50
Max. hours/wk. for services: 40
How professors are notified of LD/ADD: By both student and director

GENERAL ADMISSIONS INFORMATION

Director of Admissions: Mr. David Zuniga
Telephone: 956-381-2201

ENTRANCE REQUIREMENTS

Academic units required: 4 English, 3 math, 3 science, 2 foreign language, 3 social studies, 3 academic electives, 5 economics, 0.5 physical education, 1.5 health education, 1 fine arts, 1 speech, 0.5 technology. **Academic units recommended:** 3 academic electives. High school diploma is required and GED is accepted. TOEFL required of all international applicants, minimum paper TOEFL 500, minimum computer TOEFL 173.

Application deadline: 8/10
Notification: Rolling
Average GPA: NR

Average SAT Math: 455
Average SAT Verbal: 445
Average ACT: 18

Graduated top 10% of class: 18%
Graduated top 25% of class: 44%
Graduated top 50% of class: 75%

COLLEGE GRADUATION REQUIREMENTS

Course waivers allowed: N/A
Course substitutions allowed: Yes
In what course: On a case by case basis.

ADDITIONAL INFORMATION

Environment: The campus is in a small town near the Mexican Border.

Student Body:
 Undergrad enrollment: 12,915
 Women: 58%
 Men: 42%
 Percent out-of-state: 1%

Cost Information
 In-state tuition: $3,152
 Out-of-state tuition: $10,932
 Room & board: $4,333
Housing Information
 University housing: Yes
 Percent living on campus: 1%

Greek System
 Fraternity: Yes
 Sorority: Yes
Athletics: NCAA Division I

University of Texas—Pan American

BRIGHAM YOUNG UNIVERSITY

A-153 ASB, Provo, UT 84602-1110
Phone: 801-422-2507 • Fax: 801-422-0005
E-mail: admissions@byu.edu • Web: www.byu.edu
Support: CS • Institution type: 4-year private

LEARNING DISABILITY PROGRAM AND SERVICES

The Services to Students with Learning Disabilities program works to provide individualized programs to meet the specific needs of each student, assisting in developing strengths to meet the challenges, and making arrangements for accommodations and special services as required.

LD/ADD ADMISSIONS INFORMATION

College entrance tests required: Yes
Interview required: No
Essay required: No
Documentation required for LD: Psychoeducational evaluation
Documentation required for ADD: Yes
Submitted to: University Accessibility Program
Special Ed. HS coursework accepted: Yes

Specific course requirements of all applicants: Yes
Separate application required for program services: Yes
# of LD applications submitted each year: NR
# of LD applications accepted yearly: NR
Total # of students receiving LD services: 101
Acceptance into program means acceptance into college: Student must be admitted and enrolled in the university first and then request services.

ADMISSIONS

There is no special admission process for students with learning disabilities. Suggested courses include 4 years English, 3–4 years math, 2–3 years science, 2 years history or government, 2 years foreign language, and 2 years of literature or writing. Evaluations are made on an individualized basis with a system weighted for college-prep courses and core classes.

ADDITIONAL INFORMATION

Students may be tested at no cost for attention deficit disorder or learning disabilities. Students indentified with LD or ADD may be eligible for testing accommodations, note-takers, lecture notes, reduced course-load, staggered exam times or extra exam breaks, alternative evaluations, course substitutions, and quiet rooms for testing. Workshops are offered for non-credit. The following are some examples: math anxiety, memory, overcoming procrastination, self-appreciation, stress management, test-taking, textbook comprehension, time management, and communication. Additional services include counseling support and advising. Services and accommodations are available for undergraduate and graduate students.

Support Services Contact Information

Learning Disability Program/Services: University Accessibility Program
Director: Paul Byrd
E-Mail: uac@byu.edu
  Telephone: 801-422-2767
  Fax: 801-422-0174

LEARNING DISABILITY SERVICES

Requests for the following/services accommodations will be evaluated individually based on appropriate and current documentation.

Allowed in exams
  Calculator: Yes
  Dictionary: Yes
  Computer: Yes
  Spellchecker: Yes
Extended test time: Yes
Scribes: No
Proctors: Yes
Oral exams: Yes
Note-takers: Yes

Distraction reduced environment: Yes
Tape recording in class: Yes
Books on tape from RFBD: Yes
Taping of books not from RFBD: Yes
Accommodations for students with
  ADD: Yes
Reading machine: Yes
Other assistive technology: Yes
Priority registration: Yes

Added costs for services: No
LD specialists: Yes
Professional tutors: No
Peer tutors: Yes
Max. hours/wk. for services: Varies
How professors are notified of
  LD/ADD: By both student and director

GENERAL ADMISSIONS INFORMATION

Director of Admissions: Tom Gourley
Telephone: 801-422-2507

ENTRANCE REQUIREMENTS

Academic units required: 4 English, 3 math, 2 science (2 science lab), 2 foreign language, 2 history, 2 literature or writing. **Academic units recommended:** 4 English, 4 math, 3 science (3 science lab), 4 foreign language. High school diploma is required and GED is accepted. ACT with or without Writing component accepted. TOEFL required of all international applicants, minimum paper TOEFL 500, minimum computer TOEFL 173.

Application deadline: 2/15
Notification: Rolling
Average GPA: 3.74

Average SAT Math: 618
Average SAT Verbal: 606
Average ACT: 27

Graduated top 10% of class: 54%
Graduated top 25% of class: 86%
Graduated top 50% of class: 98%

COLLEGE GRADUATION REQUIREMENTS

Course waivers allowed: Yes
Course substitutions allowed: Yes
In what course: Foreign language and math

ADDITIONAL INFORMATION

Environment: The university is located in a suburban area 45 miles south of Salt Lake City.

Student Body:
  Undergrad enrollment: 30,847
  Women: 49%
  Men: 51%
  Percent out-of-state: 76%

Cost Information
  Tuition: $3,600 (LD's student) $5,100 (non LD's students)
  Room & board: $7,200
Housing Information
  University housing: Yes
  Percent living on campus: 20%

Greek System
  Fraternity: No
  Sorority: No
Athletics: NCAA Division I

SOUTHERN UTAH UNIVERSITY

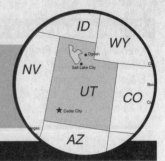

Admissions Office, 351 West Univeristy Boulevard, Cedar City, UT 84720
Phone: 435-586-7740 • Fax: 435-865-8223
E-mail: adminfo@suu.edu • Web: www.suu.edu
Support: S • Institution type: 4-year public

LEARNING DISABILITY PROGRAM AND SERVICES

The philosophy of Student Support Services (SSS) is to promote self-sufficiency and achievement. SSS assists college students with developmental classes, skills courses, academic and tutorial support, and advisement. In particular, disabled students are encouraged and supported in advocating for themselves. The university provides a full variety of services and accommodations for all disabled students. The academic support coordinator assists students with enrollment in SSS and helps them identify academic areas where they feel a need to strengthen skills to assure college success.

LD/ADD ADMISSIONS INFORMATION

College entrance tests required: Yes
Interview required: No
Essay required: No
Documentation required for LD: Diagnostic test for LD IEP's, recommendations
Documentation required for ADD: Psychological tests, diagnosis
Submitted to: Disability Support Services
Special Ed. HS coursework accepted: No

Specific course requirements of all applicants: Yes
Separate application required for program services: No
# of LD applications submitted each year: 20
# of LD applications accepted yearly: NR
Total # of students receiving LD services: 59
Acceptance into program means acceptance into college: Student must be admitted and enrolled in the university first and then request services.

ADMISSIONS

Students with learning disabilities submit the general application form. Students must have at least a 2.0 GPA and show competency in English, math, science, and social studies. The university uses an admissions index derived from the combination of the high school GPA and results of either the ACT or SAT. If students are not admissible through the regular process, special consideration by a committee review can be gained through reference letters and a personal letter. The university is allowed to admit 5 percent in flex admission. These applications are reviewed by a committee consisting of the director of support services and representatives from the admissions office. Students are encouraged to self-disclose their learning disability and submit documentation.

ADDITIONAL INFORMATION

Student Support Services, a project funded by the U.S. Department of Education, assists college students with developmental classes, skills courses, academic and tutorial support, and advisement. Tutoring is available in small groups or one-to-one, free of charge. Basic skills classes, for credit, are offered in English, reading, math, math anxiety, language, and study skills. The English writing support that SSS offers is a section of English 1000 which students take in conjunction with English 1010. This class is recommended for any student entering SUU with a score of 16 or lower on the ACT English subset or those needing additional support in writing. SSS staff will also work individually with students to improve writing skills.

Support Services Contact Information

Learning Disability Program/Services: Student Support Services
Director: Carmen R. Alldredge
E-Mail: alldredge@suu.edu
  Telephone: 435-865-8022
  Fax: 435-865-8235

LEARNING DISABILITY SERVICES

Requests for the following/services accommodations will be evaluated individually based on appropriate and current documentation.

Allowed in exams
  Calculator: No
  Dictionary: Yes
  Computer: Yes
  Spellchecker: Yes
  Extended test time: Yes
  Scribes: Yes
  Proctors: Yes
  Oral exams: Yes
  Note-takers: Yes

Distraction reduced environment: Yes
Tape recording in class: Yes
Books on tape from RFBD: Yes
Taping of books not from RFBD: Yes
Accommodations for students with
  ADD: Yes
Reading machine: Yes
Other assistive technology: Yes
Priority registration: Yes

Added costs for services: No
LD specialists: No
Professional tutors: 4
Peer tutors: 6–30
Max. hours/wk. for services:
  Unlimited
How professors are notified of
  LD/ADD: By both student and director

GENERAL ADMISSIONS INFORMATION

Director of Admissions: Dale Orton
Telephone: 435-586-7740

ENTRANCE REQUIREMENTS

Academic units recommended: 4 English, 3 math, 2 science (1 science lab), 2 social studies. High school diploma is required and GED is accepted. TOEFL required of all international applicants, minimum paper TOEFL 500, minimum computer TOEFL 1.

Application deadline: Rolling
Notification: Rolling
Average GPA: 3.00

Average SAT Math: 487
Average SAT Verbal: 498
Average ACT: 22

Graduated top 10% of class: 26%
Graduated top 25% of class: 50%
Graduated top 50% of class: 80%

COLLEGE GRADUATION REQUIREMENTS

Course waivers allowed: No
Course substitutions allowed: No
In what course: N/A

ADDITIONAL INFORMATION

Environment: The university is in a small town 150 miles north of Las Vegas.

Student Body:
  Undergrad enrollment: 4,802
  Women: 55%
  Men: 45%
  Percent out-of-state: 12%

Cost Information
  In-state tuition: $3,054
  Out-of-state tuition: $9,000
  Room & board: $5,400
Housing Information
  University housing: Yes
  Percent living on campus: 13%

Greek System
  Fraternity: Yes
  Sorority: Yes
  Athletics: NCAA Division I

UNIVERSITY OF UTAH

201 South 1460 East, Room 250 S, Salt Lake City, UT 84112
Phone: 801-581-7281 • Fax: 801-585-7864
E-mail: admissions@sa.utah.edu • Web: www.utah.edu
Support: CS • Institution type: 4-year public

LEARNING DISABILITY PROGRAM AND SERVICES

The Center for Disability Services at the University of Utah provides accommodations and support for students with disabilities who have current physical or psychological documentation that qualifies them for services. The goal is to provide assistance to encourage and enhance student's independence, maintain ongoing cooperative efforts to develop and maintain an accessible physical environment, and provide educational efforts to create a supportive psychological environment for students to achieve their educational objectives. A cooperative relationship is maintained with relevant campus departments to ensure the University of Utah complies with federal and state regulations regarding students with disabilities.

LD/ADD ADMISSIONS INFORMATION

College entrance tests required: Yes
Interview required: N/A
Essay required: No
Documentation required for LD: Psychoeducational
  evaluation
Documentation required for ADD: Yes
Submitted to: Center for Disability Services
Special Ed. HS coursework accepted: No

Specific course requirements of all applicants: Yes
Separate application required for program services: No
# of LD applications submitted each year: NR
# of LD applications accepted yearly: NR
Total # of students receiving LD services: 239
**Acceptance into program means acceptance into
  college:** Student must be admitted and enrolled in the
  university first and then request services.

ADMISSIONS

There is no special application process for students with learning disabilities. All applicants to the university must meet the general admission requirements. Students who do not meet the admission requirements as a direct result of their disability may be admitted "on the condition" that course deficiencies are filled prior to earning 30 semester hours at the university. Conditional admission is determined by the Center for Disability Services and the admissions office. Students must provide appropriate information regarding their disability and any services they received in high school due to their disability. Self-disclosure is recommended only if the student needs to inform the admissions office they are working with the Center for Disability Services to consider conditional admission. Otherwise disclosure is not recommended but is left to the student to make the decision.

ADDITIONAL INFORMATION

The University of Utah is committed to providing reasonable accommodations to students whose disabilities may limit their ability to function in the academic setting. In order to meet the needs of students, and to make university activities, programs, and facilities accessible, the Center for Disability Services can provide the following services to students who provide documentation of a disability: assistance with admissions, registration, and graduation; orientation to the campus; referrals to campus and community services; guidelines for obtaining CDS services; general and academic advising related to disability; investigation of academic strengths and weaknesses; teach effective learning strategies; coordinate with academic and departmental advisors regarding program goals; coordinate reasonable accommodations of disability-related limitations with faculty and staff; act as a liaison between student and faculty or staff; provide readers, scribes, note-taker, textbooks, and printed material recorded onto cassettes; and arrange for exam accommodations. The Center for Disability Services has the right to set procedures to determine whether the student qualifies for services and how the services will be implemented. Additionally, the center has the responsibility to adjust or substitute academic requirements that unfairly discriminate against the student with a disability, and that are NOT essential to the integrity of a student's academic program. Students must provide appropriate documentation.

Support Services Contact Information

Learning Disability Program/Services: Center For Disability Services
Director: Joe Pete Wilson
E-Mail: onadeau@sa.utah.edu
Telephone: 801-581-5020
Fax: 801-581-5487

LEARNING DISABILITY SERVICES

Requests for the following/services accommodations will be evaluated individually based on appropriate and current documentation.

Allowed in exams
  Calculator: Yes
  Dictionary: Yes
  Computer: Yes
  Spellchecker: Yes
Extended test time: Yes
Scribes: Yes
Proctors: Yes
Oral exams: Yes
Note-takers: Yes

Distraction reduced environment: Yes
Tape recording in class: Yes
Books on tape from RFBD: Yes
Taping of books not from RFBD: Yes
Accommodations for students with ADD: Yes
Reading machine: Yes
Other assistive technology: Yes
Priority registration: Yes

Added costs for services: No
LD specialists: Yes
Professional tutors: 10
Peer tutors: 110
Max. hours/wk. for services: unlimited
How professors are notified of LD/ADD: By both student and director

GENERAL ADMISSIONS INFORMATION

Director of Admissions: John Boswell
Telephone: 801-581-7281

ENTRANCE REQUIREMENTS

Academic units required: 4 English, 2 math, 2 science (1 science lab), 2 foreign language, 1 history, 4 academic electives. High school diploma is required and GED is accepted. ACT with or without Writing component accepted. TOEFL required of all international applicants, minimum paper TOEFL 500, minimum computer TOEFL 173.

Application deadline: 4/1
Notification: Rolling
Average GPA: 3.51

Average SAT Math: NR
Average SAT Verbal: NR
Average ACT: 24

Graduated top 10% of class: 27%
Graduated top 25% of class: 51%
Graduated top 50% of class: 84%

COLLEGE GRADUATION REQUIREMENTS

Course waivers allowed: Yes
Course substitutions allowed: Yes
In what course: Math requirement for General Education for BS and foreign language requirement for BA.

ADDITIONAL INFORMATION

Environment: The university is located in Salt Lake City.

Student Body:
  Undergrad enrollment: 21,626
  Women: 44%
  Men: 56%
  Percent out-of-state: 8%

Cost Information
  In-state tuition: $2,986
  Out-of-state tuition: $9,495
  Room & board: $5,636
Housing Information
  University housing: Yes
  Percent living on campus: 7%

Greek System
  Fraternity: Yes
  Sorority: Yes
Athletics: NCAA Division I

UTAH STATE UNIVERSITY

0160 Old Main Hill, Logan, UT 84322-0160
Phone: 435-797-1079 • Fax: 435-797-3708
E-mail: admit@cc.usu.edu • Web: www.usu.edu
Support: CS • Institution type: 4-year public

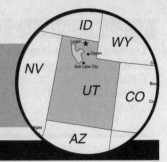

LEARNING DISABILITY PROGRAM AND SERVICES

The mission of the Disability Resource Center (DRC) is to provide support services to students with learning disabilities (and physical disabilities) in order to assist them in meeting their academic and personal goals. Staff members coordinate university support services, and help the students identify their needs, and overcome educational or attitudinal barriers that may prevent them from reaching their full educational potential. The DRC works to tailor services to students' individual needs. Many students use a combination of services to assist them academically, including campus orientation, registration referral, and academic advising to help students feel comfortable and to promote academic services.

LD/ADD ADMISSIONS INFORMATION

College entrance tests required: Yes
Interview required: No
Essay required: No
Documentation required for LD: Psychoeducational evaluation
Documentation required for ADD: Yes
Submitted to: Disability Resources Center
Special Ed. HS coursework accepted: Yes

Specific course requirements of all applicants: Yes
Separate application required for program services: Yes
# of LD applications submitted each year: NR
# of LD applications accepted yearly: NR
Total # of students receiving LD services: 150
Acceptance into program means acceptance into college: Student must be admitted and enrolled in the university first and then request services.

ADMISSIONS

All students submit the regular application. Course requirements include 4 years English, 3 years math, 3 years science, 1 science lab, 2 years foreign language recommended, 1 year history, and 4 years electives. If the admissions committee does not admit the student with a learning disability, the Disability Resource Center will consult with Admissions on special admits. Students who know they have a learning disability should contact the DRC to find out the details. Each student is assessed individually for admission. Consideration is given to waiving certain entrance requirements, such as flexibility on the GPA, course requirements, and SAT or ACT scores (lower than 17 on the ACT).

ADDITIONAL INFORMATION

Basic skills courses are offered in time management; learning strategies; and reading, math, and study strategies. The DRC has developed an assistive technology lab with computers and adaptive equipment to promote independence in conducting research and completing class assignments. General services include priority registration, note-takers, and extended time on tests. Scholarships are available.

Support Services Contact Information

Learning Disability Program/Services: Disability Resource Center (DRC)
Director: Diane Craig Hardman
E-Mail: dhardman@cc.usu.edu
 Telephone: 435-797-2444
 Fax: 435-797-0130
Contact Person: Natalie Sterling-Galloro
 Telephone: 435-797-2444

LEARNING DISABILITY SERVICES

Requests for the following/services accommodations will be evaluated individually based on appropriate and current documentation.

Allowed in exams
 Calculator: Y/N
 Dictionary: Y/N
 Computer: Y/N
 Spellchecker: Y/N
Extended test time: Yes
Scribes: Yes
Proctors: Yes
Oral exams: Yes
Note-takers: Yes

Distraction reduced environment: Yes
Tape recording in class: Yes
Books on tape from RFBD: Yes
Taping of books not from RFBD: Yes
Accommodations for students with ADD: Yes
Reading machine: Yes
Other assistive technology: Yes
Priority registration: Yes

Added costs for services: No
LD specialists: Yes
Professional tutors: No
Peer tutors: Yes
Max. hours/wk. for services: Varies
How professors are notified of LD/ADD: By student

GENERAL ADMISSIONS INFORMATION

Director of Admissions: Jimmy Moore
Telephone: 435-797-1079

ENTRANCE REQUIREMENTS

Academic units required: 4 English, 3 math, 3 science (1 science lab), 1 history, 4 academic electives.
Academic units recommended: 2 foreign language. High school diploma is required and GED is accepted. ACT with or without Writing component accepted. TOEFL required of all international applicants, minimum paper TOEFL 500, minimum computer TOEFL 173.

Application deadline: Rolling
Notification: Rolling
Average GPA: 3.57

Average SAT Math: 559
Average SAT Verbal: 547
Average ACT: 24

Graduated top 10% of class: 27%
Graduated top 25% of class: 55%
Graduated top 50% of class: 84%

COLLEGE GRADUATION REQUIREMENTS

Course waivers allowed: Yes
Course substitutions allowed: Yes
In what course: Case-by-case basis

ADDITIONAL INFORMATION

Environment: The university is located on 332 acres 96 miles north of Salt Lake City.

Student Body:
 Undergrad enrollment: 13,402
 Women: 49%
 Men: 51%
 Percent out-of-state: 27%

Cost Information
 In-state tuition: $3,372
 Out-of-state tuition: $9,700
 Room & board: $4,200
Housing Information
 University housing: Yes
 Percent living on campus: 14%

Greek System
 Fraternity: Yes
 Sorority: Yes
Athletics: NCAA Division I

CHAMPLAIN COLLEGE

163 South Willard Street, PO Box 670, Burlington, VT 05402-0670
Phone: 802-860-2727 • Fax: 802-860-2767
E-mail: admission@champlain.edu • Web: www.champlain.edu
Support: S • Institution type: 4-year private

LEARNING DISABILITY PROGRAM AND SERVICES

Champlain College does not offer a special program for students with LD. Support services and academic accommodations are available when needed. Students with LD meet individually with a counselor at the start of the semester and are assisted in developing a plan of academic support. The counselor acts as liaison between the student and faculty. The Student Resource Center offers peer tutoring, writing assistance, accounting lab, math lab, and a study skill workshop series in note-taking; mastering a college text; writing, revising, and editing papers; and personal counseling. Students must provide documentation of the disability to Support Services for Students with Disabilities, which should include the most recent educational evaluation performed by a qualified individual and a letter from any educational support service provider who has recently worked with the student would be most helpful. The letter should include information about the nature of the disability and the support services and/or program modifications provided.

LD/ADD ADMISSIONS INFORMATION

College entrance tests required: Yes
Interview required: No
Essay required: Yes
Documentation required for LD: The most recent psychoeducational evaluation, including WISC or WAIS–III and achievement testing
Documentation required for ADD: Yes
Submitted to: Support Services for Students with Disabilities
Special Ed. HS coursework accepted: Yes

Specific Couses: Yes
Separate application required for program services: No
# of LD applications submitted each year: NR
# of LD applications accepted yearly: NR
Total # of students receiving LD services: 100–130
Acceptance into program means acceptance into college: Student must be admitted and enrolled in the college first and then request services.

ADMISSIONS

There is no special admissions procedure for students with LD. Admissions are fairly flexible, although some requirements for certain majors are more difficult. Upward grade trend is very helpful and a good senior year is looked upon favorably. Recommendations are crucial. Students may elect to self-disclose the LD during the admission process and the college will take this information into consideration when making admission decisions. Students may take a reduced load of 12 credits and still be considered full-time. The average ACT for applicants is a 20 and SAT 1100 and the minimum GPA is a 2.0.

ADDITIONAL INFORMATION

Students with learning disabilities who self-disclose receive a special needs application from the coordinator of Support Services for Students with Disabilities, after they have enrolled in college courses. The coordinator meets with each student during the first week of school. The first appointment includes a discussion about the student's disability and the academic accommodations that will be needed. Accommodations could include but are not limited to tutoring, extended time for tests (in the Resource Center), readers for test, use of computer, peer note-takers, tape recording lectures, and books on tape. With the student's permission, faculty members receive a letter describing the student's disability, and discussing appropriate accommodations. The coordinator will continue to act as a liaison between students and faculty, consult with tutors, monitor students' academic progress, and consult with faculty as needed. Freshman Focus, a course designed to assist students in making a smooth transition to college, is available for students in certain majors.

Support Services Contact Information

Learning Disability Program/Services: Support Services for Students with Disabilities
Director: Allyson Krings, Coordinator & Counselor
  E-Mail: krings@champlain.edu
  Telephone: 802-651-5961
  Fax: 802-860-2764
Contact Person: Same

LEARNING DISABILITY SERVICES

Requests for the following/services accommodations will be evaluated individually based on appropriate and current documentation.

Allowed in exams	**Distraction reduced environment:** Yes	**Added costs for services:** No
Calculator: Yes	**Tape recording in class:** Yes	**LD specialists:** No
Dictionary: Yes	**Books on tape from RFBD:** Yes	**Professional tutors:** No
Computer: Yes	**Taping of books not from RFBD:** Yes	**Peer tutors:** 30
Spellchecker: Yes	**Accommodations for students with**	**Max. hours/wk. for services:** N/A
Extended test time: Yes	**ADD:** Yes	**How professors are notified of**
Scribes: Yes	**Reading machine:** Yes	**LD/ADD:** By student
Proctors: Yes	**Other assistive technology:** Yes	
Oral exams: Yes	**Priority registration:** No	
Note-takers: Yes		

GENERAL ADMISSIONS INFORMATION

Director of Admissions: Josephine H. Churchill
Telephone: 802-860-2727

ENTRANCE REQUIREMENTS

Academic units required: 4 English, 3 math, 3 science (2 science lab), 2 social studies, 4 history, 4 academic electives. **Academic units recommended:** 4 math, 4 science (3 science lab), 2 foreign language. High school diploma is required and GED is accepted. TOEFL required of all international applicants, minimum paper TOEFL 500, minimum computer TOEFL 173.

Application deadline: Rolling	**Average SAT Math:** 500	**Graduated top 10% of class:** 15%
Notification: Rolling	**Average SAT Verbal:** 500	**Graduated top 25% of class:** 35%
Average GPA: 3.0	**Average ACT:** 22	**Graduated top 50% of class:** 85%

COLLEGE GRADUATION REQUIREMENTS

Course waivers allowed: No
Course substitutions allowed: No
In what course: N/A

ADDITIONAL INFORMATION

Environment: The college is located on 16 acres in a small city surrounded by rural area mountains and Lake Champlain.

Student Body:	**Cost Information**	**Greek System**
Undergrad enrollment: 2,295	Tuition: $14,660	Fraternity: No
Women: 52%	Room & board: $9,695	Sorority: No
Men: 48%	**Housing Information**	Athletics: Intramurals only
Percent out-of-state: 44%	University housing: Yes	
	Percent living on campus: 40%	

GREEN MOUNTAIN COLLEGE

One College Circle, Poultney, VT 05764-1199
Phone: 802-287-8208 • Fax: 802-287-8099
E-mail: admiss@greenmtn.edu • Web: www.greenmtn.edu
Support: S • Institution type: 4-year private

LEARNING DISABILITY PROGRAM AND SERVICES

Green Mountain College provides accommodations for students with documented learning differences. The college believes that every student has the potential for academic success and strives to support students while teaching them independence and self-advocacy. The Learning Center (LC) functions as the primary source of information regarding academic issues relating to disabilities. Students seeking academic accommodations must self-identify and submit valid documentation of their learning needs. The LC staff determines which students are eligible for academic accommodations and works with the student and staff to develop and implement an accommodation plan that will allow the student an opportunity to succeed at college. Progress is monitored to ensure access to the necessary supports and to assist in fostering self-advocacy. The LC has 6 main functions: to provide academic support, primarily through one-on-one, small group, general content area tutoring; to serve as the campus Writing Center; to support courses specifically designed for under-prepared students; to provide support for foreign students; to be the campus center for academic issues relating to disabilities; and to provide workshops and seminars and events with the goal of improving learning skills.

LD/ADD ADMISSIONS INFORMATION

College entrance tests required: Yes
Interview required: No
Essay required: Yes
Documentation required for LD: Psychoeducational evaluation
Documentation required for ADD: Yes
Submitted to: The Learning Center
Special Ed. HS coursework accepted: Yes

Specific Couses: Yes
Separate application required for program services: No
# of LD applications submitted each year: NR
# of LD applications accepted yearly: NR
Total # of students receiving LD services: 50
Acceptance into program means acceptance into college: Students must be admitted and enrolled at the College and then reviewed for LC services.

ADMISSIONS

There is no special admissions process for students with learning disabilities. Students face the same admission criteria, which include an ACT score of 19 or SAT score of 900; 2.0 GPA; 4 years English, 2–3 years history/social studies, 2 years science (with lab), 3 years math, and 2 years foreign language. All applications are carefully considered with the best interest of both the student and the college in mind. Green Mountain College has a probationary admission that limits the course load of the new student while requiring the student to make use of support services.

ADDITIONAL INFORMATION

The Learning Center provides support services to all students. The tutoring program uses a three-tiered approach: a drop-in clinic for immediate but temporary academic assistance, individually scheduled tutoring, or a more extensive schedule of one , two, or three tutoring sessions per week for tutorial help throughout a course. The Writing Center is open during drop-in hours. All new students take placement tests to assess their achievement in reading and mathematics. Students whose work is unsatisfactory are requested to rewrite assignments with the help of the Learning Center staff. Students under prepared in math are advised to take basic math or beginning algebra, and tutoring is available.

Support Services Contact Information

Learning Disability Program/Services: The Learning Center (LC)
Director: Nancy Ruby
  E-Mail: rubyn@greenmtn.edu
  Telephone: 802-287-8287
  Fax: 802-287-8288

LEARNING DISABILITY SERVICES

Requests for the following/services accommodations will be evaluated individually based on appropriate and current documentation.

Allowed in exams
  Calculator: Yes
  Dictionary: Yes
  Computer: Yes
  Spellchecker: Yes
Extended test time: Yes
Scribes: Yes
Proctors: Yes
Oral exams: No
Note-takers: Yes

Distraction reduced environment: Yes
Tape recording in class: Yes
Books on tape from RFBD: Yes
Taping of books not from RFBD: No
Accommodations for students with
  ADD: Yes
Reading machine: Yes
Other assistive technology: No
Priority registration: No

Added costs for services: No
LD specialists: No
Professional tutors: 4
Peer tutors: 15-19
Max. hours/wk. for services:
  Unlimited
How professors are notified of
  LD/ADD: By both student and director

GENERAL ADMISSIONS INFORMATION

Director of Admissions: Joel Wincowski
Telephone: 802-287-8208

ENTRANCE REQUIREMENTS

Academic units required: 4 English, 3 math, 2 science, 1 social studies, 2 history, 6 academic electives.
Academic units recommended: 2 foreign language. High school diploma is required and GED is accepted.
TOEFL required of all international applicants, minimum paper TOEFL 500, minimum computer TOEFL 173.

Application deadline: Rolling
Notification: Rolling
Average GPA: 2.6

Average SAT Math: 203
Average SAT Verbal: 521
Average ACT: 21

Graduated top 10% of class: NR
Graduated top 25% of class: NR
Graduated top 50% of class: NR

COLLEGE GRADUATION REQUIREMENTS

Course waivers allowed: No
Course substitutions allowed: No
In what course: N/A

ADDITIONAL INFORMATION

Environment: The campus is in a small town near Rutland.

Student Body:
  Undergrad enrollment: 591
  Women: 47%
  Men: 53%
  Percent out-of-state: 91%

Cost Information
  Tuition: $19,670
  Room & board: $6,320
Housing Information
  University housing: Yes
  Percent living on campus: 90%

Greek System
  Fraternity: No
  Sorority: No
  Athletics: NCAA Division II

JOHNSON STATE COLLEGE

337 College Hill, Johnson, VT 05656-9408
Phone: 802-635-1219 • Fax: 802-635-1230
E-mail: jscadmissions@jsc.vsc.edu • Web: www.johnsonstatecollege.edu
Support: CS • Institution type: 4-year public

LEARNING DISABILITY PROGRAM AND SERVICES

Johnson State College provides services to students with learning disabilities through the Special Services Counselor. The fundamental purpose is to provide students with the appropriate services necessary to allow full participation in all Johnson State College academic programs. Students with learning disabilities are integrated fully into the college community. There is also a TRIO Program for 235 students meeting eligibility criteria, which include at least one of the following areas: enrolled in one or more basic skills courses; SAT scores below 300 on either verbal or math sections; earned a GED; has below average high school grades; not completed algebra II or its equivalent in high school; or conditionally accepted to the college. Students must also meet one of three criteria: (1) have a documented disability, (2) be a first generation college student, and (3) be economically disadvantaged. Eligible students receive intensive support services through the Academic Support Services program. The Learning Resource Center provides a friendly and supportive environment for any student who is academically struggling or under prepared to meet his or her educational goals. Services include group and peer tutoring, Math Lab, Writer's Workshop, and supplemental/instruction.

LD/ADD ADMISSIONS INFORMATION

College entrance tests required: Yes
Interview required: No
Essay required: Yes
Documentation required for LD: Follow AHEAD guidelines: cognitive measurement WAIS–R and achievement tests within three years
Documentation required for ADD: Follow ETS guidelines for ADD documentation and forms to be completed by school personnel and diagnosing physician
Submitted to:
Special Ed. HS coursework accepted: N/A

Specific course requirements of all applicants: Yes
Separate application required for program services: No
# of LD applications submitted each year: NR
# of LD applications accepted yearly: NR
Total # of students receiving LD services: 85
Acceptance into program means acceptance into college: Student must be admitted and enrolled in the college first and then request services.

ADMISSIONS

Upon consultation with the Academic Support Services Office, all students with learning disabilities who demonstrate the academic ability to be successful are accepted. Modifications to entrance requirements are accommodated if a student is otherwise admissible. Course requirements include 4 years English, 2 years science, 2 years social science, and 3 years math. High school GPA minimum is a 2.0. The SAT score range is 700–940 for the middle 50%.

ADDITIONAL INFORMATION

Academic Support Services provides tutoring, academic advising, personal counseling, career exploration, college survival skills training workshops, and assistance with establishing appropriate and reasonable accommodations. Students should be self-advocates and are responsible for notifying instructors to arrange for accommodations. The Transition Year Experience (TYE) is available to all students who are conditionally accepted to JSC. It begins one week prior to freshman year and continues through 15 weeks of the fall semester. This innovative learning experience will help make the transition from high school to college a more positive and rewarding experience for students needing strong academic and individual support. Students earn a total of four college credits through the TYE designed to teach critical inquiry, study skills, general college survival skills, and self-advocacy.

Support Services Contact Information

Learning Disability Program/Services: Academic Support Services
Director: Karen Madden, PhD
  E-Mail: karen.madden@jsc.vsc.edu
  Telephone: 802-635-1259
  Fax: 802-635-1454
Contact Person: Dian Duranleau
  E-Mail: dian.duranleau@jsc.vsc.edu
  Telephone: 802-635-1259
  Fax: 802-635-1454

LEARNING DISABILITY SERVICES

Requests for the following/services accommodations will be evaluated individually based on appropriate and current documentation.

Allowed in exams
  Calculator: Yes
  Dictionary: Yes
  Computer: Yes
  Spellchecker: Yes
Extended test time: Yes
Scribes: Yes
Proctors: Yes
Oral exams: No
Note-takers: Yes

Distraction reduced environment: Yes
Tape recording in class: No
Books on tape from RFBD: Yes
Taping of books not from RFBD: Yes
Accommodations for students with ADD: Yes
Reading machine: Yes
Other assistive technology: Yes
Priority registration: No

Added costs for services: No
LD specialists: Yes
Professional tutors: 2
Peer tutors: 15–25
Max. hours/wk. for services: Unlimited
How professors are notified of LD/ADD: By student

GENERAL ADMISSIONS INFORMATION

Director of Admissions: Penny Paradee Howrigan
Telephone: 802-635-1219

ENTRANCE REQUIREMENTS
Academic units required: 4 English, 3 math, 2 science (1 science lab), 2 social studies, 2 history. **Academic units recommended:** 4 English, 4 math, 3 science (2 science lab), 1 foreign language, 3 social studies, 3 history. High school diploma is required and GED is accepted. ACT with Writing component required or SAT Reasoning test. TOEFL required of all international applicants, minimum paper TOEFL 500, minimum computer TOEFL 173.

Application deadline: NR
Notification: Rolling
Average GPA: NR

Average SAT Math: 490
Average SAT Verbal: 500
Average ACT: 24

Graduated top 10% of class: 6%
Graduated top 25% of class: 24%
Graduated top 50% of class: 52%

COLLEGE GRADUATION REQUIREMENTS

Course waivers allowed: Yes
Course substitutions allowed: Yes
In what course: Lower math may be substituted for 1 of the 2 math requirements if there is a math LD only.

ADDITIONAL INFORMATION

Environment: The college is located in a rural area 45 miles northeast of Burlington.

Student Body:
  Undergrad enrollment: 1,441
  Women: 60%
  Men: 40%
  Percent out-of-state: 39%

Cost Information
  In-state tuition: $5,980
  Out-of-state tuition: $12,920
  Room & board: $6,454
Housing Information
  University housing: Yes
  Percent living on campus: 41%

Greek System
  Fraternity: No
  Sorority: No
Athletics: NCAA Division III

LANDMARK COLLEGE

P.O. Box 820, Putney, VT 05346-0820
Phone: 802-387-6718 • Fax: 802-387-6868
E-mail: admissions@landmark.edu • Web: www.landmark.edu
Support: SP • Institution type: 2-year private

LEARNING DISABILITY PROGRAM AND SERVICES

Landmark College is designed exclusively for high-potential students with dyslexia, specific learning disabilities, and/or ADD. It is the only accredited college in the nation for students with LD/ADD. More than 100 members of the faculty and professional staff devote their entire attention to providing the finest possible program for these students. The goal is to prepare students to enter or return to college. At Landmark, students do not bypass difficulties by using note-takers, taped books, or taking exams orally. Students must do their own work and Landmark teaches them how. Landmark's approach is unique and includes an individually designed tutorial program, very small classes, structured assignments, and an emphasis on constantly improving language and study skills.

LD/ADD ADMISSIONS INFORMATION

College entrance tests required: No
Interview required: Yes
Essay required: Yes
Documentation required for LD: Psychoeducational evaluation
Documentation required for ADD: Yes
Submitted to: Admissions
Special Ed. HS coursework accepted: Yes

Specific course requirements of all applicants: No
Separate application required for program services: No
# of LD applications submitted each year: 700
# of LD applications accepted yearly: 300
Total # of students receiving LD services: 150–250
Acceptance into program means acceptance into college: The program and the college are one and the same.

ADMISSIONS

Landmark College serves students whose academic skills have not been developed to a level equal to their intellectual capacity. Students must have average to superior intellectual potential, diagnosis of dyslexia, specific LD or ADD, and high motivation. Applicants must have a willingness to undertake a rigorous academic program that does not provide bypass methods such as note-takers, books on tape, or oral exams. Focus instead is on individualized, intensive development and honing of academic skills. Qualified students must have a testing session and interview. An admission decision is made at this time. ACT/SATs not required. There are no specific course requirements for admission, but students must take courses that lead to a high school diploma or the GED. Students may apply for admission for summer, fall, or spring semesters.

ADDITIONAL INFORMATION

Skills Development Summer Sessions ($7,300) help students develop the language and study skills needed for success in college. This program is open to students from other colleges, or recent high school graduates, as well as those planning to attend Landmark. Students can get help with writing, reading, study skills, and understanding their own learning styles. Skills classes are offered to students on campus in study skills, math, written language, oral language, and content courses.

Support Services Contact Information

Learning Disability Program/Services: Landmark College
Director: John Kipp, Academic Dean
  E-Mail: jkipp@landmark.edu
  Telephone: 802-387-4767
  Fax: 802-387-6868
Contact Person: Dale M. Herold
  E-Mail: dherold@landmark.edu
  Telephone: 802-387-6718
  Fax: 802-387-6868

LEARNING DISABILITY SERVICES

Requests for the following/services accommodations will be evaluated individually based on appropriate and current documentation.

Allowed in exams
  Calculator: Yes
  Dictionary: Yes
  Computer: Yes
  Spellchecker: Yes
Extended test time: Yes
Scribes: No
Proctors: No
Oral exams: Yes
Note-takers: No

Distraction reduced environment: Yes
Tape recording in class: Yes
Books on tape from RFBD: Y/N
Taping of books not from RFBD: No
Accommodations for students with ADD: Yes
Reading machine: Yes
Other assistive technology: Yes
Priority registration: No
Added costs for services: No

LD specialists: Yes
Professional tutors: 90
Peer tutors: No
Max. hours/wk. for services: Unlimited
How professors are notified of LD/ADD: N/A

GENERAL ADMISSIONS INFORMATION

Director of Admissions: Dale Herold
Telephone: 802-387-6718

ENTRANCE REQUIREMENTS

ACT/SAT not required. High school diploma is required and GED is accepted. TOEFL required of all international applicants, minimum paper TOEFL 200, minimum computer TOEFL 40.

Application deadline: Rolling beginning 12/1
Notification: Rolling
Average GPA: NR

Average SAT Math: NR
Average SAT Verbal: NR
Average ACT: NR

Graduated top 10% of class: NR
Graduated top 25% of class: NR
Graduated top 50% of class: NR

COLLEGE GRADUATION REQUIREMENTS

Course waivers allowed: No
Course substitutions allowed: No
In what course: N/A

ADDITIONAL INFORMATION

Environment: The college is located on 125 acres overlooking the Connecticut River Valley and the hills of Vermont and New Hampshire.

Student Body:
  Undergrad enrollment: 334
  Women: 30%
  Men: 70%
  Percent out-of-state: 94%

Cost Information
  Tuition: $37,000
  Room & board: $6,800
Housing Information
  University housing: Yes
  Percent living on campus: 96%

Greek System
  Fraternity: Yes
  Sorority: Yes
Athletics: NCAA Division III

Landmark College

NEW ENGLAND CULINARY INSTITUTE

250 Main Street, Montpelier, VT 05602
Phone: 802-223-6324 • Fax: 802-225-3280
E-mail: info@neci.edu • Web: www.neci.edu
Support: CS • Institution type: 2-year and 4-year private

LEARNING DISABILITY PROGRAM AND SERVICES

The New England Culinary Institute is in business to provide educational programs in the culinary arts, food and beverage management, basic cooking and related areas that prepare students for employment and advancement in the hospitality industry. Students with LD/ADD have found success at the institute, although sometimes it might take these students longer to finish a specific course or complete all of the graduation requirements. Some students with LD/ADD may find the production kitchen learning environment, with its intensity, pressure, and long hours, a very demanding place. Almost all of the courses have a strong academic component, which requires comprehension and retention of a great deal of new information. Students with LD/ADD often find the most success in the aassociate's degree of occupational studies (AOS) program. Additionally, students are more successful if they have a strong work ethic and have had some experience in the food industry. The Learning Services Office provides services to all students and the coordinator is available five days a week to work with students one-on-one. The goal of the Learning Services Office is to provide support to maximize culinary learning.

LD/ADD ADMISSIONS INFORMATION

College entrance tests required: No
Interview required: No-Recommended
Essay required: Yes
Documentation required for LD: Psychoeducational evaluation
Documentation required for ADD: Yes
Submitted to: Learning Services
Special Ed. HS coursework accepted: Yes

Specific course requirements of all applicants: No
Separate application required for program services: No
# of LD applications submitted each year: NR
# of LD applications accepted yearly: NR
Total # of students receiving LD services: NR
Acceptance into program means acceptance into college: Student must be admitted and enrolled in the institute first and then request services.

ADMISSIONS

There is no special admission process for students with LD or ADD. Students who are applying for the AOS program must have a high school diploma or equivalency certificate, and must submit an essay and a minimum of one to three letters of recommendation. Interviews are recommended. Applicants may also be required to spend some time in the kitchen with one of the chefs. Students interested in the BA program must complete an associate's degree first. Applicants with LD/ADD with appropriate documentation will be eligible to access accommodations once they are admitted and enrolled. Some students may wish to complete a certificate in basic cooking first to determine their commitment and skills in the culinary arts.

ADDITIONAL INFORMATION

Students with LD/ADD must provide appropriate documentation and meet with the Learning Center director in order to receive services. The director will verify the documentation, review the requests, and meet with the student to explain the learning services. Instructors are notified with student permission. Self-advocacy information is provided and a learning contract (if necessary) is written and signed by the student. Accommodations such as oral and untimed tests, alternate test sites, use of dictionary during non-vocabulary tests, note-taking, individualized tutoring, use of calculators and computers, tape recording of lectures, and paper writing assistance are available. Any student can access these services through Learning Services. These services include one-on-one tutorials, small group workshops to refresh math skills, review sessions, opportunity to retake tests, computers, software to help with writing papers, reference books,and a quiet study/work space. This is a self-serve resource and they will try to work out all requests.

Support Services Contact Information

Learning Disability Program/Services: Learning Services
Director: Jackie Burke
  E-Mail: jackieb@neci.edu
  Telephone: 802-764-2135
  Fax: 802-764-2180

LEARNING DISABILITY SERVICES

Requests for the following/services accommodations will be evaluated individually based on appropriate and current documentation.

Allowed in exams
  Calculator: Yes
  Dictionary: Yes
  Computer: Yes
  Spellchecker: Yes
Extended test time: Yes
Scribes: Yes
Proctors: Yes
Oral exams: Yes
Note-takers: Yes

Distraction reduced environment: Yes
Tape recording in class: Yes
Books on tape from RFBD: Yes
Taping of books not from RFBD: Yes
Accommodations for students with
  ADD: Yes
Reading machine: No
Other assistive technology: Yes
Priority registration: No

Added costs for services: No
LD specialists: Yes
Professional tutors: 2
Peer tutors: 5
Max. hours/wk. for services:
  Unlimited
How professors are notified of
  LD/ADD: By both student and director

GENERAL ADMISSIONS INFORMATION

Director of Admissions: Dawn Haywood
Telephone: 802-223-6324

ENTRANCE REQUIREMENTS

ACT/SAT not required. Courses recommended include 4 years English, 3 years math, 3 years science, 4 years social studies, and 2 years foreign language. Personal statement and 2 letters of recommendation are required. Interview required either in person, online, or by telephone. TOEFL required of all international applicants, minimum paper TOEFL 550, minimum computer TOEFL 213.

Application deadline: Rolling
Notification: Rolling
Average GPA: N/A

Average SAT Math: N/A
Average SAT Verbal: N/A
Average ACT: N/A

Graduated top 10% of class: N/A
Graduated top 25% of class: N/A
Graduated top 50% of class: N/A

COLLEGE GRADUATION REQUIREMENTS

Course waivers allowed: No
Course substitutions allowed: No
In what course: N/A

ADDITIONAL INFORMATION

Environment: The Institute is located in the city of Montpelier, 45 miles from Burlington.

Student Body:
  Undergrad enrollment: 625
  Women: 25%
  Men: 75%
  Percent out-of-state: 70%

Cost Information
  Tuition: $21,500–$31,00
  Room & board: $6,415
Housing Information
  University housing: Yes
  Percent living on campus: 80%

Greek System
  Fraternity: No
  Sorority: No
Athletics: Intramural

NORWICH UNIVERSITY

Admissions Office, 27 I.D. White Avenue, Northfield, VT 05663
Phone: 802-485-2001 • Fax: 802-485-2032
E-mail: nuadm@norwich.edu • Web: www.norwich.edu
Support: CS • Institution type: 4-year private

LEARNING DISABILITY PROGRAM AND SERVICES

The Learning Support Center (LSC) offers comprehensive support services in all areas of academic life. While Norwich does not have a formal program for students with learning disabilities, the university does offer support services on a voluntary basis. Students are instructed by the center staff in a wide range of study and college survival skills. The Center's staff work closely with advisors and faculty members, and are strong advocates for students with learning disabilities. The university stresses autonomy by providing a level of support that assists students with becoming responsible, thinking adults, and well-acquainted with their own needs and able to articulate them. Services are provided by a staff of professionals that includes LD specialists, study skills/writing specialists, and a basic math specialist. The professional staff is supplemented by a trained, well-supervised student tutorial staff.

LD/ADD ADMISSIONS INFORMATION

College entrance tests required: Yes
Interview required: No
Essay required: No
Documentation required for LD: Comprehensive cognitive/ achievement with full report and diagnostic conclusion with recommendation, less than five years old
Documentation required for ADD: Minimum of psychiatric/ psychological protocal targeting ADD; prefer comprehensive evaluation as for LD, less than three years old
Submitted to: Learning Support Center
Special Ed. HS coursework accepted: No

Specific course requirements of all applicants: Yes
Separate application required for program services: No
# of LD applications submitted each year: NR
# of LD applications accepted yearly: NR
Total # of students receiving LD services: 63
Acceptance into program means acceptance into college: Students must be admitted and enrolled in the university first and then request services.

ADMISSIONS

Students with learning disabilities submit a general application. Admission criteria include high school GPA of a C or better; SAT of 850 or equivalent ACT; participation in activities; and strong college recommendations from teachers, counselors, or coaches. There are no course waivers for admission. The university is flexible on ACT/SAT test scores. If grades and other indicators are problematic, it is recommended that students provide detailed information to give a better understanding the disability. A complete psychodiagnostic evaluation is required. A small number of students who do not meet the general admission requirements may be admitted if they show promise. An interview is highly recommended. In some cases the director of learning support may review the admissions file and make a recommendation. There are limited conditional admission slots. Students are required to go to a college and take courses if their high school grades and/or SAT scores are below requirement.

ADDITIONAL INFORMATION

A telephone conversation or personal meeting with the LSC support personnel is encouraged prior to the start of college, so that work can begin immediately on preparing an individualized program. Students are responsible for meeting with each professor to discuss accommodations. Services begin with Freshman Placement Testing designed to assess each individual's level of readiness for college-level reading, writing, and math. Other services include course advising in companion with an assigned academic advisor and advocacy for academic petitions. Services and accommodations are available for undergraduate and graduate students.

Support Services Contact Information

Learning Disability Program/Services: Learning Support Center (LSC)
Director: Paula A. Gills
  E-Mail: gills@norwich.edu
  Telephone: 802-485-2130
  Fax: 802-485-2684

LEARNING DISABILITY SERVICES

Requests for the following/services accommodations will be evaluated individually based on appropriate and current documentation.

Allowed in exams
  Calculator: Yes
  Dictionary: Yes
  Computer: Yes
  Spellchecker: Yes
Extended test time: Yes
Scribes: Yes
Proctors: Yes
Oral exams: Yes
Note-takers: Yes

Distraction reduced environment: Yes
Tape recording in class: Yes
Books on tape from RFBD: Yes
Taping of books not from RFBD: Yes
Accommodations for students with ADD: Yes
Reading machine: No
Other assistive technology: No
Priority registration: Yes

Added costs for services: No
LD specialists: Yes
Professional tutors: 9
Peer tutors: 15–20
Max. hours/wk. for services: N/A
How professors are notified of LD/ADD: By both student and director

GENERAL ADMISSIONS INFORMATION

Director of Admissions: Karen McGrath
Telephone: 802-485-2001

ENTRANCE REQUIREMENTS

Academic units required: 4 English, 3 math, 2 science (2 science lab). **Academic units recommended:** 4 English, 4 math, 3 science (2 science lab), 2 foreign language. High school diploma is required and GED is accepted. TOEFL required of all international applicants, minimum paper TOEFL 500, minimum computer TOEFL 173.

Application deadline: Rolling
Notification: Rolling
Average GPA: NR

Average SAT Math: NR
Average SAT Verbal: NR
Average ACT: NR

Graduated top 10% of class: 8%
Graduated top 25% of class: 21%
Graduated top 50% of class: 43%

COLLEGE GRADUATION REQUIREMENTS

Course waivers allowed: No
Course substitutions allowed: Yes
In what course: Foreign language, only with proof of inability to successfully function.

ADDITIONAL INFORMATION

Environment: The university's two campuses, located in Northfield (traditional) and Montpelier (low residency), are located 50 miles southeast of Burlington.

Student Body:
  Undergrad enrollment: 2,099
  Women: 20%
  Men: 80%
  Percent out-of-state: 80%

Cost Information
  Tuition: $20,088
  Room & board: $7,374
Housing Information
  University housing: Yes
  Percent living on campus: 98%

Greek System
  Fraternity: No
  Sorority: No
Athletics: NCAA Division III

SOUTHERN VERMONT COLLEGE

982 Mansion Drive, Bennington, VT 05201
Phone: 802-447-6304 • Fax: 802-447-4695
E-mail: admis@svc.edu • Web: www.svc.edu
Support: SP • Institution type: 4-year private

LEARNING DISABILITY PROGRAM AND SERVICES

The Learning Disability program at Southern Vermont College offers a highly supportive environment for students with special educational needs. Students who participate in the program are offered a wide range of support services tailored to their individual needs, and regularly scheduled tutorial sessions for academic support, study skills, and compensatory strategies. While support remains available throughout their college stay, students are strongly encouraged to seek support on a weekly basis, at least during their freshman year. Varying levels of support are available throughout the academic years at Southern Vermont College. There is no additional fee for services. To be eligible to participate in the Disabilities Support Program, students must provide recent documentation specifying the nature of the specific learning disability or ADD. An interview with the disabilities staff is strongly recommended.

LD/ADD ADMISSIONS INFORMATION

College entrance tests required: No
Interview required: Yes
Essay required: Yes
Documentation required for LD: WAIS–III (within two years)
Documentation required for ADD: Yes
Submitted to: Learning Differences Support Program
Special Ed. HS coursework accepted: Yes

Specific course requirements of all applicants: Yes
Separate application required for program services: No
# of LD applications submitted each year: NR
# of LD applications accepted yearly: NR
Total # of students receiving LD services: 70
Acceptance into program means acceptance into college: Student must be admitted and enrolled in the college first and then request services.

ADMISSIONS

If a student with a documented learning disability does not meet regular admissions criteria, the LD coordinator and review committee will further examine documentation and evaluation information. Each case is decided on an individual basis. Required documentation includes WAIS III–R (within 2 years) with individual sub-scores indicating at least average ability in abstract reasoning; recent individualized achievement tests indicating grade equivalents in reading skills/comprehension, math, and written language skills. General admissions criteria include a minimum GPA of 2.0, 3 years English, 2 years math, and 2 years science (can substitute). No ACT/SATs required or the student may take college placement tests in lieu of SAT/ACTs. Admissions decisions are made by the Office of Admissions.

ADDITIONAL INFORMATION

The Learning Cooperative Peer Tutorial Center is available to all students at the college. Peer Tutors are provided for most courses offered at the College. There is walk-in tutoring with trained tutors. The disabilities staff works with students and instructors to find learning strategies to help them succeed in college. Students may be placed in one of three classes: English composition and college math to master skills; literature course to improve general reading skills; and basic math, which is a self-paced course to strengthen math skills. Summer ACTion Program is available to all students accepted into the fall freshman class. This program provides an introduction to college life, dorm living, and the opportunity to earn college credits.

Support Services Contact Information

Learning Disability Program/Services: Learning Differences Support Program
Director: Todd Gerson
 E-Mail: tgerson@svc.edu
 Telephone: 802-447-6360
 Fax: 802-447-4695

LEARNING DISABILITY SERVICES

Requests for the following/services accommodations will be evaluated individually based on appropriate and current documentation.

Allowed in exams
 Calculator: Yes
 Dictionary: No
 Computer: Yes
 Spellchecker: Yes
Extended test time: Yes
Scribes: Yes
Proctors: Yes
Oral exams: No
Note-takers: Yes

Distraction reduced environment: Yes
Tape recording in class: Yes
Books on tape from RFBD: Yes
Taping of books not from RFBD: Yes
Accommodations for students with ADD: Yes
Reading machine: Yes
Other assistive technology: Yes
Priority registration: Yes

Added costs for services: No
LD specialists: Yes
Professional tutors: 2
Peer tutors: 12
Max. hours/wk. for services: Unlimited
How professors are notified of LD/ADD: By student

GENERAL ADMISSIONS INFORMATION

Director of Admissions: Elizabeth Gatti
Telephone: 802-447-6304

ENTRANCE REQUIREMENTS

Academic units required: 4 English, 2 math. **Academic units recommended:** 4 science, 2 foreign language, 4 social studies, 4 history. High school diploma is required and GED is accepted. TOEFL required of all international applicants, minimum paper TOEFL 500, minimum computer TOEFL 173.

Application deadline: Rolling
Notification: Rolling
Average GPA: 2.63

Average SAT Math: NR
Average SAT Verbal: NR
Average ACT: NR

Graduated top 10% of class: 0%
Graduated top 25% of class: 5%
Graduated top 50% of class: 35%

COLLEGE GRADUATION REQUIREMENTS

Course waivers allowed: Yes
Course substitutions allowed: Yes
In what course: Math course substitution considered only if, in spite of demonstrated efforts to master college math course material, the student has met with limited success.

ADDITIONAL INFORMATION

Environment: The college is located in a town of 17,000, 40 miles northeast of Albany, New York.

Student Body:
 Undergrad enrollment: 464
 Women: 64%
 Men: 36%
 Percent out-of-state: 66%

Cost Information
 Tuition: $12,498
 Room & board: $6,432
Housing Information
 University housing: Yes
 Percent living on campus: 53%

Greek System
 Fraternity: No
 Sorority: No
Athletics: NCAA Division III

UNIVERSITY OF VERMONT

Admissions Office, 194 South Prospect Street, Burlington, VT 05401-3596
Phone: 802-656-3370 • Fax: 802-656-8611
E-mail: admissions@uvm.edu • Web: www.uvm.edu
Support: CS • Institution type: 4-year public

LEARNING DISABILITY PROGRAM AND SERVICES

The university provides a multidisciplinary program for students with LD. ACCESS works closely with students having learning problems to ensure that campus-wide resources are used effectively. Initially, a comprehensive assessment is revised to identify students' strengths and weaknesses in learning. This information is used to carefully design classroom and study accommodations to compensate for learning problems. Through this process, students and program staff have identified a number of techniques and strategies to enable success at class and study tasks. The academic advising process for students with LD involves two offices: the academic advisor assigned by the college, and the professional staff of ACCESS who review tentative semester schedules to balance course format, teaching style, and workload with a student's learning strengths. The Learning Cooperative offers individual tutoring and assistance with reading, writing, study skills, and time management. The Writing Center assists with proofing and feedback on writing assignments. There is a developmental course called Conquering College. This is an individualized support service program designed to equalize educational opportunities for students with learning disabilities.

LD/ADD ADMISSIONS INFORMATION

College entrance tests required: Yes
Interview required: No
Essay required: NR
Documentation required for LD: Psychoeducational evaluation
Documentation required for ADD: Yes
Submitted to: Access
Special Ed. HS coursework accepted: Yes

Specific course requirements of all applicants: Yes
Separate application required for program services: No
# of LD applications submitted each year: NR
# of LD applications accepted yearly: NR
Total # of students receiving LD services: 550
Acceptance into program means acceptance into college: Student must be admitted and enrolled in the university first and then request services. Some students are reviewed by the LD program, which provides consultation to admissions.

ADMISSIONS

Students submit a regular UVM application to admissions and all documentation of their disability to ACCESS. Students are encouraged to voluntarily provide documentation of their disability. ACCESS reviews documentation and consults with admissions as to how the student's disability has effected their academic record. A clear understanding of the students' strengths and weaknesses in learning, and the influence of the disability on the current and past educational process, will enable a broader assessment of ability to meet academic qualifications, requirements, and rigors of UVM. Students with LD should submit a current educational evaluation that includes a measure of cognitive functioning and documentation of the learning problem(s). Students with ADD are encouraged to provide documentation and information on how the ADD had an impact on the educational setting. Course requirements include 4 years English, 3 years social science, 3 years math, 2 years physical sciences, and 2 years foreign language (math and foreign language can be waived with appropriate documentation). Special education courses are acceptable if the student's high school gives credit for the courses. Self-disclosing in the application is a matter of personal choice. However, at UVM, disclosing a disability will absolutely not have a negative impact on a student's admissibility.

ADDITIONAL INFORMATION

UVM provides a multidisciplinary program for students with LD, emphasizing development of academic accommodations. Services include academic adjustments including note-taking, course substitution, course load reduction, extended test time, alternate test formats, and computer/spellchecker; auxiliary services including taped tests, readers, tutoring, writing skill development, proofing services, and reading skill development; academic advising and course selection; priority registration; learning strategies and study skills training; LD support group and counseling; faculty consultation and in-service training; and diagnostic screening and evaluation referral. Students with ADD with appropriate documentation may receive help with class schedules, study activities to fit individual learning styles, support services, or accommodations in test conditions, course loads, and/or program requirements because of the severity of the disability.

Support Services Contact Information

Learning Disability Program/Services: ACCESS
Director: Margaret Ottinger
  E-Mail: Access@zoo.uvm.edu
  Telephone: 802-656-7753
  Fax: 802-656-0739

LEARNING DISABILITY SERVICES

Requests for the following/services accommodations will be evaluated individually based on appropriate and current documentation.

Allowed in exams
  Calculator: Yes
  Dictionary: Yes
  Computer: Yes
  Spellchecker: Yes
Extended test time: Yes
Scribes: Yes
Proctors: Yes
Oral exams: Yes
Note-takers: Yes

Distraction reduced environment: Yes
Tape recording in class: Yes
Books on tape from RFBD: Yes
Taping of books not from RFBD: Yes
**Accommodations for students with
  ADD:** Yes
Reading machine: Yes
Other assistive technology: Yes
Priority registration: Yes

Added costs for services: Yes
LD specialists: Yes
Professional tutors: 1
Peer tutors: 1–30
Max. hours/wk. for services: 1–2
**How professors are notified of
  LD/ADD:** By both student and director

GENERAL ADMISSIONS INFORMATION

Director of Admissions: Donald M Honeman, Director Admissions & Financial Aid
Telephone: 802)656-879

ENTRANCE REQUIREMENTS

Academic units required: 4 English, 3 math, 2 science (1 science lab), 2 foreign language, 3 social studies. High school diploma is required and GED is accepted. ACT with Writing component required or SAT Reasoning test. TOEFL required of all international applicants, minimum paper TOEFL 550, minimum computer TOEFL 213.

Application deadline: 1/15
Notification: 3/31
Average GPA: NR

Average SAT Math: 578
Average SAT Verbal: 577
Average ACT: 24

Graduated top 10% of class: 23%
Graduated top 25% of class: 57%
Graduated top 50% of class: 93%

COLLEGE GRADUATION REQUIREMENTS

Course waivers allowed: No
Course substitutions allowed: No not usually
In what course: Depends on department/college approval.

ADDITIONAL INFORMATION

Environment: The university is located on 425-acres by Lake Champlain, 90 miles south of Montreal.

Student Body:
  Undergrad enrollment: 8,143
  Women: 55%
  Men: 45%
  Percent out-of-state: 63%

Cost Information
  In-state tuition: $9,088
  Out-of-state tuition: $22,728
  Room & board: $7,016
Housing Information
  University housing: Yes
  Percent living on campus: 52%

Greek System
  Fraternity: Yes
  Sorority: Yes
  Athletics: NCAA Division I

University of Vermont

VERMONT TECHNICAL COLLEGE

PO Box 500, Randolph Center, VT 05061
Phone: 802-728-1243 • Fax: 802-728-1390
E-mail: Admissions@vtc.edu • Web: www.vtc.edu
Support: CS • Institution type: 2-year public

LEARNING DISABILITY PROGRAM AND SERVICES

The goal of Services for Students with Disabilities is to ensure equal access to all VTC programs for all qualified students with disabilities; to help students develop the necessary skills to be effective at VTC and beyond; and to further students' understanding of how their disabilities affect them in school, work, and social settings.

LD/ADD ADMISSIONS INFORMATION

College entrance tests required: Yes
Interview required: Yes
Essay required: No
Documentation required for LD: WAIS–III; WJ
Documentation required for ADD: Yes
Submitted to: Services for with Disabilities or ACT
Special Ed. HS coursework accepted: Yes

Specific course requirements of all applicants: Yes
Separate application required for program services: No
# of LD applications submitted each year: NR
# of LD applications accepted yearly: NR
Total # of students receiving LD services: 70
Acceptance into program means acceptance into college: Student must be admitted and enrolled in the college first and then request services.

ADMISSIONS

There is no special admissions process for students with learning disabilities. In general, students have a GPA of 80 percent or higher. There is no cut-off score for the SAT or ACT. The program director can make recommendations to waive certain admission criteria if they discriminate against a student with a learning disability, and other evidence of a student's qualifications exist. General course requirements include algebra I & II, geometry, and physics or chemistry for engineering programs. Many students meet with the disabilities coordinator during the application process to discuss their needs. The Summer Bridge Program, an alternative admission plan, is a four-week math/physics and language arts program used as preparation for marginal freshmen who do not require the three-year program option. The three-year alternative admission option is for engineering students who need longer than two years to complete the program.

ADDITIONAL INFORMATION

The disabilities coordinator provides a variety of services, which include assessment of students' academic needs, coordination of tutoring to provide assistance with course material, and a disabilities forum for students to share experiences and academic strategies that they have learned with other students. Individual tutoring is provided in writing and study skills, such as time management, effective textbook reading, learning strategies, and stress management. Also available are academic and career counseling and coordination of accommodations. There is a Learning Center open to all students on campus.

Support Services Contact Information

Learning Disability Program/Services: Services for Students with Disabilities
Director: RGoodall@vtc.edu
  E-Mail: Access@zoo.uvm.edu
  Telephone: 802-728-1278
  Fax: 802-728-1714

LEARNING DISABILITY SERVICES

Requests for the following/services accommodations will be evaluated individually based on appropriate and current documentation.

Allowed in exams
  Calculator: Yes
  Dictionary: Yes
  Computer: Yes
  Spellchecker: Yes
Extended test time: Yes
Scribes: Yes
Proctors: Yes
Oral exams: Yes
Note-takers: Yes

Distraction reduced environment: Yes
Tape recording in class: Yes
Books on tape from RFBD: Yes
Taping of books not from RFBD: Yes
**Accommodations for students with
  ADD:** Yes
Reading machine: Yes
Other assistive technology: Yes
Priority registration: Yes
Added costs for services: No

LD specialists: Yes
Professional tutors: Yes
Peer tutors: Yes
Max. hours/wk. for services:
  Unlimited
**How professors are notified of
  LD/ADD:** By student

GENERAL ADMISSIONS INFORMATION

Director of Admissions: Rosemary Distel
Telephone: 802-728-1243

ENTRANCE REQUIREMENTS

Admissions are based on a total picture of applicants, including transcript, ACT or SAT, recommendations, and activities. Courses required vary depending on major.

Application deadline: NR
Notification: NR
Average GPA: NR

Average SAT Math: NR
Average SAT Verbal: NR
Average ACT: NR

Graduated top 10% of class: NR
Graduated top 25% of class: NR
Graduated top 50% of class: NR

COLLEGE GRADUATION REQUIREMENTS

Course waivers allowed: No
Course substitutions allowed: No
In what course: N/A

ADDITIONAL INFORMATION

Environment: The college is located on 54 acres in a rural area.

Student Body:
  Undergrad enrollment: 1000
  Women: 25%
  Men: 75%
  Percent out-of-state: 20%

Cost Information
  In-state tuition: $7,186
  Out-of-state tuition: $13,670
  Room & board: $6,454
Housing Information
  University housing: Yes
  Percent living on campus: 79%

Greek System
  Fraternity: No
  Sorority: No
Athletics: Intramural and intercollegiate

COLLEGE OF WILLIAM & MARY

PO Box 8795, Williamsburg, VA 23187-8795
Phone: 757-221-4223 • Fax: 757-221-1242
E-mail: admiss@wm.edu • Web: www.wm.edu
Support: CS • Institution type: 4-year public

LEARNING DISABILITY PROGRAM AND SERVICES

Disability Services at the College of William & Mary is available to all students with disabilities. Reasonable accommodations upon request are evaluated on an individual and flexible basis. Program goals include fostering independence, encouraging self-determination, emphasizing accommodations over limitations, and creating an accessible environment to ensure that individuals are viewed on the basis of ability and not disability. Individual accommodations needs are considered on a case-by-case basis in consultation with the student. The staff works with students and faculty to implement reasonable supports. Students anticipating the need for academic support must provide pertinent documentation in a timely manner in order to facilitate the provision of the service. Additional documentation may be requested and accommodation requests can be denied if they do not seem to be substantially supported. Documentation for LD/ADD must include a comprehensive report of psycho educational or neuropsychological assessment. The documentation must demonstrate the impact of the disability on major life activities and support all the recommended accommodations.

LD/ADD ADMISSIONS INFORMATION

College entrance tests required: Yes
Interview required: No
Essay required: No
Documentation required for LD: Psychoeducational evaluation
Documentation required for ADD: Yes
Submitted to: Disability Services

Specific course requirements of all applicants: Yes
Special Ed. HS coursework accepted: No
Separate application required for program services: No
# of LD applications submitted each year: NR
# of LD applications accepted yearly: NR
Total # of students receiving LD services: NR
Acceptance into program means acceptance into college: Student must be admitted and enrolled in the college first and then request services.

ADMISSIONS
Students go through a regular admissions process. Students must take either the SAT or ACT and 3 SAT Subject Tests are recommended. Results of non-standardized test administrations and documentation of disability may be submitted in support of any application, but are not essential for full consideration. Once admitted, students are fully mainstreamed and are expected to maintain the same academic standards as all other students.

ADDITIONAL INFORMATION
The staff of Disability Services works with the student and the faculty to implement reasonable accommodations such as peer note-takers, alternative test forms, textbook recording services, study skills training and peer support groups. Disability Related Program Access includes assistance with priority registration, liaison to the university, assistance with academic adjustments and curriculum alternatives, advocacy, in-service training for faculty and staff, and acquisition of adaptive equipment and/or software. The staff works closely with all college departments to identify appropriate options for accommodating students with disabilities.

Support Services Contact Information

Learning Disability Program/Services: Disability Services
Director: Lisa Bickley
 E-Mail: ljbick@wm.edu
 Telephone: 757-221-2510
 Fax: 757-221-2538

LEARNING DISABILITY SERVICES

Requests for the following/services accommodations will be evaluated individually based on appropriate and current documentation.

Allowed in exams
 Calculator: Y/N
 Dictionary: Y/N
 Computer: Yes
 Spellchecker: Y/N
Extended test time: Yes
Scribes: Yes
Proctors: Y/N
Oral exams: Y/N
Note-takers: Yes

Distraction reduced environment: Yes
Tape recording in class: Y/N
Books on tape from RFBD: Yes
Taping of books not from RFBD: Y/N
Accommodations for students with
 ADD: Yes
Reading machine: Yes
Other assistive technology: Yes
Priority registration: Yes

Added costs for services: No
LD specialists: Yes
Professional tutors: No
Peer tutors: Yes
Max. hours/wk. for services: As needed
How professors are notified of LD/ADD: By student

GENERAL ADMISSIONS INFORMATION

Director of Admissions: Karen Cottrell
Telephone: 757-221-4223

ENTRANCE REQUIREMENTS

Academic units recommended: 4 English, 4 math, 4 science (3 science lab), 4 foreign language, 4 social studies. High school diploma or equivalent is required. SAT Reasoning test and 2 SAT Subject tests or ACT with Writing required. TOEFL required of all international applicants, minimum paper TOEFL 600, minimum computer TOEFL 250.

Application deadline: 1/5
Notification: 4/1
Average GPA: 4.0

Average SAT Math: 666
Average SAT Verbal: 677
Average ACT: 30

Graduated top 10% of class: 85%
Graduated top 25% of class: 97%
Graduated top 50% of class: 100%

COLLEGE GRADUATION REQUIREMENTS

Course waivers allowed: No
Course substitutions allowed: Yes
In what course: Foreign language

ADDITIONAL INFORMATION

Environment: Located 50 miles from Richmond, VA.

Student Body:
 Undergrad enrollment: 5,686
 Women: 56%
 Men: 44%
 Percent out-of-state: 33%

Cost Information
 In-state tuition: $7,096
 Out-of-state tuition: $21,902
 Room & board: $6,492
Housing Information
 University housing: Yes
 Percent living on campus: 75%

Greek System
 Fraternity: Yes
 Sorority: Yes
Athletics: NCAA Division I

FERRUM COLLEGE

PO Box 1000, Ferrum, VA 24088
Phone: 540-365-4290 • Fax: 540-365-4366
E-mail: admissions@ferrum.edu • Web: www.ferrum.edu
Support: CS • Institution type: 4-year private

LEARNING DISABILITY PROGRAM AND SERVICES

Ferrum College does not have a program for students with learning disabilities, but does provide services to students with disabilities documentation. Ferrum also does not offer a comprehensive program or monitoring services. Students motivated to accept the assistance and academic accommodations offered frequently find Ferrum's services to be excellent.

LD/ADD ADMISSIONS INFORMATION

College entrance tests required: Yes
Interview required: No
Essay required: No
Documentation required for LD: Current psychoeducational evaluation and statement of eligibility or other comparable documentation
Documentation required for ADD: Yes
Submitted to: Academic Resources Center
Special Ed. HS coursework accepted: Yes

Specific course requirements of all applicants: Yes
Separate application required for program services: No
# of LD applications submitted each year: 15-25
# of LD applications accepted yearly: 15–20
Total # of students receiving LD services: 50
Acceptance into program means acceptance into college: Students must be admitted and enrolled at the college first and then may request services. Students denied admission may appeal the decision.

ADMISSIONS

Ferrum is proactive in terms of the admissions process for students with documentation of a disability. All students first go through the admissions process. If students are not admitted through the general admissions process, the committee can be requested to reconsider with the presentation of the documentation and a recommendation from the disability service provider. Those applicants who do not meet general admission criteria are encouraged to have an interview with the Office of Admissions. General admission criteria include 4 years English, 1 year math (3 recommended), 1 year science (3 recommended), 2 years foreign language, and 3 years social studies (recommended); SAT/ACT required (average ACT is 18 and average SAT is 1040); the average GPA is 2.6.

ADDITIONAL INFORMATION

The Academic Resources Center is a learning center available for students with learning disabilities as well as all other students on campus. Some of the tutoring is provided by volunteer professors. Skills classes are offered for credit in study skills. Ferrum College offers a summer program for pre-college freshmen with learning disabilities. Accommodations include, but are not limited to, extended time for testing, oral testing, test clarification, readers, quiet testing environment, and assistive technology.

Support Services Contact Information

Learning Disability Program/Services: Academic Resources Center/Office of Academic Disability Services
Director: Nancy S. Beach
  E-Mail: nbeach@ferrum.edu
  Telephone: 540-365-4262
  Fax: 540-365-4271

LEARNING DISABILITY SERVICES

Requests for the following/services accommodations will be evaluated individually based on appropriate and current documentation.

Allowed in exams
  Calculator: Yes
  Dictionary: Yes
  Computer: Yes
  Spellchecker: Yes
Extended test time: Yes
Scribes: Yes
Proctors: Yes
Oral exams: Yes
Note-takers: Yes

Distraction reduced environment: Yes
Tape recording in class: Yes
Books on tape from RFBD: Yes
Taping of books not from RFBD: Yes
**Accommodations for students with
  ADD:** Yes
Reading machine: Yes
Other assistive technology: Yes
Priority registration: No

Added costs for services: No
LD specialists: Yes
Professional tutors: Yes
Peer tutors: 10–20
Max. hours/wk. for services:
  Unlimited
**How professors are notified of
  LD/ADD:** By both student and director

GENERAL ADMISSIONS INFORMATION

Director of Admissions: Gilda Woods
Telephone: 540-365-4290

ENTRANCE REQUIREMENTS

Academic units recommended: 4 English, 3 math, 2 science (1 science lab), 2 foreign language, 3 social studies, 2 academic electives. High school diploma is required and GED is accepted. TOEFL required of all international applicants, minimum paper TOEFL 550, minimum computer TOEFL 213.

Application deadline: Rolling
Notification: Rolling
Average GPA: 2.64

Average SAT Math: 447
Average SAT Verbal: 452
Average ACT: NR

Graduated top 10% of class: 6%
Graduated top 25% of class: 19%
Graduated top 50% of class: 46%

COLLEGE GRADUATION REQUIREMENTS

Course waivers allowed: No
Course substitutions allowed: Yes
In what course: Course substitution is discussed on a case-by-case basis and determined by the Academic Standards Committee.

ADDITIONAL INFORMATION

Environment: The college is located in a rural area south of Roanoke.

Student Body:
  Undergrad enrollment: 951
  Women: 40%
  Men: 60%
  Percent out-of-state: 18%

Cost Information
  Tuition: $16,940
  Room & board: $5,600
Housing Information
  University housing: Yes
  Percent living on campus: 80%

Greek System
  Fraternity: No
  Sorority: No
Athletics: NCAA Division III

GEORGE MASON UNIVERSITY

4400 University Drive MSN 3A4, Fairfax, VA 22030-4444
Phone: 703-993-2400 • Fax: 703-993-2392
E-mail: admissions@gmu.edu • Web: www.gmu.edu
Support: S • Institution type: 4-year public

LEARNING DISABILITY PROGRAM AND SERVICES

The university does not maintain a specific program for students with LD. George Mason is, however, committed to providing appropriate services and accommodations to allow identified students with disabilities to access programs. The Disability Resource Center is responsible for assuring that students receive the services to which they are entitled. Students must provide documentation and complete a faculty contact sheet to receive documentation. DRC must confirm student requests for services.

LD/ADD ADMISSIONS INFORMATION

College entrance tests required: Yes
Interview required: No
Essay required: No
Documentation required for LD: Psychoeducational
evaluation
Documentation required for ADD: Yes
Submitted to: Disability Resource Center
Special Ed. HS coursework accepted: Yes

Specific course requirements of all applicants: Yes
Separate application required for program services: No
# of LD applications submitted each year: NR
# of LD applications accepted yearly: NR
Total # of students receiving LD services: 400
**Acceptance into program means acceptance into
college:** Student must be admitted and enrolled in the
university first and then request services.

ADMISSIONS

Students with LD must submit the general George Mason University undergraduate application and meet the same requirements as all other applicants. Students are encouraged to self-disclose and provide documentation of their disability. Letters of recommendation are helpful for explaining weaknesses or problematic areas. Students who have deficiencies in required courses may request a waiver of the requirement. These requests are considered on an individual basis. General admissions criteria include 4 years English, 3 years math (4 recommended), 1 year science (3 recommended), 3 years foreign language, 3 years social studies (4 recommended), and 3–4 year electives; ACT/SAT; and an interview is required.

ADDITIONAL INFORMATION

Students with LD may request extended testing time or alternative formats for exams, extended time for in-class writing assignments or short-term projects, note-takers, or use of a word processor for essay exams if documentation supports these modifications. Learning Services is a resource center for all students on campus. The center offers self-help skills classes in time management, organizational skills, and test-taking strategies. A Freshman Orientation class is offered for credit and some sections of this class are geared toward academic skills.

Support Services Contact Information

Learning Disability Program/Services: Disability Resource Center
Director: Deborah Wyne
   E-Mail: dwyne@gmu.edu
   Telephone: 703-993-2474
   Fax: 703-993-4306

LEARNING DISABILITY SERVICES

Requests for the following/services accommodations will be evaluated individually based on appropriate and current documentation.

Allowed in exams
   Calculator: Yes
   Dictionary: Yes
   Computer: Yes
   Spellchecker: Yes
Extended test time: Yes
Scribes: Yes
Proctors: Yes
Oral exams: Yes
Note-takers: Yes

Distraction reduced environment: Yes
Tape recording in class: Yes
Books on tape from RFBD: Yes
Taping of books not from RFBD: Yes
Accommodations for students with ADD: Yes
Reading machine: Yes
Other assistive technology: Yes
Priority registration: Yes

Added costs for services: Yes
LD specialists: No
Professional tutors: No
Peer tutors: Yes
Max. hours/wk. for services: Unlimited
How professors are notified of LD/ADD: By student

GENERAL ADMISSIONS INFORMATION

Director of Admissions: Andrew Flagel
Telephone: 703-993-2400

ENTRANCE REQUIREMENTS

Academic units required: 4 English, 3 math, 3 science (3 science lab), 2 foreign language, 3 social studies, 3 academic electives. **Academic units recommended:** 4 English, 4 math, 4 science (4 science lab), 3 foreign language, 4 social studies, 5 academic electives, High school diploma is required and GED is accepted. TOEFL required of all international applicants, minimum paper TOEFL 570, minimum computer TOEFL 230.

Application deadline: 1/15
Notification: 4/1
Average GPA: 3.32

Average SAT Math: 559
Average SAT Verbal: 549
Average ACT: NR

Graduated top 10% of class: 16%
Graduated top 25% of class: 44%
Graduated top 50% of class: 93%

COLLEGE GRADUATION REQUIREMENTS

Course waivers allowed: No
Course substitutions allowed: Yes
In what course: Foreign language and, in some instances, analytical reasoning with specific documentation provided.

ADDITIONAL INFORMATION

Environment: The university is located on 682 acres in a suburban area 18 miles southwest of Washington, DC.

Student Body:
   Undergrad enrollment: 16,579
   Women: 55%
   Men: 45%
   Percent out-of-state: 10%

Cost Information
   In-state tuition: $5,112
   Out-of-state tuition: $14,952
   Room & board: $5,600
Housing Information
   University housing: Yes
   Percent living on campus: 21%

Greek System
   Fraternity: Yes
   Sorority: Yes
Athletics: NCAA Division I

HAMPTON UNIVERSITY

Office of Admissions, Hampton University, Hampton, VA 23668
Phone: 757-727-5328 • Fax: 757-727-5095
E-mail: admit@hamptonu.edu • Web: www.hamptonu.edu
Support: S • Institution type: 4-year private

LEARNING DISABILITY PROGRAM AND SERVICES

Hampton University is committed to assisting students with disabilities. They seek to help students achieve their academic potential within the academically competitive curriculum by providing a variety of accommodations. In the classroom students may use a tape recorder and calculator, have a note-taker, selective seating, and ask for extended time for assignments. In an examination they may have extended time, an alternate test form, a reader/scribe, an oral proctor, and a distraction-free environment. For services not available through Disability Services, referrals to other sources are made.

LD/ADD ADMISSIONS INFORMATION

College entrance tests required: Yes
Interview required: No
Essay required: No
Documentation required for LD: Psychoeducational
  evaluation. Documentation can be no older than three years.
Documentation required for ADD: Yes
Submitted to: Testing Services/504 Compliance
Special Ed. HS coursework accepted: Yes

Specific course requirements of all applicants: Yes
Separate application required for program services: No
# of LD applications submitted each year: NR
# of LD applications accepted yearly: NR
Total # of students receiving LD services: 30–40
**Acceptance into program means acceptance into
  college:** Student must be admitted and enrolled in the
  university first and then request services.

ADMISSIONS

There is no special admission process for students with learning disabilities. All students are expected to meet the same admission criteria, which include 4 years English, 3 years math, 2 years science, 2 years history, and 6 electives; ACT/SAT with a minimum SAT of 800; rank in the top 50 percent of the class; and a minimum GPA of 2.0. Each applicant should present satisfactory credentials as to ability, character, and health. Some students may be admitted through the summer Bridge Program if SAT scores are below 800 or the students are deficient in course requirements. These students take Placement Exams to determine the need for English, writing, reading, or science courses. Twenty percent of the class is admitted through Bridge.

ADDITIONAL INFORMATION

Accommodations in the classroom could include tape recorder or calculators, extended time for assignments, and note-takers. Accommodations in an examination could include: distraction-free environment, extended time, alternate test formats, reader/scribe, printed copy of oral instructions, and oral proctor. A student who would like to receive disability services must contact the Section 504 compliance officer and provide documentation of the disability not older than three years. This compliance officer is responsible for qualifying students with disabilities for reasonable academic accommodations within the university. The Pre-College Program is open to all students. Freshmen on probation may take two non-repeating courses in summer school. If they earn a C or better they may return for sophomore year.

Support Services Contact Information

Learning Disability Program/Services: Testing Services/504 Compliance
Director: Janice Halimah Rashada
  E-Mail: janice.rashada@hamptonu.edu
  Telephone: 757-727-5493
  Fax: 757-727-5998

LEARNING DISABILITY SERVICES

Requests for the following/services accommodations will be evaluated individually based on appropriate and current documentation.

Allowed in exams
  Calculator: Yes
  Dictionary: Yes
  Computer: Yes
  Spellchecker: Yes
Extended test time: Yes
Scribes: Yes
Proctors: Yes
Oral exams: Yes
Note-takers: Yes

Distraction reduced environment: Yes
Tape recording in class: Yes
Books on tape from RFBD: Yes
Taping of books not from RFBD: No
**Accommodations for students with
  ADD:** Yes
Reading machine: No
Other assistive technology: No
Priority registration: Yes

Added costs for services: No
LD specialists: No
Professional tutors: No
Peer tutors: Yes
Max. hours/wk. for services:
  Unlimited
**How professors are notified of
  LD/ADD:** By student

GENERAL ADMISSIONS INFORMATION

Director of Admissions: Angela Boyd
Telephone: 757-727-5328

ENTRANCE REQUIREMENTS
Academic units required: 4 English, 3 math, 2 science (2 science lab), 2 social studies, 6 academic electives.
Academic units recommended: 2 foreign language. High school diploma is required and GED is accepted. TOEFL required of all international applicants, minimum paper TOEFL 550, minimum computer TOEFL 213.

Application deadline: Rolling
Notification: Rolling
Average GPA: 3.00

Average SAT Math: 516
Average SAT Verbal: 526
Average ACT: 20

Graduated top 10% of class: 20%
Graduated top 25% of class: 45%
Graduated top 50% of class: 90%

COLLEGE GRADUATION REQUIREMENTS

Course waivers allowed: No
Course substitutions allowed: Yes
In what course: Foreign language; case by case basis

ADDITIONAL INFORMATION

Environment: The university is located on 204 acres 15 miles west of Norfolk.

Student Body:
  Undergrad enrollment: 5,200
  Women: 64%
  Men: 36%
  Percent out-of-state: 70%

Cost Information
  Tuition: $12,116
  Room & board: $6,424
Housing Information
  University housing: Yes
  Percent living on campus: 59%

Greek System
  Fraternity: Yes
  Sorority: Yes
Athletics: NCAA Division I

Hampton University

JAMES MADISON UNIVERSITY

Sonner Hall, MSC 0101, Harrisonburg, VA 22807
Phone: 540-568-5681 • Fax: 540-568-3332
E-mail: admissions@jmu.edu • Web: www.jmu.edu
Support: S • Institution type: 4-year public

LEARNING DISABILITY PROGRAM AND SERVICES

The Office of Disability Service (ODS) does not have a formal LD program, but students with learning disabilities are assisted individually and are eligible for appropriate accommodations. The mission of the ODS is to ensure that all students with disabilities can freely and actively participate in all facets of university life; to provide and coordinate support services and programs that enable students with disabilities to maximize their educational potential; and to assist students in the developmental process of transition to higher education, independence, and effective self-advocacy. The director functions as a liaison between students and the university community, and provides support in obtaining accommodations for equalizing academic success in the classroom. If the applicant is eligible for reevaluation through the school system, it is strongly advised to take advantage of the service before leaving high school. Current documentation with recommendations for post-secondary accommodations are crucial for providing appropriate services in college. Course substitution requests are dealt with on an individual basis. They may be appropriate for students for whom a particular subject has been a continuously documented obstacle to academic progress. Students should notify ODS upon enrollment if they want to seek a substitution for a course requirement. Substitutions are not guaranteed.

LD/ADD ADMISSIONS INFORMATION

College entrance tests required: Yes
Interview required: No
Essay required: No
Documentation required for LD: Current comprehensive psychoeducation evaluation
Documentation required for ADD: Yes
Submitted to: Office of Disability Services
Special Ed. HS coursework accepted: Yes

Specific course requirements of all applicants: Yes
Separate application required for program services: No
# of LD applications submitted each year: NR
# of LD applications accepted yearly: 90
Total # of students receiving LD services: NR
Acceptance into program means acceptance into college: Student must be admitted and enrolled in the university first and then request services.

ADMISSIONS

The admissions team at JMU is highly sensitive and knowledgeable concerning students with learning disabilities and the admissions process. Admission decisions are made without regard to disabilities. All prospective students are expected to present academic credentials at or above the minimum standards for admission as established by the admission committee. After admission to JMU, documentation will be forwarded to ODS. Current recommendations for post-secondary accommodations are crucial for providing appropriate services in college. There are no specific courses required for admission into James Madison, however students are expected to complete a solid college prep curriculum. The mid 50 percent range for the ACT is 24–28 and SAT 1110–1250 and GPA of 3.31–3.75. SAT Subject tests required in foreign language where applicable. The university uses class rank as one of the criteria reviewed, but does not use GPA.

ADDITIONAL INFORMATION

Some of the commonly used services are priority registration; the Support Lab, which houses equipment; academic advisors and academic services; and course scheduling information. Classroom accommodations include extended time for tests and written assignments, testing in a distraction-free environment, modification of exam format, volunteer note-takers, use of tape recorder in class, oral testing, scribes, use of computers for tests, and individual assistance as needed. Other university services include Reading and Writing Lab, Counseling and Student Development Center, and academic advising. Basic workshops for no credit are offered in study skills and self-advocacy. Services and accommodations are available for undergraduate and graduate students.

Support Services Contact Information

Learning Disability Program/Services: Office of Disability Services (ODS)
Director: Louis Hedrick
  E-Mail: hedriclj@jmu.edu
  Telephone: 540-568-6705
  Fax: 540-568-7099

LEARNING DISABILITY SERVICES

Requests for the following/services accommodations will be evaluated individually based on appropriate and current documentation.

Allowed in exams
  Calculator: Yes
  Dictionary: Yes
  Computer: Yes
  Spellchecker: Yes
Extended test time: Yes
Scribes: Yes
Proctors: Yes
Oral exams: Yes
Note-takers: Yes

Distraction reduced environment: Yes
Tape recording in class: Yes
Books on tape from RFBD: Yes
Taping of books not from RFBD: Yes
Accommodations for students with
  ADD: Yes
Reading machine: Yes
Other assistive technology: Yes
Priority registration: Yes

Added costs for services: No
LD specialists: No
Professional tutors: No
Peer tutors: No
Max. hours/wk. for services:
  Unlimited
How professors are notified of
  LD/ADD: By both student and director

GENERAL ADMISSIONS INFORMATION

Director of Admissions: Michael D. Walsh
Telephone: 540-568-5681

ENTRANCE REQUIREMENTS

Academic units required: 4 English, 4 math, 3 science (3 science lab), 3 foreign language, 1 social studies, 3 history. **Academic units recommended:** 4 science. High school diploma is required and GED is accepted. ACT with or without Writing component accepted. TOEFL required of all international applicants, minimum paper TOEFL 570, minimum computer TOEFL 230.

Application deadline: 1/15
Notification: 4/1
Average GPA: 3.68

Average SAT Math: 583
Average SAT Verbal: 579
Average ACT: NR

Graduated top 10% of class: 31%
Graduated top 25% of class: 79%
Graduated top 50% of class: 99%

COLLEGE GRADUATION REQUIREMENTS

Course waivers allowed: Yes
Course substitutions allowed: Yes
In what course: Foreign language

ADDITIONAL INFORMATION

Environment: The university is located in the Shenandoah Valley surrounded by the Blue Ridge Mountains and the Alleghenies, 120 miles from Washington, DC.

Student Body:
  Undergrad enrollment: 14,677
  Women: 60%
  Men: 40%
  Percent out-of-state: 29%

Cost Information
  In-state tuition: $5,886
  Out-of-state tuition: $15,322
  Room & board: $6,124
Housing Information
  University housing: Yes

  Percent living on campus: 39%
Greek System
  Fraternity: Yes
  Sorority: Yes
Athletics: NCAA Division I

LIBERTY UNIVERSITY

1971 University Boulevard, Lynchburg, VA 24502
Phone: 434-582-5905 • Fax: 800-542-2311
E-mail: admissions@liberty.edu • Web: www.liberty.edu
Support: CS • Institution type: 4-year private

LEARNING DISABILITY PROGRAM AND SERVICES

The primary purpose of the Bruckner Learning Center is to offer reading and study skills assistance to all students. The center provides individualized peer tutoring regularly or on a drop-in basis for English or math. There are three one-semester hour courses provided for students wishing to develop reading and study skills: College Study Strategies, College Reading Improvement, and Individualized Laboratory in Reading and Study Strategies. Students with a disability who self-identify may be eligible for accommodations such as priority class registration, academic advising from trained faculty, deaf interpreters, and confidential requests for classroom accommodations (additional time on tests, note-taking help).

LD/ADD ADMISSIONS INFORMATION

College entrance tests required: Yes
Interview required: No
Essay required: No
Documentation required for LD: Their latest IEP and/or psychological testing profile or other written information that describes the learning disability
Documentation required for ADD: Diagnosis from a qualified professional
Submitted to: Both Admissions and Office of Disability Academic Support
Special Ed. HS coursework accepted: No

Specific course requirements of all applicants: Yes
Separate application required for program services: No
# of LD applications submitted each year: NR
# of LD applications accepted yearly: NR
Total # of students receiving LD services: 60
Acceptance into program means acceptance into college: Student must be admitted and enrolled in the university first and then request services.

ADMISSIONS

All applicants must submit an official transcript from an accredited high school and/or college, an official copy of a state high school equivalency diploma, or an official copy of the GED test results. The minimum acceptable unweighted GPA is 2.0. All applicants must submit ACT or SAT prior to admission. The minimum acceptable scores are SAT 800 or ACT 17. Courses required for admission include 4 years of English, 2 or 3 years of college prep mathematics, 2 years of laboratory science, 2 years of social science, and at least 4 units of elective credits in subjects such as art, music, or drama. Applicants who fail to meet the minimum required GPA will be evaluated using other indicators of collegiate ability and may be admitted on academic warning.

ADDITIONAL INFORMATION

If a student's entrance test scores indicate a deficiency in English or math, then the student will enroll in a basic composition class or a fundamentals of math class. With the student's permission, instructors are provided with a written communication providing information about the student's specific disability and suggestions of appropriate accommodations. Students with a specific learning disability can be assigned to a faculty advisor who has had training in LD. This person advises students concerning academic loads and acts as a liaison between instructors and students regarding classroom accommodations. The Bruckner Learning Center provides individualized peer tutoring in most subjects on a weekly or drop-in basis.

Support Services Contact Information

Learning Disability Program/Services: Office of Disability Academic Support
Director: Mr. Denny McHaney
  E-Mail: wdmchane@liberty.edu
  Telephone: 434-582-2159
  Fax: 434-582-2468

LEARNING DISABILITY SERVICES

Requests for the following/services accommodations will be evaluated individually based on appropriate and current documentation.

Allowed in exams
  Calculator: No
  Dictionary: No
  Computer: No
  Spellchecker: Yes
Extended test time: Yes
Scribes: Yes
Proctors: Yes
Oral exams: Yes
Note-takers: Yes

Distraction reduced environment: Yes
Tape recording in class: Yes
Books on tape from RFBD: No
Taping of books not from RFBD: No
**Accommodations for students with
  ADD:** Yes
Reading machine: No
Other assistive technology: No
Priority registration: Yes

Added costs for services: No
LD specialists: Yes
Professional tutors: No
Peer tutors: 30
Max. hours/wk. for services: As
  needed
**How professors are notified of
  LD/ADD:** By Director

GENERAL ADMISSIONS INFORMATION

Director of Admissions: Richard Plyter
Telephone: 434-592-3072

ENTRANCE REQUIREMENTS

Academic units recommended: 4 English, 3 math, 2 science (2 science lab), 2 foreign language, 2 social studies, 2 academic electives. High school diploma is required and GED is accepted. ACT with or without Writing component accepted. TOEFL required of all international applicants, minimum paper TOEFL 500, minimum computer TOEFL 173.

Application deadline: NR
Notification: Continual notification
Average GPA: 3.19

Average SAT Math: 500
Average SAT Verbal: 514
Average ACT: 22

Graduated top 10% of class: 13%
Graduated top 25% of class: 33%
Graduated top 50% of class: 66%

COLLEGE GRADUATION REQUIREMENTS

Course waivers allowed: No
Course substitutions allowed: No
In what course: N/A

ADDITIONAL INFORMATION

Environment: The 5,200-acre university is located in a suburban area 45 miles east of Roanoke.

Student Body:
  Undergrad enrollment: 6,380
  Women: 51%
  Men: 49%
  Percent out-of-state: 67%

Cost Information
  Tuition: $13,700
  Room & board: $5,400
Housing Information
  University housing: Yes
  Percent living on campus: 43%

Greek System
  Fraternity: No
  Sorority: No
Athletics: NCAA Division I

OLD DOMINION UNIVERSITY

108 Rollins Hall, 5115 Hampton Boulevard, Norfolk, VA 23529-0050
Phone: 757-683-3685 • Fax: 757-683-3255
E-mail: admit@odu.edu • Web: www.odu.edu
Support: CS • Institution type: 4-year public

LEARNING DISABILITY PROGRAM AND SERVICES

Student Support Services is a TRIO Program funded by the U.S. Department of Education providing academic support. The program is oriented to meet the needs of students according to their development level. Typically, students are newly diagnosed or recently transitioning to campus. The program assists students in achieving and maintaining the academic performance level required for satisfactory academic standing at the university, thereby increasing their chances of graduating. Services include on-site orientation programs, taped materials, and tutorial services by peers, oral testing, untimed testing, and individual counseling. The students are respected as the primary source of knowledge of their needs.

LD/ADD ADMISSIONS INFORMATION

College entrance tests required: Yes
Interview required: No
Essay required: No
Documentation required for LD: WAIS–III; WISC–R; WJ: within 3 years
Documentation required for ADD: Yes
Submitted to: Disability Services
Special Ed. HS coursework accepted: Yes

Specific course requirements of all applicants: Yes
Separate application required for program services: Yes
# of LD applications submitted each year: NR
# of LD applications accepted yearly: NR
Total # of students receiving LD services: 250
Acceptance into program means acceptance into college: Student must be admitted and enrolled in the university first and then request services.

ADMISSIONS
There is no special admissions process for students with learning disabilities. Students are encouraged to include a cover letter identifying their learning disabilities and explaining weaknesses that may have affected their academic records. If students self-identify during the admissions process, the information may be used to support their application, but may not be used to their detriment. Clear and specific evidence and identification of a learning disability must be stated and the report must be conducted and written by a qualified professional. Students not meeting regular admission standards may be admitted through the Academic Opportunity Program. This is for 300 students with low test scores but high GPA. Others may be admitted through a Summer Transition Program or individual admission for non-traditional students. General admission criteria include 4 years English, 3 years math, 3 years science, 2 years foreign language, 3 years social studies, and 3 years history; ACT/SAT (with a minimum SAT of 850 and at least a 400 in the verbal and the math sections); rank in the top half of the class; and a minimum GPA of 2.0.

ADDITIONAL INFORMATION
Counseling and advising; study skills instruction; reading, writing, and math instruction; and tutorial assistance are available. Program staff design support services that focus on students' learning styles and special needs. There is a special section of Spanish for students with learning disabilities to meet the foreign language requirements as well as developmental math, reading, spelling, and writing.

Support Services Contact Information

Learning Disability Program/Services: Disability Services
Director: Sheryn Milton, MEd
  E-Mail: disabilityservices@odu.edu
  Telephone: 757-683-4655
  Fax: 757-683-5356
Contact Person: Abby Furek
  E-Mail: disabilityservices@odu.edu
  Telephone: 757-683-4655
  Fax: 757-683-5356

LEARNING DISABILITY SERVICES

Requests for the following/services accommodations will be evaluated individually based on appropriate and current documentation.

Allowed in exams
  Calculator: Yes
  Dictionary: Yes
  Computer: Yes
  Spellchecker: Yes
Extended test time: Yes
Scribes: Yes
Proctors: Yes
Oral exams: Yes
Note-takers: Yes

Distraction reduced environment: Yes
Tape recording in class: Yes
Books on tape from RFBD: Yes
Taping of books not from RFBD: Yes
Accommodations for students with ADD: Yes
Reading machine: Yes
Other assistive technology: Yes
Priority registration: Yes
Added costs for services: Yes

LD specialists: Yes
Professional tutors: Yes
Peer tutors: Yes
Max. hours/wk. for services: Varies
How professors are notified of LD/ADD: By both student and director

GENERAL ADMISSIONS INFORMATION

Director of Admissions: Alice McAdory
Telephone: 757-683-3648

ENTRANCE REQUIREMENTS

Academic units required: 4 English, 3 math, 3 science (2 science lab), 3 foreign language, 3 history, 1 academic elective. **Academic units recommended:** 3 social studies. High school diploma is required and GED is accepted. ACT with Writing component required or SAT. TOEFL required of all international applicants, minimum paper TOEFL 550, minimum computer TOEFL 213.

Application deadline: 3/15
Notification: Rolling
Average GPA: 3.30

Average SAT Math: 528
Average SAT Verbal: 529
Average ACT: 21

Graduated top 10% of class: 15%
Graduated top 25% of class: 47%
Graduated top 50% of class: 90%

COLLEGE GRADUATION REQUIREMENTS

Course waivers allowed: No
Course substitutions allowed: Yes
In what course: All students must complete three credits in math. A special one-year Spanish course is available for students registered with DS.

ADDITIONAL INFORMATION

Environment: The university is located on 46 acres in a suburban area of Norfolk.

Student Body:
  Undergrad enrollment: 13,679
  Women: 58%
  Men: 42%
  Percent out-of-state: 7%

Cost Information
  In-state tuition: $5,792
  Out-of-state tuition: $16,224
  Room & board: $5,802
Housing Information
  University housing: Yes
  Percent living on campus: 24%

Greek System
  Fraternity: Yes
  Sorority: Yes
Athletics: NCAA Division I

UNIVERSITY OF VIRGINIA

Office of Admission, PO Box 400160, Charlottesville, VA 22906
Phone: 434-982-3200 • Fax: 434-924-3587
E-mail: undergradadmission@virginia.edu • Web: www.virginia.edu
Support: CS • Institution type: 4-year public

LEARNING DISABILITY PROGRAM AND SERVICES

The University of Virginia is committed to providing equal access to educational and social opportunities for all disabled students. The Learning Needs and Evaluation Center (LNEC) is housed within the university's Center for Counseling and Psychological Services, and serves as the coordinating agency for services to all students with disabilities. The LNEC assists students with disabilities to become independent self-advocates, who are able to demonstrate their abilities both in the classroom and as members of the university community. The center provides a number of services, including review of documentation supporting the disability, determination of appropriate academic accommodations, academic support services for students requiring assistance, and serves as a liaison with faculty and administrators. Information can be shared, with the student's permission, with university personnel who have an educational need to know. Once a learning disability is documented, the center assigns appropriate and reasonable accommodations and serves as a liaison with faculty and administrators. The center's primary purpose is to support the academic well-being of students with disabilities.

LD/ADD ADMISSIONS INFORMATION

College entrance tests required: Yes
Interview required: No
Essay required: Yes
Documentation required for LD: Psychoeducational evaluation
Documentation required for ADD: Yes
Submitted to: LNEC
Special Ed. HS coursework accepted: Yes

Specific course requirements of all applicants: Yes
Separate application required for program services: No
# of LD applications submitted each year: NR
# of LD applications accepted yearly: NR
Total # of students receiving LD services: 200
Acceptance into program means acceptance into college: Student must be admitted and enrolled in the university first and then request services.

ADMISSIONS
The students with learning disabilities go through the same admissions procedure as all incoming applicants. After admission to the university, students must contact the LNEC in order to receive services. Students with learning disabilities admitted to the university have qualified for admission because of their ability. No criteria for admission are waived because of a disability. All applicants to UVA have outstanding grades, high rank in their high school class, excellent performance in Advanced Placement and Honor courses, superior performance on ACT/SAT and SAT Subject Test, extracurricular success, special talents, and interests and goals. Letters of recommendation are required.

ADDITIONAL INFORMATION
Following acceptance of an offer of admission to the university, students with an LD or ADD are advised to contact the LNEC in order to identify their need for services. All students seeking accommodations while at the university must provide acceptable documentation of their disability, including but not limited to a neuropsychological or psychoeducational evaluation report, completed by a licensed clinical psychologist or clinical neuropsychologist or clinical neuropsychologist that is current within three years of matriculation. The Learning Needs and Evaluation Center addresses such things as personal social skills, alternative speaking, reading, writing methods, and referral for tutors. Staff also consult with students about academic difficulties. Classes are offered in study skills and time management. Services and accommodations are available for undergraduate and graduate students.

Support Services Contact Information

Learning Disability Program/Services: Learning Needs and Evaluation Center (LNEC)
Director: Allison Anderson, PhD
  E-Mail: aea3f@virginia.edu
  Telephone: 434-243-5181
  Fax: 434-243-5188
Contact Person: Valerie Schoolcraft
  E-Mail: vs6r@virginia.edu
  Telephone: 434-243-5181
  Fax: 434-243-5188

LEARNING DISABILITY SERVICES

Requests for the following/services accommodations will be evaluated individually based on appropriate and current documentation.

Allowed in exams
  Calculator: Yes
  Dictionary: Yes
  Computer: Yes
  Spellchecker: Yes
Extended test time: Yes
Scribes: Yes
Proctors: Yes
Oral exams: Yes
Note-takers: Yes

Distraction reduced environment: Yes
Tape recording in class: Yes
Books on tape from RFBD: Yes
Taping of books not from RFBD: Yes
**Accommodations for students with
  ADD:** Yes
Reading machine: Yes
Other assistive technology: Yes
Priority registration: Yes

Added costs for services: Yes
LD specialists: Yes
Professional tutors: Yes
Peer tutors: Yes
Max. hours/wk. for services:
  Individualized
**How professors are notified of
  LD/ADD:** By student

GENERAL ADMISSIONS INFORMATION

Director of Admissions: John A. Blackburn
Telephone: 434-982-3200

ENTRANCE REQUIREMENTS

Academic units required: 4 English, 4 math 2 science (2 science lab), 2 foreign language, 1 social studies, 5 additional college preparatory courses (in advanced math, literature, foreign language and social science) are also required. **Academic units recommended:** 5 math, 4 science, 5 foreign language, 4 social studies. High school diploma is required and GED is accepted. TOEFL required of all international applicants, minimum paper TOEFL 600, minimum computer TOEFL 250.

Application deadline: 1/2
Notification: 4/1
Average GPA: 4.01

Average SAT Math: 671
Average SAT Verbal: 659
Average ACT: 28

Graduated top 10% of class: 84%
Graduated top 25% of class: 96%
Graduated top 50% of class: 100%

COLLEGE GRADUATION REQUIREMENTS

Course waivers allowed: Yes
Course substitutions allowed: Yes
In what course: Waivers and substitutions are allowed in foreign language.

ADDITIONAL INFORMATION

Environment: The 2,440-acre campus is located in a small city 70 miles northwest of Richmond.

Student Body:
  Undergrad enrollment: 13,231
  Women: 54%
  Men: 46%
  Percent out-of-state: 28%

Cost Information
  In-state tuition: $6,984
  Out-of-state tuition: $23,084
  Room & board: $6,600
Housing Information
  University housing: Yes
  Percent living on campus: 46%

Greek System
  Fraternity: Yes
  Sorority: Yes
Athletics: NCAA Division I

VIRGINIA INTERMONT COLLEGE

1013 Moore Street, Campus Box D-460, Bristol, VA 24201-4298
Phone: 276-466-7856 • Fax: 276-466-7855
E-mail: viadmit@vic.edu • Web: www.vic.edu
Support: CS • Institution type: 4-year private

LEARNING DISABILITY PROGRAM AND SERVICES

Student Support Services provides free supportive services to students who participate in the program. There are extensive services offered to those with LD. The objective of the services is to help students stay in school and graduate. The department consists of a director/counselor, school psychologist/LD specialist, tutor coordinator, and an administrative assistant. Students work voluntarily with the staff as individuals or as a team to develop individual plans of support. Staff members act as advocates for students with faculty and administration and provide general faculty awareness and understanding of overall student needs without disclosure of confidentiality. Virginia Intermont staff and faculty have a commitment to the significance of the individual and to the value of personalizing education. The college provides quality education with extensive support services and accommodations, rather than altering admissions criteria or course requirements. Once admitted, students are encouraged to submit documentation of any special needs. This is usually in the form of psychoeducational test data and IEP from high school. All accommodations are provided at the request of students with documentation.

LD/ADD ADMISSIONS INFORMATION

College entrance tests required: Yes
Interview required: No
Essay required: No
Documentation required for LD: Psychoeducational
assessment within past three years
Documentation required for ADD: Yes
Submitted to: Support Services
Special Ed. HS coursework accepted: No

Specific course requirements of all applicants: Yes
Separate application required for program services: No
# of LD applications submitted each year: NR
# of LD applications accepted yearly: NR
Total # of students receiving LD services: 30–40
Acceptance into program means acceptance into
college: Student must be admitted and enrolled in the
university first and then request services.

ADMISSIONS

There is no special admissions procedure for the student with a learning disability. Documentation related to a learning disability may be submitted to the Office of Admissions with the general application or may be submitted separately to the Office of Student Support Services. Testing done by a high school psychologist is acceptable. General admission criteria include average ACT of 21 or SAT 885; minimum 2.0 GPA is required; and a minimum of 15 units including 4 years English, 2 years math, 1 year lab science, 2 years social science, and 6 years electives. Virginia Intermont is more concerned with the student's quality of preparation than with the precise numerical distribution of requirements. A conditional admit may be offered if the high school GPA or SAT scores are below requirements. Students not having the proper high school preparation or not meeting the normal admissions criteria may be required, if admitted, to take developmental courses as needed in math, English, reading, and/or study strategies. These courses would not count toward graduation, and the student would be limited to 14 hours in the first semester.

ADDITIONAL INFORMATION

Students with LD will be offered appropriate accommodations recommended by the learning specialist based on the documentation. Accommodations and/or services available to eligible students include individual personal and academic counseling, Freshman Placement Test accommodations, scribes, computer tests, extended time or tests, taped tests, peer and staff tutoring emphasizing unique techniques as needed, support groups, academic advising, diagnostic testing, liaison with faculty, tape recording of classes, assistance with course selection and registration, and optional reduced course load. A few accommodations require appointments, though generally there is an open door policy. Education 100 (one credit) taught by student Support Services staff, is designed for students interested in improving academic skills. Topics covered in this course are individual learning styles, time-study management, note-taking, textbook reading, memory strategies, test-taking strategies, and test anxiety reduction.

Support Services Contact Information

Learning Disability Program/Services: Student Support Services
Director: Talmage Dobbins
  E-Mail: tdobbins@vic.edu
  Telephone: 276-466-7905
  Fax: 276-645-6493
Contact Person: Barbara Holbrook
  E-Mail: barbaraholbrook@vic.edu
  Telephone: 276-466-7905
  Fax: 276-645-6493

LEARNING DISABILITY SERVICES

Requests for the following/services accommodations will be evaluated individually based on appropriate and current documentation.

Allowed in exams
  Calculator: Yes
  Dictionary: Yes
  Computer: Yes
  Spellchecker: Yes
Extended test time: Yes
Scribes: Yes
Proctors: Yes
Oral exams: Yes
Note-takers: Yes

Distraction reduced environment: Yes
Tape recording in class: Yes
Books on tape from RFBD: Yes
Taping of books not from RFBD: Yes
Accommodations for students with ADD: Yes
Reading machine: Yes
Other assistive technology: Yes
Priority registration: No

Added costs for services: No
LD specialists: Yes
Professional tutors: No
Peer tutors: 30
Max. hours/wk. for services: Unlimited
How professors are notified of LD/ADD: By both student and director

GENERAL ADMISSIONS INFORMATION

Director of Admissions: Craig Wesley
Telephone: 276-466-7857

ENTRANCE REQUIREMENTS
Academic units required: 4 English, 2 math, 1 science (1 science lab), 2 social studies, 6 academic electives. High school diploma is required and GED is accepted. ACT with or without Writing component accepted. TOEFL required of all international applicants, minimum paper TOEFL 500, minimum computer TOEFL 200.

Application deadline: Rolling
Notification: Rolling
Average GPA: 3.13

Average SAT Math: 455
Average SAT Verbal: 490
Average ACT: 20

Graduated top 10% of class: 14%
Graduated top 25% of class: 32%
Graduated top 50% of class: 69%

COLLEGE GRADUATION REQUIREMENTS

Course waivers allowed: No
Course substitutions allowed: Yes
In what course: Decided by committee

ADDITIONAL INFORMATION

Environment: The college is located on a 16-acre campus in the Blue Ridge Mountains.

Student Body:
  Undergrad enrollment: 1,114
  Women: 71%
  Men: 29%
  Percent out-of-state: 40%

Cost Information
  Tuition: $14,500
  Room & board: $5,650
Housing Information
  University housing: Yes
  Percent living on campus: 56%

Greek System
  Fraternity: No
  Sorority: No
Athletics: NAIA

EASTERN WASHINGTON UNIVERSITY

526 Fifth Street, Cheney, WA 99004
Phone: 509-359-2397 • Fax: 509-359-6692
E-mail: admissions@mail.ewu.edu • Web: www.ewu.edu
Support: S • Institution type: 4-year public

LEARNING DISABILITY PROGRAM AND SERVICES

Although the university does not offer a specialized curriculum, personnel work with students to modify programs to meet individual needs. Disability Support Services (DSS) is dedicated to the coordination of appropriate and reasonable accommodations for students with disabilities. These accommodations are based on individual needs so that each student may receive an equal opportunity to learn to participate in campus life, to grow emotionally and socially, and to successfully complete a program of study that will enable him or her to be self-supporting and remain as independent as possible. This is facilitated through support services, information sharing, advisement, and referral when requested. Students who wish services and support need to contact DSS so that the disability can be verified, specific needs determined, and timely accommodations made. In most cases, documentation by a professional service provider will be necessary. Information is kept strictly confidential. However, it is important to share information that will enable DSS staff to provide appropriate, reasonable, and timely services tailored to individual needs.

LD/ADD ADMISSIONS INFORMATION

College entrance tests required: Yes
Interview required: No
Essay required: No
Documentation required for LD: Statement of diagnosis, tests administered and their interpretation (aptitude, achievement, information processing), functional limitations as they affect students ability to access higher education, given at age 16 or older by licensed professional in LD
Documentation required for ADD: Must be current and comprehensive (evidence of early impairment evidence of current impairment, relevant testing info, alternative diagnosis ruled out) and prepared by a professional with comprehensive training in the diagnosis and treatment of ADD
Submitted to: DDS
Special Ed. HS coursework accepted: Yes

Specific course requirements of all applicants: Yes
Separate application required for program services: No
# of LD applications submitted each year: NR
# of LD applications accepted yearly: NR
Total # of students receiving LD services: 80–90
Acceptance into program means acceptance into college: Student must be admitted and enrolled in the university first and then request services.

ADMISSIONS

Individuals with disabilities are admitted via the standard admissions criteria that apply to all students. General admissibility is based on an index using GPA and test scores. The minimum GPA accepted is a 2.0. Required courses include 4 years English, 3 years math, 3 years social science, 2 years science (1 year lab), 2 years foreign language (American Sign Language accepted), and 1 year arts or academic elective. Special education courses are acceptable if they are courses that are regularly taught in the high school. However, all applicants must complete the required core courses. Students who do not meet the grade and test score admission scale may provide additional information to the admissions office and request consideration through the Special Talent Admissions Process.

ADDITIONAL INFORMATION

Examples of services for students with specific learning disabilities include taped texts; equipment loan; alternative testing arrangements such as oral, extended time, or relocation of testing site; note-takers; tutorial assistance (available to all students); referral to Learning Skills Center, Writers' Center, Mathematics Lab; accessible computer stations; and a Kurzweil reading machine. Examples of services for students with ADD are consultation regarding reasonable and effective accommodations with classroom professors; alternative testing; books on tape; note-takers; taped lectures; equipment loans; referrals to Learning Skills Center, Math Lab, Writers' Center, and Counseling and Psychological services; information on ADD; and informal counseling. Skills classes for credit are offered in math, reading, time management, study skills, and writing skills. A Learning Skills Center and a Writing Center are open to all students. Services and accommodations are offered to undergraduate and graduate students.

Support Services Contact Information

Learning Disability Program/Services: Disability Support Services
Director: Karen Raver
  E-Mail: kraver@mail.ewu.edu
  Telephone: 509-359-6871
  Fax: 509-359-4673
Contact Person: Pam McDermott
  E-Mail: pmcdermott@mail.ewu.edu
  Telephone: 509-359-6871
  Fax: 509-359-4673

LEARNING DISABILITY SERVICES

Requests for the following/services accommodations will be evaluated individually based on appropriate and current documentation.

Allowed in exams
  Calculator: Yes
  Dictionary: Yes
  Computer: Yes
  Spellchecker: Yes
Extended test time: Yes
Scribes: Yes
Proctors: Yes
Oral exams: Yes
Note-takers: Yes

Distraction reduced environment: Yes
Tape recording in class: Yes
Books on tape from RFBD: Yes
Taping of books not from RFBD: Yes
Accommodations for students with
  ADD: Yes
Reading machine: Yes
Other assistive technology: Yes
Priority registration: Yes

Added costs for services: No
LD specialists: No
Professional tutors: 7
Peer tutors: 33
Max. hours/wk. for services: NR
How professors are notified of
  LD/ADD: By both student and director

GENERAL ADMISSIONS INFORMATION

Director of Admissions: Shannon Carr
Telephone: 509-359-2397

Entrance Requirements

Academic units required: 4 English, 3 math, 2 science (1 science lab), 2 foreign language, 3 social studies, 1 fine arts (or additional unit from above). High school diploma is required and GED is accepted. ACT with Writing component required or SAT Reasoning test. TOEFL required of all international applicants, minimum paper TOEFL 525, minimum computer TOEFL 195.

Application deadline: 9/9
Notification: Rolling
Average GPA: 3.30

Average SAT Math: 501
Average SAT Verbal: 500
Average ACT: 21

Graduated top 10% of class: 19%
Graduated top 25% of class: 44%
Graduated top 50% of class: 76%

COLLEGE GRADUATION REQUIREMENTS

Course waivers allowed: Yes
In what course: Possible waiver for foreign language, must be supported by documentation.
Course substitutions allowed: Yes
In what course: Possible substitutions in math and foreign language, must be supported by documentation.

Additional Information

Environment: The university is located on 35 acres in a small town 18 miles southwest of Spokane.

Student Body:
  Undergrad enrollment: 9,390
  Women: 58%
  Men: 42%
  Percent out-of-state: 9%

Cost Information
  In-state tuition: $3,582
  Out-of-state tuition: $12,438
  Room & board: $5,200
Housing Information
  University housing: Yes
  Percent living on campus: 20%

Greek System
  Fraternity: Yes
  Sorority: Yes
Athletics: NCAA Division I

WASHINGTON STATE UNIVERSITY

370 Lighty Student Services, Pullman, WA 99164-1067
Phone: 509-335-5586 • Fax: 509-335-4902
E-mail: admiss2@wsu.edu • Web: www.wsu.edu
Support: S • Institution type: 4-year public

LEARNING DISABILITY PROGRAM AND SERVICES

The Disability Resource Center (DRC) assists students who have a disability by providing academic services. The program may also refer students to other service programs that may assist them in achieving their academic goals. DRC will help students overcome potential obstacles so that they may be successful in their area of study. All academic adjustments are authorized on an individual basis. DRC coordinates services for students with LD. The program offers academic support in many different areas. To be eligible for assistance, students must be currently enrolled at Washington State University. They also must submit documentation of their disability. For a learning disability, the student must submit a written report that includes test scores and evaluation. It is the student's responsibility to request accommodations if desired. It is important to remember that even though two individuals may have the same disability, they may not necessarily need the same academic adjustments. DRC works with students and instructors to determine and implement appropriate academic adjustments. Many adjustments are simple creative alternatives for traditional ways of learning.

LD/ADD ADMISSIONS INFORMATION

College entrance tests required: Yes
Interview required: No
Essay required: No
Documentation required for LD: WAIS–R or WISC–R, no less than three years old
Documentation required for ADD: Yes
Submitted to: DRC
Special Ed. HS coursework accepted: Yes

Specific course requirements of all applicants: Yes
Separate application required for program services: NR
# of LD applications submitted each year: NR
# of LD applications accepted yearly: NR
Total # of students receiving LD services: 283
Acceptance into program means acceptance into college: Student must be admitted and enrolled in the university first (they can appeal a denial), and then request services.

ADMISSIONS

All students must meet the general admission requirements. The university looks at the combination of the scores on the ACT/SAT and the high school GPA. The standard admission criteria are based on an index score determined by 75 percent GPA and 25 percent SAT/ACT. Courses required include 3 years English, 3 years math, 2 years science, 2 years foreign language, 3 yers social studies, 1 year elective required. Only 15 percent of new admissions may be offered under special admission. Documentation of the learning disability and diagnostic tests given less than 3 years before are required if requesting accommodations or services.

ADDITIONAL INFORMATION

General assistance to students with learning disabilities includes pre-admission counseling; information about disabilities; referral to appropriate community resources; academic, personal, and career counseling; information about accommodations; information about the laws pertaining to individuals with disabilities; and self-advocacy. Typical academic adjustments for students with learning disabilities may include note-takers and/or audiotape class sessions; and alternative testing arrangements; textbook taping or one-to-one readers; extended time for exams; essay exams taken on computer; and computers with voice output and spellcheckers. Services and accommodations are available for undergraduate and graduate students.

Support Services Contact Information

Learning Disability Program/Services: Disability Resource Center (DRC)
Director: Susan Schaeffer, PhD
  E-Mail: schaeff@wsu.edu
  Telephone: 509-335-1566
  Fax: 509-335-8511

LEARNING DISABILITY SERVICES

Requests for the following/services accommodations will be evaluated individually based on appropriate and current documentation.

Allowed in exams
  Calculator: No
  Dictionary: No
  Computer: Yes
  Spellchecker: Yes
Extended test time: Yes
Scribes: Yes
Proctors: Yes
Oral exams: Yes
Note-takers: Yes

Distraction reduced environment: Yes
Tape recording in class: Yes
Books on tape from RFBD: Yes
Taping of books not from RFBD: Yes
Accommodations for students with
  ADD: Yes
Reading machine: No
Other assistive technology: No
Priority registration: Yes

Added costs for services: No
LD specialists: No
Professional tutors: No
Peer tutors: 50
Max. hours/wk. for services:
  Unlimited
How professors are notified of
  LD/ADD: By student

GENERAL ADMISSIONS INFORMATION

Director of Admissions: Wendy Peterson
Telephone: 509-335-5586

ENTRANCE REQUIREMENTS

Academic units required: 4 English, 3 math, 2 science (1 science lab), 2 foreign language, 2 social studies, 1 history, 1 academic elective. **Academic units recommended:** 4 English, 3 math, 2 science (1 science lab), 2 foreign language, 2 social studies, 1 history, 1 academic elective. High school diploma is required and GED is accepted. ACT with Writing component required. TOEFL required of all international applicants, minimum paper TOEFL 520, minimum computer TOEFL 190.

Application deadline: Rolling
Notification: Rolling
Average GPA: 3.46

Average SAT Math: 545
Average SAT Verbal: 527
Average ACT: NR

Graduated top 10% of class: 34%
Graduated top 25% of class: 59%
Graduated top 50% of class: 90%

COLLEGE GRADUATION REQUIREMENTS

Course waivers allowed: Yes
Course substitutions allowed: Yes
In what course: Foreign language

ADDITIONAL INFORMATION

Environment: The university is located on 600 acres in a small town 80 miles south of Spokane.

Student Body:
  Undergrad enrollment: 18,825
  Women: 53%
  Men: 47%
  Percent out-of-state: 8%

Cost Information
  In-state tuition: $5,514
  Out-of-state tuition: $14,250
  Room & board: $6,600
Housing Information
  University housing: Yes
  Percent living on campus: 37%

Greek System
  Fraternity: Yes
  Sorority: Yes
Athletics: NCAA Division I

Washington State University

DAVIS AND ELKINS COLLEGE

100 Campus Drive, Elkins, WV 26241
Phone: 304-637-1230 • Fax: 304-637-1800
E-mail: admiss@davisandelkins.edu • Web: www.davisandelkins.edu
Support: SP • Institution type: 4-year private

LEARNING DISABILITY PROGRAM AND SERVICES

Davis & Elkins offers a comprehensive support program for college students with learning disabilities. The goals blend with the college's commitment to diversity and providing a personalized education. The program goes well beyond accommodations or services by providing individualized instruction to meet each student's needs. The goal of the LD Program is to enable students diagnosed with LD/ADD to function to the best of their ability. To meet this goal each student meets at least weekly for a regularly scheduled session with one of the three experienced learning disabilities specialists. The main focus of these meetings is to develop learning strategies and academic skills. Students may request extra assistance and use the lab as a study area. There is a $2,600 fee for first year students. Applicants must submit complete and current documentation of the disability.

LD/ADD ADMISSIONS INFORMATION

College entrance tests required: Yes
Interview required: No
Essay required: Yes
Documentation required for LD: Complete psychological and academic battery, no less than three years old
Documentation required for ADD: Yes
Submitted to: Supported Learning Program
Special Ed. HS coursework accepted: No

Specific course requirements of all applicants: Yes
Separate application required for program services: Yes
# of LD applications submitted each year: 30–50
# of LD applications accepted yearly: 25–30
Total # of students receiving LD services: 35
Acceptance into program means acceptance into college: Applications are separate.

ADMISSIONS

All applications are screened by the Learning Disabilities Program director and the director of admissions. Students must be admitted to Davis and Elkins College prior to being considered for the program. The admissions counselors have been trained to recognize potentially successful students with learning disabilities. Students requesting admission to the program must meet admissions requirements; complete a separate application to the program; send complete and current documentation completed within the last 3 years; recommendation for participation in the program by a counselor or a learning specialist; copy of recent IEP, if available; a handwritten essay requesting services and indicating why services are being requested; and have a personal meting to discuss needs and expectations.

ADDITIONAL INFORMATION

Services include individual sessions with certified LD specialists; individualized programs focusing on improved writing skills, test-taking techniques, note-taking and textbook usage, and time management strategies. Specialists help students develop a personalized program focusing on improving written work, identifying class expectations and preparing work to that level of expectation, test-taking skills, using textbooks and taking notes, and managing time effectively. Students also receive advising and registration assistance based on assessment information. Personnel in the LD program also assist the students with course selection and registration; orientation to college life; monitoring of classes throughout the year and help interpreting feedback from professors; coordination of tutoring, additional counseling, and career planning; and instructional program modification as needed.

Support Services Contact Information

Learning Disability Program/Services: Supported Learning Program
Director: Dr. David Sneed
  E-Mail: sneedd@davisandelkins.edu
  Telephone: 304-637-1211
  Fax: 304-637-1371

LEARNING DISABILITY SERVICES

Requests for the following/services accommodations will be evaluated individually based on appropriate and current documentation.

Allowed in exams	**Distraction reduced environment:** Yes	**Added costs for services:** Yes
Calculator: Yes	**Tape recording in class:** Yes	**LD specialists:** Yes
Dictionary: Yes	**Books on tape from RFBD:** Yes	**Professional tutors:** No
Computer: Yes	**Taping of books not from RFBD:** Yes	**Peer tutors:** 2–10
Spellchecker: Yes	**Accommodations for students with**	**Max. hours/wk. for services:**
Extended test time: Yes	**ADD:** Yes	Unlimited
Scribes: Yes	**Reading machine:** No	**How professors are notified of**
Proctors: Yes	**Other assistive technology:** Yes	**LD/ADD:** By both student and director
Oral exams: Yes	**Priority registration:** N/A	
Note-takers: Yes		

GENERAL ADMISSIONS INFORMATION

Director of Admissions: Renee Heckel
Telephone: 304-637-1230

ENTRANCE REQUIREMENTS
Academic units required: 4 English, 3 math, 3 science (1 science lab), 1 foreign language, 3 social studies.
Academic units recommended: 4 English, 4 math, 4 science (2 science lab), 2 foreign language, 4 social studies.
High school diploma is required and GED is accepted. TOEFL required of all international applicants, minimum paper TOEFL 500, minimum computer TOEFL 173.

Application deadline: Rolling	**Average SAT Math:** 500	**Graduated top 10% of class:** 13%
Notification: Rolling	**Average SAT Verbal:** 500	**Graduated top 25% of class:** 24%
Average GPA: 3.10	**Average ACT:** 20	**Graduated top 50% of class:** 89%

COLLEGE GRADUATION REQUIREMENTS

Course waivers allowed: Yes
Course substitutions allowed: Yes
In what course: Individual requests are reviewed by the dean

ADDITIONAL INFORMATION

Environment: The college is located in a community of 10,000 in the foothills of the Allegheny Mountains.

Student Body:	**Cost Information**	**Greek System**
Undergrad enrollment: 625	**Tuition:** $15,246	**Fraternity:** Yes
Women: 62%	**Room & board:** $5,986	**Sorority:** Yes
Men: 38%	**Housing Information**	**Athletics:** NCAA Division II
Percent out-of-state: 39%	**University housing:** Yes	
	Percent living on campus: 44%	

MARSHALL UNIVERSITY

One John Marshall Drive, Huntington, WV 25755
Phone: 304-696-3160 • Fax: 304-696-3135
E-mail: admissions@marshall.edu • Web: www.marshall.edu
Support: SP • Institution type: 4-year public

LEARNING DISABILITY PROGRAM AND SERVICES

Higher Education for Learning Problems (HELP) encourages a feeling of camaraderie among the students enrolled in the program. HELP provides an individual tutoring program in coursework, exceptions in testing, and a remedial program. Students work with LD specialists one-to-one, to improve reading, writing, and language skills. Counseling is provided on-site, and the large professional staff offers a variety of additional services. This program boasts a 95% success rate with students.

LD/ADD ADMISSIONS INFORMATION

College entrance tests required: Yes
Interview required: Yes
Essay required: Yes
Documentation required for LD: A copy of the psychological and educational diagnoses; the psychological evaluation must be within the last three years; the educational evaluation must be within the last year
Documentation required for ADD: Yes
Submitted to: H.E.L.P
Special Ed. HS coursework accepted: Yes

Specific course requirements of all applicants: Yes
Separate application required for program services: Yes
# of LD applications submitted each year: 100
# of LD applications accepted yearly: 25–35
Total # of students receiving LD services: 150
Acceptance into program means acceptance into college: Students should apply to HELP first and then request admission to Marshall.

ADMISSIONS

Students with learning disabilities must follow a special admissions procedure. These students must submit an application, updated psychological and educational evaluation, one-page, handwritten, statement by the student (no assistance) regarding why college is desirable, and two recommendations stating why the recommenders feel the student should attend college. Interviews are required; minimum GPA of 2.0, ACT 17+, or SAT 810+ (tests are unimportant for LD admit); plus 4 years English, 3 years social studies, and 2 years math. Students should schedule interview before January, and submit application to HELP no less than one year in advance of the proposed entry date to college. All applications must be received by 12/31. Marshall University has a probationary admission if the reason for low GPA or test scores is convincing. There is a required five-week summer HELP Program for these incoming freshmen.

ADDITIONAL INFORMATION

The Summer Learning Disabilities Program is offered through HELP to incoming freshmen with learning disabilities. The program includes teachers with master's degrees in learning disabilities; a graduate assistant for each teacher who assists with tutoring coursework (tutors are matched to students who have a learning style compatible to the teaching style of the tutor); no more than 5 students per group; note-taking skills and study skills; test-taking strategies; organization of time; improvement of basic skills in reading, spelling, written language, and mathematics; improvement of self-esteem and self-confidence. The cost is $1,000 for West Virginia residents, $1,300 for metro area residents, and $2,000 for non-West Virginia residents. This does not include registration for classes students may take through the university. Students sign a release allowing HELP to talk to professors and parents. There is also a summer program for elementary and secondary students with learning disabilities.

Support Services Contact Information

Learning Disability Program/Services: Higher Education for Learning Problems (H.E.L.P.)
Director: Dr. Barbara P. Guyer
  E-Mail: guyerb@marshall.edu
  Telephone: 304-696-6317
  Fax: 304-696-3231
Contact Person: Lynne Weston
  E-Mail: weston@marshall.edu
  Telephone: 304-696-6316
  Fax: 304-696-3231

LEARNING DISABILITY SERVICES

Requests for the following/services accommodations will be evaluated individually based on appropriate and current documentation.

Allowed in exams
  Calculator: Yes
  Dictionary: Yes
  Computer: Yes
  Spellchecker: Yes
Extended test time: Yes
Scribes: Yes
Proctors: Yes
Oral exams: Yes
Note-takers: Yes

Distraction reduced environment: Yes
Tape recording in class: Yes
Books on tape from RFBD: Yes
Taping of books not from RFBD: Yes
Accommodations for students with ADD: Yes
Reading machine: Yes
Other assistive technology: Yes
Priority registration: Yes

Added costs for services: Yes
LD specialists: Yes
Professional tutors: 10
Peer tutors: No
Max. hours/wk. for services: Unlimited
How professors are notified of LD/ADD: By both student and director

GENERAL ADMISSIONS INFORMATION

Director of Admissions: Craig S. Grooms
Telephone: 304-696-3160

ENTRANCE REQUIREMENTS

Academic units required: 4 English, 3 math, 3 science (2 science lab), 3 social studies. High school diploma is required and GED is accepted. ACT with or without Writing component accepted. TOEFL required of all international applicants, minimum paper TOEFL 500, minimum computer TOEFL 173.

Application deadline: Rolling
Notification: Rolling
Average GPA: 3.33

Average SAT Math: NR
Average SAT Verbal: NR
Average ACT: NR

Graduated top 10% of class: NR
Graduated top 25% of class: NR
Graduated top 50% of class: NR

COLLEGE GRADUATION REQUIREMENTS

Course waivers allowed: Yes
Course substitutions allowed: Yes
In what course: Math, foreign language

ADDITIONAL INFORMATION

Environment: Marshall University has a 55-acre urban campus located 140 miles east of Lexington, Kentucky.

Student Body:
  Undergrad enrollment: 9,310
  Women: 56%
  Men: 44%
  Percent out-of-state: 17%

Cost Information
  In-state tuition: $3,818
  Out-of-state tuition: $10,128
  Room & board: $6,060
Housing Information
  University housing: Yes
  Percent living on campus: 20%

Greek System
  Fraternity: Yes
  Sorority: Yes
  Athletics: NCAA Division I

WEST VIRGINIA UNIVERSITY

Admissions Office, PO Box 6009, Morgantown, WV 26506-6009
Phone: 304-293-2121 • Fax: 304-293-3080
E-mail: wvuadmissions@arc.wvu.edu • Web: www.wvu.edu
Support: S • Institution type: 4-year public

LEARNING DISABILITY PROGRAM AND SERVICES

The Office of Disability Services is available to all students on the campus of West Virginia University. Services are provided to better enable qualified students with disabilities to maximize their academic potential. It is the student's responsibility to provide documentation for the diagnosis prior to receiving accommodations based upon that disability. Each student's academic accommodations will be determined by the university on an individual basis. In order to meet the adult criteria of "disability" under federal laws, individuals must provide documentation of how the significant impairment "substantially limits" their academic functioning. A "significant impairment" means below average functioning. An IEP is not documentation of a disability for the purposes of providing accommodations at the college level.

LD/ADD ADMISSIONS INFORMATION

College entrance tests required: Yes
Interview required: No
Essay required: No
Documentation required for LD: Recent psychoeducational evaluation
Documentation required for ADD: Yes
Submitted to: Office of Disability
Special Ed. HS coursework accepted: No

Specific course requirements of all applicants: Yes
Separate application required for program services: Yes
# of LD applications submitted each year: NR
# of LD applications accepted yearly: NR
Total # of students receiving LD services: NR
Acceptance into program means acceptance into college: Student must be admitted and enrolled in the university first (they can appeal a denial) and then request services.

ADMISSIONS

There is no special admissions process for students with LD and ADHD. In-state students must have a 2.0 GPA and out of state students must have a 2.25 GPA. Additionally, all applicants must have 4 years of English, 3 years of social studies, 3 years of math, 2 years of lab science and foreign language is recommended. Students are not encouraged to self-disclose a disability in a personal statement during the application process. Appropriate services/accommodations will be determined after the student is admitted.

ADDITIONAL INFORMATION

Requirements for the documentation of a LD include a signed, dated comprehensive psychoeducational evaluation report indicating how the LD impacts academic performance and contributes to a "significant impairment" in academic functioning. The report should address aptitude, achievement, processing, and should include the WAIS and full Woodcock—Johnson Battery. A description of the functional limitations, which impact against the educational effort, must be included in the diagnostic report. Additionally, a documented history of previous accommodations received should be included. Documentation of ADD must be in the form of a signed and dated report, by a psychiatrist, neuropsychologist or licensed psychologist trained in the differential diagnosis. Additional information is required. There are no LD specialists on staff; however, counselors are available to provide services to all students. Some accommodations that are available with appropriate documentation include priority registration, course substitutions, extended testing time, note-takers, distraction-free environments, books on tape, and assistive technology.

Support Services Contact Information

Learning Disability Program/Services: Office of Disability Services
Director: Jennifer McIntosh
  E-Mail: jmcintos@wvu.edu
  Telephone: 304-293-5496
  Fax: 304-293-3861

LEARNING DISABILITY SERVICES

Requests for the following/services accommodations will be evaluated individually based on appropriate and current documentation.

Allowed in exams
  Calculator: No
  Dictionary: Yes
  Computer: No
  Spellchecker: Yes
Extended test time: Yes
Scribes: Yes
Proctors: No
Oral exams: Yes
Note-takers: Yes

Distraction reduced environment: Yes
Tape recording in class: Yes
Books on tape from RFBD: Yes
Taping of books not from RFBD: Yes
Accommodations for students with ADD: Yes
Reading machine: Yes
Other assistive technology: Yes
Priority registration: Yes

Added costs for services: No
LD specialists: No
Professional tutors: No
Peer tutors: 65
Max. hours/wk. for services: Unlimited
How professors are notified of LD/ADD: By both student and director

GENERAL ADMISSIONS INFORMATION

Director of Admissions: Cheng Khoo, Director
Telephone: 304-293-4515

ENTRANCE REQUIREMENTS

Academic units required: 4 English, 3 math, 3 science (2 science lab), 3 social studies. **Academic units recommended:** 2 foreign language. High school diploma is required and GED is accepted. ACT with Writing component required. TOEFL required of all international applicants, minimum paper TOEFL 550, minimum computer TOEFL 173.

Application deadline: 8/1
Notification: Rolling
Average GPA: 3.3

Average SAT Math: 543
Average SAT Verbal: 528
Average ACT: 23

Graduated top 10% of class: 17%
Graduated top 25% of class: 45%
Graduated top 50% of class: 78%

COLLEGE GRADUATION REQUIREMENTS

Course waivers allowed: Yes
Course substitutions allowed: Yes
In what course: Foreign language substitution

ADDITIONAL INFORMATION

Environment: The commuteis located 70 miles from Pittsburgh, Pennsylvania.

Student Body:
  Undergrad enrollment: 18,653
  Women: 47%
  Men: 53%
  Percent out-of-state: 41%

Cost Information
  In-state tuition: $3,938
  Out-of-state tuition: $12,060
  Room & board: $6,084
Housing Information
  University housing: Yes
  Percent living on campus: 27%

Greek System
  Fraternity: Yes
  Sorority: Yes
Athletics: NCAA Division I

WEST VIRGINIA WESLEYAN COLLEGE

59 College Avenue, Buckhannon, WV 26201
Phone: 304-473-8510 • Fax: 304-473-8108
E-mail: admission@wvwc.edu • Web: www.wvwc.edu
Support: SP • Institution type: 4-year private

LEARNING DISABILITY PROGRAM AND SERVICES

The college holds a strong commitment to providing excellent support to students with documented disabilities. An individually structured program has been designed to accommodate students with varying needs. Master level professionals in the fields of learning disabilities, reading, education and counseling assist each student to design strategies for academic success. Accommodation plans are determined through a review of the documentation provided by the student and the recommendations of the student's comprehensive advisor, who works closely with each individual. Students who want to receive LD services must submit an educational assessment, completed within the last two to three years, to the director of the Student Academic Support Services (SASS). Documentation must include the WAIS and the Woodcock-Johnson Standard Achievement Battery. Alternate achievement assessment will be considered with the approval of the Director. Both numeric scores and a narrative report, which interpret a perceived or diagnosed LD, are required. A copy of the IEP would be helpful. Documentation must be submitted in a timely manner in order to plan specialized advising, preferential registration, and the implementation of the appropriate accommodations.

LD/ADD ADMISSIONS INFORMATION

College entrance tests required: Yes
Interview required: No
Essay required: No
Documentation required for LD: WAIS (in the last three years), WJ
Documentation required for ADD: A medical and/or psychological diagnosis is required, indicating how the disability interferes with the student's functioning in the academic environment, including accomodations appropriate for post-secondary education
Submitted to: Student Academic Support Services

Specific course requirements of all applicants: Yes
Special Ed. HS coursework accepted: Yes
Separate application required for program services: No
# of LD applications submitted each year: 150
# of LD applications accepted yearly: 90
Total # of students receiving LD services: 95–110
Acceptance into program means acceptance into college: Students are admitted jointly into the college and SASS.

ADMISSIONS

The director of Student Academic Support Services reviews the application of students who self-disclose a learning disability or attention deficit disorder. Applicants are encouraged to submit a psychological evaluation if they believe it will help develop an accurate picture of student potential. Interviews are encouraged but not required unless it is determined that an interview could help the admissions team gain a better understanding of the applicant. The academic dean has the authority to offer special admission to some students not admitted through the regular application process. Application decisions are made jointly by the director of admissions and the director of Student Academic Support Services. General admission criteria include a GPA no lower than 2.0; 4 years English, 3 years math, 2 years science, 2 years social studies, 1 year history, and 3 years electives. No foreign language is required for admission. The mid 50 percent range for the ACT is 18–27 and SAT 800–1400. It is to the student's advantage to self-disclose a disability. If a student chooses to self-disclose, the educational assessment is interpreted by the director of special services who may recommend admission based on the evaluation of the student's potential for success in college

ADDITIONAL INFORMATION

Support for Students with Disabilities provides the following services when appropriate: individualized support from a comprehensive advisor who plans and coordinates accommodation of student needs and acts as a liaison with other departments, annual individualized accommodation plan with yearly updates of appropriate accommodations, preferential registration and specialized academic advising for the first three semesters, extended time and separate testing location for qualified students, limited noncredit practical as needed to support composition courses, note-takers when necessary and appropriate, alternative textbook format, and individual peer tutoring. Some class offerings include "College Study Strategies", "Developmental Math", "Lindamood-Bell Learning Program" (clinical instructing in phonemic awareness, comprehension skills, and application to course work), memory techniques, note-taking, reading techniques, test taking, time management, and visual thinking.

Support Services Contact Information

Learning Disability Program/Services: Student Academic Support Services
Director: Mrs. Shawn Kuba
  E-Mail: kuba_s@wvwc.edu
  Telephone: 304-473-8563
  Fax: 304-473-8497
Contact Person: Same

LEARNING DISABILITY SERVICES

Requests for the following/services accommodations will be evaluated individually based on appropriate and current documentation.

Allowed in exams
  Calculator: Yes
  Dictionary: Yes
  Computer: Yes
  Spellchecker: Yes
Extended test time: Yes
Scribes: Yes
Proctors: Yes
Oral exams: Yes
Note-takers: Yes

Distraction reduced environment: Yes
Tape recording in class: Yes
Books on tape from RFBD: Yes
Taping of books not from RFBD: Yes
Accommodations for students with
  ADD: Yes
Reading machine: Yes
Other assistive technology: Yes
Priority registration: Yes

Added costs for services: No
LD specialists: Yes
Professional tutors: 5
Peer tutors: 18–25
Max. hours/wk. for services: 57
How professors are notified of
  LD/ADD: By student

GENERAL ADMISSIONS INFORMATION

Director of Admissions: Robert Skinner
Telephone: 304-473-8510

ENTRANCE REQUIREMENTS

Academic units required: 4 English, 3 math, 3 science (2 science lab), 2 social studies, 2 history, 3 academic electives, 7 fine arts, technology, and physical education. **Academic units recommended:** 2 foreign language, 3 social studies, 2 history. High school diploma is required and GED is accepted. TOEFL required of all international applicants, minimum paper TOEFL 500, minimum computer TOEFL 500.

Application deadline: 8/1
Notification: Rolling
Average GPA: 3.33

Average SAT Math: 525
Average SAT Verbal: 526
Average ACT: 23

Graduated top 10% of class: 23%
Graduated top 25% of class: 56%
Graduated top 50% of class: 83%

COLLEGE GRADUATION REQUIREMENTS

Course waivers allowed: Yes
Course substitutions allowed: Yes
In what course: In any course where the request is appropriate.

ADDITIONAL INFORMATION

Environment: The college is located on 80 acres 135 miles from Pittsburgh in the Appalachian foothills.

Student Body:
  Undergrad enrollment: 1,583
  Women: 55%
  Men: 45%
  Percent out-of-state: 48%

Cost Information
  Tuition: $19,450
  Room & board: $5,200
Housing Information
  University housing: Yes
  Percent living on campus: 80%

Greek System
  Fraternity: Yes
  Sorority: Yes
Athletics: NCAA Division II

ALVERNO COLLEGE

3400 South 43rd Street, PO Box 343922, Milwaukee, WI 53219
Phone: 414-382-6100 • Fax: 414-382-6354
E-mail: admissions@alverno.edu • Web: www.alverno.edu
Support: S • Institution type: 4-year private

LEARNING DISABILITY PROGRAM AND SERVICES

Alverno College is a small liberal arts college for women with approximately 2,000 students. The Instructional Services Center (ISC) provides academic support to Alverno students, and assists Alverno applicants in meeting admissions requirements. ISC offers courses in reading, writing, critical thinking, math, and algebra in order to develop academic skills as required on the basis of new student assessment results. ISC also offers tutorial support, course-based study groups, and workshops to provide an opportunity for small groups of students to study together under the direction of a peer tutor or an ISC teacher. There is also a coordinator of Support Services for Students with Disabilities who assists the student to meet her academic potential through understanding of her learning needs, development of strategies and accommodations to maximize her strengths, and development of self-advocacy with faculty.

LD/ADD ADMISSIONS INFORMATION

College entrance tests required: Yes
Interview required: No
Essay required: No
Documentation required for LD: WAIS–III; WJ WRAT–R: within 5–8 years
Documentation required for ADD: Yes
Submitted to: Disability Services
Special Ed. HS coursework accepted: No

Specific course requirements of all applicants: Yes
Separate application required for program services: No
# of LD applications submitted each year: NR
# of LD applications accepted yearly: NR
Total # of students receiving LD services: 45
Acceptance into program means acceptance into college: Student must be admitted and enrolled in the college first (they can appeal a denial), and then request services.

ADMISSIONS

Admission criteria are the same for all students coming directly from high school. General admission requirements include: 19+ ACT; 17 academic credits in college-prep courses with recommendations, including 4 years English, 2 years foreign language, 3 years math, 3 years science, 3 years social studies; a minimum of a 2.5 GPA, and rank in the top half of graduating class. There is a college transition program for students who do not meet the admissions criteria but have academic potential.

ADDITIONAL INFORMATION

Classes are offered at a beginning level in reading and writing, math and algebra. Students may not substitute courses for math courses required to graduate, but intensive assistance is provided. Tutoring is provided through ISC, and an Academic Support Group for students with LD meets every two to three weeks to discuss topics such as self-advocacy, problem solving, letter writing, and communicating with professors. The college has a Math Resource Center and a Writing Resource Center available for all students.

Support Services Contact Information

Learning Disability Program/Services: Disability Services
Director: Colleen Barnett
  E-Mail: colleen.barnett@alverno.edu
  Telephone: 414-382-6026
  Fax: 414-382-6354
Contact Person: Same

LEARNING DISABILITY SERVICES

Requests for the following/services accommodations will be evaluated individually based on appropriate and current documentation.

Allowed in exams
  Calculator: Yes
  Dictionary: Yes
  Computer: Yes
  Spellchecker: Yes
Extended test time: Yes
Scribes: Yes
Proctors: Yes
Oral exams: Yes
Note-takers: Yes

Distraction reduced environment: Yes
Tape recording in class: Yes
Books on tape from RFBD: Yes
Taping of books not from RFBD: Yes
**Accommodations for students with
  ADD:** Yes
Reading machine: Yes
Other assistive technology: Yes
Priority registration: No

Added costs for services: No
LD specialists: No
Professional tutors: 10
Peer tutors: 75
Max. hours/wk. for services:
  Unlimited
**How professors are notified of
  LD/ADD:** By both student and director

GENERAL ADMISSIONS INFORMATION

Director of Admissions: Mary Kay Farrell
Telephone: 414-382-6100

ENTRANCE REQUIREMENTS

Academic units recommended: 4 English, 3 math, 3 science, 2 foreign language, 3 social studies. High school diploma is required and GED is accepted. ACT with or without Writing component accepted. TOEFL required of all international applicants, minimum paper TOEFL 500, minimum computer TOEFL 173.

Application deadline: Rolling
Notification: Rolling
Average GPA: NR

Average SAT Math: NR
Average SAT Verbal: NR
Average ACT: 20

Graduated top 10% of class: NR
Graduated top 25% of class: NR
Graduated top 50% of class: NR

COLLEGE GRADUATION REQUIREMENTS

Course waivers allowed: No
Course substitutions allowed: No
In what course: N/A

ADDITIONAL INFORMATION

Environment: The campus is located in a suburban area on the southwest side of Milwaukee.

Student Body:
  Undergrad enrollment: 1,923
  Women: 100%
  Men: 0%
  Percent out-of-state: 3%

Cost Information
  Tuition: $15,168
  Room & board: $5,670
Housing Information
  University housing: Yes
  Percent living on campus: 13%

Greek System
  Fraternity: No
  Sorority: Yes
Athletics: NCAA Division III

BELOIT COLLEGE

700 College Street, Beloit, WI 53511
Phone: 608-363-2500 • Fax: 608-363-2075
E-mail: admiss@beloit.edu • Web: www.beloit.edu
Support: S • Institution type: 4-year private

LEARNING DISABILITY PROGRAM AND SERVICES

The goal of the Educational Development Program (EDP) at Beloit College is to provide support services and accommodations individually tailored to the needs of each student to enable the successful completion of the baccalaureate degree. EDP is a campus resource that provides opportunities for students to succeed. Beloit College students can qualify for EDP services based on any one of the following: (1) parents' educational attainment, (2) family income, (3) documented need for accommodations. EDP is funded through Beloit College in cooperation with the U.S. Department of Education. Participation is on a first-come, first-served basis for those who qualify and by the discretion of project staff.

LD/ADD ADMISSIONS INFORMATION

College entrance tests required: Yes
Interview required: No
Essay required: Yes
Documentation required for LD: Psychoeducational
  evaluation, no less than three years old
Documentation required for ADD: NR
Submitted to: Learning Support Service Center
Special Ed. HS coursework accepted: Yes

Specific course requirements of all applicants: Yes
Separate application required for program services: No
# of LD applications submitted each year: NR
# of LD applications accepted yearly: NR
Total # of students receiving LD services: 17–23
Acceptance into program means acceptance into
  college: Students must be admitted and enrolled in the
  college first and then request services.

ADMISSIONS

There is no special admissions procedure for students with learning disabilities. Each student is reviewed individually and the final decision is made by the Office of Admission. The college is competitive in admissions, but there are no cut-offs for GPA or test scores. 16 academic courses are required for admission. Courses recommended include 4 years English, 3 years math, 3 years science, 3 years science lab, 2 years foreign language, and 3 years social studies.

ADDITIONAL INFORMATION

The Beloit Learning Resource Center offers additional services to the students in the areas of tutoring, study skills and time management, math and science tutoring and study groups, improvement of writing skills, advising, mentoring, reading speed and comprehension and computer usage. Counseling services are offered in personal counseling, career guidance, and crisis intervention. Individual and self-help programs and small group workshops are available. Assessment tools are offered to help students determine individual strengths and weakness in reading rate, comprehension, and vocabulary, and there are a variety of handouts covering a wide range of academic skill areas such as studying, math, footnoting, and test taking.

Support Services Contact Information

Learning Disability Program/Services: Learning Support Services Center
Director: Diane Arnzen
  E-Mail: arnzend@beloit.edu
  Telephone: 608-363-2572
  Fax: 608-363-7059

LEARNING DISABILITY SERVICES

Requests for the following/services accommodations will be evaluated individually based on appropriate and current documentation.

Allowed in exams
  Calculator: Yes
  Dictionary: Yes
  Computer: Yes
  Spellchecker: Yes
Extended test time: Yes
Scribes: Yes
Proctors: Yes
Oral exams: Yes
Note-takers: Yes

Distraction reduced environment: Yes
Tape recording in class: Yes
Books on tape from RFBD: Yes
Taping of books not from RFBD: Yes
Accommodations for students with ADD: Yes
Reading machine: No
Other assistive technology: Yes
Priority registration: No

Added costs for services: No
LD specialists: No
Professional tutors: Yes
Peer tutors: 70-78
Max. hours/wk. for services: Unlimited
How professors are notified of LD/ADD: By student

GENERAL ADMISSIONS INFORMATION

Director of Admissions: Nancy Monnich (Vice President of Enrollment Services)
Telephone: 608-363-2500

ENTRANCE REQUIREMENTS

Academic units recommended: 4 English, 4 math, 3 science, 2 foreign language, 4 social studies, 4 history. High school diploma is required and GED is accepted. ACT with or without Writing component accepted. TOEFL required of all international applicants, minimum paper TOEFL 525, minimum computer TOEFL 197.

Application deadline: Rolling
Notification: Rolling
Average GPA: 3.46

Average SAT Math: 610
Average SAT Verbal: 640
Average ACT: 27

Graduated top 10% of class: 36%
Graduated top 25% of class: 64%
Graduated top 50% of class: 92%

COLLEGE GRADUATION REQUIREMENTS

Course waivers allowed: N/A
Course substitutions allowed: N/A
In what course: N/A

ADDITIONAL INFORMATION

Environment: The college is located 50 miles south of Madison, 90 miles northwest of Chicago.

Student Body:
  Undergrad enrollment: 1,301
  Women: 59%
  Men: 41%
  Percent out-of-state: 80%

Cost Information
  Tuition: $26,664
  Room & board: $5,924
Housing Information
  University housing: Yes
  Percent living on campus: 93%

Greek System
  Fraternity: Yes
  Sorority: Yes
Athletics: NCAA Division III

MARIAN COLLEGE OF FOND DU LAC

45 South National Avenue, Fond du Lac, WI 54935
Phone: 920-923-7650 • Fax: 920-923-8755
E-mail: admissions@mariancollege.edu • Web: www.mariancollege.edu
Support: S • Institution type: 4-year private

LEARNING DISABILITY PROGRAM AND SERVICES

The Student Development Center offers services for students with learning disabilities. The ultimate goal of the Center is to provide the academic, social, and emotional support to students in order that they may maintain at least a 2.0 GPA and persevere to earn a college degree. The Student Development Center strives to provide a "neutral" area within which students can be accepted for who they are, and can begin moving towards meeting their own personal and academic goals.

LD/ADD ADMISSIONS INFORMATION

College entrance tests required: Yes
Interview required: Yes for Excel
Essay required: No
Documentation required for LD: Psychoeducational evaluation, no less than five years old
Documentation required for ADD: Yes
Submitted to: Disabled Services
Special Ed. HS coursework accepted: No
Specific course requirements of all applicants: Yes

Separate application required for program services: No
# of LD applications submitted each year: 15–20
# of LD applications accepted yearly: 15–20
Total # of students receiving LD services: NR
Acceptance into program means acceptance into college: Students must be admitted and enrolled in the college first and then request services.

ADMISSIONS

There is no special application or admissions procedure for students with learning disabilities. Admission criteria include a 2.0 GPA, top 50 percent of class, and ACT of 18. All students, not just those with LD, are asked to meet two-thirds of these criteria. Students who do not meet two-thirds may be admitted on probation through a program called EXCEL. Students will be asked to submit three letters of recommendation supporting their ability to succeed in college-level coursework. Students also may be asked to schedule a visit to Marian for a pre-admission interview during which their skills, attitudes, motivation, and self-understanding will be informally assessed. Students admitted provisionally may be admitted with limited credit status and may be required to take a freshman seminar course. Special education coursework is accepted, but students are encouraged to be fully mainstreamed by senior year with minimal monitoring. Students who self-disclose their disability are given information on services available through the Student Development Center.

ADDITIONAL INFORMATION

The Peer Tutoring program helps students gain the confidence and skill necessary to successfully complete coursework. To receive assistance students must disclose their disability. Skill classes are offered in English, math, and study skills, as well as computer-assisted instruction in math and basic skill areas. Other services include information on community, state, and national resources; assistance in writing and proofreading papers and assignments; tutors (individual and group); liaison service; assistance in working with instructors and course scheduling. Calculators are allowed in exams for students with a documented disability in math, and dictionaries are allowed in exams for students with a documented disability in written language. Assistance is determined for each individual based on assessment. All students have access to the tutoring program, the writing lab and the computer lab. The Excel program is a support program for students admitted on probation. This is not specifically for students with learning disabilities. The Excel program offers tutoring, academic advising, help coping with transition and change, and developmental counseling.

Support Services Contact Information

Learning Disability Program/Services: Disability Services
Director: Wendy Yurk
  E-Mail: wyurk@marlancollege.edu
  Telephone: 920-923-7162
  Fax: 920-926-2113

LEARNING DISABILITY SERVICES

Requests for the following/services accommodations will be evaluated individually based on appropriate and current documentation.

Allowed in exams	**Distraction reduced environment:** Yes	**Added costs for services:** No
Calculator: Yes	**Tape recording in class:** Yes	**LD specialists:** No
Dictionary: Yes	**Books on tape from RFBD:** Yes	**Professional tutors:** Yes
Computer: Yes	**Taping of books not from RFBD:** No	**Peer tutors:** Yes
Spellchecker: Yes	**Accommodations for students with**	**Max. hours/wk. for services:**
Extended test time: Yes	**ADD:** Yes	Unlimited
Scribes: Yes	**Reading machine:** Yes	**How professors are notified of**
Proctors: Yes	**Other assistive technology:** Yes	**LD/ADD:** By Director
Oral exams: Yes	**Priority registration:** Yes	
Note-takers: Yes		

GENERAL ADMISSIONS INFORMATION

Director of Admissions: Eric Peterson
Telephone: 920-923-7643

ENTRANCE REQUIREMENTS

Academic units required: 4 English, 2 math, 1 science (1 science lab), 1 history. **Academic units recommended:** 3 math, 2 science, 2 foreign language. High school diploma is required and GED is accepted. ACT with or without Writing component accepted. TOEFL required of all international applicants, minimum paper TOEFL 525, minimum computer TOEFL 193.

Application deadline: NR	**Average SAT Math:** NR	**Graduated top 10% of class:** 10%
Notification: Rolling	**Average SAT Verbal:** NR	**Graduated top 25% of class:** 33%
Average GPA: 3.05	**Average ACT:** 20	**Graduated top 50% of class:** 68%

COLLEGE GRADUATION REQUIREMENTS

Course waivers allowed: No
Course substitutions allowed: Yes
In what course: Students have taken directed study classes to fulfill their math requirement, worked one-to-one with tutor and weekly with instructor given one year to complete semester course, but must attempt required course.

ADDITIONAL INFORMATION

Environment: Marian College is located on 50 acres in a suburb of Fond du Lac, 60 miles north of Milwaukee.

Student Body:	**Cost Information**	**Greek System**
Undergrad enrollment: 1,815	**Tuition:** $15,500	**Fraternity:** Yes
Women: 71%	**Room & board:** $5,240	**Sorority:** Yes
Men: 29%	**Housing Information**	**Athletics:** NCAA Division III
Percent out-of-state: 6%	**University housing:** Yes	
	Percent living on campus: 34%	

MARQUETTE UNIVERSITY

PO Box 1881, Milwaukee, WI 53201-1881
Phone: 414-288-7302 • Fax: 414-288-3764
E-mail: admissions@Marquette.edu • Web: www.marquette.edu
Support: S • Institution type: 4-year private

LEARNING DISABILITY PROGRAM AND SERVICES

The Office of Disability Services (ODS) is the designated office at Marquette University to coordinate accommodations for all students with identified and documented disabilities. Accommodations are determined on a case-by-case basis. In order to provide educational opportunities the student must seek assistance in a timely manner, preferably prior to the start of classes. Relevant documentation from an appropriate licensed professional that gives a diagnosis of the disability and how it impacts on participation in courses, programs, jobs, activities and facilities at Marquette is important. The student and a staff member from ODS will discuss the student's disability and how it will impact on the requirements of the student's courses. Based upon this evaluation the ODS coordinator provides a range of individualized accommodations. For students who suspect they have a disability, a free informal screening for possible LD or ADD can be provided from ODS. This screening process can determine if the student should have a formal testing battery done.

LD/ADD ADMISSIONS INFORMATION

College entrance tests required: Yes
Interview required: No
Essay required: No
Documentation required for LD: Psychoeducational evaluation
Documentation required for ADD: Yes
Submitted to: Admissions/Office of Disability Services
Special Ed. HS coursework accepted: No

Specific course requirements of all applicants: Yes
Separate application required for program services: No
# of LD applications submitted each year: NR
# of LD applications accepted yearly: NR
Total # of students receiving LD services: NR
Acceptance into program means acceptance into college: Students must be admitted and enrolled in the university first and then request services.

ADMISSIONS

There is no special admissions process for students with LD and ADD. All applicants for admission must meet the same admission criteria. Marquette requires applicants to rank in the top 50 percent of their high school class (most rank in the top 25 percent) and have 4 years of English, 2–4 years of math and science, 2–3 years of social studies, 2 years of foreign language and other additional subjects.

ADDITIONAL INFORMATION

ODS provides a number of accommodations for students with LD and ADD including taped texts and alternative testing arrangements. If a student's disability requires a backup note-taker, ODS assists students in locating or hiring note-takers. Other methods of acquiring class material may include use of a tape recorder in class for later transcription, and photocopying class notes or copies of lecture notes. Advance notice of assignments, alternative ways of completing an assignment, computer technology, assistive listening devices, taped textbooks and course or program modifications are also available. To assist students with reading-related disabilities, the Kurzweil Omni 3000 Education System is available. Students also have access to the campus Writing Center, tutors and general study skills assistance from the Office of Student Educational Services.

Support Services Contact Information

Learning Disability Program/Services: Office of Disability Services
Director: Patricia L. Almon, Coordinator
 E-Mail: Patricia.Almon@marquette.edu
 Telephone: 414-288-1645
 Fax: 414-288-5799

LEARNING DISABILITY SERVICES

Requests for the following/services accommodations will be evaluated individually based on appropriate and current documentation.

Allowed in exams
 Calculator: Y/N
 Dictionary: Y/N
 Computer: Y/N
 Spellchecker: Y/N
Extended test time: Yes
Scribes: Y/N
Proctors: Y/N
Oral exams: Yes
Note-takers: Yes

Distraction reduced environment: Yes
Tape recording in class: Yes
Books on tape from RFBD: Yes
Taping of books not from RFBD: Yes
Accommodations for students with
 ADD: Yes
Reading machine: Yes
Other assistive technology: No
Priority registration: Yes

Added costs for services: No
LD specialists: No
Professional tutors: No
Peer tutors: 50
Max. hours/wk. for services: NR
How professors are notified of
 LD/ADD: By student and director of
 services

GENERAL ADMISSIONS INFORMATION

Director of Admissions: Robert Blust
Telephone: 414-288-7004

ENTRANCE REQUIREMENTS

 Academic units required: 4 English, 2 math, 2 science (2 science lab), 2 foreign language, 2 social studies, 2 academic electives. **Academic units recommended:** 4 English, 4 math, 3 science (3 science lab), 2 foreign language, 3 social studies, 5 academic electives. High school diploma is required and GED is accepted. ACT with Writing component required or SAT Reasoning test. Minimum paper TOEFL 520, minimum computer TOEFL 190.

Application deadline: NR
Notification: 1/15
Average GPA: NR

Average SAT Math: 591
Average SAT Verbal: 587
Average ACT: 26

Graduated top 10% of class: 33%
Graduated top 25% of class: 64%
Graduated top 50% of class: 93%

COLLEGE GRADUATION REQUIREMENTS

Course waivers allowed: Yes
Course substitutions allowed: Yes
In what course: Foreign language, math

ADDITIONAL INFORMATION

Environment: Marquette University is located in the city of Milwaukee, 1 hour south of Madison and 1 hour north of Chicago.

Student Body:
 Undergrad enrollment: 7709
 Women: 55%
 Men: 45%
 Percent out-of-state: 58%

Cost Information
 Tuition: $21,550
 Room & board: $7,890
Housing Information
 University housing: Yes
 Percent living on campus: 55%

Greek System
 Fraternity: Yes
 Sorority: Yes
Athletics: NCAA Division I

RIPON COLLEGE

300 Seward Street, PO Box 248, Ripon, WI 54971
Phone: 920-748-8337 • Fax: 920-748-8335
E-mail: adminfo@ripon.edu • Web: www.ripon.edu
Support: S • Institution type: 4-year private

LEARNING DISABILITY PROGRAM AND SERVICES

The Educational Development Program (EDP) provides a wide variety of services on the campus, including academic and personal counseling, study skills information, and tutoring. Although the focus of the program is on first generation students, students of higher need, and students who are learning disabled, other students who feel they might qualify are encouraged to contact the EDP office. EDP is a voluntary program that has been in existence at Ripon College since 1974. For the many students who have used its services, EDP has provided a network of support for academic, financial, and personal concerns. A group of peer contacts serves EDP by meeting regularly with students to facilitate communication between EDP participants and the office staff. For students who qualify, EDP offers free tutoring in specific subject areas. (All-campus tutoring is also available.) The tutors are upperclass students who have been recommended by their professors and trained by the EDP staff. These tutors serve as a supplement to faculty assistance. The aim of the tutoring program is to help students develop independent learning skills and improve their course grades. Although federal guidelines require a restriction on who qualifies, the door to EDP remains open to all eligible students.

LD/ADD ADMISSIONS INFORMATION

College entrance tests required: Yes
Interview required: Yes
Essay required: No
Documentation required for LD: Psychoeducational
evaluation
Documentation required for ADD: Yes
Submitted to: Student Support Services
Special Ed. HS coursework accepted: No

Specific course requirements of all applicants: Yes
Separate application required for program services: No
# of LD applications submitted each year: NR
# of LD applications accepted yearly: NR
Total # of students receiving LD services: 10
**Acceptance into program means acceptance into
college:** Students must be admitted and enrolled in the
college first and then request services.

ADMISSIONS

Students with learning disabilities are screened by admissions and must meet the same admission criteria as all other applicants. There is no set GPA required; courses required include 4 years English, algebra and geometry, 2 years natural science, 2 years social studies, and 7 additional units. A pre-admission interview is required. Students with learning disabilities who self-disclose are referred to Student Support Services when making prospective visits to the campus in order to ascertain specific needs and abilities of the student.

ADDITIONAL INFORMATION

EDP provides tutoring in subject areas; skills classes for no credit in time management, note-taking, test-taking strategies, reading college texts, writing papers, studying for and taking exams, and setting goals; and counseling/guidance. Student Support Services provides intensive study groups, LD support groups, and internships. EDP provides students with peer contacts who provide students with one-on-one support and is useful in helping students adjust to college life, to provide a contact for the student to go to with problems or issues, organize group tutoring, and to help students open their minds and see hope in their future.

Support Services Contact Information

Learning Disability Program/Services: Student Support Services
Director: Dan Krhin
  E-Mail: krhind@ripon.edu
  Telephone: 920-748-8107
  Fax: 920-748-8382

LEARNING DISABILITY SERVICES

Requests for the following/services accommodations will be evaluated individually based on appropriate and current documentation.

Allowed in exams	**Distraction reduced environment:** Yes	**Added costs for services:** No
Calculator: Yes	**Tape recording in class:** Yes	**LD specialists:** No
Dictionary: No	**Books on tape from RFBD:** NR	**Professional tutors:** Yes
Computer: Yes	**Taping of books not from RFBD:** Yes	**Peer tutors:** 50
Spellchecker: Yes	**Accommodations for students with**	**Max. hours/wk. for services:**
Extended test time: Yes	**ADD:** Yes	Unlimited
Scribes: Yes	**Reading machine:** Yes	**How professors are notified of**
Proctors: Yes	**Other assistive technology:** Yes	**LD/ADD:** By both student and director
Oral exams: Yes	**Priority registration:** No	
Note-takers: Yes		

GENERAL ADMISSIONS INFORMATION

Director of Admissions: Michele Wittler
Telephone: 920-748-8185

ENTRANCE REQUIREMENTS

Academic units required: 4 English, 2 math, 2 science, 2 social studies. **Academic units recommended:** 4 math, 4 science, 2 foreign language, 4 social studies. High school diploma is required and GED is accepted. ACT with or without Writing component accepted. TOEFL required of all international applicants, minimum paper TOEFL 550, minimum computer TOEFL 220.

Application deadline: Rolling	**Average SAT Math:** 535	**Graduated top 10% of class:** 22%
Notification: Rolling	**Average SAT Verbal:** 550	**Graduated top 25% of class:** 57%
Average GPA: 3.43	**Average ACT:** 23	**Graduated top 50% of class:** 87%

COLLEGE GRADUATION REQUIREMENTS

Course waivers allowed: N/A
Course substitutions allowed: N/A
In what course: N/A

ADDITIONAL INFORMATION

Environment: The college is located in a small town north of Milwaukee.

Student Body:	**Cost Information**	**Greek System**
Undergrad enrollment: 885	**Tuition:** $20,490	**Fraternity:** Yes
Women: 52%	**Room & board:** $5,360	**Sorority:** Yes
Men: 48%	**Housing Information**	**Athletics:** NCAA Division III
Percent out-of-state: 28%	**University housing:** Yes	
	Percent living on campus: 83%	

U. OF WISCONSIN—EAU CLAIRE

105 Garfield Avenue, Eau Claire, WI 54701
Phone: 715-836-5415 • Fax: 715-836-2409
E-mail: admissions@uwec.edu • Web: www.uwec.edu
Support: CS • Institution type: 4-year public

LEARNING DISABILITY PROGRAM AND SERVICES

The university does not have a separate program for students with learning disabilities. However, appropriate services are provided. Documentation of a learning disability is required to receive services. Students should meet with staff in the Students with Disabilities Office 2 months before enrolling to ensure that needed documentation is in place. Academic adjustments or accommodations will be provided to meet the students' needs based on the documentation provided.

LD/ADD ADMISSIONS INFORMATION

College entrance tests required: Yes
Interview required: No
Essay required: No
Documentation required for LD: Psychoeducational evaluation, no less than three years old
Documentation required for ADD: Yes
Submitted to: SSD
Special Ed. HS coursework accepted: No

Specific course requirements of all applicants: Yes
Separate application required for program services: No
# of LD applications submitted each year: NR
# of LD applications accepted yearly: NR
Total # of students receiving LD services: 0
Acceptance into program means acceptance into college: Students must be admitted and enrolled in the university first and then request services.

ADMISSIONS

Individuals with learning disabilities complete the standard university application form and must meet the regular university admission criteria. After a student is admitted, a copy of the diagnosis and assessment of the disability including educational recommendations should be submitted to Services for Students with Disabilities. Applicants for admission should rank in the top 50 percent of their class with an ACT of 23 or SAT of 1000. Courses required include 4 years English, 3 years math, 3 years natural science, 3 years social science, 2 years foreign language, and 2 courses in any academic course or art, music, speech, and computer science. Students not admitted in the fall may find a January admission somewhat less competitive. Students must submit an ACT score and take placement tests in English, math, and other appropriate areas. Conditional student status is given during the summer and second semester of the academic year.

ADDITIONAL INFORMATION

Students must provide documentation prior to receiving appropriate accommodations. Some of the accommodations provided with appropriate documentation could include tutoring individually or in groups; readers; scribes; note-takers; taped textbooks; proofreaders; exam accommodations including extended time, readers, and separate testing rooms. The Academic Skills Center offers individualized tutoring in math preparation and background, composition, reading, and study skills. Many departments on campus provide tutors to help students with course content. Students take a form completed by SSD staff to instructors identifying appropriate accommodation requests. Students who are denied accommodations can appeal any denial by filing a complaint with the Affirmative Action Review Board. Services and accommodations are available to undergraduate and graduate students.

Support Services Contact Information

Learning Disability Program/Services: Services for Students with Disabilities (SSD)
Director: Elizabeth Hicks
  E-Mail: hicksea@uwec.edu
  Telephone: 715-836-4542
  Fax: 715-836-3712
Contact Person: Alice Bayerl
  E-Mail: bayerlam@uwec.edu
  Telephone: 715-836-4542
  Fax: 715-836-3712

LEARNING DISABILITY SERVICES

Requests for the following/services accommodations will be evaluated individually based on appropriate and current documentation.

Allowed in exams
  Calculator: Yes
  Dictionary: Yes
  Computer: Yes
  Spellchecker: Yes
Extended test time: Yes
Scribes: Yes
Proctors: Yes
Oral exams: Yes
Note-takers: Yes

Distraction reduced environment: Yes
Tape recording in class: Yes
Books on tape from RFBD: Yes
Taping of books not from RFBD: Yes
Accommodations for students with ADD: Yes
Reading machine: Yes
Other assistive technology: Yes
Priority registration: Yes

Added costs for services: No
LD specialists: Yes
Professional tutors: No
Peer tutors: 40-50
Max. hours/wk. for services: Unlimited
How professors are notified of LD/ADD: By student

GENERAL ADMISSIONS INFORMATION

Director of Admissions: Kristina Anderson, Director
Telephone: 715-836-5415

ENTRANCE REQUIREMENTS

Academic units required: 4 English, 3 math, 3 science, 2 foreign language, 3 social studies, 2 academic electives. High school diploma is required and GED is accepted. ACT with or without Writing component accepted. TOEFL required of all international applicants, minimum paper TOEFL 525, minimum computer TOEFL 197.

Application deadline: Rolling
Notification: Rolling
Average GPA: NR

Average SAT Math: 568
Average SAT Verbal: 560
Average ACT: 24

Graduated top 10% of class: 25%
Graduated top 25% of class: 60%
Graduated top 50% of class: 96%

COLLEGE GRADUATION REQUIREMENTS

Course waivers allowed: Yes
In what course: Waivers are allowed in the area of foreign language.
Course substitutions allowed: Yes
In what course: Foreign language, math

ADDITIONAL INFORMATION

Environment: The 333-acre campus is in an urban setting 95 miles east of Minneapolis.

Student Body:
  Undergrad enrollment: 9,871
  Women: 59%
  Men: 41%
  Percent out-of-state: 21%

Cost Information
  In-state tuition: $4,864
  Out-of-state tuition: $14,910
  Room & board: $4,580
Housing Information
  University housing: Yes
  Percent living on campus: 38%

Greek System
  Fraternity: Yes
  Sorority: Yes
Athletics: NCAA Division III

U. of Wisconsin—La Crosse

1725 State Street, LaCrosse, WI 54601-3742
Phone: 608-785-8939 • Fax: 608-785-8940
E-mail: admissions@uwlax.edu • Web: www.uwlax.edu
Support: CS • Institution type: 4-year public

LEARNING DISABILITY PROGRAM AND SERVICES

The goal of the Disability Resource Services Office is to provide academic accommodations for students with learning disabilities in order for them to participate fully at the university. A number of academic and personal support services are available. Students must provide documentation (completed within the last three years) to verify the disability. The mission is to identify, reduce, or eliminate barriers in education for students with disabilities within the most integrated setting possible.

LD/ADD ADMISSIONS INFORMATION

College entrance tests required: Yes
Interview required: No
Essay required: NR
Documentation required for LD: Psychoeducational
  evaluation no less than 3 years old
Documentation required for ADD: NR
Submitted to: Disability Resurces Services
Special Ed. HS coursework accepted: No

Specific course requirements of all applicants: Yes
Separate application required for program services: Yes
# of LD applications submitted each year: 30
# of LD applications accepted yearly: NR
Total # of students receiving LD services: 140
**Acceptance into program means acceptance into
  college:** Student must be admitted and enrolled in the
  university first and then request services.

ADMISSIONS

Admission criteria include an ACT of 23 and a class rank in the top 35 percent. There is limited admission for students with learning disabilities if they are close to the regular admission requirements. Students with learning disabilities are encouraged to self-disclose their disability. These applications are automatically referred to the program director who will then request a recent psychological report, three letters of recommendation, and a personal interview. The admissions office is sensitive to the director's opinions and will admit students recommended, who can succeed, even if these students do not meet standard admissions requirements.

ADDITIONAL INFORMATION

The program director writes a letter to all the student's professors explaining the student's learning disability and describing necessary modifications. The program director meets with freshmen every two weeks. A support group meets twice a month. Services include taped texts, testing accommodations, and note-takers. Students are encouraged to get tutoring through the academic departments. Tutorial assistance is offered through each department within the university. Skills classes are offered in reading, remedial English, and mathematics. Services and accommodations are available for undergraduate and graduate students.

Support Services Contact Information

Learning Disability Program/Services: Disability Resource Services
Director: June Reinert, Coordinator
  E-Mail: reinert.june@uwlax.edu
  Telephone: 608-785-6900
  Fax: 608-785-6910

LEARNING DISABILITY SERVICES

Requests for the following/services accommodations will be evaluated individually based on appropriate and current documentation.

Allowed in exams
  Calculator: Yes
  Dictionary: NR
  Computer: Yes
  Spellchecker: Yes
Extended test time: Yes
Scribes: Yes
Proctors: Yes
Oral exams: Yes
Note-takers: Yes

Distraction reduced environment: Yes
Tape recording in class: Yes
Books on tape from RFBD: Yes
Taping of books not from RFBD: Yes
Accommodations for students with ADD: Yes
Reading machine: Yes
Other assistive technology: Yes
Priority registration: Yes

Added costs for services: No
LD specialists: Yes
Professional tutors: No
Peer tutors: Yes
Max. hours/wk. for services: Unlimited
How professors are notified of LD/ADD: By student

GENERAL ADMISSIONS INFORMATION

Director of Admissions: Tim Lewis
Telephone: 608-785-8939

ENTRANCE REQUIREMENTS

Academic units required: 4 English, 3 math, 3 science (2 science lab), 3 social studies, 4 academic electives.
Academic units recommended: 4 English, 4 math, 4 science (2 science lab), 3 foreign language, 4 social studies, 2 academic electives. High school diploma is required and GED is accepted. ACT with or without Writing component accepted. TOEFL required of all international applicants, minimum paper TOEFL 550, minimum computer TOEFL 213.

Application deadline: Rolling
Notification: Rolling
Average GPA: NR

Average SAT Math: NR
Average SAT Verbal: NR
Average ACT: 24

Graduated top 10% of class: 34%
Graduated top 25% of class: 86%
Graduated top 50% of class: 98%

COLLEGE GRADUATION REQUIREMENTS

Course waivers allowed: Yes
Course substitutions allowed: Yes
In what course: Decision is made on an individual basis.

ADDITIONAL INFORMATION

Environment: The university is located on 119 acres, in a small city 140 miles west of Madison.

Student Body:
  Undergrad enrollment: 7,614
  Women: 60%
  Men: 40%
  Percent out-of-state: 16%

Cost Information
  In-state tuition: $4,895
  Out-of-state tuition: $14,941
  Room & board: $4,570
Housing Information
  University housing: Yes
  Percent living on campus: 36%

Greek System
  Fraternity: Yes
  Sorority: Yes
Athletics: NCAA Division III

U. OF WISCONSIN—MADISON

Red Gym and Armory, 716 Langdon Street, Madison, WI 53706-1481
Phone: 608-262-3961 • Fax: 608-262-7706
E-mail: onwisconsin@admissions.wisc.edu • Web: www.wisc.edu
Support: CS • Institution type: 4-year public

LEARNING DISABILITY PROGRAM AND SERVICES

The McBurney Disability Resource Center seeks to provide students with equal access to the programs and activities of the university. LD staff work with students, staff, and faculty to promote students' independence and to ensure assessment of their abilities, not disabilities. LD staff work with students to determine disability-related accommodations and academic services that will maximize a student's opportunity for success. The LD staff consists of two part-time professionals. Over 450 undergraduate and graduate students with LD/ADD are currently registered with the McBurney Center. Students with LD who tend to do well have graduated from competitive high school or college programs and are reasonably independent, proactive in seeking assistance, and use accommodations similar to those offered here.

LD/ADD ADMISSIONS INFORMATION

College entrance tests required: Yes
Interview required: No
Essay required: Yes
Documentation required for LD: Psychoeducational evaluation
Documentation required for ADD: Yes
Submitted to: McBurney Disability Resources Center
Special Ed. HS coursework accepted: NR

Specific course requirements of all applicants: Yes
Separate application required for program services: No
# of LD applications submitted each year: NR
# of LD applications accepted yearly: NR
Total # of students receiving LD services: 450
Acceptance into program means acceptance into college: Students must be admitted and enrolled in the university first and then request services.

ADMISSIONS
The admission process is the same for all applicants. Applicants not meeting regular admission criteria who self-disclose a disability can have their documentation reviewed by an admissions office liaison, and then sent to the McBurney Center. The disability could become a factor in admission when documentation is provided that clearly establishes the presence of a disability, shows it on education, and a record of academic achievement that meets guidelines suggesting potential success. Factors in the alternative admissions review process include disability information, grades, rank, test scores, course requirements completed, and potential for success. Examples of LD information include date of diagnosis or onset of disability and the ramifications of the disability on curricular requirements. If course requirements are directly impacted by the disability, resulting in low grades or the absence of courses, the GPA will be reviewed with and without those courses.

ADDITIONAL INFORMATION
The documentation must be completed by a professional qualified to diagnose a LD; must include results of a clinical interview and descriptions of the testing procedures, instruments used, test and sub-test results reported in standard scores as well as percentile rank and grade scores where useful, and interpretation and recommendations based on data gathered. It must be comprehensive and include test results where applicable in intelligence, reading, math, spelling, written language, language processing, and cognitive processing skills. Testing should carefully examine areas of concern/weakness as well as areas of strengths; documentation should include a clear diagnostic statement based on the test results and personal history. Students may be eligible for advocacy/liaison with faculty and staff, alternative testing accommodations, curriculum modifications, disability management advising, learning skills training, liaison with Voc Rehab, McBurney Learning Resource Room card, note-taker, peer support groups, priority registration, taped texts, and course materials.

Support Services Contact Information

Learning Disability Program/Services: McBurney Disability Resource Center
Director: J. Trey Duffy
  Telephone: 608-263-2741
  Fax: 608-265-2998
Contact Person: Anne Robertson
  E-Mail: amrobertson@wisc.edu
  Telephone: 608-263-2741
  Fax: 608-265-2998

LEARNING DISABILITY SERVICES

Requests for the following/services accommodations will be evaluated individually based on appropriate and current documentation.

Allowed in exams
  Calculator: Y/N
  Dictionary: Y/N
  Computer: Y/N
  Spellchecker: Y/N
Extended test time: Yes
Scribes: Yes
Proctors: Yes
Oral exams: Yes
Note-takers: Yes

Distraction reduced environment: Yes
Tape recording in class: Yes
Books on tape from RFBD: Yes
Taping of books not from RFBD: Yes
Accommodations for students with ADD: Yes
Reading machine: Yes
Other assistive technology: Yes
Priority registration: NR

Added costs for services: No
LD specialists: Yes
Professional tutors: Yes
Peer tutors: Yes
Max. hours/wk. for services: 0.5
How professors are notified of LD/ADD: By student

GENERAL ADMISSIONS INFORMATION

Director of Admissions: Robert Seltzer
Telephone: 608-262-3961

ENTRANCE REQUIREMENTS

Academic units required: 4 English, 3 math, 3 science, 2 foreign language, 3 social studies. **Academic units recommended:** 4 English, 4 math, 4 science, 2 foreign language, 4 social studies, High school diploma is required and GED is accepted. ACT with Writing component required or SAT Reasoning test. TOEFL required of all international applicants, minimum paper TOEFL 550, minimum computer TOEFL 213.

Application deadline: 2/1
Notification: Rolling
Average GPA: 3.68

Average SAT Math: 649
Average SAT Verbal: 611
Average ACT: 28

Graduated top 10% of class: 58%
Graduated top 25% of class: 93%
Graduated top 50% of class: 99%

COLLEGE GRADUATION REQUIREMENTS

Course waivers allowed: No
Course substitutions allowed: No
In what course: N/A

ADDITIONAL INFORMATION

Environment: The university is located in an urban area in the state capital.

Student Body:
  Undergrad enrollment: 28217
  Women: 53%
  Men: 47%
  Percent out-of-state: 29%

Cost Information
  In-state tuition: $5,866
  Out-of-state tuition: $19,866
  Room & board: $6,250
Housing Information
  University housing: Yes

  Percent living on campus: 24%
Greek System
  Fraternity: Yes
  Sorority: Yes
Athletics: NCAA Division I

University of Wisconsin—Madison

U. OF WISCONSIN—MILWAUKEE

PO Box 749, Milwaukee, WI 53201
Phone: 414-229-3800 • Fax: 414-229-6940
E-mail: uwmlook@des.uwm.edu • Web: www.uwm.edu
Support: CS • Institution type: 4-year public

LEARNING DISABILITY PROGRAM AND SERVICES

The Learning Disabilities Program offers a wide range of support services. The goal of the program is to provide an environment that encourages the development of the unique talents of each student. This program is well suited for those who can function independently with some academic support. There is an emphasis on mainstreaming and participation to the fullest extent in the total life of the university community. Services provided include taped textbooks, tutorial services, and special arrangements for test taking, note-takers, communication with professors, monitoring, and priority registration.

LD/ADD ADMISSIONS INFORMATION

College entrance tests required: Yes
Interview required: Yes for AOC
Essay required: No
Documentation required for LD: Comprehensive and current psychoeducational or neuropsychological assessment; recommended testing instruments include the WAIS–III and the WJ–R
Documentation required for ADD: Preferred is a comprehensive and current psychoeducational or neuropsychological assessment. Also accepted is completion of the UWM'S LD Program's form of certification of ADD by a psychiatrist or psychologist
Submitted to: Learning Disabilities Program
Special Ed. HS coursework accepted: Yes

Specific course requirements of all applicants: Yes
Separate application required for program services: Yes
# of LD applications submitted each year: 50
# of LD applications accepted yearly: 25–50
Total # of students receiving LD services: 100–125
Acceptance into program means acceptance into college: Students must be admitted and enrolled in the university first and then request services. Some students may apply directly through AOC.

ADMISSIONS

Admission into UWM is necessary for participation in the LD Program. Students apply directly to the admissions office. Course requirements include 4 years English, 3 years math, 3 years science, 1 science lab, 3 years social studies, and 4 years electives. The LD Program does not make admission decisions. Students should send documentation to the LD Program, and once admitted to the university, the students will be contacted by the LD Program. The director of the LD Program can assist students with the admission process, and can make informal recommendations to the admission office on an individual basis. Students not regularly admissible, who are serious about continuing their education, and show potential for university study, may apply through the Academic Opportunity Center (AOC). Students should submit a UWM application; send transcripts; take AOC placement tests; submit ACT/SAT; and schedule an interview. Approximately 60–75 students submit applications yearly through AOC. There is no limit to the number of students who can be admitted through the AOC each year.

ADDITIONAL INFORMATION

Students, who may not be regularly admissible based on low GPA, ACT, SAT, or rank in class or who lack academic units, or those who would benefit from intensive advising, may want to apply directly to AOC on their UWM application. Students will need to take the AOC test series, including math, English, and the Nelson Denny Reading Test to identify which accommodations can be requested. Students must also have an interview with an advisor in the AOC. The AOC will evaluate the student's potential in making an admission decision. AOC offers intensive advising, basic skills courses, and additional academic support.

Support Services Contact Information

Learning Disability Program/Services: Learning Disabilities Program
Director: Laurie Petersen
 E-Mail: lauriep@uwm.edu
 Telephone: 414-229-6239
 Fax: 414-229-2237

LEARNING DISABILITY SERVICES

Requests for the following/services accommodations will be evaluated individually based on appropriate and current documentation.

Allowed in exams		
Calculator: Yes	**Distraction reduced environment:** Yes	**Added costs for services:** No
Dictionary: Yes	**Tape recording in class:** Yes	**LD specialists:** Yes
Computer: Yes	**Books on tape from RFBD:** Yes	**Professional tutors:** No
Spellchecker: Yes	**Taping of books not from RFBD:** Yes	**Peer tutors:** Yes
Extended test time: Yes	**Accommodations for students with**	**Max. hours/wk. for services:** 3
Scribes: Yes	**ADD:** Yes	**How professors are notified of**
Proctors: Yes	**Reading machine:** Yes	**LD/ADD:** By student
Oral exams: Yes	**Other assistive technology:** Yes	
Note-takers: Yes	**Priority registration:** Yes	

GENERAL ADMISSIONS INFORMATION

Director of Admissions: Beth Weckmueller
Telephone: 414-229-3800

ENTRANCE REQUIREMENTS

Academic units required: 4 English, 3 math, 3 science (1 science lab), 3 social studies, 4 academic electives. Academic units recommended: 4 English, 3 math, 3 science (1 science lab), 2 foreign language, 3 social studies, 4 academic electives. High school diploma is required and GED is accepted. TOEFL required of all international applicants, minimum paper TOEFL 500, minimum computer TOEFL 173.

Application deadline: 8/1	**Average SAT Math:** NR	**Graduated top 10% of class:** 8%
Notification: Rolling	**Average SAT Verbal:** NR	**Graduated top 25% of class:** 29%
Average GPA: NR	**Average ACT:** 22	**Graduated top 50% of class:** 69%

COLLEGE GRADUATION REQUIREMENTS

Course waivers allowed: No
Course substitutions allowed: Yes
In what course: Determinations will be made for course substitutions on an individual basis, generally in math and foreign language courses

ADDITIONAL INFORMATION

Environment: The university is located on 90 acres in a residential area 90 miles north of Chicago.

Student Body:	Cost Information	Greek System
Undergrad enrollment: 19,785	**In-state tuition:** $4,439	**Fraternity:** Yes
Women: 55%	**Out-of-state tuition:** $17,190	**Sorority:** Yes
Men: 45%	**Room & board:** $4,320	**Athletics:** NCAA Division I
Percent out-of-state: 1%	**Housing Information**	
	University housing: Yes	
	Percent living on campus: 13%	

U. OF WISCONSIN—OSHKOSH

Dempsey Hall 135, 800 Algoma Boulevard, Oshkosh, WI 54901
Phone: 920-424-0202 • Fax: 920-424-1098
E-mail: oshadmuw@uwosh.edu • Web: www.uwosh.edu
Support: SP • Institution type: 4-year public

LEARNING DISABILITY PROGRAM AND SERVICES

Project Success is a language remediation project that is based on mastering the entire sound structure of the English language. These students are academically able and determined to succeed, in spite of a pronounced problem in a number of areas. Help is offered in the following ways: direct remediation of deficiencies through the Orton-Gillingham Technique, one-to-one tutoring assistance, math and writing labs, guidance and counseling with scheduling coursework and interpersonal relations, extended time on untimed exams, and by providing an atmosphere that is supportive. The goal is for students to become language independent in and across all of these major educational areas: math, spelling, reading, writing, comprehension, and study skills. As full-time university students they will acquire language independence by mastering the entire phonetic structure of the American English language.

LD/ADD ADMISSIONS INFORMATION

College entrance tests required: Yes
Interview required: No
Essay required: Yes
Documentation required for LD: Full psychoeducational testing no less than three years old
Documentation required for ADD: Yes
Submitted to: Project Success
Special Ed. HS coursework accepted: Yes

Specific course requirements of all applicants: Yes
Separate application required for program services: No
# of LD applications submitted each year: 50–70
# of LD applications accepted yearly: 40
Total # of students receiving LD services: 200
Acceptance into program means acceptance into college: Students are accepted jointly to Project Success and the university; however they must submit separate applications for the program and the university.

ADMISSIONS

Students should apply to Project Success in their sophomore year of high school. Applicants apply by writing a letter, in their own handwriting, indicating interest in the program and why they are interested. Applications are processed on a first-come, first-served basis. Those interested should apply at least 1–2 years prior to desired entrance. Students and parents will be invited to interview. The interview is used to assess family dynamics in terms of support for the student, and reasons for wanting to attend college. The director is looking for motivation, stability, and the ability of the students to describe the disability. Acceptance into Project Success does not grant acceptance into the university. Admission to the university and acceptance into Project Success is a joint decision but a separate process is required for each. General admissions procedures must be followed before acceptance into the special program can be offered. ACT/SAT or GPA are not critical. Accepted students for Project Success are required to register for a summer term prior to freshman year. 3 years of Math are required for admission

ADDITIONAL INFORMATION

Incoming freshmen to Project Success must participate in an eight-week summer school program consisting of simultaneous multi-sensory instructional procedures (SMSIP). This procedure is used to teach study skills, reading, spelling, writing, and mathematical operations. Students are eligible for tutoring services and extended time testing opportunities. The Project Success program offers enrolled students the following services at no cost: organizational tutors at least once a week, math tutors, remedial reading and spelling courses, and tutoring for English and written expression. An important component of Project Success is the social habitation program, which focuses on learning about dyslexia.Services and accommodations are available for undergraduate and graduate students.

Support Services Contact Information

Learning Disability Program/Services: Project Success
Director: William R Kitz, PhD
   E-Mail: kitz@uwosh.edu
   Telephone: 920-424-1033

LEARNING DISABILITY SERVICES

Requests for the following/services accommodations will be evaluated individually based on appropriate and current documentation.

Allowed in exams
  Calculator: Yes
  Dictionary: Yes
  Computer: Yes
  Spellchecker: No
Extended test time: Yes
Scribes: No
Proctors: Yes
Oral exams: No
Note-takers: No

Distraction reduced environment: Yes
Tape recording in class: Yes
Books on tape from RFBD: NR
Taping of books not from RFBD: Yes
Accommodations for students with
  ADD: Yes
Reading machine: No
Other assistive technology: Yes
Priority registration: Yes

Added costs for services: No
LD specialists: Yes
Professional tutors: Yes
Peer tutors: 80
Max. hours/wk. for services: NR
How professors are notified of
  LD/ADD: By both student and director

GENERAL ADMISSIONS INFORMATION

Director of Admissions: Jill Endries
Telephone: 920-424-0202

ENTRANCE REQUIREMENTS

 Academic units required: 4 English, 3 math, 3 science (3 science lab), 3 social studies, 1 history, 4 academic electives. **Academic units recommended:** 4 math, 4 science. High school diploma is required and GED is accepted. ACT with or without Writing component accepted. TOEFL required of all international applicants, minimum paper TOEFL 525, minimum computer TOEFL 193.

Application deadline: 8/1
Notification: Rolling
Average GPA: 3.1

Average SAT Math: NR
Average SAT Verbal: NR
Average ACT: 22

Graduated top 10% of class: 8%
Graduated top 25% of class: 32%
Graduated top 50% of class: 81%

COLLEGE GRADUATION REQUIREMENTS

Course waivers allowed: Yes
In what course: UW—Oshkosh has special accommodations in place relating to the foreign language requirement
Course substitutions allowed: Yes
In what course: Foreign language and several other in selected areas

ADDITIONAL INFORMATION

Environment: The campus is located 3 hours north of Chicago and 2 hours northeast of Madison.

Student Body:
  Undergrad enrollment: 9,692
  Women: 59%
  Men: 41%
  Percent out-of-state: 2%

Cost Information
  In-state tuition: $4,616
  Out-of-state tuition: $14,662
  Room & board: $4,630
Housing Information
  University housing: Yes
  Percent living on campus: 25%

Greek System
  Fraternity: Yes
  Sorority: Yes
Athletics: NCAA Division III

U. OF WISCONSIN—STEVENS POINT

Student Services Center, Stevens Point, WI 54481
Phone: 715-346-2441 • Fax: 715-346-3957
E-mail: admiss@uwsp.edu • Web: www.uwsp.edu
Support: S • Institution type: 4-year public

LEARNING DISABILITY PROGRAM AND SERVICES

The university does not have a formal program or a specialized curriculum for students with LD; rather it provides all of the services appropriate to ensure equal access to all programs. Their philosophy is to provide what is mandated in order to enhance the student's academic success, and also to convey their concern for the student's total well-being. The director is a strong advocate for students. Students are encouraged to meet with the director prior to admissions for information about the services. A full range of accommodations are provided. The services provide a multisensory approach developing compensatory skills, not remediation, and utilize a developmental model for advising as well as psychosocial adjustment. Student success is contingent on many factors; some responsibilities belong to the student, others belong to the university, and others are shared by both. Students should make an appointment at the beginning of each semester; should not miss appointments; register with RFBD for taped texts; make their needs known; and be a self-advocate. The Office of Disability Services (ODS) provides students with accommodations that are appropriate for the disability. Together, ODS and the student can work toward effective accommodations and utilization of support services and establish a working relationship based on trust and communication.

LD/ADD ADMISSIONS INFORMATION

College entrance tests required: Yes
Interview required: No
Essay required: No
Documentation required for LD: WAIS or WISC R, WJ, ETS as appropriate
Documentation required for ADD: Yes
Submitted to: ODS
Special Ed. HS coursework accepted: No

Specific course requirements of all applicants: Yes
Separate application required for program services: No
# of LD applications submitted each year: NR
# of LD applications accepted yearly: NR
Total # of students receiving LD services: 160
Acceptance into program means acceptance into college: Student must be admitted and enrolled in the university first and then request services.

ADMISSIONS

There is no separate admission procedure for students with learning disabilities. However, students are encouraged to make a pre-admission inquiry and talk to the director of ODS. Students with learning disabilities who do not meet the combined class rank and ACT test score criteria of 64 should send a letter of recommendation from the high school LD specialist or counselor. Students should also meet with the director of disabled student services at Stevens Point if support is needed in the application process. The director of admission does have the flexibility to admit students with learning disabilities on a case-by-case basis. General admission requirements include 4 years of English (3 credits of college preparatory composition and literature; 4th year may be any non-remedial English course that meets DPI requirements); 3 years of social science; 3 years of mathematics (algebra 1 and other college preparatory courses with an algebra and/or geometry prerequisite); 3 years of natural science; 2 years of academic electives (from the above areas, foreign language, fine arts or computer science, excluding keyboarding); and 2 years of other electives (from the above areas or other academic or vocational courses); students who rank in the top 25 percent of their high school graduating class or have an ACT score of 21 or higher (SAT Reasoning test 990) and have a GPA of 3.25 or higher (on a 4-point scale) or have a 21 or higher on SAT Reasoning test and rank in the top 50 percent of their high school graduating class. Applicants who meet one of the following requirements will be considered on an individual basis: rank in the top 50 percent of the high school graduating class, have a high school grade point average of 3.00 or above, or earn an ACT composite score of 21 or higher (SAT SAT Reasoning test 990).

ADDITIONAL INFORMATION

ODS provides accommodations that are appropriate to the disability, orientation assistance, taped textbooks, note-takers, proctors and scribes, adaptive testing, priority registration, assistance with life skills and advising, referral to tutoring and writing assistance, time management and study strategies training, notification to faculty/staff regarding necessary accommodations, assessment and referral services for those not yet diagnosed, and a commitment to keeping scheduled appointments and a corresponding commitment to being timely. The Tutoring-Learning Center schedules 30-minute tutoring sessions and small-group tutoring; tutoring is free for students wanting help with reading or writing assignments. Tutoring in subject areas is done in groups and there is a $10 enrollment fee; however, for most students, the fee is covered by various support programs.

Support Services Contact Information

Learning Disability Program/Services: Office of Disability Services (ODS)
Director: Jim Joque
  E-Mail: jjoque@uwsp.edu
  Telephone: 715-346-3365
  Fax: 715-346-2558

LEARNING DISABILITY SERVICES

Requests for the following/services accommodations will be evaluated individually based on appropriate and current documentation.

Allowed in exams	**Distraction reduced environment:** Yes	**Added costs for services:** No
Calculator: Yes	**Tape recording in class:** Yes	**LD specialists:** No
Dictionary: Yes	**Books on tape from RFBD:** Yes	**Professional tutors:** 3
Computer: Yes	**Taping of books not from RFBD:** Yes	**Peer tutors:** 5
Spellchecker: Yes	**Accommodations for students with**	**Max. hours/wk. for services:** 2
Extended test time: Yes	**ADD:** Yes	**How professors are notified of**
Scribes: Yes	**Reading machine:** Yes	**LD/ADD:** By director
Proctors: Yes	**Other assistive technology:** Yes	
Oral exams: Yes	**Priority registration:** Yes	
Note-takers: Yes		

GENERAL ADMISSIONS INFORMATION

Director of Admissions: Catherine Glennon
Telephone: 715-346-2441

ENTRANCE REQUIREMENTS

Academic units required: 4 English, 3 math, 3 science, 3 social studies, 4 academic electives. **Academic units recommended:** 2 foreign language, High school diploma is required and GED is accepted. ACT with or without Writing component accepted. TOEFL required of all international applicants, minimum paper TOEFL 550, minimum computer TOEFL 193.

Application deadline: Rolling	**Average SAT Math:** 526	**Graduated top 10% of class:** 15%
Notification: Rolling	**Average SAT Verbal:** 536	**Graduated top 25% of class:** 47%
Average GPA: 3.40	**Average ACT:** 23	**Graduated top 50% of class:** 97%

COLLEGE GRADUATION REQUIREMENTS

Course waivers allowed: No
Course substitutions allowed: Yes
In what course: Both

ADDITIONAL INFORMATION

Environment: The University of Wisconsin at Stevens Point is located on 335 acres 110 miles north of Madison.

Student Body:	**Cost Information**	**Greek System**
Undergrad enrollment: 8,536	**In-state tuition:** $4,000	**Fraternity:** Yes
Women: 55%	**Out-of-state tuition:** $14,046	**Sorority:** Yes
Men: 45%	**Room & board:** $4,094	**Athletics:** NCAA Division III
Percent out-of-state: 6%	**Housing Information**	
	University housing: Yes	
	Percent living on campus: 36%	

U. OF WISCONSIN—WHITEWATER

800 West Main Street, Baker Hall, Whitewater, WI 53190-1791
Phone: 262-472-1440 • Fax: 262-472-1515
E-mail: uwwadmit@uww.edu • Web: www.uww.edu
Support: CS • Institution type: 4-year public

LEARNING DISABILITY PROGRAM AND SERVICES

The University of Wisconsin—Whitewater offers support services for students with learning disabilities including tutoring, teaching strategies for long-term success, test-taking accommodations, and note-takers. The program is based on the philosophy that students with learning disabilities can learn specific strategies that will enable them to become independent learners who can be successful in a college setting. Project ASSIST offers a four-week high school to college program for incoming freshmen during the summer prior to first year entry into the university. The intent of this program is to help students make a smooth transition from high school to university life. Any student with a learning disability who is accepted to UW—Whitewater is eligible to attend the summer program. There is a charge for room and board for the four weeks (residence and meal plan), the three credit course based on the university's fee schedule for in and out-of-state tuition, and a separate fee for Project ASSIST.

LD/ADD ADMISSIONS INFORMATION

College entrance tests required: Yes
Interview required: Yes
Essay required: Yes
Documentation required for LD: WAIS–III; WJ
Documentation required for ADD: Yes
Submitted to: Project Assist
Special Ed. HS coursework accepted: No

Specific course requirements of all applicants: Yes
Separate application required for program services: Yes
# of LD applications submitted each year: 125
# of LD applications accepted yearly: 80
Total # of students receiving LD services: 200
Acceptance into program means acceptance into college: Students must be admitted and enrolled in the university first and then request services. Project ASSIST reviews some applications and makes recommendations to admissions.

ADMISSIONS

All applicants must meet the same criteria for admission. General criteria include ACT 18 or a lower ACT if the student is in the top 50 percent of the class. Students apply to the university admissions first; after a decision is made to admit or deny the director of Project ASSIST reviews the file to decide whether to make an exception for admission or whether the student may use services. If the director needs to make an exception for admissions, then the Summer Transition program is required and students receive 2 years of support. Summer Transition Program is only offered to students with learning disabilities.

ADDITIONAL INFORMATION

Students may have LD assessments on campus for $250. Skills courses are offered for no credit in reading comprehension and writing. The Summer Transition program offers a three credit study skills class that emphasizes such things as note-taking skills, test taking strategies, time management skills, word processing skills, and verbal and written language skills. The students also write a research paper during which time they become proficient on the word processor, as well as, learning how to use the library. This course is a "developmental" course, which means that although the students get a grade for the course and the grade is averaged into their cumulative grade point average, the course does not count toward the total hours needed for graduation. Students in the Summer Transition Program also take a Project ASSIST class where students learn about their learning disabilities-both strengths and weaknesses-as well as their learning styles and how these affect their success in the classroom. Students begin to practice advocating for themselves with their professors and receive help with registration for the fall semester. Focus is also on time management, organization and various learning strategies.

Support Services Contact Information

Learning Disability Program/Services: Project Assist
Director: Nancy Amacher
 E-Mail: amacher@uww.edu
 Telephone: 262-472-4711
 Fax: 262-472-4865

LEARNING DISABILITY SERVICES

Requests for the following/services accommodations will be evaluated individually based on appropriate and current documentation.

Allowed in exams
 Calculator: Yes
 Dictionary: Yes
 Computer: Yes
 Spellchecker: Yes
 Extended test time: Yes
 Scribes: Yes
 Proctors: Yes
 Oral exams: Y/N
 Note-takers: Yes

Distraction reduced environment: Yes
Tape recording in class: Yes
Books on tape from RFBD: Yes
Taping of books not from RFBD: Yes
Accommodations for students with
 ADD: Yes
Reading machine: No
Other assistive technology: Yes
Priority registration: Yes

Added costs for services: 1400 (per year)
LD specialists: Yes
Professional tutors: No
Peer tutors: 35
Max. hours/wk. for services: Unlimited
How professors are notified of LD/ADD: By student

GENERAL ADMISSIONS INFORMATION

Director of Admissions: Mr. Stephen J. McKellips
Telephone: 262-472-1440

ENTRANCE REQUIREMENTS

Academic units required: 4 English, 3 math, 3 science, 2 foreign language, 3 social studies, 4 academic electives.
Academic units recommended: 4 English, 4 math, 4 science, 2 foreign language, 4 social studies, 4 academic electives. High school diploma is required and GED is accepted. ACT without Writing component accepted. TOEFL required of all international applicants, minimum paper TOEFL 500, minimum computer TOEFL 214.

Application deadline: Rolling
Notification: Rolling
Average GPA: NR

Average SAT Math: NR
Average SAT Verbal: NR
Average ACT: 22

Graduated top 10% of class: 10%
Graduated top 25% of class: 34%
Graduated top 50% of class: 81%

COLLEGE GRADUATION REQUIREMENTS

Course waivers allowed: No
Course substitutions allowed: Yes
In what course: Math and foreign language

ADDITIONAL INFORMATION

Environment: The university is located in a small town southwest of Milwaukee.

Student Body:
 Undergrad enrollment: 9,239
 Women: 51%
 Men: 49%
 Percent out-of-state: 4%

Cost Information
 In-state tuition: $4,370
 Out-of-state tuition: $14,965
 Room & board: $4,210
Housing Information
 University housing: Yes
 Percent living on campus: 40%

Greek System
 Fraternity: Yes
 Sorority: Yes
Athletics: NCAA Division III

University of Wisconsin—Whitewater

SHERIDAN COLLEGE

3059 Cofeen Avenue, Sherdian, WY 82801
Phone: 307-674-6446 • Fax: 307-674-4293
E-mail: admissions@sheridan.edu
Web: www.sheridan.edu
Support: S • Institution type: 2-year public

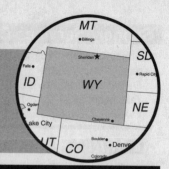

LEARNING DISABILITY PROGRAM AND SERVICES

Sheridan College has limited services available for students with learning disabilities. Students who have been enrolled in special education classes in high school may find that the college does not have the extensive services necessary for them to be successful. Students need to be self sufficient, because only a small percentage of the time of the two advisors/counselors are available to work with students with disabilities. Students requesting accommodations must provide psychoeducational evaluations and have these sent to the counseling/testing offices. The college reserves the right to evaluate whether it can serve the needs of students.

LD/ADD ADMISSIONS INFORMATION

College entrance tests required: No
Interview required: No
Essay required: No
Documentation required for LD: Psychoeducational evaluation
Documentation required for ADD: Yes
Submitted to: Learning Center
Special Ed. HS coursework accepted: Yes

Specific course requirements of all applicants: No
Separate application required for program services: Yes
# of LD applications submitted each year: 10
# of LD applications accepted yearly: 8
Total # of students receiving LD services: 10
Acceptance into program means acceptance into college: Students must be admitted and enrolled in the college first and then request services.

ADMISSIONS

There are no special admission procedures or criteria for students with learning disabilities. The college has open admissions and any student with a high school diploma or GED is eligible to attend. All students are treated the same and must submit the general college application for admission. Any information on learning disabilities provided is voluntarily given by the student. Students with learning disabilities must submit psychoeducational evaluations. The admission decision is made by the director of the program.

ADDITIONAL INFORMATION

The college offers tutoring, quiet places to take tests, readers, extended testing time, recorders, note-takers, and the availability of a few Franklin Spellers. Remediation courses are offered in arithmetic skills, spelling, vocabulary, reading, writing, and algebra. Other aides for students with learning disabilities include test-taking strategies, books on tape, tutoring one-on-one or in small groups in the Learning Center, and GED preparation and testing. Support services include career testing and evaluation, peer counseling and personal and career development.

Support Services Contact Information

Learning Disability Program/Services: Advising/Learning Center
Director: Zane Garstad
 E-Mail: zgarstad@sheridan.edu
 Telephone: 307-674-6446
 Fax: 307-674-7205
Contact Person: Lisa Wallace
 E-Mail: lwallace@sheridan.edu
 Telephone: 307-674-6446
 Fax: 307-674-7205

LEARNING DISABILITY SERVICES

Requests for the following/services accommodations will be evaluated individually based on appropriate and current documentation.

Allowed in exams
 Calculator: Yes
 Dictionary: Yes
 Computer: Yes
 Spellchecker: Yes
Extended test time: Yes
Scribes: Yes
Proctors: Yes
Oral exams: Yes
Note-takers: Yes

Distraction reduced environment: Yes
Tape recording in class: Yes
Books on tape from RFBD: Yes
Taping of books not from RFBD: Yes
Accommodations for students with ADD: Yes
Reading machine: No
Other assistive technology: Yes
Priority registration: No

Added costs for services: No
LD specialists: No
Professional tutors: Yes
Peer tutors: Yes
Max. hours/wk. for services: Unlimited
How professors are notified of LD/ADD: By student

GENERAL ADMISSIONS INFORMATION

Director of Admissions: Zane Garstad
Telephone: 307-674-6466

ENTRANCE REQUIREMENTS

High school diploma is required and GED is not accepted. Open door admissions. TOEFL required for all international applicants, minimum paper TOEFL 500, minimum computer TOEFL 173.

Application deadline: Rolling
Notification: Rolling
Average GPA: NR

Average SAT Math: NR
Average SAT Verbal: NR
Average ACT: NR

Graduated top 10% of class: NR
Graduated top 25% of class: NR
Graduated top 50% of class: NR

COLLEGE GRADUATION REQUIREMENTS

Course waivers allowed: Yes
Course substitutions allowed: Yes
In what course: On a case-by-case basis

ADDITIONAL INFORMATION

Environment: The college is located on 64 acres in Sheridan.

Student Body:
 Undergrad enrollment: 3,500
 Women: 60%
 Men: 40%
 Percent out-of-state: 6%

Cost Information
 In-state tuition: $1,723
 Out-of-state tuition: $4,371
 Room & board: $3,720
Housing Information
 University housing: Yes
 Percent living on campus: 5%

Greek System
 Fraternity: No
 Sorority: No
Athletics: NJCAA

UNIVERSITY OF WYOMING

Dept 3435, 1000 E University Ave, Laramie, WY 82071
Phone: 307-766-5160 • Fax: 307-766-4042
E-mail: Why-Wyo@uwyo.edu • Web: www.uwyo.edu
Support: CS • Institution type: 4-year public

LEARNING DISABILITY PROGRAM AND SERVICES

University Disability Support Services (UDSS) offers academic support services to students with learning disabilities and physically handicapped students. The goals are to promote the independence and self-sufficiency of students, and to encourage the provision of equal opportunities in education for students with disabilities. Any student enrolled at UW who has a documented disability is eligible for assistance. UDSS provides disability-related accommodations and services, technical assistance, consultations, and resource information. Recommended documentation includes a clear statement of the LD (documentation should be current, preferably within the last three years); a summary of assessment procedures and evaluation instruments used to make the diagnosis and a summary of the results, including standardized or percentile score that supports the diagnosis (LD testing must be comprehensive, including a measure of both aptitude and achievement in the areas of reading, mathematics, and written language); a statement of strengths and needs that will impact the student's ability to meet the demands of college; and suggestions of reasonable accommodations that might be appropriate. Accommodations are collaboratively determined by the student and the assigned disability support service coordinator.

LD/ADD ADMISSIONS INFORMATION

College entrance tests required: Yes
Interview required: No
Essay required: No
Documentation required for LD: A comprehensive diagnostic report completed by an appropriate professional. Report must specifically state what the diagnosed condition is and how it currently affects the individual
Documentation required for ADD: A current, diagnostic report from a qualified professional that provides a specific diagnosis, how that diagnosis was determined, and the functional impact of the ADD on that individual
Submitted to: UDSS
Special Ed. HS coursework accepted: Yes

Specific course requirements of all applicants: Yes
Separate application required for program services: Yes
# of LD applications submitted each year: 50–75
# of LD applications accepted yearly: NR
Total # of students receiving LD services: 50–75
Acceptance into program means acceptance into college: Students must be admitted and enrolled in the university first and then request services.

ADMISSIONS

Students with learning disabilities must meet general admission requirements. If the of UDSS students are borderline and have a documented learning disability, they are encouraged to self-identify to the director. Students who were diagnosed late in high school or began utilizing services late may be able to explain how this had an impact on academics. Students with learning disabilities who meet the general admission criteria request LD services after being admitted. Conditional admission is granted with GPA of 2.5 or GPA of 2.25 and 20 ACT or SAT of 960. Students with learning disabilities not meeting admission criteria and not qualifying for assured or conditional admission may have their applications reviewed by the LD program director. The LD director will make a recommendation to the Office of Admission.

ADDITIONAL INFORMATION

Services include priority registration, readers, assistance with study skills, note-taking, test preparation, word processing orientation, equipment loan assistance, tutor referral, and advocacy for students via university committee on campus access for the disabled. Auditory systems are also used to provide access to print mediums for persons with LD. Synthesized speech reinforces visual cues; grammar checking software is available to proof documents and to improve writing skills; writing skills may be improved through the use of word prediction software; and Dragon Dictate, a voice recognition program, may benefit those students who have learning disabilities that affect written expression. All students must take one course in math or quantitative reasoning to graduate.

Support Services Contact Information

Learning Disability Program/Services: University Disability Support Services (UDSS)
Director: Chris Primus
  E-Mail: cfprimus@uwyo.edu
  Telephone: 307-766-6189
  Fax: 307-766-4010

LEARNING DISABILITY SERVICES

Requests for the following/services accommodations will be evaluated individually based on appropriate and current documentation.

Allowed in exams
  Calculator: Yes
  Dictionary: Yes
  Computer: Yes
  Spellchecker: Yes
Extended test time: Yes
Scribes: Yes
Proctors: Yes
Oral exams: Yes
Note-takers: Yes

Distraction reduced environment: Yes
Tape recording in class: Yes
Books on tape from RFBD: No
Taping of books not from RFBD: Yes
Accommodations for students with ADD: Yes
Reading machine: Yes
Other assistive technology: Yes
Priority registration: Yes

Added costs for services: No
LD specialists: Yes
Professional tutors: Yes
Peer tutors: Yes
Max. hours/wk. for services: As available
How professors are notified of LD/ADD: By both student and director

GENERAL ADMISSIONS INFORMATION

Director of Admissions: Sara Axelson
Telephone: 307-766-5160

ENTRANCE REQUIREMENTS

Academic units required: 4 English, 3 math, 3 science (3 science lab), 3 cultural context electives. **Adademic units recommended:** 3 behavioral or social sciences, 3 visual or performing arts, 3 humanities or earth/space sciences. High school diploma is required and GED is accepted. ACT with or without Writing component accepted. TOEFL required of all international applicants, minimum paper TOEFL 525, minimum computer TOEFL 197.

Application deadline: 8/10
Notification: Rolling
Average GPA: 3.40

Average SAT Math: 544
Average SAT Verbal: 535
Average ACT: 23

Graduated top 10% of class: 21%
Graduated top 25% of class: 48%
Graduated top 50% of class: 77%

COLLEGE GRADUATION REQUIREMENTS

Course waivers allowed: No
Course substitutions allowed: Yes
In what course: Foreign language, math

ADDITIONAL INFORMATION

Environment: The university is located on 785 acres in a small town 128 miles north of Denver.

Student Body:
  Undergrad enrollment: 9,102
  Women: 52%
  Men: 48%
  Percent out-of-state: 27%

Cost Information
  In-state tuition: $3,300
  Out-of-state tuition: $9,200
  Room & board: $5,953
Housing Information
  University housing: Yes
  Percent living on campus: 20%

Greek System
  Fraternity: Yes
  Sorority: Yes
  Athletics: NCAA Division I

QUICK CONTACT REFERENCE LIST

ALABAMA

College	Location	Contact	Service	Phone
Auburn U.	Auburn U., AL 36849	Dr. Kelly Haynes	Students w/ Disabilities	334-844-2096
Auburn U.	Montgomery, AL 36124-4023	Tamara Massey	Special Services	334-244-3754
Gadsden St. C.C.	Gadsden, AL 35999	Dr. Judy Hill	Student Services	256-549-8271
Jacksonville St. U.	Jacksonville, AL 36265	Daniel Miller	Academic Center for Excellence	256-782-5093
Samford U.	Birmingham, AL 35229	Anne Sherman	Counseling Services	205-726-4078
U. of Alabama	Birmingham, AL 35294-1150	James Saski, PhD	Disability Support Director	205-934-4205
U. of Alabama	Huntsville, AL 35899	Rosemary Robinson	Services for Students with Disabilities	256-824-6203
U. of Alabama	Tuscaloosa, AL 35487	Judy Thorpe	The Office of Disabilities	205-348-4285
U. of Montevallo	Montevallo, AL 35115	Deborah S. McCune	Services for Students w/ Disabilities	205-665-6250
U. of South Alabama	Mobile, AL 36688-0002	Bernita Pulmas	Special Student Services	251-460-7212

ALASKA

College	Location	Contact	Service	Phone
Sheldon Jackson C.	Sitka, AK 99835	C. Carlyle Haaland	Learning Assistance Program	907-747-5222
U. of Alaska	Anchorage, AK 99508-8046	Kaela Parks	Disability Support Services	907-786-4535
U. of Alaska	Fairbanks, AK 99775-7480	Mary Mathews	Disability Services	907-474-5655
U. of Alaska—Southeast	Juneau, AK 99801-8681	Michele Federico	Disability Coordinator	907-465-1298

ARIZONA

College	Location	Contact	Service	Phone
Arizona St. U.	Tempe, AZ 85287-3202	Deb Taska	Disability Resource Services	480-965-1234
Coconino C.C.	Flagstaff, AZ 86004	Nancy Elliot	Disability Resources	928-226-4243
Embry—Riddle Aero. U. (AZ)	Prescott, AZ 86301-3720	Rosemary Carr	Student Success Program	928-777-3700
Gateway C.C.	Phoenix, AZ 85034	Emily Bluestine	Special Services	602-392-5049
Mesa C.C.	Mesa, AZ 85202	Mora Shahan	Disability Resources and Services	480 461-7447
Northern Arizona U.	Flagstaff, AZ 86011-4084	Chad Loberger	Disability Support Services	928-523-8773
Phoenix C.	Phoenix, AZ 85013	Gene Heppard	Special Services	602-285-7477
Pima C.C.	Tucson, AZ 85702	Eric Morrison	Disabled Student Resources	520-206-6688
U. of Arizona	Tucson, AZ 85921	Dr. Diane Quinn	SALT	520-821-1427

ARKANSAS

College	Location	Contact	Service	Phone
Arkansas St. U.	State Univ., AR 72467	Dr. Jenifer Rice Mason	Disability Services	870-972-3964
Harding U.	Searcy, AR 72149	Dr.Jim Johnston	Student Support Services	501-279-4197
Henderson St. U.	Arkadelphia, AR 71999-0001	Vickie Faust	Disability Services	870-230-5453
NW Arkansas C.C.	Bentonville, AR 72712	Mike Kurk	Learner Development Center	479-619-4384
S. Arkansas U.	Magnolia, AR 71753-5000	Paula Washington-Woods	Student Disability Special Services	870-235-4145

Institution	Contact	Location	Service	Phone
U. of Arkansas	Dr. Timothy King	Fayetteville, AR 72701	Disability Services	479-575-3104
U. of Arkansas	Susan Queller	Little Rock, AR 72204	Disability Support Services	501-569-3143
U. of Arkansas	MikeWashington	Pine Bluff, AR 71601-2799	Office of Veterans & Disability Services	870-575-8512
U. of Central Arkansas	Crystal Hill	Conway, AR 72035	Disability Services	501-450-3135
U. of the Ozarks	Julia Frost	Clarksville, AR 72830	Jones Learning Center	479-979-1403

CALIFORNIA

Institution	Contact	Location	Service	Phone
Bakersfield C.	Shannon White	Bakersfield, CA 93305	Support Services Program	661-395-4334
Biola U.	Tim Engle	La Mirada, CA 90639	Services to the Disabled	562-944-0351 ext. 5851
Butte C.C.	Richard Dunn	Oroville, CA 95965	Services for Students with Disabilities	530-895-2455
Cabrillo C.	Frank Lynch	Santa Cruz, CA 95060	Disabled Student Services	831-479-6390
Cabrillo C.	Deborah Shulman	Aptos, CA 95003	Learning Skills Program	831-479-6220
Calif Polytechnic St. U.	William Bailey	San Luis Obispo, CA 93407	Disability Resource Center	805-756-1395
Calif St. Polytechnic U.	Dr. Micki Bryant	Pomona, CA 91768	Disabled Student Services	909-869-3333
California St. U.	Lee Bettencourt	Turlock, CA 95832	Disabled Student Services	209-667-3159
California St. U.—Bakersfield	Janice Clalussen	Bakersfield, CA 93311	Services for Students with Disabilities	661-664-3360
California St. U.—Chico	Billie Jackson	Chico, CA 95929-0720	Disabilities Support Services	530-898-5959
California St. U.—Fullerton	Paul Miller	Fullerton, CA 92634	Disabled Student Services	714-278-3112
California St. U.—Hayward	Mary Cheng	Hayward, CA 94542	Learning Disabled Resources	510-885-3868
California St. U.—Long Beach	David Sanfilippo	Long Beach, CA 90840	Disabled Student Services	562-985-5401
California St. U.—Northridge	Mary Ann Cummins Prager	Northridge, CA 91328-1286	Students with Disabilities Resource	818-677-2684
California St. U.—Sacramento	Patricia Sonntag	Sacramento, CA 95819	Services for Students With Learning Disabilities	916-278-6955
Calif. St. U.—San Bernardino	Laurie Flynn	San Bernardino, CA 92407	Services to Students with Disabilities	909-880-5238
California St. U.—San Marcos	John Segoria	San Marcos, CA 92096-0001	Disabled Student Services	760-750-4905
Cerritos C.C.	Bob Hughlett	Norwalk, CA 90650	Disabled Students Programs & Svcs	562-860-2451 ext. 2335
Chapman U.	Dr. Lynn Mayer	Orange, CA 92866	Center for Academic Success	714-997-6828
Citrus C.C.	Vince Mercurio	Glendora, CA 91741	Disabled Student Program	626-914-8578
City C. San Francisco	Kathleen Kerr Schocket	Orinda, CA 94563	Disabled Student Services	415-452-5481
C. of Redwoods	Sandra Nightingale	Crescent City, CA 95531	Disabled Student Spec.	707-465-2324
College of the Siskiyous	Karen Zeigler	Weed, CA 96094	Disabled Student Services	530-938-5297
Columbia C.C.	Suzanne Patterson	Sonora, CA 95370	Disabled Student Programs & Services	209-588-5133
Cuesta C.	Ellen Young	San Luis Obispo, CA 93403	Academic Support	805-546-3148
De Anza C.	Benita Rashall, MS	Sunnyvale, CA 94087	Educational Diagnostic Center	408-864-8959
East Los Angeles C.	Grace Marillo Hernandez	Monterey Pk, CA 90025	DSPS	323-265-8787

College	City, State ZIP	Contact	Service	Phone
El Camino C.	Torrance, CA 90506	Lucinda Aborn	Special Resource Center	310-660-3296
Foothill C.	Los Altos, CA 94022	Margo Dobbins	STEP	650-949-7038
Grossmont C.	Ramona, CA 92065	Carl Fielden	Disabled Students Programs & Services	619-644-7112
Humboldt St. U.	Arcata, CA 95521-8299	Ralph McFarland	Disabled Student Services	707-826-4678
John F. Kennedy U.	Orinda, CA 94563	Lisa Noshe-Pitro	Student Disability Services	925-969-3447
Lake Tahoe C.C.	So. Lake Tahoe, CA 96150	Bob Albrecht	Disability Resource Center	530-541-4660 ext. 249
Laney College	El Sobrante, CA 94803	Carol Dalissio	Disabled Student Program Services	510-464-3432
Long Beach City C.	Long Beach, CA 90808	Mark Matsui	Disabled Student Program Services	562-938-4111
Los Angeles City C.	Los Angeles, CA 90039	Susan Matranga	LD Services	323-953-4000 ext. 2270
Loyola Marymount U.	Los Angeles, CA 90045	Robert Scholz	Disability Support Services	310-338-4535
Master's C.	Newhall, CA 91322	Marion McElwee	Disability Services	661-253-3540 ext. 3209
Menlo C.	Atherton, CA 94027	Janet Miller	Academic Success	650-543-3854
Occidental C.	Los Angeles, CA 90041	Raul Villa	Center for Academic Excellence	323-259-2545
Oxnard C.	Oxnard, CA 93033	Leo Orange	Disabled Students Program & Services	805-986-5830
Pasadena City C.	Pasadena, CA 91106	Lisa Paiz	Disabled Student Services	626-585-7127
Reedley College	Reedley, CA 93654-2099	Dr. Janice Emerzian	Disabled Students Programs & Services	559-638-0332
Saddleback C.	Carlsbad, CA 92008	Randy Anderson	Special Services	949-582-4885
San Diego City C.	San Diego, CA 92101	Barbara Mason	Disabled Student Program & Service	619-230-2513
San Diego St. U.	San Diego, CA 92182	Margo Behr	Disabled Student Services	619-594-6473
San Francisco St. U.	San Francisco, CA 94132	Deidre De Freese	Disability Programs & Resource Center	415-338-6356
San Jose St. U.	San Jose, CA 95192	Cindy Marota	Disability Resource Center	408-924-6000
Santa Barbara City C.	Santa Barbara, CA 93109	Janet Shapiro	Disabled Student Services	805-965-0581
Santa Clara U.	Santa Clara, CA 95053	Ann Ravenscroft	Disability Resources	408-554-4111
Santa Monica C.	Santa Monica, CA 90405	Mary Jane Weil	Disabled Student Services	310-434-4265
Santa Rosa Junior C.	Santa Rosa, CA 95401	Patie Wegman	Disability Resource Department	707-527-4278
Sierra C.	Rocklin, CA 95677	Delecia Nunnelly	Learning Opportunities Center	916-781-0592
Sonoma St. U.	Rohnert Park, CA 94928	Linda Lipps	Disabled Student Services	707-664-2677
Stanford U.	Stanford, CA 94305-3005	Joan Bisagno	Disability Resource Center	650-723-1066
Taft C.	Taft, CA 93268	Jeff Ross	Disabled Student Services	661-763-7776
U. of California—Berkeley	Berkeley, CA 94720-4250	Ed Rogers	Disabled Students' Program	510-642-0518
U. of California—Davis	Davis, CA 95616	Keltie Jones	Learnining Disability Center	530-752-3184
U. of California—Irvine	Irvine, CA 92717	Karen Myers	Office of Disability Services	949-824-7494
U. of California—Los Angeles	Los Angeles, CA 90095	Dr. Julie Morris	Office for Students with Disabilities	310-825-1501

Institution	Location	Contact	Service	Phone
U. of California—Riverside	Riverside, CA 92521	Marcia Theise Schiffer	Services for Students w/ Disabilities	909-787-4538
U. of California—San Diego	La Jolla, CA 92093-0337	Roberta Gemblett	Office for Students with Disabilities	858-534-4382
U. of California—Santa Barbara	Santa Barbara, CA 93106	Diane Glenn	Disabled Student Program	805-893-2182
U. of California—Santa Cruz	Santa Cruz, CA 95064	Sharyn Martin	Disability Resource Center	831-459-2089
U. of Redlands	Redlands, CA 92373-0999	Judy Bowman	Academic Support Services	909-335-4079
U. of San Diego	San Diego, CA 92110-2492	Margo Behr	Disabled student Services	619-594-6473
U. of San Francisco	San Francisco, CA 94117	Tom Merrell	Student Disability Services	415-422-6876
U. of Southern California	Los Angeles, CA 90089	Dr. Mattie Grace	Disability Services & Programs	213-740-0776
U. of the Pacific	Stockton, CA 95211	Lisa Cooper	Office of Services for Students with Disabilities	209-946-2879
Whittier C.	Whittier, CA 90608	Joan Smith	Disability Services	562-907-4825

COLORADO

Institution	Location	Contact	Service	Phone
Colorado Mt. C.	Glenwood Springs, CO 81601	Ida Burnaman	Developmental Education	970-945-8256
Colorado School of Mines	Golden, CO 80401-1869	Ron Brummett	Student Development & Career Center	303-273-3297
Colorado St. U.	Fort Collins, CO 80523	Dr. Charles Davidshofer	Resources for Disabled Students	970-491-6385
Fort Lewis C.	Durango, CO 81301	Dian Jenkins	Learning Assistance Center	970-247-7459
Mesa St. C.	Grand Junction, CO 81502-2647	Sandra J. Wymore	Education Access Service	970-248-1801
Northeastern Junior C.	Sterling, CO 80751	Lori Gill	Study Skills Services	970-521-6670
Regis U.	Denver, CO 80221-1099	Joie Williams	Disability Services	303-964-3666
U. of Colorado, Boulder	Boulder, CO 80309-0107	Cindy Donohue	Disability Services	303-492-8671
U. of Colorado, Col. Springs	Colorado Springs, CO 80933	Kaye Simonton	Disability Services	719-262-3354
U. of Colorado—Denver	Denver, CO 80217	Lisa McGill	Disability Support Department	303-556-8388
U. of Denver	Denver, CO 80208	Ted May	LEP	303-871-4293
U. of Northern Colorado	Greeley, CO 80639	Nancy Kauffman	Disability Access Center	970-351-2289
Colorado State University - Pueblo	Pueblo, CO 81001	Pam Chambers	Disabilities Resources Office	719-549-2584
Western St. C. of Colorado	Gunnison, CO 81231	Jan Edwards	Learning Assistance Center	970-943-7056

CONNECTICUT

Institution	Location	Contact	Service	Phone
Briarwood C.	Southington, CT 06489	Cynthia Clark	Services for Students with LD	860-628-4751
Central Connecticut St. U.	New Britain, CT 06050	Dr. George Tenney	Special Student Services	860-832-1957
Eastern Connecticut St. U.	Willimantic, CT 06226	Pamela Starr	Counseling for Students w/ Disabilities	860-465-5573
Fairfield U.	Fairfield, CT 06430-5195	Rev. W.L. O'Neil SJ	Student Support Services	203-254-4000 ext. 2445
Housatonic C.	Bridgeport, CT 06608	Lynn Langella	Disability Support Services	203-332-5000
Mitchell C.	New London, CT 06320	Dr. Peter Troiano	Learning Resource Center	860-701-5141

CONNECTICUT

College	Location	Contact	Office	Phone
Quinnipiac C.	Hamden, CT 06518	John Jarvis	Learning Services	203-582-5390
Southern Connecticut St. U.	New Haven, CT 06515	Suzanne Tucker	Disability Resource Office	203-392-6828
U. of Connecticut	W. Hartford, CT 06117	Nadine Brennan	Disability Support Services	860-570-9232
U. of Connecticut	Storrs, CT 06269	David Parker	UPLD	860-486-0178
U. of Hartford	West Hartford, CT 06117	Susan Fitzgerald	Learning Plus	860-768-5129
U. of New Haven	West Haven, CT 06516	Linda Copney-Okeke	Disability Services & Resources	203-932-7331
Wesleyan U.	Middletown, CT 06459-0265	Vancenia Rutherford	Learning Disabilities Services	860-685-2600
Western Connecticut St. U.	Danbury, CT 06810	Barbara Barnwell	Disability Services	203-837-8277
Yale U.	New Haven, CT 06520	Carolyn Barrett	Resource Office for Disabilities	203-432-2324

DELAWARE

College	Location	Contact	Office	Phone
Delaware Tech C.C.	Georgetown, DE 19947	Bonnie Hall	Student Support Services	302-856-5400 ext. 3360
U. of Delaware	Newark, DE 19716-6210	Barbara Lewis-Kuszyk	Academic Services	302-831-2805

DISTRICT OF COLUMBIA

College	Location	Contact	Office	Phone
American U.	Washington, DC 20016	Melissa Scarfone	Academic Support Center	202-885-3360
Catholic U. of America, The	Washington, DC 20064-0001	Bonnie McClellan	Disability Support Services	202-319-5211
Gallaudet U.	Washington, DC 20002	Patricia Tesar	Prog for Students w/ Other Disabilities	202-651-5256
George Washington U.	Washington, DC 20052	Christy Willis	Disability Support Services	202-994-8250
Georgetown U.	Washington, DC 20057	Marcia W. Fulk, M.Ed.	Learning Services	202-687-8354
Trinity C. (DC)	Washington, DC 20017-1094	Heather Petrelli	Career Services	202-884-9647

FLORIDA

College	Location	Contact	Office	Phone
Barry U.	Miami Shores, FL 33161-6695	Vivian Castro	Center for Advanced Learning	305-899-3461
Beacon C.	Leesburg, FL 34748	Carolyn Scott	Director of Admissions	352-787-7660
Broward C.C.	Ft. Lauderdale, FL 33301	Beverly Cranmer	Disability Services	954-201-7655
Edison C.C.	Fort Meyers, FL 33906	Kathy Doyle	Disability Services	239-489-9112
Embry-Riddle Aeronaut. U. (FL)	Daytona Beach, FL 32114	Vanessa Lloyd	Disability Services	386-226-7916
Florida A&M U.	Tallahassee, FL 32307	Dr. Sharon Wooten	Learning Development & Evaluation Ctr.	850-599-8474
Florida Atlantic U.	Boca Raton, FL 33431	Nicole Rokos	Office for Students with Disabilities	561-297-3880
Florida International U.	Miami, FL 33199	Beverly Paben	Disability Services	305-348-3532
Florida St. U.	Tallahassee, FL 32306	Lauren Miller	Student Disability Resource Center	850-644-9566
Gulf Coast C.C.	Panama City, FL 32401	Linda Van Dalen	Disability Support Services	850-872-3834
Hillsborough C.C.	Tampa, FL 33631-3127	Denise Giarrusso	Disabled Services	813-253-7914
Indian River C.C.	Fort Pierce, FL 34981	Rhoda Brant	Disability Services	772-462-4700

Institution	Contact	Service	Location	Phone
Jacksonville U.	Dr. John Balog	Disabled Students Services	Jacksonville, FL 32211	904-256-7070
Lynn U.	Marsha Glines	Institute for Achievement	Boca Raton, FL 33431	561-237-7881
Pensacola Jr. C.	Linda Sheppard	Disability Support Services	Pensacola, FL 32504	850-484-1637
Saint Thomas U.	Maritza Rivera	Academic Enhancement	Miami, FL 33054	305-628-6713
Santa Fe C.C.	Claudia Munnis	Disability Resource Center	Gainsville, FL 32606	352-395-5948
Seminole C.C.	Dorothy Paishon	Disabled Support Services	Sanford, FL 32773	407-328-2109
St. Petersburg Jr. C.	Dr. Linda Giar	Disability Services	St. Petersburg, FL 33733	727-341-3721
U. of Central Florida	Dr. Philip Kalfin	Student Disability Services	Orlando, FL 32816	407-823-2371
U. of Florida	John Denny	Disability Resources	Gainesville, FL 32611	352-392-1261
U. of Miami	Judith Antinarella	Office for Students w/ LD	Coral Gables, FL 33146	305-284-2374
U. of South Florida	Dr. Server	Student Disability Services	Tampa, FL 33620	813-974-4309
U. of Tampa	Robert Ruday	Student Disability Services	Tampa, FL 33606-1490	813-253-6204

GEORGIA

Institution	Contact	Service	Location	Phone
Andrew C.	Sherri Taylor	FOCUS	Cuthbert, GA 31740	229-732-5908
Armstrong St. C.	Amelia Castilian	Disability Services	Savannah, GA 31419	912-927-5271
Brenau U.	Dr. Vincent Yamilkoski	Learning Center	Gainesville, GA 30501	770-534-6134
Clark Atlanta U.	Ricky Robinson	Student Assistance	Atlanta, GA 30314	404-880-8771
Columbus C.	Joy Norman	Disability Services	Columbus, GA 31907	706-568-2330
Darton C.	Tanya Anderson	Disabled Student Services	Albany, GA 31707	229-430-6867
Georgia Perimeter College	Bonnie Martin	Ctr. for Disability Services	Clarkston, GA 30021	404-299-4038
Emory U.	Gloria Weaver	Disability Services	Atlanta, GA 30322	404-727-6016
Gainesville C.	Carolyn Swindle	Disability Services	Gainesville, GA 30503	770-718-3855
Georgia Institute of Tech.	Denise Johnson	Disabled Student Services	Atlanta, GA 30332-0320	404-894-9191
Georgia Southern U.	Wayne Akins	Disabled Student Services	Statesboro, GA 30460	912-871-1566
Georgia St. U.	Caroline Gergely	Disability Services	Atlanta, GA 30302-4009	404-463-9044
Life U.	Dr. Lisa Rubin	Academic Assistance Center	Marietta, GA 30060	770-426-2725
Oglethorpe U.	RoseMary Watkins	Learning Resources Services	Atlanta, GA 30319	404-364-8869
Reinhardt C.	Sylvia Robertson	Academic Support Office	Waleska, GA 30183	770-720-5567
Southern Polytechnic St. U.	Frida Castleberry	Counseling & Disability Services	Marietta, GA 30060	678-915-7226
Spelman C.	Merrine McDonald	Student Disability Services	Atlanta, GA 30314	404-223-1444
U. of Georgia	Dr. Noel Gregg	Learning Disabilities Center	Athens, GA 30602	706-542-4589
Valdosta St. U.	Kimberly Godden	Access Office for Students with Disabilities	Valdosta, GA 31698	229-245-2498

HAWAII

College	Location	Contact	Department	Phone
Chaminade U. of Honolulu	Honolulu, HI 96816	Don Kopf	Student Affairs	808-735-4845
Hawaii C.C.	Hilo, HI 96720	Karen Kane	Ha'awi Kokua Program	808-933-0702
U. of Hawaii—Hilo	Hilo, HI 96720-4091	Susan Shirachi	Disability Services	808-933-0816
U. of Hawaii—Manoa	Honolulu, HI 96822	Ann C. Ito	KOKUA Program	808-956-7511

IDAHO

College	Location	Contact	Department	Phone
Boise St. U.	Boise, ID 83725	Blaine Eckles	Special Services	208-426-1583
Idaho St. U.	Pocatello, ID 83209-8270	Dennis Toney	ADA Disabilities Center	208-282-3599
Lewis-Clark St. C.	Lewiston, ID 83501	Debbie Mundell	Recruitment and Retention	208-792-2378
U. of Idaho	Moscow, ID 83844-4140	Gloria R. Jensen	Disability Support Services	208-885-7200

ILLINOIS

College	Location	Contact	Department	Phone
Aurora U.	Aurora, IL 60506	Susan Lausier	Disability Services	630-844-5267
Barat C. of DePaul U.	Lake Forest, IL 60045	Debbie Sheade	Learning Opportunities Program	847-574-4312
Benedictine U.	Lisle, IL 60532-0900	Tina Sonderby	Academic Resource Center	"630-829-6512
Chicago St. U.	Chicago, IL 60628	Carlos C. Drazen	Abilities Office	773-995-4401
C. of Du Page	Glen Ellyn, IL 60137	Jacqueline Reuland	Special Student Services	630-942-2567
C. of Lake County	Grayslake, IL 60030	Beth Remedi	Disability Student Services	847-543-2473
Columbia C. (IL)	Chicago, IL 60605-1996	Suzan Snook	Services for Students with Disabilities	312-344-8134
DePaul U.	Chicago, IL 60604	Stamatios Miras	Productive Learning Strategies	773-325-4239
Eastern Illinois U.	Charleston, IL 61920-3099	Kathy Waggoner	Disability Services	217-581-6583
Elgin C.C.	Elgin, IL 60123	Annabelle Rhoades	Disability Services	847-697-1000
Harper C.	Palatine, IL 60067	Tom Thompson	Center for Students with Disabilities	847-925-6266
Illinois Institute of Technology	Chicago, IL 60616	Gleann Kehr	Center for Disability Resources	312-567-5744
Illinois St. U.	Normal, IL 61790	Ann Caldwell	Disability Concerns	309-438-5853
Ivy Tech St. C.	Evansville, IL 47710	Peg Ehlen	Special Needs	812-429-1386
John Wood C.C.	Quincy, IL 62301	Rose-Marie Akers	Support Services Center	217-224-6500
Joliet Junior C.	Joliet, IL 60436	Jewell Dennis	Project Achieve	815-729-9020 ext. 2455
Kankakee C. C.	Kankakee, IL 60901	Joylenne Keiser	Special Population & Instruc. Support	815-802-8482
Lake Forest C.	Lake Forest, IL 60045	Laura Panko	Dean's Office	847-735-5200
Lakeland C.	Mattoon, IL 61938	Emily Hatke	Special Needs Office	217-234-5259
Lincoln C.	Lincoln, IL 62656	Tony Schilling	Director—Admissions Office	800-569-0556
Loyola U. of Chicago	Chicago, IL 60611	Maggie Rogers	Services for Students w/ Disabilities	773-508-2741
McHenry C.C.	Crystal Lake, IL 60012	Bev Albright	Special Needs	815-455-8676

Institution	Location	Contact	Office/Service	Phone
Morraine Valley C.C.	Palos Hills, IL 60465	Debbie Sievers	Center for Disability Services	708-974-5330
Morton C.	Cicero, IL 60650	Chris Martin	Special Needs	708-656-8000
National-Louis U.	Evanston, IL 60201	Jady Piper	Center for Academic Development	312-261-3300
North Central C.	Naperville, IL 60566	Deanne Wiedemann	Learning Disability Services	630-637-5264
Northeastern Illinois U.	Chicago, IL 60625	Victoria Amey-Flippin	HELP Program	773-442-5495
Northern Illinois U.	DeKalb, IL 60115	Darth Rubin	Ctr. for Access-Ability Resources	815-753-1303
Northwestern U.	Evanston, IL 60204	Margie Roe	Services for Students with Disabilities	847-467-5530
Oakton Community C.	Des Plaines, IL 60116	Linda McCann	ASSIST	847-635-1759
Parkland C.	Champaign, IL 61821	Norman Lambert	Disability Services	217-353-2620
Roosevelt U.	Chicago, IL 60605	Nancy Litke	Learning Support Services Program	312-341-3810
Saint Xavier U.	Chicago, IL 60655	Sue Zientara	Student Success/Learning Assist. Ctr.	773-298-3308
Schl. of Art Inst. of Chicago	Chicago, IL 60603	Heather Walsh	Learning Center	312-345-9478
Shimer C.	Waukegan, IL 60079-0500	Alan Solid	Admissions Office	847-249-7173
SIU—Carbondale	Carbondale, IL 62901-4710	Sally DeDecker	Achieve Program	618-453-2369
SIU—Edwardsville	Edwardsville, IL 62026	Jane Floyd-Hendey	Disability Student Services	618-650-3782
U. of Chicago	Chicago, IL 60637	Aneesah Ali	Assistance for Disabled Students	773-702-5671
U. of Ill.—Urbana-Champaign	Urbana, IL 618-1	Brad Hedrick	Division Rehab-Education Services	217-333-4600
U. of Illinois—Chicago	Chicago, IL 60680	Joy Hesney	Disability Services	312-413-2183
Waubonsee C.C.	Sugar Grove, IL 60554	Iris Hansen	Access Ctr. for Students w/ Disabilities	630-466-2564
Western Illinois U.	Macomb, IL 61455-1390	Joan Green	Disability Support Services	309-298-2512

INDIANA

Institution	Location	Contact	Office/Service	Phone
Anderson U.	Anderson, IN 46012	Rinda Vogelgesang	Disabled Student Services	765-641-4226
Ball St. U.	Muncie, IN 47306	Richard Harris	Office of Disabled Students	765-285-5293
Butler U.	Indianapolis, IN 46208	Michele Atterson	Student Disabilities Center	317-940-9308
DePauw U.	Greencastle, IN 46135	Diane D. Hightower	Academic Services	765-658-4027
Earlham C.	Richmond, IN 47374	Donna Keesling	Center for Academic Enrichment	765-983-1200 ext. 1341
Goshen C.	Goshen, IN 46526-4794	Margot Zahner	Academic Support Center	219-535-7576
Indiana St. U.	Terre Haute, IN 47809	Rita Worrall	Student Support Services	812-237-2301
Indiana U. SE	New Albany, IN 47150	Hannah Wallace	Disabilities Services	812-941-2243
Indiana U. East	Richmond, IN 47374-1289	Sheryl Stafford	Student Support Services	765-973-8319
Indiana U.—Bloomington	Bloomington, IN 47405-7700	Jody Ferguson	Disabled Student Services	812-855-3508
Indiana U.—Purdue Univ.	Indianapolis, IN 46202-5143	Pamela King	Adaptive Educational Services	317-274-3241

Institution	Location	Contact	Service	Phone
Indiana U.—South Bend	South Bend, IN 46634-7111	Mark Dosch	Division of Disabled Student Services	574-237-4479
Indiana Wesleyan U.	Marion, IN 46953-4999	Todd Ream	Student Support Services	765-677-2256
IPFW—Ft. Wayne	Ft. Wayne, IN 46805	Susan Borror	Services for Students with Disabilities(SSD)	260-481-6950
IVY Tech	Fort Wayne, IN 46805	Debra Clarke	Disability Services	260-480-4207
Manchester C.	N. Manchester, IN 46962	Denise Howe	Services for Students w/ Disabilities	260-982-5076
Marion C.	Indianapolis, IN 46222	Marge Batic	Learning and Counseling Center	317-955-6150
Purdue U.—Calumet	Hammond, IN 46323-2094	Michaeline Florek	Student Support Services	219-989-2455
Purdue U.—West Lafayette	West Lafayette, IN 47907	Marvin Schlatter	Adaptive Program	765-494-1247
St. Joseph's C.	Rensselaer, IN 47978	David Weed	Counseling Services	219-866-6116
Taylor U.	Upland, IN 46989	Edwin Welch	Academic Support Services	765-998-5523
Tri-St. U.	Angola, IN 46703	Marline Sweet	Special Students	260-665-4172
U. of Evansville	Evansville, IN 47722	Sylvia Buck	Counselling & Testing Center	812-479-2663
U. of Indianapolis	Indianapolis, IN 46227	Deborah Spinney	BUILD Program	317-788-3536
U. of Notre Dame	Notre Dame, IN 46556	Scott Howland	Office for Students w/ Disabilities	574-631-7141
U. of Saint Francis	Fort Wayne, IN 46808	Michelle Kruyer	Student Learning Center	260-434-7677
U. of Southern Indiana	Evansville, IN 47712	James Browning	Counseling Center	812-464-1867
Valparaiso U.	Valparaiso, IN 46383	Christina Grabarek	Disability Support Services	219-464-5790
Vincennes U.	Vincennes, IN 47591	J. Kavanaugh	STEP	812-888-4485
Wabash C.	Crawfordsville, IN 47933	Julia Rosenberg	Writing Center-Academic Support	765-361-6024

IOWA

Institution	Location	Contact	Service	Phone
Coe C.	Cedar Rapids, IA 52402	Lois Kabela-Coates	Academic Achievement Program	319-399-8547
Cornell C.	Mount Vernon, IA 52341	John Harp	Dean's Office	319-895-4234
Des Moines Area C.C.	Ankney, IA 50021	Pamela Parker	Special Needs	515-964-6850
Drake U.	Des Moines, IA 50311	Chrystal Stanley	Student Disability Services	515-271-1835
Graceland U.	Lamoni, IA 50140	Cathie Hosie	Student Support Services	641-784-5211
Grand View C.	Des Moines, IA 50316-1599	Carolyn Wassenaar	Academic Success	515-263-2971
Grinnell C.	Grinnell, IA 50112	Joyce Stern	Academic Advising Office	641-269-3702
Hawkeye C.C.	Waterloo, IA 50704	Barbara Hill	Student Development	319-296-4014
Indian Hills C.C.	Ottumwa, IA 52501	Mary Stewart	Academic Services	641-683-5218
Iowa Central C.C.	Ft. Dodge, IA 50501	Heather Lundberg	Special Needs	515-576-7201
Iowa St. U.	Ames, IA 50011-2011	Beatrice Awoniyi	Disability Services	515-294-6624
Iowa Wesleyan C.	Mount Pleasant, IA 52641	Kay Brouwer	Learning Center	319-385-8021
Iowa Western C.C.	Council Bluffs, IA 51502	Sara Hollowell	Special Needs	712-325-3479

Institution	Location	Contact	Service	Phone
Loras C.	Dubuque, IA 52001	Dianne Gibson	Learning Disabilities Program	563-588-7134
Mount Saint Clare C.	Clinton, IA 52733-2967	Dean Gary Cooper	Student Affairs	563-242-4023
Saint Ambrose U.	Davenport, IA 52803-2898	Ann Austin	Students with Disabilities	563-333-6161
Scott CC E. Iowa CC	Bettonderf, IA 52722	Peggy Garrison	Student Support Services	563-441-4072
Southeastern C.C.	W. Burlington, IA 52655	Brenda Wilkins	Office for Students with Disabilities	319-752-8251
U. of Dubuque	Dubuque, IA 52001-5050	Jesse James	Admissions Office	319-589-3214
U. of Iowa	Iowa City, IA 52242	Dau-shen Ju	Student Disability Services	319-335-1462
U. of Northern Iowa	Cedar Falls, IA 50614	Jane Slykhuis	Disability Services	319-273-2676
Waldorf C.	Forest City, IA 50436	Michelle Murray	LD Program	641-585-8207
Wartburg C.	Waverly, IA 50677	Alexander Smith	Student Life	319-352-8260

KANSAS

Institution	Location	Contact	Service	Phone
Baker University	Baldwin City, KS 66006	Cindy Novelo	Learning Resource Center	785-594-8352
Benedictine College	Atchison, KS 66002	Kelly Vowels	Admission and Financial Aid Office	800-467-5340
Bethel C.	N. Newton, KS 67117	Daniel Quinlin, PhD	Center for Academic Development	316-284-5333
Butler City C.C.	Eldorado, KS 67042	Teresa Eastman	Special Needs & Services	316-322-3166
Colby CC	Colby, KS 67701	Monica Kane	Student Support Services	785-462-3984
Emporia St. U.	Emporia, KS 66801-5087	Trudi Benjamin	Project Challenge	620-341-5097
Hutchinson C.C.	Hutchison, KS 67502	Jill Crank	Disability Services	620-665-3554
Johnson County C.C.	Overland Park, KS 66210	Holly Dressler	Student Access Center	913-469-8500
Kansas City C.C.	Kansas City, KS 66112	Valerie Webb	Academic Resource Center	913-288-7670
Kansas St. U.	Manhattan, KS 66506	Gretchen Holden	Disabled Student Services	785-532-6441
Pittsburg State U.	Pittsburg, KS 66762-5880	Dr. Jamie Wood	Learning Center	620-235-4193
Pratt C.C.	Pratt, KS 67124	Kim Evert	Student Success	620-672-5641 ext. 215
U. of Kansas	Lawrence, KS 66045	Mary Ann Rasnak	Services for Students with Disabilities	785-864-2620
Wichita St. U.	Wichita, KS 67260	Grady Landrum	Resource Center for Independence	316-978-6970

KENTUCKY

Institution	Location	Contact	Service	Phone
Bellarmine C.	Louisville, KY 40205	Dr. Claudia Beeny	Office of Student Affairs	502-452-8150
Bluegrass Comm. & Tech. College.	Lexington, KY 40506-0235	Veronica Miller	Disability Support Services	859-257-4872
Brescia C.	Owensboro, KY 42301	Dr. Dolores Kiesler	Student Support Services	270-686-4259
Eastern Kentucky U.	Richmond, KY 40475	Teresa Belluscio	Disability Services	859-622-2933
Lexington C.C.	Lexington, KY 40506-0235	Veronica Miller	Disability Support Services	859-257-4872
Morehead St. U.	Morehead, KY 40351	Debra Reed	Disability Services	606-783-5188
Murray St. U.	Murray, KY 42071	Annazette Fields	Office of Equal Opportunity	270-762-3155

Institution	Location	Contact	Office	Phone
Northern Kentucky U.	Highland Heights, KY 41099	A. Dale Adams	Disability Services	859-572-5180
Southeast C.C.	Cumberland, KY 40823	Ruth Lewis	Student Support Services	606-589-2145 ext. 2080
Thomas More C.	Crestiew Hill, KY 41017	Barbara Davis	Student Support Services	859-344-352
U. of Kentucky	Lexington, KY 40506	Jake Karnes	Disability Resource Office	859-257-2754
U. of Louisville	Louisville, KY 40292	Cathy Patus	Disability Resource Center	502-852-6938
Western Kentucky U.	Bowling Green, KY 42101	Huda Melky	Director Equal Opportunity/504/ADA Compliance	270-745-5121

LOUISIANA

Institution	Location	Contact	Office	Phone
Louisiana C.	Pineville, LA 71359-0560	Betty Matthews	Disability Services	318-487-7629
LSU—Baton Rouge	Baton Rouge, LA 70803	Benjamin Cornwell	Office of Disability Services	225-578-4401
Loyola U. New Orleans	New Orleans, LA 70118	Sarah Smith	Acad. Enrichment and Disibility Svcs.	504-865-2990
Nicholls St. U.	Thibodaux, LA 70310	Gerald Sanders	Disability Services	504-448-4430
Southeastern Louisiana U.	Hammond, LA 70402	Sharon Eaton	Disability Services	504-549-2247
Southern U. of New Orleans	New Orleans, LA 70126	Dr. Zelma Frank	Student Support Services	504-286-5106
Tulane U.	New Orleans, LA 70118-5680	Dr. Jillandra Rovaris	Disability Services	504-862-8433
U. of New Orleans	New Orleans, LA 70148	Dr. Janice G. Lyn	Office of Disabled Student Services	504-280-6222
Univ. of Louisiana Lafayette	Lafayette, LA 70504	Page Salley	Services for Students w/ Disabilities	337-482-5252

MAINE

Institution	Location	Contact	Office	Phone
Bates C.	Lewiston, ME 04240-9917	Celeste Branham	Dean's Office	207-786-6219
Bowdoin C.	Brunswick, ME 04011-8441	Joanne Canning	Dean's Office	207-725-3866
Colby C.	Waterville, ME 04901-8840	Mark Serdjenian	Dean's Office	207-872-3106
Eastern Maine Tech. C.	Bangor, ME 04401	Elizabeth Warden	Student Affairs	207-974-4658
Kennebec Valley Tech	Fairfield, ME 04937	Karen Normandin	Students With Disabilities	207-453-5019
N. Maine Tech C.	Presque Isle, ME 04769	Laura Flagg	Student Affairs—TRIO	207-768-2793
Southern Maine C. C.	South Portland, ME 04106	Mark Krogman	Disability Services	207-741-5629
Unity C.	Unity, ME 04988-0532	James Horan	Learning Resource Center	207-948-3131
U. of Maine—Augusta	Bangor, ME 04401-4367	Phil Watkins	Cornerstone Program	207-621-3157
U. of Maine—Farmington	Farmington, ME 04938	Claire Nelson	Acad. Svcs. for Students w/ Disab.	207-778-7295
U. of Maine—Orono	Orono, ME 04469-5757	Ann Smith	Onward Program/Disabilities	207-581-2319
U. of Maine—Presque Isle	Presque Isle, ME 04769	Myrna McGaffin	Student Support Services	207-768-9613
U. of Maine—Machias	Machias, ME 04654	Jean Schild	Student Resources	207-255-1228
U. of New England	Biddeford, ME 04005	Susan McDevitt Church	Disability Services	207-283-0171 ext. 2815
U. of Southern Maine	Portland, ME 04104	Joyce Branaman	Support for Students with Disabilities	207-780-4706

MARYLAND

College	Location	Contact	Service	Phone
Allegheny C.	Cumberland, MD 21502	Carol Davis	Student Support Center	301-784-5551
Anne Arundel C.C.	Arnold, MD 21012	Mimi Stoops	Disabled Student Services	410-777-2306
Baltimore City C.C.	Baltimore, MD 21215	Nicole Wilson	Disability Support Services Center	410-462-8585
Carroll C.C.	Westminster, MD 21157	Joyce Sebian	Student Support Services	410-386-8329
Catonsville C.C.	Catonsville, MD 21228	Jill Hodge	Special Student Population	410-455-4718
Cecil C.C.	North East, MD 20901	Russ Davis	Academic Advising	410-287-6060 ext. 551
College of Southern MD—La Plata	La Plata, MD 20646	Glennis Daniels-Bacchus	Academic Support Services	301-934-2251 ext. 7614
Essex C.C.	Baltimore, MD 21237	Beth Hunsinger	Office of Special Services	410-780-6741
Frostburg St. U.	Frostburg, MD 21532	Leroy Pullen	Disability Support Services	301-687-4483
Goucher C.	Baltimore, MD 21204-2794	Frona Brown	Disability Specialist	410-337-6178
Harford C.C.	Bel Air, MD 21015	Lorraine Peniston	Learninng Support Services	410-836-4414
Hood C.	Fredrick, MD 21701	Tom Kranz	Disability Services	301-696-3421
Howard C.C.	Columbia, MD 21044	Joan King	Learning Assistance Center	410-772-4822
Loyola C. (MD)	Baltimore, MD 21210	Michelle Brewer	Center for Academic Services and Support	410-617-2663
McDaniel College	Westminster, MD 21157	Kevin Selby	Student Academic Support Services	410-857-2504
Montgomery C.	Rockville, MD 20850	Brenda Williams	Disability Support Services	301-279-5050
Morgan St. U.	Baltimore, MD 21251	Melanie Cosby	Counseling Center	443-885-3130
Towson U.	Towson, MD 21252-0001	Susan Willemin	Disability Support Services	410-704-2638
U. of Baltimore	Baltimore, MD 21201	Jacquelyn Truelore	Disability Support Services	410-837-4775
U. of Maryland—C. Park	College Park, MD 20742-5235	Dianne Halliah	Disability Support Services	301-314-9969
U. of Maryland—Eastern Shore	Princess Anne, MD 21853	Dorling Joseph	Disabilities Coordinator	410-651-6461

MASSACHUSETTS

College	Location	Contact	Service	Phone
American International C.	Springfield, MA 01109-3184	Prof. Mary M. Saltus	Supportive Learning Services	413-205-3426
Amherst C.	Amherst, MA 01002	Francis Tuleja	Services for Students with LD	413-542-2529
Anna Maria C.	Paxton, MA 01612	Livvy O.Tarleton	Learning Center	508-849-3356
Assumption C.	Worcester, MA 01615	Sister Ellen Guerin, RSN	Disabled Students Services	508-767-7487
Babson C.	Babson Park, MA 02157-0310	Aaron Evans	Disability Services/Office of Class Dean	781-239-4508
Bentley C.	Waltham, MA 2452	Christopher Kennedy	Counseling & Student Development	781-891-2274
Berklee C. of Music	Boston, MA 02215	Pablo Vargas	Learning Center	617-747-2667
Berkshire C.C.	Pittsfield, MA 01201	Pamela Farron	Services for Disabled Students	413-499-4660
Boston C.	Chestnut Hill, MA 02167	Kathleen Duggan	Academic Development Center	617-552-8093

College	Address	Contact	Service	Phone
Boston U.	Boston, MA 02215	Alan Mawrdy	Learning Disability Support Services	617-353-3658
Brandeis U.	Waltham, MA 02254	Laura Lindon	Dean's Office-Academic Affairs	781-736-3470
Bridgewater St. C.	Bridgewater, MA 02325	Joanne Eno	Office for Students with Disabilities	508-531-1214
Clark U.	Worcester, MA 01610-1477	Sharon DeKlerk	Disability Services	508-793-7468
C. of the Holy Cross	Worcester, MA 01610-2395	Dr. Matthew Toth	Disability Services	508-793-3363
Curry C.	Milton, MA 02186	Dr. Susan Pratt	Program for Advancement in Learning	617-333-2250
Dean C.	Franklin, MA 02038	Anne Smith	The Center for Learning	508-541-1764
Emerson C.	Boston, MA 02116-1511	Ronn Beck	Special Asst to Director -Ugrad Admissions	617-824-8449
Endicott C.	Beverly, MA 01915	Laura Rossi-Le	Student Support Program	978-232-2292
Fitchburg St. C.	Fitchburg, MA 01420-2697	Willa Peterson	Disability Services	978-665-3427
Framingham St. C.	Framingham, MA 01701	Elizabeth Smith-Freedman	Academic Support	508-626-4905
Gordon C.	Wenham, MA 01984-1899	Ann Seavey	Academic Support	978-927-2306
Hampshire C.	Amherst, MA 01002	Joel Dansky	Center for Academic Support and Advising	413-559-5423
Harvard and Radcliffe C.s	Cambridge, MA 02318	Louise Russell	Student Disability Resource Center	617-496-8707
Holyoke C.C.	Holyoke, MA 01040	Maureen Conroy	College Disability Services	413-552-2582
Lesley C.	Cambridge, MA 02138	Laura Patey	Disability Services	617-349-8194
Mass Bay C.C.	Wellesley Hills, MA 02181	Rita Heywood	Disability Services	781-239-2626
Massasoit C.C.	Brockton, MA 02402	Andrea Henry	Disability Services	508-588-9100
Mt. Ida C.	Newton, MA 01259	Jill Mehler	Learning Opportunities Program	617-928-4648
Mt. Wachusett C.C.	Gardner, MA 01440	Mike Sidoti	Students with Disabilities	978-632-6600
N. Adams St. C.	N. Adams, MA 01247	Theresa Miller	Learning Center	413-662-5309
North Shore C.C.	Danvers, MA 01923	Carolyn Bailey	SSC - Disabilities Services	978-762-4000 ext. 4036
Northeastern U.	Boston, MA 02115	Ruth K. Bork	Disability Resource Center	617-373-2675
Pine Manor C.	Chestnut Hill, MA 02167	Mary Walsh	Learning Resource Center	617-731-7181
Quinsigamond C.C.	Worcester, MA 01606	Lori Corcoran	Disabilities Services	508-854-4471
Simmons C.	Boston, MA 02115	Todd Herriott	Academic Support	617-521-2471
Smith C.	Northampton, MA 01063	Laura Rauscher	Office of Disability Services	413-585-2071
Springfield C.	Springfield, MA 01109	Deborah Dickens	Student Support Service	413-748-3768
Springfield Tech C.C.	Springfield, MA 01105	Mary Moriarty	Office of Disability Services	413-755-4785
St. C. at N. Adams	N. Adams, MA 01247	Terry Miller	Ctr. for Acad. Advancement Learning	413-662-5309
Stonehill C.	Easton, MA 02357-5610	Richard Grant	Academic Services	508-565-1306
Suffolk U.	Boston, MA 02114-4280	Christopher Giordano	Dean of Students Office	617-573-8239
Tufts U.	Medford, MA 02155	Sandra Baer	Academic Resource Center	617-627-5571

Institution	Location	Contact	Office	Phone
U. Mass.—Amherst	Amherst, MA 01003	Cheryl Howland	Learning Disabilities Support Services	413-545-4602
U. Mass.—Boston	Boston, MA 02125-3393	Renee Goldberg	Roth Center for Disability Services	617-287-7430
U. Mass.—Dartmouth	North Dartmouth, MA 02747	Carole J. Johnson	Disabled Student Services	508-999-8711
Wellesley C.	Wellesley, MA 02481	Barb Burke	Learning & Teaching Center	781-283-2641
Western New England C.	Springfield, MA 01119	Bonnie Alpert	Student Disability Services	413-782-1257
Wheaton C. (MA)	Norton, MA 02766	Marty Bledsoe	Academic Support Services	508-286-8215
Wheelock C.	Boston, MA 02215	Paul Hastings	Disability Services	617-879-2304
Williams C.	Williamstown, MA 01267	Pettengill Fahnestock	Assoc. Dean for Student Services	413-597-4264
Worcester Poly. Institute	Worcester, MA 01609	Joann VanDyke	Office of Academic Advising	508-831-5381
Worcester St. C.	Worcester, MA 01602-2597	Dennis Lindblom	Disability Services Office	508-793-8000

MICHIGAN

Institution	Location	Contact	Office	Phone
Adrian C.	Adrian, MI 49221-2575	Jane McCloskey	EXCEL	517-265-5161
Albion College	Albion, MI 49224	David Hawsey	Disability Services	517-629-0756
Alma C.	Alma, MI 48801-1599	Patricia Chase	Center for Student Development	989-463-7225
Aquinas C.	Grand Rapids, MI 49506-1799	Jackie Sweeney	Academic Achievement Center	616-632-2166
Calvin C.	Grand Rapids, MI 49546	Dr. James Mackenzie	Student Academic Services	616-526-6113
Central Michigan U.	Mount Pleasant, MI 48859	Carol Wojcik	Academic Assistance	989-774-3018
Delta C.	Universal City, MI 48710	Michael Cooper	Learning Disabilities Services	989-686-9322
Ferris St. U.	Big Rapids, MI 49307	Eunice Merwin	Disabilities Services	231-591-3772
Finlandia U.	Hancock, MI 49930	Kirsti Arko	Retention and the Teaching Learning Center	877-202-5491
Grand Rapids C.C.	Grand Rapids, MI 49503	Anne Sherman	Disability Support Services	616-234-4140
Grand Valley St. U.	Allendale, MI 49401	Kathleen Vanderveen	Office of Academic Support	616-331-2490
Hope C.	Holland, MI 49422-9000	Jacqueline Heisler	Academic Support Center	616-395-7830
Itaska C.C.	Grand Rapids, MI 55744	Anne Vidovic	Support Services	218-327-4167
Kellogg C.C.	Battle Creek, MI 49017	L. Marshall-Washington	Support Services	269-965-3931 ext. 2627
Lansing C.C.	Lansing, MI 48901	Jennifer Lack	Counseling Services	517-483-5263
Madonna U.	Livonia, MI 48150-1173	Michael Meldrum	Educational Support Services	734-432-5641
Marygrove C.	Detroit, MI 48221	Veronica Killebrew	Support Services	313-927-1200 ext. 1427
Michigan St. U.	East Lansing, MI 48824	Michael Hudson	Resource Center for Disabilities	517-353-9642
Michigan Tech U.	Houghton, MI 49931	Dr. Gloria Melton	Handicapped Services	906-487-2212
North Central Michigan C.	Petoskey, MI 49770	Katherine Flewelling	Educational Opportunity Program	231-348-6687
Northern Michigan U.	Marquette, MI 49855	Carolyn Stabenow	Disability Services	906-227-1737
Oakland C.C.	Auburn Hills, MI 48309	Mary Jo Lord	PASS Office	248-232-4080

College	Location	Contact	Service	Phone
Oakland U.	Rochester, MI 48309	Linda Sisson	Disability Support Services	248-370-2100
Saginaw Valley St. U.	University Ctr, MI 48152	Cynthia Woiderski	Disability Services - Student Affairs	989-964-4168
Schoolcraft C.C.	Livonia, MI 48152	Dr. Debra Daiek	Academic Assessment Services	734-462-4436
SW Michigan C.	Dowagiac, MI 49047	Susan Sullivan	Special Populations	269-687-4801,
U. of Michigan—Ann Arbor	Ann Arbor, MI 48109	Stuart Segal	Services for Students with Disabilities	734-763-3000
U. of Michigan—Flint	Flint, MI 48502	Paula Pollander	Student Development Center	810-762-3456
Wayne St. U.	Detroit, MI 48202	Jane DePriester-Morandini,	Education Access Service	313-577-1851
Western Michigan U.	Kalamazoo, MI 49008	Beth denHartigh	Disabled Student Resources and Services	269 387-2116

MINNESOTA

College	Location	Contact	Service	Phone
Augsburg C.	Minneapolis, MN 55454	Emily Nugent	CLASS Program	612-330-1053
Bethel C.	St. Paul, MN 55112	Gretchen Wrobel	Disability Services	651-638-6403
Bimidji St. U.	Bimidji, MN 55601	Kathy Heagen	Disability Services	218-755-3883
Carleton C.	Northfield, MN 55057	Hudlin Wagner	Support Services	507-646-4075
Century C.	White Bear Lake, MN 55110	Ed Sapinski	Access Center	651-779-3354
C. of Saint Benedict	Saint Joseph, MN 56374	Michelle Sauer	Academic Advising	320-363-5011
C. of Saint Catherine, The	Saint Paul, MN 55105	Barbara Mandel	Resources for Disabilities - O'Neill Center	651-690-6563
C. of Saint Scholastica, The	Duluth, MN 55811-4199	Jay Newcomb	Academic Support Services	218-723-6552
Concordia C. (Saint Paul, MN)	Saint Paul, MN 55104-5494	Annette Carpenter	Students with Disabilities	651-641-8272
Fond du Lac C.C.	Cloquet, MN 55720	Bill Kallis	Office of Students with Disabilities	218-879-0815
Gustavus Adolphus C.	St. Peter, MN 56082	Henry Toutain	Academic Advising: Dean of Students	507-933-7526
Hamline U.	Saint Paul, MN 55104	Deb Holtz	Disability Services	651-523-2521
Hibbing C.C.	Hibbing, MN 55746	Bonnie Olson	Disability Services	218-262-7246
Inverhills C.C.	Invergr Hgts, MN 55076	Tim Boyer	Disabled Student Services	651-450-8628
Lake Superior C.	Duluth, MN 55811	Georgia Robillard	Disability Services	218-733-7650
Century College	White Bear Lk, MN 55110	Ed Sapinski	Access Center	651-779-3354
Macalester C.	St. Paul, MN 55105	Micheal Dickel	Learning Center	651-696-6118
Mesabi C.C.	Virginia, MN 55792	Carrie Thomas	Disability Services	218-749-0325
Minneapolis C.C.	Minneapolis, MN 55403	Jane Larson	Office for Students with Disabilities	612-659-6730
Minnesota State U.—Mankato	Mankato, MN 56002	Gael Meicle	Center for Academic Success	507-389-5902
Minnesota State U.—Moorhead	Moorhead, MN 56563	Greg Toutges	Disability Services	218-236-2652
N. Hennepin C.C.	Brooklyn Pk, MN 55445	Connie Sherman	Disability Access Services	763-493-0556
Normandale C.C.	Bloomington, MN 55431	Debbie Tillman	Office for Students with Disabilities	952-487-7035
Riverland C.C.	Austin, MN 55912	Sharon Stiehm	Student Success Center	507-433-0646

Institution	City, State ZIP	Contact	Office	Phone
Rochester C.C.	Rochester, MN 55904	Travis Kromminga	Disability Services	507-280-2968
Saint Cloud St. U.	Saint Cloud, MN 56301-4498	Owen Zimpel	Student Disability Services	320-308-3117
Saint John's U.	Collegeville, MN 56321-7155	Susan Douma	Academic Advising	320-363-3246
Saint Mary's U.	Winona, MN 55987-1399	Joe Dulak	Academic Skills Center	507-457-1414
Saint Olaf C.	Northfield, MN 55057-1098	Linne Jensen	Academic Support Center	507-646-3288
Southwest St. U.	Marshall, MN 56258	Pam Ekstrom	Learning Resources	507-537-7672
U. of Minnesota	Crookston, MN 56716	Laurie Wilson	Office for Students w/ Disabilities	218-281-8587
U. of Minnesota—Duluth	Duluth, MN 55812-2496	Penny Cragun	Learning Disability Program	218-726-8727
U. of Minnesota—Minneapolis	Minneapolis, MN 55455	Sheila Fox-Wassink	Disability Services	612-624-2893
U. of Minnesota—Morris	Morris, MN 56267	Ferolyn Angell	Academic Assistance Office	320-589-6163
U. of St. Thomas	St. Paul, MN 55105-1096	Kimberly Schumann	Enhancement Program	651-962-6315
Winona St. U.	Winona, MN 55987	Nancy Dumke	Disability Services	507-457-2391

MISSISSIPPI

Institution	City, State ZIP	Contact	Office	Phone
Mississippi St. U.	Mississippi, MS 39762	Debbie Baker	Student Support Services	662-325-3335
U. of Mississippi	University, MS 38677	Ardessa Minor	Services for Students with Disabilities	662-915-7128
U. of Southern Mississippi	Hattiesburg, MS 39406	Suzy Hebert	Office of Svcs. for Stdnts w/ Disabilities	601-266-5024
William Carey C.	Hattiesburg, MS 39401-5499	Stacey Kimbro	Student Support Services	601-318-6209

MISSOURI

Institution	City, State ZIP	Contact	Office	Phone
Blue River C.C.	Blue Springs, MO 64015-7242	Lea Shelton	ACCESS Office	816-655-6077
Columbia C.	Columbia, MO 65216	Amy Brundage	Student Support Center	573-875-7624
Drury C.	Springfield, MO 65802-9977	Jenifer Murphy	Assistive Student Services	417-873-7419
Evangel U.	Springfield, MO 65802	Sheri Phillips	Academic Development Center	417-865-2815
Fontbonne C.	St. Louis, MO 63105	Jane Snyder	Academic Resource Center	314-719-3627
Kansas City Art Institute	Kansas City, MO 64111-1762	Dr. Bambi Burgad	Academic Resource Center	816-802-3376
Lindenwood U.	St. Charles, MO 63301-1695	Tonie Isenhour	Disability Services	636-949-2000
Longview Comm. C.	Lee Summit, MO 64081-2105	Connie Flick-Hruska	ACCESS Office	816-672-2254
Maple Woods C.C.	Kansas City, MO 64156	Kim Fernandes	ACCESS Office	816-437-3192
Mineral Area C.	Park Hills, MO 63601	Lisa Leftridge	Special Services	573-518-2152
Missouri Southern St. C.	Joplin, MO 64801-1595	Melissa Loger	Learning Center	417-625-9516
Missouri Valley C.	Marshall, MO 65340	Linda Kanagawa	Student Support Services	660-831-4210
Missouri Western St. C.	Saint Joseph, MO 64507	Ellen Smither	Non-Traditional Student Services	816-271-4280
Northwest Missouri St. U.	Maryville, MO 64468	Phil Kenkel	Director Student Support Services	660-562-1861

College	Location	Contact	Office/Service	Phone
Penn Valley C.C.	Kansas City, MO 64110	Connie Spies	Access Office	816-759-4152
Saint Louis U.	Saint Louis, MO 63103	Charles Murphy	Student Disabilities Center	314-977-2930
Southwest Missouri St. U.	Springfield, MO 65804	Dr. Steve Capps	Learning Diagnostic Clinic	417-836-4787
St. Charles City C.C.	St. Peters, MO 63376	Pam Bova	Disabled Student Services	636-922-8247
St. Louis C C.—Florissant Valley	St. Louis, MO 63135	Suelaine Matthews	ACCESS Office	314-595-4549
St. Louis C.C.—Forest Park	St. Louis, MO 63110	Claudia Felsen	ACCESS Office	314-644-9260
St. Louis C.C.—Meramec	St. Louis, MO 63122	Linda Nissenbaum	ACCESS Office	314-984-7654
Three River C.C.	Poplar Bluff, MO 63901	Dr. Joseph Mick	Student Support Services	573-840-9650
Truman St. U.	Kirksville, MO 63501	Vicki Wehner	Disability Services	660-785-4478
U. of Missouri—Columbia	Columbia, MO 65203	Sarah Weaver	Office of Disability Services	573-882-4696
U. of Missouri—Kansas City	Kansas City, MO 64110-2499	Scott Laurent	Services for Students with Disabilities	816-235-5696
U. of Missouri—Rolla	Rolla, MO 65409	Connie Arthur	Disability Support Services	573-341-4568
U. of Missouri—Saint Louis	Saint Louis, MO 63121	Marilyn Ditto-Pernell	Disability Access Services	314-516-6554
Washington U.	Saint Louis, MO 63130-4899	Dr. Fran Lang	Disability Resource Center	314-935-4062
Westminster C.	Fulton, MO 65251-1299	Hank Ottinger	Learning Disabilities Program	573-592-5304
William Jewell C.	Liberty, MO 64068	Shawn Anderson	Counseling and Testing	816-415-5946

MONTANA

College	Location	Contact	Office/Service	Phone
Montana St. U.	Billings, MT 59101-0298	Trudy Carey	Disability Support Services	406-657-2283
Montana St. U.	Bozeman, MT 59717	Brenda York	Disability Services	406-994-2824
Montana Tech. College	Butte, MT 59701	Lee Barnett	Disability Services	406-496-3730
Northern Montana C.	Harve, MT 59501	William Linier	Assistant Dean of Students	406-265-4113
Rocky Mountain C.	Billings, MT 59102	Dr. Jane Van Dyk	Services for Academic Success	406-657-1128
U. of Montana	Missoula, MT 59812	James Marks	Disabiltiy Services for Students	406-243-2243
The U. of Montana—Western	Dillon, MT 59725	Dr. Eric Murray	Disability Services	406-683-7565

NEBRASKA

College	Location	Contact	Office/Service	Phone
Concordia C.	Seward, NE 68434	Margene Schmidt	Academic Support	402-643-7365
Creighton U.	Omaha, NE 68178	Wade Pearson	Educational Opportunity Program	402-280-2195
Dana C.	Blair, NE 68008	Lori Nielsen	Academic Support Services	402-426-7334
Doane C.	Crete, NE 68333	Sheri Hanigan	Academic Support	402-826-8554
Metropolitan C.C.	Omaha, NE 68103	Melinda Classen	Special Needs Program	402-457-2700
Southeast C.C.	Lincoln, NE 68510	Suzy Dunn	Disability Services	402-323-3413
Union C.	Lincoln, NE 68506-4300	Debbie Forshee-Sweeney	Teaching Learning Center	402-486-2506

Institution	Location	Contact	Office	Phone
U. of Nebraska	Omaha, NE 68182	Kate Clark	Disability Services	402-554-2896
U. of Nebraska	Lincoln, NE 68588-0417	Veva Cheney	Services for Students w/ Disabilities	402-472-3787
Wayne St. C.	Wayne, NE 68787	Dr. Jeff Carstens	Disability Services Office	402-375-7500
West Nebraska C.C.	Scottsbluff, NE 69361-1899	Norm Stephenson	Counseling Center	308-635-6090

NEVADA

Institution	Location	Contact	Office	Phone
Truckee Meadows C.C.	Reno, NV 89512	Lee Geldmacher	Disabled Student Services	775-673-7286
U. of Nevada—Las Vegas	Las Vegas, NV 89154	Anita Stockbauer	Learning Enhancement Services	702-895-0866
U. of Nevada—Reno	Reno, NV 89557	Mary Zabel	Disability Resource Center	775-784-6000
Western Nevada C.C.	Carson City, NV 89703	Susan Hana	ADA Support Services	775-445-3275

NEW HAMPSHIRE

Institution	Location	Contact	Office	Phone
Colby-Sawyer C.	New London, NH 03257	Jennifer Zotalis	Academic Development Center	603-526-3714
Dartmouth C.	Hanover, NH 03755	Nancy Pompian	Student Disabilities Center	603-646-2014
Franklin Pierce C.	Rindge, NH 03461-0060	Trish Moore	Academic Services	603-899-4107
Keene St. C.	Keene, NH 03435	Jane Warner	Office of Disability Services	603-358-2353
New England C.	Henniker, NH 03242	Anna Carlson	Pathways Center	603-428-2218
New Hampshire Tech	Concord, NH 03301	Beverly Boggess	Support Services	603-271-7723
Rivier College	Nashua, NH 03060	Kate Ricci	Office of Special Servcies	603-897-8497
Southern New Hampshire U.	Manchester, NH 03108	Hyla Jaffe	Disability Services	603-668-2211
U. of New Hampshire	Durham, NH 03824	Maxine Little	The Access Office	603-862-2607

NEW JERSEY

Institution	Location	Contact	Office	Phone
Bergen C.C.	Paramus, NJ 07652	Nancy Carr	Office of Special Services	201-612-5270
Brookdale C.C.	Lincroft, NJ 07738	Elaine Foley	Director of Disability Services	732-224-2730
Caldwell College	Caldwell, NJ 07006-9165	Abbe Benowitz	Office of Disability	973-618-3645
Camden County C.	Blackwood, NJ 08012	Anne-Marie Hoyle	PACS Program	856-227-7200
Centenary C.	Hackettstown, NJ 07840	Jeffrey Zimdahl	Disability Services	908-852-1400 ext. 2251
C. of New Jersey, The	A. Degennaro, NJ 08650-4700	Terri Yamiolkowski	Office for Students w/ Differing Abilities	609-771-2571
County C. of Morris	Randolph, NJ 07869	Dr. David Nast	Horizons Program	973-328-5284
Drew U.	Madison, NJ 07940	Edye Lawler	Academic Dean's Office	973-408-3514
Fairleigh Dickinson U.	Teaneck, NJ 07666	Dr. Mary L. Farrell	Reg. Ctr. for College Students with LD	201-692-2087
Georgian Court C.	Lakewood, NJ 08701	Patty Cohen	The Learning Center	732-364-2200
Kean U.	Union, NJ 07083-0411	Dr. Marie Segal	Project Excel	908-737-5400
Middlesex C.C.	Edison, NJ 08818	Elaine Weir-Daidone	Project Connections	732-906-2546

College	Location	Contact	Service	Phone
Monmouth U.	W. Long Branch, NJ 07764	Carolyne Chirchello	Disability Services for Students	732-571-3460
New Jersey City U.	Jersey City, NJ 07305	Jennifer Aitken	Project Mentor Regional ctr for students w/ LD	201-200-2091
Ocean County C.	Toms River, NJ 08754	Maureen Reustle	Disability Resource Center	732-255-0456
Princeton U.	Princeton, NJ 08544-0430	Maria Flores-Mills	Disability Services	609-258-3054
Ramapo C. of New Jersey	Mahwah, NJ 07430	Jean Balutanski	Office of Special Servcies	201-684-7514
Raritan Valley C.C.	Somerville, NJ 08876	Cathy Doyle	Disability Services	908-218-8860
Rider U.	Lawrenceville, NJ 08648	Barbara J. Blandford	Education Enrichment Program	609-895-5492
Rutgers U.	Piscataway, NJ 08854-8097	Altyman Brown	Learning Center	973-353-5608
Rutgers U.	Newark, NJ 07102-1896	James Credle	Dean's Office	973-353-5300
Salem C.C.	Carneys Point, NJ 08069	Richard Duffy	Special Population	856-299-2100
Seton Hall U.	South Orange, NJ 07079	Linda Walter	Disability Support Services	973-313-6003
Sussex C.C.	Newton, NJ 07860	Kathleen Okay	LD Program	973-300-2153

NEW MEXICO

College	Location	Contact	Service	Phone
C. of Santa Fe	Santa Fe, NM 84505	Donna Collins	Disability Services	505-473-6552
Eastern New Mexico U.	Portales, NM 88130	Bernita Nutt	Services for Students with Disabilities	505-562-2280
New Mexico Junior C.	Hobbs, NM 88240	Cynthia Zambrelli	Special Needs Services	505-392-5041
N.M. Inst. of Mining & Tech.	Socorro, NM 87801	*Dr. Judith Raymond	Services for Students with Disabilities	505-835-5443
New Mexico St. U.	Las Cruces, NM 88003	Michael Armendariz	Services for Students with Disabilities	505-646-6840
Santa Fe C.C.	Santa Fe, NM 87502	Jill Douglas	Special Services	505-428-1331
U. of New Mexico	Albuquerque, NM 87131	Juan Candelaria	Special Services Program	505-277-3506

NEW YORK

College	Location	Contact	Service	Phone
Adelphi U.	Garden City, NY 11530	Susan Spencer	Program for Students with LD	516-877-4710
Alfred State College	Alfred, NY 14802	Heather Meacham	Services for Students with Disabilities	607-587-4122
Barnard C.	New York, NY 10027	Susan Quinby	Disability Services	212-854-4634
Binghamton U./SUNY	Binghamton, NY 13902	Jean Fairbairn	Services for Student with Disabilities	607-777-2686
Bronx C.C./CUNY	Bronx, NY 10453	Melissa Kirk	Disability Services	718-289-5874
Brooklyn C./CUNY	Brooklyn, NY 11210	Roberta Adleman	Services for Students with Disabilities	718-951-5538
Broome C.C./SUNY	Binghamton, NY 134902	Lisa Hughes	Learning Disabilities	607-778-5316
C. of New Rochelle	New Rochelle, NY 10805-2339	Joan Bristol	Student Services	914-654-5364
C. of Staten Island/CUNY	Staten Island, NY 10314	Margaret Venditti	Disability Services	718-982-2510
Canisius C.	Buffalo, NY 14208	Ann-Marie Dobies	Disabled Student Services	716-888-3748
Cayuga C.C./SUNY	Auburn, NY 13021	Helene Stapleton	Office of Disability Services	315-255-1743

Institution	City, State ZIP	Contact	Service	Phone
Colgate U.	Hamilton, NY 13346	Lynn Waldman	Academic Program Support	315-228-7225
C. of Saint Rose, The	Albany, NY 12203	Kelly Hermann	Office of Students with Disabilities	518-454-5299
Columbia Greene C.C./SUNY	Hudson, NY 12534	Catherine Tretheway	Dean of Students	518-828-4181 x3437
Concordia C. (NY)	Bronxville, NY 10708	George Groth	The Concordia Connection	914-337-9300 x2361
Cornell U.	Ithaca, NY 14850	Mathew Tominey	Student Disability Services	607-254-4545
Corning C.C.	Corning, NY 14830	Judy Northrop	Counseling for Students with Disabilities	607-962-9262
Culinary Institute of America	Hyde Park, NY 12538	Jack Rittel	The Learning Strategies Center	845-451-1219
Daemen C.	Amherst, NY 14226	Dr. Kathleen Boone	Disability Support Services	716-839-8301
Dowling C.	Oakdale, NY 11769-1999	Dr. Dorothy Stracher	College Students with LD	631-244-3306
D'Youville C.	Buffalo, NY 14201	Isabel Vecchio	Disability Services	716-881-7728
Eastman School of Music	Rochester, NY 14627	Phyllis Wade	Office of the Dean of Students	585-274-1200
Farmingdale/SUNY	Farmingdale, NY 11735	Malka Edelman	Support Svcs. for Stdnts. w/ Disabilities	631-420-2411
Finger Lakes C.C./SUNY	Canandaigua, NY 14424	Amy Nichols	Services for Students with Disabilities	585-394-3500 ext. 70390
Fordham U.	New York, NY 10458	Christina Bertsch	Disabled Student Services	718-817-4362
Hamilton C.	Clinton, NY 13323	Louise Peckingham	Disabled Student Services	315-859-4305
Hofstra U.	Hempstead, NY 11549	Dr. Linda DeMotta	PALS Program	516-463-5059
Houghton C.	Houghton, NY 14744	Dr. Susan M. Hice	Student Academic Services	716-567-9239
Hudson Valley C.C./SUNY	Troy, NY 12180	Jennifer Miller	Disability Resource Center	518-629-7552
Hunter C./CUNY	New York, NY 10021	Don Cohen	Office of Students with Disabilities	212-772-4857
Iona C.	New Rochelle, NY 10801	Madeline Packerman	College Assistance Program	914-633-2582
Jamestown C.C./SUNY	Jamestown, NY 14702	Nancy Callahan	Disability Support Services	716-665-5220
Jefferson C.C./SUNY	Watertown, NY 13601	Sheree Trainham	Learning Skills Center	315-786-2288
Keuka College	Keuka Park, NY 14478-0098	Dr. Joanne Desotelle	Academic Support Program	315-279-5615
Kingsborough C.C./CUNY	Brooklyn, NY 11235	Anthony Colarossi	Special Services	718-368-5175
LaGuardia C.C./CUNY	Long Island City, NY 11101	Matthew Joffre	Office for Students with Disabilities	718-482-5278
Le Moyne C.	Syracuse, NY 13214	Roger Purdy	Academic Support Center	315-445-4118
Lehman C/CUNY	Bronx, NY 10468	Marcos Gonzalez	Disability Issues	718-960-8441
Long Island U.—C.W. Post	Brookville, NY 11548-1300	Cynthia D'Arpino	Academic Resource Center	516-299-2937
Manhattan C.	Riverdale, NY 10471	Dr. Ross Pollack	Learning Disabilites Program	718-862-7101
Manhattanville C.	Purchase, NY 10577	Eleanor K. Schwarz	Higher Education Learning Program	914-323-5313
Marist C.	Poughkeepsie, NY 12601-1387	Linda Cooper	Office of Special Services/LD Program	845-575-3274
Marymount C.	Tarrytown, NY 10591	Polly Waldman	Learning Services	914-332-8310
Marymount Manhattan C.	New York, NY 10021	Dr. Ann Jablon	Program for Academic Access	212-774-0721

College	Contact	Location	Office	Phone
Mercy C.	Terry Rich	Dobbs Ferry, NY 10522	Support Services	914-674-7416
Mohawk Valley C.C./SUNY	Lynn Igoe	Utica, NY 13501	Services for Students with Disabilities	315-792-5413
Molloy C.	Sister Barbara	Rockville Centre, NY 11570	STEEP Program	516-678-5000
Nassau C.C./SUNY	Janice Schimsky	Garden City, NY 11530	Center for Students with Disabilities	516-572-7138
NY Institute of Technology	Alice Heron Burke	Old Westbury, NY 11568-8000	Student Services	516-686-7683
New York U.	Lakshmi Clark	New York, NY 10011	Henry & Lucy Moses Ctr for Stnts with Disabilities	212-998-4980
Niagara U.	Dianne Stoelting	Niagara University, NY 14109	Office of Academic Support	716-286-8076
NYU Para Educator Ctr	Dr. Jane Herzog	New York, NY 10003	Para Educator for Young Adults	212-998-5800
Onondaga C.C.	Elizabeth Bellen	Syracuse, NY 13215	Svcs. for Students w/ Special Needs	315-469-2190
Paul Smith C.	Carol A. Lamb	Paul Smith's, NY 12970	Special Services	516-327-6415
Rensselaer Polytechnic Inst.	Debra Hamilton	Troy, NY 12180	Disability Services	518-276-2746
Roberts Wesleyan C.	Dr. Jennifer Kehoe	Rochester, NY 14624	Learning Center	585-594-6270
Rochester Inst. of Technology	Lisa Fraser	Rochester, NY 14623	Disability Services/LSS	585-475-5296
Rockland C.C.	Marge Zemek	Suffern, NY 10901	Office of Disability Services	845-574-4316
Saint Bonaventure U.	Nancy Mathews	St. Bonaventure, NY 14778	Services for Students with Disabilities	716-375-2065
Saint John's U. (NY)	Jackie Lochrie	Jamaica, NY 11439	Director of Student Services	718-990-6568
Saint Lawrence U.	John Meagher	Canton, NY 13617	Academic Svcs for Students with Special Needs	315-229-5104
Saint Thomas Aquinas C.	Richard Heath	Sparkill, NY 10976	The STAC Exchange	845-398-4230
Schenectady C.C.	Tom Dotson	Schenectady, NY 12305	Disabled Student Services	518-381-1344
SUNY at Albany	Carolyn Malloch	Albany, NY 12222	Learning Disabled Student Service	518-442-5490
SUNY at Canton	Veigh Mehan Lee	Canton, NY 13617	Accommodative Services Department	315-386-7392
SUNY at Delhi	Linda Weinberg	Delhi, NY 13753	Center for Academic Services	607-746-4593
SUNY at Stony Brook	Joanna Harris	Stony Brook, NY 11794	Disabilities Support Services	631-632-6748
SUNY C. at Brockport	Vivian Vanderzell	Brockport, NY 14420-2915	Office for Students with Disabilities	716-395-5409
SUNY C. at Buffalo	Marianne Savino	Buffalo, NY 14222-1095	Disability Services	716-878-4500
SUNY C. at Fredonia	Carolyn Boone	Fredonia, NY 14063	Disabled Student Support	716-673-3270
SUNY C. at Geneseo	Kelly Clark	Geneseo, NY 14454-1471	Multicultural & Disability Services	585-245-5620
SUNY C. at New Paltz	Portia Lillo	New Paltz, NY 12561	Disability Resource Center	845-257-3020
SUNY C. at Oneonta	Craig Levins	Oneonta, NY 13820	Learning Support Services	607-436-2137
SUNY C. at Oswego	Starr Knapp	Oswego, NY 13126	Office of Disabled Student Services	315-312-3358
SUNY C. at Plattsburgh	Ms. Michele Carpentier	Plattsburgh, NY 12901-2681	Student Support Services	518-564-2810
SUNY C. at Potsdam	Sharon House	Potsdam, NY 13676	Accommodative Services	315-267-3267
SUNY C. at Purchase	Ronnie Mait	Purchase, NY 10577	Special Services	914-251-6035

Institution	Location	Contact	Department	Phone
SUNY C. of Technology	Cobleskill, NY 12043	Lynn K. Abarno	Disability Support Services	518-255-5282
SUNY C. at Cortland	Cortland, NY 13045	Ute Gomez	Disabilities Services	607-753-2066
Syracuse U.	Syracuse, NY 13244	Stephen Simon	Office of Disability Services	315-443-4498
Tompkins Cortland C.C.	Dryden, NY 13035	Catherine Wunderlich	Baker Center for Learning	607-844-8211 ext. 4375
U. of Buffalo	Buffalo, NY 14260	Randall Borst	Office of Disability Services	716-645-2608
U. of Rochester	Rochester, NY 14627-0251	Vicki Roth	Learning Assistance Services	585-275-9049
Union C.	Schenectady, NY 12308	Shelly Shinebarger	Director- Student Support Services	518-388-6061
Utica C. of Syracuse U.	Utica, NY 13502-4892	Mr. Patterini	Academic Support	315-792-3032
Vassar C.	Poughkeepsie, NY 12604	Belinda Guthrie	Office of Disability Services	845-437-7584
Wagner C.	Staten Island, NY 10301	Christine Hagedorn	Academic Advisement Center	718-390-3340
Westchester C.C.	Valhalla, NY 10595	Marcia Kalkut	Disabled Students	914-785-6552

NORTH CAROLINA

Institution	Location	Contact	Department	Phone
Appalachian St. U.	Boone, NC 28608	Suzanne T. Wehner	Office of Disability Services	828-262-2291
Ashville Buncombe Technical C.C.	Ashville, NC 28801	Annie Clingenpeel	Special Needs	828-254-1921 ext. 141
Belmont Abbey C.	Belmont, NC 28012	Jennie Latimer	Academic Assistance	704-825-6776
Brevard College	Brevard, NC 28712	Susan Kuehn	Office for Stnts w/Special Needs & Disabilities	828-884-8131
Central Piedmont C.C.	Charlotte, NC 28235	Patricia Adams	Services for Students with Disabilities	704-330-6556
Davidson C.	Davidson, NC 28036	Kathy Brey Merrell	Services for Students with Disabilities	704-894-2225
Duke U.	Durham, NC 27708	Jim Baker	Dean of Students Office	919 668 1267
East Carolina U.	Greenville, NC 27858	Liz Johnston	Services for Students with Disabilities	252-328-6799
Elon University	Elon, NC 27244	Priscilla Lipe	Disability Support Services	336-278-6500
Guilford C.	Greensboro, NC 27410	Sue Keith	Disability Services	336-316-2200
Guilford Tech C.C.	Jamestown, NC 27282	Angela Leak	Academic Skills Center	336-334-4822 ext. 2325
Lenoir-Rhyne C.	Hickory, NC 28603	Sherry Proctor	Academic Support Services	828-328-7296
Mars Hill C.	Mars Hill, NC 28754	Barbara Mc Kinney	Services for Students with LD	828-689-1464
Nash Community C.	Rocky Mount, NC 27804	Cynthia Hinnant	Student Support Services	252-443-4011 ext. 315
North Carolina St. U.	Raleigh, NC 27695	Cheryl Branker	Compensatory Education Department	919-515-7653
Richmond C.C.	Hamlet, NC 28345	Dr. John Wester	Disability Services for Students	910-582-7117
Rockingham C.C.	Wentworth, NC 27375	LaVonne James	Student Development	336. 342.4261 ext. 2243
St. Andrews Presbyterian C.	Laurinburg, NC 28352	Dorothy Wells	Student Development	910-277-5331
Southwestern C.C.	Sylva, NC 28779	Cheryl Contino-Conner	Disability Services	828-586-4091
U. of N. Carolina—Chapel Hill	Chapel Hill, NC 27599	Jane Byron	Student Support Services	919-962-7227
U. of N. Carolina—Charlotte	Charlotte, NC 28223-0001	Joanne Ferneld	Learning Disabilities Services / Disability Services	704-687-4355

Institution	City, State ZIP	Contact	Service	Phone
U. of N. Carolina—Greensboro	Greensboro, NC 27402-6170	Patricia Bailey	Disability Services	336-334-5440
U. of N. Carolina—Wilmington	Wilmington, NC 28403	Dr. Peggy Turner	Disability Services	910-962-3746
Wake Forest U.	Winston-Salem, NC 27109	Van D. Westervelt	Learning Assistance Center	336-758-5929
Wake Tech C.C.	Raleigh, NC 27603	Janet Kilhen	Disability Support Services	919-662-3615
West Piedmont C.C.	Morgantown, NC 28655	David Collins	Disabled Student Services	828-438-6044
Western Carolina U.	Cullowhee, NC 28723	Carol Mellon	Student Support Services	828-227-7127
Wingate U.	Wingate, NC 28174	Linda Stedje-Larsen	Disability Services	704-233-8269
Winston-Salem St. U.	Winston-Salem, NC 27110	Myra Waddell	Academic Resource Center	336-750-2000

NORTH DAKOTA

Institution	City, State ZIP	Contact	Service	Phone
Bismarck St. C.	Bismarck, ND 58506	Marlene Swenson-Seaworth	Disability Support Services	701-224-5554
Dickinson St. U.	Dickinson, ND 58601-4896	Dr. Mary Jo Gonzales	Student Support Services	701-483-2029
Minot St. U.	Minot, ND 58707	Jan Nahinurk	Learning Center	701-228-5479
North Dakota St. C.	Wahpeton, ND 58076-0002	Joy Eichhorn	Study Svcs. for Students w/ Disabilities	701-671-2623
North Dakota St. U.	Fargo, ND 58105-5226	Bunnie Johnson-Messelt	Disability Services	701-231-7671
United Tribes Tech C.	Bismarck, ND 58504	Royce Irwin	Student Support Services	701-255-3285
U. of North Dakota	Williston, ND 58801	Penny Powell	Disability Support Services	701-774-4220
U. of North Dakota	Grand Forks, ND 58202	Deb Glennen	Disabled Student Support Services	701-777-3425

OHIO

Institution	City, State ZIP	Contact	Service	Phone
Antioch C.	Yellow Spring, OH 45387	Liz England Kennedy	Academic Support Services	937-769-1166
Ashland U.	Ashland, OH 44805	Suzanne Salvo	Disability Services	419-289-4142
Baldwin-Wallace C.	Berea, OH 44017	Carol Templeman	Svcs for Students w Disabilities	440-826-2188/419 289-5904
Bowling Green St. U.	Bowling Green, OH 43403	Robert D. Cunningham	Office of Disability Services	419-372-8495
Capital U.	Columbus, OH 43209	Lydia Block	Disability Concerns	614-236-6284
Case Western Reserve U.	Cleveland, OH 44106	Susan Sampson	Disability Support Services	216-368-5230
Central Ohio Tech C.	Newark, OH 43055	Dr. Phyllis Thompson	Office for Disability Services	740-366-9246
Clark St. C.C.	Springfield, OH 45505	Marie Ann Kaiser	Office of Student Services	937-328-6019
Cleveland St. U.	Cleveland, OH 44115	Mike Zuccaro	Disability Services	216-687-2015
C. of Mount Saint Joseph	Cincinnati, OH 45233-1630	Jane Pohlman	Project Excel	513-244-4623
C. of Wooster	Wooster, OH 44691	Pamela Rose	Learning Center	330-263-2595
Columbus St. C.C.	Columbus, OH 43216	Wayne Cocchi	Disability Services	614-227-2629
Cuyahoga C.C. Western	Parma, OH 44130	Mary Sender	Access Office for Accommodation	216-987-2052
Denison U.	Granville, OH 43023	Jennifer Grube Vestal	Office of Academic Support	740-587-6224
Franklin U.	Columbus, OH 43215-5399	Carla Marshall	Student Services - Advisor for Disability Services	614-341-6256

Institution	Location	Contact	Service	Phone
Hiram C.	Hiram, OH 44234	Dr. Lynn B. Taylor	Counseling	330-569-5952
Hocking C.	Nelsonville, OH 45764	Kim Forbes Powell	Access Center	740-753-3591 ext. 2230
Kent St. U.	Kent, OH 44242-0001	Anne Jannarone	Student Disability Services	330-672-3391
Kenyon C.	Gambier, OH 43022	Erin Salva	Academic Advising	740-427-5145
Lakeland C.C.	Kirtland, OH 44095	Alan Kirsh	Services for Students with Disabilities	440-953-7245
Lorain City C.C.	Elyria, OH 44035	Theodora Scott	Office for Special Needs Services	440-366-4058
Lourdes C.	Sylvania, OH 43560	Kim Grieve	Disability Services	419-885-3211
Marietta C.	Marietta, OH 45750	Dr. Michael Harding	Counseling Center	740-376-4784
Miami U.—Hamilton	Hamilton, OH 45011	Mary Vogel	Special Services	513-785-3211
Miami U.	Oxford, OH 45056	Doug Green	Learning Disabilities Services	513-529-8741
Muskingum C.	New Concord, OH 43762	Dr. Ilene Henry—Director	PLUS Program	740-826-8280
North Central State C.	Mansfield, OH 44901	Sandra Luckie	Disability Services	419-755-4727
Oberlin C.	Oberlin, OH 44074	Jane Boomer	Off. of Serv. for Students w/ Disab.	440-775-8467
Ohio Dominican C.	Coumbus, OH 42319	Amy Spencer	Academic Development	614-251-4511
Ohio Northern U.	Ada, OH 45810	Anne Lippert	Student Affairs	419-772-2034
Ohio St. U.	Marion, OH 43302	Margaret Hazelett	Learning Disabilities Services	740-389-6786 ext. 6247
Ohio St. U.—Columbus	Columbus, OH 43210-1200	Patty Carlton	Office for Disability Services	614-292-3307
Ohio St. U.—Newark	Newark, OH 43055	Dr. Phyllis Tompson	Learning Assistance Services	740-366-9246
Ohio U.—Athens	Athens, OH 45701	Katherine Fahey	Off. for Institutional Equity/Disab. Svcs.	740-593-2620
Ohio Wesleyan U.	Delaware, OH 43015	Dr. Blake Michael	Academic Advising	740-368-3275
Otterbein C.	Westerville, OH 43081	Ellen Kasulis	Academic Support Center	614-823-1362
Owens C.C.	Toledo, OH 43699	Beth Scheffert	Disability Resource Services	419-661-7007
Raymond Walters C.	Cincinnati, OH 45236	John Kramer	Disability Services	513-729-8625
Shawnee St. U.	Portsmouth, OH 45662	Scott Douthat	Office of Special Needs Services	740-351-3276
Sinclair C.C.	Dayton, OH 45402	Robin Cooper	Disability Services	937-512-5113
Terra St. C.C.	Fremont, OH 43420	Gina Staccone-Smeal	Disability Services	419-334-8400
U. of Akron	Akron, OH 44325-2001	Sally Gamauf	Services for Students with Disabilities	330-972-7928
U. of Cincinnati	Cincinnati, OH 45221-0091	Debra Merchant	Disability Services	513-556-6823
U. of Dayton	Dayton, OH 45469-1611	Timothy King	Disabled Student Services	937-229-3684
U. of Findlay	Findlay, OH 45840	Lori Colchagoff	Supporting Skills System	419-424-5532
U. of Toledo	Toledo, OH 43606-3390	Kendra Johnson	Office of Accessibility	419-530-4981
Ursuline C.	Pepper Pike, OH 44124-4398	Eileen D. Kohut	Program for Students w/ LD	440-646-8123
Walsh U.	Canton, OH 44720	Ellen Kutz	Disability Services	330-490-7302

College	Location	Contact	Office	Phone
Washington St. C.C.	Marietta, OH 45750	Jill Bancheri	Student Development	740-374-8716
Wright St. U.	Dayton, OH 45435	Jeff Vernooy	Office of Disability Services	937-775-5680
Xavier U.	Cincinnati, OH 45207-2612	Ann Dinan	Learning Assistance Center	513-745-3280

OKLAHOMA

College	Location	Contact	Office	Phone
Cameron U.	Lawton, OK 73505	Samantha Thomas	Vice President for Student Services	580-581-2244
Oklahoma City C.C.	Oklahoma City, OK 73159	Pat Stowe	Services to Students with Disabilities	405-682-1611
Oklahoma St. U.	Stillwater, OK 74078	Michael Shuttic	Student Disability Services	405-744-7116
Southeastern Oklahoma St. U.	Durant, OK 74701-0609	May Susan Dodson	Student Support Services	580-745-2254
Tulsa Junior C.	Tulsa, OK 74119	Yolanda Williams	Disabled Student Resource Center	918-595-7115
U. of Oklahoma	Norman, OK 73019	Suzette Dyer	Office of Disability Services	405-325-3852
U. of Tulsa	Tulsa, OK 74104	Dr. Jane Corso	Center for Student Academic Support	918-631-2315

OREGON

College	Location	Contact	Office	Phone
Blue Mountain C.C.	Pendelton, OR 97801	Amy Spiegel	Services for students with disabilities	541-278-5840
Chemeketa C.C.	Salem, OR 97309	Rebecca Woods	Office for Students with Disabilities	503-399-5192
Lane C.C.	Eugene, OR 97405	Nancy Hart	Disabled Student Services	541-463-3000
Linn-Benton C.C.	Albany, OR 97321	Adero Allison	Disability Services	541-917-4789
Mt Hood C.C.	Gresham, OR 97030	Liz Johnson	Disability Services	503-491-7650
Oregon Institute of Technology	Klamath Falls, OR 97601	Ron McCutcheon	Campus Access and Equality	541-885-1031
Oregon St. U.	Corvallis, OR 97331-2133	Tracy Bentley-Townlin	Services for Students with Disabilities	541-737-4098
Portland St. U.	Portland, OR 97207	Dan Spero	Disability Resource Center	503-725-4150
Rogue C.C.	Grants Pass, OR 97527	Bonnie Reeg	Support Services	541-956-7337
Southern Oregon State U.	Ashland, OR 97520-5032	Margaret Dibb	Disabled Student Services	541-552-6214
Umpqua C.C.	Roseburg, OR 97470	Barbara Stoner	Disability Services	541-440-4600
U. of Oregon	Eugene, OR 97403-1217	Steve Pickett	Disability Services	541-346-1162
Western Baptist C.	Salem, OR 97301	Daren Milionis	Academic Services - dir	503-375-7012
Western Oregon U.	Monmouth, OR 97361	Phil Pownall	Office of Disability Services	503-838-8250
Willamette U.	Salem, OR 97301	Deb Loers	Disability Services	503-370-6471

PENNSYLVANIA

College	Location	Contact	Office	Phone
Albright C.	Reading, PA 19612	Tiffenia Archie	Learning Center - Academic Support	610-921-7662
Bryn Mawr C.	Bryn Mawr, PA 19010-2899	Stephanie Bill	Dean's Office	610-526-7351
Bucknell U.	Lewisburg, PA 17837-9988	Elaine Garrett	Admissions Svcs. for Disabled Students	570-577-1301
Bucks County C.C.	Newton, PA 18940	Marie Stevens Cooper	Program for Students with Disabilities	215-968-8463

Institution	City, State ZIP	Contact	Service	Phone
Cabrini C.	Randor, PA 19087	Amy Wildey	Disabilities Support Services	610-902-8572
California U. of Pennsylvania	California, PA 15419	Cheryl Bilitski	Office for Students with Disabilities	724-938-5781
Carlow C.	Pittsburgh, PA 15213	Andrea Beranek	College Learning Center	412-578-6136
Carnegie Mellon U.	Pittsburgh, PA 15213	Larry Powell	Equal Opportunity Services	412-268-2012
Chatham C.	Pittsburgh, PA 15232	Janet James	College Learning Center	412-365-1611
Clarion U. of Pennsylvania	Clarion, PA 16214	Jennifer May	Disability Support Services	814-393-2095
C. Misericordia	Dallas, PA 18612	Dr. Joseph Rogan	Alternative Learning Project	570-674-6347
C.C. of Allegheny County	Pittsburgh, PA 15212	Mary Beth Doyle	Support Svcs. for Stdnts. w/ Disabilities	412-237-4614
C.C. of Philadelphia	Philadelphia, PA 19130	Joan Monroe	Educational Support Services	215-751-8478
CCAC C. North	Pittsburgh, PA 15237	Kathleen White	Support Services	412-369-3686
Delaware Valley C.	Doylestown, PA 18901	Sharon Malka	Learning Support Services	215-489-2490
DeSales U.	Center Valley, PA 18034	Dr. Rosalind Edman	Learning Center	610-282-1100 ext. 1293
Dickinson C.	Carlisle, PA 17013-2896	Keith Jervis	Learning Support	717-245-1485
Drexel U.	Philadelphia, PA 19104	Robin Stokes	Office of Disability Services	215-895-1401
Duquesne U.	Pittsburgh, PA 15282	David Lachowski	Learning Skills Center	412-396-6035
East Stroudsburg U. of PA	East Stroudsburg, PA 18301-2999	Dr. Edith Miller	Office of Disability Services	570-422-3954
Edinboro U. of Pennsylvania	Edinboro, PA 16444	Dr. Robert McConnell	Office for Students with Disabilities	814-732-2462
Franklin & Marshall C.	Lancaster, PA 17604-3003	Kenneth John, PhD	Counseling Services	717-291-4083
Gannon U.	Erie, PA 16541	Sr. Joyce Lowrey, S.S.J.	Program for Students w/ LD	814-871-5326
Gettysburg C.	Gettysburg, PA 17325	Dr. GailAnn Rickert	Academic Advising	717-337-6579
Harcum Jr C.	Bryn Mawr, PA 19010	Kathleen Nadler	AccESS Development	610-526-6036
Indiana U. of Penn	Indiana, PA 15705	Dr. Catherine Dugan	Advising and Testing Center	724-357-4067
Kutztown U. of Pennsylvania	Kutztown, PA 19530	Patricia Ritcher	Services for Students with Disabilities	610-683-4108
Lebanon Valley College	Annville, PA 17003-0501	Ann H. Hohenwarter	Office of Disability Services	717-867-6158
Lehigh U.	Bethlehem, PA 18015	Cheryl A. Ashcroft	Dean's Office	610-758-4152
Lock Haven U. of Pennsylvania	Lock Haven, PA 17745	Dr. Reynol Junco	Student Support Services	570-893-2926
Luzerne Cty. C.C.	Naanticoke, PA 18634	Anna Mary McHugh	Learning Support Services	570-740-0771
Lycoming C.	Williamsport, PA 17701	Daniel Hertsock	Academic Resource Center	570-321-4294
Mercyhurst C.	Erie, PA 16546	Dianne Rogers	Program for Students with LD	814-824-2450
Messiah C.	Grantham, PA 17027-0800	Dr. Keith Drahn	Disability Services	717-796-5358
Montgomery College C.C.	Blue Bell, PA 19422	Saul Finkle	Services for Students with Disabilities	215-641-6574
Muhlenberg C.	Allentown, PA 18104-5596	Wendy Cole	Academic Support Services	484-664-3433
Northampton C.C.	Bethlehem, PA 18017	Laraine Demshock	Services for Disabled Students	610-861-5342

College	Location	Contact	Service	Phone
Penn St. U.—Delaware	Media, PA 19063-5596	Sharon Manco	Support Services	610-892-1461
Penn St. U.—Mont Alto	Mont Alto, PA 17237-9703	Nanette Hatzes	Learning Center	717-749-6045
Pennsylvania St. U.—U. Park	Univ. Park, PA 16802-3000	Bill Welsh	Office for Disability Services	814-863-1807
Robert Morris C.	Moon Township, PA 15108	Cassandra L. Oden	Center For Student Success	412-262-8349
Saint Joseph's U. (PA)	Philadelphia, PA 19131	Jim Scott	Services for Students with Disabilities	610-660-1774
Seton Hill University	Greensburg, PA 15601	Teresa A. Bassi	Disability Services	724-838-4295
Shippensburg U. of Penn.	Shippensburg, PA 17257-2299	Dr. Lois Waters	Office of Social Equity	717-477-1161
Slippery Rock U. of PA	Slippery Rock, PA 16057	Linda M. Smith	Office for Students with Disabilities	724-738-4877
Temple U.	Philadelphia, PA 19122-6096	Dr. Dorothy Cebula	Disability Resources & Services	215-204-1280
U. of Pennsylvania	Philadelphia, PA 19104	Jerome F. Knast	Student Disability Services	215-573-9235
U. of Pittsburgh—Johnstown	Johnstown, PA 15904	Theresa Horner	Learning Resources Center	814-269-7001
U. of Pittsburgh—Pittsburgh	Pittsburgh, PA 15260	Noreen Mazzocca	Disability Resources & Services	412-648-7890
U. of Scranton	Scranton, PA 18510-4699	Mary Ellen Pichiarello	Learning Enrich. Spclst—Learning Resources Cntr	570-941-4039
Washington & Jefferson C.	Washington, PA 15301	Catherine Sherman	Student Resource Center	724-250-3533
West Chester U. of PA	West Chester, PA 19383	Martin Patwell	Disability Services	610-436-3217
Widener U.	Chester, PA 19013-5792	Dr. Rebecca Corsey-Mckeogh	ENABLE	610-499-4179
Wilkes U.	Wilkes-Barre, PA 18766	Thomas Thomas	Learning Center	570-408-4154

RHODE ISLAND

College	Location	Contact	Service	Phone
Brown U.	Providence, RI 02912	Catherine Axe	Disability Services	401-863-9588
Bryant C.	Smithfield, RI 02917	Laurie Hazard	Academic Center for Excellence	401-232-6746
C.C. of Rhode Island	Warwick, RI 02856	Tracy Karasinski	Student Access and Mentoring	401-825-2402
Johnson & Wales	Providence, RI 02903	Meryl Berstein	Center for Academic Support	401-598-4689
Providence C.	Providence, RI 02918	Nicole Kudarauskas	Office of Academic Services	401-865-2494
Rhode Island College	Providence, RI 02908	Anne Roccio	Disability Services	401-456-8061
U. of Rhode Island	Kingston, RI 02881	Pamela Rohland	Disability Services	401-874-2098

SOUTH CAROLINA

College	Location	Contact	Service	Phone
Citadel, The	Charleston, SC 29409	Dr. Barbara Zaremba	Academic Support Special Services	843-953-6877
Clemson U.	Clemson, SC 29634	Jane Greenawalt	Student Disability Services	864-656-6848
C. of Charleston	Charleston, SC 29424	Bobbie D. Lindstrom	Center for Disability Services	843-953-1431
Francis Marion U.	Florence, SC 295001	Rebecca Lawson	Counseling & Testing	843-661-1828
Limestone C.	Gaffney, SC 29340	Dr. Eric Heinrick	Program for Alternative Learning Styles (PALS)	864-488-4534
Southern Wesleyan U.	Central, SC 29630-1020	Carol Sinnamon	Disabilities and Special Services	864-644-5130

Institution	Location	Contact	Service	Phone
USC—Lancaster	Lancaster, SC 29721	Charleen Mungo-Perry	Academic Success Center	803-313-7063
USC—Aiken	Aiken, SC 29801	Kay Benitez	Disability Services	803-641-3609
USC—Columbia	Columbia, SC 29208	Deborah Haynes	Office of Disability Services	803-777-6142
USC—Spartanburg	Spartanburg, SC 29303	Jim Gorske	Disability Services	864-503-5199
York Tech C.	Clover, SC 29730	Sally Herlong	Disability Services—Special Resources Office	803-325-2896

SOUTH DAKOTA

Institution	Location	Contact	Service	Phone
Augustana C. (SD)	Sioux Falls, SD 57197	Susan Bies	Svcs. for Students with Special Needs	605-274-5503
Black Hills St. U.	Spearfish, SD 57799	Joan Wermers	Student Support Services	605-642-6294
Dakota St. U.	Madison, SD 57042	Robert Jackson	ADA Academic Services	605-256-5823
Dakota Wesleyan U.	Mitchell, SD 57301-4398	Amy Novak	Student Support Services	605-995-2902
National American U.	Rapid City, SD 57709	Dr. Sam Kerr	HR Services	605-721-5214
Northern St. U.	Aberdeen, SD 57401	Karen Gerety	Office of Disability Services	605-626-2371
South Dakota St. U.	Brookings, SD 57007-1198	Nancy Schade	Office of Disability Services	605-688-4504
U. of South Dakota	Vermillion, SD 57069	Elaine Pearson	Disability Services	605-677-6389

TENNESSEE

Institution	Location	Contact	Service	Phone
Chattanooga St. Tech C.C.	Chattanooga, TN 37406	Kathy Lutes	Disability Services	423-697-4452
Cleveland St. CC.	Clevland, TN 37320	Amy Derrick	Disabilities Support Services	423-472-7141 ext. 288
East Tennessee St. U.	Johnson City, TN 37614-0731	Martha Edde-Adams	Disability Services	423-439-8494
Lee U.	Cleveland, TN 37311	Gayle Gallaher	Academic Support Program	423-614-8181
Middle Tennessee State U.	Murfreesboro, TN 37132	John Harris	Disabled Student Services	615-898-2783
Pellissippi St. Tech C.	Knoxville, TN 37933	Sarah McMurray	Services for Students with Disabilities	865-539-7091
Rhodes C.	Memphis, TN 38112	Melissa Butler	Disability Services	901-843-3994
Tennessee St. U.	Nashville, TN 37209-1561	James D. Steely	Disability Services	615-963-7400
Tennessee Tech U.	Cookeville, TN 38505	Sammie Young	Disabled Services	931-372-6318
U. of Memphis	Memphis, TN 38152-6687	Susan TePaske	Student Disability Services	901-678-2880
U. of Tenn. at Martin	Martin, TN 38238	Audra Lindsey	Student Academic Support	731-881-7195
U. of Tenn.—Chattanooga	Chattanooga, TN 37403	Debra Anderson	College Access Programs	423-425-4006
U. of Tenn.—Knoxville	Knoxville, TN 37996	LaRosia Davis	Disabled Student Services	865-974-6087
Vanderbilt U.	Nashville, TN 37203-1700	Sarah Ezell	Opportunity Development Center	615-322-4705

TEXAS

Institution	Location	Contact	Service	Phone
Abilene Christian U.	Abilene, TX 79699	Gloria Bradshaw	Alpha Academic Services	325-674-2667
Amarillo C.	Amarillo, TX 79178	Brenda Wilkes	Accessibility	806-371-5436

Institution	Location	Contact	Office	Phone
Austin C.C.	Cedar Park, TX 78613	Amber Kelly	Students Services	512-223-2012
Central Texas C.	Killeen, TX 76540	Geneva Weedon	Disability Support Services	254-526-1293
El Paso C.C.	El Paso, TX 79998	Jan Lockhart	Center for Students with Disabilities	915-831-2426
Lamar U.	Beaumont, TX 77710	Callie Trahan	Services for Students with Disabilities	409-880-8026
Lamar U.—Orange	Orange, TX 77630	Judy Shoate	Disability Services	409-882-3379
Laredo C.C.	Laredo, TX 78040	Sylvia Trevino	Special Population	956-721-5137
Lee C.	Baytown, TX 77522	Dr. Rosemary Coffmann	Disabilities Services	281-425-6384
Midwestern St. U.	Wichita Falls, TX 76308-2099	Debra Higginbotham	Counseling & Disabilities Services	940-397-4618
Saint Edward's U.	Austin, TX 78704	Lorrain Perea	Student Disability Office	512-448-8660
Schreiner U.	Kerrville, TX 78028-5697	Jude Gallick	Learning Support Services	830-792-7256
Texas State Universtiy—San Marcos	San Marcos, TX 78666	Tina Schultz	Office of Disability Service	512-245-3451
Southern Methodist U.	Dallas, TX 75275-0355	Rebecca Marin	Services for Students w/ Disabilities	214-768-4557
Stephen F. Austin St. U.	Nonacogdoches, TX 75962	Chuck Lopez	Disability Services	936-468-3004
TCU	Fort Worth, TX 76129	Marsha Ramsey	Student Disability Services	817-257-7486
Texas A&M U.	Kingsville, TX 78363	Dr. Dianne Brown	Services for Students with Disabilities	361-593-3302
Texas A&M U.—C. Station	College Station, TX 77843	Anne Reber	Services for Students with Disabilities	979-845-1637
Texas Tech U.	Lubbock, TX 79409-5005	Frank Silvas	Disabled Student Support	806-742-2405
Texas Woman's U.	Denton, TX 76204-5679	Joanne Nunnelly	Disability Support Services	940-898-3835
Tyler Jr. C.	Tyler, TX 75711	Vickie Geisel	Suport Services	903-510-2615
U. of Houston	Houston, TX 77204-3022	Cheryl Amoruso	Center for Students with Disabilities	713-743-5400
U. of Houston—Downtown	Houston, TX 77002-1001	Duraese Hall	Disabled Student Services	713-221-8430
U. of North Texas	Denton, TX 76203-5358	Ron Venable	Office of Disability Accommodations	940-565-4323
U. of Texas at Austin	Austin, TX 78712	Jennifer Maedgen	Services for Students with Disabilities	512-471-6259
U. of Texas—Dallas	Richardson, TX 75083-0688	Kerry Tate	Disability Services	972-883-2098
Univesity of Texas at El Paso	El Paso, TX 79968	Susan Lopez	Disabled Student Services	915-747-5148
U. of Texas—Pan American	Edinburg, TX 78539	Esperanza Cavazos	Off. of Serv. for Persons with Disabilities	956-316-7005
U. of Texas—San Antonio	San Antonio, TX 78249-0617	Lorraine Harrison	Disability Services	210-458-4157
West Texas A&M U.	Canyon, TX 79016	Eric Lathrop	Student Disability Services	806-651-2335

UTAH

Institution	Location	Contact	Office	Phone
Brigham Young U. (UT)	Provo, UT 84602-1110	Paul Byrd	University Accessibility Program	801-422-2767
C. of Eastern Utah	Price, UT 84501	Dede Howa	Disability Support Services	435-613-5670
Snow C.	Ephraim, UT 84627	Mike Anderson	Student Support Services	435-283-7393
Southern Utah U.	Cedar City, UT 84720	Carmen Alldredge	Student Support Services	435-865-8022

Institution	Location	Contact	Office	Phone
U. of Utah	Salt Lake City, UT 84112	Joe Pete Wilson	Center for Disability Services	801-581-5020
Utah St. U.	Logan, UT 84322	Diane Craig Baum	Disability Resource Center	435-797-2444
Utah Valley State College	Orem, UT 84058	Kimberly Beck	Accessibility Services	801-863-8747
Weber St. U.	Ogden, UT 84408-1103	Jeff Morris	Disabilities Center	801-626-6413

VERMONT

Institution	Location	Contact	Office	Phone
Burlington C.	Burlington, VT 05401	Michael Watson	Educational Resource Center (ERC)	802-862-9616
Castleton St. C.	Castleton, VT 05735	Kelley Gilmour	Academic Support Center	802-468-1321
Champlain C.	Burlington, VT 05402-0670	Becky Peterson	Support Services	802-865-6425
Green Mountain C.	Poultney, VT 05764-1199	Nancy Ruby	Learning Center	802-287-8287
Johnson St. C.	Johnson, VT 05656	Katherine Veilleux	Academic Support Services	802-635-1259
Landmark C.	Putney, VT 05346	John Kipp	Landmark College	802-387-6865
Lyndon St. C.	Lyndonville, VT 05851	Margaret Hunter	Academic Support Services	802-626-6210
Marlboro C.	Marlboro, VT 05344	Lydia Greene	Advising	802-258-9235
Middlebury C.	Middlebury, VT 05753-6002	Jodi Litchfield	ADA Office	802-443-5936
New England Culinary School	Montpelier, VT 05602	Laura Wisniewski	Learning Services	802-225-3327
Norwich U.	Northfield, VT 05663	Paula Gills	Learning Support Center	802-485-2130
Saint Michael's C.	Colchester, VT 05439	William Wilson	Dean's Office	802-654-2466
Southern Vermont C.	Bennington, VT 05201	Todd Gerson	Disabilities Support Program	802-447-6360
U. of Vermont	Burlington, VT 05401	Margaret Ottinger	ACCESS	802-656-7753
Vermont Technical C.	Randolph Center, VT 05061	Robin Goodall	Services for Students with Disabilities	802-728-1278

VIRGINIA

Institution	Location	Contact	Office	Phone
Blue Ridge C.C.	Weyers Cave, VA 24486	Beth Styers	Disability Services	540-234-9261
Christopher Newport U.	Newport News, VA 23606	Debbie Witt	Services to Students with Disabilities	757-594-8763
C. of William and Mary	Williamsburg, VA 23187-8795	Lisa Bickley	Disability Services	757-221-2510
Eastern Mennonite U.	Harrisonburg, VA 22801	Joyce Coryell Hedrick	Disability Support Services	540-432-4233
Ferrum C.	Ferrum, VA 24088	Nancy Beach	Academic Resource Center	540-365-4262
George Mason U.	Fairfax, VA 22030-4444	Paul Bousel	Disability Resource Center	703-993-2470
Hampton U.	Hampton, VA 23668	Janice Rashada	Off of Sec 504 Compliance—Disability Services	757-727-5493
Hollins C.	Roanoke, VA 24020	Rita Foster	Student Support Services	540-362-6298
James Madison U.	Harrisonburg, VA 22807	Louis Hedrick	Office of Disability Services	540-568-6705

Liberty U.	Lynchburg, VA 24502	Dr. Dennis McHaney	Office of Disability Academic Support	434-582-2159
Longwood C.	Farmville, VA 23909	Susan Rood	Office of Disability Support Services	434-395-2391
Lynchburg C.	Lynchburg, VA 24501	Jessica Baldwin	Academic Advising	434-544-8152
Mary Baldwin C.	Staunton, VA 24401	Beverly Askegaard	Learning Skills Center	540-887-7250
Mary Washington C.	Fredericksburg, VA 22401	Stephanie Smith	Academic Services	540-654-1266
Marymount U.	Arlington, VA 22207	Kelly Desenti	Disabled Student Services	703-284-1615
New River C.C.	Dublin, VA 24060	Jeananne Dixon	LEAP Center	540-674-3600 ext. 4358
Old Dominion U.	Norfolk, VA 23529-0050	Sheryn Milton	Disability Services	757-683-4655
Patrick Henry C.C.	Martinsville, VA 24115	Scott Guebert	Student Support Services	276-656-0257
Radford U.	Radford, VA 24142	Joann Stephens-Forrest	Disability Resouce Office	540-831-6350
Randolph-Macon C.	Ashland, VA 23005	Jack Trammell	Disability Support Services	804-752-7343
Roanoke C.	Salem, VA 24153-3794	Greg Wells	Academic Services	540-375-2248
Saint Paul's C.	Lawrenceville, VA 23868	Walter Dean	Student Support Services	434-848-6453
Sweet Briar C.	Sweet Briar, VA 24595	Laura Symons	Academic Resource Center	434-381-6278
Thomas Nelson C.C.	Hampton, VA 23670	Nancy Bailey	Disabled Student Services	757-825-2833
Tidewater C.C.	Portsmouth, VA 23703	Sue Rice	LD Services	757-822-1213
U. of Richmond	Richmond, VA 23173	Hope Walton	Academic Skills Center	804-289-8626
U. of Virginia	Charlottesville, VA 22906	Valerie Schoolcraft	Learning Needs & Evaluation Center	434-243-5180
U. of Virginia-College at Wise	Wise, VA 24293	Narda Porter	Student Support Services	276-328-0177
Virginia Commonwealth U.	Richmond, VA 23284	Joyce Knight	Disability Support Services	804-828-2253
Virginia Intermont College	Bristol, VA 24201-4298	Talmage Dobbins	Student Support Services	276-466-7906
Virginia St. U.	Petersburg, VA 23806	Rosezelia W. Roy	Students with Disabilities Program	804-524-5061
Virginia Tech	Blacksburg, VA 24061	Susan Angle	Services for Students with Disabilities	540-231-3788
Virginia Western Comm C.	Roanoke, VA 24038	Martha Richardson	Reach Student Support Services	540-857-7286

WASHINGTON

Bates Tech C.	Tacoma, WA 98405	Daniel Eberle	Special Needs	253-596-1698
Central Washington U.	Ellensburg, WA 98926-7463	Robert Campbell	Disability Support Services	509-963-2171
Eastern Washington U.	Cheney, WA 99004	Karen Raver	Disability Support Services	509-359-6871
Everett C.C.	Everette, WA 98201	Kathy Cook	Center for Disability Services	425-388-9273
Evergreen St. C., The	Olympia, WA 98505	Linda Pickering	Student Access Services	360-866-6000
Gonzaga U.	Spokane, WA 99258	Kathy Shearer	Disabilities Support Services	509-323-4134
North Seattle C.C.	Seattle, WA 98103	Suzanne Sewell	Educational Access Center	206-527-7307
Pacific Lutheran U.	Tacoma, WA 98447-0003	Leslie Foley	Academic Assistance	253-535-7520

Institution	City, State ZIP	Contact	Service	Phone
Pierce C.	Tacoma, WA 98446	Brenda McKinney	Disability Support Services	253-964-6526
Saint Martin's C.	Lacey, WA 98503	Karen McSwain	Access Services	360-438-4580
Seattle Pacific U.	Seattle, WA 98119	Sara Wetzel	Center for Learning	206-281-2272
Seattle U.	Seattle, WA 98122	Carol Schneider	Student Learning Center	206-296-5740
Spokane Falls C.C.	Spokane, WA 99204	Ben Webinger	Support Services	509-533-3437
Tacoma C.C.	Tacoma, WA 98465	Catherine Hilt	Services for Students with Disabilities	253-566-5339
U. of Puget Sound	Tacoma, WA 98416	Ivey West	Disability Services	253-879-2692
U. of Washington	Seattle, WA 98195-5840	Dyane Haynes	Disabled Student Services	206-543-8924
Washington St. U.	Pullman, WA 99164-4122	Dr. Susan Schaeffer	Disability Resource Center	509-335-1566
Western Washington U.	Bellingham, WA 98225	David Brunnemer	Disabled Student Services	360-650-3844
Whatcom C.C.	Bellingham, WA 98226	Bill Culwell	Disabled Student Services	360-676-2170 ext. 3320
Yakima Valley	Yakima, WA 98907	Bob Chavez	Disability Services	509-574-4968

WEST VIRGINIA

Institution	City, State ZIP	Contact	Service	Phone
Davis & Elkins C.	Elkins, WV 26241	Judith Sabol McCauley	Learning Disability Program	304-637-1229
Marshall U.	Huntington, WV 25755	Dr. Barbara Guyer	H.E.L.P.	304-696-6317
West Virginia St. C.	Institute, WV 25112-1000	Kelly Toledo	Collegiate Support Services	304-766-3000
West Virginia Tech	Montgomery, WV 25136	Kitty Polaski	Student Support Services	304-442-3498
West Virginia U.	Morgantown, WV 26506-6009	Dr. Richard Strasburger	Disability Services	304-293-6700
West Virginia Wesleyan C.	Buckhannon, WV 26201	Shawn Kuba	Student Academic Support Services	304-473-8563

WISCONSIN

Institution	City, State ZIP	Contact	Service	Phone
Alverno C.	Milwaukee, WI 53234-3922	Nancy Bornstein	Instructional Service Center	414-382-6353
Beloit C.	Beloit, WI 53511	Diane Arnzen	Learning Support Services	608-363-2572
Cardinal Stritch C.	Milwaukee, WI 53217-3985	Marcia Laskey	Academic Support	414-410-4168
Carroll C. (WI)	Waukesha, WI 53186	Amy Kallas	Disability Services	262-524-7333
Carthage C.	Kenosha, WI 53140	Diane Schowalter	Office of Academic Advising	262-551-5802
Concordia U. (WI)	Mequon, WI 53097	Jean Timpel	Learning Resource Center	262-243-4216
Edgewood C.	Madison, WI 53711	Elizabeth Watson	Disability Services	608-663-8347
Gateway Technical C.	Kenosha, WI 53144	Jack Sullivan	Special Needs	262-564-2320
Lawrence U.	Appleton, WI 54912-0599	M. Hemwall	Disability Services	414-832-6530
Marian C. of Fond Du Lac	Fond du Lac, WI 54935	Wendy Yurk	Academic Support Services	920-923-7162
Marquette U.	Milwaukee, WI 53201-1881	Patricia Almon	Disability Services	414-288-1645
Milwaukee Inst. of Art & Des.	Milwaukee, WI 53202	Jennifer Crandall	Academic Support	414-847-3344

Institution	City/State	Contact	Service	Phone
Milwaukee School of Eng.	Milwaukee, WI 53202-3109	Shawna Fuller	Student Support Services	414-277-7281
Northland C.	Ashland, WI 54806	Judi Holevatz	Office of Special Needs	715-682-1340
Ripon C.	Ripon, WI 54971	Daniel J. Krhin	Student Support Services	920-748-8107
Saint Norbert C.	De Pere, WI 54115	K. Goode-Bartholomew	Academic Support Services	920-403-1326
U. of Wisconsin Oshkosh	Oshkosh, WI 54901	Dr. William Kitz	Project Success	920-424-1033
U. of Wisconsin—Eau Claire	Eau Claire, WI 54701	Elizabeth Hicks	Services for Students with Disabilities	715-836-4542
U. of Wisconsin—Green Bay	Green Bay, WI 53411-7001	Nora Kanzenbach	Director Educational Research	920-465-2671
U. of Wisconsin—LaCrosse	LaCrosse, WI 54601-3742	June Reinert	Disability Resource Services	608-785-6900
U. of Wisconsin—Madison	Madison, WI 53706	J. Trey Duffy	McBurney Disability Resource Center	608-263-2741
U. of Wisconsin—Milwaukee	Milwaukee, WI 53201	Laurie Peterson	Learning Disabilities Program	414-229-6239
U. of Wisconsin—Oshkosh	Oshkosh, WI 54901-8662	Bill Kitz	Project Success	920-424-1033
U. of Wisconsin—Parkside	Kenosha, WI 53141	Renee Sartin Kirby	Learning Disabilities Support Services	262-595-2610
U. of Wisconsin—Platteville	Platteville, WI 53818	Bernie Bernhardt	Student Support Services	608-342-1817
U. of Wisconsin—River Falls	River Falls, WI 54022	Carmen Croonquist	Challenge Program	715-425-3884
U. of Wisconsin—Stevens Pt.	Stevens Point, WI 54481	Jim Joque	Disability Services	715-346-3365
U. of Wisconsin—Stout	Menomonie, WI 54751	Debroah Shefchik	Disabilities Services	715-232-2995
U. of Wisconsin—Superior	Superior, WI 54880	Karen Strewler	Special Services	715-394-8185
U. of Wisconsin—Whitewater	Whitewater, WI 53190	Nancy Amacher	Project Assist	262-472-4788
Viterbo C.	La Crosse, WI 54601	Jane Eady	Learning Center	608-796-3085
West Wisconsin Tech. C.	La Crosse, WI 54602	Kristina Puent	Disability Services	608-785-9875
Wisconsin Indianhead Tech.	Shell Lake, WI 54871	Anne Freagon	Disability Services	715-246-6561 ext. 4348

WYOMING

Institution	City/State	Contact	Service	Phone
Laramie County C.C.	Cheyenne, WY 82007	Lisa Digman	Resource Center	307-778-1359
Sheridan C.	Sheridan, WY 82801	Elizabeth Stearns-Sims	Learning Center	307-674-6446
U. of Wyoming	Laramie, WY 82071	Chris Primus	University Disability Support Services—Student Educational Opportunity	307-766-6189

CANADA/ALBERTA

Institution	City/State	Contact	Service	Phone
Grace MacEwan C.C.	Edmonton, AB T51 2P2	Abigail Parrish-Craig	Counseling & Special Services	780-497-5811
Lethbridge C.C.	Lethbridge, AB T1K 1L6	Julie Deimert	Support Services	403-320-3244
N. Alberta Inst. Tech.	Edmonton AB T5G 2R1	Wendy Marusin	Services to Disabled Students	780-471-8874
S. Alberta Inst. Tech.	Calgary AB T2M 0L4	Lois Hayward	Disability Support Services	403-284-8125
U. of Alberta	Edmonton AB T6G 2E8	Marion Vosahlo	Disabled Student Services	780-492-3381

CANADA/BRITISH COLUMBIA

Institution	Contact	Address	Service	Phone
Camosun C.	Susan McArthur	Victoria BC V8P 4X8	Adult Special Education	250-370-3325
Capilano C.	Jolene Bordewick	N. Vancouver BC V71 3H5	Disability Support Services	604-983-7527
C. of New Caledonia	Fran Miller	Pr. George BC V2N 1P8	Disability Support Services	250-561-5848 ext. 250
Kwantlen College	Susanne Dadson	Surrey V3T BC 5H8	Services for Stud. With Disabilities	604-599-2003
Langara C.	Wendy Keenlyside	Vancouver BC V5Y 2Z6	Disability Services	604-323-5635
Okanagan C.	Fiona Neal	Kelowna BC V1Y 4X8	Disability Services	250-762-5445 ext. 4477
Simon Fraser U.	Andrea Wareham	Burnaaby BC V5A 1S6	Centre for Students with Disabilities	604-291-3112
U. of N. British Colum.	Maureen Hewlett	Prince Grge BC V2L 5P2	Disability Services	250-960-6355
U. of British Columbia	Ruth Warick	Vancouver BC V6T 1Z1	Disabilities Resource Center	604-822-5844
U. of Victoria	David Clode	Victoria BC V8W 3P2	Student & Ancillary Services	250-721-8024

CANADA/MANITOBA

Institution	Contact	Address	Service	Phone
U. of Manitoba	Janalee Morris-Wales	Winnipeg MB R3T 2N2	Disabilities Services	204-474-6213
U. of Winnipeg	Jess Roebuck	Winnipeg MB R3B 2E9	Disability Resource Center	204-786-9771

CANADA/NEW BRUNSWICK

Institution	Contact	Address	Service	Phone
Mt. Allison U.	Jane Drover	Sackville NB E0A 3C0	Center for Learning Assistance	506-364-2527
U. of New Brunswick	Sandra Latchford	Fredericton NB E3B 6E3	Disability Services	506-452-6021

CANADA/NEWFOUNDLAND

Institution	Contact	Address	Service	Phone
Mem. U. Newfoundland	Dr. Donna Hardy-Cox	St. John's NF A1G 5S7	Student Development	709-737-3057

CANADA/NOVA SCOTIA

Institution	Contact	Address	Service	Phone
Dalhousie U.	Lynn Shokry	Halifax NS B3H 4J2	Student Accessibility Services	902-494-2836
St. Mary's U.	David Leitch	Halifax NS B3H 3C3	Support for Disabled Students	902-420-5449

CANADA/ONTARIO

Institution	Contact	Address	Service	Phone
Algoma U. C.	Barbara Muio	S. Ste. Marie ON P6A 2G4	Special Needs	705-949-2301
Cambrian C.	Susan. Alcorn MacKay	Sudbury ON P3A 3V8	Disability Services	705-566-8101 ext. 7420
Canadore C.	Dawson Pratt	N. Bay ON P1B 8K9	Special Needs Services	705-474-7600 ext. 5213
Carleton U.	Dr. Nancy McIntyre	Ottawa ON K1S 5B6	Paul Menton Centre for Students w Disabilities	613-520-6608
Centennial C.	Irene Volinets	Scarborough ON M1K 5E9	Special Needs	416-289-5000 ext. 8022
Durham C.	Willona Blanche	Oshawa ON L1H 7L7	Special Needs—(REACH)	905-721-3123
Fanshawe C.	Lois Wey	London ON N5V 1W2	Counseling & Student Life	519-452-4304
George Brown C.	Stephanie Burke	Toronto ON M5T 2T9	Special Needs	416-415-5000 ext. 6370
Humber College	Ollie Leschuk	Toronto ON M9W 5L7	Services for Students with Disabilities	416-675-6622 ext. 4151

College	Location	Contact	Service	Phone
Lakehead U.	Thunder Bay ON P7B 5E1	Donna Grau	Learning Assistance	807-343-8087
Loyalist College	Belleville ON K8N 5B9	Catherine O'Rourke	Stnt Office for Alternative Resources	613-969-2256
Mohawk College	Hamilton ON L8N 3T2	Rachel Mathews	Disability Services	905-575-2389
Nippissing U. College	N. Bay ON P1B 8L7	Bonnie Houston	Disability Services	705-474-3450 ext. 4235
Ontario C. of Art	Toronto ON M5T 1W1	Ionka Van Steenwyk	Services for Students with Disabilities	416-977-6000 ext. 288
Queen's U.	Kingston ON K7L 3N6	Allyson Harrison	Disability Services	613-533-6311
Seneca College	N. York ON M2J 2X5	Arthur Burke	Special Needs	416-491-5050
St. Clair C.	Windsor ON N9A 6S4	June Egan	Disability Services	519-966-1656
St. Lawrence C.	Brockville ON K6V 5X3	Doug Hone	Special Needs	613-345-0660 ext. 3235
Sheridan C.	Oakville ON L6H 2L1	Mary Foley	Special Needs	905-845-9430
Trent U.	Peterborough ON K9J 7B8	Eunice Lund-Lucas	Special Needs	705-748-1011 ext. 1637
U. of W. Ontario	London ON N6A 3K7	Denise Dunleavey	Services for Students with Disabilities (SDC)	519-661-2147
U. of Waterloo	Waterloo ON N2L 3G1	Rose Padacz	Services for Disabled Persons	519-888-4567 ext. 5231
U. of Windsor	Windsor ON N9B 3P4	Brooke White	Special Needs Office	519-253-3000
York U.	N. York ON M3J 1P3	Marc Wilchesky	LD Programs—Counseling & Development Center	416-736-5297

CANADA/PRINCE EDWARD ISLAND

College	Location	Contact	Service	Phone
Holland College	Charlottetn PE C1A 4Z1	Frank Morrison	Counseling	902-566-9515

CANADA/QUEBEC

College	Location	Contact	Service	Phone
Concordia U.	Montreal PQ H4B 1R6	Leo Bissonnette	Office for Students with Disabilities	514-848-2424 ext. 3518
Dawson C.	Montreal PQ H3Z 1A4	Alice Havel	Centre for Students with Disabilities	514-931-8731
John Abbott C.	St. An. Belvue. PQ H9X 3L9	Brenda Rowe	Special Needs Learning Center	514-457-6610
McGill U.	Montreal PQ H3A 1X1	Joan Wolforth	Special Services	514-398-6009

CANADA/SASKATCHEWAN

College	Location	Contact	Service	Phone
SIAST-Kelsey	Saskatoon SK S7K 6B1	Tony Kessler	Dept. of Disabilities Services	306-933-6445
U. of Saskatchewan	Saskatoon SK S7N 0W0	Maxine Kinakin	Disabled Student Services	306-966-5673

CANADA/YUKON

College	Location	Contact	Service	Phone
Yukon C.	Yukon YT Y1A 5K4	Catalina Colaci	Learning Assistance Center— Service for Students with Disabilities	867-668-8785

ALPHABETICAL LIST OF COLLEGES BY LEVEL OF SUPPORT SERVICES

College/University	State	Support
Adelphi University	New York	SP
American International College	Massachusetts	SP
American University	District of Columbia	SP
Anderson University	Indiana	SP
Augsburg College	Minnesota	SP
Barat College of DePaul University	Illinois	SP
Barry University	Florida	SP
Beacon College	Florida	SP
Brenau University, The Women's College	Georgia	SP
College Misericordia	Pennsylvania	SP
College of Mount Saint Joseph	Ohio	SP
Concordia College	New York	SP
Curry College	Massachusetts	SP
Davis & Elkins College	West Virginia	SP
Dean College	Massachusetts	SP
Dowling College	New York	SP
Fairleigh Dickinson University	New Jersey	SP
Finlandia University	Michigan	SP
Gannon University	Pennsylvania	SP
Hofstra University	New York	SP
Iona College	New York	SP
Landmark College	Vermont	SP
Long Island University—C.W. Post	New York	SP
Loras College	Iowa	SP
Louisiana College	Louisiana	SP
Lynn University	Florida	SP
Manhattanville College	New York	SP
Marist College	New York	SP
Marshall University	West Virginia	SP
Marymount Manhattan College	New York	SP
Mercyhurst College	Pennsylvania	SP
Mitchell College	Connecticut	SP
Mount Ida College	Massachusetts	SP
Muskingum College	Ohio	SP
New Jersey City University	New Jersey	SP
Northeastern University	Massachusetts	SP
Reinhardt College	Georgia	SP
Rochester Institute of Technology	New York	SP
Saint Thomas Aquinas College	New York	SP
Schreiner College	Texas	SP
Southern Illinois University—Carbondale	Illinois	SP
Southern Vermont College	Vermont	SP

Southwest Missouri State University	Missouri	SP
Union College	Nebraska	SP
University of Arizona	Arizona	SP
University of Denver	Colorado	SP
University of Indianapolis	Indiana	SP
University of the Ozarks	Arkansas	SP
University of Wisconsin—Oshkosh	Wisconsin	SP
Ursuline College	Ohio	SP
Vincennes University	Indiana	SP
Waldorf College	Iowa	SP
West Virginia Wesleyan College	West Virginia	SP
Westminster College	Missouri	SP
Wright State University	Ohio	SP

CS: COORDINATED SERVICES

College/University	State	Support
Abilene Christian University	Texas	CS
Adrian College	Michigan	CS
Appalachian State University	North Carolina	CS
Arizona State University	Arizona	CS
Binghamton University (SUNY)	New York	CS
Black Hills State University	South Dakota	CS
Boston College	Massachusetts	CS
Boston University	Massachusetts	CS
Brevard College	North Carolina	CS
Brigham Young University	Utah	CS
Brown University	Rhode Island	CS
Bryant College	Rhode Island	CS
Caldwell College	New Jersey	CS
California Polytechnic State University—San Luis Obispo	California	CS
California State Polytechnic University—Pomona	California	CS
California State University—Chico	California	CS
California State University—Northridge	California	CS
California State University—San Bernardino	California	CS
Calvin College	Michigan	CS
Catholic University of America	District of Columbia	CS
Central Ohio Technical College	Ohio	CS
Clarion University of Pennsylvania	Pennsylvania	CS
Clark University	Massachusetts	CS
Colby-Sawyer College	New Hampshire	CS
Colgate University	New York	CS
College of St. Catherine	Minnesota	CS
College of the Siskiyous	California	CS
College of William and Mary	Virginia	CS
Cornell University	New York	CS

Davidson College	North Carolina	CS
DePaul University	Illinois	CS
Dickinson College	Pennsylvania	CS
Drexel University	Pennsylvania	CS
Duke University	North Carolina	CS
East Carolina University	North Carolina	CS
East Stroudsburg University of Pennsylvania	Pennsylvania	CS
Eastern Kentucky University	Kentucky	CS
Edinboro University of Pennsylvania	Pennsylvania	CS
Elon University	North Carolina	CS
Emerson College	Massachusetts	CS
Emory University	Georgia	CS
Evangel College	Missouri	CS
Fairfield University	Connecticut	CS
Farmingdale State University	New York	CS
Ferris State University	Michigan	CS
Ferrum College	Virginia	CS
Florida A&M University	Florida	CS
Florida Atlantic University	Florida	CS
George Washington University	District of Columbia	CS
Georgetown University	District of Columbia	CS
Georgia Southern University	Georgia	CS
Georgia State University	Georgia	CS
Georgian Court College	New Jersey	CS
Grand View College	Iowa	CS
Harding University	Arkansas	CS
Hocking College	Ohio	CS
Illinois State University	Illinois	CS
Indian Hills Community College	Iowa	CS
Indiana University—Bloomington	Indiana	CS
Iowa State University	Iowa	CS
Jacksonville State University	Alabama	CS
Johnson & Wales University	Rhode Island	CS
Johnson State College	Vermont	CS
Kansas City Art Institute	Missouri	CS
Kansas State University	Kansas	CS
Kean University	New Jersey	CS
Kent State University	Ohio	CS
Keuka College	New York	CS
Kutztown University of Pennsylvania	Pennsylvania	CS
Lee University	Tennessee	CS
Lenoir-Rhyne College	North Carolina	CS
Liberty University	Virginia	CS
Limestone College	South Carolina	CS
Louisiana State University	Louisiana	CS

Loyola University—Chicago	Illinois	CS
Manchester College	Indiana	CS
McDaniel College	Maryland	CS
Miami University	Ohio	CS
Michigan State University	Michigan	CS
Middle Tennessee State University	Tennessee	CS
Minot State University	North Dakota	CS
Monmouth University	New Jersey	CS
Montana Tech of the University of Montana	Montana	CS
National-Louis University	Illinois	CS
New England College	New Hampshire	CS
New England Culinary Institute	Vermont	CS
New York University	New York	CS
North Carolina State University	North Carolina	CS
Northern Illinois University	Illinois	CS
Northwestern University	Illinois	CS
Norwich University	Vermont	CS
Ohio State University—Columbus	Ohio	CS
Old Dominion University	Virginia	CS
Pine Manor College	Massachusetts	CS
Pittsburg State University	Kansas	CS
Providence College	Rhode Island	CS
Reedley College	California	CS
Regis University	Colorado	CS
Rhode Island College	Rhode Island	CS
Rider University	New Jersey	CS
Rocky Mountain College	Montana	CS
Roosevelt University	Illinois	CS
Saint Ambrose University	Iowa	CS
St. Bonaventure University	New York	CS
St. Lawrence University	New York	CS
San Diego State University	California	CS
San Francisco State University	California	CS
San Jose State University	California	CS
Santa Clara University	California	CS
Santa Monica College	California	CS
Santa Rosa Junior College	California	CS
Seton Hall University	New Jersey	CS
Sierra College	California	CS
Southern Connecticut State University	Connecticut	CS
Southern Illinois University—Edwardsville	Illinois	CS
Southern Methodist University	Texas	CS
Southern Wesleyan University	South Carolina	CS
Southwest Texas State University	Texas	CS
Springfield College	Massachusetts	CS

Stanford University	California	CS
SUNY at Albany	New York	CS
SUNY at Stony Brook University	New York	CS
SUNY College at Potsdam	New York	CS
SUNY College of Technology at Delhi	New York	CS
Syracuse University	New York	CS
Temple University	Pennsylvania	CS
Texa State University—San Marcos	Texas	CS
Towson University	Maryland	CS
Unity College	Maine	CS
University of California—Berkeley	California	CS
University of California—Los Angeles	California	CS
University of California—San Diego	California	CS
University of California—Santa Barbara	California	CS
University of Central Florida	Florida	CS
University of Colorado—Boulder	Colorado	CS
University of Colorado—Colorado Springs	Colorado	CS
University of Connecticut	Connecticut	CS
University of Delaware	Delaware	CS
University of Dubuque	Iowa	CS
University of Florida	Florida	CS
University of Georgia	Georgia	CS
University of Hartford	Connecticut	CS
University of Houston	Texas	CS
University of Illinois—Urbana-Champaign	Illinois	CS
University of Iowa	Iowa	CS
University of Kansas	Kansas	CS
University of Maryland—College Park	Maryland	CS
University of Maryland—Eastern Shore	Maryland	CS
University of Massachusetts—Amherst	Massachusetts	CS
University of Memphis	Tennessee	CS
University of Michigan—Ann Arbor	Michigan	CS
University of Missouri—Columbia	Missouri	CS
University of Nevada—Reno	Nevada	CS
University of New Hampshire	New Hampshire	CS
University of North Carolina—Chapel Hill	North Carolina	CS
University of North Carolina—Charlotte	North Carolina	CS
University of North Carolina—Greensboro	North Carolina	CS
University of North Carolina—Wilmington	North Carolina	CS
University of North Texas	Texas	CS
University of Oregon	Oregon	CS
University of Pittsburgh	Pennsylvania	CS
University of Rhode Island	Rhode Island	CS
University of Saint Francis	Indiana	CS
University of San Francisco	California	CS

College/University	State	Support
University of South Dakota	South Dakota	CS
University of Southern California	California	CS
University of Tennessee—Chattanooga	Tennessee	CS
University of Tennessee—Knoxville	Tennessee	CS
University of Toledo	Ohio	CS
University of Tulsa	Oklahoma	CS
University of Utah	Utah	CS
University of Vermont	Vermont	CS
University of Virginia	Virginia	CS
University of Wisconsin—Eau Claire	Wisconsin	CS
University of Wisconsin—LaCrosse	Wisconsin	CS
University of Wisconsin—Madison	Wisconsin	CS
University of Wisconsin—Milwaukee	Wisconsin	CS
University of Wisconsin—Stevens Point	Wisconsin	CS
University of Wisconsin—Whitewater	Wisconsin	CS
University of Wyoming	Wyoming	CS
Utah State University	Utah	CS
Utica College	New York	CS
Vermont Technical College	Vermont	CS
Virginia Intermont College	Virginia	CS
Wake Forest University	North Carolina	CS
Washington University in St. Louis	Missouri	CS
Western Carolina University	North Carolina	CS
Western Connecticut State University	Connecticut	CS
Western Illinois University	Illinois	CS
Wheelock College	Massachusetts	CS
Widener University	Pennsylvania	CS
Wingate University	North Carolina	CS
Xavier University	Ohio	CS

S: SERVICES

College/University	State	Support
Alfred State College	New York	S
Alverno College	Wisconsin	S
Beloit College	Wisconsin	S
Bowling Green State University	Ohio	S
California State University—Fullerton	California	S
Case Western Reserve University	Ohio	S
Champlain College	Vermont	S
Clemson University	South Carolina	S
College of Santa Fe	New Mexico	S
Colorado State University—Pueblo	Colorado	S
Drake University	Iowa	S
Eastern Illinois University	Illinois	S
Eastern Washington University	Washington	S

Emory University	Georgia	S
Florida State University	Florida	S
Frostburg State University	Maryland	S
George Mason University	Virginia	S
Grand Valley State University	Michigan	S
Green Mountain College	Vermont	S
Grinnell College	Iowa	S
Guilford College	North Carolina	S
Hampton University	Virginia	S
Indiana Wesleyan University	Indiana	S
James Madison University	Virginia	S
Lamar University	Texas	S
Lexington Community College	Kentucky	S
Lincoln College	Illinois	S
Loyola Marymount University	California	S
Marian College of Fond du Lac	Wisconsin	S
Marquette University	Wisconsin	S
Messiah College	Pennsylvania	S
Midwestern State University	Texas	S
Minnesota State University—Moorhead	Minnesota	S
Montana State University—Billings	Montana	S
New Mexico Institute of Mining & Technology	New Mexico	S
New Mexico State University	New Mexico	S
Nicholls State University	Louisiana	S
North Dakota State University	North Dakota	S
Northern Arizona University	Arizona	S
Northern Michigan University	Michigan	S
Oberlin College	Ohio	S
Ohio University—Athens	Ohio	S
Oklahoma State University	Oklahoma	S
Oregon State University	Oregon	S
Penn State—University Park	Pennsylvania	S
Ripon College	Wisconsin	S
Rivier College	New Hampshire	S
St. Andrew's Presbyterian College	North Carolina	S
St. Olaf College	Minnesota	S
Seton Hill University	Pennsylvania	S
Sheridan College	Wyoming	S
Shimer College	Illinois	S
Smith College	Massachusetts	S
Sonoma State University	California	S
South Dakota State University	South Dakota	S
Southern Maine Technical College	Maine	S
Southern Utah University	Utah	S
SUNY College of Technology at Alfred	New York	S

SUNY College of Technology at Canton	New York	S
Texas A&M University—College Station	Texas	S
Texas A&M University—Kingsville	Texas	S
Texas Tech University	Texas	S
Thomas More College	Kentucky	S
University of Alabama—Huntsville	Alabama	S
University of Alabama—Tuscaloosa	Alabama	S
University of Alaska—Anchorage	Alaska	S
University of Alaska—Fairbanks	Alaska	S
University of Cincinnati	Ohio	S
University of Idaho	Idaho	S
University of Kansas	Kansas	S
University of Maine—Machias	Maine	S
University of Montana—Missoula	Montana	S
University of Montana—Western	Montana	S
University of Nebraska—Lincoln	Nebraska	S
University of Nevada—Las Vegas	Nevada	S
University of New England	Maine	S
University of New Haven	Connecticut	S
University of New Orleans	Louisiana	S
University of Northern Colorado	Colorado	S
University of Northern Iowa	Iowa	S
University of Notre Dame	Indiana	S
University of Oklahoma	Oklahoma	S
University of Redlands	California	S
University of Saint Thomas	Minnesota	S
University of South Carolina—Columbia	South Carolina	S
University of Southern Colorado	Colorado	S
University of Southern Indiana	Indiana	S
University of Southern Mississippi	Mississippi	S
University of Tennessee—Martin	Tennessee	S
University of Texas—El Paso	Texas	S
University of Texas—Pan American	Texas	S
University of the Pacific	California	S
University of Wisconsin—Stevens Point	Wisconsin	S
Washington State University	Washington	S
Wayne State College	Nebraska	S
West Virginia University	West Virginia	S
Western Kentucky University	Kentucky	S
Western Oregon University	Oregon	S
Western State College of Colorado	Colorado	S
Wheaton College	Massachusetts	S
Whittier College	California	S
Winona State University	Minnesota	S

ADDENDUM: INDEPENDENT LIVING OPTIONS

The following programs are options for students who may have LD/ADHD or other disabilities, but who want to continue to pursue independent living skills and education beyond high school.

Allen Institute Center for Innovative Living	85 Jones Street PO Box 100 Hebron, CT 06248-0100 www.alleninstitute.info mchaloux@alleninstitute.info Phone: 866-666-6919 Fax: 866-228-9670
Anchor to Windward	66 Clifton Avenue Marblehead, MA 01945 www.anchor-to-windward.com anchortowinward@aol.com Phone: 781-693-0063 Fax: 781-639-9184
Bancroft	Hopkins Lane PO Box 20 Haddonfield, NJ 08033-0018 www.bancroft.org/html/contact.html Phone: 856-429-0010 ext. 297
Berkshire Center	18 Park Street Lee, MA 01238 www.berskshirecenter.org Phone: 413-243-2576 Fax: 413-243-3351
Brehm Preparatory School Options Program at Brehm	1245 E. Grand Carbondale, IL 62901 www.brehm.org Phone: 618-457-0371 Fax: 618-529-1248

Center for Adaptive Learning	3350-A Clayton Road Concord, CA 94519 www.centerforlearning.org Phone: 925-827-3863
Chapel Haven	1040 Whalley Avenue Westville, CT 06515 www.chapelhaven.org Phone: 203-397-1714
Cloister Creek	1280 Highway, 138 Southwest Conyers, GA 30094 http://yp.bellsouth.com/sites/cloistercreek/ Phone: 770-483-0748 Fax: 770-918-8217
Evaluation and Developmental Center	500-C South Lewis Lane Southern Illinois University Carbondale, IL 62901 www.siu.edu/~rehabedc/ Phone: 618-453-2331
Foundation for Independent Living	5311 NE 33rd Avenue Fort Lauderdale, FL 33308 www.filinc.org/fjaug2001.html csutherland@filinc.org Phone: 916-325-1690
The Horizons School	2111 University Boulevard. Birmingham, AL 35233 www.horizonsschool.org Phone: 205-322-6606 or 800-822-6242 Fax: 205-322-6605
Independence Center	3640 South Sepulveda Boulevard, Suite 102 Los Angeles, CA 90034 www.independencecenter.com Phone: 310-202-7102 Fax: 310-202-7180

Life at Cape Cod	550 Lincoln Road Hyannis, MA 02601 http://www.lifecapecod.org/application.html Phone: 508-790-3600
Life Development Institute	18001 N. 79th Avenue, Suite E71 Glendale, AZ 85308 www.life-development-inst.org/ ldomaroz@aol.com Phone: 623-773-2774 Fax: 623-773-2788
Life Skills Inc.	100 Highlands Way Oxford, GA 30054 www.independentlivingga.com Phone: 770-385-8913
Living Independently Forever, Inc. Life Group Living	175 Great Neck Road South Mashpee, MA 02649 Phone: 508-539-6979 or 508-477-6670 www.lifecapecod.org/groupliving.html
Maplebrook School	5142 Route 22 Amenia, NY 12501 www.maplebrookschool.org mmbsecho@aol.com Phone: 845-373-9511 Fax: 845-373-7029
Minnesota Life College	7501 Logan Avenue South, Suite 2A Richfield, MN 55423 www.minnesotalifecollege.com Phone: 612-869-4008 Fax: 612-869-0443
Moving Forward Toward Independence	1350 Elm Street Napa, CA 94559 www.moving-forward.org/ Phone: 707-251-8603

New York Institute of Technology Independent Living Program	Central Islip Campus Central Islip, NY 11722 info@vip-at-nyit.org Phone: 631-348-3354 Fax: 631-348-0437
Pace Program	National-Louis University 2840 Sheridan Road Evanston, IL 60201 www2.nl.edu/PACE Phone: 847-256-5150
G.R.O.W. Project at Riverview School	549 Route 6A East Sandwich, MA 02537 grow@riverviewschool.org Phone: 508-888-3699 Fax: 508-833-7628 fax
Riverview School	551 Route 6A, Suite 1 East Sandwich, MA 02537 www.riverviewschool.org admissions@riverviewschool.org Phone: 508-888-0489 Fax: 508-833-7001
Threshold Program at Lesley University	29 Everett Street Cambridge, MA 02138 www.lesly.edu threshld@mail.lesley.edu Phone: 617-349-8181 or 800-999-1959 ext. 8181
Vista Vocational & Life Skills Center	1356 Old Clinton Road Westbrook, CT 06498 www.vistavocational.org/contact.html Phone: 860-399-8080 Fax: 860-399-3103

RECOMMENDED WEBSITES

Council for Exceptional Children
www.cec.sped.org

Council for Learning Disabilities
www.cldinternational.org

Independent Educational Consultants Association
www.IECAonline.com

LDA of America
www.ldanatl.org

National Center for Learning Disabilities
www.NCLD.org

INDEX